PUBLIC PAPERS OF THE PRESIDENTS
OF THE
UNITED STATES

PUBLIC PAPERS OF THE PRESIDENTS
OF THE
UNITED STATES

William J. Clinton

1993

(IN TWO BOOKS)

BOOK II—AUGUST 1 TO DECEMBER 31, 1993

UNITED STATES GOVERNMENT PRINTING OFFICE
WASHINGTON : 1994

Published by the
Office of the Federal Register
National Archives and Records Administration

Foreword

During the second half of 1993, the American people continued to confront vast changes around the world and here at home. We found the courage to move forward as a Nation, striving to build better lives for ourselves and our children and to chart America's course into the 21st century.

As these papers document, we continued to make the changes necessary to empower the American people to move ahead with confidence. The Congress enacted our Administration's economic plan, providing the largest cut in the Federal budget deficit in history and increasing investments to help hardworking Americans meet the challenges of the world economy. After a vigorous debate, the Congress enacted the North American Free Trade Agreement with Canada and Mexico, forging ties among our countries that will help us all compete and win around the world.

As business responded favorably to the changes in our country's economic policy, we strove to change the way our government does the people's business as well. Following Vice President Gore's recommendations in the National Performance Review, we began to reinvent our government to make it more efficient and more effective for the American people, streamlining the Federal workforce, giving more responsibility to frontline workers, and making the regulatory process less costly, more accountable, and more efficient.

We recognized, too, that government can only do so much. The greatest responsibility for renewing the American Dream and restoring our spirit of community belongs to the American people themselves. In signing legislation creating a new national service program, AmeriCorps, I asked all Americans to seize the opportunity "to reach beyond themselves and to reach out to others and to make things better." In the final analysis, the most lasting changes must come from the individual acts of all Americans. At the Church of God in Christ in Memphis, Tennessee, where the Reverend Martin Luther King, Jr., had delivered the last speech of his lifetime, I asked our fellow citizens to remember that, without spiritual renewal, "none of the things we seek to do will ever take us where we need to go."

We all were reminded of the hopeful possibilities of our times when we witnessed an historic act of reconciliation that American diplomacy helped foster. The Prime Minister of Israel and the Chairman of the Palestine Liberation Organization came to the White House for a handshake of hope and a declaration of principles to put an end to their ancient conflict. America and the world saw how much we can all accomplish when we decide to move forward together.

Preface

This book contains the papers and speeches of the 42d President of the United States that were issued by the Office of the Press Secretary during the period August 1–December 31, 1993. The material has been compiled and published by the Office of the Federal Register, National Archives and Records Administration.

The material is presented in chronological order, and the dates shown in the headings are the dates of the documents or events. In instances when the release date differs from the date of the document itself, that fact is shown in the textnote. Every effort has been made to ensure accuracy: Remarks are checked against a tape recording, and signed documents are checked against the original. Textnotes and cross references have been provided by the editors for purposes of identification or clarity. Speeches were delivered in Washington, DC, unless indicated. The times noted are local times. All materials that are printed full-text in the book have been indexed in the subject and name indexes, and listed in the document categories list.

The Public Papers of the Presidents series was begun in 1957 in response to a recommendation of the National Historical Publications Commission. An extensive compilation of messages and papers of the Presidents covering the period 1789 to 1897 was assembled by James D. Richardson and published under congressional authority between 1896 and 1899. Since then, various private compilations have been issued, but there was no uniform publication comparable to the Congressional Record or the United States Supreme Court Reports. Many Presidential papers could be found only in the form of mimeographed White House releases or as reported in the press. The Commission therefore recommended the establishment of an official series in which Presidential writings, addresses, and remarks of a public nature could be made available.

The Commission's recommendation was incorporated in regulations of the Administrative Committee of the Federal Register, issued under section 6 of the Federal Register Act (44 U.S.C. 1506), which may be found in title 1, part 10, of the Code of Federal Regulations.

A companion publication to the Public Papers series, the Weekly Compilation of Presidential Documents, was begun in 1965 to provide a broader range of Presidential materials on a more timely basis to meet the needs of the contemporary reader. Beginning with the administration of Jimmy Carter, the Public Papers series expanded its coverage to include additional material as printed in the Weekly Compilation. That coverage provides a listing of the President's daily schedule and meetings, when announced, and other items of general interest issued by the Office of the Press Secretary. Also included are lists of the President's nominations submitted to the Senate, materials released by the Office of the Press Secretary that are not printed full-text in the book, and proclamations, Executive orders, and other Presidential documents released by the Office of the Press Secretary and published in the *Federal Register*. This information appears in the appendixes at the end of the book.

Volumes covering the administrations of Presidents Hoover, Truman, Eisenhower, Kennedy, Johnson, Nixon, Ford, Carter, Reagan, and Bush are also available.

The Public Papers of the Presidents publication program is under the direction of Frances D. McDonald, Director of the Presidential Documents and Legislative Division. The series is produced by the Presidential Documents Unit, Gwen H. Estep, Chief. The Chief Editor of this book was Karen Howard Ashlin, assisted by Margaret A. Hastings, Carolyn W. Hill, Susannah C. Hurley, Albert Kapikian, Rachel Rondell, Cheryl E. Sirofchuck, and Michael J. Sullivan.

The frontispiece and photographs used in the portfolio were supplied by the White House Photo Office. The typography and design of the book were developed by the Government Printing Office under the direction of Michael F. DiMario, Public Printer.

Martha L. Girard
Director of the Federal Register

Trudy Huskamp Peterson
Acting Archivist of the United States

Contents

Foreword . . . v

Preface . . . vii

Cabinet . . . xi

Public Papers of William J. Clinton,
August 1–December 31, 1993 . . . 1297

Appendix A
Digest of Other White House Announcements . . . 2209

Appendix B
Nominations Submitted to the Senate . . . 2219

Appendix C
Checklist of White House Press Releases . . . 2231

Appendix D
Presidential Documents Published in the Federal Register . . . 2239

Subject Index . . . A–1

Name Index . . . B–1

Document Categories List . . . C–1

Cabinet

Secretary of State .... Warren M. Christopher

Secretary of the Treasury .... Lloyd Bentsen

Secretary of Defense .... Les Aspin

Attorney General .... Janet Reno

Secretary of the Interior .... Bruce Babbitt

Secretary of Agriculture .... Mike Espy

Secretary of Commerce .... Ronald H. Brown

Secretary of Labor .... Robert B. Reich

Secretary of Health and Human Services .... Donna E. Shalala

Secretary of Housing and Urban
Development .... Henry G. Cisneros

Secretary of Transportation .... Federico Peña

Secretary of Energy .... Hazel Rollins O'Leary

Secretary of Education .... Richard W. Riley

Secretary of Veterans Affairs .... Jesse Brown

United States Representative to the
United Nations .... Madeleine Korbel Albright

Administrator of the Environmental
Protection Agency .... Carol M. Browner

United States Trade Representative .... Michael Kantor

Director of the Office of Management
and Budget .... Leon E. Panetta

Assistant to the President and
Chief of Staff .... Thomas F. McLarty III

Chair of the Council of Economic
Advisers .... Laura D'Andrea Tyson

Director of National Drug
Control Policy .... Lee Patrick Brown

Administration of William J. Clinton

1993

Exchange With Reporters Prior to a Meeting With the Progressive Caucus
August 2, 1993

Bosnia

Q. Mr. President, could you clarify U.S. policy towards Bosnia? Is the U.S. prepared to unilaterally use military force to break the siege of Sarajevo and get humanitarian supplies in? Or will it work only in conjunction with the NATO allies?

The President. Well, let me say, I think the stories this morning perhaps exaggerate our position a bit. Our position is we are working with the allies. We're going to try to work through to a common position. We believe we will be able to work through to a common position. And I don't think it serves much of a purpose to speculate what might otherwise happen.

I don't believe that the allies will permit Sarajevo to either fall or to starve. I just don't believe that will happen. So I think we'll have a common position. There are some concerns; there always have been by those who have forces on the ground there, particularly those in the exposed positions. And I think we'll work it through, and I want the talks to continue. My goal has always been to work with them and to proceed together, and I think we'll be able to do that.

Q. Are you concerned about the reports that the talks may be delayed because the Bosnians expect you to come in on their side militarily?

The President. No, I don't think that will happen. Let me say this: I think peace has been delayed by the reverse perception that because the allies have not done anything to try to stabilize the position. The situation has until very recently gotten much worse since they were all in Athens talking—because the allies did nothing. Now, I think it's getting a little better again because, in part, because we're talking about what ought to be done for humanitarian reasons and to protect our own forces there, the U.N. forces.

So I'm very hopeful. I think they've made real progress in the peace talks, and I'm hopeful that will go on. I don't think the Bosnian Government will pull back.

Economic Program

Q. Are you going to win?

The President. America is going to win. Not me, it's not about me; it's about the country.

NOTE: The exchange began at 10:14 a.m. in the Roosevelt Room at the White House. A tape was not available for verification of the content of this exchange.

Interview With Newspaper Editors
August 2, 1993

The President. Hello?

Economic Program

Q. Mr. President, I want to give you the first question and to point out that the attention you've given our Senator Herb Kohl in the last couple of days has raised his level of notoriety to a point that he hasn't known since he was elected. Now, I know you wouldn't trade a vote, but is there anything that you and Senator Kohl mutually want in terms of legislation or other benefits for Wisconsin that you have an interest in?

The President. The main thing that Senator Kohl was concerned about—he was interested in two things, to be fair, and there was—in the national interest. One was to minimize the burden on middle class taxpayers. And when he looked at the whole package and saw that working families with incomes under $30,000 were held harmless and that working families with incomes of $50,000 and $60,000 were looking at a $33-a-year burden with the spending cuts, I think that really made a big difference to him.

The other thing that he was interested in that I think is certainly as significant over the long run is he wanted a program that had some real economic growth incentives, that had some business help in it. And this program does a lot for small businesses. Over 90 percent of the small businesses in the country are eligible for a tax reduction if they reinvest more money in their businesses. It does more for research and development. It does more for revitalizing homebuilding and real estate. It does more across a whole range of issues. For the heavy industry in Wisconsin, under this plan, there will be more incentives to invest in new plant and equipment in Wisconsin to be competitive there as opposed to going overseas. So all those things were important.

And then the third issue that he raised, which I certainly agree with him on, is that we need to bring this deficit down to zero. And in order to do that, we're going to have to cut more. But to do that, we have to reform the health care system. So the next issue is how to bring down health care costs so we can get this budget deficit down to zero and not just take $500 billion off of it.

Q. Have you convinced him, Mr. President, that these changes are enough to get his vote on this issue?

The President. Well, I hope so. I've worked hard on that. That's going to be up to him, not me, and I don't think I should speak for him. But let me say this: I think he has really done a good job here, and he has been very important in bringing a business, pro-jobs perspective to the whole debate. So we'll just see. But we've got a $495, $496, $497—something in that range—billion dollar deficit reduction package. We're now going to have more cuts than tax increases in the package. The top 1.2 percent of the American people, of people with incomes over $200,000 will pay more than 75 percent of the burden now. And there are quantifiable spending cuts now in excess of $250 billion across the whole range of Federal programs. So it is a very important first step here.

Q. Mr. President, you haven't had quite as good a success with our Senator Boren, who, I think, like many people in Oklahoma are concerned that the spending cuts to come later—when we went through that in 1990, and they never came. Why should things be different this time?

The President. Well, for one thing I'm going to have a trust fund and all the money will have to be put into the deficit reduction package, both the spending cuts and the tax increases. What actually happened in 1990, Jim, to be completely accurate about it, is that the Congress adopted a plan based on the previous administration's rosy revenue estimates. And no one really thought the revenues would grow that much; so they didn't. And then spending increased because the recession went on and more people were entitled to Medicare and Medicaid. And between those two things, they were in deep trouble.

Now, let me just address the major objections Senator Boren has, because I think what he says is right, but it's not a good reason to vote against this program. What he says is that in order to take the deficit from where we're taking it down to zero, you have to do something about the entitlement programs, especially about Medicare and Medicaid. Now, that is true. But the problem is if you don't reform the health care system, that is, if you don't fundamentally restructure the system of the way health care is insured against and the way the—cutting out a lot of the paperwork and a lot of the things that are more expensive in America than anywhere else that have nothing to do with health care, and you cut the medical expenses of the Federal Government, all in the world you're going to do is have a hidden tax on the private sector because the providers will do what they always do. They'll pass their costs on to people that have insurance. So that, for example, the Daily Oklahoman would have its medical premiums go up more than otherwise would be the case because the Government's not paying the full cost of its health care.

So I don't disagree that we have to do something about health care costs and entitlements. But the time to do that is in the context of a health care reform debate, which we're going to start as soon as we can get this budget out of the way. If we don't adopt the budget, we'll never get there. Everybody who looks at it can see that this budget's a lot better deal than the one in 1990. The numbers are more realistic. The growth package is realistic. We've got new business capital gains tax in there and all kinds of other incentives for small businesses to grow. Over 90 percent of the small businesses can get a tax reduction under this plan because of it. This is going to create some jobs, too. So it's a better package.

But you can't solve all the problems of the world in this bill. That's my quarrel and dispute with Senator Boren. He's right, you've got to get the entitlements if you want to go to zero, but we're going to have to do it in two steps, not one.

Q. Mr. President, a lot of people are concerned with, out here, the fact that the spending reductions, the major ones, seem to come so late in the plan, and the tax increases come so early. Wouldn't it be better to go back in and make another slash, even if this means delaying the budget a little bit?

The President. Here's the problem with it: First of all, there are going to be more spending reductions all the way along. The House of Representatives has already approved $10 billion in spending reductions over and above what's in this budget, but working with me. I've encouraged them. The Vice President is going to have a reinventing Government report out sometime next month, which will provide a lot more savings. So we're just getting started on the spending reductions. And then as I said, we'll be able to project a decade of spending controls in the health care area if we do health care reform.

The problem is that no matter what you do with that, the budget we have now and the budget we're going to have next year—we're already preparing to cut more off next year right now. But that is not an excuse not to act now. Still the big reductions in spending are those that aggregate up over time. That is, if I cut $10 billion this year and $10 billion next year, then that's $20 billion over this year's figure and then $30 billion and $40 billion. You see what I mean? So the spending cuts are always going to look bigger in the out-years because they compound one another.

Small Business

Q. Mr. President, we're relaying some of our readers' questions. One of them was, how can the job market grow when small businesses are afraid new taxes and the health plan will put them out of business?

The President. Well, first of all, new taxes and the health plan won't put them out of business. We've tried to send a clear signal to the small business community that there won't be a tax problem here. But if they have to have a premium to cover their own employees, we will limit how much of their payroll it can be, and it will be phased in over a period of years.

But let me flip it over to you on the other side. Seventy percent of the small businesses in America provide some health care coverage for their employees, and almost all of them pay much more than they should because we're the only country in the world that forces employers who cover their employees to subsidize employers who don't, and that's what happens. Everybody in this country gets health care, but if you don't have health insurance and you can't pay for it, you get it too late when it's too expensive. You show up at the hospital; you get cared for, and then the providers, the doctors and the hospitals, in effect, raise their costs to everybody else. So you could argue that the small business community as a whole in this country is more hurt by the system we have than by the one we're moving to.

Also, let me make one other point. We spend about 10 cents on the dollar more than any other country in the administrative costs of our health care system because we have 1,500 separate health insurance companies writing thousands of different policies, all with different rules and regulations, so that the cost of compliance is staggering, and then the Government aggravates it.

So I think the small business community will wind up ahead on this. But we've tried to send some clear signals that we're not going to pop them with a big payroll tax, and I do think employers who don't provide anything for their employees should bear some responsibility through the private insurance system. But it ought to be limited and phased in so that nobody goes broke doing it.

Economic Program

Q. Mr. President, on Friday, last Friday we had a conversation with Roger Altman about your budget plan, and one of the questions we asked him was what the administration would have done differently to sell this plan. And he was very frank about it. He said, "We would have started a lot earlier." And I'm curious in terms of your strategy why you didn't really start giving everybody the hard sell a lot earlier.

The President. You mean not in the Congress

but in the country?

Q. Yes, talking to the people.

The President. Well, actually we did a lot of that, but we didn't have our war room set up, and we were, frankly, just overwhelmed by the day-to-day news coverage of Republicans carping about taxes and unable to kind of break through about what the facts of the program were.

I worked hard—for 2 months after I made my State of the Union Address I went out into the country once a week. I did my best to talk about the program. But we didn't have the kind of organized disciplined effort we've had for the last few weeks in reaching out to local newspapers and television and radio stations and bringing in opinion leaders and doing all these things we're doing now. And I think we did lose control of the debate. Also, to be fair to them, to Roger Altman and the others, an issue like this tends to go through cycles. I told the people about it on February 17th, and they liked it. Then the sort of negative rhetoric took over. Now we're kind of coming back to reality, and all the surveys show we're bringing it back our way now.

Interest Rates

Q. Mr. President, Alan Greenspan has been giving some subliminal signals about raising interest rates. Wouldn't that sort of derail your plan for reducing the deficit if the interest rates went up? And are you worried about that?

The President. Yes, I am. I don't think you should raise interest rates until there's real economic growth that brings on real inflation. I mean, there's no real inflation in this economy, and we can have growth without inflation. And I think we may be reading too much into his remarks.

Q. Have you talked to him directly about what he did mean since he made those remarks?

The President. No, but I talk to him fairly often, and I'm scheduled to have another session with him pretty soon. I know him pretty well, and my read on what he said was if inflation warranted it, he might raise interest rates. But if you think about it, what we're trying to do in bringing the deficit down is to justify keeping the interest rates down even when there's economic growth because the Federal Government will be taking less capital away from the markets, and therefore, there won't be as much competition for it, and we ought to be able to keep lower interest rates. That's our theory.

He has constantly and consistently supported the deficit reduction efforts of this administration in very explicit terms. So I would be surprised to see him raise interest rates when we're doing something to support the reverse. If we were having 4 or 5 percent growth and inflation was getting out of hand, I could understand it. But there's no grounds for it now.

Economic Program

Q. Mr. President, obviously, in this part of the country it would have been more popular to cut spending first, raise revenue later. You used the early year forecast of the deficit to go back on your pledge for a middle class tax cut. Since, there have been other estimates, why haven't you gone back to a cut spending first program?

The President. Well, first of all, we are cutting spending. We are cutting spending. This idea that we're raising taxes—taxes come in constant amounts, whether it's a fuel tax or an income tax.

This is a dodge. David Stockman, who pioneered Reagan's program in 1981, has now admitted in repeated interviews that they cut taxes twice as much as they meant to because they got into a bidding war with Congress, that there is no way to restore any kind of fairness to the Tax Code or reduce the deficit to zero unless there is a revenue component. So if I were to say, "Okay, we'll put these spending cuts in for a couple of years, and then we'll raise taxes," all we would do by doing that is basically have a bigger deficit in the first years because we'd have the spending cuts but not the taxes, and we would have higher interest rates, and we'd have slower economic recovery.

Let me just say, in the year that I'm in now—which I'm not even responsible for this budget until October the 1st—our deficit is going to be about $25 billion less than it was predicted to be when I became President.

But to go back to the middle class tax argument, after the election but before I took office, the previous administration said, "Oh, by the way, the deficit's going to be $165 billion bigger over the next 5 years." So I always in that campaign said I am not going to say "read my lips" because I've run a government long enough at the State level to know that sometimes circumstances can change on you. I've been very candid with the American people about that. I think most people with incomes of $50,000 a year don't think $33 a year is too much to pay. I think what most people have believed is, they've been told that they're going to be paying a fortune. And——

Q. Mr. President——

The President. Now, wait a minute. Let me just finish this. I want to make this point. I'm going to be President 4 years. We've got opportunities to have even more fairness in the Tax Code if we're bringing down the deficit and we are opening up economic growth. There are all kind of options to do things over the next 4 years. But the most important thing now is to do something about the deficit. The truth is that all these people who say they want to cut spending now, what they really want is an accounting practice which still would have all the spending cuts come in the 3d, 4th, and 5th year of this budget cycle.

What they're really saying is let's pass a bill that says it's going to cut spending later now before we raise taxes. They don't propose more spending cuts in these first years than I do, none of them do. And to go back to Senator Boren's bill, particularly the one he offered in the Senate didn't have nearly as much support as the one I offered, because it didn't have the kind of deficit reduction unless you did what he proposed to do, which was to take more out of Medicare for middle class people. And even then it wasn't going to happen for the 3d, 4th, or 5th year, most of it.

So the people that say cut spending now are saying, "We don't want to cut any more spending than Bill Clinton does right now, but we want to pass a bill that cuts spending in the 3d, 4th, and 5th year in health care without health care reform and then talk about whether we should tax the wealthiest Americans later." That's what they're really saying.

Q. Is there any chance, do you think, that this bill will go down? Is there any chance that it will not pass in the Senate?

The President. Well, sure there is. But I think it will pass. And the reason I think it will pass is this: I think most of those people are going to say, is this a better bill than we've ever had before and better than we had in 1990? And the answer to that will be, yes. Is this fairer

to average Americans than the ones we've been considering? The answer to that will be, yes. Does this restore some economic growth incentives for small business, for new high-tech businesses, for housing, for real estate that we haven't had in the Tax Code for 7 or 8 years? And the answer to that will be, yes. Does this bill lift the working poor out of poverty and encourage people to get off welfare, not with a Government program but by using the tax system to reward people who work, even at very low wages? The answer to that will be, yes. And then the last question is, do we want to hang around here in Washington for 60 or 90 more days and debate this, and either come back here and pass something very like it or something that's so much weaker that we'll have higher interest rates, more uncertainty, and we'll waste 2 or 3 months when we could be dealing with health care, with welfare reform, with a crime bill, with things that will grow this economy with a new world trade agreement, all these things we need to get on about the business of doing.

We are literally paralyzed here. We can't get anything else done. The only other major initiative that's going to come out of this is the national service bill that I've been working on for a long time. Other things cannot even be dealt with.

And again I want to say to those of you interested in the cut issue, keep in mind the Vice President is going to issue our reinventing Government report within 60 days. The Congress is still cutting some other spending with my strong support. We are going to have more cuts even than we have now. But to delay this program is a great mistake. All it will do is paralyze the Government, paralyze the financial markets, and leave us with uncertainty. We've been talking about this since February. It's time to move.

NOTE: The interview began at 3:25 p.m. The President spoke via satellite from Room 459 of the Old Executive Office Building. Participating in the interview were the editorial page editors of the Milwaukee Sentinel, the Milwaukee Journal, the Arizona Republic, and the Reno Gazette Journal.

Interview With Newspaper Editors
August 2, 1993

Economic Program

Q. As you are well aware, Louisiana's Senator, Bennett Johnston, is or was at last report among the small, key group of Democrat Senators who've indicated reluctance to vote for your deficit reduction package. What are you doing or what can you do to get Senator Johnston's vote? And do you think you will ultimately get it?

The President. I don't know the answer to the last question, but what I've done is to try to take the strengths of both House and Senate versions of the bill and try to put them together. The strength of the Senate version was it had fewer overall taxes and was even more progressive. The strength of the House version was it had much more economic incentives, more economic growth incentives, for research and development, for investment in new firms, for small business, the things of that kind.

So the argument that I'm going to be making to all these Senators is that this plan now clearly has $500 billion in deficit reduction; it will now have more spending cuts than tax increases in it; it will have over 75 percent of the new tax burden now borne by people with incomes above $200,000; that the middle class tax burden is now down to $33 a year; and that the economic growth incentives qualifying, for example, 90 percent plus of the small businesses in the country for a reduction in taxes if they invest more in their companies; and enabling the working poor through the earned-income tax credit to lift themselves above poverty by working full time, these are very, very important things. And the time has come to act.

Now, let me say just as a generic thing, since this may help to shape some of the other questions: The people who are leaning against this program or have announced against it—not the Republicans, that's almost entirely a political deal; the Republicans have even opposed the conservative amendments to our budget to control entitlements and impose discipline. But the Democrats basically fall into two categories: There are those who think it's the right thing for the country, but they're afraid there's been so much misinformation out there about it that they'll get beat if they vote for it. And then there are those who think that it's a good first step, but it doesn't go far enough.

The only thing I would say to the latter group is that we do have to do something on entitlements, but we can't get there until we do something to reform health care spending overall, and that this is a major step that will stabilize the financial markets, keep interest rates down, and enable us to move on to health care reform, to getting a world trade agreement, to welfare reform, to the crime bill, to all these things that are out there crying for attention that we can't even address if we don't go ahead and get this budget out of the way. And also, there will be further budget cuts. The Vice President's report on reinventing Government is due next month. It will have many more suggested budget cuts. And the House of Representatives has already cut another $10 billion off the budget that we can't fully count yet because the Senate hasn't acted. But when they do, we'll have even more cuts.

Q. Mr. President, good afternoon.

The President. Good afternoon.

Q. Let me pass on to you a question I'm getting increasingly from Constitution readers. How can you assure that your tax increase package does not have the same result as Mr. Bush's 1990 tax increase package, which is to say no result at all except higher taxes?

The President. I can do that in two ways. First of all, let's look at what happened in 1990. Why did the deficit reduction package in 1990 not produce the deficit reduction it was intended to? There were basically two or three reasons. But one big reason is that they overestimated how much the revenues would bring in; that is, they had some very, very liberal revenue estimates, and those revenues did not materialize. So that within 60 days after the package passed, they revised downward the amount of deficit reduction by $130 billion. Now, we have instead taken the most conservative revenue estimates we could get.

The second thing is that I have pledged to the Congress that by Executive order, I will put all of this money, the spending cuts and the revenue increases, into a trust fund and that every year if we miss the deficit reduction target, I will come forward to the Congress and give them a plan to meet the target, that is, to have further cuts to meet the target, and ask them to vote on it. I might say that we had those requirements in the law, and through the parliamentary rules of the Senate, the Republicans took it out of the law. One hundred percent of the Republicans agree with that budgetary discipline, and they took it out because they thought it was good politics for them to take it out and weaken the bill further. So I'm going to do it by Executive order. So it is different.

Now, let me say, there was one other thing different from 1990. Because this plan has been taken much more seriously by the financial markets, it has already had a big impact in bringing down long-term interest rates, and that has led millions of people to refinance their homes and their business loans. And I'm convinced once we actually pass the plan, we'll release a lot of investment into the economy. The other thing we do that was not done in 1990 is have investment incentives: the 75-percent in small business expensing—that will qualify over 90 percent of the small businesses in the country for a tax cut if they invest more in their business; a new business capital gains tax which will really help in high technology areas; we've got incentives to reinvest in homebuilding and to reinvest in new plant and equipment through changes in the alternative minimum tax. So there are a lot of pro-growth incentives in this plan that were not there in 1990, and those are the principal differences.

Q. Mr. President, good afternoon. Ross Perot is saying that this proposal should be rejected so Members of Congress can go back home, visit with their constituents, get a better feel for the spending cuts that would be accepted, come back in September and cut some more. Why should that not be done?

The President. Well, because we've already got more spending cuts than revenue increases, number one; because we're going to keep cutting spending, as I have said. But no one who looks at this budget deficit believes it can seriously be brought under control unless there are some revenue increases. And you know, I think it's pretty funny—I mean, I've got a 4.3 cent gas tax in my plan. Ross Perot proposed a dime a year for 5 years or a 50 cent gas tax increase in his plan, something he was running from yesterday on television. I have more verifiable spending cuts than he proposed in his plan.

We have done what we need to do here to get a budget out.

Here is the problem: Nothing precludes us from cutting more spending. We're going to cut more spending. But until we pass this budget, we are paralyzed from going on to the next big problem with the deficit, which is health care costs and entitlements there. And that's got to be dealt with in the context of health care reform. We can't get to health care reform; we can't consider the next big round of spending cuts through reinventing Government; we can't do the crime bill, which is very, very important; we can't do welfare reform; we can't do anything until we pass a budget. And we've debated this from February to August. These Members have been going home every weekend. There will be more spending cuts. There will be more spending cuts in every year I'm here. But the time has come to pass this budget and get on with it. The tax burden is fair. Spending cuts now will exceed the tax increases. And we're going to put it all against the deficit. And we've just got to do this so we can go on and do the rest of it. To keep wallowing around in it won't serve anybody very well.

Q. What do you do about Mr. Perot?

The President. Well, nothing. He doesn't have a vote in Congress. I think what was done yesterday was wonderful. The press kept saying, "Well, what would you do? Here's your plan; how can you criticize the President? Yours was off by $400 billion. You're going to raise the gas tax by 50 cents." And so I don't have to do anything. I think, you know, it was nice to see him answer some questions for a change. There's nothing for me to do. I've got a plan, and it'll work, and I want to pass it. And it's good for the country.

Let me just say this: We had 67 business executives here from big and small companies last week, 4 energy company executives—half of them were Republicans, one of them was President Bush's cochairman—supporting this plan. And every one of them said we've got to do it because we've got to bring the deficit down, we've got to keep interest rates down, we've got to stabilize the economy, we need some incentives to grow—every one of them. I mean, there is very broad support for this program among people who really understand it.

When I went to Tokyo to meet with the leaders of other industrial nations at the G–7 summit, for 10 years the statement coming out of that meeting had criticized the United States for its budget deficit. For the first time in 10 years, they complimented the United States. And they agree with me that we ought to go and try to get the 111 countries that are in the General Agreement on Tariffs and Trade to lower tariffs on a whole range of issues, eliminate them on a lot of other products. And everybody concedes, who's studied this, that this could add hundreds of thousands of jobs to the American manufacturing sector this year. Why? Because we're doing something about our deficit.

We have got to move. We don't need to delay this another month or 2 months or 3 months. That's what they did in 1990, by the way. One of your questions was what didn't work in 1990. In 1990 they said, well, we just can't make up our mind, so we'll delay. So instead of adopting it in August, they adopted it at the end of October. That's 90 precious days almost from the first week in August to the end of October, 90 days we could be dealing with health care; we could be passing the Vice President's recommendations on reinventing Government, which would be even more spending cuts; we could be passing a crime bill to help make our streets safer; that we could be dealing with welfare reform; all these things to strengthen the economy. None of this can be done unless we get this out of the way.

Q. Sir, there's been a good bit of discussion about the timing of the spending cuts, particularly saying that they mostly come in the later years. Could you please comment on the timing of the spending cuts?

The President. Well, they weren't timed to do that. The fact is that we have more control—when I took over this budget—these budgets are done on a 5-year cycle. If you're going to make deep cuts, it's easier to plan for them if you have a little time to plan for them. And also under the previous budget that we inherited, the budgets were already tighter in the early years, and they were much looser, I thought, in the later years.

But I assure you, we're not waiting for that. I've already given instructions to my Cabinet to prepare more budget cuts for the coming year. We have reduced the deficit in this year since I've been in office, mostly because of lower interest rates, by about $25 billion over and above where it was projected to be. So

there are budget cuts in the early years, but it's like planning anything else. If you're going to take big whacks out of a large organization, the longer time goes on, the more you have to plan, the bigger the cuts you can make.

Now, let me say one other thing. Other people talk about "cut first and tax later;" most of their cuts are in the later years, too. They just want to pass them first and then avoid the tough decisions on the taxes. But if you look at the cuts that are proposed by others, if you look at Senator Boren's cuts on entitlements, almost all of them come in the later years, the meaningful ones. That's where they come, except the proposals that would have raised the costs of health care to middle class Medicare recipients or upper class ones. I'm not against, for example, raising the premiums on Part B. That's what he called a spending cut. But if you're going to do it, it ought to be done in the context of overall health care reform and not just trying to get more money from those folks. I think we need to reform the health care system.

The people who talk about spending cuts first are basically saying this. If you ask the people who say they're opposed to this but they understand the budget, they will tell you the following things: We are cutting defense sharply and about all we can. I'm concerned that we should not do more. We've cut it quite deeply. There is an overall freeze on domestic spending. For example, that means every dollar we increase Head Start, every dollar we increase education and training for workers that have been displaced by defense plants closing down, every dollar we put into new technologies for defense conversion—those are the three areas where we basically have increased—we have to cut in veterans affairs, in agriculture, in all these other areas. Already we have a budget that will reduce the Federal work force by over 100,000 people in the next 5 years, and there will be more cuts coming to that, so that's flat.

The only thing that's increasing in this budget are the so-called entitlements, and that's basically Medicare and Medicaid and Social Security cost of living. We have restrained Federal pay increases and Federal pension increases below where they have been under the previous administrations. They are getting some cost of living, but less than they ordinarily would, and I called for a freeze in the first year. So the real growth is in Medicare and Medicaid, in the health care programs. If you put a lid on them now without reforming the health care system, you must do one of two things that I think are not good. One is to charge middle class elderly people more for their Medicare and much more if you're going to make them pay it all. Or the second is to not charge them any more, just limit how much the Federal Government pays, and force the doctors and hospitals to shift all the costs to the private sector, which would raise the health insurance premiums of every newspaper on this telephone. That's what's been going on for years.

I guess I need to say this as clearly as I can: I do not dispute those who say if you want to take the deficit from where I take it to down to zero, you have to deal with entitlements. And it will require more spending cuts, not more tax increases beyond where we are. I agree with that. But my point is you don't get to that until you do this first. You've got to pass the budget first, then reform the health care spending in the country. Otherwise, what's going to happen with health care cuts, it's going to be very, very unfair to the elderly on Medicare or to people who are paying private insurance. They're going to bear the costs.

Space Station and Super Collider

Q. Mr. President, down here you're talking about budget cutting in Texas; that means two things basically, the SSC and the space station. How do you see their future? Are they going to hang in there? And if push comes to shove, how would you put them in priority of importance if you have to keep one and get rid of one?

The President. Well, let me just say this. They're both very important to me for different reasons. And I think they're both important to the country. I think, if you're asking how they're doing now, I think the space station is more secure than the super collider, because the space station passed a House vote. It was a narrow vote, as you probably know, the first time. The second time we got some more votes. But the first time we only carried it by a couple of votes when two good friends of mine who went down to vote against it stayed to the end and changed their vote so we could save it because they knew it was important to me and, I think, to the country, as I said.

So we have redesigned the space station after a serious review by an eminent team of national scientists. It is very important to maintain our leadership in space technology. It's very important in terms of new partnerships with Russia to keep them involved in this kind of technology, to reduce the incentive they have to sell weapons and keep them taking their nuclear force down. But most important, it's a big economic boom to us. If we get out of this, the Europeans will move right in, take this over, and have a lot of those high-wage jobs that Americans should have. So I think it is critically important.

The super collider is important, in my judgment, for science and for research, not so much for applied technology now. We don't know for sure what it will produce, but we know that it has the potential to produce a great deal, and we know that other major science research projects like this have often had unintended benefits.

It's in more trouble now. And frankly, whether we can save it or not depends entirely on whether we can save it in the Senate. And the climate's not as good as it was last year when it was saved. I think then-Senator Bentsen clearly saved it in the Senate last time. It got beat by 70 more votes in the House this time than it did last year. I really don't know whether that's the real sentiment of the House or not. And then I don't know how much that had to do with the fact that, at the moment they were voting on the super collider, your Senators and Mr. Perot were out on the steps of the Capitol screaming at them to cut more spending, at the very moment the bill came up. I don't know whether that had anything to do with it or not, but I know it lost by 70 more votes than it did last year.

And you know, it's pretty tense in the Senate now over a lot of these issues. But I am strongly supporting it. I'm going to do what I can to pass it, and I think we've got a chance to pass it. The key to passing it, frankly, is asking the Senate to look at the national interest and look at the fact that we have to make a significant investment in nondefense research and development and technology. Now that we've cut defense a great deal and we have not offset all the cuts in technology with domestic investments in technology, and that's where a lot of these high wage jobs of the future come from, we can't permit this to become a debate where the people in California took 40 percent of the base closing cuts last time and they complained that Texas took no cuts and that they're voting for new revenues and the Texas Senators want—I mean, if it becomes a deal, you know, a State-by-State deal, I think it's gone. The only way we can save it is if people will recognize that it is in the national interest to do so. I'm hoping we can do it.

Q. There's time for one more question.

The President. I can't believe all these editorial writers don't have another question. [*Laughter*]

Economic Program

Q. You spoke about now having more spending cuts than tax increases. I wonder if you could give us the figures, the current state of affairs.

The President. Well, you know, they're still negotiating. It could change, but the last time I talked to Senator Mitchell it was about $254 billion in spending cuts and about $242 billion or $241 in taxes, or something like that. They were at about $496 billion. And like I said, it could change in the next few days, but—I mean in the next day or so. You know, let me close by, if I might—you asked me a question when you started, and I didn't really give you a very good answer about how I could get Senator Johnston's vote. I think, frankly, he's worried about looking like he reversed himself from voting against it the first time, and I can understand that.

But let me say, without identifying anybody, if you look at the people who have opposed the program or the people who voted for it with reluctance, their basic objections break down into two categories. One is a political one, pure and simple: "I think this is the right thing to do for the country, and I hope it passes, but I'm scared I'll get beat if I vote for it." And we have tried to help in several ways: first of all, by recreating an aggressive communications strategy, more like what we did in the campaign, to try to combat what we think are false claims against this plan and just to get the information out about it; and secondly, to ask everybody to imagine what it's going to be like, not the day after the vote but after we've had a chance to continue our spending cut program through the Vice President's reinventing Government initiative and through other cuts that will come when we've got a chance to deal with health care and welfare reform and the crime bill and these other issues.

Then there's a whole second category of people who say that this is okay, this is a legitimate and honest effort to do better, and it does, but it doesn't do enough. Senator Nunn, for example—we've got the Atlanta Journal on here—Senator Nunn is sort of in that category, you know, said you've got to deal with entitlement costs, too. And my argument to that group of people—and that's the argument that Senator Boren made yesterday—is that you're right, it doesn't do enough. But that's not a good reason to vote against this because what it does is very good, indeed. And unless you do this, you can't get to the second stage. That is, I completely agree we have to control entitlement costs and that that begins overwhelmingly with Medicare and Medicaid costs. I just don't think it's fair or right to do it unless it's part of an overall health care reform plan which brings down the cost of health care to all Americans and stops cost-shifting and doesn't impose unfair burdens on elderly people on Medicare. And my argument is, we're just beginning this process; we're not ending it. But if we don't pass this budget now, we'll fool around here for 60 or 90 more days debating the same old thing. We'll wind up with a program that may be marginally different than the one we've got, but it will in all probability have much less deficit reduction if we have to go into some sort of situation where we're paralyzed on this.

So the real issue here—I think the reason that we've had so many Republican as well as Democratic business leaders supporting this is that they want a decision, they want certainty, they want real deficit reduction, and they think this meets all those criteria and also has some real incentives to grow the economy, and it will free us to move on to these other things. That's what I keep emphasizing to Members of Congress who say this is not perfect. I say, look, we've got a 4-year contract here to deal with all these problems, and you can't expect this one bill to solve all the problems of the country. It won't carry that much water. But this is very, very important, but only a first step.

Health Care Reform

Q. Mr. President, since you brought up health care reform, what do you say to reassure Americans—looming over this budget package with its various tax increases is the specter of more increases to pay for health care. How can you reassure Americans that they're not getting ready to get hit by a one-two punch?

The President. First of all, I think we tried to be pretty clear from the beginning that a cigarette tax was just about the only thing we had under consideration to deal with the Government's part of this responsibility, which is how to provide health care for the unemployed uninsured.

Now, the other big question that the small business community raised is what's going to happen to the employed uninsured, virtually all of whom work for small businesses. And I don't, myself, think that it's right to raise everybody else's taxes to cover those people because everybody else is paying too much already. I do think that if we're going to join the ranks of every other advanced country in the world and we're going to bring our costs down, we've got to cover everybody. An employer should bear some responsibility for their employees. And the employee should bear some responsibility, too. But my own view of that is that the best way to do that is to limit the ultimate cost to small business and phase any new requirements in over a period of years so that nobody is adversely affected too much.

But let me say on that point, it's important to remember that 70 percent of the small businesses in America already provide some coverage to their employees. Most of them pay too much for too little coverage because of the way our insurance market is organized. Most of them, in other words, are disadvantaged by the present system. For those who don't provide any coverage for themselves or their employees, they still get health care. But if they can't pay for it, the cost of that health care is simply shifted onto everybody else by the providers.

So my argument there is that we're going to do this with extreme sensitivity to the economy. I think that most business groups will like this program. I think most provider groups will like the program. And I think everybody recognizes that there's something badly wrong when we're spending over 14 percent of our income as a country every year on health care and no other country in the world except for Canada is even over 9. They're just barely over 9. We're competing with the Germans, who are at 8, and the Japanese, who are 8 percent of their income. And with no discernible effect on our life expectancy or anything else—we've got some serious problems they don't have.

Now, we'll never get down to where they are because we have more poor people, more violence, and because for good reasons we emphasize more technology and breakthroughs. So we'll never get down to where they are, but we have got to bring these costs under control or the deficit will never get down to zero, and we can't really restore the competitiveness of our private sector.

So I would say that people should look forward to this with eagerness. Also, this is not going to be jammed through the Congress overnight. We're going to have an honest and open debate on this. I want the American community to sit down and really visit about this health care thing and talk it through. This is not going to be some sort of a blitzkrieg deal. We're going to take some time and really discuss it and debate it, just as we have for the last 6 months.

Thank you very much.

NOTE: The interview began at 3:49 p.m. The President spoke via satellite from Room 459 of the Old Executive Office Building. Participating in the interview were the editorial page editors of the New Orleans Times-Picayune, the Atlanta Journal, the Daily Oklahoman, the Dallas Morning News, the Houston Chronicle, and the Houston Post.

Message to the Congress Reporting on the National Emergency With Respect to Iraq
August 2, 1993

To the Congress of the United States:

I hereby report to the Congress on the developments since my last report of February 16, 1993, concerning the national emergency with respect to Iraq that was declared in Executive Order No. 12722 of August 2, 1990. This report is submitted pursuant to section 401(c) of the National Emergencies Act, 50 U.S.C. 1641(c), and section 204(c) of the International Emergency Economic Powers Act, 50 U.S.C. 1703(c).

Executive Order No. 12722 ordered the immediate blocking of all property and interests in property of the Government of Iraq (including the Central Bank of Iraq), then or thereafter located in the United States or within the possession or control of a U.S. person. That order also prohibited the importation into the United States of goods and services of Iraqi origin, as well as the exportation of goods, services, and technology from the United States to Iraq. The order prohibited travel-related transactions to or from Iraq and the performance of any contract in support of any industrial, commercial, or governmental project in Iraq. U.S. persons were also prohibited from granting or extending credit or loans to the Government of Iraq.

The foregoing prohibitions (as well as the blocking of Government of Iraq property) were continued and augmented on August 9, 1990, by Executive Order No. 12724, which was issued in order to align the sanctions imposed by the United States with United Nations Security Council Resolution 661 of August 6, 1990.

Executive Order No. 12817 was issued on October 21, 1992, to implement in the United States measures adopted in United Nations Security Council Resolution 778 of October 2, 1992. Resolution 778 requires U.N. member states temporarily to transfer to a U.N. escrow account up to $200 million apiece in Iraqi oil sale proceeds paid by purchasers after the imposition of U.N. sanctions on Iraq. These funds finance Iraq's obligations for U.N. activities with respect to Iraq, including expenses to verify Iraqi weapons destruction, and to provide humanitarian assistance in Iraq on a nonpartisan basis. A portion of the escrowed funds will also fund the activities of the U.N. Compensation Commission in Geneva, which will handle claims from victims of the Iraqi invasion of Kuwait. The funds placed in the escrow account are to be returned, with interest, to the member states that transferred them to the United Nations, as funds are received from future sales of Iraqi oil authorized by the United Nations Security Council. No member state is required to fund more than half of the total contributions to the escrow account.

This report discusses only matters concerning the national emergency with respect to Iraq that was declared in Executive Order No. 12722 and matters relating to Executive Orders Nos. 12724 and 12817 (the "Executive Orders"). The report covers events from February 2, 1993, through August 1, 1993.

1. There have been no amendments to the Iraqi Sanctions Regulations during the reporting period.

2. Investigations of possible violations of the Iraqi sanctions continue to be pursued and appropriate enforcement actions taken. These are intended to deter future activities in violation of the sanctions. Additional civil penalty notices were prepared during the reporting period for violations of the International Emergency Economic Powers Act and Iraqi Sanctions Regulations with respect to transactions involving Iraq.

3. Investigation also continues into the roles played by various individuals and firms outside Iraq in the Iraqi government procurement network. These investigations may lead to additions to the Office of Foreign Assets Control's listing of individuals and organizations determined to be Specially Designated Nationals of the Government of Iraq.

4. Pursuant to Executive Order No. 12817 implementing United Nations Security Council Resolution 778, on October 26, 1992, the Office of Foreign Assets Control directed the Federal Reserve Bank of New York to establish a blocked account for receipt of certain post-August 6, 1990, Iraqi oil sales proceeds, and to hold, invest, and transfer these funds as required by the order. On May 18, 1993, following the payment of $1,492,537.30 by the Government of the United Kingdom to a special United Nations-controlled account, entitled United Nations Security Council Resolution 778 Escrow Account, the Federal Reserve Bank of New York was directed to transfer a corresponding amount of $1,492,537.30 from the blocked account it holds to the United Nations-controlled account. Future transfers from the blocked Federal Reserve Bank of New York account will be made on a matching basis up to the $200 million for which the United States is potentially obligated pursuant to United Nations Security Council Resolution 778.

5. Since the last report, there have been developments in two cases filed against the Government of Iraq. Another ruling was issued in *Consarc Corporation* v. *Iraqi Ministry of Industry and Minerals et al.,* No. 90–2269 (D.D.C., March 9, 1993), which arose out of a contract for the sale of furnaces by plaintiff to the Iraqi Ministry of Industry and Minerals, an Iraqi gov-

ernmental entity. In connection with the contract, the Iraqi defendants opened an irrevocable letter of credit with an Iraqi bank in favor of Consarc, which was advised by Pittsburgh National Bank, with the Bank of New York entering into a confirmed reimbursement agreement with the advising bank. Funds were set aside at the Bank of New York, in an account of the Iraqi bank, for reimbursement from the Bank of New York if Pittsburgh National Bank made a payment to Consarc on the letter of credit and sought reimbursement from the Bank of New York. Consarc received a down payment from the Iraqi Ministry of Industry and Minerals and substantially manufactured the furnaces. No goods were shipped prior to imposition of sanctions on August 2, 1990, and the United States asserted that the funds on deposit in the Iraqi bank's account at the Bank of New York, as well as the furnaces manufactured for the Iraqi government or the proceeds of any sale of those furnaces to third parties, were blocked. The district court ruled on December 29, 1992, that the furnaces or their sales proceeds were properly blocked pursuant to the declaration of the national emergency and blocking of Iraqi government property interests. However, according to the court, due to fraud on the part of the Ministry of Industry and Minerals in concluding the sales contract, the funds on deposit in an Iraqi bank account at the Bank of New York were not the property of the Government of Iraq. The court ordered the Office of Foreign Assets Control to unblock these funds, and required Consarc to block the proceeds from the sale of one furnace and to hold the remaining furnace as blocked property. On January 27, 1993, the Office of Foreign Assets Control complied with the court's order and licensed the unblocking of $6.4 million plus interest to Consarc. On March 9, 1993, the court affirmed its ruling in response to Consarc's motion to clarify the December 29 order and the Office of Foreign Assets Control's motion to correct the judgment to conform to the December 29 opinion. The Office of Foreign Assets Control and Consarc have each appealed the district court's ruling.

In *Brewer* v. *The Socialist People's Republic of Iraq,* No. 91–5325 (D.C. Cir., 1993) the United States Court of Appeals for the District of Columbia Circuit affirmed the district court's ruling denying appellant's motion to attach U.S.-located assets of the Government of Iraq and its state tourism organization. Following the holding of *Dames & Moore* v. *Regan,* 453 U.S. 654 (1981), the court upheld the power of the President to freeze foreign assets and prevent their attachment by private litigants in times of national emergency.

6. The Office of Foreign Assets Control has issued a total of 391 specific licenses regarding transactions pertaining to Iraq or Iraqi assets since August 1990. Since my last report, 54 specific licenses have been issued. Licenses were issued for transactions such as the filing of legal actions against Iraqi governmental entities, for legal representation of Iraq, and the exportation to Iraq of donated medicine, medical supplies, and food intended for humanitarian relief purposes.

7. The expenses incurred by the Federal Government in the 6-month period from February 2, 1993, through August 1, 1993, that are directly attributable to the exercise of powers and authorities conferred by the declaration of a national emergency with respect to Iraq are estimated at about $2.5 million, most of which represents wage and salary costs for Federal personnel. Personnel costs were largely centered in the Department of the Treasury (particularly in the Office of Foreign Assets Control, the U.S. Customs Service, the Office of the Assistant Secretary for Enforcement, and the Office of the General Counsel), the Department of State (particularly the Bureau of Economic and Business Affairs, the Bureau of Near East and South Asian Affairs, the Bureau of International Organizations, and the Office of the Legal Adviser), and the Department of Transportation (particularly the U.S. Coast Guard).

8. The United States imposed economic sanctions on Iraq in response to Iraq's invasion and illegal occupation of Kuwait, a clear act of brutal aggression. The United States, together with the international community, is maintaining economic sanctions against Iraq because the Iraqi regime has failed to comply fully with United Nations Security Council resolutions, including those calling for the elimination of Iraqi weapons of mass destruction, the inviolability of the Iraq-Kuwait boundary, the release of Kuwaiti and other third country nationals, compensation for victims of Iraqi aggression, long-term monitoring of weapons of mass destruction capabilities, and the return of Kuwaiti assets stolen during Iraq's illegal occupation of Kuwait. The U.N. sanctions remain in place; the United States will

continue to enforce those sanctions under domestic authority.

The Baghdad government continued to violate basic human rights by repressing the Iraqi civilian population and depriving it of humanitarian assistance. The United Nations Security Council passed resolutions that permit Iraq to sell $1.6 billion of oil under U.N. auspices to fund the provision of food, medicine, and other humanitarian supplies to the people of Iraq. Under the U.N. resolutions, the equitable distribution within Iraq of this assistance would be supervised and monitored by the United Nations. The Iraqi regime so far has refused to accept these resolutions and has thereby chosen to perpetuate the suffering of its civilian population. Discussions on implementing these resolutions resumed at the United Nations on July 7, 1993.

The policies and actions of the Saddam Hussein regime continued to pose an unusual and extraordinary threat to the national security and foreign policy of the United States, as well as to regional peace and security. Because of Iraq's failure to comply fully with United Nations Security Council resolutions, the United States will therefore continue to apply economic sanctions to deter Iraq from threatening peace and stability in the region, and I will continue to report periodically to the Congress on significant developments, pursuant to 50 U.S.C. 1703(c).

WILLIAM J. CLINTON

The White House,
August 2, 1993.

Remarks on Signing the Government Performance and Results Act of 1993 and an Exchange With Reporters
August 3, 1993

The President. Thank you very much. Thank you. Ladies and gentlemen, when I took this office with a real determination to engage in what we've come to call reinventing Government around here, it was really encouraging to me to see that there were Members of the Congress who had been examining these questions for years and seriously trying to address them. I want to say a special word of thanks to Senator Glenn, in his absence, and to Senator Roth; to my friend Congressman Conyers and Congressman Clinger and the other Members who have worked so hard to try to put us on the road to seriously reexamining how this Government works. It is important to restore the confidence of the American people in their Government. It is important because, to the extent that our Government works with greater efficiency and effectiveness and less unnecessary cost, it will strengthen the American economy as well as the bonds of our citizenship.

This law holds a lot of promise to do both things. The legislation itself mainly involves the inner workings of Government, things that most people don't think about and maybe don't ever want to think about. It requires the formulation of strategic plans, of setting yearly goals and targets for every program, of measuring and reporting how well programs actually perform compared to the targets set for them, and more accountability for achieving results. But we should view this structure in much simpler terms, terms that every American should be able to identify with. The law simply requires that we chart a course for every endeavor that we take the people's money for, see how well we are progressing, tell the public how we are doing, stop the things that don't work, and never stop improving the things that we think are worth investing in.

Earlier this year I met with our staff to discuss this. The Vice President and I were both enthusiastic about this bill, and I am very, very pleased that it has passed so rapidly. I do want to point out that it is, as the Vice President said, an important first step in the efforts to reform the way the Federal Government operates and relates to the American people. It may seem amazing to say, but like many big organizations, ours is primarily dominated by considerations of input, how much money do you spend on a program, how many people do you have on the staff, what kind of regulations and rules are going to govern it, and much less by output, does this work, is it changing people's lives for the better, can we say after we take money and put it into a certain endeavor that it was worth actually having it away from the taxpayers, into this endeavor, and their lives are better? These may seem like simple questions, but for decades they haven't been answered in a very satisfactory way. We are determined to do that.

I think it's fair to say that most Americans will understand that no organization as large and complex as the National Government can be transformed overnight. I also want to say that a lot of the things that this Government does, it does pretty well, and there are a lot of dedicated employees out there who do their jobs well. But everyone who has ever spent any time looking at how we do things, how decisions are made, how they tend to pile one on top of the other, year-in and year-out, without ever being examined in total or in terms of their effect would say that this is an effort that is long, long overdue.

So I ask, as I sign this bill, for the support of the American people to continue the work of reinventing Government and for their careful attention to the report that the Vice President will present to me next month. I ask for the support of the Congress in being willing to reexamine all of our assumptions and to try to take a fresh look at the way we spend the people's money. And I ask for the support of the fine people who work for the Federal Government to try to find a new spirit of renewal and change that I think will make their jobs more satisfying, and I know will help to restore the credibility and confidence of the American people in the public enterprise.

Thank you very much.

[At this point, the President signed the bill.]

Income Tax Increases

Q. Mr. President, sir, on the subject on which you're not getting bipartisan support, on the budget, can you respond to Republican, very sharp Republican criticism of the retroactivity of the income tax increases?

The President. Well, as you know, we had supported moving it up for 6 months. But in the conference committee there was a very strong demand to do some other things that made it very difficult not to put it back retroactively, apparently. For example, the conference wanted to raise the income threshold to which Social Security recipients were subject to higher income taxes so that now no one on

Social Security, and I think it's about the bottom 90 percent, will not be subject to any higher taxes.

And the people that we have to get votes from asked for the following: They said, we want the economic incentives in, we want $495 billion of deficit reduction, and we don't want a higher energy tax number. And I think the conferees— I don't think any of them were very happy about that, but I think they thought that since that had been announced in January, or February, since a lot of people were already making adjustments on the basis of that, that that was a fairer way to do it than to run the risk of dropping below $490 billion in deficit reduction and, frankly, not being able to pass the program.

Q. Won't it be underwithheld, and won't it be a drag on the economy——

The President. It depends on what else we do. We think we have some options to offset it, but it is ironic that the same people who filibustered the jobs program earlier this year are worried about a drag on the economy. They had a chance to put a half a million Americans to work and turned away from it.

This money will be spent to reduce the deficit and to provide economic incentives to many of those same people who will provide the higher taxes. So I think that, on balance—I understand the decision the conferees made. I wish it hadn't been necessary. But part of it was just dictated by the size of the deficit reduction package we wanted and the low energy number. I think it is a good package; it's solid; it's clearly real numbers. It's very different from the 1990 package in many ways. So I feel quite good about it.

Bosnia

Q. Mr. President, what message is being sent to Bosnian Serbs and Muslims with this agreement that NATO has reached?

The President. The message is, first of all, that the allies are determined to protect the United Nations forces there, determined to secure the humanitarian relief program. And the other message is that we would very much— all of us—like to see a successful agreement and a fair peace agreement that can then be enforced. We'd like to see an end to the fighting. There should be an end to the shelling of Sarajevo, an end to the misery before we go through another winter with grave, grave difficulties ahead. And I hope the message will be there. I feel very good about what happened yesterday, and I appreciate the support of the allies for the United States position.

Q. How long do the Serbs have before air strikes would begin?

The President. Thank you very much.

Spending Cuts

Q. Did you notice they kept the honeybee subsidy, the one thing you had promised to get rid of?

The President. We'll eventually get it.

The Vice President. Phil Lader and I are going to get rid of that.

The President. Let me tell you, there will be many more budget cuts. This is the beginning, not the end. The House has already embarked on that course. There will be more.

NOTE: The President spoke at 9:43 a.m. in the Roosevelt Room at the White House. S. 20, approved August 3, was assigned Public Law No. 103–62.

The Office of the Press Secretary issued a statement on August 2 concerning the NATO decision on air strikes against the Bosnian Serbs, with the text of the NATO resolution attached.

Remarks With Supreme Court Associate-Justice-Designate Ruth Bader Ginsburg and an Exchange With Reporters
August 3, 1993

The President. Good afternoon. My fellow Americans, today we heard the sound of gridlock breaking in Washington, and I liked what I heard. Today the Senate passed our national service program, one of my top legislative priorities. Within months, thousands of young people will be at work in their communities helping our country and helping to pay for their own education. And middle class students everywhere will have an easier time affording college.

Also today, the Senate Judiciary Committee voted unanimously to confirm Judge Louis Freeh to be Director of the FBI. This support for a crime fighter of iron will and unshakable integrity affirms that he is clearly the right person for the job.

But I am most gratified today by the overwhelming vote in the United States Senate to confirm Judge Ruth Bader Ginsburg to be Associate Justice of the United States Supreme Court. Too often in the past, judicial nominations have prompted a partisan brawl and generated more heat than light. Today we've put aside partisanship, and the national interest won out.

I have no doubt that Ruth Ginsburg will be a great Justice. She has the opportunity to move the Court not left or right but forward. Her legal brilliance, wisdom, and deep devotion to justice has brought our Nation together around her nomination. When I announced her appoint-

ment, she spoke about her grandchildren. Someday, I believe my grandchildren will benefit from and learn from the contributions she is about to make.

We've done some good work today, but there's more to do. Tonight I will address the Nation about my plans to put our economic house in order. I hope that my remarks will be persuasive. But this afternoon, I just wanted to take a few moments to congratulate now Justice Ginsburg and to give her a chance just to say a sentence or two about this very important day in her life and the life of our Nation.

Judge Ginsburg. I am so glad to be part of what has been a very good day for the country. And last time I was here I don't think there was an opportunity for any questions. So if one of you has a question, I'll do my best to respond.

Q. Justice Ginsburg, what do you think that you'll bring to the Court that has not been present before in the Court? What insights, what experience, what background?

Judge Ginsburg. I think you must reserve judgment. I'll do the very best I can in this job, and then you can write a review of my performance in a year or so from now.

Q. You've been called a liberal; you've been called a conservative; you've been called a moderate. What are you?

Judge Ginsburg. I think you could report on

that, too. But I don't believe that every child that's born alive is either a little liberal or else a little conservative, except in Gilbert and Sullivan.

Q. But you're not a child.

Judge Ginsburg. That's every child that grows to become a woman or a man, yes.

Economic Program

Q. Mr. President, even though this is Justice Ginsburg's moment, could we ask you what you hope to accomplish with your speech tonight? What persuading do you need to do? What misperceptions perhaps are there?

The President. Well, I think there is still a continuing job to do to make sure the American people know again exactly what is in this program and why I think it is good for the country, and what it means in terms of our long-term economic health and well-being to regain control over our economic destiny; to keep interest rates down; to have these economic incentives to create jobs; to lift the working poor out of poverty; to enable us to move on to deal with health care, with welfare reform, with an important crime bill. All these things will help to strengthen our efforts at economic recovery. And therefore, this moment in this debate is very, very important because it's decisionmaking time, not delay time. And I hope that I can persuade the American people that that time has come.

Q. Mr. President, throughout the budget process, people have seemed to be able to roll you and get away scot-free. Senator Boren, the prime example, got you to back away from the broad-based energy tax and now says he won't support the deal. That begs the question, sir, how can you expect people to support a very— or take a very politically difficult vote when there doesn't seem to be any penalty for those who won't?

The President. How can you expect me to answer a question which is not credibly put? He had a veto on the Senate Finance Committee, didn't he, because the Republicans refused to engage in responsible budgetary discussions? So I didn't agree to do anything. He didn't roll anybody. He exercised his vote, and his vote was enough. And that's the way the legislative process works, near as I can tell, from the beginning of the country. Now, perhaps you know more than I do.

You know, I saw a lot of people talking about Lyndon Johnson. When Lyndon Johnson was the Senate majority leader, a Senator could not introduce a bill unless he signed off on it. Would you like to return to that system? Would the press favor that? That would give us a little more party discipline around here if no Republican or Democrat should introduce a bill unless they signed off on it. I've done the best I can. I think we've got a very good program.

Look at the principles that we've got. Look what we started with. We've got $500 billion in deficit reduction. We've got a very progressive tax program that asks, now, 80 percent of the money will come from people with incomes above $200,000. The middle class, that is, couples with incomes of under $180,000 down to $30,000, will be asked to pay this gas tax. It's about $33 a year. Families with under $30,000 of income will be held harmless.

We have the economic incentives that we have long asked for: for small business, over 90 percent of them getting a tax break; the working poor lifted out of poverty; new investments for children and for families. This is a very good program very much like what I recommended and very different from what we've been doing for the last 12 years. And if it passes, I will be very glad. And to do it with no help from the opposition party will be remarkable.

Q. Do you have the votes yet for this plan? And you've been waging this full-court press now for several weeks, and it doesn't seem to have persuaded any Senators to come to your side. Do——

The President. We'll wait—watch and see. See if we win.

Q. Why do you think you've had such a hard time persuading the Democrats in your own party?

The President. Well, I think for one thing, I think we've shown a lot more party cohesion than the Republicans have. You know, more Republicans voted against the House Republican budget than Democrats voted against mine. And last year, 75 percent of the Republicans voted against President Bush's budget. So I think we've done pretty well. And also they've had to do it against a withering barrage of misinformation from the Republicans, trying to convince people there were no budget cuts, no deficit reduction, all the taxes on the middle class, all things that were totally untrue that they just kept saying. I think that the Democrats that are with us have shown a remarkable amount of political courage.

It's hard to get people to be brave when they see for 12 years we took the debt from $1 to $4 trillion and reduced investment in our future. And people made those decisions and were rewarded by them by just always taking the easy way out. I'm not asking them to do something easy. I'm asking them to do something hard. And I'm proud of the ones that are doing it. And I think when they vote, there will be a majority. I feel very good about it.

Partisanship

Q. Mr. President, I don't want to detract from your beautiful day, but you said that partisanship had been set aside; but almost unprecedented is the way the Republican Party in both Houses has united against you on this bill. Do you think it's personal? Do you think that there is some— over and beyond the political implications?

The President. No, I think it's all politics. I think that the guiding spirit there is incredible partisanship. I think they think their job is to hurt the Democrats in Congress politically and hurt the President politically on this bill. I don't think it has anything to do with principle, and I don't think it's personal.

But I'll tell you this: I don't think it will happen again. I think if you look at Judge Ginsburg's vote; if you look at the national service vote and the fact that they didn't sustain the filibuster all the way through until we voted on the economic program; if you look at the genuine dialog that's occurred on health care; if you look at the bipartisanship we'll have on trade issues, on the crime bill, on welfare reform, and I think on future budgets; if we prove we can take the tough decisions now and we're rewarded for it by resuming control of our own destiny, I don't think we'll have this level of partisanship on any other issue.

Q. Why not?

The President. Because there will be no incentive for them to do it. The only way they can win with this strategy is if the Democrats don't adopt the program. Once this is done, all the rhetoric goes away and the reality takes place. People will see that the middle class are not burdened, that they're benefited by the program. They'll see that the wealthiest Americans who can afford to pay are carrying the lion's share. They'll see the spending cuts. They'll see the working poor rewarded. They will see the reality.

The only thing that benefits them now is delay and denial and more of what we've had for too long. And I think if we move tonight and move tomorrow and move the next day and move this week on this program, then we'll get this country back on a forward movement. The momentum will be there to face the health care crisis, to face the welfare crisis, to face these other problems. And I believe we will do it in a bipartisan manner. I'm very, very hopeful about it.

Thank you.

Address to the Nation

Q. So have you finished the speech already? Are you still writing or is it done?

The President. I'll fool with it some more, but I'm done.

Q. Is it a good speech, sir?

The President. I'll give the Judge Ginsburg answer: That's for you to determine. It's what I believe.

NOTE: The President spoke at 4:44 p.m. in the Rose Garden at the White House.

Statement on Senate Action Confirming Ruth Bader Ginsburg as a Supreme Court Associate Justice
August 3, 1993

I am extremely pleased at the swift and determined action by the U.S. Senate in overwhelmingly confirming Ruth Bader Ginsburg to the United States Supreme Court. I want to thank Chairman Biden, Senator Hatch, and their colleagues on the Judiciary Committee and the Senate as a whole for prompt consideration of her nomination.

As President, I am proud of having nominated such an outstanding jurist who demonstrated in the confirmation process tremendous intellect, integrity, comprehension of the law, and com-passion for the concerns of all Americans. I am confident that she will be an outstanding addition to the Court and will serve with distinction for many years.

Statement on Senate Action on National Service Legislation
August 3, 1993

I am extremely pleased by action taken today by the Senate in passing the National and Community Service Trust Act. I am also gratified that Republicans and Democrats were able to work together to turn this landmark legislation into reality.

National service will take on our Nation's most pressing unmet needs while empowering a new generation to serve as leaders of change. National service is about enhanced educational opportunity and rebuilding the American community. Most importantly, national service is about getting things done.

A number of Senators played crucial roles in helping pass this bill. In particular, I would like to thank Senator Kennedy for the leadership and dedication he has shown throughout this process. Thanks to the efforts of the Senate today and the House last week, young people will soon be serving their country in their communities here at home.

I've always said national service is the American way to change America. I commend the United States Congress for taking action that will prove that true.

Interview With the Nevada Media
August 3, 1993

The President. Thank you, Gary, and thank you, Paula. First of all, let me thank all of you for giving me a few moments of your time today in order that we might together communicate directly with the citizens of Nevada about a whole range of issues, but especially about the economic program that the United States Congress will be voting on in the next few days.

I've worked hard to put together a program that would achieve the very important principles I outlined when I became President. We want to reduce the deficit by $500 billion. We want to do it in a way that focuses on specific spending cuts, over 200 of them, and has at least as many cuts as new taxes. We want the new tax burden to be fair. And in this program, now over 80 percent of the burden will be borne by people with incomes above $200,000. The average cost for a middle class family with an income of about $60,000 a year will be $33 a year in the 4.3 percent fuel tax. Working families with incomes of under $30,000 will be held harmless. The fourth thing we want to do is to make sure that this program promotes jobs and growth. After all, that's the objective. If we pass the program, we'll keep interest rates down and that will make it possible for people to refinance their homes and businesses and invest at low interest rates for high growth.

We also have incentives in this program that I think are very important. Number one, over 90 percent of the small businesses in America will be eligible for tax reductions if they invest in their businesses and in new jobs and growth and opportunity. Number two, we support research and development. Number three, we support new firms, especially new high-tech firms, and their attempts to get new capital by giving a capital gains break of 50 percent for people who invest in these new and small firms for 5 years or more. And finally, this program lifts up work and family, supporting most importantly the working poor. For the first time ever if this program passes, through the tax system, people who work hard, have children in their homes, and are still below the poverty line will be lifted above poverty, not by a Government program but by reductions in the tax system. This is a program that will get America on the move.

Finally, I want to say that if we do what others ask and just delay, we might run the risk of what happened in 1990, fooling around for 3 months, wasting valuable time when we ought to be dealing with the health care crisis, with welfare reform, with a new crime bill, with urgent matters that will bring more jobs into this economy, and winding up with a program as in the 1990's that doesn't work. This is a good, fair bill. It will make a good difference to America. And I hope that the Senators and the Congressman from Nevada will support it. I hope, most importantly, that the people of Nevada will support it.

I'll be glad to answer your questions.

Economic Program

Q. Mr. President?

The President. Yes.

Q. Hi, Mr. President. Greetings from Nevada.

The President. Thank you.

Q. First of all, many Nevadans appear to be losing some trust in Washington. At the same time, too, Nevada has been a State that has created quite a few jobs over the past few years. But now you offer a budget package that seems to hurt our big business, in other words, tourism, with the gas hike. Why should Nevadans buy into this gas hike?

The President. Well, for several reasons. First of all, it is a modest one, and gasoline is at its lowest real price in 30 years. In other words, if you adjust for inflation, gas is cheaper now than it has been for 30 years. This fuel tax increase is quite modest and, for example, will be a much lower burden on fuel than the Btu tax which the House of Representative originally passed.

Secondly, there are offsetting benefits to the job-generating engine that Nevada has become. As I said, over 90 percent of the small businesses are eligible for an actual tax reduction. Bigger businesses will be able to get incentives to invest in new plant and equipment. There are all kinds of other things that really help the business community. That's why the Home Builders, the Realtor Association, the American Electronics Association, any number of business

groups have endorsed this program, because it will create jobs. And keeping interest rates down while there's so much building going on in Nevada is very important because you have to borrow money to finance construction. So that also will have a big boon to the Nevada economy. You will get a lot more out of it than the 4.3 cent gas tax will cost.

Q. Mr. President, we've been taking phone calls from our viewers for the past 24 hours, and the overwhelming percentage have been asking, why not cut spending more first before raising these taxes?

The President. Well, first of all, we do cut spending at the same time. There are $255 billion in spending cuts over a 5-year period and about $241 billion in taxes over a 5-year period. They are going into a trust fund so the money can't be spent on anything else. And if we miss the reduction targets, every year I will be bound by the system we're now following to come in and correct this. Secondly, there will be more spending cuts. We are going to have a report in September from the Vice President's Commission on Reinventing Government, which will recommend some substantial increases in spending cuts. And finally, as we deal with health care, we'll be able to deal with the exploding costs of entitlement spending on health care to our Federal budget. But the only fair way to do that is to provide health security and to reform the health care system. So I assure you, there will be more spending cuts coming up.

But let me finally say that no person who's studied this believes that we can bring this deficit down and eventually get it down to zero unless we also ask primarily those people who got most of the income gains in the 1980's, that is, the top 1½ percent of our income earners; they got most of the benefits of the eighties, and they got the tax cuts of the eighties. All we're trying to do here is to restore some fairness and ask those who can pay to do so. Together these things will make a balanced package. We can't get there with just spending cuts. If I were, for example, to take all the revenue increases out, just have the spending cuts, and wait for the others to trigger in, I believe what would happen is that you'd have a substantial increase in interest rates as all these people who thought we were serious about reducing the deficit will say, well, there they go again. So we are going to cut spending more and more and more, but we need the revenues, too.

Q. Mr. President, are you disappointed that a moderate Democrat like Dick Bryan is not supporting your budget? And what message does that send?

The President. Well, I'm always disappointed if we don't get 100 percent of the votes. But I think that Senator Bryan had some questions about the bill that was in the Senate last time that I hope that this conference report will answer. And let me just mention a few things that I think will make the bill more attractive to him, and I hope may still secure his vote.

For one thing, there are clearly more spending cuts and tax increases in this bill. For another, there is a provision in this bill that— it does something that many of the people in the hotel business, the restaurant business have wanted for some time, which gives them a credit against the Social Security taxes they have to pay on their waiters' tip income, which is an important thing that's been passed by the Congress before but never actually written into law because it was vetoed previously. Thirdly, the economic incentives that were in the House of Representatives bill that were not in the Senate bill have now been put back in, for research and development, for high-tech industry, new business capital gains. We almost double the expensing for 94 percent of the small businesses in America.

A lot of things that are in this final bill in much greater degree than they were in the bill that Senator Bryan voted against. So I'm hopeful that these things plus the fact that we are going to have this trust fund, which was not in the Senate bill, to guarantee that the money goes to deficit reduction, will be enough for him to say that the bill has improved to the point where he can join Senator Reid and Congressman Bilbray in supporting it.

Reaganomics

Q. Mr. President, can you respond to former President Reagan, who wrote in today's New York Times that he felt your budget plan was unwise and would plunge the economy into the deep doldrums?

The President. Sure. When President Reagan became President, we had a $1 trillion debt. We now have a $4 trillion debt. For the last 10 years under Presidents Reagan and Bush, we have pleaded with our allies to work with us to support a higher rate of growth to create more jobs in all the rich countries of the world,

and they have said publicly for 10 years the biggest problem is the American deficit: "You won't do anything to get your own house in order; don't tell us what to do." This year, the allies, Germany, Japan, all these other countries, for the first time in 10 years when I met with them complimented the United States for finally doing something about our deficit and said now we're going to be able to work together to grow the economy and create jobs.

And finally, we saw the end of Reaganomics in the last 3 or 4 years, where we had 4 years with only a million new jobs coming into the economy. And the record came in on the eighties, where 60 percent of the economic growth went to the top one percent of the people. And we didn't grow very many jobs compared to previous decades.

So my answer is that President Reagan's program, which was to cut taxes and increase spending and have a huge deficit and try to borrow and spend our way out of our economic problems worked pretty well in 1983 and 1984, but after that, it began to have serious problems. And for 6 or 7 years, it's now apparent that we can no longer borrow and spend our way to prosperity. We have to have some more discipline in our national life.

Taxes

Q. Good afternoon, Mr. President. You've said that your plan will create 8 million jobs, but half of the proposed deficit reduction package comes in the way of new taxes. How do you plan to reconcile those two, when history has proven that increased taxes does not create new jobs?

The President. I don't know that history has proven that. Under President Bush's administration, where he railed against taxes and finally signed a program in 1990 which was basically a middle class tax increase that had 2½ times the burden on the middle class that this program does, we didn't have new jobs. There were times in American history when we had much higher tax rates than we will have under this program, much, much higher, where we were creating any number of jobs.

I think what has killed this economy is that so much of our money is going to deficit financing that that has kept interest rates high. People have not been able to afford money to borrow and to invest, and we have seen ourselves losing control of our financial future. So I don't think all taxes are by definition bad for the economy. Do I think you can overtax the economy? Sure I do. But we still are going to have, on the whole, lower taxes than our major competitors and much lower taxes than we've had at times past when we created more jobs. I think we will lose more if we do nothing now and let this deficit get out of hand and run the interest rates back up. I think that will be much worse. If I didn't, I wouldn't recommend this.

Let me just make one point here by way of just kind of trying to establish my credibility on this issue. Before I became President, I was Governor of a State for 12 years where we never had to raise taxes to balance the books, where I routinely cut spending—I ran a tight balanced budget—and where, in every year I was Governor, our State was in the bottom five in the country in the percentage of our people's income taken up by State and local taxes. The only time we ever raised any new taxes was when we had heavy majority support for dedicated support for either schools or roads. That's it.

Now, what we're facing now in this country is a situation not of my own making. I wasn't in Washington the last 12 years, in either party, voting to run the debt from $1 trillion to $4 trillion. But I have to face the fact that that's where it is. And we're either going to do something to regain control of our own destiny, or we're going to let the economy continue to spin out of control and we'll be helpless to influence it. So it's just a question of whether we're going to do this for the long run or not.

And let me just make one final comment, because it relates to the last two questions. If you go back and look at Japan in the mid-1970's, they had a deficit about as big as ours now, a big part of their income. They decided they would balance their budget over a 10-year period. They brought it down with a disciplined balance of tax increases and spending cuts. It did not hurt their economy; it strengthened their economy. And I think if we take the long view, we will see we've got to get ourselves out of debt and invest in job growth and our future.

And keep in mind, most new businesses and most existing businesses can have their taxes reduced under this program. Only the top 4 or 5 percent of the businesses and the top 1½ percent to 2 percent of the income earners are going to pay any substantial income tax increases under this program. There are no income tax increases for businesses earning under $180,000 or for couples earning less than that.

Environmental and Economic Policy

Q. Good afternoon, Mr. President. Nevada poses some interesting possibilities here in terms of the jobs and growth that you've talked about. But there are also a number of environmental concerns. We have it at Yucca Mountain and also at the Nevada test site in nuclear terms. Then in northeast Nevada, there is a mine whose reopening has been delayed because of environmental concerns. What can Nevadans expect from the White House in terms of any overall policy whenever the environment clashes with the economy?

The President. You can expect an honest attempt to do what the Secretary of the Interior, Bruce Babbitt, and the EPA Director, Carol Browner, are doing all over the country, to try to do our best to reconcile the two in ways that are good for the economy, in that if the environment has to foreclose some economic activity, we believe the Federal Government has a responsibility to try to help open another avenue of activity.

You mentioned those three things, so let me run through them quickly. With regard to the magna site, I have asked the EPA to accelerate review of that. It's in an economically depressed area. If we can find a way to permit that in an environmentally responsible way, I think we ought to do it sooner rather than later. And if we can't do it, we ought to tell the people sooner rather than later. So I've asked the Government to expedite review of that.

With regard to the nuclear testing site, as you know, I have called upon the other nuclear powers of the world to observe a moratorium on nuclear testing. If that holds up, I think we have an obligation to work with you to try to find ways for the resources there and the people there to find other forms of economic activity. And with regard to Yucca Mountain, we've already ordered an independent financial management review. We're working on an independent management review. And the Governor and your congressional delegation have also talked to me very often about the question of the scientific basis on which Yucca Mountain was selected, and we have under review what we ought to do about that.

So I think we're on top of all three of those issues. And I believe ultimately, sound environmental policy is good for the economy, and I think we'll find a way to create more jobs than we lose out of it if we do it right.

Next question.

Nuclear Testing Sites

Q. Mr. President, you just mentioned the Nevada test site. And as you know, the Nevada congressional delegation has several suggestions for different types of activity that would go on there. There's 8,000 jobs at stake. They have all kinds of ideas, from solar energy research facility to plutonium storage. Could you be more specific about what plan you have for the test site?

The President. No, I can't, because I didn't know until just a few weeks ago, as you know, that we would not be resuming nuclear testing. I had not made a final decision on that, and I had not had a chance to consult with our allies.

I can tell you this—let me say this again as clearly as I can. I think that your congressional delegation and your Governor will come up with some very good ideas. I believe we have a strong obligation to work with them to develop alternative economic activities for the site. First of all, the United States has a great investment there. And secondly, we have an obligation to the people of Nevada.

And let me say, for 2 or 3 years now, long before I even started running for President, I was complaining that the Federal Government started cutting defense spending way back in 1987 with no plan for helping the people affected to convert and succeed in a domestic economy. We are now trying to deal with that and play catch up on defense cuts. I don't want the same thing to happen in Nevada at the nuclear testing sites. So I'll do what I can to help and to be there and work with your local leadership.

Next question.

Immigration

Q. Mr. President, I'd like to know a little bit about what you plan to do about illegal aliens coming into our country. There's been a big hue and cry about that nationwide, people settling into California, Arizona, and Nevada. It's becoming an increasing problem. I'd like to know if you have a plan for getting these people either legal or helping to keep them from our shores and our borders.

The President. I do, and about 10 days ago I announced a plan and presented it to the Senate. And I'm very proud of the fact that this is one of those issues where we haven't had any gridlock. The Senate passed a major part of our immigration reform bill, 87 to 13, just a couple of days ago.

Let me tell you essentially what we're dealing with. Basically, there are three substantial alien problems. There is the problem of access to our country by terrorists or potential terrorists or people who will work with terrorists. And we have enacted some reforms to change the way we exercise security at airports here in the United States and security at other airports.

Secondly, there's the problem of all these people being smuggled in in, in effect, slave boats, all the folks coming in from China, for example. We have a plan designed to deal with that now and to impose a much stiffer penalty on those who do that kind of thing and also to process those people much more quickly than they have been in the past.

Then the third problem is just the problem of large numbers of illegal aliens coming. The big States that receive them now are California, Texas, and Florida, but many, many other States also have a large number of illegal aliens. We're going to have 600 more border patrol operations, faster review, and expedited review and return of people that we find who are illegal. We will observe their constitutional rights. We will be as precise and fair as we can, but we're going to expedite the review.

I support legal immigration. I think immigrants have made an enormous contribution to this country and have made us a stronger nation and a much better prepared nation to face the 21st century because we have so many different racial and ethnic groups in America. But you can only keep America safe for legal immigration if you do something firmer than we've been doing for years on illegal immigration. So that is the basic outline of the plan. We're proceeding with vigor to implement it. And we're looking at what other options we have to do more.

Yes, sir.

Economic Program

Q. Mr. President, if I might, sir, I'd like to revisit a question or perhaps broaden the scope a bit of a question a moment ago. You hold the distinction, sir, of being the first Democratic candidate to run for President who won the

State of Nevada in 28 years. That said, why then do you deserve the continued support of Nevadans when your budget package adversely affects tourism here by increasing fuel taxes, asking more money for resort companies, the engine of job growth here, and lowering deductions for meal expenses?

The President. Because Nevada will also benefit from this. Every small business in your State has a chance to lower its tax burden by investing more in its business. Every person who wants to invest in a new business in Nevada capitalized at $50 million or less has a chance to cut their tax burden by 50 percent by investing for 5 years in such a business. There are all kinds of incentives to grow jobs in Nevada. And the most important thing is all Americans benefit when we reduce this deficit and keep our interest rates down.

If you look at what has happened to long-term interest rates since I've proposed the deficit reduction plan and it started making its way through Congress and since Alan Greenspan, the head of the Federal Reserve Board and a Republican, consistently said that this is what we need to do more than anything else to get control of our deficit. The cost of borrowing to all those Nevada businesses you just mentioned are going—by and large, for any of them that have to borrow any substantial amount of money or who can go out and refinance their business debt, they will save much more than they will be hurt by the extra burdens imposed by the changes here. So there are national interests at stake which will benefit people in Nevada, and there are specific things which will benefit people in Nevada. We have to decide—if we're going to do something about this deficit, we're all going to have to contribute.

You know, I come from a State which has the highest, or second or third highest amount of gasoline usage per vehicle in the United States of America. But the fact remains that gasoline is at its lowest price in 30 years and that the average person's annual bill is going to be around $35 for this. And I don't think that's going to keep anybody from coming to Nevada to vacation.

Single Parent Families

Q. We took calls this morning from our audience to find out what to ask you, and we had so many different calls about, "Hey, ask him to come and play his saxophone for us in Las Vegas, the entertainment capital of the world." But——

The President. I'd love to do that.

Q. ——on a more serious note, we did get a lot of calls from single parents that wanted to know what your economic plan will do to help reward them; say, they are raising a child, a full time job, and you alluded to that earlier in the opening. Could you be more specific on this topic, please?

The President. Sure, very specific.

If I might, I'd like to answer that question, but I'd like to also say one other point in response to the young man who asked the previous question about the fuel tax. I believe that most people or at least a huge percentage of people who come to Nevada to vacation or to convention, fly there. And one of the things that Congress and the administration were very concerned about was the impact of this on an already troubled airline industry, on whether that would lead to big increases in fares, which really might have had an adverse impact on you. And as a result of that, relief was granted from airline fuel from this tax. So I think that was a big concession that I think will be very helpful to you and will avoid any adverse damage.

Now, to go back to the other question, most working parents, single parents who work and have children in the home, have family incomes of under $30,000, all of them will be held harmless from the impact of the fuel tax by an offset in their income tax. Those who are at or near the poverty line may actually get a refund on their income tax to make sure that they will be lifted above the poverty line if they're working 40 hours a week and they have children in the home.

Interestingly enough, this expansion of the earned-income tax credit, which has received relatively little attention, is probably the most significant social reform that is pro-family and pro-work that the Congress has enacted in 20 years, because it will say to people like the very person you're talking to: We know you're out there working hard. We know you don't need any more taxes. We know you're doing everything you can to support your children. And because of the way the income tax system will be changed, if you're making a pretty good income, that is, let's say $29,000, $28,000, $27,000, something like that, you'll be held harmless from this. We'll give you an income tax offset for the gas tax increase. But if you make lower wages and if you're down around the poverty line, we will give you a tax refund so you can be lifted above the poverty line and support your children in dignity. Now, this will really help us to encourage people to move off welfare and into work.

One of the next things that I want to take up, along with health care, when this is over, is a fundamental reform of the welfare system that will literally end welfare as we know it. In order to do that, you've got to take all the incentives out of welfare and put them into work and enable people to be successful parents and successful workers. So this is a very, very important part of this provision. And that's one reason I would hope all the single parents in America will support it. Almost all of them will benefit from it.

Administration Accomplishments

Q. Mr. President, this will be the last question. I know we're supposed to be Mike Wallace here and ask you all these important questions. But it's been a pretty rough first 6 months for you. Is it what you expected, and are you having fun?

The President. I am having a great deal of fun. I'm excited by this job. I knew it would be rough if we came in and tried to change a bunch of things at once, because it's easier if you don't try to do much and you just kind of take it easy; then you can make sure you don't have so much rough sledding.

But I feel good about it. I mean, today my appointee to the Supreme Court, Ruth Bader Ginsburg, was confirmed by a 96-to-3 vote in the Senate. I think she will be an historically important Justice. Today the United States Senate on a bipartisan basis adopted one of the heart-and-soul ideas from my 1992 campaign,

the national service bill, which will enable hundreds of thousands of our young people, as we get it up and going, to earn credit against their college costs by doing service for their communities, enable people at the grassroots level in Nevada, for example, to work with their friends and neighbors to solve problems and earn credit against college while doing it. I am very excited about that. We passed the family leave law, which becomes effective this week, which protects the right of people to go home if their child is sick or their parents are ill without losing their jobs. We've gotten an awful lot done.

So I think we're moving in the right direction. And we've got a health care bill, a crime bill, and a welfare reform bill ready to go when we get the budget out of the way. So change is always hard, but I am very excited about it, and I am having a good time. And believe it or not—Governor Miller will be glad to know this—I'm trying to find a way to play golf once a week, in spite of all this work I'm doing. And most weeks I get it done. And maybe I can come out there and enjoy some of your courses once I get a little of this work out of the way.

Q. We have some great courses. Thank you, Mr. President. I've always wanted to say that.

The President. Thank you.

Q. Thank you, Mr. President, for spending this half hour with us. I think this is the best kind of television there is, and we get a little longer than the sound bite that we're used to.

NOTE: The interview began at 5:09 p.m. The President spoke via satellite from Room 459 of the Old Executive Office Building. In his remarks, he referred to Nevada journalists Gary Wadell and Paula Francis.

Address to the Nation on the Economic Program
August 3, 1993

Good evening. Tonight I want to report to you on the progress we've made and to ask for your help on our Nation's most urgent priority, reviving the American dream by restoring the American economy.

It's been at least 30 years since a President has asked Americans to take personal respon-

sibility for our country's future. It's been 25 years since our Government had a balanced budget. For at least 20 years, middle class incomes have been nearly stagnant, with too many Americans working nights, weekends, and holidays just to make ends meet. For at least 10 years costs in our health care system have exploded while millions of Americans go to bed each night worrying that if they lose their jobs or their children get sick, their health insurance will be taken away. And for the last several years our economy has failed to generate jobs, good jobs that pay enough to own a home, buy a car, pay the bills, educate your children, and retire with dignity.

For too long, our Government has failed to tackle these problems. We've been given the politics of entitlement, Government handouts without asking anything in return. And we've been given the politics of abandonment, cutting taxes on the well-off and asking nothing of them in return either, while raising taxes on the middle class to pay more for the same Government, instead of investing in our jobs and our future. The results: fewer jobs, stagnant incomes, a massive debt for ourselves and our children, higher cost and greater insecurity in health care, and a host of problems simply neglected.

Well, tonight we're on the verge of breaking out of that old false choice between tax-and-spend and trickle-down, between abandonment and entitlement; on the verge of a new way of doing things grounded in our most enduring values, a philosophy that says America owes all of us an opportunity if we'll assume responsibility for ourselves, our communities, and our country. No more something for nothing. We're all in this together.

This means we must make Government work for the people who pay the bills. All of us have been awed in the last few weeks by the vast power of the Mississippi River breaking its banks and the devastation that has followed. But we've also been awed by the courage of the flood victims and the compassion of other Americans who've joined them in fighting back the waters and trying to restore normal life. I'm especially proud that this time the Federal Government has been fighting alongside the people.

That is what we must do on all fronts. We must do more, much more, to turn this country around. And now we have the chance to change. We're on the eve of historic action. This week, Congress will cast a crucial vote on my plan for economic recovery. In a comprehensive economic plan, there are always places for give and take, but from the first day to this day, I have stood firm on certain ideas and ideals that are at the heart of this plan.

Tonight I can report to you that every one of those principles is contained in the final version of the plan: first, the largest deficit reduction in history, nearly $500 billion, with more spending cuts than tax increases. Rather than the games and gimmicks of the past, this plan has 200 specific spending cuts, and it reduces Government spending by more than $250 billion. We cut more than 100,000 positions from the Federal payroll by attrition. We freeze discretionary spending for 5 years. We limit pay increases for Federal employees.

Why must we take extraordinary action now? Well, this chart shows you why. America faces a choice. We can continue on the path of higher deficits and lower growth, or we can make a fundamental change to improve our Nation's economy by adopting my economic plan.

Now, it won't be easy, and it won't be quick. But it is necessary. Without deficit reduction, we can't have sustained economic growth. Economists and business leaders alike warn us that growth will falter if we don't take dramatic steps to tame this deficit, and soon. With so much at stake it would be irresponsible not to take decisive action. With this plan in place, the economy will grow, and more than 8 million new jobs will be created in the next 4 years. Without it, we put the economy and our standard of living at further risk. If we take this important first step now, over the long run we will see deficits go down and jobs go up.

The second principle of this plan is fairness. Those who have the most contribute the most. As this chart shows, we asked the well-off to pay their fair share, requiring that at least 80 percent of the new tax burden fall on those making more than $200,000 a year and very little on any other Americans, not to punish the successful but simply to ask something of the very people whose incomes went up most and whose taxes went down during the 1980's. For working families making less than $180,000 a year, there will be no income tax increase. I repeat: For working families making less than $180,000 a year, there will be no income tax increase.

The third principle is that we must protect older Americans from punitive cuts in Social Security, Medicare, and veterans benefits that some have proposed. While all Americans must do their part, I will not balance the budget on the backs of older Americans while protecting the wealthy. Every alternative offered by the opponents of change begins with deep cuts in the health care of older Americans. I believe we must build a better future for our children without sacrificing the security of their grandparents. We can control health care costs, but only by reforming the health care system, not simply by hurting the elderly.

The fourth principle is that we must keep faith with the hard-working middle class families who are the heart and strength of our Nation. We've worked hard in this plan to ensure the lowest possible tax on the middle class. The plan asks an average working family to pay no more than $3 a month in new taxes, less than a dime a day, with a 4.3-cent-a-gallon increase in a gas tax. This is the only new tax working people will pay.

Let me be plain about where the deficit reduction comes from. Look at this chart: Out of every $10 in deficit reduction, $5 and actually a little more comes from spending cuts, $4 comes from taxes on incomes of those with more than $200,000 a year in income, and just $1 comes from everyone else. This plan is fair. It's balanced. And it will work.

Finally, we must have an economy that creates jobs and lifts up the American people. In the past, deficit reduction efforts have failed because they neglected incentives for business growth and investments to make Americans smarter and stronger and safer. This plan is very different. It generates jobs. In fact, over 90 percent of the small businesses in this whole country are eligible for tax reductions, tax cuts, if they invest in their future and create new jobs.

If you have the courage to invest in a new business and the vision to hold that investment for 5 years, this plan will cut your capital gains tax in half. If your business invests in research and development, this plan will reward you. If your small business creates new jobs and buys new equipment, this plan will provide incentives for growth by nearly doubling the expensing provision for new investments.

While we make deep cuts in spending, we also make room for some needed investments. Our plan invests in people and makes special investments in our children and in our families through Head Start, nutrition for pregnant mothers, and immunizations for poor children. These things pay for themselves in healthy, growing, strong children.

We will revolutionize the student loan program so that all Americans can better afford to finance a college education. And we make

bold changes in worker training so that high school graduates can get high-skilled, high-wage jobs.

Perhaps most important, this plan rewards work over welfare by lifting out of poverty every parent with children at home who chooses full-time work over lifetime welfare. We do this through the earned-income tax credit, which reduces taxes for 20 million working families and households earning less than $27,000 a year. It does this without creating a new Government bureaucracy and simply using the Tax Code.

This sends an enormously powerful message to the people who struggle against great odds to raise themselves and their families. It empowers them. It says we're on the side of people who work and care about their children. It's pro-work. It's pro-family. And it is a critical first step to one of my most important priorities, ending welfare as we know it.

Every element of this plan is a departure from business as usual. And if there's anything our country needs, it's to put business as usual out of business. I know full well that Americans are very skeptical of any claim by the Government. You must wonder if these cuts are for real and whether the taxes will really be used to pay down the deficit. Well, our plan is fundamentally different from business as usual. Here's why:

First, the plan is based on conservative estimates of future revenues. It presents, line by line, year by year, specific cuts in Government spending. And it offers new incentives so we can expand the economy and generate jobs. It minimizes the burden on the middle class and asks the wealthy to pay their fair share. And finally, it puts into place two clear safeguards to keep a watchful eye on future Federal spending while protecting the savings produced by this plan.

All the money we save will be locked away in a deficit reduction trust fund so the savings will not be spent on politicians' pet projects. Because some in the Senate have used technicalities to block Senator DeConcini's amendment to create the deficit reduction trust fund and frustrated the efforts of many other Senators and a clear majority of the House of Representatives who support it and who support controls on annual spending and entitlement programs, I will sign Executive orders tomorrow putting both these safeguards in place so that you know the money must be spent on deficit reduction. And if we miss our deficit reduction targets over the next 5 years, I will be obliged to present a plan to correct the course to make sure we keep doing what we're telling you we're going to do. Now, this is a new direction.

This plan has been carefully examined by the most conservative and skeptical critics of all, those who run our Nation's financial markets. They've studied the plan and determined that over the long term, paying down the deficit will be good for the country. And as we have made progress in enacting this plan, the markets have lowered interest rates. Lower interest rates, in turn, make it easier to own a home, finance a business, buy a car, pay off credit cards, and borrow for college. For example, if you are a middle class family with a $100,000 mortgage at 10 percent interest, you should be able to refinance the mortgage today down to 7.5 percent and save $175 a month right away, as millions of Americans have already done.

The chief executive officers of 80 of our country's most successful companies, Republicans and Democrats alike, have also supported this plan. So do many small business organizations, from the National Small Business United and the National Association of the Self-Employed to the National Venture Capital Association. The men and women whose business it is to create jobs and growth have been solid in their support of this historic endeavor.

At this exceptional moment of promise, why are so many in Washington so reluctant to take action? Why is it so hard for so many in this city to break the bad habits of the past and take the steps we all know we have to take? For 5 months our critics had the chance to offer alternatives, and all the major plans came up with the same thing: less deficit reduction or more paying for older Americans or both, protections for the wealthy from paying their fair share of the taxes, and no new incentives for business to create jobs or investments in the American people. And every one of these alternatives was soundly rejected in the Congress. Now there are only two choices, our plan or no plan.

Our opponents want to bring the plan down. The guardians of gridlock will do anything to preserve the status quo, to serve special interests, and to drag this thing out. They practice partisanship when we need progress. They call for delay when we've been waiting for 12 years and working on this project for months. They

talk and talk about what to do, instead of doing what must be done.

When I was the Governor of Arkansas, our State had one of the lowest tax burdens in the country. I inherited this big Federal deficit just like you did. And I don't like taxes any more than you do, but our Nation is in economic danger, and now we've got to take this problem we inherited, you and I, and do something about it. We have to take responsibility for change. Passing this plan will be a bold step and the first step on a longer journey toward giving our Nation a comprehensive national economic strategy.

This economic strategy begins with putting our house in order, but it cannot end there. We must also have the courage to reform our health care system, so never again will a family be denied health care or a business be bankrupted by health care costs.

Let me show you this first chart one more time. If you look at this deficit, under our plan we can bring the debt down solidly for 5 years. If you want the deficit to go down to zero, as I think almost all of you do, we have got to challenge the health care system. It is bankrupting the private sector, bankrupting the public sector, and millions of Americans live in insecurity and constant fear of losing their health care. So dealing with health care is good for the economy, good for bringing the deficit down further, and good for the American people.

We also have to end welfare as we know it. We can move millions of idle Americans off the welfare rolls and on to the work rolls if we'll change the system. And we've got to revolutionize Government itself, cleaning out waste, corruption, bringing state-of-the-art management that will give more saving to the taxpayers, have Government work better, and put it back in charge of the people who are paying the bill. And we must continue to work to open foreign markets to create American jobs.

All of these things come together to form an economic strategy that will give opportunity to every American and ask responsibility from every American. But we can't take any of the steps if we don't take the first step.

That's why the decision Congress must make this week is so terribly important. We cannot afford not to act. I need your help. I need for you to tell the people's representatives to get on with the people's business. Tell them to change the direction of the economy and do it now, so that we can start growing again, producing jobs again, and moving our country forward again.

In the last 6 months, we've won some important battles here: a new family and medical leave law just taking effect that allows young parents to take time off to care for a new baby or a sick child or an ill parent without losing their jobs; a new national service corps that will help tens of thousands of our young people to pay for college through service to their country in their communities; a new Supreme Court Justice confirmed just today without partisanship or rancor; new policies to develop high-technology jobs and to convert defense facilities and plants to productive civilian purposes, expanding jobs and opportunity. And, from a summit in Vancouver, Canada, to help save Russian democracy, to a summit in Tokyo to help revive the world economy, there are now new opportunities for Americans and a new respect for America's leadership.

We Americans are a people both privileged and challenged. We were formed in turbulent times, and we stand now at the beginning of a new time, the dawn of a new era. Our deeds and decisions can lift America up so that in our third century we will continue to be the youngest and most optimistic of nations, a people on the march once again, strong and unafraid. If we are bold in our hopes, if we meet our great responsibilities, we will give the country we love the best years it has ever known.

Good night, and may God bless you all on this journey.

NOTE: The President spoke at 8 p.m. from the Oval Office at the White House. The Executive orders of August 4 on budget control and the deficit reduction fund are listed in Appendix D at the end of this volume.

Statement on an Agreement on Pacific Northwest Timber Sales
August 3, 1993

We are committed to working to enhance the long-term economic and environmental health of the region. That commitment means a responsible forest management plan and a responsible but determined effort to get timber moving back into the mills. We have offered an innovative, comprehensive, and balanced plan to solve a difficult set of problems. Now we are taking steps to implement that plan and get timber to the mills.

NOTE: The President's statement was included in a White House statement announcing the agreement.

Nomination for Posts at the Department of Health and Human Services
August 3, 1993

The President announced his intention today to nominate Texas Woman's University president Shirley Chater to be the Commissioner of Social Security and Nobel laureate Harold Varmus to be the Director of the National Institutes of Health at the Department of Health and Human Services.

"It gives me great pleasure to announce these nominations today," said the President. "Shirley Chater is an accomplished administrator with a strong background in health care issues. I am convinced that she will do an outstanding job of running this enormous and enormously important Agency. Likewise, as one of the world's leading medical researchers, Harold Varmus will bring great strength and leadership to the National Institutes of Health."

NOTE: Biographies of the nominees were made available by the Office of the Press Secretary.

Remarks and an Exchange With Reporters on the Economic Program
August 4, 1993

The President. Thank you very much. Let me just briefly say I had the opportunity to meet with the House caucus today. We have been informed that several Members who voted no when the bill came up the first time for different reasons had decided to vote yes on the bill this time. Some of them are here with us today, and others are not. It was a very good meeting.

I told them that for the last couple of months, and even last night in speaking to the American people, I felt much as I did when I was a young man in school and I belonged to all these little clubs who would try to earn money for club events by washing cars. I felt like a lot of what I was doing was trying to clean dirt off of windshields so that the American people could see out of the windshield again. There has been so much misinformation put out about this plan, about who bears the burden of it and whether it reduces the deficit, exactly how it's going to be done, that a lot of what we have been doing in the last 6 weeks or so was just trying to get the facts out. All the evidence is that the more facts we get out, the better we do. And so I am encouraged on what has happened in the last few days. I'm very hopeful.

The fact remains that every other plan which has been raised has gotten more opposition and less support than the administration's plan. Every other one had less fairness and/or less deficit reduction. And now the choice is whether we're going to do this, or do nothing and flail around for another 60 to 90 days.

I think it is clear that the Congress will vote to act and to move forward and to make this enormous downpayment on solving the deficit problem and giving some incentives to the economy to grow. I'm very hopeful about it, very optimistic today. And I want to thank the Speaker and the leadership and the members of the House caucus for hearing me today.

Mr. Speaker, you may want to say another word or two before we take questions. But this was a very, very good meeting this morning.

[*At this point, House Speaker Thomas S. Foley made brief remarks.*]

Q. Mr. President, what would you say to those economists who say that this deal had been so diluted with compromises and deals that it would be ineffective?

The President. I don't believe any economists are saying that. My response is, look what happened to interest rates after the speech last night and then after the progress we were making yesterday. I mean, the interest rates once again were lowered in anticipation of the plan's successful passage.

The economic incentives that were in the House bill are in the final conference for job growth. They have been slightly scaled back because we reduced the tax burden by over $40 billion in reducing the energy tax. And that's another that some of the economists said that we ought to do.

So I think that you've got the same deficit reduction. You've got the economic growth incentives. You have real fairness in the Tax Code, and you made 90 percent of the small businesses in this country eligible for a whole wide range of tax reductions if they invest in their businesses. So I think it's a good plan, and I think that they're wrong.

Q. You're not concerned about the number of deals that have been cut to get this through?

The President. No, absolutely not. Since when has a big piece of legislation like this ever moved through the Congress unamended? I mean, give me one example of that. Most things of this magnitude, when you turn the country around, take years to get done. We put it together in just a few months.

I think that the things that I cared about are there. The plan has $500 billion in deficit reductions. There are now more spending cuts than taxes. The tax system is very fair, indeed, more progressive than it was when I presented it. Now 80 percent of the burden falls on couples with incomes above $200,000. There are enormous incentives in here for business growth which were not in any of the Republicans' plans—a new business capital gains tax; there are research and development incentives; we nearly double the expensing for small businesses in this country. Then finally, the thing which I think will really have a huge difference in terms of our society: The earned-income tax credit lifts working families out of poverty. It's a huge incentive to leave welfare and go to work. So the big guts of the things that I proposed way back in February have survived this whole legislative process. And I feel good about it.

Q. Mr. President, you've apparently padded the margin here on the House side. But obviously the really, really close vote is going to come on the other end of this building. What are your feelings at this point? Does it still come down to that one vote over there? Is there any other outlook for you at this point?

The President. I think it depends upon, obviously, what happens in the next couple of days. I think if we carry the House, I think we'll carry in the Senate. I don't think the Senate will let this plan go down. I don't think they will do that to the country.

There are two groups of Senators that basically are either declared against or leaning against, some who have said forthrightly to me, "This is the right thing for the country, but there's been so much misinformation about it, people will never know the real truth, and I will never recover politically if I vote for it, even though it's good," and others who say that "This is a very good first step, but it doesn't do everything that needs to be done. Therefore, I won't vote for it."

And my argument to the second group is going to be that this bill cannot possibly be expected to carry the burden of solving all the problems of the last 12 years; that we do have to control entitlement spending; we do have to control health care spending. I will be for such controls in the context of reforming the health care system, and I still think we've got a shot to get a lot of those.

Also, the spending reductions, for those who say there ought to be more spending cuts, I remind them that the House of Representatives has already adopted over $10 billion in spending cuts in excess of those in a reconciliation bill which the Senate will have a chance to adopt. The Vice President's report on reinventing Government is coming up, and the health care debate is coming up. There will be further spending reductions by this Congress and this administration.

So I'm going to keep making that argument to them, and I think we'll prevail.

Q. What's it going to take for you to get in the Senate the security that you apparently now feel in the House?

The President. I don't know if that will ever happen. [*Laughter*] We need the votes to win over there, and as I said, I believe that the Senate will pass the plan if the House does. I think that there clearly is a majority in the Senate who know that this is far better than the alternative—there is no other available alternative—and that the worst thing this country could do would just be to flail around for 60 to 90 days, instead of moving on with all the things that are there before us: the health care issue, further efforts to deal with the budgetary problem.

Helen Thomas. Mr. President, did you hear Senator Dole's rebuttal, and what did you think of it?

The President. My response to Senator Dole's rebuttal is to wish you a happy birthday. [*Laughter*]

Ms. Thomas. Oh, no. [*Applause*] Thank you.

The President. I would like to respond to a couple of those things. First of all, Senator Dole says too many of our budget cuts are in the latter half of our plan. My response to that is he has a higher percentage of his budget cuts in the last 2 years than we do. That is a smokescreen to continue the intransigent Republican position that we should not ask the wealthiest Americans to pay their fair share of the burden, even though they got the tax cuts in the eighties and received well over half the economic gains of the eighties.

Secondly, my response to Senator Dole's claim that this bill imposes burdens on people who are no longer living—you heard all that— that implies that somehow the Democrats are voting to raise the estate taxes on people who have—estate taxes are not imposed on people who have no estate, that is, who have not yet died. But that is totally misleading. All the Congress did was to extend the estate tax rates imposed back in the late eighties. And I haven't checked this this morning, but I believe Senator Dole voted for that. I believe that this bill extends the estate tax rates that Senator Dole voted for. I believe that. In any case, the Congress voted for it. He knows that this bill does not somehow increase taxes on citizens after they die. That is totally misleading.

Let me see what else he said. Oh, he said we didn't cut the deficit enough. My answer to that is we don't cut it all the way to zero, but we will. And we cut the deficit much more than the Dole plan did, and we do it specifically.

We have a lot more deficit reduction than he did, and in his plan he had $66 billion in, quote, unspecified cuts. He wouldn't even say where the tough cuts were coming from.

Q. Retroactivity is what he——

The President. Well, the retroactivity, my answer to that is twofold. Number one, on the merits, it applies to the same couples with incomes above $200,000, individuals with incomes above $150,000 to $160,000; that they will be given 3 years without penalty, a subsequent 3 years to pay the taxes; that all the tax cuts are retroactive and some of the tax incentives go back to the middle of 1992, not just to the first of '93.

So those would be my answers to the attacks he made on the program.

NOTE: The President spoke at 10:07 a.m. in Statuary Hall at the Capitol. A tape was not available for verification of the content of these remarks.

Remarks to the National Urban League
August 4, 1993

Thank you very much. Reg Brock, John Jacob, distinguished dais guests, and ladies and gentlemen. It was just about a year ago that we were together at the Urban League convention in San Diego. What a difference a year makes.

Many of you in this audience have been friends of mine for a very long time. Those of you from my home State of Arkansas have worked with me in partnership there for many years. I know what the Urban League can do to make a difference in the lives of people and in the minds and hearts of people.

I want to say at the outset today that while I came here to talk about what we're trying to do in Washington, what we can do in Washington is in no small measure determined by what lives in the hearts and minds and visions of Americans throughout this land. I know that the Urban League, for more years than I have by far, has struggled to remind Americans that, without regard to our race or creed or station in life, we must go forward together; that there is no place for hatred or division.

And yet we know today that we are challenged by that on every hand. When people would bomb the NAACP headquarters in Tacoma or in Sacramento, when people would threaten your own John Mack in Los Angeles, when people would seek again to divide us by race instead of to take the hard and difficult path of making the changes we all need to make together as a country, we need the Urban League. America needs it. The President, the Congress, the politicians alone cannot do nearly as much as you can do to reach to the truth of the human heart and stand up against bigotry. But there are things that we can do. I know the Attorney General appeared before you in this conference, along with at least four other members of my Cabinet. No wonder I couldn't find any of them this week. They were over here. [*Laughter*]

But I tell you, one of the reasons that we picked Judge Louis Freeh from New York to head the FBI is that he was not only committed to continuing the long overdue work of opening the FBI to women and minorities but also because he had successfully, heroically, and determinedly prosecuted the criminals who murdered a Federal judge and a civil rights leader in the South when others had given up and thought it could not be done.

I am especially in debt to the Urban League because the Urban League not only gave to the Nation such great leaders as Whitney Young, but you gave to me a lifelong friendship and the service in this administration of Vernon Jordan and Ron Brown. I would have never met either one of them if it hadn't been for the Urban League.

I also want to say to all of you that it is terribly important as we seek to bring America together that we continue our struggle to remind the doubters and the naysayers that we can go forward together.

There was an especially reassuring article, at least to me, in the Washington Post a few days ago by the distinguished columnist William Raspberry in which he pointed out that when I said I wanted a Cabinet that looked like America, I was subject to ridicule in many quarters who claimed that I was about to diminish the quality of the Government by imposing some sort of quota system on the Cabinet. Well, it turned out that I produced a Cabinet with more women and more minorities than had ever served in a President's Cabinet. And most people think it's one of the best Cabinets that ever served the United States of America.

And as Mr. Raspberry pointed out, when Janet Reno speaks as Attorney General now, people don't think of her as the first woman Attorney General. When Mike Espy's out there up to his ears in mud in the middle of the Mississippi River Valley flooding, and people are saying we've got the best response to a national emergency they've ever seen, nobody says he's the first black Secretary of Agriculture; he's somebody out there helping the farmers to put their lives back together.

In the last 6 months, a great deal has happened in this town. The pace of change has been dizzying. And with all change, there has been strong opposition, and it's been a little ragged around the edges from time to time. But let me ask you this: If on Inauguration Day someone had told you that this administration, with the most diverse Cabinet in history, would work with the Congress and with our allies in the country and around the world to produce the Family and Medical Leave Act, twice vetoed by the previous administration, which became effective this week, to guarantee that working people can take a little time off when a baby's born, a child's sick, or a parent's ill, won't lose their jobs; would produce the motor voter bill, which is a significant advance in voting rights for the young, the poor, and the dispossessed; would produce a bill with the National Institutes of Health which would take the politics out of medical research and finally do what ought to be done in medical research with regard to women and their health care problems; would produce a dramatic change in environmental policy which would be applauded all around the world for putting the United States back in the forefront of energy conservation, of responsible efforts to deal with the population explosion, of all kinds of efforts to reconcile the conflicts between the environment and the economy; if someone had told you that we would take the lead in trying to keep democracy alive in Russia in ways that would be good for ordinary Americans by continuing to reduce

the threat that nuclear weapons will ever be used and by opening up future markets there; that the United States would be able to go to a meeting of the great industrial nations of the world in Tokyo and for the first time in a decade not be attacked because we are a drag on world growth because of our deficit, and instead, we would be complimented and they would agree with us to lower tariffs on goods in a way that every American analyst concedes will add hundreds of thousands of jobs, good, high-paying manufacturing jobs, to the world economy if we can get all the other nations to agree with it; and that in the middle of this budget debate we would pass the program for national service which will give Americans a chance to bridge the gaps of race and income and earn credit against their college education by dealing with the human problems of Americans at the grassroots level—I'd say that's a pretty good record for 6 months, and I think the American people ought to be proud of it.

But let me say to you that there is much, much more to be done. And whether we can get about the business of doing it will be determined in the next 48 hours or 72 hours or so by how the Congress of the United States responds to the challenge presented by the economic plan.

I thank the Urban League for its early endorsement and support of this plan, and I would remind you here briefly why you did it, what is in it, how it makes a difference to ordinary Americans. Remember that for 20 years now, literally 20 years in 1993, most working Americans have seen the power of their incomes eroded. Wages for wage earners have been virtually stagnant for 20 years as the cost of health care, housing, and education has exploded.

In 1980, we had a Presidential election which said that this problem that the American people were having paying their bills and dealing with global economic forces was a problem of too much Government in America and what we needed to do was to cut taxes, get Government out of the way, and everything would be wonderful. What that rhetoric masked was an old-fashioned attempt to cut taxes and increase spending, except it was done in a different way. We cut taxes on the wealthiest Americans, increased primarily defense spending, and got out of the way.

And for a couple of years it worked. We had a couple of years in which jobs came into the economy because we were spending a lot more than we were taking in and putting a lot of people to work in defense industries. But after that, the patterns imposed on the United States by the realities of the global economy returned with a vengeance and were made worse by the decisions made in the early eighties where we cut taxes on the wealthy, ran the deficit up.

What happened later? When the Congress and the President started going back at it, we had a decade in which taxes were cut on the wealthy, and the top one percent got more than half of the income gains on the 1980's. Taxes were raised on the middle class whose incomes were going down. We reduced our investment in our children, their education, our economy, and our future. We cut defense spending without reinvesting in California, Connecticut, Massachusetts, and the other States that were hurt. And all of the money went to pay more for the same health care, to pay more interest on the massive debt, and to deal with the fact that we were creating a whole new class of poor people. It reached the point that by 1992, 1 in 10 Americans was on food stamps.

So I say to you, that path didn't work very well. We now have evidence that it didn't work. In the last 4 years, only a million new jobs came into the economy. We are 3.5 million jobs behind where we would have been in a normal economic recovery.

And so I presented a plan to the Congress— and I have asked them to adopt it, and I asked the American people to support it last night— which brings down the deficit by $500 billion over the next 5 years. Why should liberals be for that? Why should people in urban constituencies be for that? I'll tell you why. Because as long as that deficit keeps getting bigger, we'll spend more and more of your tax money, hardworking middle class people's tax money, paying bond payments to wealthy bond holders instead of investing in reinvigorating the American economy. Interest rates will go back up, and we won't be able to provide the things that people need.

If we pay the deficit down—look what happened again yesterday: It looks like we're going to pass the plan; the interest rates dropped to an all-time low. I'm telling you, folks, we need to have a consensus in America without regard to race or political philosophy that we have to gain control over our economic destiny again and stop being paralyzed. If we don't do something about this, within 5 years we'll be spending all of our money paying more for the same health care and interest on the debt. And there will be nothing to grow America and grow our people and bring us together. That is the first issue.

The second thing is that this plan is fair. This plan is fair: Eighty percent of the new revenues will come from people with incomes above $200,000—80 percent, 80 percent; no income tax increases on couples with incomes below $200,000, actually $180,000 in adjusted gross income. The 4.3-cent gas tax that is in this plan amounts to about $35 per year for a family of four with an income of $50,000. Working families with incomes of under $30,000 are held harmless. This is a fair plan. In 1990 when there was virtually no burden on the wealthiest Americans in the budget plan, the burden on the middle class was 2½ times as great as this.

The third point I want to make is, unlike 1990 and unlike the other plans which have been offered to the Congress this year, this plan has real incentives for economic growth that will affect a lot of you in this room. Every small business in America will be eligible to increase their expensing provision by almost double. What does that mean in plain terms? It means that over 90 percent of the small businesses in this country are going to get a tax cut out of this bill if they reinvest more money in their business. Now, that's something the Republicans haven't told you in the last few weeks: Over 90 percent will get a tax cut.

For those of you who live in California and are worried about the economy out there, this plan increases the incentives for companies out there to invest in research and experimentation. That's where a lot of it is going on. That will create more jobs. For those of you who live in Michigan, Ohio, other States with heavy industry, this plan gives those big companies some relief from the minimum tax provisions if, but only if, they invest in new plant, new equipment, and they do things that will make them more competitive and able to hire more people and create new jobs.

This plan gives a sweeping new investment incentive for people with the courage to invest in new and small businesses. It says if you do it and hold the investment for 5 years, you get a 50 percent cut in the tax you'd otherwise have to pay to get people into that. This plan will grow the economy.

Finally, let me say this plan is fair to people who deserve our support. There is some more money in this plan for Head Start, to help pregnant mothers, to start people off well, to invest in the apprenticeship training of our young people, to help to pay for national service, and for more access to college education. And the most important thing of all, which has received very little attention until the last few days, this plan arguably has the most important piece of social reform in the last 20 years because it puts $21 billion into the earned-income tax credit program, which means we can say to the working poor, if you have children in your house and you work 40 hours a week, you will be lifted out of poverty. We are tired of seeing people work their heads off and work their fingers to the bone and be in poverty.

That is something that every conservative in this country who's talked about how bad the welfare system is for years ought to embrace with tears of joy. Think about it. For the first time in the history of the country we can say, "If you go out and work hard and play by the rules and you're still living in poverty"—and almost one in five, 18 percent of the workers in this country work for a wage that will not support a family of four above the poverty line— this says "the tax system, not a Government bureaucracy, not a program, the tax system will lift you out. You will be rewarded for your work."

That is a dramatic advance. It will change the lives of millions of Americans who are out there just killing themselves to raise their kids and to obey the law and to do what is right. And that, too, is in this program.

But when they say, our opponents, "This thing doesn't do anything for jobs. It doesn't do anything to cut the deficit. It taxes the middle class, not any different from what we've done before," it is just not so. And I ask you in these closing hours, if you have a Senator or a Representative who is potentially a vote for this, call them and tell them you'll be with them.

I've spent a lot of time talking to the Members of Congress. I hear two arguments from people who say they may not or they won't vote for the program. Argument number one is a terrible indictment of democracy, but a lot of them have said it: "This is a good program; it's good for America; it's good for my district,

but our people don't believe it. So much misinformation has been put out. They don't believe there's any deficit reduction. They don't believe there's any spending cuts. They believe the middle class is paying the taxes. They don't think there's any incentives for growth. And we'll never convince them of that. So even though it's good for America, I can't vote for it because my people are not capable of hearing the truth." I think that is wrong.

As soon as this bill passes, we will clear away the murky fog of misinformation and reality will take over. And we've been doing a better job of that in the last month. But you need to give courage to those people.

There are others who say, quite rightly, that "This bill doesn't solve every problem America has, and therefore, I won't vote for it." Well, we'll never vote for any bill if that's the test.

It is true, this bill brings the deficit down for 5 years, and then it will start going up again unless we do something about health care costs. But the time to do that is when we reform the health care system and provide affordable health care to all Americans and control health care costs in the private sector as well as the public sector. It is not fair to say we're going to control health care costs and doing it by slashing Medicare benefits to middle class elderly people or by simply shifting the costs onto the private sectors.

Now, I want to say this again. This is something we all have a common interest in. We do spend too much on health care. We spend it in the private sector and in the public sector. We spend over 14 percent of our income on health care. Only Canada, of all the other countries in the world, spends as much as 9 percent of their income on health care. Everybody else is less. And we spend it partly because the whole system costs too much to administer— it is a bureaucratic nightmare—and because we are the only advanced country that doesn't provide some quality coverage to all of our citizens and security of people so that they'll have health care coverage even if they lose their jobs or if they move jobs or if somebody in their family has been sick before. We have to deal with this.

But if we did what these folks are saying and tried to solve the health care problem now by slashing what we spend on Medicare and Medicaid without reforming the system, you know what would happen? We'd either hurt the middle class elderly or the poor, or we'd keep on doing what's been done in this country now for about 15 years: We'd be sending the bill to the private sector. All of you who are in the private sector—most of you are paying health insurance premiums that cost too much already. If we just cut what the Government pays, you'll pay more.

So I say to those people who say we have to do something about these entitlement programs and health care, you are right. Let's do it right. Let's not use that as an excuse not to move forward with this program. There's too much good in it.

Finally, let me say we have a lot more to do. We have to move on to health care. We have to move on to welfare reform. We have to move on to the crime bill, which will do a great deal to help us to put more police officers on the street in community policing settings where we will be working with people in the community to make them safer and to prevent crime from occurring in the first place. We need to pass the Brady bill. We have fooled around with this too long. It is time to pass it.

I had a heartbreaking conversation over the weekend with a friend of mine who is a Member of Congress who had a friend whose son was shot in one of these blind, mad encounters between children over the weekend, where four young boys got in a fight with four others, and they didn't know the other guys had guns. And finally they just took out the guns and started shooting them. This is crazy. This is crazy.

Our television news is filled at night with horrible incidents of violence in Bosnia and other places in the world that break our heart. Twenty-four people were killed in this town, our Nation's Capital, in one week last month. We have to get on with that.

You had Hugh McColl here the other day, my friend Hugh McColl, one of the most enlightened bankers in America, a supporter of our community development banking proposal. We've got to prove we can bring free enterprise and investment back to distressed urban and rural areas in this country. That is out there waiting for action. None of this stuff is going to be addressed until we get this budget economic plan passed and get it behind us and move forward.

The Vice President is going to present a stim-

ulating plan to reorganize the Federal Government in ways that serve you better at the grassroots level and still save the taxpayers money. We are not done with trying to control the budget. But we cannot move forward unless we act on this now.

And so I say to you, my fellow Americans, we have tried delay, denial, gridlock. We've had all this tough talk and easy action. I've been criticized in some quarters for not talking tough enough. My theory is if you do the tough things, your actions can speak louder than your words. We've had too many words that didn't mean a thing in this town for too long.

So I ask you as Americans to continue your support of these endeavors. I ask you for your partnership for the future. Let's make the national service program work and make it an instrument of healing and unity and real problemsolving, just what the Urban League has always been about. Let's prove we can deal with the health care issue in America, that we don't have to be the only advanced country in the world that can't seem to find a way to either control health care costs or provide security to our families. Let's prove that we can bring our deficit down and grow our economy.

In short, let us prove that together we will assume more responsibility, create more opportunity, and come together again in this great American community. I am tired of hearing about all the things we cannot do. I am tired of hearing about cynicism and skepticism being the excuse for inaction and paralysis. This is a very great country. And when you travel abroad and you see the problems that these other nations are having and you see all these other rich countries with higher unemployment than we have, you know that there is nothing before us that we cannot deal with if we simply have the vision and the will to do it.

We are being given a chance now to demonstrate that vision and that will. It is consistent with everything the Urban League has ever stood for or done. I ask for your prayers, your support, and your memory that—President Kennedy once said it better than I ever could, "Here on Earth, God's work must truly be our own." Our work is before us. I'm trying to do my part. I hope you will do yours.

Thank you, and God bless you all.

NOTE: The President spoke at 10:48 a.m. at the Washington Convention Center. In his remarks, he referred to Reginald K. Brock, Jr., chairman and chief executive officer, Time, Inc.; John Jacob, president and chief executive officer, National Urban League, Inc.; and John W. Mack, president, Los Angeles Urban League.

Remarks on Signing the Executive Orders on Budget Control and the Deficit Reduction Fund and an Exchange With Reporters
August 4, 1993

The President. Before I sign these orders, I'd like to make a brief statement, if I might. Nothing has done more to erode the confidence of the American people in our Government than our chronic failure to manage our finances and to stabilize the economy so that it can create jobs. Year after year, the public has been told that sustained economic growth and deficit reduction would come from actions taken here. And as deficits have grown larger and incomes have shrunk, the people have become more and more skeptical, even cynical, about everything that is said and done here even with the best of intentions.

We have a budget deficit, we have an investment deficit, and we clearly have a trust deficit in America. I am determined to do something about all three. I know the American people are doubtful about any claim by our Government, and I know they wonder if the cuts that we are proposing are real and if the taxes will really be used to pay down the deficit. That's why I want to go the extra mile to ensure that this plan is fundamentally different from what has been done in the past.

This plan is based on conservative revenue estimates of future revenues, with year-by-year, line-by-line specific spending cuts; new incentives to expand the private sector's contribution to economic growth; minimizes the burdens on the middle class; and now creates two safeguards to keep a watchful eye on future spending, especially in entitlements, while protecting the savings produced by the plan.

We owe the Executive orders I am about to sign to the hard work of the Members of Congress who are here today. The House included both provisions in its version of the reconciliation bill. The Senate would have done the same with similar amendments supported by Senator DeConcini, Senator Feingold, recommended publicly by Senator Bradley and others, but for the procedural maneuvering by people who feed the public cynicism by talking about deficit reduction on the one hand and nonetheless have prepared to block action for these needed reforms on the other. The fact that the Senate rules required these Executive orders today, that we could not do it by statute, is something that should be debated at a later time. But I want to make it clear that the Senators who are here and others strongly support what is being done.

These orders are almost completely identical to the provisions adopted by the House and approved by a majority in the Senate. The deficit reduction order creates a deficit reduction trust fund, an account in the Treasury that guarantees that the savings from the reconciliation bill are dedicated exclusively to reducing the deficit. This locks in deficit reduction and mandates all members of the executive branch to follow these procedures.

The entitlement and review order requires that entitlement spending be limited to the estimated levels included in the reconciliation bill. If those levels are exceeded, I will present recommendations to Congress on corrective action. No longer can we permit entitlement spending to soar out of control without some concrete action being taken to restrain it.

These Executive orders are the product of years of hard work by the men and women represented here today. I am grateful to them for their inspiration and their tenacity in getting this work done.

As important as this plan is for reducing the budget and investment deficits, these Executive orders deal also with the trust deficit. They are the assurance to the American people that our good words about deficit reduction and economic growth will be matched by good works as well.

[*At this point, the President signed the Executive orders. Senator Dennis DeConcini then made brief remarks.*]

Economic Program

Q. Mr. President, what have you offered him to—[*inaudible*]

The President. Good Government. [*Laughter*]

Q. Can you have the—will you have the vote without him?

The President. I guess I ought to say one other thing about this. I still think these things should be adopted in the law. And I would be prepared to support, as quickly as we can get it up and voted on, a separate piece of legislation to do these things. And I do want to emphasize that.

These Executive orders are identical, virtually identical, word for word, for what the Congress, the majority in the Congress, wanted. They clearly bind the executive branch just as much as an act of Congress. But I think it would be better, from the point of view of the public trust and also more binding on Congress, if we can pass a separate piece of legislation.

So I do want to make it clear that while I support these ideas strongly and I will faithfully adhere to them in the Executive order, I have also told the Members of Congress who care about this that I am prepared to strongly support a separate legislation to achieve these objectives in the law. And I'd like to see it brought up just as quickly as we can after the August recess is over.

Thank you.

Q. Mr. President, did you know it before now that Senator DeConcini had not made up his mind yet?

The President. Senator DeConcini and I agreed that this press conference would be about this, and not——

NOTE: The President spoke at 12:39 p.m. in the Oval Office at the White House. The Executive orders are listed in Appendix D at the end of this volume.

Interview With the Louisiana Media
August 4, 1993

Economic Program

Q. Do you have a commitment from Bob Kerrey, or did DeConcini do it for you?

The President. I think I should always let the Senators speak for themselves. I've always believed that if the program passed in the House, it would pass in the Senate. I don't think they will let it go down.

If you listen to the criticisms of—for the people who are voting no, they all basically say, at least in private what they say, they say one of two things: They either say that this is a good program; it's serious deficit reduction; it's progressive; it has incentives for growth and new jobs; 90 percent of the small businesses in the country get a tax break if they invest in their businesses; the working poor are lifted out of poverty. That affects 390,000 taxpayers in Louisiana, working families. But they say that the adversaries have put so much bad news on the people and they've convinced so many people that it doesn't reduce the deficit, it doesn't cut spending, and it taxes the middle class, that we can't ever fix it. So it's just bad politics even though it's good for the country.

The other argument is that it doesn't solve every problem. We still have to control health care costs. We still have to deal with that to bring the deficit down to zero. That is true, but you can't do that in this bill. You have to reorganize and reform the health care system to do that. You've got a classic example with Charity Hospital or with any of your health care providers that get Medicare funds. If we did what some of our critics say here and we just slash Medicare, put a cap on it without reforming the underlying health care system, one of two things would happen: We would either really hurt middle class Medicare recipients plus the hospitals and other providers of Medicare, or those providers would take the shortfall and pass it on to your employers so that everybody who has private health insurance would pay more.

So I think most people know this is a good program. It's good for the country, and I think it'll pass.

Q. So that means that DeConcini did lock it up for you, then?

The President. I believe it will pass. I'm not going to—all the Senators will have to speak for themselves. I believe if the House passes it, the Senate will pass it, I believe. But we haven't passed the House yet. That's tomorrow's test.

Q. We've heard all day about how good this plan is for Louisiana. Yet, many Louisiana Democrats, two in the House, maybe three, and of course Senator Johnston, plan to vote against it. Disappointed, considering that——

The President. Sure, I'm disappointed, But you know, they took a terrible licking on all the sort of negative attacks on the plan early on. Senator Johnston told me, he said, "I know there are a lot of good things in this plan, but the people of Louisiana don't know it. And I don't think they will know it."

I don't know how in the world we could ever make any decisions in this country if we made decisions on that basis. But you know, the truth is that 15,000 Louisianians, according to our research, will pay the higher income tax rates, and 390,000 Louisianians will benefit from the earned-income tax credit reductions for the working poor, and over 90 percent of the small businesses will be eligible for substantial tax reductions if they invest in their businesses. I mean, those are the facts. And the average family of four with an income of $50,000 will pay $35 a year under this program, and all the money goes to reduce the deficit. And there are now more spending cuts than tax increases in the deficit.

All I can do is take the people who have not declared and keep hammering home the facts. And I hope we will get those—but a lot of your House Members said the same thing to me. They said they were just afraid that the public had been so misinformed that it would never get all straightened out. My argument is that it will get straightened out if it passes, because once the bill passes, reality takes over and the rhetoric shrinks. I mean, either you are affected by it, or you aren't. You know how it works, or it doesn't.

Q. Mr. President, what about Congressman——

The President. No, go ahead. I've got to give

other questions.

Q. How do you expect the Congressmen to go along with the spending cuts in the long run? I mean, if they vote tomorrow yes, they're voting for, what, $255 billion——

The President. Billion dollars, that's right.

Q. ——in tax cuts. I mean, down the road, you know—I mean, we've seen this happen before.

The President. Well, I want to make two points about it and what's different about it this time.

The first point is that today I issued an Executive order which is legally binding on my Government, which requires all the tax increases and all the spending cuts to be spent on deficit reduction for the 5-year life of the budget. And that has the force of law. So if any of our people divert from that, they are breaking the law.

The second thing is that if we miss the target in any given year, because it's impossible for any of us to calculate to the dollar what's going to happen to our enterprises for 5 years, any year we miss it I have to come back in with a plan to fix it.

In addition to that, I told the House Members today that we were going to try to pass these requirements as a separate piece of legislation in September, and I feel confident we will. The Republicans essentially—we could have put it on the budget, but the Republicans in the Senate threatened to filibuster it if we did. I don't know why, because they were for it, I thought.

Now, the other point I want to make about the spending cuts: There are three other opportunities we're going to have to cut spending to continue to drive the deficit down. Opportunity number one is in the health care debate. If we reform the health care system properly, over this decade we will spend less money on Medicare and Medicaid than we otherwise would. But if we do it right, then we'll be saving money for the private sector as well as the public sector. For example, we spend about 10 cents on the dollar in administering the health care system, because of all the various insurance and governmental regulations that no other country spends. We can do better. We can cut health care spending.

Second, the Vice President has a reinventing Government report coming to me next month which will recommend a substantial amount of reorganization of the Government to eliminate both waste and corruption, that will bring us new savings. The Government is just like any other big company. It needs to go through a period of restructuring now. But this Government has not fundamentally been reexamined since Herbert Hoover's civil service report in the late fifties. So there will be more cuts coming there.

The third thing I want to say, because I know there's a lot of skepticism about the Congress that you should know, that Congress will have further opportunities between now and September 30th to cut spending in the regular appropriations process. In other words, what this bill says is they have to cut at least this much spending, at least $255 billion. That's what this bill does. But they can cut more. The House of Representatives has already approved more than $10 billion in spending cuts over and above what we require and sent it on to the Senate. And I've been working for the last 2 days on trying to organize a Senate-House effort to continue to cut spending when this is over. So, we're just getting started. This is the first step, not the end of this road.

Q. Congressman Stenholm announced that he would not vote for the plan. Mr. McLarty said don't cut him out yet. He may be—put him in a middle column. My first question is, are you going to try to attempt to persuade Mr. Stenholm to join the yes voters? And the second question is, do you think Mr. Stenholm can pull away enough conservative Democrats who were perhaps going to vote for the plan if Stenholm did, so they could say, "A good conservative Democrat like Stenholm voted yes, so I can, too"—do you think he can pull away enough that will threaten passage in the House?

The President. I don't think he can. I think he could, but I don't think he will. That is, I think he is in a very unique position. I like and admire him very much. He was very disappointed when the parliamentary maneuvers by the opposition party in the Senate made it impossible for us to put these budget control mechanisms on the final bill. But he came over today to the White House when I issued the Executive orders, and he said he would do everything he could to pass it.

He made a statement that he's sort of stuck with now. And I think it's a statement that he thought was responsive to his constituents. He said, "Look, I voted for the Btu tax, and I'm from Texas, but it raised $70 billion. If you're

going to have this gas tax, which only raises $23 billion, that's the only thing the Republicans can claim we're doing to the middle class. Why don't we just get rid of it?"

The problem is with getting rid of it is that we also have a whole lot of Democrats who will only vote for deficit reduction if it's the biggest package in history and if it's over $495 billion. They want it to be real deficit reduction. And we couldn't ever get a majority way to make up that $23 billion to get rid of the fuel tax. So I think Stenholm has taken some public positions which narrow his options. And he knows that several people who voted no before have declared yes today. We had three of them in a press conference today, including Charlie Wilson from Texas. But there are at least two others from Texas who are changing from no to yes.

So I believe we'll have enough to pass it in the House. But I will say again to you, to respond to your question, the key in my judgment is the House. I do not believe the Senate will let the bill fail and let the whole thing come apart if the House passes it. But we've got to keep our focus on first things first.

Q. How disappointed are you that all 215 members of the GOP delegation in Congress are united against your plan?

The President. Oh, I'm terribly disappointed. Let me give you an example. There are 20 to 30 Republicans in sort of a moderate caucus in the House who told me in the beginning that they didn't mind voting for taxes on upper income Americans, that their problem was the Btu tax and the Social Security tax, you know, extending the income tax to some Social Security income.

So we took the Btu tax out, and now Social Security tax only affects the upper 10 percent of Social Security recipients who have a net worth, average net worth in excess of $1 million, and who will still get what they put into the Social Security system plus interest back without taxation. So I wish they would come with us, because I know that there are Republicans who want to vote for this.

I have talked to Republicans in the Senate who tell me they think that this is a good plan and better than the alternatives anyway. And I regret it. But, you know, the leadership basically has said they were all going to go on strike, and that's what they've done.

But let me say this. I think if we pass this

plan tomorrow and the next day, I do not believe this will ever happen again, because then the dynamics of every other debate favor broadening the base of the country and the party. If you look at health care, the crime bill, the welfare reform bill, the trade issues, there will be supporters and perhaps opponents in both parties on all issues. We will really be able to have a more bipartisan coalition. And every budget issue we have to deal with in the future that I can foresee will be nontax spending control issues. And they won't have the maneuverability, I don't think, to control all those Republicans. I think you'll see more of what we saw in the national service bill, which Senator Breaux and I worked very hard on, where we did get Republicans who broke the filibuster in the Senate, got a big Republican vote in the House, and a nice group of Republicans supporting us in the Senate. I think you'll see more of that.

Q. Mr. President, tell me—people that we see in our polls just don't believe that higher taxes and Government cutting is going to help them. I mean, that's what the polls show, and obviously you're trying to change that. Can you tell people in Shreveport, Louisiana, and Hope, Arkansas, and Longview how directly their lives will be better next year than they are right now because of this?

The President. Yes, and I can tell you three or four specific reasons. Number one, if we bring down this deficit, we will be able to keep these interests rates down at historically low levels. Interest rates started to drop from the minute we announced this program. And every time we've made progress on it, they dropped some more. And every time there was some rumor that we were going to lose control of it, interest rates spiked up a little bit.

If you have low interest rates stable for a couple of years, what happens is people refinance all this huge debt from the eighties, their home loans, their business loans. That lowers their cost of carrying that debt, puts money directly in their pocket. And if they know it's going to be stable, then they turn around and reinvest it. So there are already millions of Americans who have refinanced their home loans because of these low interest rates that the deficit fight has brought about. If we can keep it back down for a year, then a lot of that money will be reinvested. So they will benefit directly if they refinance their homes or their

business loans or take out a lower loan for consumer credit or college or a car or if they reinvest it.

The second thing is that, I will say again, 90 percent of the small business people in this country are eligible—which is probably more than 90 percent in Arkansas and Louisiana— are eligible for significant and retroactive tax reductions if they invest in their business. We almost doubled the expensing provision for small businesses. That means that over 90 percent will have a net tax cut if they reinvest.

We increase incentives for people to invest in new businesses and small businesses. If you hold the investment for 5 years, you cut your income tax rate by half. And the smaller businesses, the newer ones, are the ones that are creating the jobs. So that will directly affect them.

Then, the last thing I want to say is that over a quarter of the working families of Louisiana will be eligible for relief under the earned-income tax credit, because they earn less than $30,000 a year. And working families with children with earnings of less than $30,000 a year will be held harmless from the gas tax through income tax cuts. And if they're much lower than that, they'll actually get a tax break out of it.

So there will be more cash in Louisiana, in Shreveport and more economic incentives to invest in the economy. And a lower deficit helps everybody.

Otherwise, let me say what happens if we don't do this. If we don't do it, this deficit will move up toward $500 billion and $600 million a year, and every year more and more of our tax money will go to pay interest on the debt instead of to invest in education and other things.

The other thing this plan does, I think it's worth pointing out, that's very helpful to Louisiana and Arkansas is it invests more money in Head Start; in early childhood health programs, which are real problems in our two States; in job training programs; in defense conversion programs for people who have been hurt by military cutbacks to train them for new jobs and to help communities adjust; and in making college more available to young people. So those are the specific ways that people will be benefited by it.

Q. Certainly, Mr. President, there's an antitax sentiment out there. The Btu tax was scrapped. Now we have a 4.3-cent gas tax. Why should

Louisianians feel good about that?

The President. They shouldn't necessarily feel good about that; they should think it's a price worth paying to get the deficit down and to get these incentives for the economy to grow. If you look at it, gasoline in real dollar terms—that is, adjusted for inflation—is at its lowest price in 30 years. So this is the least burdensome time to put this on. Let me compare it. If you compare the tax burden imposed on the middle class in the 1990 tax bill and this one, that bill imposed a burden 2½ times greater than this one. So we tried to minimize the burden on the middle class, hold working families with incomes under $30,000, which is a big percentage of Louisiana and Arkansas, harmless from the tax increase and asked the people in the upper 1½ percent, people with incomes above $200,000, to pay 80 percent of the taxes, because they got a majority of the income gains of the 1980's; literally the top 1 percent got over 60 percent of the income gains and got a tax cut.

So I think this is a fair program. The main thing is, we're going to lock all this money up and put it to bringing the debt down. And we all win if that happens.

Q. Mr. President, why are so many of your spending cuts postponed for 4 or 5 years? And will they really ever take place?

The President. Oh, yes. They're legally bound to take place. But let me say this in response to what Senator Dole said last night. You ought to go study the program he presented the Senate. A higher percentage of his cuts occur in the last 2 years than mine. The reason for that is that these cuts tend to be cumulative. That is, if you start right now and you want to shave a program—let me give you a program that I tried to shave that we are going to cut, the subsidy for people who grow wool and mohair, you know? The wool and mohair subsidy is $600 million. It's money that can't be justified. It goes back to the Korean war. Because the people that represent those farmers didn't want to eliminate it altogether, we're phasing that in. If you cut farm subsidies, which we're doing, it's fairer to phase that in. You want to give people time to prepare for that.

The other reason, frankly, is that we have already gotten for next year and the year after in our budget virtually flat spending from this year. So if you want to go from flat spending to big cuts, you've got to give people time to adjust to that. But these cuts are absolutely real, and they have to be put in.

The only thing that could derail this budget is if there's a big recession and the revenues don't come in or we don't with discipline, deal with the health care issue, which I intend to do.

Deficit Reduction

Q. You said the debt would be going down just a second ago. But isn't it true it will actually be going up but at a slower rate?

The President. No, the deficit, the annual deficit will go down. But since there will be a deficit, the national debt will go up but at a much lower rate.

What we need to do is to work toward bringing the deficit down to zero. If you look at my little chart that I was showing last night, what it shows—and by the way, all charts show this. Anybody else's chart would show the same thing, the other plans would show the same thing. You can bring this deficit down substantially in 5 years, but because of the exploding cost of Medicare and Medicaid and because health care spending is going up at twice the rate of inflation or more, after 5 years that becomes such a big percentage of the budget, unless you control that, the deficit starts to go up again.

If you want to bring it down to zero, what we have to do is to make sure we reform the health care system and do it in a way that by the time this budget ends it cycle in the 5th year, you start having health care costs go down. And believe me, health care costs—in this budget, what that means is health care would go up at the inflation rate plus population. Or in other words, if we could take it up to 6 percent a year instead of 9 percent a year, we could bring the deficit down to zero in about 9 years.

And let me say, that would be a very good thing. You can contract the economy too much. Let me just say there are a lot of economists who say, not conservative economists but traditional progressive economists, who say in all periods of slow growth you should cut taxes and increase spending. The problem is our debt is so big we can't do that, that's crazy. So how can we reduce the deficit and grow the economy? By keeping the interest rates down and having people refinance. But you can't do it too fast.

So if you go back and look, we're about where

Japan was in 1975. They were in the same fix we're in now. They had a deficit that was about the same percentage of their income. And they said, "We're going to bring this thing down to zero. We're going to do it in 10 years." And 10 years later they did it. And now they've run a balanced budget or had a small surplus for the last 5 years as a result of that, even though their economy is growing slower than ours. They have more flexibility to deal with their system than we do. So we've got to do this. And I feel very good about it. I think it's going to work. But we've just got to realize we didn't get into this fix overnight; we're not going to get out of it overnight.

Let me just close with this. There are two issues here. One is, what's the condition of the economy and what caused it? The second is, what's the proper response from Government? The economic problems we face have been developing over a 20-year period. Average workers' wages in this country peaked in 1973, if you adjust for inflation. Since '73 more than half of the American people have been working harder for the same or lower wages, while they paid more for health care, housing, and education. That's because of all these changes in the global economy. That's run through Republicans and Democrats. That's a fact of this age and time.

The Reagan response, which was continued by President Bush, was cut taxes, tilted heavily to the wealthiest Americans on the theory that they would reinvest it, and spend more money on defense because that will balloon the high-tech economy at home. What happened was, when we had to start bringing down defense at the end of the cold war, by that time health care costs were going up faster than defense was going down. We had to keep spending money on the same health care and interest on the debt. And because they were unwilling to cut other spending or to ask the wealthiest Americans who got the big tax cuts in the eighties to just restore some—we don't even restore all of it. Tax rates are still going to be lower than they were in 1980 before this happened. Because we were unwilling to do that, we had this big imbalance.

So what I'm trying to do is to say—I'm not blaming anybody for the larger economic things. These are 20 years in the making. We can turn it around, but we have to have a different response. We have to change from trickle-down economics to an invest-and-grow economics. And that means bringing the deficit down and targeting investments for business, because that's what we're trying to do.

Public Works Projects

Q. One last question, Mr. President. I cover Eldorado and Monroe, and you've inflated a lot of people's appetites with all the talk of the interstate coming through there, I–69. Eldorado doesn't have one. Northeast Louisiana would like to get more than its share because it's through Senator Johnston's wording in the bill— the proposal's going through Shreveport. What assurances can you give us in northeast Louisiana and southern Arkansas that we get a fair share of the public works project?

The President. Well, the Congress, of course, will ultimately approve the route. But I can tell you that basically if you look at my record at home, I've always supported those things. And that's one way that we're going to keep jobs and incomes up in this country. We're going to have to continue to invest—that's a Government program, if you will, that in my judgment is not waste. We have to continue to invest in these things. And I will do what I can to see that we keep the investments on schedule. Especially because of where I'm from, I can't be in the position myself of picking the routes. But I think the Congress will do that, and it looks to me like you're in pretty good shape on that score.

Deficit Reduction

Q. Mr. President, an old friend of yours and a man who many Louisianians admire very much said today at noon, I heard him: "His deficit reduction plan just won't work," unquote, Buddy Roemer. What can we take back—*[laughter]*.

The President. Spoken like a good Republican. Let me say, I believe first of all that what the Republicans have done, they ran this Government for 12 years. We went from a $1 trillion to a $4 trillion deficit. Now, the Democratic Congress has voted for that, but you need to know that under both the Reagan and Bush administration Congress actually appropriated a little bit less money than the Presidents asked for.

My answer to you, sir, is that not very long ago one of our Nation's newspapers, the Philadelphia Inquirer, went around and interviewed what you might call neutral experts on the deficit reduction plan, basically the budget analysts for the big accounting firms and other big finance firms. And they all concluded that my budget was the most honest one presented in a decade, the first Presidential budget to be taken seriously by Congress since the first Reagan budget. And the budget analyst for Price Waterhouse, the big accounting firm, whom I have never met and don't know and obviously doesn't work for me, said that my budget was the best budget in more than a decade, and the only thing I was wrong about is that it would reduce the deficit more than I was saying, not less. So let's just hope he's right. I think he is.

Thank you.

NOTE: The interview began at 5:32 p.m. in the Red Room at the White House.

Statement on the Executive Order on Federal Pollution Prevention
August 4, 1993

With this Executive order, the Federal facilities will set the example for the rest of the country and become the leader in applying pollution prevention to daily operations, purchasing decisions, and policies. In the process, Federal facilities will reduce toxic emissions, which helps avoid cleanup costs and promotes clean technologies.

NOTE: The President's statement was included in a White House statement announcing the signing of the Executive order of August 3, which is listed in Appendix D at the end of this volume.

Remarks Honoring Teachers Hall of Fame Inductees and an Exchange With Reporters
August 5, 1993

The President. Thank you, Mr. Secretary, and good afternoon to all of you. I'm sorry we started a little late, but I think you know I've been in there on the telephone to the Congress.

It's a great pleasure to welcome all of you here, especially the inductees into the National Teachers Hall of Fame. I'd also like to thank the representatives of Emporia State University, the Emporia public schools, and the city of Emporia, Kansas, for all their hard work in establishing the National Teachers Hall of Fame. Recognizing our teachers is a wonderful idea, and I hope I can help to do it every year I'm here.

We're here to honor the spirit and the dedication of teaching that motivates this wonderful group of educators, people who every day in small towns and large cities bring to our young people the gift of learning. Every one of us has a memory of a teacher who literally changed our lives. A good teacher does more than pass on information. A good teacher inspires a thirst for learning that lasts a lifetime, instilling confidence, conveying values, shaping our understanding of the world around us. I'm reminded of a quote from Henry Brooks Adams: "A teacher affects eternity; he can never tell where his influence stops."

The 10 men and women we recognize today, chosen from hundreds of nominees, are examples of our Nation's finest teachers. Not only do they bring a special gift for teaching, they've all made other contributions to their communities. Each of them has a unique style of teaching and a vision for the role of education that must be played now and well into the 21st century.

I'd like to acknowledge each of these inductees, beginning with the ones from 1992. First, Sheryl Abshire from Lake Charles, Louisiana. She served—I'm going to see if I can pronounce this, and I'm from Arkansas, I should be able to pronounce this—she served the Calcasieu—is that right?—Calcasieu Parish schools for 18 years as an elementary school teacher and library/media specialist. Today she is the principal of Westwood Elementary in Westlake, Louisiana. She's made technology a part of the total elementary curriculum and has brought such innovative learning projects to her State that the president of the Louisiana Association of Teachers credits her for setting the standard in Louisiana for instructional technology.

The second winner is Anna Alfiero of Norwichtown, Connecticut, who has taught science and math at Clark Lane Junior High in Waterford, Connecticut, for 31 years. She has found new ways to bring economics to the classroom and to make math real to her enthusiastic students. This is particularly important because one of our Nation's most pressing educational challenges is to improve the math skills of the next generation.

Third is Helen Case from El Dorado, Kansas. She attended a one-room rural school in the early 1900's. I hate to say that. [*Laughter*] And she has dedicated her life to serving others. She began teaching at the tender age of 17 and went on to teach in the Kansas public school system for 45 years. She integrated innovative teaching methods into her curriculum long before they became widely popular. I hear she used to hold mock sessions of Congress, national party conventions, and elections in her classes. Maybe she can give me a tip or two today. [*Laughter*]

I'd next like to acknowledge Shirley Cunningham Naples from Detroit, Michigan. During each of her 23 years in the schools of Ferndale, Michigan, Mrs. Naples issued a challenge to her students to be the best. And every year they did just that, because she did. Parents in Ferndale started planning as early as kindergarten for their children to be in her class because of the personal commitment she made to the education of each and every one of her students. She also contributes her teaching skills to help immigrant boat children become successful English-speaking members of the school community.

Next is Joseph York of Memphis, Tennessee, who teaches senior English at Adamsville Junior-Senior High School. Practically no one in his community is beyond his reach. In addition to teaching his regular students during the day, he tutors other teachers and children and teaches 4 nights a week at area universities, including the regional State prison. This incredible energy and devotion to teaching stems from his belief that a student's learning ability is directly related to his or her self image.

Let's give them all a hand. [*Applause*]

And now, the 1993 inductees: Leslie Black from Northport, Alabama. During her 25 years of teaching, Mrs. Black has been recognized for her efforts to strengthen and encourage a better link between home and school, something that I believe very strongly in, as I had experience in my State with a preschool program that my wife brought to Arkansas called the home instruction program for preschool youngsters. Mrs. Black has brought individualized instruction to the classroom and has worked to integrate music, the arts, and cultural awareness into the daily curriculum. She was also awarded the 1992 Presidential Award for Excellence in mathematics.

Next is Stewart R. Bogdanoff of Yorktown Heights, New York. For 28 years a physical education teacher for the Lakeland Central School District in Thomas Jefferson Elementary School, he's helped develop the physical fitness curriculum and after-school programs that not only enriches the lives of students but also provides stimulating learning environments as well. He's dedicated countless hours to working with disabled athletes and received the Point of Light award from President Bush for his dedication to community projects.

I'd like to say just parenthetically, I become more and more concerned about the physical health of our people as we enter into this great debate about national health care. I think it is very important that we not overlook the fact that it is my judgment a real mistake to cut back on physical education for all students in schools at a time when we're trying to build better health habits in all the American people.

Next, Ida Daniel Dark of Philadelphia, Pennsylvania. During 31 years of teaching music, she has been dedicated to providing a culturally rich learning environment to all of her students, including physically and mentally challenged children. She's developed a music curriculum for severely and profoundly impaired children which is now being used throughout the United States and Canada and has established a program that allows inner-city students to attend theater, art, and music presentations on the weekends.

Next is James K. Jackson, Sr., of Wauconda,

Illinois, a true visionary, an industrial education teacher at Mundelein High School who's made students and parents part of his dream of building and flying airplanes. He's found imaginative ways to teach technology-advanced subjects that can help students prepare for the rigors of a rapidly changing world. His students built the airplane that he flew to the National Teachers Hall of Fame induction ceremony in Emporia. Now, that's real confidence in your students. [*Laughter*] Is that true?

And finally, Christine Lungren-Maddalone of Long Beach, California, an elementary teacher at John Greenleaf Whittier Elementary School in Long Beach. After the Los Angeles riots in 1992, she set up after-school self-esteem enhancement classes for her students and talked to them about the need for a responsible change in the aftermath of the riots. She tries to teach her students to learn from life's experiences and has proven that all children, when given the chance, can succeed.

Let's give them a hand, too. [*Applause*] Good for you.

I do want to say that in recognizing and honoring these teachers, I know they would want us to, through them, honor the contributions of teachers throughout our Nation. These teachers are reminders that we must allow teachers to do what they do best, to teach. And we must struggle here in Washington and in every State capital and in all the central offices of all the school districts to empower teachers to teach and not to break them down with the burdens of bureaucracy and requirements that have nothing to do with whether their children can learn. We have to allow teachers and principals and parents to make more of their own decisions, to set the agendas and to chart the future course of their schools and their children's education with clear standards so they can know whether our children are doing as they should in a tough, global environment.

We in Washington are trying to recommit ourselves to making the Federal Government a real partner in education. That's why Secretary Riley and I have worked so hard to make the national education goals the foundation of true reform. We have to make sure that our children start school ready to learn and have the opportunity to succeed. And we have to challenge all of them to meet rigorous, world-class standards of learning. We owe this to them, to their future, and to all the rest of us as well. That's

why I'm so proud to be here to honor the achievements and dedication of these wonderful teachers.

I thank them for coming, and I'd now like to invite here Robert Glennen, the president of the National Teachers Hall of Fame, to the stage to make a few remarks. Mr. Glennen.

[*At this point, Mr. Glennen made brief remarks.*]

Economic Program

Q. Mr. President, can we ask you what you're telling these Congress Members you're on the phone with, what appeals are you making, and what more can you do?

The President. Well, we've done a lot of work today to try to sketch out what will happen in the next couple of months after this process. And the argument I'm making is that this is the beginning, not the end, of our efforts to have responsible budgeting. There will be one more round of budget cuts. There will be the unveiling of the Vice President's report on reinventing Government, which will have billions of dollars in further savings that can be achieved. There will be the opportunity to control health care costs in the context of the health care reform bill in a way that will not be unfair to older people on Medicare.

So, what I am suggesting to them is that this is clearly the best chance for real deficit reduction, for a fair apportionment of the spending cuts and revenue increases, and for an economic plan that will grow the economy. And no one I have talked to, including people who say that they may not vote for it, has suggested that anybody believes seriously that a better result will occur if the bill does not pass. So I feel pretty good.

Q. [*Inaudible*]—convene a special conference to find more budget cuts or a session of Congress, similar to what Kerrey is proposing?

The President. I've been working with them for 2 or 3 days. And I'm very much open to that. We have to do something like that anyway to deal with the Vice President's reinventing Government report. And what we had planned to do was to suggest that there be a bipartisan commission, including Members of both parties of Congress, to review these recommendations. So we can certainly accommodate this.

What I keep trying to tell all the Members is this is the beginning of this process, not the end. There's a whole lot more work to be done.

We've just been here 7 months. You know, finally they've got somebody here who's serious about responsible budgeting instead of just talking about it. And the argument I'm making to them is there is no alternative. And every alternative we saw from the other side had less deficit reduction, more bogus spending cuts, and did not ask the wealthy to pay their fair share. And there were no economic growth incentives. And after all, the whole purpose of this is to generate jobs and revitalize the economy. So I feel pretty good about it.

Q. Have you spoken to Senator Kerrey, sir? And whether you have or not, do you know where he is on this?

The President. I'm going to follow my ironclad rule on this. I'm going to let the Members speak for themselves. Yes, I have spoken to him.

Bosnia

Q. [*Inaudible*]—Sarajevo, it looks like the siege is getting worse and may not be able to wait until Monday. Do the allies—[*inaudible*]—need to move it up to protect the city before it falls?

The President. I can't answer that now, because I haven't been briefed on it. But I may have something to say about it later. I'm sorry.

Economic Program

Q. Have any of the Members you've spoken with made it a prerequisite that there be a so-called budget session or whatever for them to vote for this package?

The President. Well, let me say, I have offered a whole series of things that are consistent with what I have believed in all along. I mean, a lot of the Members want a separate bill which contains the budget control measures that the House adopted, that the Senate rules wouldn't permit. They want further opportunities to shave the budget, which I have committed to and which I strongly support, have from the beginning. They want opportunities for other issues to be debated between now and the end of

the year relating to the structure of the budget, all of which I have agreed to. So I think there is no question here—there is no serious suggestion that we could get a better result if this bill does not pass. So I think that we've got a very good chance to pass it. But you know, I never predict until they vote.

Thank you.

Q. Any Republican votes, Mr. President?

The President. A lot of them want to vote for it.

Q. How do you know that?

The President. I've had several of them say they'd like to vote for it—— .

Q. Who did you talk to today—round number?

The President. I don't know, a bunch.

Family and Medical Leave Act

Q. ——today, what do you say to the people, the businessmen who are now complaining about this new mandate?

The President. That if we're going to be pro-work and pro-family, we have to make it possible for people to succeed as parents and as workers. We cannot force people to choose between the two. Most parents have no choice but to work. But parenting is still the most important job of society.

And all these nations with which we compete provide for those kind of family supports. We were one of the very few nations in the world that had achieved any kind of standard of living that didn't provide this basic protection for families. I think it will increase productivity in the work force, increase the morale of workers, and people will make a lot more money out of it than it will cost them by sticking up for the families.

NOTE: The President spoke at 4:20 p.m. in the Rose Garden at the White House. A portion of the exchange could not be verified because the tape was incomplete.

Remarks on House of Representatives Action on the Economic Program
August 5, 1993

Thank you very much. I want to congratulate the Members of the House and their leaders

for breaking gridlock tonight and entering a new era of growth and control over our destiny. In the future, the American people will thank them for their commitment to moving away from the horrendous legacy of debt, underinvestment, and slow growth of the 1980's and putting the national interest ahead of the narrow interest, putting tomorrow ahead of today's pressure.

The margin was close, but the mandate is clear. I will continue to fight for this economic package with everything I have. And I urge the Members of the Senate to act on it in a positive way tomorrow. The fight is still on, and we have just begun to fight.

This economic plan represents an important first step in changing America. For the first time in a very long time we are making a meaningful downpayment on the Federal deficit, with deep spending cuts locked away in a trust fund that cannot be spent for anything else. For the first time in a dozen years the tax burden that is a part of the deficit reduction trust fund will be borne largely by those best able to bear it, with 80 percent of the new revenues coming from those with incomes above $200,000. And still, there will be shared contributions. The middle class is asked to make a modest contribution to paying down the deficit and growing the economy. For the first time in a decade we are making a serious effort to invest in our children, reward work over welfare, strengthen our families, and give genuine incentives to business to grow new jobs. These incentives are very, very important because the purpose of bringing the deficit down is to keep interest rates down, be able to control our financial destiny, and permit people with the right incentives to put the American people back to work.

Finally, as I said, this is just a first step to putting our financial house and our economic house in order. This program is shared sacrifice for shared benefit. We're all in this together, but we have just begun.

If the Senate acts favorably tomorrow, and as soon as the August recess is over, I am committed to further steps for discipline in the Federal budget, in getting rid of unnecessary spending and waste, including reenacting the controls that the House originally passed and that I embodied in my Executive orders of yesterday. After that, we will move on to the Vice President's report on reinventing Government, which will contain a myriad of exciting possibilities for making the Government more efficient and reducing unnecessary and inefficient spending.

Then we will move on to deal with the health care issue, to provide the security of affordable health care to all families and to lower the growth in health care costs over the long run, without which we will never bring this budget into balance or restore real financial health to the private sector. Then there is the process of ending welfare as we know it, making our streets safer, and most important of all, putting all this together in a program to restore jobs and growth for the American people.

We have set our sights high, but for 20 years our people have struggled harder on stagnant wages with too little investment and too few new jobs and exploding debt. For 12 years we have tried trickle-down economics while the debt went up and investment went down. Now we want a new direction to invest and grow this economy.

We began by seizing control of our destiny on a daily basis with this heroic vote today by the House of Representatives. I congratulate those who voted. I urge the Senate to follow their lead. And I look forward to continuing the battle tomorrow.

Good evening.

NOTE: The President spoke at 10:55 p.m. in the Rose Garden at the White House.

Nomination for an Assistant Administrator at the Agency for International Development
August 5, 1993

The President announced his intention today to nominate career Foreign Service Officer John F. Hicks to be Assistant Administrator of the Agency for International Development, U.S. International Development Cooperation Agency, and Director of AID's Africa Bureau.

"John Hicks is a dedicated and capable professional who is one of the Foreign Service's leading experts on African development," said the President. "I expect him to do an outstanding job in this position."

NOTE: A biography of the nominee was made available by the Office of the Press Secretary.

Nomination for President of the Government National Mortgage Association
August 5, 1993

The President announced today that he intends to nominate Dwight P. Robinson to be the President of the Government National Mortgage Association in the Department of Housing and Urban Development.

"Throughout his career in Michigan and here in Washington, DC, Dwight Robinson has distinguished himself as a leader in the housing field. I am grateful for his service," said the President.

NOTE: A biography of the nominee was made available by the Office of the Press Secretary.

Message to the Senate Transmitting a United Nations Convention on International Trade Law
August 6, 1993

To the Senate of the United States:

With a view to receiving the advice and consent of the Senate to accession, I transmit herewith the United Nations Convention on the Limitation Period in the International Sale of Goods done at New York on June 14, 1974, and the Protocol amending the Convention done at Vienna on April 11, 1980. Also transmitted for the information of the Senate is the report of the Department of State with respect to the Convention.

This is the second Convention in the field of international sales of goods law produced by the United Nations Commission on International Trade Law (UNCITRAL) that has been transmitted to the Senate for its advice and consent. The first, the 1980 United Nations Convention on Contracts for the International Sale of Goods, was ratified by the United States and entered into force for this country on January 1, 1988. Both of these Conventions establish uniform international standards in the commercial law of sales of goods in order to facilitate commerce and trade. Both benefit the United States by removing artificial impediments to commerce that arise from differences between the national legal systems that govern international sales of goods.

The Secretary of State's Advisory Committee on Private International Law, on which 11 national legal organizations are represented, in May 1989, and the House of Delegates of the American Bar Association, in August 1989, endorsed U.S. accession to the Convention and amending Protocol, subject to a U.S. declaration permitted under Article XII of the Protocol. The declaration is set forth with reasons in the accompanying report of the Department of State.

I recommend that the Senate promptly give its advice and consent to accession to this Convention together with its amending Protocol.

WILLIAM J. CLINTON

The White House,
August 6, 1993.

Remarks on Senate Action on the Economic Program
August 6, 1993

Thank you. Thank you very much. What we heard tonight at the other end of Pennsylvania Avenue was the sound of gridlock breaking. It was the sound of progress and change which can now resound throughout every corner of our great and beloved Nation.

I want to thank the United States Senators who voted for change tonight, especially the Senate majority leader, George Mitchell, for his untiring efforts, and all the others who worked so hard for so long to see this night come about. I want to thank the Vice President for his unwavering contribution to the landslide. I thank the economic team who worked so hard on this from last November: Leon Panetta, who is here; Secretary Bentsen; Mr. Rubin; and all the people who work with them. I thank Mr. McLarty and all the members of the White House staff. I thank Mr. Altman and the war room for the work they did in the last several weeks. I thank especially Howard Paster and Steve Ricchetti and all those who worked for us in the Senate. I hope that they will get some well-deserved rest.

After 12 long years, we can say to the American people tonight we have laid the foundation for the renewal of the American dream. The days of endless gridlock, rising deficits, and trickle-down economics are over. The days of economic growth and real opportunity for the working families of this country have begun.

This was not easy, but real change is never easy. It is always difficult. It is always easier to sustain the status quo and to talk as if you were changing. But that is not why I was elected President, nor is it why we were sent here.

When we came here, our national debt had quadrupled in 12 years, and the incomes of our forgotten working families had been stagnant for nearly 20 years. Our heritage of investment in our people and our economy had been gradually forsaken and the people of our Nation questioned whether anyone here in this city would take responsibility for our future, change the direction of our country, and ensure a better life for them and their children.

After a long season of denial and drift and decline, we are seizing control of our economic destiny. To be sure, as I have said repeatedly, this is just the beginning, just the first step in our attempts to assert control over our financial affairs, to invest in our future, and to grow our economy, to deal with the health care problems, the welfare reform problems, the problems of crime in the streets, and the other things that deal with the daily fabric of life for our people. But make no mistake about it, this is a very, very important beginning.

The economic program that Congress passed tonight puts $500 billion into a trust fund locked away for deficit reduction; $255 billion in specific, real, enforceable spending cuts; tax cuts for 20 million working Americans with marginal incomes who are trying to raise their children. This will reward their desire to choose work over welfare. It is an important advance in the fabric of opportunity and responsibility in this country.

This new direction includes new opportunities for the sons and daughters of middle class families to go to college because it reforms the student loan programs in ways that make student loans more accessible to more people and cuts the cost in the program through waste reduction. It provides immunizations to give a healthy start to millions of American children. It provides significant new incentives for small businesses to grow and expand. In this sharp departure from business as usual, this program will create jobs, reduce the deficit, and put the American people first.

In the lifetime of this country, the courage and wisdom of the American people in difficulty have always prevailed when we faced a challenge and needed a change. Sometimes in the past they have prevailed by the narrowest of margins in the beginning but always picking up steam, always marching confidently toward the future. That will be true in this time as well.

We are determined not to let the American dream founder. We are determined to stop avoiding our problems and start facing them, to embrace them as challenges, to turn them into opportunities, to seize the future that rightfully belongs to every American willing to work hard, play by the rules, and take care of their children. We are determined that the next generation of Americans will inherit a brighter future than we have known, just as we did from our parents. For more than two centuries, that has been the promise of the American dream. Tonight, because of the bold action taken by courageous men and women in the House and the Senate, that dream will not be deferred but rather be fulfilled.

I am profoundly grateful tonight for the opportunity to stand here not simply as President but as an American citizen seeing our Nation once again roll up our sleeves together, tackle our problems, and march to tomorrow.

Thank you, and God bless you all.

NOTE: The President spoke at 11:05 p.m. at the North Portico at the White House.

Statement on Meeting With Mario Chanes de Armas
August 6, 1993

I am honored to welcome to this house and to this country one of the heroes of our time. Mario Chanes de Armas was freed from prison in Cuba after having spent three decades as a political prisoner of the Castro regime. He is a living testimony to the unbending will to strive for liberty and dignity.

He sacrificed the best years of his life to the ideal that he and his fellow citizens will be free. The full might of dictatorship was brought to bear against him. Yet, it could not break his spirit. It is men and women like him who have built our land into a beacon of freedom and hope for the oppressed peoples of the world.

Our meeting today is a symbol to those brave Cubans who remain in prison on political charges or who struggle daily, risking their lives, for the twin causes of human rights and democracy. Our message to these courageous people is simple: The United States will not rest until all of the peoples of this hemisphere enjoy the fruits of freedom and democracy.

The President's Radio Address
August 7, 1993

It's a bright, sunny day in Washington in more ways than one. The political fog that has surrounded this town for so long is at long last lifting. For months we've all been working for this day, a day when we can say to the American people that our Government is getting on with the business of creating jobs, expanding the economy, and doing better by all the American people.

Members of the House and the Senate showed our Nation how Government for the people can actually work for the people. They took the courageous step of breaking gridlock, passing my economic plan, and putting our Nation on the road to long-term growth.

This plan plants us firmly on the path to getting so many good things done for our people. For the first time in a long time, we'll be making a meaningful downpayment on the massive Federal deficit, and as we reduce that deficit by nearly $500 billion over 5 years, with more spending cuts than tax increases, we'll be strengthening the foundation for our future at home and our position in the world economy.

For the first time in a dozen years the weight of the tax burden will be shifted so that it is borne more fairly. Middle class working families will pay about a dime a day to bring the deficit down in the form of a 4.3-cent gasoline tax—no hidden taxes, no games, no gimmicks.

But 80 percent of the new revenues will come from those who can best afford to pay, with family incomes over $200,000 a year. Those people got over half the economic gains, over half the economic gains of the 1980's and big tax breaks besides. We don't want to punish success. We want to reward it. But in order for all Americans to have a chance to succeed, we have

1347

to bring the deficit down, and it's only fair to ask those best able to pay to do so. If family income is less than $200,000 a year, there will be no increase in income taxes.

For the first time in a decade, we're also making a serious effort to invest in our children, to reward work over welfare, to strengthen our families, and to give real incentives to businesses to grow new jobs. Analysts project that our economy will create 8 million new jobs now in the next 4 years. We're keeping interest rates down and giving real, real incentives for people to invest in new business, research and development, and new plant and equipment.

For all these reasons this plan is an urgent step. But I want to emphasize, it is only the first step. We're well on our way, but our work is far from finished. We'll continue to look for ways to further cut unnecessary spending and trim waste. On that front, we will remain tireless, responsible, and accountable to you.

Soon we expect the Vice President's report on reinventing Government. It will help make your Government leaner, smarter, more efficient. It will show you that we're trying to have a Government here that actually works for the people who pay the bills and takes how their money is spent very seriously.

We want to end welfare as we know it and restore dignity to millions of idle Americans who have been dependent too long. We'll do that by changing the system so it's a path to a job, not a way of life. The economic plan went a long way toward doing that by lifting all the people in this country, millions of them, who work 40 hours a week and have children in their homes, out of poverty, not through a Government program but through the tax system, saying we won't tax people into poverty, we'll use the tax system to lift those out of poverty who are pro-work, pro-family, and doing their part.

And we cannot rest while millions of Americans do without affordable health care and many, many millions more worry that they won't be able to afford the cost of their health care policy or that they'll lose their health care coverage if they lose their job or someone in their family gets sick. It's not right. And until we give all Americans health care that's always there and control the cost, the health care crisis will continue to bankrupt our businesses, our families, and eventually our Nation.

So we'll keep moving as fast as we have in these first 6 months of the administration and keep taking new ideas to the American people for making our country better and putting our people first. With your support we've already moved on several fronts to ensure the principles that I fought for during the last campaign: providing opportunity, encouraging personal responsibility, and rebuilding our communities.

Just this week, our national service program cleared its final hurdles and now will clearly become law. That means 100,000 young people will have the chance to help America's communities while helping themselves pay for a college education. Also this week the Family Leave Act went into effect. And now millions of American workers will be able to take some time off to care for their newborn children or an ill family member without fearing loss of their jobs. In our Nation, where most people have to work, we cannot force people to choose between being a good parent and a good worker. Now millions more will be able to do both.

We've also won passage of a new motor voter law to make voter registration more easy, more open, more accessible. We've eased the credit crunch for small businesses all across America, making student loans easier to get and less costly to repay and working to open markets overseas to create jobs here at home. We've also changed the environmental policies of this administration so that once again America is a leader, not a follower, in the effort to preserve the global environment and our environmental issues here at home. We've made medical research more sensitive to the needs of women and more helpful to people with diabetes, Parkinson's, and other diseases where political bias kept research that was very needed from going on for too many years. We changed the ethics of the executive branch with the toughest ethics restrictions in American history, restricting people from lobbying for foreign governments or lobbying at all for years after they leave top positions in our Government.

There is more political accountability and more political reform on the way. Campaign finance reform, lobby reform, the line-item veto, all three of these things have passed at least one House of Congress. We're going to work hard to make them law. With these and other measures to better the lives of our people, we're putting business-as-usual out of business in Washington. That's what you ordered in the last election.

This week the majority of the lawmakers on Capitol Hill joined us to break gridlock. They voted to move us forward together, to leave behind the shameful legacy of debt and deficits, and to give our Nation control over our own economic destiny. I congratulate those lawmakers for the courage they've shown in winning this tough fight in the face of all kinds of charges and misinformation that fill the airwaves. These people stood firm. They stood together. And they stood for you.

As we fought for this plan, we brought together business and labor, the cities and the heartland, Americans from every generation. Now, on the threshold of a new era of growth and prosperity and a new direction for our Nation, it's time for all of us to stand together. And that includes those who opposed my plan on Capitol Hill.

To our critics there I say, all Americans, whatever their political stripe, can reap the benefits of the change we can begin today. I say to those critics, we must now put aside bitterness and rancor, move beyond partisanship, and work together to give the country we all love the new direction it needs. In the future, people will not ask whether we were Democrats or Republicans, whether we were conservatives or liberals. They will ask what we did to face our problems, meet our challenges, seize our opportunities, and secure a better future for our children. Let us begin that together.

Thanks for listening, and Godspeed.

NOTE: The President spoke at 10:06 a.m. from the Oval Office at the White House.

Statement on White House Staff Changes
August 7, 1993

I appreciate the outstanding work Regina Montoya has done as the Director of the Office of Intergovernmental Affairs.

When I asked Regina to join my administration, I knew she was sacrificing a great deal to leave a successful legal career and her family in Dallas. When she informed me she was contemplating returning to Dallas because of the difficulty the commute has placed on her family, I was supportive of her decision to reunite her family.

I applaud her decision and thank her for the hard work and dedicated service she gave her country and wish her happiness and success in the future. And I look forward to calling on her for her insight in the future.

I am also very pleased that Marcia Hale has agreed to take on this new responsibility. Marcia has been a strong team player, a dedicated worker, and a valued adviser in her capacity as Director of Scheduling and Advance. Her background in State government and experience in consensus-building and solving local issues will make her a forceful advocate for local and State interests. I look forward to Marcia's trusted counsel, analysis, and judgment in this new and exciting endeavor.

NOTE: The White House press release also included statements by Regina Montoya and Marcia Hale.

Nomination for United States Court of Appeals Judges
August 7, 1993

The President yesterday nominated three U.S. Court of Appeals judges: Martha Craig Daughtrey for the sixth circuit, Pierre N. Leval for the second circuit, and M. Blane Michael for the fourth circuit. In addition, the President also announced the nominations of U.S. District Court judges for Maryland, South Dakota, Nebraska, New Mexico, the Eastern District of New York, the Eastern District of Virginia, the Eastern District of Kentucky, and the Eastern

District of Arkansas.

"There are few things that I will do that will have more lasting effect than the appointment of Federal judges," said the President. "Along with Ruth Bader Ginsburg on the Supreme Court and the many other judges yet to be named, this outstanding group of jurists will change the face of the Federal courts and help move our country forward."

NOTE: Biographies of the nominees were made available by the Office of the Press Secretary.

Nomination for Chair of the National Endowment for the Arts
August 7, 1993

The President today announced his nomination of award-winning actress, producer, and author Jane Alexander as Chair of the National Endowment for the Arts, National Foundation on the Arts and the Humanities.

"The arts play an essential role in educating and enriching the lives of all Americans, and the National Endowment is integral to helping arts thrive throughout the country. The NEA helps enhance our children's learning, serves as an economic catalyst for local communities, and makes the arts a more accessible and vital part of people's everyday lives," said the President.

"The Endowment's mission of fostering and preserving our Nation's cultural heritage is too important to remain mired in the problems of the past. It is time to move forward, and Jane Alexander is superbly qualified to lead the Endowment into a new era of excellence. Just as she has brought the power of performance to regional theaters throughout the country, she will be a tireless and articulate spokesperson for the value of bringing art into the lives of all Americans.

"More than 30 years ago, President John F. Kennedy said, 'I see little of more importance to the future of our country and our civilization than full recognition of the place of the artist.' With those words as her challenge, I am confident Jane Alexander will work tirelessly and courageously to make the arts a full and productive partner in our Nation's future," the President said.

NOTE: A biography of the nominee was made available by the Office of the Press Secretary.

Remarks to the Community in Charleston, West Virginia
August 9, 1993

Thank you very much, and hello, West Virginia. It's good to be back again.

I want to thank my longtime friend, Senator Jay Rockefeller, for that wonderful introduction. And I want to thank Jay and Sharon for the work they have done for the people of West Virginia and the people of our country. I thank my friend Governor Caperton for being here and Mayor Hall and Congressman Rahall and Congressman Wise. I'd like to thank Congressman Mollohan and your fine Senator Robert Byrd in their absence for their support of our program.

I learned something about West Virginia that I already knew, but I saw it writ large in the last few days of the debate in the Congress when we really had to make tough decisions, when people who talked tough and they talked about talking tough, and they talked about talking about talking tough, finally had to act tough. West Virginia was there. And there was no wiggle or wobble or waffle or wonder. They were just there. They said, "This is good for America. I know it's tough. I know we'll be criticized. I know there are people who will find fault, but we're going to do what is right for the people of West Virginia, right for the people of America. Sign us up. We're moving toward the future." And I appreciate that.

I want to thank all the people who made

this rally possible today. And I want to thank you and the people of this great country, who have endured hard times with hope, for helping us to break the gridlock in Washington. Now we can truly say change has come to America.

Last week Congress voted for the values of the American heartland, the values of the middle class, the values of the small business economy, the values of the small towns in the hills and hollows of West Virginia and my native State. They voted for work and family, for reducing our deficit and increasing our investment in our people and their future, for jobs and growth for those who work hard and play by the rules.

After 20 long years of stagnant incomes, after 12 years of exploding deficits and reducing investment in our people, after 12 years of partisan gridlock and talking tough and acting soft, we reversed the direction. Now there is a new direction in America: opportunity for those who are responsible; no more something for nothing; a sense of community again. We're all in this together, and everyone must do his or her part.

And again I say to you, I am very grateful to the West Virginia delegation and to all the others who voted for this program because they remembered amidst the withering fog of misinformation that surrounded it that, after all, none of us were sent to Washington to keep our jobs; we were sent to Washington to help you keep your jobs.

And so we have taken, my fellow Americans, a first but major step to regain control of our economic destiny. We cut the deficit. We cut spending. We reward work. We ask those who can pay more to pay their fair share. We give the private sector incentives to grow jobs and invest in the future of our people. This is a good beginning.

This plan will help our Nation's economy to create 8 million new jobs over the next 4 years. Just last month in calendar year 1993 we saw the one millionth job come into the American economy. That's about as many as were created in the previous 4 years. We are beginning.

Is it enough? Of course it isn't. West Virginia still has the highest unemployment rate in the Nation, although you may have the highest percentage of willing workers in the Nation. If ever there was a place where people wanted to go to work, this is it.

We cannot turn this around overnight, but we can never turn it around unless we show

a willingness to change, and that is what last week was all about. In the last 12 years we added $3 trillion to our national debt. That's right. From the beginning of our Nation until 1980, we had a $1 trillion national debt. By 1992 it was $4 trillion. We were running annual deficits in the range of $300 billion a year over 5 percent of our annual income going to Government deficits.

When that happens, interest rates are too high, businesses cannot expand, and we cannot spend the money we need to spend to educate people, to create jobs, to deal with all the military cutbacks from California to Connecticut and help those people start a new life, to deal with the declines in mining and manufacturing in a State like West Virginia. It takes more money. And if you're up to your ears in debt paying more every year on interest in the debt, more for the same health care with an out-of-control budget, it cannot be done.

This plan cuts the deficit more than ever before by about $500 billion. There are $255 billion in specific spending cuts—no rhetoric, no hot air, no plugs, no "we'll think about it later"—specific cuts. And by the Executive order that I have signed, we will lock both the new taxes and the spending cuts away in a deficit reduction trust fund, an idea so long championed by Congressman Bob Wise. And when the Congress returns in September, with the help of Nick and Bob and Jay, I hope we will be able to persuade the entire Congress to create that trust fund in law.

The rest of the deficit reduction comes largely from asking those who received most of the economic gains in the 1980's to pay their fair share. Every serious economic analysis shows that the top one percent of our earners got over half the economic benefits of the last decade and a tax cut as well. We asked them to pay more not because we wish to punish success but because in America people who work hard deserve to be treated fairly, and we have to have a fair burden.

Eighty percent of these new revenues will come from those with incomes over $200,000 a year. Families with incomes of under $180,000, including 99 percent of all West Virginians, will not pay more in income taxes. For the first time in the history of this country, people who work 40 hours a week and have children in their homes will be lifted, not by a Government program but by the tax system, out of poverty—no bureaucracy, but a tax refund for people who do it.

I have heard for years and years and years the politicians make pious speeches about how bad welfare is and how we ought to move people from welfare to work. But if people with low education who can only get low-wage jobs can stay on welfare and have health care for their kids and they don't have to come up with child care, is it any wonder that some do? Now we say, "Go to work, and we'll spend tax money lifting you out of poverty because you work." That is what we ought to be doing.

I want to say to all of you that this idea of the earned-income tax credit being expanded to lifting the working poor and their children out of poverty was first championed by the National Commission on Children chaired by Jay Rockefeller. It was a good idea then, and it's a good idea now. Just think of it, 105,000 West Virginia working families being eligible to get some help to clothe their children and feed them and pay the medical bills and reinforce the values of work and family. It is one thing to talk about these things, my fellow Americans, and quite another to do it. This does it.

There's another very important part of this plan I want to emphasize here today because of your high unemployment rate. For the last 12 years most of the new jobs in America have been created by smaller businesses. And yet, very little attention has been given to what policies might help them. In fact, more and more, laws may be passed which affect them adversely whether in terms of more regulation or more taxes, without any thought being given to how we can create more jobs. This is the most pro-small business economic plan adopted in many a year in Washington, DC.

Over 90 percent of the small businesses in this country will get a tax break under this plan if they invest more in their businesses. There is a 75 percent increase in the expensing provision in the Tax Code for small businesses to reinvest in their own businesses, the biggest incentive for people in 1-, 2-, 5-, 10-, 20-, 25-employee operations to reinvest in making their businesses more modern that I have seen in the last 12 or 15 years. It is a good provision. It will help everybody in Charleston, West Virginia, and Casper, Wyoming, and throughout this country.

There is another provision in this code which enables people here in West Virginia to take a bigger chance to start new businesses. It says if you invest your money, however modest, in a new business that is capitalized up to $15 million and you hold that investment for 5 years, you will get a 50 percent cut in the tax you owe from the gain you earn. Now, that's how to get a tax cut, invest and put people to work. That's when we should lower people's taxes, when they're putting the rest of America to work to move this economy forward.

The last thing I want to say is that we do our best in this plan to invest in our people. I was attacked during the course of this budget debate because there was some new spending in this program, and I plead guilty. There's a lot more spending cuts than spending, but there is some new spending. In every area I challenge you to prove that it doesn't make sense.

We spend some more money on the Head Start program to get poor children off to a good start in school; to help poor pregnant mothers while they are carrying their children to be well-nourished so their children are born at normal birth weight in good condition, to save the taxpayers money, not to cost them money; to immunize our children against serious childhood diseases. You tell me why the United States of America has the third worst record of all the countries in the Western Hemisphere in immunizing children against diseases. You are all paying for it in higher medical bills for everybody else because we don't immunize the kids. It's a good investment. It pays off. And yes, we spent some money to do it.

We spend a modest amount of money in this plan to provide more apprenticeship training programs for young people who don't go on to college but need a skill so they can earn a decent income. That will pay itself back, and you know it. And this plan makes it much, much easier for young people from working families to finance a college education: lower interest college loans, better repayment terms. You can pay it back based on a percentage of your income even if you borrow a lot of money, but you must pay the loan back now. It is a good change. It will educate more people.

My fellow Americans, Friday night we began to put our economic house in order. The specifics of the day may soon fade from our memories; even the closeness of the vote will someday fade. But what will endure is that it was at this moment that we finally decided that change had to come, that we must finally face our problems, meet our challenges, build a better future, and stop just talking about it.

Now, last week was more partisan than I had hoped. And as I say, I'm very deeply grateful to the West Virginia delegation and to many others who put the national interest ahead of their personal interest. There were some Democrats, because of the partisan nature of the debate, who came from districts where the people were not nearly so personally advantaged, who voted for it anyway even though they put their own political futures on the line. I think of Congresswoman Marjorie Margolies-Mezvinsky from Pennsylvania, for example, from one of the most prosperous congressional districts in America, who voted yes and said this is in the national interest. And even people who pay higher income taxes will benefit if we have lower interest rates. If their interest payments go down more than their taxes go up, they'll still create more jobs, and America will go forward. There were people like that in this Congress who literally put their necks on the line. But I say to you, we have to do better. We have to do better.

We cannot have every great issue of the day decided on the basis of partisanship, scheduled around the next trip to New Hampshire for a primary still 4 years away. We have got to do some of these things together.

This administration is devoted to change. But I don't care if it's called liberal or conservative or Democratic or Republican. I'm interested in tomorrow versus yesterday in solving the real problems of the country. You can see what we can do when we work together. Just last week with bipartisan support, the family leave act became effective so that people now don't have to lose their jobs if they go home and take care of a sick child or a sick parent. We can do more of that.

And I challenge the Congress when they return to pass with bipartisan support the national service act to give so many tens of thousands of our young people a chance to work off their college loans through serving their communities. Jay Rockefeller came here through national service. This is very, very important. It can open up a whole new area of solving our problems at the grassroots level. And we ought to do it without regard to partisanship.

But finally, we have to deal with the greatest continuing threat to our economic security and to the personal security of most American families, an issue that your Governor has dealt with, an issue that Senator Rockefeller has dealt with, an issue that your Congressmen have dealt with, particularly as it affects the coal miners here, and that is the question of health care.

Unless we reform the health care system of this country, we can never take the deficit down to zero. We can never assure that millions of working families will have their health insurance even if someone in their family gets sick and they have to change jobs. We can never assure that a small business will be able to continue to afford to cover its employees and never have to choose between going broke or going without health insurance. We can stop, if we do it, the pattern of the last 12 years where in workplace after workplace after workplace American working men and women had to give up their wage increases because of the increased cost of the health care package. We have got to do something to provide health security to all Americans in a way that is good for the private sector, good for our employers, and controls the cost without sacrificing quality. Can we do it? Of course we can.

And there is more to do. The Vice President will have a report next month on reinventing our National Government to further eliminate unnecessary Government wasteful spending. We will have a plan to continue our efforts to end welfare as we know it. We will have a crime bill to put more police officers on the street, not only to catch criminals but to prevent crime from happening. All of these things must be done in a different way, and we need bipartisan support. We need to put an end to the partisan rancor and put the American people first again.

My fellow Americans, when I got off at the airport, someone gave me this, a picture of President Kennedy when he was here 30 years ago in the rain in this spot in which he said, "The sun does not always shine in West Virginia, but the people always do." Well, today the sun shone, and so did you, and I am very grateful. If it hadn't been for West Virginia, John Kennedy probably would not have been elected President of the United States. When he was here 30 years ago on his last visit, he reflected the eternal optimism, the unbending confidence that we could solve our problems that is his enduring legacy and his enduring lesson to those of us who come behind.

I tell you, throughout all the difficulties we have, the biggest problems we have are those that are inside our minds: the limitation on our vision, our will, and our heart and our willingness to put aside the old divisions and work together to build a better America. There is nothing before us that cannot be cured if we have the willingness to open our ears, lower our voices, roll up our sleeves, and make our words speak through our deeds. That is what we must do from now on.

Thank you for giving me a warm welcome. Change has come to America. Let's keep it going. God bless you all.

NOTE: The President spoke at 1:15 p.m. at the State Capitol. In his remarks, he referred to Mayor Kent Strange Hall of Charleston. The Executive order of August 4 on the deficit reduction fund is listed in Appendix D at the end of this volume.

Nomination for Associate Directors at the Office of Science and Technology Policy
August 9, 1993

The President today announced his intention to nominate Marci Greenwood Associate Director for Science and Jane Wales Associate Director for International Affairs and National Security in the Office of Science and Technology Policy.

"I am pleased today to name these two experienced individuals to our team at OSTP," the President said. "Marci Greenwood's work in

both science teaching and university administration will be invaluable as she takes the lead at the Science Division. I am equally confident that Jane Wales' experience in the foreign policy arena will be used well as our staff at OSTP continues to pursue joint science and technology ventures with other countries around the world."

NOTE: Biographies of the nominees were made available by the Office of the Press Secretary.

Remarks on the Swearing-In of James J. Blanchard as Ambassador to Canada and an Exchange With Reporters
August 10, 1993

The President. Good morning, ladies and gentlemen. I'm delighted to have you here today at the White House for the swearing-in of my longtime friend and a very able public servant, Governor Jim Blanchard, to be our Nation's next Ambassador to Canada. I have known and respected Jim for many years now. We've worked on many things together both as Governors and as fellow partisans in political wars. I can tell you that he is one of the ablest Governors with whom I ever worked, one of the most creative and innovative people I have ever met in public life.

As a Governor and earlier as a Member of Congress, Jim Blanchard was known as someone who would innovate, listen, and act. Those are capabilities which will be indispensable in his

new assignment. His service in Ottawa will also benefit from his insights and his personal ties to Canadian leaders gained from being Governor of a State with a large border and close ties to Canada.

When I nominated Jim Blanchard for this post, it was a sign to me, and I hope to the Canadians as well, of the immense importance I place on our relationships with Canada. For that relationship is unquestionably one of the most important in the world to us. Canada is our largest trading partner. Over $200 billion in goods and services cross our borders annually. That amount increased significantly after the passage of the free trade agreement. And I believe it will increase again after implementation of the North American Free Trade Agreement.

Our relations with Canada are far more than economic, however. The fact that we share the world's longest undefended border is one of our greatest security assets. And Canada's cooperation on a host of international security efforts is absolutely invaluable. Canada has been our partner in efforts toward the former Soviet Union, Haiti, Somalia, and many other areas. With Canada we founded the United Nations and NATO. We work closely together today in the Group of Seven, in GATT, in international peacekeeping operations, just to name a few of the arenas that are important to us because of what we are able to do together.

Today the United States and Canada share a challenging list of opportunities for mutual progress. We can work together to promote greater economic growth in our own hemisphere and throughout the world. We can work together to protect the air, the water, the environmental quality that is significantly shared by our two peoples. We can work together to improve the security of both our nations in this new era of world affairs.

In all this I have greater confidence in the ability of Canada and the United States to make that kind of progress knowing that we will be represented in Ottawa by Jim Blanchard. I appreciate the fact that Jim and Janet are willing to accept this assignment. We all wish them great success.

And now, Mr. Vice President, I would like to ask you to do something I cannot do, administer the oath of office.

[*At this point, the Vice President administered the oath of office.*]

NAFTA

Q. Mr. President, have you given up on NAFTA?

The President. That's ridiculous. No.

Q. Some people say that the administration isn't fighting hard enough for it.

The President. We don't have an agreement yet. We have to wait until we finish. The Trade Ambassador has not finished with the negotiations.

NOTE: The President spoke at 11:48 a.m. at the North Portico of the West Wing at the White House.

Remarks on Signing the Omnibus Budget Reconciliation Act of 1993
August 10, 1993

Thank you very much. Thank you. Ladies and gentlemen, the Vice President has given me a very generous introduction and has fairly characterized the struggle in which we have been engaged. I might say also, for all of you sports fans, he's given a whole new meaning to the term "tie-breaker." [*Laughter*]

But I think it would really be unfortunate if this event were to come and go without recognizing the fact that the people in Congress who voted for this plan had to labor under historically difficult circumstances. They had to reverse a plan of trickle-down economics in which it was the accepted path always to say the right thing but never to do it, and in which, if you tried to do the right thing, people would say the wrong things about you and cloud the debate with a fog of misinformation.

In this incredible series of events that have unfolded, there were many Members of Congress who never appeared on the evening news, whose names never appeared in the newspapers simply because of their quiet courage and determination to do what they thought was right and to see this process through to the end. And I think I would be remiss, therefore, if on this occasion I did not ask at least all the sitting Members of the United States Congress who are here to stand and to receive a round of applause. Would you all please stand? I also want to explicitly thank all the many members of the Cabinet and the administration who are here who worked so hard on this program, as well as the many citizens throughout the country who helped us to lobby it through.

Today we come here for more than a bill signing. We come here to begin a new direction for our Nation. We are taking steps necessary and long overdue to revive our economy, to renew our American dream, to restore confidence in our own ability to take charge of our own affairs. This was clearly not an easy fight. When I presented this program to Congress, I had hoped for something quite different: I had hoped that it would spark a genuine, open, honest, bipartisan national debate about the serious choices before us, about the world economy we face as we move toward the 21st century, about the problems we have here at home and all the people whose lives and potential we lose and what economic consequence that has for all the rest of Americans. I had hoped that we could discuss whether and to what extent the revival of the competitive skills of our work force could raise incomes and generate jobs; how we could both reduce the deficit and increase investment in our future; whether we could escape the trap that has afflicted so many wealthy countries, that even when their economies are growing now they don't seem to be creating jobs; how we could escape the policies of the seventies and the eighties which led middle class Americans to work longer work weeks for lower pay while they paid more for the essentials of life; whether we could bring the power of free enterprise to bear in the poor inner cities and rural areas of this country and lift people up with the force of the American dream; whether the short-term consequences of bringing the deficit down would be more than overweighed by the short-term benefits of lower interest rates and the long-term benefits of being in control of our economic destiny.

These are the kinds of things that I wanted to see debated. And to be sure, to some extent, we did debate them. But for 5 months the American people heard too little about the real debate and too much from those who oversimplified and often downright misrepresented the questions of tax increases and spending cuts because they had narrow economic or political or personal reasons to do so.

So today, as we sign this landmark legislation, I say again, now we can talk about the national interests, how this plan will begin to bring the change we need in America, how we can have economic revival and hope if this is a beginning and we move forward from here. After all, after 12 years of the most rapid increase in deficits in our country's history, when the national debt went from $1 to $4 trillion in only 12 years, this is the largest deficit reduction plan in history, with $255 billion in real enforceable spending cuts in very specific areas, not generalized

hot air and tomorrow's promises but specific cuts. After 12 years of trickle-down economics where taxes were lowered on the wealthiest Americans, raised on the middle class, hoping that investments would be made which would reverse the trends of the last 20 years, we now have real fairness in the Tax Code with over 80 percent of the new tax burden being borne by those who make over $200,000 a year, with the middle class asked to pay only $3 a month, and with a tax cut to working families with children who make under $27,000 a year. By expanding this earned-income tax credit to working families and especially to the working poor, this Congress has made history by enabling us to say for the first time now, if you work hard and you have children in your home and you spend 40 hours a week at work, you can be a successful worker and a successful parent, and you will be lifted out of poverty.

Every elected public official in America sometime in the last 10 years has given someplace between one and a thousand speeches decrying the welfare system, extolling the values of work and family. But finally, the people who voted yes on this plan put a down payment toward ending welfare as we know it by finally doing something to reward work and family instead of just talking about it.

Everybody in this debate talked about small business, and the people who opposed this plan said it was bad for small business. But in truth, the opposition plan actually increased the burden on small business people who took out their own health insurance by taking away their deduction for it, while this plan increases by 75 percent the expensing allowance for small businesses in ways that will give over 90 percent of the small businesses in America a tax cut if they do what they ought to do, invest more money in their business. Others talked about it; we did it. And we should be proud of it, and we should tell the small business community about it.

Others talked about the importance of small business as a job generator. This plan passed a pro-jobs capital gains tax that reduces tax rates by 50 percent for people who invest their money in new and small businesses and hold those investments for 5 years or more, the most dramatic incentive we have ever had to encourage people to take money out of their savings and take a chance on the free enterprise sector in America in the places where the jobs are being created, in the small business sector. That's what this plan does. Instead of talking about doing something for small business, this plan actually did it. And all of you need to be proud of that.

The plan offers incentives to Americans to invest to revive the homebuilding market; to invest in research and development, something that especially helps high-tech companies; to invest in new plant and equipment. Even the biggest companies in America now will be able to have tax incentives if they are willing to invest in growing more jobs here at home. These are the right ways to cut taxes, my fellow Americans, cutting taxes for people because they spent their money in growing this economy and putting their fellow Americans to work. And that's what this plan does.

This plan was criticized in some quarters because it did spend some new money on some new things. I would argue to you that anybody who thinks that all Government spending is the same might just as well say all kinds of bread taste the same. We did not come here to leave our judgment and our knowledge about the global economy at the city borders of Washington, DC.

So yes, I plead guilty: We reformed the student loan program to lower the interest rates on student loans and make it easier for people to take out college loans and to repay them. We did, finally, after 6 long years of reducing defense spending at rapid rates, at throwing people in the street from California to Connecticut, we finally did put some more money in here for defense conversion to give those people a chance to go back to work in a peacetime economy, to contribute to the American dream. We did spend some more money on Head Start and on poor pregnant mothers to try to get their children into the world in good shape, to try to lower the tax burden on other people and increase their productivity. We did spend some money to try to give 6 million more children inoculations, because no one can explain to me why the United States of America has the third worst immunization record in the Western Hemisphere and we're paying a fortune for it.

This plan has already begun to work. Ever since it was clear that we were working to bring down the deficit and every time we made progress along the way, long-term interest rates dropped, enabling millions of Americans to refinance their home either to lower their monthly payments or to build up their own savings, enabling businesses to refinance their loans and, over the long run, lowering the cost of new investment in new jobs.

Because of the leadership of the Speaker of the House, Senator Mitchell, Congressman Gephardt, the hard work of the committee chairs, Senator Moynihan, Congressman Rostenkowski, Senator Sasser, Congressman Sabo, the committee chairs in all the other committees in the Congress, and as I said earlier, the simple courage of millions of Americans in supporting this plan and the quiet courage of so many Members of Congress who literally put their careers on the line, this country has begun to take responsibility for itself.

I say to those Members who took a big chance in voting for this, with all the rhetoric that was thrown against them, if you go home and look your people in the eye and tell them you were willing to put your job on the line so that they can keep their jobs, I think they will understand and reward you with reelection.

This plan is only the beginning. As I said on February 17th and would like to say again today as we close, this administration views job creation and deficit reduction, expanding international trade and providing health care at affordable rates to all Americans, training and educating our work force, making our families healthier and our streets safer, reforming our welfare system and reinventing our Government not as different challenges requiring disparate solutions in different coalitions but part of the fabric of reviving the dream that we were all raised with.

We cannot simply say, "This is a complicated time, and we're unequal to the challenge. So we'll do this, and 4 or 5 years from now we'll worry about that." We have to think about what it takes to build the fabric of community, to rebuild the fabric of our families, to give our children a good shot, and to have sensible economic policies at home and with our allies around the world. Toward this end let me say again, in the long run we cannot succeed in an endless season of partisan bitterness and rancor and bickering. If some of us have to make hard choices while others stand aside and hope that the house collapses, nothing will in the end get done.

And so I ask today of the American people and the American people's representatives, without regard to your party or philosophy, when the August recess is over, let us join again in the common work of American renewal. There is so much to be done that can only be done if we're all willing to carry our share of the load. Clearly, that is what the American people want us to do.

In the very first week when the Congress comes back, the Senate will have a chance to demonstrate that bipartisan spirit by passing the national service plan that the House has already passed and opening up the opportunity for hundreds of thousands of young Americans to pay their college way by serving their communities and rebuilding a sense of community in this country. And then we will move on to the other great issues of the day. And move on we must. We cannot stand still.

I remember every time I do something like this who we're really working for: I remember the people that Senator Moynihan and I saw lined along the long way from the airport to Hyde Park in New York; the people who stood out in 3-degree weather in Chillicothe, Ohio, to visit with me about their hopes for America; the young people I saw at Rutgers in New Jer-

sey, in New Orleans, and in Boston, so deeply committed to the idea of national service because they want to be in a position to give something back to their country and to believe that their country can work for them again; high school students in Chicago who for the first time are dreaming of an affordable college education; and inner-city youths I saw at the playground in Los Angeles who believe that there's no reason they can't live in a neighborhood that is free of crime and full of opportunity. These are the people that we all came here to work for. These are the people that we celebrate for today.

This is a beginning. Let us resolve when this recess is over to come back with a new determination to finish the work. And let us again hold our hands out to those who were not part of this process and say, "America needs us all. Let us go forward together."

Thank you, and God bless you all.

NOTE: The President spoke at 12:33 p.m. on the South Lawn at the White House. H.R. 2264, approved August 10, was assigned Public Law No. 103–66.

Remarks on the Swearing-In of Supreme Court Associate Justice Ruth Bader Ginsburg
August 10, 1993

The President. Please be seated. Welcome to the White House. It is my distinct honor to introduce the Chief Justice of the Supreme Court.

[At this point, Chief Justice William Rehnquist administered the oath of office, and Justice Ginsburg then made brief remarks.]

The President. Ladies and gentlemen, before we adjourn to the reception in honor of Justice Ginsburg, I'd like to acknowledge the presence here today of Senator Moynihan, who sponsored her so strongly in the Senate, Senator Larry Pressler of South Dakota, Senator Strom Thurmond of South Carolina, and the chairman of the House Judiciary Committee, my good friend Jack Brooks from Texas. It's good to see all of you here.

This was a very important appointment to me.

In one of my former lives I had the great joy and responsibility of teaching the United States Constitution and the decisions of the Supreme Court under it to aspiring but not always interested law students. *[Laughter]* I have learned over the course of a lifetime of practical experience what I knew then: We breathe life into the values we espouse through our law. It gives to every American, including the most illiterate among us, the most totally unaware of how the legal system works, a fair measure of our ideals and some reality that comes into life from the speeches given by the rest of us. There is no one with a deeper appreciation of this fact than Ruth Bader Ginsburg. This is a moment, this historic moment, therefore, that all Americans can celebrate. For no one knows better than she that it is the law that provides the rules that permit us to live together and that permit us to overcome the infirmities, the bigotry, the prejudice, the limitations of our past and our present.

Her nearly unanimous confirmation by the United States Senate was the swiftest in nearly two decades. Much credit must go to her own brilliance and her thoughtful, balanced reasoning. But I thank Senators Moynihan and D'Amato for their sponsorship and assistance. I thank Chairman Biden and Senator Hatch for their contributions and all the other Senators, including those here present, who supported her.

Ruth Bader Ginsburg does not need a seat on the Supreme Court to earn a place in our history books. She has already secured that. As a brilliant young law school graduate she became an early victim of gender discrimination when as a woman and mother she sought nothing more than that which every one of us wants, a chance to do her work. She met this challenge with character and determination. She took on the complex challenges of winning what seems now to be such a terribly simple principle, equal treatment for women and men before the law. Virtually every significant case brought before the Supreme Court in the decade of the seventies on behalf of women bore her mark. Today, virtually no segment of our society has been untouched by her efforts.

In the 1980's, Ruth Bader Ginsburg ended her career as a scholar and advocate and began a new one as a judge on the United States Court of Appeals here in the District of Columbia. She has emerged as one of our country's finest judges, progressive in outlook, wise in judgment, balanced and fair in her opinions. She defied labels like "liberal" and "conservative," just as she did in her hearing before the Senate, to earn a reputation for something else altogether, excellence.

And through it all she has proved that you can have what most of us really want, a successful work life and a successful family life. That is due in no small measure to her husband of 39 years, himself a distinguished lawyer and now, I hasten to say, for all the rest of us fast becoming a national model of what a good husband ought to be. [*Laughter*] Marty Ginsburg, please stand up and take a bow.

Her children, Jane and James, are here. And she became a proud grandmother of Paul and Clara and in her announcement made them two of the most famous grandchildren in the entire United States.

Now Ruth Bader Ginsburg's greatest challenge lies ahead, a challenge to which she brings a powerful mind, a temperament for healing, a compassionate heart, a lifetime of experience. Her story already is a part of our history. Now her words and her judgments will help to shape our Nation today and well into the 21st century.

Most of us know that the inscription above the main entrance to the Supreme Court reads: Equal Justice Under Law. But carved into the marble above the Court's other entrance is another telling message: Justice, the Guardian of Liberty. In Ruth Bader Ginsburg, I believe the Nation is getting a Justice who will be a guardian of liberty for all Americans and an ensurer of equal justice under law. We are all the better for that.

Thank you for being here. We're adjourned to the reception in Justice Ginsburg's honor. Thank you.

NOTE: The President spoke at 2:43 p.m. in the East Room at the White House.

Nomination for Ambassador to Spain
August 10, 1993

The President announced today that he intends to nominate Columbia University professor Richard N. Gardner to be Ambassador to Spain.

"Professor Gardner is an internationally recognized authority on international law, international economic problems, and U.S.-European relations," said the President. "He will serve our country well as Ambassador to this important ally and trading partner."

NOTE: A biography of the nominee was made available by the Office of the Press Secretary.

Nomination for Director of the Institute of Museum Services
August 10, 1993

The President today announced his intention to nominate Diane B. Frankel to be Director of the Institute of Museum Services, National Foundation on the Arts and the Humanities.

"Diane Frankel has spent her career strengthening the commitment to teaching in the museums in which she has worked and fostering closer ties between museums and their local communities," the President said. "With her unique background as the founder of her own museum, I am confident she will do an excellent job directing the IMS in its efforts to support America's museums, historical sites, and zoos."

NOTE: A biography of the nominee was made available by the Office of the Press Secretary.

Nomination for Deputy Administrator of the Small Business Administration
August 10, 1993

The President today announced his intention to nominate small business entrepreneur Cassandra Pulley Robinson as Deputy Administrator at the Small Business Administration.

"As someone who has started a business herself, Cassandra Robinson understands the challenges new business people face. I am confident she will do an excellent job assisting Erskine Bowles at the head of SBA as we work to better opportunities for small and growing businesses," the President said.

NOTE: A biography of the nominee was made available by the Office of the Press Secretary.

Nomination for Inspector General of the Department of Labor
August 10, 1993

The President announced today that he intends to nominate Charles C. Masten, a former FBI agent and Deputy Inspector General at the Labor Department, to be that Department's Inspector General.

"I am very pleased to be naming Charles Masten, an experienced investigator with a thorough understanding of the Department of Labor, to this position. I think he will continue to serve well," said the President.

NOTE: A biography of the nominee was made available by the Office of the Press Secretary.

Remarks Announcing the Anticrime Initiative and an Exchange With Reporters
August 11, 1993

The President. Thank you very much. Mr. Vice President and Attorney General, distinguished Members of the Congress, the law enforcement community, and concerned American citizens. I'm glad to have all of you here in the Rose Garden today for this important announcement. I want to say a special word of appreciation to Senator Biden and to Chairman Brooks, who have worked for a long time to try to get a good crime bill through the United

States Congress. I hope today is the beginning of that.

I'm proud to be here with representatives of the Nation's police and prosecutors and States' attorneys general with whom we have worked closely to fashion this bill. And it gives me particular pleasure to be here with some of the brave men and women who risk their lives every day to protect the people of this country and to preserve the law.

The first duty of any government is to try to keep its citizens safe, but clearly too many Americans are not safe today. We no longer have the freedom from fear for all our citizens that is essential to security and to prosperity. The past 4 years have seen 90,000 murders in this country. Last month in this city, our Nation's Capital, in one week 24 murders were committed. When our children must pass through metal detectors to go to school or worry that they'll be the victim of random drive-by shootings when they're playing in the swimming pool in the summertime, when parents are imprisoned in their own apartments behind locked doors, when we can't walk the streets of our cities without fear, we have lost an essential element of our civilization.

Many of you have heard me tell many times over the last year and a half or so of the immigrant worker in the New York hotel who said that if I became President he just wanted me to make his son free. And when I asked him what he meant, he meant that his son couldn't walk to school two blocks without his walking with him, his son couldn't play in the park across the street from their apartment house without his father being there. He said his son was not free.

It's time we put aside the divisions of party and philosophy and put our best efforts to work on a crime plan that will help all the American people and go beyond the cynicism of mere speeches to clear action.

Today I'm proud to be here with the chairs of the House and the Senate Judiciary Committees to announce this plan. The plan is not— it's tough. It is fair. It will put police on the street and criminals in jail. It expands the Federal death penalty to let criminals know that if they are guilty, they will be punished. It lets law-abiding citizens know that we are working to give them the safety they deserve. It is the beginning, just the beginning but a major beginning, of a long-term strategy to make America a more law-abiding, peaceful place and to make Americans more secure and to give our young people, wherever they live, a better chance to grow up, to learn, to function, to work, and to have a decent life.

This bill first addresses the most pressing need in the fight against crime. There simply are not enough police officers on the beat. The plan is designed to make the major downpayment on the pledge that I made in the campaign to put 100,000 police officers on the street. Thirty years ago there were three police officers for every violent crime. Today the ratio is reversed, three crimes for every police officer.

Like so many of the best ideas, community policing was spawned in the laboratories of experimentation on the streets of our cities and towns. Then-commissioner Lee Brown of New York, now my Drug Director, sent some 3,000 additional police officers onto the streets of New York City, launching community policing in every precinct. Then shortly thereafter, for the first time in 36 years, crime rates went down in every major category. It's worked from Boston to St. Louis, to Los Angeles.

The crime bill that will be introduced next month will include $3.4 billion to fund up to 50,000 new police officers to walk the beat. It will also create a police corps to give young people money for college, train them in community policing, and ask them to return to their communities to serve as police officers in return for their education. This will add to the numerous community policing initiatives we have already undertaken. For example, earlier this year I signed a jobs bill that will make $150 million available right away to hire or rehire police officers. And I'm happy to report that the Labor Department will allocate $10 million to retrain newly discharged troops from the United States Armed Forces to become police officers. After defending our freedom abroad, they'll be given a chance to do so at home.

Second, we must end the insanity of being able to buy or sell a handgun more easily than obtaining a driver's license. The Brady bill, which requires a waiting period before the purchase of a handgun, is simply common sense. I have said so before Congress and before the American people. It is long past time to pass it. If the Congress will pass it, I will sign it. I believe now that Congress will pass it. There is no conceivable excuse to delay this action one more day.

The effort to keep handguns out of the hands of criminals cannot and should not wait for the passage of this legislation. Today I will sign two Presidential directives that fight gun violence. I am ordering that the rules governing gun dealers be reviewed to make sure that only legitimate gun dealers are in the business of selling guns. And I am ordering the Treasury Department to take the necessary action to suspend the importation of foreign-made assault pistols, which have become the weapons of choice for many gangs and drug dealers. Too many weapons of war are making their way onto our streets and turning our streets into war zones. Let me also say that this effort against crime will not be complete if we do not eliminate assault weapons from our streets. No other nation would tolerate roving gangs stalking the streets better armed than the police officers of a country. Why do we do it? We shouldn't, and we ought to stop it.

Finally, if we are to take back the streets of America from the gangs and the drug dealers, we must do what has not been done before: We must actually enact a crime bill. This legislation will be introduced by Chairmen Biden and Brooks, and it will build upon a lot of good ideas from around the country, including one I worked hard on when I was Governor, community boot camps for young offenders, boot camps which give young people the discipline, the training, the treatment they need for a second chance to build a good life. When it comes to hardened, violent criminals, society has the right to impose the most severe penalties, but I believe we should give young people a chance to make it.

As I said during the campaign and as I said during my tenure as a Governor, I support capital punishment. This legislation will reform procedures by limiting death-row inmates to a single habeas corpus appeal within a 6-month time limit but also guaranteeing them a higher standard of legal representation than many have had in the past. Both elements are important if this is to be genuine reform. And it will provide the death penalty for some Federal offenses, including killing a Federal law enforcement officer.

As I said, this is just the beginning of our efforts to restore the rule of law on our streets. To do this we must work with thousands of law enforcement officials around the country who risk their lives every day. We must work

with the mayors, with the Governors; we must work with the people who deal with children before they become criminals. We must have a broad-based assault on the terrible things that are rending the fabric of life for millions of Americans.

But we in Washington must work together, too. For too long, crime has been used as a way to divide Americans with rhetoric. It is time—and I thank the Republican Members of Congress who are here today—it is time to use crime as a way to unite Americans through action. I call on the Democrats and the Republicans together to work with us and with the law enforcement community to craft the best possible crime legislation.

Last week we began to break the gridlock with a new budget and an economic plan. Now we can do so again in ways that unite us as Americans. And I pledge to you my best and strongest efforts to pass this bill at the earliest possible time. There are good things in it. It will make our people safer. It will shore up our police officers. It will move America in the right direction.

May I now introduce the person who has done a great deal to do all those things just in the last few months, our distinguished Attorney General, Janet Reno.

[At this point, Attorney General Janet Reno, Senator Joseph Biden, Representative Jack Brooks, Mississippi attorney general Mike Moore, National Association of District Attorneys president William O'Malley, and Boston, MA, police commissioner William Bratton made brief remarks.]

Meeting With Pope John Paul II

Q. [*Inaudible*]—your visit with the Pope tomorrow, what you anticipate from it?

The President. [*Inaudible*]—I'm really very, very excited. I'm looking forward to the visit, and I'm honored that he's come to the United States.

Gun Control

Q. Mr. President, there are all sorts of attempts to water down the Brady bill. Are you one of those purists that Chairman Brooks talked about, or would you consider amendments to water it down?

The President. That bill shouldn't be amended. It's a modest bill, and I think it ought to be passed like it is. We would like to see the

Senate go on and do it. I feel very strongly about it. I also associate myself with the other remarks of the Attorney General. I think it's the beginning. It's not the end of the process by any means.

Q. What would you like to see on handguns?

The President. Well, I think extending the ban on imported handguns is important, which I will do today. Then Congress is debating this whole issue of assault weapons generally, broad definition, and we'll see what we can come out with. But you know, there's a bill in the House; there's a bill in the Senate. And I'd like the crime bill to pass, and then I'd like for that to be debated.

Q. Would you do the Brady bill separate?

Q. Yes, would you do the Brady bill separately or as part of the crime——

The President. It's fine with me, whatever— [*inaudible*]—done. I would prefer to get it as quickly as possible, but I think the important thing is that it be passed in a strong and clear and unambiguous form.

NOTE: The President spoke at 9:43 a.m. in the Rose Garden at the White House. The memorandums on gun dealer licensing and importation of assault pistols are listed in Appendix D at the end of this volume.

Remarks Announcing the Nomination of General John Shalikashvili To Be Chairman of the Joint Chiefs of Staff
August 11, 1993

Good afternoon, ladies and gentlemen. It's a great honor for me to be here today with the Vice President, Secretary Aspin, and General Powell to introduce to you and to our Nation the person whom I have selected to replace Colin Powell as the Chairman of the Joint Chiefs of Staff, General John Shalikashvili. He's widely known to his friends as General Shali. And since we're going to be seeing a lot of each other and you're going to have to write a lot about him, I think I'll just start using the shortened version of his name.

General Shali is superbly well qualified for this position. He is a soldier's soldier, a proven warrior, a creative and flexible visionary who clearly understands the myriad of conflicts, ethnic, religious, and political, gripping the world, as well as the immense possibilities for the United States and for the cause of freedom that are out there before us.

He has shown a proven ability to work with our allies in complex and challenging circumstances. He has shown me a real concern for the ordinary men and women who have enlisted in our armed services and who are living through this difficult and challenging period of downsizing. He understands how to downsize the Armed Forces and still maintain the strongest military in the world, with the equipment and, most important, the trained force with the morale we need to always fight and win when we have to.

And finally, I am convinced that he is in a unique position to be an advocate for the men and women in the armed services and for the national security of the United States to the Congress, to the country, and to our military allies throughout the world.

General Shali entered the United States Army as a draftee and rose through the ranks to his current position of Supreme Allied Commander in Europe and the commander in chief of all United States forces there. He's demonstrated his outstanding military talents repeatedly throughout a distinguished career from the day he was first drafted into the Army. He's a decorated Vietnam veteran. He ran Operation Provide Comfort in Iraq. He served on the Joint Chiefs of Staff as General Powell's assistant. He has the deep respect of both the troops who have served under him and the military leaders who have worked with him.

I selected him because I believe he has the ability to lead and to win any military action our Nation might ask of him. Above all, I am confident that in every instance he will give me his absolutely candid and professional military advice, which as President I must have.

He is also a shining symbol of what is best about the United States and best about our armed services. There is much more to his life than most Americans now know. It is a great American story. It began as so many American stories do, in another land. General Shali was born in Warsaw, Poland, the grandson of a Russian general in the Czar's army, the son of a Georgian army officer—that's the Georgia over there not over here—the heir of a family caught in a crossfire of the kinds of ethnic and national rivalries that now trouble so much of our world. In 1944, when he was 8 years old, his family fled in a cattle car westward to Germany in front of the Soviet advance. He came to the United States at the age of 16, settled in Peoria, Illinois, and learned English from John Wayne movies so that he could take a full course load from his first day in school. Now I intend to nominate this first generation American to the highest military office in our land, on the strength of his abilities, his character, and his enormous potential to lead our Armed Forces. Only in America.

I intend to nominate him, in particular, because his skills are uniquely well suited to the security challenges we face today. He helped revamp NATO to be a more flexible military and political force. He created a NATO Rapid Reaction Corps to undertake peacekeeping missions that are significantly different from our cold war challenges. He's been a leader in persuading NATO members to consider missions outside traditional alliance boundaries, a very, very important step in the recently announced NATO posture with regard to Bosnia. The end of the cold war has created many opportunities for our security and many new threats that lurk among the world's continuing dangers. General

Shali is the right man to lead our forces in this challenging era.

Our Nation is blessed with the finest military on the face of the Earth and the best military we have ever had. That was made clearer to me than ever as I approached this selection, for the top ranks of our Nation's military are an impressive bastion of talent, patriotism, and vision. Nothing illustrates that better than the great soldier whom General Shali will replace as Chairman of the Joint Chiefs of Staff. And I want to take this opportunity before all of America to personally thank General Colin Powell for the magnificent service and leadership he has rendered to this country for so many years, to thank him especially for the last several months of difficult and challenging decisionmaking we have done together, for always giving me his most candid advice, and for the wonderful job he has done of working with the other service chiefs to come to consensus on challenging and very difficult issues. He has contributed a great deal to a grateful Nation. And I know that we all wish him well.

I think there is no greater way for me at least to express the respect we all feel for General Powell than to name as his successor such a outstanding leader of such caliber, General John Shalikashvili.

I now invite him to the podium for whatever remarks he might wish to make. General Shali.

NOTE: The President spoke at 5:40 p.m. in the Rose Garden at the White House. Following his remarks, General Shalikashvili made brief remarks and responded to questions from reporters.

Letter to Congressional Leaders on Trade With Peru
August 11, 1993

Dear Mr. Speaker: (*Dear Mr. President:*)

Pursuant to section 203 of the Andean Trade Preference Act (ATPA) (19 U.S.C. 3202), I wish to inform you of my intention to designate Peru as a beneficiary of the trade-liberalizing measures provided for in this Act. Designation will entitle the products of Peru, except for products excluded statutorily, to duty-free treatment for a period ending on December 4, 2001.

Designation is an important step for Peru in its effort to fight against narcotics production and trafficking. The enhanced access to the U.S. market provided by the ATPA will encourage the production of and trade in legitimate products.

My decision to designate Peru results from consultations concluded in July 1993 between this Administration and the Government of Peru regarding the designation criteria set forth in section 203 of the ATPA. Peru has demonstrated to my satisfaction that its laws, practices, and policies are in conformity with the designation criteria of the ATPA. The Government of Peru has communicated on these matters by a letter to the Office of the United States Trade Representative and in so doing has indicated its desire to be designated as a beneficiary.

On the basis of the statements and assurances in Peru's letter, and taking into account information developed by the United States Embassy and through other sources, I have concluded that designation is appropriate at this time.

I am mindful that under section 203(e) of the ATPA, I retain the authority to suspend, withdraw, or limit the application of ATPA benefits from any designated country if a beneficiary's laws, policies, or practices are no longer in conformity with the designation criteria. The United States will keep abreast of developments in Peru that are pertinent to the designation criteria.

This Administration looks forward to working closely with the Government of Peru and with the private sectors of the United States and Peru to ensure that the wide-ranging opportunities opened by the ATPA are fully utilized.

Sincerely,

WILLIAM J. CLINTON

NOTE: Identical letters were sent to Thomas S. Foley, Speaker of the House of Representatives, and Albert Gore, Jr., President of the Senate. This letter was released by the Office of the Press Secretary on August 12. The related proclamation of August 11 is listed in Appendix D at the end of this volume.

Remarks on Signing Flood Relief Legislation at a Tribute to Flood Heroes in St. Louis, Missouri
August 12, 1993

Thank you very much. Please be seated, and good morning, to our distinguished host, Governor Carnahan; and majority leader of the United States House, Dick Gephardt; Secretary Espy; Secretary Shalala; James Lee Witt; the distinguished other Members of Congress who are here, Congressmen Jim Talent, Alan Wheat, Jerry Costello, Ike Skelton, and Bill Emerson. To the distinguished Governor of Kansas, Joan Finney, my good friend, welcome, and to all of you from all the States who were affected by this terrible flood.

We're going to begin today by awarding 19 outstanding Americans Presidential Certificates of Commendation. These recipients are everyday people, but what they did was most extraordinary. Hillary and Chelsea and I just had the opportunity to meet them all and to talk with them a little bit about their experiences during the flood. Because of their efforts, lives were saved and larger disasters were averted. In some cases, they provided the support that kept all the other volunteers going, and that's what made the difference.

In their communities, they are mothers and fathers, business owners, police officers, and neighbors. But in this time of crisis, they risked their lives to save children and parents, to pull people from troubled waters or trapped vehicles, to feed the hungry, to provide water to people who literally could not have had safe living conditions otherwise. And most importantly, a lot of them are committed to staying involved in this for the long haul. It is so easy to forget that much of the work is still to be done.

Today we salute them and others like them. And to be sure, there are hundreds, indeed thousands of others that we might have just as well recognized today who took on the raging rivers to stick up for their friends and neighbors and total strangers.

Now I'd like to ask the FEMA Director, James Lee Witt, to come here and present the commendations to the individuals as they are introduced and to thank him and all the State FEMA directors and all the local emergency management people for the wonderful work that they have done also in dealing with this flood.

Mr. Witt.

[At this point, Director Witt presented the Presi-

dential Certificates of Commendation. Gov. Mel Carnahan and Representative Richard Gephardt then made brief remarks.]

Thank you very much, ladies and gentlemen. Please be seated. I want to thank my friend Congressman Gephardt for that generous introduction and Governor Carnahan for his fine remarks. I acknowledged Governor Finney here. I thank all the others from the other States who are here. We have the Lieutenant Governor of Nebraska, the heads of various States' National Guards and emergency management programs, representing all those who worked.

I have been now to the Midwest four times since this flood began. The Secretary of Agriculture, who was up here with me, Mike Espy, has been here probably twice that many times, if not more. And I have charged him with being responsible for the long-term cleanup efforts, so I wanted him standing up here. So when you get frustrated with the Federal Government 30 days from now, call him—[*laughter*]—and harass him. He'll be good at it.

I thank also the Secretary of Health and Human Services, Donna Shalala, who has come here with me today. Many members of my Cabinet have been here to the Midwest, and many of them have a role to play.

We are here for two reasons. The first was to honor these fine people who have received their just recognition. The second is to sign the relief package which will permit the rebuilding to begin with a significant dose of support from the Federal Government.

Throughout human history it has been the way of nature to visit us on occasion with disaster, without apparent cause, without explanation, often without mercy, always reminding us that we need to live our lives with a little more humility and always understanding that we are not in full control. How we face these misfortunes tells us a lot about ourselves and our friends. We know we cannot contain the fury of a river. But we can and we must allow our humanity to overflow as well, to help to reclaim the lives that are shattered. That is what I have seen happen here in the Midwest, from official responses and from individual responses.

The other day I had a young girl from Wisconsin in the Oval Office. You may have seen her story written up. She's 13 years old, but she's only 4 feet tall. She weighs about 60 pounds. She was born with a rare bone disease which resulted in over two dozen bone-breakings in her body before she was born. Years ago she would never have been able to live any kind of life, but because of the medical miracles of the National Institutes of Health, which she has visited once every 3 months since she was an infant, she is able to function as a student. She is able to have a semblance of a normal life. She is a delightful young person. But she still can easily break major bones in her body. And yet, she implored her parents to let her leave Wisconsin—she lives in Milwaukee—and come to Iowa to help to fight the floods, knowing that she had an imminent risk just by carrying a can of water around.

That is the sort of thing that I have seen happen. When people say to me, "Well, FEMA really did a great job this time. The Federal Government was here all the way," I say, what else could we have done in the face of that kind of contribution by ordinary Americans?

One of the reasons, frankly, that FEMA did such a good job, I think, is that the Director of FEMA has actually spent several years helping ordinary people fight disasters. He is a friend of mine. He was a county judge in a county where all the Clintons came from. But he was not a political appointment to FEMA, he was somebody who knew what it was like to see people there risking their lives, their businesses, their livelihoods, putting sandbags against a swollen river. We need more people like that in our National Government, people who are related at the grassroots level to the real concerns of people. And we're going to try to give you that.

In this disaster, more than 45 lives were lost; 70,000 people had to be evacuated. But you all know it could have been a lot worse if it hadn't been for folks like you and the many tens of thousands who fought to make it as good as possible.

In just a minute I will sign this disaster relief bill, $6.3 billion in Federal assistance to the victims of the flood here in the Midwest and other disasters. This is an extraordinary measure taken under extraordinary circumstances with real speed, moving through Congress with the help of suffering citizens from the Midwest and eloquent advocates for the Midwest. I would be remiss if I did not commend the legislators of both parties who put aside partisan differences and put the people of this area first in passing this bill: people who are not here, like Senator Tom Harkin from Iowa and Senator Paul Wellstone of Minnesota; people who never seek the headlines, like Senator Jim Exon of Nebraska; people who are here represented, who quietly work for you day in and day out, again, without regard to party. We finally even found something that Senator Dole and I could agree on, in this bill. [*Laughter*]

These funds will be used across a wide spectrum and delivered quickly. They'll help farmers who lost their crops. Secretary Espy will see to it that payments are made at the rate of 100 percent of approved 1993 crop losses as defined by the 1990 farm bill. The funds will also be used to repair public facilities, bridges, highways, levees, and flood control networks; to provide for the health and social service needs of flood victims, and they will be significant. I hope we will have heroes who will be attending to those who will inevitably suffer from depression, from an undefinable and almost uncontainable sense of loss as they go back and see their life savings gone, the work of their lifetime washed away, even their family albums no longer available to them in times of sorrow. They'll be used to provide housing for the displaced; to help homeowners and businesses to clean up and rebuild; to help our dislocated workers to find new work, hopefully with even better skills.

Two billion dollars will go to the Federal Emergency Management Agency, FEMA, for relief of the floods and other disasters and to provide for emergency cash relief for those who qualify for that. I'm proud to say that FEMA has enjoyed a new respect as a result of their efforts in this flood. I was especially heartened by the praise given FEMA by the Mayor of Quincy, Illinois, Chuck Scholz. His city's brave stand against the rising waters made all Americans proud. And they didn't win all their battles.

All of the help in this relief package will come free of the bonds of redtape. Disasters provide enough grief without more coming from Washington, so we've worked as hard as we could to streamline the paperwork, to cut out unnecessary delays, to work on flexibility and fairness, to help in every way that we can.

A good example of this flexibility and willingness to cut redtape is contained in another bill that I will also sign this morning, called Depository Institutions Relief Act. It doesn't mean a thing, does it? Washington language. But what the act will do is important. It will allow Federal regulators to waive certain legal requirements for financial institutions serving areas hard hit by flooding, by relaxing a few regulations in response to this emergency. We'll allow local banks to make local decisions on how best to speed up aid and credit to those who really need it.

Just this week I signed into law the largest deficit reduction package in the history of America, almost $500 billion. There were a lot of things in that bill, which will become apparent over time, which really help ordinary Americans, including tax relief for people who work 40 hours a week and have children in their homes and still are living below the poverty line. One part of that bill is especially important today. Under it, flood victims will have more time and flexibility in replacing their homes and personal property. At the same time, the IRS will ease tax collection requirements on those who now have to live on their insurance proceeds.

You can be sure that we will continue to review the help needed by people in this region. We are in it for the long run. As I said, Secretary Espy is our designated leader on long-term Federal involvement in the rebuilding. And if there are further problems, we'll depend upon you, directly or through your elected representatives, to let us know.

Will Rogers once said, "We can't all be heroes because somebody has to sit on the curb and clap as everybody else goes by." [*Laughter*] Well, that may be true. And today we have applauded 19 heroes. But we have acknowledged also that they simply represent the best of what thousands of people demonstrated. I think that we can all be heroes if we learn something from this that we carry over into the rest of our lives.

Think about Reverend Donna Harris and the people of Niota, Illinois—the spiritual nourishment and the groceries, meals, and fresh water that she provided in that tiny town of 200 for flood victims. Or Al Vogt in Glen Haven, Wisconsin, who risked his life to save a teenager, a boy being dragged by flood waters through the street when Al saw him and pulled him to safety. The town I grew up in had a flash flood once where waters 10 feet high rushed at 30 miles an hour down the main street of town. I saw people pull babies flying in that kind of water. It is a terrifying experience. He braved it. He could have been drowned; he could have been pulled away. Sheriff Ken White helped to rescue two people, in two separate operations, from drowning. Once he had to tie himself to a truck so he could save a woman hanging onto a telephone pole.

Hearing these people, I'm reminded of what President Kennedy said of his own heroism in World War II. He said, "It was involuntary; they sank my boat." [*Laughter*] To be sure, for all these people heroism was involuntary. Maybe that's why the courage of daily life, in a way, is all the more to be admired, when there is no life-threatening danger, when we just are required to get up every day and to go about our business and to try to face our challenges and seize our opportunities. That, in a way, is the enduring heroism of the American people.

It's the heroism that I believe will be embodied when the Congress comes back to town next month and passes the national service corps bill to give young people a chance to serve their communities and earn some credit toward a college education, the heroism embodied in people like the local VISTA volunteers here in St. Louis. I want to single out Delores Despiwa. She's here somewhere. Please stand, Delores. Stand up there. Her home's under water, and she's still working for other people. I want to recognize the Iowa Conservation Corps. There are some members here from the Iowa Conservation Corps. Would they stand? I think they're here. Yes. Thank you.

That is the sort of sustained service that all of us need to think about providing to our country, and the attitude of cooperation, the determination to bridge the gaps that divide us, gaps of party and religion and philosophy, to struggle for common values. In the face of a 500-year flood, that's what millions of you did here in the Middle West. And you gave us an enduring vision of your courage.

The best way for the United States to reward that courage is not only for me to sign this flood relief bill and to work with you for the long haul but for all of us to try to learn something that we can take into our daily lives from the example you set in this emergency.

A couple of nights ago, Hillary and I had the incredible honor of hosting at the White House all the commanders in chiefs of all of our military commands all over the world, all the four-star generals and admirals that—someone said it was a 76-star dinner, but I don't think it was because I'm not sure you can divide 76 by 4 and get an even number. [*Laughter*]

But at the dinner, the Vice Chairman of the Joint Chiefs of Staff, Admiral David Jeremiah, who's become quite a good friend of mine, came up to me and said, "You know, you can't roll up your sleeves if you're wringing your hands." An interesting statement, isn't it? When the floods were coming no one had time to wring their hands, so they just automatically rolled up their sleeves. When the floods go away, we have time to wring our hands, so a lot of us don't roll up our sleeves. Let us honor the heroes here today by firm resolve to go back about the business of our daily lives as Americans, rolling up our sleeves and not wringing our hands.

Thank you very much.

I would like now to ask the Members of the United States Congress who are here to come up on the stage and join me as I sign this bill.

NOTE: The President spoke at 10:20 a.m. at the Henry VIII Hotel. H.R. 2667, approved August 12, was assigned Public Law No. 103–75.

Statement on Signing Flood Relief Legislation
August 12, 1993

Today I have signed into law H.R. 2667, the "Emergency Supplemental Appropriations for Relief From the Major, Widespread Flooding in the Midwest Act of 1993." This Act provides $6.3 billion of Federal assistance to the victims of the Midwest floods and other disasters. I commend the Congress for acting expeditiously to develop a bill that helps those who are suffering as a result of the Midwest floods.

H.R. 2667 provides an estimated $2.35 billion for disaster payments to farmers through the Commodity Credit Corporation. Pursuant to this Act, I am informing Secretary of Agriculture Mike Espy that extraordinary circumstances exist and that he is to make payments for 1993 crop losses at a 100 percent payment rate for each eligible claim, as authorized in the 1990 Farm Bill and this Act.

The Act also provides $2.0 billion for Federal Emergency Management Agency (FEMA) operations for disaster relief, both for the Midwest floods and for other disasters. This FEMA funding will provide for the repair of public facilities and for housing and other assistance to those affected by the Midwest floods. $235 million is provided to the Army Corps of Engineers for repairing damage to Federal and non-Federal levees and other flood control works.

The Act provides $389 million in Small Business Administration (SBA) loans and $200 million for long-term recovery efforts through the Economic Development Administration (EDA). The low-interest SBA loans will be made available primarily to homeowners, renters, and business owners to assist in their recovery from physical damage caused by the flooding in the Midwest. In addition, some of the loans will be made to firms engaged in agriculture-related activities that have suffered substantial economic injury due to farm damage. The Act also provides $10 million for additional SBA staff in order to facilitate the processing of loan applications. The EDA disaster assistance grants will be provided to State and local units of government for economic recovery strategy, technical assistance, and public works grants.

The Act includes $75 million for the Public Health and Social Service Emergency Fund of the Department of Health and Human Services for the repair and renovation of community health centers and migrant health centers damaged by the Midwest floods and for social services for flood victims. The Act also provides $200 million for disaster recovery planning with State and local agencies and for disaster-related community development. This $200 million is provided through the Department of Housing and Urban Development's Community Development Block Grant program.

The Act includes $42 million for the Department of Agriculture's Agricultural Stabilization and Conservation Service. This includes $12 million to hire temporary employees to accelerate processing of applications for crop disaster claims. It also includes $30 million to assist farmers with debris cleanup and the restoration of damaged farmland. Sixty million dollars is provided for the watershed and flood prevention

operations program in the Department of Agriculture. These funds will be used to repair levees, dikes, and other flood-retarding structures and to open water courses plugged with sediment and debris. Under certain conditions, this funding could also be used to enroll eligible cropland in Agriculture's Wetlands Reserve Program. In addition, $270.5 million is included for rural development and housing loans, emergency water grants, very low income housing repair grants, and for the Extension Service.

Also included in H.R. 2667 is $175 million for highway repair. This will allow the Secretary of Transportation to provide immediate assistance to States whose highways and bridges have been damaged by flooding. In addition, $21 million is provided for local rail assistance to help restore rail service in the flooded regions of the Midwest, and $10 million is provided for the Coast Guard.

The Act provides $54.6 million for title III of the Job Training Partnership Act, which authorizes assistance to dislocated workers. This additional funding will be available for the Secretary of Labor to finance temporary jobs to repair damage caused by the floods, clean up affected areas, and provide public safety and health services. Participants would include workers who have been dislocated by the floods, other displaced workers, and the long-term unemployed.

The Act provides $1 million to repair and replace National Oceanic and Atmospheric Administration (NOAA) facilities and equipment damaged during the Midwest floods. This includes repair and replacement of critical weather and flood warning systems.

H.R. 2667 provides $70 million for disaster assistance to schools affected by the floods. Also provided is $30 million to supplement Federal Pell Grant awards. College financial aid officers have the authority to adjust award amounts to assist students who, due to the flood, lose income or documentation of income.

The Act provides $50 million for the HOME Investment Partnerships Program in the Department of Housing and Urban Development. This funding will provide for a range of housing activities, including acquisition, rehabilitation, tenant-based rental assistance, and new construction in areas affected by the flooding in the Midwest.

Five programs in the Department of the Interior receive a total of $41.2 million: the U.S.

Geological Survey, the Fish and Wildlife Service, the National Park Service, the Historic Preservation Fund, and the Bureau of Indian Affairs. These funds will allow the Department to repair facilities on Indian reservations and to rehabilitate national wildlife refuges, fish hatcheries, dikes, roads, trails, and several national monuments and historic sites damaged by the Midwest floods.

The Act provides $34 million for the Environmental Protection Agency (EPA). These funds will be used for environmental damage assessment; for identifying, collecting, and disposing of pesticides and other contaminants; and for cleanup actions at eligible leaking underground tank sites that have been affected by the Midwest floods.

The Legal Services Corporation is provided $300,000 to assist those harmed by the flood with legal matters. Also provided is $4 million for State youth and conservation corps programs involved in disaster cleanup activities.

In addition to amounts previously designated as emergency requirements in accordance with the applicable provisions of the Balanced Budget and Emergency Deficit Control Act of 1985, as amended, I am today designating as emergency requirements the following appropriations and authorities provided by this Act:

Department of Agriculture, Commodity Credit Corporation fund: $300,000,000;

Department of Agriculture, Commodity Credit Corporation fund: all costs associated with raising to 100 percent the payment rate to farmers for 1993 crop losses;

Department of Education, Impact Aid: $70,000,000;

Department of Labor, Job Training: $11,100,000;

Department of Transportation, Local Rail Freight Assistance: $21,000,000;

Federal Emergency Management Agency, Disaster Relief: $862,000,000 for FY 1993, which replaces the July 29, 1993, emergency designation of these funds, which were originally requested for FY 1994; and

Legal Services Corporation, Payment to the Legal Services Corporation: $300,000.

WILLIAM J. CLINTON

The White House,
August 12, 1993.

NOTE: H.R. 2667, approved August 12, was assigned Public Law No. 103–75.

Remarks Welcoming Pope John Paul II in Denver, Colorado
August 12, 1993

Your Holiness, I think you can see from the wonderful reception you have received that the United States is honored to have you in Denver. I thank you for coming to Denver, to this historic gathering of young people from across the world.

I want to extend a special thanks to the cosponsors of World Youth Day, Archbishop Keeler and the National Conference of Catholic Bishops and the Pontifical Council for the Laity. I'm especially gratified that so many leading Catholic Americans could join us today. And I'd like to pay special tribute to one, my good friend, the former Mayor of Boston and our Ambassador to the Vatican, Ray Flynn. I also thank my friends Governor Roy Romer, Mayor Willington Webb, the members of the city council, and Congresswoman Patricia Schroeder, in whose district we now stand—or sit, as the case may be.

I want to thank the people of Denver who have opened their hearts and their homes to these young people and say a few words of appreciation, Holy Father, to American Catholics especially.

As the Catholic Church prepares to enter its third millennium, our Nation prepares to enter its third century. It is altogether fitting that such a young country would host World Youth Day. America has maintained its youth by always being able to change while holding fast to its fundamental values: a determination to support family and work; to the proposition that all children matter and we don't have a one to waste; to the proposition that in every corner of the world, race or creed should not deter any young boy or girl from growing up to the fullest of their God-given capacities.

Your Holiness, even though I am not myself a Roman Catholic, I was educated as a young boy by nuns and as a young man by Jesuit priests. And I might add, since we're in the business of paying compliments, I appointed a man born in Poland to be Chairman of the Joint Chiefs of Staff yesterday. But all Americans without regard to their religious affiliation are grateful to the Catholics of this country for the standards they have set for citizenship and service, for supporting their families and working well at their assigned tasks, and for caring about the less fortunate.

And all Americans without regard to their religious faith are grateful to you, Your Holiness, for your moral leadership. For we know that you were the force to light the spark of freedom over communism in your native Poland and throughout Eastern Europe, that you have been an advocate for peace and justice among nations and peoples, a strong voice calling for an end to hatred and to hunger everywhere and reminding people blessed with abundance that they must offer special comfort to the poor and the dispossessed. Your presence here is welcome. America is a better, stronger, more just nation because of the influence that you have had on our world in recent years and because of the influence that American Catholics have had on our Nation from the very beginning of our birth.

If we were to find one sentence that would sum up the Catholic social mission, the work that Catholics have done as citizens, it would be the great line from our only Catholic President's inaugural speech when President Kennedy said, "We must always remember that here on Earth God's work must be our own."

In 1987, Your Holiness, when you came to Detroit, you said that each of us must be instrumental in promoting a social order that respects the dignity of persons and serves the common good. That is what we must all be about. America today is striving to achieve that goal. We have many problems here, and we are trying to address many problems abroad. We dare not turn away from our obligations to one another. Your presence here today will remind us all of those obligations, of the values by which you have lived, of the causes for which you have worked.

I ask you now to come to this platform to welcome a grateful nation and many tens of thousands of young people from all across the world who are privileged to be in your presence here today.

NOTE: The President spoke at 2:45 p.m. at Stapleton International Airport. In his remarks, he referred to Archbishop William H. Keeler of Baltimore, president, National Conference of Catholic Bishops.

Remarks Following Discussions With Pope John Paul II in Denver
August 12, 1993

Good afternoon. It was a great pleasure and a great honor for me to be able to spend some time with the Holy Father. We had a cordial and productive meeting, and I believe we laid the basis for a productive and constructive relationship in the future.

We shared many values and perspectives: a commitment to today's young people in the United States and throughout the world; a belief in work and family and the importance of pursuing policies that support them; a commitment to correcting the social problems that give rise to so many problems for our people in this country, violence, drugs, and other things; and a recognition that we need in this Nation and throughout the world both more individual responsibility and more community action.

We talked about a wide range of international problems. We discussed Bosnia at length, as you might imagine. We talked about the peacekeeping mission in Somalia. We talked about the efforts of nations working together through the United Nations to reduce violence and support human rights and democracy throughout the world, in Cambodia, for example, and other places. We talked about the former Soviet Union and conditions in many countries. We talked about the Holy Father's native Poland and the progress that they are making there. We talked about Haiti and what the United States has tried to do there to restore democracy and freedom.

And throughout, I, like every other person who has ever met him, was profoundly impressed by the depth of His Holiness' conviction, the depth of his faith, and the depth of his commitment to continue on his mission.

I very much welcome the Vatican's commitment to human rights, including religious freedom for all. I welcome the progress that is being made in forging relationships and closer ties between the Vatican and Israel. That can only help as we seek to pursue peace in the Middle East.

We both are worried about the conditions in Somalia, the Sudan, Haiti, and Bosnia. We both are concerned about the problems that have always been with us, but we believe that we can make progress in dealing with them.

Finally, let me just say once again how very grateful I am to the Holy Father for coming

to World Youth Day here in Denver and for the Catholic Church's decision to bring World Youth Day to the United States and to Denver. It is my hope that the success of this extraordinary gathering of young people will create a greater spirit of unity and community among them and renewed commitment among those who are Americans to work for greater justice and opportunity here at home.

At the end of our meeting the Holy Father presented me with a Bible. And so, I close with a verse from it that I think characterizes his work and I hope in due time will characterize the work that we are doing here, the exhortation in St. Paul's letter to the Galatians, "Let us not grow weary while doing good, for in due season we shall reap if we do not lose heart."

Thank you, Your Holiness, for your heart and your efforts.

NOTE: The President spoke at 5:20 p.m. at Regis University.

Remarks to the Community in Alameda, California
August 13, 1993

Thank you very much, Secretary Perry, Admiral Ruck, Admiral Briggs, Secretary of the Navy Dalton, Acting Secretary of the Army Shannon. The other people on this platform with me are essential to the partnership that I seek to establish and continue here today: Secretary of Commerce Ron Brown, who has been instructed by me to head the administration's efforts to develop a specific strategy to revitalize the California economy; the United States Senators from California, Dianne Feinstein and Barbara Boxer; and your Congressman and the chairman of the House Armed Services Committee, Ron Dellums. I am glad to be here with all of them.

To the distinguished military officers to my right and most of all to those of you who are here from the United States Navy, from the Marine Corps, the United States Army, and from the Coast Guard, it is an honor to be here with you in the shadow of this magnificent aircraft carrier, the U.S.S. *Carl Vinson*, and just off to my left here, a ship that I helped to launch, the U.S.S. *Arkansas*, back in a former life of mine. It's wonderful to see the ship again

and to see the flag of my State and the flag of my country waving there.

I come here, first of all and foremost, to thank all of you, those of you in uniform and those of you who have worked to support those in uniform, for being genuine patriots, for helping to win the cold war, for making a difference in the lives of all Americans and billions of people around the world. You have done the right thing by your country.

As a result of that, it has become possible, indeed it has become necessary, to downsize the defense establishment of the United States and to, more importantly, reorganize so it can maintain its dominance in a world that is new and different but still quite dangerous and very much uncertain.

The one thing we must never do is to lose the ability to recruit and maintain the best trained, the best educated, most highly motivated men and women in the Armed Forces in the entire world. The other thing we must never do is to lose our capacity to train them and to give them the finest, most technologically advanced weaponry of offense and defense available in the world.

In order to accomplish those tasks, it is inevitable that as we downsize defense, we must not only reduce the numbers of people coming into the Armed Forces, not only reduce some of the money we have been spending on weapons systems, we have to reduce the base structure of our Armed Forces. If we do not do it at an appropriate level, we will wind up underspending on the education and training and support systems for the men and women in the service, underspending on the important research and development and weaponry we must have in order to maintain our own national security and our capacity to lead the world.

Nonetheless, when a base closing is announced, it means a difficult transition for the people in uniform and, very often, even more for the people in the community. I know that because I have been through a very traumatic one in my own State, when an Air Force base was closed in a community that had 15 percent unemployment when the closing was announced.

I come here today not only to say what I have said about why these things are happening but also to talk about what we can do together to help all of you cope with this change and to help this place and all these people come out winners in the end.

The wave of change that has washed over our shores has caused this shifting military structure. It has also opened up dramatic new opportunities in a global economy, if we have the vision and courage to seize those opportunities.

One of the things that we have not done very well is to frankly face the future and to plan aggressively for change, to give every person in this country a chance to live up to his or her God-given potential even in the face of change. You heard Secretary Perry quoting President Kennedy, "Those who think only of the past and the present will miss the future." That has happened. In a world that is changing as rapidly as ours is, people lose the opportunities they now have not just because of defense cutbacks but because of other changes in the global economy. It is absolutely critical if we are going to secure a better future for these young boys and girls that the Navy and the Marine Corps have helped to get off to a better start in life, to stay off drugs, in school, to be learners. We have got to learn to adapt to change and plan for it.

Let us first say clearly what you already know. This base and others like it, announced in the last round of base closings, will not actually shut down for several years. But if we wait until then to plan what happens to the people in and out of uniform and to the resources here, we will absolutely ensure a period of economic dislocation that need not occur.

Those of you in the military face the uncertainty of relocation. Others are wondering whether they will find a new job or what the future will bring. As I said, as Governor I went through this when we lost several thousand jobs in the Arkansas delta, which was the poorest area in the United States with the highest unemployment rate. I can report to you that if there is a good, aggressive partnership, good things can happen. There are hundreds of new and different and higher paying jobs in that community today because of what the local folks did working with the State and making the most of what we were given by the National Government. But I think we can do even better.

I make this pledge to you. The men and women who won the cold war will not be left out in the cold by a grateful Nation. If we are smart, imaginative, and creative, if the Federal Government listens to people at the grassroots level and moves this vast national bureaucracy in the interests of the people rather than the priorities and the prerogatives of those who govern the bureaucratic levers, we can move forward.

Nobody knows better what kind of future you can build than your own people. Just this morning, I found imaginative ideas in your local newspaper for urging the base to form closer ties to the growing economies of Asia. That's a good idea, the fastest growing region of the world.

Our plan for reusing military bases is community centers. The vision for the future is up to you. Our job is to give you the tools to build a future, whether you are individual service men and women who deserve a right to a good relocation or, if you leave the service, an adequate opportunity to increase your skills, your income, and your future, or whether you're staying behind here in this community and you want to grow the economy and find opportunity.

Last month, as Secretary Perry said, I announced a five-part, $5 billion action plan to help to turn closing military bases into engines of economic opportunity. We will respond rapidly and spend money wisely. We will not just give speeches. We will act.

Indeed, before I came here today I met with your local community commission devoted to revitalizing the economy of the area, and I listened to them. Presidents would do better if they spent more time listening to people at the grassroots levels. And that's one of the lessons I'm trying to learn and teach to Washington.

When a base closes, henceforward our first priority will be to create jobs and promote economic development. Every one of the changes will be directed toward providing jobs for the people who live here and their neighbors. Believe it or not, putting jobs first is a change in Federal policy. Even though we have been downsizing the defense establishment since 1987, that has not been the priority until this administration passed a new policy.

Right now, believe it or not, the law actually requires the Government to charge communities full price for a closed military base if it is used for job creation and economic development. But the Government can give away a military base if it's used for recreational purposes. Well, people who are out of work have too much time for recreation. Let's put people to work first and then provide for their recreation.

Earlier today I met with this community commission representing you so well and announced an example of our jobs-first policy. For years the port of Oakland has been trying to lease 200 acres of Navy property at the Oakland Naval Supply Center so that it could expand. For years there was a stalemate. Today I announced that that property will be rented out, much of it for $1 a year. That will create hundreds of good jobs.

To make the port a magnet for shipping and commerce we must deepen the channel. For years environmental concerns have slowed this process. I have directed the Army Corps of Engineers, the EPA, and all other concerned agencies to get on with it and to act as quickly as possible to resolve the issues so that we can dredge the channel and bring more opportunity to the people who live here.

Under the leadership of your Congressman, Ron Dellums, the people who formed the East Bay Conversion and Reinvestment Commission, with whom I met this morning, are already planning for a better and a brighter and a much more different future. Our administration has already provided $70,000 to hire staff and start the work of this commission. Now we can say that we will provide up to $3.5 million to plan for the East Bay of tomorrow. And we will begin now. We will not wait until the dislocations occur.

We've got to avoid the problems that others have faced in the past, problems that I faced when I was a Governor. Environmental cleanup is often dragged on for years. But my EPA Administrator, Carol Browner, has already met with this commission and has set firm deadlines for the cleanup. We've appointed local coordinators here in the East Bay to bust the bureaucracy, to slash through the redtape.

The East Bay has the potential to be a magnet for technology, for aviation, for manufacturing. Alameda County is the home of some of the world's finest research laboratories, Lawrence Livermore, Lawrence Berkeley and the University of California at Berkeley. We have a technology reinvestment project for defense conversion that is already drawing high-tech firms into partnerships with these institutions. If we succeed, this military axis could be transformed into a thriving, high-tech commercial hub, a high-tech gateway to Asia and beyond.

Here at the Naval Air Station you already have a wealth of facilities that can be converted into commercial use: an aircraft painting facility that meets Federal and State pollution rules. Now they paint fighter jets. Why not commercial planes? You have a state-of-the-art hush room used to test jet engines. Why not private jet engines? If we use our imagination, our energy, our creativity, this naval base and those around it now serving our freedom can and will thrive in the pursuit of commercial excellence.

In the technology reinvestment initiative, we have already received over 8,000 new proposals to put the American people to work in a peacetime economy, and almost 3,000 of them have come from the State of California alone. The future is out there waiting for us, if we have the courage and vision to seize it.

Within 60 days after the Congress finalizes the base closing list, the Departments of Labor and Commerce will have a SWAT team on the ground here in Alameda, specialists whose marching orders will be to work with people, train them, counsel them, and help them find a future. When the time comes, we will put into place a reemployment center here on the base to help with everything from job training to résumé writing, to create a new jobs data base so that for the first time people can actually call on a computer and find all the jobs available in the near area. And they will make sure that you have access to as much training in high-tech fields as you need.

I have directed the Navy to hold a special west coast conference here in the Bay area on October 26th and 27th to help community leaders plan for base reuse in their future. At that meeting there will be leaders from communities throughout the country which have already gone through base closures and have actually come out creating more jobs than they have lost. And they did it without the kind of support that we are now providing.

None of these changes will be easy, but we only have one choice. We can make this work to help people, or let the future take its course. I think the choice is clear. The world of global competition which we now face requires us, in order to make our next century a great one, to put our economic house in order. That means we live in an economy where capital, money, is mobile—can fly all over the world in a second—where commerce is global. Our wealth depends more than anything else on the skills of our people and our ingenuity in working together and investing in areas of high return.

That's why I fought so hard to get control of our economy again by the record deficit reduction package that the Congress passed last week. That's why I will propose a health care plan next month to provide affordable health care and security to all American families, because it's bad for business for us to spend 35 percent more on health care than any other nation in the world, insure 40 million fewer of our people than we would if we had any other system in the world, and constantly risk the security of millions of families and at the same time put our business in bad shape. In the private sector most American workers have given up their wage increases for the last several years just to hold on to their health benefits, and it will happen for 10 more years unless we have the courage to change the system. It's good for bringing the deficit budget down. It's good for the American economy.

That's why I will fight for expanded trade opportunity, to secure by the end of the year a world trade agreement through the General Agreement on Tariffs and Trade that every analyst says will add hundreds of thousands of man-

ufacturing jobs to America by the end of the decade, and why I can say today, finally, that we have concluded what I believe is a very successful negotiation with the Mexican Government on the North American Free Trade Agreement, one that will now guarantee that a port city like Oakland will be able to send ever-increasing quantities of American-made goods to sell in Mexico and beyond.

I am pleased that the United States, Mexico, and Canada have reached this agreement and have done it in a way that for the first time ever in a trade agreement requires another nation, in this case Mexico, not to use lower environmental standards, not to use lower labor standards just to get jobs here at America's expense but to actually have mutual trade based on increasing environmental standards, increasing wages and incomes in Mexico, and fair trade between the two nations so that both of us can win, create more jobs, and build a better future. That's the kind of future we all need.

My fellow Americans, I am determined not to let the American dream founder. What a tragedy it would be if the aftermath of winning the cold war were a legacy that we left millions of Americans who won that war out in the cold. What a tragedy it would be if because we did not have the discipline and will to change, we hung on to outmoded ways of doing things under the guise of being good to our men and women in uniform, and we wound up weakening our national security because we didn't have the money to invest in continued technology and training in support of the men and women in uniform.

There is another and better way. And it is the way we are pursuing here. I do want this county, I do want these facilities, I do want this area to be a national model.

On the surface you have paid an enormous price here. The largest impact of the last round of base closings came in the Bay area and in northern California. Everybody knows that. But if you look around you at the people, if you look around you at the resources, if you imagine the future toward which we are tending, if we do the right thing, it means a better future for our people. It means a brighter future for this area, and it means a stronger, stronger America.

I thank you again for your service to your Nation. The best way we can demonstrate honoring your patriotism is to take steps now that are aggressive, tough, unrelenting, and worthy of what you have done for your country. I will do my best to do just that.

Thank you, and God bless you all.

NOTE: The President spoke at 12:05 p.m. at Wharf #3 at the Alameda Naval Air Station. In his remarks, he referred to Rear Adm. Merrill W. Ruck, USN, Commander, Naval Base San Francisco; and Rear Adm. Steven R. Briggs, USN, Acting Commander, Naval Air Force, U.S. Pacific Fleet.

Statement on North American Free Trade Agreement Supplemental Accords
August 13, 1993

I am pleased that the United States, Mexico, and Canada have reached agreement on the supplemental accords to the North American Free Trade Agreement.

Last fall, I pledged that I would not submit NAFTA to Congress until my administration addressed shortfalls in the areas of environmental protection, worker rights, and import surges. Early this morning we fulfilled that promise. Today I pledge my strongest commitment to a major effort this fall to secure NAFTA's passage.

With the completion of the side accords, we have turned NAFTA into a pathbreaking trade agreement. NAFTA is strongly in the interest of the United States. This agreement helps our workers, our environment, our businesses, and our consumers.

With these agreements on environmental quality and labor standards, the North American Free Trade Agreement has become a fair trade agreement as well.

NAFTA will create thousands of high paying American jobs by unlocking access to Mexico, a growing market of 90 million people that thirst for American products and services. The old rules marked by high trade barriers and preferences for companies manufacturing in Mexico have been pushed aside. In their place NAFTA establishes a level playing field, low tariffs, and a tough mechanism for resolving environmental and labor problems.

NAFTA is part of my broad economic strategy to gear the American economy for a changing world, to channel change for the benefit of working men and women. I look forward to working with the Congress and the American people to make NAFTA a reality.

Remarks on Signing the Colorado Wilderness Act of 1993 in Denver
August 13, 1993

Thank you very much. Thank you very much, Senator Campbell, ladies and gentlemen. I am delighted to be back in Colorado. I'll be back tomorrow and the next day and the next day. I really wanted to come here for this bill signing because not only of the wilderness, and it's important to me personally, but also because this effort reflects what I think our country needs more of: people who are willing to go after something and stay after it as long as it takes, and people in the end who are willing to sit down and reason together and work together and feel that they're stronger when they reach

agreement rather than weaker. I hope, as Senator Brown characterized this process, I'd like to bring it to more of the problems our great Nation faces, although I hope none of them take 12 years to resolve. [*Laughter*]

I do want to thank all of the members of the Colorado delegation, without regard to party, for their work here. I especially thank Congressman Skaggs, my good friend Pat Schroeder, and Senator Campbell, and Senator Brown. And there are others who are not here. I want to say a special word of thanks to my friend of now more than 20 years, Senator Gary Hart, and to Tim Wirth, who has done a magnificent job now in the State Department taking his environmental passion global. Even when I get bad press, Tim Wirth gets good press. He has been almost universally acclaimed for the breath of fresh air he has brought to the efforts of the United States to promote responsible policies to preserve and enhance life throughout this planet. And I'm glad to be here with him today. And I want you to know that even though he's not a Senator from Colorado anymore, he is serving the people of Colorado in an exemplary way.

Almost 100 years ago to the day, not far from here, another visitor to Colorado was moved by what she saw, and she wrote a poem. She wrote of spacious skies and fruited plains and amber waves of grain. On that day Katherine Lee Bates described America the Beautiful. Today we return to reaffirm the beauty and the majesty of the land that she fell in love with and that we all hold dear. Today I come back to sign H.R. 631, the Colorado Wilderness Act, which designates a total of 612,000 acres, 19 separate areas in our national forests, as components of the National Wilderness Preservation System. The Act also protects five areas totaling over 150,000 acres under management plans that are slightly less restrictive but still important. It protects rugged and roadless expanses, sets aside glacier-chiseled valleys and jagged peaks, preserves the calm of still mountain meadows and the cathedrals of magic old-growth groves.

The names of the places we are preserving today provide more than ample proof of their majesty. Sangre de Cristo range is a haunting and painful image of a barren peak washed in sunset colors. Fossil Ridge speaks of wide-eyed children stumbling upon ancient relics, hopefully not as they turned out in "Jurassic Park." [*Laughter*] Oh Be Joyful is surely a peak that will be noticed on any topographical map.

At the same time as it protects these treasures, the Act releases about 115,000 acres of Forest Service lands in Colorado for other purposes, balancing the goal of preserving our environment with the need to provide for a healthy economy for the people who live and work here.

It's been a dozen years since the last legislation designating wilderness in Colorado, a dozen since an administration has been committed to expanding wilderness delegations. In those years wilderness designations were questioned by those who wonder why these things must be set apart and saved. We save our wilderness because it reflects the diversity of the gifts of God that go with the diversity of our people and our culture and because many, many of us believe that its sheer grandeur offers us the clearest evidence we have here on Earth of divine providence. The great conservationist John Muir said, "Everyone needs beauty," and that's why we save wilderness.

I'd like to close today with a short message from Wallace Stegner to acknowledge his passing this past spring and to acknowledge the wilderness area of which he wrote so eloquently. "The remainder and the reassurance that is still there is good for our spiritual health even if we never once in 10 years set foot on it," he wrote. "It is good for us when we are young because of the incomparable sanity it can bring briefly, as vacation and rest, into our insane lives. It is important to us when we are old simply because it is there. Important, that is, simply as an idea." That idea, an essentially American idea, is embodied in this act of Congress. I thank all of you who made it possible. And I am proud to have the opportunity to sign it into law.

Thank you very much.

NOTE: The President spoke at 5:35 p.m. at Stapleton Airport. H.R. 631, approved August 13, was assigned Public Law No. 103–77.

Statement on Signing the Colorado Wilderness Act of 1993
August 13, 1993

I am pleased to sign into law H.R. 631, the "Colorado Wilderness Act of 1993." This Act designates 19 areas within the National Forests and public lands of Colorado, encompassing 612,000 acres, as components of the National Wilderness Preservation System. This Act also protects five areas, totalling some 155,000 acres, under management plans that are slightly less restrictive than wilderness designation.

Enactment of this bill ends a long debate regarding wilderness designation in the National Forests of Colorado. Key to resolving this debate is the compromise language on the protection of wilderness water resources. Because all of the areas designated as wilderness lie at the headwaters of river watersheds, wilderness water resources can be protected by restricting new diversions of water from within these areas. Existing water rights and water diversions are also protected by this Act. In short, the Colorado delegation has found an innovative solution to a very complicated water resources issue, and for this they are to be commended. However, the circumstances in Colorado are unique and this compromise language may have to be refined if it is to be used to protect wilderness water resources in other States.

By signing this bill into law today, we further the protection of unique and sensitive lands within the National Forests of Colorado. The areas designated in this Act are outstanding additions to the National Wilderness Preservation System. These areas join the 2.6 million acres of outstanding National Forest System (NFS) lands in the State that have already been designated as wilderness. At the same time, this Act releases about 115,000 acres of NFS lands in Colorado for other purposes, balancing the goal of environmental protection with the need to provide for a healthy economy.

Today, we complete the decade-long process of reviewing wilderness study areas in Colorado that were designated in earlier legislation. I commend the Colorado delegation for their diligence and bipartisan leadership in making this Act a reality. This balanced approach to wilderness designation preserves opportunities for economic development in Colorado, while maintaining the quality of life that makes Colorado such a wonderful place to live and work.

WILLIAM J. CLINTON

The White House,
August 13, 1993.

NOTE: H.R. 631, approved August 13, was assigned Public Law No. 103–77. This statement was released by the Office of the Press Secretary on August 14.

Statement on Signing the Small Business Guaranteed Credit Enhancement Act of 1993
August 13, 1993

Today I am signing S. 1274, the "Small Business Guaranteed Credit Enhancement Act of 1993." This legislation will inject new life into many small businesses by significantly increasing the availability of loans that can be guaranteed by the Small Business Administration (SBA).

My Administration and the Congress recognize that SBA is an increasingly critical component of our efforts to end the credit crunch by making sufficient capital available for small businesses to grow and prosper. The demand for SBA loan guarantees has increased over the past several years at a 35 to 40 percent annual rate, as banks have increasingly turned to SBA for assistance in small business lending.

S. 1274 increases the amount of loans that may be guaranteed per dollar of credit subsidy. This will allow SBA to more than double its Section 7(a) General Business Loan Guarantee program from a range of $3 billion to $4 billion to a range of $7 billion to $8 billion in fiscal year 1994, based on anticipated appropriations. This higher program level will provide an uninterrupted source of credit for small businesses, something that has been lacking over the past few years. And it will do so while providing significant savings to the taxpayers. The savings will be about $180 million in the first year and $748 million over four years relative to appropriations that would be needed to meet expected demand for the 7(a) program absent the reforms.

Perhaps most importantly, the lending authority provided by S. 1274 will assist firms in maintaining and creating more than 600,000 jobs over the next four years.

S. 1274 also makes technical changes to other small business programs in order to improve SBA's administration of the Small Business Development Center Program and the Microloan Demonstration Program, and to facilitate planning and execution of the White House Conference on Small Business.

I am pleased to sign legislation that helps small businesses and their employees.

WILLIAM J. CLINTON

The White House,
August 13, 1993.

NOTE: S. 1274, approved August 13, was assigned Public Law No. 103–81. This statement was released by the Office of the Press Secretary on August 14.

The President's Radio Address
August 14, 1993

Good morning. This week we took a big step toward restoring opportunity and prosperity to the people of our Nation when I signed into law our economic growth plan. It puts our house in order with the largest deficit reduction measure in our history, mandating more than $250 billion in spending cuts, with substantial cuts in more than 200 specific spending programs. It makes over 90 percent of our small businesses eligible for tax cuts if they invest to spur job creation. And it provides new incentives to lift people who work full time and have children in their homes but still live in poverty above the poverty line. That's a real incentive for the working poor to stay at work and a downpayment on our plan to end the welfare system as we know it.

With this economic plan in place, private analysts believe more than 8 million jobs will be created over the next 4 years. Already the plan has brought interest rates to historic lows and the stock market to historic highs. People are refinancing home loans and business loans, saving a lot of money, money that can be invested to grow this economy. And we've had about a million new jobs come into the economy in the last 6½ months. This plan will help us to restore the economy and revive the American dream.

But there's another threat to our security, to our economic revival, and to our most basic values. It's the crime that's ravaging our neighborhoods and communities. There were 90,000 murders in America in the last 4 years and a startling upsurge in gang activity, drive-by shootings, and bloody car-jackings. There's a virtual war on many of our streets, and crime has become a national security issue to millions of Americans. I've worked to fight crime as an attorney general and a Governor. I've worked with law enforcement officers, community leaders, victims groups. I know we can make our streets safer and our children's future more secure.

This week I announced my administration's anticrime plan, and law enforcement officers from all over America came to support it. People from Massachusetts to Mississippi spoke up. William O'Malley, a district attorney in Massachusetts, said the murder rate in Plymouth County had doubled, and the age of defendants in court is getting younger. One of the law enforcement officers said that in his area the average age of a killer was now under 16 years of age. Police commissioner Bill Bratton of Boston spoke of the fear that grips his city where homicides have gone up 60 percent this year because of gangs and domestic violence. The attorney general of Mississippi pointed out that the crime wave has now reached small towns and rural areas, and we can't leave them out of our solution.

These facts could be repeated by any prosecutor, any police officer in the United States. We have to give these people the help they need to seize the control of our streets. And that's precisely what I'm determined to do.

Our new crime initiative goes back to basics: toughening criminal laws and disarming criminals, putting more police on patrol, protecting students, restoring order to our streets. It also emphasizes some good ideas that do work: community policing, working with citizens to prevent crime and catch criminals, and boot camps for youthful offenders to give them a second chance to develop self-discipline and other skills to live lawful, successful lives.

Society has the right to impose the most severe penalty on the hardened criminals who commit the most heinous crimes. I support capital punishment, especially against those who kill our police officers. This legislation expands the Federal death penalty and limits the time available to criminals to appeal their sentences. The plan cracks down on the easy availability of guns. I'm eager to sign the Brady bill, which requires a waiting period before the purchase of a handgun. And I've signed a directive ordering the Treasury Department to suspend the importation of foreign-made assault pistols, the weapons of choice for many gangs and drug dealers.

Our crime bill will fund the hiring of up to 50,000 new police officers to walk the beat. It will also create a police corps to allow young people to pay for college and then ask them to return to their communities as police officers in exchange for the educational benefit. The plan expands the cop on the beat program to help pay to put more police on the street, to hire more security guards to keep our schools safe, to beef up patrol in public housing and communities where small businesses are vulnerable to crime. We ask for new Federal boot camps to provide wayward young people the discipline, the education, the training they need for a chance to avoid a lifetime of crime.

And we put these new tools into the hands of the toughest and most talented trio of crimefighters ever assembled at the Federal level: the Attorney General, Janet Reno, a seasoned prosecutor from Miami; the FBI Director, Louis Freeh, a streetwise former prosecutor and tough Federal judge with a nationally acclaimed record of crimefighting; and Lee Brown, the former police chief of New York, Houston, and Atlanta, the father of community policing, who now serves as our Director of Drug Control Policy.

But these law enforcement leaders cannot and must not wage this war alone. We in Government can start by ensuring that the criminal justice system reflects our values and restores people's confidence in the Government's ability to prevent and punish crime. But the power of every individual to influence those around them is also very strong, and it's also a power we must turn to if we're going to turn the crime problem around. Too many of our fellow citizens simply reject values like decency, order, and the respect for the rule of law. Often we can yank people like that back to what is right and what is true.

Every one of us needs to speak up and provide better role models for our young people before we lose them to the meanness of the streets. We can take simple but effective actions like taking car keys away from teenagers and adults who are under the influence of alcohol or drugs before they get behind the wheels of their cars and risk great damage to themselves and to others. We can urge broadcasters and advertisers to tone down the violence we see on television and in theaters every day and persuade them that there is a market for programs and movies that reflect and reinforce our values. We can remind people of the opportunities they have for community service so that they can express their patriotism and caring by giving something back to the country which gives us so much and helps people in need at the same time.

In short, we can work together as partners. And when we do, when the Government works with us and not against us, there is nothing the American people can't do.

With the economic plan in hand and a very tough anticrime bill on the way, we can truly say our country is headed in a new direction: more responsibility, more opportunity, a deeper sense of community, and restoring the American dream.

Thanks for listening.

NOTE: The address was recorded at 4:40 p.m. on August 13 at the Park Oakland Hotel in Oakland, CA, for broadcast at 10:06 a.m. on August 14.

Remarks to the National Governors' Association in Tulsa, Oklahoma
August 16, 1993

Thank you very much, Governor Romer, Governor Campbell, our host Governor, Governor Walters. I'm really glad to be here today. The last time the Governors met in Oklahoma was in 1981, right after I had just become the youngest former Governor in American history. I've never been to an NGA meeting in Oklahoma, so I would have showed up here even if you hadn't invited me to speak.

I want to say that Hillary and I are both very glad to be here, to be with you again. We're looking forward to our meeting after this where we can talk about the health care issue and other issues in greater detail. I treasure the partnership that I have had with so many of you and which we are trying to develop and literally embed in Federal policy today. I know that you have already received an update on the progress that we have made together, working on more rapid processing of the Governors' waiver requests in many different areas and a number of other issues, which I hope we'll be able to talk more about later.

I know too, that the Vice President has already been here and taken all my easy lines away. Even told you the ashtray story, I know, yesterday, which I understand Governor Richards said was one of those issues that her mother in Waco could understand.

Today I come to talk to you about the issue of health care. I would like to put it into some context. When I became President it was obvious to me, based on just the announcements and evidence which had come into play since the November election, that the Federal deficit was an even bigger problem than I had previously thought and that, unless we did something about it, we would not have the capacity to deal with the whole range of other issues; that forever, at least during the term of my service, we would be nibbled away at the edges in trying to deal with health care reform or defense conversion or welfare reform or any other issue by the fact that we simply were not in control of our own economic destiny.

And so we devoted the first several months of this administration to trying to pass an economic plan that would reduce the deficit by a record amount, that would have at least as

many spending cuts as new tax increases—in fact, we wound up with more spending cuts—and that would give some incentives where they were needed, particularly in the small business, in the high-tech, in the new business area, to try to grow more jobs for the American economy. That has, I believe, laid a very good foundation for the future.

This morning I was reading in the morning newspapers that long-term interest rates are now at a 20-year low, the lowest they've been since 1973. And we have the basis now to proceed on a whole range of other issues. When the Congress comes back next month, I believe that the Senate will rapidly pass the national service legislation, which many of you are very familiar with and which many of you have supported. It will pass on a bipartisan basis and will enable tens of thousands of our young people to earn credit for their college education by serving their communities at home and solving problems that no Government can solve alone.

We are working on defense conversion initiatives from northern California to South Carolina and at all points in between. I hope we can do more on that. We will have a major welfare reform initiative coming up at the first of the year, which I hope all of you will not only strongly support but will be active participants in. And meanwhile, keep doing what you're doing and asking for the waivers you think you need.

There is now before the Congress a crime bill which can have a big impact in every State here, that will add 50,000 more police officers on the street, support innovations like boot camps for first offenders, help us to pass the Brady bill, and deal with a number of other issues facing us there.

There will be initiatives to expand the economic range of Americans. As I know that you all know now—and I wish he could be here with us today—our Trade Ambassador, Mickey Kantor, successfully concluded the NAFTA negotiations just a few days ago with some historic, some historic provisions never before found in a trade agreement anywhere, including the agreement by the Government of Mexico to tie their minimum wages to productivity and economic growth and then to make their compliance with that the subject of a trade agreement, which means that it can be reviewed, that if there are violations they can be subject to fine, and ultimately the trade sanctions can be imposed. Nothing like this has ever been found in a trade agreement before. It ensures that workers on both sides of our border can benefit. And I appreciate the support of the Governors for the whole issue of expanding trade. We are now in Europe trying to get the GATT negotiations back on track, and I hope we can do that.

Finally, let me say there will be a whole push toward the end of the year on a whole range of political reform issues. One or the other House of Congress have already passed a campaign finance reform bill, a lobby limitation bill, and the modified line-item veto, which I think that 100 percent of you think that the President ought to have.

In addition to that, the Vice President will issue a report to me very shortly on the reinventing Government project, which he discussed with you in great detail yesterday. The only thing I can tell you is that everything I ever suspicioned about the way the Federal Government operates turned out to be true, plus some. The ashtray story is only illustrative. The fundamental problem is not that there are bad people in the Federal Government or that the payrolls have been swollen by people who just want to pad them. That is not true. In fact, many of the Federal agencies didn't grow at all in the 1980's. What has happened is that for the last 60 years one thing has been added on to another and people with the best of intentions have just piled one more requirement on to the Federal Government, and the fundamental systems that operate this Government have gone unexamined for too long, whether it's personnel or budgeting or procurement. And we are trying to do that in ways that I think would free up a lot of money and improve the efficiency and service that the American people are entitled to expect from all of us.

Now having said all that, I want to make two comments. I don't think that any of it will take America where we need to go unless we also reform the health care system, which is the biggest outstanding culprit in the Federal deficit and is promoting economic dislocations in this economy. And secondly, I don't think we can do it unless we do it on a bipartisan basis.

I never want to go through another 6 months where we have to get all of our votes within one party and where the other party has people that want to vote with us and they feel like they've got to stay—and the whole issue revolves around process instead of product, political rhetoric instead of personal concern for what's going to happen to this country. There's plenty of blame to go around. As far as I'm concerned there will be plenty of credit to go around. I don't much care who gets the credit for this health care reform as long as we do it.

But I am convinced that what this Nation really needs is a vital center, one committed to fundamental and profound and relentless and continuing change in ways that are consistent with the basic values of most Americans and that move all of us along a path. And I don't think you can do it unless we can sit down together and talk and work.

Many of the skills which are highly prized among you—both in your own States, where you serve and work with people who think differently than you do on some issues, who belong to different parties than you do, and the way you work around this table—those skills are not only not very much prized, sometimes they're absolutely demeaned in the Nation's Capital.

When we come here and we try to work on something like we worked on the welfare reform bill in 1988, we talked about: How does this really work? How are people really going to be affected by this? How can we deal with our differences of opinion and reach real consensus that represents principled compromise? And how can we be judged not just on what we say but on what we do?

Back east where I work, consensus is often turned into cave-in; people who try to work together and listen to one another, instead of beat each other up, are accused of being weak, not strong. And the process is a hundred times more important than the product. Beats anything I ever saw. And the people that really score are the people that lay one good lick on you in the newspaper every day instead of the people that get up and go to work, never care if they're on the evening news, never care if they're in the paper, and just want to make a difference.

And so I say to you, anything that you can do to help me and the Congress to try to recreate the mechanisms by which you have to function in order to do anything at the State level and by which we have worked together here to move forward on a whole range of issues, I will be grateful for. This country has too many words and too few deeds on too many issues, and we can do better than that.

Now, let's talk about the health care issue. We all know what's right with our health care system. For those who have access to it, it is the finest in the world, not only in terms of the incredible technological advances but in terms of having choice of our physicians, ready access to health care, and overall high quality that lasts throughout a lifetime. We can all be grateful for that.

My Secretary of Housing and Urban Development, Henry Cisneros, and I were talking the other day. His son just had a profoundly important and difficult operation. Just a few years ago he was told that about all he could hope for for his boy was a comfortable life, and eventually his time would run out, probably sooner rather than later. And because of the relentless progress of medical technology, his son now has a whole new lease on life.

Nobody wants to mess up what is good with American health care. We must preserve it and preserve it with a vengeance. But we also know what is not so good. We know that in a world in which we must compete for every job and all the incomes we can, we are spending over 14 percent of our income on health care. And only one other nation in the world, Canada, is over 9. They're at about 9.4. Our major competitors in the high-wage chase for the future, Japan and Germany, are down around 8 percent. So they're at 8, and we're at 14. More troubling, if we don't do anything to reverse the basic trends that are now rifling through our system, by the end of this decade we'll be at 19 percent of GDP on health care. No one else will be over 10, and we'll be basically spotting our competitors 9 cents on the dollar in every avenue of economic endeavor. I don't think that is something that's right.

We know that this places enormous pressure on businesses. I'll come back to some of the comments made by Mr. Motley along toward the end of my remarks, but the truth is that about 100,000 Americans a month are losing their health insurance because their employers can no longer afford to carry it under the present system we have, and others, holding on for dear life, are never giving their employees

pay raises. And it is estimated, unless we do something about this system, that the increased cost of health care between now and the end of the decade will literally absorb all of the money that might otherwise be available in this economy to raise the salaries of our working people.

We see employers unequally treated by the cruel hand of the system that we have. We know now we are spending far more money, about a dime on the dollar probably, administratively just on paperwork, pushing paper around, than any of our competitors are. A decade ago, the average doctor took home about 75 cents on the dollar that came into the clinic. Today that's down to 52 cents on the dollar, in only 10 years, because we are awash in paperwork imposed (a) by the Government and (b) for the fact that only the United States has 1,500 separate health insurance companies writing thousands and thousands of different policies.

I have a doctor friend in Washington who recently hired somebody not even to do paperwork but just to stay on the phone to call insurance companies every day to beat them up to pay what has already been covered—money right out of the pockets of the nurses that work in his clinic. And there's a story like that in every health care establishment in America today.

We know we still have almost 40 million people uninsured, and more every month, not fewer. We know that State governments are literally being bankrupt by the rising costs of Medicaid—money that used to go to education, money that used to go to economic development, money that could have gone to law enforcement going every year, just shoveling out the door, not for new health care, more money for the same health care. And even when we control the price of certain things, that extra utilization, or more people coming into the system because the rest of it is broken down, are driving the costs up. We know that there are still serious access problems.

And we know, as I said, that the Federal deficit is in terrible shape because of health care. If you look at this budget the Congress just adopted, defense goes down, discretionary spending is flat. That means we spend more money on defense conversion, on Head Start, on pregnant women, on a few other things— every dollar that we spend more on, that something else was cut. The only thing that's going up are the retirement programs—and Social Security taxes produced a $60 billion surplus for us even with the cost-of-living allowances—and health care. Everything else is either flat or down. And under all scenarios proposed by all people who presented any budgets last year, the deficit went down for 4 years and then started going up again because of health care. So the only way we can keep our commitments, you and I, to the American people to restore real control over this budget is to do something about health care.

Now, I would argue that if you know you've got a list of what's right and you know you've got a list of what's wrong and what's wrong is going to eventually consume what's right, you cannot continue to do nothing. And I don't think most people want to continue to do nothing.

I want to thank the NGA and especially the Governors who have worked with us throughout this process. Many of you have met with the First Lady and Ira Magaziner and the people, literally hundreds and hundreds of people, who have worked with them on a bipartisan basis to try to craft a health care reform package that will ensure that the States are real partners in our efforts to preserve quality, cover everyone, control costs, and enable the States and the Federal Government to regain some control over their financial futures.

No one embodied that spirit of bipartisanship on this issue more than our late friend, George Mickelson. And I just want to take a word here to say how very much I appreciated him as a friend, as a Governor, and as someone who had the sort of spirit that if it could embrace this country on this issue, we could solve this problem in good faith.

The National Government has a lot to learn from the States in the tough decisions that some of you have made already. I can honestly say that along toward the end of my tenure as Governor, the most frustrating part of the job was simply writing bigger checks every year for the same Medicaid program when I didn't have the money that all of us wanted to spend on education and economic development and the other important issues before us.

There have been phenomenally important contributions made to this debate already by the Governors of many States in both parties. I won't mention 1, 5, or 10 for fear I'll leave out someone I should have mentioned, but let me say that I am very grateful to all of you

for the work that you have already done. I also want to say a special word of regret about the absence here of the Governor from my home State, Jim Guy Tucker, who himself has been getting some world-class medical care. And I talked to him last night. He's feeling quite well, and he promises to be at the next meeting.

But all of you have a role to play in what we're about to do. Over the last 8 months, I've met with many of you personally in Washington. Many of you have lent your staffs to the efforts that we're making on health care reform. And we've learned clearly that what works in North Dakota may not work in New York. Just yesterday your executive committee pledged to support health care reform within a comprehensive Federal framework that guarantees universal coverage and controls costs. We will work with the States to phase in reform, and we will help you to work out problems as they arise. And we have to have an honest discussion about what that framework ought to look like.

I want today to tell you what I think we should do. Next month I will outline a plan to Congress that will offer real hope for all Americans who want to work and take responsibility and create opportunities for themselves and their children. I think the elements of that plan ought to be as follows:

One, we've got to provide health care security to people who don't have it. That means not just those who don't have health insurance coverage now but those who are at risk of losing it. I don't know how many people I met last year all over this country, all kinds of people, who knew they would never be able to change jobs again because someone in their family had been sick. I don't know how many other people I met who couldn't afford their health insurance package because there was someone in their job unit that they needed to get rid of in order to be able to afford it. We have got to have a system of universal coverage that provides security to Americans.

Second, I think we have to have a system of managed care that maintains the private sector, organizes Americans in health alliances operated within each State, contains significant new incentives for prevention and for wellness and against overutilization, and that has a budget so that the competition forces should keep things within the budget. But ultimately, especially in the early years, there must be some limit. I will say again, if we don't change this, we're going to go from 14 to 19 percent of our income going to health care by the end of the decade. It is going to be very difficult for us to compete and win in the global economy with that sort of differential.

Second—third, excuse me, there must be insurance reform. There has to be a basic package of benefits. There needs to be community rating. There has to be some opportunity—I heard Governor Wilson talking about this before I came out—for pooling for small employers. We cannot permit price differentials that exist today to get worse instead of better simply because of the size of the work units.

Finally, in this connection, if we do these things, there will be massive cuts in paperwork because you won't have to have every health unit in this country trying to keep up with thousands of different options and all the myriad complexities that flow from that. We won't have another decade when clerical employment in the health care area goes 4 times faster than health care providers. No one believes that that is a very sound investment in our Nation's future.

Next, we have to have significant, significant increases, not decreases, in investment and research and technology.

Next, in my judgment, we should attempt to take the health care costs of the workers' comp system and the auto insurance system into this reform. That might be the biggest thing we could do for small businesses. It would also perhaps be the biggest thing we could do to reduce some of the inequalities—some of you might not like this, and others would love it—but the inequalities in economic incentives that various States can offer because of dramatic differences in workers' comp costs from State to State, occasioned more than anything else by the health care burden of workers' comp.

Next, I think that we should have 100 percent tax deductibility, not 25 percent tax deductibility, for self-employed people. And that will be a part of the plan we will offer to Congress, something that will increase the capacity of people who are self-employed to maintain health insurance, whether they're farmers or independent business people.

Finally, I think the States must have a strong role and essentially be charged with the responsibility and given the opportunity to organize and establish the health groups of people who will be able to purchase health care under the managed care system. I think we should expand options for people of low incomes on Medicare but not poor enough to be on Medicaid to get a prescription drug benefit phased in over a period of years. Similarly, I think we must do the same thing with long-term care. But as we provide more long-term care opportunities for the elderly and for persons with disabilities, we must also expand the option so that they can get the least cost, most appropriate care. We must remove the institutionalized biases that are in the system now, which keep a lot of people from having access to home care, for example.

And finally, I think there has to be some responsibility in this system for everyone. There are a lot of people today that get a free ride out of the present system who can afford to pay something. I think there should be individual responsibility. I think every American should know that health care is not something paid for by the tooth fairy, that there is no free ride, that people should understand that this system costs a lot of money. It should cost a lot of money; it ought to be the world's best. But we should all be acutely aware of the costs each of us impose on it.

But I also believe that in order to make individual responsibility meaningful and in order to control the cost of this system, there has to be some means of achieving universal coverage. If you don't achieve universal coverage, in my judgment, you will not be able to control the costs adequately. Why? Well, for one thing, you will continue to have cost shifting. If you have uncompensated care, the people who give it will shift the cost to the private sector or to the Government. And that will create significant economic dislocations.

Now, it seems to me we have four options. If you believe—you have to decide—if you believe everybody should be covered, you have only four options. And I would argue that three of them are not, at least based on what I have seen and heard, very good options in practice as opposed to in theory.

Option number one is to go to a single-payer system, like the Canadians do, because it has the least administrative cost. That would require us to replace over $500 billion in private insurance premiums with nearly that much in new taxes. I don't think that's a practical option. I don't think that is going to happen. That would be significantly dislocating in the sense that overnight, in a nation this size, you'd have all the people who are in the insurance business out of it unless they were in the business of managing the health care plans themselves, as more and more are doing.

Option number two would be to have an individual mandate rather than a mandate that applies to employers and to employees, saying that every individual's got to buy health insurance, and here are some insurance reforms to make sure you can get it. This approach has found some favor in the United States Congress, primarily among Republicans but not exclusively, because it has the appeal of not imposing a business mandate, which has a bad sound to it.

Here's the problem with that, it seems to me. If you have an individual mandate, on whom is it imposed? And don't you have to give some subsidy to low-income workers, just the way you'll have to give some subsidy to low-income businesses if there's an employer mandate? Who gets it and who doesn't? And if you impose an individual mandate, what is to stop every other employer in America from just dumping his employees or her employees, to have a sweeping and extremely dislocating set of—a chain of events start? So it seems to me that there are a lot of questions that have to be asked and answered before we could embrace the concept of an individual mandate.

The third thing you could do is not worry about it. You could just say, well, we'll have all these other reforms, and just hope that if you could lower the cost of insurance and simplify the premiums and have big pools, that sooner or later somehow everybody will be covered.

The problem is that there is a lot of evidence that some people will still seek a free ride. And make no mistake about it, people that never see themselves as free riders still ride the system, because everybody in this country who needs health care eventually gets it. It may be too late. It may be too expensive. But if someone who works in a workplace where there is no insurance has a child that gets hit in a car wreck or just gets sick or has an acute appendix or something happens, they'll get health care. And that will be paid for by someone else.

And indeed, even for the employers and employees that may go a whole year and never use the health care system, it's there waiting for them. It's an infrastructure just as much as the Interstate Highway System is. Every medical clinic, every hospital, every nursing home, all these things are the health care infrastructure of the country, all being paid for by someone else but still available to be used for those folks. So I don't think we can rationally expect to stop cost shifting or to have a fair system if we say we're going to organize all this and just hope everybody will get into it.

That leaves the fourth alternative, which is to build on the system we now have. The system we now have works for most Americans. Most Americans are insured under a system in which employers pay for part of the health insurance and employees pay for part of the health insurance, and it's worked pretty well for them except for the laundry list of problems that we talked about. But most Americans are covered under it.

What are the problems with doing this? Well, first of all, if you just passed an employer mandate and did nothing else, there would be a ton of problems in doing it, because the most vulnerable businesses would have the highest premiums and a bunch of them would really be in deep trouble. No one proposes to do that. In other words, an employer mandate itself would not be responsible unless you also had significant insurance reforms, a long period of phase-in, and a limitation on how much the premium could be for very small businesses or businesses with very low-wage workers that obviously are operating on narrow profit margins.

But I would argue to you that based on my analysis of this—and I've been thinking about this seriously now for more than 3 years, ever since the Governors' Association asked me and the then-Governor of Delaware, now a Congressman from Delaware, to look at the health issue. And I have thought about it and thought about it. There may be some other issue, but I see only those four options for dealing with this. And it seems to me the shared responsibility, in a fair way, of employer and employee, building on the system we have now which works, taking proper account of the need to phase in and to maintain limits on lower income and lower wage employment units, is the fairest way to go.

Now, it seems to me that all this will be discussed and debated in the Congress; the Governors will be a part of it. The first decision we have to make is whether we can fool around with this for another 10 or 20 years or whether the time has come to act. Just consider this one fact: If health care costs had been held in check—that is, to inflation plus growth—since 1980, State and local governments would have, on average, 75 percent more funding for public school budgets. In 1993, fiscal year 1993, States spent more on Medicaid than on higher education for the first time. And State spending on Medicaid is expected to jump from $31 billion in 1990 to $81 billion in 1995 if we don't change this system.

I believe that health care reform will boost job creation in the private sector if it is done right. I believe it will offer a level playing field to all those small employers who are covering their employees right now and paying too much for it. I believe it will be a critical first step in rewarding work over welfare.

When we did the Family Support Act in 1988, those of you who were here then will all remember what all of us concluded—and the Governor of South Carolina, since he had once been the ranking member of the appropriate subcommittee on the House Ways and Means Committee, played as big a role in understanding this as anybody else—that a lot of people stayed on welfare not because of the benefits, because the benefits had not kept up with inflation; they did it because they couldn't afford child care for their kids and because they were going to lose health insurance for their children.

We have gone a long way, I think, toward reducing incentives to stay on welfare with this new economic plan, because the earned-income tax credit has increased so much that now people that work 40 hours a week and have children in the home will be lifted above the poverty level. That was the most major piece of economic social reform in the last 20 years. But we still have to deal with the health care issue.

I recently had a very sad conversation with a woman who became a friend of mine in the campaign who was a divorced mother of seven children, and her youngest child had a horrible, horrible and very expensive health care condition. The only way she could get any health care for this kid was to quit a job where she was making $50,000 a year, proudly supporting these children, to go on public assistance so she could get Medicaid to take care of her child. And the young child just recently passed away. And so I called and talked to the woman, and I was thinking about the incredible travail that she had gone through and wondering if now she would ever be able to get another job making that kind of money to support her remaining

children and to restore her sense of dignity and empowerment.

Let me say one last thing about this. I think if we do this right, it will restore our sense of individual and common responsibility. I will say again, I do not believe anybody should get a free ride in this deal. I think we have all—at least I've been part of it—have made a mistake in trying to say that people should pay absolutely nothing for their health care if they could afford to pay something. People ought to pay in proportion to what they can afford to. But I think that the system we have is so riddled with those who don't have any responsibility at all that it is chock full of loopholes.

And let me say again, everybody who says, "Well, this is just too complicated, and it's too much trouble, and it's too hard to think about," ought to consider the consequences of doing nothing. Doing nothing means more people lose their coverage, and those who don't will pay too much for their coverage. Doing nothing means that all those uninsured and underinsured Americans will be covered by vast outlays by State, local, and Federal governments. The rest of us will pay more at the doctor's office, the hospital, and our own businesses. Doing nothing means insurers will continue to be able to charge prices that are too high to those who don't have the good fortune of being in very large buying cooperatives, and that the paperwork burden of this system, I will say again, will continue to be a dime on the dollar more than any other country in the world. We cannot sustain that sort of waste and inefficiency. More than 60 cents of every new dollar going to the Federal Treasury over the next 5 years under our reduced budget will go to health care, after we had a $54 billion reduction in Medicare and Medicaid expenses over the estimated cost of the previous budget; 12 to 15 percent added costs every year for large businesses; 20 to 30 percent for small businesses; no wage increases for millions, indeed tens of millions of workers; and continued fear and insecurity. Policing the system against incompetence will be left to a flawed system of bureaucrats, of insurance oversight and malpractice that rewards things that don't deserve to be rewarded and ignores legitimate problems.

Now, let me talk about this jobs issue one more time. If you just imposed a mandate and did nothing else, would it cost jobs? Yes, it would. Any study can show that. That is not what we propose. If you reform the insurance system and all these big employers that are paying way too much now and all these small employers that are paying way too much now, wind up with reductions or no increases in the years ahead, that is more money they're going to have to invest in creating new jobs in the private sector. If you reform the insurance system, you phase in the requirements, and you limit the amount of payroll that someone can be required to put out in an insurance premium, you're going to limit the job loss on the downside while you're increasing it dramatically on the upside. If you reduce the paperwork burdens, yes, you won't have this huge growth in people doing clerical works in doctors offices and hospitals and in insurance offices. But you will have more people going into old folks' homes and giving them good personal health care, trying to keep them alive in ways that are more labor intensive but less expensive. So there will be shifts here.

But who can say, if you trust, if you trust the private sector to allocate capital in ways that will make America most competitive and to take advantage of lower health care costs by reinvesting it in this economy, who could possibly say that if we move closer to the international average in the percentage of our income going to health care, it wouldn't lead to more productive investment and more jobs in America? I think that is clearly what would happen.

We have focused this debate only on the minority of people who don't have health insurance and don't cover their employers and assume that we would lay some mandate on them and make no other structural changes. I wouldn't be for that. You couldn't be for that, although at least that would stop the cost shifting. It would not be enough. That is not what we propose. But if you do this right and we phase it in so that as we deal with problems, we find them, we can correct them; if the States are dealing with the management side of this through these health alliances, we can make this work.

It just defies common sense to say that we can't maintain the world's finest health care system, stop all this cost shifting, bring our costs back at some competitive level, cover everybody, and create jobs. No matter what happens we'll be spending a lot more than any other country on health care at the end of the decade. But we'll be protecting people, and we'll be working with them.

I'm convinced that the biggest problem we've got right now is the fear of the unknown and the exaggeration into the unknown of what, in fact, is already known. To say that we're talking about some untried, untested thing ignores the experience of Hawaii, ignores the experience of every other country that we're competing with, ignores what we know about how our private sector could actually manage the problem better in some ways than Germany and Japan have managed it, and basically, is rooted in somehow our lack of belief that we can overcome all the ideological divides and the rhetorical barbs and the fears that are gripping us.

So I will say again, I don't pretend to have all the answers, but I am absolutely sure this is the problem that America cannot let go, that we cannot walk away from. And I am absolutely convinced that we can solve it if we can meet around a table without regard to party and listen to the facts and work through it. I am convinced of that.

I want to close by telling you a story. When the Pope came to Denver and I was given the opportunity to go out there and meet him and have a private audience that I will remember and cherish for the rest of my life, we arranged for a young girl to come there and just stand in the audience. And all she did was have the Pope put his hand on her head and say a word of blessing. This child is 13 years old. She's from Wisconsin. Her father we met in the course of the campaign. She was born with a rare bone disease which caused the bones in her body to break continuously so that by the time she actually came out of her mother's womb she had already had about more than a dozen bones break in her body.

Just a few years ago, anybody like that could never have grown up and had anything like a normal life. They just would have been helpless, just continually crumbling. Now, this girl has gone to the National Institutes of Health every 3 months for her entire life. And even though she's just 13 years old, if she were here talking to you, she would speak with the presence, the maturity, the command of someone more than twice her age. And she looks a little different because the bones in her skull have broken, the bones in her legs have broken, the bones in her back have broken. But she can walk and she can function and she can go to school. And even though she's only 4 feet tall and weighs only 60 pounds, she can function.

And she asked her father to take her to Iowa so she could help people in Iowa to fight the flood. And she went to Iowa and loaded sand in the sandbags, knowing that any one of those bags could have broken her leg above the knee, could have put her away for a year. She said, "I cannot live in a closet. This is something that's there. I want to live. I want to do my life. I want to do what other people do." And I was so overcome by it, I brought the girl to see me, and then we just quietly arranged for her to be there when the Pope was there.

I say that to make this point. I asked her why in the world she would have done that, why she would have risked literally breaking her body apart to be there with all these big, husky college kids fighting this flood. And she said, "Because I want to live. And it's there, and I have to go on. I have to do things." If a child like that can do something like that, surely

to goodness, we can stop wringing our hands and roll up our sleeves and solve this problem. And surely we can do it without the kind of rhetoric and air-filling bull that we hear so often in the Nation's Capital. We can do it.

I miss you. I miss this. I miss the way we make decisions. I miss the sort of heart and soul and fabric of life that was a part of every day when I got up and went to work in a State capital. Somehow we've got to bring that back to Washington. Think about that little girl, and help us solve this health care problem.

Thank you.

NOTE: The President spoke at 10:50 a.m. at the Tulsa Convention Center. In his remarks, he referred to John Motley, vice president, National Federation of Independent Business, and Gov. George S. Mickelson of South Dakota, who died April 20 in an airplane crash.

Remarks on Naming William M. Daley as NAFTA Task Force Chairman and an Exchange With Reporters
August 19, 1993

The President. Good afternoon, everyone.

Audience member. Happy birthday!

The President. Well, thank you very much. Thank you, Helen [Helen Thomas, United Press International].

Ladies and gentlemen, I am pleased to announce that my good friend, Bill Daley of Chicago, has agreed to be the Chair of the administration's Task Force on the North American Free Trade Agreement. This agreement means more trade, more exports, and more jobs for the United States. I think it is very much in our national interest.

I also think it means the opportunity to go not only to Mexico but beyond Mexico into other nations in Latin America to develop stronger trading relationships that will boost our economy, the jobs, and the incomes of the American people well into the 21st century.

Thanks to the hard work done by Ambassador Mickey Kantor and the other members of the U.S. Trade Representative's staff, we have now seen in the last several days the conclusion of a remarkable set of side agreements to guarantee real investments in environmental cleanup and a dramatic and unprecedented commitment by the Government of Mexico to tie their minimum wage structure to increases in productivity and growth in the Mexican economy and to make that a part of the trade agreement, so that failure to do that could result in fines and ultimately trade sanctions, meaning that Mexico is serious about making this a trade agreement that benefits Mexican workers, raises wage levels, increases their ability to buy American products, and decreases the impetus for continued illegal immigration across the Mexican border. I am very, very encouraged by this.

I also want to say that as we move into this campaign vigorously now—and it's something that we've not been able to do because we didn't have an agreement until just a few days ago—Mr. Daley will be working with Ambassador Kantor, with the Secretary of Treasury, with the Director of EPA, with the Labor Secretary, and with other members of the Cabinet, including the Commerce Secretary, to present a strongly united front. Furthermore, we will be reaching out to involve in the national leadership of this task force prominent Republicans,

Democrats, and independents who have a common interest in promoting the NAFTA and what it can do for our economy.

I believe, as I said repeatedly, that if we could get these side agreements which have now been concluded, this trade agreement means a better future for America's workers, for American industry, for the American economy. I think it is very much in our interest to adopt it. I believe the fact that Bill Daley has agreed to take a leadership role enhances the chances of its adoption, and I know that the Vice President, Mr. McLarty, and others in our administration join me in expressing our thanks to Bill Daley. And he'll be here soon, and we'll be going to work.

Would you like to say a few words?

[At this point, Mr. Daley made brief remarks.]

NAFTA and Job Creation

Q. Mr. President, how can you convince American workers that NAFTA is good for them when major corporations are laying off thousands of people? Where are the jobs going to come from?

The President. Well, major corporations are laying off thousands of people in part because they don't have enough work for them. Part of this downsizing is an inevitable part of the reorganization of some of those big employers. But what has happened is that for the last 12 years—for a long time—we had more jobs created in small business, in medium-sized businesses than were being lost in large businesses. The Fortune 500 laid off more than 100,000 people a year every year of the 1980's.

So, this trend is something that has been going on for some time. Whether we gain jobs or not, and gain good jobs, depends on whether there is more demand for American products and services. And there is ample evidence that the only way a wealthy country grows wealthier in a global economy is to increase the volume of trade. And it is a clear, elemental principle of economics that if you want more people to go to work in a competitive economy, you have to have more people to sell to. So that's what we're trying to do. I feel very strongly about it.

I also believe that by raising the incomes of Mexicans, which this will do, they will be able to buy more of our products, and there will be much less pressure on them to come to this country in the form of illegal immigration. So I think this will be a very stabilizing, economically healthy agreement.

I believe, to be fair, that a lot of the people who are against this agreement were against the original agreement and may not have had the chance to evaluate the side agreements that we've worked so hard since January to conclude with the Mexican Government. And I think that that will make a difference.

I also think that it's important that this Government, our Government, make a good-faith effort to make sure that we provide adequate retraining and other opportunities for people who fear they will be subject to dislocation under this agreement. In my mind, there is no question that this agreement is a significant net plus for the American economy.

Justice Department Reorganization

Q. Mr. President, what do you think about this proposal to merge the DEA with the FBI? And what kind of signal would that send about U.S. commitment to drug interdiction?

The President. Well, first of all, I've not had a chance to view the proposal. The Vice President's task force has under review a number of proposals. I'm not sure they've even finalized their own decisions. You might want to ask him about that. But he'll be making a presentation to me early in September. And when and if that recommendation comes to me, I'll evaluate it. I'll talk to him, and I'll talk to the Attorney General about it. But I will say this: Anything we do will be designed to enhance our efforts to combat drugs, not to weaken it. And any decision I make will be made with that in mind.

NAFTA

Q. Do you and Mr. Daley have any idea how you are going to overcome or circumvent the leadership of the House, the majority leader and the chief whip, both of whom are opposed to NAFTA?

The President. Well, the chief whip is clearly opposed to it, and I think he and I—I admire him immensely, but we just have an honest disagreement about this. And I might say, since he's from Michigan, I would just point out to you not very long ago General Motors announced that they were moving 1,000 jobs back from Mexico to the United States to be closer to the market and because of the higher productivity of the American worker.

I'd like to make one point about that, and then I'll say something about the majority leader. I have governed a State where people shut their plants down and went to Mexico for low wages. I have been there. And my belief is that if we defeat NAFTA, nothing will stop. NAFTA won't stop people. If you beat NAFTA, it will not stop people who want to go to Mexico for lower wages from going there. But more and more, smart manufacturers are deciding that they should locate where they're going to have a highly productive work force and where they'll be reasonably close to the market and where they'll be very flexible to change product lines on a rapid basis. I think that this will help the American economy.

I also think that the kinds of investments you'll see in Mexico, if NAFTA passes, are not those investments along the American border that produce more products to come back into America but investments further down into Mexico to put Mexican people to work to produce products for their own market, which, again, will stabilize their incomes, stabilize their population movement, increase their ability to buy American products. So that's the argument I'm going to make to others. I don't think I can change Mr. Bonior's mind, but I think perhaps I can change others.

Mr. Gephardt has a different set of concerns. He wants to make sure that we're going to adequately fund the training programs, that we're going to adequately fund the environmental pro-grams, and that the Mexican commitment to raise minimum wages means that manufacturing wages will in fact go up as their incomes go up. And I still have high hopes that things that will happen between now and the time the implementing legislation is presented to Congress in several weeks will persuade him to support this. I do believe it will be difficult for us to prevail if both of them are opposed. But Mr. Gephardt has some high standards for this agreement, but I'm not sure they can't be met.

And I also say, I want the Members of Congress who have not announced their positions to review these agreements. There has never been a trade agreement with this kind of environmental protection in it. There has certainly never been a trade agreement where one country committed to raise its wages when its productivity increases and to make that wage increase a subject of the trade agreement so that they can be subject to fines for trade sanctions that they don't keep. This has never happened before. Mexico was serious about trying to raise the living standards of its own people in ways that help stabilize American wages and American jobs.

Thank you.

NOTE: The President spoke at 12:57 p.m. in the Oval Office at the White House. A tape was not available for verification of the content of these remarks.

Statement on Naming William M. Daley as NAFTA Task Force Chairman
August 19, 1993

I am pleased to announce that William Daley has agreed to serve as Chairman of the administration's Task Force on the North American Free Trade Agreement. His willingness to serve—on behalf of expanded exports, expanded jobs, and expanded trade—is a further measure of his commitment to public service.

For the next several months, the Congress of the United States will debate and determine the fate of NAFTA. With the leadership of the United States Trade Representative, Mickey Kantor, and the help of others in our administration, new supplemental agreements have been completed that will transform NAFTA into a force for job creation, environmental cleanup, greater American competitiveness, and higher labor standards.

The case for NAFTA is strong, and in Bill Daley I have found the strongest possible advocate to make that case. Bill will work effectively and closely with Ambassador Kantor, Treasury Secretary Bentsen, Commerce Secretary Brown, Labor Secretary Reich, EPA Administrator Carol Browner, and other members of the Cabinet to conduct a positive, bipartisan campaign to explain the benefits of the NAFTA to the country and to the Congress.

NAFTA is a pathbreaking trade agreement because its implementation will bring a better deal for American workers, companies, and consumers, while acting as a spur for a cleaner environment and a better climate for workers on all sides of the border. Passage of the NAFTA is a high priority of our administration,

and the appointment of Bill Daley to coordinate our efforts for its adoption should be viewed as a signal of my personal commitment. I am grateful to him for accepting this appointment and this challenge.

NOTE: A biography was made available by the Office of the Press Secretary.

Statement on the Report of the National Commission to Ensure a Strong Competitive Airline Industry
August 19, 1993

Today I received with great interest and enthusiasm the report of the National Commission to Ensure a Strong Competitive Airline Industry. For the past 3 months, Governor Baliles and his colleagues have worked tirelessly to identify ways to revive this critical industry. The Commission has done its work well.

Now my administration and the Congress must take the next steps to ensure that Government policy encourages a prosperous airline industry. Aviation provides high-wage jobs and is a leading exporter of American products and services. In the past, this industry has provided good jobs for millions of Americans, while meeting and beating our competition abroad. In recent years, however, both airlines and aerospace manufacturers have suffered financial losses and have laid off some of our most skilled and productive workers.

We have already taken the first and most important steps toward strengthening the aviation

industry. This sector's problems are intertwined with our Nation's broader economic challenges. By reducing the deficit and providing incentives for economic expansion, the recently enacted budget creates the climate for economic growth that is a precondition for the revival of aviation.

The Commission's report recommends several additional steps to achieve an air transport system that is efficient, technologically superior, and financially strong. Under the leadership of Transportation Secretary Federico Peña and Council of Economic Advisers Chair Laura Tyson, my administration will consider these proposals and develop an administration plan. We will work with Congress to respond to the industry's problems in a manner consistent with our deficit reduction and economic goals.

I look forward to meeting with Governor Baliles and the Commission members upon my return to Washington.

Statement on Democratic National Health Care Campaign Chair Richard Celeste
August 19, 1993

In selecting Governor Celeste to chair the national health care campaign, David Wilhelm has made a superb choice. I had the pleasure of working side-by-side with Governor Celeste for 8 years as a fellow member of the National Governors' Association. I learned then what the people of Ohio know well: Governor Celeste

is a strong, effective, charismatic leader, and a remarkable motivator of people.

Governor Celeste's proven ability to forge bipartisan consensus will be a great help as Democrats and Republicans work together to reform our health care system. I am heartened to know that Governor Celeste will help in our fight to bring health security to every American. Health care reform is a complex issue, and it is critically important to our lives.

I know that Governor Celeste accepted this new challenge because he wants to serve all the people, and I compliment David Wilhelm on his leadership in making this appointment.

Memorandum on the Combined Federal Campaign
August 19, 1993

Memorandum for Heads of Departments and Agencies

The Combined Federal Campaign is an avenue through which thousands of Federal employees voluntarily express their concern for others each year. Public servants working in nearly every corner of the globe not only contribute to the campaign but assume leadership roles to assure that the campaign is a huge success.

I am delighted to inform you that Secretary of Commerce Ronald H. Brown has agreed to serve as the chair of the 1993 Combined Federal Campaign of the National Capital Area. I ask you to support Secretary Brown by personally chairing the campaign in your agency and appointing a top official as your vice chairman.

Your commitment and visible support will help to guarantee another successful campaign this year. Together, we must do everything we can to encourage Federal employees everywhere to do their part by participating in the 1993 Combined Federal Campaign.

WILLIAM J. CLINTON

Letter to Congressional Leaders Reporting on the Cyprus Conflict
August 19, 1993

Dear Mr. Speaker: (Dear Mr. Chairman:)

In accordance with Public Law 95–384 (22 U.S.C. 2373 (c)), I am submitting to you this report on progress toward a negotiated settlement of the Cyprus question. The previous report covered the period from November 13, 1992, through February 14, 1993, the date of the election of Glafcos Clerides to succeed George Vassiliou as President of the Republic of Cyprus. The current report covers the remainder of February through July 15, 1993.

On February 22, Secretary of State Warren Christopher, while enroute between Beirut, Lebanon, and Cairo, Egypt, met with President-elect Clerides and then-President Vassiliou at the airport in Larnaca, Cyprus. During this short meeting, the Secretary of State assured them of the continued high level of U.S. interest in U.N. Secretary General Boutros-Ghali's efforts to find a fair and permanent solution to the Cyprus problem.

President Clerides was sworn in on February 28.

On March 2, the U.S. Special Cyprus Coordinator, Ambassador John Maresca, met in Rome with his counterpart from the Government of Turkey, Mr. Tugay Ulucevic. Ambassador Maresca also met with the U.N. Secretary General's Deputy Special Representative, Mr. Gustave Feissel in Rome. At both meetings, Ambassador Maresca stressed the necessity of an early resumption of the Cyprus negotiations.

Also on March 2, in Nicosia, Mr. Oscar Camilion, the Secretary General's Special Representative, informed the parties that he was resigning the position to return to the service of the Argentine Government as Minister of Defense. Mr. Camilion left Cyprus in mid-March after participating in another round of preparatory talks on the island. During Minister Camilion's tenure as the Secretary General's Special Representative, substantial progress was made toward resolution of the Cyprus dispute, and I would like to take this opportunity to add my appreciation for his long and distinguished service.

U.N. Under-Secretary General Marrack Goulding and Mr. Feissel arrived in Nicosia for a round of preparatory talks on March 7 and, during the course of the talks, obtained commitments from President Clerides and Mr. Denktash to come to New York for a short face-to-face meeting on March 30. On March 10, the two Cypriot leaders met for dinner at the invitation of Mr. Camilion, the first face-to-face meeting on the island of the leaders of the two communities in several years.

At the end of the preparatory meetings in Cyprus, Goulding and Feissel returned to New York where they met on March 15 with Ambassador Maresca to discuss their plans for the March 30 meeting.

On March 25, on the occasion of the National Day of the Hellenic Republic of Greece, I publicly restated the strong U.S. interest in the U.N. Secretary General's efforts to reach a fair and permanent solution of the Cyprus problem.

In preparation for the face-to-face meeting between the two Cypriot leaders scheduled for March 30, the members of the U.N. Security Council authorized the President of the Security Council to issue a statement that called on the parties to cooperate fully with the U.N. Secretary General and reaffirmed the determination of the Security Council members to remain seized of the Cyprus question and to lend their support to the Secretary General's efforts. (The full text of the Security Council President's statement is enclosed.)

On March 29, the U.S. Permanent Representative to the United Nations, Ambassador Madeleine Albright, met with President Clerides and Mr. Denktash to reiterate the U.S. position that both sides should work with the U.N. Secretary General to reach an equitable and lasting solution for the benefit of all Cypriots. She presented letters to the two leaders from Secretary of State Christopher and me.

At the March 30 face-to-face meeting, the leaders of the two communities agreed to return to New York for substantive discussions on May 24. The Under-Secretary General's summation of the meeting stated that the sides had agreed to resume their discussions "using the set of ideas for the purpose of reaching freely a mutually acceptable overall framework agreement" after a preparatory process on the island (full text enclosed). The summation also welcomed the parallel process of private meetings (that is, not under U.N. auspices) between the two

leaders. There was another such meeting between the two leaders in New York on the margins of the U.N. talks.

Also on March 30, U.N. Secretary General Boutros-Ghali issued a report on the United Nations Operation in Cyprus in which he requested a major restructuring and reorganization of the U.N. Peace-keeping Force in Cyprus (UNFICYP) due to reductions, withdrawals, and announcements of plans for further withdrawals of troops by troop contributors. (The full text of that report is enclosed.) Informal consultations among members of the Security Council on this subject continued throughout the remainder of this reporting period, ultimately resulting in changes in the way UNFICYP is financed. Information on the U.N. Security Council resolutions through which this was done will be found later in this report.

On March 31, the five Permanent Members of the U.N. Security Council held separate meetings with the leaders of the two communities to urge them to cooperate with the representatives of the Secretary General and to prepare for the substantive talks, which were to resume on May 24.

In mid-April, Mr. Feissel, who had been named as the new resident representative of the Secretary General on Cyprus, began the preparatory talks in Nicosia working on both the U.N. "set of ideas" and on confidence-building measures developed by the U.N. Secretariat, in accordance with the suggestions of the Secretary General at the end of the October-November session of the New York talks.

On April 24, I again publicly stated the strong U.S. commitment to a fair and permanent solution of the Cyprus problem. On the same day, President Turgut Özal of Turkey, who had strongly supported the efforts of the Secretary General to find such a solution, died after a strenuous effort to resolve serious disputes in south-west Asia.

Mr. Feissel concluded the first phase of his preparatory work in Nicosia on May 6, and, on the same day, the State Department's Director of Southern European Affairs, Mr. David Ransom, arrived in Nicosia. He was joined there on May 10 by Special Cyprus Coordinator Maresca, and both met with the leaders of the two communities to urge them to cooperate with the U.N. effort. Ambassador Maresca departed Cyprus on May 12 and Director Ransom departed on May 13 after meeting with Mr.

Feissel, who had returned to Nicosia for additional intensive preparation for the May 24 meetings in New York.

A U.N. Security Council resolution sponsored by the United Kingdom on the structure and financing of the U.N. Peace-keeping Force in Cyprus was vetoed by Russia on May 11 because it appeared to eliminate voluntary contributions as a preferred way of financing U.N. peace-keeping operations. (Another resolution was successfully negotiated during the two weeks that followed, and it was passed on May 27, after the end of this reporting period.)

Mr. Feissel's intensive preparations for the May 24 New York negotiating round focused on a package of confidence-building measures, which included a plan to reopen the fenced area of the city of Varosha and the Nicosia International Airport under U.N. auspices.

In my view, the package of confidence-building measures is fair and balanced, offers significant benefits to both sides, and should be accepted by both sides as a means of improving the atmosphere for negotiation of a fair and permanent resolution of the Cyprus problem. More specifically, I urge Mr. Denktash, the leader of the Turkish-Cypriot community, to accept this package in order to establish a better climate for negotiations based on the U.N. "set of ideas." I believe that the Government of Turkey also should exercise its special responsibility to urge him to accept this package. This is an historic opportunity for the Turkish-Cypriot community and for all Cypriots. It would be tragic if this opportunity to move forward were missed.

Following these developments, the U.N. Secretary General's resident representative in Cyprus was engaged in intensive talks in Nicosia with the leaders of the two Cypriot communities, which focused on a package of confidence-building measures, including the reopening, under U.N. auspices, of both the Nicosia International Airport and the city of Varosha, on the eastern coast of Cyprus. These consultations ended, and Mr. Feissel returned to U.N. Headquarters on May 20 to begin final preparations for the May 24 New York negotiating session.

That session opened, as scheduled, with a meeting chaired by the U.N. Secretary General and attended by the leaders of the two Cypriot communities, Mr. Joseph Clark, the Secretary General's newly appointed Special Representa-

tive; Cyprus Coordinator John Maresca; and U.S. Ambassador to Cyprus Robert Lamb.

During the next five days it became apparent that Mr. Denktash, the leader of the Turkish-Cypriot community, was not prepared to accept the package of confidence-building measures. He asked for additional time to consider the package and consult with his community. The Secretary General initially granted Mr. Denktash four additional days. At a meeting on June 1, chaired, in the absence of the Secretary General by Mr. Clark, Mr. Denktash was granted an additional postponement until June 14, with the approval of the representatives of the permanent members of the Security Council, also present, on condition that Mr. Denktash would seek a positive response from his community on the proposed package of confidence-building measures, including the proposals for Varosha and the Nicosia International Airport.

On June 8, the State Department released a statement (copy attached) that supported the U.N. Secretary General's package of confidence-building measures, including his proposals for Varosha and the Nicosia International Airport, stated that we believe the package is fair and balanced and that it offers real economic and practical benefits to both sides and that the package should be accepted quickly and in its entirety, and stated our belief that Turkey should be helpful in ensuring an agreement on this package.

Also on June 8, in an airport statement on his arrival in Turkey, Mr. Denktash made it clear that he was not seeking a positive response from his community to the Secretary General's package. On the same day, Secretary Christopher spoke with Turkish Foreign Minister Cetin, who, like Secretary Christopher, was in Athens for the meetings of the North Atlantic Council and the North Atlantic Cooperation Council, about the developing situation.

On June 9, a letter on the Cyprus situation and the U.N. Secretary General's confidence-building package from Secretary Christopher was delivered to Foreign Minister Cetin. In a speech to the Turkish Grand National Parliament, in Ankara, on the following day, and in follow-up statements to the media, Mr. Denktash said that he could not accept the confidence-building package and would not return to New York as scheduled on June 14.

Secretary Christopher discussed the Cyprus situation with President Demirel and Foreign

Minister Cetin in meetings in Ankara on June 12. In New York, a spokesman for the U.N. Secretary General issued a statement (copy attached) the same day that stated that the Secretary General had been informed by Mr. Denktash that he would not be able to return to New York as planned on June 14 and that a representative of Mr. Denktash would come in his stead "to explain the situation that has arisen." The statement said that the Secretary General regretted that Mr. Denktash had unilaterally departed from the agreement of June 1, and that, as a consequence, the joint meetings would not resume at U.N. Headquarters as planned on June 14. The Secretary General undertook to submit a report to the Security Council.

On June 14, Mr. Kenan Atakol, representing Mr. Denktash, arrived in New York and started a series of meetings with Mr. Feissel and members of the diplomatic missions to the U.N. of the five Permanent Members of the Security Council. Mr. Atakol was not prepared to discuss "practical problems" concerning the Secretary General's confidence-building package, to which Mr. Denktash had referred in Nicosia and Ankara. On June 25, before returning to Cyprus, Mr. Atakol met with Ambassador Edward Walker, the U.S. Deputy Representative to the U.N.

On July 1, the Secretary General issued the report (copy attached) that he had promised on June 12. In the report he reviewed his efforts since November 1992, explained in detail the confidence-building package that he had proposed, including his proposals for Varosha and the Nicosia International Airport, and provided observations on the current state of the negotiations. The gist of those paragraphs is that: (paragraph 45) all concerned have a special responsibility to bring to a positive conclusion an effort that has already produced "significant progress"; (paragraph 46) the Secretary General was particularly gratified that the preparations in Nicosia for the May 24 New York negotiating session had brought his confidence-building proposals to an advanced stage; (paragraph 47) the Varosha/Nicosia International Airport proposals would bring considerable and proportionate benefits to both Cypriot communities; (paragraph 48) beyond the economic gains to both sides, the package would open avenues of contact between the communities and engender the kind of goodwill that should exist in a federation; (paragraph 49) the Secretary General is dis-

appointed that, despite his assurances of June 1, Mr. Denktash neither promoted the acceptance of the package during his consultations in Nicosia and Ankara, nor did he honor his agreement to return to New York on June 14; (paragraph 50) the Secretary General hopes that the merits of the package will commend themselves to all concerned once they have been fully presented; and (paragraph 51) the Secretary General intends to continue his efforts and, to that end, has asked his Special Representative (Mr. Clark) to visit Cyprus, Greece, and Turkey in the following few weeks. The Secretary General also attached, as an annex to his report, a list of the confidence-building measures that his representatives had proposed to the two sides (including the Varosha/Nicosia International Airport proposals, which were detailed in the body of the report).

The Security Council, on July 7, approved a letter (text attached) from its President to Secretary General Boutros-Ghali that endorsed the conclusions of the Secretary General's report and underlined the obligation of both parties to cooperate fully with the Secretary General in promptly reaching an overall framework agreement and, in the first instance, in reaching an agreement on the Secretary General's confidence-building package.

The letter welcomed the Secretary General's decision to send Mr. Clark to Cyprus, Greece, and Turkey, and requested a report from the Secretary General in September 1993, and, if necessary, his recommendations for action by the Security Council.

Mr. Clark and Mr. Feissel arrived in Nicosia on July 13 on the mission outlined in the Secretary General's report. On the same day, the U.S. Special Cyprus Coordinator, Ambassador Maresca, arrived in Ankara for discussions with the Government of Turkey on the Cyprus question.

On June 11, the Security Council extended the mandate of the U.N. Peace-keeping Force in Cyprus (UNFICYP) for an additional six-month period until December 15, 1993. As noted in the last report, the Council had reached agreement on the future mission and funding of UNFICYP on May 27, during the New York negotiating session outlined above. The U.N. Secretariat continues to seek forces to replace the Canadian contingent that began its previously planned withdrawal in the week following June 15. (The Secretary General's report of June 9 on U.N. operations is attached.)

As I noted in the conclusions of my last letter to you on this subject, I believe that the Secretary General's package of confidence-building measures is fair and balanced. I believe that its acceptance by both sides, promptly and in its entirety, would certainly improve the atmosphere and could speed the acceptance of an overall framework agreement based on the Secretary General's "set of ideas." I want to reiterate the strong support of the U.S. for the efforts of the Secretary General to carry out his good-offices mandate and to reach a conclu-

sion acceptable to both Cypriot communities and which is for their mutual benefit. It is time for all concerned to build on the substantial progress noted by the U.N. Secretary General in his July 1 report and to resolve this long-standing problem.

Sincerely,

WILLIAM J. CLINTON

NOTE: Identical letters were sent to Thomas S. Foley, Speaker of the House of Representatives, and Claiborne Pell, chairman of the Senate Committee on Foreign Relations.

Letter to Congressional Leaders Reporting on Proliferation of Chemical and Biological Weapons
August 19, 1993

Dear Mr. Speaker: (Dear Mr. President:)

On November 16, 1990, in light of the dangers of the proliferation of chemical and biological weapons, President Bush issued Executive Order No. 12735, and declared a national emergency under the International Emergency Economic Powers Act (50 U.S.C. 1701 *et seq.*). Under section 202(d) of the National Emergencies Act (50 U.S.C. 1622(d)), the national emergency terminates on the anniversary date of its declaration unless the President publishes in the *Federal Register* and transmits to the Congress a notice of its continuation. On November 11, 1992, the previous Administration extended the emergency, noting that the proliferation of chemical and biological weapons continues to pose an unusual and extraordinary threat to the national security and foreign policy of the United States.

Section 204 of the International Emergency Economic Powers Act and section 401(c) of the National Emergencies Act contain periodic reporting requirements regarding activities taken and money spent pursuant to an emergency declaration. This report is made pursuant to those provisions. Additional information on chemical and biological weapons proliferation is contained in the report to the Congress provided pursuant to the Chemical and Biological Weapons Control and Warfare Elimination Act of 1991.

The United States has continued to control the export of items with potential use in chemi-

cal or biological weapons or in unmanned delivery systems for weapons of mass destruction through the 3 export control regulations issued under the Enhanced Proliferation Control Initiative. The United States has also continued to address the problem of the proliferation and use of chemical and biological weapons in its international diplomatic efforts.

In January 1993 the Chemical Weapons Convention (CWC) was opened for signature in Paris. In addition to banning chemical weapons among its parties, the Convention will also require parties to restrict, and ultimately cut off, trade in certain chemical weapons-related chemicals with nonparties. The United States was an original signatory of the Convention and has sought to encourage other countries to sign as well. To date, over 145 nations have signed the CWC, which is expected to enter into force in early 1995.

The United States is playing a leading role in the work of the CWC Preparatory Commission, which is meeting in The Hague to work out the procedural and administrative details for implementing the Convention.

The membership of the Australia Group (AG) of countries cooperating against chemical and biological weapons proliferation has grown from 22 to 25, with the group admitting Argentina, Hungary, and Iceland to membership at its December 1992 meeting. At the same meeting, all AG-member countries agreed to impose export controls on a common list of biological organisms, toxins, and equipment.

In December 1992, Hungary hosted a seminar on Australia Group practices for non-Australia Group countries from Eastern Europe and the former Soviet Union. The AG plans further outreach programs to nonmembers. Progress also was made in the steps taken by countries outside the Australia Group to expand chemical weapons export controls. India announced that it would control all chemicals on the Chemical Weapons Convention schedules even before the CWC enters into force, and China indicated that it would

do the same.

Pursuant to section 401(c) of the National Emergencies Act, there were no additional expenses directly attributable to the exercise of authorities conferred by the declaration of the national emergency.

Sincerely,

WILLIAM J. CLINTON

NOTE: Identical letters were sent to Thomas S. Foley, Speaker of the House of Representatives, and Albert Gore, Jr., President of the Senate.

The President's Radio Address
August 21, 1993

Good morning. In the past few weeks, our Nation has taken a bold first step toward a new economic destiny. The economic program I signed into law earlier this month reduces the deficit and embraces the core values of America: the values of the middle class, of small business, of rewarding hard work and giving the next generation as bright a future as our parents gave to us. This was a crucial first step in strengthening the quality of life all across our Nation.

With the passage of the economic plan, Americans will be assured of lower deficits, lower interest rates, and real economic growth rooted in incentives for small and new businesses and new investment incentives which bring better jobs, better wages, and new economic opportunities.

Now we must take the next step. We must reform our health care system so that you and every American will be assured not only of economic security but the security of knowing that health care is always there for you. We also have to reform health care because we're spending tens of billions of dollars on things that do not make us healthier but instead endanger our economy further.

Unless we provide quality and affordable health care, we can't bring this Federal deficit down to zero and balance the budget. We can't guarantee quality health care to many U.S. citizens. We can't guarantee health for U.S. businesses who are spending too much on health care today. And we can't guarantee that millions

of workers won't be deprived of their wage increases because they'll have to pay more and more and more every year for the same or less health coverage.

To be sure, a lot is right with the American health care system. Our hospitals, doctors and nurses, our technology and research make us the envy of the world, and we intend to stay that way. But at the same time, there's clearly a lot wrong. Health care costs are draining the Nation's coffers and robbing too many Americans of the security they need and deserve. Millions of our friends and neighbors have lost their health coverage simply because they switched jobs, moved to a different city, or got sick. Many of them can't change jobs because someone in their family has been sick, and they're locked into the health coverage they have or none at all.

Now we have an historic opportunity to change all that. Next month I'll outline a health care plan to Congress that offers hope for all Americans who want to work and take responsibility and create opportunities for themselves and their children. The plan will be built on three guiding principles: security, savings, and simplicity.

First, it will guarantee all Americans the security of knowing they won't lose their health coverage even if they switch jobs, lose a job, get sick, have a family member who gets sick, move to a new city, or start a small business.

Second, the plan will generate savings by introducing real competition into the health care market. We'll limit the growth of expensive premiums and costs that can't be justified, such as drugs made in America costing 3 times more here in the United States than they do overseas. We'll root out fraud and abuse which now eat up to 10 percent of every health care dollar. And we'll reform a malpractice system that drives up prices for doctors and patients. And we'll make it more rewarding for doctors to practice preventive medicine than to perform expensive tests and procedures that aren't necessary.

Third, the plan will be simpler for consumers and health care providers. We spend about 10 cents on the dollar more for administrative and paperwork costs than any other nation in the world. That's probably why health care takes up more than 14 percent of our income while no other country, except Canada, spends over 9 percent, and they're just a little over that.

Only the United States has 1,500 separate health insurance companies writing thousands of different policies, requiring millions of people to keep up with the paperwork in doctors' offices, in hospitals, in the insurance companies themselves. We're going to have one basic insurance form instead of thousands. We'll reduce nightmarish paperwork that now requires 4 times as many clerical workers to be hired as new health care providers, just to keep up with the mountains of redtape.

Reforming our health care system is not only the best way to reduce costs, rein in our Federal deficit, and provide security for our citizens, it's also good for our economy. This plan will boost the private sector by generating savings for businesses which they can use to create jobs and by creating jobs in health care, not for more paperwork but to provide new, innovative ways to people to stay healthy or be well.

When we talk about health care reform, we mean giving businesses who don't currently provide insurance plenty of time to phase-in coverage for their employees. We mean asking those employees to pay something for their own health insurance so they'll know that it doesn't come free. We mean establishing a system that gives small businesses lower insurance rates instead of pricing them out of the market. We mean providing the very smallest firms and the lowest wage firms with some modest subsidies to help them cover the costs of insuring their

workers. And we mean allowing the self-employed a 100-percent deduction for their health care costs.

With health care reform, our economy will be more productive; our companies will be more competitive; our workers will be more secure in their jobs and, therefore, more productive in them; and our families will be more confident about their future. If we want to really straighten out this economy and live more prosperous lives, we have to improve the Nation's health care system.

And we know something else: The price of doing nothing about health care is far too high. Doing nothing means more and more Americans losing their coverage. Doing nothing means allowing insurers to dictate prices, charging whatever they want to whomever they want. Doing nothing means continuing a system in which anonymous bureaucrats peer into every hospital and doctors' offices and second-guess medical decisions. Doing nothing means no wage increases for millions of workers, not to mention the most important thing of all: more fear, anxiety, and insecurity on the part of our citizens. And amazingly, doing nothing is the most expensive thing of all. It means about 100,000 Americans a month will join the nearly 40 million already without health insurance, and we will continue to spend much, much more of our income on health care, than any other people on Earth.

As we work for reform in the months ahead, we can't let this health care issue fall victim to partisan bickering. This is not a Democratic challenge, not a Republican challenge, not a liberal or a conservative challenge; it's an American challenge we must all face together.

I am pledged to work with all who have a commitment to change, Republicans as well as Democrats in the Congress, with the Governors and others throughout the country, with doctors and nurses and hospitals and other health care providers, with responsible drug companies who've committed to help keep their costs within inflation and are already giving critically needed drugs to public health clinics across the country.

These are the kinds of things we need more of. This is a cause in which all Americans must enlist, a cause in which special interest must put aside a broken system and become a lobby for the American people and a lobby for the

American future. We've got to roll up our sleeves, make the tough decisions now, and get on with this. With your help, I know we can succeed.

Thanks for listening.

NOTE: The address was recorded at 11:30 a.m. on August 19 in the Roosevelt Room at the White House for broadcast at 10:06 a.m. on August 21.

Nomination for Ambassador to Norway
August 27, 1993

The President today announced his intention to nominate Thomas A. Loftus to be the U.S. Ambassador to Norway. Mr. Loftus is the director of WisKids Count and served in the Wisconsin State Legislature for 14 years, including 8 years as its speaker.

"I am pleased today to announce my intention to nominate Tom Loftus as the Ambassador to Norway," said the President. "Tom will bring to this position the same energy and commitment to public service that characterized his leadership in the Wisconsin Assembly. He will strengthen our already strong ties with the Government of Norway and will serve this Nation with pride."

NOTE: A biography of the nominee was made available by the Office of the Press Secretary.

The President's Radio Address
August 28, 1993

Good morning. Thirty years ago today a great American spoke about his dream for equality, brotherhood, and the need to make real the promises of democracy. His voice thundered from the steps of the Lincoln Memorial, across the great Mall in Washington, and into our homes, our heart, and our history. That man, of course, was the Reverend Martin Luther King, Jr.

He lived and died in a great struggle to close the gap between our words and our deeds, to make good on good intentions, to see that none of us can be fully free until all of us are fully free, to make us all agents of change.

In the 30 years since Martin Luther King gave what I believe is the greatest speech by an American in my lifetime, we've come a long way. But clearly, we've got a long way to go before realizing his dreams. We owe it to him, to his work, to his memory to rededicate ourselves today to the causes of civil rights, civic responsibility, and economic opportunity for every American. In the last 7 months, we've made some great strides on that road.

To begin to turn good words into better deeds, we first had to get our economic house in order. That's what we did by breaking gridlock and passing a tough economic program to cut our deficit by nearly $500 billion over 5 years, to give new incentives to businesses to expand, to individuals to invest, and to create millions of new high-wage jobs here at home.

Already we've felt some of the good side effects of getting serious about our economy. Unemployment has dipped to its lowest level in 22 months, and interest rates are at their lowest rates in 20 years. We've also won some important battles for working families. The Family Leave Act now permits people to take some time off from work to care for a sick family member or a newborn child without losing their job. And changes in the tax laws now provide that no one who works 40 hours a week with children in the home will 'live in poverty. That's a big first step in welfare reform and in ending welfare as we know it. It's pro-work and pro-family.

We're moving to open the doors of college education to all Americans at a time when education is more important than ever to getting good jobs. We've reorganized the student loan program so that there will be lower interest rates, and repayments will be tied to income and, therefore, easier to make. We're on the verge of passing the national service program to give our young people the chance to use their energies and talents to rebuild our communities and, at the same time, to help pay for their college educations.

We've been moving on a massive program of defense conversion to help defense workers, military personnel, and communities who won the cold war build a brighter future even in the face of defense reductions. And because we want America to be a safer place, I've sent to Congress a crime bill that, among other things, will put tens of thousands more police officers on the streets and will pass the Brady bill to provide for a waiting period before handguns can be bought.

We're moving to change politics as usual. The Senate has passed a campaign finance reform bill that gives less influence to political action committees and opens the doors of communication to all candidates. And they've passed a lobby reform bill to reduce the influence of lobbyists. Now we have to get the House to pass these bills, too.

So in the quiet of this August day, as we reflect on what's happened over the last several months, we can say that together we've made a good beginning, but the job has just begun. There are still great challenges out there for Americans. There aren't enough jobs, incomes are too stagnant, and there is too much insecurity for too many families.

Our biggest challenge is to reform health care. It's the main reason millions of people can't get pay raises. It's the chief cause of insecurity for millions of families. It's the biggest culprit in the Federal deficit. And it's a threat to America's business growth because we're spending over 14 percent of our income on health care. Our competitors, the Germans and the Japanese, are spending just over 8 percent of their income on health care, and they have every bit as good a health care system, in most ways, as we do.

Soon the First Lady's task force will make its recommendations on what we need to do to ensure that every American has access to good, affordable health care, a plan that keeps what's good about our health care system—our doctors, our nurses, our health care providers, our medical research, our great technology— but a plan that changes what's wrong: an increasingly expensive and unjustifiable system of finance, one that's too bureaucratic, one that has runaway costs.

Another urgent task for our country is to pass the North American Free Trade Agreement. Last year I told the American people this agreement with Mexico and Canada could mean more jobs for Americans if it could be strengthened to ensure that our jobs would not be lost because of low environmental standards or depressed wages in Mexico. Today I can tell you we've won unprecedented provisions in this agreement that will help to guarantee that it will benefit all Americans. When it's in place, we'll open up a whole new world of job opportunity for Americans here at home by trading more with Mexico and ultimately with the rest of Latin America, the second fastest growing area in the world.

We're also dedicated to fixing our own Government, to reducing unnecessary bureaucracy, eliminating waste, increasing the quality of service, and giving you more value for your dollar. We haven't reexamined the way our Government works or doesn't work for a very long time. But for the last several months, Vice President Gore has been studying the problem with the best experts in the country, and early next month we'll have his recommendations on how our Government can serve you better and save you money. Quite simply, we've still got a lot to do in a town where change is hard and words too often substitute for real action. Congress, however, has already spent about 40 percent more time on the job than it did last year.

Many people say I'm pushing too hard for change. Well, 30 years ago today Martin Luther King said, "This is no time to engage in the luxury of cooling off or the tranquilizing drug of gradualism. Now is the time to make real the promises of democracy." As our children go back to school and, after a great family vacation, I go back to work, I have faith that together we can do just that, make real the promises of democracy for all Americans.

Thanks for listening.

NOTE: The address was recorded at 9:45 a.m. on August 27 at a private residence on Martha's Vineyard, MA, for broadcast at 10:06 a.m. on August 28.

Statement on the 30th Anniversary of the March on Washington for Jobs and Freedom
August 28, 1993

On this day 30 years ago, almost a quarter million Americans gathered in the shadow of the Lincoln Memorial to ask our Nation to uphold its founding ideals of equal justice and equal opportunity for all.

As he looked at the crowd, Martin Luther King, Jr., must have been inspired by what he saw: people of every color, united in mutual respect and common purpose, representing America as it was meant to be and as it must be. In the words of A. Philip Randolph, whose vision of a multiracial movement for social justice inspired this historic demonstration, those who marched on August 28, 1963, were "the advance guard of a massive moral revolution for jobs and freedom."

Three decades later, we remember how far we have come on freedom's trail, and we rededicate ourselves to completing the journey. As a son of the South, I have seen in my own lifetime how racism held all of us down and how the civil rights movement set all of us free. We must never forget the hard-earned lesson that America can only move forward when we move forward together.

That is why we rededicate ourselves to vigorous enforcement of the civil rights laws, to eradicating discrimination of every kind, and to opposing intolerance in all its forms. And we firmly believe that, as such visionary leaders as Martin Luther King, A. Philip Randolph, and Bayard Rustin understood three decades ago,

jobs and freedom are inextricably linked. Human dignity demands that each of us have the opportunity to use our God-given abilities, to support ourselves and our families, and to produce something of value for our fellow men and women.

In everything we do, we are guided by that vision of economic empowerment. That is why we have struggled to lift the working poor out of poverty. That is why we have struggled to expand the opportunities for education, training, and national service. That is why we have struggled to bring new jobs, new opportunities, and new hope to communities all across this country, from our smallest towns to our oldest cities. That is why we will spare no effort to provide every family in America with health care they can count on, health care that's always there. And as we pursue the timeless goals of opportunity for all and responsibility for all, let us follow the example of those who marched 30 years ago and work together, regardless of race or region or religion or party.

As we honor the past and build the future, let us listen again to the words of Martin Luther King, Jr., "Now is the time to make real the promises of democracy . . . now is the time to make justice a reality for all God's children." Together, we can make that dream a reality. Together, we can make the country we love everything it was meant to be.

Remarks Prior to Departure From Martha's Vineyard, Massachusetts
August 29, 1993

The President. Can you hear me? Good. Well, first of all, let me thank you all for coming. I'm astonished by this crowd, but it is what we have seen all week. I can't thank you enough on behalf of all of us for the wonderful hospitality we've had here. My family never needed a vacation more, and it's hard to imagine how this one could have been better. We are going home immensely grateful to all the people who

have been here, for your hospitality, your warmth, your understanding of the problems we caused on occasion and very much refreshed, renewed, and ready to go back to work for the American people.

We have a lot of work to do. We're going to take up the health care issue, which I think is the most important thing out there facing our country right now and any number of other things that you will read about in the days ahead.

I don't want to give a political talk tonight. I just want to tell you that, at a very personal level, this was a wonderful 10 days for us, and we are grateful to all of you. This has been a great time. This is a great family place. I wish everyone in America could see it, but at times I thought everyone in America was here already. [*Laughter*]

I'd like to ask Hillary to come up and say a word on behalf of our family, and I want to thank you again. And we want to get out here and shake a few hands before we leave, but I want Hillary to say a word or two.

[*At this point, Hillary Clinton expressed her thanks.*]

The President. Thank you very much. Bless you. I hope we'll see you again. Thank you so much.

NOTE: The President spoke at 9:36 p.m. at the Martha's Vineyard Airport.

Remarks at a White House Interfaith Breakfast
August 30, 1993

Thank you. Thank you very much. I want to once again, as the First Lady did, welcome all of you to the White House on behalf of Vice President and Mrs. Gore and Hillary and myself. We're delighted to have you all here.

We wanted to make this new beginning by beginning with a group of religious leaders from all faiths and parts of our country to come here today as we rededicate ourselves to the purposes for which we're called here.

I wanted to make just a couple of brief remarks. We've had an immensely interesting conversation at our table about some of the things which are dividing Americans of faith as well as those which are uniting them. I would say to you that I am often troubled as I try hard here to create a new sense of common purpose. All during the election I would go across the country and say that we're all in this together. Unless we can find strength in our diversity, our diversity of race, our diversity of income, our diversity of region, our diversity of religious conviction, we cannot possibly meet the challenges before us. That does not mean, in my view, that we have to minimize our diversity, pretend that we don't have deep convictions, or run away from our honest disagreements. It means that we must find a way to talk with respect with one another about those things with which we disagree and to find that emotional as well as the intellectual freedom to work together when we can.

A couple of days ago, when I was on vacation—let me say, the most important religious comment made to me this morning was that several of you gave me dispensation for my vacation. You said I did not need to feel any guilt for taking a little time off, so I appreciate that. [*Laughter*] But I bought a book on vacation called "The Culture of Disbelief" by Stephen Carter, a professor at our old alma mater, Hillary's and mine, at the Yale Law School. He is himself a committed Christian, very dedicated to the religious freedoms of all people of faith, of any faith, in the United States. And the subtitle of the book is "How American Law and Politics Trivialize Religious Devotion." And I would urge you all to read it from whatever political as well as religious spectrum you have because at least it lays a lot of these issues out that I am trying to grapple with.

Sometimes I think the environment in which we operate is entirely too secular. The fact that we have freedom of religion doesn't mean we need to try to have freedom from religion. It doesn't mean that those of us who have faith shouldn't frankly admit that we are animated by the faith, that we try to live by it, and that it does affect what we feel, what we think, and what we do.

On the other hand, it is very important that, as Americans, we approach this whole area with a certain amount of humility, that we be careful when we say that because we seek to know and do God's will, God is on our side and therefore against our opponent. That is important for two reasons. One is, we might be wrong. [*Laughter*] After all, we're only human. The other is that the thing that has kept us together over time is that our Constitution and Bill of Rights gives us all the elbow room to seek to do God's will in our own life and that of our families and our communities, and that means that there will be inevitable conflicts; so that there will never be a time when everything that we think is wrong can also be illegal. There will always be some space there because there will have to be some room for Americans of good faith to disagree.

I think we need to find areas where we can agree and work together on. The restoration of religious freedoms acts is a very important issue to me personally. And this administration is committed to seeing it through successfully. And I think virtually every person of faith in this country, without regard to their party or philosophy or convictions on other issues, agrees with that. So we are hopeful that that will happen. But there must be other areas in which we can meet together and talk together and work together and frankly acknowledge our agreements and our disagreements.

If people of faith treat issues about which they disagree as nothing more than a cause for a screaming match, then we also trivialize religion in our country. And we undermine the ability to approach one another with respect and trust and faith. And I say that not just to those who disagree with me on some of the particularly contentious issues but also to those who agree with me. Every person in this country who seeks to know and do the will of his or her Creator is entitled to respect for that effort. That is a difficult job, difficult to know, even harder to do. That is hard work.

But people that have that level of depth, that aren't totally carried away by the secular concerns of the moment must, it seems to me, find a way to talk and work with one another if we're ever going to push the common good. We can't pass a health care program without a conviction that this is in the common interest, that over the long run we will all win. If this becomes some battle where I'm trying to slay some dragon of special interest and that's all it is, we'll never get where we want to go. The American people have to open their hearts as well as their minds and figure out, this is this horrible problem. We have to solve it. But we have to solve it in a way that enables us to be united together.

We can't work our way through a lot of these economic problems unless we frankly admit that we're moving into a new age where no one has all the answers. We may have to modify, all of us, our specific policy positions. But our goal should be to enable every person who lives in this country to live up to his or her God-given potential. And if we look at it that way and frankly admit we're in a new and different era, then we can go forward.

We can't possibly do anything for anybody in this country unless they're willing to also do something for themselves. There has to be a new ethic of personal and family and community responsibility in this country that should unite people across the lines of different faiths and even different political philosophies. And the people of faith in this country ought to be able to say that, so that if you say that you've got to have that sort of revitalization at the grassroots, person by person, that the Democrats can feel comfortable with saying that; no one says, "Oh, you're just being a rightwinger." It's just simply true, it is self-evidently true: You cannot change somebody's life from the outside in unless there is also some change from the inside out.

So these are the kinds of things that I've had a lot of time to think about over the last few days. And I have felt in the last several months during my Presidency that we oftentimes get so caught up in the battle of the moment, the heat of the moment—how are you going to answer this charge and make that change or deal with this difficulty—that sometimes we forget that we are all in this because we are seeking a good that helps all Americans. There must be some sense of common purpose and common strength and, ultimately, an end which helps us all, that revels in the fact that there are people who honestly disagree about the most fundamental issues but can still approach one another with real respect, without assuming that if you disagree on issue X or Y, you've jumped off the moral and political cliff and deserve to be banished to some faraway place.

So I wanted to have you here today because I wanted you to hear this direct from your President. I wanted to ask you to continue to pray for me and for our administration, and I wanted to invite you to be part of an ongoing dialog, which we will come back to all of you later on, talk about how we can continue to involve people who care about their citizenship as well as about their relationship to their God and how we can work through these things.

There are no easy answers to this. The Founding Fathers understood that; that's why they wanted us to have the first amendment. There are no simple solutions. But I am convinced that we are in a period of historic significance, profound change here in this country and throughout the world and that no one is wise enough to see to the end of all of it, that we have to be guided by a few basic principles and an absolute conviction that we can recreate a common good in America.

But it's hard for me to take a totally secular approach to the fact that there are cities in this country where the average murderer is now under the age of 16. Now, there may not be a religious answer to the policy question of whether it's a good thing that all these kids can get their hands on semiautomatic weapons. But there certainly is something that is far more than secular about what is happening to a country where we are losing millions of our young people and where they shoot each other with abandon and now often shoot total strangers for kicks, shoot at them when they are swimming in the swimming pool in the summertime.

So I believe that we have enormous possibilities. I think we have enormous problems. There will always be some areas of profound disagreement. What I would ask you today to do is to, as I said, to pray for us as we go forward, to be willing to engage in this dialog, to reach out to others who may disagree with us on particular issues and bring them into the family of America, and to give us a chance to find common ground so that we can build a common good and do what all of us in our own way are required to do. For I believe that each of us has a ministry in some way that we must play out in life and with a certain humility but also with deep determination.

So I thank you for being here. This has been a wonderful morning for me and for all of us. And I ask you to think about these things and to be willing to continue to engage in this dialog. We have a lot of work to do to lift this country up and to pull this country together and to push this country into the 21st century. And we have serious responsibilities beyond our borders. Every day there is some good news in the press about that—some of you have been talking about the Middle East, how many times we thought we had good news and been disappointed, but better than the bad—and every day there is some frustration. So we have to go forward with a much deeper sense of shared values and togetherness toward the common good than we've had so far. That is what I seek to do and what I ask for your prayers and guidance and support and involvement, active involvement, to achieve.

Thank you very much.

NOTE: The President spoke at 10:03 a.m. in the State Dining Room at the White House.

Remarks and an Exchange With Reporters Prior to a Meeting on Flood Relief and Hurricane Emily
August 30, 1993

The President. Let me say, I asked that James Lee Witt to come in this morning to provide to me and to the Vice President and to our senior staff a briefing on Hurricane Emily and what provisions we're making to be ready for that and as well as to give me an update the—how we're handling the aftermath of the flood damage in the Midwest. And as you know, there was more flooding in Iowa yesterday.

So those are the two things we're going to be talking about, and I thought I would maybe just let Mr. Witt say a word or two and then you may have a couple of questions.

[*At this point, Federal Emergency Management Agency Director Witt made brief remarks.*]

Middle East Peace Talks

Q. Mr. President, changing the subject for a second. The Palestinians and the Israelis appear to have some historic breakthrough involving perhaps mutual Israeli-PLO recognition. If the Israelis and the PLO recognize each other, will that result in the U.S. resuming its dialog with the PLO?

The President. Well, first, let me say I am very much encouraged by what is happening there and very hopeful. The administration has worked hard to facilitate it. But ultimately, whatever happens will have to be done by the parties themselves. If there is a new and different landscape in the Middle East, then I might be willing to entertain some questions. But I can't say now. I can't answer your question now. It's hypothetical, and it would only interfere with the discussions now going on. I don't think it's appropriate for the United States even to consider its own position here until the parties have a chance to work out a resolution of this.

Q. But the U.S. did have intervention in this, didn't it? I mean——

The President. Oh, absolutely. I don't know if I would call it an intervention, but we've certainly worked hard to be a handmaiden or whatever the appropriate term is——

Q. So you are involved?

The President. We are involved, but our position has not been at issue here and should not be discussed until the parties themselves worked out their differences.

NAFTA

Q. Mr. President, Senator Dole suggested the prospects for NAFTA would be better were you to take it up to the Senate first. Do you agree?

The President. Yes, I think I do. At least my preliminary—I haven't talked to Mr. Daley about this or to the congressional leadership. But if you mean by that there's a far greater likelihood that today that NAFTA would pass in the Senate than the House, that's clearly correct.

Q. What's going to be your strategy for winning over the House Democrats? David Bonior says that 75 percent of them right now are against NAFTA.

The President. Well, not all of them have reached a position on it. And I want to do two or three things. First of all, as I told the Governors when I met with them in Tulsa, I'd like for all the Governors who support this to ask their Members of Congress to take no position until they actually read the agreement and see the implementing legislation itself.

Remember, my position, going back to 1992, was that I was not for the NAFTA agreement as originally concluded but that I would support it if certain conditions were met. Those conditions have been met as far as our agreements

with the Mexicans. We still have to have a training program, but we're going to have the first trade agreement in history that's got strong environmental requirements and that has Mexico committing to raise its minimum wage as its economy grows.

So these are very encouraging and very different things. So my strategy for Democrats and Republicans who have not declared for but have not adamantly planted their feet in cement against, would be to ask them to read the agreement and wait until they see the implementing legislation, because that will tell them where we're going with the job training, and then make a judgment. And I think if that happens, we can prevail because, again I will say, Latin America is the second fastest growing part of the world. Mexico is just the beginning of this process. And I think it means more jobs for Americans. And I think I'll be able to persuade——

Q. Should Bonior remove his hat as your whip, and——

The President. No. I think that's a decision that the leadership in the House has to make. You know, Presidents and their Members of Congress are going to differ on some things. I heard the other day—I don't know that this is true—but I heard that so far, the Democrats in the Congress have voted for me more consistently than the last two or three Democratic Presidents. I have not checked that. That's just what I heard.

Q. You don't believe that, do you?

The President. I think yes, I think they have with remarkable consistency and very high percentages. But I think that we have an honest disagreement here. He has worked his heart out for me. This is the first issue on which we have disagreed. I think he's wrong; he thinks I'm wrong. I think in the end that my position will prevail.

Hurricane Emily

Q. I want to get this question—the people in the Carolinas are remembering still in their mind not only the devastation, of course, but the response of the Federal Government after—that they consider that largely a nightmare as well. What do you say to them to let them know that you're prepared, well prepared, in case it does, of course, hit them?

The President. I would say two things. First of all, we're here looking at this map today trying to get ready. That's what we're doing here. And secondly, if you look at the way FEMA and the Agriculture Department and the other Departments handled the flooding in the Middle West, it's obvious that while we don't control what Mother Nature does, we're going to be on top of it with all the resources and effort that we can possibly marshal as quickly as possible.

NOTE: The President spoke at 11:13 a.m. in the Roosevelt Room at the White House. In his remarks, he referred to William M. Daley, Chairman, NAFTA Task Force. A tape was not available for verification of the content of these remarks.

The President's News Conference With Caribbean Leaders
August 30, 1993

President Clinton. Good afternoon. Today I had the great honor of welcoming five outstanding leaders from the English-speaking Caribbean to the White House: President Cheddi Jagan of Guyana, Prime Minister Erskine Sandiford of Barbados, Prime Minister Patrick Manning of Trinidad and Tobago—Tobago, excuse me; I'm still hoarse from our luncheon—Prime Minister P.J. Patterson of Jamaica, and Prime Minister Hubert Ingraham of the Bahamas. I'm impressed by the intelligence, the dynamism, and the dedication of the Caribbean leadership.

The end of the cold war has altered the nature but not the depth of our interest in the Caribbean. Our concern for the region is firmly rooted in geographic proximity, the resultant flows of people, of commodities and culture, and in our shared interest in fighting drug trafficking and projecting our economic interests and in protecting fragile ecosystems.

As with U.S.-Mexican relations, U.S.-Caribbean relations dramatically demonstrate the absolute inseparability of foreign and domestic issues. More than ever before, our Nation is a Caribbean nation. In our discussions, we recognize the concerns that NAFTA may adversely affect the Caribbean and Central American nations by diverting trade and investment flows to Mexico. Therefore, I want to announce today that I have asked Ambassador Mickey Kantor to study the impact of NAFTA on these small economies and to consult with them on new measures to increase regional trade.

American workers have a direct interest in the prosperity of the English-speaking Caribbean. The $2 billion in United States exports to those countries creates at least 40,000 American jobs. Our warm and productive luncheon meeting covered many other areas as well. These nations are all vibrant democracies striving to adapt their economies to new global realities while maintaining a full respect for individual freedoms and human rights.

In the Organization of American States and in the United Nations, they consistently take strong stands in favor of the collective defense of democracy. They have all been firm supporters of multilateral efforts to restore President Aristide in Haiti. And we discussed cooperative security and economic measures to assist Haitian democracies. I thank them for their support of the restoration of President Aristide and, of course, we all enjoyed a recounting of President Aristide's swearing-in of his new Prime Minister today.

The Caribbean community will be an important building block of a hemispheric community of democracies linked by growing economic ties and common political beliefs. That will happen, I believe, in no small measure because of the leadership of the five people who are here with us today. And I'd like now to ask them each in turn to come to the microphone and say a few remarks.

And I think President Jagan is going first. He was here first in 1961. Is that right? The microphone is yours, sir.

President Jagan. Thank you, Mr. President. As you just pointed out, I was here in 1961. Those were difficult, different times. I'm happy to be here now with my colleagues jointly at this invitation of the President and to say that we definitely have problems, you in the United States and we in the Caribbean. Your problems are big; ours are critical. And I think it will be necessary for us to work closely together to solve these problems because at one time Caribbean was described as a third border of United States, and some have said it's the Achilles' heel. And I believe 10 years ago, the Caribbean was described as one of the world circles of crisis.

We have deteriorated somewhat; our economies are in trouble. But nevertheless we are optimistic that if we work together with the United States in a feeling, in a spirit of genuine partnership and interdependence, we can together resolve these problems. We have to, because increasingly we see developments taking place around the world in megablocs, and we in this hemisphere have to chart out our own destiny and work together in order to alleviate the problems of our people—they are many— and to bring about economic progress and human development.

Thank you.

Prime Minister Sandiford. We in Barbados and the rest of the Caribbean believe that we in this region have great opportunities to deal with the problems facing our region. We see these problems as relating to the achievement of greater levels of growth, providing more jobs for our people, keeping inflation low, and also dealing with the issues of competitiveness and productivity in our economies. Within this framework we believe that the United States, the Caribbean, and all other countries of our region have an opportunity to work through a new conceptualization of our region based on what I am calling a twin continent concept, involving the countries of North America, the countries of South America, linked on the one side by the countries of Central America and on the other side by that string of lovely tropical islands called the Caribbean, of which Barbados, forgive me, is the most beautiful. And then there are all the countries that are in between. [*Laughter.*]

The opportunity of discussing with the President and his high-level delegation the issues involved and how we can do this, I think, is a most welcome one. And we believe that we can do it on a sustainable basis, sustainable in the sense that we have to provide an acceptable standard of living for our people, taking into account that those who are disadvantaged or deprived are not left to waste away and taking into account also that we have to make provision for our children and our children's children so that they, too, can live in an environment that

can enable them to achieve adequate standards of living. We believe that we must now sit down and work as partners in order to achieve these objectives. And that is what we have been discussing, and that is what we will be working for.

Prime Minister Manning. Thank you very much, ladies and gentlemen. We were very pleased today to have a chance to talk with the U.S. President and a team of his closest advisers. The CARICOM countries are situated on the doorstep of the United States of America. And it would be a great error to conclude that now that communism has come virtually to an end, that the CARICOM countries and the Caribbean territories on the whole are no longer of significance to the United States of America. That would be a great mistake, indeed.

All of these countries are going through a structural adjustment, and in that context, we are all experiencing relatively high—relative on absolute terms—high levels of unemployment. It will be a great tragedy if in seeking to pursue sustainable development for our countries, it takes place at such a rate that the domestic populations begin to see as one of the options available to them a greater involvement in drug and drug-related activities. That's an option, ladies and gentlemen, that we are trying our best to avoid already. There's a drug problem in the Caribbean, and many of our countries have been transshipment points for the transfer of cocaine from South America to the United States and Canada and to the north.

And so there is an urgency in the way we deal with development, and there's an urgency in the strategies that we pursue, the urgency in identifying these strategies and pursuing them as expeditiously as possible to ensure that we satisfy the aspirations of our populations.

That is a point that was discussed at length today. And in particular we discussed with the President and his advisers this whole question of access to aid in the transition period, as our economies go from one state to the next, and in particular the use of per capita income as an indicator, a trigger indicator, an indicator for accessing concessional rates of funding and of assistance. Really, the populations of countries don't see per capita income. What they see is the change in per capita income. So no matter where you are, as long as there's a significant change downwards in the per capita income of any country, then it results in social problems in that particular country. And that is a point of view that we advocated today as perhaps an alternative for mechanisms for giving aid to countries and for allowing countries to access concessional funding. I think that the point was taken. And our discussions were in fact very pleasant and, I believe, very fruitful.

Thank you.

Prime Minister Patterson. When I heard the Prime Minister of Barbados asserting the claims of his country, I thought of making a simple rejoinder and then reflected that it ran the risk of being misunderstood here. I had intended to say, good wine needs no bush. [*Laughter*]

May I, Mr. President, thank you on behalf of the Government and people of Jamaica, and indeed on behalf of all the governments and people of the CARICOM member countries, for having invited us to participate in a timely discussion with you as your administration seeks to chart a relevant Caribbean policy in the context of the developments in the world and the hemisphere to which we belong.

I think out of our discussions has emerged a recognition of the need to take that further step in forging a closer and more effective working partnership. As has been mentioned, the United States, Canada, and Mexico are on the verge of completing the signatories for the NAFTA agreement. For us in the Caribbean, we note that the whole world is moving towards larger and larger trading blocs. And we envisage a time when eventually there is going to be a free trade that extends throughout the hemisphere to which we belong.

We in the Caribbean, particularly in CARICOM, have already started to prepare for that process. But we recognize that there is going to be the need for special transitional arrangements, taking into account certain products and exports which are very sensitive to us and certain areas of industrial activity that are so important to ensuring that employment levels are maintained, indeed, that unemployment is reduced so that social stability is maintained in all our respective countries.

To these objectives, the strengthening of democracy, the enhancement of social mobility, and for economic progress in our region, all of us are firmly committed. And we are very happy that we are agreed to work in a collaborative exercise to make the dreams of all us as proud, independent people in this hemisphere a reality in our times.

Prime Minister Ingraham. Mr. President, colleagues, ladies and gentlemen. When I heard the Prime Minister of Barbados and Jamaica— [*laughter*]—and I speak for the Bahamas, the undisputed leader in tourism in the entire region. [*Laughter*]

We are delighted to have the opportunity to be in Washington, DC, at the White House and to have been so warmly welcomed by President Clinton and his administration. And in my capacity as Chairman of CARICOM and as Prime Minister of the Bahamas, let me say thank you very much for the opportunity to exchange views, which we found most useful.

We had the opportunity to talk about the further steps which we may take as a group of nations to strengthen democracy in our region and to ensure that there is great accountability to our citizens and transparency in the governance of our respective countries. We were able to share views on Haiti and the progress which is being made in relation to the restoration of democracy to that country and to express our appreciation to the United States of America for the work which it is doing in that regard. We were also able to discuss our desire to do all we can to assist in helping to create an atmosphere in this region where all countries in the region will be democratic countries in the not too distant future, including Cuba.

We were able to put before the administration of the United States the items of highest priority for the Caribbean region, and they are the inclusion in NAFTA, provisions to preserve and enhance CBI benefits to small CARICOM countries, the convention tax deduction benefits, and tourism development, which is most important to countries in the region like the Bahamas and elsewhere. We were able to point out the need for continual support for agriculture and banana, particularly for the countries of St. Vincent, Dominica, and St. Lucia.

We were also able to focus on the joint cooperation in the antidrug effort and to point to the fact that one of the most successful, if not the most successful, drug interdiction program which has taken place anywhere takes place between the United States of America and in the Bahamas where some 26 percent of all cocaine seizures are captured.

And lastly and finally, we were able to focus upon the need for the continuing promotion of democracy in our region.

We all leave Washington, DC, reinvigorated

and determined to continue our efforts in this region to work together as partners to ensure better quality of life for all of our citizens. We are most hopeful of the benefits that will come to our region through the administration of President Clinton, and we thank you very much.

President Clinton. Thank you. Let me also say, before you ask the question, if there are people here representing your nations, I want to make sure that I give them a chance to ask their questions also, but we'll start with Helen [Helen Thomas, United Press International].

NAFTA

Q. Mr. President, since you have a better chance of passing NAFTA in the Senate, will you push for the Senate consideration first? And did it come as a surprise to you that the Caribbean would feel adversely affected by NAFTA? I mean, was it news?

President Clinton. No. Well, let me answer the first question first. I haven't made a decision on that yet, and I don't think I should until I consult with the supporters of the agreement. It can't pass in either House until the legislation is developed, which is now going on to embody the agreement. But I'm certainly open to that. I just simply haven't had the opportunity to sit down and visit with the supporters and see what they want to do. I have no objection to going that way.

With regard to the Caribbean, it didn't come as a surprise to me. I think in general what these leaders said was that they thought it was a good idea but that it shouldn't adversely affect existing relationships. Our administration has worked hard to have a positive mutually beneficial relationship with the CARICOM nations to faithfully carry out the laws of Congress, including one that was passed late last year designed to stop a previous problem with our efforts there. And I said, as I said today, I asked the Ambassador for Trade, Mickey Kantor, to look into this and see whether we can provide some assurances that there will not be a disadvantage to the Caribbean nations.

Cuba

Q. Mr. President, can you be more specific about what the dialog was on Cuba and bringing it into a more democratic society?

President Clinton. Actually, we had a general conversation about it. As you know, the position

of CARICOM and the position of the United States with regard to trade with Cuba is different. I just simply reiterated that the Cuban democracy act does not sanction any trade with Cuba unless it is somehow subsidized by governments. That is not contemplated, so the difficulty issue we just got off the table, and then we talked a little bit about what the prospects were for economic and political reform in Cuba, something that is devoutly to be hoped for by the peoples of all the nations here represented. But there was nothing more specific than that.

Bosnia

Q. Mr. President, if the Bosnian peace agreement is reached in Geneva, how many American forces would you be willing to offer to help enforce that agreement? How long would they be required to serve? And what would be the risk to those forces?

President Clinton. Well, first of all, whether I would be prepared to do that or not depends on whether I'm convinced that the agreement is both—is fair, fully embraced by the Bosnian government, and is enforceable. That has been a source of concern for our military planners all along—about, you know, whether we could have something that would be enforceable.

But I made clear last February, and I will reiterate again, the United States is prepared to participate in a multinational effort to keep the peace in Bosnia. But I want to see what the details are. I want to get the briefing on it. I want to know that it will be enforceable. But I'm certainly open to that, but I also want to know whose responsibility it is to stay, for how long.

It's a little bit different than the situation in Somalia, for example, where you really have two problems that relate to one another. There needs to be a lot of nation-building in Somalia from the ground up, a lot of institution-building. We did go there to stop the starvation and the violence and the bloodshed. But it's also true that the absence of order gave rise to all those problems.

And so we're still trying to fulfill our original mission in Somalia. This is a very different sort of thing, but I certainly think it can work. A multinational effort to keep the peace, if it is enforceable and the understandings are there, can clearly work. You can see that in the longstanding success we've had in our participation in the aftermath of the Camp David agreement.

Cuba

Q. Mr. President, my question is for Prime Minister Patterson, if you could step to the microphone. Going back to Cuba, what is the position of CARICOM in regards to Cuba? And do you think you can do anything to bring Cuba back into the democratic fold?

Prime Minister Patterson. First of all, what we are seeking to establish with Cuba is a joint commission that discusses the range of matters no different from those presently covered by a joint commission with Mexico, with Venezuela, with Colombia. It is not an agreement that provides for subsidized trade with Cuba and therefore does not offend any existing legislation in the United States or elsewhere.

We feel that the time has come for all countries in the hemisphere to work towards a normalization of relationships among them. There are differences between the political systems in Cuba and those in the CARICOM countries. We remain firmly committed to the democratic tradition. But Cuba unquestionably is a Caribbean country. That is a reality which we must face, and we believe that the joint commission should assist in the process of inducing Cuba towards the sorts of policies and programs that are compatible with those of other independent nations in the hemisphere.

Q. Would you like to see the U.S. do the same thing?

Prime Minister Patterson. What the U.S. does is a matter for the U.S. to determine. If we can assist anywhere in the process of contact or mediation, we are always prepared to do so.

Somalia

Q. Mr. President, in Mogadishu some of the humanitarian relief workers say that the U.S. raid early this morning was a blunder, and in fact, the U.S. military is making their job more difficult. What do you say to those who are there to help? And will the U.S. forces remain there long enough to capture Aideed? Is that a target for you?

President Clinton. Well, the United Nations operation set that as their objective, and they asked us for our help in that regard.

I would remind you that I understand the problems with this, but the United Nations be-

lieves and has ample evidence to support the fact that the supporters of Aideed murdered a substantial number of Pakistani peacekeepers and are behind the deaths of four Americans. So we have to deal with that. And I am open to other suggestions. I think the United Nations should be open to other suggestions.

To date, we have tried to be cooperative with the policies that have been jointly developed. We have not been just simply driving this. We have really tried to work within the framework of the U.N. to prove that this thing could work over the long run. We've also tried to make sure that everyone understood that this is not all of Somalia we're talking about. We're talking about one part of Mogadishu. In much of the rest of the country, the U.N. mission has continued unimpeded and successfully. I don't think anyone wants to change the fundamental character of it.

And so, would I be willing to discuss that with our people and with anyone else? Of course, I would. But I think it is very important to point out that what provoked this was people involved with Aideed killing the Pakistanis first and then the four Americans.

Caribbean-U.S. Relations

Q. Mr. President—[*inaudible*]—talked about the need for—[*inaudible*]. Is there a need to ensure the dialog continues through the establishment perhaps of U.S.-CARICOM policy machinery? What are you prepared to do?

President Clinton. Well, I think there is a need for a continuing dialog. One of the things that I pledged today to these leaders is that next year when the conference on the sustainable development in smaller nations is held in the Caribbean, that the United States would send a high level delegation there. And we didn't discuss any specific mechanism. But I think it is very important. You know, all these nations, and others not here present, in the Caribbean, are at different points in their history with different challenges. And I think that what we need to do is to make it clear that the United States is committed to democracy, to market economics, and to economic growth of this region over the long run. Here even at home we find great difficulty in predicting with precision what's going to happen economically, because we're in a period of real profound economic change. And I think it's important that we make these commitments over the long run and that we keep the doors of communication open, and that's exactly what we intend to do.

Thank you very much.

NOTE: The President's 24th news conference began at 2:09 p.m. in the East Room at the White House.

Exchange With Reporters on Cuba
August 30, 1993

Q. Mr. President, are there any conditions that would be met that you would be able to end the U.S. embargo on Cuba?

The President. We've had the press conference. [*Laughter*]

I support the Torricelli bill, as you know. I did when it was passed, and I still do. But I said before, I could just reiterate what I said again: We all hope that there will come a time when democracy and an open economy will come to Cuba. And it will be a cause of enormous celebration in this country when it happens.

NOTE: The exchange began at 2:36 p.m. in the Blue Room at the White House. A tape was not available for verification of the content of this exchange.

Exchange With Reporters Prior to a Meeting With the Joint Chiefs of Staff
August 30, 1993

Defense Review

Q. Is this a crisis meeting, Mr. President?

The President. I hope not. [*Laughter*] The Secretary of Defense and the Joint Chiefs say it's a meeting to discuss their review of the defense needs of the country and how we're going——

Somalia

Q. Was the Somalia raid bungled?

The President. I don't think I would characterize it in that way.

NOTE: The exchange began at 4:16 p.m. in the Cabinet Room at the White House. A tape was not available for verification of the content of this exchange.

Remarks at the Summer of Service Forum in College Park, Maryland
August 31, 1993

The President. You know, I really love Senator Mikulski, if she just weren't so laid back and passive and soft-spoken, you might figure out what's on her mind. [*Laughter*] She was terrific.

I'd like to begin by introducing some other people who are here, and I hate to do this always because I know I'm going to miss someone that I should introduce. But I want to begin anyway by introducing the distinguished Gov-

ernor of Maryland, Governor Don Schaefer, one of my former colleagues when I was a Governor; one of the most important leaders in the House of Representatives, Congressman Steny Hoyer from Maryland. I want to introduce a man who came all the way from his State of Connecticut to be here with us today, the first Republican sponsor we had for the national service legislation, Representative Chris Shays from Connecticut. Thank you very much.

I see my good friend Senator Mike Miller there, the head of the Democratic majority in the Senate of Maryland. A former Congressman from Maryland and now the Cochair of the President's Council on Physical Fitness—when he stands up you'll see why—distinguished former professional basketball player, Mr. Tom McMillen, my friend in the back. I was really— Tom and I ran 4 miles together the other day, and he's almost 7 feet tall, and he ran at a pace I had difficulty maintaining. So I was very impressed. He convinced me he was qualified for the job I gave him.

And finally, I'd like to acknowledge the president of the University of Maryland, President William Kirwan, who is here. And in some ways most important of all, the person who I put in charge of creating and carrying out the national service program, my friend of nearly 25 years, Mr. Eli Segal; I'd like to ask him to stand.

I'll tell you, I just saw—there's one other person way in the back I've got to introduce because he and I started working on this concept of national service a few years ago through an organization I was involved in called the Democratic Leadership Council. And he's a professor here at the University of Maryland, but he's on leave. He's working in the White House for me now, Professor Bill Galston. Thank you, Bill, for your help.

I came here mostly to listen to you today and to thank you, but I wanted to just say a few words. This campus has a special meaning in my life. The first time I ever came to the University of Maryland was 30 years ago this summer when I was a delegate from my home State of Arkansas to the American Legion Boys Nation program. We stayed here and then went to Washington frequently to learn about the Government. I met President Kennedy then. I saw Members of Congress, members of the Cabinet, and really had my eyes opened to a whole world of possibility. But the thing that I remember I think most clearly after all these years is that President Kennedy said in his Inaugural that we should not ask what our country could do for us but what we could do for our country. And he also said that we must always remember that here on Earth, God's work must truly be our own. That's what all of you have done.

I just finished a 2-week vacation, which I needed very badly because I've worked pretty hard the last several years. But you just finished 2 months of very important work. The summer of service ends today, and I hope you feel refreshed by the time you gave to other people and the service you rendered. And we are about to begin, as Senator Mikulski said, when the Senate passes the national service bill next week, we'll start the first full year of national service at the community level. I always believe that you and tens of thousands, eventually hundreds of thousands of young people like you could change the future of America and, in the process, could change your lives.

I ran for President for two big reasons. One is, I thought our country was not going in the right direction; and the second, I thought our country was coming apart when it ought to be coming together. I wanted to get the country moving again, and I wanted to bring the country together again. I wanted people to have a sense of the common good. I wanted us to draw strength from our diversity and to face our problems honestly and to seize our opportunities. I wanted people to recognize again that we don't have a person to waste and that too many of our young people are being lost.

And I believed that we could do it. I never thought the Government could do all these things alone. I just don't believe that. And for too long our country has been in the middle of this great debate where some people say, well, the Government ought to solve these problems, and other people say the Government ought to walk away. And I don't believe either is right. The Government basically has to be a partner. In order for Government to work, it has to be a partner.

And I have now, for the last several years, long before I started running for President, tried to capture this idea in three simple words. It's those of us in Government, it's our responsibility to try to help create opportunity. So our watchword should be opportunity. That's what the economic program's all about. That's what trying to reform the health care system's all about. That's what creating a national service bill is all about, trying to create opportunity. Then citizens have to recognize that all the opportunity in the world doesn't amount to a hill of beans unless there is someone there to seize responsibility, personal responsibility, for themselves, their families, their communities, and for their neighbors. And finally, out of that we can build a new American community.

There are so many people lost today because they don't think anybody really cares about them, because they can't imagine the future, because they have never been the most important person in the world to anybody else. We have got to create a sense of community in this country where we're prepared to take responsibility for each other, not just to point the finger at each other and tell each other what we ought to do but to offer a helping hand.

So I say all these things to you because I think you represent that. You represent the best of the opportunity you were given to be in the summer of service, of the personal responsibility you displayed by doing your work, and of the sense of the community that you helped to create by what you have done.

If every American did what you did for the last 2 months, if we all could do that for several years, we could revolutionize our country. There are no problems we could not solve. There is no future we cannot have. And I hope with all my heart that what you have done here will set the standard for the national service projects in community after community that young people will engage in when this bill becomes law.

I told Eli on the way up here today I'm convinced now there are tens of thousands of young people who could do this every summer who may not need to, want to, or be able to do it during the year. And I'm not sure we shouldn't go back to the Congress, Senator Mikulski and Representative Hoyer and Representative Shays, and at least file a report on this summer of service and consider having a special summer program over and above the year-long program we do because so many young people could do it just during the summer.

I just want you to remember that you are this country. You are America. You are this country. And so now I want to hear from you, but I want you to know that not just your President but your country is grateful to you for showing what America can be at its best. And I hope that we'll see it repeated hundreds of thousands of times over the course of my Presidency. And I hope it will become a permanent part of American life. If it does, the whole country will be stronger.

Greg, shall we begin?

[At this point, Greg Ricks, facilitator of the event, discussed the Summer of Service project and the group's overall accomplishments. A participant then discussed her experience working in an immunization program.]

The President. Thank you so much. That was a terrific presentation. Let me just make one comment about the immunization issue because your presentation pointed it up more clearly than my words could, but you all should know that in spite of the fact that America is a very wealthy country we have the third worst record in the Western Hemisphere of immunizing our children. One problem is the cost of vaccines. We make vaccines in this country which cost more money here than they do in many foreign countries. That's a long story, and we don't have to go through it, but one of the things that Congress did, and I want to thank those here who supported it, was to pass the economic program which included several hundred million dollars for the Federal Government to buy vaccines in bulk to make them available to clinics like the ones with which you were working. Even if you have the vaccines there it won't increase the immunization rate if people don't know about the service, don't feel comfortable about it, don't want their kids to be immunized. And one of the things that we clearly need is more people going out doing door-to-door work, doing community work, and it's obvious that there's not enough money in any local government, particularly an area with a lot of poor people and a lot of diversity, to hire people to do that unless you have a service project like this. So the national service whole idea really carries within it the seeds of lifting the immunization rates of America to those of other advanced nations in the world and changing the whole health care future of thousands and thousands of young children. Thank you.

[A participant from ICARE-Philadelphia asked if the health care reform plan would subsidize immunization programs.]

The President. Yes, the health care plan that will be announced in the next few weeks will have a big component of preventive care in it and will also provide the resources necessary to support the community-based clinics.

I think it's very important that—we have spent too little on preventive and primary care, causing us to have to spend too much on emergency care and care in later stages. So we're going to try to invest more in preventive and primary care and in those neighborhood clinics both in urban and rural areas. I think it will make a huge difference. The Philadelphia program is very, very impressive.

Yes. Nice hat. [*Laughter*]

[*A participant asked about the role of medical students and health care professionals in the health care reform plan.*]

The President. Yes, actually, of course, all the students in all the health care professions will be eligible to actually participate in some of these programs through the national service initiative, so there will be a continuing opportunity there both during the school year and during the summer to do that.

Secondly, we have tried over the last several months, through the task force that the First Lady has headed, to engage in dialog medical students, nursing students, other people studying in the health care professions to try to make sure that the incentives we have in this program produce the kind of health care system we want and give young people who really want to serve in the problem areas a chance to do it. For example, as compared with all other advanced countries, the United States has far more specialists and far fewer family practitioners—dramatic difference, huge difference from any other country. That means it's much harder to get people out in the basic clinics doing the basic services. So what we tried to do was to construct a program which would provide more incentives for medical schools and for students themselves, financial incentives and others, to go out and practice family medicine but at the same time would not frighten the American people into thinking we're backing off of medical technology. So there's going to be more invested in medical research under this program. So I think that it will be good, and I hope you will be able to take advantage of that and continue to participate.

[*Participants described their experiences working on environmental service projects.*]

The President. Thank you very much. I thought they both did a terrific job. I'd just like to make one comment again to try to reinforce the importance of the whole service concept in the environmental area.

When you talk to most people, maybe even a lot of you, and certainly in my mind when you mention environmental issues, often you think of policies that ought to be changed. So, for example, after I became President, I had promised to take some different policies. So we committed ourselves to signing the Biodiversity Treaty that other nations signed after the world conference in Rio de Janeiro last year, or we committed ourselves to reducing the amount of greenhouse gases in the environment to the 1990 levels by the year 2000, or last week we committed ourselves to no net loss of wetlands.

But as you can see, when you pass a law, it's one thing to say these things and another to do it, just like you did the wetlands restoration project. An enormous number of the environmental things that need to be done in this country require the same amount of labor intensity that it does to go door-to-door and try to immunize children. The lead paint example in New York is just one, but it is a very good one. That's a serious problem in many of the major cities in America, exposing some of the most vulnerable children.

That's another irony that you brought out here in your environmental presentation. A lot of people think of the environment as preserving distant areas that most people never see. But the truth is that the people in this country who need a better environment than most may be those who live in inner cities, who are most subject to pollution from dumps that are there, from lead in the paint, from any number of other threats.

So I really appreciate this because I hope that we can come to see the environment not only in terms of the sweeping national policies that the Vice President and I have committed ourselves to but also in terms of things that preserve the culture of Native Americans and that literally may preserve the lives of people not only in rural areas but in the cities as well. So I thank you for that.

Anybody got any questions on that subject?

[*A participant asked about increased funding for energy conservation programs.*]

The President. Yes. You know, having been a Governor—and the States operate those programs, Congress provides the funds but the States specifically operate them—I have seen firsthand how many jobs they create and also how much good they can do. I mean, I didn't make that point before, but a lot of this weatherization work for poor people, especially for a lot of elderly people who are stuck in these old houses that have holes in the walls literally, a lot of them, or in the floor not only make them warmer in the winter and cooler in the summer, they also save money on their utility bills. They literally do. They conserve energy, and they put more money in the pockets of people who have just barely enough to get by. So I strongly support them.

I also think that, in general, we should move to more energy resources that are within our own control. We have vast amounts of natural gas, for example, in this country that are environmentally cleaner than a lot of the fuels we burn, and we ought to move to develop them.

So the short answer to your question is yes. It's interesting, it's kind of a hard sell in the Congress now because the price of oil is so low and energy is so cheap. It's much cheaper in America than it is in any other major country. But if you just have enough to get by on, you're living on a Social Security check or you're living on a minimum wage, it's still very, very expensive and a big part of your budget.

Thank you. Yes?

[A participant commented on lead paint and other housing conditions and asked about extending the national service program to community members who are not in college.]

The President. Good question. That's a good question not only on the housing issue but on a number of other issues. And I wish I had a very good, complete answer for you today. I can tell you that that question is one that we have seriously discussed, and I have asked Henry Cisneros, who is the Secretary of the Department of Housing and Urban Development, to try to come up with a proposal for me that would help to do that, where the Federal Government could basically help local communities trying to engage the energies of people who are prepared to volunteer, work part-time, do whatever it takes to solve some of these problems. They are also very labor-intensive.

I'm hoping, beyond that, that some of the things that were in this economic program we passed, for example, extending the low-income housing tax credit and some other things that we put in there, will help State governments and local communities to work with developers to try to rehabilitate a lot of these houses and try to put people to work in doing it.

If you look at the building structure of the United States, we still have a lot of commercial overbuilding. We haven't worked through that. And a lot of people are in a position now to finance or refinance their home mortgages or buy new homes because interest rates are low. But the population growth in America of people who can buy homes has kind of slowed down. So the real economic opportunity may be in rehabilitating existing housing structures. And we are looking at what can be done to try to deal with that terrible problem.

We went for 12 years without any kind of serious housing program in America, and it led to a lot of these difficulties. And now I hope that, through Henry's work, working in partnership with people at the local level, we can come up with a better idea. So I don't have an answer for you today, but I can tell you we're working on the problem. And I see it as a real area of economic opportunity for people, the rehabilitation of existing housing structures. It's a better opportunity than building new commercial real estate buildings in many places and a better opportunity than building even new houses in some places where there's no population growth and no demand for it. So I hope we can come up with an answer to the problem you've posed.

[A participant asked about homeownership programs.]

The President. The most important thing we can do is get the mortgages down, which we've done. I mean, we have now the lowest mortgage rates in 25 years, so that people can buy housing at lower costs. The other thing that we did in this last economic program was to extend something called the low-income housing tax credit which basically gives people real incentives to build low-cost housing that is affordable. The final thing that we're doing is having Mr. Cisneros, the Secretary of the Housing and Urban Development Department, work with developers and people in local community groups all across the country to try to figure out how we can either build or rehabilitate more low-income housing so that those three things together I think should permit more people—particularly low-income working people who have virtually given up on the idea of owning their own home over the last 15 years as the price of housing outstripped inflation dramatically—I think you're going to see that kind of turn around now. And I believe that in the next 5 years the percentage of people owning their own homes, including lower income working people, will go up rather dramatically, but only if we work on all three of those areas.

[*A participant discussed his experience as a teacher's assistant.*]

The President. Thank you very much. I think you could see we were all very moved by the presentation.

Before I ran for President, I was Governor for 12 years, and I spent during that time more time in schools and with children and with teachers and watching people learn and watching people struggle, not just in my State but around the country, I guess than anything else I did. What I saw there emphasizes some very basic things that, again, I would say, the whole country could learn from and mobilize young people.

Number one, the one-room schoolhouses in New York proved that children can help other children learn dramatically. There's a lot of evidence of that, by the way. If we had time I could give you lots of other examples. But at phenomenal levels, phenomenal levels, there's evidence of—there's a school in Boston where, in order to get in the school, the seniors and juniors had to agree to tutor the seventh and eighth graders. And these kids were all basically from average or low-income families and most of them had average IQ's, and they all did very well, and there was almost no dropout—nearly everybody went to college, nearly everybody finished. And one of the key things was—and they had a very, very hard curriculum, very hard. But the older kids all did the tutoring for the younger kids—made a big difference.

Second point that your slide show pointed out and your presentation, was that learning should be fun for children, especially if they come from disadvantaged backgrounds. Instead of making it a pain, it should be fun, and they should be taught to believe that they can learn things. That New Orleans project I'm familiar with—it is astonishing that kids that once would be given up as—you know, you'd be lucky if they could read at the 7th-grade level when they got out of high school—are now being exposed to physics and computer technology and all that.

The third point I want to make—and this is something that all of you should remember, too—and that is, there's a lot of research in America which shows that kids that grow up in educationally disadvantaged homes or poor homes may work like crazy in school, but they're always afraid that they're not going to do as well as other kids, so they're always afraid to say what they don't know. But most of the best learning occurs in groups.

There was a huge study done a couple of years ago—and a lot of you going to college, you'll remember this—a huge study done in California a couple of years ago which showed that different groups of kids going into the University of California at Berkeley were studied based on how well they did academically and the connection to how hard they studied. The kids that actually spent the most time studying did the least well because they were afraid to study with each other because they were ashamed to say what they didn't know. The kids that studied in groups and talked with each other about what they didn't know and didn't understand, who worked together in a family, learned like crazy.

All of these things could be affected nationwide, these learning patterns could be affected nationwide by programs like this. You could literally revolutionize the educational system of the country if there were enough service volunteers like you to reach these kids.

The last thing I want to say is a lot of this stuff was done one on one. Every serious study of kids that grew up in difficult circumstances and succeeded against all the odds show that every one of them has got a different story, and there's only one constant that's almost always there: Nearly every child had some sort of a relationship with a caring adult, which you qualify for, for these little bitty kids. Keep in mind if you're 18 years old and you're helping some kid that's 5, you are the caring adult. Right?

So those are the points I want to make. Again, I would say, I hope this work will somehow register on people throughout the country that may not be within our program, because these four simple things that you have shown here could change the face of American education.

Yes, sir? I've been wanting you to talk because I wanted to get a good look at that hat. [*Laughter*]

[*A participant from Harlem Freedom Schools asked about plans to focus on diversity in schools.*]

The President. Under our system of government, basically, public education from kindergarten through 12th grade is the province of the State government and the local school districts. The Federal Government provides extra help, by and large, to help poor kids through nutritional programs or extra educational resources. So the New York City School Board would have to decide to change that.

It's an issue, by the way, that you might want to see what you could do to get it made an issue in the coming mayor's race. There's going to be a mayor's race in New York. That's what politics is for, to debate these things. That's what elections are for, to discuss these.

But I want to try to support what you're saying in this way: When cultures lived separately from one another, you didn't have to worry about any of this being done at school because it was always communicated at home, and besides, everybody was just like everybody else. Now that we're crashing in on each other— Los Angeles County, for example, has 150 different racial and ethnic groups living in one county—this has become a very important thing. And I was very moved by what you said about the kids that wouldn't get on the bus with other kids, that wouldn't go in the classroom with other kids. You know, it seems when you think about it, it's perfectly logical that people coming to another country would be terribly frightened by people very different from them, and maybe the only image they had of them was something they saw in some cheap thrills gangster movie or one of those. So I think it's important.

But I think the only thing that we can do at the national level besides talk about it—the President can talk about it—is to try to make sure that we run the national service program all year round like you said, not just in the summertime, all year round to make sure that we have volunteers available for programs like this and that if a program, for example, in your community is set up to do this year round, that we would give that a priority through national service so we could direct our people and say, you can earn your college grade, you can do it if you'll become a part of this program. We can support that, and we will.

So you can say, look, to New York, you won't have to pay for all of it; the national service people will get you the volunteers if you will let the program go forward. And that's what I think we should do.

[*A participant asked about the long-range future of the national service program.*]

The President. Ten years from now I believe this will be a major fixture of our national life. I don't believe it will be 10,000 kids a year or 50,000 or 100,000; I think that the program will become so popular and will so capture the imagination of the country that, in effect, anybody who wants to be a part of it, to help defray their college costs or just because they want to serve, will be able to do it. I think it will become a very, very big part of American life.

Just look at what we've seen already, and look at what your experience is. This country simply has—first of all, we've got all these young people full of energy and passion and belief and without any cynicism and all this talent out there dying to serve, at a point in your life when you don't have to support a lot of other people so you can work for a fairly modest wage, particularly if you get some educational credit out of it. And secondly, we've just got an unbelievable number of problems out there that have to be solved in a personal, highly labor-intensive way that neither the Government nor the private sector could otherwise afford. So I believe 10 years from now, you will look back 10 years from now and say, I was a pioneer in something that changed America for the better.

[*A participant asked about the role of the national service program in educational reform and innovation.*]

The President. First, let me tell you what I think the innovation should be in general. We have a bill now that we're trying to pass through the Congress which would write into law the national education goals that the Governors and President Bush's administration agreed on back in 1989. And I care a lot about them, because at that time I was the Democratic Governor representing the Governors to write the goals, so I believe in them.

One of the things that we learned, after years and years in studying schools, is that all the magic of education and the learning occurs not in the White House, not in the Statehouse, but in the schoolhouse and in the school room between the teacher and the students and then among the students and then at home, if the student is lucky. We have to find more individual ways of reaching kids, and we've got to make our education system far less bureaucratic, and we've got to give school by school much more flexibility to principals and teachers and students to design their learning programs and to be flexible and to be creative.

So I believe that the role that the national service program will have in the revolution of American education will be very large if, but only if, we can persuade the schools of our country, in effect, to restructure themselves to give more flexibility and authority to the principals, the teachers, and the students on a school-by-school basis.

[*A participant asked about school system accountability for education.*]

The President. Well, I think community service should help, but I think the school system should be held accountable for it. The answer to your question is, we will start doing that when we start evaluating our schools based on the results they get rather than the input.

For example, let me just give you one simple example. We evaluate teachers for whether they can get hired in most school districts in this country based on whether they've got an education degree from a certified college of education, right? So there are all kinds of Americans who are retired from the military. Right now, we will take, from 1987 to 1998, the United States military will go from having 3.5 million people to 1.5 million people, 2 million folks out there walking around among the best educated, best trained, most highly motivated people in the world, with the best values, that know how to get things done, right? You can have one of these people, a graduate of the United States Military Academy and a massive amount of knowledge in chemistry, and they can't teach in most of the schools of the country. Most States now have some sort of exception, but it's a real problem. Why? Because we evaluate people not on whether they're good teachers but on whether they've got good—the qualifications. We evaluate schools based on how many kids are in the classroom, what the schoolbook certifications are, or what does the building look like. All these things may be important, but we don't have any way of evaluating our teachers, our schools, and our school systems in most States based on the results they get. What do the kids know when they started; what do they know when they finished? What happened to them? What kind of problems did they have, and did they get services—that goes back to

your question—did the school actually serve the problems they had instead of the problems that some kids had a generation ago? And we're still doing it the way we used to do.

So that's what I'm trying—I'm trying to be a part of a movement, at least, that will decentralize authority, let the principals, the teachers, the kids, and the parents, in effect, design more and have more flexibility over their own school year and then measure them by the results they achieve. So that if you don't get results, you stop doing what you're doing and you do something else. But we don't measure—anything funded by tax dollars is normally measured by rules and regulations on the front end, instead of results on the back end. We need less rules and regulations and more results, and we need it in schools.

[*A participant spoke about her work to increase literacy.*]

The President. Greg said you had been a VISTA volunteer for 20 years, is that right? 20 years ago you did it?

Q. Twenty years ago this summer.

The President. Good for you. That's another answer I'll give you. Ten years from now I hope you'll be wanting to do this just like she did after 20 years. That's great.

[*A participant spoke about her work to improve housing and encourage safe neighborhoods.*]

The President. I just would make one point about that. When we had a commission to study the needs of the Lower Mississippi River area, starting in southern Illinois and going all the way to New Orleans—that is still the poorest part of America. And one of the things that you forget—we always think of public safety as an urban issue, but one of the things that's easy to forget is it becomes a big rural issue. And at periodic times in this country you will see crime waves will sweep across rural America. And one of the reasons is that a lot of people are just out there, and nobody can even find them.

The story she told you about the county in our State where people are literally unidentified, where they don't have an address, where they called for help—you know, it would take you 5 minutes to explain where they were—this is a serious problem in all of rural America. And I appreciate the work you did on it.

[*A participant asked if the President could give*

concrete examples of welfare reform.]

The President. Yes, I can. That's a good question. I will give you three concrete examples, but let's talk about what's wrong with the system now, very briefly. Again, it goes back to the question the young man from Harlem asked me about education, where a lot of the schools are being run for a time that no longer exists instead of a time that does exist. The original welfare system was set up to deal with an American society that existed about 50 years ago, where nearly everybody who wanted to work could find some kind of job at some low level, but they could find some kind of job. There were very few women in the work force, if they were in the home and they had children. And the typical welfare recipient in the beginning was, let's say, a West Virginia miner's widow, 60 years ago. The husband gets killed in the mines. They live up in the hills and hollows of West Virginia. The woman has a fourth-grade education. She's got three or four kids, no way to go to work, no job to find, and the welfare supports the kids.

Then there was another typical welfare recipient that represents about half the people on welfare today, for whom welfare should exist, the people who hit on hard times. Suddenly a spouse dies, and there's two little children in the home, and you can't work. Or you lose a job, and you can't get another one, and you run out of unemployment benefits. In other words, about half the people on welfare only stay for 4, 5, 6 months, and then they get off. Those are the people we would all want a welfare system for, because they fall through the unemployment system cracks or they need support or they have little children. They can't be working because they have a whole slew of them or whatever.

Increasingly, however, there are people on welfare whose parents were on welfare, whose grandparents were on welfare, who never have worked, and who basically can stay on forever as long as they have children under a certain age, because welfare's proper name is Aid to Families with Dependent Children, AFDC, that's what it means.

So, why do people stay on welfare? To know how to fix it, you have to know why they stay. The benefits aren't all that great in most States. In fact, over the last 20 years, benefits have not kept up with inflation. Why do people stay?

They stay for one reason: because they, by and large, have very little education, may not know how to get into the system; if they did get a job, their job would pay low wages and they would lose two things they have on welfare, medical coverage for their kids under the Medicaid program and they would then have to pay for child care that they themselves are providing.

Now, I see the Governor paying close attention. Maryland's done a lot of work on this whole issue in this State. He can maybe give a better answer than I can. But if you look at the system—and by the way, I have spent hours and hours in my life talking to people who are on welfare, and nearly all of them want to get off quick as they can. So what would you do to fix it?

First thing you've got to do is make sure work pays. Eighteen percent of the American work force, almost one in five, work for a wage that will not lift a family of four out of poverty. In the last economic program that we passed just before the Congress went on recess, one of the most important parts of it was to increase something called the earned-income tax credit, which is a refund you can get from the Government on your tax system to say to the working people of this country, if you work 40 hours a week and you have a child in your house, you will be lifted above poverty by the tax system. We will not tax you into poverty. If you're willing to work hard, play by the rules, and raise your kids, we'll lift you out of poverty. That's the first thing. That's one specific thing, very important to do.

The second thing you have to do is to provide medical coverage for all Americans without regard to whether they're working or not. Seventy percent of all the people in this country who don't have health insurance are working for a living. So if you're on welfare, let me just give you an example. This is something that actually happens now. I helped work on a welfare reform program which Congress passed and President Reagan signed in late 1988 right before he left office. And to try to deal with this medical coverage program, we said, if you get a job that doesn't have health insurance we will provide you health insurance for 6 or 9 months, to get you off welfare. That's great, but guess what happens? You've got two people working side by side, one of them that used to be on welfare has got health insurance for her kids for 9 months, working next to somebody who has never been on welfare that doesn't have any health insurance. So the second thing you have to do if you want to end welfare as we know it is to provide a system, like every other advanced country has, that has affordable health care for all Americans. If you don't do it, you're going to continue to have these problems.

The third thing you have to do is to make sure that all the States that run the welfare programs have the resources they need and the incentives they need to actually train people for jobs that it will exist.

And then there's one final thing, there's a fourth thing you have to do. If you want to end the welfare system as you know it, you have to say, if you have health care for your kids and yourself, and you have the education and training, after a certain amount of time, if you don't go to work there will be some sort of community service job provided for you by the local government, and that's what you have to do if you want to get an income. In other words, there has to be an end of it. Finally, you have to move people to independence and away from dependence.

If we did those four things, we could end the welfare system as we know it, and we could leave welfare for the people that really need it. And all of you would feel good about the program instead of bad about it.

[*A participant from Habitat for Humanity asked about easing restrictions in Federal housing programs in favor of homeownership.*]

The President. Yes, I do support that. I don't know if I can prevail, but I do support that. There's a reason why there's been a longstanding debate in the Congress about this. And a lot of the Members of Congress who really believe in providing affordable housing to people are afraid if you move away from—if you have a really strong bias in favor of homeownership, that the good things that would be done by Habitat for Humanity, for example, would be offset by people being, in effect, cut loose in these public housing units that then they won't have the resources to maintain. So we have to do it in a delicate way, but I think you're absolutely right. And I think it has to be done.

By the way, for those of you who don't know about—we talked about it a couple of times, but Habitat for Humanity is arguably the most successful continuous community service project in the history of the United States, started by two wonderful people, Millard and Linda Fuller, who I was lucky enough to meet in another life before I ever thought about doing this job. It is organized on a community service basis, community by community. They never take any Government money. And it has revolutionized the lives of—how many houses has Habitat built now?

Q. ——are we building now?

The President. No, I mean where are they now in the cumulative total? Does anybody know? How many?

Q. Twenty-one thousand around the world.

The President. Yes, that's how many they're building right now. They've built more, though. But anyway, it's an amazing thing. And I think— I wish I knew. I did know a couple of months ago, but I've forgotten.

You're absolutely right. What we need to do— that's one way we can have a partnership with Habitat, if we use the HOME program to favor more homeownership. And I think we can do it in a way that will satisfy the legitimate concern of Members of Congress that we not be in a position of handing over big housing units to people who don't have the capacity, the resources to maintain them. That's the real problem there.

[*A participant asked if former participants in the national service program could advise in the development of new projects.*]

The President. I'll let Mr. Segal answer that. Eli.

Mr. Segal. We've learned so much in the course of the last 8 weeks, I think. Had we not thought of it, we would have said yes to you right now. It's a great idea, and we certainly need to make certain we're enjoying all the benefit of all the wisdom you've learned, and it certainly should be part of the program going forward.

The President. Let me make a suggestion. If you have a specific idea about how we can do that and how we should do that, if you would write it up and send it to Mr. Segal, I'd really appreciate it. I hadn't thought of it before, and it is self-evidently the right thing to do. So why don't you think about it a little bit and write him a proposal on it.

[*At this point, a participant presented the President with a T-shirt.*]

The President. I'll get it. He'll bring it to

me. Go ahead. Thanks, Chris. Nice color.

[*A participant asked if national service would be mandatory and part of the school curriculum.*]

The President. A different question—those are two different questions. I don't believe that participation in this program, the national service program, which we are proposing is, by definition, voluntary, but you get something for it. You get credit toward college.

I believe that it is a very good thing for States or local school districts to mandate community service for kids at certain levels in the public schools. A few years ago I had the opportunity to serve on a commission on middle schools, and we recommended two things that didn't get done but I thought should be. One is that there ought to be a set of basic civic values that are taught in the schools, and the second was that community service ought to be a part of the curriculum. So yes, I think that every State should include community service as a part of the curriculum at some appropriate point, where students, young people, as a part of their education, get the experience of doing what you've done, the thrill of it and learn from it and see—don't you find that you see the world in a different way once you do this? I mean, you know what the problems are, but you also have a sense that you can solve them and make a difference. Yes, that's what I think should be done.

Yes, over in the corner.

[*A participant asked what could be done about the high number of young people in jail.*]

The President. Yes, there are a huge number of young people in jail. We have now the unfortunate distinction of having the highest percentage of our people in prison of any country in the world. Did you know that? America has the highest percentage of its population behind bars of any country in the world, and most of them are young. Most of them are under 25 years of age.

I think, in a way, all of you are doing something about it. I think that if you go to the prisons and talk to these people and get the story of their lives and figure out how they got there. And most of them never met anybody like you on a consistent basis, that is, had a chance to be part of what you are doing. And so, I think there are a lot of things we can do about it, but in the end, what we have to

do about it is to continue to touch more of them at the earliest possible point in their lives so they don't wind up doing what they're doing later, and keep something in their mind about tomorrow. Let them always believe there is a tomorrow, that there is a future, that there is something they can do that makes them feel good, that makes them important, that makes their lives meaningful, that doesn't require them to do what they do to get in prison.

I also think that a lot of kids who wind up getting in trouble because they're in gangs do it because—it goes back to what I said about studying—everybody wants to be in a gang. You just hope it's a good gang and not a bad gang, right? You're in a gang. That's what all these T-shirts mean. Right? See what I mean?

So I think the whole point of what you do is to try to gather them up before it happens. Also, there's a whole lot of law enforcement strategies that work and antidrug strategies, and we could talk about that. But from your point of view, giving people something to say yes to as well as something to say no to and to be part of a group that matters, I think that would do more over the long run. If you gave every kid in America that chance, every one of them that chance, you would see the prison population go down dramatically over 10 or 15 years, not overnight but over a 10- or 15-year period.

[*A participant asked about initiatives to help African-American and Latino males.*]

The President. What I think I can do—again, I will say—I gave this answer to another question, but one of the things that I like about this national service concept is that we can go out and recruit African-American and Latino males, and then we can give priority to projects, community-by-community, that we know have a good chance of succeeding and put people in there and help to pay for it. That's what we can do. And that will be a major, major thing. That's what you did, I mean, without maybe thinking about it in that way. But that's what we can do.

But what you've also got to do is to make sure that those things which are in the control of the State or those things which are in the control of the local government or those things which the private sector ought to be doing in your community, that they're doing that, too. For example, I still think you could rescue a bunch of kids that are in trouble if you have the right kind of court programs, if you have alternatives to incarceration for first offenders.

We've got another program that is separate from this now. I'm really proud of it. I signed a bill in June, another one of my passions, where we're using empty military bases and National Guard volunteers to work with high school dropouts to give them a chance to do what they once might have done in the military but can't now because we've phased the military down so much, to recover their future and get a GED.

So we're going to continue to do programs like that that are highly targeted toward people that otherwise might get in trouble. But I will say what we want to do at the national level is to provide a vehicle for people like you to serve. But you still got to get people at the local level to say, "Hey, this is a problem in our community; will you give us the folks to do it?" And then we can say yes.

[*At this point, the facilitator introduced a participant from south central Los Angeles.*]

Q. How are you doing?

The President. I'm doing better since I spent the last couple of hours with you.

[*The participant discussed his experience working with children in the neighborhood he grew up in.*]

The President. If I might just respond to you. You know, I've spend a lot of time in your community over the last—and I started going there before I ran for President and before the riots. I first went to south central L.A., over 3 years ago now, just to sit and talk with people. My wife and I went and talked with a bunch of sixth graders, and we met with the people from Uno and SCOC, the community organizations out there, and others. And one of the things I think Americans who don't live in these really troubled communities often forget is that most people who live in places like that do not break the law, get up and go to work every day, want their children to do well, are doing the best they can. And a lot of the kids who wind up in gangs do it almost out of self-defense because they don't think they have any alternatives.

I was out there the other day—you probably don't remember this, but I visited that sporting goods store in south central L.A. run by the two guys who used to be in gangs. We played basketball in the backyard there—the parking lot of the sporting goods store. But I think that is so important.

Now again, we have a job to do. We, the government and the private sector, have got to put more opportunity into places like that.

One of the things that the Congress did in this economic program I really hope will work—at least we've got a chance to see now—is to pass a bill which will enable us to identify six really troubled, big, urban areas and say to people in the private sector, "Look, we'll give you a whole lot of extra incentives if you'll put you money there, create jobs there, and put people to work." I mean, it is nuts if you go into some of these areas and you think about all these people just walking around without jobs. That's an enormous resource going to waste. If those people were working, they'd have money to buy things from other people. They would create jobs. We've allowed this economy to shrink.

But over and above that, we have to put in a lot of volunteers, people like you who can do that. I mean, I'm convinced that the economy is one thing we have to address, but all these social problems have to be addressed one-on-one.

And let me just close with this sentence. I was talking to somebody I've known since I was 6 years old the other day, and we were talking about all the kids in trouble. And she said, "You know, a guy asked me the other day what are we going to do about all these kids? How are we going to save all these kids?" And she said, "We've got to save them the same way we lost them, one at a time." And so you can have an enormous impact on the future of your community. And it's up to me to try to make sure that we can keep programs like this going so that you and people like you will have a chance to do that.

It's also important that you be an advocate for all those people and not let us forget about them. I mean, it's crazy just to pay attention to a city when all the buildings burn down. Then it's often too late. We need to pay attention to them when the kids are growing up and they're trying to do the right thing. And I hope that in south central L.A. and in a lot of the other places that are represented here today, we're going to be able to do that. Not that we'll solve the problems overnight, but if everybody knows we're trying, everybody knows we're working together, everybody knows we're going in the right direction, that is the feeling

I think people want. That's what gets people going.

What breaks people is not the problems they face; what breaks people is that they think tomorrow is not going to be any better than today. And what this national service is about is making people believe that it will be different. And you have proved that. Thank you.

Q. And finally, Mr. President, nowhere have we seen service so urgently needed——

Q. Excuse me, Mr. President. I've got a really important question to ask and a really important observation. I'm from Ohio Wesleyan University, and I'm under the direction of John Powers. And I'd like to take time to ask you to recognize the program directors and the community leaders who are here and who have come so far to—[*applause*]——

The President. Would they stand up? Will you have them stand up?

Q. ——to make sure that your vision has gone through.

The President. Stand up. Stand up. Good for you. Good for you. Thank you.

[*A participant asked how the national service program would address rural problems.*]

The President. It is true that this summer, because we were basically doing a test program this summer and we wanted to plug into programs that were established and that had a real chance of working—the program you mentioned in Philadelphia, the City Year Program that Greg's involved with—that we knew were working. So we did that, and we did it deliberately, and I still think it was the right thing to do.

On the other hand, there were some nonurban projects, the Red Lake project, the one in south Texas that was done. And as I said earlier, I come from a rural background, a State full of small towns and rural areas, and I know that all the problems that are in the big cities are also there. So we are going to appoint this board to run the national service program that is fully representative of the rest of the country, and one of their missions will be to allocate the resources in a way that are fair to the whole country so that we don't forget about the small towns and the rural areas. They're not much different, except in size, in the scope of the problems that they face today. And I thank you for saying that. Give them a hand. [*Applause*]

[*At this point, the facilitator introduced participants who discussed their experiences in restoration of disaster areas.*]

The President. First, let me just say a simple thank you to all of you.

I was in the Midwest during the floods on four occasions, and I saw a lot of young people there working hard and really giving it all they had. But one of the things I think being a Governor is a good preparation for President is dealing with natural disasters, because when you see them occur—first of all, it's just breathtaking to see a flood take away a town or a tornado or a hurricane blow away a place. But the other thing, you know, is just what you got through saying, that everybody pours out their heart when it's happening, and they come and help. But a year from now there are still people who don't have their lives together. And the stresses on the families and the communities are staggering.

One interesting thing we have done is to—as soon as I got in office, I named Henry Cisneros as the administration's coordinator for dealing with the long-term relief of Hurricane Andrew. Then I named Mike Espy, the Agriculture Secretary, as the administration's coordinator for dealing with the long-term relief of the flood in the Midwest. These are the kinds of things that we have to do. We've got to stay with it for the long run. And I hope that the national service project can provide volunteers next year in the Midwest if they are needed and next year in south Florida if they are needed, so that we don't forget about those people. It takes a long time to recover from a disaster of the magnitude of Andrew or a 500-year flood, which is what we just had in the Midwest. And I really thank you for it.

Thank you.

NOTE: The President spoke at 11 a.m. in the Adele H. Stamp Student Union at the University of Maryland.

Nomination for Director of the Indian Health Service
August 31, 1993

The President today announced his intention to nominate Dr. Michael Trujillo, a physician who has spent his career working to better health care delivery to Native Americans across the country, as Director of the Indian Health Service within the Department of Health and Human Services.

"Many Americans are without adequate health care, but access to care for our country's Native Americans has been particularly poor," the President said. "Dr. Trujillo has a well-earned reputation for working to change that situation, and I am confident he will work hard to improve the delivery of health care to Native Americans in our cities and reservations."

NOTE: A biography of the nominee was made available by the Office of the Press Secretary.

Nomination for Posts at the Departments of Agriculture, Defense, Labor, and Veterans Affairs and the Agency for International Development
August 31, 1993

The President today announced his intention to nominate the following individuals to posts in his administration:

Department of Agriculture

Michael Dunn, Administrator of the Farmers Home Administration

Department of Defense

H. Allen Holmes, Assistant Secretary for Special Operations and Low-Intensity Conflict

Department of Labor

J. Davitt McAteer, Assistant Secretary for Mine Safety and Health

Preston Taylor, Jr., Assistant Secretary for Veterans Employment and Training

Department of Veterans Affairs

Kathy Jurado, Assistant Secretary for Public and Intergovernmental Affairs

U.S. International Development Cooperation Agency

Mark Schneider, Assistant Administrator for Latin America and the Caribbean, Agency for International Development

The President applauded his new nominees. "These individuals, experienced in each of their fields, are important additions to our administration," the President said.

"Michael Dunn's work at the National Farmers Union will serve him well as he takes the helm on issues important to rural Americans. H. Allen Holmes brings an extensive knowledge of foreign affairs and previous State Department experience to his new role. Mr. McAteer's important work in mine safety will assist him as he works to ensure the safety of our country's mine workers.

"I am confident General Taylor will be an effective advocate for veterans in the Labor Department as will Kathy Jurado in the Department of Veterans Affairs. Mark Schneider's experience in pan-American issues will also bode him well as he takes his post at AID," the President said.

NOTE: Biographies of the nominees were made available by the Office of the Press Secretary.

Announcement of Senior Executive Service Appointments
August 31, 1993

The President today announced his appointment of 38 men and women to Senior Executive Service posts in his administration.

"I am proud today to name these hard-working men and women to posts in my administration," the President said.

Asian Development Bank

N. Cinnamon Dornsife, Alternate Executive Director

Department of Commerce

Gary Bachula, Deputy Under Secretary for Technology Administration

Keith Calhoun-Senghor, Director of the Office of Space Commerce

Michele C. Farquhar, Director of the Office of Policy Coordination and Management, National Telecommunications and Information Administration

Katherine W. Kimball, Deputy Assistant Secretary for the National Oceanic and Atmospheric Administration

Paul L. Rosenberg, Deputy Assistant Secretary for Planning for the International Trade Administration

Jonathan M. Silver, Assistant Deputy Secretary

Department of Defense

Cheryl P. Bowen, Executive Director of the National Committee for Employer Support of the Guard and Reserve

Joan Kelly Horn, Chair of the Reinvestment Assistance Task Force

Josephine S. Huang, Assistant Deputy Under Secretary for Environmental Security

Clark A. Murdock, Deputy Assistant Secretary for Policy and Plans

David Ochmanek, Deputy Assistant Secretary for Resources and Plans

Department of Education

Eugene E. Garcia, Director of the Office of Bilingual Education and Minority Languages Affairs

Thomas Hehir, Director for Special Education Programs

Jana Sawyer Prewitt, Special Assistant to the Director for Communications, Office of Public Affairs

European Bank for Reconstruction and Development

Lee Jackson, Alternate Executive Director

General Services Administration

Cynthia A. Metzler, Associate Administrator

Department of Health and Human Services

Faye Baggiano, Associate Administrator for Communications, Health Care Financing Administration

Lavinia Limon, Director of the Office of Refugee Resettlement, Administration for Children and Families

Donald Sykes, Director of the Office of Community Services, Administration for Children and Families

Sally R. Richardson, Director of the Medicaid Bureau, Health Care Financing Administration

Michael S. Wald, Deputy General Counsel

Robert Williams, Director of the Administration for Developmental Disabilities, Administration for Children and Families

Department of the Interior

Robert P. Davison, Deputy Assistant Secretary for Fish and Wildlife and Parks

Cynthia L. Quarterman, Deputy Director of the Minerals Management Service

Michael J. Anderson, Associate Solicitor for Indian Affairs

Peace Corps

Patricia Wilkerson Garamendi, Administrative Director of Volunteer Recruitment

Small Business Administration

Richard Hernandez, Counselor to the Administrator

John T. Spotila, General Counsel

Department of State

Bennett Freeman, Deputy Assistant Secretary for Public Affairs

Cathy Elizabeth Dalpino, Deputy Assistant Secretary of the Bureau of Human Rights and Humanitarian Affairs

Mark R. Steinberg, Counselor on International Law, Office of the Legal Adviser

Department of the Treasury

Jose R. Padilla, Associate Customs Commissioner for Congressional and Public Affairs, U.S. Customs Service

Floyd L. Williams III, Senior Tax Adviser for Public and Legislative Affairs

Thrift Depositor Protection Oversight Board

Dietra L. Ford, Executive Director

U.S. International Development Cooperation Agency

Michael Mahdesian, Senior Advisor for the

Bureau of Food and Humanitarian Assistance, Agency for International Development

Alejandro J. Palacios, Deputy Assistant Administrator for the Bureau of Legislative Affairs, Agency for International Development

U.S. Information Agency

Robert L. Schiffer, Director of the Office of Special Projects

NOTE: Biographies of the appointees were made available by the Office of the Press Secretary.

Remarks on the Swearing-In of Federal Bureau of Investigation Director Louis Freeh
September 1, 1993

Thank you very much, General Reno, for that fine introduction and for your exemplary work. I want to thank, as the Attorney General did, Floyd Clarke for his distinguished work over a lifetime for the FBI and his work as the Acting Director. Also, I think bound to thank Judge Freeh's family, his wife, his children, his parents, who are here, for their willingness to support him and for the work they did to make him what he is today.

Finally, let me say by way of introduction, I am profoundly honored to be here in the presence today of the person Judge Freeh picked to swear him in, Judge Frank Johnson. To those of us who grew up in the South, Frank Johnson was a symbol of respect for law, the determination to live by it, and the belief that all of us who live in this country, without regard to the color of our skin, are entitled to a fair shot at life's brass ring. And I thank you for being here today, Judge.

I am also honored to be here today among the thousands of brave men and women who make up our FBI, people who continue to be our elite force in the fight against crime. You should know that I have special respect for FBI agents. When I was Governor of my State, a former agent served as my chief of staff, and other former agents served in my administration.

Today we come to celebrate the elevation of a genuine law enforcement legend, Judge Louis

Freeh, to take the reins of this great Agency. It is a new day for the FBI. Judge Freeh has agreed to take on a difficult task, but no job is more important. And I want to thank the leaders of the Congress on a bipartisan basis, beginning with Senators Biden and Hatch and Mitchell and Dole, for their historic and rapid move to confirm Judge Freeh virtually as soon as I nominated him.

The FBI's mandate is broad. Its reach is sweeping. Its 24,000 employees track down violators of civil rights, people who defraud the health care system, those who run drugs ultimately into the veins of our children. The FBI scientists and technicians perform feats of investigative wizardry that can find wrong-doers through a fragment of a fingerprint or a shard of a bomb. Its agents show commonly that bravery is uncommon everywhere but the FBI, the Armed Forces, and a few other places in our country.

There are many heroes that do their work in the ordinary course of business: people like Special Agent Daniel Miller of Minneapolis, who subdued an armed bank robber by hand to ensure that no one else got hurt; Special Agent Neil Moran of New York, who was severely injured when he used his car to block a suspect's getaway vehicle rather than risk wounding his colleagues with gunfire; people like the 45 others who received Agency medals over the past

3 years. All of you have served well, and America is justly proud of you.

Today's FBI operates in a new and challenging world, without that part of the Agency's mission that was driven by the cold war but with new and even more immediate threats. Terrorism once seemed far from our shores, an atrocity visited on people in other lands. Now, after the attack on the World Trade Center, we know that we, too, are vulnerable. Violent crime has been frightful but limited. But now armed drug gangs stalk the streets of our cities, equipped like mercenary armies, randomly cutting down innocent bystanders in a primitive struggle for territory.

The FBI has already begun to meet these challenges head on. Through the safe streets program, the Agency has begun working with State and local police forces to combat drug gangs and to reclaim our neighborhoods. But we must do more, and we will. Today, I was given a pin which I am wearing that commemorates the FBI's drug prevention program. In churches, in schools and Scout troops all across this country, agents work with young people to stop drug use before it starts.

The FBI has always worked at the cutting edge of law enforcement technology. Today, the scientists and technicians are exploring new frontiers, pioneering the use of DNA analysis to ferret out the guilty and to protect the innocent. And in the interest of justice and effectiveness, the Agency has begun to open its doors to full equality for minorities and for women. We must do more, and we will.

Now, amid this swirl of change, a new era at the FBI is about to begin. The FBI has passed through some troubled times, but I believe those times are over. The men and women who work day and night to protect the public never let us down. And now, a vigorous new Director is going to lead the FBI into the next century so that the men and women who work for the FBI will be led and not let down.

In a few moments, Judge Freeh will take the oath of office. He is, as has been widely chronicled and now is as widely known by his fellow Americans, a brilliant investigator, a tough prosecutor, a born leader. He has the unique combination of experience, courage, and prudent judgment that I believe the directorship of the FBI demands. A career as the scourge of drugrunners and terrorists, tempered by his service as a Federal judge, in my judgment makes him the ideal Director of the FBI. He does have, as the Attorney General said, both humanity and humility to go with experience and brilliance and toughness and judgment. Even those who serve with him respect him and also notice all these qualities. I must say, I have been overwhelmed by the outpouring of support for Judge Freeh, and I have to tell you one example which may surprise even the biggest supporters of the judge. One fellow wrote in and told us that he'd had a lot of experience with the criminal justice system. I'd like to paraphrase the letter we received—the judge received. He said, "Earlier this year you sentenced me to 20 years in prison. But I want you to know that of the five judges who have sentenced me to prison, you have been by far the fairest"—[*laughter*]—"and I endorse your nomination to be the Director of the FBI." With all the problems we've got in this country, I hope he'll be getting a lot more of those letters in the next few years.

I believe that under the leadership of this dynamic, young Director, the FBI will capture the imagination of the American people once again and will enlist once again the millions of ordinary Americans in the work of keeping our streets safe and fighting our crimes for us in partnership with the FBI and with State and local law enforcement officials. I want the men and women of the FBI to look back on the 1990's as a decade in which the FBI became well-known and well-loved for its successes in cracking down on terrorists and drug lords, just as much as the G-men of the thirties were successful in cracking down on racketeers and mobsters.

And to Judge Freeh I say, keep showing the vision and integrity that brought you here, that earned you the esteem of all your colleagues, your countrymen and -women, and even those you sent to jail. To the men and women of the FBI I say, you are the finest we have. Just keep on doing your best, and we will stand behind you. And to the American people I say, we know that our people value law and order and safety. We are working to pass a crime bill that will put more police officers on the street. We are working to get guns out of the hands of criminals. We are working to expand the toughness of our law enforcement. Our frontline crime fighters, Attorney General Reno, Drug Policy Coordinator Lee Brown, and now the FBI Director, Louis Freeh, are putting decades of grassroots experience to work for you.

You, the American people, have a right to freedom from fear. Your families have a right to security and to safety. We won't rest until you have those rights. We ask only for your support and your cooperation as this fine Director launches what I believe will be a legendary

career in the legendary Federal Bureau of Investigation.

Thank you very much.

NOTE: The President spoke at 10:16 a.m. at FBI headquarters. Following the President's remarks, Judge Frank Johnson administered the oath of office, and Director Freeh made remarks.

Nomination for an Assistant Secretary of Energy
September 1, 1993

The President today announced his intention to nominate Wyoming energy commissioner Dr. Bil Tucker as Assistant Secretary for Fossil Energy at the Department of Energy.

"Through his years of work in the energy field in both the public and private sectors, Bil Tucker has demonstrated he has the technical

understanding and commitment to hard work that will make him an asset at the Department of Energy," the President said. "I am pleased he has agreed to join our team."

NOTE: A biography of the nominee was made available by the Office of the Press Secretary.

Remarks Prior to Discussions With Prime Minister Viktor Chernomyrdin of Russia and an Exchange With Reporters
September 2, 1993

The President. I would like to make just a brief comment, if I might, and then I'll take a couple of questions.

I want to welcome Prime Minister Chernomyrdin here to the United States. We clearly recognize that his support for President Yeltsin's reform program has been essential to its success and will continue to be essential to its success. And we're very grateful that he's here.

I also want to express my appreciation to the Prime Minister and to Vice President Gore for successfully concluding the first round of talks and agreements under the Commission on Economic and Technological Cooperation that grew out of my meeting with President Yeltsin in Vancouver. They have signed just now, as all of you know, some very exciting agreements which will permit us to cooperate with Russia in space. Russia has agreed to observe the principles of the Missile Technology Control Regime, which is something the United States very much appreciates. We are going to work to-

gether on matters of energy and environmental protection, which I think will be very helpful to Russia's long-term development and also help with American business. And in general, I think this is the beginning of a lot more opportunities for mutual trade and investment between our two countries.

So I'm personally very happy about this. And because of the efforts of the Prime Minister and the Vice President, this first step has exceeded my expectations considerably, and I'm very, very appreciative.

Health Care Reform

Q. Sir, on health care, are short-term price controls now dead?

The President. Well, they never were alive. I never embraced them. They have been discussed. What I think you have to acknowledge is that the pharmaceutical companies and the industry as a whole and other segments of the health care providers have voluntarily offered, during the course of this debate, to keep their prices within inflation for a year or two as we get up and get going the health care reform package. And I think they should be given the opportunity to adhere to the commitment that they've made.

And so, my own view is—I've never been particularly hot on price controls. I believe in budgets, and I believe we have to limit the amount of growth and the revenues we're spending on health care, both public and private. So I want to point out that, as all of you know, in the last budget, you've got a decline in defense, flat domestic spending. Medicare and Medicaid is going up. It's someplace between 11 and 15 percent in the first year, down to 9 to 11 percent in the 5th year of the budget, and still going up way too much. So we're going to bring it down. But I don't think we have to have a bureaucratic system of price controls to do it.

Q. Sir, what about the senior citizens groups that are afraid that Medicare is going to be squeezed under the plan that will be announced?

The President. Under our plan, as you know because we've talked about it for a long time, we want to phase in a more comprehensive plan of long-term care for the elderly as well as access to medicine for people on Medicare who aren't quite poor enough to be on Medicaid and can't afford their drug bills. We're having a lot of extra costs in our health care system because senior citizens can't get the drugs that they need. So senior citizens will come out way ahead.

It is not logical, with inflation at 3 percent and the population growth of Medicare and Medicaid between 1 and 1½ percent, to have those programs going up between 12 and 16 percent a year. That's not right and it's not necessary, and we can do much, much better. And from those savings in the rate of increase—we're not talking about cutting the programs, we're talking about slowing the rate of increase—we can fund the drug and long-term care programs, which is what I propose to do.

Bosnia

Q. With the collapse of the Bosnian peace talks, are you going to repropose lifting the arms embargo on the Bosnian Muslims and the air strikes?

The President. Let me answer the question in two parts, if I might. First of all, they are stalled. I don't believe they are collapsed. The United States will do everything we can in the next few days to get the parties to resume the talks in good faith.

Secondly, if while the talks are in abeyance there is abuse by those who would seek to interfere with the humanitarian aid, attack the protected areas, and resume the sustained shelling of Sarajevo, for example, then first I would remind you that the NATO military option is very much alive. And secondly, I would say, as you know, I have always favored lifting the arms embargo. I think the policy of the United Nations as it applies to that government is wrong. But I am in the minority; I don't know that I can prevail. But our allies have said repeatedly that they don't want to totally eliminate the arms embargo if the present state of play is sufficiently abused by other parties. So yes, it's still on the table, but I think that the sequence should be let's try to get the peace talks started again. Let's remember that there is a NATO option that is very much alive if there is an interruption of the present state of play that is sufficiently severe.

[At this point, a question was asked and answered in Russian.]

Russia-U.S. Relations

Q. Mr. President, a Russian journalist.

The President. A Russian journalist?

Q. Yes. When can be expected the lifting of these old restrictions and barriers to the trade and cooperation between Russia and the United States back from the cold war period?

The President. When the Congress comes back into town next Tuesday, we have a list of approximately 60 pieces of legislation that we would like to see repealed. And we believe there will be broad bipartisan support from both Republicans and Democrats in the Congress for moving this legislation through. So I think you will see quick legislative action on a whole broad range of issues to recognize the fact that Russia is a democracy, is working with us, and that we are moving forward together. And I look forward to pushing that package very aggressively.

Vietnam

Q. You mentioned the Bosnia arms embargo. Within the next couple of weeks people expect you to lift the embargo against Vietnam. Have you made a decision, sir, and have you discussed with the Prime Minister—what have you discussed about the possibility of American POW's in the Soviet Union?

The President. We're going to go visit. We haven't discussed anything about anything yet. We're just about to start our meeting. And I've reached no further decisions about Vietnam.

Middle East Peace Talks

Q. On the Middle East, you will be discussing, I'm sure, that with Russia, that played a major role. What is the latest development that you know of? Are you very optimistic on the Middle East?

The President. I'm still hopeful. The parties, I think, have been quite candid with the public and the press about some continuing difficulties. But they're really working hard and with great candor, I think, with one another. I'm hopeful. We've been up the hill and down the hill before with the Middle East, but these people are really working at it, and I think their hearts as well as their minds are in it. I think we should keep our fingers crossed. The United States will continue to do what we have done. We're just a sponsor of this process. They will have to make the agreement. And I think there's reason for hope.

Thank you.

NOTE: The President spoke at 12:15 p.m. in the Rose Garden at the White House. A tape was not available for verification of the content of these remarks.

Remarks to Nobel Prize Recipients and an Exchange With Reporters
September 2, 1993

The President. Ladies and gentlemen, I am here this afternoon to honor these winners of the 1992 Nobel Prize. I take great pride in their being recognized in their lifelong efforts to contribute to science and technology and to better the human condition.

Dr. Gary Becker received the Nobel Prize in Economic Science for his expansion of economic analysis to aspects of human behavior that had not before been analyzed with economic principles of our other social science disciplines. For example, in the 1950's, Dr. Becker made a groundbreaking proposal by concluding that racial and ethnic bias could exist only where markets were not fully competitive. Dr. Becker currently is a professor at the University of Chicago. He is to my immediate left.

To my right are Dr. Edmond Fisher and Dr. Edwin Krebs. They are joint winners of the Nobel Prize in Physiology of Medicine. In the 1950's they discovered a cellular regulatory mechanism that controls a variety of metabolic processes. The Nobel selection committee stated that this discovery, and I quote, "concerns almost all processes important to life and opened up one of the most active areas of scientific research." Dr. Fisher and Dr. Krebs are professors at the University of Washington in Seattle.

To my left, Dr. Rudolph Marcus received a Nobel Prize in Chemistry for his mathematical analysis of the cause and effect of electronic changes among molecules. The Nobel committee said that this work helped to explain many complicated chemical reactions, including photosynthesis, that are fundamental to life's processes. Dr. Marcus currently is a professor at the California Institute of Technology. He told me that it took 20 years to actually prove the theories that he developed. And I told him that I was beginning to think that being President was more and more like being a scientist. [*Laughter*]

We are very proud of these Nobel laureates. I salute their successes and their contributions, not only as President but clearly on behalf of all the American people. And I thank them and their spouses for coming to the White House today.

Thank you very much.

Do you, any of you, want to give a speech?

Q. What does it feel like to win a Nobel Prize?

Edwin Krebs. A big surprise.

Q. [*Inaudible*]—better if it could be your economic policies, Mr. President.

The President. You got me, but at least it's more people-centered.

Health Care Reform

Q. Might you ask Dr. Becker whether your health care plans are economically feasible?

The President. He probably wants to read it first.

Gary Becker. I haven't seen them yet. I'm looking forward to it. But clearly we need a great deal of reform in the health care area. So I'm looking forward with anticipation to see what they're like.

Q. Will a sin tax be part of that, sir——

Q. ——my segue.

The President. I'm against sin, aren't you? [*Laughter*]

Let me say one thing, since you asked Dr. Becker the question. There has been an assumption in many of the business articles about the health care plan that it was necessary because too many people don't have health insurance and in any given 2- or 3-year period about one in five or one in four Americans will be without it. But the assumption is that it will be a job drain. That assumes that we will pile costs on top of what is already the most expensive system in the world by a good long ways.

I believe that this will be a job generator if we implement it sensibly and gradually and over time we slow the rate of growth of health care costs. Right now we have to compete with other countries that are spending under 9 percent of their income on health care and covering everyone with outcomes and life expectancy and health that are as good or better than ours, and we're over 14 percent. If we don't change, we'll be up to 19 percent by the end of the decade without covering everybody and with no improvements in the present problem.

So my judgment is that if we do this right, it will be a job creator. So I think you have two things here, we have better health care and more security for American families and a better economic environment over the long run.

I've already talked more than I meant to. Maybe I'll win a Nobel Prize for that theory. [*Laughter*]

Q. Is the assumption about costs on top incorrect, Mr. President?

The President. I don't know what the assumption is.

NOTE: The President spoke at 4:11 p.m. in the Blue Room at the White House. A tape was not available for verification of the content of these remarks.

Remarks at the Opportunity Skyway School-to-Work Program in Georgetown, Delaware
September 3, 1993

Thank you. I want to say how delighted I am to be back in Delaware. You know, when I saw Governor Carper here I was reminded of the time back during the election when Senator Biden and I had a big rally in Wilmington. And I was pleased to say that I was delighted to be in a place where it was not a disadvantage to be the Governor of a small chicken-growing State.

I am delighted to be here today. I can tell all of you are happy, too. How could you not be when you see students like Chrissy and Francis making those presentations? Weren't you proud of them? They were great. Let's give them another hand. [*Applause*]

I also want to thank Governor Carper and my former colleague and longtime friend, now your Congressman, Mike Castle, and Senator Biden—without whom I don't think I could function as President—all of them for being here today. He is not responsible for the mistakes I make, only for the things that go right. [*Laughter*]

I want to thank all your State officials for coming here today and many of the local officials and all of you from the various groups. I want to say a special word of thanks to the two persons who also spoke on the program, Dorothy Shields from the AFL–CIO and my longtime friend Larry Perlman who came from a long way away. He lives in Minnesota, and he thought enough of this project to come here to represent the American business community. This is the sort of partnership that I want us to have in America. I'd like to say, too, how much I appreciate the work that has been done by this education program, and to Diane and to all the others who are here, Carlton Spitzer and others, I thank you for the work you have done.

I came here today not just to showcase these fine students but to make the point that every student in America needs the opportunity to be in a program like this. I got into the race for President because I was very concerned about the direction of my country, a direction that had been underway for 20 years under the leadership of people in both parties in Washington with forces that are beyond the reach of ordinary political solutions. In 1973, real hourly wages for most working people peaked in this country, if you adjust them for inflation. For 20 years, most Americans had been working a longer work week for the same or lower wages, once you adjust them for inflation, while they've paid more for health care, housing, and education.

We have tried a number of things to deal with this issue, to deal with the whole question of how do you keep alive the American dream; how do you offer each generation of young people a better future than their parents had. It is clear to me that we have to revive our economy, all right, and we also have to pull our people back together. And the two things are inseparable. We need to offer our people more opportunity, insist that they assume more responsibility. We need to all be reminded that we are in this together. We have to recreate the American community. That's why when you see here business and labor and government, when you see young people of different racial and ethnic groups, when you see people reaching across their party lines, you really see the future of America—if it's going to be a good future.

I picked the two Cabinet members who are here with me today because I thought they could help us to create that future. The Secretary of Labor, Bob Reich, has been a friend of mine for 25 years and I think has written more thoughtfully than any other person I know about the future of the American work force and what's happening to us in this global economy. The Secretary of Education, Dick Riley, has been my friend for about 15 years now, was my colleague and one of the best Governors I ever served with on the issues of education and economic development. In other words, one of them is at the Labor Department, the other

is at the Education Department, but they both understand that if you want a good economic future, there can be no simple division between work and learning. We must do both.

In the last several months and in the months ahead, you will see a lot of publicity about other initiatives of our administration: the economic plan that reduced the deficit, increased incentives to invest, offered 90 percent of our small businesses a chance to reduce their tax burden but only if they reinvest in their businesses and gave tax relief to 20 percent of the working poor families in the State of Delaware; the reinventing Government program that the Vice President will announce next week that will help us to virtually revolutionize a lot of the things about the Federal Government to eliminate waste and inefficiency and give all of you better value for your tax dollar; the health program that the First Lady has worked on so hard for several months now, which will finally give every American family the security of knowing they won't lose their health care if they lose their jobs or someone in their family is born with a serious medical condition and will give the American business community the assurance that we're not going to bankrupt the country and wreck the economy by continuing to spend more and more and more for the same health care.

I will ask the Congress to approve, with the amendments that we secured, the trade agreement between the United States and Canada and Mexico because I believe it will create more jobs. And we'll have a vigorous debate about that, but I will tell you this: The real problem we've got right now in America in creating more jobs is rooted at least in part in the fact that our exports are not selling abroad because we have too many trade barriers in the world and slow economic growth everywhere. Latin America is the second fastest growing part of the world. They can buy more of our things, and they should.

And finally, Senator Biden and I are going to work on a new crime bill that will put more police officers on the street and take more guns out of the hands of our children.

All of these are critical to restoring opportunity, insisting on more responsibility from our people, and giving America the sense that we are one community again. But none of them will work unless we maintain a steadfast determination to educate and train our people at world-class standards. We are living in a world where what you earn is a function of what you can learn; where the average 18-year-old will change jobs seven times in a lifetime; where there can no longer be a division between what is practical and what is academic. Indeed, one of the young students back there said, "I'm learning a lot more than I used to because this is fun." Now, that sounds funny, and a lot of you clapped when Chrissy talked before, but the truth is there's a lot of very serious academic research which indicates that significant numbers of our people actually learn better in practical circumstances than they do in classroom settings. It's different for different people.

For two centuries our education system has always been adequate to the task and has helped us to keep alive the American dream—an awful lot of people here today who wouldn't be doing what you're doing if you hadn't had the opportunity to get a good education. But on the eve of this new century, when we are struggling so hard to get and keep good jobs; when we are struggling hard to reestablish the premise that people that work harder and are more productive should earn more money year-in and year-out; a world of instant communication, supersonic transportation, worldwide technologies in global markets, and a veritable explosion of knowledge and invention, we have to face the fact that we, while we still have the best system of higher education in the world, are the only advanced country without a system to guarantee that every student that doesn't go on to a 4-year college institution has the opportunity to be in this program or one like it that we're celebrating here today. We don't do that.

So what happens? We see these young people talk and we see these young people demonstrate their skills, and our hearts are filled with joy, and we're proud, and we know they're going to have a decent future. What we don't see here today is that 50 percent of the high school graduates in this country do not go on to college, 75 percent of the high school graduates in this country don't finish college, and nowhere near all of them are in programs like this which should start when they are in high school. That is what this is all about today.

During the 15-year period from 1975 to 1989, the wages of young high school graduates, that is, young people who are under 25 who had only a high school diploma, dropped about 40 percent in real terms. The wages of young high

school dropouts, that is, people who are working full-time, dropped even more. Why? Because of the downward pressure on those wages caused by global competition, caused by mechanization, caused by all the pressures that you all know. But young people who got at least 2 years of post-high school training related to a workplace skill for which there is a demand in this global economy were overwhelmingly more likely to get good jobs with rising incomes.

And when you look at the American economy, when you see the unemployment rate or you see the income statistics, you know that they're grossly oversimplified. If the unemployment rate is 6.8 percent, what it really means is that the unemployment rate among people over 40 with college educations is about 3.5 percent, which is almost zero. You've got almost that many people walking around at any given time. But the unemployment rate among young people who drop out of high school may be 20 percent. And if they happen to live in a place where there's already high unemployment, it may be 40 or 50 percent.

This issue that we're meeting here about today may never acquire a great deal of public attention because we're not fighting about it. The bill that I introduced shortly before the Congress left has Republican as well as Democratic cosponsors. There are labor as well as business people up here. We are not having the old fights, but the old fights have not provided the new solutions that America desperately needs. And that is what we are here today to seek.

Change is going to happen in this country. No President can promise to shield the American people from the changes going on. And anybody that tries to is simply not being candid. The real question is whether change is going to be the friend of these young people and the rest of us or our enemy. And that depends on whether we can adapt to change.

This program today is an example of what America has to do to adapt to change. We can no longer afford to be the only advanced nation in the world without a system for providing this kind of training and education to everybody who doesn't go on and get a 4-year college degree. We can do better. We can have programs like this everywhere. And that's what our legislation is designed to do.

This legislation basically will support learning in the workplace, learning in the schoolroom, and connections between the workplace and the schoolroom. It will involve all kinds of programs that are working. It is not a big Federal top-down program, but we will have some common standards: a certificate that means something when you finish a program, meaningful learning in the workplace and in the schoolroom, a real connection between work and school, and a real chance to get a job. And when combined with the other major piece of education legislation that we have in the Congress, the Goals 2000 program, which seeks to enshrine in the law the national education goals that the Governors adopted along with the previous administration of President Bush back in 1989, that legislation will establish for the first time a national system of skill standards so that you will actually know whether you're learning what you're supposed to learn by national standards and whether they stack up with the global competition. That is what we seek to achieve, not with a new Federal bureaucracy but by building on successes like this.

This bill involves a historic partnership, too, between the Departments of Education and Labor. They will sort of operate like venture capitalists. They will provide seed money to States, set the goals and the standards, give waivers to communities to give them more flexibility as they set up new programs, and require that the graduates attain real skill certificates that verify the quality of their training. But the design and planning of the programs will be left to States and communities and educational institutions who know best how to address the local possibilities. Finally, the school-to-work legislation will enable our Nation for the first time to create the kind of partnership that we so desperately need between schools, businesses, labor, and communities, so that we can connect our people to the real world. That's why the Business Roundtable, the National Association of Manufacturers, the United States Chamber of Commerce, the National Alliance of Business, the AFL–CIO, and leading Republican and Democratic legislators all support this legislation.

If we are going to prosper in the world toward which we are heading, we have to reach out to every one of our young people who want a job and don't have the training to get it. We don't have a person to waste. And believe you me, when we waste them, the rest of us pay. We pay in unemployment. We pay in welfare. We pay in jail costs. We pay in drug costs.

And when we make education come alive, as it has for these young people who showed me their plane, when we enable students to apply English, history, and science to the practical problems of the workplace, we are building a future that all of us will be a part of. We must—I will say it again—we must learn to integrate serious academic study into the workplace, starting in high school and continuing for at least 2 years thereafter, for everyone who needs it. If we do it, if we do it, we are going to do as much as anything else we could do to guarantee most Americans a real shot at a good future. And if we don't, all of our other, all of our other economic initiatives will be consigned to less than full success.

I got into this issue when I was a Governor of a State not unlike Delaware and I saw too many people working their fingers to the bone for less and less and less, too many people who were dying to go to work who could never find a job, too many people who didn't have impressive academic accomplishments but were plenty smart enough to learn anything they needed to know to compete and win in this global economy. I determined then as a Governor that if I ever had a chance to do something about this in this country, I would. And that's what we're here doing today.

I want you to support this legislation just like you support Opportunity Skyway. I want you to support the idea that the public and private sectors all over America can do for all of our young people who need it what this program has done for the young people we've heard from today: provide a smooth transition from school to work. So far, 900 high school students have participated in Opportunity Skyway. Many of them are en route to careers in aircraft maintenance, avionics, and airline piloting. Now they'll find out how much algebra and geography they've learned. And I'll say this, I'm on my way back to Washington now using a flight plan that the students prepared. Three or four hours from now, if I'm wandering out over the Atlantic somewhere—[*laughter*]—I'll know I wasn't very persuasive today.

There are programs like this one all over the country; we're going to build onto them. But we need your help. Next week when the Congress comes back, I hope each one of you will do what you can to encourage the United States Congress, without regard to party, to embrace this new approach to a new economy to give these young people a new future and give America a better future. We can make a real difference, folks, a real difference if we'll pass this legislation and get about providing every young people the opportunity to be as self-assured, as knowledgeable, as skilled as the two young people you heard from today. That's an important legacy we ought to leave to them.

Thank you, and God bless you all.

NOTE: The President spoke at 10:47 a.m. in the Delmarva Aircraft Hangar at Sussex County Airport. In his remarks, he referred to Opportunity Skyway participants Chrissy Thomas and Francis Orphe; Larry Perlman, chairman and CEO of Ceridian Corp. and chairman of the Business Roundtable working group on workforce training and development; and Carlton Spitzer, director, Opportunity Skyway.

Remarks on Naming Bill Frenzel as Special Adviser to the President for NAFTA and an Exchange With Reporters
September 3, 1993

The President. Good afternoon, ladies and gentlemen. A few days ago, as all of you know, I announced that Bill Daley in Chicago would be Special Counselor to the President to coordinate our effort to pass the North American Free Trade Agreement in the Congress. It is my great pleasure today to announce that Bill will be joined in our team by the gentleman to my left—probably an uncomfortable position for him—*[laughter]*—the distinguished former ranking minority member of the House Ways and Means Committee, Bill Frenzel from Minnesota, who for 20 years in Congress established a well-deserved record and is a genuine expert on this use of trade. He is now a guest scholar at the Brookings Institution, and he has agreed to come aboard as Special Adviser to the President for NAFTA while we work through this effort in Congress.

I also want to point out that we have just received a letter signed by 283 economists, among them liberals and conservatives and 12 Nobel laureates, reinforcing the position that I have taken strongly for over a year now, which is that this agreement, especially coupled with the side agreements, means more jobs, not fewer jobs, for the American people. This is a jobs issue.

Since the late 1980's, over half of our net new jobs have come from expanding exports. And one of the biggest deterrents to our expanding the job base in America today is declines in exports because of the flat economy in Europe, the flat economy in Japan. Latin America, as a whole, is the second fastest growing area of the world. Mexico is leading that

growth. I believe this is a very good move for the United States. It means more jobs. And I want to thank Bill Frenzel for his willingness to come aboard to make clear to all of America that this is a truly bipartisan effort and also to make it clear that we are serious about getting as many votes from Members of both parties as we can in the United States Congress. I thank you.

Congressman, I invite you to make a few remarks.

[At this point, Representative Frenzel thanked the President and reaffirmed his commitment to NAFTA.]

Q. Mr. President, do you think it will pass? And also, is there some intramural fight on whether health care should go first or you should focus on NAFTA first?

The President. Yes, I think it will pass, and no, there isn't one. We believe that it is the challenge, obviously, to present any kind of a major initiative to the Congress. But there is quite a difference between the two issues. Once the bill is ready for introduction under the laws governing NAFTA, it must be voted on in a certain amount of time. So there is a legislative timetable that will control that. The health care issue—the timetable for that will be largely determined by how quickly a consensus can be reached and by how much time the individual Members of the Congress are willing to put into mastering what is clearly the most complex public policy issue facing the United States today.

Nevertheless, I continue to believe strongly that the two issues complement each other; I do not think they conflict. I think that there is an enormous amount of bipartisan interest in doing something to control health care costs as a way of stimulating the economy as well as providing health security to all Americans. And it gives people something to be for, and it puts in the larger context that all these things are being done to try to provide the American economy and bring the American people into a stronger position as we face the 21st century. So I just don't buy the conflict argument. I feel good about this.

Health Care Reform

Q. Mr. President, do you think that the fact the Congress won't let you go forward with any additional broad-based taxes to pay for health care reform, that that's going to force you to so scale back the universal health care that you once envisaged that it won't have the kind of effect that you thought it would originally?

The President. No, not at all. If you go back to my February address, I have never wanted to have any big, broad-based taxes to pay for health care. I have never thought that was right, and I've never understood why you can justify taxing the American people as a whole to pay to cover those who aren't covered, when more than half of the American people are paying more for their health care than they'll be paying today. And when we are paying now almost 40 percent more of our income for our health care than any other advanced nation, I just don't think you can justify that. So I'm quite comfortable with that, and I think when we put

out our ideas and others put theirs out, that the American people will see pretty quickly we can do comprehensive coverage and without a big, new tax.

Q. Do you think Mr. Kantor is big enough to take on Mr. Perot?

The President. Yes, he's wanted to—show them your—he's already wounded, but even wounded, Mr. Kantor is a formidable fighter. Now he's got a lot of good help, too.

Oval Office Redecoration

Q. What do you think of your new surroundings?

The President. I like them very much. I think it's a beautiful rug. I like the couch. I like it.

Q. How much input did you have in this? I mean, is this you?

The President. I like it a lot. A little input. I thought a darker rug would be pretty and would lift the room, and something other than white couches. I like it.

You ought to sit on the couches. He also made them stronger so people don't sink in when they come in here. Did you ever go into an office and sink into the couch, you know? I don't think that's very good, so I wanted people to feel good.

Helen [Helen Thomas, United Press International], when Mickey opened his coat, did you think of President Johnson? [*Laughter*]

NOTE: The President spoke at 2:37 p.m. in the Oval Office at the White House. A tape was not available for verification of the content of these remarks.

Message on the Observance of Labor Day, 1993
September 3, 1993

On this important occasion of Labor Day, we take time out of our active schedules to honor the working men and women of America whose diligence and energy have made this country great.

These are the men and women whose sweat and toil built this nation from the ground up. They laid the railways, highways, and runways that brought this far-flung land together. They created an industrial machine that became and

still remains the envy of the world. They answered the call in every time of need and forged the military might of a superpower. And, more recently, they have led the world into a new age of communications and services. Their labors have fed, clothed, and housed this nation in good times and in bad.

Despite labor's tremendous contribution to the growth and success of our country, those who worked hard and played by the rules were once frequently unrecognized and exploited. Yet the cause of labor has advanced greatly in this century because of the determined efforts of brave labor leaders who risked their own security to bring about fair working conditions and a decent standard of living for the rank and file men and women of this country. Labor Day gives us all an opportunity to recognize the pivotal role that working men and women have played in our history.

We are now at the dawn of a new era of prosperity. On this Labor Day, let us dedicate ourselves to the idea that hard work should be justly rewarded. We still have much to do. The challenges of remaining competitive in a global economy make it all the more imperative that we continue to embrace the ideas of innovation and industry. All of us have our own contribution to make to the success of America. We don't have a single person to waste. Recognizing this, we can celebrate this day by reflecting upon the dignity of labor and the pride felt in a job well done.

Best wishes for a wonderful holiday.

BILL CLINTON

Announcement of Senior Executive Service Appointments
September 3, 1993

The President today appointed eight individuals to Senior Executive Service posts in the Departments of Agriculture and Transportation.

"I am pleased that these eight men and women have agreed to join our team and certain they will each work hard to support the great work being done by Secretaries Espy and Peña to make their Departments work better for the American people," the President said.

Department of Agriculture

Grant B. Buntrock, Administrator, Agricultural Stabilization and Conservation Service
Wayne H. Fawbush, Deputy Administrator, Farmers Home Administration

Lon Shoso Hatamiya, Administrator, Agricultural Marketing Service
Patricia A. Jensen, Deputy Assistant Secretary for Marketing and Inspection Services
Bonnie Luken, Deputy General Counsel
Wilbur T. Peer, Associate Administrator, Rural Development Administration

Department of Transportation

Antonio Califa, Director of Civil Rights
Frank Weaver, Director of Commercial Space Transportation

NOTE: Biographies of the nominees were made available by the Office of the Press Secretary.

Nomination for the Assassination Records Review Board
September 3, 1993

The President today announced his intention to nominate three historians and an attorney to the Assassination Records Review Board, convened to review Government records related to the assassination of President John F. Kennedy. Named were Princeton University librarian William L. Joyce, University of Tulsa dean Kermit L. Hall, American University history professor Anna Kasten Nelson, and Minnesota chief deputy attorney general John R. Tunheim.

"I am pleased these talented people, recommended by our country's leading historical groups, have agreed to take on this important task," the President said.

NOTE: Biographies of the nominees were made available by the Office of the Press Secretary.

The President's Radio Address
September 4, 1993

Good morning. On this Labor Day weekend, we honor the working men and women who are the strength and the soul of America. For people who work hard all year, this weekend offers the opportunity to relax with our families at a picnic, a barbecue, a beach, or just in our own homes. In the calm and the quiet of these last days of summer, there will be a moment when most of us think about our families and our future. Maybe it will come during a walk on the beach, a stroll through a park, or when we watch a son or a daughter take a swing at a softball or build a castle in the sand.

We'll think of the faith of our parents that was instilled in us here in America, the idea that if you work hard and play by the rules, you'll be rewarded with a good life for yourself and a better chance for your children. Filled with that faith, generations of Americans have worked long hours on their jobs and passed along powerful dreams to their sons and daughters. Many of us can remember our own parents working long hours on their jobs and then coming home and helping us with our homework. The American dream has always been a better life for people who are willing to work for it.

In 7 months as your President, I've been deeply inspired by the people I've met who are working hard and studying hard, building their futures in a time of turbulence and change. I'll never forget a woman I met from Detroit who had to support her children after her husband died. Determined not to be on welfare, she enrolled in a 6-year advanced training program and found a job as a machinist. I'll never forget the men and women I met at Van Nuys Community College in California, people who had lost their jobs as aerospace workers and auto workers and were learning new skills from film production to computer science. And just yesterday in Delaware, I spoke with young people who are combining their high school education with specialized job training for highly skilled jobs in the aviation industry. Young and old, these people are the heroes we honor on Labor Day, people who take personal responsibility for making their lives better and making our Nation stronger.

Every morning when I go to work in the Oval Office, I think about how we can offer our hard-working Americans the opportunities they deserve, opportunities too many have been denied for too long.

When Congress passed our economic plan last month, America took an important step toward building the high-wage, high-skill, high-growth economy where hard work is rewarded. We're beginning to pay down the deficit we inherited, get our economic house in order, cut wasteful spending, and invest in education and training and new technologies. We changed the tax laws to make sure that no one who works 40 hours a week with children at home will live in poverty. That means tax cuts for millions of American families with incomes below $27,000 a year. It's a pro-work, pro-family approach that's not about building bureaucracies but about encouraging people to keep doing the right things.

We've also made it possible for over 90 percent of the small businesses in this country to reduce their taxes, but only if they invest more in their businesses. And we've opened the doors of college education to millions more Americans with lower interest loans and easier repayment terms and the opportunity for tens of thousands of our young people to pay off their college loans or earn credit against college through the national service program and building their communities at the grassroots level. These policies too are pro-work and pro-family. We're taking the values that are central to our own lives, values of work and family, and putting them at the center of our public policies. We've got to keep America moving, and we've got to pull America back together.

In just 7 months we've done a lot. But for 20 years, because of the pressures of the global economy and problems here at home, Americans have been working harder for less. And after 12 years of trickle-down economics, which worked for just a little while but then left us with no fundamental change except a huge, huge national debt and a massive annual deficit, we've still got a lot more to do.

In the weeks ahead we'll be taking three new steps on the journey of change toward a new American economy and a stronger American community. First, we'll reform the health care system to provide health care security to all Americans and affordable costs so that this health care system doesn't bankrupt the economy while failing to cover millions of Americans. Second, we'll try to create more jobs through expanded trade through the North American Free Trade Agreement and a general agreement with the other trading nations of the world. And third, we'll try to give you more value for your tax dollar by reinventing Government to make it more efficient and less expensive. These are the things we can do to give our people the tools they need to build a stronger economy. Health security, expanded trade, and reinventing Government really aren't separate goals. They're part of a comprehensive strategy to promote long-term growth, increased incomes, more jobs, and a stronger American community, part of our effort to make all these changes our friend and not our enemy.

In our own lives we understand that we often have to do several things to reach one goal. Think about the talk at your kitchen table when you discuss the challenges facing your own families. You might be talking about whether you can afford to buy a home or send your youngest child to college or whether to build a new business of your own or go to night school to learn a new skill. Of course, these are separate questions, but they all add up to one challenge: building a better life for you and your family.

It's the same with building our country's future. These pieces must all fit together. To con-

trol the deficit, we have to reform health care and give families more security. To create new jobs for our workers, we have to open new markets for our companies and our products. And for Government to be a help and not a hindrance in economic growth, we must make it less bureaucratic and more productive. Business and labor and Government must work together as partners to achieve these goals.

This Labor Day weekend is a good time to remember that a free society needs a strong and a vibrant labor movement. From the struggle against communism in Poland to the struggle against apartheid in South Africa to the struggle for social justice in our own Nation, we have seen what working men and women can accomplish when they work together in the spirit of solidarity. Now more than ever America needs the spirit of solidarity and the courage to change, the understanding that we're all in this together and that we have to move forward together.

Together we can make the changes that our people deserve and our times demand. And then on Labor Day weekends years from now, our children and our children's children will look back on the work we did, and they will say with gratitude and pride that we kept faith with the American dream.

Thanks for listening.

NOTE: The President spoke at 10:06 a.m. from the Oval Office at the White House.

Nomination for Commissioner of the Rehabilitation Services Administration
September 4, 1993

The President today announced his intention to nominate rehabilitation counselor Bobby Charles Simpson Commissioner of the Rehabilitation Services Administration at the Department of Education.

"Bobby Simpson has dedicated his life to

helping people with disabilities, and I am grateful that he has agreed to lend his commitment and experience to our administration," the President said.

NOTE: A biography of the nominee was made available by the Office of the Press Secretary.

Remarks to the Community in Homestead, Florida
September 6, 1993

Ladies and gentlemen, I have had a great tour of Florida City and Homestead today, and we just had a wonderful community meeting where I heard from a lot of people who have been through the last year and who have suffered, but who triumphed.

I want to give you just one message on this Labor Day. This is a day where we honor the men and women of our country who work and keep this country going. What we have proved is that the Government and the people in their own lives can work together as partners, can labor together to pull this community together and rebuild this community and come back. And I want you to know that I am very proud of the work that all of you have done. I'm very grateful for the presence here today of several members of the Florida congressional delegation, several House Members and Senator Graham, for your Lieutenant Governor, for the people here on the Dade County Commission, and all the local leadership, but also for the citizens here.

I ran for President because I really believed we could make Government work again. I believed that things could happen that could change the lives of people. And I knew that a lot of it would have to be done by people at the local level, by the State legislators that are here in large numbers, by people who have actually lost their homes and seen things go away here. But I also knew the National Government had a responsibility. I asked Henry Cisneros, the Secretary of Housing and Urban Development, to coordinate our long-term commitment to helping people here deal with the aftermath of the hurricane. We hired Otis Pitts,

who's done a terrific job down here as the Deputy Under Secretary of HUD, to work with all of you. And I just want to say to all of you, we are in this for the long run. I heard today about some things that still need to be done. And we will not have our work done until everybody in this part of our country who wants a job has one, until people are back in their homes, until these communities are rebuilt.

One other thing I want to say to you is that, as you know, huge numbers of people in the Middle West have been displaced by what amounted to a 500-year flood on the Mississippi River. And I want those people to see you on television tonight. I want them to read about you in their newspapers tomorrow. And I want them to believe that you really can bring an area back if you work together and stay together and rebuild a sense of community and give people a chance to take responsibility for themselves. We'll be there with you. I'm glad to be here today, and I thank you for spending a little time with your President on Labor Day.

Hillary and I both are delighted to be back. It was almost exactly a year ago—it was a year ago this week that I came down here, and you have done very well. I'm glad we could be your partners for a year, and we will be until the job is done.

Thank you very much.

NOTE: The President spoke at 11:45 a.m. at the intersection of 17th and Krome. In his remarks, he referred to Otis Pitts, HUD Deputy Assistant Secretary for Federal Relief—South Dade County. A tape was not available for verification of the content of these remarks.

Remarks to the Community in Cutler Ridge, Florida
September 6, 1993

The President. Thank you so much. I want to thank Marty Urra and my longtime friends Governor Chiles and Senator Graham, Secretary Reich and Secretary Cisneros, who have done such a fine job coordinating our National Gov-

ernment's response to Hurricane Andrew over the long run down here. I'd also like to introduce a few people even on this hot day. First of all, the First Lady's here; my wife, Hillary, is down there. There she is. In addition to Senator Graham, we have four other members of your congressional delegation here: Representative Carrie Meek—five, five—Representative Peter Deutsch, Representative Ileana Ros-Lehtinen, Representative Lincoln Diaz-Balart, and Representative Alcee Hastings. Let's get them all up here. Your Lieutenant Governor Buddy MacKay's been with me all day. I think he's back in the crowd again. We also have a large number of State legislators, Dade County commissioners, and other local leaders here. Let's give them all a hand, all the ones that are over here. [Applause] All the legislators and commissioners who want to come up, come on up. You've got some——

Audience member. Where's Chelsea?

The President. Chelsea's playing today. We have legislators and commissioners who lost their homes in the hurricane; they deserve to be up here, I think. Bring Larry Hawkins up here. He lost his house; he deserves to be here. That's good.

Ladies and gentlemen, one year ago this week I came here to south Dade County to see what Hurricane Andrew had wrought. A year later I come back as President, honored to see much of the work done that I ran for President to do, honored to see that people here are working together to make Government work on the real problems of real people. I want to thank again Henry Cisneros for taking the lead in coordinating our response. And I want to thank Otis Pitts from Miami for representing the administration so well and helping people overcome the impact of the flood. [Applause] Thank you.

You know, Dade County has done a lot for the Clinton administration. I got the EPA Director, Carol Browner, from Dade County. I got Jeff Watson, who used to work for the Mayor of Miami. There are a number of other people, but I guess the most famous Dade County citizen I now have is Janet Reno, your Attorney General. I want to tell you that you can be very proud of the work that she has done, and all the others. And you need to know that about three times a day, when Janet Reno says something that makes real good sense, she says that she learned it from the people of Dade County that she represented for so long.

One of the things that I wanted very much to do as President was to reestablish a partnership among business and labor and Government. I thought we had been divided for too long. I think in order to rebuild America, we have

got to reunite America. We've got to reach across the barriers of race and region and income and party, and we've got to prove that we can work together on the things that we all have to deal with, if we're going to make this country what it ought to be.

I am proud of the work that has been done by the Department of Housing and Urban Development and the AFL–CIO in creating a partnership to invest in our communities. Now, you heard Secretary Cisneros mention it, but I want to talk a little bit more about that.

This new partnership between Government and labor will make possible the building of 102 moderate and low income housing units here in Cutler Ridge. And let me tell you how this is going to work. We'll also make it possible for a lot of people to be trained to learn the jobs of today and tomorrow, because the Labor Department is going to give the AFL–CIO some money to subsidize apprenticeship programs at this site so that we can give skill training and meaningful jobs to people who live here and need work, too.

All across the country, the AFL–CIO, supported by two Government Agencies with the funny names that many of you probably never heard of before of Fannie Mae and Freddie Mac, are going to establish a housing investment trust fund that will provide an additional $600 million to rebuild and create affordable housing across this country, with a significant percentage of that money going to regions like this one which have been struck by hurricanes or the middle western communities devastated by the floods.

This is the kind of thing that we ought to be doing together. The Government can guarantee the security of the pension funds. The unions can put up those pension funds to invest in houses. The Labor Department can help to provide the funds to train people. We'll have more houses, more investment, more jobs, and a better America starting right here in this community. That's the sort of thing we ought to be doing.

You know, this is a day of rest and relaxation for most Americans, looking forward to going back to work tomorrow, and many of our young people are going back to school. Well, tomorrow when you return to work, you can know that in this year over one million jobs have been added to our economy. That's about as many as were added during the previous 4 years in

America. We've still got a long way to go, but it's a pretty good beginning, and it's something we can build on.

President Harry Truman, who came from a State that neighbors mine, in Missouri, once said this: If the working people of our country are well off, whether they work in factories or on the farms, in offices or in stores, this country will get along all right. The reverse is also true. When the working people of our country are not all right, the rest of the country is in deep trouble.

We have got to make sure that we have policies in this Government that reward work and family for hard-working middle class people that are doing everything they can to raise their kids and make this country a better place. Since you gave me this job, that's what I've tried to do. You heard someone mention earlier the Family and Medical Leave Act. What that means is that for a change—since that law became in effect, now if somebody has a baby born or a sick parent or a child gets sick, you can take a little time off from your job without losing it. It's high time we provided for that sort of protection in America.

In the economic program that Congress just passed, we see not only the biggest reduction in the Federal deficit in the history of this country, something that will lift a burden off the children in this audience and the grandchildren, something that will make us freer to invest in our future and take control of our destiny, something that has brought us the lowest interest rates in 25 years, that is enabling young people all across America for the first time to even think about buying a home. That economic program also actually did something that, from your point of view, may be more important. It lifted the working poor out of poverty by saying: If you work 40 hours a week and you have children in the home, we will not tax you into poverty; we will use the tax system to lift you out of poverty even if it requires a refund. I haven't looked at all the figures, but I can tell you that in Carrie Meek's congressional district, for example, that means over one-third of the working families in that congressional district will be eligible for a tax reduction under the economic program that the Congress passed to promote work and family.

Over 90 percent of the small businesses in the entire United States of America are eligible for a tax cut to encourage them to hire more people, because most of the new jobs are being created by small business people. That is pro-work; it is pro-family; it is not bureaucratic. It is the sort of thing that we need to be doing in this country.

Now, my fellow Americans, on this Labor Day I want to ask you, as we move ahead to other challenges, to recognize that this is a new and different world. We have here in this county people from all over the world coming here to live, trying to make a new life for themselves in an America trying to move into the 21st century. We are doing it against a backdrop where all the wealthy countries in the world are having trouble creating new jobs and raising people's incomes and giving people security. We have a lot of things we have to do, and I can tell you one thing: We will never get there unless we ask ourselves not just "What's in it for me?" but "What's in it for us?" How can we move together to make this country what it ought to be for everybody who's willing to work hard and play by the rules. That's what I saw today in Florida City and Homestead, people who said, "What's in it for us?", who worked together to rebuild our communities and put the lives of families back together. That is what we have to do as a nation.

In the next few weeks you're going to see the Congress deal with an enormous number of issues, but they all have one thing in common: We've got to deal with them to pull our country together and move our country forward. If we don't control health care costs and provide affordable health care to every American family, we'll never be the nation we ought to be.

If we don't open the doors of college education to all Americans and give all Americans who don't go to college the chance to get good training programs so they can get good jobs, we'll never be the nation we ought to be.

If we don't open new avenues of trade so that we can sell our products around the world and reinvest in this country, where the bases have been closed and the defense plants have been shut down, in putting those people back to work, we will never be the nation we ought to be.

And finally, if we don't decide once and for all we are going to have secure, strong, safe communities, free of violence and guns, where we promote independence and work, not welfare, and where everybody has a chance to raise their children in a decent, secure, safe environment, we will never be the nation we ought to be.

On Labor Day, you are doing your part by working for America. And I pledge to you that our administration will do its part by working for these goals to make this country what it ought to be.

Thank you, and God bless you all.

NOTE: The President spoke at 1:50 p.m. at the Caribbean West Apartments. In his remarks, he referred to Marty Urra, president, South Florida AFL–CIO, and Jeffrey H. Watson, Deputy Assistant to the President and Deputy Director of Intergovernmental Affairs.

Remarks Announcing the Report of the National Performance Review and an Exchange With Reporters
September 7, 1993

The President. Mr. Vice President and members of the Cabinet, distinguished guests, Mrs. Gore, Senator Gore, thank you for coming. To all of you from the Federal Government and from the private sector who worked on this report and all of you who care about seeing it implemented, I think we all owe an enormous debt of gratitude to the Vice President for the difficult and thorough work which has been done and for the outstanding product which has been produced. My gratitude is great also to the staff of the National Performance Review and to the employees of the Federal Government and the people in the private sector who helped us to do this and to the Cabinet members who have supported it.

I will say I had the opportunity to read this report in draft over the weekend. I read it very carefully. I read some sections of it more than once. And if the report is any indication of where we're going, then the future looks bright indeed, because this is an oxymoron; this is a Government report that's fun to read. [*Laughter*] It's well written. It's interesting. It's compelling, and it is hopeful.

I ran for President because I wanted to get America on the move and I wanted to pull our country together. And it became quickly apparent to me in the campaign that the feelings I had developed not only as a citizen but as a Governor over the previous 12 years were widely shared by others. It's hard for the National Government to take a leadership role, even a partnership role, in bringing America together and putting America on the move when people have no confidence in the operations of the Government, when they don't believe they

get good value for the dollars they give to the Government in taxes, when they don't believe that they're being treated like customers, when they don't really feel that they are the bosses in this great democratic enterprise.

And so, 6 months ago, I asked the Vice President to embark on a risky adventure, to see if we could make the Government work better and cost less, to serve our people better, and to, as important as anything else, rebuild the confidence of the American people in this great public enterprise.

Our Founders clearly understood that every generation would have to reinvent the Government, and they knew that long before the Government was nearly as big or cumbersome or bureaucratic or far-reaching as it is today. Thomas Jefferson said, laws and institutions must go hand in hand with the progress of human mind as that becomes more developed, more enlightened, as new discoveries are made and new truths discovered and manners and opinions change. With the change of circumstances, institutions must advance also to keep pace with the time.

That is what the Vice President and this group tried to do, to listen and to learn from people who best understand how to make Government work better. This report reflects the practical experiences of Federal employees whose best efforts have too often been smothered in redtape, business people who have streamlined their own companies, State and local officials who are reinventing government at the grassroots, and concerned citizens who deserve and demand more value for their tax dollars.

To meet the challenges of the global economy and to better use new technology, our most successful companies have been through this process, many of them starting more than a decade ago: eliminating unnecessary layers of management, empowering frontline workers, becoming more responsive to their customers, and seeking constantly to improve the products they make, the services they provide, and the people they employ.

Meanwhile, I have seen too little of this happen nationally. I do want to say that there are many reasons for this. Government, as we all know, has too often a monopoly on the money of the American people and on those who have to be its customers. Government also does not have the pressure from time to time to change that the private sector does, so that what we have today, as the Vice President said, is a lot of good people trapped in bad systems. We still have a Government that's largely organized on a top-down, bureaucratic, industrial model when we're in an information age. And very often, it is just easier to keep on doing what you have been doing.

I want to say, though, that we not only have the models that the Vice President mentioned— the terrific work done in Texas by Governor Richards and the comptroller, John Sharp, who's here with us today; the work that I started when I was Governor of my State, and we had the first comprehensive statewide quality management program in the country—but also we have something else to be even more hopeful for and that is that in spite of all the obstacles, there are stunning examples of Federal employees succeeding in this environment. The thing I want to encourage all of you to do is to actually read this report. It's not very long. It is fun to read, and it will reassure you that there are people out here who are making productivity improvements, who are giving you value for dollar, who are trying to save money, and who are proving, most important of all, that we can do this on a sweeping basis all across the Government.

Make no mistake about this: This is one report that will not gather dust in a warehouse. I will challenge every concerned American to read it. I will discuss it in great detail with the Members of the Congress. I will ask people to help us to pass those programs which have to be passed through Congress and to implement those things which must be done by the executive branch. This program makes sense. It's going to work. We're going to do it.

There are a lot of places in this report where it says "the President should," "the President should," "the President should." Well, let me tell you something, I've read it, and where it says "the President should," the President will.

You know, everybody knows that we've got a big budget deficit. Most of us know we, ironically, also have got an investment deficit. The two are not unrelated. We don't have enough money to invest in the growth of the economy and the development of our people because we've spent too much money on other things and because we have refused to change. The key to remedying both the budget deficit and the investment deficit is to overcome the performance deficit in the Federal Government. And we intend to make a beginning on that.

There's no reason that we can't have a post office where you always get served within 5 minutes of the time you walk up to the counter; why you can't have an IRS that always gives you the right answer and takes your phone call; why you can't have a Government that pays no more for a hammer or a pair of pliers, or more importantly, for a personal computer than you'd pay at a local commercial outlet.

The Vice President and I are going to work with the Cabinet to find ways to make the Government more responsive and to implement this report. We're going to rely on the innovations of our leaders in the Cabinet. For example, under Secretary Cisneros' leadership, the Department of Housing and Urban Development is finding new ways to empower citizens not to expand bureaucracy. The Department is determined to eliminate 75 different rules and statutes that make it more difficult to build housing and to redevelop communities and determined to do more to help people who live in public housing have control over their own destinies instead of being controlled by mindless rules and regulations and decisions made by people an awful long way from where they live.

We have other community initiatives that we are supporting for States and cities and towns: community policing, citizens patrols, and other special programs to keep young people out of trouble. All those things have to spring up from the local level, and there shouldn't be Federal rules and regulations getting in the way. States and cities and towns applying for funds for community development and assistance to the homeless will be required now to submit only one application and one report, not the seven that have been required.

Under the Attorney General's leadership, the Justice Department is finding new ways to collect more than $14 billion that delinquent debtors owe the Government. Those who are able to pay, should. About 20 percent of the money owed the Federal Government today is delinquent. It's time we collected on the bills.

Under Secretary Bob Reich's leadership, the Labor Department will offer one-stop career service centers to help their customers make better use of the presently bewildering array of 150 different employment and training programs. There is a gripping story in this report of someone who lost their job in a company because of global competition, then got hired again by the same company and lost this job a second time because of cutbacks in the defense budget. If the person had quit the first time, they could have gotten job training under the Trade Adjustment Assistance Act, but because they quit and went back to work, which was the right thing to do, and lost their jobs a second time before there was a defense conversion plan in place to train people who lost their jobs—the second time, the same guy couldn't get any job training.

I could give you lots of examples of that. We are going to fix that. We're going to put these programs together and recognize that all Americans need job training. The Labor Department ought to provide it. Instead of providing people to push papers around to figure out how to keep people out of 150 different programs, there ought to be one that all Americans can participate in.

Under Secretary Mike Espy's leadership, the Agriculture Department is concentrating on six key functions: commodity programs, rural development, nutrition, conservation, food quality, and research. This will allow the Agriculture Department to consolidate from 42 to 30 Agencies and cut administrative costs by more than $200 million a year.

This just isn't about changing our Government; it's about changing our country. We reinvent the Government. We're doing something that is essential to reviving our economy, restoring our confidence in Government, and therefore, permitting us once again to be one American community.

Last month, we passed an important milepost when Congress passed the economic plan that will begin to pay down an enormous deficit we inherited, cut wasteful spending, and make investments we need in our people, our jobs, our educational and technological future.

In the weeks ahead, we have other challenges to face from reforming our health care system to provide security for every family, to opening new markets for our products and services abroad so that we can start creating jobs again. But to accomplish any of these goals, we have to revolutionize the Government itself so that the American people trust the decisions that are made and trust us to do the work that Government has to do. The entire agenda of change depends upon our ability to change the way we do our own business with the people's money. That is the only way we can restore the faith of our citizens. An effective Government can offer people opportunities they need to take greater responsibilities for their own lives and to rebuild their families, their communities, and our beloved country.

We ask the support of Americans from every walk of life, from every party, from every region. The Government is broken, and we intend to fix it. But we can't do it unless we all understand that this isn't a Democratic goal or a Republican goal. This is an American imperative, and we all need to be a part of it.

I look forward to the day when every American can cite some example that he or she has personally experienced in this revolution in the way Government works, a program that is paid for not by stopping something worthy or raising new money or increasing the deficit but by stopping something that didn't need to be done anymore. I look forward to a day when you call the IRS and ask a question, and they give you an answer, and you know it's the right one; when you ask your children what they think about the Government and they can all cite something the Government has done to make their lives better and done in a good and efficient way.

If that happens, we'll all be in debt for a long time to the Vice President and his staff and to all the others who participated in this report. I think they did a great job. Now it's time for the rest of us to do a great job and implement the recommendations so that we can change the way the American people feel about their Government and change the role that the Government plays in our lives for the better.

Thank you very much. God bless you.

Q. Mr. President, why do you think this is going to be any more successful than other attempts that have been made in the past and failed?

The President. I think there are two or three reasons. First of all, frankly, this is a better report. It's not just a report in which one group of Americans tells another group of Americans, "Here are big things we don't need to do anymore. Let's just stop doing." This is a report which says, "The whole way the Government operates is incompatible with the world in which we're living, and we can change it."

I think if you read it, this is qualitatively different from past reports. This is a real generational change in the attitude about what should be done in Government and how it should work. So I think that will make a big difference.

Secondly, I think there is more public support for this than there has been in the past that runs across all partisan lines, Republicans, Democrats, independents.

And thirdly, there is a President here who will do more than talk about it. I intend to do what I can to implement it. I've asked the Vice President to give me a set of recommendations, starting immediately about which things we can change by Executive order, which things we need to go to Congress with, and how we're going to go to Congress with these recommendations and push them through. So it's a very different thing.

Finally, I think there's a lot more support in the Congress than there has been in the past. I think a lot of people in the Congress now realize that if we're going to close the investment deficit, if we're going to close the budget deficit, we've got to close the performance deficit in Government, that it just doesn't work. And the harder they work—and let me just say this: The Congress, for example, has spent about 40 percent more time on the job this year than they did last year. But you can work hard and hard and hard, and if the American people don't have confidence in the ulti-

mate enterprise, it's still hard for the Members of Congress to get credit for the work they're doing because the ultimate product is not going to function very well. So I think those are the reasons that this won't be like past reports.

Q. Do Members of Congress know about this yet, Mr. President, and what are they telling you back when you tell them about this proposal?

The Vice President. Let me respond to that. We're getting a lot of tremendous support from the Congress. Let me point out that some of the pioneers in this effort have been in the Congress. The chairmen and ranking members of the two principal committees on how the Government operates are all very supportive.

There will be some opposition. You know that, and we couldn't change what needs to be changed without running into opposition. But the ground has shifted. The world has changed. The American people are demanding that we change the way the Federal Government operates. It doesn't work well now. It costs too much money; it performs very poorly. We want to make it work better and cost less by implementing the recommendations of this report. We fully intend to do that.

Q. What about—get Congress to go along with the biennial budget? Will you be able to get Congress to go along with the biennial budget?

The President. I hope so. Well, in times past, over a majority of the Congress has supported a biennial budget. It can't be very satisfying for them to have to spend all their time doing that when they can spend more time evaluating how these programs work.

Q. What about the unions, Mr. President?

The Vice President. They've been very supportive. They've been very supportive. All three of the principal ones have endorsed it.

NOTE: The President spoke at approximately 10:20 a.m. on the South Lawn at the White House. The exchange portion of this item could not be verified because the tape was incomplete.

Statement on Senate Action Confirming Joycelyn Elders as Surgeon General
September 7, 1993

I am extremely pleased and gratified by the Senate's action today in confirming Dr. Joycelyn Elders as the Nation's next Surgeon General. Dr. Elders has consistently demonstrated a high level of intellect, courage, and wisdom in dealing with the wide range of health and social problems facing our country. Her dedication to improving the lives of all Americans, especially the children of America, won her the strong backing of a bipartisan majority of the Senate. I look forward to working with her in confronting the pressing issues facing the public health of our Nation.

I am especially grateful to Senator Kennedy for his steady leadership during the Labor and Human Resources Committee's consideration of Dr. Elders' nomination. Senator Kennedy's dedication to this nominee was extraordinary.

Statement by the Press Secretary on the President's Telephone Conversation With President Boris Yeltsin of Russia
September 7, 1993

President Clinton spoke by phone today with President Boris Yeltsin of Russia for about 40 minutes to discuss several bilateral and foreign policy issues.

President Clinton reiterated strong U.S. support for Russian political and market reform and the work of President Yeltsin and the Russian Government to keep those reforms on track. They discussed the status of existing and prospective U.S. assistance for the reform process.

The President agreed that last week's meeting in Washington of the Joint Commission on Energy and Space, led by Vice President Gore and Russian Prime Minister Chernomyrdin, was a great success. They also agreed on the need for further progress, particularly on a number of U.S. private sector energy investment projects.

Turning to the Middle East, the Presidents welcomed the historic progress in negotiations between Israel and the PLO in recent weeks and pledged to work together to promote peace in the Middle East region.

On other foreign policy issues, President Yeltsin briefed the President on his recent trip to Ukraine. President Clinton welcomed the progress achieved by President Yeltsin and President Kravchuk, particularly regarding the nuclear weapons now deployed in Ukraine. The President affirmed U.S. interest in working with both parties to assist in the resolution of outstanding issues.

The President congratulated President Yeltsin on the withdrawal of Russian forces from Lithuania last week and reaffirmed U.S. support for a rapid and complete withdrawal of forces from Latvia and Estonia. The two leaders also discussed their support for the ongoing effort to promote peace in Bosnia.

Statement by the Press Secretary on the President's Telephone Conversation With Chancellor Helmut Kohl of Germany
September 7, 1993

President Clinton spoke by phone today with Chancellor Helmut Kohl of Germany for about 40 minutes.

The two leaders discussed a number of bilateral and foreign affairs issues. On the Generalized Agreement for Tariffs and Trade (GATT), the two leaders agreed on the need for successful conclusion of the Uruguay round by the end of 1993 and undertook to remain in contact throughout the autumn for that purpose.

President Clinton and Chancellor Kohl dis-

cussed developments in the Middle East, both indicating their deep satisfaction over the prospects for historic breakthroughs in ongoing talks. They reviewed progress in the political and economic reform process in Russia and discussed their efforts to assist that process. They also agreed on the need to cooperate on issues related to the former Yugoslavia.

Announcement of White House Office Appointments
September 7, 1993

White House Chief of Staff Mack McLarty today announced the appointment of Joe Velasquez as Deputy Assistant to the President and Deputy Director of Political Affairs and Keith Mason as Deputy Assistant to the President for Intergovernmental Affairs.

Mr. Velasquez is deputy to Political Affairs Director Joan Baggett, and Mr. Mason is deputy to Director of Intergovernmental Affairs Marcia Hale. The President praised the new members of his team. "Joe Velasquez understands the importance of increasing voters' involvement in the political process, and I am confident he will

ensure Americans of all concerns have a voice in our Government," the President said.

"From his experiences in Georgia, Keith Mason knows firsthand the needs and concerns of State and local governments today. I know that he will work hard to forge strong bonds between Washington and our States and cities so that we can all work together in the best interest of the American people," the President said.

NOTE: Biographies of the appointees were made available by the Office of the Press Secretary.

Message to the Congress Transmitting the Armenia-United States Investment Treaty
September 7, 1993

To the Senate of the United States:

With a view to receiving the advice and consent of the Senate to ratification, I transmit herewith the Treaty Between the United States of America and the Republic of Armenia Concerning the Reciprocal Encouragement and Protection of Investment, signed at Washington on September 23, 1992. Also transmitted for the information of the Senate is the report of the Department of State with respect to this Treaty.

The Treaty will establish an agreed-upon legal basis for the protection and encouragement of investment. This Treaty thus forms an integral part of the framework for expanding trade and investment relations between the United States and the countries of the former Soviet Union. It is designed to encourage economic oppor-

tunity—for investment, trade, and growth—in both countries. It will assist Armenia in its transition to a market economy by strengthening the role of the private sector and by encouraging appropriate macroeconomic and structural policies.

The Treaty is fully consistent with U.S. policy toward international and domestic investment. A specific tenet, reflected in this Treaty, is that U.S. investment abroad and foreign investment in the United States should receive fair, equitable, and nondiscriminatory treatment. Under this Treaty, the Parties also agree to international law standards for expropriation and compensation for expropriation, free transfers of funds associated with investments, freedom of investments from performance requirements, and the investor's freedom to choose to resolve disputes with the host government through international arbitration.

I recommend that the Senate consider this Treaty as soon as possible, and give its advice and consent to ratification of the Treaty at an early date.

WILLIAM J. CLINTON

The White House,
September 7, 1993.

NOTE: This message was released by the Office of the Press Secretary on September 8.

Message to the Congress Transmitting the Kyrgyzstan-United States Investment Treaty
September 7, 1993

To the Senate of the United States:

With a view of receiving the advice and consent of the Senate to ratification, I transmit herewith the Treaty Between the United States of America and the Kyrgyz Republic Concerning the Encouragement and Reciprocal Protection of Investment, signed at Washington on January 19, 1993. Also transmitted for the information of the Senate is the report of the Department of State with respect to this Treaty.

The Treaty will establish an agreed-upon legal basis for the protection and encouragement of investment. This Treaty thus forms an integral part of the framework for expanding trade and investment relations between the United States and the countries of the former Soviet Union. It is designed to encourage economic opportunity—for investment, trade, and growth—in both countries. It will assist Kyrgyzstan in its transition to a market economy by strengthening the role of the private sector and by encouraging appropriate macroeconomic and structural policies.

The Treaty is fully consistent with U.S. policy toward international and domestic investment. A specific tenet, reflected in this Treaty, is that U.S. investment abroad and foreign investment in the United States should receive fair, equitable, and nondiscriminatory treatment. Under this Treaty, the Parties also agree to international law standards for expropriation and compensation for expropriation, free transfers of funds associated with investments, freedom of investments from performance requirements, and the investor's freedom to choose to resolve disputes with the host government through international arbitration.

I recommend that the Senate consider this Treaty as soon as possible, and give its advice and consent to ratification of the Treaty at an early date.

WILLIAM J. CLINTON

The White House,
September 7, 1993.

NOTE: This message was released by the Office of the Press Secretary on September 8.

Message to the Congress Transmitting the Kazakhstan-United States Investment Treaty
September 7, 1993

To the Senate of the United States:

With a view to receiving the advice and consent of the Senate to ratification, I transmit herewith the Treaty Between the United States of America and the Republic of Kazakhstan Concerning the Reciprocal Encouragement and Protection of Investment, signed at Washington on May 19, 1992. Also transmitted for the information of the Senate is the report of the Department of State with respect to this Treaty.

The Treaty will establish an agreed-upon legal basis for the protection and encouragement of investment. This Treaty thus forms an integral part of the framework for expanding trade and investment relations between the United States and the countries of the former Soviet Union. It is designed to encourage economic opportunity—including investment, trade, and growth—in both countries. It will assist Kazakhstan in its transition to a market economy by strengthening the role of the private sector and by encouraging appropriate macroeconomic and structural policies.

The Treaty is fully consistent with U.S. policy toward international and domestic investment. A specific tenet, reflected in this Treaty, is that U.S. investment abroad and foreign investment in the United States should receive fair, equi-table, and nondiscriminatory treatment. Under this Treaty, the Parties also agree to international law standards for expropriation and compensation for expropriation, free transfers of funds associated with investments, freedom of investments from performance requirements, and the investor's freedom to choose to resolve disputes with the host government through international arbitration.

I recommend that the Senate consider this Treaty as soon as possible, and give its advice and consent to ratification of the Treaty at an early date.

· WILLIAM J. CLINTON

The White House,
September 7, 1993.

NOTE: This message was released by the Office of the Press Secretary on September 8.

Message to the Congress Transmitting the Moldova-United States Investment Treaty
September 7, 1993

To the Senate of the United States:

With a view to receiving the advice and consent of the Senate to ratification, I transmit herewith the Treaty Between the United States of America and the Republic of Moldova Concerning the Encouragement and Reciprocal Protection of Investment, with Protocol and related exchange of letters, signed at Washington on April 21, 1993. Also transmitted for the information of the Senate is the report of the Department of State with respect to this Treaty.

The Treaty will establish an agreed-upon legal basis for the protection and encouragement of investment. This Treaty thus forms an integral part of the framework for expanding trade and investment relations between the United States and the countries of the former Soviet Union. It is designed to encourage economic opportunity—including investment, trade, and growth—in both countries. It will assist Moldova in its transition to a market economy by strengthening the role of the private sector and by encouraging appropriate macroeconomic and structural policies.

The Treaty is fully consistent with U.S. policy toward international and domestic investment. A specific tenet, reflected in this Treaty, is that U.S. investment abroad and foreign investment in the United States should receive fair, equitable, and nondiscriminatory treatment. Under this Treaty, the Parties also agree to international law standards for expropriation and compensation for expropriation, free transfers of funds associated with investments, freedom of investments from performance requirements, and the investor's freedom to choose to resolve disputes with the host government through international arbitration.

I recommend that the Senate consider this Treaty as soon as possible, and give its advice and consent to ratification of the Treaty, with Protocol and related exchange of letters, at an early date.

WILLIAM J. CLINTON

The White House,
September 7, 1993.

NOTE: This message was released by the Office of the Press Secretary on September 8.

Remarks to General Services Administration Employees in Franconia, Virginia
September 8, 1993

Thank you very much. Mr. Vice President, Roger, Senator Robb and Congressman Moran, Congresswoman Byrne, and, most important, to all of you who have worked so hard here at this center to give the American people the Government they deserve. I want to begin by once again thanking the Vice President for the incredible amount of work that was done by the Vice· President, by his staff, by hundreds and hundreds of volunteers, and by people like you who gave us the ideas that went into the National Performance Review report.

I also want to say to all of you something that you all know, because you are both public employees and private citizens. If we can reform these procurement practices, we can probably do more there than in any other area of our national life in the short run to restore the confidence of the American people in their Government. Every taxpaying citizen who goes out in the summertime has bought insect repellant, and no rational person could possible believe that Federal employees need specially designed insect repellant. Everybody's bought aspirin. Everybody's filled out a form they wished they hadn't filled out. Everybody's bought things like folders and computer tapes. And at a time when we are now 20 years, 20 years into a period in our history where most American wage earners are working longer work weeks for stagnant wages, it is outrageous for the Government to have rules and regulations which take those people's money from them and spend it on things that cannot be justified.

You heard the Vice President say some of these things. But our Government employs 142,000 people in the procurement system alone. We know we have 900 detailed procurement laws, and we're going to ask the Congress to change a lot of that. I've asked myself many times, as I've heard these stories from coast to coast, how this occurred. And I think there are many reasons.

I was out the other day in a particularly wrenching encounter in Alameda, California, at the naval station there, which is one of the military facilities that's going to be closed in the base closings. And I talked to this man who

had been an enlisted person in the Navy for 19 years, raised a family as a Navy enlisted person. He said, "Look, I hope I can stay. But," he said, "I'll tell you one thing. I just tried to buy a personal computer for our operations." And he said, "Thank the Lord we had some sort of waiver, because," he said, "under the rules and regulations, I was going to have to spend $4,500 on a computer that had half of the capacity that I got for $2,200 at the local store where people buy their computers." And he said, "You know, if you're going to ask people like me to leave the armed services because we have to cut back the defense budget, people who are willing to serve and willing to put their lives on the line, it is wrong to do that and keep spending twice as much for computers with half the capacity." The American people know this.

I think there are a lot of reasons why this happens over time. Number one, Government rule writers never made a distinction between a very specialized product that was made only for the Government, like a bomber, for example, and insect repellant. You have to have rules for both. Number two, the distribution system in America has changed dramatically so that ordinary Americans can now access economies of scale because of discount distribution centers for items small- and medium-sized. That was not true 10 years ago. Number three, there's no way rulemaking can keep up with technology cycles. The Vice President mentioned that as it relates to computers.

And finally—and this is the most important thing of all, I think, because this pervades everything we're trying to do—we spend too much time in Government, in my judgment, trying to keep bad things from happening with rules and regulations that eventually prohibit sensible public employees from making good things happen. If you spend all your time trying to keep something bad from happening—*[applause]*— now, I want to make it clear what we're talking about here. I'm not talking about a system with no accountability. I'm not talking about what happens when we change all the financial rules affecting S&L's and then had no accountability, so we got what was predictable. There was a middle ground. We didn't have to overregulate them to death. We don't want to overlearn the lessons of that. We're not talking about what happened in the scandals in the Housing and Urban Development Department where there was no oversight and accountability of what was actually being done, but that is different from trying to micromanage and superregulate every decision that you and every other public employee makes before he or she makes it.

And one of the things that I hope very much that the Vice President and I will be able to communicate through the national media to the American people is that we're going to have to give our public employees some more elbow room to make sensible decisions to save people money and yet hold them accountable so that if errors are made, they're pointed out; if somebody does something dishonest, it's found out. But we are now paying far more for the system of protecting ourselves from things than we ever would by the occasional mistake that will be made by an honest, creative public employee.

There are all kinds of accountability systems that can be built in out there that still don't strangle people when they go to work every day. That is what we are committed to. I think it will make it more fun to work for the Federal Government. I think it will be more exciting for people to get up and go to work every day knowing that they have the capacity to treat the dollars within their control, given to them by hardworking taxpayers, the same way the taxpayers would their own money in their own purchases in their own homes and businesses. That is our objective, and we are determined to achieve it.

The other thing I want to say to you is that this rulemaking problem is not just a problem in procurement. For example, you know that diabetics can have trouble with circulation and sometimes that can result in an amputation of the limb. It's shocking, but a veteran with diabetes in some cases can't qualify for a special shoe that would help the circulation and maybe even save his foot from an amputation, but he would qualify for an artificial limb and, by the way, the cost of the surgery. Now, which costs more? What makes more sense? Nobody ever did this on purpose. But the failure to analyze this, the fact that our Government has basically been unexamined for so long, has led to thousands and thousands of examples which cannot

be defended. We just want to make sense out of this. We want to modernize this system so that you can take advantage of the best products, the best technology, the best pricing. We want you to be able to decide to buy Off so you won't go buggy when you need insect repellant. [*Laughter*]

I also want to say that I'm very grateful to those of you who helped us get this far, and I'd like to ask you to help us one more step. In the appropriate way, Mr. Johnson will be testifying before committees of Congress. But I think, as citizens, anything any of you can do, just write and say, "Look, this is our life. We know how this works. And we want to change it. And we can be trusted to make a lot of these decisions. And there are also easily establishable accountability systems so that if we make a mistake it can be corrected."

When I was in the campaign last year, I often quoted a line my wife read to me from a psychology book, which is that insanity was doing the same thing over and over and over again and expecting a different result. [*Laughter*] Well, we're trying to stop doing the same thing over and over again. We believe we can do better by our people. We believe we can do better by our public employees. Our responsibility, I know, is to take the knowledge that you have given to the Vice President and to the National Performance Review and change the way Government works. In the process, change the way we spend the taxpayers' money and change the way we impact on people.

I will end where I began. The central tenet of every democracy in the end is trust. It's trust. When people elect Members of Congress and Presidents and empower them to establish institutions like the GSA, what they are basically saying is, "There is no way in the world I can do all this for myself, and I certainly can't make all these decisions. So just for the privilege of having a check at election time, I trust you to make these decisions in the meanwhile."

That's what this is all about. And I've said more and more, we have all kinds of deficits in our country. We've got a budget deficit; we've got an investment deficit; we have a performance deficit, and that has led to a trust deficit. The profound sense of alienation so many people feel in our country has got to be healed, because we've got to do a lot of things to get America into the 21st century, to restore a sense of opportunity, to be able to create jobs, and to be able to support incomes again that justify the hard work people do. And that no society will be able to do it unless there is a real partnership between Government and people in their private lives. And a partnership, whether it's a marriage, a business, or a Government-private partnership, requires trust.

So in the end, this is about more than dollars, it's about more than the pain of filling out those forms. It's even about more than making you happier and more productive on the job. It is about whether together we can restore the trust of the American people in their Government so that we can move on to these large tasks that we have to embrace to make the changes that are going on in the world friendly rather than dangerous for the American people.

I do not think you can underestimate the importance of the work that you and I are engaged in. Because if we can reestablish that trust, we can regenerate opportunity, we can restore a sense of community in this country, we can make other people willing to take responsibility for their own actions because we are doing it, and we are setting an example. This is a big, big thing. We must do it together. And I thank you for your contribution to this important effort.

Thank you very much.

NOTE: The President spoke at approximately 9:30 a.m. at the GSA Franconia Distribution Center. In his remarks, he referred to Roger W. Johnson, Administrator, General Services Administration.

Exchange With Reporters Prior to a Meeting With Congressional Leaders
September 8, 1993

The President. Let me say, first of all, I'm delighted to have the Congressional leadership here today. And we're going to begin our conversations by talking about the reinventing Government initiative. The Vice President's going to give the leadership a briefing. And I'm very much looking forward to this new phase of the congressional session and of a bipartisan effort on a lot of issues. And I hope we will center it on this, because I think this effort can do as much as anything else to build the trust of the American people and what we're doing on a whole range of other issues.

Q. Mr. President, on health care, some of the people who have briefed, Democrats and Republicans, believe that the Medicaid and Medicare cuts are too large, too politically difficult, and too nonspecific. Can you reassure them?

The President. At the appropriate time.

Q. There is some concern, sir——

Q. What about the chance that the health care, though—do you think that you can handle

all of these things, reinvent Government, trade?

The President. Absolutely. I don't think we have an option because I think the country can't walk away from this problem. But I think we should begin with this because this is something that will unify Americans and will unify the Congress and will prove that we can spend the money we have in appropriate ways and stop wasting so much of it.

Q. What will be the chances of bipartisanship on some of these issues, like health care?

The President. Good.

Q. Why so, given the experience you had in the first part of this administration?

The President. These are different issues with different constituencies, and they can be presented in a different way. I think the chances are really good.

NOTE: The exchange began at 11:16 a.m. in the Cabinet Room at the White House. A tape was not available for verification of the content of this exchange.

Remarks and an Exchange With Reporters Prior to Discussions With President Alija Izetbegovic of Bosnia
September 8, 1993

Q. Mr. President, are you going to ask President Clinton for air strikes?

President Izetbegovic. I have to thanks to Mr. President Clinton to receiving me, on behalf of me and of my colleagues here, and then thanks to the United States and to the peoples of the United States for the support, for the very beginning of the independence of the Bosnia-Herzegovina.·

And just now, I have thought to say that I have some issues to discuss with Mr. President, but one point is of essential importance for us. It's we are now hard working for the peace, to make a peace, to reach an agreement about peaceful solution in Bosnia-Herzegovina. But one point is very important: It's a problem of guarantee for the agreement. We will ask and request from the President Clinton that the United States participate in these guarantees, of course, between NATO forces and so on. But for us, it's essential, of essential importance that the United States participate in these guarantees.

President Clinton. I'd like to make a brief statement, in view of what President Izetbegovic has said. First of all, I want to welcome him again to the White House and to express, as I have so many times in the past, my admiration for the leadership that he has shown in this very difficult period. I want to encourage the peace process. The United States has done what it could to mobilize the forces of NATO to stop the attempt to overcome Sarajevo and the areas in the east and to push the Serbs and the Croats to make reasonable decisions in this peace process.

If they can reach a fair agreement, I would support, as I have said since February, the United States participating along with the other NATO nations in trying to help keep the peace. Of course in the United States, as all of you know, anything we do has to have the support of the Congress. I would seek the support of the Congress to do that. But I think these peo-

ple that the President represents—the Vice President was here, others have been very courageous and brave, and they're trying to now make a decent peace. And I think we ought to support that process, if there is an agreement that is not forced on them but one that is willingly entered into and is fair. And if we can get the Congress to support it, then I think we should participate.

Q. Would you agree to a date certain, Mr. President, by which the Serbs would have to withdraw from Sarajevo, free the city, after which you would use air strikes?

President Clinton. I believe that all that has to be part of the negotiating process. I don't think the United States can simply impose an element of it. I think they know what the conditions are that NATO has imposed and that we have certainly taken the lead in for avoiding air strikes. They know how to avoid the air strikes. And so far they've done that, and I presume they will continue to do that.

Q. Are you willing to go along with the President's request for a guarantee?

President Clinton. I've been willing to do that since February. But in order to do it, we have to have a fair peace that is willingly entered into by the parties. It has to be able to be enforced or, if you will, be guaranteed by a peacekeeping force from NATO, not the United Nations but NATO. And of course, for me to do it, the Congress would have to agree.

But I'm glad that the President has said what he has said, and I think the Congress and the American people need to know that the Bosnian government would look to the United States to be a part of any attempt to guarantee the peace.

NOTE: The President spoke at 5:25 p.m. in the Oval Office at the White House. A tape was not available for verification of the content of these remarks.

Statement on Senate Action on National Service Legislation
September 8, 1993

I want to thank and congratulate Members of the United States Senate today for passing a landmark piece of legislation, the National and Community Service Trust Act of 1993.

Many times I have talked about how national service will bring together Americans from a wide variety of backgrounds, expand their educational opportunity, and empower a new generation to take on our Nation's most pressing domestic needs. Thousands will spend a year or two serving their country and their communities, working as teachers, as health care workers, or on environmental projects, while helping to pay for school.

In the best sense of reinventing Government, the new Corporation for National and Community Service will emphasize decentralization in favor of empowering local initiatives that devise local solutions to local problems. It will be bold and it will be entrepreneurial in its quest for excellent programs and quality participants. Its business plan will be an unwavering mandate to get things done in our communities and our country.

Today's Senate action is yet another opportunity for change for the American people. National service will be the American way to change America.

Statement by the Press Secretary on Democracy in South Africa
September 8, 1993

The President welcomes the historic decision in South Africa to establish a transitional executive council in anticipation of South Africa's first democratic election next April. He commends all those who achieved this important step along the road to a peaceful transition to democracy in South Africa and looks forward to the ratification of the agreement by South Africa's Parliament next week.

In separate phone calls this afternoon to State President F.W. de Klerk and African National Congress President Nelson Mandela, President Clinton congratulated the two leaders on the historic breakthrough and said, "The historic agreement on the transitional executive council paves the way for the transition to a multiracial, democratic South Africa. The United States will remain a partner in the process of building democracy and promoting economic development in South Africa." President Clinton indicated that the United States looks forward to announcing a number of new initiatives to support the smooth transition to democracy.

Nomination for Four Ambassadors
September 8, 1993

The President announced his intention today to nominate Alan John Blinken to be Ambassador to Belgium, Swanee Hunt to be Ambassador to the Republic of Austria, and William Lacy Swing to be Ambassador to the Republic of Haiti. In addition, the President announced that he has nominated Richard Wallace Teare to be Ambassador to the Republic of Papua

New Guinea, the Solomon Islands, and Vanuatu.

"These four individuals have all exhibited the level of accomplishment and excellence that Secretary Christopher and I have pledged that our Ambassadors would have," said the President. "I am very proud of these choices."

NOTE: Biographies of the nominees were made available by the Office of the Press Secretary.

Remarks on the Israeli-Palestinian Agreement and an Exchange With Reporters in Cleveland, Ohio
September 9, 1993

The President. I just got off the telephone with Prime Minister Rabin. I called him to congratulate him on the agreement that he has reached today.

When we first met, he told me that he was prepared to take risks for peace, and I told him that it was the responsibility of the United States to do everything we could to minimize those risks. And I reaffirmed that today. They have reached a general agreement, but the process of implementing it will be quite complicated. And we expect to be closely involved in the process all along the way. I am extremely happy that it has finally happened. I am very, very hopeful for the future. And this is a very brave and courageous thing that has been done.

Q. Will there be a signing ceremony Monday——

Q. Will the U.S.—with the PLO as part of this deal, Mr. President?

The President. Well, let me answer you in this way. Later today we will see what the statements of the parties are, and then I will have another formal statement later in the day. If the PLO's statement today meets the criteria we have repeatedly set down, renouncing terrorism, acknowledging Israel's right to exist, those things, then we will resume our dialog with them and then we'll go forward from there. And we'll have an announcement probably today, perhaps tomorrow, about what happens next with regard to this agreement.

Q. Will that constitute formal recognition of the PLO?

The President. I don't want to say any more today. Let's wait until their statement comes out. For the moment, for the next few hours let's savor the fact that they have made this agreement. As Prime Minister Rabin said, it's the first time in 100 years that the Israelis and the Palestinians have agreed on something fundamental and important.

Q. Why do you think the time was right now for such an agreement, sir?

The President. I think that there are many reasons. I think, frankly, the major leaders in Middle East, beginning with Prime Minister Rabin and Mr. Arafat, were at a point in their lives, their careers, their experiences, where for all kinds of reasons they thought the time had come. And I also want to compliment Foreign Minister Peres; I think he deserves a lot of credit.

I think the circumstances were propitious. I think most people thought they had exhausted their reasonable alternatives, and they didn't want to go on in this manner anymore. And I hope we can keep this process going.

But I want to remind you that there are a lot of things that still have to be done to make this really happen, and the United States is committed to doing our share.

Q. Was the U.S. cut out of this deal, Mr. President?

The President. No. You know the facts, but let me briefly reiterate them. We sponsored, along with the Russians, the resumption of the talks. We put on the table a set of basic principles. About 70 percent of them were in the ultimate agreement that came out of the secret channel in Oslo. Our job was to keep these talks going in Washington, and the Secretary of State did a masterful job on two different occasions, once with the deportations and once with the conflict in the Bekaa Valley, when they were in danger of being derailed. And he worked hard. He went to the Middle East. We've worked hard to do that.

We were made aware in the most general terms of what was happening in Norway, but we didn't know a lot of the details, nor should we have known. I think this matter was so volatile and so difficult that it may be that the only way the final agreements could have been reached on the principles was in a secret and totally unknown channel. I think it gave both sides the freedom to reach out to one another.

So I think we did everything we could have, and a lot of our work is still to be done now that the agreement has been made and is public and has to be implemented. And we're prepared to do our part. But I'm pleased about this, and I hope that it means more good things in the future.

Q. Will the U.S. find the money, sir, to support this kind of agreement? Because after all, there's going to be a lot of aid needed.

The President. [*Inaudible*]—a lot of work, a lot of economic reconstruction that has to be done. I believe we'll do our part. I believe the Congress will be willing, and I think the American people will be willing. I think that our people will appreciate the absolutely historic significance of this. This is a huge development in the——

Q. Did you offer to sponsor a signing ceremony or have some kind of official recognition in Washington?

The President. We've been discussing that for the last several days, but I think that I should wait until there is a formal statement by the Israelis and the PLO later today, and then we'll have more to say about that.

Thank you.

Q. But you will——

The President. Later today.

NOTE: The President spoke at 10:50 a.m. upon arrival at the Park Corp. I–X Jet Center. In his remarks, he referred to Prime Minister Yitzhak Rabin and Foreign Minister Shimon Peres of Israel and Yasser Arafat, Palestine Liberation Organization Chairman.

Remarks to the Community in Cleveland
September 9, 1993

The President. Thank you so much. Thank you very much. It is great to be back in Cleveland. I've never had a bad day in Cleveland. [*Laughter*] But I felt so good about coming here today that I wore a necktie I bought in Cleveland the last time I was here.

I want to say first how very grateful I am to all of you for being here, how much I appreciate——

[*At this point, audience members interrupted the President's remarks.*]

The President. I can't hear. Can you hear me?

Audience members. Yes!

The President. Well, I can't hear them, and you can hear me, so that's good.

Let me say, first of all, I want to thank Senator Glenn, Congressman Stokes, and Congressman Hoke for coming down from Washington with us. I want to tell you that Senator Glenn especially is going to have a big role in passing these Government savings initiatives we proposed because he's the chairman of the Government Operations Committee. So if we want it to operate, he has to help us make it operate. And I'm grateful for his support. I thank the Congressmen for being here.

And Mayor White, I'm delighted to be back here and glad you had somebody out there screaming you were the best mayor. That's good. [*Laughter*] I also want to acknowledge attorney general Lee Fisher and your State treasurer, Mary Ellen Withrow, two good friends of our administration in this effort.

Let me say as briefly as I can what all this celebration is about from the point of view of the Federal Government. We give the State and local governments over $220 billion of your tax money every year. That means that you give it to us; we turn it around and give it to the States and the cities. If we make a mess of it, we waste a lot of your money; and if we don't do it right, the mayors and the Governors, the city councils, the county commissioners can't do what you hired them to do.

So a huge part of this National Performance Review, in attempting to make the Government work better at less cost, has to involve a better relationship between the National Government and the States and the local government. If we don't do it, then nothing we do in Washington will overcome the things that you don't have happen here at the local level.

There's a real slogan now going around, and I think a lot of slogans aren't any good, but this one is appropriate for our time. It is: Think globally, but act locally. What does that mean? It means my job is to tell you as President what the sweeping problems and challenges of our age are and to help us to deal with all this change that's happening, to help make the changes our friends and not our enemies, and to talk about them in terms of big things, like providing affordable health care or bringing the deficit down or opening new opportunities for jobs through trade or reinventing the Government. But it has to mean something to you here. It has to mean a job in that store or better services or better housing or safer streets. It has to mean something where you live.

I've said many times we've got a lot of deficits in this country. We've got a budget deficit and an investment deficit and a performance deficit in the Government. But you all know we've also got a trust deficit, where people no longer really believe that anything we do in Washington can change their lives for the better in Cleveland. And I believe that is clearly wrong.

These three Cabinet members who came here today have something in common with me and with the Mayor. Two of them, Secretary Peña, the Secretary of Transportation, and Secretary Cisneros, the Secretary of Housing and Urban Development, were mayors. The Secretary of Education, Secretary Riley, was the Governor of South Carolina. We believe we have to reinvent Government and reinvent education and make it work. And we think Washington has often gotten in the way instead of helping. So we are here to tell you what we intend to do to change the way the National Government works, so you can have more shopping centers like this, more safe streets, more housing projects, more people working. That's what this is all about.

Now, to do that we propose to do a number of things, but I'll just mention three of them. The first thing we want to do is to say, if a mayor like Mike White has got an idea like this, and they need a little money to make it go, they ought not to have to hire somebody to go through Washington's file after file after file of hundreds and hundreds of grants and figure out if we can somehow write some little grant proposal that goes through all these hoops and clears all these bureaucrats and gets the money. We spend a fortune, literally billions of dollars—to be exact, we spend $19 billion a year of your money administering the $220 billion of Federal grants. I don't know whether you think that's right or not; that strikes me as a waste of money.

So what are we going to do about it? The first thing we're going to do is to give the States, the counties, and the cities the right to design what we call bottoms-up initiatives. In other words, you decide what it is you need, tell us what you need, and if it's in a grant proposal that's anywhere under $10 million or over $10

million if you get approval for it, we will design something to give you the money you need instead of you having to figure out how to walk through the hoops of all the rules and regulations of the hundreds and hundreds of grants in the Federal Government. It will make a difference.

The second thing we're going to do is to do something that the States have been asking for for years, and that is to take 55 of these big grant programs and break them down into six big ones, so that we will have more flexibility. Instead of worrying about every little last detail, if you've got something you want to do in transportation, you ought to be able to get it from a transportation program. If you have something you want to do in the environment or highway safety or water quality or education or defense conversion, we want to help you do that without you having to figure out how to comply with all these rules and regulations. We think that you know what needs to be done to change the way your schools operate.

In the States that have lost lots of jobs from defense conversions, they know what they can do to retrain people to find new jobs, in what areas, better than people in Washington do. Why should they have to figure out how to comply with five or six or seven or eight different programs just to do it? So that's the second thing we're going to do.

The third thing we're going to do is to try to have the National Government operate on problems of people in Cleveland and Dallas and Seattle and Tampa and you name it, just the way this city government did, cooperating with the county government to figure out how to move all the property that made the shopping center and so many of the housing efforts and other things possible.

I am going today, as soon as I finish talking, to sit down here and sign a new order to my Cabinet to create a community enterprise board from the Cabinet, not a domestic policy group to tell people what to do but a community enterprise board. What is the practical impact of that? It will be for us to identify neighborhoods in trouble all across America. They will say what they want done. Then my Cabinet will sit down and work together and figure out how to do it, not how to tell them how to comply with our rules but how to do what people need done at the local level.

Now, we know that by doing this, just by

eliminating a lot of the rulemakings, a lot of the regulations, a lot of the paperwork, we will actually save billions of dollars over the next 5 years. But guess what? The States and the localities will actually get more money more quickly, with fewer strings attached, more able to solve the problems that the people have identified.

We are dealing globally with a big problem: Government's not working, and Government must be a partner with the private sector in order to revitalize our economy. That's the big problem. We are dealing locally. You get to decide how to solve the problem. As long as you don't waste the money and you're willing to be accountable for it, you decide. You define the future. And we'll have a lot more projects like this. That's the significance of what we're doing here today.

Let me say finally that we have a lot of work still to be done, but this administration is committed to changing America and to making America friendly to the changes that are going on in the world so that we can win in the face of change. Some days I wake up and I wish I could tell you, let me be President and I'll make it the way it was 10 or 20 or 30 years ago. You know better than to think anybody can do that. All these changes that are rifling through the world are going to happen whether we want them to or not. The test for us is whether we can win in the face of change instead of lose in the face of change, whether change will be our friend or our enemy.

And there can be no Government program that works to solve these problems unless you trust the Government, unless the Government performs, unless we repeal the problems of the past and face the future with confidence. And we have to be willing to change before we can ask any of you to change. So today in Cleveland, we are signaling a new era in the relationship with the National, the State, and the local governments to help make more projects like this possible. That's our commitment to change, and we're going to see it through.

Thank you and God bless you all.

NOTE: The President spoke at 12:33 p.m. at the Church Square Shopping Center.

Memorandum Establishing the President's Community Enterprise Board
September 9, 1993

Memorandum for the Vice President, the Secretary of the Treasury, the Attorney General, the Secretary of the Interior, the Secretary of Agriculture, the Secretary of Commerce, the Secretary of Labor, the Secretary of Health and Human Services, the Secretary of Housing and Urban Development, the Secretary of Transportation, the Secretary of Education, the Administrator of the Environmental Protection Agency, the Director of National Drug Control Policy, the Administrator of the Small Business Administration, the Assistant to the President for Domestic Policy, the Assistant to the President for Economic Policy, the Chair of the Council of Economic Advisers, the Director of the Office of Management and Budget

The Vice President and I strongly believe that the best way to serve distressed communities in urban and rural America is through a comprehensive, coordinated, and integrated approach that combines bottom-up initiatives and private sector innovations with responsive Federal-State support. Today, I direct the Federal agencies to work cooperatively to implement this approach in a way that reflects the principles of the Vice President's National Performance Review—i.e., meeting the needs of local communities through a performance-measured, customer-driven philosophy and a cross-agency approach. I also hereby establish the President's Community Enterprise Board ("Board") to advise and assist me in coordinating across agencies the various Federal programs available (or potentially available) to distressed communities and in developing further policies related to the successful implementation of our community empowerment efforts.

The Vice President has agreed to chair this Board, and the Assistant to the President for Domestic Policy and the Assistant to the President for Economic Policy have agreed to serve as Vice-Chairs of the Board. I request the following Administration officials to serve on this Board: the Secretary of the Treasury, the Attorney General, the Secretary of the Interior, the Secretary of Agriculture, the Secretary of Commerce, the Secretary of Labor, the Secretary of Health and Human Services, the Secretary of Housing and Urban Development, the Secretary of Transportation, the Secretary of Education, the Administrator of the Environmental Protection Agency, the Director of National Drug Control Policy, the Administrator of the Small Business Administration, the Director of the Office of Management and Budget, and the Chair of the Council of Economic Advisers.

The first task of the Board is to assist in the successful implementation of the Administration's empowerment zone legislation, Subchapter C of Title XIII of the Omnibus Budget Reconciliation Act of 1993, Public Law 103–66, "Empowerment Zones, Enterprise Communities, and Rural Development Investment Areas." This Act authorizes the Secretaries of HUD and Agriculture to designate certain localities as empowerment zones and enterprise communities, thus enabling them to receive certain Federal funds and other benefits from the Federal Government.

Other programs, old and new, are similarly beneficial to local communities. These programs, however, form an overly complex, categorical, unworkable, and ineffective response to the needs of distressed communities. I hereby direct the Board to review these programs in order to ascertain how we can make the entire Federal effort more responsive to the needs of distressed communities. In addition, with respect to the empowerment zones and enterprise communities, I direct the Secretary of the Treasury, the Attorney General, the Secretary of the Interior, the Secretary of Agriculture, the Secretary of Commerce, the Secretary of Labor, the Secretary of Health and Human Services, the Secretary of Housing and Urban Development, the Secretary of Transportation, the Secretary of Education, the Administrator of the Environmental Protection Agency, the Director of National Drug Control Policy, and the Administrator of the Small Business Administration to (1) identify, within 15 days of this directive, existing programs that further the goals and objectives set forth in this memorandum and the Act and (2) make available, to the extent permitted by law, funds from those programs for use in implementing the strategic plans of the

designated empowerment zones and community enterprises.

In order to advise and assist me regarding issues that relate to community development and empowerment, I request that each Board member—

(a) Provide me with recommendations, consistent with Section 13301 of the Omnibus Budget Reconciliation Act of 1993 ("OBRA" or "the Act"), on the criteria to be used for selection and designation of empowerment zones and enterprise communities, as set forth in Section 13301 of the Act;

(b) Identify additional legislative mandates that further the goals and objectives set forth in this memorandum and the Act and, where appropriate, develop for my consideration recommendations for further action;

(c) Identify legislative mandates that may be impeding State, local, and tribal governments from meeting the goals and objectives set forth in this memorandum and the Act, and, where appropriate, develop for my consideration recommendations for further action; and

(d) Consult with the Board regarding exemptions from regulatory mandates for which the member agency has jurisdiction and inform his or her decisions regarding any such exemptions with the recommendations of the Board.

In addition, I direct each of the agencies to cooperate fully with the Chair, the Vice-Chairs, and the Secretaries of HUD and Agriculture in assisting designated zones and enterprise communities in successfully implementing their strategic plans under Section 13301 of the Act. This interagency effort shall, among other things, coordinate Federal assistance and support within each empowerment zone and enterprise community.

In order to meet the goals and objectives set forth above, I also request the Secretary of HUD and the Secretary of Agriculture to consult with the Board regarding (1) the designation, under Section 13301 of the Act, of empowerment zones and enterprise communities and (2) possible revocation of designations, as set forth in Section 13301 of the Act.

Finally, I direct the Secretaries of HUD, Agriculture, and HHS (in consultation with the Board) to take, by November 1, 1993, the appropriate regulatory measures to ensure that the use of all Title XX grants awarded under the Act meets the criteria of Section 13761 of the Act, including, specifically, that portion of Subsection C that requires, among other things, localities to use Title XX grants (1) in accordance with the strategic plans approved by the Secretaries of HUD and Agriculture, (2) for activities that directly benefit the residents within the designated empowerment zones and enterprise communities, and (3) to promote economic independence for low-income families and individuals.

With the Board members' commitment to achieving community empowerment and to providing our local communities with a single Federal forum, we will be able to assist distressed communities and American families all across urban and rural America in obtaining economic self-sufficiency.

WILLIAM J. CLINTON

Message on the Observance of Rosh Hashana, 1993
September 9, 1993

Rosh Hashana is a time of reflection and hope—thoughtful reflection on the year just past and hope for a good year to come.

The days between Rosh Hashana and Yom Kippur are the most solemn of the Hebrew calendar. But in the midst of heartfelt repentance and prayer, it is the promise of life—the rich possibility of realizing our most compelling dreams—that inspires the soul and lifts the spirit.

The ancient customs that are handed down to each new generation in this season are re-minders of life's enduring sweetness and its perpetual renewal. The Jewish people celebrate Rosh Hashana above all as a time to rejoice in God for giving us life, for sustaining us, and for again enabling us to reach this season.

May this holiday season be filled with good health and happiness for you and your families, and may the year ahead be one of peace for the people of the United States, Israel, and all the world.

Best wishes for a wonderful New Year.

BILL CLINTON

Nomination for a United States Tax Court Judge
September 9, 1993

The President announced today that he has nominated Judge Herbert L. Chabot to continue as a judge on the United States Tax Court. Chabot has served on that court since 1978.

"Judge Chabot's service on the Tax Court for the past 15 years has been commendable," said the President. "I am pleased that he has accepted my nomination to remain on the bench."

NOTE: A biography of the nominee was made available by the Office of the Press Secretary.

Nomination for the Overseas Private Investment Corporation
September 9, 1993

The President named his choices today for four positions on the Board of Directors of the Overseas Private Investment Corporation, U.S. International Development Cooperation Agency, announcing that he has nominated Gordon Giffin to serve on that Board and that he intends to nominate John Chrystal, George J. Kourpias, and Lottie Shackelford.

"These nominations will strengthen this important foreign assistance Agency," said the President. "I look to these four individuals to provide leadership in helping American busi-

nesses compete more effectively overseas."

NOTE: Biographies of the nominees were made available by the Office of the Press Secretary.

Exchange With Reporters Prior to a Meeting With Congressional Leaders
September 10, 1993

Israeli-Palestinian Declaration

Q. Mr. President, are you going to invite Arafat and Rabin to the ceremonies on Monday?

The President. The parties will decide, as they've made all the other decisions, who will come to the ceremony. Whatever their decision is is fine with me.

Q. Can you give us an idea of what the United States is prepared to do to help this agreement work?

The President. I'll be talking a little more about that later, and I'll have a statement as soon as this meeting is over. I want to talk to the Members here about it first.

Q. Well, can you give us an idea of what this meeting is all about?

The President. Well, we're going to brief them on—the Secretary of State and I are—about, obviously, our strong support for the agreement, what America's responsibilities will be, what our allies and friends around the world are interested in doing about it, and where we go from here.

NOTE: The exchange began at 9:18 a.m. in the State Dining Room at the White House. A tape was not available for verification of the content of this exchange.

Remarks on the Israeli-Palestinian Declaration of Principles and an Exchange With Reporters
September 10, 1993

The President. Ladies and gentlemen, today marks a shining moment of hope for the people of the Middle East and, indeed, of the entire world. The Israelis and the Palestinians have now agreed upon a declaration of principles on interim self-government that opens the door to a comprehensive and lasting settlement.

This declaration represents an historic and honorable compromise between two peoples who have been locked in a bloody struggle for almost a century. Too many have suffered for too long. The agreement is a bold breakthrough. The Palestinian Liberation Organization openly and unequivocally has renounced the use of violence and has pledged to live in peace with Israel. Israel, in turn, has announced its recognition of the PLO.

I want to express my congratulations and praise for the courage and the vision displayed by the Israeli and Palestinian leadership and for

the crucially helpful role played by Norway.

For too long the history of the Middle East has been defined in terms of violence and bloodshed. Today marks the dawning of a new era. Now there is an opportunity to define the future of the Middle East in terms of reconciliation and coexistence and the opportunities that children growing up there will have whether they are Israeli or Palestinian.

I want to express the full support of the United States for this dramatic and promising step. For more than a quarter of a century our Nation has been directly engaged in efforts to resolve the Middle East conflict. We have done so because it reflects our finest values and our deepest interests, our interests in a stable Middle East where Israelis and Arabs can live together in harmony and develop the potential of their region, which is tremendous. From Camp David to Madrid to the signing ceremony that will take place at the White House on Monday, administration after administration has facilitated this difficult but essential quest. From my first day in office, Secretary Christopher and I have made this a priority. We are resolved to continue this process to achieve a comprehensive Arab-Israeli resolution.

In 1990, the United States suspended the U.S.-PLO dialog begun 2 years earlier following an act of terrorism committed against Israel by a faction of the PLO. Yesterday Yasser Arafat wrote to Prime Minister Rabin, committing the PLO to accept Israel's right to exist in peace and security, to renounce terrorism, to take responsibility for the actions of its constituent groups, to discipline those elements who violate these new commitments, and to nullify key elements of the Palestinian covenant that denied Israel's right to exist. These PLO commitments justify a resumption of our dialog. As a result and in light of this week's events, I have decided to resume the dialog and the contacts between the United States and the PLO.

The path ahead will not be easy. These new understandings, impressive though they are, will not erase the fears and suspicions of the past. But now the Israelis and the Palestinians have laid the foundations of hope. The United States will continue to be a full and an active partner in the negotiations that lie ahead, to ensure that this promise of progress is fully realized.

All the peoples of the Middle East deserve the blessings of peace. I pledge to join them in our help and our support to achieve that objective. I look forward to joining with Russia, our cosponsor in the Middle East peace process, and with the people of the world in witnessing the historic signing on Monday.

I also want to say I am very grateful for the overwhelming support this agreement has generated among members of both parties in the United States Congress. I especially thank leaders in the Congress from both parties who have foreign policy responsibilities who have come to meet with me this morning in the White House, many of whom have stayed on for this statement.

This is a time for bipartisan support for this agreement and, indeed, a bipartisan effort to reassert and define America's role in a very new world. We were talking today in our meeting about how this period is not unlike the late 1940's, a time in which America was the first nation to recognize Israel, in which we formed the United Nations and other international institutions in an attempt to work toward the world which everyone hoped would follow from World War II.

Once again we must develop a strong philosophy and a practical set of institutions that can permit us to follow our values and our interests and to work for a more peaceful, a more humane, and a more democratic world. This is an enormous step toward that larger goal. And I think all Americans should be grateful for the opportunity that we have been presented to help to make this historic peace work.

Helen [Helen Thomas, United Press International].

Q. Mr. President, does the start of the dialog with the Palestinians also mean that you will recognize the Palestinians as Israel has?

The President. Well, it means that we're going to——

Q. I mean the Palestinian entity.

The President. I understand that. We expect to work with the Palestinians and the Israelis in implementing the agreement. And we expect the dialog to produce further and clearer expressions of our policy on that.

Andrea [Andrea Mitchell, NBC News].

Q. Mr. President, are there any circumstances under which Yasser Arafat might come to the ceremony? And if not, when would you expect that he might come to the United States and might meet with you or your representatives?

The President. Well, let me say in terms of the ceremony, the people who will be here representing the United States and Israel—I mean, excuse me, the PLO and Israel—are the people that the PLO and Israel decide will come. That is entirely up to them. We are a sponsor of the peace process, and we understand that we must play a major role in trying to ensure its success. And the Secretary of State worked very hard to keep it going at difficult moments along the way in the last few months. But the thing that made it work was: They got together and agreed; they made decisions for themselves, face to face, on matters that they could never have taken an intermediary suggestion on because they were so sweeping. I think that's the system that works.

So what I have said and what I communicated personally to Prime Minister Rabin is that they should decide who is going to show up and sign, and whoever they decide will be here is fine with us, and we will welcome them.

The gentleman from Norwegian Television. I think we ought to——

Q. Mr. President, could you please elaborate on the Norwegian mediating role in this process? And then, one more question: How and when were you informed about the secret process going on in Oslo?

The President. Well, we had been aware for some time. I don't remember the exact date, but we've known for quite a while about the discussions in Norway. But frankly, we didn't want to know much of the details because the people were talking to each other.

I will say again, I think that's what made this agreement possible. If they had tried to do some of the things they had done in public, I think the constituencies of both sides would have made it virtually impossible for the agreement to be made. And I think that the world is indebted to Norway for providing a genuine opportunity for face-to-face and totally private and honest and open consultations.

It was made possible, I think, by the fact that we were able to keep the formal process going here. Many of the ideas embraced by the parties directly were ones discussed here, but which could not be agreed to in a public forum. So I think the world owes Norway a great debt of gratitude, and I think the people of the Middle East do as well.

Brit [Brit Hume, ABC News].

Q. Mr. President, you spoke of the need for a strong philosophy to guide the United States and its friends in this new atmosphere. Can you give us a sense of what some of the touchstones, some of the essence of that strong philosophy in your view should be?

The President. Well, first of all, after the end of the cold war, we know from just a cursory reading of any morning newspaper that the end of danger and misery and difficulty and oppression has far from passed from the face of the Earth. The United States still has interests and values which compel us to support peace, the absence of oppression, the recognition of human rights both on an individual and a group basis and, wherever possible, democracy. And I believe that while we must work with our friends and neighbors and allies through multilateral organizations as much as possible, the leadership of the United States is still absolutely essential to bring many of these conflicts to a successful conclusion.

That does not answer all the specific details about any particular area, but it is clear to me that for the foreseeable future, we have a unique role which we must assume, and it is very much in our interests as well as consistent with our values to do it.

Rita [Rita Braver, CBS News].

Q. Mr. President, can you tell us what you might do to discourage radical elements that might try to sabotage this agreement?

The President. Well, I think I should answer that in more affirmative terms. What we're going to try to do is to generate as much support for this agreement as possible, not just in the United States and throughout the world but also in the Middle East, within the Arab States, within the Palestinian communities, within our friends in Israel. We believe that to the extent we can show leadership and work with others who are interested in supporting this—and I want to emphasize we've gotten clear expressions of interest and support for implementing this agreement from the Europeans, from the Japanese, from Norway and the other Scandinavian countries, from the Gulf countries, from many of the Arab States—to whatever extent we can show that this can work and can lead from here to a more comprehensive resolution of the other issues still rending the Middle East, I think that will tend to undermine the ability of any specific group to derail this process.

Press Secretary Myers. One more question.

Q. Can I follow on that?

The President. Yes.

Q. Will the United States support a U.N. force in the Gaza Strip if necessary, and specifically, what will the U.S. do to help ensure the security of Israel and the Palestinian entity?

The President. Well, that has to be worked out by the parties. There will plainly be some peace guarantees. Through what mechanism it's not clear. There were some after Camp David, and I would point out that they worked very, very well. Most people are probably not even aware of the longstanding presence of American forces in a multilateral context in the Middle East in the aftermath of Camp David because it did work so well. But no specific decisions have been made. That has to be worked out with the parties, and they'll bring a proposal to us, and we'll be working with them all along the way. And you will know it as it develops. But we've not made a specific decision, and it would be inappropriate for me to speculate about it now.

Thank you very much.

NOTE: The President spoke at 10:16 a.m. in the Rose Garden at the White House.

Remarks to the North Valley Job Training Partnership in Sunnyvale, California
September 10, 1993

Thank you very much, Mr. Vice President and Madam Mayor and ladies and gentlemen. It's a great pleasure for me to be here today. And we want to spend most of our time listening to you, but I'd like to take just a few minutes to explain what it is we're trying to do with this reinventing Government project and how it relates to the future of the California economy and the ability of this State to come back.

When I ran for President it was apparent to me that America had not done very well in dealing with all these terrific challenges and changes that are sweeping through our world. And you know from your own personal life when you're confronted with a change and a challenge, you basically have two options: You can kind of hunker down and deny it and pretend it's not there and hope it'll go away—and about one time in a hundred it will work out all right, and the other 99 times it's not a very satisfactory response—or you can take a deep breath and embrace the change and determine to make something good happen. And that's what we have to do as a country. We have to make change our friend again and not our enemy.

Of all the States in America, the State that's had the toughest time lately is California. Your unemployment rate's about 3 percent higher than the national average. Because you had 21 percent of the country's defense budget, you've taken the lion's share of the defense cuts, not only in base closings but costing even more jobs, I would argue, contract cutbacks, which have affected people in this part of the State in particular. And you've had a lot of other manufacturing job losses and other problems. And as a result of that, there have been other kinds of pressures forcing the society apart when we need to be coming together.

Now, I believe that in order to remedy that,

there are a number of things we have to do. We know we've got—the Vice President and I always talk about all the deficits we have— we know we've got a budget deficit, but if you know anybody who's out of work, you know we've also got an investment deficit. And the Government has a performance deficit, which means we've got a trust deficit with the people. That is, people want me to do things all the time, but they're not sure they trust the Federal Government to do it, whatever "it" is, because people have worried so long.

So what I would say to you is that if you just look at it from the point of view of California, there are certain policies we need to change if we're going to generate more jobs and bring people together. We know that. We have an economic program, for example, that gives people big capital gains incentives now to invest in new high-tech companies like those that have generated so many jobs here. We have some changes in our economic program which will encourage other kinds of investments that will create jobs here. We've got a new defense conversion program, and this is an amazing story, where we put out bids on about, oh, $475 million of matching funds for people who had ideas to convert from defense technologies or convert businesses to domestic technologies. We received 2,800 proposals of a total of $8.5 billion, and one-quarter of them came from California.

Now the interesting thing is, one-quarter of all the unemployed people in America today live in California. Right? What does that tell you? That says there's a big mismatch. You've got all these people with ideas and brains and new technologies and ways to create jobs who are trying to close that gap. So just in the last 24 hours we have reached agreement with the United States Congress to put another $300 million into this program, because the demand was so much greater than the supply. It's great.

Now, so there's the policy aspect. Then there's the whole idea about how we from the top down can cut through the bureaucracy. One of the things that I did when I became President was to decide I needed to put one of my Cabinet members in charge of devising a strategy for California. And I asked the Secretary of Commerce, Ron Brown, to do it. And now thankfully he's got a Deputy Secretary who is from Silicon Valley, which won't hurt him any in making good decisions.

And so we thought a lot about what can we do for California. For example, by the end of the month we're going to announce a new policy, that we probably would not have done this fast if it hadn't been for the demands of the people right here in Silicon Valley, to change some of the old cold war rules that keep a lot of our high-tech companies from selling products overseas to countries that used to be our enemies but aren't anymore. So we did that. But we found over and over again that even if we had good policies and even if we tried to go around our own bureaucracy, until we made a commitment to make this Government work better, which means do more, cost less— and both are important—we could never really serve you as we ought to.

And let me just mention that the one specific thing that I want to talk about—I have been just overwhelmed by the work that's been done here in Sunnyvale basically to continuously provide more services at lower cost, but I want to talk just a minute about this job training issue. You told me you'd been on the job for 2 years, and you explained how your company closed down and moved to another State. That is unfortunately going to become a more typical experience for people.

The average 18-year-old will now change jobs about eight times in a lifetime, which means job security does not necessarily mean having the same employer. What it means is having the ability to always get a job as good or better than the one you've got today, which means that we have to make a commitment to the lifetime education and training of everybody in our country. And people in our country have to make a commitment to be willing to have that lifetime education and training into their fifties, into their sixties, as long as they're in the work force, because nobody can repeal all of these sweeping changes that are going on.

We're either going to face them and try to make the most of them or hope they'll go away. And like I said, that only works about one in a hundred times.

Now, here's the problem: Your Federal Government is not organized to help you very well. The NOVA program works because it is not like the way the Federal Government set the job training program up. It works in spite of the fact that it gets Federal money, not because of it. I mean, that's what you need to know. It works in spite of the fact that it gets Federal money.

Here's how the job training program of your country is organized. There are 14 departments spending $24 billion a year on job training, which is a pretty good chunk of money, in 150 separate programs. Now, if you're unemployed and you need a new training program, you don't give a rip which one of those 150 programs you fit into. And a lot of people fall between the cracks. The Vice President uncovered this incredible story of a person who was working for a company and he lost the job that he had because of foreign trade, lower cost competition from overseas. So he took another job with the same company instead of just quitting, you know, and going on unemployment. And then he lost that job because the defense budget was cut. At the time, there was a program to retrain people who lost their jobs for foreign trade, but not to retrain people who lost their jobs because of defense cuts. So the poor guy was punished for going back to work by losing funds to get his training. That's crazy.

So what we're going to try to do through the Secretary of Labor—he'll say more about that later—is to merge the unemployment system and the job training system, determine immediately who's not likely to get that job back or one just like it, and give you access to all the training opportunities that the Federal Government is funding. It is crazy. You're paying for this out of your pocket. I mean, you're paying for $24 billion worth of training, and I'm sure that there's not a person here who could name 10, much less 150, of the separate training programs available. Am I right? Not only that, you shouldn't have to know that. It is irrelevant.

So the reason we came here is because this NOVA program is what we want to do all across the country. Yes, we want to make the Government cost less, but if it doesn't work better, you still don't get what you need. And the people who are training who work in this fine company that we just toured are examples of what we want to provide for the whole country.

And I thank you for spending a little time with us today. Thank you.

NOTE: The President spoke at 2:55 p.m. in the courtyard of the Sunnyvale Community Center. In his remarks, he referred to Mayor Patricia Castillo of Sunnyvale.

Message to the Senate Transmitting the Ecuador-United States Investment Treaty
September 10, 1993

To the Senate of the United States:

With a view to receiving the advice and consent of the Senate to ratification, I transmit herewith the Treaty Between the United States of America and the Republic of Ecuador Concerning the Encouragement and Reciprocal Protection of Investment, with Protocol and related exchange of letters, signed at Washington on August 27, 1993. Also transmitted for the information of the Senate is the report of the Department of State with respect to this Treaty.

This is the first bilateral investment treaty with an Andean Pact country, and the second such Treaty signed with a South American country. The Treaty is designed to protect U.S. investment and encourage private sector development in Ecuador, and support the economic reforms taking place there. The Treaty's approach to dispute settlement will serve as a model for negotiations with other Andean Pact countries.

The Treaty is fully consistent with U.S. policy toward international and domestic investment.

A specific tenet, reflected in this Treaty, is that U.S. investment abroad and foreign investment in the United States should receive fair, equitable, and nondiscriminatory treatment. Under this Treaty, the Parties also agree to international law standards for expropriation and compensation for expropriation, free transfers of funds associated with investments, freedom of investments from performance requirements, and the investor's freedom to choose to resolve disputes with the host government through international arbitration.

I recommend that the Senate consider this Treaty as soon as possible, and give its advice and consent to ratification of the Treaty, with Protocol and related exchange of letters, at an early date.

WILLIAM J. CLINTON

The White House,
September 10, 1993.

The President's Radio Address
September 11, 1993

Good morning. Today I'm in Houston with Vice President Gore. This week we've been talking with Americans in Ohio and California and Texas about our plan to reinvent Government, to make Government work better and cost less.

We're living in truly revolutionary times, with profound changes sweeping the entire world. On Monday, Israel and the PLO will come to the White House to sign a courageous and historic peace accord, the first step in replacing war

with peace and giving the children of the Middle East a chance to grow up to a normal life. Here at home, we're trying to face the future with confidence and to face the changes that have confronted us by owning up to our problems and seizing our opportunities.

We've sharply broken with the past of trickle-down economics and huge deficits by adopting an economic program that drives down the deficit, increases investment incentives to small businesses and high-tech businesses, and helps our people to move from welfare to work.

We seek other fundamental reforms, including a new trade agreement with Mexico with historic protections for labor rights and improvements in the environment. And we're putting the finishing touches on a health care reform proposal that will restore peace of mind and financial security to homes and to businesses all across America by providing health care that's always there at an affordable price.

In this world of dramatic change, one of the biggest obstacles to our changing is the machinery of Government itself. It's frankly been stuck in the past, wasting too much money, often ignoring the taxpayer, coping with outdated systems and archaic technology, and most of all, eroding the confidence of the American people that Government can make change work for them.

Reforming, indeed, reinventing Government is essential to make our economic, health care, and trade efforts succeed. For the last 6 months, Vice President Gore has been studying the problems in the Federal Government. His National Performance Review has found more than $100 billion in savings that we can claim through serious and lasting management reforms over the next 5 years, reforms that will at the same time make the services we provide to you, the taxpayer, our customers, more efficient and more effective.

Now, I want to ask the Vice President to tell you more about what he's found in this historic review.

Mr. Vice President.

[*At this point, the Vice President discussed the findings of the National Performance Review.*]

The President. And thank you, Mr. Vice President, for the excellent National Performance Review. It is important for all the reasons you've said and for this one: We need to earn the trust of the American people. Until we do that, it's going to be hard to move on these other problems, for the Government has to be a partner in many of the things the American people need to do. We not only have a budget deficit and an investment deficit, we've got a real performance deficit in this Government. And that's led to the trust deficit that you're doing so much to help us overcome.

I am determined that these changes will come about. Where Executive action is recommended to bring change, I will take that action. Where legislation is needed to bring change, I will work with the Congress, with members of both parties, to win that legislation. Those of us in the business of Government owe the American people no less than making it the best it can be. Make no mistake about it, we've got a lot of work ahead of us. But we're all going to win on this.

Again, I thank you, Mr. Vice President, and I believe the American people do too, for a job very well done.

Thanks for listening.

NOTE: The President spoke at 9:06 a.m. from Room 810 of the Wyndham Warwick Hotel in Houston, TX.

Remarks and a Question-and-Answer Session on the National Performance Review in Houston, Texas
September 11, 1993

The President. Thank you very much. Mr. Vice President, Governor Richards, Mayor Lanier, and my good friend Gary Marrow and all the rest of you who are here.

The first thing we decided to do was to reinvent common sense by coming to Houston and having a meeting in a building that wasn't air conditioned. [*Laughter*]

When I heard John Sharp—I want to brag

on ol' John Sharp—when I heard John Sharp saying that, you know, he had been involved in this program to promote humility in Texas and that we had ruined it by giving you so much credit, which is justly deserved, for what we're trying to do, I began to wonder if the cost benefit was worth it. And then I realized that there are some things that even a President can't do, and promoting humility among folks like John Sharp is one of them. [*Laughter*]

Let me tell you, I am very proud to be here today and deeply grateful to John, to Billy, to all the people who played a role in this, and also profoundly grateful to the people that I have known over the years in State and local government who have done what folks wanted them to do. You can go all over America, you know, and take some surveys among people, and they'll tell you: I trust my mayor; I trust the Governor; I trust them to solve this, that, or the other problem, in various places based on personal experiences.

As soon as Bob Lanier got in office, he told me what he was going to do with police officers. He did it, and the crime rate went down. That's what people want to see happen. We talked the other day about a program he's got to promote more housing here, not just for people that can afford nice houses but for low-income people who were working, and he'll get that done. And when that happens, people will feel good about it without regard to their incomes, to know that people who are trying to play by the rules have a decent place to go home to at night.

But this country has a big trust deficit in the National Government. And that is a huge problem, because we're living in a time of profound change, and the American people absolutely cannot meet the challenges of the future unless the National Government can take initiative, can be partners with the private sector and partners with State and local government and seize by the throat some of these things that have been bedeviling us for so long.

You heard the Mayor talk about how much money the City of Houston is going to save because we passed the deficit reduction program that's driven interest rates to their lowest level in 25 years. Millions of Americans have gone out and refinanced their homes at lower interest rates or at shorter mortgage terms because the deficit's going down.

We are going to be able to do all kinds of things we couldn't do otherwise. But all over the country we found widespread cynicism, when I was trying to pass that economic program, that the Federal Government could do anything right; people didn't believe the deficit was going down, even though the interest rates are dropping like a rock, that "I cannot believe the National Government will spend my money to bring the deficit down and to really invest

in long-term economic growth."

So what happens is, we're facing a time where we not only have a budget deficit and an investment deficit, but because of the performance deficit in the Federal Government, there is a huge trust deficit in the American people. And unless we can cure that, it's going to be very hard for us to face these other issues.

You know, I'll just say Texas is probably the only State in America right now where there's overwhelming public support for the trade agreement with Mexico and Canada, which I strongly support. But let me just give you an example. One of the problems we've got—that trade deal has two aspects that no other trade agreement's ever had. It's got a commitment on the part of both countries to dramatically increase their spending on environmental cleanup along the border, and it's got a commitment on the part of Mexico to raise their wages every time their economy goes up. Nobody has ever agreed to that in a trade agreement before. And it's a blip on the screen. Why? Because a lot of people in this country whose jobs are at risk do not trust the National Government to do anything right. So what Al Gore is trying to do here affects that.

We've got to fix the health care system in this country. Do you know that we are spending 35 percent to 40 percent more on health care than any nation in the world, and yet we're the only advanced country that leaves tens of millions of people uninsured? Do you know that we're spending about a dime on the dollar more in administrative costs for health care, blind paperwork, than any other major country? The only way it can get fixed is if we take initiative. But a lot of people say, "Oh, my God, can they be trusted to do anything right?" So what we have to do with this reinventing Government thing is not only save you money and give you better services but restore the trust of the American people that, together, through our elected officials, we can actually solve problems.

This is a big deal, and it goes way beyond just the dollars involved. I kind of backed into it when I was Governor, because we just started, just every 2 years to see if we could do it, we'd eliminate some government agency or department and see if anybody squealed, and no one ever did. It was amazing. We didn't eliminate the department of education or anything; we took a little something, but it was just interesting, just sort of an acid test to see if that ever happened.

Then, we were working with all of our businesses in the tough years of the eighties on quality management and improving productivity, and I realized after a while I was hypocritical, providing the services to the private sector if I didn't try to do that in the public sector. And one day, we found out we could give people their licenses that they ordered by mail in 3 days instead of 3 weeks. And we found out that the people that are on the public payroll badly wanted to do it. But there was nothing wrong with them except poor systems and poor management and a lot of political decisions that no one had ever thought through.

So we are doing this not to fill the trust deficit, and we are trying to do three things. And that's why I want to get back to the Texas report and why we wanted to come here today to wrap up this tour. When John Sharp issued that report, I got a copy of it in a hurry, and I sat down and read it. And I was exhilarated when I read it, and that was before I was a candidate for President, before I ever knew I'd be here doing this today, because it put together all the things I had been feeling as a Governor for a decade.

And so there is a way to save money, make people on the public payroll happier on the job, and improve the services you're giving to the taxpayers all at the same time. It can be done. And that's very important.

And I'm going to tell you one story, I'm going to announce what I'm going to do, and we're going to spend the rest of the time listening to you. The other day I went out to Alameda, California, near Oakland, where there's a big naval base that's about to be closed. It's a very traumatic time for them. California has 12 percent of the country's population, 21 percent of the military budget, taken a 40 percent almost of the cuts in the last round of the base closings. It's a very difficult time. And their unemployment rate is over 9.5 percent.

And I'm sitting there talking to—I had lunch on the aircraft carrier *Carl Vincent* with one admiral and four naval enlisted personnel, wonderful people. And the guy sitting to my right had been in the Navy for 19 years, raised his two children, had a wonderful life, and told me why he'd stayed in the Navy. And I started asking him about the Government procurement process. And his eyes started dancing, you know, because we were there to cut a base and to short-circuit a lot of military careers that we had to do.

And this guy says to me, he said, "Let me tell you something." He said, "if I had to go through the Government procurement process to get a computer we were supposed to buy last week, I'd wait 1½ or 2 years to spend $4,500 for a computer that has half the capacity that I could buy for $2,200 at the local computer discount store." And he said, "You know something, Mr. President, I understand this defense downsizing. You have got to do it. But we've still got to have a defense. And it is wrong to ask people like me who are prepared to give our lives for our country to get out of the service if you're going to keep wasting money like that. Clean that up; then if we have to go, we'll go."

Now, that is the kind of thing that is out there that is confronting us every day. So, I say to you, we wound up our week on reinventing Government in Texas because we owe you a debt of gratitude, and we are grateful to you. And we want you to know we're determined to do this.

Let me just say one other thing. People ask me all the time, "Well, what's the difference in this report and all these other reports? The Government's just full of reports at the national level that never got implemented." I'll tell you why. Because there was never a system that the President was behind to push the thing through. If the Governor of Texas had been against John Sharp's report, could it have passed? I doubt it. Will there be opposition in Congress? Of course there will be. But there will also be a lot of support, won't there, Gene? And if the people make their voices heard and we stay at it, we can do this.

Now, what I've tried to do is to determine what I can do by Executive order or directive and what I have to have the Congress' help on. And I'm going to do everything I can possibly do by Executive orders. So today, basically as a thank-you to Texas, I'm going to issue the first Executive orders here, and I want to tell you what they are.

The first order directs the Federal Government to do what successful businesses already do: Set customer service standards, and put the people that are paying the bills first. It tells the Agencies to go to their customers, analyze their needs, evaluate how well the Government meets the needs, and operate like a customer service center.

Now, the second order will respond to what you saw when we announced this report. Do you remember when the Vice President gave me the report, we had the two forklifts full of paper? Almost all those regulations were regulations of the Government regulating itself. They were intergovernmental regulations on personnel and things like that, costing you billions of dollars a year for things that happen just within the Government. Now, today, the Executive order I'm signing on that will make the Federal agencies cut those regulations on Government employees in half within 3 years.

Now, remember, these regulations don't guard things like the safety of our food or the quality of the air we breathe. They regulate the Federal Government in their walking-around time every day. We're going to cut them in half within 3 years, save a lot of money and a lot of folks. The Government employees can then spend less time worrying about rules and more time worrying about results.

And finally, I'm going to sign a directive today that tells everybody in my Cabinet that they have to take responsibility for making the personnel cut that I've outlined, and more than half of the personnel cut has to come from people who are basically in middle management, handing down rules and pushing up paperwork.

Today, the National Government, on the average, has one supervisor for every seven employees. There are some Government Agencies that have one supervisor for every four employees. And the directive I'm signing today directs the Federal Government agencies under the control of the President of the United States to slash that ratio, in effect, to cut in half the number of management for employees within the next couple of years. So we're going to go on average in the Government from one manager to seven employees to one to fifteen. I think we can do better than that. That'll be a good start, and that alone when it is done will account for more than half of the 252,000 personnel reduction we seek to achieve.

As we do these things, I hope you folks in Texas will take a lot of pride in the contribution you made. And I hope you will see that it will make it possible for us, then, to gain the confidence of the American people so that we can restore the economy, fix the health care system, expand trade, give opportunities to our people, and make people believe this country works again.

If we can do it, you can take a lot of credit for it. Thank you very much.

The Vice President. Ladies and gentlemen, we would now like to hear from you. And we call this approach a reverse town hall meeting because we want to ask questions about how you have done it here in Texas in the Texas Performance Review, other parts of the State government, the land office, and the city of Houston.

Let me ask a couple of questions here first. How many people here are from, or worked on, the Texas Performance Review? Could you raise your hands? All right. Very good. How many people here work in the land office? Raise your hands. How many people here work for other parts of State government? Could I see your hands? How many people here work for the city of Houston? Can I see your hands? Okay, all of you. There you go, Mayor.

The President. Good for you, Mayor. [*Laughter*]

[*At this point, a participant discussed the improved response time of the Houston police department and its impact on crime in the city.*]

The President. Thank you. Let me say, this is one message I hope goes out across the country today. Millions of Americans have given up on the ability of their law enforcement resources to get the crime rate down. You can walk lots of streets in lots of places. People don't think it'll ever happen. You can reduce crime if you have the resources and if you direct them properly.

And you heard the Mayor say, I'm trying to pass our crime bill which, in the crime bill alone, goes halfway toward the 100,000 more police officers on the street goal that I have set. But they also—the resources have to be properly deployed in every community in this country. When you do it, you can bring crime down. It is simply not true you can't do it. But you have to target the resources and have them. And I applaud you, and I thank you for that.

[*The Vice President and the participant discussed direct involvement of workers in increasing efficiency and identifying goals to be accomplished.*]

The President. Give her a hand. That was great.

[*A participant discussed how the Texas perform-ance reviews led to State and local cooperation in efforts to keep criminals off the streets and in jail without raising taxes.*]

The President. I'll bet, too—you must have done this—but I'll bet you that you have—if you calculate how much money the people save by reducing the crime rate 20 percent in Hous-ton, I'll bet it's a heck of a lot more than it costs you to hold the people.

Q. On just purely a cost basis, it costs us roughly $1,000 per major crime reduced here in the city. To put that in context, car theft costs $4,000 or $5,000; of course, murder and rape are just infinite, but $1,000 per major crime reduced is pretty much a bargain, I think, for the taxpayers.

The Vice President. Thank you. Could we hear from some of the employees of the Texas Per-formance Review? What lessons did you learn in going through your performance review work here in Texas that surprised you the most, and what do you think is the most important way to identify waste and inefficiency and cut it out? Anybody want to—there's one, there's a volun-teer back there.

[*A participant discussed Texas health and human services initiatives to centralize access to avail-able services.*]

The President. I'd like to ask you a question; really, two questions. First of all, I'd like to ask you—my belief is that this is one of the biggest problems in Government, trying to re-form the delivery of human services all over the country. And while the services are largely delivered at the State level or by private provid-ers, a lot of the money comes from the Federal level.

So I would like to ask you two questions: Number one is, what do you think the biggest obstacles to doing what you want to do are? And, number two, how much of a problem has the Federal Government been through its rules and regulations?

Q. There's probably other folks who could answer that better, Mr. President, but I think for Texas, let me give you an example. For our 2-year spending budget right now in health and human services, $13 billion out of $23 bil-lion is Federal money. We obviously have to keep on top of how we report to the Federal Government and how we use that money. I

think there are probably some—I noticed in the summary of your report, Mr. Vice President, that there's talk about empowering the employ-ees to make some decisions. There are some real boring kind of things that we have to get into in terms of cost accounting, in terms of how we account for the funds. And when we talk about one-stop connection, we're talking about collapsing funding sources, a lot of fund-ing sources.

If you can give us a little trust, a little flexibil-ity on how we account for those dollars, we'll account for them, but we may not be able to get down to each sticky pad in terms of which funding source it came from. We'll account for the money, we'll be able to provide the services, and I think we have some work going on in Texas which can provide you some examples of that.

So I guess in summary it would be, trust us and keep on keeping on, and I appreciate it.

[*The Vice President discussed a National Per-formance Review recommendation for a bottom-up grant consolidation program to allow more flexibility at the local level and promote Federal, State, and local cooperation toward agreed-upon goals. A participant then discussed a Harris County initiative to use prison labor to reclaim wetlands and suggested the creation of a Federal corrections conservation corps.*]

The President. Let me say before you sit down, first of all, we didn't really know who was going to stand up and what they were going to say, but I can't tell you how much I appre-ciate what you just said. The United States— I agree, by the way, with what Governor Rich-ards and the Mayor said. You've got to keep more people in prison that you know have a high propensity to commit crimes.

The flip side of that is that we now rank first in the world in the percentage of our peo-ple behind bars. And we know who people be-hind bars normally are, right? They're normally young. They're normally male. They're normally undereducated. More than half of them have an alcohol or drug abuse problem. And they're wildly unconnected basically to the institutions that hold us together and conform our behavior, whether it's church or family or work or edu-cation. And it's the most colossal waste of human potential that in the Federal and the State systems, most prisoners—not all, there are some that do really useful work and get training—but a phenomenal number of prisoners either do useless work that they can't make a living at when they get out and don't feel good about and don't learn anything from, or don't do anything at all. And if you're looking for something the taxpayers are already paying for, we're already out that money. And you have just said something of enormous importance, and I thank you, sir.

[*A participant praised a Texas initiative using magnetic strip cards for transferring AFDC and food stamp benefits to recipients. The Vice President concurred and cited a National Performance Review recommendation for electronic benefits transfer.*

A participant then discussed Texas initiatives for innovative use of natural gas. Another participant discussed a Casey Foundation grant for local, State, and Federal cooperation to expedite services to the community.]

The President. Thank you. Let me just say one thing to you. Because I try to follow the work of the Casey Foundation, I'm a little familiar with what you're doing. One of the most frustrating things to me as a public official is that I have been a Governor, now President, having oversight of programs that people are supposed to fit their needs to. It is absurd. You've got a lot of poor people in this country who are absolutely dying to get out and get some job training, go to work, get off welfare, you name it. If they've got troubled kids or three or four different problems, they're liable to have three to four different programs, three or four different caseworkers. I mean, you feel sometimes like you're a laboratory animal almost if you get help from the Federal Government because you've got so many different people that are on your case. It is absurd.

Now, you should have, if you're in trouble, somebody to help you. But there ought to be one person to help you. You shouldn't be up there dissecting people the way these programs do. It is awful. And I really hope you make

it and get it done. Thank you.

[*A participant discussed the need for a program for crime victims. Another participant asked about funding for education, and the Vice President discussed recommended reforms to education grant programs.*]

The President. Let me just say one other thing. I asked a couple of questions—he's told you, right? We're going to try to change the funding of Chapter 1, and if what you're saying is right, that you have an enormously high percentage of eligible people, your district and your school would benefit. But the problem is that this is—that's one of those things we have to pass through Congress. And when the dollars follow the child, that is, if a rich district that has poor kids—when that happens, then every Congressman gets a little of the money.

So I asked a couple of you what the biggest obstacle to implementing your changes are. We need your support when we come up here and we present these legislative packages. And we're trying to figure out now how—we want as few bills as we can in Congress. But we really need your support to ask the Members of Congress to do this in the national interest, to make some of these changes so that we can do this. I need your help to do that. People in Washington need to think the American people want this. They don't need to think it's Bill Clinton and Al Gore's deal; they need to think it's your deal. And if they think it's your deal, then we can pass it.

NOTE: The President spoke at 10:39 a.m. at the Texas Surplus Property Agency. In his remarks, he referred to Mayor Bob Lanier of Houston; Gary Marrow, Texas land commissioner; John Sharp, Texas State comptroller; Billy Hamilton, Texas deputy comptroller and National Performance Review Deputy Director; and Representative Gene Green. Following his remarks, the President signed the Executive orders and the memorandum, which are listed in Appendix D at the end of this volume.

Appointment for the White House Conference on Small Business Commission
September 12, 1993

The President today appointed 11 members to the White House Conference on Small Business Commission and designated New York businessman Alan Patricof to be the Commission's Chair. The Commission is responsible for developing recommendations for Executive and legislative action to encourage the economic viability of small business and for convening the 1994 White House Conference on Small Business.

"I am very proud to have put together this outstanding group of people to serve on this Commission," said the President. "I am committed to expanding opportunities for small business and look forward to receiving this Commission's advice."

In addition to the Chairman, the members of the Commission are: Merle Catherine Chambers; Rudolph I. Estrada; Clark Jones; Mary Francis Kelly; Peggy Zone Fisher; Larry Shaw; C. Hough Friedman; Brian Lee Greenspun; Josie Natori; and Gary M. Woodbury.

NOTE: Biographies of the appointees were made available by the Office of the Press Secretary.

Remarks at the Signing Ceremony for the Israeli-Palestinian Declaration of Principles
September 13, 1993

The President. Prime Minister Rabin, Chairman Arafat, Foreign Minister Peres, Mr. Abbas, President Carter, President Bush, distinguished guests.

On behalf of the United States and Russia, cosponsors of the Middle East peace process, welcome to this great occasion of history and hope.

Today we bear witness to an extraordinary act in one of history's defining dramas, a drama that began in the time of our ancestors when the word went forth from a sliver of land between the river Jordan and the Mediterranean Sea. That hallowed piece of earth, that land of light and revelation is the home to the memories and dreams of Jews, Muslims, and Christians throughout the world.

As we all know, devotion to that land has also been the source of conflict and bloodshed for too long. Throughout this century, bitterness between the Palestinian and Jewish people has robbed the entire region of its resources, its potential, and too many of its sons and daughters. The land has been so drenched in warfare and hatred, the conflicting claims of history etched so deeply in the souls of the combatants there, that many believed the past would always have the upper hand.

Then, 14 years ago, the past began to give way when, at this place and upon this desk, three men of great vision signed their names to the Camp David accords. Today we honor the memories of Menachem Begin and Anwar Sadat, and we salute the wise leadership of President Jimmy Carter. Then, as now, we heard from those who said that conflict would come again soon. But the peace between Egypt and Israel has endured. Just so, this bold new venture today, this brave gamble that the future can be better than the past, must endure.

Two years ago in Madrid, another President took a major step on the road to peace by bringing Israel and all her neighbors together to launch direct negotiations. And today we also express our deep thanks for the skillful leadership of President George Bush.

Ever since Harry Truman first recognized Israel, every American President, Democrat and Republican, has worked for peace between Israel and her neighbors. Now the efforts of all who have labored before us bring us to this moment, a moment when we dare to pledge what for so long seemed difficult even to imagine: that the security of the Israeli people will be reconciled with the hopes of the Palestinian people and there will be more security and more hope for all.

Today the leadership of Israel and the Palestine Liberation Organization will sign a declaration of principles on interim Palestinian self-government. It charts a course toward reconciliation between two peoples who have both known the bitterness of exile. Now both pledge to put old sorrows and antagonisms behind them and to work for a shared future shaped by the values of the Torah, the Koran, and the Bible.

Let us salute also today the Government of Norway for its remarkable role in nurturing this agreement. But above all, let us today pay tribute to the leaders who had the courage to lead their people toward peace, away from the scars of battle, the wounds and the losses of the past, toward a brighter tomorrow. The world today thanks Prime Minister Rabin, Foreign Minister Peres, and Chairman Arafat. Their tenacity and vision has given us the promise of a new beginning.

What these leaders have done now must be done by others. Their achievement must be a catalyst for progress in all aspects of the peace process. And those of us who support them must be there to help in all aspects. For the peace must render the people who make it more secure. A peace of the brave is within our reach. Throughout the Middle East, there is a great yearning for the quiet miracle of a normal life.

We know a difficult road lies ahead. Every peace has its enemies, those who still prefer the easy habits of hatred to the hard labors of reconciliation. But Prime Minister Rabin has reminded us that you do not have to make peace with your friends. And the Koran teaches that if the enemy inclines toward peace, do thou also incline toward peace.

Therefore, let us resolve that this new mutual recognition will be a continuing process in which the parties transform the very way they see and understand each other. Let the skeptics of this peace recall what once existed among these people. There was a time when the traffic of ideas and commerce and pilgrims flowed uninterrupted among the cities of the Fertile Crescent. In Spain and the Middle East, Muslims and Jews once worked together to write brilliant chapters in the history of literature and science. All this can come to pass again.

Mr. Prime Minister, Mr. Chairman, I pledge the active support of the United States of America to the difficult work that lies ahead. The United States is committed to ensuring that the people who are affected by this agreement will be made more secure by it and to leading the world in marshaling the resources necessary to implement the difficult details that will make real the principles to which you commit yourselves today.

Together let us imagine what can be accomplished if all the energy and ability the Israelis and the Palestinians have invested into your struggle can now be channeled into cultivating the land and freshening the waters, into ending the boycotts and creating new industry, into building a land as bountiful and peaceful as it is holy. Above all, let us dedicate ourselves today to your region's next generation. In this entire assembly, no one is more important than the group of Israeli and Arab children who are seated here with us today.

Mr. Prime Minister, Mr. Chairman, this day belongs to you. And because of what you have done, tomorrow belongs to them. We must not leave them prey to the politics of extremism and despair, to those who would derail this process because they cannot overcome the fears and hatreds of the past. We must not betray their future. For too long, the young of the Middle East have been caught in a web of hatred not of their own making. For too long, they have been taught from the chronicles of war. Now we can give them the chance to know the season of peace. For them we must realize the prophecy of Isaiah that the cry of violence shall no more be heard in your land, nor wrack nor ruin within your borders. The children of Abraham, the descendants of Isaac and Ishmael, have embarked together on a bold journey. Together today, with all our hearts and all our souls, we bid them *shalom, salaam*, peace.

[*At this point, Foreign Minister Shimon Peres of Israel and Mahmoud Abbas, PLO Executive Committee member, made brief remarks. Following their remarks, Foreign Minister Peres and Mr. Abbas signed the declaration, and Secretary of State Warren Christopher and Foreign Minister Andrey Kozyrev of Russia signed as witnesses. Secretary Christopher and Foreign Minister Kozyrev then made remarks, followed by Prime Minister Yitzhak Rabin of Israel and Chairman Yasser Arafat of the PLO.*]

The President. We have been granted the great privilege of witnessing this victory for peace. Just as the Jewish people this week celebrate the dawn of a new year, let us all go from this place to celebrate the dawn of a new era, not only for the Middle East but for the entire world.

The sound we heard today, once again, as in ancient Jericho, was of trumpets toppling walls, the walls of anger and suspicion between Israeli and Palestinian, between Arab and Jew. This time, praise God, the trumpets herald not the destruction of that city but its new beginning.

Now let each of us here today return to our portion of that effort, uplifted by the spirit of the moment, refreshed in our hopes, and guided by the wisdom of the Almighty, who has brought us to this joyous day.

Go in peace. Go as peacemakers.

NOTE: The President spoke at 11:15 a.m. on the South Lawn at the White House.

Interview With the Arab News Media on the Middle East Peace Process
September 13, 1993

Q. Mr. President, thank you very much for this chance to speak to the Arab nation and Arabic television through NBC television on this very historic day. What would you like to say to the Arab world at the——

The President. I would like to say that I hope all the people in the Arab world will support this agreement. It is the beginning of a new relationship not only between Israel and the PLO and the Palestinians, but I hope it will lead to a comprehensive peace in the Middle East. And if that occurs, it would mean a whole range of presently unimaginable opportunities for the nations of the Middle East to work together and for the United States to work with all of them and for us to work together to help people in other parts of the world who are troubled and need our help.

Q. You pledged during the signing ceremony your full support for the peace process in the Middle East. How involved are you prepared to stay in this process?

The President. Extremely involved. After the ceremony I met for a few moments with Mr. Arafat. And then I came back here and had a quick meal with Prime Minister Rabin. And I told both of them clearly that I wanted to begin immediately to help to implement the peace accord. I think the United States can help them in the practical ways to shore up the political decisions that have to be made. I think that clearly we can assist in raising funds necessary to carry this out. I believe that we can continually reassure the people of Israel about their security. And they must feel more secure in this in order to go forward. And again, I hope that over the long run we can fulfill the objective of a comprehensive peace.

Q. Mr. President, you spoke recently to President Asad of Syria and King Hussein of Jordan. Are you hopeful of any breakthrough on the Jordanian, Syrian tracks?

The President. Of course. As a practical matter, I think it's easier now for a breakthrough on the Jordanian track. And I would hope that would come quickly. But I believe we'll have continued and very serious negotiations with Syria coming out of this process. And I believe that over time the parties will come together. We're going to have to focus now on getting this agreement implemented and on making sure that the parties affected by this agreement feel secure in it.

Q. Mr. President, any Palestinian entity that might come up as a result of this agreement is going to be pretty expensive to establish and even more expensive to maintain. How far can you help in the establishment of such an entity, and how do you plan to fund it?

The President. Well, first of all, there has to be an economic committee established under the agreement. And they will presumably be able to give us all some guidance about exactly how we should channel funds. But I have spoken and my Secretary of State has spoken with many nations. I think if you look at the foreign ministers who came today—the Foreign Minister of Japan came all the way from Tokyo to be here today. The Japanese, the Western Europeans, the Scandinavians, the Gulf states, all have expressed an interest in supporting this. King Fahd of Saudi Arabia told me in particular that he thought that the cause of peace required his nation to support this effort. And of course, the United States will support it.

Q. So you are satisfied with the support you got from leaders?

The President. So far, I'm eminently satisfied. But we have to work out the details, you know, how much money do we need when, for what purposes, who's going to give in what order. I mean, all these details still have to be worked out.

Q. Talking about King Fahd, how important is the Saudi role in the future of the peace process?

The President. Well, I think it's quite critical not only because the Saudis are willing to contribute financially but because they have been friends of the United States. They have been somewhat estranged from the PLO in the aftermath of the Gulf war. I think that their involvement is a part of the overall healing that I see coming out of this and what I hope will be an increasing solidarity among the Arab peoples.

Q. During these recent telephone calls with leaders of the Gulf, did you get any guarantees on lifting the embargo on Israel?

The President. No. But I didn't ask for them in this conversation. I told them I would be back to them on that. I have discussed it obviously with many of the leaders in the past. I do believe it is a logical step to take in the fairly near future. But I think the first and most important thing was to secure their support for this agreement.

Q. Arabs are asking, Mr. President, that the United States has been paying billions of dollars to Israel over the years; will you be willing to divert some of the aid to a new Palestinian entity?

The President. Well, I think that that's not the question. The real question is not whether we should divert from our support for Israel. Keep in mind, all the progress yet to be made depends upon the conviction of the people of Israel that they are secure and that making peace makes them more secure. So I don't think anyone in the Arab world should want me to do anything that makes the Israelis feel less secure. And I have no intention of doing that. But I do intend to support financially the development of an economic infrastructure for the

Palestinians and their self-rule. And I also intend to ask many other nations to contribute. And I think the United States clearly will be taking the initiative on that.

Q. There will be even more Israeli security concerns when it comes to a deal with the Syrians, that's if the Israelis decide to withdraw from the Golan Heights. What security guarantees are you prepared to give both sides?

The President. Well, first of all, let's get this agreement implemented. Let's start on that. And let's see what the Israelis and the Lebanese and the Syrians decide to do in their continuing discussions. I think we should focus on and savor this moment. I have made it clear to President Asad, Prime Minister Hairi, to Prime Minister Rabin, to everyone that I was committed to continuing this process until we achieve comprehensive peace. But I don't think we ought to jump the gun. We are now in this moment, and we ought to focus on it and sort out our responsibilities to implement this agreement.

Q. During your meetings with Mr. Arafat and Mr. Rabin, how genuine did you feel their quest for peace was today?

The President. Oh, I felt it was quite genuine. Just before we walked out—you know, they had never spoken before—and they looked at one another and immediately got down to business, no pleasantries. One said, you know, "We have a lot of work to do to make this work," the Prime Minister. And Chairman Arafat said, "I know, and I'm prepared to do my part." I mean, that was the immediate first exchange. And I thought they were both serious.

Q. And the famous handshake?

The President. I was pleased by it.

Q. Mr. President, will Secretary Christopher be back in the region to try to push some progress on the Syrian, Israeli track?

The President. Well, I expect Secretary Christopher to be in the region aggressively on a whole range of issues. He's already been there twice, and I expect him to be there quite a lot more.

Q. In view of some of the financial programs that you have in your national development programs, how is the U.S. administration going to cope with any extra financial burden that the peace process might bring about?

The President. Well, for us, I think, two things will make it possible for us to contribute. First, as a practical matter, we'd been given so many assurances by other nations that they wish to contribute that ours will probably be a minority contribution to an effort that while it will be sizable, will not be overwhelming and as much as the number of people living in Gaza and in the Jericho area, however it is ultimately defined, will not be so great.

And secondly, I think most Americans expect us to do this. They understand how important to the United States making this peace might be with all of its possible future implications. And I think the American people also understand that this is a genuinely historic opportunity, one that comes along at most once in a century and that we have to seize it.

Q. Mr. President, your Russian aid bill went through some difficulties to pass through the Congress. There are lots of laws that prohibit any American aid to the PLO. Is there any plan of revoking these laws?

The President. Well, our dialog has just begun. And presumably that's one of the things we'll be discussing. The Russian aid program I expect to be successfully concluded. But we have, because our budget deficit has gotten so large, we have now very strict laws about how we spend money and how we account for it. So we take great care before we spend any new money. But there's a lot of support for the Russian aid package, and I expect it to pass soon.

Q. How do you see the relationship between the peace process and the spread of fundamentalism in parts of the Middle East?

The President. And beyond.

Q. And beyond?

The President. I think if we carry through the peace process in good faith and we give the Palestinian people a chance to enjoy a normal life with a sense of place, that it will remove one of the great causes of fundamentalism and political extremism. Doubtless there will be other causes. And a lot of the groups are very well organized and very well financed and are furthering political objectives that have no longer anything to do with the grievances of the Palestinian people. But still, that was at the root of it all in the beginning. I also believe if we can do it, it will show the Islamic peoples of the world that the United States and all of the nations which help us, respect and honor the religious and cultural traditions of the Muslims wherever they are and are prepared to work with and support Islamic nations as long as they are willing to adhere to the international rules

governing human rights and peace and democracy.

Q. Mr. President, in your call with President Asad of Syria, you asked him for some more active role in the peace process. And you are negotiating and taking part in talks with the Syrians. Is it not a bit weird to still have Syria's name on the blacklist of states supporting terrorism?

The President. Well, the countries that get on that list are put on the list under American laws based on factual inquiries and evidence in certain particular cases. That is an issue which has to be resolved in the course of our common negotiations. I think the important thing is that as an American President I have had several exchanges of letters with President Asad, and the Secretary of State has been to see him. I had a very good, long conversation with him on the telephone. And we are talking. And that is important.

Q. Mr. President, in your interview yesterday with the New York Times and today in the Washington Post, there were some implications that you were blaming the Palestinians for throwing stones at the Israelis. We have the whole Arab world watching us now that would say, is it not at least a two-way street? Why don't you blame the Israelis for also punishing the Palestinians?

The President. Well, the context of the Washington Post story this morning was quite different. It was with reference to the specific incidents. You know, yesterday, we had Israeli soldiers killed, we had one driver killed, we had the attempted destruction of the bus.

Q. And three Palestinians.

The President. And so—that's right—but what I was asked about were those incidents, those particular instances. So I expect both sides to keep the commitments they made in this peace agreement. But one of the things that Mr. Arafat did, to his credit, was to renounce terrorism and to recognize the existence of the state of Israel and to say that he would take responsibility within the areas of self-governance for promoting the law. And that's all I said, was I thought he ought to do that.

Q. Isn't there a difference, Mr. President, between terrorism and freedom fighting? I mean, someone, a terrorist in someone's eyes might be a freedom fighter in the other's. What is the defined line that divides between these two?

The President. Well, I suppose it's like beauty,

it may be in the eyes of the beholder. But from the point of view of the United States, there are clear definitions of terrorism, and one of them clearly is the willful killing of innocent civilians who themselves are not in any way involved in military combat. That is what we seek to prevent.

Q. Mr. President, today has been an historical day with the signing of the agreement, with the very first interview by an American President on an Arabic television. Once again, we thank you very much for this interview and for this time, and we say congratulations on the agreement that's been signed today.

The President. I hope there will be more of these.

NOTE: The interview began at 3:30 p.m. in the Oval Office at the White House. A tape was not available for verification of the content of this interview.

Interview With the Israeli News Media on the Middle East Peace Process
September 13, 1993

Q. Mr. President, thank you for granting this interview to the Israeli television. I wanted to ask you first, with your permission, after having Mr. Arafat and Prime Minister Rabin shake, reluctantly, sort of, each other's hand, did you manage to get them to talk to each other?

The President. Yes, indeed. They talked a little bit before they came out and before they had shaken hands. I understand the many decades of events which have divided them and the awkwardness of this moment for both of them. And I understand, I think, why this is different from the agreement reached by Israel and Egypt at Camp David. This was an agreement that will require not just the concurrence of two governments but tens of thousands of people who will literally be living in close proximity to one another. So it was a very challenging moment.

But before we came out, Mr. Rabin and Mr. Arafat were alone in the Blue Room upstairs with me, and we walked down together when everyone else had left. And they had not spoken during the time of the reception. But they looked at each other really clearly, in the eye, for the first time, and the Prime Minister said, "You know we're going to have to work very hard to make this work." And Arafat said, "I know, and I am prepared to do my part." And they immediately exchanged about three sentences, right to business, no pleasantries but went right to business. But I thought they were both quite serious.

And you saw what happened on the stage. They did shake hands. A lot of people thought that would never happen. And I thought the fact that they did it and that they said what they did, each trying to speak to the people represented by the other, was an important gesture.

Q. How involved, Mr. President, do you plan to get in getting this accord off the ground?

The President. Very involved. I spent about 10 minutes with Mr. Arafat today after the occasion and made it clear to him that I was prepared to take a the lead in trying to organize the finances necessary to carry this through and to try to build the political support for it but that it was imperative that he honor the commitments made to Israel's security, to denouncing terrorism, to assuming responsibility within the areas of self-government for maintaining law and order.

And then I came over here to the Oval Office and went into my dining room and had lunch with the Prime Minister. And we had a good, long talk about what the next steps are. And I reaffirmed to him my determination to use the influence and the power of the United States and the resources of the United States to make sure that the people of Israel feel more secure, not less secure, by this agreement. And we talked a little about that, and we agreed that we would move immediately to begin to implement it.

Q. Were you disappointed with the contents of Mr. Arafat's speech, if I may ask, since many Israelis feel that he did not repeat those commitments that he was undertaking in writing. That is, to publicly denounce terrorism, say "no more violence," repeat what the late President

Sadat was saying here during the ceremony of Camp David: "No more war, no more bloodshed." He was probably the only speaker who didn't say it explicitly. It is not the way we wanted to hear him say that.

The President. Well, he did say the time had come for an end to war and bloodshed, but he did not reaffirm the specific commitments he made in writing. And yes, I think I would have liked the speech better had he done so. But when I listened to it in Arabic, it seemed to be delivered with great conviction and passion, more than the translation would imply. And I think you have to have a certain discount factor really for both of the speeches because of the ambivalence of the supporters of both men about this agreement. I mean, Arafat, after all, did not get a unanimous vote in his council for this agreement. You know, what he was trying to do is to reach out to the Israeli people to establish his good faith without further weakening his position.

And by the same token, I think the Prime Minister did a terrific job of reaffirming to the Israeli people how difficult this was for him, how strongly committed he is to the welfare of the people of Israel and why, that he is doing this because he thinks it's better for them.

I wasn't perhaps as disappointed as you were, because I thought it was so important that Arafat came and spoke directly to the people of Israel, reaffirmed in general the commitments he had made, looked at me and thanked the United States in ways that he—I mean, he has to know, because I've made it so clear publicly and privately, that the United States is committed to the security of Israel and that therefore if he wants us to help him, he's going to have to honor every last one of the commitments he made, which in private again today I asked him to do, and he reaffirmed that he would.

Q. Do you feel, Mr. President, that in view of the new circumstances in the Middle East, the American commitment to Israel's security will have to take a different shape, other forms?

The President. Well, I think we may have to do some more different things. We may wind up doing more in terms of economic development; we may wind up doing more in terms of shared technology. I think we've agreed already, the Prime Minister and I have, in our previous meeting that we want to do some more joint strategic thinking just to recognize the fact that military technology itself has changed the

dimensions of what Israel has to do to protect its security. But I would leave it with you this way: I have no intention of doing anything on my own which would in any way raise the question in the mind of any citizen of Israel that the United States is weakening in support for the security of Israel. The only way we can make this work is if every day more and more and more Israelis believe that they will be more secure if there is a just peace. That's why I went out of my way not to try to impose terms in these negotiations but only to create the conditions and the process and the environment within which agreement could be made and why I have constantly, since it was announced, reaffirmed my commitment to the security of Israel.

Q. In a conversation with Mr. Arafat last night, he was asking me—he doesn't need me as an intermediary, of course—to ask you on this interview today whether the United States would be willing to help the Palestinians create those institutions and establish this police force which——

The President. Absolutely. Absolutely, I would be willing to help him do that. And I think that is very much in Israel's interest. And my clear impression from the Prime Minister and from the Foreign Minister and from our contacts back and forth is that that's what you want me to do, that's what Israel wants me to do.

There are all kinds of practical questions left unanswered by this agreement. This agreement has very specific commitments on Israel's security and sovereignty and right to exist, on denouncing terrorism, on the Palestinians being willing to assume responsibility for conduct within the areas of self-governance. But it doesn't say how is a police force going to be set up, funded, and trained. How are elections going to actually be conducted? How will the candidates be able to get out and campaign? All these things have not been worked out. These are areas where the United States can genuinely help the process to work.

Q. Is there any change in the U.S. position on the establishment of a mini-Palestinian independent state at the end of the road?

The President. No. Our position on that has not changed. That is something that the parties are going to have to discuss and agree to. The United States is not going to change its position. That is something to be left to the parties to make and discuss.

Q. Mr. Arafat was speaking last night about his wish to have some form of confederacy with Jordan. Mr. President, will the United States support moves in this direction, linking up whatever Palestinian entity will finally emerge into—West Bank and Gaza with the national kingdom of Jordan?

The President. Well again, let me say the first step there is for Israel and Jordan to make peace and to reach an agreement. And I think a general agreement is forthcoming very soon. Then the three of them can get together, and they can discuss those things, and we'll see whether there is agreement among the parties to the peace process. If all the parties agreed, then the United States would be supportive. We want to facilitate the debate. We want ideas to remain on the table. But we don't want to impose a settlement of any kind. And so we'll just see what happens.

Q. The agreement between Israel and the Palestinians was reached through Norway, as an honest broker, mediator. We could not hope, I believe, to arrive at any conclusion of our negotiations with Syria without your administration playing a major role in bringing the two sides together. Do you think the time is right now to embark upon a similar effort in getting the Israelis and the Syrians together?

The President. I think we have to keep the talks going, but I think first we need to focus on implementing this agreement. And if you look at what happened in Norway—I mean, I think it was quite important. But if you go back and look at how it fit with the talks going on here in Washington, the question of the relationship of Israel to the PLO is such a volatile one that I doubt seriously that this agreement ever could have been made in Washington with anybody's involvement because of the intense publicity surrounding everything that happens here.

The thing that Norway did that was so important was to provide a representative of Israel and a representative of the PLO a chance to talk over an extended period of time in absolute secrecy so that they were free to say things to one another and to explore ideas without having to read about it in the paper the next day. And I think it was very important.

Our job during this time was to keep this process going, not to let the deportation crisis and the crisis occasioned by the raids in the Bekaa Valley or anything else derail this. And I was pleased with the agreement which came out which was very like the original principles the United States put on the table and that it included the Gaza-Jericho resolution which we were very pleased by.

Q. Finally, Mr. President, there are probably five million Israelis watching us now and five million Palestinians and who knows how many other Arabs across the border, whatever you would like to tell them on this day.

The President. I would like to tell them that this is a great day for the Israelis, for the Palestinians, for the Middle East, but it must be followed up. We must make good the promises of this agreement. And the United States has a terrific responsibility first to make Israel feel secure in making peace; second, to help the Palestinians to set up the mechanisms of self-government and of growth, of economic opportunity; and third, to keep the overall peace process going. And I intend to meet my responsibility. But in the end, whether it succeeds depends upon what is in the minds and the hearts of the people who live in the area.

I believe with all my heart that the time has come to change the relationships of the Middle East and that the future is so much brighter if we can abandon the polarization, the hatred, not just the war but the constant state of siege which prohibits and prevents both the Israelis and the Arabs from having anything resembling a normal life. I think the Middle East can bloom again. It can be a garden of the world if we can put aside these hatreds. And I'm going to do what I can to help.

NOTE: The interview began at 3:45 p.m. in the Oval Office at the White House. A tape was not available for verification of the content of this interview.

Remarks on the Israeli-Palestinian Declaration of Principles
September 13, 1993

Thank you very much. I never thought I would enter what may well be the first meeting of its kind in the history of our country—[*applause*]—that I would enter this meeting hearing our erudite Vice President quote Lao Tse. But today, I think we could solve all our problems with China, too, and everything else. All things are possible today.

I do want to acknowledge the presence, also, of a person here who has done a lot of wonderful work on this and the other foreign policy efforts we've made since I've been President, my National Security Adviser, Tony Lake.

I want to thank all of you for the work that so many of you have done, many of you for years and years and years, to help make this day come. I know well that there were a lot of people—I couldn't help when I was looking out at that crowd today, I thought there were so many people I wish I had the luxury of just standing up and mentioning, because I knew of the things which have been done to help this day come to pass. And I thank you all.

I know that most of what needs to be said specifically has already been said, so let me just say this: I am convinced that the United States must assume a very heavy role of responsibility to make this work, to implement this agreement, and that means I must ask you for two or three things, specifically. First of all, this is a difficult time for our country and with our own borders, and a lot of our own people are very insecure in a profoundly different way than the insecurities about which we just talked today.

We simply cannot afford to sort of fold up our tent and draw inward. We can't afford to do it in matters of trade, we can't afford to do it in matters of foreign policy, and we certainly can't afford to do it when we have been given a millennial opportunity and responsibility in the Middle East. And so I ask you, together and individually, to do what you can to help influence the Members of Congress whom you know, without regard to their party, to recommit themselves to the engagement and leadership of the United States in the Middle East.

I have been profoundly impressed by the broad, and deep bipartisan support in the Congress for this agreement. But everyone must understand that this agreement now has to be implemented. A lot of the complicated details are left. And frankly, even beyond the financial issues, the United States is perhaps in the best position of any country just to help with the mechanics of the election, with the mechanics of the law enforcement issue, with a whole series of complex, factual issues, which have to be worked through. And if we are leading, then we can send American who are Jewish or Arab to go there to work with this process. So the beginning is a sense that there is still the work to be done and a commitment to do it in the Congress.

Secondly, there is an enormous amount of work that can be done by private citizens. Many of you have been doing that and giving of your time and money for a very long time. Now, you'll be given the chance to do it in a different context, and I hope we will explore ways that this group can stay together, work together, and define common projects, because I think that that will help to shape the attitudes of the people who live in the region, what we do here as Americans together in specific terms as private citizens as well as through Government channels.

And finally, let me say that if there's one lesson I learned in my own life in politics here in America and one that I relearn every time I leave the White House and go out and talk to ordinary citizens in this very difficult time, it is that no public enterprise can flourish unless there is trust and security. Indeed, one of the reasons that I think the Vice President's work on the National Performance Review is so important—if I might just veer off and then come back to this subject—is that because our Government for so long has had not only a budget deficit and an investment deficit but a general performance deficit, there is this huge trust deficit in America, which makes it difficult for us to do what we ought to do. And when millions and millions of our people are profoundly insecure, it is even more difficult for them to restore their trust.

If that is true in America, how much more difficult must it be in the Middle East when the very issues of survival have been confronting people for a very long time now? On the other hand, unless the political leadership which made this agreement winds up stronger for doing it, we won't be able to succeed and move on to the next steps and ultimately conclude this whole process in a way that will really get the job done.

And so the last thing I want to ask you to do is, again, individually and collectively, to make as many personal contacts as you can with people in the region to tell them you support this, the United States is going to stand for peace and security and progress, and they should give their trust to this process. It is clear to me now that the major threat to our success going forward is not necessarily all those who wish to wreck the peace by continuing the killing of innocent noncombatants but the thin veneer of hope which might be pierced before it gets too deep and strong to be broken.

So we, you and I, we have a big responsibility to strengthen the support for the people who did this among their constituents, not to interfere in the internal affairs of Israel or the PLO but simply to make it clear that we are going to be there and that we believe in it, and that we believe it will enhance security and make trust more possible and make all the parties ultimately over the long run more reliable. I think this is a very big deal. Any many of you in some ways are in a unique position to manifest your belief in that.

So those are the things we must do. We have to have the support in the United States for our Government to take the lead in implementing the agreement. We have to have you and people like you, more of you, willing to undertake projects individually, as groups, and perhaps jointly as citizens, private citizens, that will reinforce what has been done. And we must begin immediately to make it absolutely clear that we support this decision and the people who made it for making it and that we will have more security for doing it.

If we can do those three things, then we can honor what happened here today, and we can validate the feelings we all had. And instead of just being a magic moment in history, it will truly be a turning point. That's what I think it is.

Thank you.

NOTE: The President spoke at 4:24 p.m. in Room 450 of the Old Executive Office Building.

Remarks at a Dinner Honoring Former Presidents
September 13, 1993

Ladies and gentlemen, may I have your attention please. The microphone's not on, so I'll just speak.

First, let me welcome you all to the White House and thank you all for being part of a great and promising day for the United States and for the Middle East and for the entire world.

I am so pleased that we could end this magnificent day with a gathering of many of the great American leaders who made this day possible. I want to salute all my predecessors who are here: President Ford, President Carter, President Bush, and especially acknowledge the contributions of President Carter at Camp David and President Bush in starting the peace talks in Madrid, President Ford for his wise leadership during a pivotal time in the history of the Middle East. I want to thank the Secretaries of State who worked tirelessly over many years for peace in the Middle East: Henry Kissinger, George Shultz, Cyrus Vance, James Baker, Larry Eagleburger, and of course, my own Secretary and good friend, Warren Christopher. I thank the Congress for the essential role that it plays in providing the guidance, the resources, and the bipartisan support. The Speaker is here and our majority leader, Dick Gephardt, the Senate and House whips, Senators Ford and Simpson, Congressmen Bonior and Gingrich. And I want to thank all the rest of you who are here who have made a contribution to the remarkable events that are unfolding today.

In this room we represent both political parties and, I think it's fair to say, a fairly wide array of views about public events. But we do have this in common: We agree that the United States must continue to exert its leadership if there is to be hope in this world of taking advantage of the end of the cold war, great hunger of people all over the world for democracy and freedom and peace and prosperity.

In the days ahead I ask you all to be willing to provide counsel to our administration and bipartisan support to sustain the role that the United States must pursue in the world. In the face of difficulties and dangers and in the pursuit of a better world, we must lead.

One of our efforts begins tomorrow when all the Presidents and former Secretaries of State who are here join me in the formal kickoff of our efforts to secure passage of the North American Free Trade Agreement. I know that will require great effort and bipartisanship, but I believe we will succeed because of the stakes for ourselves economically and politically in this hemisphere.

Tonight, however, let us for the moment rest on the laurels of the United States of America and toast peace and progress and the prosperity of the American people.

NOTE: The President spoke at 9:15 p.m. in the Blue Room at the White House.

Message to the Congress Transmitting the District of Columbia Budget and Supplemental Appropriations Request
September 13, 1993

To the Congress of the United States:

In accordance with the District of Columbia Self-Government and Governmental Reorganization Act, I am transmitting the District of Columbia Government's fiscal year 1994 budget amendment request and fiscal year 1993 supplemental budget amendment request.

The District of Columbia Government has submitted a request to decrease its fiscal year 1994 general fund spending authority by $36.968 million with a reduction of 832 FTE positions.

In addition, the District's fiscal year 1993 supplemental amendment request includes an increase of $7.367 million in general fund spending authority. The amendments are needed to address a projected operating deficit for fiscal year 1993 and fiscal year 1994 that was not addressed in the District's original budget submission pending congressional action.

WILLIAM J. CLINTON

The White House,
September 13, 1993.

Remarks at the Signing Ceremony for the Supplemental Agreements to the North American Free Trade Agreement
September 14, 1993

Thank you very much. Mr. Vice President, President Bush, President Carter, President Ford, ladies and gentlemen. I would like to acknowledge just a couple of other people who are in the audience because I think they deserve to be seen by America since you'll be seeing a lot more of them: my good friend Bill Daley from Chicago and former Congressman Bill Frenzel from Minnesota, who have agreed to lead this fight for our administration on a bipartisan basis. Would you please stand and be recognized.

It's an honor for me today to be joined by my predecessor, President Bush, who took the major steps in negotiating this North American Free Trade Agreement; President Jimmy Carter, whose vision of hemispheric development gives great energy to our efforts and has been a consistent theme of his for many, many years now; and President Ford, who has argued as fiercely for expanded trade and for this agreement as any American citizen and whose counsel I continue to value. These men, differing in party and outlook, join us today because we all recognize the important stakes for our Nation in this issue.

Yesterday we saw the sight of an old world dying, a new one being born in hope and a spirit of peace. Peoples who for a decade were caught in the cycle of war and frustration chose hope over fear and took a great risk to make the future better.

Today we turn to face the challenge of our own hemisphere, our own country, our own economic fortunes. In a few moments, I will sign three agreements that will complete our negotiations with Mexico and Canada to create a North American Free Trade Agreement. In the coming months I will submit this pact to Congress for approval. It will be a hard fight, and I expect to be there with all of you every step of the way. We will make our case as hard and as well as we can. And though the fight will be difficult, I deeply believe we will win. And I'd like to tell you why. First of all, because NAFTA means jobs, American jobs and good-paying American jobs. If I didn't believe that, I wouldn't support this agreement.

As President, it is my duty to speak frankly to the American people about the world in which we now live. Fifty years ago at the end of World War II, an unchallenged America was protected by the oceans and by our technological superiority and, very frankly, by the economic devastation of the people who could otherwise have been our competitors. We chose then to try to help rebuild our former enemies and to create a world of free trade supported by institutions which would facilitate it. As a result of that effort, global trade grew from $200 billion in 1950 to $800 billion in 1980. As a result, jobs were created and opportunity thrived all across the world. But make no mistake about it, our decision at the end of World War II to create a system of global, expanded, freer trade, and the supporting institutions, played a major role in creating the prosperity of the American middle class.

Ours is now an era in which commerce is global and in which money, management, technology are highly mobile. For the last 20 years, in all the wealthy countries of the world, because of changes in the global environment, because of the growth of technology, because of increasing competition, the middle class that was created and enlarged by the wise policies of

expanding trade at the end of World War II has been under severe stress. Most Americans are working harder for less. They are vulnerable to the fear tactics and the averseness to change that is behind much of the opposition to NAFTA.

But I want to say to my fellow Americans, when you live in a time of change the only way to recover your security and to broaden your horizons is to adapt to the change, to embrace it, to move forward. Nothing we do, nothing we do in this great capital can change the fact that factories or information can flash across the world, that people can move money around in the blink of an eye. Nothing can change the fact that technology can be adopted, once created, by people all across the world and then rapidly adapted in new and different ways by people who have a little different take on the way the technology works. For two decades, the winds of global competition have made these things clear to any American with eyes to see. The only way we can recover the fortunes of the middle class in this country so that people who work harder and smarter can at least prosper more, the only way we can pass on the American dream of the last 40 years to our children and their children for the next 40 is to adapt to the changes which are occurring.

In a fundamental sense, this debate about NAFTA is a debate about whether we will embrace these changes and create the jobs of tomorrow, or try to resist these changes, hoping we can preserve the economic structures of yesterday. I tell you, my fellow Americans, that if we learned anything from the collapse of the Berlin Wall and the fall of the governments in Eastern Europe, even a totally controlled society cannot resist the winds of change that economics and technology and information flow have imposed in this world of ours. That is not an option. Our only realistic option is to embrace these changes and create the jobs of tomorrow.

I believe that NAFTA will create 200,000 American jobs in the first 2 years of its effect. I believe if you look at the trends—and President Bush and I were talking about it this morning—starting about the time he was elected President, over one-third of our economic growth and in some years over one-half of our net new jobs came directly from exports. And on average, those exports-related jobs paid much higher than jobs that had no connection to exports. I believe that NAFTA will create a million jobs in the first 5 years of its impact. And I believe that that is many more jobs than will be lost, as inevitably some will be, as always happens when you open up the mix to a new range of competition.

NAFTA will generate these jobs by fostering an export boom to Mexico, by tearing down tariff walls which have been lowered quite a bit by the present administration of President Salinas but are still higher than Americas'. Already Mexican consumers buy more per capita from the United States than other consumers in other nations. Most Americans don't know this, but the average Mexican citizen, even though wages are much lower in Mexico, the average Mexican citizen is now spending $450 per year per person to buy American goods. That is more than the average Japanese, the average German, or the average Canadian buys; more than the average German, Swiss, and Italian citizens put together.

So when people say that this trade agreement is just about how to move jobs to Mexico so nobody can make a living, how do they explain the fact that Mexicans keep buying more products made in America every year? Go out and tell the American people that. Mexican citizens with lower incomes spend more money—real dollars, not percentage of their income—more money on American products than Germans, Japanese, Canadians. That is a fact. And there will be more if they have more money to spend. That is what expanding trade is all about.

In 1987, Mexico exported $5.7 billion more of products to the United States than they purchased from us. We had a trade deficit. Because of the free market, tariff-lowering policies of the Salinas government in Mexico, and because our people are becoming more export-oriented, that $5.7 billion trade deficit has been turned into a $5.4 billion trade surplus for the United States. It has created hundreds of thousands of jobs.

Even when you subtract the jobs that have moved into the *maquilladora* areas, America is a net job winner in what has happened in trade in the last 6 years. When Mexico boosts its consumption of petroleum products in Louisiana—where we're going tomorrow to talk about NAFTA—as it did by about 200 percent in that period, Louisiana refinery workers gained job security. When Mexico purchased industrial machinery and computer equipment made in Illi-

nois, that means more jobs. And guess what? In this same period, Mexico increased those purchases out of Illinois by 300 percent.

Forty-eight out of the 50 States have boosted exports to Mexico since 1987. That's one reason why 41 of our Nation's 50 Governors—some of them who are here today, and I thank them for their presence—support this trade pact. I can tell you, if you're a Governor, people won't leave you in office unless they think you get up every day trying to create more jobs. They think that's what your job is if you're a Governor. And the people who have the job of creating jobs for their State and working with their business community, working with their labor community, 41 out of the 50 have already embraced the NAFTA pact.

Many Americans are still worried that this agreement will move jobs south of the border because they've seen jobs move south of the border and because they know that there are still great differences in the wage rates. There have been 19 serious economic studies of NAFTA by liberals and conservatives alike; 18 of them have concluded that there will be no job loss. Businesses do not choose to locate based solely on wages. If they did, Haiti and Bangladesh would have the largest number of manufacturing jobs in the world. Businesses do choose to locate based on the skills and productivity of the work force, the attitude of the government, the roads and railroads to deliver products, the availability of a market close enough to make the transportation costs meaningful, the communications networks necessary to support the enterprise. That is our strength, and it will continue to be our strength. As it becomes Mexico's strength and they generate more jobs, they will have higher incomes, and they will buy more American products.

We can win this. This is not a time for defeatism. It is a time to look at an opportunity that is enormous. Moreover, there are specific provisions in this agreement that remove some of the current incentives for people to move their jobs just across our border. For example, today Mexican law requires United States automakers who want to sell cars to Mexicans to build them in Mexico. This year we will export only 1,000 cars to Mexico. Under NAFTA, the Big Three automakers expect to ship 60,000 cars to Mexico in the first year alone, and that is one reason why one of the automakers recently announced moving 1,000 jobs from Mexico back to Michigan.

In a few moments, I will sign side agreements to NAFTA that will make it harder than it is today for businesses to relocate solely because of very low wages or lax environmental rules. These side agreements will make a difference. The environmental agreement will, for the first time ever, apply trade sanctions against any of the countries that fails to enforce its own environmental laws. I might say to those who say that's a giving up of our sovereignty: For people who have been asking us to ask that of Mexico, how do we have the right to ask that of Mexico if we don't demand it of ourselves? It's nothing but fair.

This is the first time that there have ever been trade sanctions in the environmental law area. This ground-breaking agreement is one of the reasons why major environmental groups, ranging from the Audubon Society to the Natural Resources Defense Council, are supporting NAFTA.

The second agreement ensures that Mexico enforces its laws in areas that include worker health and safety, child labor, and the minimum wage. And I might say, this is the first time in the history of world trade agreements when any nation has ever been willing to tie its minimum wage to the growth in its own economy. What does that mean? It means that there will be an even more rapid closing of the gap between our two wage rates. And as the benefits of economic growth are spread in Mexico to working people, what will happen? They'll have more disposable income to buy more American products, and there will be less illegal immigration because more Mexicans will be able to support their children by staying home. This is a very important thing.

The third agreement answers one of the primary attacks on NAFTA that I heard for a year, which is, "Well, you can say all this, but something might happen that you can't foresee." Well, that's a good thing, otherwise we never would have had yesterday. I mean, I plead guilty to that. Something might happen that Carla Hills didn't foresee, or George Bush didn't foresee, or Mickey Kantor or Bill Clinton didn't foresee. That's true. Now, the third agreement protects our industries against unforeseen surges in exports from either one of our trading partners. And the flip side is also true. Economic change, as I said before, has often been cruel to the middle class, but we have to make change

their friend. NAFTA will help to do that.

This imposes also a new obligation on our Government, and I'm glad to see so many Members of Congress from both parties here today. We do have some obligations here. We have to make sure that our workers are the best prepared, the best trained in the world.

Without regard to NAFTA, we know now that the average 18-year-old American will change jobs eight times in a lifetime. The Secretary of Labor has told us, without regard to NAFTA, that over the last 10 years, for the first time, when people lose their jobs most of them do not go back to their old job; they go back to a different job. So that we no longer need an unemployment system, we need a reemployment system. And we have to create that. And that's our job. We have to tell American workers who will be dislocated because of this agreement, or because of things that will happen regardless of this agreement, that we are going to have a reemployment program for training in America. And we intend to do that.

Together, the efforts of two administrations now have created a trade agreement that moves beyond the traditional notions of free trade, seeking to ensure trade that pulls everybody up instead of dragging some down while others go up. We have put the environment at the center of this in future agreements. We have sought to avoid a debilitating contest for business where countries seek to lure them only by slashing wages or despoiling the environment.

This agreement will create jobs, thanks to trade with our neighbors. That's reason enough to support it. But I must close with a couple of other points. NAFTA is essential to our long-term ability to compete with Asia and Europe. Across the globe our competitors are consolidating, creating huge trading blocs. This pact will create a free trade zone stretching from the Arctic to the tropics, the largest in the world, a $6.5 billion market with 370 million people. It will help our businesses to be both more efficient and to better compete with our rivals in other parts of the world.

This is also essential to our leadership in this hemisphere and the world. Having won the cold war, we face the more subtle challenge of consolidating the victory of democracy and opportunity and freedom. For decades, we have preached and preached and preached greater democracy, greater respect for human rights, and more open markets to Latin America.

NAFTA finally offers them the opportunity to reap the benefits of this. Secretary Shalala represented me recently at the installation of the President of Paraguay. And she talked to Presidents from Colombia, from Chile, from Venezuela, from Uruguay, from Argentina, from Brazil. They all wanted to know, "Tell me, is NAFTA going to pass so we can become part of this great new market—more, hundreds of millions more of American consumers for our products."

It's no secret that there is division within both the Democratic and Republican Parties on this issue. That often happens in a time of great change. I just want to say something about this because it's very important. Are you guys resting? I'm going to sit down when you talk, so I'm glad you got to do it. [*Laughter*] I am very grateful to the Presidents for coming here, because there is division in the Democratic Party and there is division in the Republican Party. That's because this fight is not a traditional fight between Democrats and Republicans and liberals and conservatives. It is right at the center of the effort that we're making in America to define what the future is going to be about.

And so there are differences. But if you strip away the differences, it is clear that most of the people that oppose this pact are rooted in the fears and insecurities that are legitimately gripping the great American middle class. It is no use to deny that these fears and insecurities exist. It is no use denying that many of our people have lost in the battle for change. But it is a great mistake to think that NAFTA will make it worse. Every single solitary thing you hear people talk about, that they're worried about, can happen whether this trade agreement passes or not, and most of them will be made worse if it fails. And I can tell you it will be better if it passes.

So I say this to you: Are we going to compete and win, or are we going to withdraw? Are we going to face the future with confidence that we can create tomorrow's jobs, or are we going to try against all the evidence of the last 20 years to hold on to yesterday's? Are we going to take the plain evidence of the good faith of Mexico in opening their own markets and buying more of our products and creating more of our jobs, or are we going to give in to the fears of the worst-case scenario? Are we going to pretend that we don't have the first trade agreement in history dealing seriously with labor

standards, environmental standards, and cleverly and clearly taking account of unforeseen consequences, or are we going to say this is the best you can do and then some?

In an imperfect world, we have something which will enable us to go forward together and to create a future that is worthy of our children and grandchildren, worthy of the legacy of America, and consistent with what we did at the end of World War II. We have to do that again. We have to create a new world economy. And if we don't do it, we cannot then point the finger at Europe and Japan or anybody else and say, "Why don't you pass the GATT agreement; why don't you help to create a world economy?" If we walk away from this, we have no right to say to other countries in the world, "You're not fulfilling your world leadership; you're not being fair with us." This is our opportunity to provide an impetus to freedom and democracy in Latin America and create new jobs for America as well. It's a good deal, and we ought to take it.

Thank you.

[*At this point, the President signed the NAFTA supplemental agreements.*]

I'd like to ask now each of the Presidents in their turn to come forward and make a statement, beginning with President Bush and going to President Carter and President Ford. And I will play musical chairs with their seats. [*Laughter*]

[*At this point, President Bush, President Carter, and President Ford made remarks in support of NAFTA.*]

I wanted you to welcome Mrs. Carter. [*Applause*] Let me again express my profound thanks on behalf of all of us to President Bush, President Carter, and President Ford and close the meeting by invoking a phrase made famous last year by Vice President Gore: "It's time for us to go."

Thank you very much.

NOTE: The President spoke at 10:39 a.m. in the East Room at the White House. In his remarks, he referred to William M. Daley, NAFTA Task Force Chairman, and Bill Frenzel, Special Adviser to the President for NAFTA. The President was introduced by the Vice President.

On September 14, Press Secretary Dee Dee Myers issued the following statement:

Due to a staff error, the President incorrectly stated that NAFTA would create 1 million new jobs over 5 years.

The NAFTA will create 200,000 new export-related jobs in the first 2 years after it is passed.

By 1995, 900,000 U.S. jobs will be dependent on exports to Mexico. NAFTA will help secure those jobs, and trade with Mexico will help create even more jobs in future years.

Remarks and an Exchange With Reporters Prior to Discussions With Prime Minister Paul Keating of Australia
September 14, 1993

The President. Good morning. First, I want to welcome Prime Minister Keating here and his colleagues from Australia. We're looking forward to having a very good discussion, and we'll have some comments later, as you know.

I also want to applaud the announcement today of the common agenda established between Jordan and Israel, as well as the historic stop that Prime Minister Rabin and Foreign Minister Peres have made in Morocco, seeing King Hassan. I applaud King Hassan, and I hope that other Arab leaders will follow that example. And we will continue now rapidly to break down the barriers between Israel and other nations. And I'm looking forward to beginning work immediately on the United States part of implementing this agreement.

NAFTA

Q. Do you agree, sir, with President Carter and President Bush in their characterization of Ross Perot as a demagog?

The President. I'm going to try to pass NAFTA. And they're perfectly capable of speaking for themselves. I don't agree with Mr. Perot on this, and some of the assertions are not accurate that he has made. But, you know, I'm going to be out here. My job is to try to pass this. And I don't want to overly personalize it. I'm just trying to pass it. I think it's good for America; it's good for jobs.

Q. Are you going to work as hard for health care as you are for NAFTA, or vice versa?

The President. I'm going to try to pass them both. I'm going to try—you know, I work at

everything I do. I just get up in the morning and go to work. I think that's what I got hired to do.

[*At this point, one group of reporters left the room, and another group entered.*]

The President. As you know, we're going to have a joint statement afterward, and we'll answer your questions then. But I do want to welcome the Prime Minister and his colleagues here. I want to say to all of you how very important the relationship that the United States has with Australia is to me and to our administration. And I look forward to discussing a whole wide range of things, especially the upcoming APEC conference in Washington State in November. And I want to thank the Prime Minister publicly for his leadership in helping to put that together and helping to bring the leaders of the other countries there. We'll have more to say about it later, but I'm anxious to get on with the meeting.

Q. Will you get a chance to visit sometime, perhaps for the Olympics in Sydney?

The President. Why, I hope so. I've always wanted to come. I had one other chance to go to Australia, and I had to turn it down because of when I was a Governor. And I've been jealous of every friend of mine who ever went there. So I sure hope I can come.

NOTE: The President spoke at 12:48 p.m. in the Oval Office at the White House. A tape was not available for verification of the content of these remarks.

The President's News Conference With Prime Minister Paul Keating of Australia
September 14, 1993

The President. Good afternoon. It's a great pleasure for me to welcome the Prime Minister of Australia, Mr. Keating, to Washington and to have this opportunity to make a couple of statements and then answer some of your questions.

Despite that vast ocean which separates us, Australia and the United States share essential values and interests rooted in our frontier heritages, our shared commitment to democracy, our status as Pacific trading nations, and our efforts across the years to ensure and strengthen our common security. It's a pleasure for me to have the opportunity to personally reaffirm those bonds today.

The Prime Minister and I exchanged views on a wide variety of issues. I'd like to emphasize the importance of one in particular, the Uruguay round of multilateral trade negotiations. We agreed that strengthening GATT's trade rules is a top priority for both our countries. As a founder of the Cairns Group of free trading agricultural nations, Australia is working closely with us to bring the Uruguay round to conclusion this year. So that we can achieve agreement this year, the Prime Minister and I strongly urge the European Community not to reopen the Blair House accord on agricultural trade as has been suggested. We need to move forward, not backward, to complete the round and to give the world economy a much-needed boost.

We also discussed the importance of economic relations in the new Pacific community that both our nations are committed to help build. We discussed the building blocks of that community: bilateral alliances, such as the one we share; an active commitment to supporting the spread of democracy; and support for open and expanded markets. We discussed the important role of the Organization for the Asian Pacific Economic Cooperation, APEC. Both the U.S. and Australia are members. Both of us have been active proponents of regional trade liberalization. And I look very much forward to working with Prime Minister Keating to make the November APEC ministerial meeting and the leaders conference in Seattle, Washington, a big success.

Australia and the United States also share mutual security interests. Australia has been our ally in every major conflict of this century. Today we share an interest in bolstering the region's security and in supporting its movement toward democracy. I expressed my particular admiration for the crucial role Australia has played in fashioning and implementing the international effort to promote reconciliation in Cambodia. I told the Prime Minister that we look forward to many similar partnerships in the years ahead.

This meeting was to have occurred yesterday, but Prime Minister Keating and I agreed that we should delay it because of the signing of the Israeli-Palestinian peace agreement. That historic breakthrough reminds us that we live in a momentous time when the old walls of division are falling and new vistas are opening. Our success in seizing these opportunities will depend in large measure on how well the community of democracies can respond to work together towards shared goals. Today this meeting with the Prime Minister reaffirms that our two nations will continue to work together closely to turn the promise of this era into reality.

Mr. Prime Minister.

Prime Minister Keating. Thank you, Mr. President. Well, I'd like to say firsthand that our meeting was most worthwhile, from my point of view and Australia's point of view, for the quality of our discussions. And our close agreement on a wide range of issues I think demonstrates the vitality and the relevance of the Australia-U.S. relationship at a time of great change internationally. Let me say, I'm very favorably impressed by the vigor and imagination with which the President and his team are addressing the new challenges we now face in the world.

Australia is a country which puts great importance on its relationship with the United States. Our longstanding friendship which the President has just referred to is based on shared values of democracy and freedom. And as he remarked, we fought in five major conflicts together over the course of this century. And in the post-cold-war period, I'm happy to say that our alliance remains very strong, indeed. In commerce and diplomacy we do a great deal together.

I was impressed in our discussions today by the priority which now attaches to fundamental questions of international trade structures. I welcome the strong support that President Clinton has given to APEC as an organization for promoting trade and investment in the Asia-Pacific area. I congratulated him on his truly historic initiative of inviting other APEC leaders to join him at an informal meeting in Seattle this November. This will allow APEC leaders to discuss ways of moving towards an Asia-Pacific community which brings benefits of closer economic integration to all members. This step also recognizes the increased importance of the Asia Pacific in world affairs.

We agreed on the importance of achieving a successful and balanced outcome of the Uruguay round by the mid-December deadline. No other joint action by governments this year could do more to boost the prospects of world growth and jobs, both subjects which the President and I are intensely interested. We agreed that any move by the European Community to reopen the Blair House accord on agriculture seriously risks jeopardizing the whole Uruguay round. The Blair House accord already represents a minimum outcome acceptable to those countries seeking to establish fair rules of trade for agriculture.

Finally, I should like to thank the President for his gracious hospitality and to congratulate him on the leadership he is showing on the United States international and domestic agendas.

Mr. President, thank you very much for having us in the White House from Australia. And we appreciated the arrangements, particularly the difficulties of the—the opportunity presented by signing the Middle East accords and the arrangements today. It's been great to be here with you.

The President. Terry [Terence Hunt, Associated Press], I'd like to call on you first, and then if we could, I'd like to alternate between one question from an American journalist and one question from an Australian journalist. So we'll have to go on the honor system, although I think most of the Australians are here on the right. Okay, Terry, go ahead.

NAFTA

Q. Mr. President, you said today that you don't want to personalize the NAFTA fight, but I'd like to ask you about remarks made today in this room by Presidents Carter and Bush. They both spoke about demagoguery in NAFTA, and President Carter spoke about a demagog with unlimited financial resources, obviously Mr. Perot. Do you think that Mr. Perot is playing loose and fair with the facts?

The President. Well, I'm going to reiterate what I said before. I am for this agreement because I think it will create more jobs. I think anyone who wants to enter the debate should do so. I think we should be very careful that if we make an assertion, that we know that it has some factual basis. And if any of us make a mistake we ought to say so.

You know, my office has already put out a statement because I inadvertently made a factual error today, not a big one, but it was an error, and we corrected it. And I just think that the people of this country and of most of the wealthier countries in the world have seen such enormous pressure on the middle class—our folks have really been hurt—that they want this to be an open debate. But we don't need to prey on their fears, we need to really work through all the various arguments and the issues and the facts. And I'm going to do my best to do that, and I'll be glad to argue, debate, or discuss with anyone who has a different opinion. But I think, as President, I should take the position that I'm going to try to bring this country along with this and leave that other business to others to fight.

Someone from Australia. Yes?

Pacific Community and Human Rights

Q. Mr. Clinton, could you comment on Australian concerns that the U.S. push on human rights in countries such as China and Indonesia could threaten Asia-Pacific economic cooperation? Could Mr. Keating also comment on that? And Mr. President, could you also flesh out exactly what you want to see coming out of the leaders summit in Seattle in November?

The President. Let me mention, first of all, the United States does have a very strong position on human rights, and I think we should. I also think your government has a good position on human rights, which it has not been reluctant to express in dealing with other nations. But that has not undermined our relationships, commercial relationships and political relationships with countries that we think are making an honest effort to shoot straight with us and to work with us.

You mentioned Indonesia. I went out of my way to ask President Soeharto to come to Japan and meet with me when I was there, because he's the head of the nonaligned nations. Indonesia, I think, is one of the most underestimated countries in the world. Most people have no idea how big it is, that 180 million people live there, that it is a vast, enormous potential partner in a global economy. We have questions about the issues of East Timor, as you know, and I think you do, too—your country does, too. But we have had good contact with Indonesia.

With regard to China, the United States has, after all, an $18 billion trade deficit with China. It would be hard to say that we are not doing our part to aid the Chinese economic revival. We have very strong commercial relationships with them. But it is our responsibility in the world in which we live, I think, to try to restrain the proliferation of weapons of mass destruction, to try to stand up for human rights, and to try to engage the Chinese across a whole broad range of issues, so that we can't simply have a commerce-only relationship.

I am going to do what I can to build the Pacific community and not to undermine it, and that's what your Prime Minister spoke so eloquently about today.

I think you wanted him to comment on this, too.

Prime Minister Keating. Neither the United States nor Australia will ever compromise its shared sense of democracy, its commitment to human rights and the respect of human values. And we put them forthrightly wherever we see those values under threat or seeking to be compromised. And this is true in Australia's case with Indonesia. It's been true in respect of China, as has been the case with the United States. But I think it's true for me and I'm certain for the President that we see these issues as part of a total relationship where we seek to have an influence on these countries and where the influence may be diminished if the totality of the relationship only involves the human rights questions, and beyond that, that is on these other issues like proliferation and other issues and commercial questions, where the relationship must be seen in its totality.

Middle East

Q. Mr. President, a day after the historic sign- ing ceremony here on the South Lawn yesterday, the Israelis appear to be establishing a relationship with Morocco, a formal relationship, and there is this agreement between Israel and Jordan. What specifically are you doing now, to try to promote the establishment of formal diplomatic relations between Israel and other Arab nations, Saudi Arabia, Kuwait, good friends of the United States? And do you think that is in the cards in the immediate future?

The President. Well, let me first say that I am very, very pleased that Prime Minister Rabin and Foreign Minister Peres have been received by King Hassan in Morocco. When we learned of this development yesterday, and we talked about it in some detail—Prime Minister Rabin and I talked about it—I was very pleased, because I think that the King may have set an example, which I hope other Arab states will consider following now, to try to continue now to just establish dialog.

We are at this moment focusing on three or four aspects of what we can do to implement this relationship. One is, what about all the practical problems that are still out there? You know, elections have to be held. Economic endeavors have to be undertaken in the Gaza, and there are lots of things that just have to be done practically. So we have a team now looking at all these practical problems to see what can the United States do to facilitate this.

The second thing we're doing is looking at what we can do to try to organize an appropriate level of investment. And in that regard, we're looking primarily at maybe having a donors meeting and trying to bring in the interested European countries and Asian countries and Arab countries to talk about how we can put together the kind of package we ought to have. Yesterday I met with a couple of hundred American Jewish and Arab leaders from around the country, and I asked them to participate from the point of view and private sector and partnerships and helping to develop these areas so we could really move this relationship forward.

And then the third thing that we're going to do is to discuss on a political level what we should do to try to facilitate further political contacts. The announcement between Israel and Jordan today is very helpful. And I hope that will give further encouragement to other Arab countries.

Is there another—yes?

Agricultural Subsidies

Q. Mr. President, you made a very eloquent appeal for support for your NAFTA proposals today, asking for the middle class to understand what it could provide in jobs for your NAFTA initiative. Yet you're still providing massive subsidies, $90 billion a year, in the agricultural sector. When are we going to see some change in that? Because that is hurting free traders like Australia.

The President. I'm sorry, I didn't hear—change in what?

Q. Your agricultural subsidies, particularly the Export Enhancement Program.

The President. Well, perhaps the Prime Minister would like to comment on this, too, but what we are trying to do with the Export Enhancement Program is to have it run, if you will, only against or in competition with countries that have done things that we believe constitute unfair trade by governmental action. That is, we intend to do what we can to avoid using the program in ways that undermine Australia's interests. And we're going to work very hard on that because Australia basically is a free trading country in agriculture. And in a larger sense, if we could get a new GATT agreement that includes agriculture, that would be of enormous benefit to Australia, to the entire Cairns Group, and to the whole principle of reducing subsidies in agricultural trade and opening up more competition.

So I think if you will just watch the way that thing is applied, that program over the next year, you will see that we are going out of our way not to have it conflict with the trade targets and interests of Australia, which is a country that does practice what it preaches in terms of free trade and agriculture.

NAFTA

Q. Mr. President, what is your estimate now of how many jobs would be lost, net jobs lost, under the North American Free Trade Agreement? Can you better describe your proposal for reemployment? Is it job training? Are they subsidies? What kind of proposal——

The President. First of all, our administration is convinced that, net, more jobs will be gained than lost. If we didn't think that, we wouldn't be pushing it. But we know that some jobs will be lost. How many will be lost really depends upon things that are almost impossible to calculate. Let me just give you one example.

We know right now that certain agricultural sectors will be helped and others over a period of time will lose some of their tariff protections in America over a period of several years. We know right now that certain manufacturing sectors, particularly high-end manufacturing sectors—higher wage, more sophisticated manufacturing will be helped. Other manufacturing will be subject to more competition and fewer import limits.

What we don't know, and this is why it's hard to answer your net question, is how many jobs will move to Mexico from somewhere else and will then use American products. Let me just give you one example. Someone told me yesterday about a company that's making toys now—no offense, Prime Minister—in China that intends to open a plant in Mexico because it will cost so much less to send the toys from Mexico to the U.S. than China to the U.S. And if they do, they will all of a sudden begin to buy all their plastic, which is over 80 percent of the component parts, from Du Pont or some United States company.

So it is hard to know how many jobs will be lost. Net, we believe, there will be a big plus. But there will be jobs lost. There are now jobs being lost in defense cutbacks. And what I want to do is to completely reorganize the unemployment system into a reemployment system in which people who lose their jobs who are not likely to get that same job back within a reasonable amount of time can get a wide range of training opportunities based on two things: What do they want to do, first, and secondly, based on the best information we have, what are they most likely to get a job doing? And so we are now—the Secretary of Labor is designing a program. We intend to present it to the Congress, and I think it will have broad bipartisan support.

Q. How will you finance it?

The President. We plan to finance it now through economies associated with implementing the reinventing Government report.

An Australian journalist. Yes, sir?

Q. You've just acknowledged that some of the gains of NAFTA might be at the cost of East Asia. How do you see NAFTA, which seems to be essentially a preferential arrangement within the North American context, being able to operate within that broader APEC framework, which is meant to be nondiscriminatory?

I would ask Mr. Keating to also respond,

please.

The President. If you look at it from our point of view, what we're trying to do is to further lower our trade barriers against Mexico and against Canada. They're going to lower more of theirs against us. That's not inconsistent with what my overarching goal is, which is to get a freer trading system worldwide, which is why we're pushing the GATT round. But meanwhile, it is very much in the interest of the United States to have a stronger, more stable, more democratic, and more prosperous Mexico on our southern border, able to buy more of our products. And most of what we do there would have marginal or no impact one way or the other on anything that could happen, for example, in Southeast Asia in the next 4 or 5 years. I would also say that if this works, what I think you'll see is more open trading systems and fewer tariffs in many other Latin American countries which are changing politically and economically as well.

So I am not for a discriminatory system, but what I am trying to do is make those systems less closed in their relationships with us now in the hope that over the long run, the GATT round and the worldwide trading rules will really come to dominate the trading policies of all nations. And then, when we have regional groups like APEC, they'll be for the purpose of putting more arrangements together that create jobs rather than dealing with trade rules and regulations.

Yes, would you like to answer that?

Prime Minister Keating. I don't think that there is anything necessarily inconsistent between either the United States trading into the Asia Pacific, Canada trading with the Asia Pacific, or Mexico trading with the Asia Pacific individually or collectively as part of NAFTA. I think what is important in terms of the view of the Asia-Pacific economies of NAFTA is that there is perhaps more flesh on the bones of APEC before NAFTA goes beyond Mexico, perhaps into South America. But the concept of NAFTA integrating with the Asia Pacific is one where I don't think there is any conflict of concepts. And as the President has said, both things are going to increase the velocity of trade, both within the Americas and within the Asia Pacific.

APEC Meeting in Seattle

Q. Mr. Keating, could you tell us if you've determined who will represent China at the leaders conference that follows the ministerial meeting and if you've given the President any idea of other issues that might be discussed at that time and what the objectives actually are at that conference?

Prime Minister Keating. Well, I think the President naturally is the host of this conference, and therefore, the invitees and the acceptances are primary a matter for him. But I know that China is now considering who they might send.

The key thing about the conference is that it provides definition to a new world economic community, and that is the Asia-Pacific economic community. So by having a leaders conference, by the APEC member states attending at leadership level, it's providing a definition of that area that formerly wasn't so.

APEC, in terms of its intrastate trade, is in fact more integrated than is the European Community or even NAFTA. So there's a great naturalness about APEC, and I think the President's historic initiative of inviting the leaders together gives it form, substance, and as we ourselves adopt an agenda, a work program for the trade-liberalizing agenda of APEC. Not only is that body having form and definition, but it will actually proceed along the path of trade liberalization, the very thing that the President is committed to.

The President. If I might, let me just say, first of all, on the economic issues, Asia is the fastest growing part of the world. Latin America is the second fastest growing now. About 40 percent of our exports are now going to Asia. And more and more of our trade-related jobs are tied there. It is a very important thing that we are not only hosting this economic conference, that—and the Prime Minister has been too modest. He played a major role in convincing all these countries that their leaders should come to Seattle to be a part of this. But the fact that all these leaders are going to come here and we're going to have a chance to sit one-on-one and in groups with no sort of bureaucratic apparatus, no preset agenda, nothing to weigh us down, and talk through a whole range of economic and political issues, is an enormous opportunity for me to follow up on what we did at the G–7, where we reestablished clearly and publicly the dynamics of our relationship with Japan which we're working on now, our security obligations in Korea. Now we'll have a chance I'm not sure a United States President has ever had before, to talk to the leaders of all these countries at one time and to try to map out an agenda. But I don't want to prewrite what's going to happen there because it might get a little better as we go along.

Q. Who will represent China, sir?

The President. Well, we don't know yet. But I'm hoping that they'll be very well represented, and I kind of think they will be.

We owe the last question to an Australian journalist because we promised 50/50. Go ahead.

Q. I appreciate it. For both of you gentlemen, do you see that the NAFTA——

The President. He's not an Australian journalist. [*Laughter*]

Q. No, for the ABC, the Australian Broadcast Corporation.

The President. Oh really? Okay, go ahead.

Q. You talked a lot about——

The President. I thought we'd get an American trying to mimic an Australian accent. [*Laughter*] I didn't realize we had—go ahead.

Multilateral Trade Negotiations

Q. You've talked a lot about the NAFTA process and GATT. And for both of you, do you see any positive impact of having alternatives of NAFTA and APEC for the GATT process? Is there a certain political leverage that you get out of it? I believe Ambassador Kantor had talked about that during one of the congressional hearings. Is there a positive impact going back to the GATT process?

Prime Minister Keating. Well, I think APEC and NAFTA, too, end up being GATT-plus options. They are GATT plus. But in the event that GATT did fail, they do define themselves as freer trade areas, in the case of NAFTA, in the case of APEC, defining an area which has got enormous mass, an enormous weight— economic mass and economic weight and economic growth. So the United States locking into that, all of us locking into that, lifting the velocity of that means that in defining a new economic and trading community, in getting that growth up, this is at least some alternative than where we'd have been in the unhappy position of the GATT round failing.

Now, frankly, I don't think the GATT round will fail. I don't think the Europeans can let the French decide that the world's trading round should fail. I don't think the French will want to carry the odium of the round failing at their expense. And therefore, I believe there's much in the GATT round succeeding. But I do see NAFTA and APEC as GATT-plus overlays or overlays to the GATT. But you can also see them in place thereof, in part, as discrete area communities where we can all benefit by freer trade.

Q. [*Inaudible*]

Prime Minister Keating. Well, I think you've got to say this, that APEC equals growth, equals jobs. I think NAFTA equals growth, equals jobs. And that's the point the President was making earlier.

The President. I couldn't give a better answer than that. Thank you very much.

NOTE: The President's 25th news conference began at 3:11 p.m. in the East Room at the White House.

Remarks and a Question-and-Answer Session on the North American Free Trade Agreement in New Orleans, Louisiana
September 15, 1993

The President. Thank you. I'm glad you didn't let a little rain and a change of venue dampen your spirits. You may all still be excited after the Saints game last week. But I'm glad to be here.

I want to thank Mr. Brinson and Senator Breaux and Congressman Jefferson for what they have said. I'm glad to be here again with your Governor, your Lieutenant Governor, your State treasurer, and others, and Mayor Barthelemy. And I want to thank the Members of Congress who came here from other States, took time out of their busy schedules in Washington just to travel down to express their support on a bipartisan basis and from States all across this country for the North American Free Trade Agreement.

It really is, I think, not only a job winner

for the United States but the opportunity for us to get off the defensive in our economic policies and go on offense and try to build a world in which there are more opportunities for Americans not only for good jobs but for growing incomes.

For 20 years we have been buffeted by the fortunes of global competition and mechanization and all the things that you know about, and more and more working people have been pressured in their daily lives, finding it harder and harder to make ends meet. It is obvious that what we have been doing has not worked very well. We know what makes more jobs in a wealthy country: Expanding trade makes more jobs; educating your people better makes more jobs; providing more investment makes more jobs. These are the things that I am committed to.

There have been a lot of things said about the North American Free Trade Agreement. We came down here to New Orleans today to listen to people who know how the trade with Mexico works and who will be affected by it, talk about it. But I want to just say one or two general things to all of you today.

Three decades ago this port was dedicated by President Kennedy, a person who had a vision of America that knew no limits, who believed that we ought to face our challenges, that we ought to look outward to the world, that we shouldn't hunker down, that we could compete and win with any people anywhere on Earth. It is time that we reestablish that belief, that conviction, that commitment.

Today we come to New Orleans because I believe you face the rest of the world with confidence. We heard Senator Breaux and Congressman Jefferson talk about the Port of New Orleans. We heard Mr. Brinson say it's the most important thing in strategic planning for the future of this port to pass this new trade agreement with Mexico.

Well, yesterday I signed a couple of side agreements that strengthen that, agreements that do the following things: number one, that commit the Government of Mexico, as well as the Government of the United States to invest more money in environmental cleanup. Now, that means two things: number one, more opportunities for American companies who do that kind of work. Number two, it means that there will be less difference in the cost of production on either side of the border because of different environmental regulations.

The second agreement commits the Mexican Government to enforce its own labor laws. And you should know what that really means. It means that for the first time in history a government has committed itself to raise the minimum wage as its economy grows, thereby raising the wage structure throughout the country, because the President of Mexico has made a personal commitment to me, to the United States, and to this process that Mexico from now on will raise its minimum wage every time its economy grows on a regular basis, which means that more rapidly than before and much more rapidly than if we don't pass this trade agreement, the wage gap between their workers and ours will close, and there will be less incentive to move our plants to Mexico but more ability by the Mexicans to buy American products that we ship from places like the Port of New Orleans.

Why do I believe this will work? Well, for a couple of reasons. First of all, because in the last few years Mexico has begun to lower its tariffs and open their markets to more American products. You know that because you've been shipping more out of here. In 1986—these boxes basically represent where we are—but in 1986 our exports to Mexico were a little over $12 billion, represented by this first crate here. At that time we had about a $5.7 billion trade deficit with Mexico. Because they've lowered tariffs, already we've got a $5.6 billion trade surplus with them now. And we estimate that by 1995, just a couple of years after the pact goes into effect, we'll have about $60 billion in trade with Mexico, represented by this big crate. You don't have to be Einstein to figure out if you're an American it's better to have four crates than one. That's what this is all about.

Let me just say a couple of other things. It's not just Mexico, especially for the Port of New Orleans. If we can make this trade pact work, and we will, because keep in mind—I want to make one other point to all those people that say this is a job-loser—that tariffs in Mexico, in spite of our trade surplus, are still 4 times as high as the tariffs in America against Mexican products. The average Mexican spends $450 a year buying American products, more than anybody in the world except the Canadians, more than the Japanese, more than the Germans, more than a lot of countries where the people are much wealthier. This will work because their tariffs are still higher than ours. If you lower the tariffs down to where they're as low as ours and then we eventually eliminate them, again it just stands to reason that we're going to have more sales and more products and more opportunities.

What I want to say to you finally is that this is the beginning of this process, because I can tell you that I have heard from the leaders of countries all over Latin America. They are looking at the Congress; they are looking about whether we're going to adopt this trade agreement. And if we do, then Chile, then Venezuela, then Argentina, then many other countries that are becoming more democratic and more free-market, free-enterprise oriented are going to want to have more trade with the United States and have more of our products. And that means still more, more trade going out of the Port of New Orleans because there are hundreds of millions of people in Latin America committed to democracy now, committed to free markets, and hungering for the benefits of a free economy. We can help them to get it and put the American people to work as well. And we know that trade-related jobs pay, on the average, higher wages than jobs not related to trade. So I ask all of you to support this. Now, let me just say that—thanks. [Applause]

There was a time when all the working people in America were for more trade, when people realized that if you didn't expand trade you couldn't keep expanding jobs. I want to say as a word of respect and partial regret, as we're here, there's a funeral going on in New Orleans for a labor leader named Lindsey Williams who helped to build this port. And Lindy Boggs, your former Congresswoman, wrote me a note about it, because I think she is there today. But she was reminding me in this note about how New Orleans had always been a place that pushed for more trade and a place where labor and management and Republicans and Democrats, African-Americans and whites and Hispanics and everybody got together because they looked outward to the world.

I'm telling you, folks, we cannot afford to look inward. We cannot repeal the force that is driving the world economy together. We can run away from it and get beat by it, or we can embrace it, do what we have to do, and win with it to create more jobs, more incomes, and more opportunity. That's what I think we want to do.

And as I sit down, I want to thank these men and women who are behind us. They work for and run companies that benefit from trade with Mexico today and who would flourish even more if we pass NAFTA. They ship their products through this port every day. And I thank them for coming here. They're not professional politicians or seasoned speakers, but they're the people that really count. They're the people that really count. They're the people who represent the future of this economy. And all the people who are arguing around this thing in politics, a lot of them won't be affected one way or the other. You need to assess who is going to be affected. Are they going to win or lose? The answer is this is a good deal. It's a winner. We ought to take it. And these folks are about to tell us why.

Thank you very much.

[At this point, a participant stated that NAFTA will create 15 to 20 more jobs in a local rice mill.]

The President. So you'll put together 15 or 20 more people, and the rice farmers in my home State of Arkansas will send you rice down here to go out of the Port of New Orleans. That's what you're saying, right?

Q. Well, I'd like for it to be that way, but unfortunately, I'm sure your mills will benefit from it too in Arkansas.

The President. Thank you. I appreciate that. Who's next?

[An Amoco employee discussed the environmental benefits of exporting natural gas liquids to Mexico.]

The President. I think we ought to talk about this a minute for people who don't know. One of the most closed aspects of the Mexican economy has been the whole energy sector. And the Mexicans, as you know, have their own oil company, and their own oil reserves, but they have flared off their natural gas. They never have saved it, distributed it. And as a consequence, they have a lot of problems, which you just mentioned, especially in Mexico City.

It may well be that in the short run the fastest growing economic opportunities will be in the energy area, particularly if we can figure out a way to get large volumes of compressed natural gas down there and get it into the stream of usage, as well as the other petrochemical products. So I thank you for talking about that.

That's a huge issue and a big short-term winner for us.

Who's next?

Q. I am all for the idea of the NAFTA because it means more security for our jobs and our families.

The President. What do you sell to Mexico?

Q. Hot sauce, canned beans——

The President. That's pretty good, they sell hot sauce to Mexico. I think we ought to clap for that, don't you? [*Applause*] Canned goods?

Q. Canned beans.

Q. We have five factories that produce processed food products in America, several of them in Louisiana and Texas. We're vitally interested in NAFTA because basically it opens the Mexican market to our company and our products. We have a processing plant in El Paso, Texas, that virtually has been unable to sell any of our manufactured food products into Mexico because of their closed-market situation, which began to change some 4 years ago under the Salinas government. What we need now is we need that to change and that opening to be completed under NAFTA so that the market will be totally open to us, and we will be able to compete on an even basis with the Mexican industry that we compete with.

The President. Do you have any idea what it will do to your sales? Have you done any estimates on how much it will increase your markets?

Q. Yes, we are talking millions of dollars of increased sales. And we're talking hundreds of jobs, possibly thousands in time to come. But Mexico has 80 million people, 80 million consumers who have a natural affinity to our products. And we think it's a great potential market for our products and will be enhanced greatly under NAFTA.

The President. Good for you. So you don't have—I want to get this straight—you have plants near the Mexican border on the American side; you don't have any intention of moving them. And in fact, you know you're going to hire more people to work there if this trade agreement is passed.

Q. That's exactly right.

The President. Thank you very much.

[*A participant explained how NAFTA will benefit companies that are helping to alleviate environmental problems in Mexico.*]

The President. What do you produce?

Q. We produce specialty polymers for water purification, wastewater treatment. We produce a lot of products and services to help our customers minimize pollution and to prevent pollution. And we produce superabsorbent polymers. We produce products that are used in the pulp and paper industry. All of these things would face a dramatic increase if the NAFTA agreement were ratified.

The President. Have you done any estimates on how much your sales might increase if it passes?

Q. I'm sure we do, but from the numbers I've seen, we know that for about every million dollars increase in sales resulting from NAFTA, that would generate about five additional jobs at NALCO, and most of those would be in manufacturing. And again, the Garyville plant here in Louisiana is our biggest plant, so it would have the most dramatic impact in that area.

The President. Thank you. Go ahead.

[*A participant expressed support for NAFTA because the reduction in tariffs would create more jobs.*]

The President. You know, I'm really glad that some of you are coming here who work for these companies, because we know that the only way a wealthy country like America can grow wealthier is if we have more customers, if we sell more. We know we can't just sell to each other. We have to open up our borders.

And the point I want to make to the working people who are worried about whether they are against this or not is that anybody who wants to move a plant to Mexico because wages are lower or because the environmental standards are low can do that today. They can do it tomorrow. They can do it if NAFTA fails. And in fact, if the NAFTA agreement fails, it will be easier to move a plant to Mexico because wages will be lower down there and environmental standards will be laxer. But it will be harder for them to buy our products because they won't be making as much money and because we won't be able to send as many products in there.

So I appreciate all of you being here, especially because in the end what my job is, is to find ways in a very tough world economy, where Europe's economy is not growing, where Japan's economy is not growing, I have to find ways to try to help our economy grow to create more jobs and higher incomes. Mexico's economy is growing. Latin America is the second fastest growing part of the world, next to Asia. And so I really appreciate the working people coming here because, in the end, the reason we're doing this is to provide greater security to the working families of this country.

I told the Members of Congress on the way down here, and I guess I ought to tell all of you, as many of you know I was the Governor of your neighboring State to the north for 12 years. I have known people whose plants shut down and moved to Mexico. I've seen that happen. Believe me, this agreement will not make that any easier. That's going to happen or not happen, regardless. This agreement will make it harder because it will change the economics in ways that benefit both sides of the border. If I didn't know that, I wouldn't be out here pushing for this agreement.

So I thank all of you for coming here today. Ron, would you like to say something?

[*At this point, J. Ron Brinson, president and CEO, Board of Commissioners, Port Authority of New Orleans, stated that increased trade with Mexico would continue to produce jobs in Louisiana and that NAFTA might lead to a hemispheric trade agreement in the future. Gov. Edwin W. Edwards of Louisiana then endorsed NAFTA, stating that Louisiana industries would benefit from it.*]

The President. We are going to wrap up, but before we do, I would like to ask all of you to give all of these people who came up here and spoke a hand, because they are what this whole thing is about. [*Applause*]

In the weeks and months ahead we are going to try to do a number of events like this to highlight the importance of NAFTA. But I'd like to ask all of you who are here from Louisiana to write to Members of Congress and your Senators and tell them that you support this, it means more jobs for your State, and you would appreciate their voting for it. They need to hear from you. The people who are afraid of this agreement are quite well organized. Some of them have a dollar or two, as you may know, and they need to hear from you. We just tried to give these folks a chance to make a direct plea today. I want everybody within the sound of my voice to also make your opinion known to your Representatives in Congress. It is up to them now.

We need your help. It means more jobs for America. Thank you very much.

NOTE: The President spoke at 12:03 p.m. at the Port of New Orleans. In his remarks, he referred to Lt. Gov. Melinda Schwegmann and State treasurer Mary Landrieu of Louisiana, and Mayor Sidney Barthelemy of New Orleans.

Remarks in Response to Letters on Health Care Reform
September 16, 1993

The President. Good morning. Please be seated. Welcome to the Rose Garden. I'm glad the rain has stopped, but we put up the tent just as a precaution.

Nine months ago, when I asked the American people to write to us to send their thoughts about the health care system and the need to reform, I had no idea what I was doing to our already overworked correspondence staff. Today, more than 700,000 letters later, I am happy to be able to join Hillary and Al and Tipper in welcoming a few of you here who wrote to us.

In the weeks and months ahead, health care will often be topic number one at dinner tables, at offices, at medical clinics, and in the Halls of Congress. But before we launch into the debate I wanted to invite you here to remind everyone that, as Hillary says, there are 250 million health care experts in our Nation, and everyone has a different story.

If you read some of these letters as I have, the picture very quickly becomes clear. Even the millions of Americans who enjoy health care coverage are afraid it won't be there for them next month or next year. They want us to take action to give them the security that all Americans deserve. Let's start then with four people whose stories speak volumes about our health care system.

In order, they are Jermone Strong, Nelda Holley, Stacey Askew, and Margie Silverman.

[At this point, the participants read their letters.]

The President. These letters are representative of tens of thousands that we received telling stories like the ones you've heard: people who can't go back to work, people who can't take job advancements, people who have no coverage because they're young and they're unemployed, all the other things that you have heard here.

There is one particular problem in our health insurance system in America that I'd like to focus on by asking for two more people to read letters, something that's a part of the everyday vocabulary now of most working men and women in this country: the preexisting condition, the thing which if you have it you either can't get health insurance or you can never leave the job you're in. So I'd like to hear from two people from California and Illinois, Suzy Somers and Jean Kaczmareck.

[The participants read their letters, and Hillary Clinton responded.]

The President. Let me just say one thing about this to try to hammer home what I think is a very important point. All the stories you've heard today have nothing to do with the quality of American health care but everything to do with the system of insurance we have. And in the weeks and months ahead you may hear a lot of stories about that, but the bottom line is this: If you lived in any other advanced country in the world, you wouldn't have this problem, none of these problems. But it's not a reflection on our doctors, our nurses, our health care providers; it is the system by which we insure against risk. It can be different.

I want to go on now to the next issue, because every time I say this, people say, "Well, how are you going to pay for this? This is going to cost a fortune." I have an answer to that, but I want to hear from people who are talking already about the exploding costs of health care in this country. Next to the problem of security, we hear more about cost.

And of course, Miss Holley talked a little bit about costs, and some of the rest of you did, too. But we have some people here who want to read letters. They're from Georgia, Pennsylvania, and California: Karen Nangle, Mary Catherine Flyte, and Brigitte Burdine. Would you please read your letters to us, or say what you'd like to say?

[The participants read their letters, and Tipper Gore responded.]

The President. I wish I could say something to each of you, but I want to hear the other letters. But let me just say one thing to you, Karen. One of the things that really has upset me now that I am at least nominally in charge of the Federal Government—I say nominally— is how many programs, like the Supplemental Security Income program, were designed with the best of intentions, but because we have this crazy little patchwork health care system with a little done here, a little done there, a little done the other place, a system that was designed to help your family is actually wrecking your health care plan—and one that works—and costing the taxpayers more money to boot. That's one of the things that we think, just by rationalizing the system, we can handle.

One other thing I want to say to you, Brigitte. I want to make it clear, there will be some difficult choices in this decision. But let's not kid ourselves: There's a lot of waste in this system which we can squeeze out. But there will be some difficult choices, and your family represents one. And I want to just try to describe this to you.

Most countries that insure people either directly by tax dollars or indirectly, as in Germany, through employers—and more and more American States that are looking at this are looking at something called community rating. Hawaii has had it since 1974, where 98 percent of the people in the work force are covered and they have lower than average overall premiums. But it's because they put all people in big, big insurance pools.

Now consider this, in the case of your family, how much better off your family would have been if your sister could never lose her insurance, certainly as long as she was at work, and then if she wasn't she'd be picked up under a general system. Even though she got sick her employer would not have to worry about going broke by covering her under the insurance package because he or she and all the employees would be in a big, big pool, say, a couple of hundred thousand people. So if one person gets AIDS, it only adds marginally to the cost of this big pool. Same thing with you.

Now, I just want to tell you what the tough choice is. The tough choice is that someone like you in the same pool, because you're young and healthy and strong and unlikely to get sick, might have to pay a little bit more in insurance premiums so that everybody in the big pool could always be covered and no one would be kicked out. I think most young, healthy, single Americans would be willing to do that to avoid the kind of horror stories we've heard today. Same thing would have helped you.

But I do want to say, there are a lot of things that can be done to this system, but I don't want to kid you, the American people will have to be willing to make some changes. And this is one change that we think most young Americans would like to make, because they are all presumably going to be older some day or going to be sicker some day. And that is one thing that I think we've just got to do. If we were all in these big pools, then you wouldn't have had half the problems you had, and your family would be better off.

Let's go to the next issue that nobody in America understands this, the crisis of American health care, more than small businesses. Small business owners often have the worst of both worlds. They want very much to cover their employees, but they can't afford the coverage, again because they can't buy into large pools. Their premiums are much, much more expensive. So you have this situation where a lot of small businesses don't cover their employees. Then when they get sick, they don't get care until they are real sick and they show up in the emergency room. Or they provide coverage, but the deductibles or the copays are astronomical, often as much as $2,500 a year.

So I thought we should hear from a couple of people who can share their stories, Mabel Piley from Kansas and Karl Kregor from Texas.

[The participants read their letters. Mr. Kregor concluded by thanking his wife for having the courage to support his career change.]

The President. I feel the same way about my wife. *[Laughter]*

First, let me thank both of you for coming. And let me say that this is another one of these areas where I think a change can offer enormous hope and deal with the problems that you have outlined, but where we'll also have to take some disciplined, different action that will require some people to do more. And let me describe that.

Most small business people, both employers and employees and people who are self-employed, do have some kind of health insurance.

But it often provides inadequate coverage or has astronomical deductibles or, in any case, costs a fortune. You said that your premiums, I think, quadrupled in 3 years, from '89 to '92. Now, during that time the cost of health care was going up at about 2½ times the rate of inflation. But that would not lead to the amount of increase you had. You had that increase because you owned your own business and you were probably in a very small pool of people, probably 100, 200, 300, something like that.

Under our plan, two things would help you. You would be in a very large pool with a community rating—the same thing that would help your sister and family—and also as a self-employed person, because you'd still have to pay relatively more, you'd get 100 percent tax deductibility for your premiums instead of 25 percent today. So it is almost certain that your costs would go down. It is certain. Your costs would go down. Under our system, what would happen to you is if you developed your own consulting business, you would become like Mable. You'd have 100 percent deductibility for your premium, and you'd be able to buy into a very large pool, just as if you were an employee in a company that had 5,000 people insuring its own employees.

Now, the flip side of that is, the only way we can make that work is for the small business people today who don't provide any insurance coverage at all to their employees to make some contribution to the health care system and for the employees to do it.

Now, it will be better than the present system because we're going to lower premiums for small businesses by putting them in big pools. I just explained that. We also propose to provide a subsidy to keep the premiums even lower for several years for the employers that have low-wage employees and therefore are very low-margin businesses.

So we're going to try to help there. But you have to understand that all the employers in the country who don't provide any insurance to their employees, they basically are getting a free ride in some ways from the rest of you because if their employees or they show up at the hospital, it's there. It's just like driving on the road without paying a gas tax. I mean, the infrastructure is there. The clinics are there. The hospitals are there. The tests are there. The nurses are there. And until everyone is willing to make some contribution to his or her own health care, and until we get all the employers in the system even at a modest rate, we won't have a fair system where we can apportion the costs fairly, and we can keep everybody else from being overcharged.

So that's one of the most controversial parts of this program. But it is true that a lot of small businesses simply could not afford to get into the insurance market today without going broke. That's absolutely true. And since most jobs are being created by people like you who are starting small businesses, we know we can't afford to do that. But it's also true that a lot of big businesses can't afford to hire anybody else and always work their people overtime or hire part-time workers because they can't afford health insurance premiums because they're paying too much. It's also true that a lot of people who work for employers that have health insurance never get a raise anymore because all of the money is going to the health insurance premiums.

I don't want to pretend that this is all going to be easy, but it seems to me that it is a fair thing to say: Everyone in America should make some contribution to his or her own health insurance. And all employers should make some contribution, but if they have a very low margin, we're going to subsidize them for several years while we work into this system. And if we do that and give you 100 percent deductibility and you 100 percent deductibility and put you in great big pools, then more Americans will live without the kind of blackmail that you just outlined. I think it is the only fair way to work it. It's the only way any other country has solved this problem. And I don't think we can reinvent this wheel.

You've heard a little about this already because of the so-called preexisting condition problem, but there are literally millions of Americans who are locked into the jobs they're in. This is a very tough thing in a country where job mobility is important, and the average young American going into the work force will change jobs eight times in a lifetime. To be locked into a job at a time when many people who've lost a job here can tell you, you don't get that same job back, you have to get a new job, is a very, very hazardous thing.

Judy Dion and Shelly Cermak are here to tell us about this problem with our health care system that's come to be known as job lock. They're from Maine and Maryland. Judy and Shelly.

[The participants read their letters.]

The President. We agree. And we don't think taking care of your beautiful, young daughter should keep you from ever taking a better job, either.

The bottom line on this is that if we change the rules so that no one can be denied insurance coverage because of a preexisting condition, we also have to change the system so that no business goes broke for giving that insurance coverage. In other words, we can't afford to cut off our nose to spite our face. We have to make it possible.

So again, what we hope to do is to give you the protection of knowing you can always have health insurance; that if you change your jobs, you'll be able to get it; that no one will be able to turn you down; but that your employer won't go broke, either, because they will be in these large pools so that the risk will be fairly spread across a significant percentage of the American citizenry. And it seems so simple. You must wonder why it hasn't been done before. But it's wrong not to do.

And probably this and the cost issue will probably affect more Americans than any other single issue because a lot of you, even who have talked about other problems, are indirectly affected by this whole job lock issue. Also, it affects everybody in all kinds of different ways. So we must do this. We must do this.

And let me also say that it's bad for the American economy. Every healthy person in America is disadvantaged if you two can't take a better job. Because when Americans with talents and gifts can't fulfill their God-given abilities to the maximum extent, then that makes our whole economy less productive, less competitive. It hurts everybody. So it's not just all the people who have your life stories. All the rest of us are really disadvantaged if you get locked into a job. Also, somebody coming along behind you who would get that job, and that's a better job than they have, those folks are disadvantaged, too.

Let me just say in 'ntroducing the last set of letters that there are a lot of people in this system who are very frustrated by the incredible bureaucracy of the American system. It is the most bureaucratic health care system in the world of all the advanced countries. The expense is staggering. It probably costs at least a dime on the dollar more in sheer paperwork than all competing systems. That not only has financial consequences; it has terrible personal consequences. We've found some people here who have been lost in that maze, and I wanted you to hear their stories.

So let me ask now James Heffernan from Florida—I'm going to try to pronounce this right—Carol Oedegeest—close enough?—from California to read their letters, and the Vice President will respond.

[*The participants read their letters and Vice President Gore responded.*]

The President. Let me say that I hope all of you are familiar with—at least have heard about the Vice President's brilliant report on reinventing Government. And he's given us suggestions that will save the taxpayers $100 billion over the next 5 years, if we can implement them all, and free up that money to reduce the deficit or invest it in needed programs. But the health care system needs that, too. And our strongest allies in this, I think, will be doctors and nurses.

To illustrate what he said, let me just give you two statistics with this nurse sitting here. The average hospital in America has hired clerical workers at 4 times the rate of health care providers in the last 10 years. Think about it. Another thing: In 1980, the average doctor took home 75 percent of the money that came into his or her clinic. They just took it home. By 1990, that figure had dropped from 75 to 53 cents on the dollar, the rest of it going to paperwork. You wonder why the bills are going up? So this is a huge deal.

I also want to thank publicly, I think—I've not had a chance to do this—I want to say a special word of thanks to Tipper Gore for being such an active member of the Health Care Task Force and being such a passionate advocate for the interests of the mentally ill and the interest that the rest of us have in dealing with it in a more sensible and humane fashion.

And I'd also like to thank the First Lady for the work this task force has done, not only for receiving 700,000 letters but for meeting with literally 1,500 different interest groups and involving thousands and thousands of people in the health care system itself.

In the months ahead, as we debate health care reform, you will hear numbers and arguments fly across America. I hope that this beginning will help us to remember that fundamentally this is about people, about all of you that have read your letters, about all of you who wrote us letters who are out here today whose letters couldn't be read. I invite all of you to speak to the members of the press who are here about your stories.

I just want to thank you for coming and for having, particularly these people, for having the courage to tell us their personal story and to tell America their personal stories. We can do this. We can do this if we recognize that even though it's complicated, we can work through it, if we will listen to the voices of the real people who know it has to be better and different.

Thank you very much.

NOTE: The President spoke at 8:10 a.m. in the Rose Garden at the White House.

Remarks and a Question-and-Answer Session With Small Business Leaders on Health Care Reform
September 16, 1993

The President. Thank you very much. First of all, I want to echo what Erskine Bowles said. I thank you for taking some time off today to come in here and just visit with me about this whole health care issue and about what we're trying to do and about your personal situations and whether we're responding adequately to them.

Let me tell you that one reason we're a little late this morning is that I started the morning—some of you may have seen it on television—I started the morning with about 15 people of the 700,000 people who have written letters since I asked my wife to chair this health care group. Seven hundred thousand Americans have written us about their personal situation. A lot of them were small business people. Some of the people who were there today at our morning meeting in the Rose Garden were small business people. A lot of them were people with sick family members, people who were locked into jobs they couldn't ever change, all the things that you know about. But I wanted to leave that group—and we had another 100 people who've written letters who just were asked to come and be in the audience—I wanted to leave that group and come straight here because it is the small business community that, as business people, will arguably be most immediately affected, although there will be an impact on larger businesses, too.

First, I'd like to thank our hosts, the Siegels, for letting us come to this great small business which goes back to 1866. Most of us weren't around back then. I really appreciate you doing that. I want to thank Mayor Kelly and so many of the DC City Council members for being here. And we're delighted to be here. Harry, I think we're in your district, aren't we? Your ward. We're glad to be here.

Let me just make a few opening remarks, and then I'd like to hear from all of you. We have a lot of problems in this health care system. There are a lot of things that are right about it. Most all Americans get to pick their doctors. And we have high quality care if you can access it. But every month, hundreds of thousands of people lose their health insurance and over 100,000 of them lose it permanently, so that each year more and more people are without health care coverage. We're the only advanced country in the world that doesn't have a system to provide a basic health care package to all of its citizens.

The second thing that happens is that the cost of health care, particularly since 1980, but really before that, but especially since 1980 has being going up much more rapidly than inflation, 2 and 3 times the rate of inflation.

The third thing is it's hitting small businesses and self-employed people much harder than bigger employees now because they tend to be in much smaller insurance pools. So if one person gets sick in that pool or one person gets sick in the employment unit, it can rocket your costs. We were with a person today earlier who between 1989 and 1992 had their premiums quadruple, from something like $200 and some a month to over $900 a month.

The third thing is that very often small busi-

ness people, to get any insurance coverage at all, have to have astronomical copays and deductibles, so that it becomes almost dysfunctional for their employees. And more and more small businesses every month are having to drop their coverage.

Now, the flip side of that, believe it or not, is that many big businesses have been able to maintain generous benefit packages but only at the expense of never giving their employees a pay raise. And we're looking at a situation now that for the rest of this decade we could, in effect, take away all the pay raises for the work force of this country to go into higher health insurance premiums, unless we do something. So it's a very, very serious problem.

You also have a health care system that is wildly inefficient. None of you could run your businesses and stay in business with a system that had the administrative overhead and the paperwork burden and the bureaucracy that the health care system does. The average hospital is hiring clerical workers at 4 times the rate of health care providers. The average doctor in 1980 took home 75 percent of the money that came into the medical clinic; by 1990 it had dropped from 75 cents on the dollar to 53 cents on the dollar—going to bureaucracy, paperwork, the way the insurance system is organized.

So what we tried to do is to come up with a plan that would require every employer and employee to contribute something; would have a cap of 7.9 percent of payroll as a maximum that anyone could be required to pay; would provide some subsidies for employers with under 50 full-time employees, which means you could have more if some of them were part-time, all the way down to 3.5 percent of payroll, depending on the wage rates; and would lower the cost increases of health insurance to all Americans.

The most controversial aspect of this is requiring all employers and employees to contribute some portion of the cost of health care. The problem is if you don't do that, it's going to be very hard to get costs under control because unless everybody contributes, there will always be a lot of cost shifting in the system. That adds a lot of administrative costs. It also means that the people who are paying for health insurance are paying more than they would otherwise pay, because they alone pay for the infrastructure of health care, the hospitals, the clinics, the people that are there. And they alone pay for the emergency rooms and the uncompensated care in that regard.

So we're trying to work this out in a fair way that's bearable. But I believe it will aid the American economy and will help small business growth if we do it properly. That will be a big point of controversy as we debate this over the next few months.

So I wanted to start on the first day right from the get-go, if you will, hearing from the small business community. And I'd like to—who wants to go first? Our host. And make sure that you've got the microphone close enough to you.

[At this point, a participant asked if the economic situation would not be compounded as the new health care plan would force small businesses to raise prices.]

The President. It would be, except most small businesses under this system will actually have lower costs. Keep in mind, most small businesses are providing some health coverage to their employees now at astronomical costs. Many small business families are self-employed and insure themselves as self-employed. Self-employed people, under our plan, will get much lower premiums, much lower, because they'll be in big insurance pools. And they'll also get 100 percent deductibility for their insurance premiums, not 25 percent, for the first time. So those will go down. All employers who offer anything will have their employees go down now. Employees with groups under 50 will start out, most of them, paying less than $1 a day per employee for health insurance under our system.

[Administrator Bowles stated the new plan would enable small business owners to provide comprehensive, low cost coverage.]

The President. I don't mean to minimize this, but let me tell you what the flip side of this is. Every year one of the things that adds to the cost of health care in America is cost shifting. So every time the Government doesn't pay for the people we're supposed to cover or somebody else doesn't pay and somebody shows up in an—somebody without health insurance normally won't get health care in a preventive and primary way where it's cheapest, but they'll get it when it's too late, when they're really sick, often showing up at the emergency room. All those costs get shifted onto someone else. And

then their competitiveness is eroded, so they eventually drop their health insurance. And more and more people keep dropping it. It's just sort of in a death spiral every year where more and more people drop their insurance, more and more people are uninsured. And then the people who are insured are paying for all of them when they finally access the system.

And as I said, we're the only country in the world that does it this way. We're the only country in the world with 1,500 separate health insurance companies writing thousands of different policies and trying to divide little small businesses up into smaller and smaller groups. Some of these groups are so small that the overhead, that is, the insurance company administrative costs and profit, is up to 40 cents on the dollar. We can't sustain the system.

I don't pretend that even a dollar a day per employee won't be more difficult for some small businesses. It's just that we can't figure out any other way to fairly apportion the cost of this system and keep everybody covered and finally get the cost under control. The costs are spiraling out of control.

The other alternatives are nobody gets coverage, or the taxpayers pay it. And if the taxpayers pay it then, in effect, we're raising taxes on people who are already paying way too much for their health care to pay for people who aren't paying anything.

So I think this is a fair way. And what I would ask you to do and everybody in your circumstances is when we produce the copy, the final copy of this health care plan, because we're still in extensive consultations on it, but in the next several days, I'd like to ask you to go over it, calculate exactly how it will affect you, and then draw a conclusion about how you think it will impact you. Look at the specific facts and get back in touch with Erskine Bowles and tell him how you think it will affect you.

[A participant asked who would be responsible if the new plan is overutilized and costs begin to rise.]

The President. I'll answer your question, but let me say first of all, you're much more likely to have overutilization and exploding costs if we keep on doing what we're doing than if we adopt our plan. In other words, particularly for smaller employers, costs have been going up on average anywhere from 20 to 50 percent a year. Only the very biggest employers that are able, in effect, to bargain more toughly with their own insurance providers have been able to hold their costs in line, and they've been able to do a little bit better job in the last few years simply because of their size.

So under our system you would not only start out with a lower premium than you're paying now so you would get an immediate savings, you'd be part of a big alliance of employers and employees who would have some say over the governing of your big health care group. And if the evidence of every other country is any guide, if the evidence of the places which have started it in this country is any guide, the cost is going to go up much less rapidly under this system than it will if we stay with what we've got. In other words, the worst alternative that we can conceive is to continue to do what we've got for small business.

Now, in addition to that, we've proposed to have a backup budget cap so that if by pure competition you can't keep costs as low as we think that—you know, basically to inflation plus the growth in people participating, we'll still have a budget to limit it.

So the answer to your question is, there is no conceivable scenario, at least that I can conceive of, where you would wind up paying more under this plan than another. Also there are more incentives in this plan not to overutilize the system, not just for your employees but for the American people as a whole. Under our plan all the employees in the country would have to pay something towards their own health care up to 20 percent, which is something that many don't now. And if they wanted a more generous plan than we cover, which is quite adequate, they would have to pay even more. So there will be a lot of incentives not to overutilize the system and not to run the cost through the roof.

Let me also point out that over the next 5 years, since you mentioned the short-term period, that's the period over the next 5 years where we'll be realizing a lot of the administrative savings. Our country stands approximately a dime on the dollar more in paperwork than all of our competitors. That's a bunch of money in an $800 billion health care system. So if— let me just say this—if what we've tried to do in implementing this health care system is to phase it in over a period of years, to build in corrections so if something goes wrong, we will find another way to control the costs, not

to increase your costs for this health care.

We are spending—let me say—I want to drive this home. Today, America spends 14.2 percent of its gross domestic product on health care. Canada spends 9.4 percent. No other advanced country in the world is over 9. None. Not Germany, not Japan. And in the German system, which is about 8.6, 8.7 percent of their gross domestic product, the benefits are as generous as the best plans, more generous than most, and contain a lot of primary preventive health care. So unless we just all go to sleep at the switch, this is—you know, there is no way that you can't be better off under this new system.

But there are protections. The way we've got it written, there are basically opportunities to recalculate, to avoid imposing undue burdens on employers 3 and 4 and 5 years down the road. The way it's written, we'll have to have opportunities to readjust it.

The bottom line is, sir, none of us are going to do anything which put more small businesses out of work than are already doing it now, because most of the new jobs in this country are being created in units of under 50. So I wouldn't be doing this if I didn't think it was not only better for the health care of the country but also would tend to stabilize the environment for small business so we could get back to generating new jobs.

[Administrator Bowles reaffirmed that the new plan would be beneficial to small businesses. A participant then asked about employees with catastrophic or preexisting illnesses.]

The President. First of all, as you know, this is not an unusual condition. This has happened to millions of employers in America and millions of employees. For the employer, the burden is just what you suggested, you're put in this awful situation of having to fire somebody who may be a good employee and making their lives miserable or paying enormously increased premiums.

For the employee, there's another problem for the American economy that's now come to be known under the rubric of job lock. We now live in a country where labor mobility is quite important. The average 18-year-old will change jobs eight times in a lifetime now. And we've got all kinds of folks who can never change jobs again because they or someone in their family's been sick. What we propose to do about it is to reorganize the insurance market so, first of all, nobody can be denied coverage or dropped from coverage because of a preexisting condition, and secondly, so that small business employers of people with preexisting conditions don't have undue rises in their premiums because they are in very, very large buying pools. So that the preexisting condition that one of your employees or a family member has, say you've got 30 employees—or how many employees do you have? So you've got 14. That could wreck you if you're in a buying group with a couple of hundred or even a couple of thousand. But if you're in a huge buying pool with 100,000 people or more, or 200,000, then each preexisting condition would only have a marginal impact on you.

We propose to go to what is called community insurance rating. It puts you in a large pool so that that will only have a marginal impact on the increased costs to the total people in the pool. All of them will be represented in bargaining for the package of health insurance benefits with the people who provide it. So it will provide a lot of protection for you, as well as protection for the employees. And it is, by the way, the way it is typically handled in other countries and the way it is generally handled in Hawaii, where 98 percent of the employees are covered by the requirement and where they have a community rating system.

[*A participant asked about the role of private insurance companies.*]

The President. Well, let me say that you have that in every country where you have universal coverage, because there are some people who may want a little extra coverage on this, that, or the other thing. But you also have that here, frankly. And a lot of even the better employer-employee plans here—there may be employers, for example, who go out and buy another policy. You see it in Germany also. You see it in nearly every country. But what you might call the customized insurance policy that covers an additional extra risk, you find everywhere. But that's mostly to guarantee more personalized care. Under our system, people who run out of that will have a Government back-stop, if you will, to take care of people and those kinds of problems.

One of the reasons, however, we elected not to try to go to the Canadian system, even though the Canadian system is administratively the simplest, that is, they have the lowest administrative

costs of any system we studied; the Australian system may be about there, and the British system is, but it's all government-owned. No one wanted to get that. The Canadian system is a private health provider system, publicly financed system where all insurance premiums are abolished. Everybody pays a tax, and you just pay it out. It's like Medicare, but everybody's on it. And there's no administrative costs to speak of. It's very low. We decided not to do that for two reasons. One is we thought there would be a lot of aversion to canceling all the premiums and converting it into a tax. And people probably distrust Government about as much as they do big insurance companies. Secondly, if you look at the German system, for example, which is more similar to what we're trying to do, we have private insurance companies with bigger pools for small businesses. We thought that more likely you'd have lower costs and better service if you could put some competition in it and give the employers and the employees some leverage and in effect bargaining with the health care providers for the comprehensive services that will be provided. And that, I think, will tend to keep costs down and keep services more comprehensive.

But there is no country, including the United States, where there is not some what you might call third insurance market, over and above what the government does and what the employers do for speciality coverage. We expect that, in effect, there will be less of that here under this plan than would otherwise be the case.

[*A participant asked if the employer contribution for Social Security would increase and if the national health board would take the place of private insurance companies.*]

The President. No. First of all, the answer to your first question is none of us can totally perceive the future. What I can assure you of— and that's what I've said to Barry before—is that under this system, costs will rise much more slowly than they otherwise would.

Let me tell you, we're at 14.2 percent of gross domestic product now. It is estimated that the United States will be at 20 percent of gross domestic product on the health care by the end of the decade and that no other country will be over 10. Canada might be a shade over 10. If we get to the point where we're spotting all of our competitors a dime on the dollar on health care, we're going to be in trouble sure enough. It's bad enough where it is.

So costs of health care will continue to rise. What we're going to try to do is to bring the health care system's cost in line with inflation plus additions to population. That is, if the population gets older and more people need different kinds of health care, of course, that will go up. But what we can't afford to do is to let health care continue to go up at 2 or 3 times the rate of inflation.

The answer to your second is, the national health board is not going to replace insurance companies, but insurance companies will—if the little ones want to continue to do this they'll have to find a way to join with one another to get into big bargaining units because we've got to let the small business people be in bigger units, otherwise they can't get their costs down. The national health board will be responsible for making sure that there is a reasonable budget to keep the costs in line and for making sure that we have developed reasonable quality standards to make sure that there is no erosion of quality of health care in the prescribed services.

[*A participant asked if small businesses should be limited to obtaining insurance from an alliance program only.*]

The President. Well, each State will have the right to certify how many alliances they approve, and my presumption is, given just what you said, is that most States will choose to certify a number of alliances and then you can choose whichever one you want. You'll have the three basic policies that you can choose plus however many alliances there are in any given State or the District of Columbia. You can pick the one that you think will provide the highest quality care and perhaps the one that gets the better price. Keep in mind, we're talking about ceiling on payroll costs, and if they get a better price you get a better price.

[*Administrator Bowles reaffirmed the importance of alliance programs in driving down the cost of health care and stated that businesses will still be able to choose what kind of alliance they want.*]

The President. But as an employer, if there are more than one alliance covering your State, you would choose the alliance you wanted to be a part of.

Q. Will those alliances compete with each other for prices, or will they——

The President. Absolutely. What we're trying to do is get the maximum amount of competition in the system for the services that have to be provided at——

Administrator Bowles. Harnessing the power of the marketplace to drive the price down, to put power in your hands instead of in the hands of insurance companies.

The President. We are trying not to turn this into a system where the Government has to regulate it all or the Government tries to just fix the prices. We are trying for once to get marketing power. What happens now is the Government doesn't do it, but the private sector doesn't do it either. There's no effective competition except for big buyers.

And let me just say, our estimated costs, which are dramatically less than the system's now but more than inflation, may be too high if you really get competition. The California public employees, for example, have a huge buying unit. And they can bargain for themselves. They got a 3 percent increase this year or something like that.

Companies with over 5,000 employees that are in a position of bargaining for themselves have averaged 6 percent premium increases in the last 2 or 3 years. They've been able to do what we now want small business to be able to do by allowing them to join together. My own personal preference is you should have an option of different alliances to be in. But under the plan as it now is, that is a judgment that will have to be made on a State-by-State basis. And the reason we did that is that the States are in different circumstances. I mean, for example, availability of the number of alliances may be quite different in Wyoming, our least populous State, than it would be in California, our most populous State. So we think it has to be a State-by-State decision.

[*Administrator Bowles added that businesses will save money because they will no longer have to take the time to negotiate with insurance companies.*]

The President. Yes, sir. I like your tie, Save the Children tie. I've got one just like it.

[*A participant asked if small business employees would have the same coverage as Federal employees, whether the Government could help small businesses receive credit more easily, and if employees would have to pay 20 percent of their salary on health care.*]

The President. First of all, let's start with your first question. We propose to put the public employee groups in buying alliances, just like people in the private sector. And in fact, we hope we'll have a lot of these alliances. We'll have both public and private folks within the same alliance.

In effect, the employees and the employers that have preexisting comprehensive health benefits where the benefits equal or exceed what they're providing now, we don't propose to take those away from them, those that are paying more and do it, but even many of them will be better off.

For example, General Motors—I don't think I'm talking out of school here. I believe it's General Motors—is now paying about 19 percent of payroll on health care costs, about two-thirds for existing employees, one-third for retirees. They will actually, over a period of years, have a very steep drop in their payroll costs, which will enable them to hire more people and also invest more money and do more business with their smaller contractors around the country. That's just one example.

The short answer to your question is, yes, we want the public employees to be in the alliances as well.

With regard to your second question, we believe that the credit system should be opened up. You may know, I've been trying since I first got in office to simplify the banks' regulatory system and to get them to be able to make more good faith loans again and to do a lot of that. I must say, we're trying to do a canvass of the country now. We're getting wildly uneven reports. I had three Congressmen, for example, from the heartland of the country the other day tell me they just had lunch together, and they were all three spontaneously talking about how much different it was and how banks were loaning money to small businesses again. But as I talked to most bankers and most business people in California, New England, Florida, just to give you three examples, I hear basically no difference. So maybe Erskine would like to address that. I do think that the general availability of credit to small business is still a big problem in this country.

The third thing I would say is that most employees with modest wages will not be paying a great deal for their health care. If they get sick and have to get health care without any insurance, they may face a much bigger bill. Meanwhile, all the people who are paying something for their health care are in effect paying to keep the infrastructure of health care there for them.

If I were to propose to you, for example, the following proposition, that it is unfair to make some people pay the gas tax because it's tough on them, there would be a riot in this country, because people think that we should all pay for the infrastructure of the highways. But there is an infrastructure of health care. And those of you who pay something for your health care have paid for it. You have paid just to have the hospitals there and the emergency room there and the doctors there when someone else needs it.

It seems to me, if you want to simplify the system and control costs, one of the things that you've got to do is stop the cost shifting. So I would argue that even though it might be tough, that to ask employees to pay 20 percent of the cost of health care, if you're controlling the cost and—not only you're controlling it today and providing it to them cheaper than they could otherwise get it but also make sure that the cost goes up more in line with inflation instead of 3 or 4 times the rate of inflation, that that is a fair thing to ask people to do.

Do you want to talk about the credit issue for a minute?

[*Administrator Bowles discussed caps in the plan to prevent employees from paying too much and efforts to make credit more available.*]

The President. I guess I'd be remiss if I didn't say this. Most everybody in this room will be a net beneficiary from the fact that the recent economic plan increased the expensing provision from $10,000 a year to $17,500 a year. For people who don't have any insurance now and are going to provide some, that increased expensing provision will probably for many thousands of small businesses more than cover the increased cost of the premiums. They access it.

Administrator Bowles. Mr. President, I did promise that I would get you back very quickly, so we don't have much more time.

[*A participant asked how preventive care would be addressed in the new plan.*]

The President. Yes, wasn't that great? First of all, what I know about your situation, you will benefit, I think, considerably from this, from the premium cap. But secondly, one of the things that we built into this coverage was a preventive and primary care component.

I don't want to pretend that the only reason health care is more expensive in America is because of the insurance system and the administrative costs, although that's a big reason, and because you don't have any buying power. But another reason is, we go way heavy on specialty care and high-technology care, which is great if you need it. And it will keep us from every get down to what some other countries have. That's why I think we're all willing to pay a premium because we know someday we or some loved one of ours may need that extra operation or that fancy machine.

But it's important to recognize that in America, for example, only about 15 percent of the graduates coming out of our medical schools now are general practitioners. In almost all the other countries with which we're competing, about half the doctors are general practitioners. They do primary and preventive care.

So we have done two things that I think are important. In this plan we will increase the money for medical research. But at the same time we will provide more incentives to the medical schools of our country to produce more primary care physicians, more family doctors, if you will. And in the health care plan, we will cover more preventive services, because it is just clear that the more you do preventive medicine, the more you lower the cost of health care and the healthier you keep your folks.

[*A participant expressed concern that the cost of the new plan would prevent some small businesses from competing in a global economy.*]

The President. Well now, I think the numbers do add up. Some small businesses will pay more, plainly. Those who aren't paying anything and those who are paying less than they would otherwise pay under the initial premiums set unless we are able to—our estimate unless in the bargaining power they'll even be able to bargain for lower prices, which is conceivable. But we have to start out with something.

But there's a lot of talk about these numbers not being—I'd just like to tell you what we've done over the last 7 months. Number one, for the first time we've got four Government De-partments that agree on the numbers, that the numbers are accurate at least, and we have run these numbers through 10 actuarial firms, private sector firms. So we have tried to get at least the first set of numbers that have ever been through this sort of vetting process from any private or public agency on health care. No one else has ever done as much work as we have tried to do to make sure the numbers work out. Keep in mind, we proposed for the Government to cover the uninsured who are unemployed.

We believe you can't get costs under control and stop cost shifting unless you have some means of insuring everybody else. We believe employers should do something. There are those who may have to pay more because their premiums are quite low, and we're going to increase the coverage substantially. But all of our surveys show that is a distinct minority of the people who provide any insurance now, that many people who provide insurance now will actually get, unbelievably enough, lower premiums and more coverage. But some will pay more. I don't want to minimize that; some will. What I think all of you are going to have to do is two things. You're going to have to read the plan when you get the details, when we finally produce it, and say, "How's this going to affect me, and can I live with it?" And then you're going to have to say, "How will it affect the small business sector of the economy as a whole, and are we net better off?"

And more importantly, I would argue to you that even those of you—let's suppose there's an employer here in this group who will go from 6 percent of payroll to 7.9 percent of payroll. If you look at where you've come in the last 5 years, if we don't do something to bring these costs under control, you're facing one of two decisions. You're either going to have to drop your coverage altogether with all the attendant insecurities and anxieties and problems that presents for your employees, or your costs are going to go through the roof.

So my argument is—I really believe this, this goes back to the very first question Barry asked—my argument is that in 5 years from now, even the people who pay slightly more now will be better off because the overall system's costs will be controlled for the first time, and we're not going to be strangled with it. That's why we tried to at least do a phase-in for the smaller employers.

[*A participant claimed the new plan would result in job loss due to increased health care costs for small businesses.*]

The President. How can it possibly triple your health care costs?

Q. We're paying currently about 2.9.

The President. To do what?

Q. For major medical benefits—of payroll costs.

The President. What does it cover?

Q. What are they covering?

The President. Yes.

Q. Major medical, 80/20. Catastrophic care.

The President. Well, we tried to have a catastrophic package, remember, a few years ago? And the whole country rose up against it.

All I can say to you, sir, is that if we don't do something like this, then everybody's going to be going in the same direction you are. I mean, we are looking at a situation now where we're going to give the pay raises of American workers to the health care lobby. That's where we are now. We are looking at a situation, if we don't do something—maybe Erskine's got a specific answer to you. But if we keep on doing what we're doing, more small businesses will go bankrupt, more people will do without health insurance. We're basically going to give our economic growth to health care for the next 7 years if we keep on doing what we're doing.

And if we don't require some uniformity of coverage, then everybody will want the lowest common denominator, and the Government will wind up picking up the bill for all the other health care costs. I mean, there is no way we can, I don't think, solve every problem. But if there is something we can do for people like between 50 and 100 employees, if there's something else we need to look at, we ought to do it. But I still believe—I will say to you—every study shows, the National Small Business United study shows, that the vast majority of small business people will come out way ahead economically on this. So the question is, are we going to lose more jobs doing what we're doing? Are we going to lose more jobs with the alternative? I argue to you that we have killed this economy now unconscionably for the last 12 years by letting health care costs go up as they have.

[*Administrator Bowles again stated that the new plan would enable business owners to provide comprehensive, low cost coverage. A participant then asked about low-profit small businesses, as compared to his own highly profitable restaurant.*]

The President. First of all, let's just take somebody's running a family restaurant and they make $20,000 a year. The following things will happen to them: First of all, they'll be capped at 3.5. Secondly, their expensing provision of the Tax Code went from $10,000 to $17,500. Thirdly, they're going to get a tax cut under the new tax bill because their family's working for a living and because of their low income.

So those folks are going to do fine. The people that I'm concerned about here are people who have—people like him, say people who net between $50,000 and $100,000 income, have more than 50 employees, and aren't eligible for the cap the way the bill's now drawn. Anybody who is under 50 employees with anything like in the wage range we're talking about, I think will probably recover between the caps and the expensing provision, will probably be able to manage through this okay in the early years. The people that I'm most worried about are the people in the category of this gentleman here who spoke.

Q. Won't there still be a cash flow problem for these small businesses, though? And how will that be addressed? Is this a percentage of their salary that will be withdrawn every paycheck, or how will that work?

[*Administrator Bowles stated that the cost increase per employee would not be appreciable.*]

The President. One of you asked a question about the employees, too, about how they could pay and whether they could pay. Don't forget that under this tax bill that just passed, most families, working people with children with incomes of under $27,000 a year, are going to get a tax reduction which will help them to deal—if they have no health care costs now—with the upfront cost of this. Most of them will have a tax reduction that exceeds what their 20 percent cost of the premium will be.

I think the real problem, by and large, there may be some—I can conceive of economic circumstances under which these problems will occur that you talked about. But I think the real problem here in the way the plan is drawn now is the people in his category.

Administrator Bowles. Can we close with one——

The President. Well, let's take two more. These folks in the back, and then our hosts ought to be able to close up.

[*A participant asked if the plan would address behavioral causes for increased health care costs.*]

The President. Yes, well, let me sort of reinforce what she said. I'm going to back off one step and then I'll come right back to your question. If someone asks me, is there any conceivable way America could get its contribution, that is, the percentage of our income we pay going to health care down to Canada's or Germany's, I would say no. And I would say no for some good reasons and then no for some not so good reasons.

One good reason, though, that we probably all agree on is that we spend more money on medical research, advanced technology, trying to break down barriers, trying to help people live longer and better lives than any other country. And I don't think any of us would want to give that up. Let's just say that adds 1 or 2 percent to our contribution to health care. It also employs a lot of people, by the way, who make basically high incomes and make our economy stronger. So I don't think any of us would want to give that up.

But here, to go back to your point, are the down sides. We have a lot of people who smoke, a lot of people who are overweight. We also have a higher percentage of teenage births which are far more likely to be low birth weight births, far likely to be very costly, and far likely to lead to children with mental and physical limitations. We have the highest percentage of AIDS of any advanced nation, and that's extremely expensive. And as, thank God, we find drugs to keep people alive and their lives better longer, it will be more expensive. We have to have a preventive strategy there. And perhaps most important of all, and here in Washington I think I could say it and get a cheer from the Mayor, this is the most violent advanced country on Earth. We have the highest percentage of our people behind bars of any country, which means that every weekend we've got more people showing up at the emergency room cut up or shot than any other country, and the rest of you are all paying for it.

So yes, we need a strategy to change those behaviors. We could start by passing the Brady bill and taking semiautomatic weapons out of the hands of teenagers. It would change the environment. Nobody ever talks about it that way, but if you did something about this, it would lower health care costs. I mean, if you could get a spreadsheet on the cost of health care in Washington hospitals, you would see that an awful lot of it goes to the emergency room.

So the answer to that is yes. One of the reasons I made the appointment I did to the Surgeon General's office is so that we could have a broad-based, aggressive, preventive strategy to change group behaviors as well as individual ones.

[*A participant asked what decisions were still to be made before the plan could be implemented.*]

The President. Well, there are a lot of hurdles that exist. But I think some of those hurdles are good hurdles. That is, I have been working on this issue for 3 years, over 3 years. Long before I ever thought of running for President, I agreed to head a project for the Governors on health care. And I started off by interviewing 900 health care providers in my own State. I then interviewed several hundred business people and employees about their particular circumstances. This is the most complicated issue that the United States has had to face in a long time. It has a very human face when you deal with the human dimensions of it. But it's extremely complex.

So the first hurdle is to try to get everybody singing out of the same hymnal, as we say at home. For example, in the next few days, Congress is going to sponsor a 2-day health university for Republicans and Democrats just to try to get information and facts out, just to try to get the evidence so people will get a feel for all of your different circumstances and what are the problems, and how does the system presently work, and what are the costs, and where are we out of line, all things we've been talking about today. So getting the information out, I think is significant.

Then I think the next big hurdle will be trying to make sure that we make decisions based on the real issues and not illusory ones. I've not tried to mask the fact today, and I won't in the debate, that there are some tough choices to be made and that in the short run we can't make 100 percent of the people winners. For example, if you want to end job lock and preexisting conditions and really smooth out things for small business, you have to go to broad-based community rating. That is plainly the best for small business and plainly the best for most Americans. If you do that, young, single, super healthy people may pay slightly higher premiums, because what you do is you merge them in with middle-aged people who get cancer but still can go back to work, for example. So there are tough choices to be made.

Then thirdly, if you really clean out the administrative waste in this system and you go to a more preventive-based system, you will shift the way you are spending money. You will shift the dimensions of the health care system, and you'll shift money drastically away from administration and insurance costs into the provision of basic health care. And so there will be people who won't favor that and will fight it.

You will also tend to favor either bigger providers of health care, and these big alliances are people who have joined together and do it jointly to provide an alliance. So then we'll fight through the winners and losers. That'll be the toughest part in the Congress. There is a real spirit of cooperation, I think, in the Congress now. A willingness to try to face this terrible problem, do something sensible about it, take our time and really listen to people, and do more good than harm. And I think that's very hopeful. We should all be very glad about that.

[*A participant asked how the Government could prevent the plan from becoming underfunded due to population age.*]

The President. Well, the way you can—arguably, Medicaid is underfunded now, although the truth is that it's wrongly funded. That is we're spending money on the wrong things. The Medicaid budget is still going up, over the next 5 years is projected to go up somewhere between 16 percent next year and 11 percent in the 5th year, in other words, over 4 times the rate of inflation next year.

Social Security, believe it or not, is now overfunded. That is, it got underfunded 10 years ago. If people hadn't made the right projections for the—it is now overfunded, but the overage is all being used to make the deficit look smaller. So we're going to have to stop spending Social Security on the deficit if you don't want the payroll tax for Social Security to bankrupt

small business. Because when I, people my age—I'm the oldest of the baby boomers, people born from '46 to '64—when we start retiring in the next century, we cannot at that moment still be using the Social Security tax to make the deficit look smaller, which is another reason it's so important to get control of this deficit now. We just can't do it.

The answer to your question, sir, is Social Security is basically under control if we bring the deficit down. The problem with the Medicare and Medicaid system is that it can't control its membership since the system, the private system, is hemorrhaging. And it is based on a fee-for-service system where there is no regularization of benefits and where many of the beneficiaries don't assume any responsibility for themselves.

So what we're going to try to do is to increase the amount of personal responsibility in the system as well as put some cost controls. Then, instead of just paying a fee-for-service system, what we want to do is put Medicare and Medicaid—starting with Medicaid because Medicare actually works pretty well, it's adequately funded and well-administered—but Medicaid, we want to put those folks in the same kind of health alliances so they'll be in competition, to go back to what you guys said, so there will be some competition for the services.

Florida has started to do that, and their preliminary indications are there's going to be a big reduction in the cost of Medicaid if we do it. In other words, I think the mistake has been not to have Medicaid subject to the same sort of competitive environment that the bigger private sector employers are. If you put small business and the Medicaid in where a lot of the bigger employers are now and the public employees, you're going to see a real modification of the cost trends in the outer years in ways that will help you all as taxpayers as well as employers.

Thank you very much. They say we've got to go. I wish we could stay. You were great. Thanks.

NOTE: The President spoke at 10:15 a.m. at the W.S. Jenks and Sons hardware store. In his remarks, he referred to DC City Council member Harry Thomas, Sr.

Remarks Honoring the All-American Cities Award Winners
September 16, 1993

The President. Thank you very much, please be seated—everybody except you. [*Laughter*]

I want to say first of all, whenever I am with a group from our Nation's small towns and cities, I always feel at home. I've just come from a number of meetings. Mayor Cisneros, you should have been with me. We just had a health care briefing with leaders from cities and counties and States around the country. And then I met with the Association of Black Mayors. But I'm especially glad to be here, because one of the cities represented here is from my previous hometown of Little Rock—and I'm glad to see Mayor Sharon Priest here and Lottie Shackleford from the City of Little Rock, Congressman Thornton, and a lot of my other friends are here—along with all the other cities who won in 1992 and who are being recognized in 1993.

Before he became the chairman of the Housing and Urban Development—or the Secretary of the Housing and Urban Development Department, Henry Cisneros was the chairman of the National Civic League. And as we recognize that League for this program today, I'd also like to thank the group for generously surrendering Mr. Cisneros to the administration. [*Laughter*]

Last week in Cleveland with Mayor Mike White, who's also here to be recognized, the Vice President and I announced how we want to change the way our National Government works and how we work with State and local government to encourage more of the kinds of successes we salute today. We believe if we can streamline Federal grant programs so that mayors can worry more about what works for their community rather than what works for grant administrators in the Federal bureaucracy, our country will work better, and we'll get more for our tax dollars. We believe that by cutting paperwork, we'll get the money to the local level more quickly and save the taxpayers money at the same time.

I also want to commend our mayors for the struggle to provide health care to the citizens of our cities in spite of the barriers to access, in spite of skyrocketing costs, in spite of underfunded public health clinics and overtaxed institutions and not very much leadership from this capital for quite a long time. With the mayors' help, we can bring about comprehensive, affordable health care for all Americans and free up more of our strapped State and local budgets to invest in jobs and growth and opportunity for our people.

I want to now congratulate the mayors and the delegations from each of our All-American Cities. This prestigious award recognizes America's heroes who have taken responsibility for their communities, who form partnerships among citizens, local government, and private businesses to ensure that we meet the urgent needs of our people and open new opportunities for our neighbors.

The 1992 winners are here along with the 1993 winners because there was no ceremony last year. So very briefly I am going to recognize all the 1992 winners, and I think they are to my right, is that right? I will acknowledge the mayor and the city, and then if anybody is here from the city I call out, I want you to stand up, too.

First of all, Mayor John Williams from Kenai, Alaska. Anybody else here? How many people live there, Mayor?

Mayor Williams. Seven thousand.

The President. Seven thousand, that's a lot bigger than the town I was born in. [*Laughter*]

Mayor Sharon Priest from Little Rock, Arkansas. Would the group from Arkansas please stand? Thank you. Mayor Gerald Roberts from Delta, Colorado. Would the group from Colorado please stand? Mayor Charles Box from Rockford, Illinois. Mayor Joseph Steineger from Wyandotte County, Kansas City, Kansas. Mr. Charles Tooley—is that right?—from Billings, Montana. Anybody else here from Billings? Thank you. Beautiful place.

Mayor George Jones from Jacksonville, North Carolina. Mayor George Christensen from Minot, North Dakota. Mayor Gregory Lashutka—is that right?—from Columbus, Ohio. Great city. Mayor Bill Card from Harlingen, Texas. I've been there.

Now I want to recognize this year's winning communities in alphabetical order.

Cleveland, Ohio, wins this award for the fifth

time for fostering cooperation between police and citizens, for addressing Cleveland's school system in the Cleveland Summit on Education, and for its innovative efforts, which I have personally observed, to direct investments to needy neighborhoods. As I said last week when we kicked off our reinventing Government campaign, the Vice President and I went to Cleveland because of the astonishing success Mayor White is having in moving property that has been abandoned or where the taxes haven't been paid into the hands of his citizens and into the hands of developers and putting jobs back into the inner city. Congratulations to you, sir.

Believe it or not, inadvertently somebody let me come out here without all the names of all the winners, so we're going to have to— Have you got the list of the names of the people who are here? Who else is here from Cleveland? Anybody else? Stand up there.

The next winner is Dawson County, Nebraska. Mr. Ed Cook, and who else is here from Dawson County? Thank you—an All-American County for countywide cooperation among seven separate communities on regional economic development, solid waste disposal and recycling, and for improving the awareness of the diverse cultural backgrounds of the people of his county.

Next is Delray Beach, Florida, Mayor Thomas Lynch—anybody else here? Thank you. For community policing—thank you—increased public involvement in the local schools and for turning an underused former high school into a useful community cultural center for all the people of Delray Beach.

Fort Worth, Texas, Mayor Kay Granger. Who else is here from Fort Worth? Anyone else? That's good, a big delegation. Welcome. For its crime fighting program, Code Blue, for neighborhood planning efforts, and for the Vision Coalitions Town Hall Meeting. That must have been some gathering. I've been conducting town hall meetings for 2 years, and I never won an award for one yet. [*Laughter*] I guess I won an election for one, maybe that's just as well. [*Applause*] Thank you. One thing I will say, they work. They tell you what people think, and it gives people a chance to reestablish connections with their political leaders.

Laredo, Texas, for community-wide efforts for better health care, for the Poncho de la Garza Housing Development Program, and a new branch library to serve community needs. Who's here from Laredo?

Mayor Ramirez. Saul Ramirez.

The President. Oh yes, Mayor Ramirez. Who else is here? There they are. I've been there. I was with the Mayor over a year ago in Laredo. It's also a good place to jog in the early morning.

Oakland, California, Mayor Elihu Harris, Congressman Ron Dellums, and others. Please stand up, all the people from Oakland, whose residents came together across the lines of race and class to rebuild after the fire of 1991. Its Safe Streets Now program has brought 3,500 people together to get tough with landlords responsible for 250 properties used to traffic drugs. They have also established a health center to meet the special needs of Oakland's American Indian population. And I can say, based on recent knowledge, it's a very good place to spend the night. Thank you very much. Congratulations.

Pulaski, Tennessee, Mr. Daniel Speer. Who else is here from Pulaski, Tennessee? Please stand up. For industrial development that attracts new jobs, for the rehabilitation of public housing, for Pulaski's annual Brotherhood Observance, which shows how people can take their city back and send a moving message of hope all across our Nation.

Washington, North Carolina. Mayor Floyd Brothers. How are you, Mayor? Good to see you. [*Applause*] Thank you. Anyone else here from Washington? Thank you for coming. For efforts to revitalize the West Fourth Street neighborhood, for addressing the quality of drinking water, for waste water treatment and protection of surrounding rivers, and for bringing more of the community together through increased cultural outreach programs.

Wichita, Kansas, Mayor Elma Broadfoot. Anybody else here from Wichita? [*Applause*] Thank you. For its Summer Youth Academy to get young people more involved in learning and less involved in gangs, for a partnership that encourages troubled youths to seek treatment for their problems and rewards them with improved self-esteem and for a project to restore the quality of life within a Wichita neighborhood.

Wray, Colorado, Ms. Roberta Helling. How are you? Anybody else here from Wray, Colorado? For the town's first rehabilitation center, a family counseling center and a new hospital, the only multiple-physician facility in a 100-mile radius, all this done by a town with a population of just about 2,000 people. If we had the people from this Colorado town here in the Nation's Capital, we'd probably lick our problems in no time. [*Laughter*]

While I have mentioned these places by name, the awards really belong to the people in the communities, even those who weren't able to come here today. To be an All-American City, it doesn't matter how big you are or how much money you have. It's not the racial composition or the region in which the community is located. What matters is the commitment of the people, the innovation of the leaders, and the cooperation of people across all the lines that too often divide us in America.

Now to say a few words on behalf of the All-American City program, is Mr. Wayne Hedien—come on up here—chairman and CEO of Allstate Insurance, representing the Allstate foundations, whose generosity has made these awards possible.

[*At this point, Mr. Hedien made brief remarks.*]

The President. A generation ago, Robert Kennedy spoke of America's cities and towns and said, "The time has come to bring the engines of government, of technology, of the economy fully under the control of our citizens, to recapture and reinforce the values of a more human time and place."

We honor leaders who have done that. But I hope also we look at the challenges still facing all of us. I asked Henry Cisneros to join this Cabinet because I thought he was not only a brilliant and committed person but because I thought he understood how we could help instead of hinder the energies of people who live at the grassroots level. We're trying to reform a lot of our housing programs to help you do that.

I asked Bob Reich to come into the Labor Department because I thought he understood that cities and local groups committed to training our work force and helping unemployed people go back to work weren't doing very well with 150 separate education and training programs. We want to allow you to consolidate them and spend the money in ways that will best put your own people back to work.

I have done everything I could to support the brilliant work done by the Vice President to try to reconceive the whole relationship between the Federal and the State and local government. We have a lot of work to do.

And I just want to say one thing in closing. One of the things that we have to do is to impress upon the people who live here in Washington, and not just the United States Congress but also the people who run all of these Departments, that we don't have a day to waste. You see every day where you live what can happen if you do something right. You also see the enormous consequences of continued neglect, of continuing to do things the way they are.

And let me just say, there are a lot of things that I want to do as President that will just help you to do what I know you'll do anyway if we can find a way to give you the power to do it.

I hope you will help us to pass the kind of health care reform that will liberate you and make your citizens healthier. I hope you will help us to pass this reinventing Government program. I hope you will support the innovations of Henry Cisneros and Bob Reich and the other members of the Cabinet. I hope you will come up to this city and demand that we finally do something to help you get guns out of the hands of people who are behaving irresponsible with them. We need to pass the Brady bill. And we don't need to have a situation that we have in many of our cities where the average person committing a murder is under the age of 16 and has access to semiautomatic weapons. There's no reason children should have those in the cities of this country. We have work to do. We need your help. Bring your ideas, your innovation, your energy back to Washington and give us a chance to do it.

Thank you very much.

NOTE: The President spoke at 5:10 p.m. in the East Room at the White House.

Remarks to the Congressional Hispanic Caucus Institute
September 16, 1993

Thank you all, ladies and gentlemen, for that wonderful welcome. And thank you especially, my good friend Congressman Serrano, for that warm introduction and for not telling them that you are, after all, much faster than I am. [*Laughter*]

I also have to tell you, I just left my daughter at home. She's home working on her homework. Hillary's still working on health care. She summoned me. She said, "Dad, when you get the monkey suit on, come in and let me look at you." [*Laughter*] She always checks to see if I've taken all the shaving cream off my face. I was so proud of her because she is working on her accelerated Spanish course. When I heard Joe up here introducing me, I thought I should go ahead and confess that I asked my daughter if she would let me learn along with her. And she said, "I doubt if you can keep up, Dad, but you're welcome to try." [*Laughter*]

I am deeply honored to be here tonight with the Hispanic Congressional Caucus Institute. Since the time this institute was founded and I was Governor of Arkansas, I have admired your work. Your programs are helping to pass the baton to a new generation of leaders, grooming them in the halls of Congress and in Federal Agencies and encouraging them to pass along what they've learned to others. It's important work for young people and for our country. I want to say thank you for that. One day, it will produce a President of the United States.

I want to compliment the Institute's executive director, Rita Elizondo. Her hard work may help to inspire other children to pursue the lofty achievement of those whom you honor tonight: Ellen Ochoa, the first Hispanic woman in space, and Lucille Becerra Roybal, who has done so much to set an example for everyone in bringing urgent change to our country at the grassroots level. I would also like to honor and acknowledge Mrs. Roybal's husband, former Congressman Edward Roybal, and their daughter who has followed so well in her footsteps, Congresswoman Lucille Roybal-Allard.

There are a few people here from our administration tonight; I'd be remiss if I did not acknowledge them. First of all, our brilliant Secretary of Housing and Urban Development, Henry Cisneros, and his wife, Mary Alice. And I want to say a public and personal thank you to Henry Cisneros for what he did this week to prove that we're still behind the enforcement of civil rights in housing in this country. I want to acknowledge the presence of our outstanding Secretary of Transportation, Federico Peña, and his wife, Ellen. Unlike me, they may be faster runners than Congressman Serrano.. Nelson Diaz, the General Counsel at HUD; Aida Alvarez, the Director of the Office of Federal Housing Enterprise Oversight at HUD; Norma Cantu, the Assistant Secretary for Civil Rights at the Department of Education; Fernando Torres-Gil, the Assistant Secretary for Aging at HHS; Maria Echaveste, who runs the Wage and Hour Division at the Department of Labor; Joe Velasquez, the Deputy Assistant to the President for Political Affairs; Isabelle Tapia, the Deputy Assistant to the President for Scheduling and Advance; Patti Solis, the Deputy Assistant to the President who directs the scheduling for the First Lady; Lillian Fernandez, my Special Assistant in the House Liaison Office; and Carolyn Curiel, who is with Communications and Speechwriting and helped me write all the things that I may not be able to say properly tonight. I want to say a special word of thanks, too, to a former member of our staff, the Assistant to the President for Intergovernmental Relations, Regina Montoya, who went home to Dallas. But she's here with us tonight. I thank her for her service.

The people now who serve in this administration, from the White House to the Cabinet departments, the people who serve on Capitol Hill, the people who are full-time public servants, have set an example that will be important to the whole country. All the people who are now in the unprecedently large Hispanic Caucus in the Congress can now honestly help to represent the hopes, the dreams of the Hispanic people of the United States and equally important, perhaps, to ensure that we make Hispanic-Americans full partners so that we move forward and do it together.

I had an awesome experience earlier this week, as all of you know and some of you have already commented on it, when I hosted the Prime Minister of Israel and the Chairman of the Palestine Liberation Organization in signing an historic peace agreement that, if you had asked just one month before, probably 90 percent of the American people and 90 percent of the informed opinion in the world would say could never come to pass.

It was an amazing thing, you know, once I realized it was going to happen and they wanted to come here to Washington to consummate the signing and make sure that the President didn't forget that the signing was the beginning, not the end, of the process, and then trying to work out how these two men who had fought each other literally for decades, who had put their whole lives into spilling the blood of one another's family and friends and allies, how they could somehow undergo this transformation to see each other as problems but not as necessary enemies. Someone said—I don't want to claim credit for that phrase—that this whole thing happened because, for some reason, at this magic moment in our history, those people looked at each other and saw enemies no more, but only problems. Problems can be solved. Progress can be made. Enemies don't talk to each other.

Tonight I want to talk to you from the heart for just a moment about possibilities. Because what that moment reminded me of, again, is that if we can imagine it, it can happen. If we can somehow engage the thorniest problems, if we can somehow unlock the ears and the hearts of the toughest adversaries, it can happen.

Tonight I ask you, my fellow Americans, to think about what it is we would like our children and our grandchildren to say we did with this moment in history, a moment in which many, many good things are happening and many, many bad things are happening at a bewildering rate of speed. The cold war comes to an end when the Berlin Wall drops and the Eastern European countries abandon communism and Russia abandons communism, revealing there a whole new set of problems, economic problems, social problems, religious and ethnic conflict but still, to be sure, taking away the threat of nuclear annihilation. We see people hungering in Latin America for democracy and seizing it and trying to build free economies where free people can work hard and be rewarded for their labors, trying to escape from the dark years of political repression and economic depression.

We see so much to be hopeful about. Here in this country, we see the wonders of technology opening up worlds we would never have imagined. That's all true. But we also see a world in which none of the rich countries can figure out how to create jobs, a world in which most Americans are working harder than they were 10 years ago for roughly the same wages in real dollar terms they were making 20 years ago to pay more for education and health care and in taxes, wondering whether ever they will be able to pass along to their children the dream that they had as children.

We have to face the fact that, in spite of the fact that people look to us all over the world to make peace, they wish us to go in and stop the starvation and the oppression in other countries, we of all the countries in the world have the highest percentage of people in prison because we are so violent. We have cities where the average age of murderers is now under 16, where teenagers carry weapons that are better than those police officers have. So we have this anomalous situation. If you are well-off in this country, you have the best health care in the world, but if you're one of the 35 million or so who don't have it, you're in a real fix. If you work for a living and you lose your job, you might lose your health care. If your child ever gets sick, really sick, you may never be able to change jobs without losing your health care.

We have a Government desperately needing more funds to grow the economy and to deal with the real problems we face at home and abroad, mired in the operating patterns of 60 years ago. And it is no wonder that so many of us are distrustful of our Government and afraid of our future and unwilling to take the kinds of chances that Americans have always taken in expanding trade beyond our borders, in reaching out to establish closer ties with our neighbors, in believing that the future belongs to us and can be bright and broad and deep if we do what we should.

So I ask you tonight not to take the shine off a perfectly wonderful and happy evening, to simply search your heart and say if Itzhak Rabin and Yasser Arafat could come here and sign away the legacy of the last four or five decades of hatred, to try to make a new beginning, can we not also make a new beginning in this time of sweeping change?

My dreams for this country are not very complicated. I believe that, in a time of change, you can do two things: You can hunker down and turn away from it and hope it'll go away, and that works about one time in a hundred. About once in a hundred it'll work. Or you can say there has to be a way I can make this change my friend. There has to be a way that the most basic traditional values I harbor, to have a good family life, to live in a safe community, to see my work rewarded, to give my children a good education, there has to be a way for me to enhance those values and hopes and dreams in the face of all this change. What is it I must do to do that?

And if I ever do anything, whether you agree with it or not, and you want to know, "Why in the world did that fool do that?" all you have to do is to remember what I just told you, because I believe in this time of momentous change, it is my job not to turn away from it and hunker down but to embrace it with gusto and figure out how to preserve those basic values by making the changes that will make all these trends our friend and not our enemy.

I do not pretend for a moment that I am always right or that I have all the answers. Indeed, sometimes I am so perplexed it is almost heartbreaking. But I know that the people who walk the dusty roads of south Texas or the hard streets of the South Bronx, the people who were in the Adelante Con Clinton army that got me 70 percent of the Hispanic vote in the last election, hired me to change things in this country.

And so I ask you to be part of that change. Everything that we have done is a part of that. The motor voter bill is important. Why? Because it makes it easier for more people to vote who aren't represented. Why should you trust people in politics to make changes if you're not a part of electing them?

The family leave law is part of that. Why? Because in a world in which more than half the mothers of children under 5 are in the work force, we have to make it possible to be a successful parent and a successful worker. We cannot force people to choose.

The economic program was part of that. Why? Because it is criminal for us to leave another decade where we quadruple the national debt and we load it onto our kids. And then the Congress, 10 years from now, comes to town, and they have no money to spend on education, no money to spend on the economy, no money to spend on new technology, no money to spend

defending the country, no money to spend on anything except paying checks, more money for the same health care, writing checks for retirement, and writing checks on interest on the national debt. There will be no ability to create the future unless we do something to release the burden of the debt.

The economic program was also important because, for the first time in history, we changed the tax laws so that millions of families, including millions of Hispanic families, can be told, if you work 40 hours a week and you have a child in your home, you will no longer be in poverty. The tax system will lift you out of poverty, not drive you into it. That was a profoundly important thing.

But there is more work to be done. We began today the formal campaign to try to pass a drastic reform of the health care system. Look at the Americans without health care. Look at the Americans in peril of losing their health care. Look at the businesses going broke or at least not able to hire anybody else because they can't afford the cost of health insurance for extra employees, so they work their present employees overtime or work part-time people because they can't pay for health insurance. Look at the number of people who live in our cities who don't have access to public health facilities that ought to be open around-the-clock and that ought to be engaging in primary and preventive care. Look at the number of children who are born with low birth weight. Look at all these things, and ask yourself how in the world can we justify continuing a system which costs our people 40 percent more than any other people on Earth pay and does less with it because we insist on funneling money into things that have nothing to do with the health of the American people and everything to do with undermining the future of this economy. I tell you, we cannot do it.

We are spending more money every year on the same health care. And I'm having trouble preserving funding for the space station, something which provides high-tech employment to Hispanic Americans from Texas to Florida to California and made possible future astronauts like Ellen Ochoa. Why? Because we have not faced our obligations. So I ask you to join me in this great effort to provide affordable health care to all Americans. We can do it, and we must do it.

Now, I ask you too—and I know, you know,

one of the worst things you can do at a dinner is talk about something where people at the dinner disagree. But I have to do this on the NAFTA issue, and I want to tell you why. I don't care if I change a single mind tonight, but I want you to think about this. I want you to think about—now, wait a minute. Wait a minute. You all can all speak and argue with each other when I'm gone. That's what I want you to do. [*Laughter*] I want you to think about this: The argument against the treaty is that it will lead to the movement of American jobs to Mexico because their wages are lower than ours. That's true. That's the argument, right?

There are 2,100 companies now in the *maquilladora* area. I governed a State where people shut down and moved their plants to Mexico, and I knew the people who lost their jobs. The only thing I want you to know is I would not knowingly do anything to make more people like that. So you say, why is this nut doing this if he's had personal experience? I'll tell you why. Because if we beat this thing, they can keep on doing that.

I'll give you another thing that I think is important. Because of the immigration laws passed before I became President, 2½ million Hispanics will have the opportunity to become legal citizens of this country. I believe that immigration has enriched and strengthened America. But the rising tide of illegal immigration in States like California is sparking a disturbing hostility to the diversity that is clearly the future of America. And I hear people in California say, "Well, I'm against this because of all this illegal immigration problem." What I want to tell you is anybody who wants to go to Mexico for low wages can go regardless of NAFTA. If we don't raise incomes in Mexico and incomes in America by strengthening our ties, the illegal immigration problem will get worse, not better. And then you will have more of this highly destructive, emotional, counterproductive feeling rifling throughout our political system. And I don't think that's good.

I think America ought to revel in its diversity. We ought to embrace our diversity. When people go to Los Angeles County, they ought to be happy that there are 150 different racial and ethnic groups there, not worried about somebody else who might show up tomorrow. So we, we should produce the policy, whatever it is; we should pursue the policy that will reduce illegal immigration, keep legal immigration going, and make Americans feel better about the diversity. Because without it, we'll never be what we ought to be, moving into the 21st century.

And let me say one last thing. A rich country in the world we're living in only grows richer, a rich country only grows richer by expanding its economic contacts beyond its borders. And we do not have the option to do what our friends across the Pacific and Japan did to build their economy—they don't even have the option of doing it anymore; they're going to have to quit—which is to sell everything to other people and not buy any of their stuff. We don't have that option.

So when I look at what's happening in the world and I see that Asia is the fastest growing part of the world and Latin America is the second fastest growing part of the world and Latin America is just here handy and starts on the south of our border with Mexico, the reason I want to do this over the long run is I want to keep the movement to democracy, I want to keep the movement for economic growth, I want Americans to prosper by helping our friends and neighbors in this hemisphere to build a stronger world. I think over the long run it will protect America's economic future.

Now, you don't have to agree. You don't have to agree. But I ask you if you disagree, don't win just because people are scared today, because we all know they're scared of losing their jobs. We all know people are alienated. But somebody's got to explain to me how people would be more likely to move their jobs to a place where they can move their jobs now if all they want to do is chase lower wages when the wages will be coming up, the environmental standards will be coming up, and people will be buying more American products. I believe it is in the interest of this country, again, not to turn away from the change but to embrace it, not because it will be easy, not because nobody will be hurt but because on balance we'll be better. We can never make in a world in which we live, which is always imperfect—we cannot make the perfect solution the enemy of the better solution. That is why I have embraced this course and why I hope others will as well.

Now let me just say one or two other things. I am excited about the upcoming referendum in Puerto Rico. Whatever they're for, I'm for. And I hope you are. I am excited about the prospects we have been given to promote democracy from Russia to the Middle East to Haiti. I am excited about the promise of change. I am profoundly disturbed about the problems we have.

The only thing I ask you to do is, even if you disagree with me, never run away from the problems. I don't understand why in the United States of America, when we've got the violence we've got on our cities, we can't pass the Brady bill in the Congress and take these assault weapons out of the hands of teenagers. I don't understand why we can't do that. I don't understand why we don't have an education and training system that from the moment someone loses their job—because now people don't normally get the jobs they lost back; they have to find another job—is no longer an unemployment system, but is a reemployment system, and from the get-go, from the first day, from the first week, people are told, "Here are the new jobs of the future, and here are funds to train for them." I don't understand that. But if you will help me and you leave me in, I'll fix those two problems, because you will fix them, not me. We'll do it together.

And I could give you example after example

after example of this. The thing I always love about being in the presence in any form or fashion of the Hispanic culture is that it is so life-affirming. It is so passionate. It is so real. It is so straightforward. I tell you, my friends, think about that event last Monday. Think about the passion, the feelings, the strength you have, what you worry about for your children and what you want for the future and say, if they can make peace, how can we in America walk away from our challenges? We're going to walk into them. We're going to conquer them. And the Hispanics in America are going to lead the way, lead the way in partnership with our administration and on every street and in every community of this country. I love what we can do, but I am troubled by the fact that we're not doing it. Let's seize every day we have to make the most of it. And always remember that peace agreement in the Middle East as a spur to us to make this country what it ought to be for our children.

Thank you, and God bless you all.

NOTE: The President spoke at 8:30 p.m. at the Washington Hilton.

Nomination for Assistant Secretaries of Commerce
September 16, 1993

The President today announced his intention to nominate Raymond E. Vickery, Jr., as Assistant Secretary for Trade Development and Charles Meissner as Assistant Secretary for International Economic Policy at the Department of Commerce. The President also nominated Lauri Fitz-Pegado as Assistant Secretary and Director General of the Office of the U.S.

and Foreign Commercial Service at Commerce.

"These talented individuals, experienced in their fields and committed to hard work, will offer strong support to Secretary Brown's team at Commerce," the President said. "I am pleased to have their help."

NOTE: Biographies of the nominees were made available by the Office of the Press Secretary.

Nomination for Deputy Director of the Peace Corps
September 16, 1993

The President today announced his intention to nominate U.S. Ambassador to the Republic of Djibouti, Charles R. Baquet III, a former Peace Corps volunteer, as Deputy Director of

the Peace Corps.

"Like Peace Corps Director Carol Bellamy, Charles Baquet is a former volunteer who knows firsthand the possibilities and problems facing the Peace Corps," the President said. "I am confident his experiences both as a volunteer and as a Foreign Service officer will serve him well as he works to ensure the Peace Corps meets its mission of helping others around the world."

NOTE: A biography of the nominee was made available by the Office of the Press Secretary.

Remarks at the Children's National Medical Center
September 17, 1993

The President. Thank you. Well, Dr. Beard, I promise to free you of the paperwork if you will promise not to use your free time to run for President. [*Laughter*]

Mr. Brown and Ms. Freiberg, Dr. Beard, to all of you who helped to make our visit here so wonderful today, I want to thank this Children's Hospital for bringing us together this morning, for giving us a chance to see some of your patients and their parents and their friends and to witness the miracles you are working. I want to thank Ben Bradlee and Sally Quinn for calling Al and me and telling us to hustle more money for the hospital.

In my former life, when I was a Governor, my wife and I worked very hard for the Arkansas Children's Hospital. Some of you know it's one of the 10 biggest hospitals in the country, and every year we finished first or second in the telethon, even though we come from a small State. There's a lot of grassroots support for people who are doing what you're doing.

We built a tertiary care nursery at our hospital with State funds, the first time anything like that had been done. And I have spent countless hours in our Children's Hospital at home with my own daughter, with the children of my friends, sometimes their last day, sometimes their best day. And I am profoundly grateful to you.

I think the people in the press and maybe some others might have wondered today why in the wide world we would come to a children's hospital, with all of its gripping, wonderful, personal stories, to have an event about bureaucracy and paperwork. After you listen to a nurse say why she couldn't care for a sick child and a doctor plead for more time to be a doctor, maybe you know. There is an intensely human element behind the need to reform the system we have.

When we were upstairs and Dr. Grizzard and Ms. Mahan were showing us some forms, we looked at four case files that they said had $14,000 worth of work in them that were absolutely unrelated to the care of the patient. The doctor said he estimated that each doctor practicing in this hospital, 200 in total, spent enough time on paperwork unrelated to patient care every year to see another 500 patients for primary preventive care—times 200. You don't have to be a mathematical genius to figure out that's another 10,000 kids who could have been cared for, whose lives could be better.

People say to me, how in the world do you expect to finance universal coverage and cut Medicare and Medicaid? Let me say first of all, nobody's talking about cutting Medicare and Medicaid; we're talking about whether it doesn't need to increase at 16 percent or 12 percent or 15 percent a year anymore. And it wouldn't if we had some simplification so people could spend the time they have already got on this Earth doing what they were trained to do.

I've got a friend who is a doctor that I grew up with who happens to live in the area, who calls me about once every 3 months to tell me another horror story. And the other day, he called me and he said, "You had better hurry up and get this done." He said, "You know, I'm in practice with this other guy. We've got all of these people doing paperwork. Now we've hired somebody who doesn't even fill out any forms. She spends all day on the telephone beating up on the insurance companies to pay for the forms we've already sent in. We actually had to hire somebody to do nothing but call on the phone." He said, "I'm lost in a fun house here." [*Laughter*] He said, "I went to medical school to try to practice medicine. Now I've got to hire somebody who does nothing but call people on the phone to pay the bills they're supposed to pay, after I've spent all this time filling out these forms?"

People complain about doctor fees going up. I'll give you one interesting statistic. In 1980, the average physician in America took home 75 percent of the revenues that were generated in a clinic. By 1990, that number had dropped from $.75 on the dollar to $.52. Where did the rest of it go? Right there. Most of it went to forms.

Now you know, when we were up in that medical records room, we saw all these forms. We were told that by the time the room was done, the room was already too small because the paper kept coming faster than you could make space for it in this hospital. A lot of you are nodding about that. Now they have records flowing on into a room that is beneath us in the garage, and these files are still growing at the rate of 6.5 feet a week.

We know, of course, from what Dr. Beard and Ms. Freiberg said, that's just some of the story. There are departments in this hospital that spend all their time trying to satisfy hundreds of different insurers. There are 1,500 in America, by the way. No other country has that many. This hospital I think deals with over 300. Each of them want a slightly different piece of information and in a slightly different way; so that even if you try to have a uniform form, it's not uniform by the time you finish customizing it.

How did this happen? Hospitals like this one treat people who are most vulnerable, weak, ailing, and in pain. To make sure that sick patients were getting the best care, Government regulators and private insurers created rules and regulations, and with them came forms to make sure you were following the rules and regulations. To make sure doctors and nurses then didn't see the patients that were getting the best care too often, keep them in the hospital too long, or charge them too much, there were more rules and regulations and along with them, more forms.

As more and more insurance agencies and private companies got into the business of selling health insurance—and as I said, there are now more than 1,500 insurers in this country; no other country in the world has anything like that many—each of them had their own forms and their own different list of what they would cover. And so what are you left with? Instead of all this paper and all these medical forms

assuring that the rules are followed and people get healthy, we're stuck in a system where we're ruled by the forms and have less time to make children and adults healthy.

When doctors and nurses are forced to write out the same information six different times in seven different ways just to satisfy some distant company or agency, it wastes their time and patients' money, and in the end, undermines the integrity of a system that leaves you spending more and caring for fewer people.

Just think about the patients. I don't know if you've read the stories in the morning paper about the people we invited to the Rose Garden at the White House yesterday. We invited about 100 people who had written us letters. We let 15 of them read their letters. They are part of the 700,000 letters that my wife and her group have received since we started this health care project. And they were all saying more or less the same thing: We want coverage. We don't want to be locked into our jobs, preexisting conditions shouldn't bankrupt families.

But there was one gentleman there from Florida, Jim Heffernan, who told us that he is a retiree on Medicare who spends his time working in hospice programs with people who are much sicker than he is. And he talked about how all the regulations, the reimbursement forms, all the complexities sap the energy and the morale and the vitality of the people that he was trying to help. He describes mountains of paperwork that older Americans face. He told how he now volunteers his time helping these patients to decipher their forms instead of helping them to feel better about their lives and think of something interesting to do every day to make every day count.

The biggest problem with all this, of course, is the waste and inefficiency. We spend more than 20 cents of every health care dollar on paperwork. And after about 4 years of studying this system, long before I even thought of running for President, I got interested in this at home, and I've tried to honestly compare our system with systems in other countries. And it appears to me that we spend about a dime on the dollar more than any other country in the world on bureaucracy and paperwork.

In a medical system that costs $880 billion, you don't have to be a mathematical genius to figure out what that is. What could we do in this country with that money? How many people could we cover? How many things could we do? How much more preventive care could we do to lower the long-term cost of the system? How many more children could we care for?

In the last 10 years, our medical providers have been hiring clerical help at 4 times the rate of direct health care providers. That is a stunning statistic. They spend resources that should go into care on other things.

What we want to do with this health security plan is to do away with all of that, to streamline the rules, reduce the paperwork, make the system make sense, and do nothing to interfere with the private delivery of care system that we have now. And we believe we can do it. We think we can do away with the different claims forms, with all the confusing policies, and put the responsibility for measuring quality where it belongs, with you on the front-lines and not with examiners that work for Government or the insurance company thousands of miles away.

Here's how we propose to do it. First, we want to create a single claim form, one piece of paper that everyone will use and all plans will accept. We've already started moving in this direction now. There are some standard forms used by Medicare and others that are aimed at cutting back on all this craziness. But as you know here at Children's, a single form is no good if every insurer uses it differently. You might as well have different forms.

So we will now introduce a single form which we have a prototype of here today. I've got one here, or you can see one here, a single form which would go to every hospital, every doctor's office in the country, which would deal with the basic benefits package and which would replace that and worse. Think of what that will do. Think of how many hours it will free up for all of you.

Now, when we do this, that won't be enough. We'll have to standardize how the forms are used, building on what has been done in other contexts in private industry, building on what we know from the professional associations in health care. We'll ask doctors and nurses and health care plans to decide together on what information absolutely has to be given to guarantee the highest quality and most cost-effective care.

Secondly, in order to make this form work, we'll have to create a single comprehensive benefit package for all Americans. We'll allow consumers of the health care, the employees and others in our country, to make some choices between the packages. But it will essentially be one comprehensive package. No longer will hospitals and doctors have to keep track of thousands of different policies. No longer will they have to chase down who has which insurance and what's covered under what circumstances. If it's covered, it's covered no matter who you are or what plan you're in, no matter whether you have a job or whether you don't. It will simply be covered.

It will simplify your life. And it will also provide security to the American people who worry that if they switch jobs, they'll lose their health care coverage, or it will be so different it will take them 6 months to figure out what's covered and what isn't. They won't have to know—the American people won't—enough jargon to fill a phone book just to come down here and see you. It will mean that more of the money we all pay for health care will go for health care and not bureaucracy.

And finally, the Government will try as hard as we can, and I say that because I've found as President I have to work extra hard to change the culture of the Government when I want to get something done. But our rules are going to be that we are going to rebuild the trust between doctors and hospitals and patients and the Government that is funding some, but by no means all, of the health care.

Federal programs, let's face it, are a big part of the paperwork problem. We will simplify and streamline Medicare reimbursement and claims processes, and we'll refocus clinical laboratory regulations to emphasize quality protection. And we will reduce a lot of the unnecessary administrative burden that the National Government has put on them now.

If we do this right, those of you on the front-lines will spend less time and money meeting the paperwork requirements, and more time and energy treating patients. You'll face fewer crazy rules and regulations, worry less about which insurers cover what, have better tools and information to help actually protect people and promote quality, rather than constantly having to prove you've done nothing wrong.

You'll hear a lot more about this proposal in the weeks ahead. As the debate evolves, I want to tell the people about these children, these brave children I met upstairs, about the wonderful people who are caring for them, and about how they deserve the opportunity to care more and spend less time with paper and forms.

I value what you do here at this hospital and what people like you do all over America. If the American people really knew what nurses and doctors have to go through today just to treat people, they would be up in arms, they would be marching on Congress, demanding that we do something to solve this problem.

I hope that, by our coming here today, we have made a very real and human connection between these magnificent children and all of the wonderful people who care for them and this awful problem represented by this board up here. If we move here, it means more for them. And that's why we came here.

Thank you very much.

NOTE: The President spoke at 10:20 a.m. in the Atrium. In his remarks, he referred to Lillian Beard, M.D., Washington, DC, pediatrician; Debbie Freiberg, R.N., pediatric cancer nurse; Michael B. Grizzard, M.D., vice president for medical affairs; Michelle Mahan, vice president of finance; Ben Bradlee, vice president at large, Washington Post; and author and journalist Sally Quinn.

Exchange With Reporters Prior to Discussions With Prime Minister Carlo Azeglio Ciampi of Italy
September 17, 1993

The President. Hi, Helen [Helen Thomas, United Press International].

Somalia

Q. Hi. How are you? What do you think of Aideed's proposal, Mr. President, concerning Somalia and straightening out his position?

The President. Well, I think we have to— my main concern is not to allow Somalia to deteriorate to the condition which it was in before the United Nations went there. I look forward to talking with the Prime Minister about Somalia today.

Obviously, we would like it if some political initiative could be taken to stop the current violence, but we certainly can't afford to do anything that would permit the country, after all of the efforts the United Nations has made, to deteriorate to its former condition where hundreds of thousands of people are killed or starved at random. So we'll just see—we're discussing it. We're going to discuss it today, and we have it under active discussion here what we should do, and we're looking at our options.

Q. Have you resolved your differences between U.S. and Italy on the question of Somalia?

The President. Well, I hope we have, but we haven't had a chance to talk about it.

NOTE. The exchange began at 11:15 a.m. in the Oval Office at the White House. A tape was not available for verification of the content of this exchange.

The President's News Conference With Prime Minister Ciampi of Italy
September 17, 1993

The President. Good afternoon. It is a great pleasure for me to welcome Prime Minister Ciampi to the White House and to see him again after our very successful meeting in Tokyo this summer. I deeply value the opportunity to exchange thoughts on all the challenges that we face today with one of Europe's most respected figures.

The domestic reforms which have been undertaken during the Prime Minister's tenure are truly impressive, and I salute him for that. And I congratulate the people of Italy on achieving greater financial stability and laying the foundations for future growth. Our two nations share a wealth of cultural, historical, and personal ties. From the voyage of Columbus to the contributions that millions of Italian-Americans make today to our Nation, those ties form a foundation for a common understanding of common objectives.

I salute, too, the Prime Minister for the contributions Italy is making around the world. No country has stood more solidly for NATO or is doing more now to ensure the health and the vitality of our transatlantic alliance.

Italy is in the forefront of efforts to build an integrated Europe also, a goal the United States strongly supports, and to draw Europe's many nations, East and West, closer together. In places as far-flung as Somalia, Mozambique, Albania, Nagorno-Karabakh, and the Middle East, Italy shoulders major responsibilities. Over the coming year Italy will have an even more important role to play as the chairman of the G–7. Italy will host the 1994 G–7 summit in July and will soon assume the chairmanship also of the Conference on Security and Cooperation in Europe. I welcome the opportunity to work with Italy to promote our common values and interests while Italy upholds these important leadership positions.

Of the issues we discussed today, I'd like to underscore one in particular, the need to stimulate global economic growth and create jobs in all of our countries by concluding by year's end the Uruguay round of trade negotiations. I emphasized to the Prime Minister and asked him to convey the message to his partners in Europe that the European Community must uphold the Blair House accord on agricultural trade. When the EC meets in a few days' time, it must resist reopening this hard-struck bargain and avoid standing in the way of efforts to bring the round to a rapid and successful conclusion.

The Prime Minister and I pledged that our nations will continue to work closely together to enhance trade, as well as to enhance peace, stability, and democracy. In particular, we agreed on the critical need for a peace settlement in Bosnia and discussed plans for the implementation of such a settlement should it be achieved.

I expressed our appreciation for the important role Italy has played in our efforts to secure a just peace in Bosnia, especially the role of its air bases. We also discussed the prospects for peace in the Middle East following the historic events of last Monday. We agreed on the need to help all parties in the Middle East make steady progress toward a comprehensive peace

settlement, and I discussed with the Prime Minister the possibility of having a donors conference among the major nations who will be asked to contribute to implementing the details of the peace accord. Italy and the United States will work together to raise the resources to assist Palestinian self-government, while in Somalia and Mozambique we cooperate with the United Nations to assist peacekeeping and to promote civil society. We also discussed Iran and Libya, and I stressed the need to continue to press these nations to abide by international law.

I want to say a few words, if I might, on the subject with which I began, the profound political changes now underway in Italy. America has historically been in the forefront of such change and has supported it. As a people, we have always believed our Nation had only one direction, forward. Change, a vigorous and healthy process, is now at work to an astonishing degree in Italy. I want to again commend the Prime Minister for successfully guiding Italy's impressive electoral and financial reforms, and I stressed that between democracies such as ours, change can never be a source of concern but instead always should be a source of reassurance that democratic renewal is at work.

I wish Prime Minister Ciampi, his government, and the Italian people success in their own endeavors at self-renewal. My nominee as Ambassador to Italy, Reginald Bartholomew, one of our finest professional diplomats, will help to maintain strong ties between our countries during this critical period. I want to assure the Italian people that as both our countries undergo domestic transformations, a key bond endures, the abiding friendship between our nations and our peoples.

Mr. Prime Minister.

Prime Minister Ciampi. Thank you, Mr. President. First of all I wanted to thank President Clinton for giving me the possibility to be here today. And the discussion with President Clinton will fully confirm the atmosphere of a deep and intense trust that emerged during our meeting in Tokyo last July. They were given new momentum by the event taking place just a few days after the historic event that on these very grounds opened a new chapter of dialog and hope in the relations between the people of Israel and Palestine, which Italy as a Mediterranean country has always advocated. Europe, too, stands ready to make its contribution to consolidating this position through political support and through an economic effort toward a reconstruction of the territories and development of the region.

During the course of our discussions, I briefed President Clinton on the deep process of transformation underway in Italy. I stressed that this process is taking place in an atmosphere of democratic order and a wide public consensus. The priority of the Italian Government is economic recovery and job creation. Our action will range from reducing the public debt and the public deficit and keeping inflation under control to reshaping the industrial system also by means of privatization.

Results have already been achieved. They are confirmed by the renewed confidence of domestic and international financial markets. While we are aware that this renewed confidence doesn't mean that our problems have been solved, it does indicate that we are on the right road. We must persevere. It is a long journey; this we know.

The Italian Government's strong commitment to its domestic affairs is sped forward also by its awareness that the changes in the international arena following the end of the cold war require it to play an operative role in the new set of common responsibilities of the largest industrialized economies of the Western World. Italy intends to proceed on the road toward European integration for the creation of the community that is a strong partner in an open system of international trade and a new system of international security, the excitement of the prospect for revolution of transatlantic relations in the area of security and of economic collaboration.

We brought one another up today and organized our perspective on the situation in the former Yugoslavia and in Somalia. On this last topic, my government, the Italian people harbor a legitimate and special concern heightened by the most recent tragic developments.

President Clinton and I recognize the problems of operating in a completely devastated institutional, social, and economic context, as is the case in Somalia. This very reality, unacceptable as it is, was the source of our common participation in Restore Hope. But the experience of these past months leads us today to recommend a concrete program to be proposed jointly to the United Nations for the revival of a political initiative in Somalia. It is a matter, in particular, of supporting the humanitarian and the security mission on the ground, with a more decisive management of the process of a national reconciliation among so many factions. This is the precondition for an effort to reconstruct the country, institutionally and materially.

I confirmed to President Clinton Italy's determination that the Uruguay round be brought to a global and equitable solution by December 15th. The GATT agreement is indispensable, not only because of its merits but also as a message of the confidence to economic operators. We both attach the utmost importance to the Atlantic summit of next January, and we hope that this alliance, which has proved so effective against the threats of the cold war will be capable of expressing a renewed vitality in this phase of a transition of a post-Communist system to democracy and to a worldwide market economy.

At the doorway to Italy and that of Europe, the dramatic events in the former Yugoslavia stand as an insult to our civil conscience and as a challenge to the leadership ability of the international community. In this framework, President Clinton and I both agreed that Atlantic solidarity must play a central role under the aegis of the United Nations. On my part, I confirmed to President Clinton that Italy's strongly committed to ensuring that the summit of the seven of the most industrialized nations, which will be hosted by Italy in July of next year in Naples, regain its driving force toward partnership on the broad themes of economic growth and international collaboration.

In closing, I would like to express the hope that, even before this event takes place, President Clinton will be able to visit Italy. And to this end, I was happy to convey a letter of invitation addressed to him from the President of the Italian Republic.

Somalia

Q. Mr. President, there is a growing feeling in Congress that you should declare a victory and pull out of Somalia. And also, are you any closer to a way to have a negotiated peace in Somalia as a result of your conversations today?

The President. Prime Minister Ciampi and I started this conversation in July in Tokyo, and we resumed it today. Both of us believe that some renewed political initiative in Somalia is important because in the end there has to be a political settlement that leaves the Somalis in control of their own destiny. The trick is how to do it without in any way rewarding the kind of behavior that we have seen that could spread among all of the other warlords, who have been essentially playing by the rules and trying to work out a peaceful life for the people who they represented when everybody was fighting over there. So we're looking at what our options are, and we hope that we'll be able to see some sort of political initiative. There plainly was never intended to be nor could there be some ultimate military solution to Somalia.

Is there an Italian journalist here?

Q. He had to leave.

The President. He had to leave so we will go on.

Go ahead, Terry [Terence Hunt, Associated Press].

Health Care Reform

Q. You're just a few days away from announcing your health care legislation. Can you tell us at this point how you plan to finance this plan, how much you plan to increase cigarette taxes and other sin taxes, and whether or not you plan to raise taxes on beer and wine?

The President. No. [*Laughter*] I'll tell you why, though. Let me tell you why. The reason why is that I still have another round of meetings to attend that will go through one last time what our best estimates of costs are, what our options for phasing in those costs are, what our best estimates for the Medicare and Medicaid savings are. And we're working through that.

I will say this about the dollars, because I read in the press reports that others have questioned it: For the first time ever, at least, we got all the Agencies of the Government together to hammer out agreed upon costs. That had never been done before. Then we went to, I think, 10 outside actuaries, including big firms who represent major players in health care in America.

So we have done our best and certainly it is literally an unprecedented effort to try to come to grips with what the real costs are and what the real dollars are in potential savings. And when I make those final decisions, they'll be announced. You have to give me something to announce next week. I mean, everything else I've already read in the newspapers, the news magazines. I see it on the evening news. There has to be something.

Go ahead, Gwen [Gwen Ifill, New York Times].

Somalia

Q. Back on Somalia for a minute. As you talk with allies like the Prime Minister here about the renewed political initiative you're talking about, do you have any way of drawing lines or reassuring the people who Helen [Helen Thomas, United Press International] referred to on the Hill and elsewhere that this won't be a situation that America just can't get out of?

The President. Well, it's not going to be a situation we just can't get out of. But on the other hand, we don't want to leave under conditions that will cause things to immediately revert to where they were before the United Nations entered. And so there has to be some sort of political initiative. And the Congress worked with me on their resolution on Somalia, gave me a reasonable amount of time to come up with a renewed initiative in cooperation with our allies. And I think by the time, you know, the time comes to go back to Congress, I will be able to answer those questions.

Q. Can I follow?

The President. Sure.

Q. [*Inaudible*]—a commitment of troops?

The President. No. No, no. We have the troops there, and it certainly doesn't mean more troops there. It means what we can do to stop the fighting and enable the U.N. to continue or at least the U.S. to continue to reduce its troop presence without seeing the whole country consumed in the kind of violence we've seen in one small part of Somalia recently.

Andrea [Andrea Mitchell, NBC News].

Q. On the subject of——

The President. And then we'll take some Italian journalists afterward. Let's give the Italians a couple of questions after Andrea asks hers.

Health Care Reform

Q. On the subject of health care, do you think it will be necessary to phase out the small business subsidies after a decade or so, in order to prevent large corporations from gaming the system by spinning off their low-wage workers? And is it now your expectation that there would be a one percent payroll assessment on large corporations who opt to not be part of the health alliances?

The President. Well, the answer to your second question is I haven't decided yet, but there's a very good case for that, and there's a very good case for the fact that they will be still much better off financially having all this happen, because they have been having exploding costs dumped on to them. And we're also, under our plan, going to relieve them of a lot of the burden of carrying their own retirees. So they would still come out well ahead, even if we did that.

The answer to your first question is, I don't think it's possible to foresee what will happen 10 years from now, which is why I wouldn't think we should make a commitment. Mr. Magaziner was quoted in the press; he's often said we could do that if, in fact, people decided to game the system.

What I think will happen is that we will finally have some genuine control over cost. This is basically the only area of our national life where it's been taken as a given that it was okay for costs to go up to 3 or 4 times the rate of inflation. I think when that happens, that the system we have will become more widely accepted; it won't be gamed, and people will continue to think it's acceptable to give a break to the very small businesses and the ones with very low payroll costs. That's what I think will happen. I can certainly say that no decision has been made to do that. He just was saying in response to people who say, "Well, what are you going to do if someone. starts to game the system," one option that we might pursue.

Italian journalists. Let's take a couple of questions.

Somalia

Q. Let me ask you to elaborate a little bit farther on this political initiative on Somalia. Is that an initiative you agreed with Mr. Ciampi right now? Does it have something to do with the letter by Aideed? Is that initiative a U.S. initiative, a U.S.-Italian initiative, a U.N. initiative?

The President. We discussed the letter that Mr. Aideed wrote to President Carter. And we discussed some of the options that we might pursue. And we agree that both of us would go back with our respective folks and see if we could come up with something to take to the United Nations. We did not reach agreement today on what to do. We agreed that we needed a political initiative but that the political initiative should further the original United Nations initiative and not undermine it.

The Prime Minister perhaps would like to respond also.

Prime Minister Ciampi. First of all, hearing

the questions that have been asked to the President, I was wondering whether in Washington or in Rome, because leaving aside Somalia, which is a common problem to both of us, the questions on health care, which is keenly felt in Rome, too, and so I wasn't sure where I was, whether I was in Rome or in Washington, because our domestic problems obviously are very similar.

Having said this, concerning Somalia, what I meant to say was that, having discussed the issues alluded to by President Clinton, we have a full agreement on this, keeping in mind the original goals of the mission in Somalia. And we agree that we must promote with the U.N. a political and diplomatic initiative which would fully highlight the fundamental goals and reasons for it being in Somalia. The military presence must complement the goals, the political goals, the humanitarian goals. This is what we agreed on. But what we must do must be done with a U.N. decision. What Italy does, or what the U.S. can do is to make proposals within the U.N.

Q. Are you contemplating an international mediation through, for instance, ex-President Carter? Are you going to make a proposal like that to the U.N.?

The President. We made no specific decision today, nor do I think we should speculate about them. I don't want to think out loud about them. We have agreed that there ought to be a political initiative, that it ought to be an initiative which furthers the original U.N. mission of enabling the Somalis to take control of their own affairs in peace, in dignity, and without starvation and murder. That is, we don't want to do something that rewards the very conduct we went to Somalia to put an end to. And that's the only decision that was made.

Unemployment

Q. I have a question for both of you, actually, on the jobs losses, because this is a problem for both countries on the road to economic reform or economic recovery. It seems to me that the two countries give two answers: The Americans lay off people; Italians keep subsidizing them, as in the latest accord in southern Italy on the chemical industry. Have you talked about it? Is there a way that this problem could be tackled differently from these two extremes?

Prime Minister Ciampi. If you are referring to the Crotone case, this has been resolved.

Keeping in mind the principles of economics, all factories have their economic worth. This is the agreement that we have reached the other day, the other night in Italy at the Chigi Palace, with the leadership of Senator Maccanico, who is here with us today, who is one of my members of the staff and Under Secretary of the Council of Ministers.

So there was no implementation of measures which were not coherent with the respect of economic principles. So the companies that don't do well will be closed, and what we have to do is to give birth to companies that can make an economic contribution and to implement as appropriately as possible those measures which we call social assistance measures, which will help the unemployed so that we can alleviate the negative effects of unemployment until they are reemployed. But what I would like to emphasize is that we will not implement anti-economic solutions.

The President. If I might just comment briefly, I'm not in a position to comment on the specific Italian case which you mentioned, but I believe that if we want to create more jobs again—and I would point out that the problem of job creation is a problem for Europe, for Japan, for the United States, for all the wealthier countries—it is clear that each country who shares this goal among the wealthier countries must first of all be committed to increasing growth in the global economy. Unless there is global growth we cannot hope to see growth in our own countries because of all the competition from lower wage countries doing things that our people used to do.

Secondly, there must be increased trade in the context of global growth because that's the only way a wealthy country can grow wealthier.

Thirdly, within each country there must be economic policies that promote adequate investment, encourage people to hire new employees, and provide dramatic opportunities for continuous lifetime retraining since most people will change their work a lot of times over a lifetime. That is what we have to do to generate new jobs, and we have to do it together. You can protect this industry or that industry for a while, but in the end if you want to grow jobs, we have to have a lot of changes in the international network and a lot of changes within our countries. They're not easy ones to make, but they have to be made.

Nuclear Testing by China

Q. Mr. President, China reportedly is preparing to conduct a nuclear test, and you have previously said that if the moratorium on nuclear testing is broken, that you would direct the Energy Department to resume testing. Will you do that if the Chinese proceed?

The President. Well, let me say first of all, let's wait and see what they do. I'm still very hopeful that the Chinese will not do that. And I have asked other nations that have relationships with China to also encourage them not to do it.

The Chinese are finding their strength. today, their real strength, in the same way that any other country at the end of the cold war finds theirs, in economic growth. There is no reasonable threat to China from any other nuclear power. Every other nuclear power has forsworn the use of testing. The United States is certainly a major trading partner of China. We have our second biggest trade deficit with China. We are doing more than our fair share to contribute to their economic renewal. And I would hope that the Chinese would see their future in terms of their economic strength and step away from this. And until they make a final definite decision and it happens, I don't want to cross any more bridges. I want to keep trying to persuade them not to do it.

Yes, sir.

Somalia

Q. Mr. President, you said you don't want to discuss your methods until you go to the U.N., but you seem to be describing a goal of establishing a government, a functioning government in Somalia. Would you confirm that you're thinking in those terms and any timetable you might have?

The President. No, I won't, because our position is not well enough formed yet to be characterized fairly in the way that you just characterized it.

I've been very disturbed, frankly, as many Members of Congress, many Americans, have, in the last several days by the turn of events in Somalia. Although I'm disturbed not only that our troops under the U.N. banner have been increasingly embroiled in conflict which have led to the deaths of Somalis, but I'm also disturbed that this is plainly part of a strategy by supporters of General Aideed to make the presence of the U.N. more unpopular there in all the member countries. And if that is all that is achieved, then when we leave, the chances that they will revert to exactly the same horrors that got us there are very large.

I have to remind my fellow Americans and all of the people in the world who have an aversion to the events of the last 2 weeks not to forget that over 300,000 people lost their lives there, were starved, were murdered, were subject to incredibly inhumane conditions because of the chaotic and lawless behavior of the people who had authority.

Now, many of those warlords have changed their behavior, have been cooperating with the United Nations, have enabled at least the conditions of orderly life to remain. On the other hand, it is plain to me that it was never an option for us to continue to pursue a military solution or to be obsessed with Aideed or anybody else, to the exclusion of trying to build a peaceful society.

So what the Prime Minister and I have recognized is that we have to do more to try to develop a political initiative that will enable not only the United States to withdraw but for the United Nations to remain as long as is necessary and in a more peaceful and constructive role. That is the only decision we have made to date.

Prime Minister Ciampi. I have nothing to add to what President Clinton said, and I already said before what the Italian position was, which is to give a new political dimension which prevails over a U.N. intervention of Somalia. Therefore, our action is with the U.N., and I am very happy that this coincides with the President's feeling and that is to promote this action. And without this, a purely military action would not make any sense.

The President. Thank you very much.

Bosnia

Q. Mr. President, on Bosnia——

The President. I will take one question on Bosnia.

Q. Mr. President, with the cease-fire agreement now apparent in the former Yugoslavia, will this lead to the sending of 25,000 U.S. troops there as peacekeepers? And what is your opinion of this peace agreement?

The President. Well, first of all, keep in mind what was agreed to. What is was agreed to was a cease-fire and the agreement to begin talking again. We are hopeful about this but also properly wary. I mean, there's been no territorial agreement, and that is the nub of the controversy. So we hope very much that next week there will be real progress to provide a humane and decent life in the future for the Bosnians.

I have said all along that—going back to February—that the United States would be prepared to participate in a multinational peacekeeping effort there if there were a fair settlement, generally and freely entered into by the Bosnian Government, which we have supported. But while the signs of the agreement are hopeful, it is important not to overread them. There has not been an agreement in the major areas of contention yet.

So next week, or soon thereafter, if an agreement is reached that the United States can evaluate and act on, I can answer that question, but I can't answer that question until there is an agreement that we know is a full and fair agreement that we have some sense is enforceable.

Thank you very much.

NOTE: The President's 26th news conference began at 1:43 p.m. in the East Room at the White House. Following his opening remarks, Prime Minister Ciampi spoke in Italian, and his remarks were translated by an interpreter.

Appointment for Chair of the Commission on Civil Rights
September 17, 1993

The President today announced his appointment of Mary Frances Berry to be Chair of the Commission on Civil Rights. Berry is the first woman to be appointed to the chair since its inception.

Ms. Berry, the senior member of the Commission, having served as Vice-Chair under President Carter, is currently the Geraldine R. Segal professor of American social thought and professor of history at the University of Pennsylvania.

"Mary Frances Berry is a civil rights scholar as well as an advocate," said the President. "I am proud to make this historic nomination, and I have every confidence in the commitment and abilities of Ms. Berry. Her distinguished life and career uniquely qualify her for this new leadership role."

NOTE: A biography of the appointee was made available by the Office of the Press Secretary.

Nomination for Secretary and Under Secretary of the Army
September 17, 1993

The President today announced his intention to nominate Togo Dennis West, Jr., a veteran of the Defense Department and a former Army officer, as Secretary of the Army. The President also announced his intention to nominate Joe R. Reeder Under Secretary of the Army.

"I am pleased today to announce my nomination of Togo West as our new Secretary of the Army," the President said. "Togo is a seasoned veteran of the Defense Department who knows firsthand the challenges facing our fighting men and women. I am confident he will do an excellent job of leading our Army as we adapt to the changes forced by the end of the cold war, while continuing to ensure that our fighting force remains number one in the world."

NOTE: Biographies of the nominees were made available by the Office of the Press Secretary.

Nomination for Ambassador to Brunei
September 17, 1993

The President today announced his intention to nominate career Foreign Service officer Theresa Anne Tull as Ambassador to Brunei.

"Theresa Anne Tull has spent her entire life serving our country in the Foreign Service," the President said. "I am certain she will use that experience to represent America well overseas and am proud that she has accepted this challenge."

NOTE: A biography of the nominee was made available by the Office of the Press Secretary.

The President's Radio Address
September 18, 1993

Good morning. This week we've seen inspiring examples of people reaching across their differences, having the courage to change, to achieve what is best for everyone.

On Monday, I had the great honor of hosting Israeli Prime Minister Rabin and PLO Chairman Arafat for the signing of the historic peace agreement between two peoples who have been engaged in a century of bitter conflict. Their unforgettable handshake holds the hope of a normal and more secure life for Israelis and Palestinians. And with American leadership we can build on this historic agreement to promote peace throughout the region and beyond.

On Tuesday, I signed agreements strengthening the North American Free Trade Agreement protecting labor and environmental standards in Mexico, Canada, and the United States. I was joined by former Presidents from both parties: President Bush, President Carter, and President

Ford. We stood together because NAFTA will create jobs here in the United States, 200,000 jobs by 1995.

This week, Americans began a new chapter in our national discussion about one of our greatest challenges, how to preserve what's right and fix what's wrong with our health care system. In the Rose Garden on Thursday, the First Lady and I and Vice President and Tipper Gore met with a few of the people from all across America who had written to us about their experiences with health care and their growing insecurity.

Nine months ago, when I asked Americans to send us their thoughts about health care, I had no idea we would receive over 700,000 letters. If you read some of those letters, as I have, the picture becomes clear: Even the millions of Americans who enjoy good health care coverage today are concerned that it won't be there for them next month or next year. Their stories make me even more determined than ever to provide health security to every American.

On Thursday morning, I spoke with Mabel Piley from Iola, Kansas. She and her husband own a small garden shop. After they each had minor surgery, their insurance premiums more than tripled in 4 years, until they hit $900 a month. They finally had to drop the coverage. Since then they found new coverage but with a $2,500 annual deductible. She told me, "My concern now is for my children and grandchildren. I sincerely hope our Government can do something about this runaway nightmare of a problem."

And I heard a heartbreaking story from Margie Silverman of Miami, about her 28-year-old daughter who lives in California. Last year, her daughter had a serious operation. And now, at a time when her daughter needs to be with her family, she can't move back home. That's because she's insured through a company that doesn't operate in Florida. And no other company will cover her because of her preexisting condition.

These problems and many others like them affect us as Americans, not as Democrats or Republicans, and frankly, not as people who consume health care and those who provide it. I talked to doctors and nurses today who are heartsick at the burden of unnecessary paperwork. At the Children's Hospital here in Washington, the doctors told me that $2 million a

year is spent on paperwork that has nothing to do with caring for patients, that the average doctor has to give up the chance to see 500 more patients a year just to fill out forms.

I know we can work together, across the lines of partisanship, to solve these problems and find an American answer to this American challenge.

On Wednesday night, when I speak before a joint session of Congress, I will ask the Congress to provide every American with comprehensive health care benefits that cannot be taken away. I'll ask Congress to work with me to reduce costs, increase choices, improve quality, cut paperwork, and keep our health care the finest in the world. And I'll ask members of both parties to work together for this important purpose.

We have to work together because there is so much that is good about American medicine that we must preserve. We have the best doctors and nurses, the finest hospitals, the most advanced research, the most sophisticated technology in the world. We cherish this as Americans, and we'll never give them up, nor will we give up our right to choose our doctors, our hospitals, and our medical treatments. That is especially true for older Americans, who've worked their whole lives and deserve this security. I want to say to those older Americans listening today: Our plan offers you more peace of mind.

First—and this is something I feel strongly about—we will maintain the Medicare program. If you're happy with Medicare, you can stay in it. And we're going to increase your choices and give you the chance to join a less expensive plan, but it'll be your choice. We're also going to maintain your right to choose your own doctor, and you'll continue to get the benefits you get now.

Second, we must do something about the human tragedy of older Americans who are forced to choose, literally choose every week between medicine and food or housing. Prescription drugs, currently the largest out-of-pocket expense for older Americans, will be covered under this proposal.

Third, our initiative will expand services for older Americans with serious illnesses or disabilities. Today, about 75 percent of elderly Americans with serious illness receive care from their families. But often these families can't afford the services they really need. Now, for the first time, all older Americans with serious impairments will be eligible for care in their homes or in community-based settings that they choose. This will help them be near their families while receiving the care they need.

Finally, this initiative will offer tax incentives that will make private insurance more affordable for older Americans seeking coverage for long-term care.

Sixty years ago, in the midst of the Great Depression, America provided Social Security for all Americans so that a lifetime of work would be rewarded by a dignified retirement. Now it's time to provide health security for all Americans so that people who work hard and

take responsibility for their own lives can enjoy the peace of mind they deserve. To reach this goal, I want to work with everyone, doctors and patients, business and labor, Republicans and Democrats. At a time when the world is filled with new hope and possibility, let's work together for a great goal worthy of our great Nation.

Thanks for listening.

NOTE: The address was recorded at 6:04 p.m. on September 17 in the Roosevelt Room at the White House for broadcast at 10:06 a.m. on September 18.

Remarks at the Congressional Black Caucus Foundation Dinner
September 18, 1993

Thank you very much. Senator Carol Moseley-Braun, I'll never forget the first time I saw you campaigning in Chicago in the spring of 1992. I told Hillary that night when I called her on the phone that I didn't know if you could be elected to the Senate, but whatever it is you have to have in politics to make it, you've got it. I saw it that night. I knew it then. And now, Jesse Helms knows it, too.

I have had a wonderful time tonight seeing friends from all over America, all kinds of people, people in politics, people in private life. It's been a great joy to see so many of you here. I also had a wonderful time tonight listening to the music. I just want to say again, as a child of the sixties, I love listening to Shanice and Crystal and Penny Wilson. I love seeing the Boyz 2 Men, knowing they could sing some songs that were alive in my childhood and before they were born. And I love hearing Martha Reeves and the Vandellas again. I did play with them 6 years ago, just as she said, up in Michigan, and I'm sorry I was disabled from playing with them tonight, but maybe I can have a raincheck.

I want to thank the chairman of the Congressional Black Caucus, Congressman Mfume; the Caucus Foundation chairman, Alan Wheat, and my neighbor, the honorary chairman of this weekend, Harold Ford. I also want to acknowledge the presence of two people I understand are here, but I have not seen them tonight,

the chairman of the Southern Governors' Conference, Governor Doug Wilder of Virginia, and the next Mayor of New York City, David Dinkins.

I have many friends in the Congressional Black Caucus: Some I never met before I was elected President; some I have known for years and years; some I've just had the opportunity to work with; some who walked the long and hard road with me from the beginning of my long and sometimes lonely quest to win the Presidency. But I can tell you this: As a group, they are a group of truly outstanding and committed leaders who do their best to think independently but to act together when it's in the interest of their people.

Tonight, from the bottom of my heart, more than anything else I just wanted to come here and say to them, thank you. Thank you for your support. Thank you for your constructive criticism. Thank you for your vigor and your caring. Thank you for the consistency with which you approach your work. I wish every one of you could see them working, working every day up here on these problems, problems that are as profound as have confronted our country in a very long time. I hope you will be patient with them and maybe a little with your President when we can't work miracles. We don't always have an operating majority, but they are a ferocious crowd, and they get things done, and they have made a difference.

I also would like to thank Senator Moseley-Braun for acknowledging the members of my Cabinet: the Secretary of Commerce, Ron Brown; the Secretary of Agriculture, Mike Espy; the Secretary of Energy, Hazel O'Leary; the Secretary of Veterans Affairs, Jesse Brown; and our Drug Policy Coordinator, for the first time in history a member of the President's Cabinet, Lee Brown, formerly the police chief of New York and Houston and Atlanta.

There are many other African-Americans in this administration at the sub-Cabinet level. I hesitate to begin to mention them for fear I will hurt some others; I saw a lot of them are here in the crowd tonight. But I do want to say a word about a couple of people who are in somewhat nontraditional positions: the person who argues America's case before the Supreme Court, our Solicitor General, Drew Days; the person who is in charge of protecting the President, the Assistant Secretary of the Treasury for Enforcement, Ron Noble, over at the Secret Service, the Customs Department, and the Alcohol, Firearms and Tobacco; and one of my most recently confirmed administration officials, someone I believe will be recognized by all Americans as a great national treasure, and my dinner partner tonight, the new Surgeon General, Dr. Joycelyn Elders from Arkansas. Please stand up. Stand up, Joycelyn.

When I asked Joycelyn Elders to become the director of the department of health in Arkansas, she said, "Well, what do you want me to do?" And I said, "Not much. I want you to cut the rate of teen pregnancy, get the infant mortality rate below the national average, put our State ahead of the curve in dealing with the curse of AIDS, do something about environmental health, and bring health services into the schools where poor children can get them." And she said, "What else? I'll do that." And when her nomination generated a little controversy, as I hoped it would—[*laughter*]—I called our senior Senator, Dale Bumpers, who's got a great reputation as a humorist. And he said, "Well, you know, every now and then Joycelyn may be a little too outspoken, but you've got to say one thing for her: She plants the corn where the hogs can get at it." [*Laughter*]

I was glad, too, to see this slide show tonight acknowledge the contributions of the new United States Ambassador-designate to Jamaica, Shirley Chisholm. And I want to acknowledge the two people whom I believe to be the two highest-ranking African Americans ever to serve in the Office of the White House: the Assistants to the President for Public Liaison and the Chief of Staff to the First Lady, Alexis Herman and Maggie Williams. I thank them for what they do. And yesterday, I appointed to be the Chair of the U.S. Commission on Civil Rights an old friend of many of yours, Mary Frances Berry.

My friends, these and hundreds of other Americans are part of our partnership to fighting battles on old and new fronts. As President, that's my job. As an American, I think it is my moral obligation. As your partner, it is my privilege.

A few days ago, we fought a battle in Vidor, Texas. Henry Cisneros, the Secretary of Housing and Urban Development, went there to deliver our message loud and clear: No more discrimination and segregation in public housing. That message has also been delivered by the Attorney General, Janet Reno, in the areas of employment, education, hate crimes, and voting rights. And we believe that districts drawn to increase the empowerment of minorities are good for America, not bad for America.

If I might say tonight, the end of the cold war imposes on us new responsibilities to fight for democracy and freedom and peace for peoples around the world where we can, consistent with our resources, our reach, and our interests. I am disturbed from time to time to read articles as I did last week, someone who said that President Clinton's problem is he thinks that foreign policy is about helping the weak, when foreign policy is really about dealing with the strong. Well, I thought it was about both. And I remember a time when this country was weak in its beginning, and weak became strong. The United States can never stop worrying about the weak and dealing only with the strong. That's not what we're about, not at home and not abroad.

I would also say, my fellow Americans, there is more than one way to define strength. Tonight I would like to introduce someone I consider to be quite strong; the duly elected President and soon to be returned President of Haiti, President Aristide. Please stand up, sir.

I also want to thank Congressman Mfume, Congressman Rangel, and others who are going to lead a delegation to Haiti in the next few days to make it clear that we deplore the violence of the last few days and we are still intent on working with our allies in the United Nations to restore real democracy, freedom, and peace to the people of that troubled land.

You know, when I look out at all of you tonight and I see so many people here of different racial and ethnic backgrounds supporting this caucus, I am reminded that in 1992, one of the hot political books that was written and widely read by everyone involved in that campaign argued that the Democratic Party had been reduced to permanent minority status because we believe in the empowerment of minorities, and especially African-Americans; that unless we could somehow rid ourselves of our affection for, our allegiance to, and our deep and profound ties to racial minorities, the wide majority would never give us any support again and we could never elect a President again.

Well, I hope that one of the things the 1992 election proved was that most Americans want this country to pull together, not be pulled apart. Most Americans believe that we really are all in this together. Most Americans believe and want the same things: greater opportunity for people who work hard and play by the rules and for their children, a renewed sense of responsibility for ourselves and for our fellow brothers and sisters, a deepened sense of the American community.

Most people really do think we're going up or down together. I remember the first time I went to Detroit, and then I went to Macomb County, which was supposed to be the symbol of the Reagan white flight of the 1980's and seventies, and intentionally gave the same speech to both crowds. Some people thought I had slipped a gasket. But I kind of liked the way it felt, and so before the campaign was over, I went back and did it again. And I found out that most people thought it was kind of nice to have someone who tried to preach to white folks that they couldn't run from black folks, and to black folks that they ought to embrace their allies in every community they could find them.

I confess when I got here tonight, I was sort of tired. I was up for about 22 hours on that magnificent Monday of this week, when the history of the world was changed with a magic handshake between Yitzhak Rabin and Yasser Arafat. When I saw that happen, so close at hand, with a little nudge from their friends, I felt a surge of emotion that I have felt in the last few years only one other time, and that was when my daughter and I, on a Sunday morning, watched from a very long distance as Nelson Mandela walked out of his jail cell for the first time in 27 years.

I thought to myself: If those two old warriors, after decades of fighting against each other, decided it was better for them to put aside their hatred and just call them problems, to no longer allow their enemies to dictate their own energies but instead to think about the long-term interests of their people, then surely we can do what we have to do here at home. Surely those of us who have taken too many years avoiding one another can sit down and work out the plain and present and pressing problems which threaten to rob our children of the American dream.

Oh, I know in the last few months we have made a lot of progress. And I appreciate the things that have been said. But make no mistake about it, my fellow Americans, we still stand at the crossroads in a time of swirling change, generational change, engulfing not just the United States but the entire world. We cannot simply blame on the last 12 years economic difficulties that are more than two decades in building, every wealthy country in the world having difficulty creating jobs, wages stagnant in this country, for more than two decades most families working harder for less and paying more for the basic things in life. Then for the last 12 years, trying trickle-down economics and finding not much trickled down, but the deficit exploded upward. So that now when we need most to invest more in jobs and education and in our future, we are mired in a debt and frozen in a pattern of practice that will never take us where we need to go. We now have to break out of our patterns, just as Israel and the PLO did this week.

I thank the Black Caucus for making the beginning, for helping us finally to get the motor voter law, a genuine expanse of civil rights, for helping working families to be able to take a little time off when there's a baby born or a parent sick without losing a job. I thank them for enacting empowerment zones to see if we can get the private sector to invest in our most distressed areas again. I thank them for reversing the tide and helping to expand women's rights and helping to expand the protection of our environment and helping to pass the national service bill and a dramatic reformation of student loans which will open the doors of college education to all. I thank them for that.

And I thank the Congressional Black Caucus for voting for a budget that, for the first time in the history of our country, will use the tax system to lift the people who work for a living and to have children in the home and have modest wages out of poverty, so that we will tax them out of poverty, not into poverty, using the income tax credit. That is the most significant piece of income reform in 20 years, and every member of the Congressional Black Caucus voted for it.

But it is just the beginning. We must find a way to create more jobs in this economy. I believe we can't do it unless as President, I have the freedom to work with other nations to expand world growth. I believe we can't do it unless we can expand global trade. But I know we can't do it unless we invest more in putting our people to work here, in converting from a defense economy, in training people who lose their jobs, in changing this unemployment system to a reemployment system and revolutionizing the whole notion that when people lose their jobs, we should just wait around and hope something good happens to them. From now on, since most people don't get back the same job they lose, from the minute they're unemployed they should be in a new training program, and people should open up the vistas of the future to them.

I believe that African-Americans want to do something about crime. But it's important that we don't just think of crime as punishment. You can't go around telling people they should say no to things unless they have something to say yes to. People should have something to say yes to. And the best police force is the community police force that prevents crime, not just catches criminals.

And while we're at it, folks, why in the world don't all politicians stop making speeches about crime until they at least pass the Brady bill and take assault weapons out of the hands of teenagers in this country? You can't drink legally until you're 21. And there are cities in this country when the average age of people who commit killing is under 16. And we are giving aid and comfort to the continued disintegration of this society because the grown-ups won't take the guns out of the hands of the kids, because they are afraid to stand up to the gun lobby. It's time to change that, and we ought to do it this year.

And finally, let me say, with all my heart I believe we will never restore health to our budget, we will never restore health to our economy until we provide health to all of our people, comprehensive, affordable health care to all the American people.

This week, we kicked off the administration's efforts to work with Congress, without regard to party or region, to overhaul this country's health care system. We are spending 40 percent more of our income than any country in the world. We have 35 million Americans uninsured. We have an atrocious infant mortality rate. Only two nations in this hemisphere have a worse immunization rate of children. There are millions of people who never get primary and preventive care. There are millions who can never leave the job they're in because someone in their family has been sick.

And I went to the Children's Hospital in this city this week and heard a nurse say that she had to turn away from a child with cancer who wanted her to play with him because she had to go to a school to learn how to fill out yet another new form in the most insane bureaucratic maze of financing that any country on the face of the Earth has. I heard a doctor plead with me—you may have seen her on television—a pediatrician, a native of this city, plead with me to do something to lift the burden of the present health care financing and regulatory system off her back. The Washington Children's Hospital said that the 200 doctors that have privileges at that hospital could see another 500 children a year each, 10,000 more children, if we just had the courage to make the simple changes in our health care system that other nations have already made. I tell you, we can do better, and we must. And we must do it together.

My fellow Americans, and especially the members of the Congressional Black Caucus whom I honor tonight: I ask you to think about how in 5, 10, or 20 years you want to look back on this period. One of your colleagues complained to me the other night that the Congress has already met 40 percent more this year than they did last year. I said, "That's good. That's what we were hired to do." We need to look back on this time and say: In this time of change, when so much was threatened and so much was promised, we beat back the threats and we seized the promise. We revived the

American dream. We did right by the people who sent us here. We honored the deepest traditions of America, and we gave our children and the children of the world a better future.

Thank you all, and God bless you.

NOTE. The President spoke at 9:40 p.m. at the Washington Convention Center.

Remarks to Physicians and Supporters on Health Care Reform
September 20, 1993

Good morning. I thank you for coming here, and I thank Dr. Koop for his stirring remarks. He always makes a lot of sense, doesn't he? And the Nation is in his debt for his work as Surgeon General and now, for the work he is about to undertake in behalf of the cause of health care reform.

I also want to thank the many physicians from all across America, from all walks of medical life who have made a contribution to the debate as it has progressed thus far. I got very interested in this subject years ago when, as the Governor of my State, I noticed I kept spending more and more for the same Medicaid and had less and less to spend on the education of our children or on preventive practices or other things which might make a profound difference in the future.

In 1990 I agreed to undertake a task force for the National Governors' Association, and I started by interviewing 900 people in my State who were involved in the delivery of medical care, including several hundred doctors. Some of them are in this room today. I thank them for their contributions, and I absolve them of anything I do which is unpopular with the rest of you. [*Laughter*]

I'm glad to see my dear friend and often my daughter's doctor, Dr. Betty Lowe, the incoming President of the American Academy of Pediatrics; my cardiologist, Dr. Drew Kumpuris, who pulls me off a treadmill once a year and tells me I'm trying to be 25 when I'm not— [*laughter*]—and Dr. Morriss Henry from Fayetteville, Arkansas, back here, an ophthalmologist who hosted the wedding reception that Hillary and I had in Morriss and Anne's home almost 18 years ago next month; Dr. Jim Weber, formerly president of the Arkansas Medical Society. We started a conversation with doctors long before I ever thought of running for President, much less knew I would have an opportunity to do this.

This is really an historic opportunity. It is terribly important for me. One of the central reasons that I ran for President of the United States was to try to resolve this issue, because I see this at the core of our absolute imperative in this sweeping time of change to both give the American people a greater sense of security in the health care that they have, and call forth from our people—all of our people, including the consumers of health care—a renewed sense of responsibility for doing what we all ought to do to make this country work again.

I am determined to pursue this in a completely bipartisan fashion. And I have reached out to both Republicans and Democrats, as well as the thoughtful independents to help. There is one person in the audience I want to introduce, a longtime friend of mine who has agreed to help mobilize support for this approach among the Democrats of the country, the distinguished former Governor of Ohio, my friend Dick Celeste, who's here. Thank you for being here.

When Dr. Koop talked about the ethical basis of this endeavor, he made perhaps the most important point. If I have learned anything in these years of public endeavors, or anything in the last several months of serving as your President, it is that once people decide to do something, they can figure out how to do it.

When, one week ago today, on the South Lawn of the White House, Yitzhak Rabin and Yasser Arafat signed that peace accord, they did not even know what the ultimate map-drawing of the city of Jericho would be, or how all the elections would be held, or how the Palestinians' candidates would advertise on the radio since the radio stations don't belong to the Palestinians. I could give you a hundred things they did not know the answer to. They knew one thing, they couldn't keep going in the direction they were going, and so they decided to take a different direction.

When President Kennedy's administration challenged this country to go to the Moon, they didn't have a clue about how they were going to go. The Vice President knows more about science than I, so he can tell it in a funnier way about they didn't understand what kind of rocket they were going on and what their uniforms would be like and on and on and on. But the ethical imperative is perhaps the most important thing. We have to decide that the costs, not just the financial costs but the human costs, the social costs of all of us continuing to conduct ourselves within the framework in which we are now operating is far higher than the risk of responsible change.

We have certainly tried to do this in a responsible way. I want to thank the First Lady and all the people who work with her. I want to thank Tipper and Ira and Judy and everybody who was involved in this. We have really worked hard to reach out to, literally, to thousands and thousands of people in this great medical drama that unfolds in America every day.

I want to thank Donna Shalala and the Department of Human Services for the terrific work they have done. We have really tried to do this in an embracing and a different way, almost a nonpolitical way. If you look around this room, we have doctors from Maine to Washington, from Minnesota to Florida. Some of you are patients in rural Virginia, some in public hospitals, others of you devote your lives to training the next generation of physicians.

But I think every one of you is committed to seeing that we provide the finest health care in the world. That means as we undertake this journey of change, we clearly must preserve what's right with our health care system: the close patient-doctor relationship, the best doctors and nurses, the best academic research, the best advanced technology in the world. We can do that and still fix what's wrong. In fact, we can enhance what's right by fixing what's wrong.

If we reduce the amount of unnecessary paperwork and governmental regulation and bureaucracy, that will by definition enhance the doctor-patient relationship. If we spend less money on paying more for the same health care and the incentives to churn the system, we will have some more money, for example, to invest more in medical research and advanced technology and breaking down the barriers which

still limit our ability to solve the remaining problems before us. We need a discussion. We need constructive criticism. We need constructive disagreement on some points. This is a very complex issue.

I worked at this for over a year and realized when I was a Governor I was just beginning to come to grips with it. When we started this great enterprise and I asked Hillary to undertake this task and she looked at me as if I had slipped a gasket—[*laughter*]—I knew more about it than she did. Now, she knows a lot more about it than I do.

This is a learning effort. We are going to start today, as many of you know, this health care university, we call it, for Members of Congress, and about 400 Members of Congress have signed up for 2 intensive days of learning. That is an astonishing thing. I have never seen anything like it: these Members, without regard to their party and completely without respect to the committees they are on, since most of them are on committees that would not have direct jurisdiction over this, hungering to know what you go through every day, hungering to learn, wanting to avoid making an irresponsible decision but determined that they should make some decisions to change this system. I think that is a terrific cause for hope.

For patients, the reform we seek will mean more choices. Today, employers are too often forced by rising health care costs to decide which plans to offer their employees, and often they are inadequate or too costly. The decision is usually based on the bottom line, and is a moving bottom line as more and more Americans every month actually lose their health insurance for good. Our plans give consumers the power to choose between a broad range of plans within their region, giving them more freedom to find and to stay with a doctor they like.

For doctors, reform will mean the flexibility to choose which networks or providers you want to join. If you want to be involved with one, that's fine. If you want to be involved with more than one, that's fine. So that whatever you want to do to continue to see the patients you see today, you will be able to do it. It's your choice.

We intend to see a reform that drastically simplifies this system, freeing you from paperwork and bureaucratic nightmares that have already been well discussed. I cannot tell you how moved I was when we were at the Washington Children's Hospital the other day and we heard not only the statistics that the hospital has calculated that they spend $2 million a year on paperwork unrelated to patient care and keeping up with the procedures, but the human stories. I mean, we had a nurse actually tell us about being pleaded with by a young child with cancer to play with the child, and she couldn't do it because she had to go to a little seminar on how to learn how to fill out a new set of forms that they were being confronted with, and she said, that really was a picture of what their life was like; an eloquent doctor who said she wanted to live in Washington, DC, she wanted to care for the poor children in the area. She did not go to medical school to spend her life poring over a piece of paper. And all of you have had that experience.

We can do better than this. We also know we're going to have to trim back Government regulations that get in your way and do little to protect the patients or provide better care. If we simplify the system, we will reduce the apparently insatiable bureaucratic urge that runs through administrations of both parties and seems to be a permanent fixture of our national life to micromanage whatever aspect of tax dollars they have some jurisdiction over. We are determined to undo much of that. We want to respect your training, your judgment, and your knowledge and not unduly interfere with what you do.

We also are determined to preserve the quality of health care that our people receive. Today, part of the reason we have the finest doctors in the world are the academic health centers. For years they have been the guardians, the guarantors of quality, training doctors and health care professionals and reaching into surrounding communities to provide help for those in need. In the coming years, these centers, if our plan passes, will have even greater responsibility to turn out high quality physicians, particularly primary care physicians who will work in underserved areas, and to create a system of lifelong learning for health care professionals. And they must continue to expand their partnerships with communities around them.

The initiative I am offering offers the possibility of giving real building blocks to this Nation's health care system to fill in a lot of the gaps which exist for millions of Americans, not just universal coverage gaps but also organizational problems and the lack of adequate access.

I want this plan to be fair, compassionate, and realistic, and I believe it is. Health security can be provided to the American people so that you don't lose your health care when you lose your job; you don't get frozen into a job because someone in your family has been sick and you're in the grip of the preexisting condition syndrome, which is literally undermining labor mobility in a world where the average 18-year-old American must change work eight times in a lifetime to be fully competitive, when security means the ability to continuously learn and find new and evermore challenging work, not to stick in the same rut you're in anymore. We don't have that option. We are literally rendering people insecure through job lock, undermining their potential, keeping them from moving on, and also keeping others from moving up into the positions they previously held. This is a serious economic problem.

This plan will guarantee that every patient who walks in your door is covered. It will make sure you are paid to keep your patients healthy as well as to treat them when they're sick. It will give you the flexibility and freedom you need to do your jobs. In return, it must demand more responsibility from all of us. We must have a new generation of doctors which has a recommitment to primary care. We don't have enough primary care physicians in America, and I think we all know it. We have to care about family practice, pediatrics, and preventive medicine. And we all have to work together to get medical costs under control.

But I'm convinced with your leadership we can do that. Without your help, we could not have covered as much ground as we have covered so far. I thank Dr. Koop for what he said. But the attention to detail by this project is the direct result of the painstaking effort and the hours that have been provided by physicians and other health care providers who have come to this town and spent day after day after day after day almost always at their own expense just to do something to help their country as well as to improve the quality of their own practice. We know that this will not be done overnight. We know that we will have to have a long-term commitment from individuals, from Government, from businesses, and from health care professionals. But we know that we have to begin now. This is a magic moment.

Let me just say two things in closing. There are a lot of other things we haven't discussed, and I know that, but we didn't come here for a seminar on the details of it. We are trying some innovative approaches to the malpractice problem, which I think will find broad favor. We are going to do some things that will increase public health clinics' ability to access people who are otherwise left out of the system and try to deal with these horrible statistics on immunization and the absence of prenatal care. There are a lot of those things that are going to be dealt with.

But I want to make two points in closing. First of all, there are a lot of disconnects as you might imagine between Washington, DC, and the rest of America, which everybody loves to talk about when they get alienated from the Federal Government. But one of the most amazing in this has been the following thing: I don't talk to any doctor or any hospital administrator or any nurse with any seniority in nursing who doesn't believe that there's a huge amount of waste in this system, that has nothing to do with caring for people, which can be gotten rid of. I don't talk to anybody in Washington who thinks you can do it. [*Laughter*]

Our friends in the press are laughing because you know I'll finish this talk, then they'll go talk to somebody on the Hill who will say, "Aahh, they can't save that money in Medicare and Medicaid. It's got to be that way. We really need a room under the garage in the Children's Hospital in Washington, DC, which is piling up paper 6½ feet a day. We've got to have that. How would we function?"

Hillary goes to the Mayo Clinic; they've already got their annual average cost increases now down under 4 percent. And we talk about, you know, maybe getting it down over the next 3 or 4 years to inflation plus population plus 2 percent, and they talk about how we are slashing Medicare and Medicaid, when what we really want to do is take the same money and not take it out of health care, but use it to cover the uninsured, unemployed, use it to cover some new services to do more preventive primary health care. So this is an interesting thing. Dr. Koop said: In the past, reform has been imposed on the doctors. You might have to come up here and impose it on the politicians and the bureaucrats. You may have to do that.

I say that not to be critical of the Congress. We are all—all of us see the world—[*laughter*]—no, no, no, I don't—all of us see the world through the prism of our own experience, don't we? You do. I do. We all do that. And they are so used to believing that the only way they can be decent stewards of the public trust, to take care of the poor on Medicaid and the elderly on Medicare, they are so used to believing that the only way they can do it is just to write out a check to pay more for the same health care, never mind if it's 2 or 3 or 4 times the rate of inflation; never mind if there's a 16-percent increase in the Medicaid budget for the coming year, when we estimate no more than a 2-percent increase in the enrollments in Medicaid.

We're just so used to believing that in this town that we have to have your help to believe that it can be different, and you can enhance the care people get, not undermine it. I don't want to minimize it. Yes, we need your critical scrutiny of the specific plan the administration will propose. Yes, we do. But we also need for you to convince the people who live here, who believe we are trapped in this system, that it can be different. And you are the ones who have responsibility for caring for people. If you can believe it can be different, you can convince the Congress that it can be different, that they are not going to hurt, they are going to help by making some of these changes.

The second point I want to make in closing is this: This is really a part of a great national discussion we have to have about what kind of people we are and what kind of country we're going to be. And Dr. Koop said it better than I could, but we can't really get the kind of health care system we need until there is a real renewed sense of responsibility on the part of everyone in this system. It is terribly important to recognize that we have certain group behaviors in this country that, unless they are changed, we will never get health care costs down to the level that our competitors have.

It's not just high rates of AIDS and excessive smoking; it's high rates of teen pregnancy, of low birth weight, of poor immunization of children. It's outrageous rates of violence that we willfully refuse to deal with by taking away the main cause of it, which is the unrestricted access that young people in our most violent areas have to guns that give them better weapons than the police.

Yes, within the health care system, doctors shouldn't perform unnecessary procedures, patients shouldn't bring frivolous malpractice suits, people who use the health care system now, who aren't in it now, are going to have to pay a little for their health care, so they realize there is a price for everything instead of when all of the money just comes from a third-party source they don't know. There needs to be more responsibility within this system but we also have got to remember that if we can plant the ethical roots that Dr. Koop talked about, we may then be able not only to change this system but to use this success to try to change some of the destructive group behavior that is tearing this country apart.

But believe me, it all begins here. If we can give the security of decent health care to every American family, it will be the most important thing that the Government has done with—not for but with—the American people in a generation. And it can only happen if people like you lead the way.

Thank you very much.

[*At this point, Hillary Clinton invited participants to breakfast.*]

Q. Mr. President, is Senator Moynihan wrong?

The President. [*Inaudible*]—you heard what he said yesterday? What he said was absolutely right. I mean, based on the experience of the last decade, you can't get the cost down to zero,

but that's not what we proposed. We proposed working over a 5-year period to move the Government's cost to inflation plus population growth. And in the beginning—we have inflation plus population growth plus another 2 or 3 percent. Where this group care is working well, like at the Mayo Clinic, they now are down to less than inflation plus population growth. So I believe that if you give us 5 years to do it, we can get there. But it will require some substantial changes.

What I said was true. People in Washington can't imagine that it can be different because of the experiences they've had over the last 5 years. But to say we're trying to cut Medicare and Medicaid, it's not true. We propose never to take it below inflation plus population growth.

NOTE: The President spoke at 8:45 a.m. in the East Room at the White House. In his remarks, he referred to C. Everett Koop, former Surgeon General; Ira Magaziner, Senior Adviser to the President for Policy Development; and Judith Feder, Principal Deputy Assistant Secretary for Planning and Evaluation at the Health and Human Services Department. The exchange portion of this item could not be verified because the tape was incomplete.

Nomination for Posts at the Department of the Treasury
September 20, 1993

The President today announced his intention to nominate Joan Logue-Kinder as Assistant Secretary for Public Affairs and Public Liaison at the Department of Treasury. The President also announced his appointment of Darcy Bradbury as Deputy Assistant Secretary for Federal Finance.

"Secretary Bentsen and I are pleased to have these two talented individuals on board," the President said. "I am sure they will work hard to ensure the Treasury Department works well for the American people."

NOTE: Biographies of the nominees were made available by the Office of the Press Secretary.

Remarks on Signing the National and Community Service Trust Act of 1993
September 21, 1993

Thank you very much, Mr. Vice President. I always wanted to be introduced by the host

of the David Letterman Show. [*Laughter*] I was thinking about what my top 10 list would be, the best things about having Al Gore as Vice President. He educates me on things great and trivial, and that's 10. And numbers nine through one are, he has a vote in the United States Senate. He said, "And I'm always on the winning side when I vote." [*Laughter*]

I want to welcome you all to America's backyard, a fitting place to come to celebrate the opportunity to serve our neighbors and the opportunity to rebuild the American community. I have harbored this dream for years. It was stoked in me by so many thousands of experiences, I cannot even recall them all.

When the Vice President and I went across this country last year, I was deeply moved by forces that were both good and bad that kept pushing me to believe that this was more important than so many other things that all of us do in public life. I saw the wreckage, the insanity, the lost human potential that you can find now not only in our biggest cities but in every community. And yet, I saw even in the most difficult circumstances the light in the eyes of so many young people, the courage, the hunger for life, the desire to do something to reach beyond themselves and to reach out to others and to make things better.

I listened and learned from so many people. I saw the examples of the service programs that you have represented here on this stage. I watched people's dreams come to life. I watched the old and the young relate in ways they hadn't. I watched mean streets turn into safer and better and more humane places. I saw all these things happening, and I realized that there was no way any Government program could solve these problems, even if we had the money to spend on them, which we don't, but that the American people, if organized and directed and challenged and asked, would find a way.

I am in debt to so many people, all of whom have been at least referred to. But I would like to say a particular word of thanks to those who sponsored previous legislation for a limited basis. I want to say a special word of thanks to the Republicans and the Democrats who joined together in the Congress to make sure that this would know no party and that we would somehow reach beyond the normal debate and dialog to unify this country, starting with the Congress. I thank the people who helped me before I became President to understand more about national service, the people who wrote books and articles, the people who

worked with me in the DLC and other organizations. I thank all of you because all of you played a role in this day. But most of all, I want to thank the young people of this country who were so wonderfully represented by these three young people, Reshard and Derek and Priscilla. Weren't they terrific? Let's give them another hand. [*Applause*]

I don't believe there was a stop on our bus tour across the country when the Vice President and I didn't mention our commitment to national service as a part of our drive to make college education affordable to all but also as part of our deeper desire to bring the American community back together.

I have to say a special word of appreciation to Eli Segal. I have known him for about half my lifetime. I can still remember when we were young with the dreams and the enthusiasms that these young people on this stage have today. I could not have known when we first met in our attempt to do the best we could by our country so long ago, that someday we would be standing here on this stage to do this. But I know this: This national service bill and this project would not be in the form it is and we would not be here celebrating today in the way we are if it had not been for his brilliant, dedicated leadership. And I thank him for that. Relying on the ancient adage that if it ain't broke, don't fix it, I am today forwarding to Senator Kennedy and the United States Senate the nomination of Eli Segal to be the Chief Executive Officer of the Corporation for National and Community Service.

I also want to acknowledge, as has already been referred to, the roots of our history in all this day and people who have contributed to this day because of what they did in their time. Twice before in this century Americans have been called to great adventures in civilian service. Sixty years ago in the depths of depression, Franklin Roosevelt created the CCC and gave Americans the chance not only to do meaningful work so that they could feed themselves and their families but so that they could build America for the future. And down to this day there is not a State in this country that is untouched by the continuing impact of the good work done by the people who labored in the CCC.

Today we have two veterans of President Roosevelt's Civilian Conservation Corps, William Bailey and Owen Davis. Would they please stand wherever they are? There they are. Thank you. It is with special pride that I will use President Franklin Roosevelt's pen set, with which he signed nearly every piece of legislation as President, to sign our bill here today.

We also point with pride, as the Vice President said, to the enduring legacy and the continued vitality of John Kennedy's Peace Corps, created by legislation which President Kennedy signed 32 years ago tomorrow. I want to acknowledge, as the Vice President did, the wonderful work of Sargent Shriver not only as the first Director and guiding spirit of the Peace Corps but for what he did with the VISTA program. And I want to acknowledge—[*applause*]— thank you—and to say with some pride that it was my privilege, influenced by people like the Vice President whose sister served with such distinction in the Peace Corps, to appoint the first Peace Corps volunteer to actually direct the Peace Corps, Carol Bellamy. And I thank her for her leadership. Thanks to the generosity of Sargent Shriver, I will also use the pen President Kennedy used 30 years ago—32 years ago to sign the Peace Corps legislation, to create a new national service corps for America. We will call it AmeriCorps.

When I asked our country's young people to give something back to our country through grassroots service, they responded by the thousands. You heard a couple of them here today. Eli's office was literally swamped with letters asking to serve. These two young people today represent 20,000 young people next year and 100,000 young people 3 years from now. And I hope, believe, and dream that national service will remain throughout the life of America not a series of promises but a series of challenges across all the generations and all walks of life to help us to rebuild our troubled but wonderful land. I hope that some day the success of this program will make it possible for every young American who wishes to serve and earn credit against a college education or other kinds of education and training, to do that. And I believe it will happen.

This morning our Cabinet and the heads of our Federal Agencies were directed to redouble their efforts to use service, community grassroots service, to accomplish their fundamental missions. We want them to help reinvent our Government, to do more and cost less, by creating new ways for citizens to fulfill the mission of the public. We believe we can do that. Already

departments have enlisted young people and not so young people to do everything from flood cleanup to housing rehabilitation, from being tour guides in our national parks to being teachers' aides in our schools. In the coming months we will also challenge States and nonprofit organizations to compete for AmeriCorps volunteers. We'll ask our friends in higher education and the foundation world and in business to continue their leadership in the growing movement of national service.

But beyond the concrete achievements of AmeriCorps, beyond the expanded educational opportunities those achievements will earn, national service, I hope and pray, will help us to strengthen the cords that bind us together as a people, will help us to remember in the quiet of every night that what each of us can become is to some extent determined by whether all of us can become what God meant us to be.

And I hope it will remind every American that there can be no opportunity without responsibility. The great English historian Edward Gibbon warned that when the Athenians finally wanted not to give to society but for society to give to them, when the freedom they wished for most was freedom from responsibility, then Athens ceased to be free.

My fellow Americans, there are streets and neighborhoods and communities today where people are not free. There are millions of Americans who are not really free today because they cannot reach down inside them and bring out what was put there by the Almighty. This national service corps should send a loud and clear message across this country that the young people of America will preserve the freedom of America for themselves and for all those of their generations by assuming the responsibility to rebuild the American family. That is the dream which drove this idea to the reality we find today.

I am so proud of all of you who are a part of this. I am profoundly grateful to you. I ask you only now to remember that as we move toward the 21st century, the success of our great voyage—of this, the longest experiment in free society in human history—to remember that it is at the grassroots, in the heart of every citizen, that we will succeed or fail. Today we are taking a stand in this country for the proposition that if we challenge people to serve and we give them a chance to fulfill their abilities, more and more and more we will all understand that we must go forward together. This is the profoundest lesson of this whole endeavor. And it will be the great legacy of the wonderful people who make it come alive.

Thank you, and God bless you all.

NOTE: The President spoke at 11:15 a.m. on the South Lawn at the White House. In his remarks, he referred to Summer of Service participants Reshard Riggins, Derek Gottfried, and Priscilla Aponte. H.R. 2010, approved September 21, was assigned Public Law No. 103–82.

Interview With Tabitha Soren of MTV
September 21, 1993

National Service Program

Q. Obviously, this is a huge success, getting national service passed so quickly. One of the goals of national service is to have kids have a multicultural experience. But yet, in the pilot program, Summer of Service, within a couple of days, the black kids were in black caucuses, there were Hispanic caucuses and gang groups. How are you going to make sure during national service, when it gets going, that they serve side by side?

The President. Well, those are the kinds of projects we'll favor. But I think if you look all across the world today, there's always going to be some ethnic cohesion. People are going to pull together, talk together, feel a greater initial comfort level. That's just true worldwide.

But what we also saw in the Summer of Service is that people really were working together across racial and ethnic groups to an extent greater than they had before. I think what we have to do is let people be themselves but favor those programs that have multiracial makeup, and we will do that.

Health Care Reform

Q. Okay. As far as health care is concerned, isn't it true that because your health care plan is community based that many young people, because they're young and healthy and they get discounts on insurance now, may end up paying more with your plan?

The President. Yes, in the first year, those who have insurance may pay more, depending on whether they work for small or big businesses. Very young people who are basically in plans that have big businesses insuring them may pay some more in the first year. Even they, however, within 5 years should be paying less, because we slow the rate of growth in these premiums.

Young people who work for small businesses probably won't pay more because they're paying too much already, all small businesses. And they'll be in great big groups. But I would also point out that an awful lot of young people who don't have health insurance—and some young people do have access; some young people do get sick; some young people even have serious illnesses—so it will help them. And I would say, also, to all these young people, if we change it in this way so that we're all rated as a community, what it means is, is that some family gets a sick child, it means that they won't lose their health insurance if they change jobs, or they won't be locked into the job they're in. And all of the young people—I can certify because I was one once—will someday be middle-aged, will someday be older, and they will then benefit from that.

So the fair thing for America to do is to do what Hawaii has already done, what a couple of other States have already done, and what other nations do, which is to have the nation in big pools of people so that we can keep overall costs down.

Abortion

Q. In terms of the health care plan, last time I spoke with you, you said you wanted abortion to be covered under the health care plan. And now I understand the language says "medically necessary, pregnancy-related services" are covered.

The President. That's what it says——

Q. Does that mean that anyone who wants an abortion can get one and have it covered under the plan?

The President. It means that it will be just like it is today in most private plans. Most private plans absolutely cover it. But no insurance plan specifically mentioned any surgical procedure. The surest way to eliminate any kind of abortion coverage from this act would be to mention it specifically, because no other surgical procedure, none, are mentioned specifically. And all private insurance plans which cover abortion may cover pregnancy-related services, and the doctor and the woman make the decision. So what we propose to do is to put low-income people who are covered by the Government today into these big pools with people who are privately insured, give everybody a private plan.

Q. I'm sorry, I don't—is it more than the Hyde amendment in terms of——

The President. Oh, yes, absolutely.

Q. How so? I don't——

The President. Because the Hyde amendment prohibits any public funding for abortions, except when the life of the mother is at risk.

Q. But I thought the Hyde amendment was self-certifying now, and you could say, I have a heart condition, therefore——

The President. Well, I don't know about that, but you have to prove that your life is at risk.

Q. Or rape and incest.

The President. Not in the Hyde amendment.

Q. No? Okay.

The President. No. We tried to expand it and broaden it, but this would simply put people who get Government funds into big private insurance pools, and they would then be treated like other people in private insurance pools. It's just what we did for the public employees this year; we got rid of the Hyde amendment for public employees this year.

Q. You couldn't have just put "abortion" instead of "pregnancy-related"?

The President. Absolutely not. And it would have been wrong to do that. Then people would say, "Well, why don't you put brain surgery in there; why don't you put appendectomies in there; why don't you put other surgeries in there?" And that would have sparked a whole reaction. They would say, "Why are we giving special preference to one kind of procedure over all others?" This will guarantee that most plans will cover abortions.

Now, there will be religious exemptions, which there are today. Catholic churches or other religious groups that have health plans don't have to cover it; doctors who have religious—don't have to do it. But if a doctor and a woman decide that that is an appropriate preg-

nancy-related service under this plan, then it can be provided.

Health Care Cost Estimates

Q. In terms of paying for universal health care, why are you trying to sugar-coat it? Why not just give us the bitter medicine of how much it's going to cost us in taxes?

The President. I'm not trying to sugar-coat it. I have worked harder to get better cost estimates on this than anybody ever has. Moynihan—in all respect to Senator Moynihan, he's a very brilliant man, but he and his committee staff have not done anything like the work that I've done on this. Now, they may not want to pass Medicare cuts; they should say that. It doesn't mean the numbers aren't right. We have had——

Q. ——some people say——

The President. No. We have had four different Government Agencies, for the first time, working together to verify these numbers. We have had outside actuaries from people who work for private business working to verify these numbers. It may be difficult to pass because the Congress will not want to make the administrative changes necessary to lower the rate of increase. But I want to tell—first of all, there are no Medicaid cuts in this. The inflation rate in this country today is about 3 percent. Medicaid's going up this year at 16 percent. We're talking about, over an 8-year period, bringing down the rate of inflation in health care costs to the rate of inflation in the economy plus the number of people who are increased into the program. That's all we're talking about doing.

For the next 5 years, health care costs will still go up more than prices as a whole in this economy. I don't think that is fantasyland, if you have a systematic change. Other countries do it. The Mayo Clinic, which is normally thought of as having some of the finest care in the world, is now charging less for many basic services than an awful lot of ordinary health care plans all across America today because they manage their business better.

So it is not fantasy to say that the numbers are right and they can be achieved. Will it be politically difficult to do? You bet. Why? Because there are a lot of people who make a lot of money out of the inefficiencies of the system today. And because there are a lot of people who honestly don't believe you can ever do more with less. But I do, and I think there's a lot of evidence of that.

So, Senator Moynihan is right, it's going to be tough to pass. I don't think that the numbers are wrong. And let me also say something nobody else has noticed. There are 85 Members of the House of Representatives who want the Government to basically eliminate the private health insurance companies, get out of it altogether, have a huge tax increase to pay for health care but eliminate the premiums. They propose bigger cuts in Medicare and Medicaid than I do. So I just think that the numbers are entirely defensible, and I think we'll be able to persuade the Congress.

Entertainment at Signing Ceremony

Q. I forgot to ask you about—why Soul Asylum?

The President. They were supportive in the campaign, and they made that wonderful song about runaway children, which had a big impact on young people throughout the country. We just thought they'd be a good group to be here.

Q. Does Chelsea like them?

The President. Yes. I do, too. I heard them play last night, you know. So I sort of got caught up on my music last night, listening to them practice.

Q. Have people that looked like that ever walked into your Oval Office before?

The President. Oh, sure. [*Laughter*] This is everybody's Oval Office. I'm just a tenant here.

Q. I see.

The President. Thanks.

Q. Most people here tend to bathe, however. [*Laughter*] Thanks.

The President. Thanks. Bye.

NOTE: The interview began at 12:02 p.m. in the Colonnade at the White House. The band Soul Asylum played at the beginning of the signing ceremony for the National and Community Service Trust Act of 1993. A tape was not available for verification of the content of this interview.

Interview With Radio Talk Show Hosts
September 21, 1993

The President. Thank you very much, and welcome to the Executive Office Building and to the White House, and thank you for coming today. I—what did you say, nice tie? [*Laughter*] That's a Save the Children tie.

Audience member. All right!

The President. I wore it for the national service signing today.

It's interesting, we just had a lunch with a number of columnists——

Audience members. Lunch? Lunch? [*Laughter*]

The President. Lunch? I'm sorry. I'm sorry. Would it make you feel better if I said I didn't enjoy it? I mean—[*laughter*]—anyway, and they knew you were all here, and we had 700 or 800 people out on the lawn for the national service signing. And four or five of these folks that have been covering Washington for 20 years said they had never seen the White House so busy. I didn't know if they were happy or sad about it, but anyway, it's busy.

I thank you for coming today. I hope this will be the first of a number of opportunities we have to provide people who have radio talk shows and who communicate with millions of Americans on an intimate basis, daily, to come to the White House to have these kinds of briefings. You've already heard all the basic approaches that the administration is going to take on health care and that will be hopefully crystallized in a compelling way in my address to the Congress and to the country tomorrow evening.

So, I thought what I would do is make a general statement about how this fits into the overall approach the administration is taking and then answer your questions. I'd rather spend time just answering your questions.

But let me just make a general comment, that I think you can—that runs through the thread of debate that we had on the economic program, on the health care issue, on NAFTA, on the crime bill that's coming up, on the welfare reform issue, on all the major things we're trying to come to grips with.

It is now commonplace to say that we are living through a time of profound change, not only in our country but around the world. People are trying to come to grips with a rate and nature of change that comes along less frequently than once a generation.

You may know that just since you've been sitting here, Boris Yeltsin has dissolved the Russian Parliament and called elections for that Parliament in December, and his major opponent has apparently declared himself President. I mean, they are going through these things, trying to come to grips with what it means to be a democracy and what it means to try to change the economy.

In our country, if we're going to continue to be the leading power of the world, not just militarily but economically, socially, the shining light of the world, this has to be a good place for most Americans to live. Most people have to know that if they work hard and play by the rules that they can make the changes that are sweeping through this country and the world their friends and not their enemies. They have to believe that as citizens they can work together and trust the major institutions of our society to function well, to meet these changes, to respond to them.

We confront this bewildering array of challenges: the size of the deficit, the fact that we have an investment deficit, too, in many critical areas, the health care crisis, at a time when most people are quite insecure in their own lives and most Americans have worked harder for stagnant or lower wages for the last 10 to 20 years, when they're paying more for the basics in life, when they have lost faith in the fundamental capacity of political institutions to represent them and to solve problems.

I think you can see that in the 700,000 letters we got on health care. The number of people who would say, you know, "What's wrong with me? I worked hard all my life, and I lost my health insurance," or "My child got sick, and now I can never change my job," or "My wife and I spend 60 hours a week running our business. And our health insurance was $200 a month 4 years ago, and it's over $900 a month today," you know that things are out of control. I say that because I believe providing security in the health care area and in meeting the other objectives we talked about, quality and choice and cost controls and all, is a necessary precondition, not only to improve the health care of the American people but to help root the American people again in this moment, to make

them freer to face the other challenges that we face. I see in this debate over NAFTA—which I have wrestled with in my own mind, that is, the whole nature of our trade relations with Mexico and other countries and where we are going for far longer than I've been President, I had to deal with it when I was a Governor. I see people, some of them looking ahead with confidence in the future that we can triumph in the world of the 21st century, that we can compete and win, that we can create tomorrow's jobs, and others so uncertain about it, just trying to hold on to today and to yesterday's jobs.

So, what I am trying to do is to give the American people a greater sense of security over those things that are basic to their lives that they can control and at the same time challenge our people to assume responsibility for dealing with our problems and for marching confidently into the future. That's what this national service issue is all about that we celebrated today on the White House lawn.

And therefore, the health care issue is about more than health care. It is about restoring self-confidence to America's families and businesses. It's about restoring some discipline to our budget and investment decisions, not only in the Government but in the private sector. It's about giving us the sense that we actually can move forward and win in the face of all these changes. I cannot under—or I guess I cannot overstate how important I think it is, not only on its own terms but also for what it might mean for America over the long run.

Yes.

Health Care Reform

Q. Does anybody really know whether this will work, from the administration? Have you parsed the numbers that fine, that you can say if this is passed in toto, it will indeed do what you say, cut costs, maintain quality of care, cover everybody?

The President. We know it will do that, but that's not exactly what you asked. That is, we know that if this plan is adopted, it will provide universal coverage, that it will achieve substantial savings in many areas where there is massive waste.

Dr. Koop, who was, you know, President Reagan's Surgeon General, who was with us yesterday, and the doctors that we had, said that in his judgment, there was at least $200 billion of waste, unnecessary procedures, administrative waste, fraudulent churning of the system, at least, in our system. So, we know that those things will achieve those objectives? We do. Do we know that every last dollar is accurate, or that there will be no unintended consequences, or that the timetable is precisely right? No we don't know that because nobody can know that exactly.

But I would like to make two points. Number one, our administration has gone further to get good health care numbers than anyone ever has before. Until I became President I didn't know this, but the various Agencies in the Federal Government responsible for various parts of health care financing and regulation had never had their experts sit down in the same room together and agree on the same set of numbers and the same methodologies for achieving them. So that's the first thing we did. No wonder we had so much fight over what something was going to cost and the deficit was going crazy. The Government had never gotten its own act together.

Then the second thing we did was to go out and solicit outside actuaries from private sector firms who made a living evaluating the cost of health care and asked them to review our numbers. Now, that is very important that you understand that, because there is going to be— there should be a debate over whether the course I have recommended is the best course to achieve the goals we all want to achieve, whether there is a better course, whether we can achieve the Medicare and Medicaid cuts that we say we can achieve without hurting the quality of care. That's fine. But I want you to understand that we really have killed ourselves at least to get the arithmetic right, to give people an honest starting point, a common ground to start from, so that we can have the arguments over policy.

Yes, sir.

Q. Do you feel that your plan places undue hardship on business with the employer mandate versus an individual plan that has been proposed with other proposals?

The President. No, and I'll say why. First of all, let's just look at the employer mandate. Most employers cover their employees. I like your question in the sense that the question assumes that we should have universal coverage, and that's a good assumption. If you don't have universal coverage, you can never really slow the

rate of waste in cost, because you'll always have a lot of cost shifting in the system. That is, people who aren't covered will still get health care, but they'll get it when it's too late, too expensive, somebody else will pay the bill, and it will have real inefficiencies and distortions, as it does today.

If you want to cover everybody, there are essentially three ways to do it. You can do it the way Canada does. You can abolish all private health insurance premiums, raise taxes to replace the health insurance premiums, and have a single-payer system, just have the Government do it. That's the most administratively efficient. That is, the Canadian system has very low administrative costs, even lower than Germany and Japan. The problem is, it's not very good for controlling costs in other ways, because the Government makes all the cost decisions. The citizens know they've already paid for this through government. So they make real demands on the system. Whereas if you have a mixed system where employers and employees are actually in there knowing what they're spending on health care and lobbying for better management and to control costs, like in Germany, you don't have costs go up as fast. So the Canadian system, even though it's administratively the cheapest, is the second most expensive in the world. We're spending 14 percent of our income; they're spending 10 percent of theirs. Everybody else is under 9.

Now, the second system is the individual mandate. It's never been tried anywhere. The problem with the individual mandate is that it could—and again, I want a debate on this. I think the Republicans are entitled to their day in court on this, and I want them to have it. Really, I do. I mean, I want an honest, open discussion on this. I am so impressed with the spirit that is pervading this health insurance— we had 400 Members of Congress show up for 2 days at our health care university just trying to get everybody to have enough information to be singing out of the same hymnal when we talk to one another.

The dangers of the individual mandates are that it could cause the present system we have for most Americans, which is working well for most Americans, to disintegrate. That is, you have to have some subsidies with an individual mandate. So will companies that now cover their employees basically start covering their upper income employees or not their lower income employees? Will they dump all their employees and make them go under the individual mandate system? How are you going to keep up with all these individuals when you realize who you've got to subsidize or not? In other words, we believe it has significantly more administrative burdens, and it has the potential to cause the present system to come undone. But they deserve their day in court on it, and we'll debate it.

Let me just say this. Our system for small businesses, I'd like to make the following points: We propose to keep lower the premiums of small businesses with fewer than 50 employees, including all those that are just starting up. And they get more if their wages of their employees are low, and low-wage workers also get a subsidy to try to make sure nobody goes out of business. But the point I want to make is, most small businesses who do cover their employees, and that's the majority of them, are paying too much for their health insurance. They are being burdened by it. That's one reason 100,000 Americans a month permanently lose their health insurance, as well as at any given time in a year, as many as one in four may be without it.

So what we propose to do will actually help more small businesses than it will hurt. And over the long run, they'll all be better off, because if you put everybody under this system, then the rate of increase in health care costs will be much lower. And it's just not fair, at some point, for anybody who can pay something to get a free ride, because keep in mind, we all get health care in this country. But if we're not insured, we get it when it's too late, too expensive. Usually we show up at the emergency room, the most expensive of all, and then somebody else pays the bill. That's one of the things that's driving these costs out of sight.

Yes, sir.

Q. We've heard a lot about every group today, except for the doctors. And from the doctors that I'm hearing from, they're saying that this is going to hit them in their pockets. In my experience before in being in operating rooms and seeing doctors after the diagnostic related groups started setting some prices of procedures back in the eighties, a lot of doctors that went into business for themselves were either multi-using single-use items or resterilizing items that were made for single-use so that they wouldn't lose any of the money that was going to be coming to them, so they wouldn't take a per-

sonal hit out of it. How does your plan guarantee us an uncompromised medical plan?

The President. Well, for one thing, the quality standards that govern medical care today will still be in effect. That is, most of them are professional standards, and they're not enforced by the Government today.

Q. They're talking about doing more procedures to make up the money. They're saying, "Well, I'm going to have to see more patients and spend less time with them."

The President. Yes, but that's what's happening today. I mean, the truth is that as we've tried to control the costs of Medicare and Medicaid, particularly Medicare, by holding down costs, you see dramatically increased numbers of procedures. What we want to do is to remove the incentive for having large numbers of procedures by having big blocks of consumers pay for their annual health care needs in a block, so that you won't have so much fee-for-service.

I would also point out to you that one of the big problems we've had with doctor costs going up is that doctors are having to negotiate their way through the mine field of 1,500 separate health insurance companies writing thousands of different policies, having to keep up with it in ways that no doctors anywhere in the world but our doctors have to deal with.

We've already had the American Academy of Family Practice and a lot of other doctors groups have endorsed our plan. The AMA has been quite interestingly supportive in general terms. They say they want to see all the details. They believe there ought to be universal coverage. Dr. Koop has agreed to come in and sort of moderate this discussion. But we had a couple hundred doctors here yesterday, most of whom were extremely supportive. And let me just give you one big reason why. This is the flip side of the argument you made.

In 1980, the average doctor was taking home 75 percent of the money generated by a clinic. In 1990, the average doctor was taking home 52 cents on the dollar, 52 percent of the money generated by a clinic. Twenty-three cents on the dollar increase in the amount of money the doctor was having to spend on people, basically to do clerical work in the clinics.

The Children's Hospital at Washington told us last week that the 200 doctors on staff there spent enough time in non-health-care-related paperwork every year because of the administrative cost of this system—a dime on the dollar more than any other system in the world—to see another 500 patients each a year, 10,000 more kids a year. So, a lot of doctors are going to feel very liberated by this because they are going to be freer to practice medicine, and the incentives to churn the system just to pay for all their paperwork will be less.

Yes, sir.

Mr. Strauss. Time for one more question.

Q. I guess I have the opportunity, I'll make it a two-part question because it's a rare opportunity, and I appreciate it. First of all, if you receive everything that you want, that you're hoping for, and we hear about the 37 million uninsured and the many underinsured people, I'm wondering if there's anybody that will be disappointed with the new system——

The President. Oh yeah.

Q. ——if you get everything you want, and who those people might be? And secondly, I hear very little about medical fraud and medical malpractice problems, as if it isn't a major problem, and we are led to believe that it is.

The President. It is a big problem. Maybe I should answer that question first, because it's a quicker one. Then let me try to tell you how to sort through the winners and losers. Okay?

First of all, in this system if you put consumers of health care, employers and employees, particularly the small businesses, in large buying groups where they will have more market power and more oversight authority, you will inevitably—we are going to change the economic incentives as well as the private sector oversight to reduce fraud and abuse—we are definitely going to see big savings there.

Secondly, what was the other thing you asked me?

Q. The medical malpractice.

The President. Medical malpractice. Doctors——

Q. Doctors spending—[*inaudible*]——

The President. Well, doctors——

Q. [*Inaudible*]

The President. One of the things that we don't know is how much extra excess procedures and tests are done as defensive medicine or to churn the system, to go back to your other question. The economic incentives to churn the system will be dramatically reduced under these kind of payment plans.

It will be more like the way the Rochester, New York, system works, the way the Mayo Clinic system works. More and more people will be in a system where they pay up front, and then they take what they need. And the doctors are going to get paid out of that.

But the malpractice issue is a problem. We will propose some significant reforms, including limiting the percentage of income lawyers can get in contingency fees in lawsuits. But I have to tell you, what I think the most significant—and alternative dispute resolution mechanisms—but I think the most important one will be permitting the professional associations to draw up medical practice guidelines which, when approved, will protect the doctors to some extent, because if they follow the guidelines in any given case, it will raise a presumption that they weren't negligent. And that will be a real protection against just doing an extra procedure because you're trying to hedge against a lawsuit.

The State of Maine pioneered this because they wanted more general practitioners in rural Maine to do more things for people like help deliver babies because they didn't have anybody else to do it. So, the idea of giving people practice guidelines I think is very good.

Now, you asked who's going to win and who's going to lose. Can we talk through that?

Q. Yes, sir.

The President. I'll tell you who will have to pay more. You know, there will be some people who will have to pay more. The news magazines this week did a pretty good job of analyzing this.

If we go to community rating, so that we can allow people, for example, who have had a sick child not to be bankrupt by their insurance costs and to move from job to job, and you put everybody in a broad community, it means young, single, super healthy people will pay more in the first year of this than they would have otherwise. Now, here's why I think that's a good deal for young, single, super healthy people. Number one, all young, single, super healthy people will get insured, and they aren't now. Number two, they'll all be middle-aged someday, too, and they'll win big. Number three, their cost will go up less every year. So even though they might pay more this year, within 5 to 8 years, if this plan goes through, everybody will be paying less than they would have. So, they would pay more.

Secondly, there are some businesses who don't insure at all. They'll have to pay something. There are others who insure but only for catastrophic. They will have to pay more, but they'll get much better benefits, and their rates will go up less. So, there will be some people who will pay more now than they were paying. But I believe that if we can—keep in mind, if we can stop the cost of health care from going up at 2 and 3 times the rate of inflation, if we can get it down where the rate of increase is much lower, by the end of the decade everybody will be way better off than they were.

Russia

Q. Mr. President do you approve of—Boris Yeltsin's announcement that he's going to dissolve the Parliament, and does the United States support him in his power struggle with his opponents?

The President. Well, first of all, let me say I have had only a sketchy briefing about this, and I have not talked to President Yeltsin yet. I would like to reserve the right to issue a statement after I attempt to talk to President Yeltsin. In any case, I will issue a statement before the end of the day, but I think at least I should have a direct briefing.

Yes sir, one more. Go ahead.

Health Care Reform

Q. President Clinton, tomorrow you'll be speaking before a joint session of Congress and there are 535 people, individuals, in Congress that will have their own specific plans of what

they want——

The President. Yes.

Q. If you could say that you could put your name on one or two or three specific parts of this that you want to say, "This is my health care plan," that you want to see no matter what 535 other people want to see, that you feel you want to be part of your Clinton health care program, what two or three items, specifically?

The President. Number one, every American would have security in their health care system. You would be able to get health insurance, there would be adequate benefits, and you wouldn't lose them. Number two, the system would impose a far higher level of responsibility for managing costs than it does now on all the players, including the consumers. Number three, people would keep their choice of physicians and medical providers. And number four, we would guarantee adequate access to preventive and primary care so we could stop some of the big things that are happening to us before they get going. And five, we would have market incentives to bring costs down. Those are the things that I want to be the hallmark of our program.

I wish I could stay all day. I'm sorry, but thank you very much.

NOTE: The President spoke at 3:06 p.m. in Room 450 of the Old Executive Office Building. Richard Strauss was the White House radio services coordinator.

Statement on the Situation in Russia
September 21, 1993

From the beginning of my administration, I have given my full backing to the historic process of political and economic reform now underway in Russia. I remain convinced that democratic reforms and the transition to a market economy hold the best hope for a better future for the people of Russia.

The actions announced today by President Yeltsin in his address to the Russian people underscore the complexity of the reform process that he is leading. There is no question that President Yeltsin acted in response to a constitutional crisis that had reached a critical impasse and had paralyzed the political process.

As the democratically elected leader of Russia, President Yeltsin has chosen to allow the people of Russia themselves to resolve this impasse. I believe that the path to elections for a new legislature is ultimately consistent with the democratic and reform course that he has charted.

I called President Yeltsin this afternoon to seek assurances that the difficult choices that he faces will be made in a way that ensures peace, stability, and an open political process this autumn. He told me that it is of the utmost importance that the elections he has called be organized and held on a democratic and free basis.

In a democracy, the people should finally decide the issues that are at the heart of political and social debate. President Yeltsin has made this choice, and I support him fully. I have confidence in the abiding wisdom of the Russian people to make the right decision regarding their own future.

Message to the Congress Transmitting the Report on Mine Safety and Health
September 21, 1993

To the Congress of the United States:

In accordance with Section 511(a) of the Federal Mine Safety and Health Act of 1969, as amended ("the Act"), 30 U.S.C. 958(a), I transmit herewith the annual report on mine safety and health activities for fiscal year 1992. This report was prepared by, and covers activities occurring exclusively during the previous Administration. The enclosed report does not reflect the policies or priorities of this Administration.

My Administration is committed to working with the Congress to ensure vigorous enforcement of existing mine safety and health standards. We are also intent on improving these rules where necessary and appropriate to better protect worker health and safety.

WILLIAM J. CLINTON

The White House,
September 21, 1993.

Message to the Congress Transmitting the Report of the Saint Lawrence Seaway Development Corporation
September 21, 1993

To the Congress of the United States:

I transmit herewith the Saint Lawrence Seaway Development Corporation's Annual Report for fiscal year 1992. This report has been prepared in accordance with section 10 of the Saint Lawrence Seaway Act of May 13, 1954 (33 U.S.C. 989(a)), and covers the period October 1, 1991, through September 30, 1992.

WILLIAM J. CLINTON

The White House,
September 21, 1993.

Message to the Congress Transmitting the Report of the National Science Foundation
September 21, 1993

To the Congress of the United States:

In accordance with section 3(f) of the National Science Foundation Act of 1950, as amended (42 U.S.C. 1862(f)), I am pleased to send you the annual report of the National Science Foundation for Fiscal Year 1992. This report describes research supported by the Foundation in the mathematical, physical, bio- logical, social, behavioral, and computer sciences; engineering; and education in those fields.

Achievements such as the ones described in this report are the basis for much of our Nation's strength—its economic growth, national security, and the overall well-being of our people.

As we move toward the 21st century, the Foundation will continue its efforts to expand our Nation's research achievements, our productivity, and our ability to remain competitive in world markets.

WILLIAM J. CLINTON

The White House,
September 21, 1993.

Remarks Prior to a Meeting With Congressional Leaders and an Exchange With Reporters
September 22, 1993

The President. Ladies and gentlemen, I want to say, in the presence here of the press, this is the last meeting I will have a chance to have with the large bipartisan leadership in Congress on health care issues. But I do want to say a profound word of thanks on behalf of not only myself but the entire administration for the work that has been done by people in both parties in the Congress since the first bipartisan leadership meeting I had on January 26th, when I asked that people be designated to work with us from both parties on this health care issue.

I'm not sure that any consultative process like this has ever been carried out before where there's been so much common work, not only between and among ourselves but also with people in the country who are interested in this issue. We have met with over 1,100 groups, with literally thousands of doctors, nurses, and other affected folks in this process. But the most important thing to me has been the spirit of genuine searching and determination that I have seen from leaders in both parties on this issue.

I just want to say, as I prepare to give this speech tonight, how much I appreciate that and how much I look forward to continuing that process in the weeks and months ahead. I'm very grateful to you, and we're going to talk for about an hour here, and then the Senate has to go make a vote, I think. But we're going to have a chance to talk about health care one more time before I speak tonight.

Health Care Reform

Q. Mr. President, you're about to start something tonight that has been tried and failed several times in recent years. Why is this——

The President. Throughout the whole century.

Q. Throughout the whole century. Why is this different?

The President. Well, I think, you know, if you go back and look at the history of health care, I think there are two things that are different. One is, there is almost unanimous consensus that the cost of continuing on the present course is greater than the cost of change. With health care costs rising at more than twice the rate of inflation and rising much faster than that for small businesses, with more people losing their coverage every month so that we're paying more for less health care, with the range of choices available for Americans dropping dramatically and the administrative cost to the system escalating at a breathtaking rate, that the cost of going on is greater than the cost of change. I don't think that there has ever been that much consensus before.

The second thing is, I think you've got all of the people trying to work together now. If you go back through the whole history of the 20th century, you can find times when Republicans wanted to do something about health care and Democrats didn't, some when Presidents wanted to do something and the Congress didn't. There's one example when, early in this century, when the American Medical Association wanted to have a national health care bill and the labor movement didn't.

I mean, these things have been flip-flopped. If you read the history of health care, it's like people, you know, passing each other in the night. And I think now you've finally got everybody in the country focused on it. So I think we have a moment in history when we can seize it and move forward if we can maintain this determination to stay in touch with the real problems of our people and with this sort of spirit that we have now of working together.

Taxes

Q. Can you tell us what the sin taxes are going to be for people to help pay for this?

The President. Tonight.

Q. [*Inaudible*]—tell us tonight—[*inaudible*]—an hour and a half.

Q. Are you purposely avoiding that topic today?

The President. No, no. Lord, no.

Q. Are you concerned about the story tomorrow——

The President. No. There will be less than you think, I'll say that.

Russia

Q. Mr. President, do you have anything on the situation in Russia? Are you more reassured now than yesterday?

The President. Well, the situation is calm, and I am hopeful. You know what my position is on it, and I still think the United States has to be on the side of reform and democracy in Russia, and President Yeltsin represents that. But I know nothing more today than I knew last night when we talked, except that I've obviously gotten my morning briefing, and the situation is calm, and we're hopeful.

Q. Are you trying to contact world leaders, sir, to encourage them to come out in support of him as well?

The President. I called Mr. Kohl last night, and we communicated in other ways with Prime Minister Major and President Mitterrand, Prime Minister Balladur in France, and others. I noted that Prime Minister Major came out today in support, and I know Chancellor Kohl issued a statement yesterday. So I very much appreciate that.

NOTE: The President spoke at 11 a.m. in the State Dining Room at the White House.

Address to a Joint Session of the Congress on Health Care Reform
September 22, 1993

Mr. Speaker, Mr. President, Members of Congress, distinguished guests, my fellow Americans, before I begin my words tonight I would like to ask that we all bow in a moment of silent prayer for the memory of those who were killed and those who have been injured in the tragic train accident in Alabama today.

Amen.

My fellow Americans, tonight we come together to write a new chapter in the American story. Our forebears enshrined the American dream: life, liberty, the pursuit of happiness. Every generation of Americans has worked to strengthen that legacy, to make our country a place of freedom and opportunity, a place where people who work hard can rise to their full potential, a place where their children can have a better future.

From the settling of the frontier to the landing on the Moon, ours has been a continuous story of challenges defined, obstacles overcome, new horizons secured. That is what makes America what it is and Americans what we are. Now we are in a time of profound change and opportunity. The end of the cold war, the information age, the global economy have brought us both opportunity and hope and strife and uncertainty. Our purpose in this dynamic age must be to make change our friend and not our enemy.

To achieve that goal, we must face all our challenges with confidence, with faith, and with discipline, whether we're reducing the deficit, creating tomorrow's jobs and training our people to fill them, converting from a high-tech defense to a high-tech domestic economy, expanding trade, reinventing Government, making our streets safer, or rewarding work over idleness. All these challenges require us to change.

If Americans are to have the courage to change in a difficult time, we must first be secure in our most basic needs. Tonight I want to talk to you about the most critical thing we can do to build that security. This health care system of ours is badly broken, and it is time to fix it. Despite the dedication of literally millions of talented health care professionals, our health care is too uncertain and too expensive, too bureaucratic and too wasteful. It has too much fraud and too much greed.

At long last, after decades of false starts, we must make this our most urgent priority, giving every American health security, health care that can never be taken away, health care that is always there. That is what we must do tonight.

On this journey, as on all others of true consequence, there will be rough spots in the road and honest disagreements about how we should proceed. After all, this is a complicated issue. But every successful journey is guided by fixed stars. And if we can agree on some basic values and principles, we will reach this destination, and we will reach it together.

So tonight I want to talk to you about the principles that I believe must embody our efforts to reform America's health care system: security, simplicity, savings, choice, quality, and responsibility.

When I launched our Nation on this journey to reform the health care system I knew we needed a talented navigator, someone with a rigorous mind, a steady compass, a caring heart. Luckily for me and for our Nation, I didn't have to look very far.

[*At this point, audience members applauded Hillary Clinton, and she acknowledged them.*]

Over the last 8 months, Hillary and those working with her have talked to literally thousands of Americans to understand the strengths and the frailties of this system of ours. They met with over 1,100 health care organizations. They talked with doctors and nurses, pharmacists and drug company representatives, hospital administrators, insurance company executives, and small and large businesses. They spoke with self-employed people. They talked with people who had insurance and people who didn't. They talked with union members and older Americans and advocates for our children. The First Lady also consulted, as all of you know, extensively with governmental leaders in both parties in the States of our Nation and especially here on Capitol Hill. Hillary and the task force received and read over 700,000 letters from ordinary citizens. What they wrote and the bravery with which they told their stories is really what calls us all here tonight.

Every one of us knows someone who's worked hard and played by the rules and still been hurt by this system that just doesn't work for too many people. But I'd like to tell you about just one. Kerry Kennedy owns a small furniture store that employs seven people in Titusville,

Florida. Like most small business owners, he's poured his heart and soul, his sweat and blood into that business for years. But over the last several years, again like most small business owners, he's seen his health care premiums skyrocket, even in years when no claims were made. And last year, he painfully discovered he could no longer afford to provide coverage for all his workers because his insurance company told him that two of his workers had become high risks because of their advanced age. The problem was that those two people were his mother and father, the people who founded the business and still work in the store.

This story speaks for millions of others. And from them we have learned a powerful truth. We have to preserve and strengthen what is right with the health care system, but we have got to fix what is wrong with it.

Now, we all know what's right. We're blessed with the best health care professionals on Earth, the finest health care institutions, the best medical research, the most sophisticated technology. My mother is a nurse. I grew up around hospitals. Doctors and nurses were the first professional people I ever knew or learned to look up to. They are what is right with this health care system. But we also know that we can no longer afford to continue to ignore what is wrong.

Millions of Americans are just a pink slip away from losing their health insurance and one serious illness away from losing all their savings. Millions more are locked into the jobs they have now just because they or someone in their family has once been sick and they have what is called the preexisting condition. And on any given day, over 37 million Americans, most of them working people and their little children, have no health insurance at all.

And in spite of all this, our medical bills are growing at over twice the rate of inflation, and the United States spends over a third more of its income on health care than any other nation on Earth. And the gap is growing, causing many of our companies in global competition severe disadvantage. There is no excuse for this kind of system. We know other people have done better. We know people in our own country are doing better. We have no excuse. My fellow Americans, we must fix this system, and it has to begin with congressional action.

I believe as strongly as I can say that we can reform the costliest and most wasteful system on the face of the Earth without enacting new broad-based taxes. I believe it because of the conversations I have had with thousands of health care professionals around the country, with people who are outside this city but are inside experts on the way this system works and wastes money.

The proposal that I describe tonight borrows many of the principles and ideas that have been embraced in plans introduced by both Republicans and Democrats in this Congress. For the first time in this century, leaders of both political parties have joined together around the principle of providing universal, comprehensive health care. It is a magic moment, and we must seize it.

I want to say to all of you I have been deeply moved by the spirit of this debate, by the openness of all people to new ideas and argument and information. The American people would be proud to know that earlier this week when a health care university was held for Members of Congress just to try to give everybody the same amount of information, over 320 Republicans and Democrats signed up and showed up for 2 days just to learn the basic facts of the complicated problem before us.

Both sides are willing to say, "We have listened to the people. We know the cost of going forward with this system is far greater than the cost of change." Both sides, I think, understand the literal ethical imperative of doing something about the system we have now. Rising above these difficulties and our past differences to solve this problem will go a long way toward defining who we are and who we intend to be as a people in this difficult and challenging era. I believe we all understand that. And so tonight, let me ask all of you, every Member of the House, every Member of the Senate, each Republican and each Democrat, let us keep this spirit and let us keep this commitment until this job is done. We owe it to the American people. [*Applause*]

Thank you. Thank you very much.

Now, if I might, I would like to review the six principles I mentioned earlier and describe how we think we can best fulfill those principles.

First and most important, security. This principle speaks to the human misery, to the costs, to the anxiety we hear about every day, all of us, when people talk about their problems with the present system. Security means that those who do not now have health care coverage will

have it, and for those who have it, it will never be taken away. We must achieve that security as soon as possible.

Under our plan, every American would receive a health care security card that will guarantee a comprehensive package of benefits over the course of an entire lifetime, roughly comparable to the benefit package offered by most Fortune 500 companies. This health care security card will offer this package of benefits in a way that can never be taken away. So let us agree on this: Whatever else we disagree on, before this Congress finishes its work next year, you will pass and I will sign legislation to guarantee this security to every citizen of this country.

With this card, if you lose your job or you switch jobs, you're covered. If you leave your job to start a small business, you're covered. If you're an early retiree, you're covered. If someone in your family has unfortunately had an illness that qualifies as a preexisting condition, you're still covered. If you get sick or a member of your family gets sick, even if it's a life-threatening illness, you're covered. And if an insurance company tries to drop you for any reason, you will still be covered, because that will be illegal. This card will give comprehensive coverage. It will cover people for hospital care, doctor visits, emergency and lab services, diagnostic services like Pap smears and mammograms and cholesterol tests, substance abuse, and mental health treatment.

And equally important, for both health care and economic reasons, this program for the first time would provide a broad range of preventive services including regular checkups and well-baby visits. Now, it's just common sense. We know, any family doctor will tell you, that people will stay healthier and long-term costs of the health system will be lower if we have comprehensive preventive services. You know how all of our mothers told us that an ounce of prevention was worth a pound of cure? Our mothers were right. And it's a lesson, like so many lessons from our mothers, that we have waited too long to live by. It is time to start doing it.

Health care security must also apply to older Americans. This is something I imagine all of us in this room feel very deeply about. The first thing I want to say about that is that we must maintain the Medicare program. It works to provide that kind of security. But this time and for the first time, I believe Medicare should provide coverage for the cost of prescription drugs.

Yes, it will cost some more in the beginning. But again, any physician who deals with the elderly will tell you that there are thousands of elderly people in every State who are not poor enough to be on Medicaid but just above that line and on Medicare, who desperately need medicine, who make decisions every week between medicine and food. Any doctor who deals with the elderly will tell you that there are many elderly people who don't get medicine, who get sicker and sicker and eventually go to the doctor and wind up spending more money and draining more money from the health care system than they would if they had regular treatment in the way that only adequate medicine can provide.

I also believe that over time, we should phase in long-term care for the disabled and the elderly on a comprehensive basis. As we proceed with this health care reform, we cannot forget that the most rapidly growing percentage of Americans are those over 80. We cannot break faith with them. We have to do better by them.

The second principle is simplicity. Our health care system must be simpler for the patients and simpler for those who actually deliver health care: our doctors, our nurses, our other medical professionals. Today we have more than 1,500 insurers, with hundreds and hundreds of different forms. No other nation has a system like this. These forms are time consuming for health care providers. They're expensive for health care consumers. They're exasperating for anyone who's ever tried to sit down around a table and wade through them and figure them out.

The medical care industry is literally drowning in paperwork. In recent years, the number of administrators in our hospitals has grown by 4 times the rate that the number of doctors has grown. A hospital ought to be a house of healing, not a monument to paperwork and bureaucracy.

Just a few days ago, the Vice President and I had the honor of visiting the Children's Hospital here in Washington where they do wonderful, often miraculous things for very sick children. A nurse named Debbie Freiberg told us that she was in the cancer and bone marrow unit. The other day a little boy asked her just to stay at his side during his chemotherapy. And she had to walk away from that child because she had been instructed to go to yet another

class to learn how to fill out another form for something that didn't have a lick to do with the health care of the children she was helping. That is wrong, and we can stop it, and we ought to do it.

We met a very compelling doctor named Lillian Beard, a pediatrician, who said that she didn't get into her profession to spend hours and hours—some doctors up to 25 hours a week—just filling out forms. She told us she became a doctor to keep children well and to help save those who got sick. We can relieve people like her of this burden. We learned, the Vice President and I did, that in the Washington Children's Hospital alone, the administrators told us they spend $2 million a year in one hospital filling out forms that have nothing whatever to do with keeping up with the treatment of the patients.

And the doctors there applauded when I was told and I related to them that they spend so much time filling out paperwork, that if they only had to fill out those paperwork requirements necessary to monitor the health of the children, each doctor on that one hospital staff, 200 of them, could see another 500 children a year. That is 10,000 children a year. I think we can save money in this system if we simplify it. And we can make the doctors and the nurses and the people that are giving their lives to help us all be healthier a whole lot happier, too, on their jobs.

Under our proposal there would be one standard insurance form, not hundreds of them. We will simplify also—and we must—the Government's rules and regulations, because they are a big part of this problem. This is one of those cases where the physician should heal thyself. We have to reinvent the way we relate to the health care system, along with reinventing Government. A doctor should not have to check with a bureaucrat in an office thousands of miles away before ordering a simple blood test. That's not right, and we can change it. And doctors, nurses, and consumers shouldn't have to worry about the fine print. If we have this one simple form, there won't be any fine print. People will know what it means.

The third principle is savings. Reform must produce savings in this health care system. It has to. We're spending over 14 percent of our income on health care. Canada's at 10. Nobody else is over 9. We're competing with all these people for the future. And the other major countries, they cover everybody, and they cover them with services as generous as the best company policies here in this country.

Rampant medical inflation is eating away at our wages, our savings, our investment capital, our ability to create new jobs in the private sector, and this public Treasury. You know the budget we just adopted had steep cuts in defense, a 5-year freeze on the discretionary spending, so critical to reeducating America and investing in jobs and helping us to convert from a defense to a domestic economy. But we passed a budget which has Medicaid increases of between 16 and 11 percent a year over the next 5 years and Medicare increases of between 11 and 9 percent in an environment where we assume inflation will be at 4 percent or less. We cannot continue to do this. Our competitiveness, our whole economy, the integrity of the way the Government works, and ultimately, our living standards depend upon our ability to achieve savings without harming the quality of health care.

Unless we do this, our workers will lose $655 in income each year by the end of the decade. Small businesses will continue to face skyrocketing premiums. And a full third of small businesses now covering their employees say they will be forced to drop their insurance. Large corporations will bear bigger disadvantages in global competition. And health care costs will devour more and more and more of our budget. Pretty soon all of you or the people who succeed you will be showing up here and writing out checks for health care and interest on the debt and worrying about whether we've got enough defense, and that will be it, unless we have the courage to achieve the savings that are plainly there before us. Every State and local government will continue to cut back on everything from education to law enforcement to pay more and more for the same health care.

These rising costs are a special nightmare for our small businesses, the engine of our entrepreneurship and our job creation in America today. Health care premiums for small businesses are 35 percent higher than those of large corporations today. And they will keep rising at double-digit rates unless we act.

So how will we achieve these savings? Rather than looking at price control or looking away as the price spiral continues, rather than using the heavy hand of Government to try to control what's happening or continuing to ignore what's

happening, we believe there is a third way to achieve these savings. First, to give groups of consumers and small businesses the same market bargaining power that large corporations and large groups of public employees now have, we want to let market forces enable plans to compete. We want to force these plans to compete on the basis of price and quality, not simply to allow them to continue making money by turning people away who are sick or old or performing mountains of unnecessary procedures. But we also believe we should back this system up with limits on how much plans can raise their premiums year-in and year-out, forcing people, again, to continue to pay more for the same health care, without regard to inflation or the rising population needs.

We want to create what has been missing in this system for too long and what every successful nation who has dealt with this problem has already had to do: to have a combination of private market forces and a sound public policy that will support that competition, but limit the rate at which prices can exceed the rate of inflation and population growth, if the competition doesn't work, especially in the early going.

The second thing I want to say is that unless everybody is covered—and this is a very important thing—unless everybody is covered, we will never be able to fully put the brakes on health care inflation. Why is that? Because when people don't have any health insurance, they still get health care, but they get it when it's too late, when it's too expensive, often from the most expensive place of all, the emergency room. Usually by the time they show up, their illnesses are more severe, and their mortality rates are much higher in our hospitals than those who have insurance. So they cost us more. And what else happens? Since they get the care but they don't pay, who does pay? All the rest of us. We pay in higher hospital bills and higher insurance premiums. This cost shifting is a major problem.

The third thing we can do to save money is simply by simplifying the system, what we've already discussed. Freeing the health care providers from these costly and unnecessary paperwork and administrative decisions will save tens of billions of dollars. We spend twice as much as any other major country does on paperwork. We spend at least a dime on the dollar more than any other major country. That is a stunning statistic. It is something that every Republican and every Democrat ought to be able to say, we agree that we're going to squeeze this out. We cannot tolerate this. This has nothing to do with keeping people well or helping them when they're sick. We should invest the money in something else.

We also have to crack down on fraud and abuse in the system. That drains billions of dollars a year. It is a very large figure, according to every health care expert I've ever spoken with. So I believe we can achieve large savings. And that large savings can be used to cover the unemployed uninsured and will be used for people who realize those savings in the private sector to increase their ability to invest and grow, to hire new workers or to give their workers pay raises, many of them for the first time in years.

Now, nobody has to take my word for this. You can ask Dr. Koop. He's up here with us tonight, and I thank him for being here. Since he left his distinguished tenure as our Surgeon General, he has spent an enormous amount of time studying our health care system, how it operates, what's right and wrong with it. He says we could spend $200 billion every year, more than 20 percent of the total budget, without sacrificing the high quality of American medicine.

Ask the public employees in California, who've held their own premiums down by adopting the same strategy that I want every American to be able to adopt, bargaining within the limits of a strict budget. Ask Xerox, which saved an estimated $1,000 per worker on their health insurance premium. Ask the staff of the Mayo Clinic, who we all agree provides some of the finest health care in the world. They are holding their cost increases to less than half the national average. Ask the people of Hawaii, the only State that covers virtually all of their citizens and has still been able to keep costs below the national average.

People may disagree over the best way to fix this system. We may all disagree about how quickly we can do the thing that we have to do. But we cannot disagree that we can find tens of billions of dollars in savings in what is clearly the most costly and the most bureaucratic system in the entire world. And we have to do something about that, and we have to do it now.

The fourth principle is choice. Americans be-lieve they ought to be able to choose their own health care plan and keep their own doctors. And I think all of us agree. Under any plan we pass, they ought to have that right. But today, under our broken health care system, in spite of the rhetoric of choice, the fact is that that power is slipping away for more and more Americans.

Of course, it is usually the employer, not the employee, who makes the initial choice of what health care plan the employee will be in. And if your employer offers only one plan, as nearly three-quarters of small or medium-sized firms do today, you're stuck with that plan and the doctors that it covers.

We propose to give every American a choice among high quality plans. You can stay with your current doctor, join a network of doctors and hospitals, or join a health maintenance organization. If you don't like your plan, every year you'll have the chance to choose a new one. The choice will be left to the American citizen, the worker, not the boss and certainly not some Government bureaucrat.

We also believe that doctors should have a choice as to what plans they practice in. Otherwise, citizens may have their own choices limited. We want to end the discrimination that is now growing against doctors and to permit them to practice in several different plans. Choice is important for doctors, and it is absolutely critical for our consumers. We've got to have it in whatever plan we pass.

The fifth principle is quality. If we reformed everything else in health care but failed to preserve and enhance the high quality of our medical care, we will have taken a step backward, not forward. Quality is something that we simply can't leave to chance. When you board an airplane, you feel better knowing that the plane had to meet standards designed to protect your safety. And we can't ask any less of our health care system.

Our proposal will create report cards on health plans, so that consumers can choose the highest quality health care providers and reward them with their business. At the same time, our plan will track quality indicators, so that doctors can make better and smarter choices of the kind of care they provide. We have evidence that more efficient delivery of health care doesn't decrease quality. In fact, it may enhance it.

Let me just give you one example of one

commonly performed procedure, the coronary bypass operation. Pennsylvania discovered that patients who were charged $21,000 for this surgery received as good or better care as patients who were charged $84,000 for the same procedure in the same State. High prices simply don't always equal good quality. Our plan will guarantee that high quality information is available in even the most remote areas of this country so that we can have high quality service, linking rural doctors, for example, with hospitals with high-tech urban medical centers. And our plan will ensure the quality of continuing progress on a whole range of issues by speeding research on effective prevention and treatment measures for cancer, for AIDS, for Alzheimer's, for heart disease, and for other chronic diseases. We have to safeguard the finest medical research establishment in the entire world. And we will do that with this plan. Indeed, we will even make it better.

The sixth and final principle is responsibility. We need to restore a sense that we're all in this together and that we all have a responsibility to be a part of the solution. Responsibility has to start with those who profit from the current system. Responsibility means insurance companies should no longer be allowed to cast people aside when they get sick. It should apply to laboratories that submit fraudulent bills, to lawyers who abuse malpractice claims, to doctors who order unnecessary procedures. It means drug companies should no longer charge 3 times more per prescription drugs, made in America here in the United States, than they charge for the same drugs overseas.

In short, responsibility should apply to anybody who abuses this system and drives up the cost for honest, hard-working citizens and undermines confidence in the honest, gifted health care providers we have. Responsibility also means changing some behaviors in this country that drive up our costs like crazy. And without changing it we'll never have the system we ought to have, we will never.

Let me just mention a few and start with the most important: The outrageous costs of violence in this country stem in large measure from the fact that this is the only country in the world where teenagers can rout the streets at random with semiautomatic weapons and be better armed than the police.

But let's not kid ourselves; it's not that simple. We also have higher rates of AIDS, of smoking and excessive drinking, of teen pregnancy, of low birth weight babies. And we have the third worst immunization rate of any nation in the Western Hemisphere. We have to change our ways if we ever really want to be healthy as a people and have an affordable health care system. And no one can deny that.

But let me say this—and I hope every American will listen, because this is not an easy thing to hear—responsibility in our health care system isn't just about them. It's about you. It's about me. It's about each of us. Too many of us have not taken responsibility for our own health care and for our own relations to the health care system. Many of us who have had fully paid health care plans have used the system whether we needed it or not without thinking what the costs were. Many people who use this system don't pay a penny for their care even though they can afford to. I think those who don't have any health insurance should be responsible for paying a portion of their new coverage. There can't be any something for nothing, and we have to demonstrate that to people. This is not a free system. Even small contributions, as small as the $10 copayment when you visit a doctor, illustrates that this is something of value. There is a cost to it. It is not free.

And I want to tell you that I believe that all of us should have insurance. Why should the rest of us pick up the tab when a guy who doesn't think he needs insurance or says he can't afford it gets in an accident, winds up in an emergency room, gets good care, and everybody else pays? Why should the small business people who are struggling to keep afloat and take care of their employees have to pay to maintain this wonderful health care infrastructure for those who refuse to do anything? If we're going to produce a better health care system for every one of us, every one of us is going to have to do our part. There cannot be any such thing as a free ride. We have to pay for it. We have to pay for it.

Tonight I want to say plainly how I think we should do that. Most of the money will come, under my way of thinking, as it does today, from premiums paid by employers and individuals. That's the way it happens today. But under this health care security plan, every employer and every individual will be asked to contribute something to health care.

This concept was first conveyed to the Congress about 20 years ago by President Nixon.

And today, a lot of people agree with the concept of shared responsibility between employers and employees and that the best thing to do is to ask every employer and every employee to share that. The Chamber of Commerce has said that, and they're not in the business of hurting small business. The American Medical Association has said that.

Some call it an employer mandate, but I think it's the fairest way to achieve responsibility in the health care system. And it's the easiest for ordinary Americans to understand because it builds on what we already have and what already works for so many Americans. It is the reform that is not only easiest to understand but easiest to implement in a way that is fair to small business, because we can give a discount to help struggling small businesses meet the cost of covering their employees. We should require the least bureaucracy or disruption and create the cooperation we need to make the system cost-conscious, even as we expand coverage. And we should do it in a way that does not cripple small businesses and low-wage workers.

Every employer should provide coverage, just as three-quarters do now. Those that pay are picking up the tab for those who don't today. I don't think that's right. To finance the rest of reform, we can achieve new savings, as I have outlined, in both the Federal Government and the private sector through better decision-making and increased competition. And we will impose new taxes on tobacco. I don't think that should be the only source of revenues. I believe we should also ask for a modest contribution from big employers who opt out of the system to make up for what those who are in the system pay for medical research, for health education centers, for all the subsidies to small business, for all the things that everyone else is contributing to. But between those two things, we believe we can pay for this package of benefits and universal coverage and a subsidy program that will help small business.

These sources can cover the cost of the proposal that I have described tonight. We subjected the numbers in our proposal to the scrutiny of not only all the major agencies in Government—I know a lot of people don't trust them, but it would be interesting for the American people to know that this was the first time that the financial experts on health care in all of the different Government agencies have ever been required to sit in the room together and agree on numbers. It had never happened before. But obviously, that's not enough. So then we gave these numbers to actuaries from major accounting firms and major Fortune 500 companies who have no stake in this other than to see that our efforts succeed. So I believe our numbers are good and achievable.

Now, what does this mean to an individual American citizen? Some will be asked to pay more. If you're an employer and you aren't insuring your workers at all, you'll have to pay more. But if you're a small business with fewer than 50 employees, you'll get a subsidy. If you're a firm that provides only very limited coverage, you may have to pay more. But some firms will pay the same or less for more coverage.

If you're a young, single person in your twenties and you're already insured, your rates may go up somewhat because you're going to go into a big pool with middle-aged people and older people, and we want to enable people to keep their insurance even when someone in their family gets sick. But I think that's fair because when the young get older they will benefit from it, first, and secondly, even those who pay a little more today will benefit 4, 5, 6, 7 years from now by our bringing health care costs closer to inflation.

Over the long run, we can all win. But some will have to pay more in the short run. Nevertheless, the vast majority of the Americans watching this tonight will pay the same or less for health care coverage that will be the same or better than the coverage they have tonight. That is the central reality.

If you currently get your health insurance through your job, under our plan you still will. And for the first time, everybody will get to choose from among at least three plans to belong to. If you're a small business owner who wants to provide health insurance to your family and your employees, but you can't afford it because the system is stacked against you, this plan will give you a discount that will finally make insurance affordable. If you're already providing insurance, your rates may well drop because we'll help you as a small business person join thousands of others to get the same benefits big corporations get at the same price they get those benefits. If you're self-employed, you'll pay less, and you will get to deduct from your taxes 100 percent of your health care premiums. If you're a large employer, your health care costs won't go up as fast, so that you will have more money to put into higher wages and new jobs and to put into the work of being competitive in this tough global economy.

Now, these, my fellow Americans, are the principles on which I think we should base our efforts: security, simplicity, savings, choice, quality, and responsibility. These are the guiding stars that we should follow on our journey toward health care reform.

Over the coming months, you'll be bombarded with information from all kinds of sources. There will be some who will stoutly disagree with what I have proposed and with all other plans in the Congress, for that matter. And some of the arguments will be genuinely sincere and enlightening. Others may simply be scare tactics by those who are motivated by the self-interest they have in the waste the system now generates, because that waste is providing jobs, incomes, and money for some people. I ask you only to think of this when you hear all of these arguments: Ask yourself whether the cost of staying on this same course isn't greater than the cost of change. And ask yourself, when you hear the arguments, whether the arguments are in your interest or someone else's. This is something we have got to try to do together.

I want also to say to the Representatives in Congress, you have a special duty to look beyond these arguments. I ask you instead to look into the eyes of the sick child who needs care, to think of the face of the woman who's been told not only that her condition is malignant but not covered by her insurance, to look at the bottom lines of the businesses driven to bankruptcy by health care costs, to look at the "for sale" signs in front of the homes of families who have lost everything because of their health care costs.

I ask you to remember the kind of people I met over the last year and a half: the elderly couple in New Hampshire that broke down and cried because of their shame at having an empty refrigerator to pay for their drugs; a woman who lost a $50,000 job that she used to support her six children because her youngest child was so ill that she couldn't keep health insurance, and the only way to get care for the child was to get public assistance; a young couple that had a sick child and could only get insurance from one of the parents' employers that was a nonprofit corporation with 20 employees, and

so they had to face the question of whether to let this poor person with a sick child go or raise the premiums of every employee in the firm by $200; and on and on and on.

I know we have differences of opinion, but we are here tonight in a spirit that is animated by the problems of those people and by the sheer knowledge that if we can look into our heart, we will not be able to say that the greatest nation in the history of the world is powerless to confront this crisis.

Our history and our heritage tell us that we can meet this challenge. Everything about America's past tells us we will do it. So I say to you, let us write that new chapter in the American story. Let us guarantee every American comprehensive health benefits that can never be taken away.

You know, in spite of all the work we've done together and all the progress we've made, there's still a lot of people who say it would be an outright miracle if we passed health care reform. But my fellow Americans, in a time of change you have to have miracles. And miracles do happen. I mean, just a few days ago we saw a simple handshake shatter decades of deadlock in the Middle East. We've seen the walls crumble in Berlin and South Africa. We see the ongoing brave struggle of the people of Russia to seize freedom and democracy.

And now it is our turn to strike a blow for freedom in this country, the freedom of Americans to live without fear that their own Nation's health care system won't be there for them when they need it. It's hard to believe that there was once a time in this century when that kind of fear gripped old age, when retirement was nearly synonymous with poverty and older Americans died in the street. That's unthinkable today, because over a half a century ago Americans had the courage to change, to create a Social Security System that ensures that no Americans will be forgotten in their later years.

Forty years from now, our grandchildren will also find it unthinkable that there was a time in this country when hardworking families lost their homes, their savings, their businesses, lost everything simply because their children got sick or because they had to change jobs. Our grandchildren will find such things unthinkable tomorrow if we have the courage to change today.

This is our chance. This is our journey. And when our work is done, we will know that we have answered the call of history and met the challenge of our time.

Thank you very much, and God bless America.

NOTE: The President spoke at 9:10 p.m. in the House Chamber at the Capitol.

Statement on the Cost-Share Adjustment for Midwest Flood Recovery
September 22, 1993

I have been in the Midwest four times since early summer when the floods first began to exact their steep toll on the lives and livelihoods of thousands of hardworking Americans. I've seen firsthand the magnitude of the damage, the submerged towns, and the drowned fields, shops, and farms—some temporarily out of business, some permanently destroyed.

I promised that when the Midwest asked the Federal Government for help, the Federal Government would answer swiftly and strongly. And I'm very proud of the speed and efficiency with which our Government, led by FEMA, has met this challenge.

But the job is far from done. The extraordinary duration and force of the floods caused an unprecedented degree of damage to the economies in the Midwest, damage that will take dozens of months and billions of dollars to repair. And as I pledged, the Federal Government will not leave the people of the Midwest to handle this alone.

That's why earlier I announced that in States where the cost of flood damage was at least $64 a person, the Federal Government would adjust the requirement that States assume 25 percent of the cost of FEMA-provided relief. Instead, the National Government would pay fully 90 percent of those costs.

. However, as the damage toll continues to mount, it's becoming increasingly clear to me that we must not view flood relief as local assistance only. The scope of this disaster is so great that it has the potential to have a dampening effect on our entire national economy, and we must respond accordingly.

Therefore, today I have established a second standard that will be used to address those disasters with wider economic impact. In multiple State disasters with significant impact on the national economy, the alternative threshold has been established at .1 percent of the gross domestic product. That means I have approved the reimbursement of eligible public FEMA assistance disaster costs for the nine Midwest States affected by this summer's catastrophic flooding at a 90 percent Federal/10 percent non-Federal cost-share basis.

As the families of the Midwest struggle to restore order to their lives and rebuild their communities, I want them to know that this administration plans to be with them every step of the way. And I'm determined that our commitment remains as clear in our actions as it is in our words and our prayers.

Remarks at a Rally for Health Care Reform
September 23, 1993

The President. Thank you very much, Tipper and Vice President Gore and to the First Lady and all of you. This has been an incredible 10 days on the lawn of the White House, in the Nation's Capital, and in the life of your President, for me as a citizen as well as the President.

After the Middle East peace signing, we had just a couple of days ago the signing of the national service bill here, with hundreds of young people, a bill I believe literally has the capacity to change not only the lives of hundreds of thousands of young people but the fabric of life and the strength of community all across America. I signed the bill with two pens: one, the pen that President Roosevelt used to sign his bills with, and the other, the pen that President Kennedy signed the Peace Corps bill with 32 years ago. And I thought to myself, this is why I went to the snows of New Hampshire. This is why I wanted to be President, because together we can make this democracy work.

And then last night, speaking to the Congress and sensing the incredible, historic opportunity we have to reach across party and regional lines, to unite people who are worried about universal coverage and people who are worried about cost control and people who are worried about the disabled and people who are worried about men and women with AIDS and people who are worried about mental health and people who are worried about elderly, to get everybody together to try to find a solution that will permit us at once to provide comprehensive lifetime health care benefits to all the people in our country and at the same time to stop the waste, the bureaucracy, and the unconscionable increase in cost that is putting a terrible burden on our economy and our Government's budget—to have the opportunity literally of a generation to see the American people come together around a common goal and achieve it—that's truly awesome.

But what I want to remind you of today is this: First, we should be grateful that the moment has come when vast margins of our fellow citizens understand in their gut, even if they don't know all the details of this complex system, that the cost of staying with what we have is far greater than the cost and the risk of change; secondly, that for the first time in the 20th century, we sort of have everybody in the same place at the same time.

Believe it or not, in the first two decades of this century there was one instance in which the American Medical Association wanted a national health program, and the AFL–CIO opposed it. It didn't take long until that turned around. Then there were times when Democrats wanted to do it but Republicans didn't. And then there was President Nixon who offered an employer mandate to get universal coverage, and the political consensus for it wasn't there. It's almost like for this whole century someone would decide that this was a terrible problem, that someone ought to do something about it,

but all the other players were like ships passing in the night. Now you have big business and small business and health care providers and health care consumers, families who have been broken and workers who are trapped in their jobs all agreed that the time has come to act.

I think my job today is to tell you that as much as I wish this to be a celebration to thank you for everything you've done, it's to remind you that our work is beginning, that the real celebration will be when you come back in even larger numbers to this lawn when I sign a bill to solve these problems.

In the next few days the Congress will begin in earnest to take this issue up. It is, as all of you know as well or better than I, a matter of mind-boggling complexity on the one hand and simple truths on the other. Even all of us in this audience do not agree on every detail about how to reach the goal that we all share.

So, just for one minute I would like to reiterate what I said last night: Let us at least commit ourselves to the principles which must shape the final legislation. First and most important is security. We have simply got to provide for every American, for a lifetime, health care that is comprehensive, that is always there and cannot be taken away.

Second, we must make this system more simple, more simple because it will have more integrity and more support, because it will free up doctors and nurses and other medical professionals to do the work that they hired out to do in the first place, and thirdly, because we will never get real savings out of massive parts of this system until we simplify it.

Next, we must insist that through simplicity and other mechanisms, we actually get savings. And I've said this before, I want to say it again, we had a couple hundred doctors in here the other day, and I said, you know, one of the most controversial parts of the argument we're making is that we can finance health care for the unemployed uninsured through savings in the system. Most people in Washington don't believe it, but everybody I've talked to outside of Washington who is in health care believes it because they live awash in the waste every day. Everybody I talked to believes that.

I say to all of you who know something about this, we must continue to hammer the points of opportunity to save money so we can free up funds to do the things we all know we ought to do: to cover the unemployed uninsured through public funds; to provide savings to the private sector that will permit them to cover the employed uninsured without going broke; to extend coverage to prescription drugs for all Americans, including the elderly; to bring in long-term care for the disabled.

I want to point out again, if you look at this system, all of you know but it is still sinking in on our fellow citizens that we are already spending 35 percent more than any other nation on Earth as a percentage of our income, 40 percent more than our major competitors as a percentage of our income. They cover all their folks and we don't, and their standard benefit package is better than most of our people have. We can achieve savings, but it will require discipline and concentration and effort and belief. And you can help make that happen. Our dream of security can be undermined unless we have the courage and the discipline to keep fighting for savings.

Fourthly, we have to guarantee choice. The American people simply won't put up with it if they think they have no choices in their health care. But again, I ask for an injection of the real world. Most of the decision-makers here may have choice, but fewer and fewer Americans have any real choice in their health care. So under this system we do propose to give all persons a choice between three plans, three options that they can buy into. We also propose to give physicians more choices about the plans in which they participate, because unless they have choices, obviously the consumer's choice is limited as well. We have to do that. It's an American value, and we can do it without adding to the cost of the system.

Next, we have to ensure quality. And quality means value for service. You heard me say last night that the task force that Hillary headed uncovered among other things a remarkable effort in Pennsylvania to just publicize to health care consumers the quality and cost of various services and found out that for heart surgery, the same operation could cost between $21,000 and $84,000 in Pennsylvania with no discernible difference in health outcomes. If there's no difference in health outcomes, you might argue it's healthier to pay $21,000 than $84,000. This is an important issue. We have a friend in our home State who showed us two different bills for the same surgery he performs—a bill sent out from the hospitals, from two different hospitals—wildly different prices, exact same procedure and exact same outcomes.

So I say to you, we must tell the American people we believe in quality. And we must provide quality in other ways. We must provide quality by understanding that by depriving ourselves of certain kinds of services, we inevitably undermine the quality as well as raise the cost of health care. And I just want to reiterate how thrilled I was last night to get a good response when I pointed out that our package would cover the whole range of preventive services because that is an important part of quality health care.

And finally, let me say that we must all have responsibility, too. Everyone of us has pointed our finger at someone else and told them they should be responsible. It's that old saying, do as I say, not as I do. You know, we all know that there are sometimes when doctors order unnecessary procedures. We all know that some malpractice claims are frivolous. We all know that some practices of pharmaceutical companies can't be defended. We can all cite somebody else in the health care system. We all know that sometimes the insurance premiums go up or people get cut off in ways that are unconscionable. But it's time for us to admit that the vast mass of Americans have some responsibility problems, too.

None of the people I just mentioned are responsible for the fact that we have higher AIDS rates than any other advanced nation. None of the people I just mentioned are responsible for the fact that we have much higher teen pregnancy rates than anybody I just mentioned— than any other country we're competing with, or higher rates of low-birth-weight babies. And they're certainly not directly responsible, the public isn't, for the fact that we have the third worst rate of immunization in the Western Hemisphere. And they're not responsible for the fact—that got such a nice line of applause last night—that we literally are raising tens of thousands, indeed millions, of children in war zones in which other children have access to weapons more sophisticated than police. No one can imagine, in other countries, why we would let that happen.

Now, neither are those people responsible, or any of other actors in the health care system, when we behave in ways that are personally irresponsible. They don't control it if we drink too much, if we smoke. They don't control it if we don't take care of ourselves. They don't control it if we don't even give a second thought to the way we access the health care system and pretend that it doesn't cost anything just because it's not coming out of our pocket. And it is too easy for us to blame the people who are providing the services, when we do things that are also wrong and unjustifiable. And it is very important that those of you who have worked so long for this effort also say that an essential principle of this health care plan will be responsibility from all Americans including us, not just them but us. I want you to stay with me on that.

Now, there's still a lot of people that don't think we're going to get this done. You know, Roosevelt tried it; Truman tried it; Nixon tried it. President Johnson wanted to do it. President Carter wanted to do it. But we are going to get it done because things are different. Circumstances are more dire; it is more obvious to people that we must change. The system itself is hemorrhaging. Not only do one in four Americans find themselves without adequate coverage at least at some point in every 2-year period but about 100,000 Americans a month are losing their coverage permanently. It is hemorrhaging. We can't go on. But we have to do it right. And we have to do it right now. We don't want to rush this thing; it's too complicated. But we don't want to delay it using complexity as an excuse.

So, I ask you to leave here today not simply celebrating what happened yesterday or lauding the work of the First Lady's task force for the last 8 months but leaving here determined to help the Congress keep the commitment that it made last night across party lines to get this done, to do it right, to do it for America, to make this opportunity of a generation a reality in the lives of every man and woman, every boy and girl in this country. Leave here with that dedication, and we'll be back here, sure enough, for a celebration in the future.

Thank you, and God bless you all.

NOTE: The President spoke at 2:16 p.m. on the South Lawn at the White House.

Remarks in the ABC News "Nightline" Town Meeting on Health Care Reform in Tampa, Florida
September 23, 1993

Ted Koppel. Welcome. A standing ovation. It's got to be downhill from here on in. [*Laughter*]

The President. A lot of the work is still to be done.

Mr. Koppel. Indeed. I'm going to begin with what may seem like a rather trivial thing, although I'll tell you it wasn't trivial to you yesterday. There you were. You were in front of the joint session of Congress. You had the Joint Chiefs of Staff there. You had your Cabinet there. You were talking to tens of millions of people. And you step up to the podium, and if you'd be good enough to take a look at one of those monitors out there, we're going to run—[*applause*].

[*At this point, the audience watched television monitors which showed videotape from the previous evening.*]

The President. You can see the teleprompters there. You can see them. I am telling the Vice President, "Al, they've got the wrong speech on the teleprompter." He said, "That's impossible." I said, "You're not reading it. Read it." That's what I said. [*Laughter*]

So it turned out that the people with our communications department had typed in the speech for the teleprompter on the disk that also had my State of the Union speech in February. And when the disk was called up, it started at the State of the Union instead of at the health care speech. And I thought to myself, that was a pretty good speech but not good enough to give twice. [*Laughter*] So that's what happened.

Mr. Koppel. When I was looking at the First Lady there—you must have talked to her later on—it was almost as though she was telepathic. She looked worried. She knew there was something wrong.

The President. She knew there was something wrong. My daughter, actually, watching at home, told me she also sensed that there was something wrong. And I just decided to go on and give the talk. I mean, I had, you know, I'd internalized it. I'd worked hard on writing it with our folks. The only problem is when you have to go through a lot of points, and you can't just read it. So I would just look at the first line and try to recall from memory. I didn't want to miss anything.

And the other problem is if the teleprompter goes off, that's one thing; you just look at the audience just like I'm looking at you. But imagine if I've got these teleprompters here, and I'm trying to speak to you, and the wrong words are going up on the screen, which is what we started out to do.

So I had to ignore all these words and try to look through the words to the people. But about 8, 9 minutes into the speech, the fellow figured out what was wrong, pulled up the right speech and then whizzed through it to figure out where I was. And from then on in it was reasonably normal.

Mr. Koppel. Well, I've got to tell you, Mr. President, as a communications specialist—and it may be the last nice thing I say to you or for you this evening—you have my admiration. I can't tell you how tough that is when you've got the wrong speech going by. You did an extraordinary job.

Let us take at look at how the speech played. We've got some phone numbers there. Before the speech you can see, we took a poll and 43-percent approval of your health care plan, 41-percent disapproval. Let's take a look at after the speech: up to 56-percent approval; 24-percent disapproval. You're too good a political pro to put too much faith in that sort of kick that you get right after a speech. How tough is it going to be to hold onto that?

The President. I think it depends upon how good a line of communication we can maintain with the American people and how open we can be in working this process through Congress. There will be a lot of people who will honestly disagree with certain things I have recommended. There will be a lot of other people who will not want it to happen because they will make less money out of the system that we propose or because it will require them to change. And they will all be heard. So the important thing is that everyone understand that this is an extremely complicated thing. You interviewed me before, and I saw you showed

it out here. I've been working on this issue seriously for 3½ years, and I've been dealing with health care as a Governor and attorney general and a citizen for a long time, but really working on the systematic problems for 3½ years and talking to hundreds of doctors, of other experts all around the country. It's a complex thing.

But I think if the American people know that Hillary and I and our administration, that we're listening to people and that we're really shooting them straight, then I think we can maintain support for change. Because the reason there's so much support for change among Republicans and Democrats and all the people in the health care system is that those who know the most, know we cannot afford to continue with the system we have. It's bankrupting the country and not helping people.

Mr. Koppel. Mr. President, we've got an awful lot of people here who I know want to ask questions. I just want to show you one more poll result. Take a look. "I worry my future health care costs won't be taken care of." Now, look at how many people agree——

The President. They should worry.

Mr. Koppel. ——with that statement. That's after hearing your speech.

The President. They should worry about that.

Mr. Koppel. Why do you think it's still so high? Two-thirds of the American public still worry that their future health care costs won't be taken care of.

The President. Because health care costs have been going up at twice the rate of inflation, or more. For people insured in small businesses, more than twice the rate of inflation. Because in any given 2-year period, almost one in four Americans don't have any health insurance, because about 100,000 Americans a month lose their health insurance permanently. So how could people not? And even if that hasn't happened to you, almost every one of us knows someone that it's happened to.

Mr. Koppel. Let me ask you a favor, Mr. President. I've already talked to the audience out here and asked them the same favor. They're going to introduce themselves to you, tell you their names and who they are. We've got so many people who want to talk to you, to the degree that we can, let's zip through as many questions and answers as we can.

[*A homemaker said that she and her husband*

had the best insurance coverage available to cover the costs of weekly treatment for her son, who had nearly drowned, and asked if that coverage would be lost under the new health care plan.]

The President. Well, first of all, it won't get any worse. That is, if you're paying for it now and you have coverage that covers that, there's nothing to prevent that from continuing in our system. Anybody, for example, who's got a situation at work where your employer is paying 100 percent of your premiums, that can continue. So you shouldn't worry about that.

But in all probability, because of the changes in our plan, you will have more secure coverage. That is, if this plan passes, you will know that the coverage you have can never be taken away from you and that we will cover primary and preventive services, and those kinds of long-term care services for children are very important.

Also what we want to do—it's very important, especially in the event your husband has to change jobs—we're going to rate all families in America under a broad-based community rating system so that people go into big pools. Insurance companies make money like grocery stores do, a little bit of money on a lot of people, instead of a lot on a few, and we all share the risks in ways that will guarantee that you'll always be able to get insurance at lower rates than would otherwise be the case.

Mr. Koppel. All right, let me move right on. And forgive me, I know that none of you is going to be completely satisfied and would like to ask follow-up questions, but we are going to try and move around.

Go ahead, sir.

[A psychiatrist asked about coverage for mental health out-patient services.]

The President. It depends. The reimbursement rate will depend upon what plan the person joins who wants the mental health care. For example, each individual will choose what health plan they belong to. If you choose, for example, a preferred provider organization where a lot of doctors get together and offer to give services, they will prescribe what the reimbursement rate will be and what the cost of the plan will be.

If a person joins a fee-for-service plan, then the reimbursement rate will be published on the front end, and it will be agreed to by the

doctors in the beginning. But the Government won't set the rate. So there will be some more flexibility there.

And let me also say, because I don't want to overpromise in this thing, I really believe it's important for us to cover mental health benefits. But we're not going to be able to cover the full range of mental health benefits because we don't know how to cost them out very well, as much as I think we should, until the year 2000. So there won't be unlimited visits, for example, until the year 2000. But we'll start with some hospitalization that's significant and a number of visits per year and then build up to full coverage over the rest of the decade.

Mr. Koppel. Mr. President, we also have our financing plan here. We have to take some commercial breaks. We're going to take the first of them right now. We'll be back with President Clinton and our audience here in Tampa in just a moment.

[At this point, the network took a commercial break.]

Mr. Koppel. If you take a look at the poll— I don't know if you can read—your eyes are probably better than mine. I can't read those results from here. Can we put it up on the big screen? Can we see the poll up there?

The President. Yes, I see it.

Mr. Koppel. Can you read it? Well, will you be good—there we go. They think your plan versus the present system: 64 percent think it's better; 17 percent think it's worse; 3 percent think it's the same. Again, that's pretty good. I mean, you can't expect it to do much better.

The President. Sixty-four percent are right. [*Laughter*] They're right.

Mr. Koppel. Just to keep things from getting too dull, let's see if we can get a question from one of the 17 percent. Go ahead.

[A homemaker said that she provides care to her mother and husband, who both have Alzheimer's disease, and asked what the new plan would do for caregivers.]

The President. It will do three things. First of all, for people with Alzheimer's and other problems that require institutional care, we will continue to cover that. And we will cover it at least as well or better as now.

But secondly, over a period of years—now, we can't do all this at once, because we have to phase-in the coverage as we realize more savings from the waste in the existing system. But over a period of years, we will also reimburse people for in-home care, because often times it's less expensive to maintain people in homes than in nursing homes. So we will, for the first time, have a system by which people can actually have coverage for in-home care. And that will include respite care, too. If, for example, you are taking care of a parent or a spouse, you're doing an incredible service for a society. You're keeping your family together, and you're saving money for the system, but you're entitled to a little time off. And so under this system, over a period of years we'd actually set up a reimbursement system so you could be reimbursed or covered to bring in a nurse, for example, if you wanted to take a 4-day weekend or something just to get away from the pressure of your duties.

And over the long run, this will enable more people to keep their families together, lower the cost of care by keeping more people out of institutions and make for, I think, a better quality of life in our country.

Mr. Koppel. To the degree that you can, Mr. President, can you give a sense of what the progression of years is going to be? In other words, you keep saying we're not going to be able to do all of this right away.

The President. Sure. Yes. Let me say, first of all, we assume that it will take a period of several months for the Congress to work through this. But I must tell you, this is the best spirit I have ever seen in the Congress, at least in modern times, among Democrats and Republicans, first to learn everything they can and second, to work together. We're in Florida tonight. We have six members of the Florida delegation up here, three Democrats and three Republicans who came down here with me tonight, and that's sort of the attitude that's going on.

So, let's assume we pass a bill sometime next year. The first and most important thing we have to do is to lock in basic security for everyone; so we want to get that done by 1996. That is, everybody's covered with comprehensive benefits. And then, between 1996 and the year 2000, we want to phase in each year more of these long-term care benefits. So it'll be about a 5-year period after the basic benefits come out.

Mr. Koppel. You have got to be concerned, because I mean, there's a little thing called "re-

election" that has to kick in before you can be sure that you're going to be able to continue doing these things into a second term. You must feel tremendous pressure to get a lot of this done by the end of your first term.

The President. What I feel the pressure to do is to at least pass the legislation and get the security in. I want everybody to have their health security card so I know they'll have comprehensive benefits that can't be taken away, that they can't lose. If that happens, I believe that the public feeling for this will sweep across America without regard to party, to region, to age, and that the American people will see this as a decent, humane thing that we have waited too long to do, and that it will then be a tide that no one can turn back, and no one will really want to turn back.

Mr. Koppel. Let me ask you to swivel around. And I know you wanted to acknowledge the Attorney General, who is sitting up there. If we can just do that.

The President. Say hello to Attorney General Reno. [*Applause*] She wanted to come home with me—you know, Janet Reno is from Florida—for two reasons. First of all, we're going to do an event tomorrow dealing with young people and crime and the costs that that imposes on our health care system, and because she also is deeply concerned about what she can do to help deal with some of the issues here. The Attorney General must enforce the Americans With Disabilities Act, for example. The Attorney General has the power to reach and deal with our young people in ways that can have a direct impact on the quality of their lives and health care in this country. So she came down here, and I'm glad she's here.

Mr. Koppel. Swivel your attention over to the left, the gentleman up there at the microphone. Go ahead, sir.

The President. Yes. sir.

Q. Good evening, Mr. President.

The President. Good evening, sir.

[*A retired educator with AIDS discussed the difficulty of getting treatment under Medicaid.*]

Mr. Koppel. Do me a favor, if——

The President. I know what you're—can I get to the—I know the question. First of all, there are a lot of doctors who don't treat Medicaid patients because it's an incredible paperwork hassle fooling with the Federal Government, and because often the reimbursement rates are so much below regular insurance reimbursement rates for Medicaid. People with AIDS at some point have to quit working, and often times don't have insurance on the job, so they quit working just so they can get Medicaid.

Two things will happen under this system that will really help you and people like you all over America. There are one million Americans that are HIV or AIDS today:

Number one, because you will be covered with health insurance while you're able to work, including a drug benefit that will make you able to work longer, along with everybody else, you will always have health insurance, and it won't break your employer because you'll be part of a big community pool. So your rates will be the same as everybody else. So the first thing is, more people with HIV positive will be able to work longer without bankrupting their employers.

Number two, if you do have to quit work and you go onto what we now—now the Medicaid program, it won't be a separate Medicaid program. Medicaid patients will be in these big health alliances with self-employed people, small business people, the employees of big corporations, everybody will be in there together. Everybody will pick their plans together. And the plan will treat you just like everybody else, because the reimbursement for you will be just like everybody else, and there will be one form to fill out for you, just like everybody else. So there will no longer be an incentive or the option to turn you down. They won't even know, for all practical purposes, whether you're Medicaid or not, because you'll just be in the plan with everyone else.

That's a huge thing. It's a very important thing.

Mr. Koppel. I told our audience before we went on the air, let me take this opportunity to tell our audience at home, we have three panels of experts: One in Boston; they're experts on public finance from Harvard's Kennedy School of Government group. In Chicago, they're practicing physicians; they're professors of medicine at the University of Chicago. And I'd like to turn now to a panel in Los Angeles. They're three experts on public health policy at UCLA.

Only one of them, if you would be kind enough, gentlemen, but I know you have some thoughts on what we've discussed thus far. And I need all the help I can get, please.

[*Dr. Robert Brook praised the new health care plan's universal coverage but asked how the plan would assure quality care.*]

The President. We will basically have, I think, two assurances of quality of care. First of all, the plans that will be provided and the prices that will be offered in these plans will be influenced heavily by the physicians and the other caregivers. But there will be a lot of incentive to lower cost, because your administrative cost would be so much lower.

Secondly, the National Government, as happens now with the Government in different ways, will prescribe certain quality standards, and then each State will offer information to people in these plans about not only the price of services but the outcomes.

For example, as you probably know, Pennsylvania now has a program in which they presently publicize the price of certain services and the outcomes. And it enables people to make judgments about both quality and price that they couldn't otherwise make. So we're going to give consumers more information, we're going to give professionals more capacity to figure out how to manage the system while maintaining quality, and we will have ultimately, Government standards as the guarantor of quality practice.

Mr. Koppel. Go ahead, Doctor, if you want to make one more quick comment. Then we've got to go to a break.

[*Dr. Brook asked about flexibility to allow different family members to receive care from different medical sources.*]

The President. That's a good question. Let me try to answer it. First of all, every person will have at least three choices. Most people will have more choices, but every person will have at least three. And so let me try to say what they would be.

You can choose to stay in a traditional fee-for-service medicine. That is, you pick your doctor, and they charge you by the service. That may be more expensive, but it may not be if big networks of doctors get together to offer these services together. In that case, you would have a cardiologist and a pediatrician working together.

Secondly, you could go into what's called a "preferred provider organization" which is normally an organization that is organized by health care managers but that have all kinds of specialists in them.

Thirdly, you can go into an HMO which will have a range of specialists, but it'll be a closed panel. That is, the people that work there will be on salary. So you may not have the specialists you want.

In the first two cases, you'll probably be able to do exactly what you want for the price that you pay up front. In the third case, if you're in an HMO, you'll still be able—if you say, "Look, my child is really sick, and I want this child to see a pediatrician who is not in this HMO who is in another State," you'll still be able to go to that other State, but that pediatrician will be reimbursed by your insurance plan only at the rate that the HMO pediatrician will be reimbursed, then you would pay the difference. But that plan will be the cheapest, so you'll come out about the same, no matter what.

Mr. Koppel. We're going to take another short break.

The President. Least expensive. I don't like that word "cheap." [*Laughter*]

[*At this point, the network took a commercial break.*]

Mr. Koppel. Now, you see the results of that poll. New taxes to pay for the health plan, you were being a little bit cagey in your speech last night. You were saying no broad-based taxes——

The President. That's right.

Mr. Koppel. You are going to have taxes on cigarettes. You haven't yet decided whether you're going to have taxes on alcohol, liquor.

The President. But let me tell you what—[*applause*]. I know you all have a lot of questions. Let me just make some general points about this. Our analysis shows—and let me say, we have consulted with health care finance experts in Fortune 500 companies, in big accounting firms. We have talked to everybody we can talk to who have dealt with the health system for years. They believe that if we can get the kind of savings we know are there—keep in mind, in the American health care system, we spend 10 cents on the dollar more on paperwork. That's more than $80 billion a year more than any other country, a dime on the dollar more just on shuffling paper. If we can get the savings that I talked about last night, they believe that 63 percent of Americans that have health insurance will pay the same or less for the same or better coverage, that the people

that have virtually no insurance but just a skeleton policy will pay a little more, and that young single workers, because they'll go into community ratings with people who are older and sicker, will pay about $6 more a month. Now, that's what they think. Why?

With only a modest—I mean, a cigarette tax, not modest but a little under $1—and a fee on the big corporations who opt out of the system and continue to self-employ——

Mr. Koppel. You haven't decided on alcohol yet——

The President. Self-insure.

Mr. Koppel. ——whether to put a tax on it.

The President. No, I don't think it's necessary. Our numbers show that with a cigarette tax and if the big employers who opt out of the system because we let them self-insure, they should be asked to pay a little more, because they should pay for medical education, the health education centers, the preventive care networks, all the things that all the rest of us will pay for in our premiums.

They still, by the way, will be big winners. Their premiums will drop a lot anyway, because big employers are paying way too much now because they're bearing the cost of the uninsured. That is, when people who are uninsured get real sick, they get health care, and then the rest of us pay the bill in higher hospital bills and higher insurance premiums. So we think that the larger employer fee plus the cigarette tax plus the savings, plus—keep in mind—requiring the people who are presently uninsured, but employed, and their employers to pay something, that those things will pay for it. I don't think we should raise a big general tax on people to pay for the uninsured when most people are paying too much for their insurance already. Keep in mind, 63 percent of the people under this plan will pay the same or less for the same or better coverage.

Mr. Koppel. You know that much of the criticism is coming from small businessmen. I know because this gentleman came up and asked a question before the program started. Go ahead, sir, and ask it. If you'd be good enough to identify yourself, too.

[*A small business owner paying 4 percent of payroll for health insurance asked about coverage for dependents of his 10 employees.*]

The President. First of all, let me ask you a question. How many of your employees have a spouse which also works?

Q. Three.

The President. Okay. Then, here's the short answer. The seven, you will have to provide a family plan under mine; the three which have spouses at work, they will be able to decide whether you or the other employer, they'll take the children's coverage, because they'll pay more, too, keep in mind.

Now, because you are a small business person with under 50 employees, you will be eligible for a discount that could take your premiums as low as 3.5 percent of payroll, even for the family coverage. So in all probability, you will be paying about what you're paying now, even though you will be covering seven families at a minimum, in addition to the seven employees. Because, the way we set this up—in other words, we understand, and let me go back a second—we went out and interviewed hundreds of small businesses. And my Small Business Administrator took the lead in this. He's from North Carolina, and he's spent the last 20 years of his life starting small businesses.

So we were in a real dilemma here, because small businesses who cover their employees have premiums going up at roughly twice the rate that other people's premiums are going up. There's a 35 percent difference now between small business premiums and big business premiums. And I don't know what you cover, but basically that's the rule. One-third of the small businesses in America, according to a representative poll recently, said they were going to drop all their coverage if somebody didn't do something to stop the rate of cost increase.

So the only way to stop the rate of cost increase is to get everybody covered, and then put them in these big groups, so you can have the same market forces working for you that big businesses do. But it's not fair for me to put you out of business, because small businesses are also creating most of the new jobs in America. So that's why we've got the discount system. Part of what we're going to do with the money we're going to raise is to fund a discount system for people with fewer than 50 employees, so you won't have to pay the 7.9 percent of payroll, and you may pay as little as 3.5 percent. In all probability, because you only have 10 employees, you'll pay almost exactly what you do now, and you'll get more coverage for it.

Mr. Koppel. Let me just ask you quickly, though. Right now, paying 4 percent on 10 people, you're saying 3.5 percent. He would then have to pay the 3.5 percent on all the dependents, other than the three who are working.

The President. No, it's 3.5 percent of the payroll of his employees. So he would pay about——

Mr. Koppel. Total?

The President. Correct. He would pay about what he's paying now. Because he's a small business person, there would be a discount for his premiums.

Mr. Koppel. Okay. Does that answer your question? We've got to take another break; we'll be back in a moment.

[*The network took a commercial break.*]

Mr. Koppel. And let us get right to the questions again. Mr. President, if I could ask you to swivel around. We have a question back there also on money from a larger employer.

[*An IBM employee asked about the plan's effect on large businesses which self-insure.*]

The President. Well, actually, the biggest companies in the country are the ones most likely to benefit from this, because they are actually— even though they're self-insuring. When you self-insure, if you're big, the good news is that you acquire market power, and you can normally keep your rates from going up as fast as they otherwise would. The bad news is, you're still paying part of the costs of uncompensated care. That is, people are shifting the cost to you.

We estimate that for a company like IBM that self-insures, you will save, the company will save on premiums, for whatever you're doing now, you'll save about $10 a month an employee under our system, which is a huge amount, simply by stopping the cost shifting to IBM, with no change in the benefits. No, you can keep on doing exactly what you're doing.

Now, let me just give you an example of how it can get even bigger. For companies that have huge cost shifts and big retiree burdens like the big auto companies and the big steel companies, they will save even more.

But the people that will be least affected by this are big companies with over 5,000 employees that choose to continue to self-insure. You will, however, benefit by the increased competition of the system. What I want everybody else to do is to have the benefits that IBM has. You won't lose anything. Xerox has cut their costs by $1,000 an employee a year through better managed care without taking anything away from the employees. And we think we can do that for all Americans.

Mr. Koppel. Mr. President, let me be the doubting Thomas for a moment. Big companies are going to save money. The little businesses are going to save money. The 37 million people who you say are underinsured or uninsured right now——

The President. They'll pay more.

Mr. Koppel. They'll pay more, but they're going to be insured for the first time. Everybody's going to be better off——

The President. No, not everybody.

Mr. Koppel. Who's not going to be better off?

The President. Well, let me just say this. In the long run everybody will be better off if we bring health care inflation down to the regular rates of inflation.

Mr. Koppel. Who is going to get hurt in the short term?

The President. The following people will get less money, or will pay more: single, healthy workers who are insured in big plans now so they have low costs because they're at least risk, will pay more. They'll pay about $6 a month apiece more to help to cover that gentleman up there with AIDS or older people, just who get older, it costs more. They'll pay more. People who provide only the scantiest catastrophic illness—for example, I met a man, a man came into my office in the White House today with a group of folks, who travels with an entertainment group. He's got a $5,000 deductible with a modest income. He might as well not have any insurance. Now, he'll have to pay a little more, but he'll have something when he pays it.

People that don't pay anything now will have to pay more if they have jobs, and their employer will have to pay something, although we're going to try to keep the small businesses from being hurt too badly. All those people will pay more.

Who will get less under this system? You've got to squeeze—somebody's got to get less. Who will get less? The people who benefit from the paperwork explosion will get less. Hospitals in the future will hire fewer clerical workers, doctors' offices won't have to hire an extra person just to spend all day long calling insurance companies, beating up on them to pay the money

that they owe anyway. Insurance companies will not grow as rapidly, and there may be fewer of them unless they can get in here and provide these plans at competitive costs. So that's the major squeeze in the management of the system.

There will also be savings, frankly, in the provision of services. We had, in the Pennsylvania case I just cited, they published a heart procedure where the prices charged in the State of Pennsylvania varied from $21,000 to $84,000 for the same procedure, with no differences in health outcomes. When all of you get into big groups so that you have the power that the IBM employees do, you will take the $21,000 choice every time as long as there's no difference in the outcome.

And so, everybody there, there will be some losers. But, on balance, most Americans will win, and the security is worth something. And then, over the long run, we'll all win if we can bring health costs closer to inflation.

Mr. Koppel. Let me direct your attention to the balcony up there. Go ahead, sir.

[A participant asked about the effect of a tobacco tax on the tobacco industry.]

The President. Arguably, if we raise the tax, it will reduce consumption. But the answer to your question is, I don't think it's right to have a big, broad tax—I'll say again: tax everybody in America, most of whom are paying too much for what they've got to pay for those who haven't paid anything. I don't think that's right when there are savings. So, we didn't in the beginning know if there would be any tax. But we wound up with a gap in what we think the program will cost in the early years, for about 5 years before it starts to get big savings by the way, and what we had. And we had to figure out how best to make it up. And I thought that a tobacco tax and a tax on the biggest companies who will get big benefits out of this, a modest one just to make sure they contribute, as I said, to medical education, to medical research, and to preventive services like everybody else will, that those were the two fairest ways to get it.

And the truth is that smoking is one thing—unlike drinking, for example, where it's a terrible thing if you do it to excess—we know that there is some risk in any level of it and that it imposes enormous extra costs on the health care system which the rest of us have to pay. So it seemed to me that that was a fair way to get some money.

Mr. Koppel. Mr. President, I want to take advantage of one of our experts again, this time in public finance up at the Kennedy School in Harvard. Mr. Forsythe, would you go ahead, please?

[Dell Forsythe expressed concern about job losses in the health industry.]

The President. There will also be job gains in the health industry. There will be hundreds of thousands of new jobs in people providing home health care, in other kinds of preventive and primary care, so that we think even within the health industry, the job gains in direct health care providers will offset the job losses in clerical work.

Secondly, there are bound to be job gains when you lower the payroll costs that a lot of major employers are paying today. You give them more money that they will either use to give their employees pay increases, and I might say millions of people in this country have foregone any pay increases for the last 4 or 5 years, because the pay increases have gone into higher medical costs. So you're either going to have more folks hired or pay increases going back to employees for the first time. So we believe there will be a net economic benefit by shifting the way this money is spent. I don't think that all investments are equal, and I think since you're going to shift the way money is spent, and we're not going to cut, keep in mind, we are not cutting spending on health care. America at the end of 5 years will still be spending 40 percent more than any other country, maybe even a little more. But we're going to spend the money differently in ways that we think will produce more jobs, not fewer jobs.

Mr. Koppel. Let me just see if I can slip one more question in. We've only got about a minute and half left. Where is the lady who was at the microphone? You'll see—right over there. Go ahead.

[A participant asked whether a doctor or an insurance company would decide when to discharge a patient from the hospital.]

Mr. Koppel. We've got 1 minute, Mr. President.

The President. The doctor, the doctor will make the decision. The coverage will be comprehensive, and the doctor will make the decision.

Can I say one thing real quick? I want to make a specific point here. A lot of people have coverage that have lifetime limits. That is, they look real generous, but if you run up to a certain dollar amount, it's gone. Another real benefit of this—and the only way you can guarantee real security is to say there are no lifetime limits, you just have the coverage—and again, I know it's counterintuitive—a lot of people just don't believe you can ever save money on anything. But all I can tell you is that every doctor and every health care expert that we have ever consulted who has really studied this believes that there are billions and billions of dollars of savings which can be made that will enhance the quality of care, not undermine it. And that's what I urge you—I don't ask you to just take my word for it, just watch the debate unfold and listen to the people who have spent their lives working at this do it.

Mr. Koppel. Mr. President, on that note, we've got to take one more quick break, and then I'll come back with a program note. This program is going to be going on but in another form. I'll tell you about that in a moment.

[The network took a commercial break.]

Mr. Koppel. We're just about out of time now in our prime time segment. But I do want to make a quick program note. First of all, the President has indicated he wants to amend one of the answers that he gave before. We don't have enough time to do that here and now, but we will be back after your local news. Most of the country will be taking it at 11:35 p.m. Eastern Time. And the President has agreed to stay with us on an open-ended basis. Now, that means, I guess, until he gets tired or you get tired or we all get tired.

[Following the 11 p.m. news, the town meeting broadcast resumed.]

Mr. Koppel. Good evening, ladies and gentlemen. Those of you who were with us in prime time know what we're up to. Those who are just joining you now in our regular "Nightline" slot, let me point out that this is a special open-ended edition of "Nightline." Obviously, you recognize the gentleman to my immediate left, the President of the United States, who has been answering questions from a wide variety of the thousand-odd people or so that we have with us here in Tampa, Florida.

And, Mr. President, if you don't mind, we'll get right back to the questions. There are a couple of things I know you want to pick up from the last program. We'll do that in a couple of minutes. Go ahead, sir.

[A participant asked what to do about the overwhelming medical bills from his daughter's surgery.]

The President. Well, first of all, I don't think there could be a better case for changing the present system. What I think will happen before we have a change is that if your daughter has to have surgery next year, they'll probably do it, and do a good job, and that stack of bills will get higher and somehow the costs will just be spread among everybody else until we fix this system.

But let me tell you what would happen if the proposal that I have made were law now. First of all, as a self-employed person, you would be able to buy a health insurance policy for your family, even though your daughter has previously been sick, on the same terms as other self-employed people. And instead of that policy being totally out of your reach, you would be able to buy it more or less on the same terms as other small business people, because we would put you and the farmers and the other self-employed people into a big pool like everybody else. So you would be able to take advantage of an economy of scale. So you'd be able to buy a more affordable policy.

Secondly, because you're self-employed, you'd get a 100 percent deduction on your taxes for it. Today, you only get a 25 percent reduction. So it would be lower costs, comprehensive benefits, you couldn't be denied coverage because your daughter had a terrible problem, and you'd have 100 percent deductibility. That's one of the reasons we ask single, young people to pay a little more. But all those single, young people will be in your situation, too, someday, if they're fortunate.

I wish I had an answer for you right now. I don't. The answer right now is for the hospital to just step right up to the plate and the doctor and do what they did last time until we get this thing fixed. Once we get it fixed, then you won't be in this position again.

Q. Her pediatrician, Dr. Augustine Martin, knows that he's not getting paid for this, and he knows it but he's taking care of her, and he's not even worried about that, which is great.

The President. I'm really glad you said that, because we heard a sad story here before about doctors who wouldn't take Medicaid patients, which leaves the patients out in the cold, although Medicaid is a real pain. But for every case like that, there's a case like this. And those doctors need our thanks.

Q. Yes.

Mr. Koppel. Mr. President, we've got so many people who want to talk to you here. We want to move over there to the wheelchair section. Go ahead, sir, please.

[A participant described the fear disabled people have of losing Medicare and Medicaid benefits if they are employed.]

The President. First of all, by providing insurance to everyone based on a community-based rating, we would never put an employer in the position of saying, "I'd like to hire you, but you're disabled and something terrible might happen to you. And if I had to take care of it on my insurance, my premiums will go up 40 percent the next year, and I'd have to drop you anyway. So I can't do it," which is basically what happens now. A lot of disabled people are going basically to waste in our country because they could be gainfully employed, they could be making major contributions, and they're not hired because people either can't get insurance for them or because they're afraid it will bankrupt them.

Under our system, you'd be just like any other American citizen. You would pick a plan, you would go into it, and because of the community rating system, you would be insured. And therefore, there would never be a disincentive for an employer to hire you. And you would always have that insurance.

And if you needed supporting services, even at work as we build in these long-term care services, we'll be able to have not only long-term care in the home, but some support services associated with people who work. That will save this country a lot of money over the long run, because you're going to have a lot of folks who don't work now working.

But there are a lot of people who are disabled, as you know, who are on Medicaid only because they couldn't get private health insurance as workers. And just like this man who just talked to us over here about his daughter, there are people in this country who have quit their jobs and gone onto welfare and drawn Medicaid only because of the illness of their children. So that's something the disabled population has in common with people like him. That will never happen again. People will be able to keep working. It's very important.

Mr. Koppel. Mr. President, we're going to have to take another quick break. When we come back, though, we've got a public policy expert up at Harvard who is just seething at some of the numbers. He wants to have at you. And I know you want to correct a couple of things or at least make an amendment to a couple of things that you said in our prime time segment. So we have all of that ahead of us when we come back in just a moment.

[The network took a commercial break.]

Mr. Koppel. That's another one of our poll results, Mr. President: What will happen to your quality of health care? Twenty-seven percent think it's going to get better, 27 percent think it's going to get worse, and 42 percent think it's going to stay the same. You've obviously got some missionary work to do there. Do you want to comment on that poll and then get to the amendments, to what you wanted to correct?

The President. Sure. I don't blame anybody for thinking that, because while Americans know more about their own health care than almost any other subject, most of us have never had a chance to learn anything about how the system as a whole works. So it's against our common experience to believe that you can get more and pay the same or less, or that if you control costs, you won't have to give up something really valuable for it. That's against our common experience. But if you study the system, you'll find that we have, literally—I'll say again—just in paperwork alone, a dime on the dollar more waste in our system than any other system in the world, that we have more variations in prices with no differences in outcomes than any other system in the world, that there are all kinds of waste in this system that can be managed down.

You don't have to take my word for it. I saw what those folks said, but let me just give you one example. The Mayo Clinic, we would all agree that they have pretty good health care, wouldn't we? I mean, their inflation is 3.9 percent this year; that's less than half the medical rate of inflation in the country. And I could give you lots of other examples of plans with very high consumer satisfaction where people are very happy with what they have and where

they have squeezed out massive amounts of waste with no loss of quality. And so, that's what this debate ought to be about. I want that debate.

Remember what I said last night? The first thing is security, simplicity, savings, choice, quality, and responsibility. If we give up quality, the rest of this stuff won't happen, because you can't have security without quality. So we'll debate it, but I'm telling you, the more you study this, the more you become convinced that we can achieve these savings.

Mr. Koppel. President Clinton, we've got a public policy expert, John White, sitting up at the Kennedy School in Harvard. Am I misstating it, Mr. White, when I say that you don't think the figures add up?

[John White asked why the plan did not phase in benefits more slowly.]

The President. Let me answer that. First of all, the benefits that we don't phase in, basically the benefits that we start with in 1996 that are new, are primarily two: First of all, the preventive and primary services, you know, the PAP smears, the mammograms, the well-baby care, all those things, we believe that those achieve net savings fairly quickly, and almost all medical experts do. That is the relevantly low-cost, relatively quick benefits. The other major costs are the drug benefits. We provide prescription drug benefits in all health care plans, and for Medicare clients as well as Medicaid ones because there are so many older people who aren't poor enough to be on Medicaid but have huge drug bills. Now, that will cost more.

We went around, John, to all the people we could find who knew something about pharmaceutical costs and tried to pick a high figure. That is, we didn't try to lowball the cost of the drug benefit. And then, we believe that the money we're raising from cigarettes and from the fees on big corporations will cover that, and we believe that we have—all the other benefits will be phased from '96 forward over a 5- or 6-year period, and we believe during that time period, we'll be able to achieve these savings.

Now, I believe this is another decision that the Congress will have to make. But I believe that having the universal coverage—that is, getting everybody insured by '96—is critical to the savings because that's what enables people to get basic care early rather than have care when it's too expensive only at the emergency room.

[*Mr. White suggested that the system should ensure that cost savings were in place before benefits were put in place.*]

The President. I agree with that, except for the two examples I mentioned. But let me make another comment. One of the things I've asked the Congress to do is to work with me to construct a system that, in effect, has to be monitored closely every year and adjusted if the money doesn't work out right. We cannot afford to aggravate the problems we already have. But if you look, John, at the cost estimates we have, even under our plan, even under our plan we project health care costs to go from 14 percent to over 17 percent of our income between now and the year 2000. We'll still be spending a lot more than any other country. I think we'll have more savings than we estimated. But I agree, and I want to just say this about the point he made. All of us have to be prepared to face the consequences if the cost savings don't materialize. And I don't want to sign a bill, and I don't have any intention of signing a bill that doesn't at least have the process built in that I recommended. If something happens and they don't materialize, then we're going to either have to slow down the benefits or raise more money. I don't think it will happen, but he's right. And that's why we've got to phase these things in carefully so it doesn't get away from us.

[*The network took a commercial break.*]

Mr. Koppel. Let me just explain two things to you. First of all, those of you who are watching "Nightline," we just kept going after our 10 o'clock show, which ended at 11 Eastern time, and began taping so that we could save time. So technically what you're seeing right now is on tape, but we are still here live talking and it's going to go on in an open-ended fashion now.

At the end of our live segment, the prime time segment, there was a lady up there who asked you a question and you gave her a very quick answer. It was a question having to do with whether doctors or insurance companies were going to decide when you have received adequate care at a hospital.

The President. That's correct.

Q. You said under your plan, the doctor would decide.

The President. That's correct. There are two

questions that were asked that I want to clarify. One is the lady said, "Who decides when I leave the hospital, the doctor or the insurance company?" And I said the doctor. That is right with one exception. Keep in mind what I said. Mental health benefits under this plan cover limited hospital stays until the year 2000. With that single exception, the doctor decides.

The second point I want to make: You remember the gentleman who stood up over here and said he had 10 employees and he paid 4 percent of payroll, and what was going to happen. And I said he'd pay about the same amount. I want to clarify that in a couple of ways.

Number one, you're eligible for a subsidy if you have fewer than 50 employees. But you don't get the subsidy on employees with incomes of over $24,000. Almost all small businesses have incomes less. So I want to make it clear. So we're actually trying—before the end of the show, we should be able to tell him exactly what his rate will be. But let's say, for example, he had to go up to 5 percent or 6 percent from 4—got more generous benefits— two other things would happen which might make it a good deal for him anyway. Number one, we're going to fold in the health care costs of workers' comp into this system, and the health care costs of workers' comp have been going up even more than regular health care costs for most businesses.

Number two, if you have a claim against you or against your employee as a small business, your rates can go up 20 percent in a year, or 25 percent in a year just if you have a claim. Under our system, the small business would be protected from that. They'd be able to be basically on the same wavelength as some big company and would have a very marginal impact on rates because they'd be in a huge pool instead of just out there.

Mr. Koppel. Let me ask you to swivel around again if you would. We've got a question from a medical student back there. Go ahead, please.

[*A medical student asked about medical school debt deferral, malpractice reform, mandated specialties, and reallocation of funding, especially for care at the beginning and end of life.*]

The President. Let me try to remember them all. First of all, on your debt—and medical school is very costly—we propose to do two things. Number one, we have already passed a sweeping reform of the student loan program, which will enable people to borrow money without regard to their incomes at lower interest rates than have been available in the past, and then pay those loans off, not based just on the amount that you had to borrow but as a percentage of your income, which will make it easier for all people to pay their college loans off. I wouldn't call this a catch, but I have to say we're also going to be much tougher on collecting the loans than we have in the past, but they'll be easier to pay back.

Secondly, we're going to expand the health service corps concept that will enable physicians to practice in underserved areas and pay their medical loans off. And that's been constricted in the last several years. We want to expand that. That's the first question.

The second question you asked was malpractice, right?

Q. Yes, sir.

The President. We propose to do a couple of things in malpractice to—and let me just say, malpractice not only affects doctors with higher premiums but a lot of people believe it adds to the cost of the system, because doctors practice what is called defensive medicine and order procedures they otherwise wouldn't just to keep from being sued.

We propose to do three things: number one, develop more alternative-dispute-resolution mechanisms to lawsuits; number two, limit the amount of contingency fees lawyers can get in those lawsuits to one-third of the fees, not more, and number three, and I think most important, develop working with the medical specialists as well as GP's, general practitioners, a set of accepted medical practice guidelines that doctors can have that operate—to oversimplify it, almost like the checklist that you see a private pilot check off before they—if you've ever ridden in a private plane. So that if you follow the medical practice guidelines for whatever you're doing in your area, that will raise a presumption that you were not negligent. That can do more than anything else. This was pioneered for rural doctors in Maine, this whole theory. We believe it can do more than anything else to reduce the number of malpractice suits.

The third thing you asked was what about the Government trying to force you into certain specialties.

Q. Yes, sir.

The President. The truth is, if you look at

how the Government spends its money, it's heavily weighted towards specialties now. What we propose to do is to change the formula by which the Federal Government funds medical schools now to favor more—not to say you can't be a specialist but to slightly tilt more in the favor of general practice, because only 15 percent of the doctors coming out of medical school today are general practitioners. The average nation has—you know, like Germany or Japan or Canada—half the doctors will be general practitioners. We can't do what we need to do in medically underserved areas without more family doctors.

And the fourth question you asked was?

Q. The reallocation of funds.

The President. Yes. Perhaps the most important thing, long-term, in this package is that we pay for things like pregnancy visits, well-baby care visits. We pay for immunizations for all children. In other words, we try to pay for a lot of preventive and primary services starting very early, and dental care for children although not for adults, as a mandated service.

[*Following a commercial break, a dentist asked about dental benefits under the new plan.*]

The President. Let me just mention the dental issue first. Under our proposal, the comprehensive benefit package would include dental benefits for children up to 18, but not mandates for adults. That doesn't mean any employer plan that now covers dental benefits is perfectly free to keep doing so. And since they'll have all kinds of economic incentives to keep their costs down, they'll probably keep doing it. But we don't think we can, again, recognizing the costs of this, afford to do more than this at this time. But there's nothing to prohibit that.

Most people, as you know now, who have dental benefits through their employers actually buy the benefits in an override policy, and that will all still be available. The problem with the present insurance system, let me say again is that, first of all, too many people are uninsured, and the complexity of it is so great. But we are the only country in the world that has 1,500 different companies writing thousands of different policies, requiring every hospital and doctor's office to keep up with hundreds of different forms, so that we literally add about a dime to every dollar of health care cost on paperwork that has nothing to do with keeping people well.

So what we're trying to do is get down to one form, and this health security card, so that, number one, your life will be a lot simpler. The time you have to spend on forms, the time you have to hire people to spend on forms will be less; the time you spend practicing dentistry will be greater. And the time all of our medical professionals spend doing what they hired out to do in the first place will be greater. That's what we're trying to do.

Mr. Koppel. How detailed is that form going to be? I mean, that one form is going to have to be a killer form to—[*laughter*].

The President. Well, not necessarily. The form—actually I should have brought it to-night—but there will be basically a model form for the doctors and one for the hospitals and one for consumers, because they'll have slightly different information needed, and they'll have some variations because of the differences in plans. Everybody will have some choice in plans, but once you have comprehensive benefits and uniform insurance schemes, you won't have to have a lot of variations.

Let me just say this. I want to hasten to say this does not mean that physicians will stop keeping patient records on patient care. In fact, one of the ways we're going to reduce the amount of problems with malpractice, as I said, is by establishing uniform guidelines and then enabling physicians to demonstrate that they follow the guidelines and, therefore, to raise the presumption that they were not negligent.

So we're talking about paperwork over and above what is required for the basic practice of medicine. Washington Children's Hospital, where I visited last week with the Vice President, says they spend $2 million a year in that one hospital over and above the recordkeeping necessary for patient care.

Mr. Koppel. You saw that devastating study a few weeks ago that indicated that roughly 60 million Americans are—I guess the only fair word is "semi-literate," all but illiterate. You know, you're doing a terrific job here trying to explain what is obviously a terribly complex plan. How do you reach those people? Because my assumption is that the 37 million people you're talking about who are uninsured, underinsured, probably many of them will fall into that same category, and that is people who have a very hard time understanding any forms, let alone something as complex as a medical form.

The President. First, let me say that if you go back to that study, it also says that people are more literate now than they ever have been, but there are more challenges for them now than ever before. All of the research indicates that one of the things people know a lot about is the health care benefits they have and the problems with it. As a matter of fact, one of the problems that I'm having convincing you that we can save money in this system is that you know an enormous amount about your own health situation or that of your employees, and you know it costs more every year. But you've never had a chance to know about how the system itself operates; so it's hard for you to imagine that we can actually save any money—especially where the Government's involved, right?

But when you come back to the basic thing, I believe if you simplify the system and you tell everybody you get three different plans at least and here's what the plans do, I think people have had enough experience negotiating their way through the mine field of the American health care system that most of them will do quite well.

[*A participant asked if abortion would be covered under the new plan.*]

The President. It will probably become a political football because so many people feel so strongly about it on both counts. But the answer is that we are trying to privatize this system, not make it more Government-dominated. And so the answer to your question is, it will be because it is now by private plans. And what we propose to do is to fold people who get their Government health care into the private plans. That is, keep in mind, if you're on Medicaid today, you show up at the hospital, you've got all your Medicaid forms—that's why the doctors don't like to treat Medicaid patients, a whole different set of forms—and you get a specific fee for a specific service. And today, if you're on Medicaid, abortions are not covered by the Federal Government unless the life of the mother is endangered. But they are covered in some States where the States pay for it.

Under this system, people on Medicaid will join a health alliance just like other people. And then they will get to choose among plans. The plans will offer pregnancy-related services. Most private plans today that offer pregnancy-related services do offer abortions. They don't all.

There is a conscience exemption for religious reasons that covers hospitals and doctors, and that will be covered again today. And people who want to join those plans will do it. By the way, there are no specific surgical procedures guaranteed here, not knee surgery, not abortions, not brain surgery, not heart surgery. They never are. The procedures are not prescribed. The problems are covered. So you have to cover pregnancy-related services.

Let me say, since you're in Planned Parenthood, abortion under our Constitution is legal. But let me say, I also think there are too many every year, and I think this could be—[applause]—I think if you want it to be legal, safe, and rare, we have got to fund more preventive outreach.

I want to make this very clear. This plan, for the first time ever, not only acknowledges the constitutional legality of abortion but funds preventive services in ways that will reduce the number of abortions by reducing the number of unwanted pregnancies. And I want to make that—that's very important. That's part of the preventive strategy of this plan. It will do both.

[*The network took a commercial break.*]

Mr. Koppel. And we are back, once again, from Tampa. The President shaking hands with a few well-wishers here. I figured if we didn't restart the program, we'd never get you back from there, Mr. President.

The President. Tell the girls to come back later. Hey kids, I'll come back there. Later I'll be there. You wait here, and when we next take a break we'll shake hands, okay?

Mr. Koppel. What are we—come on. Shake hands. Get it over with. Come on up. Now, while we're feeling good, you might as well tell the folks what the head of St. Vincent's Hospital told you when he——

The President. St. Joseph's?

Mr. Koppel. St. Joseph's. I beg your pardon.

The President. This gentleman is the head of the hospital who took care of the daughter of the independent contractor with the $186,000 worth of bills. He said, "We took care of it before, and we'll take care of it again until we get this"—[applause]. But he also said we need to reform, because he's entitled to be reimbursed for it.

Mr. Koppel. Yes. Now, you don't expect all the questions to be that easy, do you?

The President. No.

Mr. Koppel. Okay.

The President. They've all been hard.

[*A participant expressed her disapproval of the use of taxes to fund abortion.*]

The President. Well, let me say again—let's talk about what the present law is. The present law is that there is a constitutional right to abortion, but the Supreme Court has never ruled that that meant that poor women had to have equal access to it. In other words, that if the Federal Government or a State government decided not to fund abortion services through the Medicaid program, that that was legal. So Congress for many years has said we will not specifically fund abortions unless the life of the mother is at risk. Therefore, there's no public funding for poor women to get abortion services unless each State decides to do it. Some States decide to; a majority don't. That's the law today.

I want to make clear to you what we are proposing. What we are proposing incidentally affects this: What we are trying to do is to stop the two-tiered system, to put the Medicaid patients in with the employees of small businesses and hospitals and others to provide for a common private system in which people join plans that provide services, including pregnancy-related services. Some of those plans won't cover abortion. Most of them do today. But I would just say to all of you who—if you're in a private health insurance plan today, your money is commingled with everybody else's. And if those services are covered, the money goes out from a central payment place, not necessarily for a specific service. But because people have enrolled in a plan—for example, somebody enrolls in an HMO, they don't pay for a specific thing at all necessarily on a fee-for-service basis. They pay a fee for whatever services are covered. So that is part of the limit. It would be a terrible price to pay just over this issue to keep segregating all the Medicaid patients and deny them the opportunity, and deny us the opportunity, to have the benefits of everybody being in large group health care without separating this out.

In other words, the whole system will be changed if you put everybody in a private system. There will still be also hospitals and doctors who, for religious or other reasons, for moral reasons, will not participate in this and will not have to in any way, shape, or form.

Mr. Koppel. Mr. President, this is a curious criticism to make, but sometimes I think you're so specific in your answers or so detailed in your answers that it's a little hard to know what the answer to the question was.

The President. The answer to the question is, if a person goes into a health care plan that provides pregnancy-related services, the person can ask, "Does this include abortions, or not?"

Mr. Koppel. If it doesn't, then you go to another plan?

The President. If it doesn't, they can go to another plan. If it does and they're offended by it, they can go to another plan.

Mr. Koppel. Are tax monies going to be used to support those abortions? That was——

The President. The answer is, indirectly they will. Today, it's a direct question. You know, the Government writes a check for every Medicaid procedure. Under this system, people on Medicaid would be just like any other person. They'd join a health plan. They'd sign up for certain services. The funds, the public and the private funds, would all be mixed together. They would fund certain things and not fund others.

But if our plan goes through, it will be impossible to separate out the public and the private funds, the Medicaid and the other people.

Mr. Koppel. So, implicitly, the answer is yes. There will be——

The President. That's right, they will be able to fund it. That's right. If it comes down on this issue, we keep all these Medicaid people from going into a revolutionary new system, then you're going to throw away a lot of the savings and deprive those people of a whole range of things that don't have anything to do with abortion, including higher quality care at lower cost.

Mr. Koppel. But that's clearly one of the political mine fields.

The President. That will be a big political mine field.

[*The participant reiterated her opposition to the use of her tax money to fund abortions.*]

The President. Well, let me ask you—we are also personally and morally improving preventive and primary health services, and we'll actually stop some abortions from occurring with the kind of preventive services that we're going to cover for the first time in the history of this country.

This could be a subject for a whole other program. I have a difference of opinion from you about whether all abortions should be ille-

gal. I do agree that there are way too many in the United States. I believe we need an aggressive, an aggressive plan to reduce teen pregnancy, to reduce unwanted pregnancies. One of the reasons I named the Surgeon General I did, my health department director, is because I'm committed to that. I believe we need an aggressive plan to promote adoptions in this country. If every pro-life advocate in America adopted a child, this world would be a better place.

I want this issue to be debated, and I haven't hedged with you. Most people will get this service covered because most private plans do it. And we propose for the first time ever to put Medicaid people in the big private plans to get the economies of scale. Not for the purpose of doing that, but basically to end this two-tiered system we've had. So most will be covered. But some won't if they choose to join plans that don't cover them. Most plans do today.

Mr. Koppel. I met the gentleman over there just before we went on the air. I know he wants to talk about the homeless. But we're going to take a quick break. When we come back——

The President. He's been the most patient person here. We've got to hear from him.

Mr. Koppel. We'll be back in a moment.

[*The network took a commercial break.*]

Mr. Koppel. There's another one of our poll results. Under Clinton's plan, will you pay more? Forty-nine percent think they will pay more; 10 percent think they'll pay less; 33 percent, about the same. Again, as I said earlier, you've got some missionary work to do here.

The President. But that's because people can't imagine how much waste there is in this system. Today, we spend over 14 percent of our income as a nation on health care. Canada spends 10; Germany is under 9; Japan is under 9. The German system, which is the most like what I propose, is a private system where large groups of employers and employees can work with health care providers to provide a wide range of services at low cost. But the administrative cost is much less than we have, although they cover more people and about the same number of services.

Mr. Koppel. You also know, and you've heard your critics say, they look at the Canadian system, and they start counting the Canadians who cross the border and come over to Detroit, because when it comes to optional surgery, optional procedures, they have to wait 3 months, 6 months, 9 months, a year. And they get so frenzied over this that rather than wait, they come over to the United States. Now, those people will tell you, "Whatever you do, don't exchange what you've got for what we've got."

The President. But we don't do that. In other words, keep in mind, I am not proposing to bring our cost level down to the level of Canada, much less Germany. What I am proposing is to slow the rate of increase, which if we don't slow it, by the end of the decade we'll be spending roughly 19 percent of our income on health care. Canada will be about 11, and everybody else will be under 10. And that is a huge economic disadvantage in a global economy. It also means a lot of workers just give up all their pay increases. We are not proposing to cut spending on health care. We're proposing to increase spending on health care quite briskly but not as much as we're going to if we don't change the system.

Mr. Koppel. So fundamentally, the people in that poll are right. Those who think that they're going to end up paying more, they will.

The President. They'll pay more, the system, no.

Mr. Koppel. They may get more, but they're going to pay more.

The President. The system will cost more, but they will pay much less under my plan than if we do nothing. Keep in mind, of the 85 percent of the people with health insurance, two-thirds of them will pay the same or less for the same or better benefits.

Mr. Koppel. No, I hear you. But let me try and state it one more time. You tell me if I'm wrong. Under the existing system, you're going to end up paying more.

The President. Much more.

Mr. Koppel. Under your system, you're going to end up paying more. But you're saying under your system you're going to end up paying a smaller amount more than you would in the existing——

The President. That's right. You'll pay over the next 5 years much less under my system, my proposal, much less than you'll pay if you stay with the system we've got. And you get better benefits and security. You will never lose your health care.

Mr. Koppel. This gentleman has been standing there most of the night. Go ahead, sir.

[*A participant asked if temporary workers would be included in the new plan.*]

The President. The short answer to that is somebody will be held accountable to them. For people who are temporary workers, it depends upon how they're ultimately classified under the tax system. For example, if you're a temporary worker and you work for an employer, and you're on that employer's payroll, let's say as much as 10 hours a week, then that employer would prorate his payments, or her payments, for the temporary worker. They'd have to pay a third the normal rate. If they're on the payroll for 20 hours a week, they pay two-thirds the normal rate. If the temporary employee is listed as being on the payroll of the temporary company, then they would pay. If the temporary employee is an independent contractor under the Tax Code, then the temporary employee would have to buy his or her own insurance, just like the paint contractor. But depending on the income, they'd be eligible for a discount, and they'd have 100 percent tax deductibility.

So the answer is, the temporary employees will be covered. Who pays and how depends on how they are classified under the Tax Code. But either the temp company, the company for which they're working part-time, or if they're independent contractors, they, themselves, will get coverage at an affordable rate.

Mr. Koppel. Mr. President, as I told you, we have three practicing physicians out at the University of Chicago. One of them, Dr. Mark Siegler, would like to either make a comment or ask a question.

Go ahead, Dr. Siegler.

[*Dr. Mark Siegler asked about quality of patient care under the new plan.*]

The President. If you look at the plan the way it operates, and I would urge you to read it carefully, we will actually provide more funding for medical research than we are now, more funding for health education centers than we are now. Each employee in the country will get at least three choices of plans. They might choose an HMO which, you're right, would then have a closed panel of doctors which would limit the number of doctors. But we know that there are a lot of HMO's that have very high patient satisfaction, the ones that are really well run. But they might also choose a preferred provider organization, and under our rules, no PPO can deny interest to any doctor that wanted to be a part of it. So a doctor could join a lot of different organizations so that the doctor could, in effect, be available to all his or her patients, even after this reform takes place. And finally, keep in mind, if you look at the package of comprehensive benefits here, virtually all Americans with insurance now would get the same benefits that Fortune 500 companies enjoy and much better than they have now. So we want to preserve choice; we want to preserve quality; we want to preserve a range of benefits.

Also, one of these plans, every employee will have the option today, under this plan, to choose fee-for-service medicine. Today in America, only one-third of the insured employees in this country have an option of more than one plan.

Mr. Koppel. Mr. President, let me jump in for just one moment. What I'm hearing in my ear is that some of those who have your best interest at heart, namely members of your staff, are very concerned that you not spend too much of this night with this, because you've got a big day tomorrow. So I want to let the audience know that we are in the process of winding down.

I would like to have maybe two or three more questions. Would that be all right with you?

The President. Sure.

Mr. Koppel. And then we will bring this program to a close. I suppose it's also appropriate at this point to note that, believe me, this is not going to be the last you hear on this subject. Either pro or con, the President's plan, it is just the beginning of what promises to be a long national debate. But I think you've had an extraordinary opportunity here to at least hear from the man who is behind what is clearly one of the most ambitious health plans that this country has ever seen.

[*A pharmacist asked if patients would be able to get prescriptions at the pharmacy of their choice.*]

The President. Yes, sir, you can, and that's why the Pharmaceutical Association of the United States—Association of Pharmacists has already endorsed our plan, and they were up until 2 a.m. last night sending out press releases around the country, saying that this is a good deal for your neighborhood pharmacy.

[*The mother of a boy with congenital heart defects asked if they would be denied access to quality service under the new plan.*]

The President. No.

Q. Because we can't afford to pay 20 percent of a hospital bill that is in excess of $100,000, $200,000.

The President. No, absolutely not. If you have a plan now that covers all your benefits, if anything your employer will have more incentive to continue to cover you, because their costs will go up less in the future than they would now.

Keep in mind, this 20 percent requirement for the employee to pay is for all those who don't have any coverage now. And It's not a requirement on the employee; it's a limit on how much the employee can pay. The employee cannot be required to pay more than 20 percent. If the employer wants to pay more, they can. The truth is, it's largely going in the other direction today for most folks. So if you have a good health insurance plan and it pays more than 80 percent, nothing in this plan will change that. In fact, your employer should be more willing to do it, because in the aggregate their costs will go up less in the future than they will if we stay with the same system.

I talked today to a half a dozen people who said that their contribution share was going up, up, up. And it was going to be over 20 percent before long, and they were glad to know there was a ceiling on it. All we're trying to do is to put a ceiling on it, not a floor.

Q. Thank you.

Mr. Koppel. Mr. President, we've got one more question. And you, sir, have the last question. Go ahead.

[*A participant asked if all insurance companies would be required to open their provider lists to all qualified doctors under the new plan.*]

The President. The short answer to that is yes. Keep in mind, we want to give the employee the choice. What happened to your patients was the employer made the decision to go with another health plan that closed out certain doctors. We want to give the employee the right to go with a closed panel HMO if they think that's good—health maintenance organization—if they think they get better prices and they think they get adequate services. But we also want to give the employee other options, including to continue dealing with you as a fee-for-service doctor, or working with a group of doctors in which you have an absolute legal right to be a part.

Now, if that happened today, the fee-for-service option might be a little more expensive. But what I think will happen is that you and other doctors—what I'm banking on is that the physicians of this country will get together and offer their services at reasonably competitive rates so that people will be able to maintain a maximum of individual choice. But it is legally mandated that every employee in the country will have the option to choose fee-for-service medicine or a panel of doctors, which has to remain open for any doctors who want to join so that doctors can be in multiple panels. And so we're going to increase choice of physicians, not decrease choice of physicians for most Americans. That's a very important value, and we have to pursue it.

Mr. Koppel. All right. President Clinton, please excuse my back. I just want to express a personal note of thanks to you for coming here this evening. I know there are an awful lot of people, possibly many in this audience, who wished they'd had the opportunity to pose questions to you or to criticize certain aspects of the plan. Over the course of the next year, I'd also like to say to your adversaries out there who are watching us and who have criticisms that they too will have access to this program and many others.

There is something wonderful, however, about being able to bring an American President and an audience of 1,000 of his constituents together for this kind of an exchange. And I know you'll want to express your gratitude to the President, as I do now. Thank you. [*Applause*]

The President. Thank you, folks.

NOTE: The town meeting began at 10:10 p.m. in the Playhouse at the Tampa Bay Performing Arts Center.

Nomination for United States Executive Director of the International Monetary Fund
September 23, 1993

The President announced today that he intends to nominate Columbia University professor Karen Lissakers to be the U.S. Executive Director of the International Monetary Fund. The Executive Director represents the United States on the 24-member board of executive directors, which sets policy for the IMF.

"As the largest shareholder in the IMF, the United States has a special responsibility for its operations," said the President. "Karen Lissakers has proven that she is up to the task of representing our interests. I am confident that she will shine in this position."

NOTE: A biography of the nominee was made available by the Office of the Press Secretary.

Letter to Congressional Leaders on Iraq
September 23, 1993

Dear Mr. Speaker: (Dear Mr. President:)

Consistent with the Authorization for Use of Military Force Against Iraq Resolution (Public Law 102–1), and as part of my effort to keep the Congress fully informed, I am reporting on the status of efforts to obtain Iraq's compliance with the resolutions adopted by the U.N. Security Council.

Since my last report, Iraq has informed Rolf Ekeus, Chairman of the U.N. Special Commission on Iraq (UNSCOM), that it is ready to comply with U.N. Security Council Resolution 715, which requires Iraq to implement plans for long-term monitoring and verification of its weapons of mass destruction (WMD) programs, provide new data about the suppliers of its program, and accept inspections. I appreciate Chairman Ekeus' efforts to obtain Iraq's acknowledgement of its international obligation.

We must recognize, however, that important issues remain unresolved. Although Iraq accepted the immediate installation of monitoring cameras on rocket test stands, it has not permitted the cameras to be turned on. Iraq has failed to provide a complete list of critical supplies of its WMD programs and continues to delay inspection activities, for example, by refusing flight clearance for an upcoming inspection. Saddam Hussein is committed to rebuilding his WMD capability, especially nuclear weapons, and his regime has thus far shown that it will fail to act in good faith to comply with its international obligations. Our continued vigilance is necessary.

The International Atomic Energy Agency (IAEA) and UNSCOM conducted four nuclear, chemical, and missile-related inspections since my last report. A chemical destruction group remains at Al Muthanna to monitor the destruction of thousands of chemical munitions, and a helicopter inspection team also remains in Iraq. Along with damage inflicted in combat, UNSCOM/IAEA inspections have effectively put the Iraqi nuclear weapons program out of business in the near-term and have substantially impaired Iraq's other WMD programs. Their efforts have contributed markedly to the stability of the region.

The "no-fly zones" over northern and southern Iraq permit the monitoring of Iraq's compliance with Security Council Resolutions 687 and 688. Over the last 2 years, the northern no-fly zone has deterred Iraq from a major military offensive in the region. Since the no-fly zone was established in southern Iraq, Iraq's use of aircraft against its population in the region has stopped, as have large-scale troop movements. On July 29, two Coalition aircraft in the southern no-fly zone fired on Iraqi anti-aircraft installations after detecting target acquisition radars. On August 19, aircraft supporting Operation Provide Comfort in the northern no-fly zone were fired on by an Iraqi anti-aircraft installation. In response, Coalition aircraft fired on and hit the installation, which has not displayed hostile intentions subsequently.

The United States is working closely with the United Nations and other organizations to provide humanitarian relief to the people of northern Iraq, in the face of Iraqi government efforts to disrupt this assistance. Since early August, the Iraqi government has cut off electricity to

northern Iraq, interfering with potable water supplies, impairing medical facilities, and contributing to at least 50 deaths. We are working with the United Nations to provide temporary generators and spare parts. We continue to support new U.N. efforts to mount a relief program for persons in Baghdad and the south and will ensure that the United Nations will be able to prevent the Iraqi government from diverting supplies. We are continuing to work toward the placement of human rights monitors throughout Iraq as proposed by Max van der Stoel, Special Rapporteur of the U.N. Human Rights Commission, and to work for the establishment of a United Nations Commission to investigate and publicize Iraqi war crimes and other violations of international humanitarian law.

The U.N. sanctions regime exempts medicine and, in the case of foodstuffs, requires only that the U.N. Sanctions Committee be notified of food shipments. In accordance with paragraph 20 of Resolution 687, the committee received notices of 20 million tons of foodstuffs to be shipped to Iraq through June 1993. The Sanctions Committee also continues to consider and, when appropriate, approve requests to send to Iraq materials and supplies for essential civilian needs. The Iraqi government, in contrast, has maintained a full embargo against its northern provinces and has acted to distribute humanitarian supplies only to its supporters and to the military.

The Iraqi government has so far refused to sell $1.6 billion in oil as previously authorized by the Security Council in Resolutions 706 and 712. Talks between Iraq and the United Nations on implementing these resolutions resumed briefly in July but concluded without results when the Iraqi delegation left the talks. Iraq could use proceeds from such sales to purchase foodstuffs, medicines, materials, and supplies for essential civilian needs of its population, subject to U.N. monitoring of sales and the equitable distribution of humanitarian supplies (including to its northern provinces). Iraqi authorities bear full responsibility for any suffering in Iraq that results from their refusal to implement Resolutions 706 and 712.

Proceeds from oil sales also would be used to compensate persons injured by Iraq's unlawful invasion and occupation of Kuwait. The U.N. Compensation Commission has received about 900,000 claims so far, with a total of roughly two million expected. The U.S. Government is preparing to file a sixth set of individual claims with the Commission, bringing U.S. claims filed to roughly 2,700. The Commission's efforts will facilitate the compensation of those injured by Iraq once sufficient funds become available.

Security Council Resolution 778 permits the use of a portion of frozen Iraqi oil assets to fund crucial U.N. activities concerning Iraq, including humanitarian relief, UNSCOM, and the Compensation Commission. (The funds will be repaid, with interest, from Iraqi oil revenues as soon as Iraqi oil exports resume.) The United States is prepared to transfer up to $200 million in frozen Iraqi. oil assets held in U.S. financial institutions, provided that U.S. contributions do not exceed 50 percent of the total amount contributed. We have arranged a total of over $100 million in such matching contributions thus far.

Iraq still has not met its obligations concerning Kuwaitis and third-country nationals it detained during the war. Iraq has taken no substantive steps to cooperate fully with the International Committee of the Red Cross (ICRC), as required by Security Council Resolution 687, although it has received over 600 files on missing individuals. Iraq refused to participate in a July 29 meeting under the auspices of the ICRC to consider further steps with regard to these missing persons. We continue to work for Iraqi compliance.

Iraq can rejoin the community of civilized nations only through democratic processes, respect for human rights, equal treatment of its people, and adherence to basic norms of international behavior. A government representing all the people of Iraq, which is committed to the territorial integrity and unity of Iraq, would be a stabilizing force in the Gulf region. The Iraqi National Congress (INC) espouses these goals. In August, Iraq's ambassadors to Tunisia and Canada fled to Britain and announced their support for the INC.

I am grateful for the support by the Congress of our efforts.

Sincerely,

BILL CLINTON

NOTE: Identical letters were sent to Thomas S. Foley, Speaker of the House of Representatives, and Robert C. Byrd, President pro tempore of the Senate. This letter was released by the Office of the Press Secretary on September 24.

Remarks to the Community in St. Petersburg, Florida
September 24, 1993

Thank you very much. We are delighted to be here today, all of us. I'm especially glad that Attorney General Reno came down from Washington with me. When she became the Attorney General, Florida gave the United States a great national resource, and I know you're all proud of the job that she has done.

I also want to thank my longtime friend Governor Chiles. You know, in his former life Governor Chiles was a Member of the United States Senate and was head of the budget committee. He thought arithmetic was functioning better at the State and local level, and so he decided to leave Washington. But when he left, it made it harder for the rest of us to make arithmetic work in Washington. And I'm glad to be here with him, and I especially honor the innovations that he has pushed in health care and in crime.

I want to thank Congressman Bill Young for hosting me in his district and for coming down last night on the plane. I'm also glad to see Congressman Miller here today and Congresswoman Karen Thurman from your neighboring districts.

We had a remarkable health care forum last night, as you probably know, in Tampa, with about 1,000 people there. And there were six or seven Members of Congress, roughly evenly divided between Republicans and Democrats, who came there with me in our effort to bring this country together around that issue.

I got a little briefing on St. Petersburg Beach from Mayor Horan when I was up here. He told me that we had a wide variety of ages here. I think—you said your grandson was here, and he's one year old today. Where—is the Mayor's grandson here? Hold up the Mayor's grandson. Look at that. And we have at least one of your distinguished citizens here who is in her nineties. Melita, stand up there. Thank you. In between, we've got a President; an Attorney General; a Governor; three Members of Congress; your State attorney general, Bob Butterworth, who is here; the Mayor of St. Petersburg, David Fisher; the chief of police of St. Petersburg, Darrel Stephens; a number of State representatives and county officials and representatives from community groups, Crime Watch and other groups.

I say that to make this point: If you look out across this crowd today, from that young man celebrating his first birthday to this fine lady who has seen almost this entire century come and go, you see across this crowd people of different races, different political parties, different walks of life, all of us part of the family of America, all of us caught up now in a time of sweeping and profound change, change which opens up to us vistas of opportunity that our forebears could never have imagined and change which presents us with threats and troubles that our forebears never could have imagined.

I really believe that in a time like this, my job as your President is to try to identify the challenges facing our country and then to try to offer my best ideas about a solution and then to try to energize people all across the country to work until we find a solution. Whether it's the one I suggested or some other one, we have to urgently face both the opportunities and the problems before us in a time when we have to change so much.

And that's the first decision we all have to make. Whether it's in education or the economy, we have to be willing to change. When you're confronted with a time of sweeping changes, with a bunch of things that are happening that are good that you can be part of and a bunch of things that are happening that are bad that you want to avoid, basically you have two options. You can sort of hunker down and put your arms around yourself and hope it will go away; that works about one time in a hundred. And then if you play the odds, 99 percent of the time what you have to do is take a deep breath and stick your chest out and turn right into the change and figure out what you can do.

Now, one of the things that all of us have learned in our lives, that even children learn early, is that you are more able to make changes you need to make when you are more secure. The more personally secure you are, the more you feel good about who you are and your con-

nections to other people and your roots in a community, the more you are able to change. It seems almost ironic, but the more rooted you are in the traditionally human ties and the traditional human values that make life so rich, the more you're able to change so that you can enhance what you value. The more insecure we are, the more difficult it is for us to change because we're too busy just trying to survive.

So, in a funny way, the pursuit that we must have as a people for security is tied closely to the pursuant we must have as a people for change. And I believe as strongly as I can say that that's one of the reasons that makes this campaign for health care reform so important, that it will give our people the security to change. And it's one of the things that makes our efforts to try to reduce the crime rate and enhance human decency and dignity and reduce violence and destruction in our country so important because that is the security we need, the bedrock we need to make the economic changes, to make the education and training changes, to make the other changes we need in this country.

Last night, when we had that wonderful town hall meeting, people asked dozens and dozens of questions—I don't know how long we stayed there; it was way too late. [*Laughter*] There are a lot of people in America, if they watched that whole show last night, are sleepy at work today, I'll tell you that. But what you saw there is people yearning for security.

Here in this area, the principles I announced in health care reform are very much related to the principles of this anticrime effort our administration is undertaking. Security, health care that you've always got, that can't be taken away. Simplify the system; it's a nightmare for the doctors and the nurses and the people who are getting health care. Achieve savings, because the system is too wasteful, you can't justify putting more money in a broken machine until you've fixed it. Maintain choice for consumers and have quality. One of the things that matters so much in Florida is the idea that people on Medicare as well as people on Medicaid will be able to get prescription drugs now under this program, very important for older people to maintain their quality of life. And finally, to have more responsibility in the system. And that relates directly to the crime issue because one of the reasons American health care is so expensive is that our hospitals and our emergency rooms are full of people who are cut up and shot. If you look at the amount of money the American taxpayers pay in health care for violence, it is staggering. And the more we do that, the less we have to spend on other things that make us all well and more secure.

Now, one of the things that our health care reform package and the crime initiatives that the Attorney General is leading have in common is a focus on prevention. You know, I got a great hand the other night talking to Congress, and I said, "You know how your mother said an ounce of prevention is worth a pound of cure? Well, your mother was right." Well, that's the truth. For the first time, if we pass this health care reform program, everybody will have in their health care package preventive services. We will save money and enhance the quality of life, enhance security if you give every child an immunization plan, if you have well-baby visits, if you have Pap smears and mammograms and cholesterol tests and the kinds of things that keep people well as well as help them to get well if they get sick.

The same thing is true in crime. We know from experience after experience after experience that the kind of violence that has unfortunately gripped the headlines in Florida in the last several days and grieved so many of us as Americans, when people who come to our shores are hurt or killed when they want to see our country and they want to get to know the best about it, that is far from a problem of Florida alone. And certainly not a problem for our foreign visitors alone. When Michael Jordan's father was killed recently, a nation grieved, but no one knew the names of the other 22 people who died in that county this year. This is a national problem.

When I was born in 1946, homicide wasn't even in the top ten leading causes of death in America. In fact, listen to this, throughout my lifetime homicide never made the top ten until 1989. And yet, now, homicide is the second leading cause of death among Americans age 15 to 25. And more of our teenage boys die from gunshots now than any other cause.

Now, we can decide again what to do with this. Are we going to hunker down and turn away and pretend it's not happening? Maybe it will go away; we've got a one chance in a hundred that will happen. Or we can face it, and we can face the problem in all of its human manifestations, just the way the Attorney General said.

These kids we just met out here who got in trouble and now they're in this program, pretty good kids. They've got a whole life ahead of them. They've got contributions they can make. And we need to see what we can do about preventing the life that might happen that none of us want to occur.

This initiative that we have undertaken in our administration to give more security and to make this society safer includes at least three forms of prevention I want to emphasize, because we know they work and because they are rooted in getting people at the grassroots community level more power over their own lives.

First is giving these children who get in trouble something to say yes to and some order and framework in their lives. Senator Moynihan said on television last Sunday, the distinguished Senator from New York who's been a student of American social history for 50 years, "We have gotten used to accepting a lot of behavior from people in this country that's pretty destructive. We have gotten used to the fact that a lot of kids grow up alone or almost alone in conditions that are very damaging to themselves and aren't conducive to learning good things and good habits." And we have let it happen. But all over America there are programs like the boot camp program. One of these young men just came out of the boot camp program of this program and he told the Governor that he liked the program. More people ought to be in it, because, he said, "It used to be you could"— he knew this—he said, "It used to be you could ship kids my age off to the service, but we're going down. We don't have a draft anymore. We're going down in the number of people in the service. So we've got to have a substitute where people can learn discipline and order and be able to see the future as something that happens 3 years from now, not 3 minutes from now." And we have to have programs like this Marine Institute, which now is spreading across the country. This program is giving young people a chance to take their future back, a chance to understand that there is good inside them, that they can do things that are useful and productive and profitable and a lot more fun than whatever it is that got them into this program in the first place.

Those young people told me what it was like to learn how to give CPR, to learn how to scuba dive, to learn how to repair a boat and fix it so it would sail, to learn how to deal with each other and with adults so that they could get jobs. This program now operates in partnership with grassroots people in seven other States nationwide. They've taken 20,000 young people at risk and helped them to become responsible citizens. And so far, after they leave this program 75 percent of the young people that go through this program never have any criminal convictions again. If every young person in America that got in trouble had a chance to be in a program like this, think what a difference it would make. It's very important. How many times do you pick up the paper and read about somebody finally did something terrible after they had been arrested 13 times or 15 times or 20 times. We need a system in this country, and the National Government cannot do it, but we can help you do it. We can help provide funds and support and technical expertise, but people at the grassroots level have to do it. We've got to have systems in this country where everybody in those critical young years has a chance to be in a boot camp like this, like you have in Florida, or a program like the Marine Institute or both if they need it.

We have an experimental program we started last June. Ten military facilities have been enclosed across the country where kids who are high school dropouts are able to come back and get their GED and have the benefit of military-type training. And a lot of these kids just love it. It's just changed their whole outlook on life. We have got to understand that we are raising a generation without the structure and order and predictability and support and reinforcement that most of us just took for granted. We took it for granted. And there's no use in us pretending that some National Government program and money alone will fix it. But there's no use in us pretending that just preaching at people will fix it, either. We have to actually change the conditions of opportunity for these young people.

The second thing we have to do is to recognize that our police forces can do more if they're more closely connected to the community, if there are enough of them, and if they operate in the same neighborhoods and concentrate on the problem areas. The buzzword for that is community policing. And it works. It works. I have been in cities all across America where the crime rate is dropping because of

concentrated community policing strategy where police work in partnership with the citizens who live in a community, focus their resources on the areas of greatest opportunity, respond quickly to problems. I have seen that. That works.

The chief of police of St. Petersburg, Darrel Stephens, who's here, has been one of our Nation's leading promoters of community policing. And it does move away from the old ways of trying to catch criminals after a crime occurs to doing as much as you can to prevent crime in the first place. That drives down the crime rate.

This year under Attorney General Reno's leadership, our Department of Justice will fund five community policing projects in our Nation to serve as models for the rest of the country. In a competitive process, the Justice Department tried to find rural examples and urban examples, small and medium sized towns as well as big ones. Due to the strength of the programs in your communities, the Justice Department has selected two of the five prototypes to be here in Florida, one in St. Petersburg, and the other in Hillsboro County, right next door. And these funds—not massive amounts of money, $200,000 apiece—will enable these communities to strengthen their own community policing programs and develop them in a way that can be copied by other communities.

One of the things that the Attorney General and I were talking about on the way up here is it never ceases to amaze me that nearly every problem in America has been addressed well by somebody somewhere, but we don't learn very well from one another yet. And one of the things that this Government is dedicated to doing in my administration is taking what works at the grassroots level and giving other people a chance to do it. And I thank you for that.

Now, the third thing I want to emphasize and the third thing I think we have to recognize is if you want to prevent crime in this country, violent crime, if you want to stop gunshot wounds from being the leading cause of death among young teenage boys, if you want to change the circumstance in which the average age of people killing each other is now under 16 in some of our cities, you have to change the fact that America is the only country in the civilized world where a teenager can walk the street at random and be better armed than most police forces. We have to face that fact.

The crime bill, which was introduced just a couple of days ago in both the Senate and the House, contains more funds for more police officers on the street, something I believe in, we want to put another 100,000 out there in America so everybody can adopt a community policing strategy. It also has the Brady bill which will require a 5-day waiting period before anybody can purchase a handgun. And in addition to that, there are several bills in the Congress, and I hope and pray one of them can reach my desk this year, which will ban various types of assault weapons entirely from being held in the possession of our young people.

Let me tell you something, folks. I come from a State where more than half the adults have a hunting or a fishing license or both, where most of us were in the woods by the time we were 6 years old, where some schools and some plants have to be closed on the opening day of deer season. Nobody shows up anyway. [*Laughter*] There's not a person in this country that values the culture of the outdoors and the hunting and all of that any more than I do. But neither those who love to hunt, or who love to shoot weapons in contests, nor the framers of the Constitution when they wrote the second amendment ever envisioned a time when children on our streets would illegally be in possession of weapons designed solely to kill other people and have more weapons than the people who were supposed to be policing them. And we better stop it if we want to recover our country.

Just last week the Governor of Colorado, Governor Roy Romer, signed a law that prohibits juveniles from owning handguns. He joined Governor Florio of New Jersey and 17 others who have passed that law this year.

These are things we have to do. All three of these things are preventive. They're worth a pound of cure. Have more programs like this one. Give these kids a chance to have something to say yes to, not just telling them what they have to say no to, and a chance to order their lives and to fill themselves from the inside out. A lot of these programs don't deal with people from the inside out. That's the only way you can really change people's lives.

Give our police forces a chance to succeed with a community-based strategy that prevents crimes as well as catches criminals. And get the guns out of the hands of the kids. Give our law enforcement officers a fighting chance to keep the streets safe and people secure.

These are elements of prevention that will give us the security we need to make the changes we need economically to move into the 21st century. They will have the extra benefit of dramatically lowering the costs of health care and enabling us to finance the kind of progress we need in health care which again will give us the security we need to be the people we have to be in this dynamic era.

Thank you very much, and God bless you all.

NOTE: The President spoke at 10:14 a.m. at the Pinellas Marine Institute.

Remarks on NAFTA and an Exchange With Reporters
September 24, 1993

The President. I was asked on the way out of Florida this morning to make a comment on the Court of Appeals decision involving NAFTA, where the Court of Appeals reversed the trial court and said, in effect, that NAFTA does not have to have an environmental impact statement. First, I applaud the decision. And second, I want to emphasize that if this agreement goes through, it will lead to improvements in the environment and increased investment on the Mexican side of the border in environ-mental cleanup.

I also would like to say, based on the cause and conversations that I have been having with Members of Congress, I'm beginning to feel a little bit better about this agreement. I think that more and more Members of Congress who actually listen to the arguments, pro and con, understand that the overwhelming majority of the arguments against NAFTA are complaints about things that have already happened under the existing law, all of which NAFTA will make better.

NAFTA will raise wages more quickly in Mexico than if we don't adopt it. It will raise environmental spending more in Mexico than if we don't adopt it. It will reduce illegal immigration more in Mexico than if we don't adopt it. And it will plainly lead to more high-tech jobs, high-wage jobs in this country. And also I think more of our Members of Congress understand that NAFTA stands for, in the minds of the rest of the market-oriented countries of Latin America a desire on the part of the United States to have a hemispheric trading bloc, which everyone believes will lead to more jobs and higher incomes in America; that is, NAFTA is the beginning, after which you can look at Chile, at Venezuela, at Argentina, at other of the market-oriented economies in Latin America. These things, I think, are beginning to sink in, and I'm very hopeful that we're going to be making some more progress. I think we are.

South Africa

Q. Mr. President, on another subject, Nelson Mandela today called for an end to the sanctions on South Africa. I know you've followed this issue closely for many, many years. Is the United States now prepared, are you prepared to lift the sanctions?

The President. When Mr. Mandela was here with President de Klerk, we talked about this. And then I've talked with him on the phone since he was here. And I'm looking forward to doing it again. Obviously the United States is going to be heavily influenced by the remarkable turn of events in South Africa, by the continued commitment on the part of the people of South Africa to move to a multiracial democracy. And so I will be very influenced, obviously, by what Mr. Mandela says. But I'll have a statement about that——

Bosnia

Q. Mr. President, when you go to the United Nations on Monday, can you tell us what you'll tell them about your feelings concerning Bosnia?

The President. Tune in Monday. I don't want to give the speech today.

Russia

Q. Mr. President, regarding the situation in Moscow, President Yeltsin now is clearly threatening to use force, if necessary, to disarm his opponents in the Parliament. Does that affect your attitude towards the situation in there, your support for Yeltsin?

The President. My support has not been affected by anything that has happened thus far. It is a difficult situation. I don't think we should attempt to quarterback every move from the United States. And I don't think I have anything else to say about it yet.

Anticrime Legislation

Q. Mr. President, there are a lot of people who are asking, after your comments this morning on the nexus between violence and medical costs, what your crime policies are really doing to make a change in this other than just support for gun control?

The President. Well, I've got a crime bill up there that goes far beyond support for the Brady bill and for a restriction on automatic weapons— I mean, assault weapons, although I favor both those very strongly. We also, through the crime bill and several other initiatives, are attempting to put more police officers on the street, to support boot camps and other alternative forms of punishment for young people to try to steer them away from a life of crime, and to support improvements in the criminal justice system itself to make punishment more swift and more sure.

But if you look at the crime bill, if you look at the effort to put more police officers on the street and to support community policing, and if you look at the effort to provide boot camps and alternative forms of punishment and pass the Brady bill and pass some limits on these semi-automatic assault weapons, that's a pretty broad-based anticrime strategy. I hope that the Congress will act on it and act on it this year.

NAFTA

Q. Mr. President, some people have expressed the view that NAFTA constitutes a kind of an unfortunate obstacle to you in political terms with all the focus that will be needed to pass the health care reform. How do you see the politics of the two issues fitting or not fitting together?

The President. I disagree with that, because, first of all, let's look at what has to happen now on health care reform. We're going to do one more round of intensive consultations, then we'll have some legislation to send to the Hill that embodies the principles I discussed with the American people. There will be other bills.

They will go to the committees, and then we will begin the careful and exhaustive process of reviewing this.

Meanwhile, NAFTA is on a much faster time track. The trade agreement has to be turned into legislation within a limited period of time by the Congress. And then there's a limited period of time for debate. So I will be spending a significant amount of time everyday calling Members of Congress in both parties trying to line up support and working on other people like Mr. Iacocca, to try to get them to speak out for us and working on bringing people into this debate who are selling things to Mexico and people whose jobs depend on it to show that it's a job winner as well as trying to illustrate to the Congress that the great benefits of NAFTA may well lie in its ability to be expanded to the rest of Latin America.

So I've got a big agenda. And the NAFTA issue will be over before too long. That is, under the fast track legislation on trade agreements, there is a fixed amount of time we have to do it. We're either going to do it or not. It'll be over—the health care debate is on a different timetable. So I don't see them conflicting now. We just had to get the health care debate started, or we never would have finished it.

Health Care Reform

Q. Mr. President, on health care reform, if you end up underestimating the cost of your plan, are you calling for a formal annual review mechanism that would allow for tax increases or benefit cuts, if necessary, in order to meet your target?

The President. What I think we should do is we should have an annual review process which would permit us, if we don't realize the savings through management we intend to realize, to make a decision to phase in some of the newer benefits over a longer period of time. That would control what we do—or to present them as options that can be paid for separately at the decision of the consumer until the savings enable us to phase them in completely.

I do not believe—I will say again—I do not believe you can justify taking the world's most expensive and bureaucratic system in which most Americans who have insurance pay more than they should, under any conceivable model that they'd be in, anyone besides this one, and ask them to pay taxes on top of that to pay for the uninsured. We have got to manage this system to make it simpler, to achieve the savings without sacrificing choice and quality. We can plainly do it. We know it's been done in Germany, just to take one other example. We know it's been done several places in the United States. And the administration is happy to carry the burden into these congressional hearings of demonstrating the evidence that it can be done. But if it doesn't happen just as it should, then what should happen is we should phase the benefits in more slowly or present them as options that can be paid for. We shouldn't raise general taxes on people who are already paying too much for their own health care to pay for somebody else's health care who's not paying anything for it. I just don't think that's right.

Thank you very much.

NOTE: The President spoke at 2:35 p.m. on the South Lawn at the White House, upon his return from St. Petersburg, FL. In his remarks, he referred to former Chrysler Corp. chairman Lee Iacocca.

Statement on Lifting Economic Sanctions Against South Africa
September 24, 1993

I welcome the call today by ANC President Nelson Mandela for the lifting of economic sanctions against South Africa. This call from this courageous man who has been one of the principal victims of apartheid means that the leading groups in South Africa now oppose the maintenance of economic sanctions on their country.

Yesterday's action by the South African Parliament to create a Transitional Executive Council (TEC) and today's announcement by the ANC are watershed events in the history of South Africa and its movement toward a nonracial democracy. South Africans of all races can be proud of these momentous achievements. Americans can also take pride in the role they have played through government, churches, unions, universities, activist groups, and businesses throughout America to protest the apartheid system.

We must now respect the judgment of the leaders of South Africa and move to lift our remaining economic sanctions. We will be taking steps necessary to permit lending to South Africa from the International Monetary Fund. I welcome the introduction and passage of legislation in the Senate to lift the other remaining sanctions at the Federal level and hope the House can move rapidly on the legislation as well. I also urge States, counties, and cities to move quickly to lift their sanctions.

But removing sanctions will not be enough. Americans who have been so active in breaking down the pillars of apartheid must remain committed to helping build the nonracial market democracy that comes in its wake. For this reason, I have asked that Commerce Secretary Ron Brown lead a trade and investment mission to South Africa to explore business opportunities, particularly with South Africa's black private sector. We will offer an OPIC investment encouragement agreement and propose negotiations for a bilateral tax treaty. We will consider the possibility of initiating a Peace Corps program in South Africa.

I urge private companies, investment fund managers, universities, labor unions, and other Americans to take advantage of opportunities for trade and investment in South Africa and to use their fullest talents to assist South Africa's historic transition to democracy.

Message on the Observance of Yom Kippur, 1993
September 24, 1993

My heartfelt greetings to all who are observing Yom Kippur in this momentous year of history and hope.

Yom Kippur, the Day of Atonement, is a holy day that provides the opportunity to seek forgiveness and to enter the new year with a clean conscience and a clear purpose. It is a chance to seek pardon and to ask divine guidance for self-improvement. Yom Kippur emphasizes the importance of honoring the memories of loved ones no longer living, but still remembered. Above all, Yom Kippur recognizes the need to repair personal relationships—relationships with friends and family, with God, with those who live on in our memories, and with those for whom we may have previously felt animosity.

With the recent signing of the agreement between Israel and the Palestine Liberation Organization, this Yom Kippur is particularly significant. It is my wish that people of all cultures and faiths will pledge their active support and energy to help achieve a new era of peace and hope in the Middle East and for the entire world. This will take courage and commitment. As Foreign Minister Peres so eloquently stated at the signing ceremony, "Deep gaps call for lofty bridges."

On this most solemn day, let all of us reflect on the enormous challenges that lie ahead. Let us dedicate ourselves to the next generation, and together we will usher in a true season of peace.

BILL CLINTON

Appointment for Assistant to the President and Director of Scheduling and Advance
September 24, 1993

The President has asked Ricki Seidman, currently Assistant to the President and Counselor to the Chief of Staff, to serve as his Assistant to the President and Director of Scheduling and Advance. Ms. Seidman is currently on leave and will begin operating in her new capacity

November 1.

"I am extremely pleased that Ricki will be taking on this new assignment," said the President. "Her keen political instincts, unparalleled good sense, and sincere conviction make her an invaluable part of my team."

NOTE: A biography of the nominee was made available by the Office of the Press Secretary.

Nomination for Three Federal Judges
September 24, 1993

The President announced the nominations today of three Federal judges: Rosemary Barkett for the U.S. Court of Appeals for the Eleventh Circuit, Raymond Jackson for the U.S. District Court for the Eastern District of Virginia, and Joanna Seybert for the U.S. District Court for the Eastern District of New York.

"These three individuals have all exhibited the high levels of ability and judgment that the American people deserve to expect from Federal judges," said the President.

NOTE: Biographies of the nominees were made available by the Office of the Press Secretary.

The President's Radio Address
September 25, 1993

Good morning. Last Wednesday evening, I asked Congress to take up the challenge of providing health security to every American, to help write the next great chapter in our Nation's history. Already your response has been positive and dramatic, creating what I believe will be an irresistible momentum for reform, while insisting that we be careful to do it right. And I am increasingly confident that before it adjourns next year, Congress will pass and I will sign a bill that guarantees each American comprehensive health benefits that can never ever be taken away.

In the debate between now and that day, a debate I welcome, our most urgent priority must be to ensure that we preserve what is right with American health care and fix what is wrong. So today I want to take a few minutes to talk with you about the plan that I am suggesting and how it will work for you, what will stay the same and what will change.

First, I want you to know that after considering all the options and looking at the systems in place in other countries in the world, I decided that our Nation does not need a Government-run health care system. So our plan builds upon the private system, which provides health care to the vast majority of you today. Nine of 10 of you who have private health care coverage now, get it through the place you work. In the future, you will do it just like you do now. Because that's what works now, I think it should work for everyone.

Second, under our health care plan, 63 percent, more than 6 in 10 Americans who have health insurance today, will pay the same or less than you do today for benefits that are the same or greater, including the right to choose your doctor. If you get good health care, if you like your benefits, if your employer pays 100 percent of your health care costs, nothing will change.

Let's say you work for Super Software, a small computer company that employs about 150 people, and that today your company provides you excellent health benefits, your choice of doctors, and picks up the whole tab. That won't change. You will still sign up for a health plan at work, see the doctors you want, and get the same benefits.

Now, suppose you work for a giant auto company and your union has fought hard for your benefits; you've even had to give up a wage increase or two to get them. Well, under this new plan, you will keep those benefits.

What do you get out of this plan? You get security. You get the knowledge that you'll never lose health coverage even if you lose or change your job or you get very, very sick. You also know that no matter what happens, there's a limit to what your employer can do to reduce the benefits or your choice of plans.

I know that many people also want to know whether you'll still be able to choose your doctor. Again, I say the answer is yes. And no matter what kind of plan you're in today, you will all benefit because under this new system, the cost of health care will go up much more slowly than they've been going up for the last 10 or 12 years. And you'll be able to choose from at least three plans providing comprehensive coverage. You'll also be able to choose your doctor no matter what plan you decide to join because you can follow your doctor into whatever plan he or she joins.

Now, a lot of families have more than one doctor. Say you're a working mother who values your obstetrician, and you trust your children's pediatrician. You want to know if you can see them both. There's still no need to worry, because doctors will be able to join more than one plan and keep treating the same patients they see today.

Finally, we're going to maintain the quality of American health care. We can do that by making sure that there are quality standards met by all the health care plans, by spending our money smarter, less on paperwork and unnecessary costs and more on medical research, health care centers, and preventive care; by freeing your doctors and nurses from the paperwork they've got to wade through everyday; and by giving you information, valuable information, on variations in costs and outcomes in medical procedures in your area. These are the things that are right, that make sense, that will keep the quality that we've got today.

Now, let's talk about what needs to be changed in this huge health care system of ours. We begin with the need for security. No American can be absolutely guaranteed today that he or she will never lose health care. But we begin by making that guarantee, a comprehensive package of health care benefits, the kinds of benefits that only people with the best plans and the best companies get today, that never can be taken away, even if you lose your job or move to another town or State or someone

in your family gets very sick.

Then we're going to do something, frankly, that we should have done a long time ago. We're going to provide every American, no matter what kind of plan you sign up for, with free preventive care. Things like immunizations for children, prenatal care for pregnant women, mammograms, cholesterol screenings, things that will keep us healthy and save us all a lot of money over the long run.

Many Americans will actually have more choices in the kinds of health care they get because everyone will have a choice of at least three health care plans in connection with their job. Today, only about a third of Americans have a choice of more than one plan when they're insured at work. That's a lot more than most Americans have.

We're also going to clear out the paper and the fine print. No more fighting with some insurance bureaucrat hundreds of miles away in order to get what your policy owes you anyway. And no more doctors telling stories of the hundreds of patients they could have served every year if only they weren't swamped in redtape.

This will simplify our system and literally save tens of billions of dollars a year. Don't take my word for it, ask any doctor or nurse or hospital administrator about the growth of unnecessary paperwork in the last decade, mandated by both Government and insurance companies. It adds about a dime to every single dollar we spend in health care. And it has resulted in hospitals hiring 4 times as many clerical workers as doctors being added to their staffs.

Something else is going to be different, too. We're going to ask each of you to take more responsibility. Six of every 10 of you will pay the same or less than you do now for the same or better benefits. But some people will pay more: people who are getting a free ride today, businesses that contribute nothing to cover their employees, and others who offer bare bones coverage with huge deductibles and copayments, and those employees will have to pay something for their health care. Young, single adults will pay more, too, especially those who are in the best of health and don't see any reason to buy health insurance, the ones who, when they end up in the emergency room without insurance, pass those costs on to the rest of us.

For small businesses and people on very low wages, there will be discounts to make sure we don't cost jobs or hurt people, but everybody should take some responsibility for their own health care. It's not fair to the rest of Americans when you don't. There will also be more responsibility on those in the systems, less for insurance regulation and overhead, a crackdown on fraud and abuse, fewer frivolous malpractice lawsuits, fewer unnecessary procedures done just to get the money and more responsibility for individuals for their own health, strong efforts and incentives to reduce teen pregnancy and low birthweight babies, to reduce the rate of AIDS. These are the kinds of things we have got to do.

But in the end, the most important thing that will change is this: Every American will get something that today no amount of money can buy, the security of health care that can never be taken away no matter what. No matter how good your coverage is today, you can lose it. You can lose it all at once, or it can be gradually taken away year after year.

Our goal then is health care security for all Americans. The only way to get there is to keep what's right with our system, the best medical care in the world, the best medical technology, the best medical professionals, and fix what's wrong.

We're going to protect quality and choice, but we're going to make some changes. We're going to simplify this system. We're going to get billions of dollars of savings. We're going to ask people who don't pay anything now to assume more responsibility for their own health care. That way we can give you health care security without a big tax increase.

In the weeks ahead, we'll be describing in greater details what needs to be done. But the most important thing is health security. We can do it.

Thanks for listening.

NOTE: The address was recorded at 5:21 p.m. on September 24 in the Roosevelt Room at the White House for broadcast at 10:06 a.m. on September 25.

Statement by the Press Secretary on the Situation in Somalia
September 25, 1993

The United States condemns the attack on United Nations forces in Mogadishu last night which resulted in the death of three American soldiers and injuries to several other American and Pakistani soldiers. The President offers his deepest condolences to the families and friends of these brave men who were performing a vital humanitarian mission in Somalia.

This attack underscores the need to reestablish security in Mogadishu to prevent the international humanitarian efforts from being undermined. At times like this, it is essential to remember the reasons for our engagement in the 25-nation U.N. mission in Somalia. The U.N.'s goal is to prevent the recurrence of the famine and anarchy that resulted in the deaths of 350,000 Somalis last year. We are working to create a peaceful environment in which the U.N.'s mission can be assumed by a Somali authority.

Since 28,000 U.S. troops went to Somalia last December, we have withdrawn 80 percent of our forces. Today, our troops number less than 5,000 and make up less than 20 percent of the remaining U.N. forces from over two dozen nations. As U.N. forces continue to take up the burden, the American role can continue to diminish.

Today, Somalia is on the road to recovery, especially outside of Mogadishu. District councils are reestablishing the rule of law in much of the country, hospitals and schools are operating, and crops are being planted and harvested. On Wednesday, the United Nations took important steps forward to support the reconstruction of Somalia's judicial, security, and penal systems.

We must not allow this substantial yet fragile progress to be threatened by the brutality of warlords who would profit from the suffering of others and thwart the will of the overwhelming majority of Somalis who seek peace and reconciliation.

Remarks and a Question-and-Answer Session on Health Care Reform in New York City
September 26, 1993

The President. Thank you very much, Mayor, and all my good friends in Queens. It's great to be back in this diner again. We had a terrific—was anybody here when I was here before? Well, Congressman Manton was, and Lowey was here, and you were here, and you were here when I was here before. We had a great time here. A lot of you were here. Didn't we, Antonio? We had a great time. And I felt so good about it, I brought you a cap from my food service. [*Laughter*] You can wear it here. There you go.

I came to this place during the primary as an example of a new small business and the kind of economic opportunity that I hope to support as President. In the last several months I've had the opportunity to work with the Members of Congress here present: Gary Ackerman, Tom Manton, Anita Lowey. Anybody else here from the House? I don't think so. And we've done a lot of things that I think will help the economy. We have passed the biggest deficit reduction program in history. We have record-low interest rates. We have created some empowerment zones that will help some distressed areas of our biggest cities and some of our rural areas to generate new private sector investment like this. We are pushing through some banking reforms that will make available financial institutions whose primary mission is to loan money to new small businesses, like this one was just a year or so ago. We are trying, in other words, to help to create an economy which will be connected to the future, and which people who want to work hard can win.

We are revolutionizing a lot of the educational programs of the National Government. The student loan program has been completely rewritten to provide longer term, lower interest rate student loans on better repayment terms so that young people can pay them back as a percentage of their income, no matter how much they have to borrow. We passed a national service program to allow tens of thousands of our young people to work in community programs to pay off their college loans. So we are moving ahead to create tomorrow's economy and to try to help our people adjust to it.

But one of the things that I have learned—and the reason this health care debate is so important is that it is absolutely impossible to get people to have the courage to change unless first they can be secure in their own circumstances. If you think about it, every one of you in your own personal life know that is true. Look at any child you raise up. A child, if you want a child to change his or her behavior, to try something new, the more personally secure the child is, the more the child is willing to try to do something new and different, to believe that you can change and win. The more insecure people are, the more focused they are on just surviving from day to day, the more difficult that is.

The hard truth is that this country has seen a very long period of time, about 20 years, when most working people have gotten steadily more insecure. We have, according to your senior Senator Pat Moynihan, seen almost 30 years of steady deterioration in the supports the children have in their family units. And we are now facing a great challenge in this country: How can we get the security people need so that people will have the courage to change as we move to the 21st century?

I've really thought a lot about that. That's at the core of the crime bill that's been introduced into the Congress, which will provide 50,000 of the 100,000 more police officers I want to put on the streets—will pass at long last the Brady bill, very important in New York. The Mayor told me you confiscate thousands of weapons here every year and 90 percent of them come from another State. So we've got to pass the Brady bill. And I hope that before the year's out I will have a chance to vote on one of the number of bills in the Congress now which would ban assault weapons and take them out of the hands of teenagers in our cities and give us a chance to have a saner and safer place.

That's one part of this. I want to compliment Mayor Dinkins. His program will have increased the size of the New York City police force up about 20 percent when it is completed. And New York City is one of the few big cities in America which is reporting now, for 2 years in a row, a decline in all seven major categories of crime. That's something you can be proud of. Not very many cities have done it, and you should be proud of it.

If you want people to be more secure you have to support families. And we have to make it possible for people to succeed as workers and as parents, because most parents have to work. And we have waited too long in this country to do this. That was at the heart of our party's determination, to overcome the reluctance of the last 4 years and pass the family and medical leave bill.

I want to tell you a story. I got up this morning—and my mother spent the night with me in the White House last night, and so I got my mother and my daughter and my wife up and my stepfather, and we were all bustling around on Sunday morning. And then I went out for my morning run, and when I came back in I noticed in the bottom floor of the White House a family getting a personal tour on Sunday morning—the father, the mother, and three children—three daughters, one of these young daughters desperately ill with cancer. And she had been in one of these Make-a-Wish programs, and her wish was to come to the White House and see the President. So they brought her on Sunday morning so she could see the helicopter take off as I came up here. And I got to sit and visit with her a long time. But the father of that child looked at me and he said, "My daughter has been sick a long time. And I don't know what I would have done without the family and medical leave law. I still have a job because you passed that law. Don't let anybody ever tell you it was bad for the economy."

The Members of Congress here present voted for a bill to change the tax laws so that people who work with children on lower incomes, lower wages, will be lifted above the poverty line as they work and raise their children, so that the tax system won't tax people into poverty, it will lift them out of it—the most sweeping piece of economic reform in at least two decades. Not very much noticed, but you will see it in tens of thousands of people in Queens who in the coming year will get a reduction in their income tax bill because they work for modest wages and they have children in their homes. We've got to try to do that.

But here's why we came here today. If we do all of these things, and we don't fix the health care system, we will not restore security to American life. We won't be supporting families who are trying to raise their children or take care of their parents. And we won't give people the kind of inner strength and self-confidence they need to face a world that is smaller and smaller and smaller, to support expanded trade, to support new investments in new technologies, to support the kind of things I'm going to talk about at the United Nations tomorrow.

This health care issue is uniquely a deeply personal one for every individual and every family and a massive national issue for the United States. It is inconceivable that we spend 35 to 40 percent more of our income on health care than any other country and we still have 37 million people uninsured; that in any given 2-year period, one in four people will be without adequate insurance.

This morning I was out for my morning run. This handsome young man runs by me, he says, "Mr. President, do you mind if I run with you awhile?" And I told him, not if he would slow down, I didn't. So he turned around, we're running along together, and he was an actor there involved in a play. And he said, "My wife is expecting a baby, and we're going to have our first child in April. And I'm an actor. I work as hard as I can, but my work is not constant. And every year I am not sure whether I can have health insurance. You've got to pass this program." Just a guy running along The Mall, like a lot of these people who are going to talk to us today.

We received 700,000 letters, the First Lady and her task force and I. We're still getting about 10,000 letters a week on health care alone.

Let me say, I suppose most of you either saw the address I made to Congress or the Nightline show where I answered questions for so long that everybody who watched the whole program was sleepy the next day. But I want to just reiterate one or two things real quickly. First of all, the most important thing we can do with this health care system to fix it is to keep what's right, fix what's wrong, but guarantee the benefits of it to all Americans. We are the only major country in the world where people don't have the security of knowing that they have comprehensive health care that can't be taken away if you lose your job or someone in your family gets sick or something else happens. We have got to give that sense of security. We've got to fix what is wrong and keep what is right.

What's right about the system? High quality, consumer choice. Our plan keeps them both and, in fact, increases quality by providing preventive and primary services that will save money over the long run and improve the quality of health care and increases choice for most Americans who today increasingly have only one choice of how they get their health care.

What's wrong with the health care system? Well, it costs too much, it's too complicated, and it doesn't promote personal responsibility for every American. And it has no security. There is not a soul in this country that can't lose his or her health care, nobody. So that's what is wrong with it.

Our system saves money without sacrificing quality, simplifies the system, which will elate the doctors and nurses and the people who have had to fool with it for years. We are now hiring clerical workers at 4 times the rate we are adding direct care providers in most hospitals in this country. It introduces more responsibility because it asks every employer and every employee to do what the vast majority of employers and employees are doing now, and it rewards good behavior. And finally, it provides security to everybody.

My dream is that before the Congress goes home, and after the finish of its business next year, it will pass a bill to give a security card like this to every American, so that no matter where you are and what happens to you, or whether you lose your job or whether someone in your family gets sick, you'll always be able to get health care.

Now, I know a lot of people are skeptical that this can be done. But I just ask you to remember a couple of basic facts: We are already spending 40 percent more than anybody else. We are spending at least 10 cents on the dollar in unnecessary nonhealth-related paperwork that no other country in the world is spending. Nobody. And if we have a system like the one we've outlined, that will provide discounts to small business and low-wage workers—so that a place like this, a great place, can provide some health insurance without running the risk of going broke because when businesses start and they have just a few employees, they can't all afford the market rate, and so we give them discounts to them—we can get

this done.

I just don't believe that we have to go on for another year or 5 years or 10 years being the only nation in the world that can't figure out how to give health care to everybody. I don't believe that. And I don't think you believe that.

So today we're here in Queens to hear from some of the people who wrote us from New York. A lot of you wrote us letters, but I'm going to call on eight people—and get rid of this so we can just have a conversation—who represent what I think may be the four biggest obstacles to health care security, that cause people to lose their health insurance.

So we're going to first talk about the curse of preexisting conditions that you want health insurance. And the first person who's going to talk about the letter that she wrote to us is Linda Haftel. Where are you, Linda?

[*Ms. Haftel, who was recently diagnosed with multiple sclerosis, described her fear of losing her health insurance.*]

The President. Thank you. Let's give her a hand for doing that. It was great. [*Applause*] I wanted her to go first to make a point. First of all, a lot of people who have MS now, because of medication and because of rigorous exercise, are finding that they can maintain very high levels of mobility for much longer than was previously the case. So here she is, at the peak of her capacity to give to society, wondering if she has to lie on to her insurer to keep her insurance, because again, this is the only country in the world where you can lose your insurance because you really need insurance.

So what we have to do is to change the rules of insurance to say that you cannot lose your policy because of preexisting conditions. To do that you have to make sure that insurers can't go broke, and the way you do that is to put us all in big pools called community rating, so that any person with a severe illness still adds a very small percentage to the overall cost of the operation. It's just something we've never done that we have to do.

I thank you. Marcia Calendar, where are you?

[*Ms. Calendar described the problems with the health care system that her family encountered when her son was diagnosed with a terminal illness. In spite of these problems, she and her husband decided to have another child, who was*] *in the audience asleep.*]

The President. She's the smartest person here, she's sleeping. [*Laughter*]

[*Ms. Calendar recounted her family's financial difficulty prior to her son's death and her hope for a health plan that would ensure quality of life for all children.*]

The President. Thank you, and thank you for coming and for bringing your beautiful daughter. It is hard to say anything after that, but let me just make one point that you might have missed in the heart-wrenching story of this family. When Matthew's father lost his job because of a layoff, that was the beginning of a lot of their problems with the health insurance company, if you remember the story that she told. If you go back to what I said when I first started talking about what a dynamic, changing time it is, and how people can't be expected to change if they don't have security—the average person is going to change jobs eight times in a lifetime now because of the way the economy is changing. And it is cruel, it is unconscionable that people who get caught up in the ordinary course of economic changes today, stuff we take for granted, would have to go through what they did solely because the health care system doesn't move with people from job to job, or from job to unemployment to job. It's just wrong. It is wrong because there is no comprehensive system to put prospective employers in the position of thinking that they can't hire somebody because they only have 10 employees or 15 employees, and that as a small business they can't afford to take on that risk, when most new jobs are being created by small businesses.

No one can ever stop the fact, that for reasons none of us understand, some children will be born with life-threatening and ultimately terminal illnesses. That happens, but no family should have their grief compounded and their economic misery reinforced by this kind of problem. The rest of us owe it to families like the Calendars to make sure that this does not happen anymore. Thank you.

Let's talk about what is the flip side of the preexisting conditions, where people use their health insurance, and that is they keep their health insurance at the cost of staying in a job whether they want to stay there or not. It's called the job lock syndrome. And we're going to hear first from Mary Jane Van Wick. Where

are you, Mary Jane?

[*Ms. Van Wick explained that to cover ongoing costs associated with her liver transplant, she was forced to go on medical assistance.*]

The President. Now, there are literally tens of thousands, maybe more, people like Mary Jane in this country, who can get health care only if they're on public assistance and whose children have been not necessarily covered if they're on Medicare. Just think about that.

A lot of you have seen the story of a woman I met in Ohio who has become one of the spokespersons for our campaign, named Marie Castos, who had six children, was raising them alone, had a job making a very good income. The youngest child had a terminal illness, a terrible problem. She had to quit her job and go on Medicaid and become a welfare recipient— she had a very good job—not because she wanted a welfare check but just so her children would have some health care. Her youngest child died recently. And I just saw her; she came back to the White House to see me and she's one of our health care spokespersons. And she's looking forward to going back to work.

But she was so proud of being able to support those children alone. Why shouldn't this lady be able to work? Society is going to pay for her health care anyway, right? This is—it's bad for her. She's frustrated she can't work. It's also bad for the rest of you. If society is paying for her health care—if she works and makes a contribution to society, has an income and pays taxes, number one, her child gets health care coverage and, number two, she is repaying some of the costs of her own health care.

The system we have now, everybody loses. And she's more unhappy. This will also be fixed if you have universal coverage that moves from employment to unemployment to employment again, and which includes families as well as individual workers.

Where's Jean Townsend? You're next.

[*Ms. Townsend explained that because of cutbacks in her company, she no longer worked enough hours to qualify for health insurance.*]

The President. Interestingly enough, as I'm sure all of you have noticed, in the economy around here—you see it all around the country—there are more and more part-time workers, more and more temporary workers, more and more special businesses whose whole job is to gather up folks who will work part-time and send them out to other employers. The big reason for this is the cost of health care, which then the employer can avoid.

Under our plan, even part-time workers would be covered. But we would split the difference, so that if you're a part-time worker, your employer and the employee would have the responsibility of only paying a pro rata share of what the premium would be. And the Government would pick up the rest as they do for unemployed people, as if you were unemployed because you would be sometimes. So there would be discount, if you will.

But that way you wouldn't unduly burden businesses that honestly need part-time workers. There are a lot of businesses that can't operate really functionally because of the changing demands in the schedule unless they have some full-time workers and some part-time workers. But a lot of businesses are weighing more to part-time workers now solely to avoid the health care costs.

So what we would do is we would remove the incentive to hire part-time workers solely to avoid the health care costs. And for the businesses that really have to have some part-time workers—like a lot of restaurants, for example, really need both full-time and part-time workers. It's not an attempt to avoid anything, it's just the way the workload changes.

So under our system we would be fair to those folks by saying you don't have to pay the whole cost of the premium. That's not fair; the person's not there all the time. You share in, and we'll give you a discount and then the Government will pick up the rest as if the person were unemployed. Or if a person has multiple employers, then they would all make a little contribution, as long as the part-time worker does 10 hours a week or more. I think that is a fair resolution of the problem.

Let's talk now about the fear of losing insurance related to the rising cost of it. Where is Josephine Angevine?

[*Ms. Angevine explained that her salary was frozen because her employer, a small business, covered the full cost of health insurance premiums for her son and herself, and she worried about losing her job as well as her insurance due to this cost of over $12,000.*]

The President. Wow! It takes your breath away, doesn't it? Let me make just a couple of observations about her situation. Part of it is common to millions of people in businesses large and small; part of it is—her problem—is unique to small businesses.

You heard her say she hasn't had a pay raise in 3 years. There are millions of American workers who haven't had a pay raise in 3 years because of the cost of health insurance. And it is estimated that if we don't do something to bring health care costs closer to inflation, between now and the end of the decade, most of what otherwise would have gone to pay workers' pay increases will go solely to pay for more health care costs, and not for new benefits—more health care costs for the same health care.

Now, that is something that is sweeping the country. Her premium, however, is unusual. You heard her—on a $52,000 salary with a $12,000 premium, that means she's paying over 20 percent of payroll and more than her mortgage payment.

So under our plan, we would begin with everybody at 7.9 percent of payroll for employers and a fifth of that at the most for employees. If employers want to cover their employees, they can, but it would cut that cost in half. Why? Because she's got a small business with five employees. They're probably in a very small pool with somewhere between 50 and 200 people. And under our plan she would go into a pool with other small businesses, with self-employed people. There might be 200,000 in that buying group, which would give you the economies of scale that other people have. This is unconscionable, and it's solely a function of the size of the business.

And I'll bet you anything—I haven't seen the benefit package, but I'll bet you anything it's not as good as the one that will be in the national health plan—certainly not better.

But the real problem here—this small business thing is a big deal. If we don't provide discounts for very small businesses and get all small businesses in big pools, you will see that small business will continue to have a bigger and bigger gap between their premiums and big business premiums. Right now, small business premiums are between 20 and 50 percent higher than big business premiums on average and are going up at more than twice the rate of big business premiums. And yet what we want to do is encourage people who get laid off or who get restructured or the airline industries or whatever to go out and work in or start up small businesses. So that if you look at what's going to happen in the next 10 years, a higher and higher and higher percentage of Americans will be working in smaller companies.

That is another reason we've got to do this health insurance thing now, because we cannot stop the trend of big companies toward downsizing and we don't want to stop this trend of people starting small businesses.

I am very glad you are here because even though your circumstance is somewhat extreme in terms of percentage of your payroll, it is not unusual in the kind of problem you have, and we've got to stop it.

Where is Mark Fish?

[Mr. Fish explained that he and his wife were self-employed and the cost of their health insurance was exorbitant.]

The President. What's your deductible?

Mr. Fish. It's $1,000, but it is spread out over 2 years since our medical bills are in 1993 and 1994.

By the way, I would like to tell you that I am a registered Republican who voted for you, and I think you are doing a great job.

The President. Thank you. Your problem is similar to hers. And if I were guessing, I would guess, since you're self-employed and she is in a small business and you both have family coverage for one child, but your premium is over $8,500 and hers is $12,000, my guess is, whoever your insurer is has done a better job of getting you in slightly bigger group than she has so you can spread risk.

Let me tell you, now, I've hesitated to say this in the past because, even though our books are out and have been published, what our family premium winds up being to start—this health insurance program—depends in part on what the ultimate package of benefits are. But I think I can say roughly that a family package which would be the same price starting out for everybody, whether they were self-employed or not, would be about at least $4,000 cheaper than you're paying.

And again, all that we would do is—I'd have to see the deductibles and the copays, but you'd save about $4,000 which means yours could go down about $8,000 to get a very good package of preventive and primary and comprehensive benefits.

How could we do that? Because we have the most expensive insurance system in the world.

No other country has got 1,500 insurance companies writing thousands of different policies, imposing literally tens of billions of dollars in paperwork benefits, and putting people in such small groups that company really could go broke with one bad illness. So we're just going to have to force people to rate everybody the same in a broad community basis and put people into big pools, so if something happens, God forbid, to you or someone in your family, you won't bankrupt your insurance carrier because you'll be in a big pool, not a little pool.

But now, if you were working for a company with 6,000 employees, you could get the coverage you've got now for $4,000 a year less today, maybe even less than that given what they're covering. In addition to that, if you're self-employed, today, as you know, your policy is only 25 percent deductible. Under our plan it would be 100 percent deductible for both you and your wife, which would make a big difference. So it will help.

Now I want to talk a little bit about the criteria by which insurers make these decisions. Where is Susan Berardo?

[Ms. Berardo described her problem with insurance coverage for a bone marrow transplant.]

The President. This raises a very important point. If you've read your health insurance policies, for those of you who have them, you know that they cover certain problems. They do not prescribe procedures. For example, if the health insurance policy covers pregnancy-related services, it doesn't tell you that you can—it doesn't weigh whether you can have natural childbirth with Lamaze, but you can't have a C-section if you need it, right? It doesn't say that. It doesn't say what things will happen; it just says this issue is covered, this problem is covered.

So that this lady's care is covered under her health insurance policy, but the insurance company has decided that this procedure, bone marrow transplant, shouldn't be covered even though it doesn't say that in the policy, right? It didn't say in the policy, bone marrow transplants aren't covered, did it? They decide if it's experimental.

Now, just so you don't think—I know what a lot of you must be thinking, "Well, it's probably more expensive than a regular operation." The answer to that is, in this case it probably is. But if it works, it will cost the economy a lot less money over the long run in the health care system. But just so you don't think it always applies only to more expensive procedures, I talked to a doctor just 3 days ago who talked to me about some new gall bladder technique that's done almost like arthroscopic surgery on knees which is much less expensive and is also being denied by some health insurance companies, even though the policy doesn't say so, on the theory that it's experimental, too. So that in effect, doctors are not free to practice medicine and let their patients make informed choices about what is best for their health care because of conditions not written in the insurance policy, except a general "well, if we think something is experimental, we don't have to let you do it." Big problem.

Where is Ewen Gillies? Did I pronounce your name right?

[Mr. Gillies described his problem in obtaining payment from his insurance company for his wife's intensive cancer treatment.]

The President. Give him a hand.

Mr. Gillies. May I add one postscript? A copy of the letter went to Senator Moynihan, among other people. And unasked, he got in touch with Blue Cross, who called me and said, "We're reviewing this," and 2 weeks later reimbursed us for $60,000 by placing it in a different category. *[Applause]*

The President. Let me say, first of all, what you said is a great tribute to Senator Moynihan but a pretty terrible indictment of the system, right? I must say, I'm trying to fix it so you don't have to call the White House or your Senator or your Congressman or your mayor or a Governor or anybody else to make this work. I think you've said it all in your remarks. I'm glad you're here.

How about anybody else in here? We've got some other people who wrote letters to us. Yes, ma'am.

[A participant discussed her concern that the new health care plan will not cover persons with the genetic disorder ectodermal dysplasia or other severe dental disorders.]

The President. You're right, I didn't know anything about that. I never heard of the condition before. And I will take it back and discuss it with our people. If you have something for me, I'll be glad to have it. The plan does cover in general dental benefits for children up to age 18 from the beginning.

[A participant described his problem with increased insurance costs attributed to community rating requirements.]

The President. Who is covered under your policy? You and your wife and one child. How old are you? For a family of three at your age, a community rating bill should not have raised your insurance premiums.

But let me just say this. This is the hazard. You are going to hear all of this debate when we go along. I don't want to, again, sort of prefigure the congressional debate, but you'll hear a lot of people say, well, let's just do this little part of this, or let's do that or the other thing. The problem is if you go to community rating, you also have to allow people who run accounting firms, who are self-employed, to be in very large pools so that you have a representative community in the pool. And you also have to allow them to buy their services in some sort of competitive way so you can have the leverage there of the large pool.

I hope you will all remember that when you hear this debate, when people say, well, let's do all this stuff, but don't really require universal coverage. If you don't do that, you'll have the same sort of cost shifting, the same sort of people falling through the cracks, the same sort of escalating costs you've got now, I think. I can't imagine how we could do it otherwise. And so, I appreciate what you said.

[A Medicare recipient asked about medication coverage under the new plan.]

The President. First, let me try to explain what he just said for those of you who don't understand it. If you're elderly and poor enough to be on Medicaid, that is if your income and resources are quite low, you today get drug coverage, you get medication. If you're $1 above the Medicaid line and you're on Medicare and you're elderly, you get no help for medication.

You heard this gentleman say he has a $5,000 annual bill. Let me say, if he did not take those drugs—let's say he stopped taking those drugs—he might be in the hospital 2 weeks a year extra immediately, which would cost a whole lot more than $5,000, which would be completely reimbursed by the Government.

You have all these people like him in this country today, a lot of people I have personally met, who are literally making a decision every week between buying medicine and buying food because they are just above that Medicaid line. And if they chose to buy food and get off their medicine and got real sick and went to the hospital, Medicare would pay for all of it, at a far greater expense.

So, therefore, I think it is very important to cover medicine. The answer to your question is, the medical coverage will be treated more or less as a separate benefit, and in that medical coverage there will be a deductible of about $250 and then a copay of approximately in the range of $10. But that's a lot better than $5,000.

Thank you.

[*A participant asked how the new plan would reduce hospital and health care costs.*]

The President. There are two ways, even in a State with heavily regulated hospital costs, there are two or three ways that I think it will come down. First of all, one of the things that we've learned is: In a system, if you just regulate the price of something but you don't manage the system, what happens is that people, in order to avoid having their incomes go down, increase the supply. If you lower the price, you increase the supply, you get the same income. That's a serious problem with Medicare and Medicaid all across the country.

Secondly, New York, for example, has been the beneficiary of a program called the disproportionate share. We give back to the hospitals that have very high percentages of low income people, because we have so many people who are charity cases who have to be given some care for which there is no reimbursement. The hospitals basically shift and the insurance companies shift those costs to people who are paying higher hospital bills or higher insurance premiums.

If you stop the cost shifting, and the only way to do that is to have universal coverage, then for a lot of the people who have—I'll give you an example. The best example I can think of is a big company, let's say General Motors or IBM. They may have very high insurance premiums with very good benefits, but their insurance premiums are higher than they otherwise would be because they're paying for the cost shifting. And then a small operation like this lady's operation, her insurance premiums are very high in part because she's taken out insurance, so even she or even this family with their $8,000 premium, a portion of their premium is going to pay for people who get uncom-

pensated care.

Everybody in this country gets some care sometime. If you get real sick, you show up at the emergency room. It's more expensive, it costs enormously, and then they have to recover the costs. So that will happen.

Another thing is that even in New York or New Jersey, States that have very good cost controls, or Maryland, the State with probably the best cost controls, even in those States if you look at what's happened to the manpower, health care is always going to be very labor-intensive. But in the last 12 years almost—not almost all but 80 percent of the new hires in health care have been to push paper, have been to deal with regulation, have been to deal with— the average hospital of any size will have 300 different insurers and hundreds and hundreds of different forms. And under our system if you go to one form for insurers, one form for the doctor basically, a standard care form, one form for the consumers, you will drastically cut the time and money allocated to the administrative costs of medicine.

The average doctor—let me just give you one figure; this is a stunning thing—in 1980, the average doctor took home 75 cents of every dollar that came into a medical clinic. In 1990 the average doctor took home 52 cents of every dollar that came into a medical clinic; 23 cents, boom. Where did it go? A couple of cents went to malpractice; over 90 percent of it plus went to increasing costs of administering the system.

And again, you may say this is impossible to believe. The New England Journal of Medicine did a profile of two hospitals in the last couple of years—same size hospitals, same occupancy rate, one in Canada, one in the U.S., exact same size. In the U.S. there were 220 people in the billing department; in Canada there were 6. And most of them were working to fill out American insurance forms. I mean, that's a lot—there is an enormous amount of money.

One other thing: You find within States, even with all the price controls, you find from State to State there are massive differences in the cost of caring for people on Medicare and Medicaid with the same conditions. And within States that don't have specific unit controls, there are massive differences. You know, the Pennsylvania example I cited the other night on television said that open heart surgery varied in cost between $21,000 and $84,000 with exactly the same outcomes on the study. So those are the things we're going to work through.

The money has to be going somewhere. If we're spending 14.5 percent of our income on health care—Canada's at 10, Germany and Japan are under 9, nobody else is over 9 but Canada—the nickel on the dollar is somewhere. And it's not all in higher quality health care. An enormous amount of it is in a system that is wrongly organized with too much cost shifting and a dime on the dollar, I will say again, a dime on the dollar in administrative costs no other comprehensive system in the world has.

[*At this point, a participant complained about the inadequacy of Medicaid coverage.*]

The President. We've run a little longer than I thought we were going to, but I'm glad actually we got this question, even though I've got to stop now, because this is a very important thing.

Enrollment by physicians in the Medicaid program is totally voluntary, and a lot of doctors won't treat Medicaid patients, by and large because in most States they are reimbursed at below the cost of service but the cost of dealing with the paperwork of the program is greater even than some of the insurance company paperwork, so it is a bigger hassle for a lower return. A lot of people don't do it.

One of the important aspects of the health care plan that we have presented is that people on Medicaid would be treated just like everybody else and would be mixed in with everybody else in these big groups. So if you got a security card, you'd have it whether you were an employee of a big company or a self-employed person or someone on Medicaid, and you would be involved in one of these big care networks which would give you the bargaining power to get the highest quality care you can at the most reasonable price.

Again, this is largely the way it is done in several other countries, especially in Germany, and it works pretty well. There is no reason we should have a separate Government system which then the providers can elect to participate in or not. Under this system, if it were in existence when you had your situation, it would have been totally immaterial whether you were on Medicaid or not because you would have the same reimbursement, the same paperwork coming from the same source. As a matter of fact, depending on how they set it up, the physicians

and the hospitals might not even have known you were a Medicaid patient because the Government funds will go to the health care unit you would be a part of, and they would pay the bill.

Let me talk about the freedom of choice issue very briefly. First of all, I want to say something I don't think is clear to everybody. If we pass this program—and for all the people who have better benefits, like for anybody who is in a work unit where the employer is paying 100 percent of the premium, the employer can go right on paying it. In other words, this does not require anybody—what we try to do is set some floors on coverage not ceilings. So if an employer wants to continue to pay 100 percent of the premium and have fee-for-service medicine and let people choose their doctor, they can all do that under this system. They can go right on doing that. As a matter of fact, if anything, it will be easier for them to do it. If we can lower the medical rate of inflation closer to the regular rate of inflation, it will be easier for them to do it because their premiums won't go up as much.

But under this system, people who don't have choices now will be guaranteed them. And let me explain why. Most employees in the employer-based health system we have now are losing their choices every year as the employers try to better manage the exploding cost of health care. For example, about 10 years ago 47 percent of the employees in an employer-financed health care system had some choices of plans. Now, it's down to about one in three.

So under our plan every employee would have three options with comprehensive benefits. One, you could join an HMO. And on today's facts, it would probably be the least expensive, that is, for you. And your employer pays a flat amount regardless. If you did that, you would pay a certain amount every year and then you would get those comprehensive services, but you would deal with the doctors in the HMO unless you needed a specialty help that was from a doctor not in the HMO.

Second option is, you get a lot of doctors together and they form something called a preferred provider organization. I have a friend who is a doctor in Nevada, who is in a PPO with 700 doctors—lots of choice. And they have kept their prices in the range of 2 to 3 percent up or down in the last 5 years. So big choice, big quality, low price increase.

The third option is fee-for-service medicine, which from today's facts would be more expensive, but it would be your choice and still much less. Again, 63 percent of the people in this country with health insurance would pay the same or less for the same or better coverage, if you did that. I think even that will go down in price because of the incentives in our plan to enable doctors to get together, even on a fee-for-service basis, and compete for this business.

But most Americans would have more choices than they have now under this plan. Americans who have more choices than the minimums in this plan could keep them. But there's a limit to what could be taken away. You listened to all these people talk today, you know, a lot of this stuff can be taken away from you that you think you have. All that we're doing is limiting what can be taken away.

Thank you very much. This has been great. I appreciate it.

NOTE: The President spoke at 12:17 p.m. at the Future Diner in Queens. A portion of the question-and-answer session could not be verified because the tape was incomplete.

Remarks at a Fundraiser for Mayor David Dinkins in New York City
September 26, 1993

The President. Mr. Mayor, Mrs. Dinkins, Senator Moynihan, Governor and Mrs. Cuomo, distinguished leaders of this magnificent city, other distinguished head table guests. You know, when I do a speech, because sometimes, as you will remember, I'm a little long-winded—[*laughter*]—my acute advisers always say, "Now, Mr. President, imagine what you want the headline to be." What is the headline? I think I've already heard the headline. The headline is the Mayor would very much like to have his job for 4 more years, and we ought to give it to him.

I always love to come to New York, but I certainly would have come here tonight just to listen to my Senate Finance Committee chair and your brilliant Governor and the Mayor give these speeches. And now I feel like I did the night I gave my first speech in public life, in January 1977, at the Pine Bluff Rotary banquet. It started at 6:30. There were 500 people there. Everybody in the whole place was introduced except three people; they went home mad, kind of like Dave did. And I got introduced at a quarter to 10, and the guy that was introducing me was the only person in the crowd more nervous than I was. And so everybody got awards and the whole deal had gone on, and the first words out of his mouth were, "You know, we could stop here and have had a very nice evening." [*Laughter*] And that's kind of how I feel. It is wonderful to be back in New York, wonderful to be here with all of you, and wonderful to be here on behalf of Mayor Dinkins.

I do want to thank publicly in this city, I think for the first time I've had a chance to do it, Mario Cuomo for giving the finest speech at the 1992 Democratic Convention nominating me for President. And I want to thank——

[*At this point, there was a disturbance in the audience.*]

The President. You know—let them go.

Audience members. Four more years! Four more years! Four more years!

The President. Actually, I had something to say about that. It's too bad they're going to miss it.

I do want to thank Senator Moynihan. I want all of you to remember what he said tonight because he has done a magnificent job as the chairman of the Senate Finance Committee. And if it weren't for him, I wouldn't be here tonight, because if he hadn't crafted a budget we could pass with that great landslide in the Congress—[*laughter*]—I'd be home worrying about something else, and David Dinkins wouldn't want me here. So I thank you, Pat Moynihan, for doing a great job for New York.

There was a lot of talk here tonight about the Democrat Party, and I want to tell you that I'm a Democrat by heritage, by instinct, by conviction. But I also wanted to be a part of a party that could change this country and in the process, if necessary, change itself.

Franklin Roosevelt revolutionized this country by committing himself to bold, persistent experimentation in a time of change. And a lot of people up here can tell you that I'm going around all the time just asking people for new ideas. Reverend Jackson came to see me the other day, and I pulled him off in the corner and tried to pick his brain about some new things we could do to create jobs. I called Andrew Young in a distant land, which I—having a good time—and asked him to help me to convince America to have an expansionist view of trade and how it could be used to create jobs. I do that a lot, and I listen a lot, and I tell you, my friends, it is very important that tonight we be for David Dinkins, not for just all our yesterdays but most importantly for all our tomorrows. And just once in a while I forget what this business is all about and then something will happen in a flash of an eye and bring it all back home again.

You know, we passed the family leave law in Congress, and I signed it instead of vetoing it a few months ago. And I read a column the other day that said, "You know, the President is up there passing laws, the family leave law, the earned-income tax credit, what does that mean to ordinary people, people can't identify with it." Well, let me tell you what happened to me today. I got up this morning, and I went for my customary jog on Sunday morning, and when I came back to the White House I entered through the ground floor as I normally do, and I looked up and there was a family there touring the White House on Sunday morning, a very unusual occurrence. And the woman who was giving them the tour said, "Mr. President, this is a family with three children. One of these children is desperately ill and was in the Make-a-Wish Foundation, and her wish was to come to the White House for a tour and to see you." So I went over and I shook hands with the little girl, and I talked to her for quite a while and her sisters and her parents. And then I went up and I got ready to leave to come up here and went back to see them and was taking the picture, and as I walked off, that young girl's father grabbed me by the arm, and he said, "You know, my daughter may not make it, but I've had some very important time with her because of that family leave law. And if it hadn't passed, I couldn't have taken off work. They would have taken my job away from me.

And I want you to know what it has done."

And today the Mayor and I went to Queens with Claire Shulman and Tom Manton and Gary Ackerman and a number of the other Members of Congress who are here. And we listened to people talk about the changes that still need to come, talking about this is the United States; you know we're supposed to be the leader of the world. It's the end of the cold war. I'm going to go to the U.N. tomorrow and people will say there's America, the only superpower. America is not only the only superpower, it's got the third worst immunization rate in the Western Hemisphere and is the only major country that still can't figure out how to give affordable health care to all of its citizens. And I heard those stories today in Queens.

That may sound like rhetoric here at a speech tonight, but in that diner in Queens today, which I visited running in the Democratic primary in New York, there were people talking about their lives, their jobs, their businesses going broke. Why were they paying 3 and 4 times the national average for health insurance? Why did they lose their health insurance because they got sick? That's what they bought the health insurance for. And on and on and on. And it reminded me again of why we are in this business. We are here because we hope that if we work together and we work hard and we are smart, that somehow we can enable people to live up to the fullest of their God-given potential and rebuild this fragile American community of ours. That's why I ran for President, and that's why I came here for David Dinkins tonight.

Most of this has already been said, but I—you know, I left my speech over there. I'm just sort of talking from the heart tonight, and besides that, I'll be briefer if I do that. But I was thinking to myself on the way up here tonight—today—why do you really believe this man should be reelected? And there are basically three reasons I really believe it.

Number one, you've already heard, under very difficult circumstances he's made you a good Mayor, he has been a good Mayor. I have heard all these stories about New York's financial problems for years. All I know is under difficult circumstances, with no help from Washington, you have produced four budgets and improved your bond rating. And that counts for something.

I was so proud to hear you clap for something

that really to me is what government's all about, when the Mayor talked about leaving the libraries open 6 days a week. That's a big deal, and not very many cities do it.

He started a health care program, which is consistent with what we're trying to do in Washington, not only to provide coverage for people but to guarantee access to people who need it through public health clinics that give primary and preventive services, not just expensive emergency care when it's too late and people are already sick.

And anybody can talk tough about crime. And almost every American, I want to be clear about this, almost every American desperately now is worried about the insecurity of life, the fragility of life in all of our cities and our small towns and our rural areas. So I say this not against anybody else, but it is simply a fact that your Mayor, beginning with the man who is now my drug czar, who used to be your chief of police, started this community policing program to put more police on the street, in the neighborhood, knowing their friends and neighbors, to deploy them in a different and smarter way. And it is simply true that now for 2 years in a row, in the seven major categories the FBI keeps, New York is one of the few cities in America that has had a decline in the crime rate. That should be rewarded. Are you going to punish a person for producing the results you say you want?

So I say to you, I was always worried that I never would quite fit in modern politics, which is so much television and 30 seconds and sound bite and look macho, whether you are or not, and all that sort of stuff. I hired out to do things. And here's a guy who has done things. And I came up here to say well done. I think you ought to be rewarded.

The second thing I want to say to you is that the truth is that all of us who do a good job should not on that account alone be re-elected, because that's what you paid us to do. So if you do a good job, it really only counts if it's an indication that you'll do another one if you get another term. And that's why I liked all the energy he put out tonight. He plainly wants to do it all over again in the worst way, and that's important.

But secondly, I have reviewed the Mayor's ideas. He gave me a whole list of things today I could do to help New York fulfill its potential. This jobs program is a good program, and not only that, it is consistent with what we are doing in defense conversion, in technology policy, in developing community financing institutions, in working with Congressman Rangel for the empowerment zones to get capital, private capital, back into distressed areas. It will work. So you really want in the next 4 years to have someone who will be doing things that fit with what's happening in Washington. Otherwise why did you vote for me in the first place if I can't help you?

And the last thing I'd like to say is I think you ought to vote for him because he really does believe that we have to find strength and peace and harmony in our diversity, that we cannot become what we ought to be by being divided against one another. And I think that is maybe the most important thing of all.

This has been 2 incredible weeks for me. I'm going to the U.N. tomorrow; you know, it's a bookend of that incredible day, Monday 2 weeks ago, when Yitzhak Rabin and Yasser Arafat shook hands and riveted the world. And I ask you, think of it: If after all the decades of fighting each other they finally came to the conclusion that peace in their land that they love and a normal, decent future for the children of their people required them to seek some harmony, some accommodation, some working together, and when they shook hands it was so electric that no one in the world thought that that was an act of weakness, it was instead an act of strength. Can we not learn this lesson in our multiethnic cities? Can we not see that across the lines of race and religion, those people who believe in family, those people who believe in work, those people who believe in putting their children first, those people who never violate the law and always pay their taxes and always show up for the basic things in life, have more in common than they do separating themselves, and they have to learn to vote across their racial lines, to vote across their religious lines, to reach out and make alliances that will enable us to live together. If you want to deal with the crime problems, and I do; if you want to pass a bill making illegal assault weapons so they don't get in the hands of teenagers, and I do; if you want to pass this health care reform bill and make it a right for all Americans, that can never be taken away and I do; don't we have to begin by getting the family of this country together, the people who have the same values and have the same hopes for their children and say we can do this together?

You know, let's be candid. All the way up here, I said to myself, why has Dinkins got a race? I'm going to get in a lot of trouble for saying this. I read the record, and then I actually read some of his position papers, something I bet you haven't done, some of you. [*Laughter*] And I thought about how it would fit. I know him personally inside, and I said, why has this guy got a hard race?

Let's face it. There are two reasons, I think. One is he doesn't give enough speeches like the one he gave here tonight, because he is a humble man in an age that values self-promotion. Right? Because he is a quietly tough man in an age that values loud and piercing rhetoric, and to be fair, it is sometimes necessary because so many of us are caught in the blur of events and the frustration of our times. It is a style thing, folks. Don't get the style confused with the substance. He's got the substance.

And the second reason is that too many of us are still too unwilling to vote for people who are different than we are. This is not as simple as overt racism. That is not anything I would charge to anybody who doesn't vote for David Dinkins or Bill Clinton or anybody else. It's not that simple. It is this deep-seated reluctance we have, against all our better judgment, to reach out across these lines. It is not as simple as overt racism. It's this inability to take that sort of leap of faith, to believe that people who look different than we are really are more like us than some people who look just like us but don't share our values or our interests or our conduct.

This is a big deal to me. I would not be here tonight; I would never have been reelected Governor of Arkansas in 1982; I would not have been elected President of the United States through all those tough primaries if it hadn't

been for African-American and Hispanic voters and Asians voters, people who were different from me, voting for me. I wouldn't be here.

So I read in the paper about the demographics of the Dinkins vote. And there will be some differences just because people think differently ideologically. But I want to remind you that David Dinkins, as was reminded to me tonight, when the Scud missiles were falling on Israel, went to Israel. He wants to represent all the people of New York.

Look who he had introduce him and be a part of this program tonight. This a big deal, folks. This is not just New York; this is L.A., and this is rural South. This is everyplace. We are being tested. We are going through a time of profound change. And we right now don't have the sense of personal security to make the changes we need to make. We need more confidence in ourselves and confidence that we can meet all these challenges that are out there and confidence that the 21st century will also be an American century. And in order to do it, we have to get our act together so we can feel good about the people we elect. We have to make our streets safer, our families stronger. We have to make all these economic changes, but we first must be more secure.

I ask you, think about the handshake between Rabin and Arafat. Think about what it means for the future of the Middle East if we can keep it going. And then ask yourselves, this man who has a good record, who has a good plan, who has a good heart, has earned the right to your vote, and you ought to make sure he gets it and is returned to city hall.

Thank you, and God bless you.

NOTE: The President spoke at 9:55 p.m. at the Sheraton New York Hotel. In his remarks, he referred to Claire Shulman, president of the Borough of Queens.

Message to the Congress on the National Emergency With Respect to UNITA
September 26, 1993

To the Congress of the United States:

Pursuant to section 204(b) of the International Emergency Economic Powers Act, 50 U.S.C.

section 1703(b), and section 301 of the National Emergencies Act, 50 U.S.C. section 1631, I hereby report that I have exercised my statutory authority to declare a national emergency with respect to the actions and policies of the National Union for the Total Independence of Angola ("UNITA") and to issue an Executive order prohibiting the sale or supply to Angola, other than through designated points of entry, or to UNITA, of arms and related materiel and petroleum and petroleum products, regardless of their origin, and activities that promote or are calculated to promote such sale or supply. These actions are mandated in part by United Nations Security Council Resolution No. 864 of September 15, 1993.

The Secretary of the Treasury is authorized to issue regulations in exercise of my authorities under the International Emergency Economic Powers Act and the United Nations Participation Act, 22 U.S.C. section 287c, to implement these prohibitions. All Federal agencies are also directed to take actions within their authority to carry out the provisions of the Executive order.

I am enclosing a copy of the Executive order that I have issued. The order was effective immediately upon its signature on September 26, 1993.

I have authorized these measures in response to the actions and policies of UNITA in continuing military actions, repeated attempts to seize additional territory, and failure to withdraw its troops from the locations that it has occupied since the resumption of hostilities, in repeatedly attacking United Nations personnel working to provide humanitarian assistance, in holding foreign nationals against their will, in refusing to accept the results of the democratic elections held in Angola in 1992, and in failing to abide by the "Acordos de Paz." The actions of UNITA constitute an unusual and extraordinary threat to the foreign policy of the United States.

On September 15, 1993, the United Nations Security Council adopted Resolution No. 864, condemning the activities of UNITA and demanding that UNITA accept unreservedly the results of the democratic election of September 30, 1992, and abide fully by the "Acordos de Paz." The resolution decides that all states are required to prevent the sale or supply of arms and related materiel and petroleum and petroleum products to Angola, other than through named points of entry specified by the Government of Angola. The measures we are taking express our outrage at UNITA's continuing hostilities and failure to abide by the outcome of Angola's democratic election.

WILLIAM J. CLINTON

The White House,
September 26, 1993.

NOTE: This message was released by the Office of the Press Secretary on September 27. The Executive order is listed in Appendix D at the end of this volume.

Remarks to the 48th Session of the United Nations General Assembly in New York City
September 27, 1993

Thank you very much. Mr. President, let me first congratulate you on your election as President of this General Assembly. Mr. Secretary-General, distinguished delegates and guests, it is a great honor for me to address you and to stand in this great chamber which symbolizes so much of the 20th century: Its darkest crises and its brightest aspirations.

I come before you as the first American President born after the founding of the United Nations. Like most of the people in the world today, I was not even alive during the convulsive World War that convinced humankind of the need for this organization, nor during the San Francisco Conference that led to its birth. Yet I have followed the work of the United Nations throughout my life, with admiration for its accomplishments, with sadness for its failures, and conviction that through common effort our generation can take the bold steps needed to redeem the mission entrusted to the U.N. 48 years ago.

I pledge to you that my Nation remains committed to helping make the U.N.'s vision a reality. The start of this General Assembly offers us an opportunity to take stock of where we are, as common shareholders in the progress of humankind and in the preservation of our planet.

It is clear that we live at a turning point in human history. Immense and promising changes seem to wash over us every day. The cold war is over. The world is no longer divided into two armed and angry camps. Dozens of new democracies have been born. It is a moment of miracles. We see Nelson Mandela stand side by side with President de Klerk, proclaiming a date for South Africa's first nonracial election. We see Russia's first popularly elected President, Boris Yeltsin, leading his nation on its bold democratic journey. We have seen decades of deadlock shattered in the Middle East, as the Prime Minister of Israel and the Chairman of the Palestine Liberation Organization reached past enmity and suspicion to shake each other's hands and exhilarate the entire world with the hope of peace.

We have begun to see the doomsday welcome of nuclear annihilation dismantled and destroyed. Thirty-two years ago, President Kennedy warned this chamber that humanity lived under a nuclear sword of Damocles that hung by the slenderest of threads. Now the United States is working with Russia, Ukraine, Belarus, and others to take that sword down, to lock it away in a secure vault where we hope and pray it will remain forever.

It is a new era in this hall as well. The superpower standoff that for so long stymied the United Nations work almost from its first day has now yielded to a new promise of practical cooperation. Yet today we must all admit that there are two powerful tendencies working from opposite directions to challenge the authority of nation states everywhere and to undermine the authority of nation states to work together.

From beyond nations, economic and technological forces all over the globe are compelling the world towards integration. These forces are fueling a welcome explosion of entrepreneurship and political liberalization. But they also threaten to destroy the insularity and independence of national economies, quickening the pace of change and making many of our people feel more insecure. At the same time, from within nations, the resurgent aspirations of ethnic and religious groups challenge governments on terms that traditional nation states cannot easily accommodate.

These twin forces lie at the heart of the challenges not only to our National Government but also to all our international institutions. They require all of us in this room to find new ways to work together more effectively in pursuit of our national interests and to think anew about whether our institutions of international cooperation are adequate to this moment.

Thus, as we marvel at this era's promise of new peace, we must also recognize that serious threats remain. Bloody ethnic, religious, and civil wars rage from Angola to the Caucasus to Kashmir. As weapons of mass destruction fall into more hands, even small conflicts can threaten to take on murderous proportions. Hunger and disease continue to take a tragic toll, especially among the world's children. The malignant neglect of our global environment threatens our children's health and their very security.

The repression of conscience continues in too many nations. And terrorism, which has taken so many innocent lives, assumes a horrifying immediacy for us here when militant fanatics bombed the World Trade Center and planned to attack even this very hall of peace. Let me assure you, whether the fathers of those crimes or the mass murderers who bombed Pan Am Flight 103, my Government is determined to see that such terrorists are brought to justice.

At this moment of panoramic change, of vast opportunities and troubling threats, we must all ask ourselves what we can do and what we should do as a community of nations. We must once again dare to dream of what might be, for our dreams may be within our reach. For that to happen, we must all be willing to honestly confront the challenges of the broader world. That has never been easy.

When this organization was founded 48 years ago, the world's nations stood devastated by war or exhausted by its expense. There was little appetite for cooperative efforts among nations. Most people simply wanted to get on with their lives. But a farsighted generation of leaders from the United States and elsewhere rallied the world. Their efforts built the institutions of postwar security and prosperity.

We are at a similar moment today. The momentum of the cold war no longer propels us in our daily actions. And with daunting economic and political pressures upon almost every nation represented in this room, many of us are turning to focus greater attention and energy on our domestic needs and problems, and we must. But putting each of our economic houses in order cannot mean that we shut our windows to the world. The pursuit of self-renewal, in many of the world's largest and most powerful economies, in Europe, in Japan, in North America, is absolutely crucial because unless the great industrial nations can recapture their robust economic growth, the global economy will languish.

Yet, the industrial nations also need growth elsewhere in order to lift their own. Indeed, prosperity in each of our nations and regions also depends upon active and responsible engagement in a host of shared concerns. For example, a thriving and democratic Russia not only makes the world safer, it also can help to expand the world's economy. A strong GATT agreement will create millions of jobs worldwide. Peace in the Middle East, buttressed as it should be by the repeal of outdated U.N. resolutions, can help to unleash that region's great economic potential and calm a perpetual source of tension in global affairs. And the growing economic power of China, coupled with greater political openness, could bring enormous benefits to all of Asia and to the rest of the world.

We must help our publics to understand this distinction: Domestic renewal is an overdue tonic, but isolationism and protectionism are still poison. We must inspire our people to look beyond their immediate fears toward a broader horizon.

Let me start by being clear about where the United States stands. The United States occupies a unique position in world affairs today. We recognize that, and we welcome it. Yet, with the cold war over, I know many people ask whether the United States plans to retreat or remain active in the world and, if active, to what end. Many people are asking that in our own country as well. Let me answer that question as clearly and plainly as I can. The United States intends to remain engaged and to lead. We cannot solve every problem, but we must and will serve as a fulcrum for change and a pivot point for peace.

In a new era of peril and opportunity, our overriding purpose must be to expand and strengthen the world's community of market-based democracies. During the cold war we sought to contain a threat to the survival of free institutions. Now we seek to enlarge the circle of nations that live under those free institutions. For our dream is of a day when the opinions and energies of every person in the world will be given full expression, in a world of thriving democracies that cooperate with each other and live in peace.

With this statement, I do not mean to announce some crusade to force our way of life and doing things on others or to replicate our institutions, but we now know clearly that throughout the world, from Poland to Eritrea, from Guatemala to South Korea, there is an enormous yearning among people who wish to be the masters of their own economic and political lives. Where it matters most and where we can make the greatest difference, we will, therefore, patiently and firmly align ourselves with that yearning.

Today, there are still those who claim that democracy is simply not applicable to many cultures, and that its recent expansion is an aberration, an accident in history that will soon fade away. But I agree with President Roosevelt, who once said, "The democratic aspiration is no mere recent phase of human history. It is human history."

We will work to strengthen the free market democracies by revitalizing our economy here at home, by opening world trade through the GATT, the North American Free Trade Agreement and other accords, and by updating our shared institutions, asking with you and answering the hard questions about whether they are adequate to the present challenges.

We will support the consolidation of market democracy where it is taking new root, as in the states of the former Soviet Union and all over Latin America. And we seek to foster the practices of good government that distribute the benefits of democracy and economic growth fairly to all people.

We will work to reduce the threat from regimes that are hostile to democracies and to support liberalization of nondemocratic states when they are willing to live in peace with the rest of us.

As a country that has over 150 different racial, ethnic and religious groups within our borders, our policy is and must be rooted in a profound respect for all the world's religions and cultures. But we must oppose everywhere extremism that produces terrorism and hate. And we must pursue our humanitarian goal of reducing suffering, fostering sustainable development, and improving the health and living conditions, particularly for our world's children.

On efforts from export control to trade agreements to peacekeeping, we will often work in partnership with others and through multilateral institutions such as the United Nations. It is in our national interest to do so. But we must not hesitate to act unilaterally when there is a threat to our core interests or to those of our allies.

The United States believes that an expanded community of market democracies not only serves our own security interests, it also advances the goals enshrined in this body's Charter and its Universal Declaration of Human Rights. For broadly based prosperity is clearly the strongest form of preventive diplomacy. And the habits of democracy are the habits of peace.

Democracy is rooted in compromise, not conquest. It rewards tolerance, not hatred. Democracies rarely wage war on one another. They make more reliable partners in trade, in diplomacy, and in the stewardship of our global environment. In democracies with the rule of law and respect for political, religious, and cultural minorities are more responsive to their own people and to the protection of human rights.

But as we work toward this vision we must confront the storm clouds that may overwhelm our work and darken the march toward freedom. If we do not stem the proliferation of the world's deadliest weapons, no democracy can feel secure. If we do not strengthen the capacity to resolve conflict among and within nations, those conflicts will smother the birth of free institutions, threaten the development of entire regions, and continue to take innocent lives. If we do not nurture our people and our planet through sustainable development, we will deepen conflict and waste the very wonders that make our efforts worth doing.

Let me talk more about what I believe we must do in each of these three categories: nonproliferation, conflict resolution, and sustainable development.

One of our most urgent priorities must be attacking the proliferation of weapons of mass destruction, whether they are nuclear, chemical, or biological, and the ballistic missiles that can rain them down on populations hundreds of miles away. We know this is not an idle problem. All of us are still haunted by the pictures of Kurdish women and children cut down by poison gas. We saw Scud missiles dropped during the Gulf war that would have been far graver in their consequence if they had carried nuclear weapons. And we know that many nations still believe it is in their interest to develop weapons of mass destruction or to sell them or the necessary technologies to others for financial gain.

More than a score of nations likely possess such weapons, and their number threatens to grow. These weapons destabilize entire regions. They could turn a local conflict into a global human and environmental catastrophe. We simply have got to find ways to control these weapons and to reduce the number of states that possess them by supporting and strengthening the IAEA and by taking other necessary measures.

I have made nonproliferation one of our Nation's highest priorities. We intend to weave it more deeply into the fabric of all of our relationships with the world's nations and institutions. We seek to build a world of increasing pressures for nonproliferation but increasingly open trade and technology for those states that live by accepted international rules.

Today, let me describe several new policies that our Government will pursue to stem proliferation. We will pursue new steps to control the materials for nuclear weapons. Growing global stockpiles of plutonium and highly enriched uranium are raising the danger of nuclear terrorism for all nations. We will press for an international agreement that would ban production of these materials for weapons forever.

As we reduce our nuclear stockpiles, the United States has also begun negotiations toward a comprehensive ban on nuclear testing. This summer I declared that to facilitate these negotiations, our Nation would suspend our testing if all other nuclear states would do the same. Today, in the face of disturbing signs, I renew my call on the nuclear states to abide by that moratorium as we negotiate to stop nuclear testing for all time.

I am also proposing new efforts to fight the proliferation of biological and chemical weapons. Today, only a handful of nations has ratified the Chemical Weapons Convention. I call on all nations, including my own, to ratify this accord quickly so that it may enter into force by January 13th, 1995. We will also seek to strengthen the biological weapons convention by making every nation's biological activities and facilities open to more international students.

I am proposing as well new steps to thwart the proliferation of ballistic missiles. Recently, working with Russia, Argentina, Hungary, and South Africa, we have made significant progress toward that goal. Now, we will seek to strengthen the principles of the missile technology control regime by transforming it from an agreement on technology transfer among just 23 nations to a set of rules that can command universal adherence.

We will also reform our own system of export controls in the United States to reflect the realities of the post-cold-war world, where we seek to enlist the support of our former adversaries in the battle against proliferation.

At the same time that we stop deadly technologies from falling into the wrong hands, we will work with our partners to remove outdated controls that unfairly burden legitimate commerce and unduly restrain growth and opportunity all over the world.

As we work to keep the world's most destructive weapons out of conflict, we must also strengthen the international community's ability to address those conflicts themselves. For as we all now know so painfully, the end of the cold war did not bring us to the millennium of peace. And indeed, it simply removed the lid from many cauldrons of ethnic, religious, and territorial animosity.

The philosopher, Isaiah Berlin, has said that a wounded nationalism is like a bent twig forced down so severely that when released, it lashes back with fury. The world today is thick with both bent and recoiling twigs of wounded communal identities.

This scourge of bitter conflict has placed high demands on United Nations peacekeeping forces. Frequently the blue helmets have worked wonders. In Namibia, El Salvador, the Golan Heights, and elsewhere, U.N. peacekeepers have helped to stop the fighting, restore civil authority, and enable free elections.

In Bosnia, U.N. peacekeepers, against the danger and frustration of that continuing tragedy, have maintained a valiant humanitarian effort. And if the parties of that conflict take the hard steps needed to make a real peace, the international community including the United States must be ready to help in its effective implementation.

In Somalia, the United States and the United Nations have worked together to achieve a stunning humanitarian rescue, saving literally hundreds of thousands of lives and restoring the conditions of security for almost the entire country. U.N. peacekeepers from over two dozen nations remain in Somalia today. And some, including brave Americans, have lost their lives to ensure that we complete our mission and to ensure that anarchy and starvation do not return just as quickly as they were abolished.

Many still criticize U.N. peacekeeping, but those who do should talk to the people of Cambodia, where the U.N.'s operations have helped to turn the killing fields into fertile soil through reconciliation. Last May's elections in Cambodia marked a proud accomplishment for that war-weary nation and for the United Nations. And I am pleased to announce that the United States has recognized Cambodia's new government.

U.N. peacekeeping holds the promise to resolve many of this era's conflicts. The reason we have supported such missions is not, as some critics in the United States have charged, to subcontract American foreign policy but to strengthen our security, protect our interests, and to share among nations the costs and effort of pursuing peace. Peacekeeping cannot be a substitute for our own national defense efforts, but it can strongly supplement them.

Today, there is wide recognition that the U.N. peacekeeping ability has not kept pace with the rising responsibilities and challenges. Just 6 years ago, about 10,000 U.N. peacekeepers were stationed around the world. Today, the U.N. has some 80,000 deployed in 17 operations on 4 continents. Yet until recently, if a peacekeeping commander called in from across the globe when it was nighttime here in New York, there was no one in the peacekeeping office even to answer the call. When lives are on the line, you cannot let the reach of the U.N. exceed its grasp.

As the Secretary-General and others have argued, if U.N. peacekeeping is to be a sound security investment for our nation and for other U.N. members, it must adapt to new times. Together we must prepare U.N. peacekeeping for the 21st century. We need to begin by bringing the rigors of military and political analysis to every U.N. peace mission.

In recent weeks in the Security Council, our Nation has begun asking harder questions about proposals for new peacekeeping missions: Is there a real threat to international peace? Does the proposed mission have clear objectives? Can an end point be identified for those who will be asked to participate? How much will the mission cost? From now on, the United Nations should address these and other hard questions for every proposed mission before we vote and before the mission begins.

The United Nations simply cannot become engaged in every one of the world's conflicts. If the American people are to say yes to U.N. peacekeeping, the United Nations must know when to say no. The United Nations must also have the technical means to run a modern world-class peacekeeping operation. We support the creation of a genuine U.N. peacekeeping headquarters with a planning staff, with access to timely intelligence, with a logistics unit that can be deployed on a moment's notice, and a modern operations center with global communications.

And the U.N.'s operations must not only be adequately funded but also fairly funded. Within the next few weeks, the United States will be current in our peacekeeping bills. I have worked hard with the Congress to get this done. I believe the United States should lead the way in being timely in its payments, and I will work to continue to see that we pay our bills in full. But I am also committed to work with the United Nations to reduce our Nation's assessment for these missions.

The assessment system has not been changed since 1973. And everyone in our country knows that our percentage of the world's economic pie is not as great as it was then. Therefore, I believe our rates should be reduced to reflect the rise of other nations that can now bear more of the financial burden. That will make it easier for me as President to make sure we pay in a timely and full fashion.

Changes in the U.N.'s peacekeeping operations must be part of an even broader program of United Nations reform. I say that again not to criticize the United Nations but to help to improve it. As our Ambassador Madeleine Albright has suggested, the United States has always played a twin role to the U.N., first friend and first critic.

Today corporations all around the world are finding ways to move from the Industrial Age to the Information Age, improving service, reducing bureaucracy, and cutting costs. Here in the United States, our Vice President Al Gore and I have launched an effort to literally reinvent how our Government operates. We see this going on in other governments around the world. Now the time has come to reinvent the way the United Nations operates as well.

I applaud the initial steps the Secretary-General has taken to reduce and to reform the Unit-

ed Nations bureaucracy. Now, we must all do even more to root out waste. Before this General Assembly is over, let us establish a strong mandate for an Office of Inspector General so that it can attain a reputation for toughness, for integrity, for effectiveness. Let us build new confidence among our people that the United Nations is changing with the needs of our times.

Ultimately, the key for reforming the United Nations, as in reforming our own Government, is to remember why we are here and whom we serve. It is wise to recall that the first words of the U.N. Charter are not "We, the government," but, "We, the people of the United Nations." That means in every country the teachers, the workers, the farmers, the professionals, the fathers, the mothers, the children, from the most remote village in the world to the largest metropolis, they are why we gather in this great hall. It is their futures that are at risk when we act or fail to act, and it is they who ultimately pay our bills.

As we dream new dreams in this age when miracles now seem possible, let us focus on the lives of those people, and especially on the children who will inherit this world. Let us work with a new urgency, and imagine what kind of world we could create for them over the coming generations.

Let us work with new energy to protect the world's people from torture and repression. As Secretary of State Christopher stressed at the recent Vienna conference, human rights are not something conditional, founded by culture, but rather something universal granted by God. This General Assembly should create, at long last, a high commissioner for human rights. I hope you will do it soon and with vigor and energy and conviction.

Let us also work far more ambitiously to fulfill our obligations as custodians of this planet, not only to improve the quality of life for our citizens and the quality of our air and water and the Earth itself but also because the roots of conflict are so often entangled with the roots of environmental neglect and the calamity of famine and disease.

During the course of our campaign in the United States last year, Vice President Gore and I promised the American people major changes in our Nation's policy toward the global environment. Those were promises to keep, and today the United States is doing so. Today we are working with other nations to build on the promising work of the U.N.'s Commission on Sustainable Development. We are working to make sure that all nations meet their commitments under the Global Climate Convention. We are seeking to complete negotiations on an accord to prevent the world's deserts from further expansion. And we seek to strengthen the World's Health Organization's efforts to combat the plague of AIDS, which is not only killing millions but also exhausting the resources of nations that can least afford it.

Let us make a new commitment to the world's children. It is tragic enough that 1.5 million children died as a result of wars over the past decade. But it is far more unforgivable that during that same period, 40 million children died from diseases completely preventable with simply vaccines or medicine. Every day, this day, as we meet here, over 30,000 of the world's children will die of malnutrition and disease.

Our UNICEF Director, Jim Grant, has reminded me that each of those children had a name and a nationality, a family, a personality, and a potential. We are compelled to do better by the world's children. Just as our own Nation has launched new reforms to ensure that every child has adequate health care, we must do more to get basic vaccines and other treatment for curable diseases to children all over the world. It's the best investment we'll ever make.

We can find new ways to ensure that every child grows up with clean drinkable water, that most precious commodity of life itself. And the U.N. can work even harder to ensure that each child has at least a full primary education, and I mean that opportunity for girls as well as boys.

And to ensure a healthier and more abundant world, we simply must slow the world's explosive growth in population. We cannot afford to see the human waste doubled by the middle of the next century. Our Nation has, at last, renewed its commitment to work with the United Nations to expand the availability of the world's family planning education and services. We must ensure that there is a place at the table for every one of our world's children. And we can do it.

At the birth of this organization 48 years ago, another time of both victory and danger, a generation of gifted leaders from many nations stepped forward to organize the world's efforts on behalf of security and prosperity. One American leader during that period said this: It is time we steered by the stars rather than by the light of each passing ship. His generation picked peace, human dignity, and freedom. Those are good stars; they should remain the highest in our own firmament.

Now history has granted to us a moment of even greater opportunity, when old dangers are ebbing and old walls are crumbling, future generations will judge us, every one of us, above all, by what we make of this magic moment. Let us resolve that we will dream larger, that we will work harder so that they can conclude that we did not merely turn walls to rubble but instead laid the foundation for great things to come.

Let us ensure that the tide of freedom and democracy is not pushed back by the fierce winds of ethnic hatred. Let us ensure that the world's most dangerous weapons are safely reduced and denied to dangerous hands. Let us ensure that the world we pass to our children is healthier, safer, and more abundant than the one we inhabit today.

I believe—I know that together we can extend this moment of miracles into an age of great work and new wonders.

Thank you very much.

NOTE: The President spoke at 11 a.m. in the General Assembly Hall.

Remarks at a United Nations Luncheon in New York City
September 27, 1993

[*Inaudible*]—of all the heads of state here, we thank you for your warm and eloquent words, for your gentle urging to us to do better by the United Nations, and for the hospitality and vision which you have brought to your work.

We have seen so many changes in the world in the last few years, indeed in the last few weeks. I saw the Foreign Minister of Israel here and could not help remembering again the magic ceremony on the South Lawn of the White House 2 weeks ago today and the handshake that electrified the world.

Seven months from today, black and white South Africans will join in casting their votes for a genuine multiracial democracy and a new future for that long-troubled land. New possibilities for peace and progress unfold almost daily. And the United Nations will clearly play a central role in confronting the challenges and seizing the opportunities of this new era.

Eleanor Roosevelt, a First Lady of ours who once played a vital role in the birth of the United Nations, described the United Nations as a bridge, a bridge that could join different people despite their differences. Today, the traffic across that bridge is brisk and crowded indeed. As with our own Nation and Russia, peoples who once rarely met each other halfway, now increasingly join to walk across that bridge shoulder-to-shoulder, joined in common efforts to solve common problems.

As this grand bridge reaches nearly half a century in age, we need to modernize and strengthen it, but let us not lose sight of how dramatically the view from that bridge has improved. We can see new possibilities for conflict resolution. We can look toward new breakthroughs and the efforts to make progress against humankind's oldest problems: poverty, hunger, and disease. We can envision an era of increasing peace.

Those are the sights which have driven the U.N.'s vision since its creation. Today, I suggest that we all raise our glass in a toast to make those visions new and real.

NOTE: The President spoke at 2:23 p.m. at the United Nations.

The President's News Conference With Prime Minister Morihiro Hosokawa of Japan in New York City
September 27, 1993

The President. Good afternoon. This has been an exceptional day, and both the Prime Minister and I had the honor to speak before the 48th General Assembly of the United Nations at the dawn of a new era. I'm especially pleased to have had the opportunity today to have a good conversation with Prime Minister Hosokawa. We've just renewed our acquaintance and discussed many of the issues of great importance to both our nations. I look forward to working with him in the months ahead to make sure that the issues that we're working on together bear fruit.

I want to begin by saying that I feel a great deal of respect and affinity for the Prime Minister. We are both former Governors. We were both elected by our countries with a mandate for change. Our two peoples recognized instinctively that we've entered a watershed period in our history, when both Japan and the United States must make changes that are long overdue.

My meeting with the Prime Minister persuaded me that he is indeed, as he said in his campaign, committed to change for the benefit of his people. And I hope that the changes he brings to Japan can help to redefine the relationships between our two countries in ways that improve the economic difficulties which we have had but strengthen the longstanding security and political relationships which have brought peace and security to the entire Pacific region.

The meeting that we had offered me the opportunity to reiterate my commitment for that relationship and to explore a lot of the issues that we are both concerned about. We pledged to cooperate on a whole range of global issues, especially including the Middle East peace agreement, and I thanked the Prime Minister for the announcement he made in his speech today of aid from Japan to implement that agreement.

We also shared a common sense of urgency to successfully complete the Uruguay round of GATT by December 15th. And I look forward to welcoming the Prime Minister to Seattle later this fall when we will gather to promote Asian economic integration through the APEC meeting that the United States will host.

We discussed in particular the area of U.S.-

Japan relations in need of most progress, our economic relationship. We have the largest bilateral economic relationship in the world, with our two nations representing about 40 percent of the world's GDP. It is critical in this new era that we get that relationship right. We must make significant progress regarding our bilateral trade.

At the Tokyo summit last July, the United States and Japan agreed to a framework for negotiation intended to reduce barriers to trade. Those negotiations began last week. The Prime Minister and I today reaffirmed our commitment to reach agreements as provided under the framework, which will open new trading opportunities for both our nations.

I also expressed my support for Japan's recently announced economic stimulus program. I believe it is a beneficial step. And we also discussed other things that we could do to promote greater growth in the global economy.

I was heartened by our meeting. I look forward to working with the Prime Minister in the weeks and months ahead. I'm very grateful by the enormous outpouring of popular support for the reform efforts he was undertaken in Japan. And I hope that both he and the people of Japan will be successful in their efforts at reform, change, and progress.

Mr. Prime Minister.

Prime Minister Hosokawa. Our time was very limited, but I'm very happy we were able to have a very candid meeting. At the very same juncture in history, both of us have taken on the front stage, one as President and one as Prime Minister. I believe this is not a coincidence but a necessity in history.

The President is faced with difficult tasks and exercising leadership. And I said I very much identify with him, in Japan what my Cabinet's trying to do. I explained to him what the historic mission for my cabinet is. Before anything else, we must carry through the structural reform of the systems in Japan. One is political reform, second is economic reform, and third is administrative reform. And I explained the contents of each of these, the contents of political, economic, and administrative reforms. We believe that reform in these areas will benefit not only just the Japanese but will also generate opportunities for the world as a whole. That should be beneficial for the entire world community.

On basic relations between Japan and the United States, we shall steadfastly maintain the Japan-U.S. security relationship and nurture our political as well as economic relationship as well as a global relationship affirmly. We reaffirmed that intent on both sides.

We had discussions on the economic aspects of our relationship. In July we struck that framework agreement, and in accordance with that agreement, I stated that Japan will play its part in doing its best. Also, we expressed our mutual hope, and the Japanese Government will do its best so that favorable results will emerge before the end of the year, as much as possible, for the Uruguay round.

We also discussed Russia, China, the Middle East. We also discussed North Korea. Our discussions were broad-ranging, indeed, and on each of these subjects we were able to delve into pretty much detail.

At risk of repeating myself, for the time being, our economic relationship is most important, and to improve our relations in the benefit of the world economic development is our common task, I believe. What we are trying to do should be indispensable for the development and prosperity of the United States, as well as the world. Both countries should cooperate with each other in order to open up bright prospects for both of us. And if that is done, that is beyond what I would hope for.

Thank you very much.

Bosnia and the War Powers Act

Q. [Inaudible]—what form might that agreement take and would it just be consultation of the leadership or a vote in the Congress? And could you, as a former law professor, say what you think the differences are in your view of the War Powers Act as contrasted with your predecessor, President Bush, and his predecessor, President Reagan?

The President. I feel like I've just been given an exam in law school. Let me say that I think it is clear to everyone that the United States could not fulfill a peacekeeping role in Bosnia unless the Congress supported it. And I will be consulting with all the appropriate congressional leadership in both parties to see what the best manifestation of that is.

With regard to the War Powers Act, I don't want to get into a long constitutional description of it. I had always intended to comply with it based on our best understanding of it, and I think we won't have any problem doing that. I don't believe Congress will feel that they're not being properly consulted.

In the interest of partnership, I'd like to just alternate across the aisle, take one question from a Japanese journalist and then come back to the Americans.

Japanese Government

Q. Mr. President, in the course of a few months you have dealt with two Japanese Prime Ministers representing two governments. What difference between the two Japanese leaders and the two governments in terms of how they respond to your expectations and concern for the outstanding economic issues between the two countries?

The President. How can I answer that question without getting in trouble in Japan? [*Laughter*] Let me just say that I think the real issue is that Prime Minister Hosokawa's government represents obviously a recent and fresh judgment of the people of Japan about changes in Japanese political and economic life.

I frankly, had a good relationship with the previous government. Given the fact that there was no mandate in that government for the kinds of changes that the Prime Minister and others agreed to in July, I think they thought that Japan had to take a new course.

Now, we have a government headed by a Prime Minister who himself came from a grassroots political job—he was a governor, as I was—with a mandate for change and enormous public support for that. So I think that we will be able to work together in a very constructive way over the long haul because of that mandate.

That's no criticism of the previous government. I enjoyed working with Prime Minister Miyazawa very much, and I admire him greatly. But I think having the people of Japan make a decision in an election that elevates someone who has committed himself to change and then gotten elected on that platform makes a big difference. It gives him more elbow room and a greater sense of commitment, I think.

Somalia

Q. In light of your comments today, your speech, can you give us a sense of whether you believe the right questions were asked before the United States went into Somalia and what you see as a situation that needs to occur before we can get out?

The President. I still believe—let me reiterate—I still believe President Bush made the

right decision to have the United States lead a U.N. mission in Somalia. Keep in mind, well over a quarter of a million people had died there from starvation, from murder, from illness, from famine. And there's no telling how many lives have been saved as a result of that humanitarian mission.

Because Somalia was viewed as a place where the political structure had basically disintegrated and power was broadly shared or fought over among a variety of clans with two dominant figures, I think the focus was very much on whether that could be controlled with a large number of troops, most of which were American in the beginning. And I think perhaps too little thought was given to the long-term need to develop some political alternative.

Although I do want to emphasize, in defense of the United Nations, that a lot of village councils have been developed, that a lot of Somalia is now being, in effect, governed peacefully by grassroots political organizations, that when we see the violence and the anger and the anti-U.N., anti-American expressions on television at night, that reflects a small percentage of the people in the land of Somalia. The mission has largely succeeded in its humanitarian efforts. But I think the political component of it, that is, how we end the humanitarian mission or at least turn over the political responsibility to the people of Somalia, has lagged a bit.

And so the United States wants there to be a clear commitment to the political transformation. And we want to do it in ways that make it absolutely clear we have no intention of abandoning all those people to the fate that gripped them before we got there.

I don't think when a tragedy occurs and people see on television in the United States a few Somalis jumping up and down when an American has been killed, I think it is a misrepresentation to conclude that that reflects the opinion of a majority of the people. Most Somalis are living in peace, are living in harmony, are working at reestablishing a normal life, and are not involved in what you see.

But nonetheless, it is clear that the U.N. must have a political strategy which permits us to withdraw but not to withdraw on terms that revert the people to the condition they were living in beforehand.

Japanese Economy

Q. [*Inaudible*]—did you discuss with the

Prime Minister—[*inaudible*]

The President. We did. We discussed—well, we discussed the stimulus program Japan has undertaken as well as the review the Prime Minister has ordered of what other options are available over the long run. Perhaps he would like to comment on that.

Do you have anything to say, Prime Minister Hosokawa? He's a very good politician, you see; he's staying out of all these hard questions. That's why his popularity is so high in Japan. [*Laughter*]

U.N. Peacekeeping Missions

Q. A two-part question, I wonder if you could clarify a couple things. One on Bosnia. There have been a lot of leaks lately from your administration about the conditions under which you would commit American troops to Bosnia, from exit strategies to congressional approval. I wonder if you could state from here today exactly what are the criteria you envisage for an American commitment there to a peacekeeping operation.

Then a second part, following up on your speech today, you implied in that speech that the U.N. is engaged in some peacekeeping operations now that maybe are of marginal significance. I wonder if you could specify exactly what operations are not that important and what should be the criteria for U.N. operations in the future?

The President. I wouldn't say that. I would say that there are—plainly we have gone so far so fast in peacekeeping through the U.N. that there are limits to how many new operations can be undertaken.

For example, there is no question that the United Nations could not directly manage an operation the size of the Bosnian operation, which is why we worked so hard through NATO, and the French have been involved there and others, to try to think through how we would do this.

Most of the criteria which have been discussed in the press are accurate. I would want a clear understanding of what the command and control was. I would want the NATO commander in charge of the operation. I would want a clear timetable for first review and ultimately for the right to terminate American involvement so that we—I would want a clear political strategy along with a military strategy. After all, there will be more than soldiers involved in this. And

I would want a clear expression of support from the United States Congress. Now, there are 20 other operational things I would want, but those are the big policy issues.

What was the other question?

Q. [*Inaudible*]—what criteria regarding funding of the operation.

The President. Well, we would have to know exactly what our financial responsibilities were. And of course, under our budget law, which is very strict now, we have to know how we're going to fund it and then we would have to know that others were going to do their part as well and that at least for the period of the operation that we were responsible for, that we were going to do it properly.

I wouldn't say that any of the peacekeeping operations here are ill-founded. As a matter of fact, I mentioned several that have worked very well. But there are limits to how many things we can do. There are going to be a lot of chaotic situations. We had another development in Georgia today, as you know. And we may or may not be able to see the U.N. go into every one of these circumstances. That's the only point I wanted to make. We have to really go into these things with our eyes wide open.

In Somalia, I think that we did go in with our eyes open. I think we did essentially what we meant to do. I just think that we may have underestimated the difficulty of setting in motion a political transition, which would send a clear signal to all Somalis that the United States in particular and the U.N. in general have no interest in trying to dominate or control their lives. We just want them to be able to live normal lives. We have no interest in trying to tell them how to live or what political course to take.

Security Council Membership

Q. Do you support the idea that Japan will join the additional member, a permanent member of the Security Council? And if you do so, will you give me the reason why you think so.

The President. Yes, I have long supported, even when I was a candidate for President I supported Security Council membership for Japan and for Germany. And I do so because I think that the conditions which existed at the end of the Second World War, which led to the membership of the Security Council as it was established then, have changed. Our primary adversaries in that war, Germany and Japan, have become among the major economic powers in the world. They have become great forces for democracy. They have been very generous in their support of political and humanitarian efforts throughout the world. The rest of the world community depends upon the support and the leadership of both Japan and Germany to get done much of what we will have to do in the years ahead. And so I have always felt in recognition of that that they should be offered permanent seats on the United Nations Security Council.

Thank you very much.

NOTE: The President's 27th news conference began at 4:53 p.m. at the Waldorf Astoria.

White House Statement on the President's Meeting With Baltic Leaders
September 27, 1993

The President met today jointly with President Lennart Meri of Estonia, President Algirdas Brazauskas of Lithuania, and President Guntis Ulmanis of Latvia. It was the President's first meeting with the heads of state of the Baltic countries.

The President expressed his admiration for the remarkable progress the Baltic peoples have achieved during the last 2 years in establishing democratic institutions and promoting economic reform. The President assured them of the strong U.S. interest in building close relations. The President reaffirmed U.S. support for reform and indicated the U.S. would move forward promptly on the new $50 million Baltic-American Enterprise Fund. The President also stated the United States intended to construct 5,000–7,000 housing units in Russia to facilitate the withdrawal of Russian forces from Estonia and Latvia.

The President welcomed the recent withdrawal of all Russian military forces from Lithuania. He also reiterated strong U.S. support for the early, unconditional, and rapid withdrawal of the remaining Russian forces from Latvia and Estonia. The President noted that he had raised this matter in a number of recent discussions with Russian Federation leaders. The United States intends to be helpful to all parties concerned in promoting an amicable resolution of the withdrawal issue.

The President also discussed concerns raised by the Russian Government about the treatment of ethnic Russians in Latvia and Estonia, while noting that international observers had found no evidence of human rights violations in those countries. The President expressed the hope that practical solutions could be achieved on this difficult issue. In this regard, the United States welcomes the constructive role played by the United Nations, the Conference on Security and Cooperation in Europe (CSCE), and the Council of Europe (COE) in helping to promote a resolution of all outstanding differences between Russia and the Baltic countries.

Designation of Vice Chair and Appointment of Staff Director for the Commission on Civil Rights
September 27, 1993

The President today announced he will designate Commission on Civil Rights member Cruz Reynoso as Vice Chair of the Commission and will appoint attorney Stuart J. Ishimaru as Commission Staff Director.

"With their combined experience in civil rights law, Cruz Reynoso and Stuart Ishimaru will bring strength and leadership to the cause of equality in America through their new roles on the U.S. Civil Rights Commission," the President said.

NOTE: Biographies were made available by the Office of the Press Secretary.

Exchange With Reporters Prior to a Meeting With Congressional Leaders
September 28, 1993

Somalia

·*Q.* Mr. President, have you decided to change your strategy in Somalia, perhaps not go after General Aideed out of concern, perhaps because of congressional criticisms of the mission?

The President. No. The United Nations strategy on the ground has not changed. But I have emphasized to them that every nation involved in that, from the beginning, was in it with the understanding that our first goal was to restore the conditions of normal life there, to stop the killing, to stop the disease, to stop the famine. And that has been done with broad support among the Somali people, with the exception of that small portion in Mogadishu where General Aideed and his supporters are.

So the enforcement strategy did not change, but what I wanted to emphasize at the U.N. yesterday was that there has to be a political strategy that puts the affairs of Somalia back into the hands of Somalia, that gives every country, not just the United States, every country that comes into that operation the sense that they are rotating in and out, that there is a fixed date for their ultimate disengagement in Somalia, because there's so many other peacekeeping operations in the world that have to be considered and that we owe that to all the nations we ask to participate in peacekeeping over the long run.

So there's been no change in the enforcement strategy, but I have tried to raise the visibility or the urgency of getting the political track back on pace, because in the end every peacekeeping mission or every humanitarian mission has to have a date certain when it's over, and you have to in the end turn the affairs of the country back over to the people who live there. We were not asked to go to Somalia to establish a protectorate or a trust relationship or to run the country. That's not what we went for.

Bosnia

Q. But do you have broader concerns about Bosnia? I mean, there's a similar problem there with no date certain, no exit strategy.

The President. I think there, in that case, the United States is in a much better position to establish, I think, the standards and have some discipline now on the front end. To be fair, I think that everyone involved in Bosnia is perhaps more sensitive than was the case in the beginning of this Somali operation about the— [*inaudible*]—of it, the dangers of it, and the need to have a strict set of limitations and conditions before the involvement occurs.

Somalia

Q. Given the current situation in Somalia, Mr. President, how do you go about fixing a date certain for withdrawal?

The President. I think one of the things we have to do is assess the conditions. Keep in mind, what we see every night reported now is a conflict between one Somali warlord who started this by murdering Pakistanis in a small portion of Mogadishu. It has very little to do with the whole rest of the country where tribal councils and village councils are beginning to govern the country, where most of the people are living in peace with the conditions of normal life have returned. There are lot of things that need to be sorted through there. And I think that what you'll see in the next few weeks is a real effort by the United Nations to articulate a political strategy. The country can be basically given back to the people who live there.

Q. Do you think you'll be sending troops to Bosnia?

The President. I've made it clear what I believe will happen.

NOTE: The exchange began at 11:16 a.m. in the Cabinet Room at the White House. A tape was not available for verification of the content of this exchange.

Statement on the Death of General James H. Doolittle
September 28, 1993

Lt. General James H. Doolittle's life spanned a period of American history that combined vast technological advancements with unparalleled change in our Nation's world role. At every step along the way, General Doolittle was among this Nation's trusted leaders.

General Doolittle was a pioneer in aviation. An accomplished and acclaimed airman in the years between the World Wars, he helped push the envelope of aviation and ensured that the United States was at the forefront of this emerging technology. When America entered the Second World War, General Doolittle's daring and courage emboldened an anxious and uncertain Nation. He gave the world its first example of

the steel that would allow the United States to lead the Allies to victory. In peacetime, he again served the Nation as a leader in industry and aerospace.

General Doolittle's love for his Nation will long survive him. His willingness to serve his country despite personal danger will long stand as an example of the grit and determination that has driven our Nation since its founding. Hillary joins me in mourning the loss of a patriot, a pioneer, and a hero.

NOTE: The related proclamation of September 30 is listed in Appendix D at the end of this volume.

Nomination for Ambassador to Poland
September 28, 1993

The President announced his intention today to nominate Polish-born business consultant Nicholas Rey to be the U.S. Ambassador to the Republic of Poland.

"I am very proud of this choice," said the President. "Nicholas Rey has already done much

for America in helping Poland along the road to democracy and free markets. I am confident that as our Nation's Ambassador, he will continue to further those important values."

NOTE: A biography of the nominee was made available by the Office of the Press Secretary.

Letter to Congressional Leaders on the North American Free Trade Agreement
September 28, 1993

Dear Mr. Leader:

My Administration is now making the final preparations for submitting to the Congress the North American Free Trade Agreement (NAFTA). Over the next several weeks Administration officials will sit down with Congressional Committees and their staffs to hammer out the details of implementing legislation. Let me indicate to you what I regard as a reasonable approach to Congressional consideration of this historic agreement, in hopes that we can arrive at a mutually agreed procedure for such action.

I believe strongly that the NAFTA is a good deal for the United States that warrants approval. It will benefit our country, increasing jobs and economic growth for Americans and enhancing our overall competitiveness. The NAFTA, strengthened by the agreements we have recently reached with Mexico and Canada on the environment, labor and import surges also will help to resolve problems that have existed in our relationship with Mexico. I know you share my support for this historic agreement.

As you know, in order for these agreements to take effect as scheduled on January 1, 1994, the NAFTA must be approved and implemented by Congress in accordance with procedures set out in our trade laws—the so-called "fast-track" procedures. These same procedures have worked successfully to approve and implement the results of multinational trade negotiations in 1979 and our bilateral free trade agreement with Canada in 1988. The practice has been for Congress and the executive branch to work closely together to develop a mutually satisfactory implementing bill before the President formally sends that bill to Congress. Working together in that way before introduction of the bills has resulted in rapid and overwhelming approval of the bills once introduced.

My administration is committed to the same process. We intend for the drafting of the implementing legislation to be a cooperative effort between the Administration and the Congress, in keeping with past practice. I cannot guarantee to be bound by legislation that is not yet drafted, just as you cannot commit the Congress to ap-

prove it. I can promise, however, that I will work closely with the Congress to draft legislation that best meets our mutual objectives.

I want to emphasize my strong belief that this bill should be voted on before Congress adjourns in 1993. For that to happen, I believe it is important that we conclude the joint drafting process with all Congressional Committees of jurisdiction by November 1, 1993, so that I may submit the legislation at that time. I would appreciate your efforts to enlist the cooperation of those Committees in achieving this timetable.

In the past, there has been a Congressional commitment to a vote prior to adjournment. I strongly believe that a similar commitment is called for and vital in this instance, so that this important matter can be decided this year. The national and congressional debate over NAFTA has already been long and, regrettably, rancorous.

By working together, I believe we can achieve a truly mutually satisfactory bill that will meet our obligations and enable Americans to take full advantage of the opportunities opened by these historic agreements. I greatly appreciate your efforts to this end.

Sincerely,

BILL CLINTON

NOTE: Identical letters were sent to Thomas S. Foley, Speaker of the House of Representatives; Robert H. Michel, House Minority Leader; George J. Mitchell, Senate Majority Leader; and Robert Dole, Senate Minority Leader. This letter was released by the Office of the Press Secretary on September 29.

Remarks Announcing the Clean Car Initiative
September 29, 1993

Thank you very much, and good morning ladies and gentlemen. I want to say a special good morning to the young people whose vision of the future can be seen on these great drawings they have done.

I want to begin by, as the Vice President did, acknowledging the presence here of Mr. Eaton, Mr. Poling, Mr. Smith, Mr. Bieber, and

also a lot of representatives of auto suppliers, people who supply component parts who will have a major role in this great project, I thank all them for being here, the Members of Congress. I also want to acknowledge one that we inadvertently omitted, Senator Bryan from Nevada, a longtime leader in the struggle to increase fuel efficiency.

I kind of liked the Vice President's story about the self-starter. When I first met Al Gore, I thought he had one of those implanted in him at an early age. [*Laughter*]

This is especially a happy moment for me. Some of you know that when I was a young man, when I was very young, my father was a Buick dealer in a small town in Arkansas where I was born, and he later went into business with my uncle in a larger town. I can still remember the first gainful work I think I ever did, when I was 6 years old, was trying to help my dad restore some Henry J.'s that had burned in a fire 35 miles from our home. And as a favor to the dealer, he helped him restore the cars, and we got to keep one. So until I was 18 years old, I drove a 1952 Henry J. self-made convertible. I once had an accident in it, and my jaw hit the steering wheel, and I broke the steering wheel in half. I don't know if that was an advertisement for my jaw or a condemnation of the steering wheel.

One of my most prized possessions is a 1967 Mustang convertible that I restored a few years ago. And I think when I left my home, it was the thing that I most regretted leaving behind. The other people who drove on the roads in my home State, however, were immensely relieved.

I think that all of us have our car-crazy moments and have those stories. Today, we're going to try to give America a new car-crazy chapter in her rich history, to launch a technological venture as ambitious as any our Nation has ever attempted. General Motors, Ford, Chrysler, and your National Government have agreed to accept a set of ambitious research and development goals for automobiles. We're confident that other companies outside Detroit will join in.

Our long-term goal is to develop affordable, attractive cars that are up to 3 times more fuel-efficient than today's cars—3 times—and meet strict standards for urban air pollution, safety, performance, and comfort.

Industry and Government engineering teams will work together on this. The project will involve Federal and industry funding. The Government will pick up a greater share of the high-risk projects, ones identified by an auto industry/Government team. We'll have three types of research projects: first, advanced manufacturing techniques to lower production costs and get new products on the market fast; second, research on technologies that can lead to

near-term improvements and auto efficiency safety and emissions; and third, research that could lead to production prototypes of vehicles capable of up to 3 times greater fuel efficiency.

Now, the Vice President mentioned that this brings together a number of things we are trying to do in this administration. First, there's a public-private partnership. Government can't do these things by itself, but there are a lot of things that we need to be working on that market forces alone can't do. So the third way, a partnership between the Government and the private sector to avoid the inefficiencies, the bureaucracies, and the errors of Government policy but to add the technology and the investment expertise we can bring, I think this is the way we're going to solve a lot of problems in the future. We'd be foolish not to rely on the auto industry with its clear understanding of the practical problems, and this makes sure that neither Government nor industry wastes money on projects with no real future.

The second thing we want to do is to keep America competitive. When you think of all the slogans you've heard over the years, what stands out is not just how catchy they are but how much truth there is to them. In the new Chrysler form skillfully follows—in the new Chryslers—excuse me—form skillfully follows functions. Ford has had better ideas. And there is a lot to admire if you've driven a Buick lately. We have got to do more of this.

You know, one of the great untold stories, although it's beginning to get out, is that these people up here on this stage are regaining American market share. People are buying more American cars made in America because they're doing a good job.

And since the auto industry is responsible for one out of every seven jobs in the United States, it is clearly incumbent upon all of us to support this effort and to make sure it succeeds. What better way is there to work together on a car that's practical, affordable, fun to drive, places little or no burden on the environment? We want American cars at the head of this parade, not bringing up the rear. Believe me, there will be a huge market for them.

The third thing we want to do—and this is very, very important to this administration; part of our commitment to reinventing Government—is to get rid of wasteful and costly regulation. The Government will in no way abdicate its responsibility in the search for near-term improvements in fuel efficiency, but we do want to break the wasteful gridlock in Washington over auto issues. We want a vehicle that lets us scrap a lot of the regulation in place today because it's achieved the objectives of the regulation in a much more efficient and market-based way.

This agreement represents an important peace dividend. It makes the expertise of the Department of Energy's weapons labs, as well as the research departments throughout the Department of Defense available to industry. That means all those super-strong, light-weight materials developed for weapons systems will be available here.

I told someone today right before we came out—I told the Vice President that I remember very vividly over 30 years ago standing in the showroom of the Buick dealership in my hometown and having my dad look at the new models and say, "You know, some day they'll figure out a way to make a car that weighs less than half this much, and the fuel efficiency problems will be a long way toward being solved." Now we know we'll be able to do things with engines that we never dreamed over 30 years ago.

Let me make one last point. This agreement grows out of a bedrock premise of this administration, one of the reasons that I ran for President. This agreement reflects an understanding that changes in this world are inevitable. They cannot be repealed. They cannot be rolled back. They cannot be denied. They can be avoided or delayed at our peril. What we have to do is to try to find a way to make these changes our friends. This is a visionary effort on behalf of the American people to make change our friend in one of the most important economic areas of American life. We do not have the choice to do nothing. We have to act decisively to shape change so that it matches the needs of the future. That's what we're trying to do with health care. That's what we're trying to do with economic policy. That's what we're trying to do here today.

This is the end of a long negotiation and the beginning of a great period of action and excitement in American life. Is there any risk? You bet there is. We have to condition the American people to be willing to take more risks and fail in order to ultimately succeed. Will we have setbacks? I imagine we will if we do anything. But that's no reason to give up.

Alexander Graham Bell once remarked that if he had known more about electricity, he never would have invented the telephone. We need a little more of that kind of ignorance today— to just keep walking into those solid walls until they give way.

We cannot be deterred by the difficulty. For 50 years, the companies represented here today have comprised the basic engine of American prosperity. Working together, we can make sure the freedom and convenience of personal vehicles will continue to be available to all Americans. We intend to do nothing less than to define the world car of the next century, to propel the auto industry to the forefront of world automobile production, and to make this industry the source of imagination for young people of the future, for their ideas, their careers, and their efforts.

I'm excited. But most importantly, maybe, our young people are excited. And let me just close with this story. I was greeting a number of Ambassadors the other day, including an Ambassador from one of the Baltic countries who has an American wife and a young son who is 5 years old, who speaks fluent English and German, because his father had been living in Germany. I never met a 5-year-old kid like this in my life. And when I shook hands with him, he said, "I'm glad to meet you, Mr. President. I want you to make a car that runs on electricity and doesn't pollute the air." And he said, "I intend to work on this, and I want you to tell the Vice President that I'm working on this." [*Laughter*]

So I said, "Well, you tell him." I was so impressed I went to get Al Gore, and I introduced him to this 5-year-old boy, and he said, "Hello, Mr. Vice President. I intend to spend my life working on this." And he said, "I am going to help you develop an electric car that has no pollution." And Al Gore says, "That means we're going to be partners." He said, "Yes, I guess so. But you don't understand. I'm going to spend my whole life on this." [*Laughter*]

We've got all these kids out there that are on fire about this. And I want to say again, maybe that's the most important thing in the world. We can keep them looking to the future with confidence. This country needs a good dose of old-fashioned confidence today that all the challenges we face can be met and conquered. And this ought to be a clear signal to America that the core of the American industrial economy, the auto industry, is looking to the future with confidence and that the United States Government is going to be their partner in that successful march.

Thank you very much.

NOTE: The President spoke at 10:24 a.m. on the South Lawn at the White House. In his remarks, he referred to Robert J. Eaton, chairman and chief executive officer, Chrysler Motor Co.; Harold A. Poling, chairman and chief executive officer, Ford Motor Co.; John F. Smith, Jr., president, General Motors Co.; and Owen Bieber, president, United Auto Workers.

Remarks Announcing the National Export Strategy and an Exchange With Reporters
September 29, 1993

The President. Thank you very much, and please be seated. I want to thank, first of all, the members of the Trade Promotion Coordinating Committee, all the members of my Cabinet and administration who are here, and especially the Commerce Secretary, Ron Brown, who did such a good job in chairing this effort.

I'd also like to thank the people who are involved in our national security efforts who supported these changes, a marked change from times past. And I'd like to thank the Vice President and the people who worked on the National Performance Review for a lot of the work they did to reinforce our efforts to develop a meaningful national export strategy.

Finally, I'd like to say a special word of thanks to people who are here and people all across this country who have talked to me about this issue for the last couple of years. Everywhere I went where there were people who were trying to create the American economy of the future, someone would take me aside and talk about the problems of the export control laws, which may have been needed in a former period when the technology was different and certainly the politics of the cold war were different but were clearly undermining our ability to be competitive today.

If I might just by way of general introduction say that I don't believe a wealthy country can grow much richer in the world we're living in without expanding exports. I don't believe you can create jobs—and I'm absolutely convinced you can't change the job mix, which is something we have to do in America with so many people stuck in jobs that have had flat or declining real wages. I think we have to do that.

And I don't think it can be done unless we can increase the volume of exports in this country.

And therefore, I have wanted to have a new export strategy that would deal with a whole range of issues and that would galvanize the energy, the imagination of the American private sector, not only those who are waiting to export now and just held back by laws but those that we need to go out and cultivate, especially small and medium sized businesses that could be active in international markets—their counterparts in other countries are active—but because of the system or, if you will, the lack of the system that we have had in the past, have not been so engaged.

So I want to emphasize that the announcements we make today are designed to create jobs for Americans, to increase incomes for Americans, and to create the future economy, even as we have to give up on much of the past.

I also want to say that it's very important to see this announcement today in the context of our administration's support for the NAFTA agreement. It will also open up export opportunities, not just to Mexico but throughout all of Latin America.

I just came from the United Nations earlier this week, where I had the opportunity to host meetings with the Latin American leaders who were there. The first thing every one of them asked me about was the NAFTA agreement. And every one of them said, "Look, we want to do this, too. We want to lower our barriers to American products. We want more American products in our country." No one, even the most vociferous opponents of NAFTA, would seriously urge that the proposition that if we have lowered trade barriers with Chile or Argentina or any other country, that will lead to massive loss of American jobs. It will clearly lead to massive gains in American jobs.

This is an important part of a strategy to build a hemispheric trading opportunity for Americans. I also would say that anyone who has seriously looked at the NAFTA dynamics, the specifics of the NAFTA agreement will actually alleviate all the complaints that people have who are attacking it. It will raise the cost of labor in Mexico. It will raise the cost of environmental protection in Mexico. It will lower the trade barriers in Mexico that are higher than American trade barriers. It will change domestic content rules in ways that will enable us to produce in America, sell in Mexico. And that country, with a low per capita income, already buys more American products per capita than any country in the world except for Canada.

So I think that is a very important point to make. This export strategy we announced today assumes that we have people to sell to, and we have to also keep that in mind. We have to keep reaching out to tear down these barriers, to integrate our economies in ways that benefits Americans.

Let me just basically outline in some greater detail the strategy that has been recommended by our counsel and that the Vice President summarized.

As we all know, the export controls in American law today no longer reflect the realities of the economic marketplace or the political realities. The cold war is over, and the technologies have changed dramatically. Therefore, today I am ordering sweeping changes in our export controls that dramatically reduce controls on telecommunications technologies and computers. These reforms will eliminate or greatly reduce controls on $35 billion worth of high-tech products, ultimately 70 percent of all the computers. This one step alone will decontrol the export of computers, the production of which support today—today—600,000 American jobs and now more tomorrow.

Let me be clear. As I said at the United Nations earlier this week, I am more concerned about proliferation of weapons of mass destruction than I was when I became President. Every day I have this job, I become more worried about it. And we do need effective export con-

trols to fight that kind of proliferation. But streamlining unnecessary controls will make the rest of the system more responsive and efficient in combating proliferation. And we have on too many, many occasions, for too many years, not had a coordinated, effective strategy against proliferation but have had a broad-based, highly bureaucratic policy that, in effect, cut off our nose to spite our face.

We also know we have to simplify the export process. There are 19 different export-related agencies in this Government. To say that we need more effective coordination would be a dramatic understatement. The TPCC found this, as did the Vice President's National Performance Review.

We propose to begin by creating one-stop shops in four cities, consolidating all Federal export promotion services in one place. And eventually, there will be a national network of shops linked together by computer technology. We also want to have one phone number that will serve as an information clearinghouse for any exporter of any size to learn about potential export markets.

Now, let me say why I think this is so important. Most of the job growth in America is in small and medium sized companies. Now, many of those, to be sure, are supplying bigger companies; many of those are in high-tech areas where they're already attuned to exports. But many of them are basically stand-alone operations that sell to companies in America and could sell to companies overseas but don't know how to do it, think it's too much hassle, haven't really figured out the financing, the paperwork, the market-opening mechanisms.

We have not done nearly as good a job as some countries in mobilizing the energies of these countries. I have been immensely impressed, for example, at the organization in Germany of the medium and small sized companies to make them all automatically exporting. And there's no question that the effort that they have made in that country to mobilize small and medium sized companies for export is one reason they've been able to maintain by far the most open economy in Europe and the lowest unemployment rate at the same time. We must do the same thing.

The third element of this strategy is meeting the challenge of tied aid. Now, for the benefit of those here covering this event who don't know what tied aid is, it basically is a strategy that many of our competitors have followed who say, if you want our aid you'll have to buy our products. We have worked hard to reach an agreement to limit the practice of tied aid, and we have had some success in the last few years. But unfortunately there is still way too much of it, in ways that cost Americans way too many dollars in jobs and export opportunities that we could win under any free market scenario imaginable.

Therefore, we propose to create a modest $150 million fund within the Export-Import Bank, and with the support of Mr. Brody and others who are here today, to counter the tied aid practices of our competitors. By some estimates, our companies lose between $400 million and $800 million in export sales every year because of tied aid practices.

Next, we want to focus the Government to promote private sector exports. We want an advocacy network within the Government to facilitate the efforts of our companies and to reinforce the one-stop shopping. We want a commercial strategic plan in key foreign markets to coordinate the work of Federal Agencies there, something I heard about over and over again from the U.S. business community, for example, in Japan and in Korea.

We want to ensure that our embassies play a much more aggressive role in promoting our commercial interests in a uniform way around the world. Some of our embassies, to be fair, do a very good job of this. Some are not active at all. Most are somewhere in the middle. We need a uniform policy and a deliberate mission on this, and I am very pleased at the support the State Department has given to this effort.

We want to unify the budget of all export promotion-related activities in the Government through a new process coordinated by the Economic Council, OMB, and the Trade Promotion Coordinating Committee.

Finally, let me say what we have today at long last is a coordinated, targeted, aggressive export strategy. It means growth and jobs and incomes for Americans. Compared to our competitors, we have for too long had a hands-off approach to exports. We have paid for it. We now will have a hands-on partnership, driven by the market, guided by the private sector, limited where appropriate by governmental policy, but clearly tailored to help Americans compete and win in the world of today and tomorrow.

Many people when I started thought this would never happen, especially those frustrated computer companies who have labored under the burden of the past, because it required us to think and act anew. It required disparate agencies to cooperate that had never really spoken to each other about these matters. It required Congress to work with the executive branch. It required everyone in our Government to listen to our customers, in this case the American businesses who pay so much of the tax bill. But it is working. And we have laid the foundation for a future really worth having in this country. Now, you all have to go out and make this work. We intend to support it. We intend to do what needs to be done. And we believe that Government is now going to be a good partner with the private sector in making tomorrow's economy. Thank you very much.

I want to take a question or two. But before I do, since we have a lot of folks from the private sector here, I just want to say that one of the things we have really worked hard on in Government is getting all these—look at all the Cabinet and agency heads we have here—we really try to work together. I won't say it never happens, but we have got less turfing and less infighting than any Government, I think, that's been in this town in a very long time. And it's a great tribute to them, and I want to thank them publicly in the presence of those of you who have complained about the inadequacies of the approach in the past.

Secretary of Commerce Ron Brown

Q. Mr. President, are you satisfied with Secretary Brown's explanations about his relationship to Vietnam?

The President. Well, let me say he's told me that he hadn't done anything wrong, and he's done just about everything right as Commerce Secretary. I think he's done a great job, and I have no reason not to believe him.

Q. Mr. President, are you concerned that his effectiveness as Commerce Secretary in selling programs that you're pushing, like this one and NAFTA, are undermined by this grand jury investigation?

The President. Not if he hadn't done anything wrong, I'm not. Business Week complimented him in an editorial today. I was glad to see a Democrat get complimented in Business Week. [*Laughter*]

Q. [*Inaudible*]

The President. Yes. I hope it will happen a lot more as we go along.

Russia

Q. Mr. President, did the latest events in Moscow give you pause about your previous support that you've expressed for Mr. Yeltsin?

The President. No. It is a tense and difficult issue, and how to defuse what I understand to have been the circumstances around the Moscow White House was a difficult call. I don't think that any of us should be here basically armchair quarterbacking the unfolding events.

When I talked to Boris Yeltsin a few days ago, I told him very strongly that I hoped that he would be able to manage this transition in ways that really promoted democracy, respected human rights, and kept the peace. And he said that would be exactly his policy. And so far he has done that, under very, very difficult, intense circumstances. I mean, a lot of you have talked about just the difficulty of managing this and keeping up with what's going on in the countryside and the pressures and all the various interest groups. And I think so far they've done quite well.

Now, I'm going to have a meeting with Mr. Kozyrev later today, and we'll have a chance to talk about this in greater detail. But he's already made a statement that they're still committed to a peaceful transition, and I have no reason to believe he's not. And I think that the United States and the free world ought to hang in there with a person that is clearly the

most committed to democracy and market reform of all the people now operating in Russia. Until I have some reason to believe otherwise, I'm going to hang right where we are. I think we're in the right place.

Q. What are your concerns about the human rights implications of having the Parliament building there surrounded by armed troops?

The President. I think it depends on what the facts were. If there were a lot of people armed in there and he was worried about civil disorder and unrest and people being shot, I think that when you're in charge of a government, your first obligation is to try to keep the peace and keep order. So I think so far they seem to have acted with restraint but with dispatch in trying to defuse what otherwise might have become a very difficult situation.

Now, I don't have all the facts, and neither does anyone else. But nothing has happened so far that has caused me to question the commitment that was made to me by the President and to his own people.

Thank you very much.

NOTE: The President spoke at 12:45 p.m. in the Roosevelt Room at the White House. In his remarks, he referred to Kenneth D. Brody, President, Export-Import Bank of the United States. The related Executive orders of September 30 on export controls and the Trade Promotion Coordinating Committee are listed in Appendix D at the end of this volume.

Exchange With Reporters Prior to Discussions With Foreign Minister Andrey Kozyrev of Russia
September 29, 1993

Bosnia

Q. Mr. President, is there anything the United States can now do to bring peace in Bosnia since the Bosnian Parliament has voted against the peace plan?

The President. Well, you know, this process—this goes on day by day. We're just going to have to see what happens. They want some more territory. You know, I think they're entitled to some more territory, but I don't know if they can get it. I think that the price of

passing up this peace may be very high. And I think they'll probably consider that over the next few days. But we'll just have to wait and see what happens. We haven't had time to examine what our options are.

Q. Is the only alternative more war?

The President. Well, that's up to them. All of them.

Q. Are you encouraging them then to accept this treaty, or do you think that they should go ahead with their demands for more?

The President. Well, I have encouraged them to try to make peace. That's what I've encouraged them to try to do. I hate to see another winter come on for all of them there. But that's a decision they'll have to make, their country, their lives, they'll have to make the decision.

Russia

Q. Sir, what assurances are you hoping to receive from Mr. Kozyrev about the situation, and what message might you be sending to Mr. Yeltsin through him?

The President. Well, I think he's already given the assurances that all of us hope. They're doing everything they can to preserve peace. And there's a commitment by President Yeltsin to move to a truly democratic system, through truly democratic means. That's about all the United States or anyone else could ask for.

Q. Mr. President, one more question. Is this meeting of yours with the Russian Foreign Minister, is this meeting of yours a meeting of support or is it a meeting of concern?

The President. Well, it's a meeting of support. I'm concerned about events in the sense that I hope they go well, and I hope that everything works out all right. But I am firmly in support of the efforts that President Yeltsin is making to hold democratic elections for a legislative body and to have a new constitution and to present himself for election again. I think that the United States clearly has an interest in promoting democracy and reform in Russia.

And as you know, I have aggressively supported efforts in our Congress to get more aid for the process of reform and for economic opportunity in Russia, and I will continue to do that.

NOTE: The exchange began at 4:54 p.m. in the Oval Office at the White House. A tape was not available for verification of the content of this exchange.

Nomination for an Under Secretary of Veterans Affairs
September 29, 1993

The President announced today that he intends to nominate career Veterans Affairs official Raymond John Vogel, to be the Under Secretary of Veterans Affairs for Benefits. Vogel, a disabled Vietnam-era Army veteran, would head the Veterans Benefits Administration, the VA Agency responsible for delivery of nonmedical benefits to the Nation's 27 million veterans.

In making his announcement, the President said, "John Vogel is uniquely qualified to apply his indepth expertise to the VA's new commitment to serve America's veterans during a new era of efficiency and sensitivity. He will ably assist VA Secretary Jesse Brown in his plans to modernize and streamline the VA claims process."

NOTE: A biography of the nominee was made available by the Office of the Press Secretary.

Remarks on Signing the Executive Order on Regulatory Planning and Review and an Exchange With Reporters
September 30, 1993

The President. Good morning, ladies and gentlemen. Welcome to another action-packed meeting of our action-packed administration.

Today I am signing an Executive order to create a fair, open, streamlined system of regulatory review for our Government to eliminate improper influence, delay secrecy, and to set tough standards and time limits for regulation.

It's a move in keeping with everything else we've tried to do since Inauguration Day. The philosophy of this administration has always been consistent when it comes to regulation.

We reject the "if it moves, regulate it" approach. And we reject the idea that we can walk away from regulation entirely. We have sought a third way, consistent with the philosophy behind the Vice President's reinventing Government project, with our approach to health care, to export controls, to a whole range of other issues.

We can't reject all regulations. Many of them do a lot of good things. They protect workers in the workplace, shoppers in the grocery stores, children opening new toys. But there are others that serve no purpose at all. This Executive order will provide a way to get rid of useless, outdated, and unnecessary regulations that are outdated, obsolete, expensive, and bad for business.

We're working on the impact of regulation on Government, too. That's what the Vice President's report on reinventing Government does. To improve budget, personnel, and procurements systems, we can strip away an awful lot of redtape for all of you.

All of you are working yourselves on a focused review of regulations. And that's why on September the 11th, as you'll recall, I signed an Executive order directing our Agencies to eliminate 50 percent of our internal regulations.

The next step is reforming the regulatory review process itself. That's what the Executive order today does. We've already shut down the so-called competitiveness council, which closed the back door to special interests to get out from under regulations they didn't like. In its place, we have a dramatically different approach, fair, streamlined, responsive, much more straightforward.

Under the Executive order that I am signing today, involvement by the President and the Vice President in the regulatory process is strictly limited. The order permits the Vice President's review only at the request of the Cabinet member or the OMB's OIRA office. Communications between White House staff members and the public are limited, too, on matters of regulation. In order to be utilized in the rulemaking process or the review process, they must be made in writing and put in the public record.

Just these changes alone mean the days of back-door access to undermining the regulatory process is over. But we also want to limit the number of regulations that may be reviewed by the Office of Information and Regulatory Affairs. It's very important that we let ordinary regulations be done in a more timely fashion, where the people who are going to be affected by them have more front-end involvement. This order requires written justification for rejections of regulations, mandates Sunshine provisions, requires a publicly available log, which the press will love. It has guidelines not just for review of new regulations but, this is very important, for a review of existing regulations, too. We should be eliminating regulations even as we have new ones.

This order will lighten the load for regulated industries and make Government regulations that are needed more efficient. Most of all, it will put behind us the politics of adversarialism that has divided Government and industry for too long. We saw a beginning of what that can mean for America yesterday, with the announcements between the Government and the auto industry of the project to try to triple the fuel efficiency of our cars by the end of the decade. That's the sort of thing we ought to be focusing on in our relationships with Government and industry.

In the last few weeks, we've seen a remarkable amount of progress in our Nation, a lot of things turning around. This is an important step in that process. The way the Government relates to people whom it must regulate, or decide whether to regulate or not, has an enormous amount to do with the credibility that our Government has with all of the citizens of our country and with how we're spending their tax money. I am very excited about this. I think the wind is now behind us, and I hope we can see through this project and continue on the road that we are clearly taking now.

[At this point, the President signed the Executive order.]

White House Staff

Q. Mr. President, a Member of Congress on the House floor has just characterized your claim that you've really cut the White House staff as unethical and a lie. He says that you cut people who are not political operatives and that there really hasn't been a budget savings.

The President. Well, we have cut it. I can guarantee people around here have been complaining about it because we're handling more mail, doing more work, and carrying a bigger load than this White House has carried in more than a dozen years, and we're doing it with fewer people. All you have to do is just ask people around here and they'll be glad to tell you that.

Who is the Member of Congress?

Q. Congressman Wolf.

The President. Well, the burden is on him to establish that. I don't want to get in an argument with him about the staff. The truth is we're doing more work than my predecessors did with fewer people, and it's pretty hard on these people. They're staying here real late, and they're working awful hard.

Q. Do you really have fewer political appointees than your predecessors?

The President. Well, the President has the right to replace everybody in the White House. I didn't do that, and most people don't. But to imply that someone who came here because I got elected President is somehow less valuable or not working is, I think, a pretty spurious claim.

The truth is that in the White House, at least, it's been my experience, not just for me, but for my Republican predecessors, that the so-called political appointees are the ones that have to work 60 or 70 or 80 hours a week and are making most of the decisions and doing most of the hard work. So I don't understand what

the claim is there. If Mr. Wolf wins reelection to his office, if he hires somebody to work there, they're a political appointee. But if they work hard and do a good job, they deserve to be treated like everybody else.

Q. Do you think when you talked about cutting the White House staff 25 percent, that most Americans thought that that didn't mean political appointees, it just meant career people?

The President. I don't think most Americans make that distinction. I think most Americans want to know what size Government's going to be. If we reduce the size of the Federal Government by a quarter of a million people over the next 4 years, most of those people will be career positions we won't fill again. But to say that the people that work in the White House, that work virtually around the clock all week long are somehow less significant because they work harder and longer, I think is a pretty hard argument to make.

NOTE: The President spoke at 10:45 a.m. in the Cabinet Room at the White House. The Executive order and the related memorandum on negotiated rulemaking are listed in Appendix D at the end of this volume.

Memorandum on Agency Rulemaking Procedures
September 30, 1993

Memorandum for Heads of Departments and Agencies

Subject: Agency Rulemaking Procedures

Today, I issued an Executive order setting forth the Administration's regulatory philosophy; defining a more effective and accountable role for the Executive Office of the President in regulatory planning and review; and establishing the procedures to be followed by agencies and the Office of Information and Regulatory Affairs ("OIRA") in promulgating and reviewing regulations. One primary objective of this order is to streamline the regulatory review process, thus reducing the delay in the developing and promulgating rules.

We cannot, however, reduce delay in the rulemaking process without reforms within the agencies themselves. The National Performance Re-

view team examining the issue found that many agencies require numerous clearances within the agency before a rule is submitted to OIRA for review. (Indeed, one agency found that its internal review process could only be described by using an 18-foot flow chart.) The team also learned that too often agencies use the same internal review procedures for all rules—regardless of their complexity or significance.

In order to streamline the entire rulemaking process, agencies must, consistent with any applicable laws, utilize internally the most efficient method of developing and reviewing regulations. Accordingly, I direct the head of each agency and department to examine its internal review procedures to determine whether, and if so, how those procedures can be improved and streamlined. In conducting this examination, the agency or department shall consider the number of clearances required by its review process and whether the review process varies according to the complexity or significance of a rule.

I further direct the head of each agency and department to submit to the Vice President and me, within 6 months of this memorandum, the results of its examination.

WILLIAM J. CLINTON

Memorandum on Report of Regulatory Review
September 30, 1993

Memorandum for the Administrator, Office of Information and Regulatory Affairs

Subject: Report of Regulations Reviewed

Today, I issued an Executive order setting forth the Administration's regulatory philosophy; defining a more effective and accountable role for the Executive Office of the President in regulatory planning and review; and establishing the procedures to be followed by agencies and your office in promulgating and reviewing regulations. The review process set forth in the order is designed to assist agencies in issuing better regulations by, among other things, streamlining the review process and enhancing accountability.

In order to ascertain the success of the regulatory review process, I direct you to monitor your review activities over the next 6 months and, at the end of this period, to prepare a report on your activities. This report shall include a list of the regulatory actions reviewed by OIRA, specifying the issuing agency; the nature of the regulatory action (e.g., advance notice of proposed rulemaking, notice of proposed rulemaking, interim final rule, or final rule); whether the agency or OIRA identified the reviewed regulatory action as "significant," within the meaning of the order; and the time dedicated to the review, including whether there were any extensions of the time periods set forth in the order, and, if so, the reason for such extensions. The report shall include any other information that your office may have with respect to the kind or amount of regulatory actions that were not reviewed by your office. Finally, the report shall identify any provisions of the order that, based on your experience or on comments from interested persons, warrant reconsideration so that the purposes and objectives of this order can be better achieved.

I further direct you to submit this report to the Vice President and me by May 1, 1994, and to publish the report in the *Federal Register*.

WILLIAM J. CLINTON

Remarks on Presenting the National Medals of Science and Technology
September 30, 1993

Thank you very much, ladies and gentlemen. When we schedule these wonderful things on the South Lawn, we normally do it because it's so warm at this time of year. I would give another medal to someone right now who could raise the temperature just 6 degrees. [*Laughter*]

Mr. Vice President, Secretary Aspin, Secretary Brown, Under Secretary Kunin, Dr. Gibbons, Under Secretary of Commerce for Technology Mary Good, and Acting Director of the National Science Foundation Dr. Fred Bernthal, the Director-designate of the Science Foundation Dr. Neal Lane, distinguished medal recipients and members of the National Medal of Technology Nominating Evaluation Committee, members of the President's Committee on National Medal of Science, and the 1993 Presidential Faculty Fellows, the 30 outstanding young scientists and engineers who are joining us here for this ceremony, and I congratulate all of you—where are you? They're in the back over there—and to the Foundation for the National Medals of

Science and Technology and other guests, although I hope I've named everyone by now. It's a great privilege for us to have you here today. I haven't been exposed to this much knowledge of science and technology since I named Al Gore to be my running mate last year. [*Laughter*]

I'm glad to salute all of you who are winners, whose discoveries advance our standard of living and the quality of our lives, our health, our understanding of the world and our own place in it.

I know that the achievements we honor today will improve our ability to communicate with one another, to increase the productivity of our people, and to secure our place in the global economy and hopefully to help to preserve in common our planet.

It's especially important to me that we find ways to preserve what is important to us and to succeed in this global economy, because I know we cannot win the fight that we are in by continuing to do what we have done, which is to have our working people work harder and harder for less and less.

Yesterday we celebrated two achievements of science and technology, and a great gamble besides, by announcing, as some of you noticed, an unprecedented joint research venture with the Big Three automakers, our national defense labs, and our other Federal scientific research facilities to try to triple the fuel efficiency of cars by the end of the decade. And then we announced that we were removing export controls on 70 percent of America's computers, both regular computers and supercomputers, in ways that we believe will add billions of dollars, indeed, tens of billions of dollars to our exports.

Today, we honor people who are the dreamers, the pioneers, the risk takers, who remind us that the things we celebrated yesterday were once just a gleam in the mind's eye of a brilliant scientist or an engineer. You, too, will have that pleasure some day. But today we honor people who are the new scouts in our timeless urge for adventure.

Forty years ago, J. Robert Oppenheimer said in a lecture, "Both the man of science and the man of art live always at the edge of mystery, surrounded by it. Both, as the measure of their creation, have always had to do with the harmonization of what is new with what is familiar, with the balance between novelty and synthesis, with the struggle to make partial order in total chaos." That sounds like my job. [*Laughter*] "This cannot be an easy life," he said. Well, it' may not be an easy life, but clearly it is a life worth living, and today, a life worth honoring.

I thank all of you so much for helping this country and this administration move toward the 21st century.

Daniel Boorstin wrote in his book, "The Discoverers", "All the world is still an America. The most promising words ever written on the map of human knowledge are *terra incognita*, unknown territory." Your discoveries of unknown territory are for the rest of us most promising, and your country salutes you for them.

Thank you very much.

NOTE: The President spoke at 3:05 p.m. on the South Lawn at the White House.

Remarks on the Retirement of General Colin Powell in Arlington, Virginia
September 30, 1993

Thank you very much. Secretary Aspin, President and Mrs. Bush, General and Mrs. Powell, distinguished Members of Congress, distinguished leaders of United States military forces, my fellow Americans.

Today, a grateful Nation observes the end of a distinguished career and celebrates 35 years of service and victory: a victory for the United States military that gave young Colin Powell a chance to learn and to grow and to lead; a victory for the military and political leaders who continue to elevate him based on their complete confidence and sheer respect; a victory for a Nation well served and, in a larger sense, a victory for the American dream; for the principle that in our Nation, people can rise as far as their talent, their capacities, their dreams, and their discipline will carry them.

A long time ago, Thomas Jefferson wrote, "The Creator has not thought proper to mark those in the forehead who are of stuff to make good generals." The Creator has not thought proper to mark them by the color of their skin or the station of their birth or the place they were born. Thank God for the United States that that is so.

From my first meeting with Colin Powell, before I became President, I knew that one thing I would never have to worry about was having a strong and wise, a forthright and honest Chairman of the Joint Chiefs of Staff. His knowledge and judgment were a source of constant support. The fact that he enjoyed the respect of all of his troops, from the people first entering the service to his colleagues on the Joint Chiefs of Staff; his remarkable balance of prudence and courage and his unfailing sense of humor have been there through the difficult times of now two Presidencies. And he clearly has the warrior spirit and the judgment to know when it should be applied in the Nation's behalf.

General Powell has been a rock of stability in our Nation's military during a time of profound change. He has understood more clearly than virtually any other American the enormous resource that the young men and women in our uniform have been for our Nation. He has been determined to give them the security that knowledge and skills and capacity bring, so that together they could take the changes that we have seen in the last few years.

As the Secretary has noted, he was the first Chairman to begin his tenure under the Goldwater-Nichols act, and he has clearly set a standard by which all future Chairs of the Joint Chiefs of Staff will be judged.

During his term the cold war ended. We began to grapple with the consequences of that, mostly good and some bad. We have seen world-changing events force us to reexamine our missions, our force structures, and our commands. We have also seen a leader in Colin Powell, who has not only responded to those great challenges but one who could be trusted to feel in his heart the awesome responsibility for the lives and livelihood, for the present and future of every man and woman who wore the uniform of the United States of America.

So today, General Powell, I speak for all of them who thank you for guiding and protecting their lives, even as you advance the cause of freedom around the world. I speak for their families who entrusted you with their sons and daughters. I speak for the young children who sent their mothers and fathers under your command in the Gulf, in Somalia, and elsewhere. For all of them I say you did well by them as you did well by America.

We take great pride in what you have done for your country. You have exemplified the military ethic in serving in whatever mission and in getting the job done.

When we marched around the field today, I was glad to hear the long litany of Colin Powell's career, to remind us that in the spotlight and far away from the spotlight, as a young soldier and a not-so-young soldier, he was always first and foremost a good soldier, a role model for those in our military and now a role model for all young Americans, someone we can appreciate for having done a job day-in and day-out, year-in and year-out, with ferocious dedication.

In recognition of your legacy and service, of your courage and accomplishment, today, General Powell, I was honored to present you with the Presidential Medal of Freedom, with distinction. I want to tell all those here in attendance that this was the second Medal of Freedom you have received, the first from President Bush in 1991. And today, you became only the second American citizen in the history of the Republic to be the recipient of two Medals of Freedom.

I want to thank you, too, sir, for your advice and counsel in the work I had to do in selecting your successor. It was a job I think many people were afraid to even contemplate. For you are truly a hard act to follow. I know you share my opinion that we could not have done better than General Shalikashvili.

I also want to say a special word of appreciation to Mrs. Powell for her inspiration and her support, her good-humored endurance of all the times when you could have been either with her, your daughters, or your automobiles, and had, instead, to be at the White House with me or someone else importuning on your time. I thank her, and I thank your family for their sacrifices in your public service.

When you proposed and married Alma Johnson and moved with her to Birmingham, Alabama, and before the year were already sent off as a young captain to serve in Vietnam, that year was 1962. In that same year, General Douglas MacArthur gave his famous farewell speech at West Point. He spoke the following words of praise to all those who serve in our military. I repeat them today because they apply especially well to you. MacArthur said, in reference to the American soldier, "I regarded him as one of the world's noblest figures, not only as one of the finest military characters but also as one of the most stainless."

In closing, General Powell, I am reminded of the words of another young valiant warrior, spoken when, like you, he was finishing one journey and beginning a second. John Bunyan wrote in Pilgrim's Progress of the warrior valiant at the end of his life, as he prepared to present himself to the Almighty, "My sword I give to him that shall succeed me in my pilgrimage

and my courage and skill to him that can get them. My marks and scars I carry with me to be a witness for me, to Him who shall be my rewarder."

General Powell, your reward is a grateful Nation and a bright future. Your reward is a stronger Nation, safer and better today for your sword, your courage, and your skill. From the bottom of my heart, on behalf of every man and woman, every boy and girl in this great country, I thank you and wish you Godspeed.

NOTE: The President spoke at 4:30 p.m. at Fort Myer.

Message to the Congress on Restriction of Weapons Proliferation Activities
September 30, 1993

To the Congress of the United States:

Pursuant to section 204(b) of the International Emergency Economic Powers Act (50 U.S.C. 1703(b)) and section 301 of the National Emergencies Act (50 U.S.C. 1631), I hereby report to the Congress that I have exercised my statutory authority to declare a national emergency and to issue an Executive order, which authorizes and directs the Secretary of Commerce, in consultation with the Secretary of State, to take such actions, including the promulgation of rules, regulations, and amendments thereto, and to employ such powers granted to the President by the International Emergency Economic Powers Act, as may be necessary to continue to regulate the activities of United States persons in order to prevent their participation in activities, which could contribute to the proliferation of nuclear, chemical, and biological weapons, and the means of their delivery.

These actions are necessary in view of the danger posed to the national security, foreign policy, and economy of the United States by the continued proliferation of nuclear, biological, and chemical weapons, and of the means of delivering such weapons, and in view of the need for more effective controls on activities sustaining such proliferation. In the absence of these actions, the participation of U.S. persons in activities contrary to U.S. nonproliferation ob-

jectives and policies, and which may not be adequately controlled through the exercise of the authorities conferred by the Export Administration Act of 1979, as amended (50 U.S.C. App. 2401 *et. seq.*), could take place without effective control, posing an unusual and extraordinary threat to the national security, foreign policy, and economy of the United States.

The countries and regions affected by this action would include those currently identified in Supplements 4, 5, and 6 to Part 778 of Title 15 of the Code of Federal Regulations, concerning nonproliferation controls, as well as such other countries as may be of concern from time to time due to their involvement in the proliferation of weapons of mass destruction, or due to the risk of their being points of diversion to proliferation activities.

It is my intention to review the appropriateness of proposing legislation to provide standing authority for these controls, and thereafter to terminate the Executive order.

WILLIAM J. CLINTON

The White House,
September 30, 1993.

NOTE: The Executive order is listed in Appendix D at the end of this volume.

Message to the Congress on Trade With Russia
September 30, 1993

To the Congress of the United States:

I am writing to inform you of my intent to add Russia to the list of beneficiary developing countries under the Generalized System of Preferences (GSP). The GSP program offers duty-free access to the U.S. market and is authorized by the Trade Act of 1974.

I have carefully considered the criteria identified in sections 501 and 502 of the Trade Act of 1974. In light of these criteria, and particularly Russia's level of development and initiation of economic reforms, I have determined that it is appropriate to extend GSP benefits to Russia.

This notice is submitted in accordance with section 502(a)(1) of the Trade Act of 1974.

WILLIAM J. CLINTON

The White House,
September 30, 1993.

NOTE: The related proclamation is listed in Appendix D at the end of this volume.

Message to the Congress Transmitting the Notice on Continuation of Haitian Emergency
September 30, 1993

To the Congress of the United States:

Section 202(d) of the National Emergencies Act (50 U.S.C. 1622(d)) provides for the automatic termination of a national emergency unless, prior to the anniversary date of its declaration, the President publishes in the *Federal Register* and transmits to the Congress a notice stating that the emergency is to continue in effect beyond the anniversary date. In accordance with this provision, I have sent the enclosed notice, stating that the Haitian emergency is to continue in effect beyond October 4, 1993, to the *Federal Register* for publication.

The crisis between the United States and Haiti that led to the declaration on October 4, 1991, of a national emergency has not been resolved. While substantial progress has been made toward restoring democracy pursuant to United Nations Security Council Resolution 861, all necessary conditions to that restoration have not yet been met. Multilateral sanctions have been suspended but not terminated. Political conditions in Haiti continue, therefore, to be of considerable concern to the United States. For these reasons, I have determined that it is necessary to retain the authority to apply economic sanctions to ensure the restoration and security of the democratically elected Government of Haiti.

WILLIAM J. CLINTON

The White House,
September 30, 1993.

NOTE: The notice is listed in Appendix D at the end of this volume.

Memorandum on AIDS
September 30, 1993

Memorandum for the Heads of Executive Departments and Agencies

Subject: AIDS at Work

Halting the spread of HIV/AIDS and caring for those already touched by the disease is our common responsibility. Sadly, if you do not know someone with HIV/AIDS, you soon will. Every 17 minutes an American dies of AIDS; one of every five Americans knows someone who has died of AIDS; over one million Americans are already infected with HIV.

HIV/AIDS affects everyone in this Nation. Preventing the spread of HIV/AIDS and its associated human and economic costs is crucial to the success of health care reform. Likewise, enlightened, nondiscriminatory workplace policies are essential to both our efforts at reinventing government and at lowering health costs. This Administration and this Nation must do all within our power to prevent discrimination against those infected with HIV. I am committed to facing the difficult issues raised by HIV/AIDS.

This is an Administration of action and leadership by example. Today's Cabinet meeting discussion of HIV/AIDS is the beginning. All of you are asked to develop and fully implement comprehensive HIV/AIDS workplace policies and employee education and prevention programs by World AIDS Day, 1994, beginning with your Senior Staff.

To begin this process:

- Each Cabinet Secretary shall designate a member of his/her Senior Staff to implement ongoing HIV/AIDS education and prevention programs and to develop nondiscriminatory workplace policies for employees with HIV/AIDS.
- These designees, with the Office of the National AIDS Policy Coordinator (ONAPC), shall form a working group to implement this directive.
- The Office of Personnel Management (OPM) shall review its current HIV/AIDS workplace guidelines and assist in the development of workplace policies in the departments and agencies, as directed by ONAPC. OPM should pay particular attention to ensuring that the administrative burden on the departments and agencies is minimized.
- The National AIDS Policy Coordinator shall report to me quarterly on the progress of each department and agency, beginning January 1, 1994.
- The White House Staff and the Staff of the Executive Office of the President (EOP) will participate in HIV/AIDS education and prevention training prior to World AIDS Day, December 1, 1993.

HIV/AIDS is the health crisis of this century; it cannot be allowed to extend into the next. Only through education and prevention can we stop its spread. Only through aggressive and coordinated efforts at medical research can we find a cure. Join me on World AIDS Day, 1993, to remember the hundreds of thousands of American dead and the millions of Americans infected or suffering because of this disease; help me to vividly demonstrate this Administration's commitment to end the HIV/AIDS epidemic.

WILLIAM J. CLINTON

Statement on Signing the Foreign Operations Appropriations Legislation
September 30, 1993

Today I have signed into law H.R. 2295, the Foreign Operations Appropriations Act, which includes $2.5 billion in assistance for Russia and the other new independent states of the former Soviet Union. I am grateful for the bipartisan cooperation by the leadership and many other members of Congress who acted quickly to pass this package of assistance.

Enactment of this bill marks a major advance in our strategy to enlarge the world's free community of market democracies.

This bill also contains vital support for Israel and Egypt and other measures related to the Middle East peace process. The Congress's timely passage of these provisions, soon after the dramatic advances of the past few weeks, shows our Nation's commitment to peace in the Middle East.

The elements of the bill supporting Russia, Ukraine, Armenia, and the other new independent states include: the U.S. contribution for a multilateral Special Privatization and Restructuring Program, a G–7 initiative that will support the privatization of large Russian enterprises; financing for joint projects in the energy and environmental sectors, including programs to increase the safety of nuclear reactors; expansion of the President's Democracy Corps initiative begun at the Vancouver Summit; and humanitarian assistance for those parts of the former

Soviet Union where food and medicines are still desperately needed.

Recent events in Moscow highlight the urgency of helping Russia and the other states of the former Soviet Union sustain the momentum of democratic and economic reform. This bill makes a solid investment in our own national security and prosperity, enabling us to reduce the amount we spend for national defense while offering a hand of partnership to former adversaries who are making the difficult transition to the institutions of market democracy.

WILLIAM J. CLINTON

The White House,
September 30, 1993.

NOTE: H.R. 2295, approved September 30, was assigned Public Law No. 103–87.

Statement on Signing the Continuing Appropriations Resolution
September 30, 1993

Today I have signed into law House Joint Resolution 267, a Continuing Resolution that funds the operations of the Federal Government during October 1–21, 1993.

A Continuing Resolution is necessary at this time in order to keep the Government functioning while the Congress completes the appropriations process.

I commend the Congress for presenting me with a funding measure that provides for a simple, temporary extension of normal Government

operations and is free of extraneous amendments. I urge the Congress to complete the regular appropriations process by October 21 so that a second Continuing Resolution can be avoided.

WILLIAM J. CLINTON

The White House,
September 30, 1993.

NOTE: H.J. Res. 267, approved September 30, was assigned Public Law No. 103–88.

Exchange With Reporters Prior to a Meeting With Members of Congress
October 1, 1993

NAFTA

Q. What are you going to tell them to convince them on NAFTA?

The President. We're going to have just a free-flowing conversation about NAFTA. I'm going to make the arguments that I think are important, and try to answer some questions

and try to identify the continuing concerns of these Members. I'm very heartened, I must say, by the article in the Los Angeles Times today, showing that public opinion has had a rather marked shift in favor of the agreement in the last 10 days. And I think the more people think about what happens if you don't do it as compared to what happens if you do, the problems that people associate with the agreement will seem to be associated with the status quo more than with the agreement. And that's what I believe. So we're going to talk about that, and we're just going to keep working on it, to see if we can pass it.

Middle East Peace Process

Q. Mr. President, how did you manage to convince Crown Prince Hassan and Foreign Minister Peres to come over to the White House this afternoon and have this open meeting? There have been secret meetings before, but this is the first time they've met at that kind of an open level. How important is it?

The President. I think it's quite important, because I think it's important that their people see them working together. As you know, I had hoped we would see some more states, Arab states, willing to lift the embargo. And right now, we're not making a lot of progress on that, but I think we will. I think this is an important next step. We just have to get these folks comfortable dealing with each other and being seen dealing with each other among their own people. That was the donors conference that we're having in Washington today. I think it will give a real boost to the peace process.

NOTE: The exchange began at 11:08 a.m. in the Roosevelt Room at the White House. During the exchange, the President referred to Crown Prince Hassan of Jordan and Foreign Minister Shimon Peres of Israel. A tape was not available for verification of the content of this exchange.

Remarks and an Exchange With Reporters on the Middle East Peace Process
October 1, 1993

The President. Good afternoon, ladies and gentlemen. I have a brief statement and then I want to give the Crown Prince and the Foreign Minister an opportunity to make a few remarks.

I have just had the privilege of hosting what to date has been an unprecedented meeting in the Oval Office between His Royal Highness Crown Prince Hassan of Jordan and Foreign Minister Shimon Peres of Israel. This meeting is another important step on the road toward a comprehensive peace in the Middle East.

With me in the Oval Office were Shimon Peres, a principal architect of the pathbreaking Israel-PLO agreement, and Crown Prince Hassan, a leader who has literally devoted his life to the promotion of peace and a better future for his entire region. I am grateful to both of them for accepting my invitation to further the cause of peace.

On September 13th we bore witness to an event that should serve as a turning point in the history of the Middle East. Then I spoke of my commitment to help build a new future for the Middle East and all its people. Today we have taken two additional steps to turn that hope into reality.

This morning at the State Department, in an extraordinary demonstration of international support for peace, 43 nations from every region of the world helped to usher in this new era by providing their political and financial backing to those who would make peace in the Middle East. They pledged more than $600 million in immediate needs of the Palestinians and over $2 billion over the next 5 years to help establish Palestinian self-government.

And now this meeting has just taken place in the Oval Office, coming as it does some 2 weeks after Jordan and Israel signed their agreement on a common agenda to guide their negotiations. This symbolizes a new relationship between Jordan and Israel, marked by dialog and acceptance rather than confrontation and rejection.

The special relationship between the United States and Israel is central to the pursuit of peace, and I want to emphasize the great importance the United States attaches to Jordan's critical role in achieving lasting peace in the region.

In our meeting, both the Crown Prince and the Foreign Minister spoke of their hopes for the future of peace and prosperity for Israelis, Palestinians, Syrians, Lebanese, and Jordanians all alike, indeed, for the entire region. To help to work toward this goal they discussed ways to give more energy and force to their bilateral negotiations to resolve all outstanding issues.

They also agreed today that Israel and Jordan should establish a joint economic committee, much like the one agreed to in the Israel-PLO agreement of 2½ weeks ago. And we all agreed that Israel, Jordan, and the United States should establish a working group to be convened by the United States with two representatives from each country so that Israel and Jordan can agree, together with this Nation acting as facilitator, on the next steps in economic development in their two nations. They share so much in common, as they both pointed out. Now they want a common economic agenda.

They also agreed to work through this working group on common steps to reduce the certification in the area. We want to reduce the problems of the environment and especially the problems the desert presents as a part of the long-term economic growth of the Middle East, and especially of Israel and Jordan.

And finally, they both agreed that we should all get to work as soon as possible. That's the kind of action and the kind of attitude that I hope we can keep alive, coming as it does on the heels of so many other encouraging signs in the Middle East.

Finally, let me say that they spoke of their common commitment to work in close coordination with the Palestinians as this peace process goes forward. In this way, we can all act as partners with the Palestinians and work toward our common goals.

Let me say personally that I enjoyed this meeting very much. I applaud the Crown Prince. I applaud the Foreign Minister for coming here, for being a part of it. We believe that together we can work toward a peace that benefits everyone. And we believe there are things we can be doing now to benefit the countries and the peoples economically in ways that strengthen their inner sense of security and commitment to this remarkable process.

I'd like now to offer the microphone first to the Crown Prince and then to the Foreign Minister.

[*At this point, Prince Hassan of Jordan and Foreign Minister Peres of Israel made brief statements.*]

The President. Let me say first of all, to reiterate one of the things that the Crown Prince has said, this working group that we have agreed to set up will clearly operate within the framework and the context of the peace process and not independent of it but will focus on the economic and the environmental issues I have mentioned.

Second, I appreciate what the Foreign Minister said about the Secretary of State. In the privacy of our meeting, he said that today's speech by the Secretary of State was outrageous because it was the most expensive in memory. He raised more than a million dollars for every minute he talked today, which I appreciated.

And finally, let me say, this is somewhat to my chagrin, but one of the many matters that the Crown Prince and the Foreign Minister agreed on in the meeting is that they would not take any questions today, but I could. So here I am.

Q. Mr. President, what about the Arab boycott? Can you tell us your feelings about whether the continued Arab boycott is an obstacle to the kind of economic cooperation that you gentlemen are trying to forge here today?

The President. Well, I think, first of all, they have agreed to find common economic objectives which they can pursue and seek investment for from all around the world, and they've asked us to help them do that. And so we intend to. Obviously, the region can grow more rapidly when all its partners can trade with one another and invest in one another.

I think the statement, though, of the countries in continuing their position was not altogether discouraging. Obviously, as you know, the United States wanted the boycott lifted now, but basically they were saying we have to finish the peace process. Well, we all agree with that. Israel agrees with that. No one disputes that. And so I don't want us to be deterred.

This is a really historic day. We have this meeting and the agreement coming out of it. We have the remarkable donors conference today and the results coming out of this. We are moving this process very quickly, and I am confident that in the course of time we'll get the boycott lifted.

Q. Mr. President, now that you've brought Israel and the PLO together here on the White House lawn, and Israel and Jordan today, what are the prospects of bringing Israel and Syria together here at the White House?

The President. I thought you were going to

ask me if I could get both parties together in the Congress on a health care plan.

Well, I'm hopeful. We have to take these things as we can, but I'm quite hopeful. I will say again, I am committed to finishing the peace process. I have told President Asad that. I have made it clear to Prime Minister Hariri, and we met at the United Nations and discussed Lebanon. Nothing that Prime Minister Rabin or Foreign Minister Peres has said to me leads me to believe that they have a different position.

But I will say again, the most important thing we can do at each step along the way is to build the support among the ordinary people of Israel, among the Palestinians, among the Jordanians for the agreements that have been made, for the processes that are underway, so that people all over the Middle East have a greater sense of confidence and security about what has been agreed to and what is being done. The Crown Prince made a very important point that I think needs to be reiterated.

We are trying to make our statements brief and our actions and commitments long. And that is what we have to do. And so, I understand that this whole thing has to be finished. But to finish it, to get to the end, we have to absorb the full implications of the enormity of the things which have been done and implement them in a way that keeps the support for the process going. And I am committed to finishing it with all parties, more so than when we began.

Q. Mr. President, how much of the money that was given today at the donors conference will or should go to Jordan? Or will all of this go exclusively to the Palestinians? And if so, what will Israel and Jordan be cooperating about?

The President. Well, what we are going to do, this committee is going to come up with a whole different economic agenda for Israel and for Jordan and for how to deal with the overlapping Palestinian issues. And there are some overlapping ones which might lead to some different decisions down the road about what we do with commitments that have already been made. But I think that we need a whole different economic agenda there.

I think, as you know, I'm extraordinarily excited about this group of American Jewish and Arab American business people we got together who want to see an enormous private sector commitment in the Middle East. They are particularly interested in what can be agreed upon between Israel and Jordan and whether they could play a role in that. So I wouldn't rule out anything.

But the purpose of the donors conference today was to give life and meaning and reality to the agreement we saw between Israel and the PLO. There will have to be other investments, other commitments that will help to deal with the problems of Jordan, including the enormous problem Jordan has of accumulated debt. There needs to be some debt relief for Jordan, and the United States will support that. And there are a whole lot of other things that we need to be doing on that.

Yes?

Q. Do you think that this is leading to a confederation between Jordan, Israel, and the Palestinians? Is this the beginning? Is this the basis to something like that?

The President. That's a question that I haven't answered and shouldn't answer. Anything regarding the political organization of the Middle East, that's a decision that will have to be made by the parties themselves. The United States will support the process and will support the decision of the people there.

Thank you.

NOTE: The President spoke at 3:29 p.m. on the South Lawn at the White House.

Message to the Congress Transmitting a Report on Strengthening America's Shipyards
October 1, 1993

To the Congress of the United States:

In accordance with the requirements of section 1031 of the National Defense Authorization Act for Fiscal Year 1993 (Public Law 102–484), I transmit herewith a report entitled "Strengthening America's Shipyards: A Plan for Competing in the International Market."

The U.S. shipbuilding industry is unsurpassed in building the finest and most complex naval vessels in the world. Now that the Cold War has ended, these shipyards, like many other defense firms, face a new challenge—translating their skills from the military to the commercial market. Individual shipyards already have begun to meet this challenge. The enclosed report de-scribes steps that the Government is taking and will take to assist their efforts. I look forward to working with the Congress and the industry to ensure a successful transition to a competitive industry in a truly competitive marketplace.

WILLIAM J. CLINTON

The White House,
October 1, 1993.

Statement on Emergency Assistance to Earthquake Victims in India
October 1, 1993

The people of the United States are shocked and saddened by the devastating earthquake that has taken thousands of lives and left thousands more homeless. I have directed our Government to take immediate action to help ease the suffering. I have also asked Ambassador Ray Flynn to accompany the supplies, to assess the situa-tion, and report back to me.

NOTE: The President's statement was included in a White House statement announcing that the President had directed the Defense Department and the Agency for International Development to provide humanitarian assistance to earthquake victims in India.

The President's Radio Address
October 2, 1993

Good morning. This week the good will and hopefulness that surrounded the announcement of our health security plan continued to grow. A consensus is developing that our central goal, comprehensive health benefits for you and your family that can never be taken away, is now within reach and must be achieved. For the first time in our lifetimes, the question before Congress is no longer whether to provide health security but how.

Something unique is happening here in Washington: A coalition is taking shape across political boundaries, a coalition concerned more with passing health care than with scoring political points. And when the Congress passes health care reform, it won't have a label that says Democrat or Republican, it will be delivered to you with a label that says made in America.

This week as Congress began its deliberations, health care reform and the American people have had an extraordinary advocate on their side, the First Lady. Before, in our history, only Eleanor Roosevelt and Rosalynn Carter have testified before Congress. I'm proud of the intellect and compassion and the leadership Hillary is bringing to this issue and to our country. Her commitment to health care is a human issue. She says to find a solution, it must pass the "mom test," something that she could explain to her mother and her mother would support. That certainly has cut through the heart of a very complex health care debate.

During her testimony before the Senate Finance Committee this week, something extraordinary happened: Republican Senator James Jeffords of Vermont, a leading expert on health care, stepped forward and endorsed our plan. I'm sure that after the acrimony of the budget debate, this cooperative spirit comes as welcome news to all of you as it does to me. Solving health care must remain above politics. Indeed, I hope every one of our legislative efforts in the months ahead is done in the same bipartisan spirit.

I've said since the beginning of this debate, I welcome—I need—good ideas and options from everyone. No party, no person, no segment of the health care community owns all the good ideas. After all, it was a Republican President, Richard Nixon, who first recommended over 20 years ago extending health coverage by asking every employer to take responsibility for paying some of his employees' health care costs. A current Republican Senator, Bob Packwood of Oregon, sponsored that bill 20 years ago.

Already the fruits of bipartisan cooperation are visible. In just a few months, we've moved from deep alarm over health care to designing a proposal, to crafting a solution. As I said, we don't have all the answers, and we know that. But we have to find them, and we do have a plan.

I believe this plan will work. It will guarantee comprehensive health benefits to every one of you. It's based on the notion of preserving and protecting what is best about American health care and fixing what has gone wrong.

My goal is to make the world's finest private health care system work better and work for everyone. We've rejected a big Government solution. We've rejected broad-based taxes. We've insisted that small business be protected. And I embrace the compassionate American view that no one should go without health care.

This plan will drastically cut the paperwork that now clogs the American health care system. It will maintain the highest quality health care, and it will retain your right to choose your doctors. In fact, for most of you, your choices in health care will increase, not decrease, if this plan passes.

The plan will keep health care costs down by controlling spending, by providing free preventive care that keeps us healthy and saves money in the long run. It also asks all of us to take more responsibility for paying for a health care system that all of us use but only some of us pay for.

We also ask everyone, every American, to take more responsibility for personal behavior. Just as insurance companies and doctors and lawyers and the Government must take more responsibility upon themselves to make the system work better, so must each individual. It is the common sense and shared values of our health security plan that are bringing people of all political persuasions to the cause.

I watched some of Hillary's testimony. I wish I could have seen more. We spent a lot of time talking together about what she learned from the Congress and how we can make health care a reality for each of .you. I think we've done the responsible thing by accepting this challenge, a challenge too long delayed, and by beginning a truly constructive bipartisan debate on what many have characterized as the most important piece of domestic legislation in a generation.

And I believe that once we succeed in providing health security to each of you, every family will have a chance to prosper and dream again, freed from today's fears: freed from the fear that if you lose your job, you'll lose your health care; if your business goes down, you'll never have health care coverage; if you get sick and you really need it, you won't have health care. Those fears have to be done away with.

As we move forward we'll continue to carry with us the indelible memory of the thousands of people we've talked to who have tangled with the health care system and lost, of the thousands who live in fear of losing their health care, and to the plight of so many of you who have played by the rules and lost to a system that often doesn't follow them. Once heard, no one forgets those voices.

Thank you for making this a great beginning, and thanks for listening.

NOTE: The President spoke at 10:06 a.m. in the Oval Office at the White House.

Remarks and an Exchange With Reporters on Russia
October 3, 1993

The President. Ladies and gentlemen, I have received a rather extended briefing on what we know about what is going on in Russia, and I want to make a couple of comments about it. First of all, it is clear that the violence was perpetrated by the Rutskoy-Khasbulatov forces, that there has been significant violence today in Moscow. It is also clear that President Yeltsin bent over backwards to avoid the use of force, to avoid excessive force from the beginning of this, and I still am convinced that the United States must support President Yeltsin and the process of bringing about free and fair elections. We cannot afford to be in the position of wavering at this moment or of backing off or giving any encouragement to people who clearly want to derail the election process and are not committed to reform in Russia. So we are following events moment by moment. As you know, we have access to television coverage there so you are also pretty current on it. But that is the most I know now, and that is our position.

Q. Do you think that Yeltsin can survive, Mr. President, and will you cut off aid if he is deposed?

The President. Well, I don't expect him to be deposed. I wouldn't overreact to this, now. I think the people clearly stand far more supportive of him than the Rutskoy-Khasbulatov and they seem—they don't have any organized military support that we're aware of. So we'll just have to wait for developments, but I have

no reason to believe that he would be deposed.

Q. Mr. President, have you spoken to President Yeltsin?

The President. No. I'm sure he's got more important things to do right now than to talk to me, and I don't think the United States should be involved in the moment-to-moment management of this crisis, but I do want him to know of my continued support and the support of the United States.

Q. What can the U.S. Government do right now?

The President. Well first of all, we can get as much intelligence, as quickly as possible, about what's going on, and we can do our best to look after the safety of the Americans who are there and the security of the Embassy, which has received some attention from our folks, and so far the reports on that are good.

Q. Do you have any plans to cancel your trip or postpone your trip in any way?

The President. No.

NOTE: The President spoke at 12:09 p.m. on the South Lawn at the White House. A tape was not available for verification of the content of these remarks.

Remarks to the Community in Sacramento, California
October 3, 1993

Thank you very much. Thank you for coming. Thank you for being here. Thank you for doing what you have done for the United States. It's wonderful to be here. It's wonderful to be in Sacramento, and it's great to be at McClellan, and I thank you for all being here with me today.

I'd like to say a special word of thanks to General Phillips and the people at this base for the work they have done and the work they did with your Mayor and others to keep this base alive. You are a good testimony to the wisdom of that decision, and I thank you for that.

I also want to thank General Yates, the Commander of the Air Force Materiel Division, for flying all the way across the country to be with us today. And I want to tell you one thing,

he made a real sacrifice because this is his birthday, and I thank him for spending it with us today.

I want to say, also, a special word of thanks to Congressman Hamburg, Congressman Matsui, and Congressman Fazio——

[*At this point, audience members interrupted the President's remarks.*]

You all ignore them. They don't want you to hear, but you want to hear it. Just come on. Most people in this country still believe in free speech. That's one of the things worth fighting for. I also want to say a very special word of thanks to these Members of Congress who have supported our efforts to deal with the problems of America.

I got interested in making that long and challenging race for President because I was worried about three things: I thought this country was coming apart when it ought to be coming together; I thought we were going in the wrong direction economically and we risked losing the American dream for millions of young people; and I thought that politics had become a sideshow of shouting words, instead of an instrument by which the American people could forthrightly face their problems and do something about it.

I am reminded, too, on this day, because of the events in Moscow and in Somalia, that we still live in a dangerous world. And I ask you to take just a few moments, once again, to quietly express your support for the people who are fighting for freedom in Russia and for the brave men and women in our Armed Forces, including those in Somalia today who lost their lives in a very successful mission against brutality and anarchy. My deepest condolences go to the families and the friends of those brave young Americans, and I know that all of you support them, as well.

One of the hardest things we have had to learn as a people, in the last few years, is that there is now no longer an easy division between our national security at the end of the cold war abroad and our economic and social security here at home. There's no longer an easy division between foreign policy and domestic policy, and it is perfectly clear to everyone now that if we are not strong at home, we cannot continue to lead the world. And so I have done what I could to help us to become stronger at home.

That means, as much as anything else, as we attempt to revive this economy, we have got to focus on the economy of California, the State which has 12 percent of our Nation's people but 25 percent of our Nation's unemployed. It is clear to me that we must take this problem which has developed for you over a period of years and go after it with a vengeance, step by step, with discipline and concentration.

This last week, in Washington, we made several announcements which mean more jobs and a brighter future for California. Last week, the Vice President and I announced that the United States, in recognition of the end of the cold war, would remove export controls on 70 percent of the computers and supercomputers made in the United States. That will increase exports by billions and tens of billions of dollars. It means more jobs for California. In this State, that order frees up $30 billion of exports in

computers, $2 billion in telecommunications, and $5 billion in supercomputers. In a State where one in 10 jobs depends on exports, that is very good news, indeed.

Last week, I also announced a plan to help our shipbuilders to be more competitive in the global economy. There are 124,000 Americans employed in shipbuilding, many of them in California, in places like the Nasco plant in San Diego. This plan will help them get access to foreign markets which they deserve and which they have been denied for too long.

And last week, with so many people in this country desperate for work and knowing we have to find a way to help create jobs through supporting the environment, something you've done here, we announced a ground-breaking research plan involving our defense labs, our military facilities, and the Big Three automakers to triple the fuel efficiency of our automobiles within a decade, creating tens of thousands of new jobs for Americans.

Earlier this year we announced a project very important to the future of this area, a technology reinvestment program to convert defense technology either to dual uses, defense and commercial, or purely commercial uses, something you are doing here. We have received, in return for what will soon be about $1 billion in Federal matching money, over 2,800 proposals. And guess what? Twenty-five percent of them came from the State of California. That means more jobs for California.

Tomorrow I know that Congressman Fazio and others will release the details of a new joint partnership between the Government and automakers to develop and produce electric cars, taking advantage of dual-use technology right here at McClellan. That means more jobs for California and a brighter future for America.

And let me thank you, especially here at McClellan, for the partnership you have formed with the Environmental Protection Agency and the California EPA. By streamlining Government and working together, you have performed a cleanup that, under the old rules, would have taken 6 years and $10 million. You did it in 8 weeks at a fifth of the cost. And we intend to do that all over America, copying your leadership.

Let me say to you, my fellow Americans, my biggest task as your President is to try to clearly define the time in which we live, point the way to positive change, and give the American people the security they need to make those changes. We cannot, any of us in our personal lives, in our family lives, and in our communities, make changes we need to make unless we are personally secure enough to make them. But we cannot deny the changes that are abroad in the world and pretend that they're not there.

When I leave you and walk back into this hangar, I will see some of the work that is being done here in McClellan to develop dual-use technologies. That means that the people here have decided that change will be our friend and not our enemy. When faced with a time of profound change, we can take one of two courses. We can hunker down, turn away, and pretend it's not there, and that works about one time in 100. Most of the time, you know as well as I do, when you see profound change and you want to preserve what is most important in your values, your family, your community, you have to find a way to make that change your friend. That is what this administration is dedicated to doing, both in trying to change the rules of the economic game and in trying to open up a new era of time when Americans who work hard and play by the rules have a certain basic security.

Yes, I think we ought to change our economic policies. We are giving this country the toughest trade policy it's had in years and years, demanding access to our markets. Yes, we cannot continue to have massive trade deficits with the Far East, where 40 percent of our exports are going. And yes, I favor opening up trade to Mexico and ultimately to Latin America because we have a trade surplus there and its means more jobs for Americans. I do favor it.

But let me say something. If you listen to the people who are opposed to the trade agreement, they have some very good arguments, but they're arguing against things that happened for the last 12 years. They're arguing against the insecurity of the times our people have faced and the fact that our Government has not responded to them. And so we have sought to give the American people more security by bringing this deficit down, which threatens our children and grandchildren; by changing the tax laws so that working families with children in the home, without regard to their incomes, will be lifted above poverty so there will never be an excuse to stay on welfare because work will be rewarded for people; but by reforming the student loan program so that we lower the inter-est rates and string out the repayment terms and make college available to every American for the first time; by giving tens of thousands of our young people the chance to serve their country in their community through a program of national service that will also enable them to earn credit against a college education or other education and training.

Yes, security is important, and we have other challenges before us, as well. If you look at the number of people who have been killed in this country just in the last month in drive-by shootings and mindless acts of violence, and you consider the fact that this is the only advanced country in the world where children can be in cities with no supervision, no support, roaming the streets, better armed than the police because we refuse to take automatic weapons out of their hands or pass the Brady bill, or check on it, that is wrong, and we must change that. We must change that.

But, my fellow Americans, at the root of so much of our security is the fact that we are living in a changing economy where the average young worker will change jobs eight times in a lifetime; where more and more, when people lose their jobs and they go on unemployment— it's not the way it was when I was young, where people would go on unemployment for 4 weeks or 8 weeks and then they'd get their old job back. Now most people get another job, but it's a different job. So we don't need an unemployment system anymore, we need a reemployment system to retrain our workers for the jobs that are there and for the future.

More than anything else, if you look to the heart now of our Federal budget deficit, if you look to the heart now of the economic problems of many of our leading exporters, and if you look to the heart of the gnawing insecurity that grips hardworking American families, you will find lurking behind it all the most expensive, least efficient health care system in the entire Western world.

Only in America—only in America do we spend over 14 percent of our income on health care—Canada's at 10, Germany and Japan below 9—going up more rapidly than any other country; going up twice as fast as inflation. And we still leave 35 million people, 35 million permanently without health insurance, 2 million more every month, another 100,000 every month permanently losing their health insurance.

Only in America do we have 1,500 separate

insurance companies writing thousands of different policies, creating mountains of different paperwork and always, always looking for ways not to cover the people who bought their insurance. That only happens in this country.

Only in America are the doctors who hired out to keep people well and help people who are sick spending more and more countless hours, some of them as much as 25 hours a week now, filling out forms and paperwork. Only in America has that happened. Only in America have, in the last 10 years, we seen the work of clerical workers in the hospitals grow at 4 times the rate of new doctors and health care providers. That is not happening anywhere else.

Why? Because while we have the finest doctors and nurses and technology and research in the world, we have a system of financing and delivering health care that is a nightmare. It is a nightmare for people who have lost their health insurance. It is a nightmare for people who don't get it. It's a nightmare for people who have to depend on the Government to get theirs, when not all the providers will cover Medicaid. It has been bad. And guess what? It is the primary cause of the exploding Federal deficit. It is the primary cause of many of our biggest companies' inability to compete more overseas. It is the primary cause that millions of American workers will not get a raise between now and the end of the decade because all the new profits of the companies that are trying to cover their health care will go into the exploding cost of premiums. And only in America do we spend 10 cents on the dollar in a $900 billion health care bill on paperwork that no other country has.

I say to you, my fellow Americans, it's time to give the American people health care that is always there, health care that can never be taken away, health care that is simpler and better.

Now, you know, since we're here at this magnificent air base, let me just ask you something: Can you think of a single institution in this country in the last 10 years, in the midst of all the chaos and social breakdown and violence and family troubles in America, is there any institution that has worked better than the United States military to train and educate people to perform missions, to continually give people new skills, and to provide the coherence that we need? And is there any institution that's done a better job of opening opportunities to

people without regard to race or gender? No. Why? One reason is, there is order, security, and support. Could the military have done its mission if they had the same health care system the rest of the American people have and half the people in the service could lose their health care on a given day by some accident or because a wife or a husband or a child turned out to have an illness that wasn't covered in the fine print of some policy? You know it couldn't have happened. We owe the rest of the American people that security in the face of the changing times in which we live.

Let me say, people say to me, oh, you can't slow the growth of health care costs. I say to them, look at California. I want to thank your insurance commissioner for the work he's done with my wife's Health Care Task Force to develop a health care system. You look at the California experience. Look at what happened to the health care costs of the people who had the benefit of being in the California public employee system, when the people who were providing it knew that the State was broke and didn't have a lot of money and when there were enough people there that they had bargaining power to get high-quality health care at an affordable price. What happened? The inflation rate and the premiums was less than one-third the national inflation rate in health care.

And let me say some other things about this health care system, because there's been a lot of misinformation put out there. I see all these children here. One of the things that is killing this health care system of ours is that so many people have no coverage, that when they get health care, it's when they're real sick, and it's real expensive, and they show up at the emergency room. Under this plan, for the first time in history, there will be a comprehensive package of benefits which will guarantee preventive and primary health care services to pregnant mothers, to little children, to women who need mammograms, to men who need cholesterol tests. Those are the things that will lower the cost of health care and strengthen the fabric of our economy.

Look at the burden that California alone pays because of the uninsured cost of caring for AIDS patients. Look at that. Under this system, when everybody gets covered and all people are in big pools so that one high-risk patient's cost is spread across a lot of folks, we will have coverage in the regular system and you will not have particular States going broke because they have disproportionate burdens of immigrants, of AIDS patients, or anything else. This is another important feature of this.

But finally, let me say two other things. Under this system the American people will have more choice than most Americans do now. If you have a health care plan that's better than the one we're writing into law, your company can keep giving it to you, and the cost of it won't go up as rapidly. But there's a limit for the first time to what can be taken away. If you don't have one, you will get one. And you'll have more choices today. Only one in three workers in a plant with a health insurance plan has any choice in the way they get their health care. Every American worker will be guaranteed at least three different options in the health care plan. And that's a plus for America, to give the consumers of this country more choices.

And finally, I want to say a special word of thanks to the thousands of Americans from all across this country who helped us to put this plan together and especially to the literally hundreds and hundreds of doctors and nurses and others who told us their stories, so that we found, unbelievably, we had doctors who were miserable, nurses who were unhappy, and the people who lost their insurance in the 11th hour when they didn't know what was going to hit them. So for the first time in the history, we are going to have a health care plan that has significant input on the front end from the people who provide the health care because they know, the ones who've been involved in this process, that we cannot go on.

And finally, let me just make this point: At some point in life when you have a problem, whatever it is, you have to ask yourself a pretty simple question, because every change involves taking a chance, you have to ask yourself which is greater: the cost of change or the cost of staying the same? It is clear that the greater cost is to keep on doing what we're doing and letting America go bankrupt and breaking the hearts of millions of American families.

And so I say to you, we've got a lot of work to do to turn the California economy around. But we've taken important steps that were not taken before, and there's more to come. We've got a lot of work to do to work through all the complexities of the health care issue. We've got a lot of work to do to convince Americans to have the courage and to give Americans the security they need to change. But I am telling you, folks, if we do what we ought to do, California and this country will walk into the 21st century with their heads held high, with the American dream still alive for our children, with our diversity a strength, not a weakness, in a nation that is still leading the world, if we have the courage to change and the will to give our people the security they deserve.

That is what I'm dedicated to. And I thank you for being here today to support that. God bless you all. Thank you.

NOTE: The President spoke at 5:04 p.m. at McClellan Air Force Base.

Remarks in a Town Meeting in Sacramento
October 3, 1993

The President. First of all, let me thank all of you for being here tonight, and also thank all those I can't see yet who are at the other stations, and all the people of California who are watching.

I want to talk about whatever you want to talk about tonight, but just by way of introduction, let me say that when I ran for President, I ran basically because I thought our country was headed in the wrong direction economically, because I thought our people were coming apart instead of coming together as a country, and because I thought our Government wasn't facing up to our problems. And since taking office, I've tried to address those things by changing our economic focus, by trying to bring people together across regional and racial and other lines, and by trying to just take the tough problems of the country, one after the other, starting with the deficit, trying to make some progress on it.

There are a lot of things I hope we get to

talk about, including the California economy tonight, which I spent countless hours on since I've been President. But I want to talk a minute just about the health care issue, because it relates to so much else.

We are in a time of great change. You know that out here. You've benefited from some of these changes in the last 10 years. Now you've suffered for the last 3 years from a lot of those economic changes. In order for America to make change our friend instead of our enemy, we have to have a certain base level of personal security and family security in this country. In order for us to do that, we have to be competitive with other nations, too. And both of those things bring us always back to health care, where we spend more money and have less to show for it and where we're the only advanced country that doesn't provide health security for all our people.

So the thrust of this health care effort is, first of all, to guarantee Americans security— health care that's always there, health care that can never be taken away—and to do it in a way that is fair to the American people and that lowers, not cuts health care costs but lowers the rate at which it is increasing, so that it helps the economy as well as helps the health security of American families. And it is the key to dealing with so many of our other problems and to giving the American people the security they need to face the future. I hope we get to talk more about it.

Thank you.

Russia

Stan Atkinson. Mr. President, while we are here tonight to address the matters of health care, the economy, and other domestic issues, we certainly can't ignore the events talking place today and tonight in Russia. It has been a bloody day there, with anti-Yeltsin forces fighting police and military units in the streets. Well-armed protesters won most of the battles, ramming trucks into government buildings, even launching rocket-propelled grenades. Russian President Yeltsin has issued a state of emergency, and military reinforcements in the form of his crack best troops are en route to Moscow.

Carol Bland. And before we begin tonight, Mr. President, we're wondering whether or not you could update us on the situation in Russia, in particular this Government's response to it.

The President. Well, first of all, let me say

what happened is that the opponents of reform, the people who don't want a new constitution, the people that don't want an election, basically in the person of Mr. Rutskoy and Mr. Khasbulatov, their supporters who basically started all this disorder and violence today—President Yeltsin has bent over backwards not to have the soldiers fire on anybody, not to promote any violence. And he may be thinking today he went too far in that, because they basically got up a head of steam, and the situation got out of control.

I believe that he will be successful in the end because the people support him. And I think the United States should support Yeltsin as long as he is the person who embodies a commitment to democracy and to letting the Russian people chart their own course. And he does. The people who have started this opposition are people who represent the old Communist system that Russia is trying so hard to move away from.

So I wish him success. I thank him for not trying to promote any unnecessary violence. And I hope that this will be as peaceful a resolution as possible, but it's going to be pretty tough for them for the next few days.

Mr. Atkinson. Thank you, Mr. President. Now on to our program. In addition to the audience here with you at KCRA in Sacramento, we're also going to hear from a lot of other people all over California, up and down the State, in fact. They're in cities tonight waiting to listen to you. For instance, may I do some introductions? Joining us by satellite from KRON television in San Francisco, reporter and news anchor Pete Wilson, along with a live studio audience. Moving south to Los Angeles, Paul Moyer is there with a group assembled at KNBC television. Welcome to all of you. And also, from southern California, Marty Levine. Marty and our fourth studio audience join us live from KNSD television in San Diego. And from Sacramento and KCRA, I'm Stan Atkinson. Mr. President, my partner, Carol Bland.

Health Care Reform

[*Ms. Bland introduced a participant whose insurance company refused to cover the cost of a bone marrow transplant for her son who had leukemia. She asked if the new health care plan would cover such experimental procedures.*]

The President. The answer to the question

is that in most cases the answer would be yes. And the reason I say most cases is that under our plan people will have coverage as they do in insurance today for certain conditions like leukemia. And when there is evidence that that is the best available treatment and a doctor for the child, in this case, for a child or for an adult wants to pursue that treatment, then the insurer will not take that option away. But there has to be—I don't want to mislead you, there has to be at least a doctor, there has to be some substantial evidence that the treatment might work—you never know if it will in experimental treatment—but that it might work.

So in the case of a bone marrow transplant where there is evidence that it often has been effective, it should cover that. And that's the way we tried to set it up. In other words, to be less restrictive than most insurance policies are today but still leave doctors with their considered medical judgment, some ground not to do things that don't make any sense at all.

Mr. Atkinson. Mr. President, if we can step back just a moment, let me call your attention to our screen, and we're going to see—that's a fellow whose name is Pete Wilson. Now, he's not the Governor Pete Wilson, he's the news anchor Pete Wilson from KRON television in San Francisco.

Pete.

Pete Wilson. Stan, the President and I have been over this a couple of times just in recent weeks, as a matter of fact.

The President. He always gives me that disclaimer. But I talk to Governor Wilson all the time. [*Laughter*]

Public School System

[*Mr. Wilson introduced a participant who asked what the administration plans to do to improve the public school system.*]

The President. Good question. Before I answer that, I want to thank that lady who just asked that question. It must take an awful lot of courage for her to come here within a month of losing her child, and I thank you.

Let's talk about the public schools. I have been working since I first became President to pass a new bill called Goals 2000, which will enable us to change the way we evaluate our schools and will give the schools the incentives and resources they need to perform at a much higher level.

Essentially, what we want to do is to set some national standards, not by Government employees but by educational experts, some national standards that, then, we can measure every school against every year so that parents and other interested people can tell how well the schools are doing. We want to emphasize the things that we know are important for the future, especially science, mathematics, creative thinking skills, the ability to use the language to reason through new problems, and to provide special resources for that.

The Secretary of Education has worked with the Governors of the country and educators all over the country. They're very excited about having the Government, instead of telling educators what kind of specific inputs they have, set some national standards, give the schools more flexibility over how they do it, and go forward.

The second thing we've done is to try to change the way we distribute Federal aid to education, which will be of immense benefit to California. A lot of the poorer school districts, or districts with a lot of poor kids, don't get their fair share of aid. The bill that we have in the legislature now, and the Congress passes, will be a big boon to California.

The third thing we've tried to do is to deal with the problem of the kids who don't go to 4-year colleges or don't graduate from them. Well over half of our students don't graduate from 4-year colleges, but 100 percent of our students need both a high school diploma and at least 2 years of post-high school education. So we're setting up a system now which will integrate the public schools and the 2-year institutions, the community colleges, the vocational institutions, and others, starting in high school, to let people meld work and learning and begin to do that for a lifetime.

And the final thing that we've tried to do that I think is perhaps going to have the most profound effect over the long run is to be able to tell our young people while they're in junior high and high school that they won't have to worry about paying for a college education, because we've reformed the student loan system to lower the interest rates for the loans, to string out the repayment terms, to make college affordable to everyone, and to allow, starting next year 25,000, going up to hundreds of thousands of students to repay their loan through community service at the local level.

So, start with standards instead of inputs. I spent 12 years working on the public schools, and I can tell you, we need national standards, and then we need to focus how we can give resources to the schools to meet those standards instead of telling them how to run every minute of every day in the classroom. Take account of these other things, and I think you'll see some substantial improvements.

I also will tell you that our bill provides for, I think, a better option than the option that's on the ballot out here for choice. We give States incentives to allow more choice of schools within the public school system, and we give incentives for school systems to empower people to set up schools, license them, and run them according to high standards as a part of the public school system, like you could give a group of teachers permission to start their own school, but it would be part of a school system, and it would have to meet, then, the standards of that school system and give the students and their parents the choice to go there. I think that's a better way to go than the initiative that's on the ballot out here.

Mr. Atkinson. Mr. President, we're going to switch southward now to Los Angeles. And at the studios of KNBC, there's Paul Moyer.

Violence in Schools

Paul Moyer. Stan, thank you. We're going to continue on the vein of education and schools, but this is a different aspect of the life in schools, Mr. President. I would like to introduce you to a very, very brave young man. His name is Dion Brown, he's 15 years old, and he has seen and experienced something that hopefully none of us ever will. About 3 weeks ago he was in line at Dorsey High School here in Los Angeles with his brother, simply trying to register for class. And his brother was shot in the stomach, caught in gang cross-fire. His brother was supposed to be here. He's so afraid of retaliation, we couldn't find him. We're not going to show you Dion's face because he, too, is afraid. But Mr. President, he has a question for you. He's a little nervous, so bear with us.

[*Mr. Brown explained how his brother was shot and asked what the President planned to do to prevent violence in schools.*]

The President. Thank you for coming tonight. And thank you for saying that. Let me say, first of all, the story you just heard unfortunately is becoming all too common, and not just in California and not just in big cities. And we ought to start with first things first.

This is the only country, the only advanced country in the world, the only country I know of where we would permit children access to weapons that make them better armed than police forces. So I'll tell you what we ought to do. I've asked the Congress to pass the Brady bill, which would give us a national system, a waiting period to check the backgrounds of people for age, criminal records, and mental health history before we sell weapons.

There are several bills before the Congress which would ban assault weapons, which have no purpose other than to kill. We ought to pass one. We ought to do it this year. States all over the country are looking at ownership laws which make it illegal for minors to have guns unless they're in the presence of their parents, either hunting or on a target range. And we ought to do that in every State. And we ought to look at the laws by which we regulate gun sellers. We've got to get the guns out of the hands of the children. It is imperative.

Now, in addition to that, I do have a part of this education bill that I just spoke to, safe schools initiative, which would give schools the ability to have more security forces. And in the crime bill, which includes the Brady bill, the waiting period, there are funds which would help people all over the country, cities all over the country, hire another 50,000 police officers which would allow hard-strapped cities to deploy these police officers around schools and at the places of greatest need. It makes a 50 percent downpayment on my desire and commitment from the campaign to put another 100,000 police officers on the street over the next 4 years.

Now, let me just say one final thing. I also think—make them safe first. Make the schools safe, get the guns out of the hands of the kids, put more police on the beat. Start there. Then you have to take these young people who haven't had the family supports, the neighborhood supports, the community supports that a lot of us have had, that we've taken for granted, and realize they are the tip end of a generation of change. This has been going on for 30 years, getting worse every year. And we have got to find ways to give these kids a structure, an order, a hope to their lives.

We have 10 closed military bases today around the country where we've got an experimental program going with the National Guard, teaching high school dropouts to go back and go to school and going through boot camp-like exercises. These are kids that didn't commit crimes. And we've been flooded with kids who want it, because they have no structure in their lives.

We also have more boot camps in the crime bill for first-time offenders. You've got to give these kids something to say "yes" to instead of telling them "no" all the time. But first, there has to be a reestablishment of order and safety in the schools and on the streets. And I hope if you care about this—I know I'm going on a little long, but this is a big deal—the Congress should not drag its feet. They have been debating this for 2 years. It is time to pass a crime bill, it is time to pass the Brady bill, it is time to ban assault weapons, get them out of the hands of kids so the police can do their jobs, and put more police on the street.

Mr. Atkinson. President Clinton, we're going to move even farther south. We're into San Diego now. Your audience awaits you at the studios of KNSD.

Immigration

[*Marty Levine introduced a migrant rights activist who asked about blockades to control illegal immigration from Mexico.*]

The President. Well, I think we should have more Border Patrol guards, and I think we should do more to restrict illegal immigration, I certainly do. I think the fact that we have so much illegal immigration and that half of all of the illegal immigrants in America are in California, a State with an unemployment rate 3 percentage points above the national average, is endangering the historic attitude of America that has been proimmigration. I mean, Los Angeles County has people from 150 different racial and ethnic groups alone. Immigrants made this country. But they did it, by and large, by operating within our laws. If we permit our laws to be regularly violated and flagrantly violated and impose those costs on the State that has the biggest economic problems, I think we run the risk of undermining support for immigration, which I think is a very important American value. So yes, I believe we should stiffen our efforts to control the border.

I don't think it undermines the NAFTA negotiations. The President of Mexico has never asked me to do anything illegal or to continue what is a policy that is inconsistent with our law. And as a matter of fact—I hope we get a chance to talk about this later tonight—one of the reasons that I so strongly support this North American Free Trade Agreement is if you have more jobs on both sides of the border and incomes go up in Mexico, that will dramatically reduce the pressure felt by Mexican working people to come here for jobs. Most immigrants, keep in mind, come here illegally not for the social services, most of them come here for the jobs. If they have jobs in Mexico and they pay decent wages, which this agreement will provide for, then they'll be more likely to stay there, and the immigrants who come here will be more likely to be a manageable number and legal in nature.

Health Care Reform

Mr. Atkinson. We have a health care question for you now, President Clinton. And back in KCRA, Carol Bland.

[*Ms. Bland introduced a participant who asked if she would be able to choose her doctor under the new health care plan.*]

The President. Yes.

Q. And will I have easy access to the specialists?

The President. Yes. The answer to your questions are, yes, you'll have freedom of choice; yes, you'll have easy access to specialists. And most Americans will have more choice than they have now. You heard what she said. She's on Medicare, and she's enrolled in PPO. That's a group of doctors who provide health care together so that you can get a general practitioner or a specialist. They work together.

Q. And I can go anyplace I want?

The President. And she can go anywhere she wants with any doctor who is enrolled in the PPO. And if she has an emergency, they can refer her out to a doctor.

I was just talking with a doctor in Las Vegas who helped to organize a PPO with 700 doctors in it. Under our plan, first of all if you're on Medicare, nothing will change. Secondly, every State in the country will have the power to approve every existing HMO or PPO they want to, so that the people that are already enrolled in these kinds of plans and have high consumer satisfaction will basically not see a change in their health care.

However, you should know that for people who are working for a living and who are insured through their place of work, today only one-third of them have any choice at all. Most of them have no choice, they're just told, here's your plan, and here it is. We will propose to give them at least two other choices so that everybody will have three choices. If they choose a more expensive one than their employer has chosen, they might have to pay a little more, but at least they'll have some choice. You won't be affected. And I think what you'll see is more and more doctors putting together these PPO's, so the doctors, rather than insurance companies, will be deciding the quality of health care in America.

Q. Thank you.

Mr. Atkinson. President Clinton, we're going back to San Francisco now. KRON, Pete Wilson. Pete.

Gays in the Military

[*Mr. Wilson introduced a lieutenant in the Naval Reserve who asked why the President would not allow the courts to make a decision on gays serving in the military.*]

The President. Well, the courts will decide the issue. And as you know, I don't agree with the policy of the ban, and I attempted to change it. And I did get some change, but not the change that I wanted. And there was a vote in the Senate last week, which I hope you noticed, which showed that only one-third of the Senate basically supported my position. And the reason that we had to have a compromise is we didn't have the votes to get more done.

Part of getting the agreement to stop the investigations, to not automatically throw people out who said they were gay and at least give them a chance to demonstrate that they were complying with the code of military conduct, and not using people's associations against them to investigate them, in other words, creating a big zone of privacy for gays and lesbians in the military service, was the agreement to go forward with the lawsuit. The courts know what the arguments are. The Justice Department can't just drop it because there are too many other cases. In other words, there are other cases at the same level of court, and they've all gone against the service personnel. So they're being appealed up anyway by people who lost them.

And so, it would only change the law, in other words if we changed it. It would only change the law for that circuit, that one Federal district. And if the court of appeals overturned it, it would only change the law for that one court of appeals district, and the act that Congress has enacted would still control it for everybody else. We have no reason to believe that the Supreme Court will uphold the ruling. If it does, of course, then the whole issue will be moot. I think everybody's better off in trying to get a legal resolution of it. And if we just stopped it, it would die right there with that one court. It would be nice for everybody there, but it wouldn't have national impact.

Mr. Atkinson. From Los Angeles again, Paul Moyer has another question.

Health Care Reform

[*Mr. Moyer introduced a couple whose twins were born prematurely and had to stay in the hospital for several weeks. They asked if the new health care plan would cover families who had very high medical expenses.*]

The President. I want to answer your question, but first I want to make sure that all the people that are watching this understand exactly what question he asked. You know, some health insurance policies have very good coverage, but they have a limit to how much you can draw against the coverage. They have a lifetime cap, which, if you get a really serious illness, you could use up in one time. And your lifetime cap's gone, so even though you had a real good policy, you could never use it again. That's the question he was asking.

The answer is under this plan there would be no lifetime caps. You would pay whatever you would be required to pay. If you were self-employed, you'd pay what your premium is. If you were working in a business, you would pay, if you don't have any coverage, up to 20 percent. If you have better coverage than that right now, if your employer pays everything, your employer can continue to pay everything, but there's a limit as to how much can be taken away from you under our plan.

The reason there's no need for a lifetime cap under our plan is that people will be insured in huge pools, community rating pools. You know, this is an expensive thing, but aren't you glad that they got it? They have these two beautiful children now. And so, sure, they put an extra cost on it, but instead of that cost being, say, 200 or 300 or 400 people insured, there might be 200,000 or 300,000 people insured in the same pool, so that cost spread across a big group won't be that much. And there will be no caps. Our plan abolishes the lifetime caps to keep people from being financially destroyed.

Mr. Atkinson. We're going back to San Diego now. Marty Levine has someone with another question for you.

NAFTA

[*Mr. Levine introduced a small business man who expressed concern that NAFTA would cause unemployment in California.*]

The President. Let me talk just a little about that because it is the big issue. First of all, let me tell you I was the Governor of a State that had plants shut down and jobs moved to Mexico, where people lost their jobs and their livelihoods whom I knew. And I worked very hard on stopping that and even wound up bringing one of those plants back. So I would never knowingly do anything that would put the American people's economic welfare at risk. I believe NAFTA will create jobs, not lose jobs. And I believe that the jobs we'll create will be better paying jobs. And let me explain why.

Most people who worry about NAFTA losing jobs know that there are a lot of plants that American companies own along the Mexican border with the United States in the so-called *maquilladora* area. If an American company puts up a plant down there, they can produce products in Mexico and import them back into the United States duty free. So people think, well, that happened in the 1980's, so if this agreement breaks down barriers, maybe more of that will happen. Actually, less of that will happen. Here's why.

Under the NAFTA agreement, the cost of labor and the cost of environmental investments in Mexico will go up. Under the NAFTA agreement, Mexico agrees to stop requiring so many products sold in Mexico to be made in Mexico. So, for example, we'll go from selling 1,000 American cars to 60,000 American cars in Mexico the first year, according to the auto companies. And also under the NAFTA agreement, Mexican tariff barriers are further lowered and so are Americas. The problem is theirs are 2½ times as much as ours. So as they lower barriers, we'll get a bigger benefit out of it than if we

lower barriers.

And finally, let me say this. Five years ago we had a $5.5 billion trade deficit with Mexico. Now we have a $5.7 billion trade surplus. Compare that with an $18 billion trade deficit with China, a $44 billion trade deficit with Japan. We will gain jobs out of this. We will gain incomes out of this. And finally, if we do this with Mexico, then you've got Chile, Argentina, and other countries who want the same deal. We'll make a lot of money out of it over the next 20 years if we do it.

I hope I can help you persuade the people in San Diego to support it. We're also going to get some more money for that terrible environmental problem you've got along the border there in San Diego to try to clean that up. And there will be less environmental problems and more investment of the kind you needed years ago there if we pass this agreement.

Mr. Atkinson. President Clinton, back here at KCRA, a good-looking young fellow has something he wants to ask you.

The President. Boy, he does look good.

Youth Employment Opportunities

[*Ms. Bland introduced a 13-year-old who asked what could be done to prevent youth from selling drugs in order to make money.*]

The President. Give him a hand. [*Applause*] That took a lot of guts.

Let me say, we're working on a couple of things. First of all, this last summer we were able to have a couple hundred thousand more jobs in the country for young people in the summertime. I wanted a much bigger program that I tried to pass in the Congress, but I couldn't. What I think we need to do is two things, one I mentioned earlier. I want to try in every community in the country to bring school and work closer together, so that people can learn while they're working and so that young people who need to work can work and get an educational experience at the same time. In other countries, this is much more frequent, Germany, for example. We're trying to build up those kind of programs in this country. The second thing I want to try to do is to provide opportunities for young people who need it to work part-time, but year round. And we're working on that. I tried, as I said, I tried to pass a bill through the Congress earlier this year to get more summer jobs. I couldn't pass it.

But I think there is a lot of support in the country for the idea that young people who live in economically difficult circumstances, want to work, have the chance to do it. We want to make it easier for the employers to hire them.

So we're working on that, and you've given us a little encouragement to do it.

[At this point, the television stations took a commercial break.]

Defense Conversion

Mr. Atkinson. You've had a lively afternoon. That was quite a crowd that greeted you at McClellan, a couple of thousand people. They got you going, didn't they?

The President. They did, and I love seeing them.

Mr. Atkinson. It was a hard time stopping. Just barely made it in time to get on the air here.

The President. Well, they've done so much wonderful work at McClellan. They showed me two of the electric cars that they're working with people in the area to do and some of the environmental work they've done. One of the things we're really trying to do to help California deal with all the military cuts is to emphasize the ability of the defense system, especially these bases, to develop dual-use technologies. And they showed me a lot—that is, things that can be used for defense and domestic purposes. At McClellan, they developed an electric car that goes from zero to 60 in 12 seconds, gets 80 miles per gallon at 55 miles an hour, and has a maximum speed of 100 miles an hour. And now all we've got to do is figure out how to make it economical for people to buy. *[Laughter]* But I think we'll be able to do it.

The Big Three automakers this week announced a pathbreaking research project with all of our Government and defense labs, and we're going to try to triple the mileage on cars by the end of the decade. And the auto companies have made a commitment; they're going to invest money. We're going to invest money. And it means a lot more jobs for Americans if we can do it.

Mr. Atkinson. Pretty slick.

Pete Wilson is standing by with your audience at KRON in San Francisco.

Job Training

[Mr. Wilson introduced an unemployed California resident who asked about programs to re- *train older professionals.]*

The President. You know, you're about the third person in the last 10 days that's asked me that question, and I have to tell you that we have not done anything or thought of what to do exactly that would emphasize only people above a certain age. I will tell you what we have done. Did you work in a high-tech company before?

Q. I did, sir, yes.

The President. What kind of company did you work in?

Q. It was a nuclear weapons, actually.

The President. Yes, I think even you hope we don't have to do that anymore. But let me say what we are—first thing we've got to try to do is create some more jobs in the high-tech area, so let me emphasize that. Just this week we announced, with a lot of people from California there in Washington, that we were removing from any export limitations 70 percent of the computers made in this country, in recognition of the fact that the cold war is over. We still have to worry about proliferation of weapons, but we freed up $30 billion worth of computer exports and $7 billion worth of supercomputers and telecommunications exports. That will create a lot more jobs in California, and a lot of the companies in California have already issued statements saying it will create more jobs. So I hope there will be more jobs for you to take.

Now, let me tell you what we are trying to do which will benefit older people, because very often companies don't themselves retrain them. What we're trying to do is to set up a partnership with the private sector in which we change the present unemployment system to a reemployment system. That is, you're a good example of—now, unfortunately, you're more usual than unusual. It used to be when people lost their jobs, there was a temporary downturn in the economy, and a few months later they get the same job back when their old company got new business, when the economy picked up.

Now, when people lose their jobs, most often because of what we call structural changes in the economy. That is, the jobs are lost to automation, or the demand for the jobs are no longer there, or some other country's kicked us out of the market, or we kick some other country out of the market. So the unemployment system needs to be totally changed to a reemployment system so that the minute someone is notified that they're going to lose their job, the Government kicks in with training funds, which can be used in partnership with the employer if the employer wants to keep the person and try to train them for something new. Or we show people, here's where the jobs are growing in number, here are your training options, and you start right then. Instead of waiting for their unemployment to run out and then starting it, it should start immediately at the time a person knows they're going to be unemployed and hopefully even before.

When we were in Sunnyvale, California, the other day, not too far from here, they had already started such a system, and it had resulted in a dramatic shortening of the time people were unemployed. And so that is what I think we should do.

It may be that we should give employers some extra incentive to retrain older workers. I'll be honest with you, until people like you started asking me, I had never given it much thought. If you have any specific ideas, I hope you'll write me and give them to me because, believe it or not, I normally get them. Uncle Sam's doing a pretty good job of getting your mail to me.

Mr. Atkinson. We're going back to Los Angeles.

The President. Let me—one last thing. He is really the typical American of the future. The average person will change work seven times in a lifetime now, sometimes for the same employer, sometimes for a different employer. So we simply have to establish a lifetime learning system so that people feel the same obligation to retrain the 55-year-old worker that they do the 25-year-old worker. If we don't do it, we'll never get our economy straightened out, because you can't keep the same kind of work; the nature of work is changing too fast.

[*Mr. Moyer introduced a representative of the Mexican American Grocers Association who requested help to expand the association's training program.*]

The President. Let me tell you what I want to do. Keep in mind, there are people like you all over America who may be doing different things. And the needs of every economy are different. I want to try to do two things. First of all, I think we need more funds for job training given to States, so that the States can direct

those funds in the way that they're best needed.

So in the case of California, most of the unemployed people are in the south, although the whole State has problems, but most of the unemployment is in southern California. And the people at the local level are best able to judge what programs are working. So you've got a wildly successful program; if your State had more job training funds, they could direct them to you. And that's part of what we're trying to get done in this whole reemployment system that I just described to you. And we'll be going up to Congress soon with a bill that tries to do that, to get more funds, with fewer strings attached, given to local communities for the programs that work.

The second thing that we need to do is to vigorously attempt to get more private investment into distressed inner-city areas. If you think about it, it is not rational for there not to be more locally owned businesses and more people working in these distressed inner-city areas, because most of the people who live there have jobs, make money, have checks, could spend it there, but there's no investment going into those areas. So we passed a bill earlier this year, which we're in the process of implementing, that will give big incentives for people to invest private dollars to create more jobs so that your training programs will be able to find work for people after they're trained. Those are the two things we're trying to do.

But when you see this training bill come up before the Congress in the next several weeks, I think you'll like it because it will not only provide more money but it will be with fewer strings attached, so the communities can direct it to people like you who are making things happen.

It's real impressive, 400 jobs, isn't it? It's good.

Mr. Atkinson. We're back to San Diego again.

Violence and Drugs

[*Mr. Levine introduced a church-based community organizer who asked about administration plans to combat violence and crime.*]

The President. Let me tell you, first of all, I'd like for you to have a chance to say maybe to me and to all these people what you think ought to be done. But let me begin by responding to your specific question. He is coming to see—Dr. Brown is, Lee Brown, who is the Director of Drug Policy for our country, the drug czar. He was formerly the police chief in New York, in Atlanta, and in Houston. He started a community policing program in New York. And believe it or not, New York City now, for 2 years in a row, according to the FBI statistics has had a decline in their crime rate in all seven major areas of crime.

So the first thing we've got to try to do is to make the police and the community work together better, with the proper allocation of resources with a view toward preventing crime from occurring as well as catching criminals quicker. That's why we need more police officers so cities can afford to deploy the resources that way. The second thing we've got to do, I'll say again, is to try to take the guns out of the hands of people who shouldn't have them. The third thing we're trying to do, as Dr. Brown will tell you, is we want to change the emphasis of the Federal Government's drug control efforts. And with regard to enforcement, we want to concentrate more on kingpins, really big dealers, to try to break the financial back of a lot of these networks, not just on how many arrests we can make of people in the middle but really go after big people and money networks.

Then, with people who are actual users and who may commit crimes in the course of that, we're trying to have much more comprehensive alcohol and drug abuse treatment. One of the really important things about our health care plan that I would think you would support is that it includes substance abuse treatment for people who now don't have any insurance. So that will stop a lot of these long, long delays for adequate treatment. Drug treatment works in an extraordinary percentage of the cases, not in all the cases but in a lot of the cases, if it is there.

So those are that things that we're working on. But the other thing we want to do is to listen to people like you who have actually done things that work. We have not only Lee Brown. Janet Reno, the Attorney General, was a prosecutor in Miami, one of the toughest towns in America for drug problems. And Louis Freeh, the Director of the FBI, was a U.S. attorney, a Federal judge, and an FBI agent, working principally in drug cases. He broke big international drug cases as well as dealing with drugs on the street. So we've got these three crimefighters who basically came up from the grassroots. And it's the first time we ever had

a team of grassroots crimefighters dealing with the drug issue. They want to hear from you and people like you all over the country about what would work for you.

Mr. Atkinson. Mr. President, while we have you and since you've asked, Mr. Hay does have a couple of suggestions.

The President. I want to know.

[*The participant said that education and drug treatment programs were more effective than increasing law enforcement.*]

The President. Let me say just, if you think what he said, plus what the young man said here who wanted the job for his friends, plus what the young man said whose brother got shot in school—it goes back to the bigger point: The problems you see that you're all horrified about today have been festering and developing over a generation in America.

There were poor communities in this country 30, 40, 50 years ago that had no difference in the crime rate, no difference in the drug abuse rate as the communities today. But they had locally owned businesses, coherent community organizations, and intact families, all of which you have going away today.

So if you want to do something fundamental, we have to give these kids people like him to relate to—like you, sir—people who can be almost the kind of role models you used to take it for granted that the parents would be, who can create their own kind of gang in a community organization. We all want to be in a gang, don't we? I mean, your church is a gang. Your basketball team is a gang. In other words, we have a need to be with people who are like us, who share our values, who make us feel important, who reinforce us. And there is no simple answer to this, but you've got to start with these children when they're very young, and you have to give them a way of belonging and a way of learning and a way of growing that is positive.

Let me say, I agree with you about the jails. You can build more jails and not make society safer. And we need to distinguish between people who need to be kept out of society for a very long time and others that we may be jailing we could do something else with.

There's a difference in police. More police won't necessarily make you safer, but if they relate well to the community, if their neighbors trust them, if they like them, if they're on the street, they can lower the crime rate by keeping crime from occurring, by deterring the thing from occurring. If you have the right kind of relationships, they can be an enormous weapon.

But I want you to talk to Dr. Brown. And you're absolutely right, and I thank you for giving your life to this. There is not any more important work in America today than what you are trying to do.

Health Care Reform

Mr. Atkinson. I think we're going to switch gears. This is a Sacramento physician.

Ms. Bland. Exactly. He's our first doctor of the evening, as a matter of fact——

The President. Good for you.

[*Ms. Bland introduced a doctor who asked if the new health care plan would enable struggling physicians groups to provide the best care for their patients and if independent doctors would receive assistance.*]

The President. Yes. First of all, let me say that there are things in this plan which will give much better access to data of all kinds to physicians, both business management data, health outcomes data, a whole lot of things you don't get now, particularly if you're in individual practice, and to help people to set up and operate things without losing money, without making business mistakes.

Also the plan would significantly simplify a lot of the money management and paper management problems you have today. For example, a community this size, I would imagine the average multidoctor practice would be just like a hospital, you have to deal with maybe 300 different insurance companies. And we're trying to simplify that. That will reduce the possibility of error.

Secondly, keep in mind, every person under our proposal who's not covered now would be offered the option of three different kinds of coverage, and one of which would be to keep choosing individual doctors on an individual basis. That, in the beginning, would be more expensive for the employee. But at least they'd have the choice. Today only one-third of the workers who are insured at work have multiple choices in their health plan. And what we think will happen, sir, is that a lot of independent doctors will be able to organize, but not in a HMO type thing, maybe even in a PPO thing, but at least to all say, we will serve our patients

as they need it, but we'll be able to save a lot of money doing it because the administrative costs will be lower.

Let me say, in an attempt to satisfy just your concern, we did involve hundreds of doctors in this, including people that we trusted. I asked my own doctors to help us, just from their point of view of their own practice. I figure they'd tell me the truth. They don't mind disagreeing with me or telling me I'm crazy or telling me I need to lose 10 pounds or whatever they say. [*Laughter*] So we used a lot of doctors in different specialties and family doctors, GP's, too. And we also have asked Dr. Koop, who was the Surgeon General, as you remember, a few years ago under President Reagan and did a marvelous job, to sort of be our moderator, if you will, with the physician community all over America, to try to get as much feedback as we can, so as we move forward with this plan in Congress, we address concerns just like yours and we make sure that the doctors feel very good about this when it's over.

Let me just say, as you pointed out, the independent practice is becoming rarer and rarer anyway because of the economic pressures. One of the reasons for that and one of the reasons a lot of doctors have urged us to do something, is that in 1980—just listen to this, you want to know what they're up against—in 1980, the average doctor took home about 75 percent of the money that came into a clinic. By 1992, that figure had dropped from 75 percent to 52 percent because of increased bureaucracy and paperwork and all the people they had to hire to keep up with all the things that are ballooning the cost of this system. So we're trying to simplify that and leave you the option to stay in independent practice and leave your patients the options to be covered by you.

Now, keep in mind, most of the patients you have today probably have their own health insurance. Those that are in plans now that do that, we're not going to change that. What we're trying to do is to help those who don't have coverage get some coverage. But they would also be able to choose you in either a physician group or as an independent practitioner. Another thing that they can do is to enter a PPO, and you stay out of the PPO, but when they need to see you, they see you. And then the only thing they have to pay is the difference between the reimbursement schedule in the PPO and what you would charge, which in your line of work would probably not be dramatically different.

So there are going to be all kinds of options. It should lead to a bigger patient pool, not a smaller one, and it shouldn't radically force you to change your practice, but it would give you the opportunity to do it. And if you do it, you will get the information you need to avoid losing money, and you'll have a simpler system to deal with.

Mr. Atkinson. Four out of every five people in the Sacramento metro area are in a managed health care system. We understand that Sacramento was used as something of a model for you and the First Lady. Is that true?

The President. It was. We looked at the Sacramento area because of the high percentage of people in some sort of managed care and the relatively high level of satisfaction among consumers with it. And we looked at the California public employees system because they've done such a good job of not lowering their rates but lowering the rate of increase.

We also looked at a number of other things. The Mayo Clinic system, for example, most of the people would concede that the Mayo Clinic has pretty high quality health care. Their inflation in cost this year was 3.9 percent, about a third of what the medical inflation rate was nationwide.

So there are ways to lower cost without sacrificing quality. To be fair, though, there are a lot of other things. Doctors do need a lot of information that they don't have now to deal with the system they've got. And if you give it to them and we provide it, that will also enable them to do a better job.

[At this point, the television stations took a commercial break.]

Abortion

[Mr. Wilson introduced a participant who asked if the President had changed his position on abortion.]

The President. The answer to your question is no, it hasn't changed. And in fact, if you've been following any of my rallies, all the people that protested against me in the campaign are still protesting against me. So they don't think I've changed my position.

But let me say this. When I took office I abolished the gag rule. I abolished the ban on fetal tissue research. I appointed Ruth Bader Ginsburg to the Supreme Court, who has made a career of fighting for the rights of women and believes in the constitutional right to choose. I have gotten the United States back into the effort to control worldwide population growth, which is an important human issue, not through abortion but through basic contraceptives, something that the United States had walked away from before. So I think that my record on that is clear and unblemished.

The issue that you raise is this: Federal district court judges are appointed by the President but recommended to the President by Senators, if they are Senators of the President's own party, in the States. I didn't know anything about the issue you raised until I also read it in the press. Apparently some of the Senators, two of them, I think, recommended judges to me to be appointed who have questionable positions on that issue. But they are lower court judges; they have to follow the law. So before I appoint them I will have to be satisfied that they intend to faithfully carry out the law of the United States as it now exists, or I won't do it if I think they're going to do that. So you don't have to worry about that. But I don't think I should have the same standard, if you will, or have just sort of a litmus test for every judge on every last detailed issue that might come before the court under the abortion area. I mean, there are a thousand different questions.

I think that if this is a good judge, I ought to consider appointing the judge. But I wouldn't appoint someone that I thought would just flagrantly walk away from what is clearly the law of the land, which is that a woman, within the first two trimesters of pregnancy anyway, has a constitutional right to choose. That's what the law is. That's what I believe in. I don't think it should be changed. And the judges that I appoint will have to be willing to uphold the law of the land if they want the job.

Mr. Atkinson. We're going to go back to Los Angeles, to our sister station, KNBC, and Paul Moyer.

Immigration and Border Control

[Mr. Moyer introduced a representative of the Asian Legal Center who asked about reorganization of the Immigration and Naturalization Service.]

The President. Well, let me say this, the Vice President, in his reinventing Government report, had recommended that we look at whether the border functions of Customs and the border functions of Immigration should be integrated. That was the issue. And that is something, I think, that is worth debating. We've had some instances in which—we got reports when we began to look in how the Federal Government operated, that the Immigration people and the Customs people were actually not only not cooperating but almost getting in each other's way at some border crossings in the United States.

So that's all we looked at. We would not diminish the other part of Immigration's control—function, excuse me—or defund it or underfund it or any of the things that you might be concerned about. And in fact, no decision has been made yet about the organizational issues. It's just that we have been concerned, given the kind of immigration problems we have when we want to reduce the chance that, for example, terrorists could get into this country, we want to deal with some of the problems we had where people were almost sold into bondage to come to this country. And we don't want any kind of unnecessary overlap or conflict between Customs and Immigration. So that's what we're trying to work out, not to diminish the other functions of the Immigration and Naturalization Service, which are very important.

Mr. Atkinson. Mr. President, I hope I'm not breaking the rules here, but a quick followup to that. You know that the Border Patrol says they don't have enough people.

The President. They don't.

Mr. Atkinson. They say that their equipment is falling apart. Senator Dianne Feinstein's proposed what she calls, I believe, a crossing fee of about a dollar a car to raise $400 million for more agents and better equipment. Your INS nominee testified last week that she is not philosophically opposed to that. Can we assume then that that's the administration's stand on that issue?

The President. Well, let me give you two answers. First of all, I have not endorsed the Feinstein proposal, but I am not philosophically opposed to it either. It's just we've got to think through what it means and what others might do for our crossing and whether it has any implications that we don't understand.

The main point is that Senator Feinstein and Senator Boxer and others in the California delegation want us to hire 600 more Border Patrol agents, and want us to update and modernize

their equipment, and they're right about that. We've got a bill in the Congress which will go a long way towards doing that, and I hope we can pass it and pass it soon. There are simply not enough Border Patrol agents, and the equipment that they've got is simply inadequate. And we must do better.

In terms of the fee, I wouldn't rule it out, but I just hate to embrace something before I understand all of the implications of it. But I agree with the INS Commissioner, Doris Meissner. Neither one of us are philosophically opposed to it, we just have to know what the implications of it are before we can embrace it.

But the bottom line is, what the California Senators want is results. They want more Border Patrol agents, they want modern equipment, they want them to be able to do their job, and they're right. And we're going to do our best to see that they can.

Mr. Atkinson. Appropriately enough, we're going to switch closer to the border now, to San Diego and to KNSD.

Health Care Reform and Privacy

[*Mr. Levine introduced the regional director of the National Conference of Christians and Jews, who expressed concern that the proposed national health security card would infringe on an individual's privacy.*]

The President. Well, it'll work just like a Social Security card does. It'll look something like this. This is our little mock-up that I held up on television. And you would have this, which would entitle you to health care wherever you got sick and whatever happened to you. And we have to have some sort of card like this so people can be identified. And so if, for example, if there is an emergency, their health information can be secured quickly if they're in an approved health facility or dealing with a doctor. But it will have the same sorts of protections that a Social Security card would, for example.

And if you'll remember, there was an attempt a couple of years ago to try to broaden the use of Social Security identification which was repelled, because the American people were worried about their Social Security card being used for anything other than to validate the fact that they were entitled to Social Security. So this is purely for the purposes of establishing that you belong to the health care system, that you are duly enrolled, you're properly a member, and it would function in much the same way as a Medicare card or a Social Security card.

If you have any specific suggestions, I'd be glad to have them. But I can tell you no one has ever anticipated that this would be used to sort of plunder the privacy rights of Americans, but to just increase their personal security.

Q. The concern that, as expressed, has to do with the type of information that might be magnetically made available as part of the information that that card contains and who will have access to the information that that magnetic strip would contain with regard to the individual's background.

The President. But the individual will have—the only thing you have to do is—so that the person is eligible, the person will be enrolled in a health alliance, and the alliance will know whether the person is eligible because he or she is self-employed, small business employee, a big business employee, or somebody on Medicaid. And then there will have to be some access to health data for the appropriate health professionals. But I don't think that there's going to be a lot of information just floating out there.

In fact, people will not have access to information that they don't need or that they don't have a right to know. I mean, you can't just go in and plunder somebody's files. I think the protections for the people will be quite adequate, just as they are today again with Social Security and with Medicare.

Let me just say this. If you have a list of specific questions, if you will get them to me, I will get you a list of very specific answers. Because I realize that, on this question like that, the devil is always in the details. So I know that I haven't fully satisfied you, so you send me the specific questions, and I'll send you the specific answers. And then you can decide whether you agree or not.

Mr. Atkinson. Be assured that she will. We only have 15 minutes left. It's amazing. Time has gone very quickly. We're back in Sacramento, and Carol has a guest.

Teacher Shortage

[*Ms. Bland introduced a participant who asked about efforts to deal with the shortage of teachers.*]

The President. Yes. Two things I might men-

tion. One is that you've probably noticed recently that the Congress passed and I signed the national service bill, which will, within 3 years, enable us to offer 100,000 young Americans a year the opportunity to serve their communities and either earn credit toward a college degree or, if they are teachers coming out of college, to go into teaching and teach off a significant portion of their college costs, so that the National Service Corps will have a teacher corps component.

We work with a program called Teach For America that you're probably familiar with. And a young woman named Wendy Kopp organized it to try to make sure we integrated that into the National Service Corps proposal. So young people in college today, for example, could take out loans under the National Service Corps concept and say, I'm going to be a teacher, in certain areas where there's a shortage of teachers, for a couple of years, and they can wipe off a big portion of their loans.

In addition to that, we're making a real effort to try to encourage a lot of these wonderful people who are coming out of the military, as we downsize the military, to go into teaching, to try to encourage them to do it. And we need, I might say, more cooperation from a lot of the States in passing easier ways for them to become certified to go into the classroom. But if you think about it, the military has had a stunning amount of success in educating and training people on a continuing basis. If you go back to what the gentleman said, he was an older high-tech worker that lost his job, and that's the kind of thing that we need in a lot of our schools today.

So a lot of these military people are being encouraged to go into teaching and being given, through a special program passed by Congress, some incentives to do that. And I hope we can expand that program, because I'd really like to see it. A lot of those folks are still young, they've got the best years of their lives ahead of them, and they could make a major contribution to the classroom. And a lot of them come from previously disadvantaged backgrounds and from all different races and ethnic makeups. So they can make a major contribution to what we need to do in our schools and our cities. Thank you.

Let me just say this, you didn't ask that, but since we've got a lot of doctors here, there is also the National Health Service Corps, which helped a lot of doctors to get through med school but has been shrunk in the last 10 years, will be dramatically expanded if the health care program passes. So you have a lot of doctors in urban and rural underserved areas, too, with the same plan.

Mr. Atkinson. Okay, we're going to switch back to KRON in San Francisco. Pete.

Gun Control

[Mr. Wilson introduced a participant whose brother had been murdered, and he asked what could be done to deter violent criminals who apparently do not fear punishment.]

The President. Well, a lot of the younger ones, unfortunately, aren't afraid of anything because they have no sense of the future. They're not invested in their own lives. They're not invested in what they might be doing 2 or 3 or 5 years from now. We're raising a generation of young people for whom the future is what happens 30 minutes from now or what happens tomorrow. And that's a terrible problem.

Now, I believe we should have stronger gun control measures than the Brady bill. For example, let me say again what I think we should do. I think we should pass one of a number of good bills that are in the Congress which would ban assault weapons. There are a lot of them out there for the sole purpose of killing people, and they should be banned, either at the national level or in every State. We should follow the lead of the 17 States which have now made it illegal for young people to possess handguns, unless they are, I'll say again, with their parents, hunting or at some target range, some approved place. We should have much stiffer penalties against possessing these weapons illegally. Then every community in the country could then start doing major weapon sweeps and then destroying the weapons, not selling them.

Another thing you ought to look into in your area: If the murder weapon is ever recovered, which it may not be, it would be interesting to know where it comes from and what tracking is on it. Because one of the things that I learned when I got into this is that every State of any size has hundreds of gun dealers that may be licensed only by the Federal Government for a $10 fee a year. And there are cities and States which may have other laws, but you can still be a gun dealer if you've got this little piddly Federal permit.

So another thing that ought to be done is that the price of getting into the business ought to be raised, and people ought to have to comply with the local laws and not just the Federal permitting laws. All these things would help us to deal with the sheer volume of weapons that are out there in the hands of people that are totally disconnected from our society, while we try to deal with these deeper problems that we talked about earlier.

I feel terrible about what happened to you. We have to face the fact that this is the only advanced country in the world where anybody who wants to can get any kind of gun they want to, to do anything that they want to with it. It's crazy. It doesn't happen in other countries, and we better make up our minds to change it if we want to save more lives and not have to see more people like this person on television 5 years from now. Thank you, sir.

Social Security

[Mr. Moyer introduced a senior citizen who asked why the Social Security earnings limit had not been eliminated.]

The President. Because I haven't been able to pass it yet. Specifically, what I promised to do was to raise it and not to totally eliminate it. I think that—do you know what she's talking about? Do you all know what she's talking— once you start drawing Social Security, you can only earn so much money before they start to lower your Social Security check, even if you're totally vested and you're entitled to the whole thing. And a lot of older people are finding it necessary to go back to work today, or they want to go back to work. I mean, people are standing vigorous for much longer periods of time.

And in the campaign for President, I said that I thought the earnings limit was way too low and should be substantially raised, and I do. And I don't even think it would cost a lot of money because the people who earn money pay taxes on the money they earn. And also with the population not growing as fast now, we need those older workers. And so, what I believe we should do is to raise the earning limit. We are negotiating now; we're talking about how much it can be raised, what we can pass through Congress, and what the costs will be.

One of the things that we've done is, in getting serious about the deficit, is to have to make sure before we pass anything, we have to know as precisely as we can exactly what the costs will be. I personally believe, as I told you and I said during the campaign, that it wouldn't cost much, if anything, to raise the earnings limit because the people who go to work will earn more money and pay more taxes.

But I still strongly support it. I think it should be raised, and I think it will be raised. It's just a question of how much and how quick I can get it passed in Congress. I am still committed to it, and I would like to urge you and anybody else watching this program who is in your situation to urge the Members of Congress from this State to vote to do that.

This is one of those issues that there aren't a lot of people against; it's just hard to raise it on the radar screen of the Congress. And to be fair to them—it's easy to bash Congress—they're working 40 percent more this year than last year. I'm proud of that, 40 percent more. I've put all this stuff there, and they're working hard now because of all the things we've put before them. But this has not been addressed, and you're right to bring it up. I haven't forgotten it, but I need your help in building the kind of public support we need to change it.

Mr. Atkinson. Mr. President, unfortunately we have to give way, I think, for a dolphin and "SeaQuest" here in a moment, but we wanted to save a little time for you. I think you have about a minute.

The President. Well, I wish I could take another question or two. Let me first of all thank all of you for coming. And thank you for your interest. Thank you for the very good questions you asked; I wish we could have done more. And let me urge you to keep up this level of involvement. We can get these changes made if the American people demand them. And you don't have to agree with every detail of my health care program, just demand that we pass one that has security and savings and simplicity, that preserves the kind of choice and quality these doctors talked about tonight, and that asks all of us to be more responsible.

We can do this and we can also turn the California economy around if we'll take it one day at a time, one project at a time, and keep at these things until they're done. We can do it. Thank you very much.

NOTE: The town meeting began at 6:33 p.m. at the KCRA television studio.

Remarks to the AFL–CIO Convention in San Francisco, California
October 4, 1993

Thank you very much. President Kirkland, distinguished platform guests, and to the men and women of the American labor movement, let me tell you first I am glad to be here. I feel like I'm home, and I hope you feel like you have a home in Washington.

For most of the 20th century the union movement in America has represented the effort to make sure that people who worked hard and played by the rules were treated fairly, had a chance to become middle class citizens, raise middle class kids, and give their children a chance to have a better life than they did. You have worked for that. You have done that.

For too long, in the face of deep and profound problems engulfing all the world's advanced nations, you have been subjected to a political climate in which you were asked to

bear the blame for forces you did not create, many times when you were trying to make the situation better. I became President in part because I wanted a new partnership for the labor movement in America.

Before I get into the remarks that I came here to make about all of our challenges at home and the economic challenges facing us, I have to make a few remarks this morning about developments in the world in the last 48 hours.

The labor movement has been active, particularly in the last few years with the end of the cold war, in the effort to promote democracy abroad, to guarantee the right of people freely to join their own unions, and to work for freedom within their own countries. In that context most of you, I know, have strongly supported and looked with great favor on the movement toward democracy in Russia.

The United States continues to stand firm in its support of President Yeltsin because he is Russia's democratically elected leader. We very much regret the loss of life in Moscow, but it is clear that the opposition forces started the conflict and that President Yeltsin had no other alternative than to try to restore order. It appears as of this moment that that has been done. I have as of this moment absolutely no reason to doubt the personal commitment that Boris Yeltsin made to let the Russian people decide their own future, to secure a new Constitution with democratic values and democratic processes, to have a new legislative branch elected with democratic elections, and to subject himself, yet again, to a democratic vote of the people. That is all that we can ask.

I think also, most of you know that in a military action yesterday, the United States sustained the loss of some young American soldiers in Somalia. I deeply regret the loss of their lives. They are working to ensure that anarchy and starvation do not return to a nation in which over 300,000 people have lost their lives, many of them children, before the United States led the U.N. mission there, starting late last year. I want to offer my profound condolences to the families of the United States Army personnel who died there. They were acting in the best spirit of America.

As you know, the United States has long had plans to withdraw from Somalia and leave it to others in the United Nations to pursue the common objectives. I urged the United Nations and the Secretary-General in my speech at the United Nations a few days ago to start a political process so that the country could be turned back over to Somalis who would not permit the kind of horrible bloodshed and devastation to reoccur. And I hope and pray that that will happen. In the meanwhile, you may be sure that we will do whatever is necessary to protect our own forces in Somalia and to complete our mission there.

From the struggle against communism in Eastern Europe to the struggle against apartheid in South Africa, the union movement in America has always answered the challenges of our time. It must be a source of great pride to you to see these elections unfold, to see the remarkable movement toward a genuine multiracial society within a democratic framework in South Africa.

It must, likewise, be a source of continuing frustration to you to see that even as the ideas and the values that you have espoused now for decades are being embraced around the world, here in our country and in virtually every other wealthy country in the world, middle class workers are under assault from global economic forces that seem beyond the reach of virtually any government policy.

We now know that every wealthy country in the world is having trouble creating jobs. We now know that in the last several years, inequality of income got worse in every major country. We know that we had more growing inequality in America than anyplace else because we actually embraced it. I mean, the whole idea of trickle-down economics was to cut taxes on the wealthiest Americans, raise taxes on the middle class, let the deficit balloon, and hope that the investment from the wealthy would somehow expand opportunity to everybody else.

We know that didn't work, and it made the situation worse. It left us with a $4 trillion debt. It left us with a deficit of over $300 billion a year. It left us with a legacy of weakened opportunities for workers in the workplace, too little investment, a paralyzed budget, and no strategy to compete and win in the global economy, and more inequality in America than any of the other wealthy countries. But we also know that the same problems we have are now being found in Germany, in Japan, in all of Europe, in the other advanced nations.

So we have to face the honest fact that we are facing unprecedented challenges in our own midst to the very way of life that the labor movement has fought so hard to guarantee for others around the world for decades. And therefore, it is important that we think through these issues, that we take positions on them, that we agree and that we disagree in the spirit of honest searching for what the real nature of this world is we're living in and where we are going.

The most important thing to me today is that you know that this administration shares your values and your hopes and your dreams and the interest of your children, and that together—[*applause*]—and that I believe together we can work our way through this very difficult and challenging time, recognizing that no one fully understands the dimensions of the age in which we live and exactly how we are going to recreate opportunity for all Americans who are willing to do what it takes to be worthy of it.

The labor movement, historically, has always been on the cutting edge of change and the drive to empower workers and give them more dignity on the job and in their lives. Almost a half a century ago, at the end of World War II, labor helped to change America and the world. At home and abroad, labor helped to create a generation of prosperity and to create the broad middle class that we all cherish so much today.

Now we have to do it again. We're at a time of change that I am convinced is as dramatic as the dawning of the Industrial Age. We can no longer tell our sons and daughters—we know this now—that they will enter a job at the age of 18 or 21, enjoy secure paychecks and health benefits and retirement benefits for the rest of their working lives and retire from the same job with the same company at the age of 65 or 62.

Our changing economy tells us now that the average 18-year-old will change work seven times in a lifetime even if they stay with the same company and certainly if they change; that when people lose their jobs now, they really aren't on unemployment, they're looking for re-employment; that most unemployment today is not like it used to be: When people got unemployed for decades, it was because there was a temporary downturn in the economy, and when the economy turned up again, most people who were unemployed were hired back by their old employer. Today, most people who are un-employed eventually get hired back usually by a different employer for a different job and un-less we are very good at what we do for them, often at lower wages and less benefits. So it is clear that what we need is not an unemploy-ment system but a reemployment system in rec-ognition of the way the world works today.

We know, too, that most American working people are working harder than they ever have in their lives; that the average work week is longer today than it was 20 years ago; that real hourly wages adjusted for inflation peaked in 1973, and so most people are working harder for the same or lower real wages than they were making 20 years ago.

We know that in the eighties there was a dramatic restructuring of manufacturing; that being followed in the nineties with a dramatic restructuring of the service industries. We know that for the last 12 years, in every single year,

the Fortune 500 companies lowered employ-ment in the United States in six figures, and that in the years where we have gained jobs, they've come primarily from starting new busi-nesses and from companies with between, say, 500 and 1,000 workers expanding, as the whole nature of this economy changes.

We know that the cost of health care has increased so much that millions of American workers who kept their jobs never got a pay raise because all the increased money went to pay more for the same health care. We know that some of our most powerful industrial en-gines, especially in industries like autos and steel have shown breathtaking increases in productiv-ity with deep changes in the work force sup-ported by the labor movement, and still are having trouble competing in the world, in part, because their health costs may be as much as a dime on the dollar more than all of their competitors.

We know, as I said at the beginning, that all the wealthy countries in the world are now having trouble creating jobs. If you look at France, for example, in the late 1980's, they actually had an economy that grew more rapidly than Germany's, and yet their unemployment rate never went below 9.5 percent.

So what are we to do? It seems to me that we clearly have to make some changes in the way we look at the world and the way we ap-proach the world. And in order to make those changes, we have to ask ourselves, what do we have to do to make the American people secure enough to make the changes? One of the things that has really bothered me in the late, latter stages of this era that we're moving out of is that so few people have been so little concerned about rampant insecurity among ordinary Amer-ican middle class citizens. It is impossible for people in their personal lives to make necessary changes if they are wildly insecure.

You think about that in your own life. You think about a personal challenge you faced, a challenge your family has faced. The same thing is true in the workplace. The same thing is true of a community. The same thing is true of a team. The same thing is true of our coun-try. We have to struggle to redefine a new bal-ance between security and change in this coun-try because if we're not secure, we won't change, and if we don't change, we'll get more insecure, because the circumstances of the world will continue to grind us down.

And that's what makes this such a difficult time, because we have to rethink so many things at once. I ran for President because I was tired of 20 years of declining living standards, of 12 years of trickle-down economics and antiworker policies, and rhetoric that blamed people who are working harder for the problems that others did not respond to, and because I believe that we needed a new partnership in America, a new sense of community, not just business and labor and government but also people without regard to their color or their region or anything else. I thought we didn't have anybody to waste, and it looks to me like we were wasting a lot of people and that we needed to put together. I thought the country was going in the wrong direction, and we should turn it around. But I was then and am now under no illusions that we could do it overnight or that I could do it, unless we did it together.

The beginning of the security necessary to change, I think, is in having a Government that is plainly on the side of working Americans. I believe that any of your leaders who work with this administration will tell you that we are replacing a Government that for years worked labor over, with a Government that works with labor. We have a Secretary of Labor in Bob Reich who understands that, at a time when money and management can travel across the globe in a microsecond, our prosperity depends more than anything else on the skills and the strengths of our working people. No one can take that away from us. And our people are still our most important asset, even more than they were 20 years ago.

We have nominated a Chair of the National Labor Relations Board in Bill Gould, and a new member, Peggy Browning, who believe in collective bargaining. We have a Director of the Occupational Safety and Health Administration in Joseph Dear who comes from the labor movement and believes that workers should be protected in the workplace. We have two people in executive positions in the Labor Department in Joyce Miller and Jack Otero who were on your executive council. We have two people in the SEIU in executive positions in Karen Nussbaum and Jerry Polas who are leading us to make progress.

This administration rescinded President Reagan's order banning all reemployment of PATCO workers forever. And we rescinded President Bush's orders with regard to Govern-

ment-funded contracting and one-sided information given to workers in the workplace. And this week I will sign the Hatch Act Reform Act to give Government employees political rights they have been denied for too long.

One week ago yesterday, on a Sunday morning, I came in from my early morning run, and I turned to my right as I walked into the White House, and I saw a family standing there, a father, a mother, and three daughters, one of whom was in a wheelchair. And the person who was with them who worked for me said, "Mr. President, this little girl has got terminal cancer, and she was asked by the Make-A-Wish Foundation what she wanted to do, and she said she wanted to come to the White House and visit you. So we're giving her a special tour."

So I went over, and I shook hands with them and apologized for my condition and told them I'd get cleaned up and come back and we'd take a picture. And a few minutes later I showed up looking more like my job, and I visited with this wonderful child, desperately ill, for a while. And then I talked to her sisters, and then I talked to her mother, and I talked to her father. And as I turned around to go off, the father grabbed me by the arm and he said, he said, "Let me tell you something. If you ever get to wondering whether it makes a difference who's the President," he said, "look at my child. She's probably not going to make it, and the weeks I've spent with her have been the most precious time of my life. And if you hadn't been elected, we wouldn't have had a family and medical leave law that made it possible for me to be with my child in this time."

Now, I believe, in short, that it ought to be possible to be a good parent and a good worker. I believe that it ought to be possible for people to make their own judgments about whether they want to be organized at work or not and how they're going to—[*inaudible*]. And I believe if we're really going to preserve the American workplace as a model of global productivity, we have to let people who know how to do their jobs better than other people do have more empowerment to do those jobs and to make those changes in the workplace.

That's why, as we work on the Vice President's reinventing Government initiative, we've worked so closely with Federal employees and their unions. When the Vice President spoke with business leaders and workers who had changed their companies, they all said the same thing: You've got to have the workers; you have to let them do it, tell you how to do it, tell you how to make the companies more productive.

Now, that's why yesterday I signed an Executive order—on Friday—creating a National Partnership Council. For the next several months the leaders of Federal employee unions, including John Sturdivant, the president of the American Federation of Government Employees, who is here today, will work with the leaders of our administration to make our Government more effective, cost less, and more importantly, to make the jobs of the rank and file Federal employees more interesting, more stimulating, more customer-oriented, by doing things that they have been telling us they should be able to do but that the system has not permitted them to do in the past. I applaud John and the other people in the unions representing Federal employees for what they have done. This is an unprecedented partnership that I think will benefit every American.

We want to make worker empowerment and labor-management cooperation a way of life in this country, from the factory floor to the board room. We've created a commission on the future of labor and management relations, with leaders from labor, business, and the academy, chaired by former Labor Secretary John Dunlap. And I've asked Secretary Reich to create a commission to study and improve relationships in government workplaces at every level, at the State and county and local level, as well as at the Federal level.

I believe this is something that a person like Bob Reich is uniquely situated to do. And it's the kind of thing that we ought to be promoting because we have to use this opportunity we have to try to take what has worked for workers and their businesses and spread it around the country.

For the last 12 years we've had a lot of finger-pointing and blame-placing, and we've got these stirring examples of success that we could be trying to replicate. That's what we ought to be doing, taking what works. And it always is a workplace in which workers have more say. And we're going to do what we can to get that done.

Now, on the security issue, let me just mention some other things. In addition to the family leave act, the budget bill which passed by such a landslide in the Congress contained what may well be the most important piece of economic reform for working people in 20 years, by expanding the earned-income tax credit so that you can say to people, if you work 40 hours a week and you have children in your home, you will not be poor. We are bringing new hope and new dignity into the lives of 15 million working families that make $27,000 a year or less. They'll no longer be taxed into poverty. There won't be a Government program to try to lift them out of poverty. Their own efforts will lift them out of poverty because the tax system will be changed to reward them. And there will never again be an incentive for people to be on welfare instead of work because the tax system will say, if you're willing to go to work and work 40 hours a week, no matter how tough it is, we will lift you out of poverty. That is the kind of pro-work, pro-family policy this country ought to have.

Something else that was in that bill that most Americans don't even know about yet that will benefit many, many of you in this room and the people you represent is a dramatic reform of the student loan system that will eliminate waste, lower the interest rates on student loans, make the repayment terms easier so that young people can repay their loans no matter how much they borrow as a percentage of their income, limited so they can repay it. Even though we'll have tougher repayment terms, they'll be able to do it. We'll collect the money, but people will be able to borrow money and pay it back at lower interest rates, at better repayment terms. And therefore, no one will ever be denied access to a college education because of the cost.

When you put that with our Goals 2000 program, the education reform program for the public schools, and the work that the Education Secretary Dick Riley is doing with Secretary Reich to redo the worker training programs in the country, you have a commitment to raise standards in education and open opportunities to our young people.

We need higher standards in our public schools. Al Shanker has long been a voice for that. He now has allies in the NEA and other places in the country who are saying, "Let's have national standards and evaluate what our kids are learning and how our schools are doing."

I believe we need to give our young people more choices within the public school system, and I have advocated letting States try a lot of things within districts. Let kids choose which schools they attend. Let school districts decide how they want to set up and organize schools. I think that a lot of changes need to be made in a lot of school districts. But let me say that we don't want to throw out the baby with the bath water. There are also a lot of school districts that are doing a great job under difficult circumstances. There are a lot of schools within school districts that are performing well under difficult circumstances.

And if we've learned anything, we've learned that the best way to increase the quality of education is to find better principals, get better leaders among the teachers, let them have more say over how school is run, and evaluate them based on their results rather than telling them how to do every last jot and tittle of their job every day.

We have learned these things—and if I might, since we're in California, say a special word— therefore, I believe that having worked for 12 years for higher standards, more choices and greater changes in public education, I'm in a little bit of a position to say that if I were a citizen of the State of California, I would not vote for Proposition 174, the private voucher initiative.

Now, and let me tell you why. Let me tell you why. First of all, keep in mind a lot of the schools out here are doing a good job. I can say this, you know, I never was part of the California education system. I have studied this system out here for more than a decade. They have undertaken a lot of very impressive reforms and many of their schools are doing a good job. I was interviewed last night by two people from a newspaper in Sacramento, and one of them just volunteered that he had two children in the public schools there, and they were getting a terrific education.

This bill would start by taking $1.3 billion right off the top to send a check to people who already have their kids in private schools, and who didn't need any Government money to do it, and taking it right off the top away from a school system that doesn't have enough money to educate the kids it's got in it in the first place.

Second thing it would do is to impose no real standards on the quality of the programs which could be funded: who could set up a school; what standards they'd have to meet; what tests the kids would have to pass. Just take your

voucher, and who cares whether a private school is a legitimate school or not. That is a significant issue. And all you have to do is to work in this field for a few years to understand that that is a significant issue.

Wouldn't it be ironic that at the very moment we're finally trying to find a way to measure the performance and raise the standards of the public schools, we turn around and start sending tax money to private schools that didn't have to meet any standards at all. When we're trying to get one part of our business, we're going to make the other part worse.

And finally, let me just say, I have always supported the notion that American schools ought to have competition and the fact that we have a vibrant tradition of pluralistic education and private schools and religious private schools was a good thing, not a bad thing for America. But all the years when I grew up, and all the times I saw that, and for a couple years of my life when I was a little boy, when I went to a Catholic school, when my folks moved from one place to another, and we lived way out in the country and didn't know much about the schools in the new area where we were, no one ever thought that the church would want any money from the taxpayers to run their schools. In fact, they said just the opposite, "We don't want to be involved in that." That's what the First Amendment is all about.

So I think we have to really think through— I have spent 12 years before I became President overwhelmingly obsessed with reform of the public school system, wanting more choices in the system, wanting more accountability, wanting more flexibility about how schools were organized and established and operated. But I can tell you that this is not the way to get it done, and the people will regret this if they pass it. I hope the people of California don't do that.

Now, you can educate people all you want— and I wanted to say a little more about that. The Labor Secretary and I are working on trying to take all these 150 different Government training programs and give local communities and States the power to consolidate them, working with you, and just fund the things that work on a State-by-State basis, and to set up a system of lifetime education and training.

I don't know how many of you saw the television program I did last night in California, but one man, looked to be in his early fifties, saying, "We need a training program that gives my company some incentives to retrain me, not just people who are 25, but people who are 55." And we are trying to do that. We're trying to set up a lifetime education and training program that starts when young people are in high school, so if they want to work and learn in high school they can work and learn in high school, so that we can have the kind of school-to-work transition that many of our competitors have for all those kids that won't go to college and won't get 4-year educations. We've got to do that.

But if you do all that, you still have to have someplace for people to work. We can educate and train people all we want, but we have to be able to create more jobs. How are we going to do that at a time when the Government is not directly funding the defense jobs that have kept America's job base up for so long?

Well, the first thing we've got to do is make up our mind we're going to be serious about defense conversion. Last year when I was a candidate for President—[*applause*]—last year when I was a candidate for President, I went all over the country—and I wasn't in the Congress and didn't have a vote—pleading with the Congress to pass the defense conversion bill. They did it, and the previous administration absolutely refused to spend $500 million to help convert from a defense to a high-tech domestic economy. So we have released the money. And we're going to try to get up to $20 billion spent on defense conversion and reinvestment in the jobs of tomorrow over the next 5 years. It is very important.

We have got over 2,800 proposals in this country for technology-reinvestment initiatives, to match with what will soon be about a billion dollars in Government money that can create hundreds of thousands of jobs in America. People are brimming with ideas out there to create new jobs.

I was at McClellan Air Force Base yesterday, and the airbase is working with people in the local community and the local universities and with the Federal defense labs. They have made new electric cars. They have made new manufacturing component parts to try to come up with economical ways to do it and allow those parts to be made in America. And they are targeting things that are now made overseas and imported here. That's the sort of thing that we can use our high-tech defense base to do, and we should be doing it. It's going to make for more jobs for America.

They have developed a prototype car that gets 80 miles per gallon at 55 miles per hour on the highway, goes to 60 miles per hour in 12 seconds, has a maximum speed of 100 miles an hour. That's not bad. If we can just figure out how people can afford it, we can put people to work making them. But it's a good beginning.

We announced last week that ground-breaking project with the UAW and Ford, Chrysler, and General Motors are working with the defense labs and all the Government labs on a project to triple the average mileage of American autos within the next 10 years. If they do that, that will create untold numbers of new jobs here, and we'll be selling cars to people overseas who want that instead of the reverse.

And by the way, I want to compliment the UAW. You know, this year we have regained a lot of our market share in America. People are buying more American cars in America, and we should compliment them for it.

So we have to find ways to create these new jobs. Now, I want to talk a little about health care, but before I do, I want to mention something we disagree on in the context of the trade issue. And listen to this. Since 1986, a significant portion of America's net new jobs have come from trade growth. That's something we can all find from the figures. In California, where we now are, a lot of that has come from Asia, which is the fastest growing part of the world. Asia's growing faster than any other part of the world; Latin America the second fastest growing part of the world. Everybody knows that is true.

Now, that's why, when I went to Tokyo and met with the leaders of the G-7, the seven big industrial countries, we made an agreement that we should dramatically reduce tariffs on manufactured products around the world in ways that all analysts agree would generate a lot of new manufacturing jobs here in America. There was virtually no dispute about that, because we were largely in competition with other countries that were paying the same or higher wages with the same or better benefits, with high-tech and other manufacturing products that we wanted to sell everywhere. And we're working like crazy to get that done between now and the end of the year.

What is the difference between that and the trade agreement with Mexico? And let's talk about that just a minute, because it's very important, not so you'll agree with me but so you will know what I want you to know, which is that I would never knowingly do anything to cost an American a job. That's not the business I'm in.

I was a Governor during the last 12 years, when the *maquilladora* system was in place. What did it do? It created a border zone on the other side of the border in Mexico in which people were free to set up plants, operate them by the standards that were enforced there—or not enforced, as the case may be—on labor and environmental issues, and then send their products back into this country, produced at much lower labor costs with no tariffs. That was the system set up to try to foster growth there.

But in the 1980's, because of all the economic problems we had, and because of the climate that was promoted in this country that the most important thing you could do was slash your labor costs and who cared about your working people anyway, you had the movement of hundreds of plants down there. And you didn't like it worth a flip. And you were right to be upset about what happened.

Now, I was a Governor of a State that lost plants to Mexico. And my State was so small that when people lost their jobs I was likely to know who they were. This was a big deal to me. I'm also proud of the fact we got one of them to come back before I left office. I'm proud of that, too. But I understand this.

Now, that is the system we have. You also saw this system, ironically, accelerating illegal immigration. Why? For the same reason that a lot of the Chinese boat people were coming over here after they moved to the coastal towns in China, got a job where they made a little more money than they did before, but didn't much like their life, but they got enough money to try to come here. That's what was happening along the *maquilladora* area. A lot of people would come up there, work for a while, then come on up here.

So I understand what the American working people don't like about the present system. The real issue: Will the trade agreement make it worse or better? You think it will make it worse. I think it will make it better. And I'll tell you, I think you're entitled to know why I think that. Because there is no question that, no matter what you think about the adequacy of the side agreements, they will raise the cost of labor and environmental investments above the point where they are now. There is no question that

the agreement lowers domestic content requirements in Mexico, so that we'll go from selling say 1,000 to 50,000 or 60,000 American cars down there next year. There's no question that their tariffs are 2½ times higher than ours. And there's no question that we have a trade surplus there, as compared with a $49 billion trade deficit with Japan, an $18 billion trade deficit with China, a $9 billion trade deficit with Taiwan.

We've got a trade problem, all right. It is that the Asian economies are not as open to us as we are to them. That's our huge trade problem. And we're going to have to do better there, because that's where a lot of the money is. So my reasoning is that if their tariffs are higher than ours and their costs go up faster than they're otherwise going to go up, and they're already buying $350-a-person worth of American goods, second only to Canada—replaced Japan as the number two purchaser of manufacturing products this year—and we got a $5.8 billion trade surplus, it will get better, not worse.

Is it a perfect agreement? No. But I don't want to make the perfect the enemy of the better. I think it is better than the present.

There are two other points I want to make. If the deal is not made with the United States, and instead it's made with Germany or Japan, we could lose access to an 80-million person market and cost ourselves more jobs. And if the deal is made, it could lead to further similar agreements with the emerging market economies of Latin America. And no one believes that anybody's going to invest in Argentina, for example, to export back to the American market. So all barrier dropping the further you get away from here because of transportation costs will lead to more jobs in America through greater trade.

So that's why I think it makes it better, not worse. You're entitled to know that. I don't ask you to agree, but I ask you to make the same arguments inside your own mind, because I would never knowingly do anything to cost America jobs. I'm trying to create jobs in this country.

Now, I'll tell you what I really think. What I really believe is that this is become the symbol of the legitimate grievances of the American working people about the way they've been worked over the last 12 years. That's what I think. And I think those grievances are legitimate. And I think that people are so insecure in their jobs, they're so uncertain that the people they work for really care about them, they're so uncertain about what their kids are looking at in the future, that people are reluctant to take any risks for change.

And so let me close with what I started with. I have got to lay a foundation of personal security for the working people of this country and their families in order to succeed as your President, and you have to help me do it. We have got to reform the job training system of this country, to make it a reemployment system, not an unemployment system, and to give it to kids starting when they're in high school.

We have got to have an investment strategy that will create jobs here. And that's why we removed all those export controls that were cold war relics on computers and supercomputers and telecommunications equipment, opening just this month $37 billion worth of American products to exports. That is important.

That's why I want to pass a crime bill to put 50,000 more police officers on the street, pass the Brady bill and take those automatic weapons out of the hands of the teenagers that are vandalizing and brutalizing our children in this country. And, my fellow Americans, that is why we have got to pass a comprehensive health care bill to provide security to all Americans. And we've got to do it now.

How many Americans do you know who lost their health insurance because they lost their jobs? Who never got a pay increase because of the rising cost of their health care? Who can never change jobs because they have a sick child? Millions of them. How many companies are represented in this room who could be selling more everywhere across the board, more abroad and more at home, if their health care costs were no greater than their competitors around the world?

Let's face it folks, we're spending over 14 percent of our income on health care. Canada's at 10. Germany and Japan are under nine. The Germans went up toward 9 percent of their income on health care, they had a national outbreak of hysteria about how they were losing control of their health care system. And yet they all cover everybody and no one loses their health insurance. And when I say we can do that and we can do it without a broad-based tax increase, people look at me like I have slipped a gear. [*Laughter*]

But I have spent over 3 years studying this system. And the First Lady and her task force have mobilized thousands of experts in the most intense effort to examine social reform in my lifetime. And they have recommended that we adopt a system which, first of all, builds on the system that you enjoy: an employer-based system where the employer contributes and, in some cases, the employee does and some not; a system that is focused on keeping what is good about American health care—doctors, and nurses, and medical research and technology—and fixing what is wrong—not covering everybody, kicking them off after they have a serious illness, not letting people move their jobs, having some people in such tiny groups of insurance that 40 percent of their premium goes to profit and administrative costs, and spending a dime on the dollar, a dime on every dollar in a $90 billion system goes to paperwork that wouldn't go in any other system in the world—$90 billion a year on that alone. Never mind the fraud and the abuse, and the incentives in this system to churn it, to perform unnecessary procedures just because the more you do the more you earn.

We can do better than that. So I want to just say, this system will be a good one. Everybody will get a health care security card like this. I feel like that guy in the ad; I'm supposed to say, "Don't leave home without it," when I pull it out. [*Laughter*] But I want everybody to have a health care security card like this. Just like a Social Security card. And I want people to have their health care access whether they're working or unemployed, whether they work for a little business or a big one.

Under the system we have proposed, if you've got a better deal now, you can keep it. If your employer pays 100 percent of benefits now, you can keep it. And we don't propose to tax any benefits that are above the minimum package. We told those who wanted that to give us 10 years before we put that provision in because within 10 years we'll have the minimum benefit package we start with, plus full dental benefits and full mental-health benefits and full preventive-care benefits, so it will be as good or better than any package now offered by any employer in America. Then, if somebody wants to buy something over and above that, we can talk about it. But we are not going to take anything away from you, you have.

What we are going to do is two things for you if you have a good policy. We're going to make it easier for your employer to keep these benefits you have now by slowing the rate of health care cost inflation, not by cutting health care spending, by slowing the rate of inflation in health care cost, and by removing the enormous burden of retiree benefits from our most productive companies. That will stabilize the health care benefits of working people and good plans.

The other thing we're going to do for you is to limit what can be taken away from you which is worth something. So by saying that for people who don't have any insurance now, their employer will pay 80 percent and the employees will pay 20, we are saying that no matter what happens to you, there's a limit to what can be taken away from you. So it will be easy for you to keep, easier for your employer to keep what you've got, and for you, and there will be a limit to what can be taken away.

Is it fair to ask all those employers and employees who don't have any coverage now to contribute something? You bet it is. Why? Because your premium's higher than it otherwise would be because you're paying for them now.

Can we do that without bankrupting small business? Of course, we can. We have a plan that gives a significant discount to smaller new businesses, and to smaller established businesses with lower wage employees that are operating on narrow margins.

How are we going to pay for this? Two-thirds of it will be paid for by employers and employees contributing into the system that they get a free ride in now. One-sixth of it will be paid for with a cigarette tax and with a fee on very large companies who opt out of the system so they can pay for the cost of insuring the poor and the discounts to small business, and most important, for the health education and research that makes us all richer because we are going to pay for that and for expanded public health clinics. And one-sixth of it will come from slowing the rate of growth. When you hear people say, "Oh, Clinton wants to cut Medicare and Medicaid, let me tell you something folks, we're cutting defense. We've held all domestic investment that's discretionary flat, which means if I want to spend more money on job training, on defense conversion, or on Head Start, I have to go cut something else dollar for dollar for the next 5 years. That's what we've done. We've cut defense as much as we possibly can right at the edge, held everything else flat.

You know what Medicare and Medicaid are doing? They're going up at 3 times the rate of inflation. What have I proposed to do? Let them go up at twice the rate of inflation. They say in Washington I can't do it. I don't talk to a single doctor who understands what we're going to do who doesn't think we can achieve those savings without hurting the quality of health care. If we can't get down to twice the rate of inflation from 3 times the rate of inflation, there's something wrong somewhere.

Now, that's how we propose to finance this. And I am pleading with you to help me pass this bill. No matter how good your health care plan is now, don't you believe for a minute you could never lose it, or at least get locked into your present job. And I am pleading with you to do it so that we can give to the rest of America, as well as to you and your families, the kind of personal security we have got to have to face the bewildering array of challenges that are out there before us.

You know as well as I do that we are hurtling toward the 21st century into a world that none of us can fully perceive. But we have to imagine what we want it to be like. We want it to be a world in which the old rules that you grew up believing in apply in a new and more exciting age, in which, if you don't have job security, you at least have employment security; in which the Government puts the people first, and in which people have security in their homes, on their streets, in their education benefits, in their health care benefits so that they are capable of seizing these changes and making life richer and more different and more exciting than it has ever been.

That is the great challenge before us. And if we don't adopt the health care reform, we won't get there. If we do, it will open the way to the most incredible unleashing of American energy that we have seen in more than a generation. Together we can do it, and I need your help.

Thank you very much, and God bless you.

NOTE: The President spoke at 11:30 a.m. in the Grand Ballroom of the San Francisco Hilton Hotel. In his remarks, he referred to Albert Shanker, president, American Federation of Teachers. The Executive order of October 1 on labor-management partnerships is listed in Appendix D at the end of this volume.

Exchange With Reporters in San Francisco
October 4, 1993

Russia

Q. Did Yeltsin have a choice in using force in Moscow?

The President. I doubt it. Once they were armed, they were using their arms, they were hurting people. I just don't see that they had anyplace—he had those police officers instructed not to use force, and in fact, deployed in such a way that they couldn't effectively use force, and they were routed. I don't see that he had any choice at all.

Q. Does this taint the move toward democracy in Russia?

The President. No. I think, first of all, as I said today in my remarks, clearly, he bent over backwards to avoid doing this. And I think he may even wonder whether he let it go too far. But I think as long as his commitment is clear, to get a new constitution, to have new legislative elections, and have a new election for the Presidency, so he puts himself on the election block again, I don't think it does taint it.

Somalia

Q. [*Inaudible*]

The President. The only thing that I have authorized so far—and I want to say I'll be doing a lot more work on this today, later today, when I've got some time set aside to go back to work on it—the only thing I have done so far is to authorize the rangers that are there who are wounded or exhausted or done more than their fair share to be replaced, to roll over that group and then to send some more people there with some armored support so that we can have some more protection on the ground for our people. None of this happened when we had 28,000 people there. And even though there are lots of U.N. forces there, not all of them are able to do what our forces did before. So I'm just not satisfied that the folks that are there now have the protection they need. So all I've authorized is a modest increase to provide armored support, to provide greater protection for the people over there trying to do their job.

This is not to signify some huge new commitment or offensive at this time, but I'm just not satisfied that the American soldiers that are there have the protection they need under present circumstances. So I've authorized, after consultation with the Secretary of Defense, a modest increase to get some more armored protection for them.

Q. Were any American soldiers taken hostage or taken captive by Aideed's forces?

The President. It is possible, and if it happened, we want there to be a very clear warning that those young soldiers who are there legally under international law, on behalf of the United Nations, and they are to be treated according to the rules of international law, which means not only no torture and no beating, but they're to have food and shelter and medical attention. They're to be treated in a proper way. And the United States will take a very firm view of anything that happens to the contrary. It is a very big issue. We'll probably have more to say about that later in the day.

NOTE: The exchange began at approximately 12:34 p.m. at the San Francisco Hilton. A tape was not available for verification of the content of this exchange.

Remarks to the Community and an Exchange With Reporters in San Francisco
October 4, 1993

The President. Thank you very much, ladies and gentlemen. It's wonderful to see all of you here. I thank you for coming. I want to apologize for our lateness, but I have, as you might imagine, had to spend a little extra time this morning on events around the world which have required me to be on the phone, and it pushed our schedule back a little bit. I thank you all for waiting.

I'd like to particularly acknowledge in the crowd today, once again, at the beginning, the Secretary of Energy, Hazel O'Leary, who has done a lot of work on the project that we're here to announce. I see Congresswoman Pelosi, Congresswoman Anna Eshoo, Congressman Tom Lantos here. The Mayor of Oakland, Elihu Harris, and I know Speaker Brown was here. He may have had to leave. Is he still here?

I want to thank, too, some Members of Congress who are not here who worked very hard on this issue: Senator Boxer and Senator Feinstein and Congressman Dellums and Congressman Stark. The president of Stanford is here, Gerhard Caspar; the slide director, Burt Richter; and the Stanford chairman of the board of trustees, John Freidenrich. And the Cypress Freeway area council member, Natalie Baten, is here. And there are others here, but I wanted to acknowledge them because they will be affected by some or all of what I have to say today.

I spent a lot of time in California during the Presidential campaign, and I said, if elected, I would come back and that I would remember what I saw and what I learned. This is my sixth trip to California as President, and around those visits many members of my administration have come here. Today, along with the Secretary of Energy, the Secretary of Labor, Bob Reich, is also here.

We have tried to work together in what has been an unprecedented effort, coordinated by the Secretary of Commerce, Ron Brown, to develop a strategy to revitalize the California economy. We have tried to continue to study what the problems are and what the opportunities are, given the difficulties of the Federal budget. We can't underestimate the problems of this State. Its unemployment rate is about 3 percent above the national average. About 25 percent of the total unemployed people in America are in this State, even though the State only has 12 percent of the Nation's population.

Many of the people who are out of work in California are people who helped to build the economic engine of America, people who worked in high-tech industries, people who worked in defense industries, people with very high levels of skills and major contributions to make to our future.

It is clear to me that the economy of this Nation cannot recover unless the economy of this State recovers. And it is also clear to me that if what we are doing here works, it will really change the nature of what a President's job is, because it is perfectly clear that as we move into the 21st century, the sweeping global economic changes which will affect our country will over time affect one area more than another, inevitably. That has clearly been the case for the last 15 years. So that what we try to do today for California is what me may be doing tomorrow for the New England region, or for the South where I grew up, or for the Midwest. We are going to have to focus on the fact that not every set of economic changes will affect every part of this country equally.

And that is what we have tried to do. Just in the last 7 months, we've worked on getting more infrastructure money to southern California. The biggest infrastructure announcement that has been made so far in this administration was around $1 billion for a project in the Los Angeles area.

We have worked very hard on trying to change the tax laws in the way that will benefit all of America but will especially benefit the high-tech industry here: increasing of research and development tax credit; having a capital gains tax for people who invest their money in new businesses, especially in high-tech areas; changing some of the real estate tax rules in ways that will revitalize the incredible depression that California, as well as south Florida and New England have had in their real estate industry. A lot of these things have been targeted to have a significant long-term impact on this State.

I have to say that as hard as we are working, I think that all of you know that these problems did not occur overnight, and they cannot be turned around overnight. And there is no way that there is going to be a single Government spending program that will do it. We should have strategies that target the investment of our Government in ways that are likely to produce other investments and create other jobs and other opportunities.

That's why I am particularly hopeful that the empowerment zone legislation that was adopted by the Congress in the economic program will lead to the selection of one or more sites in California that will prove that we can get private investment capital back into distressed areas in this country, both urban and rural. There is not enough Government money, with the kind of debt we've run up in the last 12 years, to solve all these problems, but they cannot be solved without Government initiative and new and different kinds of partnerships like the ones we're here to announce today. We can't be, in other words, hands off, and we can't do it all on our own.

Let me tell you the things I want to focus on today. And I want to tie them to some things that we've announced in the last week or so that will affect this economy. It's been said that you can't create genius, all you can do is nurture it. Among the many blessings this State has is a scientific and engineering genius and a high-tech infrastructure to support it. Instead of nurturing it for the last several years, we have been denurturing it because you've seen all these defense cuts since 1987 with no offsetting conversion strategy.

When I became President, I found a law on the books that the Congress passed in 1992 with my strong support as a Presidential candidate to allocate $500 million, finally, 5 years too late, but finally, to defense conversion. Not a penny of it had been spent because of the ideological opposition of the previous administration. We are releasing the money for defense conversion. That's important; it has to be done. We have to find ways for all the people who won the cold war to help to win the aftermath. And we have waited too long to begin.

There is a lot of that genius in California that is being inadequately used today. If nurtured, it will help to bring about not only an economic turnaround for California but for the entire Nation.

Now, that is the background to what leads to the first announcement. Today the Secretary of Energy, Hazel O'Leary, who is here, and my Science Adviser, Jack Gibbons, have given me their recommendation for the site of a major science project known by the deceptively simple name of the B-Factory. It doesn't have anything to do with honey. [*Laughter*] The importance of the B-Factory, however, is literally universal. It may give us critical answers on how the stars, the planets, and the heavens came to be. After much study and serious comparison of all the proposals, the Secretary and Mr. Gibbons have recommended that the B-Factory go to the Stanford Linear Accelerator Center.

There was strong competition for this project by scientists who have worked in this area for literally years, people whose contributions have, and will continue to be, outstanding. The B-Factory is a $240 million international project to create an electron/positron collider. Can you say that? [*Laughter*] Sounds good—for studying the underpinning of all science, the relationship of matter and antimatter. It will involve hundreds of scientists and build on decades of previous research at the Stanford facility.

In that same spirit of encouraging innovation as a path to prosperity, we are also moving forward with the administration's technology reinvestment project. This is a part of our general effort to convert from a defense to a domestic economy. The program is designed to support defense conversion by taking proposals and providing matching public funds to private funds from all over America.

When we put out the proposals we had an overwhelming response, over 2,800 projects with about $8 billion worth of proposed investments. One-quarter of them came from the State of California, the State with one-quarter of the unemployed people in America. An interesting parallel.

Soon we will be announcing the winners of the first round of technology reinvestment proposals for about $500 million. I'm happy to say that not long ago we reached agreement with the Congress to add to next year's projects another $300 million, which will mean that next year we'll have even more money for these projects than this year.

The Silicon Valley has been like a cradle for dual-use technology. For example, the Trimble Navigation Company developed a technology used to navigate our tanks in the Gulf war, and now it's adapted to navigate ambulances. This month when we announce the matching grants, you will see that many of the leading contenders are in California, on the merits, companies that need to have the opportunity to move from where we were as an economy to where we have to go .

I'm also pleased to be able to announce today some help for California on another front, an area we must target for further action, urban development. The Department of Housing and Urban Development today is announcing the awarding of grants totaling more than $100 million to California, here in the bay area and in southern California. About a fifth of the money is aimed for Los Angeles County. These funds will go towards housing subsidies for the working poor, housing for the elderly, the disabled, and for public housing.

This country has not had a housing policy in a dozen years, and that's one reason in the last dozen years we have seen an explosion of homelessness. So this is part of our effort not only to encourage more investment but also to restore the fabric of community in every city in this country. It is part of economic recovery. It's also a part of redefining who we are as a people.

I want to pay a special word of compliment to the HUD Secretary, Henry Cisneros, in his absence here today. We are desperately trying to find some solutions to the very complex problem of homelessness, and we are also trying to use our Nation's Capital to prove that we can not only find ways to move people off the streets but to move them from the permanent population of the homeless that has grown at such an alarming rate in our Nation over the last few years.

The severity of the economic problems here is very significant, but I hope all of you still believe that it's not as significant as the potential for renewed greatness. We have to help California rebuild in ways that are mental and ways that are physical. Today I've asked Congress, in addition to the things I mentioned above, to provide an additional $315 million to the Department of Transportation to complete repairs to the Cypress Freeway which was destroyed by the earthquake in 1989. This request clears the way for Congress to allocate money California needs and, in my view, is entitled to, to restore this vital link to the east bay. And it is the kind of thing that we need to be focusing on. You can't rebuild unless you have the materials to rebuild.

Finally, let me say that in trying to help the California economy we've also targeted increasing trade opportunities. When we can no longer count on the cold war to increase high-wage jobs, we know that we can count on increased trade to do it. A significant percentage of the net new jobs coming into the American economy in the last 5 years have come from increasing trade, increasing trade to the Pacific region, increasing trade in Latin America, increasing trade in other parts of the world. That's why I believe we should have a new General Agreement on Tariffs and Trade, which lowers the tariffs especially that all the advanced countries apply on manufacturing products and why I

have fought so hard to persuade the Congress to adopt the North America Free Trade Agreement.

I just had an interesting encounter with my friends at the AFL–CIO, who, as you know, have an opposite position, in which I made the following argument, which I will make again. The objections to NAFTA are basically objections to the system that has existed for the last 12 years, of being able to go down just across the border, set up a plant, have lower wages, lower environmental costs, export back into America with no tariffs. The question the American people should be asking is, if we adopt this trade agreement, will it make it better or worse? It will plainly make it better.

We will raise environmental and labor costs across the border. We will lower requirements to produce things sold in Mexico in Mexico. We will lower their tariffs, which are 2½ times as high as ours. They are already the second biggest purchasers of American goods. And California will be the biggest beneficiary of increased trade both to the Pacific and to Mexico and to the rest of Latin America, with the possible exception of Texas to the Mexican case. You must be first or second in any economic scenario.

So my argument is we ought to adopt this deal because it will make the problems better than they are, and it will create vast new opportunities. And it also opens the door to expanded trade on similar terms with the whole rest of Latin America, the second fastest growing part of the world, where no one expects investment will lead, to renewed trade back to America and the loss of American jobs. This is a job winner and an economic opportunity for America.

But there are other things we can do as well, and I want to emphasize them if I might. Last week I announced two projects which I think could really help this State. The first is an effort by the automakers and the UAW and all the Government labs to triple the fuel efficiency of American cars by the end of the decade. That could create hundreds of thousands of new environmentally based jobs.

The second is the most sweeping revision of our export control laws in my lifetime. We have swept away limitations on the export of American computers, supercomputers, and telecommunications equipment, comprising 70 percent of all that equipment produced in America, a potential of $37 billion worth of production now eligible for export all over the world, without increasing the dangers of proliferation. This will have an incredible impact in the State of California. It needed to be done before, but we finally got it done.

Every single high-tech executive with whom I have talked, and we developed this policy in cooperation with a lot of people from your State, including people in this room today, and every one of them believes this means a huge economic boost for this State, a huge economic boost for our country, and more jobs, the kind of good jobs that we desperately need. Companies like Hewlett-Packard and Sun Microsystems and Silicon Graphics have all said, explicitly, this policy means more jobs for California and, therefore, a better American economy.

So this summarizes where we are. Are we done? No. Have miracles occurred? No. Are we making progress? You bet we are. Is there any precedent for this kind of effort directed toward a single State or a single region? No, but I want this to set a precedent for my Presidency and other Presidents to do the same thing when other regions are troubled. We have got to bring this national economy back. Bringing down the deficit, keeping interest rates low, adopting sensible policies that help everybody, that's important. But we also have to focus on the real problems. Whether they're in California or Florida or New England or the Midwest or the South, we have to do it. And that is what today is all about.

I wish you well with the B–Factory. I want you to fix the roads, but most important, I want you to create new jobs with the economic opportunities we are committed to providing. Thank you. Good luck. And let's keep working.

Thank you. Thank you. You all wait for me, okay? I want to come out and shake hands and meet the children. You all stand right there. But I have to take a couple of questions from the press because of all the events that are unfolding today. So just—you all will get to watch a mini press conference here. We'll do it. Go ahead.

Somalia

Q. Mr. President, What more have you learned about American GI's who may have been taken captive in Somalia? Has there been any contact at all with their captors? Are you ensured of their safety? And do the incidents over the past couple of days give just still more ammunition to those in Congress who want to pull U.S. troops out of Somalia?

The President. Well, you asked me about four questions. Let me try to answer them.

First, we do have some troops who are missing, a small number. One or more may have been captured. We have issued the sternest possible warning that American troops captured in the course of doing their duty under international law for the United Nations are entitled to be treated with all the respect accorded to such troops under international law, which means not only no physical abuse but adequate medicine, food, housing, and access to personal contact by international inspectors. We are pursuing all of that even as I speak.

We have also issued the sternest warning that if anything happens to them inconsistent with that, the United States, not the United Nations, the United States, will view this matter very gravely and take appropriate action.

Now, let me go on to the second question. I think it has become clear that our forces have been subject to greater risk in the last several weeks by the coincidence of two developments. One is the drawdown of American forces. We used to have nearly 30,000 troops in Somalia. We're now down to 4,000 in part of the agreement we made with the United Nations to terminate our involvement. We have been replaced by the forces of other countries who are, I think, doing their best under the circumstances to man their various positions but are not as able to be part of a coordinated effort to protect our forces that are still the front line of defense of the policy of the United Nations.

The second is I think, ironically, the fact that the U.N. mission largely succeeded in stopping the hunger and the starvation and the death from disease and the total chaos, so that the hospitals and the schools were open and people could sleep in peace at night. And that created a circumstance in which people, forgetting how bad it was before, could be stirred up for some political activity, at least in one part of Mogadishu. So those two things have happened.

What we have done our best to do is to actually enforce the law against people who committed murder and try to continue our timetable to withdraw and get other forces in without doing anything that would let the country revert to the system of anarchy and chaos that existed before we got there.

I have no reason to believe that a majority of the Somalis really want to go back to the way it was. In fact, all the evidence we have is just to the contrary. So I can't give you any other answer than that today. I do not want to do anything which would imperil the fundamental success of one of the most successful humanitarian missions we've seen in a long time.

All I have done today is to, first of all, authorize the replacement of those people who are entitled to come home, who have done more than their fair share of the Somali peacekeeping, and to authorize a few more troops with armored capacity so that we can do a better job of protecting the people who are there while they're there as long as they are there. That is very important to me. I am not satisfied that we are doing everything we can to protect the young Americans that are putting their lives on the line so that hundreds of thousands, literally hundreds of thousands Somalis can stay alive who would not otherwise be alive, as part of the U.N. mission.

I will have more to say about this in the next few days. I am going, as soon as I leave here, immediately to Los Angeles, where I will spend a few more hours working on this during the day. And then tomorrow when I get back to Washington, we're going to spend several more hours on it. So I will have more to say about this in the next 48 hours, but I think that's all I should say at this time.

Russia

Q. Mr. President, on Russia, can you tell us, given that fact the President Yeltsin had to use force to put this down, are you concerned that you may have embraced him a little more tightly than you wished?

The President. Absolutely not. Absolutely not. What choice did he have? The truth is he bent over backwards to avoid using force, and as a result, as the only person who has ever been elected to anything by all the people of Russia, he and his forces were abused very badly. And if you look at what happened, they broke through a police line that was not as well armed as the opponents and not as willing to use force as the opponents, and things got out of hand. And I don't see that he had any choice once the circumstances deteriorated to the point that they did.

The government did not start the rioting or the shooting or the violence. If such a thing

happened in the United States, you would expect me to take tough action against it, as the only person who has been elected by the people of this country. And he did that. As long as he goes forward with a new constitution, genuinely democratic elections for the Parliament, genuinely democratic elections for the President, then he is doing what he said he would do. I am still convinced the United States did the right thing.

Q. Well, if you dismissed the Congress, as Yeltsin did, I think it would be a quite different situation in the United States, even though it's a different kind of Congress and a different kind of law. The question I have, Mr. President, is Senator Sam Nunn yesterday on television said that the United States and the IMF may have been partly responsible for the economic situation developing in Russia, that is, the privatization may create unemployment 20 to 30 percent if the shock treatment of the—[*inaudible*]—government is opposed by the Russian people. And what I wanted to know from you is what is the economic solution which is driving people in Russia to feel that their problems are not being resolved by the introduction of the market economy?

The President. Well, the United States—all Sam Nunn said was what we've said several times, which is we don't always agree that the IMF's policies are good for a country like Russia. That's been the United States position. We pushed IMF quite vigorously about it.

But all of these old command and control economies are having trouble making the transition. Even East Germany, that had the phenomenal good fortune to be integrated with the German economy and to get literally untold billions of dollars not available to Russia, not available to Poland, not available to Hungary, not available to any of these countries, is having difficulty. And they're going to have to sort through exactly how they want to do it and what they want to do. Meanwhile, we're doing what we can to support programs and policies that will reduce unemployment in Russia, not increase it, and that will give us the opportunity to help them develop their resources in ways that will put people to work.

But what Senator Nunn said about the IMF is no more than I have said on several occasions. We don't tell these people exactly what they should do or how they should do it. And we don't think the IMF is always right in trying to apply very strict standards to them that they may make their economic problems worse.

But, after all, there is no real precedent for this. We've got all these ex-Communist countries that are doing their best trying to make it as democracies and trying to develop some sort of modified market economy, and we're going to do our best to help them. And I think it's still a whole lot better and the world's a whole lot better off today that we're worrying about this problem instead of whether the Soviet Union will drop a nuclear weapon somewhere or cause some international crisis somewhere.

After all, there are always problems in the world and there will be as long as we are on this planet. I'd rather have this set of problems than the problems we might have had if the Berlin Wall hadn't fallen.

Thank you very much.

NOTE: The President spoke at 1:55 p.m. at the San Francisco Hilton.

Statement on Rebuilding the Cypress Freeway in California
October 4, 1993

Most Americans will never forget the picture of the Cypress Freeway collapsed upon itself after the Loma Prieta earthquake. As repairs‘ continue, I want the people of California to know that we will be there to get the job done. Communities around our Nation have always been able to count on the Federal Government to assume the cost of repairing Federal-aid highways hit by natural disasters. That is a commitment that we are helping to fulfill today.

NOTE: The President's statement was included in a White House statement announcing the President's request to Congress for funds to rebuild the freeway.

Statement Announcing the Supreme Allied Commander, Europe
October 4, 1993

I am pleased to announce that I have nominated and NATO has appointed Gen. George A. Joulwan, U.S. Army, to succeed Gen. John Shalikashvili as Supreme Allied Commander, Europe. I also intend to send forward to Congress General Joulwan's nomination to serve as commander in chief, U.S. European Command.

General Joulwan has had a long and highly distinguished career spanning more than three decades, with Europe as the centerpiece of his service. He has served for 14 years in Europe, beginning as a platoon commander and rising to Commanding General of the V Corps, U.S. Army Europe and 7th Army. In these postings, as well as in his current role as commander in chief of the U.S. Southern Command, Panama, he has demonstrated both the military expertise and political acumen needed to fill one of our most sensitive security postings. He has also displayed superb talents as a manager of resources and personnel and is known throughout the military as a "soldier's soldier."

General Joulwan assumes the post of Supreme Allied Commander at an important time of change for Europe and for NATO as we seek to adapt the role of NATO to the needs of post-cold-war mutual security. I will look to General Joulwan to continue the outstanding work of General Shalikashvili as SACEUR faces up to the challenge of helping guide NATO through this important period of transition. I have the utmost trust and confidence in his ability to do so.

Statement on the Retirement of House Republican Leader Robert Michel
October 4, 1993

As he noted in his statement this morning, Bob Michel has served his country—as Congressman, aide, and soldier—for close to a half century. As the eighth President to have had the pleasure of working with him, I want to express my heartfelt gratitude for his many contributions to America's strength, my profound respect for his leadership, and my sincere appreciation for the fairness and bipartisanship he has shown in his dealings with me.

For over a decade as Republican leader, Bob has exhibited the balance of partisanship and cooperation which makes our system function. He would never give my party any quarter in a partisan fight, but Bob Michel would never put his party's political interests ahead of the national interest.

I look forward to continuing to work with Bob Michel over the next 15 months as we seek to achieve a bipartisan consensus on such issues as free trade, health security, and the rest of our agenda for 103d Congress, and I wish him a long and happy retirement in his beloved Illinois.

Message to the Congress on Whaling Activities of Norway
October 4, 1993

To the Congress of the United States:

On August 5, 1993, the Secretary of Commerce certified that Norway's resumption of commercial harvesting of minke whales has diminished the effectiveness of the International Whaling Commission (IWC). The IWC acted to continue the moratorium on all commercial whaling at its most recent meeting last spring. Despite this action, Norway has recommenced commercial whaling of the Northeastern Atlantic minke, noting that it has lodged an objection to the moratorium. This letter constitutes my report to the Congress pursuant to section 8(b) of the Fishermen's Protective Act of 1967, as amended (Pelly Amendment) (22 U.S.C. 1978(a)).

The United States is deeply opposed to commercial whaling: the United States does not engage in commercial whaling, and the United States does not allow the import of whale meat or whale products. While some native Alaskans engage in narrowly circumscribed subsistence whaling, this is approved by the IWC through a quota for "aboriginal whaling." The United States also firmly supports the proposed whale sanctuary in the Antarctic.

The United States has an equally strong commitment to science-based international solutions to global conservation problems. The United States recognizes that not every country agrees with our position against commercial whaling. The issue at hand is the absence of a credible, agreed management and monitoring regime that would ensure that commercial whaling is kept within a science-based limit.

I believe that Norway's action is serious enough to justify sanctions as authorized by the Pelly Amendment. Therefore, I have directed that a list of potential sanctions, including a list of Norwegian seafood products that could be the subject of import prohibitions, be developed. Because the primary interest of the United States in this matter is protecting the integrity of the IWC and its conservation regime, I believe our objectives can best be achieved by delaying the implementation of sanctions until we have exhausted all good faith efforts to persuade Norway to follow agreed conservation measures. It is my sincere hope that Norway will agree to and comply with such measures so that sanctions become unnecessary.

WILLIAM J. CLINTON

The White House,
October 4, 1993.

Memorandum on the Freedom of Information Act
October 4, 1993

Memorandum for Heads of Departments and Agencies
Subject: The Freedom of Information Act

I am writing to call your attention to a subject that is of great importance to the American public and to all Federal departments and agencies—the administration of the Freedom of Information Act, as amended (the "Act"). The Act is a vital part of the participatory system of government. I am committed to enhancing its effectiveness in my Administration.

For more than a quarter century now, the Freedom of Information Act has played a unique role in strengthening our democratic form of government. The statute was enacted based upon the fundamental principle that an informed citizenry is essential to the democratic process and that the more the American people know about their government the better they will be governed. Openness in government is essential to accountability and the Act has become an integral part of that process.

The Freedom of Information Act, moreover, has been one of the primary means by which members of the public inform themselves about their government. As Vice President Gore made clear in the National Performance Review, the American people are the Federal Government's customers. Federal departments and agencies should handle requests for information in a customer-friendly manner. The use of the Act by ordinary citizens is not complicated, nor should it be. The existence of unnecessary bureaucratic hurdles has no place in its implementation.

I therefore call upon all Federal departments and agencies to renew their commitment to the Freedom of Information Act, to its underlying principles of government openness, and to its sound administration. This is an appropriate time for all agencies to take a fresh look at their administration of the Act, to reduce backlogs of Freedom of Information Act requests, and to conform agency practice to the new litigation guidance issued by the Attorney General, which is attached.

Further, I remind agencies that our commitment to openness requires more than merely responding to requests from the public. Each agency has a responsibility to distribute information on its own initiative, and to enhance public access through the use of electronic information systems. Taking these steps will ensure compliance with both the letter and spirit of the Act.

WILLIAM J. CLINTON

Nomination for Posts at the Department of Defense
October 4, 1993

The President announced his intention today to nominate public health expert Stephen C. Joseph to be Assistant Secretary of Defense for Health Affairs; former Pentagon official Richard Danzig to be Under Secretary of the Navy; and economic policy specialist Joshua Gotbaum to be Assistant Secretary of Defense for Economic Security.

"The people who we are adding to our Pentagon team today are recognized experts in their fields and dedicated public servants," said President Clinton. "I welcome their service at the Department of Defense."

NOTE: The President also announced the following appointments to senior Defense Department posts not requiring confirmation by the Senate:

Cliff Bernath, Deputy Assistant to the Assistant Secretary for Operations

Joel Resnick, Deputy Assistant Secretary for Reserve Affairs/Strategic Plans and Analysis

Helen Forbeck, Senior Professional, Defense Reinvestment Assistance Task Force

John Rogers, Deputy Assistant Secretary for Legislative Affairs/Plans & Operations

Mark Wagner, Special Assistant to the Assistant Secretary for Economic Security

John Goodman, Special Adviser for Defense Conversion and Technology

Sheila Cheston, Deputy General Counsel of the Air Force

Dr. Larry Caviaiola, Deputy Under Secretary/ Acquisition Operations

Audrey Sheppard, Chief of Protocol

Steven Preston, Deputy General Counsel

Sheila Helm, Special Assistant to the Secretary/Personnel

Dr. Kenneth Flamm, Principal Deputy Assistant Secretary for Acquisition (Dual Use Technology and International Programs)

Joseph Berger, Director, Peacekeeping/Peace Enforcement/Office of the Assistant Secretary for Policy (Democracy and Peacekeeping)

Robert Bayer, Deputy Assistant Secretary/ Economic Reinvestment and Base Realignment and Closure

Carolyn Becraft, Deputy Assistant Secretary/ Personnel & Readiness (Personnel Support, Families & Education)

Mary Ellen Harvey, Assistant Deputy Under Secretary/Logistics Systems Development

Roy Willis, Principal Assistant Deputy Under Secretary/Logistics

Amy Hickox, Director of Outreach America/ Office of the Assistant Secretary (Reserve Affairs)

Biographies of the nominees were made available by the Office of the Press Secretary.

Remarks and a Question-and-Answer Session With the American Association of Retired Persons in Culver City, California
October 5, 1993

The President. Good morning, ladies and gentlemen. Thank you all for coming today. I want to thank Judy Brown and the other board members of the AARP up here and the AARP nationwide for their wonderful cooperation and work with the First Lady and our health care effort over the last several months.

There is no organization in America that better represents the needs and desires of older Americans than the AARP. I've been working with them for nearly 20 years now, and it won't be long until I'll be old enough to be a member. [*Laughter*] So I have a vested interest in your lobbying on the health care plan.

I want to thank especially Mayor Mike Balkman and the people here in Culver City for their warm welcome to all of us today. I thank the Mayor. I'd also like to say a special word of thanks to your Representative in the United States Congress who's here with me, and a great Congressman, and a great ally in this fight for health care security, Congressman Julian Dixon. Congressman.

There are some people here from Congressman Waxman's district. I told him yesterday that since he had a longtime standing interest in health care I would mention today that the reason he's not here is that he's back in Washington having the next hearing on health care. So he took a redeye back last night to do the work that we have to do.

Ladies and gentlemen, as all of you know by now, we have launched a major national debate on health care, with a proposal designed to achieve a disarmingly simple but exceedingly complicated task: to provide health security for all Americans, health care that can never be taken away, that's always there, for the first time in our history and to do it by trying to fix what is wrong with our system while keeping and indeed enhancing what is right with our system.

The first and foremost thing is we have to have more health care security. There is an article today on the front page of many of the papers of the United States saying that last year there were more Americans living in poverty than at any time since 1962; that 37.4 million Americans have no heath insurance; about 2 million Americans a month lose it, about 100,000 of them permanently because the system we have is coming unraveled. It is the most expensive system in the world and yet the only advanced nation which doesn't provide basic coverage to all Americans.

We have gotten 700,000 letters to date, and

we're getting about 10,000 more every week at the White House from people describing their personal experiences and frustrations in problems with America's health care system, not only American health care consumers from parents with sick children to senior citizens who can't afford their medicine but also from doctors and nurses who can't do what they hired out to do, keep people well and treat them when they're sick, for all the bureaucracy and paperwork that's in our system.

I have personally met many older Americans who are literally choosing every month between buying food and buying medicine. And I know that many of these people are actually, in the end, adding to the cost of the health care system because eventually they wind up having to get expensive hospital care for lack of proper medication in managing whatever health condition they have.

We received a letter and then I had a chance to meet a man named Jim Heffernan from Venice, Florida, who came to the Rose Garden a couple of weeks ago. He volunteers at a local hospice trying to help people understand the tangle of forms they have to fill out just in order to get the health care they're entitled to. And he wrote the following thing to me: "I can recall one patient who was in tears and shaking because the hospital in her hometown had placed the balance of her medical charges in the hands of a collection agency and wrote that she might be sent to jail for failure to pay her hospital bill. This kind of senseless action on an elderly, terminal widow is unforgivable."

Stories like this need to be told over and over again in the halls of the Nation's Capitol until, finally, we get action. Our plan will improve what is great about our health care system: the quality of our doctors and nurses; the depth of our research and our commitment to technological advance. Those things will not be interrupted. We will strengthen them. This plan has a lot of aspects which actually strengthen the quality of the American health care system, strengthen the stream of funds going to medical research to deal with the whole range of problems that now confront us, everything from AIDS to Alzheimer's to various kinds of cancer.

We are committed to keeping what is best about this system. Indeed, more and more doctors and nurses who have had a chance to study this system say that we'll have more quality, because they'll have more time to practice their professions, they'll be able to spend less time filling out forms and hassling insurance companies.

I also want to say one thing—*[applause]*—there's one frustrated doctor starting the applause out there. [*Laughter*] There's also one thing I want to say over and over again to the AARP membership of this Nation, and that is that our plan maintains the Medicare program. It will protect your freedom to choose your doctors.

Let's face it, Medicare is one thing the Government has gotten right, it has worked. And its own administrative costs for the Government are pretty modest. There are a lot of problems with Medicare in terms of how doctors and hospitals and others have to deal with it, in light of the complexities of the health care system as a whole. But I think, on balance, the plan works well.

However, if you don't like some parts of your Medicare program today, I can say this: This plan will increase your options. It will give you a chance to pick from any of the health plans offered where you live, some of which may offer plans that are more comprehensive and less expensive than what you receive today.

Second, this health care security plan will give you the help you deserve in paying for prescription drugs. This plan, for the first time, will make people on Medicare who are not poor enough to be on Medicaid eligible for help with their prescription drugs. It also will cover prescription drug benefits for working families. We believe this is important, and if coupled with a reasonable effort to hold prices down and to stop practices that we have in America today, where some not experimental drugs but well-established drugs made in America still cost 3 times as much in America as they do in Europe—that needs to be changed. If we can change that we can afford this benefit and still do what needs to be done.

The third thing that I want to emphasize is that this plan greatly expands your options for finding long-term care services in the home, in the community, in the hospital, not simply in a nursing home. We're not going to be able to do all of this at once. We have to work in the system and make sure we have the funding before we undertake programs we can't pay for. And so we phase in the long-term care benefit between 1996 and the year 2000, and we start the drug benefit right away.

But in the end, we have to have a comprehensive set of long-term care services. And again I will say, if we do it right it will save money. It is ridiculous for the only kind of long-term care to be reimbursed by the Government, that which is most expensive and which pushes people toward institutional care at a time when the fastest growing group of Americans are people over 80 and more and more people are more active longer. I think here in California there's probably as much support for an active independent approach to long-term care as anywhere in the United States. And I want you to stay after it, and make sure we maintain the commitment to long-term care and to choice in long-term care.

Let me make one last comment that I think is very important. This program also provides for coverage for early retirees. A lot of AARP members are people between the ages of 55 and 65 who have retired early and who don't have access to adequate health care now. Under our program, those people with incomes will have to pay up to 20 percent of their coverage, just like they would if they were in the workplace and uncovered, but at least they will have access to comprehensive services, with 80 percent contributions by the Federal Government. I hope that you will all support that.

Let me say, finally, that we are interested in passing a program that meets the basic criteria that I laid down in my address to Congress. I have searched this country, and the hundreds of people working with us who searched this country for better ideas: How can we continue to simplify this plan? How can we make it even easier to administer? But we must meet certain basic principles. The first one is security. We owe it to the American people, finally, to say that America will join the ranks of the other advanced nations and give every American health care that's always there, that can't be taken away.

We have to simplify this system in order to pay for it. You live in the only country in the world that's spending at least 10 cents on the dollar—now that's a dime on a $900 billion health care bill—on every dollar, that's $90 billion a year being spent on paperwork that no other country finds it necessary to have: Hospitals hiring clerical workers at 4 times the rate of direct health care providers; doctors seeing their income from the money that comes into

the clinic go from 75 percent of what comes in down to 52 percent in 10 years, the rest of it being taken away in a vast wash of paperwork and unnecessary bureaucracy. I tell you we can do better than that. And we have to do it.

We have to maintain quality. I've already addressed that. We have to maintain choice of physicians and other health care providers. I have addressed that. We will have to ask every American to be more responsible. And those that have no health insurance today, who aren't paying anything into the system, but who can afford to pay, should be asked to pay because the rest of you are paying for those.

There are people who say—and I want to emphasize this—people say this will be terrible for small business. Folks, most small business people have health insurance. And I met a small business man yesterday in San Francisco with 12 employees whose premiums went up 40 percent this year, and he had no claims. Now, I'm worried about those small business people. They're going to go broke or have to dump their employees and make the situation worse. Those people are trying to do their part by asking everyone to do something in giving discounts to small businesses with low-wage workers, we stop the sort of irresponsible shifting of costs onto the rest of you. We also stop the practice of people getting health care when it's too late, too expensive, and when things don't work right and shift back to preventive and primary care services so people can stay well, instead of just be cared for when they get sick.

Finally, let me say this: We have to achieve some savings, and that's been one of the most controversial parts of this proposal. People say, "Oh, you can't get any savings out of Medicare and Medicaid." I hope we can talk more about this, but let me just tell you how this program is paid for. Two-thirds of the cost of this program will be paid for by contributions from employers and employees who pay nothing to this system today but still get to use it when they get sick, two-thirds of it. One-sixth of the money will come from a tax on tobacco and from asking big companies that will still have the right to self-insure, because many of them have their costs under control and have adequate benefits, they'll be able to continue to do that, but they will be asked, since their costs will go down, too, to pay a modest fee to pay for medical research and technology and to keep the public health clinics of this country open to do the work that they will have to do. And then one-sixth of it will come from what we call savings.

But I want you to understand what's happening. Today, Medicaid and Medicare are going up at 3 times the rate of inflation. We propose to let it go up at 2 times the rate of inflation. That is not a Medicare or Medicaid cut. And we have kept private sector increases so that they won't go up as much. So only in Washington do people believe that no one can get by on twice the rate of inflation. So when you hear all this business about cuts, let me caution you that that is not what is going on. We are going to have increases in Medicare and Medicaid, and a reduction in the rate of growth will be more than overtaken by the new investments we're going to make in drugs and long-term care. We think it's a good system. We hope you'll support it.

Let me just acknowledge two other people I just saw in the audience I didn't know were here. First, Congresswoman Lucille Roybal-Allard. Thank you for being here. Are there any other Members of the California Congressional Delegation here? Congressman Martinez, stand up there. It's good to see you. I'm sorry. And I want to thank your insurance commissioner, John Garamendi, for all of the work he did to try to show us what's been done in California that we put into our plan.

Thank you very much.

[At this point, Ms. Brown thanked the President and introduced Anne Jackson, chair of the health care committee of AARP's national legislative council, who discussed the AARP health care proposal and invited participants to ask questions.]

Q. [Inaudible]

The President. He said much of the program is funded with cuts in Medicare; do I really think it won't affect the recipients? Absolutely.

Let me just tell you. We just adopted a budget in Washington which cuts defense deeply, just as much as we can, and we shouldn't do a dollar more. But we have cut it dramatically. And that's one of the reasons the California unemployment rate is up, right, because defense has been cut since 1987. But there's a limit to how much it can be cut. It's cut, absolutely. It freezes all domestic discretionary spending. That is, if I want to put more money into de-

fense conversion in California, or Head Start, or public health clinics, the Congress and the Members here will tell you, they have to find for the next 5 years a dollar in cuts somewhere else for every dollar we want to spend in some new program.

The only thing we're increasing, except for the cost of living in retirement programs, is Medicare and Medicaid. Everything else is declining or frozen. And Medicare and Medicaid, under this budget that they just adopted, with an inflation rate of under 4 percent, Medicaid is projected to grow at between 16 percent and 11 percent a year, and Medicare at between 11 percent and 9 percent a year. In other words, over the next 5 year period, both will grow at more than 3 times the rate of inflation. What we propose to do is to let them grow at twice the rate of inflation, too. I think we can live with twice the rate of inflation. Yes, I do. Why? Because the rate of reimbursement increases to doctors and hospitals need not go up so fast in Medicare, because we're going to close the gap between Medicare in the private sector and what doctors and hospitals get. And they will actually save money because we're going to dramatically cut their administrative costs. So they will be getting a raise through reduced administrative expenses that they won't have to get through greater outlays of taxpayer money. And we're going to turn right around and invest that money and more into the drug benefit in the long-term care.

I don't know anybody who has really looked at this thing closely who doesn't think we can get it. Now, there may be people who try to stop us from getting it, but if we can't get a Government health care program down to the point where it can run on twice the rate of inflation, we're in deep trouble. I believe we can, and the program explicitly provides that none of the benefits can be cut.

[Ms. Brown introduced Jo Barbano, national chair of the AARP legislative council, who discussed the rate of inflation on prescription drug prices without health care reform. A participant then asked if the new health care plan would control the rising cost of prescription drugs.]

The President. Yes. We have sought and received assurances from many of the drug companies that for nonexperimental or non-newly developed drugs, which do—it costs a fortune to develop a new drug and bring it to market.

And we all know they have to be priced at very high levels early on.

The thing that has bothered me is that other countries have cost controls on their drugs, and so we have companies from America selling drugs made in America in other countries with incomes as high as our elderly people have, for prices one-third of what they're charging Americans. It's just not right. So we're trying to work through that. But a number of the drug companies, to be fair to them, have come forward and said, while you're implementing this program, we'll keep our cost increases to inflation. Then, when we get into the program, the drug services, like every other part of it, will be subject to significant pressures to stay within the rate of inflation or pretty close to it. But what the drug companies will get out of this program, they'll win big, because they will have people able to purchase drugs who never were able to do it before.

So what they give up on the rate of increase they will make back in the volume of sales, if you see what I mean. So they're not going to lose on this deal, they're just going to have to stop increasing the same drugs more and stop charging people so much more for the same health care, but they'll be able to increase their volume.

I saw one person being critical of our health care program the other night on one of these C–SPAN forums that I watched. And he said, "Well," he said, "you know in Germany, the President's always talking about Germany, and they only spend 8.8 percent of their income on health care, and we spend 14.5 percent, but they rely so much more on medicine." Yes, they do, as a result of which they don't have to go to the hospital as much.

So the way our system will work, let me just briefly say, is that the drug benefit itself for elderly people will have a $250 deductible and a copay, but no matter how serious the drug needs are, no one can be required to pay more than $1,000 a year. And obviously, income needs will be taken into account. But we will also have the same benefit for people under 65 as for people over 65. To get the drug benefit, the Part B premium will go up modestly, but it will really help to provide that service to people.

I think it's going to make a huge difference in the quality of life to millions of elderly people. And I think it's going to reduce their need

for more extensive care by giving them a maintenance schedule with the most modern medicines. And it will be good for the drug company. It will be a good swap for them to let their regular prices go up less but to be able to sell more.

Q. You were asking for information and those 25,000 older Americans that I just visited and were asking me these questions gave me a report to give to you today. Could I give that to your staff?

The President. Absolutely.

Q. Thank you.

[*Ms.. Brown introduced Mildred McCauley, member of AARP's national board of directors, who discussed the high cost of care in nursing homes. A participant then asked about funding for prevention and treatment of Alzheimer's disease and coverage for home and community-based long-term care.*]

The President. Yes. Let me first say what was said here is absolutely right. As all of you know who have ever had a family member affected by this, if you're older and you go to a hospital, you can get care covered by your policies or by Medicare. If you go to a nursing home, you basically have to spend yourself into abject poverty to get any benefits. And as a result of that, we've got a lot of folks in this country who are in trouble.

Also, the least expensive and best way to care for people might be in some community-based setting or at home, and there are relatively limited coverages available for long-term care services. And Alzheimer's is a particular example of this because a lot of people want to care for their loved ones at home, or want them to be able to stay at home for as long as possible, but can't get any help in that regard. I'll come back to the research issue in a moment.

The way this program will work, the long-term care program, is that we will permit home and community-based care to be reimbursed just like nursing home care number one. Number two, the programs will not be means-tested. That is, if people have the ability to pay something, they'll be asked to pay, but they won't be cut out of the program because their income is above a certain amount. So that solves the whole Medicare-Medicaid differential issue. Number three, in order to be eligible for Medicaid nursing home care today you have to have— there's a spend down limit of $2,000. You can only have $2,000 in assets to be eligible for 100 percent coverage under Medicaid. We're going to raise that to $12,000. And people who are in Medicaid funding in nursing homes—funded nursing homes—only get $30 a month in spending money, $30 a month. In 1977, when I entered public life and became an advocate for people in nursing homes, they got $25 a month. You can imagine—so in other words, in effect, people are getting less than half as much per month as they did in 1977. We propose to raise that to $100 which will take it back about to its 1972 levels.

So I think these things will work if we also provide better regulation and some tax preference for private long-term care insurance to supplement whatever people want or get from our Government program. But this long-term care issue is a very big issue. Keep in mind, again, elderly people are the fastest growing group of our population. Most people would prefer not to be in an institutional setting if they can be cared for at home or in a community setting.

And again, I will say to you, this is another example where sometimes we strain at a gnat and swallow a camel. Yes, it will cost more money to start this program, but over the long run, 20 years from now our health care system in the aggregate will be cheaper because we provide a wider range of care options and we don't shove everybody into the most expensive option to get any help at all. So that's how that will work.

Now, on the Alzheimer's question in particular, the way this system of funding works, we are going to develop a stream of funding that will increase our investment in medical research of all kinds, including research in the care and treatment of Alzheimer's. So you'll get more medical research. I will say again, we have been driven here not to mess up what is right with American medicine and American health care, we want to enhance what is right and only focus on what is wrong in trying to deal with it.

Q. Thank you for that response, Mr. President. I'm sure that you recognize that the issue of long-term care is one that is so very, very important to us and that we will be reminding you about it. You can be sure of that.

The President. You don't have to remind me, you've got to remind Congress. Because there will be people who say, well, now, wait a minute. And that's why I really thank the three

Members from California who are here today. They're going to have some tough decisions to make. You know, there will be a lot of people who won't want to go through some of these changes that we're recommending, and there will be a lot of people who say, well, let's just play it safe and take the—we know the least expensive course. There will be those who say, let's take these reductions in Medicare and Medicaid increases, these savings from projected increases, and put them into paying for the regular package that the President has proposed, and think about long-term care and medicine some other day.

So we need you guys to show up and be heard in the Capitol to support the Members of Congress who want to see this as a critical element of the ultimate resolution of our health care crisis.

[Ms. Brown introduced Marie Smith, chair of the economics committee of the national legislative council, who discussed cost containment. A participant then asked about cost containment provisions in the health care plan.]

The President. Thank you. First of all, as all of you know, we have runaway costs now, both in the system as a whole and for individuals who are paying into it. To keep down individual cost increases as well as systematic cost increases, we seek to do three things that we've factored in. There are a lot of things we are doing, I want to try to emphasize this; we think we'll get more cost containment than we have budgeted for, and I want to explain why.

Number one, if you simplify the system so that essentially every patient, every doctor, every insurer is dealing with a single uniform form, one for each category of people in the system, you will drastically cut the administrative cost of this health care system. We were at the Children's Hospital in Washington the other day; one hospital in one city in America estimates that they spend $2 million a year and enough time for their doctors to see another 10,000 children a year on paperwork that has nothing to do with the care of the kids or keeping up with their records necessary to monitor the care of the kids. That's the first thing.

Number two, if you cover everybody and require everybody to make some contribution to the system, that will stop a lot of the cost shifting. Keep in mind, a lot of your costs keep going up every year more and more and more because you are paying into the system, either through Medicare or through private insurance, and you pay for everybody else because the hospitals shift their uncompensated care bills to you or to insurance companies who turn around and raise the price or the Government who comes around and raises the price. So through simple administrative simplification and stopping cost shifting, you're going to have some savings.

Number three, as a backup, we also propose a cap, a limit on how much the cost of the system can increase in any given year, moving down towards inflation plus population growth over a period of years. But still, I will tell you, that we still believe—this budget is very modest. We still project over the next 5—between now and the year 2000, the American health care system will go from spending 14.5 percent of our income on health care to about 18 percent, picking up the drugs and the long-term care. If we don't do anything, we'll have no drugs, no long-term care, and be spending over 19 percent of our income on health care.

But those are very modest. Now, that means that we are calculating no savings from putting all the people in the country in these large buyer groups so that they can compete for lower prices. Look what happened to the California public employees plan. Look how little their inflation was this year. The Mayo Clinic managed care plan—most people believe Mayo Clinic provides pretty good health care—you know what their inflation was this year? 3.9 percent, and their prices before they started were lower than the national average.

We don't calculate any of those savings in our budget, the things that will come from better organizing and delivering health care and giving consumer groups the right to bargain to keep their prices lower. We have an initiative to eliminate fraud and abuse, which is significant in this system. We calculate none of those savings into our budget.

So we believe we will easily make the budget because a lot of the things we're going to do that will save money we don't even try to claim credit for to try to bend over backward to be realistic. So I think we'll get there. But you're right, you've got to have cost control.

Let me just say one other thing. There's one other thing we need to help the AARP on. There are a lot of people in the Congress who say that limitations on the rate of increases amount to some sort of price controls, and we

shouldn't have them. But look what we've had so far. If you have a third-party pay system, where the people who are working the system can get a check every time they send a bill, there are no normal market forces. You have to have some sort of discipline on the system. Now, I know the AARP favors that. And again, I want you to help us get that when this bill goes to the Congress. We believe we will more than meet the cap that we've set. We don't think we can ever necessarily even meet that cap, but we better have it in the law so people will have to know they're going to have to manage their business better, they can't keep breaking the bank.

Ms. Brown. Well, Mr. President, the time has passed so quickly. I believe it's now time, if you have some closing remarks.

The President. Let me say, first of all, I think when I leave, Mr. Magaziner is going to come up here. Ira Magaziner who has been the sort of leading light of our health care efforts in the First Lady's group on health care and who knows the answers to questions you haven't even thought of yet—at least questions I haven't thought of yet—is going to come up here and spend up to another hour answering any questions you have about the specifics of our plan. So I hope that those of you here who are interested will stay and continue to ask questions. He and some others who have come all the way to California with me, who are working in our health care effort, are going to stay. So we want to encourage all Americans to ask questions and to give us our ideas—their ideas. We don't pretend to have all the answers.

I just want to make two points in closing. Number one, I am not interested in having this become a partisan, political issue. I am profoundly grateful to the distinguished Republican Senator from Vermont, Jim Jeffords, for announcing that he intends to be a cosponsor of our initiative. That's the kind of thing we need more of, working together.

Number two, we've got to keep working on making this better, the evidence of other countries is, but you have to keep working every year. But that's why we've built this in a phased-in fashion, so that the more we learn, the more we can make adjustments and the more we can make improvements.

The point I want to make, the two of you have already made out here in these questions, is if we do nothing, it will be more costly and less satisfactory than if we take steps. And finally, let me say, we have to overcome the disbelief in America. A lot of folks don't think we can do this, but that's what they said when Social Security came in. People said we couldn't do it, but we did it.

I hold this health security card up all the time, but you just think, if everybody had a Social Security card and a health security card, what a better country this would be and how much better life would be for all the American people.

Thank you very much.

NOTE: The President spoke at 8:50 a.m. at Dr. Paul Carlson Memorial Park.

Statement on the Arts and Humanities Awards Recipients
October 5, 1993

These extraordinary individuals have made a gift to American cultural life that is beyond measure. Through these awards we celebrate their impressive achievements and extend our deepest thanks for efforts that nourish our creative and intellectual spirit.

NOTE: The President's statement was included in a White House statement announcing the awards ceremony for the National Medal of Arts and the Charles Frankel Prize scheduled for October 7.

Named by the President as 1993 National Medal of Arts recipients were:
  Walter and Leonore Annenberg, arts patrons, Wynnefield, PA
  Cabell "Cab" Calloway, singer and bandleader, White Plains, NY
  Ray Charles, singer and musician, Los Angeles, CA
  Bess Lomax Hawes, folklorist, Arlington, VA
  Stanley Kunitz, poet, editor, and educator, NY, NY/Provincetown, MA
  Robert Merrill, baritone, New Rochelle, NY
  Arthur Miller, playwright and author, New York, NY
  Robert Rauschenberg, artist, Captiva Island, FL
  Lloyd Richards, theatrical director, New York, NY
  William Styron, author, Vineyard Haven, MA
  Paul Taylor, dancer and choreographer, New York, NY
  Billy Wilder, movie director, writer, and producer, Hollywood, CA

Winners of the Charles Frankel Prize for their work in the humanities were:
  Richard E. Alegria, anthropologist, San Juan, Puerto Rico
  John Hope Franklin, historian, Durham, NC
  Hanna Holborn Gray, former University of Chicago president, Chicago, IL
  Andrew Heiskell, philanthropist, New York, NY
  Laurel T. Ulrich, author and historian, Durham, NH

Biographies of the recipients were made available by the Office of the Press Secretary.

Statement by the Press Secretary on the President's Telephone Conversation With President Boris Yeltsin of Russia
October 5, 1993

The President called President Yeltsin today from Air Force One to discuss the situation in Moscow. The two leaders spoke for 20 minutes. The President's purpose in calling was to express the continued, strong support of the United States for President Yeltsin and the Russian Government in the wake of the political crisis in Russia.

President Yeltsin thanked the President for his support during the crisis and described the events of the last few days. He reported that order had been restored to Moscow. In response to a question from the President, he also reaffirmed his intention to hold free and fair elections on December 12 and to proceed resolutely on political and economic reform in general.

The two leaders pledged to work together to continue to build close relations between the United States and Russia. The President noted in this respect his intention to implement rapidly the $2.5 billion in economic assistance funds approved by the Congress last week for Russia and the other new states. The President added that the visits to Russia this autumn of several American Cabinet officers, including Secretary of State Christopher later this month, will help to move the relationship forward.

Statement by the Press Secretary on Nuclear Testing by China
October 5, 1993

Last night China conducted an underground nuclear test at the Lop Nur test site in northwest China, despite the urging of more than 20 nations, including the United States, not to do so.

The United States deeply regrets this action. We urge China to refrain from further nuclear tests and to join the other nuclear powers in a global moratorium. Such a moratorium will contribute to the achievement of the administration's goal of completing a Comprehensive Test Ban by 1996, to which the administration is committed.

The President has today directed the Department of Energy to take such actions as are needed to put the U.S. in a position to be able to conduct nuclear tests next year, provided the notification and review conditions of the Hatfield-Exon-Mitchell amendment are met in the spring of 1994.

The President's ultimate decision on whether to test will be based on fundamental U.S. national security interests, taking into account:

—the contribution further tests would make to improving the safety and reliability of the U.S. arsenal in preparation for a Comprehensive Test Ban Treaty (CTB)

—the extent to which China and others have responded to the U.S. appeal for a global moratorium on testing;

—progress in the CTB negotiations;

—the implications of further U.S. nuclear tests on our broader nonproliferation objectives.

Administration officials will begin consultations at once with Congress and our allies on these issues.

Remarks on Signing the Hatch Act Reform Amendments of 1993
October 6, 1993

Thank you. Thank you very much, ladies and gentlemen. This is a very happy day for me. I've had lots of discussions with Senator Glenn about this bill. Bill Clay is happy as a lark. This has put 30 years on his life today. And the Vice President and I had occasion to talk about this quite a lot during the reinventing Government effort. I have some remarks I want to make, but I hope you will forgive me if, just for a moment, since this is my opportunity to speak to the national press and to the Amer-

ican people as well as to speak to you, I make a brief statement about Somalia.

Today I have had two serious meetings with my national security advisers, along with the meeting we had last night, to discuss the future course of the United States in Somalia.

Our forces went there last year under the previous administration on an extraordinary human mission: 350,000 Somalis had starved because anarchy and famine and disease had prevailed. Today we are completing the job of establishing security in Somalia that will not only permit those who are now living to enjoy the immediate fruits of our common efforts with our allies in the United Nations but also to prevent that terrible crisis from occurring as soon as we are gone. It is essential that we conclude our mission in Somalia but that we do it with firmness and steadiness of purpose.

I want to emphasize that tomorrow I will be consulting with congressional leaders in both parties and with others, and then I will report to you and to the American people. But this much I want to say today. Our men and women in Somalia, including any held captive, deserve our full support. They went there to do something almost unique in human history. We are anxious to conclude our role there honorably, but we do not want to see a reversion to the absolute chaos and the terrible misery which existed before.

I think the American people, and I hope the Congress will be satisfied that we have assessed our position accurately and that we have a good policy to pursue. I will discuss that with them tomorrow, as I said, and then I will be back to the American people and to the press as soon as that is done.

Let me say this is something of special importance to me today. When I was a 32-year-old freshman Governor, in my first year, one of the first bills I sponsored in my legislature was a bill repealing restrictions on political activities by State employees in my State. A bill that, very much like the Hatch Act, had stayed on in its present form because it was needed in a former time when, I'm a little embarrassed to say, State employees decades ago would mysteriously turn up with increases in welfare checks right before the election. Well, that hasn't happened in a long time in my State, or in any other. And so we changed the law. And I can honestly say in all the years since, not a single solitary soul ever lodged a single solitary complaint against any of our public employees for being good citizens.

Today, we put an end to a vexing contradiction in America's public life with a solution, I hasten to add, looking at the Members of Congress who are here, that is neither Democratic nor Republican but American in nature. And I thank the members of both parties who supported this important reform.

We've been supporting democracy throughout the world. We've been standing up for Boris Yeltsin in the tight he's been in and cheering when he prevailed and cheering when he reaffirmed his determination to have elections. But here in our own country, millions of our own citizens have been denied one of the most basic democratic rights, the right to participate in the political process, because of conditions that haven't existed for a very long time.

The original purpose of the Hatch Act was to protect Federal employees and other citizens from coming under improper political pressure. But now our Federal work force is the product of merit system, not patronage. We have laws to protect our citizens against coercion and intimidation. We have guarantees that the administration of Federal laws must be fair and impartial. We have an exceedingly vigilant press and people more than eager to talk to them whenever they have been abused or think they have. The conditions which once gave rise to the Hatch Act as it was before this reform bill passed are no longer present, and they cannot justify the continued muzzling of millions of American citizens.

The Federal Employees Political Activities Act, which I'm about to sign, will permit Federal employees and postal workers on their own time to manage campaigns, raise funds, to hold positions within political parties. Still, there will be some reasonable restrictions. They wouldn't be able to run for partisan political office themselves, for example, and there will be some new responsibilities, which I applaud the Federal employees' unions for embracing and supporting.

While we restore political rights to these millions of citizens, we also hold them to high standards. The Federal workplace, where the business of our Nation is done will still be strictly off limits to partisan political activity. Workers on the job won't even be allowed to wear political campaign buttons. At the same time, the reforms will maintain restrictions on the activities of workers in the most sensitive positions, in law enforcement and national security.

Because we regard good ethics as the basis of good government, this reform strengthens criminal penalties for anyone convicted of abusing his or her position. And because we want our Federal workers to be responsible, to display an integrity worthy of the public service they perform, this reform includes a provision that allows the garnishment of Federal pay to repay private debt. That's been done in the private sector for many years. And just as we now treat Federal employees like private citizens in their political activities, there's no reason Federal workers should get special protection for privately unpaid bills and obligations.

Ultimately, I believe, as Senator Glenn said, that this reform of the Hatch Act will mean more responsible, more satisfied, happier, and more productive Federal workers. When we extend the political rights of any group of Americans, we extend the political rights of all Americans. And we deepen the meaning of our own democracy.

Congress has done a lot of work on that just in the last 8 months since I've been President. We've passed the motor voter bill, which expands the franchise to people who have difficulty registering to vote. Thanks to the Vice President, we have a plan that will radically change the way Government operates. It will give rank-and-file Federal employees more meaningful jobs, more say over their work, and enable us to do more with less and increase

the confidence taxpayers have in the work we do around here.

Serious proposals on campaign finance reform and on lobbying reform have already passed the United States Senate and are now being acted on in the House of Representatives. There is a serious commitment in this Congress to try to deal with the continuing imperfections in our democracy. And I applaud them for it.

Aristotle once said that, "liberty and equality are best attained when all persons alike share in the Government to the utmost." Working together, we're closing in on that goal. And now, when I sign this bill, 3 million more Americans will have a chance to share in their beloved Government to the utmost.

Thank you very much.

NOTE: The President spoke at 3 p.m. in the East Room at the White House. In his remarks, he referred to Missouri Representative William Clay. H.R. 20, approved October 6, was assigned Public Law No. 103–94.

Statement on Signing the Hatch Act Reform Amendments of 1993
October 6, 1993

Today I am pleased to sign into law H.R. 20, the "Hatch Act Reform Amendments of 1993."

For too long, the rights of Federal and postal workers to express themselves and fully participate in our political process have been curtailed. Federal law currently penalizes public servants by limiting their political participation outside the Federal workplace. People who devote their lives to public service should not be denied the right to participate more fully in the democratic process. This law moves us in a more sensible direction.

The passage of H.R. 20 is primarily due to the steadfast efforts of many Members of Congress and the Federal and postal employees and their representatives. The Hatch Act reforms in this bill will provide Federal and postal employees the opportunity to exercise their citizenship more fully and freely for the first time in over 50 years.

At the same time, this Act spells out the rights and responsibilities of Federal and postal work-

ers. While employees will now be allowed to volunteer on their own time for the candidate of their choice, all political activity in the Federal workplace will be prohibited, including the wearing of campaign buttons.

Further, not only does H.R. 20 continue prohibitions against soliciting political contributions from the general public and subordinate employees, but it also strengthens the criminal penalties for those convicted of abusing their official position. This balanced measure will ensure Americans fair and impartial administration of Federal laws, while providing Federal and postal employees the rights that are essential to their independent exercise of personal choice.

H.R. 20 also includes a likewise overdue provision for the garnishment of Federal pay to repay private debt. We already have the authority to offset the salaries of Federal employees for Federal debt, and we use it. In presenting his National Performance Review report, Vice President Gore expressed his faith in the quality and integrity of Government employees. He and

I share that faith. This new provision of law will ensure that those few Federal workers who fail to pay their private debts will no longer be able to hide behind their Federal employment to escape their personnel financial responsibilities.

As a candidate, I strongly supported the much needed reforms contained in H.R. 20. It gives me great pleasure to sign this bill into law. I look forward to the infusion of Federal and post-al employee energy, expertise, and dedication into our political system that this bill makes possible.

WILLIAM J. CLINTON

The White House,
October 6, 1993.

NOTE: H.R. 20, approved October 6, was assigned Public Law No. 103–94.

Remarks Honoring White House Fellows
October 6, 1993

Thank you very much. Mr. Vice President and my longtime friend Nancy Bekavac, ladies and gentlemen, I want to welcome the White House fellows, their families and friends and the White House Fellowship Commission here.

This program has been largely a secret to the American people for a long time, and yet it has been one of the most important things that has been done to enrich and diversify the work of administrations for decades now.

We have a remarkable array of White House fellows this year. We have an American Indian poet and legal scholar working at the Interior Department, a basketball star and a tax expert at State, an AIDS specialist at Commerce, two doctors at the Pentagon. Several fellows work here at the White House, including an astronomer tackling environmental issues at the National Security Council, a Bronx preacher reviewing domestic policy—sometimes I think we do better praying over these problems than what we do anyway—an author and an illustrator helping to build our national service corps, and we have two heroes of the Persian Gulf war, one working for the Vice President and one for Mack McLarty, my Chief of Staff.

I am very grateful to all the people here behind me and all those who have served on the Fellowship Commission, including our birthday girl, Pauline Gore.

With all of your responsibilities, it's a credit to you that you understand the importance of this program, that you've been willing to give your time, your attention, your energies to it. I hope that you will always be very, very proud of this.

You know, Colin Powell was a White House fellow. Henry Cisneros was a White House fellow. Tim Wirth, our Under Secretary of State for Global Affairs, was a White House fellow. We don't have any idea what these young people here behind me will be doing in 5 or 10 or 15 years. But one thing is for sure, whatever it is they wind up doing, they'll do a better job of it because those of you on this Commission gave them an opportunity to serve. And I will certainly be a better President because you gave them an opportunity to serve.

This has been a truly astonishing month. A lot of incredible things have happened in the world and in our country. And all these people have been a part of that remarkable change. We're committed to continuing to do that.

I told a dinner last night there's something to be said just for showing up for work every day. Sooner or later you can make some good things happen. But it's a lot easier when you've got people with the richness, the diversity, the gifts and the commitment of the White House fellows.

So to all of you, I say thank you, and I give you my renewed commitment to this program and to honoring your service and your efforts.

Thank you very much.

NOTE: The President spoke at 5:57 p.m. in the East Room at the White House. In his remarks, he referred to Nancy Bekavac, president, Scripps College, Claremont, CA.

Message to the Congress Transmitting the Report of the National Institute of Building Sciences
October 6, 1993

To the Congress of the United States:

In accordance with the requirements of section 809 of the Housing and Community Development Act of 1974, as amended (12 U.S.C. 1701j–2(j)), I transmit herewith the 16th annual report of the National Institute of Building Sciences for fiscal year 1992.

WILLIAM J. CLINTON

The White House,
October 6, 1993.

Message to the Congress Transmitting the Report of the National Corporation for Housing Partnerships
October 6, 1993

To the Congress of the United States:

I transmit herewith the twenty-fourth annual report of the National Corporation for Housing Partnerships and the National Housing Partnership for the fiscal year ending December 31, 1992, as required by section 3938(a)(1) of title 42 of the United States Code.

WILLIAM J. CLINTON

The White House,
October 6, 1993.

Statement on the Retirement of Michael Jordan From the Chicago Bulls
October 6, 1993

As a sports fan who has had the great pleasure of watching Michael Jordan play basketball since the early 1980's, I was saddened to hear his announcement today that he was retiring from the game. But, I think we can all understand his wish to take his leave and devote himself to more private concerns.

We will miss him, here and all around America, in every small-town backyard and paved city lot where kids play one-on-one and dream of being like Mike.

His gift to us all has been in giving everything he had game after game, year in and year out. It has been our privilege for the last decade to see him gracing the hardwood, lighting up our TV screens, and brightening the lives of the young at heart all around the world.

I want to wish Michael and his family the very best. I know that the past several months have been difficult ones, and I hope that he can enjoy the peace of mind that he richly deserves.

Nomination for Director of the United States Arms Control and Disarmament Agency
October 6, 1993

The President announced today that he intends to nominate John D. Holum to be the Director of the United States Arms Control and Disarmament Agency.

"My administration has placed the highest importance on arms control and combating the proliferation of weapons of mass destruction," said the President. "A revitalized Arms Control and Disarmament Agency will play an important role in achieving new arms control agreements and fighting weapons proliferation. I can think of no finer and more dedicated person to lead ACDA than John Holum, whom I have known for 20 years and who has close working relationships with many senior officials at the State and Defense Departments, the NSC, and throughout my administration. John will be a strong voice for arms control and nonproliferation policies within the councils of Government."

NOTE: A biography of the nominee was made available by the Office of the Press Secretary.

Nomination for a Special Counsel at the Department of Justice
October 6, 1993

The President announced today that he has nominated Gerald Stern, an experienced corporate attorney and former Justice Department civil rights attorney, to be the Special Counsel for Financial Institutions Fraud at the Department of Justice.

"To preserve our people's trust in their financial institutions, it is imperative that we aggressively enforce the laws governing them," said the President. "Gerald Stern has the business experience and prosecutorial skill to make sure that we do just that."

NOTE: A biography of the nominee was made available by the Office of the Press Secretary.

Remarks on Presenting Arts and Humanities Awards
October 7, 1993

Thank you very much. To our distinguished honorees and all of you in the audience; I want to say a special word of thanks to Jane Alexander and to Dr. Sheldon Hackney for their leadership of our administration's efforts in the arts and humanities.

As a person who at various times in his life has been a frustrated writer and a frustrated musician, this is an extremely humbling event for me today. [*Laughter*] But I've been getting a lot of training in humility lately. I have a Vice President who humbles me all the time by all the things he teaches me about things great and insignificant and who unlike me actually got to go on David Letterman to prove how funny he was. [*Laughter*] And I have a wife who swept the television ratings last week talking about the arcana of health care with a passion and an eloquence. As if that weren't bad enough, USA Today had the bad grace to go out and poll the American people, and 40 percent of them said she was smarter than I am. [*Laughter*] To which I reply, "Of course, what kind of dummy do you think I am? How else would I have gotten elected President?"

And just to drive this humility home—this is the actual true part of this wonderful story— I went to southern California last week, or the first of this week, and I was looking forward to staying in the Beverly Hilton. It seemed like an exotic sort of place. And I showed up, and Merv Griffin, who owns it, shook hands with me and took me up to the floor where I was staying. There is only one person who is a permanent resident of the floor where I stayed in the Beverly Hilton, Rodney Dangerfield, who said they had put me there because we seem to belong together—[*laughter*]—and gave me 12 roses with "a little respect" on a gift card.

I am delighted to be here to honor this year's winners of the National Medal of the Arts and the Charles Frankel Prize, men and women whose achievements represent the enduring power of the arts and humanities and, in a larger sense, of the creative spirit in all of our lives.

Throughout history, the arts and humanities have been the cultural signature of this great Nation. They have enabled Americans of all backgrounds and walks of life to gain a deeper appreciation of who they are as individuals and who we all are as a society, stirring our minds and our senses, stimulating learning and collective discourse, the arts and humanities teach us in ways that nothing else can about the vastness and the depth of human experience. They are our great equalizers. We inherit them, and we can all participate in them.

Whether or not one plays an instrument, reads poetry, learns to pirouette, or spends hours alone in a local art gallery, we all have the capacity to be moved by a song, a poem, a story, a dance, a painting. We can feel our spirits soar when we see an intriguing film or the sudden illumination of a new idea or an old idea put in a new way.

At a time when our society faces new and profound challenges, at a time when we are losing so many of our children, at a time when so many of our people feel insecure in the face of change, the arts and humanities must remain a vital part of our lives as individuals and as a Nation.

For 200 years, the freedom of our artistic and intellectual imagination has contributed to the quality of our civic life. It has helped to shape American ideas of democracy, of pluralism, of tolerance. Three decades ago, President Kennedy said this: There's a connection, hard to explain logically but easy to feel, between achievement in public life and progress in the arts. The Jeffersonian era gave birth not only to the Declaration of Independence but also to beautiful Monticello. The age of Lincoln produced the Emancipation Proclamation, along

with the Hudson River school of painting and the writings of Ralph Waldo Emerson, Henry David Thoreau, and Harriet Beecher Stowe. The first half of this century gave us universal suffrage and the empowerment of American workers, as well as Charlie Chaplin, Frank Lloyd Wright, William Faulkner, Marian Anderson, and Duke Ellington. The same unbridled energy and potent imagination that took Americans to the moon inspired rock and roll, Motown, modern dance, and a new emphasis on civil and human rights.

Those of you gathered with us today are reminders that the human imagination is still the most powerful tool we have in moving forward as a civilization. You provoke our minds, you enliven our senses, endow our souls, help us to give our lives meaning. That's why public support for the arts and humanities remains essential today and for the generations to come.

Today, we are indeed fortunate to have inspiring new leaders working in Government to expand our artistic and humanistic endeavors, to carry on our heritage to future generations. I'm very proud of the work and the life that Sheldon Hackney and that Jane Alexander have lived before they came to this work. I thank them for their work here. And I tell you that we welcome all of you to give us your ideas, your suggestions, and your energy as we try to move forward together. Now it is a privilege to call forward the following recipients of the National Medal of Arts.

First, the contributions of Walter and Leonore Annenberg to American culture can literally not be overstated. The Annenbergs have enriched our appreciation of the arts through public service, publishing, and as board members of major arts institutions. They have given generously of their time and their money. And they provided among other things the magnificent portrait of Benjamin Franklin, which hangs in the Green Room at the White House, one of the most prized possessions of this, your American home.

[*At this point, the President congratulated Mr. and Mrs. Annenberg, and Hillary Clinton presented the medal.*]

The legendary vocalist and bandleader, Cab Calloway, has had indeed a remarkable career, one of the originators of American jazz. An enduring figure in popular music, Cab Calloway added "Hi-dee-ho" and the scat sound to our musical vocabulary. And for those of us who have lived a while, we can enjoy seeing the brightness of his smile in our memories going back for decades. He is an American original, and I am deeply honored that he's here with us today.

[The President congratulated Mr. Calloway, and Hillary Clinton presented the medal.]

Literally for decades, Ray Charles has been one of America's favorite singers. From his roots in Georgia, he became one of the first great truly American singers, one of the first to combine the dynamic energy of gospel music with rhythm and blues. His songs are indelibly etched in the hearts of millions of Americans.

I can tell you that it's a particular honor for me to give him this award today, because I suppose no singer ever had a bigger impact on my musical life than Ray Charles. I still remember over there in Constitution Hall a concert I attended on June 24th, 1967. I was notable for being one of a few members of my race in the audience. And Ray Charles electrified that crowd so much that that night I literally could not go to sleep until 5 o'clock in the morning. I went out and ran 3 miles to get the energy out. And I still remember to this day the date of the concert. That is testament to the enduring impact of this phenomenal American original.

[The President congratulated Mr. Charles, and Hillary Clinton presented the medal.]

Our next honoree, I believe, is part of the only brother-sister team ever to receive this great award. Bess Lomax Hawes has played a major role in the American folk movement since the 1940's as a singer, a teacher, a composer, an author of articles and books that help bring the folk arts into the lives of countless Americans. At a time when our native folk arts are largely lost to millions of our younger people, she has performed an invaluable service to our Nation in helping us to remember who we are and how we got here.

[The President congratulated Ms. Hawes, and Hillary Clinton presented the medal.]

You know what she said? She said, "I wish all the beautiful artists I've recorded and seen across the years in this country were here to receive this award for me. They were the inspiration for what I did." Thank you.

Poet and educator Stanley Kunitz has spent a life opening America's eyes and ears to poetry. He makes the ordinary become extraordinary, the everyday become timeless and significant. He was awarded the Pulitzer Prize for Poetry in 1959, and his works grace us still.

Welcome, Stanley Kunitz.

[The President congratulated Mr. Kunitz, and Hillary Clinton presented the medal.]

Robert Merrill has been acclaimed by critics as one of the great natural baritones of the century. He's appeared in 787 performances at the Metropolitan Opera over a 31-year operatic career. He's also sung on Broadway and many solo recitals and on television. And all of us who have ever heard him sing wish, as I tried to persuade him to do today, that this would be the 787th performance. He turned me down, but I still think we should give him the medal. Mr. Robert Merrill.

[The President congratulated Mr. Merrill, and Hillary Clinton presented the medal.]

Arthur Miller has given our Nation some of the finest plays of this century. His character, Willy Loman in "Death of a Salesman," caught the public's imagination by conveying the tension and drama of a common man's life. In "The Crucible," he focused on issues of conscience by probing the Salem witch trials of the late 17th century. He won the Pulitzer Prize for Drama in 1949. The thing that has always impressed me about him was the continuing energy he has brought to his work over such a long period of time, seeming forever young with something always new to say. Please welcome Arthur Miller.

[The President congratulated Mr. Miller, and Hillary Clinton presented the medal.]

Robert Rauschenberg is one of America's most innovative artists whose remarkable works have been displayed in museums and galleries around the world, and who has really helped to transform our notions of contemporary art. Modern art is often inaccessible to a lot of people who don't go to art galleries and often don't understand it. I have personally been impressed by how many people I know who don't count themselves as connoisseurs, who have seen and been moved by the works of our next honoree, Robert Rauschenberg.

[The President congratulated Mr. Rauschenberg, and Hillary Clinton presented the medal.]

He's also a pretty good comic. I said, "It's great to see you here today." He said, "Oh, I'll show up for this anytime." [*Laughter*]

Lloyd Richards has devoted his career to promoting theater in America. As dean of the Yale school of drama and artistic director of the Yale Repertory Theater, he has trained some our Nation's finest young talents, many of whom have turned into our finest, not so young talents, helping to make for him a remarkable legacy for which we are all grateful. Lloyd Richards.

[*The President congratulated Mr. Richards, and Hillary Clinton presented the medal.*]

Well, I got another little lesson in humility back there. He said, "You both have said some nice things today." And then he looked at me and he said, "And you did something for stand-up comedy also." And then he said, "Well, at least you didn't set it back." [*Laughter*]

William Styron's haunting works, including "Lie Down in Darkness," "The Confessions of Nat Turner," and "Sophie's Choice," capture our history and character with a passion and insight few others have ever achieved. His compelling prose as a fiction writer and essayist has won him readers around the world, those of us who anxiously await each new word.

I can tell you that as a young southerner, the impact of "The Confessions of Nat Turner" on me was truly stunning. And I can say that for a whole generation of us who had never quite found words to give expression to many of the things we had imagined until we read the works of William Styron.

[*The President congratulated Mr. Styron, and Hillary Clinton presented the medal.*]

Paul Taylor has been one of our Nation's pre-eminent dancers and choreographers for more than three decades. And I might say, he looks as if he could outdance most of us in this country still today. His more than 80 works explore the richness, the complexity of the American character, and graphically demonstrate the deep undercurrents of human relations in a way few other choreographers have ever been able to do. Please join me in welcoming Paul Taylor.

[*The President congratulated Mr. Taylor, and Hillary Clinton presented the medal.*]

Since coming to this country in the 1930's, Billy Wilder has helped to transform the American motion picture industry. As a writer, direc-

tor, and producer, his name attached to many classics of American film. He's won six Academy Awards and millions of fans. And perhaps most important, he's given us a lot of moving movie moments. If you've never laughed at a funny Billy Wilder picture, you have never laughed. Mr. Billy Wilder.

[*The President congratulated Mr. Wilder, and Hillary Clinton presented the medal.*]

Now, it is my great honor to introduce the winners of the Charles Frankel Prize. Ricardo E. Alegria is an historian and anthropologist who has dedicated his career to the study and public appreciation of Caribbean culture. I'm glad to see so many of his supporters from his native Puerto Rico here today, and I thank him for coming this long way to be with us. Mr. Alegria.

[*The President congratulated Mr. Alegria, and Hillary Clinton presented the award.*]

In a 50-year career as a writer and a teacher, historian John Hope Franklin has been a leading scholar of African-American studies and an active voice in the social transformation of America. He's won nearly 100 honorary degrees. He's served on the National Council of Humanities. His writings have illuminated his subject for a whole generation after generation of young readers. I was once one of them—a reader, and young—reading John Hope Franklin. And I'd like to say that one of the great moments of our 1992 campaign was when John Hope Franklin came on one of our bus trips with us; and Al Gore and Tipper and Hillary and I sat and had a chance to visit with him and really learn something from a man who has mastered the mystery of America. John Hope Franklin.

[*The President congratulated Mr. Franklin, and Hillary Clinton presented the award.*]

Hanna Holborn Gray has had a truly remarkable career. She served for 15 years as president of the University of Chicago, where she became a highly visible and widely acclaimed advocate for higher education. She has been honored for her scholarship, her words, and her work in many ways, especially in receiving the Presidential Medal of Freedom, our country's highest civilian award. She deserves greatly the award she receives today. Hanna Gray.

[*The President congratulated Ms. Gray, and Hillary Clinton presented the award.*]

After a distinguished career as chairman and chief executive officer of Time Incorporated, Andrew Heiskell was appointed founding chairman of the President's Committee on Arts and Humanities in 1982. As a leader in promoting the arts and humanities, he energetically, and I echo energetically, persuaded cultural leaders and business executives to support cultural activities and institutions. He filled a void in American life at a time when we needed him. And today we thank him for that. Andrew Heiskell.

[The President congratulated Mr. Heiskell, and Hillary Clinton presented the award.]

There are a lot of funny people. He said "All this and dinner, too?" *[Laughter]*

Historian Laurel T. Ulrich has introduced both scholarly and public audiences to the lives of ordinary people in New England's past. Her recent book "A Midwife's Tale: The Life of Martha Ballard, based on her diary," won the 1991 Pulitzer Prize for History, among other honors.

Now that I have become President, perhaps I can say this with greater authority than would otherwise be the case: We oftentimes tend to see our history too much through the lives and works of the famous and not enough through the remarkable lives of the people who are not famous. She has made a truly significant contribution to our understanding of our roots. And for that we thank her.

[The President congratulated Ms. Ulrich, and Hillary Clinton presented the award.]

And now I have one last special honor, and that is to present to Congressman Sidney Yates the Presidential Citizens Medal for his exemplary deeds of service in the area of arts and humanities. The last time Congressman Yates was here for an occasion at the White House, it happened to be on the day he and his wife were celebrating their 58th wedding anniversary. And today, we honor him for that many years and more of dedication to our common cause. Congressman Yates, please come forward.

[The President congratulated Mr. Yates, and Hillary Clinton presented the medal.]

Again, let me thank the honorees for being here today, thank all of you in the audience who have come to support them and to support the arts.

Before we go, I just can't resist saying this. Just before I came out here, I learned today that a great American writer and a friend of Hillary's and mine, Toni Morrison, was awarded the Nobel Prize for Literature today. I hope that in the years and struggles ahead we will work hard together to keep the arts and humanities alive and flourishing, not just here in the Nation's Capital or in the cultural capitals of this great land but in every community and in every neighborhood.

Remember, all the people we honor today were once in an ordinary community in an ordinary neighborhood living only with the imagination they had that brought them to this day and this honor. We have to find that imagination and fire it in the children all over America.

Thank you all, and God bless you.

NOTE: The President spoke at 2:46 p.m. on the South Lawn at the White House. In his remarks, he referred to former television talk show host Merv Griffin and comedian Rodney Dangerfield.

Address to the Nation on Somalia
October 7, 1993

Today I want to talk with you about our Nation's military involvement in Somalia. A year ago, we all watched with horror as Somali children and their families lay dying by the tens of thousands, dying the slow, agonizing death of starvation, a starvation brought on not only by drought, but also by the anarchy that then prevailed in that country.

This past weekend we all reacted with anger and horror as an armed Somali gang desecrated the bodies of our American soldiers and displayed a captured American pilot, all of them soldiers who were taking part in an international effort to end the starvation of the Somali people themselves. These tragic events raise hard questions about our effort in Somalia. Why are we still there? What are we trying to accomplish? How did a humanitarian mission turn violent? And when will our people come home?

These questions deserve straight answers. Let's start by remembering why our troops went into Somalia in the first place. We went because only the United States could help stop one of the great human tragedies of this time. A third of a million people had died of starvation and disease. Twice that many more were at risk of dying. Meanwhile, tons of relief supplies piled up in the capital of Mogadishu because a small number of Somalis stopped food from reaching their own countrymen.

Our consciences said, enough. In our Nation's best tradition, we took action with bipartisan support. President Bush sent in 28,000 American troops as part of a United Nations humanitarian mission. Our troops created a secure environment so that food and medicine could get through. We saved close to one million lives. And throughout most of Somalia, everywhere but in Mogadishu, life began returning to normal. Crops are growing. Markets are reopening. So are schools and hospitals. Nearly a million Somalis still depend completely on relief supplies, but at least the starvation is gone. And none of this would have happened without American leadership and America's troops.

Until June, things went well, with little violence. The United States reduced our troop presence from 28,000 down to less than 5,000, with other nations picking up where we left off. But then in June, the people who caused much of the problem in the beginning started attacking American, Pakistani, and other troops who were there just to keep the peace.

Rather than participate in building the peace with others, these people sought to fight and to disrupt, even if it means returning Somalia to anarchy and mass famine. And make no mistake about it, if we were to leave Somalia tomorrow, other nations would leave, too. Chaos would resume. The relief effort would stop, and starvation soon would return.

That knowledge has led us to continue our mission. It is not our job to rebuild Somalia's society or even to create a political process that can allow Somalia's clans to live and work in peace. The Somalis must do that for themselves. The United Nations and many African states are more than willing to help. But we, we in the United States must decide whether we will give them enough time to have a reasonable

chance to succeed.

We started this mission for the right reasons, and we're going to finish it in the right way. In a sense, we came to Somalia to rescue innocent people in a burning house. We've nearly put the fire out, but some smoldering embers remain. If we leave them now, those embers will reignite into flames, and people will die again. If we stay a short while longer and do the right things, we've got a reasonable chance of cooling off the embers and getting other firefighters to take our place.

We also have to recognize that we cannot leave now and still have all our troops present and accounted for. And I want you to know that I am determined to work for the security of those Americans missing or held captive. Anyone holding an American right now should understand, above all else, that we will hold them strictly responsible for our soldiers' well-being. We expected them to be well-treated, and we expect them to be released.

So now we face a choice. Do we leave when the job gets tough, or when the job is well done? Do we invite a return of mass suffering, or do we leave in a way that gives the Somalis a decent chance to survive?

Recently, General Colin Powell said this about our choices in Somalia: "Because things get difficult, you don't cut and run. You work the problem and try to find a correct solution." I want to bring our troops home from Somalia. Before the events of this week, as I said, we had already reduced the number of our troops there from 28,000 to less than 5,000. We must complete that withdrawal soon, and I will. But we must also leave on our terms. We must do it right. And here is what I intend to do.

This past week's events make it clear that even as we prepare to withdraw from Somalia, we need more strength there. We need more armor, more air power, to ensure that our people are safe and that we can do our job. Today I have ordered 1,700 additional Army troops and 104 additional armored vehicles to Somalia to protect our troops and to complete our mission. I've also ordered an aircraft carrier and two amphibious groups with 3,600 combat Marines to be stationed offshore. These forces will be under American command.

Their mission, what I am asking these young Americans to do, is the following:

First, they are there to protect our troops and our bases. We did not go to Somalia with a military purpose. We never wanted to kill anyone. But those who attack our soldiers must know they will pay a very heavy price.

Second, they are there to keep open and secure the roads, the port, and the lines of communication that are essential for the United Nations and the relief workers to keep the flow of food and supplies and people moving freely throughout the country so that starvation and anarchy do not return.

Third, they are there to keep the pressure on those who cut off relief supplies and attacked our people, not to personalize the conflict but to prevent a return to anarchy.

Fourth, through their pressure and their presence, our troops will help to make it possible for the Somali people, working with others, to reach agreements among themselves so that they can solve their problems and survive when we leave. That is our mission.

I am proposing this plan because it will let us finish leaving Somalia on our own terms and without destroying all that two administrations have accomplished there. For, if we were to leave today, we know what would happen. Within months, Somali children again would be dying in the streets. Our own credibility with friends and allies would be severely damaged. Our leadership in world affairs would be undermined at the very time when people are looking to America to help promote peace and freedom in the post-cold-war world. And all around the world, aggressors, thugs, and terrorists will conclude that the best way to get us to change our policies is to kill our people. It would be open season on Americans.

That is why I am committed to getting this job done in Somalia, not only quickly but also effectively. To do that, I am taking steps to ensure troops from other nations are ready to take the place of our own soldiers. We've already withdrawn some 20,000 troops, and more than that number have replaced them from over two dozen other nations. Now we will intensify efforts to have other countries deploy more troops to Somalia to assure that security will remain when we're gone.

And we'll complete the replacement of U.S. military logistics personnel with civilian contractors who can provide the same support to the United Nations. While we're taking military steps to protect our own people and to help the U.N. maintain a secure environment, we must pursue new diplomatic efforts to help the

Somalis find a political solution to their problems. That is the only kind of outcome that can endure.

For fundamentally, the solution to Somalia's problems is not a military one, it is political. Leaders of the neighboring African states, such as Ethiopia and Eritrea, have offered to take the lead in efforts to build a settlement among the Somali people that can preserve order and security. I have directed my representatives to pursue such efforts vigorously. And I've asked Ambassador Bob Oakley, who served effectively in two administrations as our representative in Somalia, to travel again to the region immediately to advance this process.

Obviously, even then there is no guarantee that Somalia will rid itself of violence and suffering. But at least we will have given Somalia a reasonable chance. This week some 15,000 Somalis took to the streets to express sympathy for our losses, to thank us for our effort. Most Somalis are not hostile to us but grateful. And they want to use this opportunity to rebuild their country.

It is my judgment and that of my military advisers that we may need up to 6 months to complete these steps and to conduct an orderly withdrawal. We'll do what we can to complete the mission before then. All American troops will be out of Somalia no later than March the 31st, except for a few hundred support personnel in noncombat roles.

If we take these steps, if we take the time to do the job right, I am convinced we will have lived up to the responsibilities of American leadership in the world. And we will have proved that we are committed to addressing the new problems of a new era.

When out troops in Somalia came under fire this last weekend, we witnessed a dramatic example of the heroic ethic of our American military. When the first Black Hawk helicopter was downed this weekend, the other American troops didn't retreat although they could have. Some 90 of them formed a perimeter around the helicopter, and they held that ground under intensely heavy fire. They stayed with their comrades. That's the kind of soldiers they are. That's the kind of people we are.

So let us finish the work we set out to do. Let us demonstrate to the world, as generations of Americans have done before us, that when Americans take on a challenge, they do the job right.

Let me express my thanks and my gratitude and my profound sympathy to the families of the young Americans who were killed in Somalia. My message to you is, your country is grateful, and so is the rest of the world, and so are the vast majority of the Somali people. Our mission from this day forward is to increase our strength, do our job, bring our soldiers out, and bring them home.

Thank you, and God bless America.

NOTE: The President spoke at 5:02 p.m. from the Oval Office at the White House.

Remarks at a White House Dinner Honoring Arts and Humanities Award Recipients
October 7, 1993

Ladies and gentlemen, let me welcome you all to the White House and thank you for coming and for each of your contributions to the rich cultural life of our great Nation. I want to say a special word of appreciation again to the honorees from this afternoon. I had a wonderful time with all of you this afternoon. So many of you have forgiven my ad-lib jokes, I might ask you back again next week. [*Laughter*] I may have you tell my daughter I'm funny after all.

I want you to know, that to all of you who have been honored and to all of the distinguished artists who are here as our guests tonight who didn't join us this afternoon, we are all very much in your debt. You have, each in your own way, enriched our lives and helped us to learn more and feel more deeply and to become more of the people God meant for us to be. We applaud your work. We honor your contributions, and I ask you now that all of us together raise our glasses in toast to the artists, the writers, the humanitarians who have made America the place it is today.

NOTE: The President spoke at approximately 8:30 p.m. in the State Dining Room at the White House.

Message to the Congress on Naval Petroleum Reserves
October 7, 1993

To the Congress of the United States:

In accordance with section 201(3) of the Naval Petroleum Reserves Production Act of 1976 (10 U.S.C. 7422(c)(2)), I am informing you of my decision to extend the period of maximum efficient rate production of the naval petroleum reserves for 3 years from April 5, 1994, the expiration date of the currently authorized production period.

The report investigating the necessity of continued production of the reserves as required by section 201(3)(c)(2)(B) of the Naval Petroleum Reserves Production Act of 1976 is attached. Based on the report's findings, I hereby certify that continued production from the naval petroleum reserves is in the national interest.

WILLIAM J. CLINTON

The White House,
October 7, 1993.

Remarks at a Democratic National Committee Breakfast
October 8, 1993

Thank you. Thank you very much for that wonderful welcome. This is the first time we've all been together since the day after the Inauguration at the White House. What a happy day that was. But this is a happy day, too. And in some ways a more meaningful one because, thanks to you and with your help, we have begun to fulfill the promise of the long campaign of 1992 and the commitment of our party to change America for the better.

I want to say a special word of thanks to my longtime friend David Wilhelm for all the work that he has done, even if he didn't have a top 10 list for me. After Al Gore went on David Letterman I had a top 10 list for him. I said, "The top 10 reasons I'm glad Al Gore is Vice President: No. 10 is that he has educated me in enormous detail on matters of great importance and matters entirely trivial." [*Laughter*] "And reasons nine through one are that he has a vote in the United States Senate." I told the Vice President that without blinking an eye, and he looked at me and he said, "Yeah, and every time I vote I'm on the winning side." [*Laughter*]

I want to—just think about that for a while—I want to thank Lottie Shackelford who has been my friend, as all of you know, for many years; your Vice Chair, Jim Brady, who when I was running for President was head of the State Chair's Association; my neighbor and friend, Kathy Vick, also from Louisiana. There is probably some monopoly rule they're violating, but they voted right in 1992. I want to thank my friend Roy Furman for agreeing to become the national finance chair of this party. He is doing a wonderful job, and he is wearing me out, which I guess is the test of a good job. Congressman Bob Matsui, our treasurer, is not here today, but I do want to mention him because he's been such a good friend to me and is such a good man.

And I also want to thank my good friend, Congressman Bill Richardson, who helped me to carry New Mexico and organized Hispanic voters all across America and now is one of the great leaders in the United States House. And I want to say this, people always talk about all these tough fights we're in, well, I didn't get hired to do easy things. And so if you do

hard things, they're going to be tough. But the National Journal, or one of these Washington periodicals, did a survey a couple of weeks ago which said that so far our first year success rate in Congress was second in the last 40 years only to the first year of Dwight Eisenhower's Presidency, and we've got a chance to top it if we can pass the crime bill and campaign reform before the end of the year, thanks to Bill Richardson and others like him. And I thank him.

I thank Martha Love and I thank Debra DeLee, Bob Reich's favorite DNC officer. That was really funny what she said. You know, if you stay in this job long enough you get to appreciate every little bit of humor you can squeeze out of the day.

Yesterday we had a group of people in who won arts and humanities award, and I told them a story that they thought was apocryphal, but it was actually true. After I was sort of humbled anyway last week by first of all having Al Gore go on at David Letterman and become sort of, you know, a slick magazine model again. And then Hillary became, you know, justifiably the rage of the country with her wonderful performance on health care before all those committees. Then USA Today had the bad taste to do a poll and ask people whether they thought she was smarter than me, and 40 percent said yes. [*Laughter*] And of course, they were right, which is what made it really hurt.

So I went to California, as I always do when I need a real boost, because California has been so wonderful to me, and they've got so many problems now, and they're struggling so bravely to overcome them, and we're working very hard to help them. And so I thought, this is going to be great. So I get there, I went to Sacramento and San Francisco and had a wonderful time with the AFL–CIO there, and then I came down to L.A. And I stayed at the Beverly Hilton because we were going to have a couple of events there. And I thought this is an exciting hotel. It's got a little, you know, glamour to it, and Merv Griffin owns it, and I used to watch him on TV when I was a boy. And when I walked into the hotel and there was Merv Griffin to welcome me, and I was beginning to feel like a President again, you know. [*Laughter*] I was getting over the fact that Gore was on television and Hillary was smarter than me, and I was just about to get over it. And then they took me up to the floor, and I noticed it was a high floor, which made me feel more important. We were going up, and they said, "You know, we put you on this floor because there is one person in California who is a permanent resident of that floor, and we thought this is the floor you ought to be on." So I get off the elevator and standing there to greet me is Rodney Dangerfield who had given me a dozen jungle roses and written "a little respect" on it. "A little respect."

So, let me say to all of you, this has been a remarkable time. If you look at what has been accomplished just in the last few months, we passed the largest deficit-reduction program in history, and long-term interest rates are still below 6 percent. Today's economic report indicates that this economy, even though it has been slower than we thought it would be, has been creating new jobs at a rate of about 152,000 jobs a month, which means that as of last month, there has now been more private sector job creation in the first portion of this year, the first 9 months, than in the previous 4 years.

The budget package also contained a sweeping reform of college loans, which lowered the interest rates for college loans and let people pay them back on easier terms of a percentage of their income, as well as stiffening measures for collection, something that will open the doors of college education to all Americans. There will never be an incentive not to borrow money for college now, because you can get it if you need it at a lower interest rate, and you can pay it back as a percentage of your income no matter how much you borrow. It's a dramatic change.

That budget reconciliation package had the most significant piece of reform in 20 years for lower income working families. Families with incomes of under $27,000 with children in the home will get tax relief from that bill. And we will now be able to say because of the way the earned-income tax credit was expanded in this bill, that if you work 40 hours a week in America and you have a child in the home, you will no longer be in poverty. It is a dramatic advance to the values that the Democratic Party holds dear: work and family.

We passed the family leave bill, the motor voter bill. We've got a major initiative for reform in defense conversion. We're about to announce the first winners of our technology reinvestment project, where we put up $500 million this year, and we'll put up a little more than that next year. We've already gotten 2,800 proposals from people who have ideas to convert defense technologies to domestic uses, to build the economy of the 21st century. We announced last week that we were removing $37 billion worth of high-tech computer, supercomputer, and telecommunications equipment from cold war trade restrictions, which will create many, many new jobs in our country.

We announced a proposal with the UAW and the auto companies and all the defense labs and all the other research labs of the Federal Government to try to triple the car mileage that our automobiles get by the end of the decade. If we do that we'll have sweeping gains in international markets for American produced automobiles.

We have reversed the environmental policies of the previous 12 years in ways that will be good for the economy, as well as good for the environment. We have appointed unprecedented numbers of women and members of different racial minorities to high positions in the National Government. This administration is in the process of changing this country, and you have made a profound difference.

You know, I've been a Democratic Party activist for a long time now, and I know that one of the things that gets us all into this is that we like elections, and we want to win. And one of the things that burns a lot of us out of it is that we sometimes think it's only about elections. And you can't keep doing elections after so many years unless you really believe there are some consequences to it.

So I wanted to say this to you today, to remind you that there are consequences to all the work you did and to the election that we won. And in addition to that litany I just gave you, maybe I could just tell you one story that would illustrate it better.

A couple of Sundays ago I came in from my morning run. I was on the ground floor at the White House, and I looked over down the hall, and there was a family there taking a tour of the White House, which is quite unusual on Sunday morning. But I noticed one of my staff members there had this family, and I went over to shake hands with them. It was a father and a mother and three daughters. The middle daughter was in a wheelchair. And my staff member said, "Mr. President, this is one of those Make-A-Wish families, and this little girl is desperately ill. And her wish was to come to the White House, take a tour, and meet the President."

So I went over and shook hands with the little girl and her family, and we talked a while. And I apologized for being in my running clothes. I went upstairs to change, came back down, and—looking more like my job—I then had a proper picture with them. And again, a nice visit with the wonderful child.

And as I was walking off, her father grabbed me by the arm, and I turned around and he said, "You know, my daughter is probably not going to make it. And because of that these last weeks I've spent with her are the most important times of my whole life. And because of that family leave bill I didn't have to lose my job to spend that time. But if you hadn't passed that law and signed it, I literally would have had to choose between losing my job and spending this time, or supporting my family and giving up what was the most important time of my life. Don't you ever think it doesn't make a difference who wins elections and what they do."

As you know, I believe, have believed and preached throughout the campaign of 1992 that most of the problems of America are rooted in our inability to adjust to the sweeping changes of this age. We now know that this is the 20th year—1993—since real hourly wages peaked for wage earners and that for 20 years most Americans have been working harder for less money to pay more for health care, education, housing, the basics of life. We know that that has been true through times when the economy was growing and times when it was in recession.

But there have been profound structural changes at work in this economy which have put enormous pressures on the great American middle class which was built in the 20th century and which exploded at the end of World War II and which helped to keep the American dream, that each generation could do better than their parents if they work hard and played by the rules, alive.

When you put that with the fact that we have also seen great internal changes in the structure of our society, enormous movements from one place to another—the average in America is about 20 percent of our people move every year or so now, from one place to another, extraordinary mobility—dramatic changes in the family unit, alarming pockets of profound depression where investment is not made, huge increases in the number of children born to one parent only, often to children themselves, a dramatic, breathtaking increase in arbitrary violence among young people, when you put that together with these internationally compelling economic changes, you see that if we just keep on doing what we're doing, we're in for deep trouble. Then if you look outside our borders you see also sweeping changes, many good, some troubling: the end of the cold war; the emergence of new great economic powers— China now growing at 10 to 14 percent per year; the emergence of a whole range of new democracies, and most of them hoping that they can have better relationships with us and trade with us and do business with us; the continuing difficulty of other rich countries, not just the United States, in creating jobs—Europe doing not as well as we are in creating new jobs; Japan now having trouble, even with its closed economy, creating new jobs.

And then we now know at the end of the cold war it certainly didn't mean the end of troubles and misery in the world. We've done our best to support democracy in Russia and to stick by President Yeltsin. Because I believe it's important that we have freedom and democracy in Russia, that we continue to denuclearize the world, and work hard on helping Russia to do what they're trying to do and the other republics of the former Soviet Union.

We see that there is still an enormous amount of chaos. And once the cold war was over and the Communist empire collapsed, it sort of stripped the veneer off long-simmering ethnic and religious hatreds and tensions in Bosnia and Georgia and lots of other places in the world. We know that there are countries in Africa which are not only embroiled in war but which are suffering mass famine, in Somalia where we are trying to conclude our mission and leave those people a fighting chance not to go back to times when hundreds of thousands of children died like flies in the streets. But we know that there are also troubles in other nations there. In Angola there have been as many children have their legs blown off by land mines arbitrarily planted as in any war in history that we know of.

So this is both a troubled and hopeful world. And the old rules we had for looking at the world beyond our borders were pretty simple. There was a cold war, our policy was to contain communism, our policy was to promote countries within our sphere of influence. We preferred democracy, but as long as they were anti-Communist, we'd normally stick with somebody anyway. And even if they were pro-Communist and democratic, we'd normally shy away from them. The necessity of surviving in a bipolar world gave an organizing principle to what we did and didn't do. To be sure, we had troubles and difficulties, but we knew how to do that. Now we're having to define our purposes in the world and our leadership in the world in terms of more partnership with other nations in promoting democracy and freedom and market opportunities for people that we have here, we want elsewhere. It's not easy here.

But the thing I have tried to say, with all the time that I have spent on foreign policy and military policy and trade policy, that I must say it's an absolutely fascinating time to be President, and a great honor, actually, to be President in this difficult time, to try to construct the framework for the post-cold-war world.

I spend an enormous amount of time on that, but I usually talk about what we're doing in this country because I believe you cannot be strong abroad unless you are strong at home. It is difficult to promote a concept of national security that has nothing to do with the economic strength of our Nation. That is what permits us to pay for not only defense but the other things which make us more secure.

And when we think of all these changes we need to cope with, the first thing I think we have to say, that I've been trying to hammer home and in clear, explicit terms ever since the health care speech, is that there has to be a level of security accorded to Americans if they're going to be able to change. If you think about your own life, those of you who have the privilege of raising children—on most days it's a privilege—you can watch in individual lives how difficult it is for people to change their habits, even when they know they should, if they are insecure personally.

The same is true of a family or a community or a nation. If you spend all your time waiting for the other shoe to drop, expecting something bad to happen, not expecting something good to happen, feeling that what you now have can be taken away from you by some arbitrary force, it is very difficult to have the space, the mental space and the emotional space, to think about the changes that are bearing in and what initiatives you should take.

And so an enormous part of my job as your President is not only to keep pushing this agenda of change—and getting you to help me do it, as you have so well—but to be able to explain to the American people what it is we have to change and why and then to be able to advocate those things that will give people more personal and family and community and national security so that we can have the courage and the space to change.

And if we don't do that, even our incremental progress will not satisfy people because they will be disoriented. I'm really proud of the fact that we've been creating more than 150,000 jobs a month in a tough time and that there are more new jobs now, since January, than there were in the previous 4 years. And when I say "we" I don't mean the Government. I mean "we" the American people working together, although we have played a role in it in drastically bringing the deficit down and keeping the interest rates down and targeting some investment. I'm proud of the fact that cars are selling at their highest rates since '89, and business investment is expanding at its fastest rate since '84, and all of those things. I'm proud of that.

But unless people understand this in a bigger framework, there will always be places that are behind and places that are ahead. Ten years ago, my part of the country was behind, and we had an unemployment rate 3 points higher than the national average. Today California is behind. They have 3 points higher than the national average, the center of a lot of our high-tech base, 12 percent of our population, 25 percent of our unemployed people. This is a big problem for the rest of us.

So we have to understand these things. How does it all fit together? What kind of changes do we have to make? What kind of security do we have to have? How does the change in the student loan program or passing national service and giving all these kids a chance to earn money for college by rebuilding this country at the grassroots level, or going to Tokyo and working with the Japanese and the Europeans and the Canadians to open markets, how does that all fit together? What difference will it make if we reform the welfare system early next year? How does this work?

My goal is to make individuals in this country and families in this country secure enough and strong enough to be able to face and make the changes that we must make in order to do what David Wilhelm said I talked to him about so long ago: give every American a chance to live up to his or her God-given capacity.

To do it we simply have to be able to rebuild the great middle class in this country. We can't continue to have a few people doing very well, and the bottom dropping out not just from people who are unemployed but from people who are employed. There are a lot of changes we have to make. We've begun to make some, and some I've talked about.

First of all, we've got to make a lot of economic changes. We have got to face the fact that the basis of our prosperity can no longer be an insular economy, where we don't have foreign competition, and can no longer be at least buoyed by very high levels of defense spending in high-tech because of the end of the cold war.

So what do we have to do? First of all, we have to have an investment strategy. That's why when we changed the Tax Code this year we provided for a new venture capital gains tax, which will give people a 50-percent break if they invest for 5 years, not a year but 5 years, in new businesses or smaller businesses that are growing jobs. We provided more incentives for research and development. We provided more incentives to lift off the depressed real estate market in the country. We had a theory about that, an investment theory, because there will never be enough Government money to get this country going again alone.

Secondly, we need to recognize that there are some places in this country that are profoundly depressed, and we have to do more there. So we passed some empowerment zone legislation to see whether or not with extreme incentives we could revitalize some of the really distressed areas of the country. We have a community development bank bill moving through the Congress which will set up banks that are designed to loan money to people to start self-employed businesses or very small businesses, loan money to people who live in places who ordinarily wouldn't be able to get it. We know from our experience at home, and from the

South Shore Bank in Chicago, that banks can make money loaning to poor folks if they know what they're doing. And they can make money loaning in low income areas if they know what they're doing.

These are structural changes we have to make. We have to change the entire unemployment system. You know, when I was a kid and somebody lost their job, they lost their job for 4 weeks, 5 weeks, 6 weeks, in an economic downturn. They would get hired back at the same job. That's the system that the unemployment system was designed to support, what are so-called cyclical unemployment. So you've got unemployment payments for a period of months and then you got your job back. Today most unemployment is structural. For example, we continue to lose manufacturing jobs when the economy is growing like crazy. Why? Because manufacturing productivity is going up so fast, and because we haven't gotten into enough new manufacturing areas. So we have either one of two things we have to do. We either have to train people that are manufacturing workers to do nonmanufacturing work, or we've got to make a whole lot of different things if we want to keep the employment up, because there will be an almost unlimited trend to be able to produce more with fewer people of whatever particular product you're talking about.

What does that mean? That means that instead of an unemployment system we now need a reemployment system, because people need different jobs because they're not going to get the old job back, by and large. It means that the day somebody goes on unemployment, and even before if they know they're going to go, they should know what jobs will be available within driving distance of their home. They should be able to match their skills for those jobs and where the deficiencies are they should be able to choose a training program that goes right along with that unemployment check. And it should commence immediately, so that you shorten the time in which people are unemployed.

We have to look more to a lot of other problems in our economy. We cannot avoid the responsibility to be responsible stewards of this country and this planet; so we're going to have to become more environmentally sensitive. But we have to do it in a way that creates jobs and doesn't just cost jobs. We can do that, but we have to be very creative. That requires change. We have to change the way we operate the Government. If we invest too much money in doing things in the same old way in the Government, then we don't have the money left to invest in education and training and the future. That's why the Vice President's report on reinventing Government is so important.

And Democrats have to prove they can do that. You know, if we don't hate Government, we ought to have the courage to change it. If we think Government has a critical role as partners for the private sector as we move toward the 21st century, then we have to have the courage to change it. That's really important. We can do more with less in a whole range of areas. And that's very, very important.

So all these changes need to be made. I cannot tell you how important I think it is for us to continue to push on defense conversion and invest massive amounts of money in the civilian technology possibilities of the future. We have been cutting defense since 1987, but we did not seriously begin to invest in defense conversion until 1993. The Congress last year passed a $500 million bill for defense conversion, as Congressman Richardson will tell you, and there was an ideological opposition in the previous administration to spending the money. So all the people, the scientists, the engineers, the technology workers, who had lost their jobs had to wait another year just to get these programs started.

We have got to do better on that. We have all these defense labs. We have all this research. We have all these resources. I was at McClellan Air Force Base, and at McClellan Air Force Base in California they have worked with private sector people there to produce an electric car that gets 80 miles to the gallon at 55 miles an hour. It operates alternatively on electricity and gasoline and can go from zero to 60 in 12 seconds and has a maximum speed of 100 miles an hour. If we can just figure out how to produce it at an affordable price, we'll be in great shape.

But that's the way these things are done. So I could keep you here until tomorrow morning at this time talking about the changes we need to make. But let's first talk about what the security is. What's the deal we have to make with the American working people in order to make these changes, to get them to the point where they will have to make the changes? You think about everything I just said requires the concur-

rence of millions and tens of millions of people. You change a country—now, you can't just pass a law and change it. You can't just write a bill and change it. You have to change the behavior of the whole country. People have to change their lives.

So, we can't do that unless people feel a high level of security. I think that's self-evident. The first kind of security people need is to know that in an America where the economy is tough and where most people have to work for a living, you can work and still be a good parent. That's what the earned-income tax credit was all about, to give working people with kids a break. That's what the Family and Medical Leave Act was all about. We've still got work to do to make adequate childcare supports available to people around the country. We have got to say that there has got to be a way where every American can be a good mother, a good father, and a good worker. That's the first thing.

The second thing we have to do, I would argue to you, is to give people basic security. I mean more freedom from fear. When I did my town meeting in California, there was a fine looking young Korean man who told me about how his brother had been shot and killed, an arbitrary shooting. And he asked me about it, told me the circumstances. Then there was a fine young junior high school student, a young African-American man. He told me that he and his brother just wanted to go to school. They said, "We don't want to be in a gang. We don't want a knife. We don't want a gun. We want to study. That's what we want to do, and we changed schools because we didn't think our old school was safe. So we showed up at our new school on the first day and were standing in line to register, and my brother gets shot, standing in front of me, because he's in a crossfire."

And this is not just California and New York and big cities, folks. This is my State and yours. Now, look, I live in a State where half the people have got a hunting or fishing license or both and where we have to close down whole towns on the opening day of deer season because nobody shows up at school, nobody shows up at the factory. But I think that even in my State people think it's nuts that there are places in this country where teenagers are better armed than police and people are scared to walk down the street to go to school. And so we just have to decide, you know, are we going to let all this rhetoric—you know, this country we get all—there's a lot of great things about America, but we're bad to say one thing and do another. We're pretty bad about that.

We all deplore violence, and we say punish people who do it. We are punishing people who do it. Our jails are full. We have a higher percentage of people behind bars than any country in the world today. But we won't pass the Brady bill. Now, let me say why that matters. That sounds like sort of a tepid bill now, given what else is being called for. But let me tell you why that matters.

In New York City last year, they confiscated something like 19,000 guns, whatever the figure is; 85 percent of them were from other States. So a State waiting period doesn't amount to a hill of beans when you've got the constitutional right to travel. We've got to know, how old are these people buying these guns? Who are they? Do they have a criminal record? Do they have a mental health history? It's a big deal.

The States can do something. Seventeen States have said kids can't own handguns unless they're out with their parents on a hunting trip or a target practice. A lot of States have tried to set up laws licensing gun dealers, but the Federal law will give you a license for 10 bucks, and the States can't overturn it yet.

You've got hundreds of gun dealers out there, and there's no system about it. And maybe the most important thing of all is, you've got a lot of these people, most of them very young, a lot of them with drug problems, nearly all of them with no real connection to the rest of society, who have easy access to rapid-fire assault weapons, the sole purpose of which is to kill people quicker, in greater numbers. And we have lots of bills in Congress to do something about it, and we ought to do something about it. We ought to pass one of them and do something about it and take a stand.

We have a crime bill which would put 50,000 more police officers on the street. It matters how many police officers are on the street, and I say to you, not so much for catching criminals quickly, although that is a big deal, but for preventing crime.

I'll just give you—first of all, look at New York, one of the few big cities in the country where for 2 years running, there's been a decline in the crime rate in all seven major FBI categories because they went to a community policing system. Look at Houston, where the

mayor there, Bob Lanier, got elected on a commitment to put the equivalent of 655 more police officers on the street and to concentrate them in areas of high crime, and they had a 17 percent drop in the crime rate the first year they did it. You can do this. And we ought to be about the business of helping our places become more safe. This is a huge deal. And the Democratic Party ought to do it. If we were the party of Social Security, why can't we be the party of health security and personal security and freedom from fear?

And finally let me say about the health care issue, I feel very strongly that this issue will define us not only as a party but as a people. Every day—and I don't mind a lot of this— but every day I read something about somebody saying why can't we do this, that, or the other thing? Again, we have to look at what we are doing. What we are doing, we are spending 14½ percent of our income on health care. It'll be about $900 billion this year. Canada spends a dime, or 10 percent of its income on health care, 10 percent of every dollar. Germany and Japan spend about 8.8 percent of every dollar. Nearly all of our major competitors are below that.

Now, there are some things that make the American health care system more costly that we wouldn't want to do anything about, and some things that we can't do anything about right now, at least in health care reform. What we don't want to do anything about is we have wonderful medical research and technology. We invest more in research, and we use more technology. And we don't want to change that.

What we can't do much about right now in the health care bill is that we have a higher percentage of poor people, a higher percentage of people with AIDS, a higher percentage of teenage births and low birth weight babies, and a much higher percentage of violence than any of our competitors. And that's all a health care issue. You pay for it when those folks show up every weekend all shot up and cut, and they don't have any health insurance. They pass it on to you. So, you pay for that. That's another big cost of violence. But that makes our system more expensive.

But then there's a whole lot of things that we can do something about, that it's unconscionable that we don't. I mean, we spend more than anybody else, and yet, we're the only major country that can't figure out how to give everybody basic health care, 37.4 million people, according to the last census, without health insurance. Two million people a month lose their health insurance, 100,000 of them lose it permanently. We are adding 100,000 people a month to the rolls of people without health insurance. It is hemorrhaging the system we have.

We know we spend a dime on the dollar more on paperwork and mindless administration than any other nation. We know that from studies. We know we hired 4 times as many clerical workers to work in hospitals as medical personnel in the last decade. We know that the average doctor, in 1980, brought home 75 percent of the money that came into his or her clinic. And by 1990, it had dropped to 52 cents because of the explosion of bureaucracy and paperwork.

We know we have more fraud and abuse in this system, and a system that actually encourages the performance of unnecessary procedure, and a system so complicated, it's easier to game and to milk. We know that. We know that we don't cover primary and preventive care like we ought to. We don't cover mammograms and x-rays and cholesterol tests and prenatal care and well-baby visits, and so we spend more money in the long run because we won't spend a little money now to keep people well. We spend lots of money to take care of them once they get sick.

These are things we know. This is not some idle theory. We know that a country like Germany, for example, relies more on medicine than we do, because we cover medicine for Medicaid patients, but if you're a senior citizen on Medicare—just a little bit too much income to be on Medicaid, you can't get any help with your medicine. And we know it costs a lot of money to cover medicine in a health care bill, as we propose to do. But we also know there's a whole lot of people, especially older people, who choose every week between food and medicine. And if they choose food and not medicine, eventually they get sick and wind up in the hospital. And they can spend more in a hospital in one week than they'll spend in a year on medicine. So, these are things we know. These are not sort of idle speculations.

So, when people say to me, "Well, you know, this is a big risk, this might be expensive." I say, "It's not going to be as expensive as what will happen." We're now spending 14½ percent of our income on health care. If we do nothing, if we stay with this system, by the end of the

decade we'll probably have 40 million or more uninsured, and we'll be spending 19 or 20 percent of our money on health care. You'll have doctor and hospital fees going through the roof, and miserable doctors and hospital administrators because more and more of the money they're charging you will go to pay for clerical work to hassle people to pay on insurance policies.

The time has come to put aside all the rhetoric and the reservations and realize we can't make this system any more complicated than it is. We'd have to work from now to kingdom come to make it any more expensive than it is on wasted things. And we can no longer afford the sheer insecurity that is gripping millions of Americans, not just those without health care but those who can never change their jobs because they've had somebody in their family get sick, those who are waiting for their business to fail, and they know they'll never get health care again, those who are just wrenching with the moral dilemmas of whether they need to cut their employees off health care because they can no longer afford it. I talked to a small business man in California this week, 12 employees, didn't have a single claim on his health insurance last year except for regular trips to the doctor. His premiums went up 40 percent. He said, "What am I going to do? I've got to choose between staying in business and doing right by these people who made me the money that I have today."

So, I say to you, my friends, the plan we have offered is a fair plan. We ask people who don't contribute to the system, but who work, to make a contribution, because now we're paying for them, the rest of you are. For small businesses with low wage workers, we offer a discount. So, we'll pay a little bit, but they ought to pay something. Everybody who can pay, ought to pay something into this system. It is not fair for the rest of you to pay for it. That's where two-thirds of this plan gets paid for. We asked for an increase in the cigarette tax. We asked for big companies that are going to self-insure to make some contribution to medical research and to public health facilities, like all the rest of us do. And we asked for credit for savings that will surely come in the Medicare and Medicaid program.

When you hear that I have proposed to cut Medicare and Medicaid, don't you believe it. Medicare and Medicaid are projected to go up at 3 times the rate of inflation. What we say is, "Adopt our plan, and they'll only go up at twice the rate of inflation." Now, in Washington, they think that's a cut. Where I come from, most of us would give anything to have an income increase at twice the rate of inflation, wouldn't we?

So I ask you to think about these things. The time has come to give the American people security, health care that's always there, health care that can never be taken away. The time has come to simplify the system. The time has come to prove that we can make savings. These are unconscionable areas of waste. And we can do it and preserve quality. We can do it and actually increase the choices most Americans have. We can do it and let about two-thirds of the people who have insurance get the same or better insurance for the same or less cost. But it is going to require some change in the system.

But this is a security issue. Unless we can be secure in our work and families, unless we can be secure on our streets, unless we can be secure in our health care, I'm not sure the American people will ever be able to recover the personal optimism and courage to open up to the rest of the world, to continue to lead the world, to continue to reach out and break

down the barriers of trade because we know a rich country can only create jobs through increasing the volume of trade, to make these internal educational and investment changes without which we cannot move toward the 21st century. So I ask you to keep doing what you're doing. Help us pass these bills. Get us a crime bill. Get us a health care bill. Get us the economic bills that we've got up there. Pass the Education 2000 bill, all of our education bills.

But remember what the big picture is. The big picture is, the world is trending in directions we cannot fully understand but we pretty nearly can imagine. And we have got to get to the 21st century with America still the strongest country in the world and with the American dream alive again and with a strong middle class again. That means we've got to change. And to change, we have to give our people security again. We can do it. Together, we can do it.

Thank you, and God bless you all.

NOTE: The President spoke at 10:11 a.m. at the Washington Sheraton Hotel. In his remarks, he referred to Democratic National Committee officers David Wilhelm, chairman, Kathleen Vick, secretary, and Lottie Shackelford, Martha Love, and Debra DeLee, vice chairs.

Exchange With Reporters on Departure for New Brunswick, New Jersey
October 8, 1993

Secretary of Defense Les Aspin

Q. Are you going to support Les Aspin?

The President. Well, yes. I mean, what is the question in reference to? I'm sorry.

Q. In reference to all the complaints on Capitol Hill about his performance.

The President. Well, I will say again, I asked Secretary Aspin why the extra—weren't sent to Somalia. He said to me that when they were asked for, there was no consensus among the Joint Chiefs that it should be done. And he normally relied on their reaching a consensus recommendation on an issue like that, a military—[*inaudible*]. And secondly that it was never suggested to him that they were needed for the kind of defensive purposes that it's been speculated that they're useful for during this

last raid, that it was only for offensive purposes, and that it was his best judgment that we were trying to get the political track going again, and we didn't want to send a signal that we were trying to conduct more offense in Somalia. He also said if anybody had made the defensive argument, that would have been an entirely different thing. And obviously if he had known then what he knows now, he would have made a different decision.

Q. Mr. President, did you know about the request in advance, sir?

The President. Did I know? No.

Q. Were you told—[*inaudible*]—and also do you think——

The President. No. And I was talking to General Powell on a very regular basis about this whole thing. This was not something that anybody brought to me directly.

Somalia

Q. Why won't the Somali warlords just go underground for 6 months and wait for us to get out and then declare victory? Isn't there a danger in giving them a deadline when we're going to get out?

The President. Well, it might happen. But keep in mind, we're going to wind up—by then there should be an even larger U.N. force there. And that's our objective. In 6 months, we will have been there well over a year longer than we ever committed to stay.

So we will have given them well over a year longer, more personnel, and more efforts in this endeavor. We have obligations elsewhere, including this very important effort that we've invested a lot in in Haiti, to try to support that. So, I just don't believe that we can be in a position of staying longer than that.

I also think once we send a signal to them that we're not going to tolerate people messing with us or trying to hurt our people or trying to interrupt the U.N. mission, that we have no interest in denying anybody access to playing a role in Somalia's political future. I think a mixed message has been sent out there in the last couple of months by people who are doing the right thing. Our people are doing the right thing. They're trying to keep our folks alive, trying to keep the peacekeeping mission going, trying to get the food out there. But we need to clearly state, unambiguously, that our job is not to decide who gets to play a role in postwar Somalia, that we want the political process to work. So let's give it a chance to work and see if it does.

Thank you.

NOTE: The exchange began at 12:20 p.m. on the South Lawn at the White House.

Remarks at Robert Wood Johnson Hospital in New Brunswick, New Jersey
October 8, 1993

Thank you very much, ladies and gentlemen, Governor and Mrs. Florio, Congressman Menendez, Congressman Klein, Mayor Cahill. To the distinguished participants in this program, Mr. Holzberg, Dr. Hammond, Sheriff Fontura. I hope he doesn't decide to run for President anytime soon. He gave a fine talk, I thought.

Mrs. Jones, thank you for coming here and sharing your story with us, and I thank your son sitting over here, and two other fine young men who were the victims of violence, for helping to describe their condition to Governor and Mrs. Florio and to me today and what happened to them.

I am delighted to be back here not only in New Jersey but in New Brunswick. I started one of my other crusades here not very long ago, the crusade to pass a national service bill that would give tens of thousands of our young people a chance to earn credit against their college educations by working in their communities. A few days ago, we signed that bill into law, and I think it will change the face of America.

That is one of the many changes that I hope we can make as we move toward the 21st century. But I believe very strongly that in order for us all to have the courage to make those changes, we need a higher level of personal security in this country. And I wanted to come back here to this magnificent health facility to talk today for a moment about the relationship between health care and the need for health security and violence and the need for personal security.

As you've already heard, these two things are very closely related. I'm honored to be here with my good friend and former colleague, Governor Jim Florio. You know, I was elated when Jim was awarded the John F. Kennedy Profiles in Courage Award earlier this year, because I think he really earned it. My guess is, he earned it by making even some of you in this audience mad from time to time. But I know what it's like to be a Governor and to have to work on a balanced budget, and I know what kind of trouble New Jersey was in, and you now have the best credit rating in the Northeast. I know, too, how hard it is to stand up and fight for things like an end to assault weapons, and what a long struggle it is; just passing the law is only the beginning before the final impact is felt, perhaps a year, perhaps 5 years down the road.

But we need more people in our country who will call them like they see them, who will try to identify the problems and try to get up every day and try to do something about it. And I'm just proud to be associated with Jim Florio, and I appreciate what the sheriff said about him.

Today I saw a lot of things that I have seen before over the last 3½ years since I started looking into the health care system and long before I even dreamed of running for President. I saw at this great American health institution, the very best of American health care, as well as what is wrong with America's health care. And indeed, if we want to finally, at long last, join the ranks of every other advanced country in the world and provide health care security to our people, health care that's always there and that can never be taken away, we have to work vigilantly to keep what is right with our health care system as we work to change what is wrong.

What is right is obvious about this place. I saw the care that the nurses and the doctors were giving. I saw the concern that this hospital administrator had for the way each part of this hospital worked as I worked my way through it. And I saw the way a lot of these patients, many of them very young, responded to their caregivers. I saw the gratitude in the parents' and the family members' eyes. That is the core, the kernel, the heart, the spirit of our health care system. And we can't do anything to interfere with that. Indeed, we have to be committed to enhancing that.

But I also heard three different stories about people who showed up here without health care coverage or with an insurance policy that wouldn't pay or with two different groups arguing about who owed and about long delays before the hospital got paid, and massive, massive expenditures of time and money filling out first one form and then another, and then hassling people to try to get them to pay the bill. And that is what is wrong with this health care system.

We are the only country in the world with an advanced economy that can't figure out how to cover all of our people. So what happens? They get health care all right, and then the

rest of you pay the bill or the hospital goes broke. And so many of our people get health care when it's too late and too expensive because they have no coverage; so they don't get the primary and preventive services that keep people well.

And of course, as I already said, the administrative costs are absolute nightmares. I was in the Washington Children's Hospital the other day and was told that every year they spend in that one hospital alone $2 million filling out forms that have nothing to do with keeping patient records for health care purposes, that the doctor spends so much time, the 200 doctors on staff there, on paperwork that has nothing to do with patient health care and keeping records of it, that they could see another 10,000 children a year collectively, just 200 doctors if they didn't have to do it.

So the question for us is, how do we change what's wrong, keep what's right, and how can we deal with the burden of our health care system? We now spend over 14 percent of our income in America on health care. Canada spends 10. No other nation in the world spends over 9. Even Germany and Japan, two very wealthy advanced nations, spend less than 9 percent of their income on health care, and their health outcomes are roughly similar, if not better, than ours.

Now, how did this come to be, and how can we change it? We don't want to do anything to undermine the quality of health care. If you cover everybody, if you give them primary and preventive health care services, if you do as our plan and you increase investment in medical research, you can improve quality. You certainly don't erode it. We don't want to destroy people's right to choose their health care system. Under our plan, each employee in each workplace would get at least three choices. Today, only one-third of workers who are insured in the workplace have more than one choice. Contrary to some of the complaints about it, our plan will increase consumer choice, not decrease it.

We do have to simplify the system. I said that before. And we do have to achieve savings in some areas where they can be achieved. Plainly, if you reorganize the system, you won't have as much fraud and abuse, and you'll have dramatic savings in paperwork. Your administrator was telling me that this hospital has 25 percent administrative costs. The average hospital has hired four clerical workers for every direct health caregiver in the last 10 years. The average doctor 10 years ago was taking home 75 percent of all the money that came into a private clinic. Today, that figure is down to 52 percent, 23 cents gone to a system of 1,500 separate insurance companies, thousands of different policies, thousands of different forms, and Government paperwork and bureaucracy on top of that.

And finally, we have to ask people to assume some more responsibility. Two-thirds of our plan will be paid for by asking employers and employees who don't pay anything into the system now to do their part, while giving discounts to very small businesses with lower wage workers to avoid breaking them. We have to ask people who can afford to pay, to pay, because the rest of you are paying for them. And then when they get really sick, they get their health care, and you still pay for them. So we need some more responsibility.

Now, if you did all this and you look again at this American health care system, even if you just forget for a moment about the human element—and it's very hard to do with all these wonderful young people here—and you see us way up here at 14.5 percent a year of our income, everybody else at about 9. And we're losing 100,000 people a month, permanently, who are no longer covered with health insurance and 2 million people a month lose their health insurance, but the rest of them somehow get it back. But the system is hemorrhaging.

What can we do nothing about, and what do we want to do nothing about? We wouldn't want do to anything about the fact, I don't think, that we invest more in medical research and technological advances than other countries. We should be proud of that. It contributes to our economy. The fact that we have the strongest, in this State, pharmaceutical companies in the world, and they do a lot of research to find new drugs, we shouldn't begrudge that. Indeed, in our plan I'd like to make more use of pharmaceutical treatment where appropriate by giving people on Medicare and people with health insurance policies some coverage for drugs so that they can manage their health care better, I think many times at lower cost.

Then you look at the things we plainly want to do something about, the bureaucracy, the unnecessary procedures, the fact that the system is rigged for defensive medicine, a lot of problems with it. Then you ask yourself about, what's

the rest of the difference? The rest of the difference is, this country has more teen pregnancy, low-birthweight births, AIDS rates, and other kinds of serious, highly costly illnesses and much more violence. There is nothing I can do in a health care bill that will do away with that. We have simply got to be willing to change our behavior or admit that we are going to tolerate living in a country where homicide is the second leading cause of death among Americans between the ages of 15 and 25 and the leading cause of death among teenage boys today.

We just have to say, "Well, we've just decided we're going to continue to live in the only country where police routinely find themselves outgunned by out-of-control teenagers." We'll just have to say, "We have decided that we're not going to make our streets, our parks, or even our schools safe again." You heard the story of this fine family over here that Governor Florio cited.

I was in California this week on a town meeting. We were interconnected with four big cities in California. This fine, young Korean-American businessman stood up and talked about how his brother was shot dead by somebody that wasn't even mad at him in one of these arbitrary shootings. And then a young African-American boy, a junior high school student, stood up and told me how he and his brother did not want to be in a gang, did not want to have weapons, just wanted to be good students. And they were so concerned about the lack of safety in their school that they changed schools. So they went to the newer, safer school. And on the first day of school, they were lined up registering for school, and this young man's brother, standing right in front of him, was shot down because he got caught in the crossfire in a gunfight in the middle of the safer school.

Now, there are a lot of people who say things like, "Well, people do these things. Guns don't." I'll tell you what, I'll make them a bet. You give me the guns, and I'll see if the people can get it done.

This is a huge economic problem, all right. You've already heard this. Most of the people who are victims of the $4 billion of gun violence every year in this country, 80 to 85 percent of them have no health insurance. So you pay for them. The system pays for them. It's part of the escalating cost of health care. It's part of why we can't close the gap between where we are and where other countries are. But the human tragedy is the most important thing.

Why should this young man have to worry about how well he's going to walk for the rest of his life? And let me just say this: I come from a State where over half the people have a hunting or fishing license or both. There are towns in my State where you have to shut the schools and the factories down on the opening day of deer season, because nobody's going to show up anyway. I was in the woods with a .22 when I was a kid. I love the outdoors. This has got nothing to do with people having the right to train, to learn how to use, to care for a sporting weapon and to do it under controlled circumstances. It's got nothing to do with this. But I also live in a State now where kids get shot in their schools with weapons that were designed solely for the purpose of killing people.

And Dr. Hammond told me when we were making this tour something I didn't know. He said that just in the last few years, when people go to sites where people were shot with guns, they are three times more likely to see the gunshot end in a fatality because of the use of semiautomatic and automatic weapons and multiple bullets in a body, just in the last few years.

And so, I tell you, my fellow Americans, we have a decision to make. And this is the time to make it. We can't keep saying that we deplore these things and it's terrible and keep extolling our American values on how much more law-abiding we are than other people and put up with this. We either need to say this is a level of chaos and human degradation and waste of human potential and incredible cost in society that we are willing to tolerate because we cannot bear to do something about it, or we need to get up, stand up, and be counted and do something about it.

We have to make a decision, and it's time to make it. And it directly bears on the ability of your Nation to develop a health care system that fixes what's wrong, keeps what's right, provides security, and doesn't break the bank. It is directly related.

We have a crime bill—Governor Florio mentioned it—before the Congress. It does a lot of things, but most importantly, here's what it does. It requires the Brady bill, which is a national 5-day waiting period, to establish background checks to check for age, criminal history, and mental health history. It matters. You must do it nationally. Why? Just near here in New York City, of the many thousands of weapons

confiscated last year by the police, 85 percent of them came from other States. If you don't have a national system, you will never fix this. It is a huge deal.

The second thing the crime bill does is to provide for the 50 percent of the downpayment of the commitment I made when I was running for President, that I wanted to ask the Congress to give the American people another 100,000 police officers in the next 4 years, not just to catch criminals but to deter crime. And lest you think it doesn't work, I can cite you many examples: places in New Jersey which have more police officers, where the crime rate has gone down; in New York City where the crime rate has gone down in all the seven major FBI categories where community policing has been deployed; in the city of Houston which had a 17 percent drop in crime in 1 year, because when people are there in force, it prevents crimes from occurring in the first place. So that's an important part of this.

Another part of the crime bill gives States funds to establish innovative programs for kids when they get in trouble before they do shoot somebody, to try to get them back into the mainstream of life. After all, a lot of these young people who get in terrible trouble are not really bad people. They have no structure, no order. They cannot imagine the future. There are no rules that bind them in internally to the things the rest of us take for granted. And we've got to try to get as many of them back as we can before they do something terrible which will require us to put them away for a long time.

We do have to deal with these things. And we need to pass a crime bill this year. These Members of Congress can do it. There are still people who are holding them back, and you need to urge them on. And I'll guarantee you, I'll sign it as quick as they'll put it on my desk. We have to do it.

But the second thing I want to say to you is that we need a national law to do what New Jersey has done here with the assault weapons. Again because we have a constitutional right to travel in this country. New Jersey can make a big dent in New Jersey's problems by abandoning these weapons here and then by setting up a system to try to collect them, but people are still crossing the State line all the time.

We need national legislation. There are several bills in the Congress and arguments about which one is better than which other one, but

I will guarantee you they are all better than nothing. And the Congress should pass one of those bills and send it to me this year. It would be a great Christmas present to the American people to stand up for safety.

Finally, let me just say that each of us in our own way are going to ask ourselves what we can do to deal with this. We have a culture of violence. We glorify it. I was delighted to see some of the television networks voluntarily say that they were going to do their best to try to monitor the content of violence and reduce it and degradation of people during prime time television.

We have got to take a whole generation of young people who have very short attention spans for whom the future has no claim because they cannot even imagine the future, and slowly, carefully, and one-on-one, neighborhood by neighborhood, community by community, help them to rebuild the kind of inner strength and sense of values and discipline and control and hope that will permit us to go where we need to go. No law will do that, but that is not an excuse not to pass these laws.

So I ask you today, here in this great place, let us recommit ourselves to keeping what's right about the health care system and to expand the reach of what is right when we can, with universal coverage, by giving pharmaceutical products to the elderly who are not poor enough to be on Medicaid but are on Medicare and the working people whose children may need it. Let us do that.

And let us have the courage to admit that some of these problems we will never fix until we change our ways as a Nation, and let's start with violence, begin with guns, and prove that we can do in America what you are doing here in New Jersey. Thank you and God bless you all.

NOTE: The President spoke at 3:41 p.m. in the Atrium. In his remarks, he referred to Mayor Jim Cahill of New Brunswick; Sheriff Armando Fontura of Essex County; Harvey A. Holzberg, president and chief executive officer, and Dr. Jeffrey Hammond, chief, trauma surgery and critical care, Robert Wood Johnson Hospital; and Patricia Jones, mother of a patient with a gunshot wound.

Nomination for an Assistant Secretary of Agriculture
October 8, 1993

The President today announced his intention to nominate Fred Slabach as Assistant Secretary for Congressional Relations at the Department of Agriculture.

"Fred Slabach knows how important the Agriculture Department is to rural Americans. I know he will represent their concerns fairly in Washington, with this administration and with Congress," the President said.

NOTE: A biography of the nominee was made available by the Office of the Press Secretary.

Nomination for Administrator of the Rural Electrification Administration
October 8, 1993

The President today announced his intention to nominate Wally B. Beyer, the general manager of a North Dakota electric cooperative for the past 30 years, as Administrator for the Rural Electrification Administration at the Department of Agriculture.

"With his many years working to provide electricity to rural Americans in North Dakota, Wally Beyer is exactly the type of person we need at the helm at the Rural Electrification Administration," the President said. "I am pleased he has joined our team."

NOTE: A biography of the nominee was made available by the Office of the Press Secretary.

The President's Radio Address
October 9, 1993

Good morning. For many Americans today is the beginning of a long weekend, a time to bring out the wool sweaters and coats, our security against the change of seasons. In this remarkable period of our history, our Nation is facing changes longer lasting than fall and winter. But these changes require a certain security, too.

Throughout the campaign for this office and since I became your President, I've been asking that we have the courage to change, to compete in the world economy, and to bring prosperity back home. But we can't embrace change fully unless our own people feel a high level of personal and family security, a security about our place in the world. I'm happy to report that we're making real progress on that, too. Our first job was to address economic security with a budget that seriously cuts the Federal deficit, that has led to record lows in long-term interest rates and that has led to good news in increasing bank lending and housing starts and business investments.

Since I became President, our economy has created more than a million private sector jobs, more jobs in 8 months than all those created in the previous 4 years. But it's just a beginning. Many of our people are still struggling, and we won't quit fighting for them. As long as the economy isn't working for working people, we'll be working to fix it.

We took on the issue of medical security because true security for our families and for the economy is clearly incomplete without it. Our administration's plan for health care reform will reduce waste and cost, and most importantly, will give our citizens health care that's always there, that can't be taken away.

And the blanket of security for Americans has another side to it: personal security. Our people have the right to feel safe where they live, work, play, and go to school. But too many of our people are denied that right. I've talked with parents who were afraid to send their children to schools where other kids carry guns. I've talked with children who were so afraid of becoming caught up with gangs, they didn't ever want to leave their homes. I've talked with police officers who felt anger and frustration at trying, sometimes against overwhelming odds, to stem an epidemic of violence, especially from children, better armed than police, who shoot other children. And most important, I've talked with the victims.

Yesterday, I visited a trauma center in New Jersey and saw what people with guns can do to other people. I met a woman who couldn't speak anymore because her husband shot her in the throat. I met a man who took a bullet in his chest during a robbery attempt. I met a child whose mother was killed by an assault rifle. It was heartbreaking, and it was an outrage.

These kind of attacks happen too often. They shatter lives. They destroy families. And more and more, they kill children. Violent crime crowds our emergency rooms and drains our medical resources. And it is siphoning away our humanity. Gunshot wounds are now the major cause of death among teenage boys.

My visits with these victims yesterday made me more determined than ever to win passage of our crime bill. This bill will help to restore a system where those who commit crimes are caught, those who are found guilty are convicted, those who are convicted are punished, sometimes by imposition of the death penalty for especially serious crimes. I support that.

Two months ago I asked Congress to pass a tough crime bill. This month, your lawmakers will consider it. And they should pass it this year. But what really makes this crime bill effective and different is this: more police, fewer guns. Our bill would help to prevent crime by putting 50,000 more police officers on the street in America and by expanding community policing.

Here in Washington recently, a beautiful 4-year-old girl was caught in the line of fire, and she died from a bullet wound. Her name was Launice Smith. All she was doing was watching other children at play. How did that become the wrong place at the wrong time? The fact is, with so many handguns and assault weapons flooding our streets, a lot of places can be the wrong place at the wrong time. That's why we have to pass the Brady bill. It requires a 5-day wait before a gun can be purchased, time enough for a real background check to stop guns from getting into the hands of convicted criminals. And we can't go on being the only country on Earth that lets teenagers roam the streets with assault weapons better armed than even the police.

Our crime bill also gives a young person who took a wrong turn a chance to reclaim his life by learning discipline in a boot camp. Every major law enforcement group in our country supports these measures: more police, boot camps, and alternative punishment for young people, the Brady bill, and a ban on assault weapons.

The men and women on the front lines know our country needs this kind of action on school grounds, on streets, in parking lots and homes in our biggest cities and smallest towns. The silliest of arguments, arguments that might have ended in a fist fight in bygone days, now they're too easily ended with the sound of a gun. And often, the sound of a gun leads to death.

A gunshot wound is three times more likely to lead to death today, in part because there are so many assault weapons, and the average victim of a gunshot wound now has over two bullets in him or her. It's getting hard to find a family that hasn't been touched by this epidemic of violence. Often, it means another empty chair in a classroom, an empty place at a dinner table, an empty space in the hearts of those who lost the loved ones.

Tell your Representatives on Capitol Hill you want the crime bill, and you want it now because it's important; it's long overdue. I guarantee you this: The minute I get it, I'll sign it. For we can never enjoy full economic security in our professional lives without real personal security in our homes, on our streets, and in our neighborhoods. I pledge to you today that we'll keep working to restore both.

Thanks for listening.

NOTE: The President spoke at 10:06 a.m. from the Oval Office at the White House.

Remarks at Yale University in New Haven, Connecticut
October 9, 1993

Thank you very, very much. To my good friends Guido and Anne Calabresi, President and Mrs. Levin, to Mr. Mandel, and to all the people at the head table. Let me say a special word of thanks to the artist who did that wonderful portrait, unduly flattering, also a gifted flack. You see, he's got me holding Stephen Carter's book "The Culture of Disbelief." We now know he took no money from Yale because Carter took care of him. [*Laughter*] Actually I'm deeply honored to be holding that book. I read it. I loved it. And the dean said that a person ought to be painted with a book he's read, since no one is very often.

I thank Mr. Laderman for that wonderful fanfare for Hillary and for me. I enjoyed it very much. As far as I know, it's the first piece of music ever written for someone who is a mediocre musician but loves music greatly. I want to say, too, to all of my former professors, to my classmates, and to my friends here, I thank each and every one of you for the contributions you made to my life and to Hillary's and for the work you did to make it possible for me to be here today. I thank you, Dean, for mentioning our friend Neal Steinman, who doubled the IQ of every room he ever walked into. And I thank all my classmates who are here who contributed to the last campaign in so many and wonderful ways.

I also want to say a special word of thanks to the people who taught me in class and to the people I just knew in the halls who were on the faculty in Yale Law School. It was a rich experience for me that I still remember very vividly. I was especially glad to see my fellow southerner Professor Myres McDougal out there. I'm delighted to see you here, sir. Thank you for coming today.

My wife did a magnificent job today, as she always does. This is our 20th reunion, and Monday will be our 18th anniversary. It's been a humbling experience, you know. I mean, she was so great talking about health care on television the week before last and having the country follow an issue that we have cared about for so long. And shortly after that, the U.S. News or somebody—USA Today—had the poor grace to commission a poll in which 40 percent of the American people opined, in an opinion agreed with by 100 percent of our classmates and faculty members here, that she was smarter than I am—[*laughter*]—just when I was beginning to feel at home in the job.

Then as if to add insult to injury, I went to California and did a town meeting on television and went down to L.A. And I was very excited; they put me at the Beverly Hilton. And I knew Merv Griffin owned it, and I thought, well, maybe he'll come out and say hi, and I'll begin to really feel like a President again. And sure enough, he did. He came out and said hello, and there he was. And he said, "I put you on the floor where I thought you belonged. And you have a very nice suite. But there is one permanent resident of the floor, and he'll be there to greet you when you get there." So my imagination was running wild. I got up to the floor where the suite was, and guess who the permanent resident is? Rodney Dangerfield. As God is my witness, he met me there, gave me a dozen roses with a card that said, "A little respect. Rodney." [*Laughter*]

You know, I was thinking just sitting here about the incredible events that our country has seen unfold in the last 3½ weeks at home and abroad: the developments in the Middle East and in Russia; the efforts we are making here to deal with health care; and the signing of the national service bill, which was one of the things that drove me into the campaign for President; the efforts we're making to pass the trade agreement with Mexico and Canada; the continuing troubles of Somalia. And I was thinking about what it was like 20 years ago when we were here, a time of student demonstrations when we were about to get out of Vietnam and about to get up to our ears in Watergate, when the culture of heavy rock music and drugs began to blur the sensibilities of a lot of Americans. And I noticed last night when I was reading a book on that time to Hillary that while we were at law school, the gifted singer Janis Joplin died of a drug overdose, sort of symbolic of the tragedy that was those years.

It was also a time of great hope, as Hillary pointed out, a time of advances in civil rights, a time where the environmental movement real-

ly got going in our country, a time that the real strength of the women's movement began to be felt. It was a time, too, when we assumed that if we could just fix whatever it was we thought was wrong, that everything else would be okay.

I remember at the end of my tenure here the Yale workers were on strike. And the head of the local AFL–CIO, Vinnie Sirabella, who just passed away recently, was a great friend of mine. And we were all thinking of ways we could support him and still go to class.

The idea then was that if we could divide the pie a little more fairly, everything would be wonderful. Connecticut for the last several years has been obsessed with a deeper question, which is how to get the pie to grow again and whether there will be enough for people.

Today as you look at where we are after 20 years, virtually all of us in our class have done pretty well through a combination of ability and hard work and, even though we may hate to admit it, blind luck. We have done pretty well. And we live in a world without many of the burdens that we grew up with. The most important one is that the threat of nuclear annihilation is receding, that the end of the cold war gave birth to new movements for democracy, for freedom, for market economics, not just in Russia where it has recently been reaffirmed but also in Latin America and in many new nations in Africa, all across the world.

There was someone holding a sign when I drove in here through East Haven and New Haven that said "Rabin and Arafat, Mandela and de Klerk, Clinton and Yeltsin: It's a lot to feel good about." And there is, to be sure. But it's also true that there are a lot of troubles in the world today causing the deaths of many people. Some of them we know a lot about; others we don't see very often on television, the problems of the Sudan or Angola. We now see more of what is going on in Georgia and not so much about Armenia and Azerbaijan.

We know, too, that the world hasn't quite figured out, in this post-cold-war world, how we're going to deal with a lot of these problems and whether we can actually, those of us who live in stable societies, reach into others and shape a different and more human course. And so we argue about what our responsibilities are and what is possible in Bosnia, in Somalia, in Haiti. And we do the best we can in a time of change, without some quick, easy theory like containment which helped us in the cold war.

Here at home, there's an awful lot of good, too. The movements toward opportunity for people from diverse backgrounds have continued and reached an enormous degree of success for those who can access them. We saw it when Colin Powell retired and Ruth Bader Ginsburg ascended to the Supreme Court, when there are now five African-Americans in the Cabinet of the President of the United States, when over 20 percent of our Presidential appointments are people of Hispanic or African-American origin. We are moving in the right direction in opening up opportunities in this country to all people. When we were here, there were only five women on the Federal bench. Now there are 91, and there are about to be a whole lot more.

And this is an exciting time where technology is changing the nature of work and leisure and shortening the time of decision and bringing people closer together all across the globe. It is also a time when education still largely bears its own rewards, and those who get a good education can do pretty well in this old world. It's also well to remember that with all of our problems, most people in this country get up every day, go to work, obey the law, love their families, love their country desperately, and do what is right. I saw a big slice of that coming in from the airport as there were hundreds and hundreds of people in East Haven and New Haven waving their American flags. A postman stopped and put his hand over his heart because the President of the United States went by. I still marvel every day when I travel at how much people love this Nation.

And what I want to say to you today is that the same is true even in the most distressed areas, in south central Los Angeles or the south Bronx. Most people who live there work for a living, pay their taxes, care desperately about their children, want the best for the future, and obey the law. But we also have to face the fact that we have a whole new and different set of challenges at home, some of which we could have imagined in 1973, others of which have grown all out of control.

In 1973 we now know that real average hourly wages for our working people peaked. Median family income today is only $1,000 higher than it was 20 years ago, $1,000 higher. The growth in income inequality between those who are educated and those who are not has escalated dramatically, so that even though there are 50 percent more people in the work force of minority origin with 4 years of college education or more, the aggregate racial gaps in income are deeper because the education gap has grown so great and because of the escalating inequality of income in the last several years.

We know that our country needs to invest more in creating a new world, but we're so riddled with debt it's hard to do it. And we know that like other wealthy countries—and maybe they're the company that misery loves—almost no rich country, including the United States, understands how to create more jobs at a rapid rate.

We also know that there are a lot of changes we have to make. Many of you have written about them, talked about them. A lot of you are living them. And we see the reluctance, the aversion to change in the United States at a time when we are being caught up in all the realities of the global economy. I believe that one of the reasons we haven't been able to come to grips with these great challenges is that too many of us are too personally insecure in our own lives, our family lives, our work lives, our community lives, to have the courage and self-confidence it takes to take a different course. You can see it when people are worried about losing their jobs, or they know they're working harder for less. The average working family is spending much more time on the job now than they were when we were here in law school.

I see and listen to the opposition to the North American Free Trade Agreement, something which I believe will make better the problems of the eighties that most people grieve about and clearly open a whole new world of opportunity to us with democracies in Latin America who care about us. And as I listen closely, I find that the overwhelming majority of opposition really reflects the insecurity of the people in opposition, based on the experience of the last 12 to 15 years. It has in short become the symbol, the receptacle, for the accumulated resentments of people who feel that they have worked hard and done their best and they are still losing ground. So that here is a case, which at least from my point of view, it is self-evident that we should take a course that will benefit the very people who are fighting against it. Why? Because of the insecurity people feel.

People feel rampant insecurity on our streets.

The leading cause of violence among teenage boys today is death from gunshot wounds. I learned yesterday at a trauma center in New Jersey that a person who is shot is now 3 times more likely to die from the shot than 15 years ago, because they're likely to have more bullets in them with the growth of automatic and semi-automatic weapons and the spread on the street.

We see crisis in America's families. Do you know, at the end of the World War II there was no difference in divorce rates and out-of-wedlock birth rates among the poor and the nonpoor in America, absolutely none. We were literally a pro-family society in a traditional way. Today there is a breathtaking difference in the rates of out-of-wedlock birth among the poor and the nonpoor. And that is only one symbol of the pressures on the American family today and the fact that we are creating, especially among younger people in poor distressed areas, mostly males but a lot of females, not just an underclass but an outer class, people for whom the future has no claim.

If you look across this vast sea of people today, if you look at the Democrats and the Republicans, the liberals and the conservatives, the people who identify with the whole range of speakers who have been here today, you will see that we at least all pretty much have one thing common: The future had a claim on all of us. We dreamed of what life might be. We imagined what we might become. We gave up things we would otherwise have wished to do at various stages along our lives, first for ourselves and our own future, and later for our children because we wanted them to have a future, which required us to do or not do certain things in the moment.

And now we live in a country with millions of people for whom the future is what happens in 10 or 20 minutes or maybe tomorrow, people who are often better armed than the local police, who act on impulse and take other people's lives, not so much because they are intrinsically bad but because they are totally unrooted and out of control, not bound in by the things that guided our behavior.

And I say to you today, my friends, without regard to your age or your politics, we've all done pretty well. We were really fortunate to be able to come here; I don't care how smart we were or how hard we worked. There are young geniuses in cities today whose lives are being destroyed by what they are doing or not doing. And our job in this last decade of this century is to try to give people, without regard to their station in this country, the same chance we had to live up to the fullest of their God-given capacities and in the process to revitalize the American dream in our time.

This is a challenging time. It is an interesting time. Nation states are in some ways less control over their own affairs than ever before. They have to cooperate with others to get things done in a global economy. And yet the forces of the global economy are taking away their autonomy at home. But we in America, if we are going to do our job by our people, we have got to face our problems here and get our collective acts together. And all of us, each in our way, have a responsibility for that.

I would argue that there are at least three things on which we should be able to agree. Number one, we have to have a change in the way we approach our economy. It means different economic policies, different education policies. It means reaching out to the world, not turning away from the world. We are now only 20 percent of the world's GDP, where we used to be 40 percent at the end of the Second World War. No rich country creates jobs except through expanding its relationships with others.

We also have to face the fact that a lot of our institutions are just plain old out of date. There are Members of Congress here; I appreciate their presence. They're going to have to go back next week and try to figure out how to expand or extend the unemployment benefits because so many of our Americans have been unemployed for so long. But really what they're doing—and they should do it, and I'm going to help them—but what we're doing is trying to put a Band-Aid on a seriously inadequate system because the unemployment system, just for example, was created for a time when people lost their jobs in a down economy; the economy got better; they got their jobs back. So you gave them a check in between because it wasn't their fault.

Today, more and more people never get their old jobs back. The average person changes work eight times in a lifetime. We don't need an unemployment system. What we need is what my classmate and our Labor Secretary, Bob Reich, calls a reemployment system. And as long as we keep extending unemployment benefits alone instead of turning the whole thing upside-down and aggressively starting training programs and job education programs in the beginning of the unemployment period, we're going to have a lot of very frustrated, angry Americans who desperately want to do right and who are losing their confidence and their courage to change.

The second thing we have to do is to frankly face the fact that this Nation has spoken one way and acted another when we have to organize ourselves in a different way to become more secure. And we're either going to have to make up our minds to frankly acknowledge that, or we're going to have to bring our actions and our organization as a society into line with our rhetoric. And I just would like to mention three examples.

First, family: There are now well over half the women who are mothers in this country are in the work force. We have got to make up our mind that as long as the economy mandates this—and the economic pressures of the time do—we have to find ways for people to be successful workers and successful parents. And that means we have to organize ourselves differently with regard to child care, family leave, and the incomes of people who have children and who work but they still don't make enough money to support them.

Perhaps the most important thing we did in the economic program which passed the Congress, in addition to bringing the deficit down and keeping interest rates at a historic low, was to provide an increase in tax refunds and benefits to lower income working people so there would never be an excuse to be on welfare just to support your children. And so, you can say, "You can work and still be a good parent and take care of your family."

That's why I felt so strongly about the family leave law. I'll just tell you one story, so you don't think it is just about programs. I went for my morning jog a couple of Sundays ago, and when I came in there was a family taking a tour of the White House, a rare occasion on Sunday morning. There was a father, a mother, and three children. The middle child was in a wheelchair. And my staff member said, "Mr. President, this is one of those Make-A-Wish families. That little girl has cancer and is probably not going to make it, and she wanted to come to the White House, take a tour, and see the President." So I went over and talked to the family and had a nice visit. They were fine people, dealing with their grief and their

problem with great dignity. And then I went upstairs and got cleaned up and came down and took a picture with them after I had my Presidential uniform on. And I bid them goodbye. But as I was walking away, the father grabbed me by the arm, and I turned around, and he said, "Mr. President," he said, "I want to tell you something. My little girl's having a tough time, and she may not make it. And these times I've spent with her are the most important times of my life. If it had not been for the family leave law, I would have had to choose between working at my job and supporting my family or giving up my job and my support for my family to spend this critical, precious time with my daughter. Don't ever believe it doesn't matter what decisions are made in this town." I say that not to be self-serving, but to remind you that there are real, practical consequences in the lives of families in this time in public policy.

The second thing I want to mention is violence. This is the only country in the world where police have to go to work every day on streets with teenagers better armed than they are. This is the only country in the world that would be fiddling around after all these years. How many years has it been since Jim Brady got shot in the attempt to assassinate Ronald Reagan? And we still haven't passed the Brady bill, because people are fiddling around the edges of it making parliamentary arguments because they're trying to find some way to please the people who don't like it. It's unconscionable.

I'm telling you, when I was in California earlier this week, I talked by television on this interconnected town hall meeting to a young African-American teenager. He and his brother left the school they were in because it was too violent. He said, "I don't want to be in a gang. I don't want to own a gun. I want to study. I want to do well. So does my brother. We went to a safer school." And the day they showed up at the safer school, they're standing in line to register for class, and his brother was shot down in front of him, just happened to be in the way of one of these arbitrary shootings. This is crazy, folks.

How can I preach to people about NAFTA, education, think of the future, and you've got to worry about whether your kid's going to get shot going to school? We can do something about it. And it is time to close the massive yawning gap between our rhetoric and the way we are organized in this society.

And finally with regard to security, I see this health care issue as a defining moral challenge for our people. Not in the details—maybe Hillary and I don't have it all right; I'm open to that—but in the essence. How can we justify—here we are, we talk about America and the American dream and what a great country this is. And it's all true. But we have 37.4 million people, according to last week's study, who don't have any health insurance. We have 2 million people a month who lose their health insurance; 100,000 of them lose it permanently. We have a system in hemorrhage. We find it necessary to spend 14.5 percent of our income for a health care system when Canada spends 9 percent and more appropriately Japan and Germany, which have a lot of medical research, spend less than 9 percent.

And some of it we want to spend more on, medical research and technology. Some of it we have to spend more on right now because we have more poor people, more people with AIDS, more teen births, more low-birthweight births, and a lot more violence, and that's all true. But we also have hospitals spending 25 percent of their money on paperwork. We also spend a dime on the dollar more on paperwork than any country in the world for health care. And we can't figure out how to have primary and preventive health care and give everybody health insurance. We want people to have the courage to change. We say, "Well, we'll give you a good training program; you may have to change jobs eight times in a lifetime; you'll go from a big company to a little company to a medium-sized company." And we're saying to every American, "You could lose your health insurance tomorrow." And it is not right. How can you expect people to have the courage to change if they don't know whether in the change they will be able to take care of their children's most basic needs?

The time has come for us to join the ranks of the civilized world and provide health security and comprehensive decent benefits to all of our people. We have got to do it. It is a huge problem in trying to guarantee labor mobility, high productivity in the small business workplace, and the ability of small business people to continue to function. I met a small business person this week with 12 employees whose premiums went up 40 percent this year, even though they did not have one single claim ex-

cept for normal checkups. We have to do it. This is a security issue. And if you want Americans to change—just about everybody in this room never gives a thought to your health care, but I'm telling you tens of millions of people do. And we have got to do better. We have got to quit saying this is too complicated or there's this or that or the other problem, and so maybe it'll go away. It is a security issue closely tied to whether we will change.

So there's an economic change argument. There's a security argument. The third thing I want to say to you is that we somehow have to recover, each in our own way, a sense of personal stake in the American community. We have to ask ourselves if we really believe we don't have a person to waste, if we really think everybody's important, if we really think people who follow our laws, no matter how different they are from us, should have a place at the American table, and if we really think that we all have a responsibility to do something about it.

That's why I wanted this national service program to pass so badly, because there are now millions of young people who are tired of the "me, too," "let me have it first; forget about everybody else" ethic that dominated too much of the 1980's. And they want to give something back. They need a way to do it.

But I picked up the paper today, and some of these kids I'm going to see when I leave here, school kids, were saying, "We want the President to know that we have a good school," and "We want the President to know that we're trying to be good kids," and "We're going to tell the President that we hope somebody will show up and paint the walls in our schools." Well, somebody who lives here ought to show up and paint the walls in their school. That ought to be done.

And I tell you, the reason that I have done my best to promote Professor Carter's book "The Culture of Disbelief" is that I believe a critical element of our reestablishing a sense of community in America is trying to unite the inner values that drive so many Americans with the outer compulsion we have to have to work together. The problem that I have with so much of the religious right today is not that they may differ with me about what is or is not morally right. That has always been a part of America. The problem I have is that so many of them seem to believe that their number one obligation is to make whatever they think is wrong illegal, and then not worry about what kind of affirmative duties we have to one another.

But I think there ought to be ways we can talk. Let me just give you one example. I gave a speech in Cedar Rapids, Iowa, in the campaign. And the folks that disagreed with me on the abortion issue were demonstrating, as they did during the campaign. And that's their American right, and welcome to it. And on the front row at this speech in the parking lot of the Quaker Oats Company in Cedar Rapids, Iowa, was a woman who had a pro-choice button on. But she was also holding a child of another race who had AIDS, that she adopted from another State, after she had been abandoned by her husband and was raising two kids in an apartment house. And she still adopted a child of another race, from another State, dying of AIDS, because she said it was her moral responsibility to affirm that child's life.

Now, which group was more pro-life? We have a friend who is pro-choice but adopted an Asian baby with no arms. There is a Member of Congress who has adopted six children, who is pro-life—pro-choice, I mean. The point I make here is not an attack on the pro-life. The point I make is, surely we have something to say to each other about this. Surely we do. If you look at the work of the Catholic Church and the Pentecostal Church, to mention two, in promoting adoptions—I say to you, surely there is a way we can breach these great divides and talk together about how our actions ought to affirm what we can agree on. That is the point I want to make.

Surely there is a way we can acknowledge, too, that no matter how important we Democrats think programs are, a lot of the changes we need in this country have to come from the inside out and require some personal contact with people who can give context and structure and order as well as love to a whole generation of Americans we are in danger of losing. There is a lot we have to talk about in this American community.

And I did not come here to attack any group today motivated by their own version of what they think God wants them to do but simply to say I think God wants us to sit down and talk to one another and see what values we share and see how we can put them inside the millions and millions of Americans who are living in chaos. I believe we could do better if we talked to one another more and shouted at one another less. And I hope that together we can make that decision.

Let me just say this, most everybody my age who came to Yale Law School could have gone someplace else to law school. And most of us came here at least in part because we believed that Yale would not only teach us to be good lawyers in the technical sense, not only to understand individual rights and individual contractual obligations and how particular areas of law work so that we could be successful as practitioners, but also how it all fit into the larger society. A huge percentage of our crowd came here because we thought Yale would teach us how to succeed as professional lawyers and how to be good citizens as well.

And as we look toward the 21st century with the need for America to change, with the desperate need for us to reestablish the security that most of us took for granted when we were children, with the need to rebuild the American community, I say to you, my fellow classmates, we have much to do. Yale gave us the tools to do it with. We owe it to the rest of the country because of our success to share what we know and what we can give to the future so that we can enter the next century with the American dream alive and the American family strong.

Thank you, and God bless you all.

NOTE: The President spoke at 3:05 p.m. in The Commons. In his remarks, he referred to Guido Calabresi, dean, Yale Law School, and his wife, Anne; Richard C. Levin, president of the university, and his wife, Jane; Joseph D. Mandel, president, Yale Law School Association; Ezra Laderman, dean, Yale School of Music; Neal Steinman, Yale Law School class of 1971 alumnus, who died in January; and Myres S. McDougal, Sterling professor emeritus of law.

Exchange With Reporters at Yale University in New Haven
October 9, 1993

Somalia

Q. [*Inaudible*]—with General Aideed?

Q. [*Inaudible*]—offering a cease-fire?

The President. We haven't offered a cease-fire. I expect it, that there would be a cessation of violence against the United States and the U.N. forces when I made it clear what I said at the U.N., that we wanted to support a political process in Somalia that would permit the termination of our involvement and when I made it clear I was going to send stronger forces there to reinforce our position. But there's been no direct communication. In fact, Ambassador Oakley went there to meet with President Meles and other leaders of the African nations in the region and to try to work out a political process that they would manage. We believe that over the long run, the only way that Somalians can live in peace with one another is if their neighbors work out an African solution to an African problem. So, that's just not true. We didn't extend an offer of a cease-fire. And there's been no direct negotiations of any kind.

Q. [*Inaudible*]—apparently he is offering one now.

The President. Well, if he's offering one, that's fine. He ought to stop the violence, because that's a good thing. He ought to do it. But it's not accurate to say that we have initiated it. But I welcome it. I think that he should stop the violence. And I want Ambassador Oakley to have a chance to go over there and meet with President Meles and others. And let's see what kind of political process that the African leaders themselves can get going.

Q. [*Inaudible*]—part of these negotiations, sir, or are you trying to cut them out of it?

The President. No, I didn't say that. As a matter of fact, I think the Secretary-General is going to the region just in the next couple of days, which I would welcome. So that's up to him to decide. I wouldn't say that at all. But all the nations that are there on the humanitarian mission have supported in varying degrees the idea that we didn't want to go there for nothing. We didn't want to go there, pull out, and have chaos, anarchy, starvation return.

But I think it's clear to all of us who have been involved in this that the greatest likelihood of a successful political resolution of this would be if the African leaders of the adjoining states took the initiative and they tried to work out a solution which reflected what is possible and what is desirable as they define it. And I don't think we ought to be defining it for them. I have never been for——

Q. [*Inaudible*]—your instructions been to Oakley?

The President. My instructions to Oakley were to go first to meet with President Meles, decide whether there are any other presidents of other countries in the region he needs to meet with, discuss what the role for the OAU or some other African role might be, and see what can best be done to start, really generate a lot of energy behind the political process. We think that ultimately whatever peace would be brokered, if it's brokered from forces outside Somalia, should come from the Africans. And we would hope the U.N. would be able to bless——

Q. [*Inaudible*]—prospects for the release of Chief Warrant Officer Durant? Is there any report there?

The President. Well, we're obviously encouraged by the fact that he seems to be in reasonably good shape. And we expect that he will be released. I can't give you any other specific comments now. I am very hopeful that there will be no Americans in captivity anytime soon.

Q. [*Inaudible*]—make a deal for his release?

The President. [*Inaudible*]—and I expect that that's what the rules will be. But there has been no negotiations over that at all, none.

Q. [*Inaudible*]—can't say anything now—is there some sort of sensitive process ongoing now—the process——

The President. No, I wouldn't characterize it in that way. It's just that I believe that I think that any Americans who are held captive must be released. I think they know the United States has no intention of leaving Somalia until that is done. We're going to have all of our people present and accounted for before we go home. And that's just going to be a part of whatever happens from now on in. It is the priority that we have to pursue and for our own people.

But I'm encouraged that Mr. Oakley was welcomed there by President Meles. And I'm encouraged by President—I mean, by the Secretary-General wanting to go to the region. So I think that the peace process sort of got derailed over the last several months. I think it's going to get back in gear. And I think that's a good thing for everybody.

NOTE: The exchange began at 4:30 p.m. at the Rotunda in Woolsey Hall. In his remarks, the President referred to Ambassador Robert B. Oakley, special envoy to Somalia; President Zenawi Meles of Ethiopia; U.N. Secretary-General Boutros Boutros-Ghali; and captured U.S. Army pilot Michael Durant. A tape was not available for verification of the content of this exchange.

Nomination for an Associate Director of the United States Information Agency
October 11, 1993

The President today announced his intention to nominate former City of Alexandria, VA, official Henry Howard, Jr., to be Associate Director for Management for the U.S. Information Agency.

"Henry Howard's expertise in planning and development is great and will serve him well at USIA. Our administration is fortunate to have him," the President said.

NOTE: A biography of the nominee was made available by the Office of the Press Secretary.

Exchange With Reporters on Haiti
October 12, 1993

Q. Do you have a message for the military leaders in Haiti who have——

The President. Yes.

Q. ——so far thwarted our mission?

The President. First of all, the objective of the United States is to restore democracy and President Aristide to Haiti. The instrument of that was the sanctions. It was the sanctions. We never intended, and we have no intention now, of interfering in the internal affairs of the Haitians, except to say that we want democracy and the will of two-thirds of the Haitian people to be honored.

Now, the Governors Island Agreement, which all the parties signed off on, invited the international community to come to Haiti: French speaking forces; advisers to come in and help to train the police; the Canadians and the Americans to come and help to train the army, particularly for civilian purposes. One of the reasons we have so many Seabees going in, for example, is to help the military people change their mission so they can rebuild their own country.

This is different from the other missions we have been discussing. This is not peacekeeping. This is not peacemaking. This is an agreement that has been made, that if honored, would enable our people to come in and simply serve as trainers, 600 of them. So I have no intention of sending our people there until the agreement is honored.

What I intend to do now is to press to reimpose the sanctions. I will not have our forces deposited on Haiti when they cannot serve as advisers, when they can't do what they were asked to do. So we're going to press for the reimposition of sanctions. Mr. Cédras is supposed to resign his post as soon as the parliament can pass a bill separating the military from the police. Mr. François is supposed to leave his post. And they're going to have to go through with this if they expect to have a normal existence. And otherwise the United States is going to press to reimpose the sanctions.

Q. And what else can you do to try to get Aristide back in power? Isn't this whole thing coming unraveled, sir?

The President. No, I think that what happened is they agreed to the Governors Island Agreement. They invited all these nations to come help train the police and train the military and move them away from the kind of state they've had to a democracy where they can rebuild the country.

Now, some of the people who have held onto power obviously are resisting letting it go when the pressure of the sanctions has been let up. President Aristide himself, number one, asked us to lift the sanctions, and number two, granted the amnesty to the people that were involved in kicking him out, just as he promised to do. So he has done his part. The international community has done its part. And they are reneging. There's no point in our even trying to land there until we can do what we were asked to do as advisers. This is not peacemaking, this is about restoration of democracy. So we're going back to the sanctions until those people do what they said they'd do.

Q. With those who are unarmed, is there a chance that the military will go in and then turn around and get in a hostile kind of situation once they're on the ground?

The President. The Department of Defense and our military leaders are convinced that the relatively light arms that our people were supposed to carry as advisers are more than adequate to protect themselves as long as the Governors Island Agreement is being honored. But I am not about to let them land to test it. We have to know. And we don't know yet. And so until we know, we're not going in there. We were not asked to come in there to make peace or to keep the peace. They said they would do that. All they asked us to do is to go in there and help them rebuild their country and train their forces, which we agreed to do.

Q. What's your view of the status of the Governors Island Agreement? Is it dead, has it been abrogated? What's your view of it as the legal standing of——

The President. [*Inaudible*]—do not think it is dead. I still think it will come back to life. But right now it has been abrogated by people who have decided to cling to power for a little bit longer, apparently once the pressure of the sanctions has been off. We agreed to lift the sanctions because President Aristide asked us to do it, believing that in good faith that if he honored the Governors Island Agreement, the others would. Until they do it, the rest of the international community cannot proceed.

Q. What did Cédras tell you? I mean, what have they told of why they've done this?

The President. Well, they have a lot of different explanations. Mr. Cédras basically denies that he did it, although the soldiers plainly got out of the way for the people that were staging the demonstration against the landing. And so what we want to do is we want to see action. I have no intention of asking our young people in uniform or the Canadians or the people from the French-speaking countries to go in there to do anything other than implement a peace agreement that the parties themselves agreed to. I will say again, this is very different from what we have been engaged in, even in Somalia, very different. So they're going to have to honor this agreement. Otherwise, I'm going to press very hard to put the sanctions back on and enforce them strongly.

Q. Mr. President, how about the *Harlan County*? What's going to happen to the ship? Is it going to remain offshore, is it going to move somewhere else?

The President. I'm going to remove it from the harbor and put it at a base first and then we'll see what happens. I want the Haitians to know that I am dead serious about seeing them honor the agreement they made. President Aristide has done his part. He issued the amnesty personally. They said that's what they wanted; he did it. He asked us to relieve the Haitian people of the suffering and the sanctions, and the United Nations did that. And now the time has come for the people who are clinging to their last gasp of power to honor the agreement. They made the agreement; they've got to honor it.

Q. Mr. President, does that mean that Aristide won't be coming back to power at the end of the month?

The President. No, I still think there's a chance that'll happen. But it does mean that we are going to have to reimpose the sanctions, I believe. Of course, it's up to the U.N., but I'm going to push strong for it. We've got to get this agreement honored. If the agreement is honored, he can go back without fear of his personal safety. And the Canadians, the French-speaking nations, the United States can go in there not as peacemakers, not as peacekeepers but to help to train people to rebuild their country.

We know what two-thirds of the Haitians

wanted; they voted for it. We know that President Aristide has now honored his part of the Governors Island Agreement. I still think we can get the others to honor it. But the way to do it is to press for the sanctions, to show total intolerance of this kind of behavior and not to get into a position where the Canadians, the French, the United States, anybody else's motives can be misunderstood. We are waiting to go there as we were invited by all the parties:

to be advisers. That's it. Meanwhile, we're going to push for democracy.

NOTE: The exchange began at 4:08 p.m. on the South Lawn at the White House, prior to the President's departure for Chapel Hill, NC. In his remarks, he referred to Lt. Gen. Raoul Cédras, commander of the Haitian armed forces, and Lt. Col. Joseph Michel François, chief of the Haitian police.

Remarks at the University of North Carolina in Chapel Hill
October 12, 1993

Thank you very much. Thank you. Thank you very much, President Spangler, President Friday, Chancellor Hardin, my good friend, Governor Hunt, and other distinguished platform guests, ladies and gentlemen.

I must say I have thought for a long time about what it might feel to be in a vast crowd of North Carolinians and have them do something besides root against one of my athletic teams from Arkansas. [*Laughter*]

I began to think of this moment in August when I was on vacation, and I spent an evening with a person who used to be one of your great sons, James Taylor. And I asked him to sing "Carolina in My Mind" so that I could begin to think about what this day might mean to all of us. Five other Presidents have come to this great university to speak. None has ever had the opportunity to speak to a crowd like this, on this occasion of your 200th birthday as a university.

I'd like to begin by thanking the students whom I have met and especially those who gave me this beautiful leather-bound book of essays, three of them, about the theme for this bicentennial celebration that the students chose, community. For it is in many ways what ought to be America's theme today, how we can be more together than we are apart.

This university has produced enough excellence to fill a library or lead a nation, in novelists like Thomas Wolfe and Walker Percy; in great defenders of the Constitution like Senator Sam Ervin and Julius Chambers, now one of your chancellors; and Katherine Everett, a pioneer among women lawyers; and Francis Collins,

a scientist who discovered the gene for cystic fibrosis; and journalists like Charles Kuralt and Tom Wicker and Deborah Potter and my Pulitzer Prize-winning friend, Taylor Branch; and leading business men and women like the head of the Small Business Administration in our administration, Erskine Bowles, who's here with me tonight and who, I dare say, is the ablest person ever to hold his position, probably because of the education he got here at the University of North Carolina. These are just a few of the many thousands of lives who have been brightened by what Mr. Kuralt so warmly referred to as the light and liberty this great university offers.

There are few certainties in this life, but I've also learned that when March madness rolls around, I'll be hoping my Razorbacks are there, but I know that Dean Smith's Tar Heels will always be there.

As one who grew up in the South, I have long admired this university for understanding that our best traditions call on us to offer that light and liberty to all. Chapel Hill has always been filled with a progressive spirit. Long before history caught up with him, as Mr. Kuralt just said, your legendary president, Frank Porter Graham, spoke this simple but powerful truth: "In the South, two great races have fundamentally a common destiny in building a nobler civilization, and if we go up, we go up together." What a better life we might have had if more had listened to that at a single time.

Your great State has also understood that education goes hand-in-hand with the expansion of democracy and the advancement of our own economy. Under the leadership of men like Luther Hodges and Terry Sanford and Bill Friday, this university joined with your other State's great universities, the State government, and the corporate community to begin building an advanced research center to attract new businesses and jobs. Now the Research Triangle has more than 60 companies, more than 34,000 employees; it is the envy of the entire Nation about what we can do if we strive to make change our friend.

Tonight we celebrate the day this university began, the laying of a cornerstone that marks a milestone in the entire American journey, because on this day, near this place, 200 years ago, the cornerstone was laid for the first building in the first university in a Nation that had only recently been born.

It was, to be sure, a time of hopeful and historic change, when the future was clear to those who had the vision to see it and the courage to seize it. It was a time of heroes such as William R. Davie: a fighter in the Revolution, a framer of the Constitution, a Princeton graduate who wanted a State university here to make education accessible to more than the privileged few. On October 12th in 1793, when General Davie laid the foundation for this university, he laid a foundation for two centuries of progress in American education.

Historians tell us now that there was then a joyous ceremony, that "the maple leaves flamed red in the eager air." Great joy there was, but remember now, it was in the face of great uncertainty. The wounds of the Revolutionary War had yet to heal. The debts had yet to be repaid. And the new democracy seemed still untested and unstable. Yet, in spite of all these problems, the Americans of that time had the courage to build what had never before existed, a great new republic and a public university.

In spite of the obstacles, they decided to bet on the future, not cling to the past. That is the test for us today, my fellow Americans. Alexis de Tocqueville carried this uniquely American optimism, this faith in education, this commitment to change, when he wrote in his wondrous "Democracy in America": "The Americans have all a lively faith in the perfectibility of man. They judge that the diffusion of knowledge must necessarily be advantageous, and the consequences of ignorance fatal. They all consider society as a body in a state of improvement,

humanity as a changing scene, in which nothing is or ought to be permanent, and they admit that what appears to them today to be good, may be superseded by something better tomorrow."

For two centuries now, we've held fast to that faith in the future. For two centuries we've kept the courage to change. And for two centuries we've believed with Frank Porter Graham that we must go up together. Our Founders pledged their lives, their fortunes, their sacred honor to a common cause. We fought a vast and bloody Civil War to preserve that common cause. Every battle to expand civil rights has been to deepen and strengthen that common cause, our ability to go up together.

Now, after 200 years, and after 200 years of this university, we find ourselves a people of more than 150 different racial and ethnic groups confronting a challenge in this new era which tests our belief in the future, tests our courage to change, and tests our commitment to community, to going up together. Tonight we can best honor this great university's historic builders and believers, a dozen generations after our Nation and this university began, by meeting those tests.

The cold war is over. The threat of nuclear annihilation is receding. Democracy and free markets are on the march. Mandela and de Klerk, Rabin and Arafat have given people hope that peace can come out of any conflict.

A global economy is taking shape in which information and investment move across national borders at stunning speed. And competition for jobs and incomes is intense. Expanding trade is critical to every nation's growth, and our greatest asset is no longer natural resources or material structures. It is the strength, the skills, the mind, and the spirit of our people.

This is a world America has done a very great deal to make through two World Wars, the Civil War, the cold war, the establishment of global economic and trading missions, through the attempts to build the United Nations and other instruments of peace and harmony, of progress and democracy. It is full of hope. But as we all know, it is not without its heartbreak.

There is less danger of a nuclear war between two nations but more danger of the proliferation of weapons of mass destruction in the hands of people irresponsibly prepared to use them. The oppression of Communist control has disappeared, but that disappearance has reopened ugly ethnic and religious divisions. The United Nations can do more good than ever before, but clearly there are limits to what outside forces can do to solve severe internal problems in some nations. We cannot withdraw from this world we have done so much to make, and we must face its difficulties and challenges. Through great trials we have stood with President Yeltsin for democracy, peace, and economic reform in Russia. In so doing we have helped the Russians, but we've made ourselves safer and better, too.

We have sponsored and supported the peace process in the Middle East, for which you just clapped. And so doing, of course we have contributed to a better life for the Arabs and the Jews, but we have enhanced our own security as well.

We have helped to save nearly 1 million Somalis from death, starvation, anarchy, and strengthened our argument that the world's poor and deprived need not turn to terrorism and violence for redress. In so doing we have advanced our interests, but some of our finest young soldiers have perished.

Tonight before going on, I want to express here in North Carolina my profound gratitude and deep personal sympathy to the families of the six servicemen from Fort Bragg who were killed in Somalia: Sergeant Daniel Busch, First Class Earl Fillmore, Master Sergeant Gary Gordon, Master Sergeant Timothy Martin, Sergeant First Class Matthew Rierson and Sergeant First Class Randall Schugan. May God bless their souls and their families, and may we all thank them.

Our Nation is grateful to them; so are most of the people of Somalia. I have ordered strong new steps to protect our troops, to ensure the return of our missing or captive Americans, to complete our mission in that nation in no more than 6 months, to finish that job quickly but to finish that job right.

Just as we know we cannot withdraw from the world, we know here at this great university, that we cannot lead the world unless we are first strong at home. After all, in the beginning it was our values, our ideals, our strength, our willingness to work, to make the most of what was here on this continent that made us the envy of the world.

And here at home, this new economy of ours offers much hope and opportunity. Yet every positive development seems to bring with it some jarring dislocation. The global economy not only rewards the educated, it punishes those without education.

Between 1972 and 1992, while the work year got longer for most Americans, our wages stagnated. The 75 percent of our people who don't have college degrees felt it profoundly. Those who began but didn't finish college saw their wages fall by 9 percent just since 1979. For those who didn't go on to college, wages fell 17 percent. For those who left high school, wages dropped 20 percent. We got a lot of new jobs out of international trade, but we know we also lose some every year to competition from countries with lower wages or higher quality or sometimes unfair practices. We know that our health care is the finest in the world, but millions of us are just a pink slip away from losing their health insurance or one illness away from losing a life's savings.

Most of our people are law-abiding citizens who love their families more than their own lives. But America leads the world in violent crime, has the highest percentage of its people behind bars, has 90,000 murders in the last 4 years, and more and more of our children are born into and grow up in family situations so difficult that it is hard even to make the arguments that the rest of us have taken for granted all of our lives.

More and more of our children are growing up in a world in which the future is not what happens when they graduate from the University of North Carolina but what happens 15 minutes from now. We cannot long survive in a Nation with young people for whom the people has no allure and on whom the future has no claim. All of us who come here in gratitude to this great university, and others like it, are here because we believed in tomorrow. And that must be our urgent task: to restore that tomorrow for our young people.

What is the point of all this for today? It is simply this. We are living in a time of profound change. No one can fully see the shape of the change or imagine with great precision the end of it. But we know a lot about what works and what doesn't. And we know that if we do not embrace this change and make it our friend, if we do not follow what de Tocqueville said we were about 150 years ago, if we do not follow the traditions on which this university was founded, then change will become our enemy. And yet all around our great country today I see people resisting change. I see them turning inward and away from change. And I ask myself why.

At a time when we know it's a matter of fact that every rich country in the world gains many new jobs through expanding trade, I see people saying, "Well even though my industry will get more jobs, we shouldn't have a new trade arrangement with Canada and Mexico which could one day engulf all of Latin America." And when I listen to the arguments, I hear instead of arguments against this agreement, I hear the grievances of the 1980's, the grievances of times when workers were fired without thought, when investments were not made, when people were abused. Instead of a reasoning argument about what will build America tomorrow, I hear a longing for yesterday.

But I tell you my friends, as certainly as it was true 200 years ago today, yesterday is yesterday. If we try to recapture it, we will only lose tomorrow.

But I think we can say we know some things about why we are resisting these changes and what we might do to make ourselves more like the founders of this great university, more like the founders of our great Nation, more like most of the students here on any given day at this university. When do people most resist change? When they are most insecure. Think of any child you ever raised. Think of any personal experience you ever had. Why is it that great universities provide wonderful libraries and beautiful lawns and space and time to study and to learn and to grow? So people can feel personally at peace and secure. It is that which enables us to learn and to grow and to change. And I say to you tonight, my fellow Americans, the mission of this university, the mission of every university, must be to be in the vanguard of helping the American people to recover enough personal security to be able to lead the changes that we are so urgently called on to make.

What does that mean? What does that mean? I would argue among all things, it means at least three: First, we must make Americans more secure in their families and at work. In a world transformed by trade and technology it is no longer possible for a young person to go to work and keep a job until retirement or even often to stay with the same company. The economy is creating and losing millions of jobs constantly. Most people now who are laid off from their jobs never get the same old job

back. Young people beginning their careers, on average, will change work seven times in a lifetime. The best jobs those young people here in the audience may ever have may be jobs yet to be created in companies yet to be founded based on technologies yet to be discovered.

Economic security, therefore, can no longer be found in a particular job. It must be rooted in a continuing capacity to learn new things. That means we must have a system of lifelong learning beginning with higher standards in our schools. Almost two decades ago, your Governor, Jim Hunt, began an education reform program that included higher standards in these schools. Those efforts inspired other Governors around the country, including the then-Governor of South Carolina, now our Education Secretary, Dick Riley, and me. And I thank him for that.

Now, we are trying to adopt a whole new approach in our national effort to raise standards in education. We believe the right standard for America isn't whether we are better than we were but whether we're the best in the world. This cannot be a Democratic or a Republican concern. It must be an American imperative. We know we have to expect more of our students and our schools. We have to regulate their details less but hold them to higher standards and measure whether our kids are really learning enough to compete and win in the global economy.

Then we have to ensure that every young person in this country has the opportunity to get a college education, every last one who wants it. We have already this year reorganized the student loan programs to lower interest rates and ease the repayment terms and open the doors of college education to thousands of young people by giving them a chance to be in the national service program, to rebuild their communities from the grassroots up, and earn a part of their college education.

For the three-quarters of our young people who do not get 4-year college degrees, we must merge the world of learning and the world of work to offer young people classroom training and on-the-job training. And for those who lose their jobs, the unemployment system is no longer good enough. We must create a continuous reemployment system so that people are always learning, even into their fifties and sixties and seventies, as long as they are willing to be productive citizens and to keep going and growing.

Another big part of job security that is often missed is that most workers are now parents, or at least most parents are now workers. And we can no longer force people to choose between being a good parent and a good worker. They must be able to be both. That is why people who work hard for marginal wages should not be taxed into poverty but lifted out of it by the tax system, and it is what this Government has done. For the first time ever we can say now, if you work 40 hours a week and you have children in your home, you can be lifted out of poverty.

And that is why we have said you ought not to lose your job if you have a sick child or a sick parent. You ought to be able to take a little time off without losing your job because it is important to the fabric of America to stick up for the American family.

A couple of Sundays ago when I came into the White House from my early morning run, I saw a father, a mother, and three daughters there taking a tour on Sunday morning, an unusual time. And I went over and said hello to them and learned that the family was there with the Make-A-Wish Foundation, because one of the daughters was desperately ill, and she wanted to see the President and see the White House. I talked to that family for a while, and then I came down and had my picture taken with them. And as I was walking away the father said, "Mr. President, don't you ever think it doesn't matter what goes on up here. If it hadn't been for the family leave law coming in this year, I would have had to choose between spending this time with my precious daughter who may not make it, or working to support my family so that the rest of us could go on. No parent should ever make that choice, and I don't have to now."

That is what I mean by providing the American people the personal security they need to proceed to change in this world.

The second element, after education and training, of our personal security must be health care. This is the only advanced nation in which people can lose their health care, where we don't have health care that is always there and that can never be taken away. Even though we spend 40 percent more than any place else in the world, what does that mean? Lost productivity in small businesses, people really insecure about changing jobs because they've had someone in their family sick and they know if they

change jobs that preexisting condition will keep them from getting new health insurance. So people walk around like this, millions of us all the time, 37.4 million Americans without any health insurance but many millions more knowing they could lose it like that.

How can you be secure enough to change, to take on new challenges, to start new businesses, to take new risks, if you think that you may have to let your family go without basic health care? My fellow Americans, it does not happen in any other advanced nation, and it is time for us to say as a people it will no longer happen here. No more.

And this last point I would make to you: If we are to be personally secure enough to make the changes and meet the tests of this time, we must protect our people better against the ravages of violence. Our people have the right to feel safe where they live, where they go to school, and where they work.

My fellow Americans, I was in California the other night and I talked to people all across the State in a hooked-up town hall meeting. And this young African-American boy, a junior high school student, said, "Mr. President, my brother and I, we don't want to be in gangs. We don't want to have guns. We don't want to cause any trouble. We want to learn. We want a future. And we thought our school was too unsafe. So we decided to go to another school and enroll in it because it was safer. And on the day we showed up to register for school, my brother was standing right in front of me, and he was shot," because he got in a crossfire of one of these mindless, arbitrary, endless shootings that occur among children on our streets and in our schools today. We have to stop this. We cannot let those children be robbed of their future.

I know this State grieved recently when your native son Michael Jordan's father was killed. And I know we all wish him well as Michael embarks on a new journey in his life. But let us not forget that 22 other men and women were killed in that same county in your State this year. Ten foreign tourists were killed in Florida this year, and the State grieved over it. But in our Nation's Capital, in one week this summer, more than twice that many people were killed. They were not famous, but they were the President's neighbors.

It is heartbreaking. What can we do about it? We can put more police on our streets, not to catch criminals just alone but also to prevent crime. It works. Thirty years ago there were three police for every violent crime. Today there are three crimes for every police officer. We have to give these people the help they need. And when they work the same neighborhoods and walk the same streets and talk to the same kids, they help to prevent crime.

And I say this in North Carolina, coming from a State where in my home State, half the people have a hunting license or a fishing license or both, and we have to shut down factories and schools and towns on the opening day of deer season because nobody shows up anyway. But we still ought to pass the Brady bill so we don't sell guns to people with a criminal or a mental health history.

And we should not allow in city after city after city our police officers to go to work every day knowing they will walk the mean streets of our cities with people who are better armed than they are, because this is the only country in the world where teenagers can have assault weapons designed only to kill other people and use them with abandon on the streets of our cities. We can do better than that.

Do you know, my fellow Americans, that I learned just last week that someone shot today with a bullet is 3 times more likely to perish because they are likely to have 3 times as many bullets in them as they did just 15 years ago. It is time for us to stop talking about law and order and thinking about how we can organize ourselves to protect our culture, to protect our heritage, to keep our rights as sports men and women but to protect our kids' lives and their future. The time has come to face this problem.

What has all that got to do with this? Because this is what the Founders did. They faced the problems of their time and gave the rest of us a chance to live in the most successful democracy ever known. The idea of the public university, born here in North Carolina, played a major role in revolutionizing opportunity for millions and millions and millions of Americans who never even came into this State but got that opportunity in other States because of the example set here.

This is the challenge of our time, and we must meet it so that we can change: economic security, health care security, personal security. None of us can be secure until we are prepared to take personal responsibility for making these changes, and of building a new sense of commu-

nity, each in our own way. Our jobs won't be responsible unless we are willing to learn new skills for a lifetime and until we all treat each other like indispensable partners, not disposable parts.

Our health care won't be secure, even if we pass our health care bill, until all of us practice more preventive care. Our families won't be secure until fathers and mothers begin to realize that they have to put their children first. Our communities won't be secure until people who disagree on everything else stop shouting at each other long enough to realize that we have to save the kids who are in trouble the same way we lost them, one child at a time. And it imposes a responsibility on each and every one of us.

But I tell you, my fellow Americans, I honestly believe that as you start the third century of this university's life we could be looking at the most exciting time America has ever known, if we have the security and the courage to change. We want to revitalize the American spirit of enterprise and adventure. We want to give our people new confidence to dream those great dreams again, to take those great risks, to achieve those great things.

The security I seek for America is like a rope for a rock climber, to lift those who will take responsibility for their own lives to greater and greater pinnacles. The security I seek is not Government doing more for people but Americans doing more for ourselves and for our families, for our communities, and for our country. It is not the absence of risk. It is the presence of opportunity. It is not a world without change but a world in which change is our friend and not our enemy.

We honor today the men and women who had the courage to create a new university in a new nation. We must, like them, be builders and believers, the architects of a new security to empower and embolden America and the University of North Carolina on the eve of a new century.

The only difference between America two centuries ago and America today is the difference between dawn and high noon of a very beautiful day.

In the words of your great alumnus, Thomas Wolfe, "The true discovery of America is still before us. The true fulfillment of our spirit, of our people, of our mighty and immortal land is yet to come." Let us believe in those words and let us act on them, so that 200 years from now our children, 12 generations removed, will still celebrate this glorious day.

Thank you, and Godspeed.

NOTE: The President spoke at 8:24 p.m. in Kenan Memorial Stadium. In his remarks, he referred to C.D. Spangler, Jr., president, William C. Friday, president emeritus, and Paul Hardin, chancellor, University of North Carolina; James Taylor, entertainer; and Luther H. Hodges and Terry Sanford, former Governors of North Carolina.

Statement on Support for the North American Free Trade Agreement
October 12, 1993

I am very pleased today to acknowledge the efforts of President Bush, President Carter, and President Ford in convening a group of prominent citizens for NAFTA. Never before have former Presidents joined forces to speak to the Nation about such a pressing issue.

This group includes distinguished Americans who have demonstrated achievement in such diverse fields as government, industry, and civil rights. These individuals have taken many paths to prominence, but they have come to a common conclusion that this trade pact is good for America and good for America's economic fortunes.

This debate is fundamentally about creating jobs and defining America's role in an increasingly competitive global economy. Our fundamental choice is whether we will respond to change and create the high wage jobs of tomorrow or attempt to cling to the jobs of the past. America is always at its best when we look to the future.

While I continue to be concerned about America's rate of economic growth, it is increasingly clear that exports are a key factor in boosting our economy. NAFTA represents the best immediate opportunity to expand our markets and create new jobs at home.

I am increasingly confident that this agreement will be approved by Congress. When thoughtful people look at the facts about NAFTA, they will come to the same conclusion as this group of distinguished Americans. I am hopeful that this group will elevate the debate about NAFTA and participate vigorously in the discussion about which direction America should take.

Remarks and an Exchange With Reporters Prior to a Meeting With Members of Congress
October 13, 1993

NAFTA

The President. Let me make a brief comment and then I'll answer a question or two.

I want to thank the Members of Congress who are here today. This is, as you can see, a fairly large bipartisan group of House Members who have come for one of a series of meetings I've been having to try to persuade them to vote for the North American Free Trade Agreement. I want to reiterate that the thing that has impressed me is that more and more Members are trying to look beyond the politics

of this issue and just ask what's good for America, whether it will create jobs for America, whether it opens the opportunity for more growth. I strongly believe that. I think we're making progress, and I'm looking forward to having a good discussion.

I thank Mr. Michel for coming, and the Speaker who was going to come and couldn't come at the last minute. But we've had good support there, and I'm looking forward to this discussion this morning.

Somalia

Q. Mr. President, Senator Byrd has just announced his intention to introduce an amendment which would cut off funding for the U.S. forces in Somalia February 1st, as opposed to your March 31st. (a) Do you know about this? (b) What are you going to do about it; what does it mean?

The President. Well, I just talked to him. He said that he has—he started off at December 1st as a hard deadline and now says February 1st, and the President can ask for an extension and the Congress can give. So I appreciate Senator Byrd working with me on it. I've not read it so I can't comment on the substance of it. I'm very interested in what the details are. It's not just a question of a deadline, it's also of not tying not just my hands but any President's

hands in foreign policy too much.

Our policy in Somalia, I believe, is beginning to work. I think the obvious import of what's happened in the last few days is that we're moving in the right direction, and I hope we can continue to do that. I can't comment about the specific resolution until I've read it and until I know what the alternatives are.

Q. Are you going to get Durant out? Is there a movement there—the pilot, the captive American?

The President. We're working very hard to get him out.

NOTE: The President spoke at 11:48 a.m. in the Roosevelt Room at the White House. In his remarks, he referred to Robert H. Michel, House Republican leader. A tape was not available for verification of the content of this exchange.

Message to the Congress Transmitting a Report on Somalia
October 13, 1993

To the Congress of the United States:

In response to the request made by the House and Senate for certain information on our military operations in Somalia, I am pleased to forward the attached report.

In transmitting this report, I want to reiterate the points that I made on October 6 and to the American people in remarks on October 7. We went to Somalia on a humanitarian mission. We saved approximately a million lives that were at risk of starvation brought on by civil war that had degenerated into anarchy. We acted after 350,000 already had died.

Ours was a gesture of a great nation, carried out by thousands of American citizens, both military and civilian. We did not then, nor do we now plan to stay in that country. The United Nations agreed to assume our military mission and take on the additional political and rehabilitation activities required so that the famine and anarchy do not resume when the international presence departs.

For our part, we agreed with the United Nations to participate militarily with a much smaller U.S. force for a period of time, to help the United Nations create a secure environment in which it could ensure the free flow of humani-

tarian relief. At the request of the United Nations and the United States, approximately 30 nations deployed over 20,000 troops as we reduced our military presence.

With the recent tragic casualties to American forces in Somalia, the American people want to know why we are there, what we are doing, why we cannot come home immediately, and when we *will* come home. Although the report answers those questions in detail, I want to repeat concisely my answers:

- We went to Somalia because without us a million people would have died. We, uniquely, were in a position to save them, and other nations were ready to share the burden after our initial action.

- What the United States is doing there is providing, for a limited period of time, logistics support and security so that the humanitarian and political efforts of the United Nations, relief organizations, and others can have a reasonable chance of success. The United Nations, in turn, has a longer term political, security, and relief mission designed to minimize the likelihood that famine and anarchy will return when the United Nations leaves. The U.S. military mission is not now nor was it ever one of "nation building."

- We cannot leave immediately because the United Nations has not had an adequate chance to replace us, nor have the Somalis had a reasonable opportunity to end their strife. We want other nations to assume more of the burden of international peace. To have them do so, they must think that they can rely on our commitments when we make them. Moreover, having been brutally attacked, were American forces to leave now we would send a message to terrorists and other potential adversaries around the world that they can change our policies by killing our people. It would be open season on Americans.
- We will, however, leave no later than March 31, 1994, except for a few hundred support troops. That amount of time will permit the Somali people to make progress toward political reconciliation and allow the

United States to fulfill our obligations properly, including the return of any Americans being detained. We went there for the right reasons and we will finish the job in the right way.

While U.S. forces are there, they will be fully protected with appropriate American military capability.

Any Americans detained will be the subject of the most complete and thorough efforts of which this Government is capable, with the unrelenting goal of returning them home and returning them to health.

I want to thank all those who have expressed their support for this approach during the last week. At difficult times such as these, when we face international challenges, bipartisan unity among our two branches of government is vital.

WILLIAM J. CLINTON

The White House,
October 13, 1993.

Message to the Congress Transmitting Budget Deferrals
October 13, 1993

To the Congress of the United States:

In accordance with the Congressional Budget and Impoundment Control Act of 1974, I herewith report eight deferrals of budget authority, totaling $1.2 billion.

These deferrals affect International Security Assistance programs as well as programs of the Agency for International Development and the

Departments of Agriculture, Defense, Health and Human Services, and State. The details of these deferrals are contained in the attached report.

WILLIAM J. CLINTON

The White House,
October 13, 1993.

Letter to Congressional Leaders Reporting on the No-Fly Zone in Bosnia-Herzegovina
October 13, 1993

Dear Mr. Speaker: (Dear Mr. President:)

Six months ago I provided you with my initial report on the deployment of U.S. combat-equipped aircraft to support NATO's enforcement of the no-fly zone in Bosnia-Herzegovina. I am now providing this follow-up report, consistent with the War Powers Resolution, to keep Congress fully informed on our enforcement ef-

fort.

The United Nations Security Council has been actively addressing the humanitarian and ethnic crisis in the Balkans since adopting Resolution 713 on September 25, 1991. As a significant part of the extensive United Nations effort in the region, the Security Council acted through Resolutions 781 and 786 to establish a ban on all unauthorized flights over Bosnia-Herzegovina. In response to blatant violations of these Resolutions, the Security Council adopted Resolution 816, which authorized Member States, acting nationally or through regional organizations or arrangements, to take all necessary measures to ensure compliance with the no-fly zone. NATO and its North Atlantic Council (NAC) agreed to provide NATO air assets to enforce the declared no-fly zone.

As I stated in my April 13 report, this enforcement effort began on April 12, 1993. Since that time, the participating nations have conducted phased air operations to prevent flights over Bosnia-Herzegovina that are not authorized by the United Nations Protection Forces (UNPROFOR). The United States has played a major role by contributing combat-equipped fighter aircraft as well as electronic combat and supporting tanker aircraft to these operations in the airspace over Bosnia-Herzegovina.

Militarily, enforcement of the no-fly zone has been effective. Since the operations pursuant to Resolution 816 began, we have seen no recurrence of air-to-ground bombing of villages or other air-to-ground combat activity in Bosnia-Herzegovina. Although nearly 400 violations have occurred, most have been by rotary-wing aircraft. These flights are difficult to detect because they are of short duration and are flown slowly, at low altitudes, and in mountainous terrain. Consequently, such flights sometimes can complete missions after being detected but before being intercepted. In addition, the violators appear to have learned the limits of our rules of engagement (ROE) and have become adept at playing "cat-and-mouse" games with the interceptors. When intercepted, violators heed the warnings to land, but sometimes the flights continue after the interceptors depart.

These enforcement operations have been conducted safely, with no casualties to date. Consideration has been given to strengthening the ROE to enforce the no-fly zone more aggressively. Because the violations have been militarily insignificant, however, the ROE have not been changed.

The United States continues to make extensive and valuable contributions to the United Nations efforts in the former Yugoslavia. More than 50 U.S. aircraft are now available to NATO for the continued conduct of no-fly zone enforcement operations and possible provision of close air support to UNPROFOR in the future. In addition, U.S. airlift missions to Sarajevo have numbered more than 1,900, and we have completed nearly 1,000 airdrop missions to safe areas, including Mostar. U.S. medical and other support personnel are providing vital services in support of UNPROFOR, while our U.S. Army light infantry battalion deployed to Macedonia has become an integral part of the UNPROFOR monitoring operations there. Finally, U.S. naval forces have completed more than 14 months of enforcement operations as part of a multinational effort to implement the Security Council's mandate with respect to economic sanctions and the arms embargo covering the former Yugoslavia.

Although the no-fly zone enforcement operations have been militarily effective and have reduced potential air threats to our humanitarian airlift and airdrop flights, this is only part of a much larger, continuing effort to resolve the extremely difficult situation in the former Yugoslavia. I therefore am not able to indicate at this time how long our participation in no-fly zone enforcement operations will be necessary. I have continued the deployment of U.S. Armed Forces for these purposes pursuant to my constitutional authority to conduct U.S. foreign relations and as Commander in Chief.

I am grateful for the continuing support of Congress for this important deployment, and I look forward to continued cooperation as we move forward toward attainment of our goals in this region.

Sincerely,

WILLIAM J. CLINTON

NOTE: Identical letters were sent to Thomas S. Foley, Speaker of the House of Representatives, and Robert C. Byrd, President pro tempore of the Senate.

Statement on the Withdrawal of the Nomination of Shirley Chisholm To Be Ambassador to Jamaica
October 13, 1993

I deeply regret that illness has forced Shirley Chisholm to ask that her nomination to be our country's Ambassador to Jamaica be withdrawn. As I said when I first announced my decision to nominate her, Shirley Chisholm is a true pioneer of American politics. Even before she ran for elective office, she had made her mark through her work teaching the children of New York and through the force of her remarkable personality. As the U.S. Ambassador to Jamaica, she would have been a powerful voice for cooperation and justice.

Hillary and I both wish Shirley Chisholm all the best at this difficult time. She is in our thoughts and in our prayers.

NOTE: The President's statement was included in a White House statement announcing the withdrawal of the nomination.

The President's News Conference
October 14, 1993

Somalia

The President. Good morning, ladies and gentlemen. I'm sorry I am a little late, but I just finally got through to Ambassador Oakley, and I wanted to have a chance to speak with him directly for a couple of minutes before I came out here.

I also spoke with Mrs. Durant this morning to congratulate her and to wish her well. Obviously, she is very happy. She has now had an extended conversation with her husband. And he is, as you know, in the U.N. field hospital in Mogadishu. But he will be going to Germany as soon as the doctors say that he can travel. And then, as soon as possible, he'll be back home with his family and his friends. I welcome his release, and I want to express my deepest thanks to the African leaders who pressed hard for it and to Bob Oakley, the International Red Cross, and to the United Nations, to all who have worked on this for the last several days.

Over the past week, since the United States announced its intention to strengthen our forces in Somalia, as well as to revitalize the diplomatic initiative and send Bob Oakley back, we have seen some hopeful actions: the release of Michael Durant and the Nigerian peacekeeper, the cessation of attacks on the United States and U.N. peacekeepers. That demonstrates that we are moving in the right direction and that we are making progress.

Our firm position on holding Durant's captors responsible for his well-being and demanding his release, I think, sent a strong message that was obviously heard. Now we have to maintain our commitment to finishing the job we started. It's not our job to rebuild Somalia's society or its political structure. The Somalis have to do that for themselves. And I welcome the help of the African leaders who have expressed their commitment to working with us and with them. But we have to give them enough time to have a chance to do that, to have a chance not to see the situation revert to the way it was before the United States and the United Nations intervened to prevent the tragedy late last year.

I want to also emphasize that we made no deals to secure the release of Chief Warrant Officer Durant. We had strong resolve. We showed that we were willing to support the resumption of the peace process, and we showed that we were determined to protect our soldiers and to react when appropriate by strengthening our position there. I think the policy was plainly right. But there was no deal.

If you have any questions, I'll be glad to try to answer them.

Q. Mr. President, there's still a $25,000 bounty on Mr. Aideed. Would you still like to see Mr. Aideed arrested? Do you think that's appropriate? And do you think that the United Nations now should release Mr. Aideed's forces that it's captured recently?

The President. Well, let me answer the first question. The United States position is that we have a U.N. resolution which says that there must be some resolution of the unconscionable incident which started this whole thing, which was the murder of 24 Pakistani peacekeepers who were not there in battle but were simply there doing the job that we all went there to do, the humanitarian mission. I think that it's very important to remember that.

It is further our position that we cannot afford to have any police work that we were asked to do as part of the U.N. mission be transformed into a military endeavor that, in effect, made many people believe that there was no longer a diplomatic initiative going on in Somalia. So there still has to be some resolution of that. We have a U.N. resolution, and we ought to pursue it. Now, there may be other ways to do it, and I am open to that.

As far as the release of any people is concerned, that will obviously be up to the United Nations. But they have to consider what our obligations are with regard to the murder of the Pakistani peacekeepers. That's what started this whole thing.

Q. Mr. President, isn't it pretty clear, though, that Aideed must have been given some immunity from arrest, because he talked to reporters? He seems to be pretty available. You don't seem to be laying a glove on him. Have you called off the dogs?

The President. There was no deal made, I can tell you that. We have taken account of the behavior of others on the ground there, and we will continue to do that. But for the next few days, we have to work through what the resolution will be of the U.N. requirement that got us all into the position we were in last week, which is that we have to have some means of resolving what happened to the Pakistanis, who were clearly not in anybody's combat, were just doing their jobs. And we have to do it.

Q. Well, do you hold him responsible?

The President. Well, he offered, if you remember, an independent commission to look into that. The United Nations asked the United States to attempt to arrest him and to go out of our way not to hurt him while arresting him because he was suspected of being responsible. So if he's willing to have somebody that we can all trust look into that, then that's something

I think that Mr. Oakley is certainly willing to entertain over there.

Foreign Policy Accomplishments

Q. Mr. President, despite your success today, there's been a lot of criticism that U.S. foreign policy has been run in a naive and somewhat disorganized way. What's your response to that?

The President. Well, I can tell you first of all, I've had people who were involved in the two previous administrations say that our national security decision-making process was at least as good as the two in the previous ones, perhaps better. Secondly, I think on the biggest issues affecting the future and the security of the United States, we have a good record. We have done very well with Russia, the most important issue. We have set up a system that did not exist before we came to office to deal with the other republics of the former Soviet Union and to work on nuclear issues and other issues. I think we have done quite well with the Middle East peace process and with its aftermath. I think we have done well to establish the groundwork of a new basis of a relationship with Japan and with Asia generally. We have certainly put nonproliferation on a higher plane than it was there before. I think we did very well. The United States had the most successful meeting of the G–7 in over a decade. That was clear: the first time in 10 years we were complimented instead of criticized, making real progress there.

So I think that the people who say that, because of what happened in Somalia last week, have a pretty weak reed to stand on. And in terms of Haiti,—and maybe we can get to that— when I took office, what we had was everybody in Haiti thinking about whether they could leave and come to the United States because they thought there was no way that anybody would ever stick up for the democratic process in Haiti, and the fact that two-thirds of the people voted for somebody to lead their country that was then ousted by the old regime. At least we have made an effort to try to change that. And I assure you that my determination there is as strong as ever.

It's easy to second-guess. When you get into something like Somalia, I think anybody who really thought about it at the time the decision was made—I supported it. I think it was the right thing to do. I think we went there for the right motives. But you had to know when we went there that (a) that there was no way America was going to get out in January because there was no political process in place there that could have given the Somalis a chance to survive, and (b) that there was every chance that someone, for their own reasons, at some point during this mission might kill some peacekeepers, which would complicate the mission.

We are living in a new world. It's easy for people who don't have these responsibilities to use words like "naive" or this or that or the other thing. The truth is, we're living in a new and different world, and we've got to try to chart a course that is the right course for the United States to lead, while avoiding things that we cannot do or things that impose costs in human and financial terms that are unacceptable for us. But I think that in this new world, we've made a pretty good beginning and clearly on the things that affect us most.

Haiti

Q. Mr. President, you were very clear last week in saying that you did not want your reaction to events in Somalia to be the wrong signal to the world's thugs and bullies. I wonder, sir, if it occurs to you that the events of Haiti may indicate that that signal was sent anyway?

The President. No. The problem we had in Haiti with the boat was that we sent 200 Seabees over there who were commissioned specifically to train military officers to do more work to rebuild the country. They were lightly armed; they were not in any way—they were not peacekeepers or peacemakers.

I would remind you that the Governors Island Agreement basically was an agreement among all the major parties in Haiti which clearly set forth the fact that they did not want other countries' forces or a U.N. force coming in there to provide law and order. They wanted French-speaking forces to come in and retrain the police force. They wanted French-speaking Canadians and the United States to come in and retrain the army to rebuild the country.

So those people were simply not able or ever authorized to pursue any mission other than that. I was not about to put 200 American Seabees into a potentially dangerous situation for which they were neither trained nor armed to deal with at that moment. And I did not want to leave the boat in the harbor so that that became the symbol of the debate. I pulled the boat out of the harbor to emphasize that the

Haitian parties themselves who were still there in Haiti are responsible for violating the Governors Island Agreement. We moved immediately to reimpose sanctions to include oil. We are going to do some more things unilaterally in the next day or two. And I think that we still have a chance to get this done, because the people who were there who don't want to give up power agreed to the Governors Island Agreement, and we're going to do our best to hold them to it.

Q. You don't think that those thugs on the dock there in Haiti were encouraged by the events in Somalia to try what they tried?

The President. They may or may not have been, but they're going to be sadly disappointed. I think those people on the docks in Haiti were probably the hired hands of the elites that don't want democracy to come to Haiti. So I don't think they had drawn any sophisticated interpretation from world events. But if they did, they ought to look at what else has happened in Somalia. Look at the way we have bolstered our forces. Look at the reports in the newspaper today.

What we've done in Somalia—let me go back to that—is consistent with our original mission. We did not go there to prove we could win military battles. No one seriously questions the fact that we could clean out that whole section of Mogadishu at minimum loss to ourselves if that's what we wanted to do. The reports today say that 300 Somalis were killed and 700 more were wounded in the firefight that cost our people their lives last week. That is not our mission. We did not go there to do that. We cannot let a charge we got under a U.N. resolution to do some police work—which is essentially what it is, to arrest suspects—turn into a military mission.

But the people in Haiti would be sadly misguided if they think the United States has weakened its resolve to see that democracy—the expressed will of two-thirds of the people of Haiti. I noticed Congressman Kennedy on the television this morning saying that President Aristide won an election victory with a higher percentage of the vote than any leader in the Western Hemisphere. And he can't even get into office. We're going to try to change that.

Let me just make one other comment about Haiti. This is very important to me. In addition to President Aristide, there is a government that has been struggling mightily to function in Haiti, headed by Prime Minister Malval, a business person, a person who basically did not ask for the responsibilities that he has undertaken. I want to send a clear signal today, too, that the United States is very concerned about his ability to function and his personal safety and the safety of his government. That is very important to us. Malval is key to making this whole thing work. He is recognized as a stabilizing figure, as a person who will work with all sides, as a person who will be fair to everybody. And it would be again a grave error to underestimate the extent to which this country regards him as an important part of the ultimate solution.

Somalia

Q. Mr. President, I'd like to go back to what you said about Aideed, because it appears that you've opened the door to leave him a way out this morning when you said that we have to take into account what others did on the ground there. Do you think there's a possibility that Aideed was not directly responsible for the attack on the Pakistani U.N. forces? And do you believe there's also a possibility that Aideed could now become part of the political process and indeed may someday become President?

The President. Well, let me answer the questions somewhat separately. First of all, to take the second question, what happened over the last several weeks—and let me back up and say I understood why the United States was thought to have the only capacity to pursue the police function once the Pakistanis were killed. But keep in mind what that function was: That function was to arrest people suspected of being involved in that, not to be judge and jury, not to say we know exactly what happened, not to find people guilty in advance.

So our young soldiers, at significant risk to themselves, went out of their way to capture people without killing them. As a consequence, however, because of the circumstances, as we all know, several of them lost their lives, and hundreds of Somalis who were fighting them, either with weapons or by getting in their way, lost their lives. Now, that never should have been allowed to supplant—as I said at the United Nations before this incident occurred—that never should have been allowed to supplant the political process that was ongoing when we were in effective control up through last May.

So we had to start the political process again. We have no interest in keeping any clan or subclan or group of Somalis out of the political process affecting the future of their people. The clan structure seems to be the dominant structure in the country. It is not for the United States or for the United Nations to eliminate whole groups of people from having a role in Somalia's future. The Somalis must decide that with the help and guidance, I believe, primarily of the African states and leadership around them, first of all.

Secondly, with regard to the specific incident, what I want to do is to see the U.N. resolution honored. That is, we want to know that there is some effort, honest, unencumbered effort, to investigate what happened to those Pakistanis and to have some resolution of that consistent with international law. We cannot expect the United Nations to go around the world, whether it's in Cambodia or Somalia or any of the many other places we're involved in peacekeeping, and have people killed and have no resolution of it.

Aideed, himself, as you know, offered in a letter to President Carter to have a genuinely unbiased commission look into this and have evidence presented to it. The United Nations may choose to take a different course in this, but we should honor the resolution. That is, you asked me a question about Aideed personally. I can't answer that. I can say that I believe in the strongest terms that the United States should continue to say, if you want us to be involved in peacekeeping, if peacekeepers get murdered doing their job the way the Pakistanis did, and others, there has to be an effort to look into who did it and to hold those accountable. If there is another way to do that, that's fine. What I said at the U.N., I will reiterate: The United States being a police officer in Somalia was turned into the waging of conflict in a highly personalized battle which undermined the political process. That is what was wrong, and that is what we have attempted to correct in the last few days.

Haiti

Q. Mr. President, your statement reassuring Prime Minister Malval of Haiti about his personal security raises the question, of course: Is there a threat to his personal security, and what happens if something happens to Prime Minister Malval?

The President. If something happens to him, it would be a very difficult situation for the

Haitians. It would make President Aristide's job more difficult, and it would further isolate the military and police authorities there and the people who are sponsoring them from the international community. I hope that he is not in danger. I do not have any information that he is in imminent danger. He's continuing to function, but if you know how he works down there, I mean, he has very limited security, he does a lot of work out of his home, he has not constructed a military apparatus around himself. He really is a good citizen serving his country, and he is a necessary part of the glue that would permit President Aristide to go back down there.

Keep in mind, Aristide gave these people amnesty. The truth is, a lot of them never thought he'd do it. I know there are people who have criticized Aristide, who say that, you know, maybe he's not really a political person, can't do this. All I know is that in our dealings with him, he has done what he said he would do. And I think they were disoriented by the fact that he issued the amnesty order when they didn't think he would. And I am genuinely concerned that the forces in Haiti—let me back up and say, they signed off on the Governors Island Agreement because they realized that the sanctions were having a crushing blow on them. And in the end, they and the people who were funding a lot of their activities understood that it was going to cost them more to stay with the present course than to permit this transition to democracy.

And what we're trying to do now—our policy clearly is to remind them of why they signed off in the first place in the most forceful terms and to make it absolutely clear that no one in the international community is going to walk away from our previous policy toward Haiti if they don't honor their commitments under that agreement.

Peacekeeping Missions

Q. Mr. President, would your experiences this month in Somalia and Haiti make you more cautious about sending American peacekeepers to Bosnia?

The President. Well, my experiences in Somalia would make me more cautious about having any Americans in a peacekeeping role where there was any ambiguity at all about what the range of decisions were which could be made by a command other than an American command with direct accountability to the United States here.

Now, to be fair, our troops in Somalia were under an American commander. And even though General Bir was the overall commander, it was clear always that General Hoar here in the United States was the commanding officer of General Montgomery. But because we got a general charge from the U.N. to try to arrest people suspected of being involved in the killing of the Pakistani soldiers, not every tactical decision had to be cleared here through General Hoar.

What I've made clear all along, the reason I've said that I thought that any Bosnian operation would have to be operated through NATO—the Supreme Allied Commander in Europe is an American general that talks every day to the Chairman of the Joint Chiefs of Staff, that works in very clear cooperation with the other NATO forces. They have drilled together. They have trained together. They have worked together. It is a much more coherent military operation. And I would have a far higher level of confidence about not only the safety of our troops but our ability to deal with that as a NATO operation. It's a whole different issue, Bosnia, but I would have a much higher level of confidence there.

With the U.N., let me just say, to go back to the U.N., I still believe that U.N. peacekeeping is important. And I still believe that America can play a role in that. But when you're talking about resolving longstanding political disputes, the United States as the world's only superpower is no more able to do that for other people than we were 30 years ago, or 20 years ago.

That's why if you go back and look at Somalia, what's going to happen here, and compare it to what the U.N. did in Cambodia, where the U.N. went into Cambodia first of all with this theory about what they had to do to or with the Khmer Rouge, and then they moved away from any kind of military approach and sent a lot of very brave peacekeepers, none of whom were Americans and some of whom lost their lives, Japanese and others, they worked through the politics of Cambodia by, in effect, creating a process in which the local people had to take responsibility for their own future. If we are going to do that kind of work, we ought to take the Cambodian model in Somalia and everyplace else.

Where we have to do peacekeeping, if we're

going to do that in a unified command, even if the Americans are always under American forces, we have got to make the kind of changes in the United Nations that I advocated in my speech to the U.N. We have got to have that international peacekeeping apparatus far better organized than it is now. And if you go back to the U.N. speech, it received little notice because of the momentary and important crises in Somalia and elsewhere. But the reorganization of the peacekeeping apparatus of the U.N. is an urgent mission because keep in mind, the U.N. peacekeepers, with no American soldiers there, are involved all over the world now, and they have done an awful lot of good work. But we plainly have to reorganize that and strengthen that. Got to go. Thank you.

Haiti

Q. Would you support the blockade in Haiti, President Clinton? Would you support a blockade?

The President. I support strongly enforcing the sanctions and—I want to answer that. I support strongly enforcing these sanctions, strongly. And over the next few days we will be announcing the form in which that sanctions enforcement will take place.

Thank you.

Q. Is that a yes or a no?

The President. Well, the word "blockade" is a term of art in international law, which is associated with a declaration of war, so I have to——

Q. How about patrols?

The President. I have to be careful in using that word, but I think that we have to enforce the sanctions.

NOTE: The President's 28th news conference began at 10:21 a.m. in the Briefing Room at the White House.

Statement on Action by the House of Representatives on Education Reform Legislation
October 14, 1993

I am pleased by last night's overwhelming vote in the House of Representatives in favor of my Goals 2000 education reform bill. This bill takes an important step towards codifying into law the national education goals.

Goals 2000 invites every State to participate in true systemic reform and will serve as the cornerstone of my administration's efforts to create a world-class system of education and training with high expectations and opportunities for every child.

I want to thank Chairmen Bill Ford and Dale Kildee and other Democratic members of the Education and Labor committee, whose experienced leadership and cooperation across party lines were crucial to attaining this important victory.

I am especially gratified by the broad bipartisan support that Goals 2000 enjoys. I want to thank the many distinguished Republicans, starting with Representatives Bill Goodling and Steve Gunderson, who worked hard over many months to improve this bill and who spoke out so forcefully on its behalf yesterday. And I congratulate Secretary of Education Riley and Secretary of Labor Reich, whose unswerving commitment and effective advocacy were essential.

The enactment of my comprehensive education and training agenda is crucial to achieving an economy that can compete effectively in world markets and create high-skill, high-wage jobs for all Americans. I urge the Senate to bring this legislation to the floor as quickly as possible and approve it with bipartisan support.

It will be a great day for the children of America and for all Americans when I am able to sign Goals 2000 into law.

Statement on the General Agreement on Tariffs and Trade
October 14, 1993

Audiovisual services must be included in any GATT accord. The United States does not want any special favors for American audiovisual creative works, but we also cannot accept that audio products be singled out for unacceptable restrictions. The United States is ready to sign a GATT accord that is fair and just for all. But let me make it clear that fairness and justice must apply to audiovisual works as well as other elements in a final GATT deal. This is a vital jobs issue as well as a fairness issue for America.

Finally, let me say once again that the Uruguay round is very important to the restoration of global growth, and that is why it is essential that we finish this agreement by December 15. That deadline is firm, and our trading partners must be prepared to settle with us on the many outstanding issues if we are to succeed.

Nomination for Ambassadors to Morocco, Sweden, and the Bahamas
October 14, 1993

The President announced his intention today to nominate Marc Charles Ginsburg to be Ambassador to the Kingdom of Morocco, Sidney Williams to be Ambassador to the Commonwealth of the Bahamas, and Thomas L. Siebert to be Ambassador to Sweden.

"It gives me great pleasure to make this announcement today," said the President. "Each of these three outstanding individuals has contributed in his own way to the well being of his community. Through their efforts, they will ensure that our country maintains its strong relationships with our allies in Morocco, the Bahamas, and Sweden."

NOTE: Biographies of the nominees were made available by the Office of the Press Secretary.

Nomination for Deputy United States Trade Representative
October 14, 1993

The President announced today that he intends to nominate former Washington Governor, Booth Gardner to be Deputy United States Trade Representative, with the rank of Ambassador. He will serve in USTR's Geneva, Switzerland office, representing the U.S. before the General Agreement on Tariffs and Trade, the world body on trade policies and practices among nations.

"Booth Gardner was one of the very best Governors with whom I served. He has a solid background in business and trade" said the President, "and knows firsthand the importance of free and fair trade to keeping our economy strong and creating jobs for American workers. I think he will do an outstanding job in Geneva."

NOTE: A biography of the nominee was made available by the Office of the Press Secretary.

Statement by the Director of Communications on the Death of Justice Minister Guy Malary of Haiti
October 15, 1993

The President strongly condemns the killing of Haitian Minister of Justice Guy Malary, a desperate attempt to thwart the will of the Haitian people for democracy. The United States remains firmly committed to the Governors Island accord and the return to Haiti of President Aristide. The President is currently meeting with his advisers on the situation.

Exchange With Reporters Prior to Discussions With Prime Minister Tansu Ciller of Turkey
October 15, 1993

Haiti

Q. Mr. President, have you made a decision on Haiti? Are you going to send U.S. warships to intercept boats to enforce a U.N. embargo?

The President. I'll have a statement about it later this afternoon. When the Prime Minister and I conclude our talks and our public statement, then I'll make a statement about Haiti and take questions on it.

Q. Are you concerned at all about the safety of supporters for Mr. Aristide following the assassination?

The President. I'll talk about it later this afternoon.

NOTE: The exchange began at 11:43 a.m. in the Oval Office at the White House. A tape was not available for verification of the content of this exchange.

The President's News Conference With Prime Minister Tansu Ciller of Turkey
October 15, 1993

The President. Good afternoon, ladies and gentlemen. It's a great honor for me to welcome Prime Minister Ciller to Washington today. She knows our country well from her student days and many subsequent visits. And we had a very good first meeting. We agreed to work together to strengthen our relationship and to develop an enhanced partnership between the United States and Turkey.

For centuries, Turkey has stood at the crossroads of continents, cultures, and historic eras. As the winds of change have shaped both East and West, they have often blown across the Anatolian Plateau. That is why Turkey has always offered the world such a rich and fascinating mixture of peoples, religions, art, and ideas.

Like our own Nation, Turkey is a shining example to the world of the virtues of cultural diversity. And out relationship with Turkey proves that diverse peoples, East and West, Muslim, Christian, and Jew, can work closely together toward shared goals.

Since the time 40 years ago when we stood side by side in Korea, Turkey has served the cause of freedom as NATO's southern anchor and has been a valued ally of the United States. Turkey was a steadfast member of the worldwide coalition that drove Saddam Hussein from Kuwait and instituted international sanctions against Iraq. And for that, the United States remains very grateful. We've all had to pay a price for enforcing the will of the international community, and Turkey in that regard has certainly done more than its share. And we are grateful for its contribution.

We discussed Turkey's role in helping to play a stabilizing role in a host of regional trouble spots, ranging from the former Yugoslavia, through the Caucasus, into Central Asia and, of course, toward the Southeast where Iraq and Iran both continue to pose problems for peace and stability in the world.

We also discussed the need to work for an end to the tragic conflict in Cyprus, which is dividing too many people in too many ways. I am committed to preserving and strengthening our Nation's long tradition of close cooperation with Turkey.

Our security ties must remain strong, our friendship and mutual commitment as allies unswerving. But the focus of our relationship can now shift from a cold-war emphasis on military assistance to an emphasis on shared values and greater political economic cooperation, responsive to the needs of our own peoples and the changing world.

Next month the U.S.-Turkish Joint Economic Commission will convene to work on revitalizing our economic relationship. And I look forward to the results of that effort and to supporting it. The commission will guide a process in which private enterprise will increasingly become the dynamic focus of our enhanced partnership. As an economist, the Prime Minister is ideally suited to lead this endeavor.

Today, Turkey is on the cutting edge of change once again. Its commitment to democracy fulfills the ideals of Ataturk as Turkey enters the 21st century. It's reaching out to the new states of Central Asia, even as it strengthens its longstanding ties to the West.

The Prime Minister represents a new generation of leadership in Turkish politics at a time when the world needs new leadership for a new era. And at a point when our relationship with Turkey is evolving into a new enhanced partnership, it is reassuring to me to know that someone is at the helm in Turkey who understands the needs of the ordinary citizens of that country, their hopes, their aspirations, and is pursuing policies that will give them a chance to fulfill their dreams.

It is, therefore, a great pleasure, once again, to welcome Prime Minister Ciller and to present her to you today.

Madam Prime Minister.

Prime Minister Ciller. Thank you, Mr. President. I appreciate your kind words about my country and about myself.

President Clinton and I had good talks. I believe there was a meeting of minds. And I think it's natural, since we both represent the generation of change, both of us want to do things differently and better, I hope.

Turkey and the United States have a lot in common. However, without losing my sense of dimension, since the United States is a continent and Turkey is a country, I must say that both are dynamic societies and, in some ways, both constitute a mosaic.

My visit takes place at a crucial juncture when our globe is witnessing sweeping and unprecedented changes. The collapse of communism is a victory for democracy and human rights. As representatives of a new generation of leadership, I know President Clinton joins me in welcoming these changes. Yet we both understand that they bring new uncertainties, challenges, responsibilities, and opportunities. Keeping peace is also a challenge. It is in this spirit that we have sent a unit to Somalia.

During our talks, President Clinton and I discussed at length our bilateral relations. I stressed to President Clinton that my government is strongly determined to develop, diversify, and further strengthen our relations to our mutual benefit, in our mutual interest. I am encouraged to see that the American side wishes to reciprocate our political will.

We discussed issues of mutual interest, such as the Middle East, the Gulf, the Russian situation, and the Caucasus. And I must say I am elated about the breakthrough in Arab-Israeli reconciliation. The United States, over a number of years, has shown steadfast leadership. The scene at the White House lawn with President Clinton, Mr. Arafat, and Mr. Rabin gave hope to everyone who have longed for peace in the region.

There is still substantial and difficult work ahead. On the other hand, the tragic situation in Bosnia and the aggression in Azerbaijan continue. Unilateral moves to keep peace, in particular in the Caucasus, are not acceptable.

Turkey, whose geographic position, literally centers her in the ring of fires blazing from the Caucasus and the Balkans, serves as a secular democratic model for her neighboring countries, seeking to develop pluralistic political systems. Likewise, Turkey's secularism acts to deflect the rising tide of fundamentalism. We must help consolidate the democratization process within the framework of this new era.

Turkey is totally committed to this process from Central Asia to the very heart of the European continent. And I am confident, Mr. President, that you will agree that we have the complete support of the United States to assist us in this endeavor. In the long run, strengthening democracy in my region of the world not only promotes peace and stability there but also advances the cause of global peace.

We in Turkey are naturally happy over the fact that cold war has ended. However, we didn't let ourselves be carried away by the euphoria of the times, nor did we minimize the attendant risks. Events have proved us right. The threat perception in and around Europe has changed. But it has changed in different degrees and manners for each of us. I believe the world is passing through a truly transitory phase as recent events in the former Eastern Europe and in the Caucasus have shown. During such times, it is important for the allies to stick together.

The Atlantic Alliance continues to be valid. We attach importance to the transatlantic link and to continued American engagement and leadership in global affairs. After all, in the words of President Wilson, "America was best established not to create wealth but to realize a vision, an ideal, and maintain liberty among men."

Turkey's founding father, Kemal Ataturk, shared that vision. Way back in 1923, he explained it in the following words to an American journalist, "The ideal of the United States is our ideal. Our national pact, promulgated in January 1920, is precisely like your Declaration of Independence." I believe that Turkey and the United States can work together in many ways to the benefit of not only our two countries but to the benefit of all.

I would like to conclude by thanking President Clinton for the hospitality shown to us during this visit and by expressing my satisfaction with our comprehensive and very promising discussions for a more peaceful world.

The President. Helen [Helen Thomas, United Press International].

Somalia

Q. Mr. President, aren't you weakening the Presidential power by committing Congress to set a cutoff date on a foreign policy mission, and also to cut off funding? I mean, doesn't this lead to future problems?

The President. In this case, I don't think so, because it's clear that the United States mission in Somalia—when it was announced by President Bush, the American people were told it might well be over in January, just a matter of a couple of months. It's gone on for a long time now. What I asked the Congress to do was to express itself without unduly tying my hands. And I had set a deadline of March the 31st.

The resolution adopted by the Senate last night prescribes that date, but also says if there are problems, the President can come back and ask for an extension. So under these circumstances, given the unique and traumatic events of the last several days for America, I don't have a problem with the resolution. I was gratified by the margin by which it passed.

I do caution the American people and the Congress from becoming too isolationist on economic or political fronts. This is a time period, as I have said to you before I think, that is something like the time our country faced at the end of the Second World War, when the country was weary, we had paid an enormous price, and we wanted to get back to the problems at home. Today we paid an enormous price, trillions of dollars, for the victory in the cold war. We know that as the threat of nuclear war recedes and we remain the only country in the world with a major army, our immediate physical security is not so much threatened by other nations, but we have to have a sense of where our national interests are and where our values take us.

And I strongly believe that the mission in Somalia helps to build the notion that nations working together can promote peace and freedom and can reach across religious and racial lines to build the kind of common conditions of humanity that we should be supporting.

Turkey has supported us in that. General Bir is the United Nations Commander. The Prime Minister and I had—perhaps I won't embarrass her by saying this—we had a very candid conversation at lunch in which she said the Turkish people ask the same questions of the Turkish— why the Turkish soldiers are still in Somalia— that the American people ask, and we understand that. So the answer to your question is, the exact wording of the resolution, which was carefully worked out—and I thank Senator Byrd and Senator Dole and Senator Mitchell and Senator Warner, Senator Nunn, and all those who worked on it—does not give me pause about the erosion of executive authority. What would give me pause is sort of a headlong rush into an isolationist position that the United States might live to regret.

Yes, Brit [Brit Hume, ABC News].

Somalia

Q. Mr. President, may we take it from what you've said and not said over the past week that there will be no consequences for anyone in your military chain of command as a result of the firefight that led ultimately to the loss of 17 American lives in Mogadishu?

The President. I think that when young Americans are in peril, ultimately the President has to bear that responsibility. The President is the Commander in Chief. And even if the decisions are made down the line somewhere, if they are made in good faith within a span of authority granted to a commander, when people are at risk, it sometimes doesn't work out. And I know of no reason why anyone but me should bear the responsibility for that. If I were to find out someone had disobeyed orders or displayed flagrant incompetence, that would perhaps be a different thing. I have no reason to believe that that occurred.

I have said to you many times—I said before the incident in Mogadishu that I thought the United Nations had erred, and the United States had not pushed them hard enough in resuming the political process even while we were attempting to discover who was responsible for killing the Pakistani soldiers. I still believe that.

Anyone from the Turkish press? We'll take a couple of questions from you, too.

Turkey

Q. Mr. President, is the United States inclined to help Turkey for the losses suffered over the U.N. sanctions in Iraq, and in what way?

The President. Well, the Prime Minister and I discussed that today because—and I guess I should say for the benefit of the American press something the press knows, but the American people should be reminded of—we could not have conducted the successful operation in the Gulf war, and we certainly could not have conducted Operation Provide Comfort to save the Kurds in northern Iraq, had it not been for the indispensable support of Turkey and the support of Turkey not only for Operation Pro-

vide Comfort but for the embargo on Iraq. They have paid a significant economic price.

We discussed today some ideas for helping Turkey in that regard, some of which did not involve the direct outlay of tax dollars or the transfer from one government to another. We agreed there would be further discussions between our people today and perhaps tomorrow. And I think if we reach an understanding, I should let the Prime Minister announce it at the appropriate time if we can work it out. But we're going to have a very serious dialog about that in an attempt to recognize the significant price that Turkey has paid for supporting not only the United States but the world's policies in this regard.

Q. Is the U.S. giving enough support to Turkey's fights against international terrorism threatening its territorial integrity? What is the joint policy toward countries supporting PKK's terrorism?

The President. To both of us, right? Well, that question has become far more immediate and important to the United States just in the last 24 hours as an American citizen has been taken hostage by the PKK. I guess I should start by restating our country's policies: We don't bargain or negotiate with terrorists. And we intend to work with Turkey. It's not fair for us to do, as we've done in the past, to urge Turkey to not only be a democratic country but to recognize human rights and then not to help the Government of Turkey deal with terrorism within its own borders. And so we discussed some ways today that we might cooperate further, and I think you will see some more cooperation between our two nations on this front.

Q. Actually, I had a question for the Prime Minister.

The President. Good. The more, the merrier.

Somalia

Q. As someone who has troops stationed in Somalia, does it concern you at all that the United States is now so committed to withdrawing on March 31st? Does it place you in a difficult position?

Prime Minister Ciller. Well, as Mr. President pointed out, we had a very candid conversation on that. And I pointed out to Mr. President that our people have concern over the issue as well. But if peace is to be maintained and if we will pursue the kind of cooperation we have shown in history, we should be acting together. And in that spirit and in the belief that this will help peace, we sent troops to Somalia. And we intend to have a peaceful solution there, and we hope to support that with that belief.

It is true that my people are concerned over the issue for one more reason. They feel that if our troops are in Somalia, then why aren't they in Azerbaijan as well? Why aren't we acting together in Azerbaijan where there is Armenian invasion? Of course, these are things that we further discussed, and there are ways of cooperation on this as well. And I feel that we should act together on all grounds and try to have a peaceful solution for the world in general.

Q. Are you thinking about withdrawing your troops around the same time as the U.S.?

Prime Minister Ciller. We haven't discussed the details on that during our conversation. As I said, the troops are there for the making of peace. And the sooner we make peace, the sooner we will be out of that. I know that the Congress has a firm date on that, as of yesterday. But it is not something that we have taken up in my country as of yet.

The President. Let me also remind you of one thing about this. The United States went there, as I said, with some people representing that we might even be through within a couple of months, on a humanitarian mission. The United Nations has decided to adopt the humanitarian mission and to try to help keep peace alive to avoid reverting to the conditions that existed before we went there.

That was inevitable and altogether laudable. But there are many other things that have to be done in the world. And the United States will have borne the great mass of that burden. And if we stay through March—we may be able to finish our mission before then, but if we stay all the way, we will have stayed from December of '92 through the end of March of '94, much, much longer than anyone expected us to stay in the beginning, adopting a mission that is somewhat broader than the one we undertook in the beginning. And I think it will make it easier if there needs to be a smaller and less militarily oriented United Nations force continuing to work in a peace process. I think it will be easier, not more difficult, to do.

So this is not calling a halt to the international operation itself or to the end of our involvement in global affairs, but simply to say that to stay a year and 3 months, 4 months, on a mission that was originally touted as perhaps as short as 2 months is quite a long time and enough in terms of the contribution that we have made in this area. So that among other things, we'll be free to fulfill our responsibilities in other parts of the world.

Q. Mr. President, in the last couple of days President Bush, Secretary Cheney, former Secretary Baker have all criticized this administration's handling of the Somalia policy, from a lot of different angles, from naiveté to mission creep; that they said we just went there to feed people, and that's what we should have done. I'm curious, what is your reaction to that criticism, and do you draw the lesson from your own experience in Somalia that maybe there really is no such thing as pure humanitarian intervention, that some level of political authority building or nation building is almost by definition necessary in any of these missions?

The President. First of all, I think it would be inappropriate for me to react to what they said. I will say this. It may have been naive for anyone to seriously assert in the beginning that you could go into a situation as politically and militarily charged as that one, give people food, turn around and leave, and expect everything to be hunky dory.

We tried to limit our mission by turning it over to the United Nations. We recognized that in turning it over to the United Nations we would have to stay a little while longer while the United Nations sought to bring in others to replace us, so that the feeding and the calmness of life that does pervade almost all of Somalia could continue. And what happened was, after the Pakistani soldiers were killed and the U.N. passed the resolution saying that someone ought to be held accountable, at the moment the United States was the only country capable of serving the police function.

You can say, "Well, we should have simply refused to do that and said that was someone else's problem." Then the question would have become, "Well, what kind of a friend is the United States?" The Pakistanis were there shoulder to shoulder with us; they were ready to put themselves in harm's way, just as we were. Should we walk away just because it was them that got killed instead of us? This was not an easy question.

The error that was made, for which I think all of the parties must take responsibility, including the United States, was that when the police function was undertaken, the U.N. mission lowered the political dialog so that the people that were involved over there in Mogadishu thought, "This is not police officers," to use an American analogy, "this is not police officers arresting suspects in a crime. This is a military operation designed to take a group out of a dialog about the political future of Somalia." We never intended that.

And that's where the U.N. mission went awry. And that's where if there was a mission creep, it happened there, and we did not contain it quickly enough. I thought I had done so at my speech to the United Nations. I did my best there. So I think that, if we're going to analyze the error, it seems to me that was where the error occurred.

And I think we learned a very valuable lesson there. The United States should avoid whenever possible being the police officer because it raises all these superpower military, all these other questions—and in any case, we can't go into any sort of situation like this ever and allow the political dialog to collapse, because in the end, all these folks, not just in Somalia but everywhere else in the world, ultimately have to resolve their own problems and take responsibility for their own destiny. So that's the way I would characterize what has happened and what I think we have learned.

And in fairness, I think we ought to give another question or two to the Turkish journalists who are here.

Cyprus

Q. To which extent, Mr. President—to both of you—did you discuss the Cyprus issue? To which extent?

The President. Yes, we discussed the Cyprus issue, and I would like to compliment the Prime Minister. I was encouraged. As I think you probably know, this has been an important issue to me for some time. The Prime Minister expressed her strong support for having the elections in northern Cyprus by the end of November and for resuming a dialog on confidence-building measures and her hope that she would have a constructive relationship with the new Government in Greece. And I think for a Turkish Prime Minister, that's about all I could ask right now. I was very impressed with what she said, and I look forward to our common efforts to try to resolve this in the near future.

Perhaps she would like to say something about it.

Prime Minister Ciller. Would you want me to comment on that further?

Q. Yes, please.

Prime Minister Ciller. Well, as I am having the 50th government and as a new Prime Minister, I feel that a solution in Cyprus should be found and as soon as possible. We feel that there are two communities there that need to come together. Maybe a new methodology can be searched for as well. But the fact remains that a solution should be found there at a time when other crises are emerging elsewhere in the part of the geography.

I was very happy to find out about what happened between Israel and Palestine. And I have to congratulate the leadership that was shown by the President and the United States throughout the history for that. But we are dedicated to finding a solution in Cyprus; very much so.

The only thing that might be of a retardance in that is using of this variable in domestic politics. I think we should not let that happen. We should not let that happen in Cyrus. We should not let that happen in Turkey. We should not let that happen in Greece, as well.

Russia

Q. Mr. President, on the way flying here, our Prime Minister said she has some concerns about Russian advances in the Caucasus, especially in Georgia and Azerbaijan, and that this could lead to a trend of new Russian expansionism. Do you share this concern?

The President. Well, I think Russia is like most other large countries with several million people, there are different currents and different views there. But let me say this: I believe that President Yeltsin does not want an imperialist Russia. I think President Yeltsin wants a Russia that can rebuild itself from within, economically.

As you know, in the conflict in Georgia over the last year there was all sorts of ambivalence and mixed signals from the Russian army stationed there, notwithstanding the position of President Yeltsin at times when the span of control seemed in question.

In terms of Azerbaijan, I think the Prime Minister has made a very important point, that the Russians should, of course, be involved in the resolution of that crisis, but that for the people to feel good about it within the country and Nagorno-Karabakh and beyond, they can't do it alone. Someone else should be involved also in some form or fashion. That's why the United States has strongly supported the so-called Minsk process, in the hope that we won't have an exclusive solution by anyone but that there can be a shared sense of responsibility there.

Thank you very much. Thank you.

Prime Minister Ciller. Thank you. And I have to thank Mr. President one more time for wearing the Turkish manufactured tie. Good sign of cooperation. [*Laughter*]

The President. That's right. This is my gift from the Prime Minister today, so I thought I should wear it.

Prime Minister Ciller. My people will be proud. Thank you very much again.

The President. Thank you very much.

NOTE: The President's 29th news conference began at 1:48 p.m. in the East Room at the White House. In his remarks, he referred to the PKK, the Kurdish Communist Party.

The President's News Conference
October 15, 1993

Haiti

The President. Ladies' and gentlemen, during the past few days, we have witnessed a brutal attempt by Haiti's military and police authorities to thwart the expressed desire of the Haitian people for democracy. On Monday, unruly elements, unrestrained by the Haitian military, violently prevented American and United Nations personnel from carrying out the steps toward that goal. Yesterday, gunmen assassinated prodemocracy Justice Minister Malary.

There are important American interests at stake in Haiti and in what is going on there. First, there are about 1,000 American citizens living in Haiti or working there. Second, there are Americans there who are helping to operate our Embassy. Third, we have an interest in promoting democracy in this hemisphere, especially in a place where such a large number of Haitians have clearly expressed their preference for President. And finally, we have a clear interest in working toward a government in Haiti that enables its citizens to live there in security so they do not have to flee in large numbers and at great risk to themselves to our shores and to other nations.

Two American administrations and the entire international community have consistently condemned the 1991 military coup that ousted President Aristide. In response to United States, Latin American, and United Nations sanctions and pressure, Haiti's military rulers agreed with civilian leaders on a plan to restore democracy. That plan was reached under the auspices of the Organization of the American States and the United Nations. It was concluded on July the 3d on Governors Island here in the United States.

Yesterday the United Nations Security Council, upon the recommendations of its special negotiator for Haiti, Dante Caputo, voted to reimpose stiff sanctions against Haiti, including an embargo on oil imports, until order is restored and the Governors Island process is clearly resumed.

Those sanctions will go into effect on Monday night unless Haiti's security forces put democracy back on track between now and then. I will also be imposing additional unilateral sanctions, such as revoking visas and freezing the assets of those who are perpetrating the violence and their supporters.

The United States strongly supports the Governors Island process, the new civilian government of Prime Minister Malval, and the return to Haiti of President Aristide.

I have today ordered six destroyers to patrol the waters off Haiti so that they are in a position to enforce the sanctions fully when they come into effect Monday night. I have also offered and ordered an infantry company to be on standby at Guantanamo Naval Base in Cuba just a short distance from Haiti. The purpose of these actions is this: to ensure the safety of the Americans in Haiti and to press for the restoration of democracy there through the strongest possible enforcement of the sanctions.

The military authorities in Haiti simply must

understand that they cannot indefinitely defy the desires of their own people as well as the will of the world community. That path holds only suffering for their nation and international isolation for themselves. I call upon them again to restore order and security to their country, to protect their own citizens and ours, and to comply with the Governors Island Agreement.

Q. Mr. President, you warned yesterday about maintaining the safety of the provisional government in Haiti, and yet there was this assassination yesterday of the Justice Minister. You talk about the personal safety of Americans in Haiti, is there anything the United States can do to ensure the safety of President Aristide's Cabinet? Are there any steps that you can take to help this fledgling democracy?

The President. Well we've had discussions with Prime Minister Malval. The Vice President talked to him yesterday, as well as to President Aristide. We have, as you probably know, a significant number of security forces there that we've been working to train, and there may be some things that we can do. But let me say this, we've had discussions with him. We're in constant communications with him, and we are working with him. He has been very forthright in his asking us to reinforce the sanctions strongly and to do whatever we could to try to remind people that there is no other way out for Haiti but democracy. But what we do with regard to his safety, I think, in some ways is going to have to be decided as we go along and with his heavy involvement and support.

Q. Mr. President, are the naval ships going to stop merchant ships going in and out of Haiti and maybe board them to make sure that their embargo is being complied with?

The President. That's what they're going to do. They're going to have a very wide berth to enforce the embargo, or the sanctions, very strongly. And we intend to use the six ships. One of them will be off the coast of Haiti within about an hour. They will be around Port-au-Prince by this evening, and they should all be in place by tomorrow.

Q. Mr. President, what if this embargo induces a new wave of immigrants who say they're political refugees? And what if these refugees come upon the U.S. destroyers, how will you handle that?

The President. Our policy has not changed on that. We still believe that we should process the Haitians who are asking for asylum in Haiti

and that that is the safest thing for them. So we will continue to pursue the policy we have pursued for the last several months. But the purpose of these destroyers is different. These destroyers are going there to enforce the sanctions and to do it very strongly.

Q. But if they come upon refugees, how will they handle them, though? Will they just let them go by? Will they turn them back?

The President. We have no reason to believe that what we have been doing won't work there. And I want to emphasize that our policy has not changed, and we will continue to adhere to our policy with regard to refugees as we work with Haiti and the Prime Minister and the President are restored, the democratic government. But the purpose of the destroyers is to strongly enforce the sanctions.

Q. Mr. President, are you prepared to evacuate American citizens from Haiti if the security situation there does not improve?

The President. As I said to you, we are moving an enhanced infantry company into Guantanamo so that we can be in a position to deal with whatever contingencies arise. I have taken the steps that I think are appropriate at this time. And at this time I have not made a decision to evacuate our personnel. But there are 1,000 Americans there. There are also 9,000 people who have a dual nationality. The 1,000 Americans, most of them are working. There are a handful of tourists there, not many. And there are 140 Embassy personnel there.

Q. Mr. President, since you're dealing with people who agreed to the Governors Island accords in the face of sanctions and then reneged on their promise, what in your view will be sufficient indication of compliance and future compliance so that the embargo and other sanctions will be able to be lifted?

The President. Well, I can tell you one thing that would clearly show a fundamental change, and that is if all the United Nations forces that were supposed to be there to try to help retrain the police and to retrain the army were permitted to do so in a clearly safe atmosphere where they could also be protected. That would be some evidence that we had fundamental change. Keep in mind, this is a different mission than Somalia, different from Bosnia, different from any of the existing U.N. missions.

The purpose of these people—the reason we could not even think about landing the United States forces that were there a couple of days ago is that primarily they were Seabees going there for the purpose of, in effect, helping the Haitian army to become like the Army Corps of Engineers in this country. They were helping them transform their whole mission, not to be fighters anymore but to try to rebuild one of the most environmentally plundered and devastated lands in the entire world.

So if we were seriously proceeding, evidence of that would be all these French-speaking countries being able to bring their folks back in and retrain the police force to be a professional and ordinary, not a renegade, police force and having the French-speaking Canadians and the United States in there showing the army how to build a country instead of tear up the fabric of the society.

Q. President Aristide is asking that the administration increase the Marine contingent at the U.S. Embassy in Port-au-Prince in order to protect the people in his government. Is that under consideration at this point? And if, let's say, members of his government should flee to the American Embassy, would the Embassy provide protection for them?

The President. The answer to your first question is that that is certainly something that I have not ruled out. I have not ruled out anything that I have spoken, just because I haven't spoken about it today. We had a good, long meeting this morning with Admiral Jeremiah and General Shalikashvili and others, Secretary of State, Secretary of Defense. And I am very concerned about the security and safety of the Americans there and the very brave Prime Minister and his government.

Again, I would say to you, whatever specific things we do with regard to the Prime Minister and his government, I would rather come out of statements they make, because I don't want anything I say to upset the balance of forces in Haiti now. But I wouldn't rule out a change in the deployment around the Embassy.

Our first obligation, after all, is to protect the Americans there. But I think what I have done and the announcement I have made today, based on the facts that we have as of when I came out to speak to you, is sufficient as of this moment.

Q. I'm wondering, sir, if you have thought about and considered the possibility that you

might need to have some kind of police force on the ground there in Haiti, much as has been necessary in Somalia in light of the fact that the place has been so violence-prone for so long?

The President. One of the discussions that we had when the gang showed up on the dock was the question of whether the protection for our Seabees, who were after all, as I say, not delivering food, not—their whole goal was to retrain army personnel to rebuild the country. And the agreement under which they were going there was that they would have sidearms and access to rifles—was to whether that was adequate or not. That question will obviously have to be revisited depending upon the developments in the next few days. I wouldn't rule that out, Brit [Brit Hume, ABC News], but I think we ought to—let's see what happens over the next few days.

Q. Mr. President, how does this differ from the word "blockade," which you the other day mentioned as a term of art associated with a declaration of war?

The President. Well, in a literal sense, a blockade would physically stop all traffic going in and out of the country, in this case by water. The United Nations resolution and the sanctions attempt to stop virtually all commercial traffic that could be of some commercial benefit. It does not render illegal every single entering into or exit from Port-au-Prince, Cap-Haitien, or the country in general. So there is a legal difference in that sense.

But if you use the word in the common-sense parlance, we would block any prohibited materials and goods and anything subject to the sanctions from going into the country. That is our goal.

Q. Mr. President, today was the day that Colonel François and General Cédras were supposed to resign their posts—went past. Are there any conversations between the American Embassy people and General Cédras and Colonel François going on? Has there been any attempt to have communications from both sides?

The President. Well, as you know, Mr. Pezzullo went back yesterday. And our Ambassador, Mr. Swing, is down there now. And they are working hard to make sure that everyone in the country knows that the United States is determined to see the democratic process restored. I think they've made their position clear.

NOTE: The President's 30th news conference began at 2:49 p.m. in the East Room at the White House. In his remarks, he referred to Lawrence Pezzullo, U.S. Special Envoy to Haiti.

Statement on Nobel Peace Prize Recipients Nelson Mandela and F.W. de Klerk
October 15, 1993

The Nobel Committee has made an inspired choice in selecting ANC President Nelson Mandela and State President F.W. de Klerk to share the 1993 Nobel Peace Prize. These two farsighted and courageous leaders have overcome a legacy of racial distrust to reach agreement on a framework which has set South Africa on the path of peaceful reconciliation and nonracial democracy. It is entirely fitting that, having worked so closely together for progress, they should share the most prestigious international recognition for their success in setting in motion the transition to a new political order in South Africa.

In selecting these two great leaders, the Nobel Committee has also chosen to honor the many other South Africans who have struggled for so long to achieve racial harmony and justice. It is a testament to the great strides for progress they have made and an endorsement of their hope for a free and democratic South Africa.

It is sadly ironic that just as Presidents de Klerk and Mandela receive the recognition they and their associates so richly deserve, others hesitate to join them in the creation of a new, fully democratic South Africa. Still others are committed to violence which could destroy their current and future achievements. I urge those who have withdrawn from the common political process to rethink their positions and contribute their efforts to complete the great work undertaken by Presidents Mandela and de Klerk.

The American people join me in offering their deepest congratulations to these two great statesmen and all the people of South Africa. I am certain that with similar courage and dedication they can face the challenges and tasks ahead. The many Americans from all walks of life who supported the struggle to end apartheid will be at the side of South Africans as they build a nonracial democracy.

Message to the Congress on the Determination Not To Prohibit Fish Imports From Panama
October 15, 1993

To the Congress of the United States:

Pursuant to section 8(b) of the Fishermen's Protective Act of 1967, as amended (22 U.S.C. 1978(b)), generally known as the Pelly Amendment, I am notifying you that on August 18, 1993, in accordance with section 101(a) of the Marine Mammal Protection Act (MMPA), the Secretary of Commerce certified to me that a ban on the importation of yellowfin tuna and yellowfin tuna products from Panama has been in effect since December 22, 1992. This ban is the result of a finding by the Assistant Admin-

istrator for Fisheries, National Marine Fisheries Service, that Panama's marine mammal program was not comparable to that of the United States, as required by the MMPA.

By the terms of the MMPA, such certification is deemed to be a certification for the purposes of the Pelly Amendment, which requires that I consider and, at my discretion, order the prohibition of imports into the United States of any products from the certified country to the extent that such prohibition is sanctioned by the General Agreement on Tariffs and Trade. The

Pelly Amendment also requires that I report to the Congress any actions taken under this subsection and, if no import prohibitions have been ordered, the reasons for this action.

After thorough review, I have determined that additional sanctions against Panama will not be imposed at this time. The Government of Panama is currently engaged in developing a marine

mammal program that is comparable to that of the United States. The results of these efforts should be evident in an anticipated annual report and request for a finding of comparability for 1994 from Panama.

WILLIAM J. CLINTON

The White House,
October 15, 1993.

Nomination for the Federal National Mortgage Association
October 15, 1993

The President announced his intention today to appoint five members to the Board of Directors of the Federal National Mortgage Association: William M. Daley, John R. Sasso, Russell G. Barakat, Jose Villarreal, and Thomas A. Leonard.

"These five people have consistently proven

themselves among the most capable in the country," said the President. "I welcome their commitment to the work of ensuring sound and fair management at Fannie Mae."

NOTE: Biographies of the nominees were made available by the Office of the Press Secretary.

The President's Radio Address
October 16, 1993

Good morning. I want to talk with you today about our prosperity and our strength now and in the years to come. From the beginning of our administration I promised bold action with a plan for economic growth. We moved to put our fiscal house in order, to bring the deficit down, to spur business investment, and start investing in our own people again. Our plan passed the Congress, and now good things are beginning to happen.

We still have a long way to go, but there's clearly been real progress. Long-term interest rates are at historic lows. That means more businesses investing in jobs and economic growth. Home mortgages are at a 25-year low. That's put more money in the pockets of millions of Americans who are now buying or refinancing their homes.

During the first 8 months of this administration our American economy has created 1.1 million private sector jobs, more than had been generated in the previous 4 years. Our people have been waiting for a long time for a strong

recovery. We've made progress, but we know there are other things we've got to do if we're going to put America at full strength for the long term. For one thing, we've got to have someone to buy our products and our services. To do that, we've got to look beyond our borders, to jolt our export markets so they will grow and create jobs here at home.

All wealthy nations are finding today that they can't create jobs without expanding trade. It's not just the United States, the same thing is true in Germany and the rest of Europe and in Japan. I know we can do it because, just as with the rest of the progress we've made so far, we've got a plan to increase exports. Already we've lowered cold war trade barriers, $37 billion worth of high-tech equipment which we can now sell in the export markets. We're working with Japan and with the entire international trading system to open up new markets for our manufactured products. And we've got a very important part of that plan right here in our area, called the North American Free

Trade Agreement. Perhaps you've heard it called NAFTA. The bottom line is this: NAFTA will help create export relationships that will produce jobs, 200,000 of them by 1995, and will continue to create jobs in the future. It will help our economy to grow.

Everywhere on Earth, more exports mean more jobs. And these jobs on average pay better, 17 percent better than jobs that don't have anything to do with exports. Critics may say what they will, but they can't dispute the facts. We are competing in an era of almost unimaginable economic change, where investment and information can cross the globe in the flicker of a computer screen. It's a new world. But on the trade front, America has too often been playing by old rules.

Our chief rivals in the global marketplace have been adapting. Europe has been developing its own trading bloc. Japan has cornered much of Asia. And now with NAFTA, we can adapt by using our friends and neighbors, first in Canada and Mexico and eventually in the rest of Latin America.

With NAFTA, our products will have easier access to Canada and the second fastest growing market in the entire world, Latin America. Without NAFTA, one of our best markets, Mexico, could turn to Japan and Europe to make a sweetheart deal for trade. With NAFTA, we'll be creating the biggest trading bloc in the world right at our doorstep and led by the United States. Without NAFTA, Mexico could well become an export platform allowing more products from Japan and Europe into America.

Why would we want that to happen? It's no accident that NAFTA is supported by every living former President, almost every serving Governor, and leaders of both parties. And yet, I know many Americans are worried about the agreement. They've been told that companies will head South once the ink is dry because wages are lower and environmental investments are cheaper in Mexico. But all the wishing in the world won't stop those companies from leaving today. Today companies can go to Mexico and produce for the American market with low tariffs if they want to. But NAFTA will require Mexico to enforce its own environmental laws and labor standards, to raise the cost of produc-

tion in Mexico by raising wages and raising environmental investments. That will make it less likely, not more likely, that a company will cross the Rio Grande River to take advantage of lower wages or lax pollution laws.

I say again, under NAFTA more jobs will stay at home here in America and more American exports will head to Mexico. NAFTA means exports, and exports mean jobs. I believe with all my heart the fear stirred up over NAFTA flows from the pounding the middle class took over the past decade and a half, not from NAFTA itself. But I have to tell you, as your President, I could not be for this trade agreement unless I believed strongly that we needed to ensure the economic security of our hardworking middle class families.

That's why I'm fighting in Congress to pass NAFTA when it votes on it next month. I hope you'll tell your Representatives that you want it to pass, too. If you want to create more American jobs, if you want to lower the differences in cost of production in America and Mexico, if you want to take down barriers in Mexico to exports, then you should want NAFTA.

And let me say again, America right now has a trade surplus with Mexico. Mexicans, even though their incomes are lower than Americans, are the second largest purchaser of American products per person, second only to Canada. This means greater opportunities for our people and more jobs. I hope that you will support it.

Before I close, I want to say a word about our brave helicopter pilot who was held and then released in Somalia. Tonight Michael Durant is on his way home. We are thankful beyond words that Chief Warrant Officer Durant will be reunited with his family and that he will recover from his wounds. At the same time, our hearts and the hearts of all Americans go out to the 18 families who are grieving tonight for their loved ones who were lost in Somalia and to nearly 100 others who were wounded. They and their comrades are in our prayers.

God bless you all, and thanks for listening.

NOTE: The President spoke at 10:06 a.m. from the Oval Office at the White House.

Remarks to the National Breast Cancer Coalition
October 18, 1993

Thank you very much. Secretary Shalala and Fran, Dr. Love, distinguished Members of Congress, Mrs. Cuomo, Mrs. Florio, and all of you distinguished guests. It's wonderful for me to be here today.

I was sitting here thinking that I more or less feel like the fifth wheel now. Just about everything that needs to be said has been said. But we sort of felt one man ought to talk on this program. And I won the lottery. [*Laughter*]

In the 3 minutes that will elapse at the beginning of this talk, another American woman will be diagnosed with breast cancer. If I speak for 12 minutes, another woman will die of it during the course of the remarks. And yet we know that one in every three American women does not receive the basic services, like mammographies, which can help to detect breast cancers and that the cost of not dealing with this amounts to about $6 billion a year to this country over and above all the human heartbreak involved.

Now that means that this is another one of those terrible American problems that is not only tearing the heart out of so many families but also has left us again with no excuse for why we would spend so much money picking up the pieces of broken lives when we could spend a little bit of money trying to save them.

We know all the stories; many of you here are the stories. I appreciate the reference to my brave mother, who struggles on with her breast cancer condition and who has resumed her remarkable life, but who also knows how much more we need to do. I'm glad to see Sherry Kohlenberg's husband and son here. When she came to see us in the Oval Office— Sherry was one of our 50 faces of hope, and we kind of keep up with all those folks that, to us, symbolize what we wanted this administration to be about. And when Sherry came to see us last June with Larry and with Sammy, she said, "Don't ever forget what this does to the people who are left behind." And I'm glad to see them here today, and I'm glad they had the courage to come to remind us of that.

Since we know that there are a lot of things we don't know, it's important that we focus on research as well as treatment, that we focus

on detection early as well as care. In my first budget submission, I recommended the creation of the office of research on women's health and the largest increase in funding for breast cancer research in the history of the National Institutes of Health. When you add that up to the increased funding for detection and preventive services at the Center for Disease Control, the Food and Drug Administration, and the Department of Defense, together the combined expenditures approved by this Congress, thanks in no small measure to these women who are here, amounts to about $600 million this year alone.

I also want to emphasize that in the health security plan that I have proposed to the Congress we provide for increases, not decreases in medical research and a means to fund those increases in medical research. We cannot provide basic security to all Americans and forget about the research that needs to be done on the things we don't know how to cure yet.

To help to coordinate our research and delivery efforts, in mid-December Secretary Shalala will bring together a broad range of health professionals, Government agencies, and groups like yours to develop a national action plan for the prevention, the diagnosis, and the treatment of breast cancer. A national strategy is what these petitions are all about. And while I am trying to reduce the volume of paperwork in Washington—[*laughter*]—frankly, I'm glad to see these here. We will do better, and you will help us. And we will have this national action plan.

I also want to point out that the health security plan that Hillary and I are fighting so hard for, along with the other members of our administration, will also fundamentally change the dimension of the fight against breast cancer. It is a plan that clearly shows the sign of several strong women at work, including two on this platform, based on the notion that when it comes to health care research and delivery, women can no longer be treated as second-class citizens.

We began to manifest that commitment, frankly, in this budget which was just passed, in which virtually everything was cut or frozen but which increased services for early childhood and for little children. We also believe that we have to further increase our investments in these things, in prenatal, in maternal and child health care and nutrition, and in detecting and preventing diseases.

We believe that we need a health security plan that guarantees to every American a comprehensive package of benefits that not only can never be taken away but that includes preventive services to try to keep people well as well as help them when they're sick. We believe that some of these preventive services are so important that they should indeed entail no out-of-pocket costs at all to American citizens when the considered medical judgment is that everybody should get them on a regular basis. That includes routine clinician visits and not only appropriate breast exams but also important procedures like immunizations and Pap smears.

We also know that we can reduce deaths by making mammography widely available and by encouraging its use. And this plan covers these mammograms at no additional cost to patients for all women over 50 and provides mammograms where important in the judgment of the physician and the woman in every case where there is a health care plan. So if this plan passes, for the first time everybody who's got a health insurance policy, which will be everybody in America, will have mammograms in the policy. That is a very important thing.

The unique structure of this plan, with some preventive benefits absolutely free to Americans in the highest risk categories, was based upon the best available scientific evidence expressed in the findings of the United States Preventive Services Task Force and supported by forthcoming guidelines, for example on mammograms, from the National Cancer Institute. They were based on the best available scientific evidence, I will say again. And I very much appreciate the fact that just before we came up here today, Hillary whipped out an article that had Dr. Love quoted, and she said, "Have we done it like you said we should?" and Dr. Love said, "Yes." I felt like I had gotten an A in class. [*Laughter*]

I also want to emphasize that none of this can ever be fixed in stone. You hear a whole lot of discussion as we get into the debate on the health care plan about how this or that or the other problem is not fixed. Well, my fellow Americans, this is a very dynamic thing, health care. And even the countries that have the best system, if you define "best" as high

quality results, universal coverage, preventive services at lower costs, even they have continuing problems. You have to work on this forever. This is the beginning of what we should have done a long time ago, not the end of it. And one of the things that we need to make a commitment to do now is to update all these preventive approaches as new and better studies become available, based on recommendations like those we'll soon receive from the President's Special Commission on Breast Cancer. They've worked hard for 2 years, and I'm looking forward to that report.

Finally, let me say that—and this is an important thing to women who live in inner cities or remote rural areas—the best health care coverage in a policy is no good unless you can access it. We can have great policies and coverage, but we also have to have access. So we had a whole group of people who work all across America on these problems. And I myself spent a whole 4-hour period listening to this because I've worried about it for years, coming as I do from a small rural State, to be able to say to you that if this plan passes as we propose it, we'll be able to have the latest technologies given to doctors and nurses who can practice in the smallest rural communities and the most isolated parts of our large inner cities, to allow health professionals to contribute their best to all the people of this country who need these preventive services.

As you know from your efforts to gather all these signatures, change requires that people work together. But when they work together and make their voices heard, change can come. I'll never forget the meeting I had with breast cancer advocates at a hospital during the election, and I told Hillary after it was over that if we had the energy of the women who were there at that meeting concentrated on about four major things we could turn this country around in 3½ weeks.

And so I say to you in closing, we need that energy. And we will give you a vehicle, beginning with Secretary Shalala's meeting in December, to develop a national action plan on breast cancer. But it is important that that plan be fit into a larger commitment to the health care of Americans: to put women's health concerns, from research to the delivery of health care, on an equal footing with men's; to say that it is better to focus on keeping people well than just treating them when they're sick, and when you focus on that you will find them when they're just a little sick and be able to get them well a whole lot quicker; and finally, to say that none of this will ever come to pass until we finally join the ranks of every other advanced country in this world and give every citizen of this country health care that is always there, that can never be taken away from them.

Every American can bring some weapon to this struggle, and your weapons are unique. They are not the dollars and deal-making talents of lobbyists or the stethoscopes or syringes of doctors and nurses. But they are the power of the pen and the petition and, most important of all, the power of the personal story. For in the end, America ought to be shaped by the lives of Americans, not just by the interests of Americans but by the values of Americans, not just by what we want when everything is going well but by what we need in our direst and most difficult moments.

I urge you to continue to fight in the months ahead. We can win this battle. As a part of the national drive for early breast cancer detection, tomorrow thousands of doctors and hospitals and medical centers across the country will offer discounted mammograms, thanks in no small measure to all of you.

I'm going to sign this proclamation when I finish my remarks which declares tomorrow National Mammography Day. I want to thank all the Members of Congress who pushed this through and two who are not here, Senator Biden and Congresswoman Marilyn Lloyd, who were sponsors of this legislation. And I want to remind you that you've got to continue to bring this level of intensity, of energy, of passion to this battle. You have the most powerful thing of all, personal stories. When American politics works best, it's when it reflects the lives of the American people. You can make sure on these issues we do that. And I hope you will.

Thank you, and God bless you all.

NOTE: The President spoke at 11:33 a.m. in the East Room at the White House. In his remarks, he referred to Frances Visco, president, National Breast Cancer Coalition (NBCC); Dr. Susan Love, founder of the NBCC and director of the Breast Center at the University of California, Los Angeles; Matilda Cuomo, first lady of New York; and Lucinda Florio, first lady of New Jersey. Following his remarks, the President signed the National Mammography Day proclamation, which is listed in Appendix D at the end of this volume.

Interview With Radio Reporters
October 18, 1993

The President. First of all, I want to thank all of you for coming today and for offering all of us this opportunity to have a conversation with the radio listeners around the country and beyond.

I thought I would open just by saying that I have sent a letter this afternoon to Senator Mitchell in the Senate about some potential amendments to the defense appropriation bill and one actual amendment dealing with Bosnia, Haiti, and the whole command and control apparatus of our military as it relates to cooperation with other countries in peacekeeping and other endeavors. That amendment has actually been introduced.

The letter essentially says that I oppose the amendment that affects the way our military people do their business, working with NATO and other military allies. I think it unduly gets into the details of the command and control operations of the military, which I think is an error, and that I would oppose any amendments with regard to Haiti and Bosnia that were of questionable constitutionality and unduly restricted the ability of the President to make foreign policy, and outlines some of my concerns.

In Haiti, my concerns are that there should be no restrictions that would undermine the ability of the President to protect the Americans on Haiti, that would aggravate the likelihood of another mass exodus of Haitians, or that would send a green light to the people who think they've got the best of both worlds: they got the sanctions lifted, and then they broke their word on the Governors Island Agreement.

With regard to Bosnia, the amendment simply points out that the United States has very strong NATO allies and that there were strict conditions that I have put on any kind of cooperation in Bosnia with NATO to enforce a peace agreement and that I think most Members of Congress agree with those conditions, but I don't think we should have an amendment which would tie the President's hands and make us unable to fulfill our NATO commitments, thus raising all kinds of questions about the long-term relationship of the United States to Europe.

So that's what the letter says. There is only one amendment so far that has been offered, and we are discussing with various Members of Congress other proposed amendments. We'll just have to see what happens. But I thought I ought to say clearly today that I would strenuously oppose such attempts to encroach on the President's foreign policy powers.

Now we can go to the questions. Mark [Mark Knoller, CBS News].

Haiti

Q. Thank you, Mr. President. Your opening statement raises the question of whether the United States would be willing to use military force for the purpose of removing the military leadership from Haiti and reinstalling President Jean-Bertrand Aristide in power.

The President. Let me tell you what I have done today on Haiti, first of all. I just signed the Executive order freezing the assets of any people who are supporting the military and police leaders who have continued to fight the resumption of democracy and who are responsible for the bad things that have happened down there in the last few days. I have also, with the authorization of the Haitian government, directed our ships in the area to move closer to the shore so they will be in plain sight. And that has been done today.

I think we should continue to work with President Aristide and with Prime Minister Malval. They want to go back to the sanctions. Remember, once the sanctions were tough, and they included oil, they produced the Governors Island Agreement. And what happened is that people who have an economic stranglehold on Haiti got what they wanted with Aristide's request, that is, lifting the sanctions. They got the amnesty that Aristide promised, they thought he would never give. And then, when

time came for them to deliver what they agreed to do, they didn't do it.

So I think the appropriate position for us to take at this time is to go back to those sanctions and make them as tough as possible and enforce them as completely as possible. And that is what the Prime Minister wants us to do and what President Aristide has asked us to do. I think it would be an error for me to discuss what further steps might or might not be taken. After all, we do have—I'll say again, we have 1,000 Americans there, and we have another 9,000 people with dual citizenship, and we'd have no way of knowing what will or won't happen.

But what the Haitians want is for the conditions of legitimacy to be maintained and restored. That is, the Haitian people have expressed their desires; two-thirds of them voted for President Aristide. And in terms of the questions that have been raised again in recent days about whether he could or could not govern the country, that's why he worked so hard with our support to get Mr. Malval, who plainly can run the government, as one of the ablest people in the nation to be the Prime Minister so they'd have the kind of partnership that would work. So I feel comfortable that they are capable of working with their friends and allies in the area to bring about a more democratic and a more prosperous Haiti if given the chance.

Health Care Reform

Q. Mr. President, economists are expressing some concern of late about your health care reform plan and about whether it might grow considerably larger than you envision. What assurances can you give the American public that it either will not grow out of control or that the need for universal health care is worth it ballooning to the size of, say, Medicare and Medicaid, which are 10 times larger than originally predicted?

The President. First of all, let me say that it's not a Government program. The Government will only insure the unemployed uninsured. Two-thirds of the funding for this program will come from employers and the employees who don't presently contribute anything to the American health care system.

Secondly, where have these economists been for the last 15 years? I mean, the American health care system is already 40 percent more expensive than any other one in the world and the only advanced health care system in the world that can't seem to figure out how to provide coverage to everybody while spending 40 percent more than anybody else spends.

The budget we just passed in this Government has Medicare and Medicaid going up at 3 times the rate of inflation. We proposed to reduce that in our bill. We have also ceilings on how much health care expenditures can increase in any given year if the competition doesn't cut the costs.

Now, if you look around the country at the places which have tried serious efforts at managed competition, including bringing the Medicaid program into a competitive arena, there's every indication that the rate of increase will slow down and that it will work. But the economists, they seem to want it all ways. They criticize me on the one hand for having a ceiling on how much costs could increase in any given year and then saying we don't have any guarantees, if you take it off they won't increase more. And it is difficult to imagine how we could design a system that would have costs more out of control than the one we have. I mean, the reason we have so much support here from employers in heavy industry, for example, who already cover their employees is that they're being killed by the cost increases.

The system we have is irresponsible and out of control financially, and doesn't provide health care security to Americans. So we think there are plenty of protections built in to slow the rate of increase in costs. In fact, if anything, I think we've been certainly realistic and then some, in estimating how fast we can slow costs down. That is, even under our plan, it is estimated that the percent of our income going to health care will go from about 14.5 to about 18 by the end of the decade, and that if we just stay with the system we've got, which is the alternative—in all these things, you've got to ask what's the alternative—we'll go from 14.5 to 19 to 20 by the end of the decade. We have allowed and budgeted for significant increased expenses in health care.

Republican Criticism

Q. Mr. President, in the past week or so you and your foreign policy team have come in for some pretty blistering criticism, especially from a group of prominent Republicans. Richard Lugar, Dick Cheney, Dan Quayle, James Baker, and Robert Dole have all been very, very critical of your foreign policy. And some members of

your administration have suggested that's politically motivated, these people might be running for President. What do you make of it, and how do you react to those criticisms?

The President. I think you can monitor their travel schedules and statements as well as I can. I don't have anything to say about that. I'm going to do my job as best I can. I'm going to try to support a bipartisan approach to foreign policy. I'm going to try to involve Republicans and Democrats in the process of consultation and getting as good advice as I can all the way along. And I think that you have to expect that when things go very well, as they did with Russia and the Middle East, people will say you're doing fine, and if difficulties arise, then some will say that you didn't do fine. So I just don't want to get into the politics of it.

If you want to talk about any specific policy in any specific country, I'll do my best to answer that. But I think it serves no useful purpose for me to engage any of them in this sort of debate. Whatever the political motivations are, I have a contract that runs for a specific amount of time. I'm going to do the very best I can during that time, and then when the time is up the American people can make their own judgments. I haven't even been President a year. I don't have any interest in starting a political debate now.

Administration Goals

Q. Even though it's been less than a year, Mr. President, it's been a very ambitious Presidency with a lot of projects you've taken on yourself, health care reform, reinventing Government, national service, things you inherited like Somalia, Haiti in a way, NAFTA. Is there ever coming a point, is there now a point that you just have to say, enough is enough for now, the plate is too full, we have to resolve some of these things before we get on with other things?

The President. Oh, sure. And we have taken that position. I mean, first of all, if you go back to the budget, we kept the budget front and center until that was resolved. And it plainly has worked rather well. Long-term interest rates are still below 6 percent. The budget did some remarkable things. It dramatically broadened the availability of college loans to students, and it has the most significant piece of tax reform for working families in 20 years by increasing the earned-income tax credit, so that all working families on modest incomes with children will know they'll be lifted above the Federal poverty lines. That's a lot to accomplish in a year right there.

The national service bill passed, and very well, and of course, a number of other pieces of legislation have. And now, what we're going to focus on between now and the end of the year is making as much headway as we can on the first round of reinventing Government cuts, on the crime bill, on the political reform initiatives that some of which have passed the Senate already, the campaign finance reform and lobby reform bill, and on getting the health care bill heard and setting schedules there so we'll know that it will be reviewed along with all other ideas in a prompt and timely fashion, and we'll be able to see as we wind up here a process which unfolds next year and brings us to a date-certain vote.

But we do have a lot going. We probably had more done this year than in any given first year in a long time, and there's still a lot more to do. For example, we started our welfare reform task force hearings around the country, but I don't intend to offer any legislation on that until next year. And there will be a lot of other things that will come up as we go along next year. We want, for example, to change the whole unemployment system, as you know, to a reemployment system. We don't think that will be offered until next year, to give the American people a system of lifetime education and training.

I do hope that we can pass as many bills as possible this year. I was heartened by the fact that the House passed our education reform bill, the Goals 2000 bill, with such a big bipartisan majority last week, which made me think we could probably pass that bill completely before the Congress goes home the end of the year.

Russia

Q. Mr. President, it's coming up on 2 years since the end of the Soviet Union and the declaration by the remaining states to call themselves democracies or create democracies. Secretary Christopher is headed over there. Can you tell us what the objective of his trip is? Will he be looking to set up a summit meeting?

The President. Well, there is a possibility, of course, that President Yeltsin and I will meet again early next year; I have to go to Europe

to the NATO summit. But primarily, what he wants to do is to convey the continuing support of the United States for democracy and reform in Russia, to urge the Yeltsin administration on in their efforts to complete the timetable to get a new constitution and to have legislative elections and to restore completely the conditions of democracy in Russia, and to review the progress on the Russian aid package, both the ones, the two passed by the United States Congress here with strong bipartisan support and the international package that came out of the G-7 summit. And so he'll be doing all those things. And I'm sure they'll review some of the difficulties in that part of the world, too. President Yeltsin also has his share of foreign policy problems that he can't fully solve. But we'll talk about that. We're interested very much in some of those things. Especially we'd like to see the last Russian troops withdrawn from Latvia and Estonia, as they have been from Lithuania.

Haiti

Q. Mr. President, if we could return to the Haiti issue for just a moment. Senator Dole said he didn't think it was worth any American lives to restore President Aristide. You indicated you didn't want to go too far into options. But are there conditions beyond, say, a direct physical threat to the U.S. Embassy compound in Port-au-Prince under which you would consider committing U.S. troops to Haiti? For example, attacks or killings of foreigners, a flow of refugees, or maybe just threats against foreigners? Are there any conditions for sending U.S. troops?

The President. I just think at this time it's better for me not to rule in or out options. Keep in mind, the Haitian Government, as we speak, has not asked for that and does not want that. And keep in mind that the sanctions did work once before to get this agreement, which was not honored perhaps because we raised the sanctions, we lifted the sanctions.

But let me remind you that the circumstances of this need to be focused on. Haiti is very much in our backyard. The people wanted democracy. There is the continuing issue of whether there would be another exodus of Haitians trying to come to the United States, something which I think is not in their interest or ours but is something that the present conditions could make more likely. And we do have those Americans there.

So what I want to do today is to encourage Prime Minister Malval and the brave people who are in his government and the good people of Haiti who plainly want democracy and are being pushed around by the only guys in town with guns, which I regret very much. But we are trying to preserve the legitimacy of democracy there.

Now, the truth is, as you know, there are people in this country, in the press, and in the Congress and elsewhere, who, notwithstanding the vote of the Haitian people, basically have never felt very strongly about returning Aristide anyway and have questioned his fitness to be President. You can do that with the winner of any election. But all I can tell you is that I would just like to observe just a couple of things. Number one is, unlike his adversaries, President Aristide has done everything he said he would do under the Governors Island Agreement, including giving them amnesty. And secondly, recognizing his lack of experience in politics and business, he reached out to a man like Malval, who's plainly one of the ablest people in the country and clearly a very stable and reassuring figure, asking him to run the government. So I feel that we should support the democratic movement in Haiti. And I think that the steps we're taking now are the appropriate ones.

Assistant Attorney General Nominee

Q. Mr. President, have you decided on a nominee for the position of Assistant Attorney General for Civil Rights?

The President. I don't want to give you an evasive answer, but let me tell you what happened. We had, weeks ago, a nominee who declined the position for personal reasons. And the Justice Department was asked, the Attorney General specifically was asked, to make another recommendation. I believe that she has a recommendation for me which I have not yet formally received. But I am not positive of that, but I believe so.

Gun Control Legislation

Q. Mr. President, I'd like to ask you about a subject that you've brought up in a number of your remarks lately. You've been discussing the issue of gun control, firearms violence, the extremely high cost of health care related to firearm injuries. Senator Chafee of Rhode Island has once again introduced legislation which is

pending in the Judiciary Committee now which would ban the sale, manufacture, possession, importation, or exportation of all handguns with exceptions for law enforcement, military, and licensed target clubs. You've talked about your support for the Brady bill and for a ban on assault weapons. How would you feel about Senator Chafee's bill, which I understand Dr. Sullivan, former HHS Secretary, is testifying on tomorrow?

The President. Well, I have to read it, but I think it might go a little far if it bans all handguns, just because I think that there is a lot of evidence that Americans have used handguns responsibly for sporting purposes, that they're not all used as weapons for committing crimes or killing people. I do believe, however—and let me say first—secondly, as a practical matter, I have not yet been able to get Congress to vote on the crime bill, including the Brady bill and the vote to ban a comprehensive list of assault weapons.

I also know that I heard that Senator Kohl has an amendment, which I would encourage, which would make national the ban on ownership or possession of handguns by minors unless with their parents or another supervising adult in an appropriate setting, which might be the way to go on the issue that Senator Chafee is concerned about. Nonetheless, I hold him in the highest regard. He's, I think, an extremely responsible person, and I welcome the hearings on his legislation. But I would have a little problem with a total ban on handguns. I would have a problem with that based on what my understanding of the situation is.

Again, we ought to focus on the Brady bill, the assault weapons ban, and banning possession by minors right now. Since I have been working on this in the last several months, one of the multitude of statistics that's made the biggest impression on me is the one that we were told a couple of weeks ago, that now someone shot in a criminal encounter is 3 times more likely to die from a gunshot wound because they're likely to have nearly three bullets in them, as opposed to only 15 years ago. That is a huge statistical change. And of course, as I pointed out, these wounds and the homicides put an enormous financial burden on this country, on the medical system, on the criminal justice system.

But mostly, it's an incredible human problem. We've got 90,000 people in the last 4 years murdered in America, most of them by gun-shots. That's more in any single year than were ever lost in a single year in the war in Vietnam. I think the time has come to do something about this. And I'm hopeful that both Houses of Congress will act on the crime bill and on the assault weapons bill before the end of the year. I hate to keep coming back to this, but right now I don't know that we have the votes to pass the assault weapons ban in the Congress. And I hope we can get the votes to do that and to pass the limitation on minors and posses-sion or ownership of handguns. I think if we push those now in the Brady bill, then the Con-gress could really make a dent on the exposure of Americans to lethal violence.

War Powers Resolution

Q. Mr. President, could I go back to your comments about the use of American military force and your discussions with Congress? Would you oppose, would you veto legislation which contained an amendment requiring you to ask and get the consent of Congress before you use troops in Haiti or Bosnia? And how far do you think the congressional role in the war powers area goes?

The President. Well, let me say, my letter says that I want to resist and that I urge the Senate not to vote for things which unduly in-fringe on the President's power, and certainly not things that are of questionable constitu-tionality. Before I express an opinion about a veto, I need to see a specific piece of legislation. And there are still discussions going on about the questions of Haiti and Bosnia. The whole issue of the War Powers Resolution and the role of Congress and the role of the President obviously has been the subject of virtually non-stop debate in America for the last several years, for all kinds of obvious reasons. Sometimes Con-gress has acted or attempted to act to restrict the President's authority under Presidents Reagan and Bush, and sometimes they have.

All I can tell you is that I think I have a big responsibility to try to appropriately consult with Members of Congress in both parties—whenever we are in the process of making a decision which might lead to the use of force. I believe that. But I think that, clearly, the Con-stitution leaves the President, for good and suffi-cient reasons, the ultimate decisionmaking au-thority. And I think to cut off that authority in advance of it being made without all the

circumstances and facts there before us is an error and could really lead to weakening our relationships with a lot of our allies and encour-aging the very kind of conduct we want to dis-courage in the world.

I understand what's going on here, and it's all perfectly predictable, given any reading of American history and perfectly understandable, given the aversion that Americans have always had to seeing any of our young people die when the existence of our country was not imme-diately at stake. And the President should be very circumspect and very careful in committing the welfare and the lives of even our All-Volun-teer Army. We need to have a clear American interest there, and there needs to be clearly-defined conditions of involvement, and the bur-den is on the President to provide those. But still the President must make the ultimate deci-sion, and I think it's a mistake to cut those decisions off in advance.

Advice From Previous Administrations

Q. Final question. Thank you, Mr. President. In the past week or so, President Bush himself and, as we've already discussed here today, some members of his foreign policy team have criti-cized your foreign policy team. I'm curious about the promise that has been reported that President Bush made to you. And it's also been reported in at least one commentary, that there was an implied promise from your side to go easy on any revelations about the so-called Iraqgate scandal. What can you tell us about your discussions with Mr. Bush on this?

The President. Well, first of all, with regard to the Iraqgate issue, there was no promise ex-pressed or implied. There was no discussion about that between me and President Bush. I believe he said publicly that he would not have anything negative to say about the administration for a year at least, that he thought we were entitled to that.

And again, I just don't want to get into this. This is a free country, people have free speech, they can say whatever they want to say. I think you will agree. And maybe I've been wrong to do it, but I have been pretty careful about fo-cusing on the problems we have in the future and not trying to spend a lot of time establishing partisan blame for the past. I said that in my State of the Union speech. I said it in the health care speech. I said it repeatedly. What's past is past. I'm doing the best I can with the issues that I faced when I came here. If the time comes in the future when I have to engage in a debate with any of those folks about who-did-what-when, I'll do my best to have that kind of a debate. But I just don't think—it doesn't get us very far. And I would hope that if they have a constructive suggestion to make about what America should do, I would be more than happy to take it. I'm not ashamed to ask for advice from anybody, Republicans or Democrats. I've called every living former President, I've called former Secretaries of State, I've called those that agreed and disagreed. As you know, Secretary Shultz thought that the previous administration should have done more in Bosnia, thought that we should. I mean, there are people who have—Secretary Kissinger thought just the reverse. I mean, this is a new and difficult and uncertain time. But if they have anything

to say about what they think we ought to do, I'll be glad to listen, and I'd just ask that it be constructive when they do it.

Q. I'm told by your aides that we're out of time. On behalf of the radio networks, we thank you, and we hope we can make this a regular thing.

The President. I would like to do it on a regular basis. I'm a big radio listener, you know. Except if we did it enough, we could even have Top 10 countdowns in the middle and stuff. *[Laughter]*

Q. We accept the challenge.

The President. Thank you.

NOTE: The interview began at 3:40 p.m. in the Roosevelt Room at the White House. The Executive order on Haiti is listed in Appendix D at the end of this volume.

Message to the Congress on Blocking Property of Persons Obstructing Democratization in Haiti
October 18, 1993

To the Congress of the United States:

Pursuant to section 204(b) of the International Emergency Economic Powers Act, 50 U.S.C. section 1703(b), and section 301 of the National Emergencies Act, 50 U.S.C. section 1631, I hereby report that I have again exercised my statutory authority to issue an Executive order with respect to Haiti that, effective 11:59 p.m., e.d.t., Monday, October 18, 1993, that:

(a) Blocks all property in the United States or within the possession or control of United States persons, including their overseas branches, of persons:

(1) who have contributed to the obstruction of the implementation of United Nations Security Council Resolutions 841 and 873, the Governor's Island Agreement of July 3, 1993, or the activities of the United Nations Mission in Haiti;

(2) who have perpetuated or contributed to the violence in Haiti; or

(3) who have materially or financially supported any of the foregoing; and

(b) Prohibits any transaction subject to U.S.

jurisdiction that evades or avoids, or has the purpose of evading or avoiding, or attempts to violate, the prohibitions in the new order, or in Executive Orders Nos. 12775, 12779, or 12853, except to the extent now authorized pursuant to the relevant Executive order.

I am enclosing a copy of the Executive order that I have issued.

The new Executive order is necessary to further the implementation of the Governors Island Agreement by reaching persons who are supporting the groups fomenting violence and opposing the restoration of constitutional government in Haiti. The new Executive order is to be implemented by the Secretary of the Treasury, in consultation with the Secretary of State.

WILLIAM J. CLINTON

The White House,
October 18, 1993.

NOTE: The Executive order is listed in Appendix D at the end of this volume.

Letter to Congressional Leaders on the Use of United States Armed Forces in International Operations
October 18, 1993

Dear Mr. Leader:

I am writing to express grave concern about a number of amendments that may be offered to H.R. 3116, the Defense Appropriations bill for FY 94, regarding Haiti, Bosnia and the use of United States armed forces in international operations.

I am fundamentally opposed to amendments which improperly limit my ability to perform my constitutional duties as Commander-in-Chief, which may well have unconstitutional provisions, and which if adopted, could weaken the confidence of our allies in the United States. Such amendments would provide encouragement to aggressors and repressive rulers around the world who seek to operate without fear of reprisal.

America's adversaries and allies must know with certainty that the United States can respond decisively to protect the lives of Americans and to address crises that challenge American interests. Successive administrations have found it critical in world affairs to be able to state that no option has been ruled out.

I respect and acknowledge the importance of cooperation between the executive and legislative branches. There will inevitably be give and take between the executive branch and Congress as we work to redefine our role in the post Cold War world. But it is wrong and even dangerous to allow the questions of the moment to undercut the strength of our national security policies and to produce a fundamental shift in the proper relationship between our two branches of government.

The amendment regarding command and control of U.S. forces, which already has been introduced, would insert Congress into the detailed execution of military contingency planning in an unprecedented manner. The amendment would make it unreasonably difficult for me or any President to operate militarily with other nations when it is in our interest to do so—and as

we have done effectively for half a century through NATO. It could lead to an all-or-nothing approach that causes the United States to shoulder the entire burden of a conflict even when a multinational approach would be most effective from the standpoint of military planning, burden sharing and other American national interests.

With regard to potential amendments on Haiti, let me caution against action that could aggravate that nation's violent conflict and undermine American interests. The situation on the ground in Haiti is highly unstable. Limiting my ability to act—or even creating the perception of such a limitation—could signal a green light to Haiti's military and police authorities in their brutal efforts to resist a return of democracy, could limit my ability to protect the more than 1,000 Americans currently in Haiti, and could trigger another mass exodus of Haitians, at great risk to their lives and great potential cost and disruption to our nation and others.

With regard to potential Bosnia amendments, our nation has worked with NATO to prepare to help implement a fair and enforceable peace settlement. This amendment thus could undermine our relationship with our NATO allies and frustrate the negotiation of an end to the aggression and ethnic cleansing in the former Yugoslavia. As you know, I have placed strict conditions on any U.S. involvement in Bosnia with which I believe most members of Congress would agree.

I am committed to full consultation with Congress on our foreign policy. As I have clearly stated for the record, I welcomed congressional authorization for U.S. operations in Somalia and would welcome similar action regarding U.S. efforts in Bosnia, should that become necessary. Further, as this Administration has done and is continuing to do, we will consult with and keep Congress fully informed on these and other issues that affect American national security.

Photographic
Portfolio

Overleaf: Addressing the
Congressional Black Caucus
Foundation dinner at the
Washington Convention Center,
September 18.
Left: Jogging with President Kim
Yong-sam of South Korea on the
White House track, November 24.
Right: Welcoming Pope John
Paul II in Denver, CO, August 12.
Below: Helping to prepare
Thanksgiving dinner for the
homeless at the Covenant Baptist
Church, November 24.

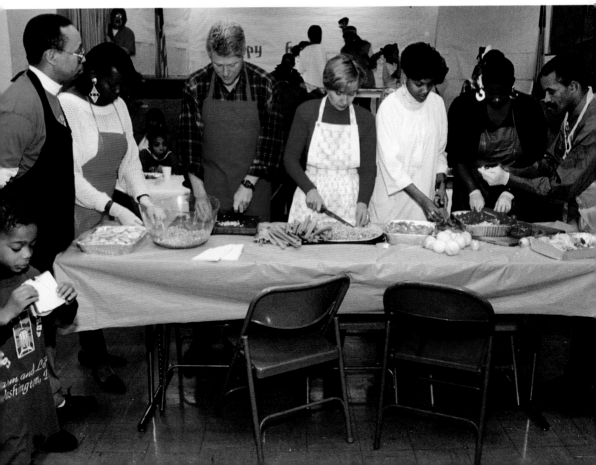

Left: With Prime Minister Yitzhak Rabin of Israel and Palestine Liberation Organization Chairman Yasser Arafat on the South Lawn, September 13.
Below: Presenting proposed health care reform legislation to the Congress in Statuary Hall at the Capitol, October 27.
Right: Giving the weekly radio address from the Oval Office, November 6.
Below right: Signing handgun control legislation with advocate James Brady in the East Room, November 30.

Above: Meeting with Presidents Gerald Ford, George Bush, and Jimmy Carter in the Residence, September 14.
Left: Signing the National and Community Service Trust Act of 1993 on the South Lawn, September 21.
Right: Holding a teleconference on the North American Free Trade Agreement at the U.S. Chamber of Commerce, November 1.
Overleaf: Walking with the Vice President on the South Lawn, August 10.

I would welcome an opportunity to engage you and others in the bi-partisan leadership in a full and constructive dialogue about the processes of executive-legislative relations regarding America's engagement in a changed world. But amendments such as these are not the right way for the American government to decide how we act in the world, and I urge the Senate to reject them.

BILL CLINTON

NOTE: Identical letters were sent to George Mitchell, Senate majority leader, and Bob Dole, Senate Republican leader.

Statement on German Ratification of the Maastricht Treaty
October 18, 1993

With the completion of Germany's ratification process last week, the way has been cleared for the entry into force of the Maastricht Treaty. The Maastricht Treaty marks a milestone in the progress of the European Community toward political and economic union, a goal which the United States strongly supports and encourages.

On behalf of the American people, I offer congratulations to the Community on this occasion and reiterate our commitment to a strong and vibrant transatlantic partnership.

Appointment for the Advisory Commission on Intergovernmental Relations
October 18, 1993

The President announced his intention to appoint 10 members to the Advisory Commission on Intergovernmental Relations (ACIR) today. Among them is former Mississippi Governor William Winter, who will serve as ACIR's Chair.

The Commission was created during the 1970's to foster better relations between all levels of government. Its primary functions are to provide an intergovernmental problem-solving forum, policy recommendations for intergovernmental cooperation, identification of emerging issues, information dissemination, and technical and international assistance.

"As a former Governor and State attorney general, I am committed to improving cooperation between governments at all levels," said the President. "When people want something done by the government, they don't care whether it gets done by the county, by the State, or by the Federal Government, they just want the job done. The talented, experienced, and diverse group of people that I am appointing to this commission, with Governor Winter taking the lead, will work to find ways to help public servants at all levels achieve that goal."

The commissioners being appointed are:

William F. Winter, former Governor of Mississippi

Carol Browner, EPA Administrator

Howard Dean, Governor of Vermont

Marcia L. Hale, White House Director of Intergovernmental Affairs

Arthur Hamilton, minority leader, Arizona House of Representatives

Michael Leavitt, Governor of Utah

Bob Miller, Governor of Nevada

Gloria Molina, member, Los Angeles County Board of Supervisors

Richard Riley, Secretary of Education

John Stroger, commissioner of Cook County, IL, and immediate past president of the National Association of Counties

NOTE: Biographies of the appointees were made available by the Office of the Press Secretary.

Nomination for an Assistant Secretary of Commerce
October 18, 1993

The President announced today that he intends to nominate GTE executive Graham R. Mitchell to be Assistant Secretary of Commerce for Technology Policy.

"I have called on the Commerce Department to take the lead in giving our country the tech-nological capability to win in a competitive world marketplace," said the President. "With his years of high-tech management experience, Graham Mitchell has the know-how that effort requires."

NOTE: A biography of the nominee was made available by the Office of the Press Secretary.

Nomination for an Associate Judge of the Superior Court of the District of Columbia
October 18, 1993

The President announced today that he will nominate Rafael Diaz to be an associate judge of the Superior Court of the District of Columbia. The President is empowered by statute to choose DC Superior Court judges from a list submitted by a local nominating commission.

"Rafael Diaz has proven himself with a decade's service to the District of Columbia," said the President. "His solid record and his reputation for competence have been widely noted, and he has been strongly recommended by a wide range of people. I expect him to be an outstanding judge."

NOTE: A biography of the nominee was made available by the Office of the Press Secretary.

Remarks and an Exchange With Reporters Prior to a Meeting With Members of Congress
October 19, 1993

NAFTA

The President. Let me say, first of all, I'm glad to have this bipartisan House delegation here, the latest in a round of several meetings on NAFTA. I want to begin by expressing my encouragement of today's housing numbers as well as the reports of increased business investment, which indicate that the economy is picking up. And I'm encouraged by that. And I know that all of us hope that that will work and that the lower interest rates and the declining deficit will help to support continued economic renewal.

But if America wants to grow more jobs, we're going to have to increase our exports. And therefore it is critical that we continue pushing and pass this trade agreement before the Congress goes home. And I'm here to—hopeful we pick up a few more votes for the NAFTA agreement today and to discuss some of the outstanding issues on it with the Members here. It's imperative: We can have an economic recovery, but if we're going to create jobs, we're going to have to increase exports. That's what wealthy countries have to do. And I hope we can do that here and pass NAFTA.

Somalia

Q. Mr. President, does the withdrawal of the Rangers from Somalia, sir, mean that you've given up on the search for Aideed?

The President. No, it means that we have 3,600 marines coming in, many of whom have similar capacities, who will be there. And it means that right now we are engaging in a political process to see how we can resolve our mission in Somalia and to do all the things the United Nations ordered to do, including working out a political solution and having a process by which the people who were responsible for killing the Pakistani soldiers—that's what started all this—that that investigation can proceed and appropriate action can be taken. There may be another way to do that. So right now we're in a stand-down position. It does mean that a final decision's been made.

Q. Mr. President, you have set a deadline of March 31st to get the troops out of Somalia. Do you have any contingency plans for Somalia at all?

The President. Well, we're doing what we agreed to do. We're pursuing negotiations to try to get a political solution. And I'm happy to say that, if anything, as you probably noted in the paper today, we're able to fulfill our mission better now than we have been for the last few months. We're delivering the safety of the— and our mission is going along as planned.

NAFTA

Q. Mr. President, this is your sixth meeting with the Members of Congress on NAFTA. So far only three Members have emerged saying that they've shifted their position—these meetings. Are you making the progress you need in order to ratify it and——

The President. I think we are. A lot of people have said things to me privately that they haven't said yet in public. And I think the Congress is still waiting to see how we're going to work out some of these other issues, including the training programs—a lot of the Democrats want to know—and they're going to have a chance to vote on that. And we still have to work through the whole issue of how we deal with the fact that if we pass NAFTA, we have to reduce tariffs. And that's a $2.5 billion tax on American consumers today, the tariffs are, that we will reduce. And under our budget laws, that has to be replacing—so we have to work through that. There are still some practical things to work out.

I believe that a majority of the Congress today believes it's the right thing to do. So our question is whether we can persuade a majority to vote, do what they think is right. I think by the end of November we'll be able to do that.

NOTE: The President spoke at 10:45 a.m. in the Cabinet Room at the White House. A tape was not available for verification of the content of these remarks.

Remarks at the White House Conference on Climate Change
October 19, 1993

Ladies and gentlemen, first let me thank you all for being here and thank the Vice President, the Cabinet, our Science Adviser, Katie McGinty, and others who worked so hard on this policy. If I might begin by just observing, I was looking at the clouds hoping we didn't have too much of a climate change this morning before the event could unfold.

This is an issue which has been of great concern to me for a long time. When I decided to seek this office back in 1991, I did it after having spent more than a decade as a Governor deeply frustrated by what seemed to me too often to be inevitable, persistent, aggravating conflicts between the impulse to promote economic opportunity for the people that I represented and the clear obligation, the moral obli-

gation, on all of us to try to preserve this planet that we all share. And anyone with eyes to see could look down the road and recognize that, even with imperfect scientific knowledge, at some point the impulse to give people something to do would have to be reconciled with the obligation to preserve the planet we all share and that if there were ways through the use of technology and partnerships and ingenuity to actually enhance economic opportunities while preserving the planet, how much better off we would all be.

That is what we have sought to do in this administration. The Vice President outlined the number of things that we have tried to do to move the environmental agenda forward and at the same time move our economy forward. I remember so well the sort of shocking but bracing and reinforcing feeling I had the first time I began to go to New Hampshire, which is what you have to do in this country if you want to ultimately become President, to find that people just living their own lives in what was in a very economically depressed State also believed that we could find a way and that we had to find a way to pursue our economic objectives and fulfill our moral responsibilities to have an aggressive and responsible program about the environment.

That cannot be done unless we change our attitude about what we put into our atmosphere and how we respect the air we breathe. That requires us to meet head-on the serious threat of global warming. I made a commitment to do that on Earth Day this year, to make a commitment to an approach that would draw on the most innovative people we could find in this country, whether they were in business, labor, government, or the environmental movement, to turn this challenge into an opportunity. And that's what this report seeks to do. It seeks to give the American people the ability to compete and win in the global economy while meeting our most deep and profound environmental challenges.

We have begun the task of linking our economy to the environment today in what I believe is a truly extraordinary fashion. And I think if all of you read the plan in its exquisite and sometimes mind-bending detail, you will see that it is a very aggressive and very specific first step; I would argue, the most aggressive and the most specific first step that any nation on this planet has taken in the face of perhaps the biggest environmental threat to this planet.

The task is accomplished primarily by harnessing private market forces, by leveraging modest Government expenditures to create a much larger set of private sector investments, and by establishing new public-private partnerships to bring out our best research and our best technologies. This plan takes the environmental debate where it should have been years ago, beyond a confrontation over ideology to a conversation about ideas, beyond polemics to real progress.

On Earth Day I made a commitment to reduce our emissions of greenhouse gases to 1990 levels by the year 2000. And I asked for a blueprint on how to achieve this goal. In concert with all other nations, we simply must halt glob-

al warming. It is a threat to our health, to our ecology, and to our economy. I know that the precise magnitude and patterns of climate change cannot be fully predicted. But global warming clearly is a growing, long-term threat with profound consequences. And make no mistake about it, it will take decades to reverse. But the first step is before us today. And because most of our recommendations do not require legislation, something which will doubtless please the Congress with all the burdens they have already on their plate, we can take action on our plan beginning today.

This plan is the result, as the Vice President has said, of genuine collaboration based on solid scientific and economic analysis, including funding to back up each and every proposal it contains. Like the announcement of our clean car initiative last month, this approach to global warming encourages public-private cooperation across a spectrum of economic, technological, and environmental questions. There are 50 separate initiatives in this plan, touching every sector of our economy because the problem, frankly, affects every sector of the economy. There are measures to improve energy efficiencies in commercial buildings and to make better household appliances. There are new agreements with public utilities to reduce greenhouse gases and new public-private ventures to increase the efficiency of industrial motors.

The plan will make it possible for all Americans to purchase appliances unlike any we own today. When your furnace dies or your washer breaks, you'll be able to go to a local store and buy a new appliance much more efficient than any you can buy today, and one that will save money in its operation. The energy savings we achieve will lower the cost of doing business in America and make us more competitive on the world market and more prosperous here at home. And the investments generated by this plan will create jobs in the sectors that make, install, and use energy efficient and pollution-cutting technologies.

Finally, to meet the challenge of global warming, as I have said with regard to cutting the deficit and reforming health care and in so many other areas, we frankly must all take some more personal responsibility. We will all benefit environmental and economically from the actions we are proposing today, and it will take all of us to make this plan work. So I say to all the American people: If your utility offers you help in conserving energy in your own home, seize it. If you own a business and the EPA offers you a chance to join the Green Lights program, do it. If you run a factory and the Department of Energy offers you a plan to help install an efficient motor system, use it. You will save money, and you will help your country and your fellow citizens.

This plan isn't designed for an archive. It's designed for action, for rapid implementation, constant monitoring, and for adjustments as necessary to meet our goals. It's part of a long-range strategy that includes the establishment of a team here in the White House to identify and implement those policies which will continue the trend of reduced emissions.

The action plan reestablishes the United States as a world leader in protecting the global climate. I urge other industrial countries to move rapidly to produce plans as detailed, as realistic, and as achievable as ours. This initiative

gives us a chance, a very, very good chance to reduce greenhouse gases, grow our economy, and create a new high-skill, high-wage job base in America.

We take pride here in this country in the love we have for our land, in our leadership among nations, in our ability to set new goals and solve new challenges. Today we have given life to those values again. And through them, we will help to build a healthier environment and a stronger economy for decades to come. We also will help to meet our moral obligation to ourselves, our neighbors around the world, and most important, to our children.

Thank you very much.

NOTE: The President spoke at 12:27 p.m. on the South Lawn at the White House. In his remarks, he referred to John H. Gibbons, Assistant to the President for Science and Technology.

Message to the Senate Transmitting a Protocol to the Israel-United States Taxation Convention
October 19, 1993

To the Senate of the United States:

I transmit herewith for the advice and consent of the Senate to ratification the Second Protocol Amending the Convention Between the Government of the United States of America and the Government of the State of Israel with Respect to Taxes on Income, signed at Washington on November 20, 1975, as amended by the Protocol signed May 30, 1980. The Second Protocol was signed at Jerusalem on January 26, 1993. Also transmitted for the information of the Senate is an exchange of notes and the report of the Department of State with respect to the Protocol.

The Second Protocol further amends the 1975 Convention, as amended by the 1980 Protocol,

in large measure to accommodate certain post-1980 provisions of U.S. tax law and treaty policy. The new Protocol also reflects changes in Israeli law and makes certain technical corrections to the Convention that are necessary because of the passage of time. It will modernize tax relations between the two countries and will facilitate greater private sector U.S. investment in Israel.

I recommend that the Senate give early and favorable consideration to the Protocol and give its advice and consent to ratification.

WILLIAM J. CLINTON

The White House,
October 19, 1993.

Message to the Congress Transmitting Transportation Department Reports
October 19, 1993

To the Congress of the United States:

I transmit herewith the 1992 calendar year reports as prepared by the Department of Transportation on activities under the Highway Safety Act and the National Traffic and Motor Vehicle Safety Act of 1966, as amended (23 U.S.C. 401 note and 15 U.S.C. 1408).

WILLIAM J. CLINTON

The White House,
October 19, 1993.

Message to the Congress Transmitting the Report of the Federal Prevailing Rate Advisory Committee
October 19, 1993

To the Congress of the United States:

In accordance with section 5347(e) of title 5 of the United States Code, I transmit herewith the 1992 annual report of the Federal Prevailing Rate Advisory Committee.

WILLIAM J. CLINTON

The White House,
October 19, 1993.

Statement on Congressional Action on Department of Commerce Appropriations
October 19, 1993

The House/Senate conference decision to bolster the Department of Commerce FY94 budget to $3.56 billion, a 12.6 percent increase over FY93 levels of $3.16 billion, represents a vote of confidence in this administration's investment priorities and in the Department of Commerce. The budget increases reflect the increased responsibilities of the Commerce Department under the leadership of Secretary Ron Brown.

Congress' decision hits a home run for this administration's civilian technology and defense conversion policies. It demonstrates the importance of our efforts to promote economic growth through civilian technology and address the aftermath of economic dislocation resulting from the end of the cold war. Their decision affirms our goal of building a stronger, more competitive private sector able to maintain U.S. leadership in critical world markets.

Highlights of the Commerce appropriations include:

• $80 million for defense conversion. These funds will provide a much needed boost to the Economic Development Administration's programs to assist communities that have been impacted by the end of the cold war.

• $520.2 million for the National Institute of Standards and Technology (NIST). NIST will be able to bolster its technology outreach programs, the advanced technology program, and the manufacturing extension partnership.

• $70.9 million for the National Telecommunications and Information Administration. The NTIA appropriation will set a speedy pace for this agency's lead role in fulfilling this administration's goal of an information superhighway, as outlined by the "National Information Infrastructure: Agenda for Action."

I commend the congressional leadership, Senator Ernest Hollings, Senator Pete Domenici,

Congressman Neal Smith, and Congressman Harold Rogers, for their foresight and support in revitalizing this country through these programs. It is a dramatic step forward for the United States toward a solid economic future.

Nomination for an Assistant Secretary of Energy
October 19, 1993

The President announced his intention to nominate Christine Ervin, currently director of the Oregon department of energy, to be Assistant Secretary of Energy for Energy Efficiency and Renewable Energy.

"We must expand our efforts to use energy more efficiently and to develop new, renewable sources of energy," said the President. "Having an Assistant Secretary of Energy with Christine Ervin's wide range of experience will help us to move that process forward."

NOTE: A biography of the nominee was made available by the Office of the Press Secretary.

Remarks at the NAFTA Jobs and Products Day Trade Fair
October 20, 1993

Thank you very much. I want to thank Harold and Bob and, of course, Lee Iacocca, who has been such an eloquent spokesperson for NAFTA. It's nice to see him on television in an ad where he's—I enjoy watching him sell Chryslers, but I like seeing him sell NAFTA even more in the television ads.

I want to thank the many Members of the United States Congress who are here today. They hold the fate of this trade agreement and in many ways the fate of America's trade future in their hands. I want to thank the members of the Cabinet who are here today: the Treasury Secretary, Lloyd Bentsen; our United States Trade Ambassador, Mickey Kantor, who negotiated the agreements on the environment, on labor standards, and some other things which make this a truly unique trade agreement in the history of world trade; the Labor Secretary, the Education Secretary, the Commerce Secretary, Bob Reich, Dick Riley, and Ron Brown. I've seen all of them. There may be other members of the Cabinet here today showing our unified support for this agreement. I also want to thank all the companies and the workers who came here today. They really showed what this trade agreement is all about. It's about the jobs of American workers and the future of American working families, people who are determined to compete and win.

Today the demonstrations in these two tents should show our country and show our Congress why we need NAFTA. In the next month before the vote, we've got to vigorously make this case to the American people. I was talking with Bob and the other steelworkers over at their exhibit over here, and I said, "You know, we figure that an enormous number of America's unions will actually pick up jobs if this agreement passes."

The NAFTA fight is an interesting one to me. Lee Iacocca has already said it pretty well, but I have to restate it for you in personal terms. Before I became President, I was a Governor of my State for a dozen years during the 1980's. When I took office in 1983, our unemployment rate was 3 percentage points above the national average. I know all about losing jobs to trade, to not being able to compete. There are a lot of companies here that have plants in my State, and I believe that every one I saw here, I have personally been in the plant. I saw companies shut down and move to Mexico in the 1980's. And when it happened, because I live in a small State, I knew who they were. I'm proud to say we brought one of them back, too, before I left office. I would not ever do anything knowingly that would cost jobs to the American economy and take opportunities from American working people. This won't do that; it will do the reverse.

The people who are fighting this are bringing to this fight the resentments that they have over what happened in the 1980's. You heard Lee talk about it: How many decent people lost their jobs? How many times did we see people shut down and move to other countries solely because of lower labor costs or higher other production costs in America? That's what happened before. But in the last 12 or 13 years we have seen productivity growth in the production sector in the United States go up at 4 percent or more a year.

You heard Lee say that you can now produce an automobile for anywhere in this part of the world cheaper in the United States than anyplace else. We've had two European companies put plants in North America. They could have gone to Mexico. Where did they go? One went to South Carolina. One is now going to Alabama. Why? Because it's cheaper. Because the labor is highly productive, even though more expensive, and that is a relatively small part of a big, complex operation, making an automobile and putting it into a showroom.

And I tell you, friends, if we can get folks in this country to focus on what this trade agreement does, it will alleviate the anxieties that so many people had in the 1980's. It raises the cost of production in Mexico by requiring greater investments in labor and in the environment. It lowers the trade barriers. On automobiles alone, the domestic content requirement will be lowered, and we'll be able to go from selling one to 50,000 American cars in one year alone. It will give us access to a Mexican market on preferential terms as compared with our Japanese and our European competitors, something that we have seen on the reverse side not only in Europe but especially in Asia. And it will create good jobs. We'll not only get more jobs out of this, but the jobs we get related to exports pay on average about 17 percent more than nonexport-related jobs in this country.

And look at the Mexicans. You know, frankly, I'm getting a little weary of hearing people criticize Mexico as not perfect. You think everybody else we trade with in the world is perfect? Look at the progress they have made. It's hard to show a country that's made a stronger commitment to open markets and a free enterprise system, coming from a long way back.

In most of my lifetime, if you wanted to be a popular politician in Mexico, the way to be popular was to badmouth the United States, blame all of the problems of the people on the United States. The last two Presidents of Mexico have started to turn that around. This President said, "We're going to compete in the global economy, and we're going to try to have open relationships. And we're going to start with the United States." And unilaterally, they have lowered a lot of their tariffs, even though they're still 2.5 times as high as ours. And now we've got the trade surplus that Lee Iacocca talked about.

We can do so much better if we adopt this agreement and we give ourselves a chance to compete in a friendly way with a country that now likes the United States, wants to be tied to the United States, full of 80 million people who spend 70 percent of the money they spend on foreign products in the United States of America. It is a pretty good deal, and it's time we started to take it.

We believe that this agreement will create 200,000 new jobs by 1995 alone. Keep in mind, as has already been said, the Mexican economy today is only about one-twentieth the size of the American economy; it's about the size of the economy of California from Los Angeles County to the Mexican border. And already these folks are accounting for a $6 billion trade surplus.

Imagine what would happen to the American economy as the Mexican economy grows, as the people there have their incomes go up, as they have more money to spend, and as they have a special trade relationship with the United States. Imagine, those of you who are involved in manufacturing, all the other things that are going to happen if we have this special relationship. One of our American toy manufacturers has already announced that they will change their plant location from China to Mexico and therefore will buy what is 85 percent of the value of the toy, the plastic parts, from an American company instead of a Japanese company. There are absolutely unforeseeable consequences of this.

Let me just tell you about a couple of the companies that we just saw. The Harris Corporation is the number one United States supplier of radio and TV broadcast equipment. Twenty-nine percent of its $3 billion in annual sales come from exports. And in the last couple of years, sales to Mexico have gone from $12 million to $40 million a year, despite 20 percent tariffs. Imagine what will happen when the tariffs drop: More people will be hired.

There's a small business from Covington, Kentucky, represented back here, the Monarch Tool and Manufacturing Company, which began to export coin slots to Mexico over the last 3 years. The company was foundering in the mideighties. Now almost 70 percent of its sales come from exports.

There's a company here from California, of which I am a satisfied customer, Golden Bear Sportswear. During the 1980's, this company, which makes among other things leather bomber jackets, moved its factory from San Francisco to Korea. And after 4 years they moved back. The lady that runs the company wrote me one of the most moving letters I've ever received, saying that she was absolutely determined to keep jobs in America and in California, to work with the people who helped to build the company and buy its products. Now the business is flourishing, and the owners are proud to put "Made in the U.S.A." on the jackets. The family-owned business with 100 employees makes 100,000 jackets a year, most marketed through retailers like Brooks Brothers, the Gap, L.L. Bean, and Lands' End. They have annual sales of $16 million. Instead of moving a plant to Korea, they'd like to move some of those jackets to Mexico. I think we ought to give them a chance to do it. That's what America is all about.

The beacon of our country's technological genius, Hewlett-Packard of Palo Alto, California, has computers which now face a 20 percent tariff in Mexico, which will drop to zero. Three years ago, Mexicans bought 120,000 personal computers. Last year they bought 390,000 personal computers. Imagine how many personal computers 80 million people could buy if there were not a 20 percent duty on those products.

Let me just say two other things about this. One person that I talked to on the line, and I wish I could remember where he was, said, "You know, Mr. President, as important as NAFTA is for Mexico and American trade, it may be actually more important for other things. It will say to the world whether we're a good trading partner. It will say to the world whether the United States Government has a constant policy of supporting expanded trade and whether the President and the trade apparatus of the country can be trusted to make deals that America adheres to." Yes, you said that. [*Laughter*] And I thank you for that. And I can tell you this, it will also say to the world and especially to the rest of Latin America whether the United States wants to be a good neighbor again, whether we want to reestablish the kind of feeling that existed 30 years ago and 60 years ago.

I tell you, my friends, democracy and the fever for a market economy is sweeping across Latin America. I dream of the day when we'll have over 700 million people in this trading bloc united in believing that we can help one another grow and flourish. But all the other countries of the world are looking at us, and all the other countries of Latin America want to know: Are we going to do this or not?

Colombia, not a very big country, has a President struggling to liberate its country from the scourge of the dominance of drugs, struggling to develop a diversified free market economy. In the last 2 years, that little country's increased their purchases of American products by 69 and 64 percent on their own. The President of Colombia says, "I want to be a part of NAFTA."

Chile, for so long a military dictatorship, is now a democratic free market economy endorsing NAFTA. They don't benefit from it. They just want it to be a symbol of something they can be a part of. Look at Argentina, once the eighth wealthiest country in the entire world, finally on the way back again. We have opportunities we cannot dream of. I don't know how long it will take us to put all that back together if we turn away from this.

The last thing I want to say is this: I have really tried to avoid talking about all the bad things that will happen if it doesn't pass because I want us to be optimistic and upbeat. And I don't want us to adopt this out of fear. There's been too much fearmongering on the other side, and all kinds of ridiculous statements made. But it is simply a fact that Mexico needs access to sophisticated goods and products, that Mexico needs access to investors who can make secure investments.

What would we do in America if we turn away from this and they make this sort of arrangement with Japan or with Europe, and they make the investments there, and then we have to deal with their products coming through the back door from Mexico? What will happen to our job base? I'm telling you, everything people worried about in the 1980's will get worse if this thing is voted down and will get better if it's voted up.

My friends in California worried about the large influx of illegal immigrants—California, a State built by immigrants but burdened by illegal immigration in volume too great for a State with a very high unemployment rate today to handle. And people are afraid there. What's going to happen if it passes, or if it doesn't pass? If NAFTA passes, you won't have what you have now, which is everybody runs up to the *maquiladora* line, gets a job in a factory, and then runs across the line to get a better job. Instead there will be more uniform growth in investment across the country, and people will be able to work at home with their families. And over the period of the next few years, we will dramatically reduce pressures on illegal immigration from Mexico to the United States.

But if you beat this, will it reduce the pressure for people looking for illegal immigration? No. It will increase the pressure on people coming here. So if you want to have the immigration problem eased, you must vote for NAFTA, not against it. We can go through issue after issue after issue, and it's the same.

So I say to you again what we started this with. I know this has been a tough time for most Americans. There's all this bewildering change in the world, and it's making people's jobs less secure. And at the same time, we've got a lot of problems here at home with violence, with the availability and cost of health care, with all the other things that are bothering our people. But we are trying to address those in this administration. We're trying to give Americans greater security in their family lives, in their education lives, with their health care, and on their streets. But we cannot create security out of an unwillingness to change.

This vote really is going to say a lot about what kind of people we expect to be. Are we going to hunker down and turn away and say, "My goodness, we're going to be overcome by a trade agreement with Mexico"? Or are we going to take this as the first step toward reaching out to the rest of the world, saying Americans can compete and win again?

We've got all the evidence we need. We know that it's not just the United States. No wealthy country in the world today can create new jobs without expanding trade. It cannot be done. Nobody is doing it. Nobody is doing it. And if you look at Europe, the most protectionist countries have higher unemployment rates. The most

open market in Europe, Germany, is the only country with an unemployment rate as low as ours. I'm telling you, this is going to define what kind of people we're going to be and whether we want to really compete and win in the global economy. I think Americans are winners. And I think when it comes down to it, the Congress will vote for us to win.

I want to say this one thing on behalf of the Members of the Congress. They have to make this vote. I'm working with them to make sure that we can get the training we need for people who will be dislocated. We need to do that for people anyway, all across America. And we will have a strategy to help those areas of the country that are already in trouble that have nothing to do with this. But the Congress tells me over and over again, they hear from the people who are against NAFTA because they're afraid and they're whipped up. They don't hear from the people who are for it, who are going to win.

So we brought you here today not only to send a message to them but so that I could ask you and companies like you and employees like your employees all across America to call or write the Members of the Congress in every State, without regard to party, to talk about this. They need to hear from people who will get jobs, who will have increased incomes, who will have increased opportunities.

I agree with Mr. Iacocca. We have no one to blame but ourselves if this thing goes down. We've got the facts on our side; they've got the fear on their side. We need to get the facts to the Congress in the faces of the people who will win from this agreement. And we have to do that.

Every time you have to face a big change in your life, you can make one of two decisions: You can hunker down and hope it'll go away, or you can sort of face it and make it turn out all right. You can make change your friend. If you hunker down and hope it goes away, that works about one time in 100. The other 99 percent of the time, you better figure out a way to make change your friend, because it's coming at you anyway. The world economy is coming at us anyway. We have already paid the price for our inadequacies. We are now competitive, and we can win. And it is time we use NAFTA to prove it to ourselves, as well as to the rest of the world.

Thank you, and God bless you all.

NOTE: The President spoke at 10:31 a.m. on the South Lawn at the White House. In his remarks, he referred to Harold Sumpter, senior vice president, H&H Industries, and steelworker Bob Scheydt.

Statement on Signing the Executive Order on Federal Acquisition, Recycling, and Waste Prevention
October 20, 1993

Families, businesses, and communities all across America know that recycling makes sense. It saves money and it protects the environment. It's time for the Government to set an example and provide real leadership that will help create jobs and protect the environment, encouraging new markets for recycled products and new technologies.

NOTE: The President's statement was included in a White House announcement on the signing of the Executive order, which is listed in Appendix D at the end of this volume.

Letter to Congressional Leaders on the Conflict in Bosnia
October 20, 1993

Dear Mr. Leader:

The violent conflict in the former Yugoslavia continues to be a source of deep concern. As you know, my Administration is committed to help stop the bloodshed and implement a fair and enforceable peace agreement, if the parties to the conflict can reach one. I have stated that such enforcement potentially could include American military personnel as part of a NATO operation. I have also specified a number of conditions that would need to be met before our troops would participate in such an operation.

I also have made clear that it would be helpful to have a strong expression of support from the United States Congress prior to the participation of U.S. forces in implementation of a Bosnian peace accord. For that reason, I would welcome and encourage congressional authorization of any military involvement in Bosnia.

The conflict in Bosnia ultimately is a matter for the parties to resolve, but the nations of Europe and the United States have significant interests at stake. For that reason, I am committed to keep our nation engaged in the search for a fair and workable resolution to this tragic conflict.

I want to express my lasting gratitude for the leadership you have shown in recent days as we have worked through difficult issues affecting our national security. With your help we have built a broad coalition that should provide the basis for proceeding constructively in the months ahead. Once again you have earned our respect and appreciation.

Sincerely,

BILL CLINTON

NOTE: Identical letters were sent to George Mitchell, Senate majority leader, and Bob Dole, Senate Republican leader.

Appointment for the Board of Governors of the American Red Cross
October 20, 1993

The President announced today that he intends to appoint seven administration officials to be Government members of the Board of Governors of the American Red Cross. The seven are:

Secretary of Defense Les Aspin
Export-Import Bank Chairman Kenneth Brody
Secretary of State Warren Christopher
Secretary of Education Richard Riley
Secretary of Health and Human Services Donna Shalala
Federal Emergency Management Agency Director James Lee Witt

Gen. John M. Shalikashvili, Chairman of the Joint Chiefs of Staff

"I have long admired and sought to support the ongoing work of the American Red Cross to bring aid to those in need both around the world and here in our own communities," said the President. "As I recently saw firsthand during the Midwest flooding this summer, their workers and volunteers are true lifesavers. I am appointing this senior group of officials to serve on their board because I want to be sure that my administration does everything that we can to support the Red Cross' important work."

Letter to Congressional Leaders on Haiti
October 20, 1993

Dear Mr. Speaker: (Dear Mr. President:)

I have directed the deployment of U.S. Naval Forces to participate in the implementation of the petroleum and arms embargo of Haiti. At 11:59 p.m. E.S.T., October 18, units under the command of the Commander in Chief, U.S. Atlantic Command, began enforcement operations in the waters around Haiti, including the territorial sea of that country, pursuant to my direction and consistent with United Nations Security Council Resolutions 841, 873, and 875. I am providing this report, consistent with the War Powers Resolution, to ensure that the Congress is kept fully informed about this important U.S. action to support multilateral efforts to restore democracy in Haiti and thereby promote democracy throughout the hemisphere.

During the past week, the world has witnessed lawless, brutal actions by Haiti's military and police authorities to thwart the Haitian people's manifest desire for democracy to be returned to their country. With our full support, the United Nations Security Council has responded resolutely to these events. On October 16, the Security Council, acting under Chapters VII and VIII of the United Nations Charter, adopted Resolution 875. This resolution calls upon Member States, "acting nationally or

through regional agencies or arrangements, cooperating with the legitimate Government of Haiti, to use such measures commensurate with the specific circumstances as may be necessary" to ensure strict implementation of sanctions imposed by Resolutions 841 and 873. The maritime interception operations I have directed are conducted under U.S. command and control. In concert with allied navies, U.S. Naval Forces will ensure that merchant vessels proceeding to Haiti are in compliance with the embargo provisions set forth in the Security Council resolutions.

The initial deployment includes six U.S. Navy ships and supporting elements under the command of the U.S. Atlantic Command. These U.S. forces and others as may be necessary, combined with those forces that other Member States have committed to this operation, will conduct intercept operations to ensure that merchant ships proceeding to Haiti are in compliance with United Nations Security Council sanctions. On the first day of the operation, one of our ships, with U.S. Navy and Coast Guard personnel aboard, carried out an interception of a Belize-flag vessel and allowed it to proceed to its destination after determining that it was in compliance with the embargo. In addition, the forces of the U.S. Atlantic Command will remain prepared to protect U.S. citizens in Haiti and, acting in cooperation with U.S. Coast Guard, to support the Haitian Alien Migrant Interdiction Operations (AMIO) of the United States, as may be necessary.

The United States strongly supports the Governor's Island Agreement and restoration of democracy in Haiti. The measures I have taken to deploy U.S. Armed Forces in "Operation Restore Democracy" are consistent with United States goals and interests and constitute crucial support for the world community's strategy to overcome the persistent refusal of Haitian military and police authorities to fulfill their commitments under the Governor's Island Agreement. I have ordered the deployment of U.S. Armed Forces for these purposes pursuant to my constitutional authority to conduct foreign relations and as Commander in Chief and Chief Executive.

Close cooperation between the President and the Congress is imperative for effective U.S. foreign policy and especially when the United States commits our Armed Forces abroad. I remain committed to consulting closely with Congress on our foreign policy, and I will continue to keep Congress fully informed about significant deployments of our Nation's Armed Forces.

Sincerely,

BILL CLINTON

NOTE: Identical letters were sent to Thomas S. Foley, Speaker of the House of Representatives, and Robert C. Byrd, President pro tempore of the Senate. This letter was released by the Office of the Press Secretary on October 21.

Remarks to the Conference of Business for Social Responsibility
October 21, 1993

Thank you very much, Helen and Arnold. The crowd would have clapped even more for you if they'd known what you were going to say before you said it. They were terrific, I thought. I have a great deal of admiration for them and for their companies and for this organization. I want to point out before I get into my remarks that I have two people here I'd like to acknowledge first: the Director of the Small Business Administration and one of the strongest supporters of our health care reform program, Mr. Erskine Bowles from North Carolina, who is here. And I believe a former board member of yours and the current Director of the Women's Bureau at Labor, Karen Nussbaum, is here.

I believe the purpose of politics is to help the American people live up to the fullest of their God-given potential and to help them to live together in strength and harmony and to fulfill their responsibilities as well as their dreams. That obligation can be met in different ways in different times. But plainly, there are some times in the history of a nation in which that obligation can only be met by the willingness to undertake the rigors of profound change. And I believe this is such a time.

The problem is that in any democracy you can only build a consensus for profound change when things have gotten pretty well off track. And by the time things have gotten pretty well off track, there are an awful lot of people who are unhappy and insecure and uncertain. And if you look around this audience at the companies here represented who have believed you could actually make money and be socially responsible, that you could actually be more productive by taking care of the people with whom you work and the people who are your customers, you see the intense dilemma we face, because people are most able to change when they are most secure. And yet, at large, it becomes possible for society to make these big changes often only when things have gotten so far off track that people are insecure. That, in a nutshell, is the larger dilemma that I face as your President today, but more importantly, that we face as a people.

If you look at the conditions that so many millions of our country men and women face, many are insecure in their jobs. Many are insecure in their ability to get new jobs, in their education levels, in their skill levels. Many, many millions are insecure in their health care. Many are insecure as children in the way they are growing up. And lamentably, at the end of the cold war, the wars that are being waged on so many streets in America have made millions of people insecure in their daily lives and movements.

And yet, we have no alternative. We have to change. We have to make economic policy changes. We have to make all kinds of real, significant different directions. And yet we live at a time of such insecurity that people distrust their institutions, their elected leaders, and even their own impulses sometimes when it comes to make these changes.

I saw that in trying to pass a budget which did some remarkable things: It reduced the deficit dramatically. It's given us the lowest long-term interest rates in 30 years. It had the most significant reform in the tax structure for working people in 20 years by saying to people with children who spend 40 hours in the work force, you won't be in poverty. No matter how low your job wage is, the tax system will lift you out of poverty, not put you into poverty. It opened the doors of college education to all Americans by expanding eligibility for college loans and lowering interest rates and making the repayment terms easier and tied to the incomes of young people when they get out of college—much of which the American people never even knew while it was going on because it was so easy to whip people up into a white heat about the word "taxes" and because people couldn't believe anyone would really do anything seriously to deal with this issue of the deficit and these other matters.

I see it now as I try to pass the North American Free Trade Agreement through the Congress. And that agreement has become the repository and the symbol of all the accumulated resentments of our people for the 1980's, of all the people who lost their jobs and all the plants that moved overseas and all the times that all the workers in this country saw that their executives were getting pay raises 4 times in percentage terms what they were, 3 times what the profits were going up; that they could lose their health care in an instant; that they could have to start over in a moment; and that no one cared about them anymore. So they associate that with expanded global trade.

So we know rationally that the only way a rich country ever grows richer is to expand its trade. And we know that wealthy countries all over the world, in Europe, in Japan, not just in the United States, are having great difficulty creating new jobs. And the only way to do that is to make more markets beyond the borders of the nation. And yet still, emotionally there is this enormous undertow rooted in the insecurities, the pain, the sense of loss, the disorientation, the feeling that nobody really looks out for me and my family.

And so we are in so many ways, on so many fronts, my fellow Americans, waging a war between hope and fear: on the streets of our cities, in our factories and workplaces, in our homes, indeed, in the hearts of perhaps a majority of our fellow country men and women. And each of us in our own way, we have a little scale inside ourselves. When I don't get enough sleep, I'm more pessimistic than I am when I get more sleep, right? You're probably like that. And I'm more optimistic. And the scales are always going up and down, even in our own lives, aren't they, inside, about how we look at the world and how we see reality.

This is a time when we must be bold, when we must be confident, in which we must have the kind of enthusiasm you exhibited when we came into this room, with a sense of possibility. We need more young people like the young man from the hotel who met me outside, who said, "Keep breaking those paradigms, Mr. President." [*Laughter*] I loved it.

But I say to you, one of the reasons that I'm so happy to see this organization growing and large and vibrant and vigorous is that you have found a way to make people feel more secure by changing by changing. You have found a way to live by the rhetoric of my last campaign, Putting People First. Putting people first.

I believe that one of the biggest problems that this country always has is trying to close the gap between what we say and what we do. I am ecstatic and honored to be here. But I want to take a few moments today to talk to you about that, how to right that balance inside every American so that hope wins out over fear; how to pursue an agenda of security so that we can pursue our agenda of change; and how, in so many profound ways, health care is right at the core of that. Because I am convinced that you have proved that the future of the American private sector, the real triumph of free enterprise, will be in proving that we can actually do right by our employees, do right by our customers, and do right by our bottom lines if we are enlightened and we do the right things.

I believe that we have set ourselves up over the last 20 years with a whole series of false choices that may work in the short run, but in the end ultimately disappoint everyone. If we have to erode the fabric of family life in America by not giving our workers health care and not providing family leave and not providing adequate child care, ultimately you wind up with less productive workers. If we can't find a way to create new jobs even as we increase productivity, then for the first time in all of human history we will have given up on technology as a job creator and given in to the age-old fears that it is a job destroyer. To be sure, it's always transferred jobs. We used to have half the people working on the farm; now only 3 percent do. But it can be either, or.

All these are questions we are dealing with. So is every other nation in the world now. We are going through a period of change. We can't see the ultimate end of it. No one knows what all these economic trends in the global economy will ultimately lead to, but we know what works. You know what works; you do it. And I came in here today as a friend and an ally to ask you to engage in this health care debate and tell the American people that this is something we have to do not because it is morally right— but it is morally right—but because it's also economically right.

The most expensive alternative of all, looking toward the future, is doing nothing. It's the most expensive financially, and it's the most expensive in human terms, and ultimately it will be the biggest drag on American productivity. It also is, as Helen said in her remarks, guaranteed to provoke the largest amount of resentment because of the uneven impact of the health care system on employees and employers and American citizens today, depending on whether you have coverage, what kind of coverage you have, and how much you're paying for somebody else's health care because we have so much uncompensated care in this system.

Now, I have watched as I have seen the Congress come to grips with many things and try to overcome even their own disbelief. When I took office, most people had been told that the country couldn't afford the family leave bill. But we did it, and the wheel hasn't run off. And I have seen the impact of that. A lot of you have heard me tell this story, but I had a family in the White House the other day with a dying child on one of these Make-A-Wish pro-

grams, that the child wanted to see the White House and the President. And the father told me that his daughter was probably not going to make it and that the time he'd spent with her was the most important time he'd ever spent, and if it hadn't been for the family leave law he would have had to choose between losing his job to be with his daughter and therefore doing wrong by his wife and his other two children, or keeping his job and letting someone else spend that precious time with his child. Now, I don't know about you, but I think that fellow is going to be a much better worker for that company than he would have been had that not been the law of the land.

So we now, I think, have a chance to keep going with this engine of change. And we've got a lot of things we need to do on the security front and the change front. We've got a world of economic changes we need to make, but we're going to have to have—if there's no more job security in this America because most people when they lose their jobs don't get it back anymore, totally the reverse of unemployment patterns of the last 60 years, we have to give employment security to Americans. If there's no job security there has to be employment security. Therefore, we have to have a whole different system of lifetime education and training. And we have to undertake that. We'll begin to do that next year. A big part of welfare reform will be doing that, making sure people really have the capacity to move from welfare to work.

We have to provide more security for families. That's what the family leave bill was all about. That's what the earned-income tax credit in the budget bill was all about, lifting the working poor out of poverty so there will never be an incentive to be on welfare and there will always be an incentive to be both a good parent and a good worker.

We have to find more security for people on their streets and in their homes and in their schools. That's why I so desperately want to do something to reduce the number of automatic weapons that are in the hands of teenagers on the streets of the city, assault weapons.

But we also have to do something about health security. You know, Hillary and I got 700,000 letters before I made my health care speech to Congress and she began to testify. And we're getting them in now at about 10,000 letters a week, more. Story after story after story: the small business that had the premium go up 40 percent a year with no claims; the business person who has to cut his or her employees back to a policy with a $2,500 or $3,000 deductible even though the employee average salary is $22,000, $23,000 a year; the person who is physically disabled but who has a fine mind who can't get a job because the only available employers are small businesses and they don't have any kind of community rating, so this person will drive the premiums out of sight; a person with the HIV virus who may have another 10 years of productive life, strong, productive life and contributions to be made, who is either not employed now and therefore won't be employed, or can't ever change jobs because of the job lock provisions of the present system; the hospitals that are out there, struggling to do a good job on modest profits, or not-for-profit hospitals who can't meet their uncompensated care burden or those that do by raising everybody else's hospital costs in ways that undermine confidence of those that pay those bills in the integrity of the system; the doctors who talk to me about how, yes, their fees have gone up a lot in the 1980's, but 10 years ago they took 75 percent of what they earned home, and now it's down to 52 percent, and all the rest of it has vanished in the sea of paperwork because they have to hassle 300 insurance companies with thousands of different policies to make sure they've crossed every "t" and dotted every "i" to get the payment they're entitled to anyway; the stories, over and over again, mounting up in every part of our country.

As you know, we spend more on health care than anybody in the world, and yet we do less with it. Now, how would you feel if you were running your business, competing with people all across the country and perhaps all across the world for jobs and incomes, if you had to spend 14 percent of your revenues covering only 86 percent of your market and all your competitors spent 8 or 9 percent of their revenues and covered 100 percent of their market? You don't have to be as bright as a tree full of owls to figure out that eventually there would be some adverse consequence to that. But we go on blithely as if that's the way it has to be. And when I propose a change, some people say, "Oh my God, we can't afford that. Look at this wonderful thing we've got going."

Now, we have in many ways the best health care system in the world. But we have in other ways the worst financed and organized health care system in the world for a country as rich as we. Otherwise, how can you explain the fact that we are plainly the capital of pharmaceuticals in the world in terms of developing new drugs and manufacturing them right here in America and we have the third worst immunization rate in this hemisphere, behind Haiti and Bolivia— I mean, ahead of them, but only ahead of them. You tell me why that happened. If we're so great, how have we permitted ourselves to go on year-in and year-out not closing that gap?

Do we have the best health care in the world, the doctors and nurses, the hospitals, the medical research, the technology? You bet we do. For people who access it, it is good. And do those people resent the burdens that are imposed on them by this crazy-quilt system? You bet they do. Some of the strongest advocates for change we've had are from doctors who are sick and tired of having to hire one more person every year because of the clerical administrative burdens of this system.

People say, "Aw, this system the President's proposed is so complex." I get tickled; it's complex compared to what? It's complex compared to zero. It's simple compared to what we have now. What is the proper standard by which you evaluate this?

If we do nothing to change the current course on which we have embarked, we'll be spending 19 percent of our income on health care by the year 2000. We will have a smaller percentage of our population covered with health insurance than we have today, because we have about 100,000 Americans a month permanently losing health insurance, 2 million every month losing it but 100,000 permanently losing it. And by the year 2000, instead of the gap being 4.5 percent to 5.5 percent between our major competitors, of our income, it'll be about 7 percent. Today, we spend 14.5 percent of our income on health care. Canada's at 10; Germany and Japan are just under 9. There is no measurable difference in the health outcomes.

Now, to be perfectly fair, there are two elements of our cost system that will always, at least for the foreseeable future, keep us above other countries. One is, we do rely more and we invest more in groundbreaking technologies and pharmaceuticals, and we should continue to do that. And we all want them for ourselves and our family if there's a chance it will prolong our lives.

The second issue is sadder. We are quite simply, as compared with other wealthy countries, more willing to endure a far higher rate of violence. We have far higher rates of AIDS. We have far higher rates of teenaged mothers and out-of-wedlock births and low birth-weight babies, and they're far more likely to cost more. So we have system-related costs that are greater than our competitors. And that's about half the gap between us and them. But the other half is our own fault. And if we don't get about the business of closing it, we're going to have a difficult time competing. And we're going to have an increasingly difficult time explaining why it is we are prepared to put up with a system that no one else on earth tolerates and to pay the human and economic cost of maintaining it.

Today I'd like to focus on two of the issues that have been raised by some people in the business community against our proposal. Some say that we propose to create a new bureaucracy by creating these health alliances, and we shouldn't do that. I say what we propose to do is to have a smaller rate of cost increases through increased competition and greater efficiency and reduce waste by giving small businesses the same bargaining power that big business and Government has today.

If you look at the Federal employees' health insurance program, for example, because of the power we have to bargain and because everybody knows the Federal Government is up to its ears in debt and doesn't have a lot of money, you look at what's happened to the rates on most of the Federal health insurance policies: very modest increases this year. Look at the California public employee system: huge people in that block, a big block of buyers, and everybody knows California is in bad shape financially, so they have a rate increase this year that's right at the rate of inflation.

Small business, however, has seen its rates go up at 2 and 3 times the rate of inflation. Why? No bargaining power. In small groups, one person gets real sick, explodes the rate structure for everybody. So what these alliances do, quite simply, is to say if you're in a firm with fewer than 5,000 employees, we will give you the option, the opportunity, to be in a big buying group. And in the course of that, we will give your employees the option of having more choices than you can probably provide for them now in health care, but none of them

will cost you any more than you would otherwise pay as an employer.

This will give smaller businesses and self-employed people access to market economics. Market economics is beginning to work in health care, that and all the Cain I think we've been raising the last year or so. It's beginning to work. The aggregate increases are beginning to slow some. But they're finding, again, as Helen said in the opening remarks, it's very uneven. You might have health care inflation at 7 percent this year or 6 percent, but you'll still have a lot of small businesses with 30 percent premium increases. Why? No market power.

So when you hear all this stuff that these alliances are big bureaucratic nightmares and Government creations, that's not true. The alliances are groups of consumers in each State in groups approved by the State, not by the Federal Government, that will have buying power presently available to governments and to big business but not to small business and often not even to medium-sized business. I think it will work.

I also believe in order to make it work we have to have insurance companies that compete not on the basis of which company is most adept at excluding people who have problems but on the basis of cost and quality. Now, to be fair to the insurance companies, you can only do that if there is a community rating system, if you don't have all the risk factors calculated into every individual purchaser of insurance. If you do that, you have nailed small business from the get-go, the people that are creating most of the new jobs in this country.

If you have a community rating system, who gets hurt, from the present system, who pays more? Young, single, healthy people will pay more, about anywhere from $6 to $8 a month more for their premiums under our estimate. They will, but it's fair. You know why? Because under our system all the young people without insurance will get insurance and because if they're young and healthy, they'll be middle-aged like me someday, and they'll get the benefit of this system. The society will be stronger. And it will be far better for the big job generators of the country, the small businesses who don't have access to health insurance now.

It also will be fairer because with community rating, you will enable people to effectively move from job to job to job. Then you can say, without breaking a company, that you can't deny someone the right to coverage when they change jobs. Under the present system that would be really tough, to say that you can't deny the coverage to someone who may be the best-qualified person you want to hire, but they have a disability which will raise the premiums of you and all your employees, your other employees, by 20 percent under the present system. That happened. We met a couple in Columbus, Ohio, that had one child with a birth defect. They were insured through the wife's community nonprofit, 20-employee group. And in order to keep that family on the rolls and keep that woman working for that business, they were going to have to raise their premiums, just the employees, every employee by another $200 a year, just the employees; the business by thousands of dollars a year. That wouldn't happen if we have community rating. And you could have free flow of workers from job to job to job, something that's quite important since we live in a time when the average worker will change jobs six or seven times in a lifetime.

Finally, and again this is a matter of some controversy in this, we believe that if you put everybody in these competitive size groups, then the businesses and the employees will be able to bargain for better prices: and they will go up far less than they've been going up. We also believe there should be some backup cap on how much business could be required to pay in any given years until we get this system up and going, and we know it is, that there ought to be some ultimate budgetary discipline in the system.

Now, a lot of people say, "Well, that's Government regulation of health care." What they really are saying is this is Government regulation of costs that might work, because it will include the public sector and the private sector. We now strictly regulate the price of particular services under Medicare and Medicaid. Do you know how much the last budget increased Medicare and Medicaid? We reduced defense; we've got domestic discretionary spending flat at a time when we ought to be investing more in education and training, in converting from a defense to a domestic economy. But Medicare, will go up 11 percent next year, Medicaid 16 percent. Why? Paying more for the same health care, that's why, more and more and more and more procedures. You have to have aggregate discipline in this system if you're going to slow the rate of increase.

I personally don't think the budgetary ceiling in our bill will ever be reached because if you give everybody the kind of competitive power that big business and Government have today, I think the cost increases will be much lower than we project them to be, and so do most of the business people I know who have worked on this plan and looked at the cost structure from the bottom up. But I don't think it's fair to say that this is some heavy-handed grab to control the private sector in health care and hurt research in the pharmaceutical industry or anyplace else.

Keep in mind, we have been so conservative or liberal, depending on how you look at it, in our budget estimates. Well, you tell me when I tell you the fact: This plan that we put in estimates that we will go to 17 percent of income spent on health care by the year 2000, as opposed to 19. And it actually will be more than 17, about 17.5 percent. I don't think that's so hot for the economy, either. And I think if we had real competition for quality and service, and if we continue to cover more primary and preventive services, we could do much better than that.

So it's not as if we propose to drive folks into poverty. All these people who are complaining about the ceilings that would be on the rate of increase, the health insurers and others, they're going to get 17.5 percent of our income instead of 14.5 percent by the year 2000. And they think it might not be enough for them to get along on.

I just want to make that clear. You need to understand when you hear all this, about how the Government's regulating this, what we did was put a big old ceiling there in case the costs continue to shoot up even after we give everybody bargaining power. The essence of this is a competitive system for price and quality. And I think it will work.

The second issue is whether or not we have to have universal coverage and whether that's bad for business, to require each business to shoulder some responsibility and each employee not covered now to at least pay some of the income of the employee to get the health care.

Now, here are the options. And here's how we came out with basically taking what we've got. We've got a system in America today that's basically an employer-based system. And when the employers are big enough or they're joined with enough others to have market-based power, the system works pretty well. They're beginning to moderate the rate of cost increases, and there are some very good health care plans out there which provide comprehensive benefits at affordable cost. Sometimes the employees don't pay anything, sometimes they pay something, but basically the systems work pretty well, and most employees are pretty satisfied with it.

The options are the following: If you want universal coverage, you could go to the Canadian system—the problem is that no one I know thinks you could pass that in Congress—which means you basically replace all the health insurance sector of the country with a tax. That's simpler on administrative costs, but since Canada is the second most expensive system, if you put the politicians instead of the people in charge of negotiating for their health care, it may not work out so well. So we rejected that alternative.

Then there are those who say, "Well, you ought to put the mandate on the employee; let the employee buy it. Make it like car insurance." The problem with that is, if you look at what they offer the employees, it's not very good. And it may encourage a total deterioration of the present system we have for those who presently have benefits where the costs are shared by employers and employees.

Then there are those who say, "Well, what we ought to do is give small businesses the right to get this market power, and the competition will lower the rate of cost, and say that no one can be denied coverage. And when you have more competition the price will go down, and everybody who doesn't have insurance who's got a job will be able to buy it. So we'll just see if it happens." The problem with that is that our experience with that is not very good. And what we know is that most employers and employees who have health insurance today are paying too much for it because they're paying for the uncompensated care that others get. And if you want to moderate the rate of increase on individual businesses' and employees' health care, you've got to make sure that everybody who accesses the system pays what they can afford to pay for the privilege of doing that. If you continue to have significant cost shifting here, then there will be continued irresponsibility in the system, which will have real uneven impacts on businesses.

In other words, most everybody in the country today who's got a good health insurance plan is paying too much for it, because they're also paying for the uncompensated care of people who always get care but they get it when it's too late and too expensive. They show up at the emergency room with appendicitis or whatever, instead of ever going in for basic checkups and basic preventive mechanisms.

So I personally don't think we'll ever get costs under control, nor do I ever think we'll be the society we ought to be, nor do I ever think we'll have the kind of personal security we need until everybody has health insurance. And if you don't have universal coverage, this idea that people are going to be able to move from job to job to job and always have it is just false. And I cannot tell you what it is doing to the families of this country who are worrying about it. It is having a devastating impact on the capacity of millions of people to function well in their jobs.

Mr. Hiatt made a very eloquent statement before I came up. When he came to our economic summit in Little Rock last December, he was then famous at having led the way on child care for his employees, and he made the following statement. He said if you do right by your employees, you, quote, contribute to a workplace that attracts good people and retains them, thereby reducing turnover. Good business.

Then there is one other issue I want to deal with on this universal coverage, and that is, a lot of people say it's not fair to ask employers to make some contribution to their part-time employees, that the taxpayers ought to pay for that. We think if there's a part-time employee that works at least 10 hours a week, a pro rata contribution should be made, a third of the total payment that would otherwise be owed, not a total contribution. And the rest will be made up from the monies we propose to raise.

Now, that can be done. Starbucks Coffee's doing pretty well, and they take care of their part-time workers as well as their full-time workers. And there are others who do that. What we want to do is to make that more economical for everyone who will do it.

Finally, let me say it also makes it affordable. The way we propose to pay for this plan, two-thirds of the money would come from premiums paid by employers and employees. But we know we're going to have to give discounts to small businesses with very low-wage employers, because we don't want to put people out of business. And we know the Government has to cover the unemployed uninsured. How will we get the money for that? Essentially from three sources: one, raising the cigarette tax by 75 cents a pack and asking the large employers who opt out of the system, as they can, to make the contribution they would make if they were in the system to medical research and to the network of public health care clinics that we will have to maintain anyway. That's another thing I want to tell you, that this plan increases the quality of health care. We're going to increase medical research, increase the reach of health clinics. That's the second source of money. The third source of money is in the savings we will achieve in the Medicare and Medicaid programs, by putting Medicaid patients, for example, into the same kind of consumer cooperative buying power that those of you who are small and medium-sized businesses will get by going into the alliance, and by drastically simplifying the paperwork of the system. So that's how it will be paid for.

I want to say again, there are these two elements. The health alliances will contribute to competition and to market-based forces getting into the health care system in a good way. It won't be a big new Government bureaucracy. The requirement of universal coverage will help to stop cost shifting and make health care security a reality and permit workers to know that even if they lose a given job, they'll be able to go on as employees. It will, in other words, give that level of personal security necessary for the American people to think about what our trade policy ought to be, what our investment policy ought to be, what our economic strategy ought to be for the 21st century, and to make the changes necessary to get that done.

And I ask you here to think about the influence that you can have on your Members of Congress, without regard to party. This ought to be an American issue. It ought to be a matter of not only the heart but of hard-headed economics. If we don't, if we don't ask everybody to assume some responsibility—and we're not talking about breaking the bank. For a small firm with an average wage of $10,000, for example, the cost would be less than $1 a day per employee for the health care plan because of the discount system.

We understand the fragility of the economy in many points. But if we don't face this now, we are not going to get a hold of the health care cost spiral. We are not going to get a hold of the fact that 100,000 Americans are losing their health insurance a month. We are not going to get a hold of the fact that a lot of these costs just involve our paying more for the same health care every year. We get nothing for it. We're spending a dime on the dollar more than any other country on sheer paperwork, 10 cents on the dollar that nobody else in the world pays.

So I would say to you it is time for us to say everybody ought to be responsible and pay something for this health care system, because we all have access to it. And when we really need it, we all get it. And it's just wrong for some people to pay for others who can pay something for themselves.

And we ought to allow the small businesses of this country and the self-employed people of this country and the medium-sized businesses in this country to have the same benefit of market power that only Government and big business have today. It isn't fair. That's what these alliances do. They are not Government entities, they are private sector entities that we're going to put the Medicaid patients in so they can have the benefit of that, too.

Now, that is the kind of thing that we need to do. That is the sort of security that we need to achieve, to build into the fabric of American life the peace of mind and the sense of fairness and justice that enables people to go home at night and look their children in the face and think they're doing a pretty good job by them, and that enables them to have the kind of personal security that will permit people like you to lead this country to make the economic changes that will enable this country to do what it needs to do as we move toward the 21st century, to keep the American dream alive, to keep this country as the foremost country in the world, to enable all of our children to live up to their God-given capacity.

This is just one of those times when we have to decide whether we're going to close the gap between our rhetoric and our reality. Desperately I hope that 30 years from now people will look back on this time just the way we look back on 60 years ago when there was no Social Security. Now we take it for granted. We think it was an easy fight; it actually wasn't. It took them a couple of years and a little blood on the floor in the Congress to get it done. And this may take a while to get done. It doesn't need to take 2 years, I'll tell you that.

You think about it, Truman, Eisenhower, Kennedy, Johnson, and Nixon all followed Roosevelt, and all of them tried to get universal coverage. Richard Nixon proposed an employer mandate. Senator Bob Packwood from Oregon, still in the United States Senate, introduced it for him. And we've been fooling around with this now for decades. Meanwhile, we just keep paying more for less. We ought to be paying less for more. That's what you do. That's why most of you are doing very well, because you have provided more for less. Why should you be stuck with a health care system that does the reverse?

I ask you to please, please engage yourself in this debate. Examine this plan. When the book comes out, go over it. If you've got a good idea, give it to us. But don't walk away from the plain obligation to have every American family with the security of health care and the plain need to let the small business people in this country and the self-employed people

in this country and the middle-size business in this country have the same bargaining power in this system that big business and Government do.

And most of all, remind the Members of the Congress that there are times when doing the right thing morally and ethically is also good business, that we can make money if we make our workers more secure and whole. When they go home at night and look at their families over the dinner table and they know they've done right by them, then America will be on its way to having the courage and the security to seize the next century and keep the American dream alive.

Thank you, and God bless you all.

NOTE: The President spoke at 11 a.m. at the Grand Hyatt Washington Hotel. In his remarks, he referred to Helen Mills, CEO of the Mills Group and Soap Box Trading Co., and Arnold Hiatt, CEO of the Stride-Rite Foundation.

Exchange With Reporters on Health Care Reform
October 21, 1993

Q. Mr. President, why is it taking you so long to draft the health care legislation?

The President. The legislation has been drafted. What we have to do—and let me say we're doing something that no administration, as far as I know, has ever done before. But the reason that we had to delay introducing it is to go back and do two more runs at higher inflation rates, because most people believe that inflation will be a little bit higher because economic growth has come back into the economy.

So we originally ran all the numbers at a 2.7 inflation rate, which was what we were asked to do, what was recommended by the Congressional Budget Office. We now went back, after consulting with our folks, and ran it at a 3.5 percent inflation rate, and then we went back and doublechecked all the numbers with all the actuaries. So unlike a lot of the other bills, we actually have, you will see when the bill comes

up, extremely detailed budgetary estimates about which part will cost how much and how it all works.

So essentially, there were no problems in drafting or the policy so much as it was trying to make sure that we had the numbers right. Also, the proposal will increase the reserve fund as a hedge in case, for example, the small business discounts cost more than we thought. We decided to go back to make the Congress and the country feel better about the costs to increase the reserve fund. So just working out the dollars is what has taken all the time, because we wanted to have good numbers ready for them when we came back.

Q. When will it be ready? When will it be ready?

The President. Oh, I think they're going to put it in early next week sometime.

Q. Next week?

The President. Yes.

Q. The 75-cent cigarette tax is final?

The President. That's what will be in the bill.

NOTE: The exchange began at approximately 11:54 a.m. at the Grand Hyatt Washington Hotel. A tape was not available for verification of the content of this exchange.

Remarks at the Executive Leadership Council Dinner
October 21, 1993

Thank you very much, Earl, and thank you, ladies and gentlemen. I actually wanted to hear him talk. I thought I've heard the speech the guy behind him has to make.

I am delighted to be here with the ELC, with Earl Washington and Buddy James and with all the rest of you. I thank you for your achievements in life, and I thank you for the work you have done. The board of this organization met at the White House, I know, last spring, and we have developed a very special relationship.

I was honored to be invited to come by the reception for a moment. I wish I could stay for dinner, but before you asked me to eat I got invited somewhere else, and it's not polite to cancel. At least that's what my mama always taught me.

I want to congratulate your honorees tonight, Suzanne de Passe and Corning Corporation and my friend Dr. Leon Sullivan. And I want to thank all of you for the efforts you're making to make America a better place.

I'd like to also say a special word of appreciation to two very important members of my team who are here tonight, a former board member and officer of this organization and your evening speaker, Hazel O'Leary, the distinguished Energy Secretary—when I saw Hazel tonight I thought nobody would be disappointed that I'm not speaking—and also the Special Assistant to the President for Public Liaison and the highest ranking African-American ever to serve in the White House, Ms. Alexis Herman. I thank her for being here.

Ladies and gentlemen, I ran for President in 1991 and 1992 because I was convinced that our country needed to change its direction and because I thought we were coming apart when we ought to be coming together.

I have always believed that the obligation of a public servant is to try to give every person

he or she represents a chance to live up to their God-given capacity and the challenge to do what is necessary to give others that chance as well. That responsibility takes on different turns and textures, depending on the moment in history when you're fortunate enough to serve. Right now, I think all of you know as well or better than I that in order for every person in this country to have a chance to live up· to the fullest of their capacity, all of us have to be committed to making some pretty fundamental changes in the way we operate our economy and the way we work together as a people and the way we relate to the rest of the world.

Whenever people are called upon to change profoundly, we all know that's difficult. I mean, I have a hard time losing 10 pounds. [*Laughter*] Change is not easy. You think about the dimensions of the changes we need to make; we know it is hard. We also know that great democracies normally only make profound changes when it is apparent to all that there is a lot of trouble. The problem with that is, when it's apparent to all that there's a lot of trouble, there are normally a lot of people who are too insecure to want to hear about much change.

If you think about your own life, every one of us has a little balance scale inside, sort of between hope and fear, between being optimistic and averse to today's changes. I know if I get less than 5 hours sleep, I'm less optimistic than I am if I get more than 6, you know. We have that. Every family has it. Every business organization has it. And every nation has it.

I am plagued by the thought of how many Americans are too insecure to feel confident in the future and to grasp the opportunities that are there before us. And so I have this duty to the country, I believe, as President to try to lay down the markers of security that our people need as well as urge them to change. And that's why we're working so hard to provide families more security with things like the Family and Medical Leave Act, to provide people more employment security in a time when you can't have a job security any more—the average person will change jobs seven times in a lifetime—we need a dramatic, radically different way of training and educating our workers; to providing health care security, without which families can't be told if they may have to be willing to change jobs, if they think they're going to have to put their kids in the poor house because they don't have any health insurance; and to try to deal with issues of personal security—ninety thousand people killed in America in the last 4 years alone, in any year more than we ever lost in any given year in the war in Vietnam. This is the only advanced country in the world where teenagers are better armed than police officers. We talk about how terrible it is and refuse to do anything about it.

But just because we are insecure, many of us, doesn't mean we can put off until tomorrow the changes we need to make. You know, whenever you're confronted with a new and challenging set of circumstances that requires you to change, you can do one of two things: You can sort of hunker down and turn away and hope it will go away, or you can face it. Now, hunkering down works about once in 100. Most of the time, it's a real loser. And what I'm trying to do as President is to also tell the American people, "Look, this Government's on your side. We're trying to lay down these elements of security for families, for safe streets, for health care, for workers. But we have to change."

The most important fight we're going to have between now and the end of the year on the change front is the fight to ratify the North American Free Trade Agreement. And most of the opposition to the agreement comes from people who have deep-seated hurts, resentments, and reservation that are legitimate based on their own experience, because the working families of this country are by and large working longer work weeks than they were 20 years ago for the same or lower wages than they were making 10 years ago—we all know that—and because many people have been in work units where they think they have been treated like so much disposable material, where they didn't feel that they were put first or even

considered. And so they look at more change in the global economy and think, "Oh, what a headache."

But rationally, NAFTA will make everything that they resent better. And the failure to pass it will make everything worse. Wages in Mexico will go up faster if we adopt NAFTA than if we don't. And the Mexican Government will make a commitment to honor their own labor code in ways that are not there now. Environmental investments in Mexico will go up more if we adopt NAFTA than if we don't. Requirements in Mexico that keep us out of the Mexican market—requirements to produce products there if we want to sell them there—will go down if we adopt it. They won't if we don't. Trade barriers, tariffs will go down if we adopt it. They won't if we don't. We have trade problems in America: $50 billion deficit with Japan; a $19 billion deficit with China; a $9 billion deficit with Taiwan. We have a $6 billion trade surplus with Mexico. And even though it's not a very wealthy country, 70 cents of every dollar they spend on products from overseas beyond their borders they spend on American products.

So I say to you, I very much hope that we'll have a wonderful open world trading system. I'm working hard to get one by the end of the year. But neither you nor I know with any certainty what the trading philosophy of Asia or Europe will be 5 or 10 years from now. We do know democracy is on the move in Latin America. We do know free markets are on the move in Latin America. And we do know that they prefer to deal with us, not just in Mexico but in other countries.

And the benefits of NAFTA come not just from new jobs being created out of the relationship between the U.S. and Mexico, although we are convinced 200,000 new jobs will be created. And on average, they'll be better paying jobs just in the next 2 years. The real benefits will come in new jobs when that agreement is the standard by which we set new agreements with Chile, with Venezuela, with Argentina, with all the other countries that want very much to be part of our family.

Every one of you here in some way or another is a profound success. All of you have had to deal with these kinds of conflicts in your own lives. Many of you have overcome enormous obstacles to get where you were, and not a single one of you is at the top of any heap today because you hunkered down or ran away from an opportunity to embrace change and embrace the future.

And so I ask you as Americans to help us in this next month convince the United States Congress that the people who are pleading with them to vote against this treaty have legitimate fears, legitimate hurt, legitimate worries. But they are imposing on NAFTA the accumulated resentment for the last 15 years, and it doesn't deserve to have it. If you look at the facts, it will make those problems better, not worse.

You have credibility with a lot of people in the Congress, in both parties, of different races and backgrounds. And if you can convince them that together we're not only going to lay down these security markers that we have to lay down, but we must have the courage to change, then we can go into 1994 having brought the deficit down, with the lowest interest rates in 30 years, with business investment going up, with housing going up, with unemployment going down, and with a view toward the future that gives us the confidence we need to make the future what it has to be for our people.

Thank you very much and God bless you all.

NOTE: The President spoke at 6:20 p.m. in the Sheraton North Ballroom at the Sheraton Washington Hotel. In his remarks, he referred to Earl S. Washington, president, and Clarence James, Jr., executive director, Executive Leadership Council.

Remarks at a Democratic National Committee Dinner
October 21, 1993

Thank you very much. David, I was hoping you'd talk a little longer; I didn't even get to finish my salad. [*Laughter*]

Ladies and gentlemen, I'm delighted to be here tonight. I've already had a chance to say hello to almost all of you, except the Members of the Senate who see me all the time. I thanked Senator Metzenbaum and Senator Levin—they came upstairs to see me, Senator Kennedy. We even had our picture taken. I came all the way to Boston to see you, and you didn't do that. [*Laughter*] I want to thank Norman Brownstein for the wonderful work he did tonight in getting you all here. Let's give him a hand. [*Applause*]

I'd also like to say a brief word if I might about this wonderful facility we are in. We have some people here who are still associated with it. The Holladays, who helped to found this, were good enough to support me early in my Presidential campaign. And a lot of our friends have been active in this wonderful place which once actually had a fine showing of artists, women artists, from my home State here. So I have been delighted to have finally the chance to come here and see this and I—Mr. Chairman, I don't know who picked this place, but whoever did is a near genius in my estimation, because I love it.

It was just about a month and a week ago when we had the remarkable signing of the Israel-PLO peace accord on the grounds of the White House. Many of you were there. I imagine all of you saw it. Hundreds of millions, perhaps over a billion people around the world saw it occur. I would like to begin my remarks by making two observations, if I might. First of all, about the peace process itself. When I traveled across this country last year and asked many, if not all of you, to support my campaign, I said that I believed the time was ripe for peace in the Middle East but that it could not be achieved unless the President of the United States understood that in the end the United States could never impose a peace on the Middle East but could only guarantee it if it were to occur. After I was elected, I met with Yitzhak Rabin in the White House, and we sat for a long time alone. And he looked at me with those soulful eyes of his and said that he was prepared to take real risks for peace, that he thought the time had come to try to make it. And I told him, if he would take the risks, we would do our best to minimize those risks. The rest is history. It was a peace made directly between Israel and the PLO, as all the best agreements are. It was a difficult thing, as we saw during the signing, sometimes from the language, sometimes from the body language. But as the Prime Minister said, "One never makes peace with one's friends. You have to make peace with your enemies."

I want all of you to know that since that day I think that we have gone forward together to try to make the peace stick, to try to make it work, and to try to expand on it. We've had a donors' conference of representatives from 43 nations raise several billion dollars in commitments from people to make this peace agreement work. We have seen now the first public meeting of leaders from Jordan and Israel. We've seen the states of Morocco and Tunisia welcome Israeli officials for the first time. We have seen real progress. There is still a lot to do. I have urged the Arab States to recognize Israel, to drop the boycott, to get rid of the hostile United Nations resolutions. And I have done what I could to keep this process going.

An especially remarkable part of it has been the unity I have seen emerging between leaders of the American Jewish community and Arab-Americans, a couple of hundred of whom met at the White House for several hours after the signing ceremony and began to explore what they can do together to try to help to bring opportunity and peace and harmony in the areas where the peace accord covered.

I believe we're moving in the right direction. I also have to tell you I don't think that we will have a complete peace until we have just that, a complete peace: one that involves Syria and Lebanon, as well as the PLO and Jordan; one that enables the people of the Middle East to live together in true security and to give the children of that area a normal life. I want to ask you tonight to help me to stay with our present policy, to be aggressive in pushing the process forward but to recognize always that in the end, there is no peace that the parties do not themselves voluntarily undertake.

When we had that signing ceremony, I wanted so much for the Prime Minister and Mr. Arafat to come, but they couldn't make up their minds whether they wanted to come for a while, for reasons that I'm sure all of you appreciate, many of you more deeply than I. In the end they decided to come because, since they had agreed to it, they might as well make the most of it. And when they did and when they reached out across decades of division and shook hands in that electric moment that was felt around the world, I think that people had a sense of possibility in so many areas that they had not had for a long time.

That's the second thing I want to say to you tonight, as I ask you on behalf of your country, on behalf of Israel, on behalf of all the peace-loving peoples of the world, to continue to help me to implement this peace process and push it forward, respecting that in the end all the parties themselves will have to voluntarily decide on the next steps.

I ask you also to help me to give that sense of possibility back to the American people. For there are so many days when I think that the biggest obstacle to the dreams I brought with me to the Presidency, the biggest obstacle is the sense that maybe we really can't change things, the sense of hopelessness so many people feel, the sense of mistrust in institutions and leaders. It is, I think, almost a truism that no great democracy can change profoundly until things are in pretty rough shape. And yet, when things get in pretty rough shape, there are so many people who have been so disappointed, who feel so injured, who feel so insecure that it is difficult to make the changes that need to be made. And so today, America, every day, gets up and presents to me a complex picture of hope and fear, a complex picture of eagerness to embrace the future, to compete and to win, and to promote the things we all believe in and a sense of insecurity that makes people sort of draw inward.

I think for the last year, hope has been winning. A sense of possibility and movement has been happening. Thanks to the people in the Congress who have supported the initiatives of this administration, including those in this audience, we have moved to really bring down the deficit. We've got the lowest interest rates in 30 years, business investment's back up, consumer spending is back up on important, big products.

We've got some real sense of movement in this economy. Thanks to this group of Congress Members who have been willing to support this administration, we signed, a week after the Middle East peace accord, the national service bill that Eli Segal did so much to shepherd through the Congress, which literally has the potential to revolutionize the way young people all across America look at their country and feel about themselves, which asks young people to give something back to their Nation and, in return, offers them a chance to go to college, no matter how meager their own income.

We have begun to face the health care crisis.

We have begun to deal with so many issues that have been too long ignored in this struggle to find our way in the world. There are those who have said, well, I haven't done everything right. For that, I plead guilty. But I'll tell you one thing: In this administration, we show up for work every day with our sleeves rolled up and a determination to face the challenges before us. And tonight I was thinking about the history of our relationships with Israel; I'm reminded that when Harry Truman recognized Israel, a long time ago now, he was still in the process of making the post-World-War II world with our allies. We had moved into the cold war, but now we all look back on that era as if it were self-evident what our domestic policies ought to be and what our foreign policies ought to be. But in truth, those of you who lived through that, particularly those of you who were adults or nearly so, then, will remember clearly that there were a couple of years after World War II when we had to work out what our foreign policy was going to be, when we had to develop the institutions necessary to carry that foreign policy out, when we had to work through in our minds what America's responsibilities at home were. And we are going through the same period now.

We know that we are the only superpower. We know we can't solve every problem in the world, but we know there are a lot of people's suffering and misery that we can alleviate. And if we believe in democracy and freedom, if we don't want to see the proliferation of terrorism and weapons of mass destruction, then we have to try.

We know that we have an interest in Russia maintaining its democratic bent and continuing to reduce its nuclear arsenal. Clearly, we know if we could bring peace to the Middle East, it might revolutionize the range of options we have with the Muslims all over the world and give us the opportunity to beat back the forces of radicalism and terrorism that unfairly have been identified with Islam by so many people.

We know some things for sure. But we also know that we are still working this out. Here at home, it is the same thing. But I can tell you this: I am convinced that if we will continue to honestly speak with one another about these issues, we'll find a way to do it.

I believe we have to find a balance between the security people need to change and the changes we need to make. I believe we will

never make America what it ought to be until we provide health care security to all of our citizens. I believe we will never have an America that is strong until we tell the American people, "You can be a successful parent and a successful worker." That's what that family leave bill was all about. That's what our budget bill was all about, which lifted the working poor out of poverty when they have children at home.

I believe we will never be able to do what we need to do as a people until we say, "Okay, if we can't guarantee you a job anymore, we can at least guarantee you employability." If the average person has to change jobs eight times in a lifetime, how can we not have a program worthy of the capacities of all Americans. It gives them a chance for lifetime education and training.

And finally, let me say, I believe we will never meet our challenges at home and abroad until the American people are more secure on their own streets again. For all the violence in the Middle East, my friends, we can read stories every day on every street in America that rivals anything you can read about in the Gaza in the toughest times. If you look at what has happened, 90,000 murders in 4 years in America, more in any given year than ever happened at the height of the war in Vietnam; you look at the fact that this is the only advanced country in the world, the only one where we don't even check your criminal record or your mental health history in some States to see if you can get a gun and where people seriously argue that that infringes on constitutional rights. This is the only country in the world where police go to work on mean streets every day and confront young people who grew up in chaotic circumstances who are often better armed than they are.

So, I say to you, we have some things to do here at home. We are breeding generation after generation of people who have no claim to the mainstream of this society and on whom the future has no claim. We are breeding so many people who are so alienated and who have no sense of all these things that you and I came here to celebrate tonight. Just 3 weeks ago, a little girl named Launice Smith was shot and killed in this city. She was on a playground 3½ miles from this wonderful building. She was 4 years old, one of 1,500 people who are shot in this town every year, our Nation's Capital. Her father could not go to her funeral because he's in prison for shooting another 4-year-old on another playground several years ago when he was 19 and got in an argument over hair barrettes. He got angry, and another kid handed him a gun, and he used it.

The point of all that I am saying is this: We've got to change in this country. And we've got to have the security——

[*At this point, there was an interruption in the tape.*]

——have to first recognize that the great power of America is the power of our ideals, our values, our institutions, and our example. And that we cannot do what we're supposed to do unless, as a Nation we are both more united and more self confident than millions of our fellow citizens are as we enjoy this great dinner tonight.

So, I ask you to remember that and to renew your commitment not only to peace in the Middle East and to American's continuing role in the world—and I thank the many of you who said as we walked through the line tonight, that you believed we did have a role of leadership in the world to alleviate suffering and to do what we can to promote freedom and democracy—but also, to rebuild this country here at home.

Most people in this country, whatever their incomes, whatever their race, whatever their walk of life, and wherever they live, are wonderful people. They get up every day. They go to work. They never break the law. They do the best they can by their kids, and they're

absolutely determined to make the most they can of their lives. But they are living in a country that has not yet made the decisions necessary to organize itself in a way that permits all of us to live up to the fullest of our God-given capacities. And until we make the decision to have an economic program, an education program, a health care program, a family policy, and a law enforcement policy, and a commitment to rescuing our kids that will permit us to do that, we will not have the security we need to lead the world and to face the future. I believe that we are on the road to changing this country. I know what I saw on September the 13th, when Arafat and Rabin shook hands, was an instant, shocking realization all across the world that things we never thought possible were, in fact, possible.

And I ask you to help me now liberate the imagination and the spirit, and the energy of the American people for the jobs that we have yet to do at home and abroad, because those things can also be done.

Thank you, and God bless you all.

NOTE: The President spoke at 8:30 p.m., at the National Museum of Women in the Arts. In his remarks, he referred to David Wilhelm, chairman of the Democratic National Committee; Norman Brownstein, attorney and Democratic fundraiser from Denver, CO; and Wilhelmina Holladay, president, National Museum of Women in the Arts, and her husband, Wallace Holladay.

Message to the Congress Transmitting the Poland-United States Fishery Agreement
October 21, 1993

To the Congress of the United States:

In accordance with the Magnuson Fishery Conservation and Management Act of 1976 (Public Law 94–265; 16 U.S.C. 1801 *et seq.*), I transmit herewith an Agreement between the Government of the United States of America

and the Government of the Republic of Poland Extending the Agreement of August 1, 1985, Concerning Fisheries off the Coasts of the United States. The agreement, which was effected by an exchange of notes at Washington June 8 and July 29, 1993, extends the 1985 agreement for an additional 2 years, from December 31, 1993, to December 31, 1995. The exchange of notes together with the 1985 agreement constitute a governing international fishery agreement within the requirements of section 201(c) of the Act.

I urge that the Congress give favorable consideration to this agreement at an early date.

WILLIAM J. CLINTON

The White House,
October 21, 1993.

Message to the Senate Transmitting the Slovak Republic-United States Taxation Convention
October 21, 1993

To the Senate of the United States:

I transmit herewith for Senate advice and consent to ratification the Convention Between the United States of America and the Slovak Republic for the Avoidance of Double Taxation and the Prevention of Fiscal Evasion with Respect to Taxes on Income and Capital, signed at Bratislava on October 8, 1993. Also transmitted for the information of the Senate is the report of the Department of State with respect to the Convention.

The Convention will be the first income tax convention between the two countries. It is intended it reduce the distortions (double taxation or excessive taxation) that can arise when two countries tax the same income. It will modernize tax relations between the two countries and will facilitate greater private sector U.S. investment in the Slovak Republic.

I recommend that the Senate give early and favorable consideration to the Convention and give its advice and consent to ratification.

WILLIAM J. CLINTON

The White House,
October 21, 1993.

Message to the Senate Transmitting the Czech Republic-United States Taxation Convention
October 21, 1993

To the Senate of the United States:

I transmit herewith for Senate advice and consent to ratification the Convention Between the United States of America and the Czech Republic for the Avoidance of Double Taxation and the Prevention of Fiscal Evasion with Respect to Taxes on Income and Capital, signed at Prague on September 16, 1993. Also transmitted for the information of the Senate is the report of the Department of State with respect to the Convention.

The Convention will be the first income tax convention between the two countries. It is intended to reduce the distortions (double taxation or excessive taxation) that can arise when two countries tax the same income. It will modernize tax relations between the two countries and will facilitate greater private sector U.S. investment in the Czech Republic.

I recommend that the Senate give early and favorable consideration to the Convention and give its advice and consent to ratification.

WILLIAM J. CLINTON

The White House,
October 21, 1993.

Statement on Signing the Agriculture, Rural Development, Food and Drug Administration, and Related Agencies Appropriations Act, 1994
October 21, 1993

Today I have signed into law H.R. 2493, the "Agriculture, Rural Development, Food and Drug Administration, and Related Agencies Appropriations Act, 1994."

The bill makes a significant shift in priorities by funding $745 million of my investment proposals, including full funding of the investment proposals for the Food Safety and Inspection initiative and for the Food and Drug Administration.

The Congress has also adopted my goal to phase in full funding for the Special Supplemental Food Program for Women, Infants and Children (WIC). This bill provides $3.2 billion for WIC, an increase of 12 percent over FY 1993.

The bill includes significant funding for my Rural Development initiative, which will provide grants, direct loans, and loan guarantees for rural residents, communities, and businesses, as well as for inducements to promote economic development.

I commend the Congress for making further progress toward reform of price-support programs for honey, wool, and mohair as recommended by the National Performance Review. The bill suspends honey subsidy payments for the 1994 crop of honey; however, payments on the 1993 honey crop will be made in FY 1994.

I am pleased that the removal of employment floors will facilitate my objective of reducing Federal employment.

WILLIAM J. CLINTON

The White House,
October 21, 1993.

NOTE: H.R. 2493, approved October 21, was assigned Public Law No. 103–111.

Statement on Signing the Departments of Labor, Health and Human Services, and Education, and Related Agencies Appropriations Act, 1994
October 21, 1993

Today I have signed into law H.R. 2518, the "Labor, Health and Human Services, and Education, and Related Agencies Appropriations Act, 1994."

This Act provides funding for the Departments of Labor, Health and Human Services, and Education, the Corporation for Public Broadcasting, and several smaller agencies. Programs within these agencies address the training and employment needs of our Nation's work force, the Federal role in our education system, and fundamental elements of our health care network.

This Act provides funding for a number of my high-priority investment proposals within the Departments of Labor, Health and Human Services (HHS), and Education. These include the Head Start program, Goals 2000 program, School-to-Work program, Immunization grants, and the National Institutes of Health.

The Act provides funding for investment initiatives for automation and disability processing within the Social Security Administration (SSA). This will help SSA improve the quality of service to millions of Americans.

I am pleased that the Act provides a large increase in funding for programs authorized under the Ryan White CARE Act. Programs authorized under this Act represent major steps forward in the battle against the AIDS epidemic.

WILLIAM J. CLINTON

The White House,
October 21, 1993.

NOTE: H.R. 2518, approved October 21, was assigned Public Law No. 103–112. This statement was released by the Office of the Press Secretary on October 22.

Statement on Signing the Continuing Appropriations Resolution
October 21, 1993

Today I have signed into law H.J. Res. 281, a Continuing Resolution that funds the operations of the Federal Government during October 22–28, 1993.

A Continuing Resolution is necessary at this time in order to keep the Government functioning while the Congress completes the appropriations process.

I commend the Congress for presenting me with a funding measure that provides for a simple, temporary extension of normal government operations and is free of extraneous amendments. I urge the Congress to complete the regular appropriations process by October 28th so that an additional Continuing Resolution can be avoided.

WILLIAM J. CLINTON

The White House,
October 21, 1993.

NOTE: H.J. Res. 281, approved October 21, was assigned Public Law No. 103–113. This statement was released by the Office of the Press Secretary on October 22.

Remarks and an Exchange With Reporters Prior to a Meeting With Members of Congress
October 22, 1993

NAFTA

The President. Ladies and gentlemen, just let me make one opening remark, and I'll answer a couple of questions. I want to thank Mr. Michel for once again bringing a group of Republicans in—that he and Mr. Gingrich have arranged for some first-term Republicans to come in and meet with me and Ambassador Kantor and Mr. Frenzel and Mr. Daley. And we're glad to have a chance to discuss NAFTA.

This has been a hard week for us, a hard working week. I have made several congressional meetings, and of course we had the great products fair with Mr. Iacocca. We're trying to work out some of the practical details now on how to deal with the reduction of the tariffs that will come from NAFTA and all that. But I feel much better than I did on Monday about where we are.

I've made, also, a large number of personal phone calls to Democrats this week, and I think we're making some good progress.

Q. Mr. President, do you think you're working hard enough so that Mr. Gingrich would no longer describe your efforts as "pathetic"?

The Vice President. He didn't say that, did he?

Q. He somehow said that, Mr. Vice President. I don't know how. [*Laughter*]

The President. He didn't——

Q. Could you——

The President. You know, one of the things that I've noticed about Washington is that when you're in a tough fight, you know, some people are always wondering about what happens if you don't make it. I'm just worried about making it. If I make it, I don't care who gets credit for it.

I'll tell you this: I'm trying to win it. And the Democrats have been—some of them have been asking me to ease up. They said every time they turn around, there's another member of the Cabinet in their office, and they're calling them at 11 o'clock at night. So I think we're doing a pretty good job. But if we win, it won't matter.

District of Columbia

Q. What do you think about sending the National Guard, or allowing the National Guard to patrol the city here?

The President. I think it should be reviewed. I've given a lot of thought to it, and I've asked our legal counsel to get with the Justice Department and look into the legality of it and what the legal hurdles are and also what the practical problems are.

Keep in mind, guardsmen are not full-time military people. They do weekend duty, by and large. And except in the summertime, again by and large, they're not on full-time duty. So if you call out the Guard in other times in any substantial numbers, you can be disrupting the normal work lives of a lot of people.

But I'm very sympathetic with the problems that the Mayor has and that Washington has. There are 1,500 shootings here a year now. It's one reason—I certainly hope that we can pass this crime bill in a hurry. If we do, we'll have another 50,000 police officers on the street, and it will reduce the pressure for National Guard officers.

But I will review it, and I think it deserves to be reviewed. It obviously is not a precedent that can easily be confined just to Washington, DC. So there are lots of questions that have to be thought through here. But I want to wait until she sends me the letter and then review the specific proposal.

I hope that we can use this moment to emphasize the need to move on the Brady bill, the crime bill, the question of whether minors should be restricted in the ownership of handguns, the questions of the assault weapons. I think all of these things are part of a rising tide of anger and fear and frustration on the part of the American people that we need to respond to.

Haiti

Q. Mr. President, are you beginning to be concerned that the sanctions won't work in time for Aristide to go back next Saturday as scheduled?

The President. I've always been concerned about that.

Q. Will it have to be today?

The President. I think that the sanctions are very tough now. And I think what the others have to think about is what it's going to be like to them a few months from now, what it is that they're fighting so hard to hold on to if these sanctions are fully implemented. We never thought that they could have an impact on their own merits within a week, although they are having some impact already. But I think that the reason we got the Governors Island Agreement in the first place is because of the sanctions. I don't know why they thought that they could ignore it and not have sanctions, but I think now they know they can.

Thank you very much.

Visit to Russia

Q. [*Inaudible*]—going to Moscow?

The President. Helen [Helen Thomas, United Press International] asked me a question about it this morning. I still don't believe we've finalized a date. But the Vice President is going next—I mean, not next month but in December. And I plan to go in January, but we haven't finalized the date. We may do it before the day's over. We don't have a date.

Thank you.

Q. It's pretty cold in January.

The President. I've been there in January. It's light about 4 hours a day. Shows you my timing.

NOTE: The President spoke at 9:17 a.m. in the Cabinet Room at the White House. A tape was not available for verification of the content of these remarks.

Remarks on the Technology Reinvestment Project
October 22, 1993

Thank you very much, Mr. Vice President. General Short, Admiral Pelaez, Dr. Alam, Dr. Dinis, Senator Mitchell and distinguished Members of Congress. And let me say a special word of thanks to my good friend, Senator Bingaman, and to Pat Schroeder, for the work they have done on this.

When I started running for President, one of the core ideas that animated my campaign and that got me really committed to the long endeavor of 1992 was the commitment that we had to find a way as we built down defenses to build up a new economy for America with new partnerships between defense technologies and the commercial future that we all seek for our country.

I'd like to put this at least briefly into a larger context. All of you know we are living in a time when all the wealthy nations of the world are having great difficulty creating new jobs. We are now in the fifth year in which the average annual growth among the wealthiest nations has been under 2 percent. And as we look toward the future and we ask ourselves what is it that will regenerate the American economic engine in a new and highly competitive global economy in which technology and money and management are mobile, and in which many people in different parts of the world will do certain things for wages our people can't live on, it is perfectly clear that there are three things we have to do: We have to better educate and train our work force; we have to find new markets for our products and services; and we have to more rapidly develop new technologies, so that technology can continue to be what it has always been for our country and for the world, a net job generator.

We know that technologies reduce the number of people necessary to perform traditional services in everything from agriculture to manufacturing. But technology has historically been a net job generator because every time it's done that, it's opened up new ways for people to make a living.

There are significant barriers to that today in this country and in all wealthy countries. The reason I believe so strongly in this project, and the reason I believe someday this will become an integral part of our economic policy, not just a way of converting from a defense to a domestic economy, is because we have to find a way to create more new applications for more new technologies more quickly so that we can create more jobs.

I am very, very happy about this day, and I want to thank all of those who had anything to do with bringing it about. I also want to say, to echo the Vice President, that the first awards in our Technology Reinvestment Project were definitely made on the merits. They were made, not surprisingly, largely in areas that had large technological bases related to defense technology where people have suffered very greatly from cutbacks and are very aggressively looking for alternatives. That provided a big incentive for those folks to be very active in trying to build a new future. But that is, after all, I'm sure what Senator Bingaman had in mind and what the Congress had in mind in funding this program.

If we're really going to guarantee the security of America—the national security of America— we have to be more economically secure. We have to invest in projects that will create these jobs with new ideas and new technologies. That is the only way, I believe, to keep our Nation strong.

This effort responds to two challenges left in the wake of the end of the cold war. The first is that you simply can't leave the men and women who won the cold war out in the cold. It is wrong to walk away from them. From southern California to Long Island to Connecticut, there are communities, companies, and employees who've depended on defense who now are desperately looking for new ways to make a living. And they can help to make America the strongest country in the world, economically, even into the 21st century.

The second challenge we have is one that is often ignored, but must not be. And that is to meet our continuing military needs in a world which still contains dangers to our interests, our values, our security in a time when we may and we want to spend a smaller percentage of our national income every year on defense but when we know we still have to maintain our lead in defense technologies. So this effort really not only helps us to create new jobs in the civilian sector, it is very good for traditional national defense concerns.

The purposes we are promoting are illustrated by the projects that are being supported today. And let me just mention a couple of them. A California-based team is seeking to demonstrate how advanced composite materials developed for high-performance military aircraft can offer major advantages for repairing and replacing our Nation's aging bridges. I have seen some of the preliminary work on a recent trip to southern California. It's a very, very impressive idea, with enormous potential in a Nation like the United States which has woefully neglected its infrastructure for 15 or 20 years now, and which has a huge number of bridges which desperately need repairing.

This technology will also help the Army Corps of Engineers build lightweight and mobile bridges in combat situations or following natural disasters such as the one we recently had in the Midwest flood, where so many bridges were wiped out and so many working people were literally cut off from their jobs or faced four-hour one-way drives just to get to their jobs.

Another example: A small defense firm is adapting its pyrotechnic technology for use in emergency rescue equipment. You might ask, "How can you have explosive technology used in rescue?" Most people are rescued from that. [*Laughter*] This effort can, nevertheless, create a whole new generation of jaws-of-life rescue devices that can save time by making hydraulic equipment much easier to operate. The reductions in weight and cost will make these devices available even to small rescue teams.

I can tell you as a former Governor of a State with a lot of rural communities, I spent an enormous amount of time just trying to figure out how to get this kind of equipment out to people and then how to make sure there were people there trained to use it. This could be a very significant thing in managing traumatic situations in rural communities, especially those that are isolated. By commercializing this technology we'll help to preserve a part of the pyrotechnic industry that is important to our Nation's defense, as well as solving the problems of Americans here at home.

We're working with a team of companies and research labs to determine how the high-powered lasers that have been developed for the military can be adapted to make civilian products. The technology will offer higher precision and greater tooling speeds. This can help American industries from automobiles to aerospace, agricultural equipment, electronics, ship building, all these industries compete and win around the world. And after more than a decade in which our machine tools have suffered significant setbacks in the global economy, this offers a real chance for us to take back a significant sector of international trade.

We're also supporting retraining programs for scientists, engineers, and other defense workers all across the country, in Alabama, Arizona, California, Michigan, New Jersey, New York, North Carolina, Ohio, and Washington. Our world is being transformed by technological, economic, and political change. This project is a part of our overall strategy in this administration to make those changes our friend instead of our enemy.

Whether we're cutting the national deficit or investing in a whole new education and training program, or reforming the welfare system, or providing health security, or expanding trade, we know that all these things have to be done if we're going to really allow the American people to live up to the fullest of their potential.

We're working hard here in the Government to set an example, under the Vice President's leadership, to give this reinventing Government effort a technological twist that maybe some of you ought to contribute to also in this project. And we want to set an example, but we also want to help lead the country to make the changes that will help us all to change our lives for the better.

We know that doing nothing is not an option. And I want to say in closing that this is one idea that has really caught on with the Congress. I think because of the debates that have been held over the last couple of years and because of the pressures that have been brought to bear in areas all across America, from the dislocations, the painful dislocations, from defense cuts, there's a real commitment. And I want to thank the Congress here that even in the closing days in our debates over the budget, when we have cut and cut and cut so many areas, this program was dramatically increased for next year so that we can maintain the pace of these projects. And I hope we'll be able to increase it year-in and year-out as long as there are new ideas, new technologies, new jobs, and new movement for the American economy.

Thank you all very much.

NOTE: The President spoke at 10:47 a.m. in Room 450 of the Old Executive Office Building. In his remarks, he referred to Lt. Gen. Alonzo E. Short, Jr., USA, Director, Defense Information Systems Agency; Rear Adm. Marc Pelaez, USN, Chief of Naval Research; M. Kathleen Alam, technical staff member, Sandia National Laboratories; and Antonio Dinis, president and chief executive officer, J. Muller International.

Interview With Stephen Clark of KGTV, San Diego, California
October 22, 1993

Technology Reinvestment Project

Mr. Clark. UCSD, University of California-San Diego, was the one you named today from this area?

The President. That's right. They have a project that will use composite materials that were part of the Stealth aircraft development to build and repair bridges. There are others; let me just tell you where the others are in southern California. We have one in Redondo Beach that Cal State-Fullerton was involved in; one at Newport Beach with Hughes Electric, G.M. Hughes; one in Torrance—two in Torrance. So if you want to mention any of them, we can.

Mr. Clark. Joining us now to talk about what is called the first wave of the Technology Reinvestment Program grant is the author of the plan, more or less, the President of the United States, Mr. Clinton. Thanks for joining us today to talk about what we here in San Diego call the defense conversion. Can you give us kind of a short definition or explanation of what it is you want to accomplish here?

The President. Yes, we're trying to take the capacities, the skills, the technologies that were developed in the big defense build-up of the 1980's, and instead of just letting those technologies and the abilities of those people go to waste, we want to give them a chance to be used in the commercial sector in a way that helps both national defense by keeping that skill and that technology alive and helps to rebuild the domestic economy and to create jobs.

Today we announced the first of what will be four announcements between now and the end of November in the technology research project, which involved 41 projects from California to Maine from former defense contractors or current defense contractors using technologies in defense for domestic purposes.

In San Diego, the University of San Diego and Muller International and a company called Trans-Science Corporation are using the composite materials developed for the Stealth aircraft to build and repair bridges. And they're working on a bridge in San Diego now. And this is just one of, as I said, over 40 projects. California got a large number of these projects but so did several other States that have been hurt by base closing and defense cutbacks. They were all given out on the merits, I assure you, and now what the companies have to do is to negotiate with our defense conversion projects to make sure that the Government and the companies all put up a fair amount of money. Then they'll start hiring people and going to work. We're very excited about it.

Mr. Clark. Mr. President, some claim that if it was a good idea, a strong company would run with that idea. Do you run a risk of propping up a bad company or a bad idea?

The President. There may be some risk of that, but it's not much of a risk. After all, in terms of the potential expenditure of money, this is mostly seed money to get these projects started. A lot of these companies are quite well-established, and these technologies have proven merit in the defense area. This is the sort of thing that our competitors in Germany, Japan, countries with lower unemployment rates and higher investment rates than we do, they do these things all the time. We know the technology, the skills, the ideas to make the conversion, but we aren't organized for it. This simply helps us to organize to make this conversion from a defense-based to a domestic economy. It will create a lot of jobs. And I think that it will be among the most efficient Government programs ever seen because, keep in mind, we don't put up all the money; if the other side doesn't put up half the money, the project doesn't get done. So, that's a pretty strong incentive to make sure whatever is done is a good project.

Mr. Clark. Mr. President, UCSD's $21 million—granted, nobody wants to look a gift horse in the mouth, but it's really a drop in the bucket when you consider what San Diego has lost so far in cutbacks in the military and defense jobs.

The President. It is, but that's the point. It starts up a new business enterprise for which there must be a market in the private sector. We believe there's a huge market. That's why all these things are helping to start up a process.

Keep in mind, too, that San Diego gained 5,200 jobs in the last round of base closings and consolidations, so those new jobs will be coming into your area over the next couple of years, and that will help some also.

Mr. Clark. Mr. President, thank you very much for joining us today.

The President. Thank you.

NOTE: The interview began at 11:50 a.m. The President spoke via satellite from Room 459 of the Old Executive Office Building.

Interview With Rolland Smith of KNSD–TV, San Diego
October 22, 1993

Technology Reinvestment Project

The President. I think we're ready now.

Mr. Smith. Mr. President, your technology reinvestment project has been funded for $472 million. You have received proposals for 2,850 projects requesting $8.4 billion. Doesn't that tell us that much more is needed?

The President. Absolutely. We just got another $500-plus million through the Congress that we'll be coming forward with next year. And in January I expect to ask for more money for this program. Much more money is needed, and I hope the Congress will now be willing to provide more money for it. There were both Democratic and Republican Members of Congress from California to the East Coast at our announcement today. And I'm very hopeful now that when Members of Congress see the incredible number of worthy projects and the potential they have to revolutionize our economy in America and to put our high-tech workers back to work and to create more jobs, that they'll be able to fund it. I'm very excited. But keep in mind, this is a big first step.

Mr. Smith. Mr. President, you said in your announcement today that we needed new training, new markets, new technologies. What do you say to the General Dynamics worker who has lost his job and lost his home, to the biotech worker who has lost his job and home, what do you say to them now? They need help now.

The President. I say that I'm doing the very best I can. We started cutting back on defense long before I became President. The defense cuts started in '87, and there was no investment in defense conversion to amount to anything until I took office. The Congress appropriated $500 million last year which was not even released by the previous administration until I took office. I believe in defense conversion. I believe in helping those people through retrain-

ing, through new investments, through new job opportunities, through things like this technology reinvestment project. And I'm going to do the very best I can to give them the opportunities that they need and that our country needs for them to have.

Mr. Smith. The UCSD project, using materials for helping to fix bridges and make new lightweight ones, how many jobs do you think that will create?

The President. Depends on what the market for bridges are. But let me just say that if you look at the evidence, at literally the thousands of bridges in America that are in disrepair, that desperately need repair, and the potential that this material has to permit that repair to be done quickly and efficiently, there may be a virtually unlimited market for it. It depends on how quickly they can make sure that this prototype bridge they're building works and then how quickly they can get out to every State in the country that controls the market for bridge repair and market this product. But I would say that there is an enormous potential to generate new jobs and incomes in your area because of this, for the simple reason that we have thousands and thousands of bridges which should have been repaired in the eighties which weren't.

Immigration

Mr. Smith. Mr. President, we've got a border war of sorts going on here in San Diego. A lot of it has to do with illegal aliens coming across taking some jobs. And now there's an "anti" feeling on both sides, including a boycott being called for against American businesses. What can you do to stop the "anti" feeling on both sides?

The President. Well, I think, first of all, from the point of view of the "anti" feeling on our side, we have to be able to enforce our immigration laws more equitably and more firmly. We welcome immigrants into this country; we always have. Southern California is, in many ways, the product of our commitment to opening our doors to immigrants. But when we have so many illegal immigrants and half of them now lodging in California at a time of economic difficulty, it undermines support for immigration in general. So first we have to try to enforce our immigration laws.

Let me just mention that just this week the Senate passed, and I will soon sign, the bill that will permit 600 more border agents and 200 others in supporting roles to help to increase our capacity to enforce our immigration laws. So that's a beginning.

The second thing we have to do in your area is get that horrible pollution problem fixed, where you're getting all the pollution coming up from Mexico and raw sewage. We've got to accelerate the construction of that sewage treatment facility down there and do what we can to make sure that people pay their fair share on the Mexican side of the border. Congressman Filner is doing a terrific job for you back in Washington on that.

The third thing we need to do on the Mexican side of the border, I guess, is to remind our friends in Mexico that we're not anti-immigration. We just want to enforce our laws. We're doing our best, I am at least, to pass the NAFTA treaty, and I hope that I'll have a lot of support in the Congress from California on that, because it will be good for easing the immigration pressures. So we have to assure the Mexicans that we want to work with them, we want to be a partner with them, but we have every right to want our immigration laws to be respected and honored.

Mr. Smith. Okay, Mr. President, thank you very much for joining us this morning.

The President. Thank you.

NOTE: The interview began at 11:56 a.m. The President spoke via satellite from Room 459 of the Old Executive Office Building.

Interview With John Culea of KFMB–TV, San Diego
October 22, 1993

Technology Reinvestment Project

Mr. Culea. All right. Well, we'll see if we can put you on the hot seat here. [*Laughter*] How do you balance a cash award in this announcement today to one company with its potential negative job impact on a competitor? Wouldn't tax incentives be more equitable?

The President. No, I disagree with that. For one thing, these awards are designed to develop defense technologies for commercial purposes. And they were the result of a competitive process. For those who were not picked, let me say we're coming back next year with over $500 million in new funds for these kinds of projects, and we will be doing more.

But the reason it's important to do it this way is that we have all these defense technologies that need to be put to work in the commercial sector. And in terms of the award in San Diego, let me remind you that there are literally thousands of bridges in this country, thousands, that need repair and a lot of new ones that need to be built. So if this technology

can be put to work in doing that, they shouldn't be able to push anybody else with a genuinely competitive product out of the market, because there are so many thousands of bridges that need repair—and cities and local governments and States are just beginning to face up to those responsibilities—and because in the 1980's this country walked away from its infrastructure needs. So, I don't see that as a problem, particularly in this sector of the economy.

Mr. Culea. You mentioned awards to Redondo Beach, Fullerton, I believe two others. Most of the awards, though, were out of State. We have 250,000 defense jobs that were lost here. What do you say to those people who need help?

The President. Most of the awards were out of State, but California got the lion's share of the awards, ran away with the contest, as well you would expect, because there are so many defense workers out of work and because there's so much technology capacity. So the State did very well on this first round, and I would expect that there will be more in the second, third, and fourth rounds.

Keep in mind, this was just the first of four rounds between now and November, and then next year we'll have another $500 million-plus to put in a whole new round of these projects. So I would say to them, I'm going to fund as many of these projects as possible; I'm working as hard as possible.

I also would point out that in the San Diego area, two other things have been done which will help in the base closing and reorganization. There will be a net gain of 5,200 jobs in the San Diego area, and we just released from export controls $37 billion worth of computer, supercomputer, and telecommunications equipment, which will open new markets and create many thousands of jobs in California; many of them will be in southern California.

So I'm moving as quickly as I can on this, and I hope that the Members of the Congress will all be as supportive as Congresswoman Lynn Schenk has been of this project, because if we had more folks like her who were willing to fund this project at higher levels, we can move even more quickly and help even more California working people.

Mr. Culea. This being a Navy-Marine town, there is concern that our military be prepared for anything in the future. What can you say to that as far as defense conversion and our ability to be prepared for future contingencies?

The President. The head of naval research was here today with me, Admiral Pelaez. He made the point that in a very profound way, this program we announced will help to keep our defense strong, because we know that the defense budget's going to be reduced. This program will help to use the commercial research and development sector to keep the defense technology strong, even as we're using defense technologies to create jobs in the commercial

sector. That is, by putting the two together, we'll be able to get a bigger bang for our defense dollar. So that even though there will be some reduction in defense spending, we'll be able to keep ahead of all of the other countries in the world and as far as we need to be on technology.

Mr. Culea. Could you give us an idea of the control of this money in some defense contractors? Jobs have been cut, profits go up, and then bonuses are given to top executives. What about the control of the money going to these firms?

The President. Well, first of all, let me explain what happens now. We have announced the projects that were worthy and that won the right to participate in this project. Now, what will happen is the group of people from our Government's side who work in this area will negotiate with each and every company to make sure that they put up their share of the money and to determine how they will spend this money.

This money, in almost every case, is not an overwhelming amount of money for these companies. What this money will be necessary for is to actually invest in developing this new product and marketing it commercially. So there won't be much of an opportunity for a rake-off here, otherwise the whole thing will collapse. And they have to agree in advance not only on a contribution schedule from their point of view but on what the money's going to be spent on. And I think we'll avoid those abuses.

Mr. Culea. All right. Mr. President, thank you so much for sharing your thoughts, and I hope you get a better seat next time.

The President. Thank you very much.

NOTE: The interview began at 12:02 p.m. The President spoke via satellite from Room 459 of the Old Executive Office Building.

Message to the Senate Transmitting the Protocol to the Netherlands-United States Taxation Convention
October 22, 1993

To the Senate of the United States:

I transmit herewith for Senate advice and consent to ratification the Protocol Amending

the Convention Between the United States of America and the Kingdom of the Netherlands for the Avoidance of Double Taxation and the

Prevention of Fiscal Evasion with Respect to Taxes on Income, signed at Washington on October 13, 1993. A related exchange of notes is enclosed for the information of the Senate. Also transmitted for the information of the Senate is the report of the Department of State with respect to the Protocol.

The Protocol will prohibit a treaty abuse otherwise permitted by the Convention, which was previously transmitted to the Senate. The Protocol will prevent a Dutch investor in the United States from evading virtually all income taxes in both the United States and the Netherlands through a permanent establishment in a third, low-income jurisdiction. The Protocol and the Convention are intended to reduce the distortions of both double taxation and tax evasion. The two agreements will modernize tax relations between the United States and the Netherlands and will facilitate greater bilateral private sector investment.

I recommend that the Senate give early and favorable consideration to the Protocol, together with the Convention, and give its advice and consent to ratification.

WILLIAM J. CLINTON

The White House,
October 22, 1993.

Nomination for Chairman of the Consumer Product Safety Commission
October 22, 1993

The President today announced his intention to nominate Ann Winkelman Brown as a Commissioner and the Chairman of the Consumer Product Safety Commission.

"Ann Brown has worked tirelessly to improve consumer product safety in America," the President said. "In her new role, I am certain she will make even further strides in this important field."

NOTE: A biography of the nominee was made available by the Office of the Press Secretary.

Appointment for Executive Director of the White House Conference on Aging
October 22, 1993

The President announced that he has appointed Robert B. Blancato as Executive Director of the White House Conference on Aging (WHCOA). The WHCOA, located at the Department of Health and Human Services, serves as a focal point for the development of national policy on aging issues.

"Robert Blancato is a leading expert in aging policy who has been recognized for his work on numerous occasions," said the President. "I look forward to his work at the White House Conference on Aging."

NOTE: A biography of the appointee was made available by the Office of the Press Secretary.

Appointment for the United Nations Human Rights Commission
October 22, 1993

The President announced his intention today to appoint former Congresswoman Geraldine Ferraro as the U.S. Representative to the United Nations Human Rights Commission (UNHRC), with the rank of Ambassador.

"In addition to earning her place in our own country's political history, Geraldine Ferraro has been a highly effective voice for the human rights of women around the world," said the President. "As alternate head of the U.S. delegation to this year's session of the UNHRC, she spoke eloquently on behalf of women in the former Yugoslavia and brought all of the parties involved to a consensus position. I look forward to her continuing her strong and much-needed advocacy in this new position."

NOTE: A biography of the appointee was made available by the Office of the Press Secretary.

Nomination for United States District Court Judges
October 22, 1993

The President announced the nomination today of his choices for four U.S. District Court vacancies: Donetta Ambrose and Gary Lancaster, both for the Western District of Pennsylvania; Wilkie D. Ferguson for the Southern District of Florida; and Charles A. Shaw for the Eastern District of Missouri.

"I am committed to giving the American people a Federal judiciary marked by excellence, by diversity, and by a concern for the personal security and civil rights of all Americans," said the President. "With these nominations today, we are giving just that to the people of Pennsylvania, Florida, and Missouri."

NOTE: Biographies of the nominees were made available by the Office of the Press Secretary.

Remarks and an Exchange With Reporters on Haiti
October 23, 1993

The President. I wanted to give you what I think is a more precise answer to your question. I was, of course, aware of the allegations; they were reported today in the press. But the question of whether he was fit to serve seems to me was reinforced by the personal experience that Ambassador Pezzullo, my Special Envoy on the subject had, plus everyone else in the administration in working with him, plus the fact that during the time when he served as President, political terrorism and abuses went down in Haiti, not up. So based on the personal experiences of the people in the administration who worked with President Aristide, we felt that they were a more valid indicator than the allegations that were reported.

Q. Mr. President, you aren't saying the allegations aren't true?

The President. No one knows whether they're true or not. They were allegations. We don't know if they were true or not. I'm just saying based on the personal experiences of a lot of people in this Government and before me even, before I became President, we had sustained experience—that the experiences of the people who were working with Aristide, plus what is the evidence that we have at least of the conduct of the administration when he was in office, tended to undermine those reports.

Q. What sort of credibility does the CIA report have then, the one that's been circulated on the Hill?

The President. Well, they were required to do what they had to do, which is to report whatever information they'd been given. And the CIA would be the first to tell you that they get a lot of information—it's not always accurate, but they have to give what they have to the intelligence committees, just as they do to the President. That's the law.

Q. Well, Mr. President, what do you think it's going to take for this to go away as far as the public is concerned and even Capitol Hill?

The President. What do you mean, for what to go away?

Q. For this whole issue about his mental stability and his mental——

Q. Jesse Helms says he's psychotic and——

The President. Well, but you know, some of those guys, they like the Government they got, I think. Sometimes some of the opposition here may come from people who were satisfied with this whole sad, recent history of Haiti. What's their alternative?

We tried to find a political solution which basically would allow democracy to return to Haiti and which has a guarantee of a more stable government by bringing in Mr. Malval, whom everybody admits was a nonpolitical business person, someone who had the best interest of his people at heart and other people who could be real stabilizing factors. The security and personal safety of the leaders of the army and the police were guaranteed. The Governors Island Agreement provided for French-speaking forces to go in and retrain the police force to make them a real police instead of an instrument of political oppression and for French-speaking Canadians and the United States to send in people who could in effect convert the army into an army corps of engineers, help them rebuild the country. And they're not seriously threatened. So I think that—and all those steps were supported by Aristide.

So when you look at the record and you look at—I would remind you—you look at the threat that we were all facing, that we continue to face, the previous administration faced from people trying to get on their boats and come to the United States, hundreds of whom have drowned in the effort, it would seem to me to—and the clear evidence that the—at least for as long as I have been President—that the hope of a return to democracy and Aristide's return was the biggest incentive for the Haitian people to stay home.

I think that we have done the right thing with our policy. We always knew there was a chance that the forces of reaction in Haiti would break the deal, but—or people in this country to try to justify the abrogation of the Governors Island Agreement based on what are now very old charges that have very little to do with the government that's operating there or with the actions of the last 9 months, I think is not very persuasive.

Q. The blockade now, according to a mission-ary, a British missionary, quoted yesterday as saying the blockade is actually hurting the people of Haiti more than it is the regime there.

The President. It always hurts the people first. The regime has access to monopolies, and they have lots of money. But the blockade is what got the Governors Island Agreement going. The blockade finally hit the regime and the elites, and in the end, they suffered, too. I think even a lot of people that have some money there must be worried about the conduct of the police and some of the military in the last few weeks.

Q. How long do you think it's going to take for it to——

The President. I don't have any idea. I don't know. But I just know that that poor country has been plundered on and off for nearly 200 years now. And the people finally thought they were going to get a shot at democracy, a chance to be embraced into the world community. It's probably the most environmentally devastated nation, at least in this hemisphere. And there are a lot of real opportunities for the people to return to a normal life and for all the people in the army and the police to find some reconciliation in a legitimate and lawful society. It's very sad.

But I would remind you that with regard to the embargo, the sanctions, that's what we were asked to do by the Government of Haiti. The government supported the return of the sanctions. But I imagine that it must be very discouraging to the people. They thought they were on the brink of having a normal government, a normal life, free of corruption and oppression, and it's frustrating to them.

I know what people are saying about Aristide; you could look at the alternatives. And we have to go based on the evidence, the conduct of people. And so far we have no—he's done everything he said he would do. And he's been more than willing to reach out to others. And he made strict guarantees as to the security of the—that his former opponents, something that they weren't willing to do, and certainly something they haven't practiced. And we even said if—the whole U.N. process was set up to reinforce that.

Q. Having said that about Mr. Aristide, is there a compromise candidate somewhere, someone who may not be Mr. Aristide but who may be a compromise with the regime there now to normalize things in Haiti?

The President. Our position is what our position is right now. Our position is we have sanctions on, because the Governors Island Agreement was violated. They have a—and he was elected to a term of office. And that's my position.

Q. When do you think Aristide may be back in Haiti? When might you get him back in there?

The President. I was hoping he'd be back on October—like I said, that country has suffered a long time. We've seen a lot of evidence, even from Haitian-Americans that the people there do not want to leave. And a lot of people who live elsewhere might go home if they just had a decent place to go home to, if they didn't have to worry about being beat up or bribed or oppressed, have a real decent chance to make a living. And that's what the world community, that's what the countries in this hemisphere wanted to help Haiti achieve. And it's unfortunate that the people down there decided they'd rather keep a stranglehold on a shrinking future than play a legitimate part of an expanding future. That's a decision they're going to have to make.

NOTE: The exchange began at approximately 8:30 a.m. on the South Lawn at the White House. A tape was not available for verification of the content of these remarks.

The President's Radio Address
October 23, 1993

Good morning. Last year I waged a campaign for President on a commitment to change our economic course in Washington, to change economic policy and put the American people first. After a long struggle we are finally seeing signs of hope in our economy. We have moved to significantly lower our Federal deficit, and now we have the lowest interest rates in 30 years. That's bringing back business investment, housing starts, purchases of expensive capital equipment. And now in the past 8 months, our economy has created more jobs in the private sector than were created in the previous 4 years.

We've still got a long way to go. We need more investment, more jobs that pay living wages, more opportunity for our students and workers to train and retrain themselves for a changing global economy. We'll never make America what it ought to be until we provide real health security for all our people, health care that's always there, that can never be taken away, that controls costs and maintains quality and coverage.

But we can't do any of those things until the American people really feel secure enough to make the changes we need to make. I see evidence of that uncertainty, that insecurity as I struggle to expand trade opportunities for our people through passing the North American Free Trade Agreement; as I struggle to convince people we should open our markets to others and force other markets open so that we can sell more of our high-tech equipment around the world; as we try to get people to accept the fact that most folks will change jobs seven or eight times in a lifetime, and therefore we can't have job security, but we can have employment security if we have a real lifetime system of education and training. All these changes require a level of confidence in our institutions and in ourselves, a belief that America can still compete and win, and that the American dream can still be alive.

One of the problems in inspiring that confidence in America is that we've become the most dangerous big country in the world. We have a higher percentage of our people behind bars than any other nation in the world. We've had 90,000 murders in this country in the last 4 years. The American people increasingly feel that they're not secure in their homes, on their streets, or even in their schools. This explosion of crime and violence is changing the way our people live, making too many of us hesitant, often paralyzed with fear at a time when we need to be bold. When our children are dying, often at the hands of other children with guns, it's pretty tough to talk about anything else. Today, there are more than 200 million guns on our streets, and we have more Federally licensed gun dealers—who, believe it or not, can get a license from your Federal Government for only $10—than we have gas stations.

It's prompted the corner grocer to shut down because he feels threatened. It's made the shopper afraid to enter a parking garage at night. It's made children think twice about going to school because classmates have been shot there. It's made parents order their children inside in broad daylight because of gunfire.

Nothing we aspire to in our Nation can finally be achieved unless first we do something about children who are no longer capable of distinguishing right from wrong, about people who are strangely unaffected by the violence they do to others, about the easy availability of handguns or assault weapons that are made solely for the purpose of killing or maiming others, about the mindless temptations of easy drugs.

This issue should be above politics. That's why I'm working closely with the leaders of Congress in urging them to pass our comprehensive anticrime legislation when it comes up in the Senate next week. The bill is based on a simple philosophy and a simple message: We need more police, fewer guns, and different alternatives for people who get in trouble.

We ask Congress to honor the struggle of Jim and Sarah Brady by passing the Brady bill, a 5-day waiting period for background checks before a person can purchase a handgun. We want to take assault weapons off the street. And we want to take all guns out of the hands of teenagers. We want more police officers on the street, at least 50,000 more. And we want them working in community policing networks so that they'll know their neighbors and they'll work with people not simply to catch criminals but to prevent crime in the first place. We want to put more power in the hands of local communities and give them options so that first-time offenders can be sent to boot camps and to other programs that we know work to rehabilitate people who use drugs and to give our children a way out of a life of crime and jail.

We also are recharting the way we fight the drug problem. Under the leadership of Dr. Lee Brown, our father of community policing in this country and now the Director of the Office of National Drug Control Policy, we are increasing our focus on the hardcore user, those who make up the worst part of the drug problem, who fuel crime and violence, who are helping a whole new generation of children to grow up in chaos, who are driving up our health care costs because of the violence and the drug use.

Our program will reach out to young people who can be saved from living a life of crime and being a burden on society, the ones who've taken a wrong turn but can still turn around. They'll have access to boot camps to learn skills and the kind of responsibility that they have to adopt if they want to turn their lives around.

Every time we feel the need to view strangers with suspicion or to bar our homes and cars against intrusion or we worry about the well-being of the child we send off to grade school, we lose a little part of what America should mean. Some of these problems were decades in the making, and we know we can't solve them overnight, but within adversity there is some hope today.

In our administration, with the Attorney General Janet Reno, our outstanding FBI Director Louis Freeh, and the Drug Policy Coordinator Lee Brown, we have a dedicated team of people used to fighting crime, determined to restore security for our people, determined to give our young people another chance. We are dedicated to restoring and expanding personal security for people who work hard and play by the rules. We're dedicated to insisting on more responsibility from those who should exercise it. We have a comprehensive crime bill that says we need more police, fewer guns, tougher laws, and new alternatives for first offenders. We're asking for a new direction in the control of illegal drugs to make our streets safer. We're asking all our people to take more personal responsibility for their health, their lives, and the well-being of their children.

I believe the American people have decided simply and finally they are sick and tired of living in fear. They are prepared to reach beyond the slogans and the easy answers to support what works, to experiment with new ideas, and to finally, finally do something about this crime and violence. If we do it together, we'll make America more prosperous and more secure. We'll have the courage, the self-confidence, the openness to make the other changes we need to make to put the American people first in the months and years to come.

Thanks for listening.

NOTE: The address was recorded at approximately 9:40 a.m. in the Oval Office at the White House for broadcast at 10:06 a.m.

Remarks on the 200th Anniversary of the Capitol and the Reinstallation of the Statue of Freedom
October 23, 1993

Thank you, Mr. Speaker, Mr. Vice President, distinguished leaders of the House and Senate, Mr. Justice Blackmun, my fellow Americans.

We come here today to celebrate the 200th birthday of this great building, the cornerstone of our Republic. We come here to watch our Capitol made whole 130 years after the beautiful Statue of Freedom was first raised above this Capitol.

This is a moment of unity in this great city of ours so often known for its conflicts. In this moment, we all agree, we know in our minds and feel in our hearts the words that Thomas Jefferson spoke in the first Inaugural Address ever given on these grounds. He said that people of little faith were doubtful about America's future, but he believed our Government was the world's best hope.

What was that hope? The hope that still endures that in this country every man and woman without regard to race or region or station in life would have the freedom to live up to the fullest of his or her God-given potential; the hope that every citizen would get from Government not a guarantee but the promise of an opportunity to do one's best, to have an equal chance, for the most humble and the most well born, to do what God meant for them to be able to do.

That hope was almost dashed in the great Civil War. When the Statue of Freedom was raised, many people questioned whether Abraham Lincoln should permit this work to go on. But he said, during the war when so many thought our country would come to an end, that if people see the Capitol going on, it is a sign we intend the Union to go on. In 1865, Abraham Lincoln gave the first Inaugural Address ever given under the Statue of Freedom.

And he said, "With malice toward none, with charity for all, with firmness in the right as God gives us to see the right, let us strive on to finish the work we are in." And in that, the greatest of all Presidential Inaugural Addresses, Abraham Lincoln gave us our charge for today, for the work of keeping the hope of America alive never finishes.

It is not enough for use to be mere stewards of our inheritance. We must always be the architects of its renewal. The Capitol is here after 200 years, this beautiful Statute of Freedom can be raised, renewed after 130 years, because our forebears never stopped thinking about tomorrow.

We require the freedom to preserve what is best and the freedom to change, the freedom to explore, the freedom to build, the freedom to grow. My fellow Americans, I tell you that perhaps the biggest of our problems today is that too many of our people no longer believe the future can be better than the past. And too many others, most of them young, have no connection to the future whatsoever because their present is so chaotic. But the future, the future has a claim on all of us.

We have, because of our birthright as Americans, a moral obligation to face the day's challenges and to make tomorrow better than today. All we really owe to this great country after 200 years is to make sure that 200 years from now this building will still be here and our grandchildren many generations in the future will be here to celebrate it anew.

Thank you, and God bless you all.

NOTE: The President spoke at 12:33 p.m. at the West Front of the Capitol.

Remarks at the B'nai B'rith 150th Anniversary Havdalah Service
October 23, 1993

Thank you very much. Mr. Schiner, Mr. Spitzer, distinguished platform guests, ladies and gentlemen. Hillary and I are delighted to be with you tonight, honored to be a part of your

150th anniversary.

When I appeared before your international convention a year ago, I said I would be honored to help you celebrate this anniversary if you would help me get into a position so that you would want me to help celebrate it. So tonight I thank you on two counts.

I am deeply honored to have been a part of your Havdalah service. It is always a great honor for me as a person of faith to be able to share the spirituality of other Americans. Far from being separate from the rest of your life, the spirituality that is renewed by you on every Sabbath infuses everything that you do.

This ceremony has been observed in captivity and exile and in freedom, on every continent and in virtually every country, and yet essentially it remains the same. And it is especially appropriate that we observe it here this evening on the occasion of your 150th anniversary on the steps of this memorial dedicated to the father of religious freedom in America, Thomas Jefferson, on the occasion of the year in which we celebrate his 250th birthday and the 50th anniversary of this Jefferson Memorial.

Jefferson attained a great deal of glory in his life. He was known and revered around the world. And yet when he died, he asked that on his tombstone it be printed only that he was the author of the Declaration of Independence, the founder of the University of Virginia, and perhaps most of all, the author of the Statute of Virginia for Religious Freedom. In other words, Jefferson understood that in the end, the deepest power of all in human affairs, the power of ideas and ideals. In words inscribed just up these steps on this memorial, he said, "Almighty God hath created the mind free . . . No man shall be compelled to frequent or support any religious worship or ministry or shall otherwise suffer on account of his religious opinion or belief, but all men shall be free to profess and by argument to maintain their opinions in matters of religion."

That simple premise on which our first amendment is based is, I believe, the major reason why here in America more people believe in God, more people go to church or synagogue, more people put religion at the center of their lives than in any other advanced society on Earth. Our Government is the protector of freedom of every faith because it is the exclusive property of none. Just as you keep the Sabbath separate to keep it holy, we all keep our faiths free from Government coercion so that they can always be voluntary offerings of free and joyous spirits. And just as the Sabbath spirit illuminates every day of your lives, Americans of every faith try to take the values we learn from our religions and put them to work in our communities. No one has done that better than the Americans who do the work of B'nai B'rith.

From your founding a century and a half ago—you may clap for yourselves; I think that's fine—[applause]—from your founding a century and a half ago on the Lower East Side of Manhattan, you've been dedicated to community service, to individual responsibility, to the struggle against every form of bigotry and injustice by investing in education and health care and helping the less fortunate, by tearing down barriers to achievement and weaving a fabric of mutuality and social responsibility. You have helped people from every faith and background to live lives of genuine accomplishment.

Even when I was growing up in Arkansas, I knew of the efforts of this wonderful organization. Back in 1914, you opened the Levi Hospital in my hometown of Hot Springs. And after all these years it still serves hundreds and hundreds every year without regard to their ability to pay. Today, the B'nai B'rith has also opened a senior citizens housing complex in my hometown. And believe it or not, those acts that help individuals are the things that I try hardest to keep in mind as President when making laws and making policies so that the spirit which animates people in their daily lives, helping each other one on one, can drive the Presidency and the Government of this great land.

It was that spirit which led me to propose and Congress to enact a new program for national service to offer tens of thousands of our young people the chance to earn their way through college by serving their communities and rebuilding this country and giving something to one another and thinking about someone besides themselves in those important and formative years of their youth. And I want to thank a distinguished member of the American-Jewish community, Eli Segal, my good friend, for being the real father of national service, for shepherding it through its creation and its enactment and now leading it along its way.

I want to thank you, too, for being there for America when tragedy strikes at home or abroad: flood victims in the Midwest; hurricane victims in Florida; earthquake victims not simply in northern California but in Mexico City, Iran, and Armenia, they are all in your debt. You helped to address the crisis in Somalia, launching your own drive to raise funds to stave off starvation when 1,000 people a day were dying there. In the cause of our common efforts, nearly a million lives have been saved.

The spirit you bring to your work explains the sense of kinship Americans of every faith have always felt for the state of Israel. It explains our yearning for peace in that land, sacred to three great religions. It explains the joy every American felt when the promise of peace for Israelis, for Palestinians, for all the peoples of the Middle East was made tangible on September the 13th in a single, stunning handshake.

I say to you tonight what you already know, that even in the joy of that moment, we must all remember that a lasting peace requires hard work, that enmity, stretching back to the founding of the state of Israel and before, cannot be made to vanish simply with the stroke of a pen. But let us not forget how far we have come. It would have been unimaginable just 2 months ago to think that between now and September 13th, the leaders of Israel have actually sat down with the leaders of Jordan, Morocco, Tunisia, and Qatar. And there is more to come. Israelis and Palestinians are engaged in intense negotiations to implement their agreements. Israel and Arab business people are meeting to lay the foundations of economic cooperation. And I am very proud of the cooperation I have seen in the United States between American Jews and Arab-Americans, working on what they can do together to make the peace agreement work.

Clearly, more must be done, and we have not a moment to waste. Just yesterday, we were reminded anew with the tragic killing of a moderate Arab leader that there are those who have a greater stake in the continuing misery of the Palestinians than in the hope of peace for all the Middle East. We have not a moment to waste.

I am committed to building on the momentum we have created to achieve nothing less than a comprehensive settlement, one in which Israel secures real lasting peace with all her neighbors. To do that we have to be able to demonstrate that when Israel takes genuine risks for peace, the Arab world responds with a similar commitment to build a new era of peace and prosperity with Israel as a partner, not pa-

riah.

The future for Israel and for the Jewish people is bright and full of promise tonight. For the first time we have the chance to achieve peace, and I am determined to see that it is real, secure, and enduring. We live in a time when ancient enmities are fading. We saw it not just in the handshake of Rabin and Arafat but in the remarkable partnership of Mandela and de Klerk, people who are giving hope that tomorrow can really be different from and better than today.

I ask all of you to think about what these times mean for us as Americans and for us as individuals. At prayer this morning many of you read the passages from the Torah where God asks Abraham not only to leave his father's house but to go forward to a new land and a new way of living and thinking.

Tonight, as we stand 7 years from a new century and a new millennium, our world is being transformed dramatically by political change, technological developments, dramatic global economic changes. We stand here tonight following the footsteps of wise men and women who faced the future with confidence, who offered a helping hand, who opened their hearts to God and asked to be led so that future generations might have better lives. That is what we, too, must do. As Thomas Jefferson did, as the founders of B'nai B'rith did, as Americans have done at every moment of change and challenge, I ask you on this occasion of your 150th anniversary to joy in the progress for peace in the Middle East, to take great pride in your own accomplishments and the givings but to resolve today that we will lay the foundation of progress and peace here at home: with health care that is always there; with an economy that serves the poor as well as those who aren't, that gives every man and woman a chance; with an end to hatred and bigotry, a commitment to make our diversity in this country a strength and not a weakness; with a commitment to engage one another in serious, moral conversations but to slow down the rhetoric of screaming and condemnation so that we can appreciate we are all the children of God.

In the end, I ask that we dedicate ourselves anew to the timeless promise of American life first proclaimed by Thomas Jefferson in whose large shadow we stand tonight, the promise of "life, liberty, and the pursuit of happiness." For all that B'nai B'rith has done to make that promise real and for all you will do in the tomorrows to come, on behalf of all the people of the United States, I say a profound thank you.

NOTE: The President spoke at 8:45 p.m. at the Jefferson Memorial. In his remarks, he referred to Kent Schiner, international president, and Jack J. Spitzer, former international president, B'nai B'rith.

Remarks at the National Italian-American Foundation Dinner
October 23, 1993

Thank you very much, President Guarini; Foundation Chair Stella; Director Rotondaro; my friend Art Gajarsa; my good friend Congressman John LaFalce, who wanted Hillary to speak tonight, I'm going to tell this on her—and John, you know John was reported in the paper saying, "I know I shouldn't say this, but every time I see Hillary I just want to hug her." [*Laughter*] So we came here tonight so he could do it in front of 3,000 people and it would seem perfectly legitimate.

Mr. Ambassador, I thank you for your eloquent remarks, and I hope you will tell the Prime Minister that I value his friendship and the friendship of your nation. I know there are about 300 of your country men and women here tonight. I thank them for their presence, and I look forward to going to Italy next year to the G–7 meeting. Hillary and I went there in 1987. It was one of the best trips we have ever made as private citizens, and I dare say, we won't have a chance to do quite as many things the next time as we did then.

You know, I was really looking forward to this tonight. I mean, last year when I came I was as nervous as a cat in a tree. It was close to the election; I had no idea if I were going to win. They put me up against Barbara Bush who had an 86 percent approval rating. [*Laughter*] I knew at least half the people here weren't going to vote for me anyway, and all I could do was think about how awful it would be if I messed up. So I thought tonight will be a gem; I'll show up as President. It'll be wonderful. First thing I have to do is take a picture of Dom DeLuise and Danny DeVito. I'm about six seats from Gina Lollobrigida and DeVito sits in my lap. [*Laughter*] This whole thing has been incredibly humbling. I'm kind of getting used to it, you know. I mean, look at this, Al Gore gets to go on David Letterman;

Hillary speaks to the Congress and a poll, taken in bad taste by USA Today, says that after she addresses the Congress for 3 days, virtually without notes, 40 percent of the American people are convinced that she is smarter than I am. I practically don't know how the other 60 percent missed it. [*Laughter*]

It was so bad the other day, I was being so humbled, I went to California seeking respite, and when I got there I thought, well, at least here they said I would go to L.A., and I would stay in the Beverly Hilton Hotel. And I knew it was kind of a jazzy place and Merv Griffin owned it, and I thought, well, I'll get there and Merv Griffin will come shake hands with me, and they'll take me up and put me in some gorgeous suite and I'll feel like the President again. This is a true story, now; I'm not making any of this up. I show up, and Merv Griffin is there and he shakes hands with me. He says he's got a gorgeous suite, and I'll feel like the President. But he says, "Before you get on the elevator, I want you to know that I've been following your activities very closely, and I've put you on a floor which does have one permanent resident. And I thought it was a place that would really fit for you." And I'm getting really excited, you know? I'm in Hollywood, I mean my mind is going crazy. And I get on the elevator, I go up to the whatever floor it was, the elevator opens and there, standing there to welcome me, as God is my witness, is Rodney Dangerfield who gives me a dozen roses with a card that says, "And a little respect." [*Laughter*]

Well anyway, there are a few good things happening tonight. I mean, Justice Scalia is to my left. And I'm about to have a victory that is the equivalent of Ronald Reagan's successful invasion of Grenada because Jack Valenti picked a fight with Janet Reno. [*Laughter*] I don't think they know about that, Jack. Yes, you did, but you'll do well.

I want to say just a few words. We've been here a long time, and you've all had a wonderful time, and I have been deeply moved by this, as I was last year. But I want to thank the honorees for what they said and who they are. Because every one of them reminded us, in a different way, of why we should be grateful to be Americans and why we should be grateful for the contribution of Italian-Americans. I want to thank Richard Grasso, and Phil Rizzuto and my good friend and supporter Danny DeVito, who shouldn't have been so shameless in expressing that, but I loved it. I want to thank our dear friend Matilda Cuomo, for everything she has been and done. I want to say to all of you, you've made me really proud just to be here tonight as a citizen of this country. Proud of what our country has been to you and to so many millions of people like you.

Most of the Italian-Americans in my administration have been mentioned: Leon Panetta and Laura D'Andrea Tyson. Matilda mentioned her wonderful son, Andrew, who has done a terrific job for us at HUD. We have a lot of other folks here tonight who are in the administration. And I won't mention them all, but I do think that I should say that I have decided to name my good friend Geraldine Ferraro as a permanent member to the U.N. Commission on Human Rights. This administration cares a lot about human rights, and so does she, and she will be terrific.

I also would like to thank a person that, in a few days, I will formally name the Executive Director of the White House Conference on Aging, someone a few of you may know, Bob Blancato.

I must say, I may be reaching the limit of the number of Italians I can have in my administration. I don't know if there's a de facto quota. I do know that when I flew out to Denver to see the Pope recently, I tried to gather up every Catholic on my staff. And I asked the Pope, I said, "Your Holiness, may I introduce you to all the Catholics on my staff?" And he said, "Yes." And practically got arthritis of the elbow shaking hands with them all. And he looked at me and he said, "Have you no Protestants and Jews for me to convert?" [*Laughter*]

You know, it's funny to me how much one of you—Danny made a joke about being from the south of Italy and not being much different from being from the South. I don't know that that's quite right, but there is something to be said for the common experiences that those of us who grew up in relatively modest circumstances in small towns in the rural South and Italian immigrants who came here. I must tell you, when I travel this great land I never feel any more at home than I do in south Philadelphia or the north end of Boston. And the other day when Hillary and I went back to New Haven for our 20th law school reunion at Yale, I was so thrilled when we drove through those Italian neighborhoods in East Haven, and all the people were still out there—this is 1993, folks—waving their American flag, not because of me but because the President was there, not me, the institution, the office and Nation. It was wonderful.

And when they asked me what I wanted to do while I was in New Haven, I said, well, I'm glad I'm going back to Yale, but I want you to call Congresswoman Rosa DeLauro and take me down to the neighborhoods again where I really feel at home. And I went down to see hundreds of people who have the stories that we've heard tonight. I say that to you because I want to make just one serious point briefly that embraces all the issues that I have sought to deal with.

In my life, when I was a child, when I was born, almost half the people in my State lived below the poverty line. Now, whatever that means, almost all the Italian immigrants, at one time in this country when they first came here were, by definition, below the poverty line. But when I was a child, we all knew, when I was being raised by my grandfather who had a fourth-grade education, all the people that moved to town—town was 6,000 people—still had a little plot of land out in the country to grow vegetables on. And all the little children could still be taught to farm, even if they weren't going to be farmers anymore. No one doubted that they were loved, that they were part of a coherent family and community, and that if they worked hard and played by the rules they would do okay.

The same is true—I have heard Mario Cuomo talk about his father, his family. I wept, like you did, when Danny DeVito told that story. Every one of you in this audience probably has a story. There was a structure of support, of love and discipline, rooted in some pretty basic ideas. Family, work, how you do in life depends more on effort and what kind of person you are than IQ and income. Just basic things. If you ask me what is wrong with this country today, I'll tell you what. Millions of people don't think it works that way anymore, and for millions of people it does not work that way anymore.

We have a whole generation of children growing up who will not be able to tell these stories, who shoot each other on the street, who have access to guns in a way they would not have access in any other country in the world. We say we're a law and order country. We're the most religious, big country in the entire world, by far, and we're the only ones that let teenagers be better armed than police, who have no structure, order in their lives, who have no identity with a future, who impulsively do things that destroy others and themselves.

When I was Governor of my State, I kept a little picture on my wall. I looked at it every day when I was 6 years old, laying on my back with a broken leg above the knee, at a time when they couldn't even figure out how to put a cast on it, so I had a steel pin put through my ankle, and my leg was hung up. And I'm there, holding hands with my great-grandfather, who lived out in the country in a house built up on stilts, hardly ever got out of overalls, and had no education at all. But he worked hard, he loved me, he did his job, and it worked, whatever it was in our family, it worked.

There are millions of people in this country today who will never even know who their great-grandparents were, who will have no pictures, who will have no nonreading parents who make sure they have books, who run them to the library. You ask me what is amiss in this country today. Well, there are a lot of changes we have to make, and we're going to make them. We're going to adjust the global economy.

Did you see what the Prime Minister of Germany said the other day? America has got it. They're working. They're going to be productive. They're going to grow again. But it won't work unless the dream that brought your families here is rekindled; unless our diversity, our religious and racial diversity becomes a strength again, not a weakness; and unless we can figure out a way to bring all those other kids back into the life that we take for granted so the future has a claim on them, just as it did on all of us when we were growing up.

So I ask you tonight when you go home, think of how Matilda Cuomo's family felt the first time they heard her give a speech. Think of what Phil Rizzuto's family felt like the first time he put on a Yankee uniform. Think of what Mr. Grasso's family felt like when they thought, "My God, he's the head of the most important financial exchange in the entire world." Think of what Danny DeVito's relatives felt like when he made it in Hollywood. Think about that. Think about what together we can do to make the children of this country have those feelings.

God bless you, and good night.

NOTE: The President spoke at 11 p.m. at the Washington Hilton. In his remarks, he referred to foundation officers Frank Guarini, president, Frank Stella, chair, Alfred Rotondaro, director, and Anthony J. Gajarsa, vice chair; Jack Valenti, CEO and president, Motion Picture Association of America; Richard Grasso, president and vice chairman, New York Stock Exchange; Phil Rizzuto, former baseball player and sportscaster; and Matilda Cuomo, first lady of New York.

Exchange With Reporters Prior to Discussions With President Hosni Mubarak of Egypt
October 25, 1993

Haiti

Q. Mr. President, all these reports are coming out of Haiti that there could be a breakthrough in the process that would bring Aristide back in. Is that optimism justified?

President Clinton. Well, there's been some movement over the weekend. I've learned in dealing with Haiti not to be optimistic ever. But there has been some movement, and it's hopeful, and we'll keep working on it.

Let me also say, President Mubarak and I will have statements to make and will answer questions later, but I'm glad to welcome him back to Washington to congratulate him on his election. And this is the first opportunity I've had face to face to thank him for the critical role that he has played in the Middle East peace process. We're looking forward to having a good discussion about that, and we'll have more to say about it later.

Q. Mr. President, over the weekend, Bob Dole said that returning Aristide to Haiti is not worth a single American life. What's your response?

President Clinton. Well, my response is that our policy is to attempt to restore democracy in Haiti, that we are doing it in the way that we think is best and that is supported by Aristide and Prime Minister Malval. We have our ships there, and you know what we're doing. And they've never asked us to run the country for them. They've asked us to help the democratic process to be restored. We hope it can be done. The United States has an interest in that, avoiding large-scale outpourings of refugees, making sure the country is not a conduit for drug deliveries to this country, and promoting democracy in our hemisphere. And we're pursuing that policy.

Palestinian Prisoners

Q. President Mubarak, can we ask about your feelings about Israel's releasing these Palestinian prisoners today?

President Mubarak. I think it's a very good act. And we have discussed this before with Prime Minister Rabin. And the man really—[*inaudible*]—in doing as far as he could to restore peace and reach a comprehensive settlement to the problem. It's a very good step forward.

Q. Mr. President, your feelings?

President Clinton. I agree. I'm very pleased. He should come every day. I can say I agree—[*laughter*]—shorten my answer.

[*At this point, one group of reporters left the room, and another group entered.*]

Invitation to Egypt

Q. Can I ask a question, Mr. President? When are you going to come and visit Egypt? [*Inaudible*]—invitation from me.

President Clinton. I think President Mubarak will have to invite me.

Discussions with President Mubarak

Q. President Clinton, which is the topic you wish to discuss with President Mubarak?

President Clinton. We have many things to discuss. I want to discuss how we can continue to work together on a comprehensive peace in the Middle East. And I want to ask President Mubarak's advice on a whole range of foreign policy issues. I want to be able to thank him personally for the absolutely indispensable role that he has played in the peace process in the Middle East so far. I don't think we would be where we are today if it weren't for President Mubarak. And we'll have our conversation, and then I'll answer your questions afterward. And I'll try to make sure you get equal time with the American press.

Q. Is Somalia on the topic of your talks with President Mubarak?

President Clinton. Oh yes, I expect to discuss Somalia, yes.

NOTE: The exchange began at 11:09 a.m. in the Oval Office at the White House. A tape was not available for verification of the content of this exchange.

The President's News Conference With President Hosni Mubarak of Egypt
October 25, 1993

President Clinton. Good afternoon. It's a great pleasure and honor to welcome President Mubarak to Washington once again.

Egypt has acted as one of our Nation's partners over a long time. They were actively involved in the Camp David peace process over a decade ago. And today, Egypt remains one of our most important global partners. We continue our partnership in working for peace and stability in the Middle East. We're also partners in a host of global efforts, from Operation Desert Storm to peacekeeping in Somalia today.

And I want to express my personal appreciation to President Mubarak for his commitment to enhance Egypt's effort in that difficult humanitarian effort as well as for his personal involvement in the recent developments between Israel and the PLO, which I am convinced would never have come about had it not been for your continuing encouragement, Mr. President.

President Mubarak has proven repeatedly that he is a leader of great courage and determination. As he enters his third presidential term he has a bold vision for his nation: to reform the economy, to build a future of full employment and free markets. This process is vital to the well-being of the people of Egypt.

The President and the government have played a crucial role in the Middle East peace process. As I said, President Mubarak was pivotal in helping Israel and the PLO reach their agreement on September 13th. And like the United States and others in the international community, Egypt has been working to help turn this agreement into reality, an effort for which I am also very grateful. Egypt is hosting the substantive talks between Israel and the Palestinians begun earlier this month, a tribute to the confidence and trust all sides place in Egypt's leadership for peace. That leadership is essential as we work for peace and as we work for a comprehensive peace.

The President and I agreed in our talks this morning that we have to keep going in this process until all the pieces are in place, until there is a full and broad and comprehensive peace in the Middle East. We discussed the next steps in the process, including our common commitment to making sure that the Israel-PLO agreement is implemented properly. We agreed that this accord can serve as a catalyst for achieving a comprehensive settlement. I'm going to work with President Mubarak and other Arab leaders to help the Arab world follow through in creating a new climate of dialog and reconciliation with Israel.

We also discussed the President's goal for his third term, and we discussed ways in which two nations can continue cooperating to address regional conflicts in Africa and elsewhere and to respond to other global challenges.

Egypt will always hold a special meaning for all of us. It is the birthplace of much of our civilization, many of our modern arts and sciences. Today, Egypt has a leadership role both as it confronts the challenges of its own

development and the challenges of building a better future for all the people in the Middle East.

The historic Egyptian experience demonstrates the importance of moderation, of tolerance, of dialog in shaping the future of the Egyptian people in the Middle East, a future marked by prosperity, by coexistence, and by stability. President Mubarak has been an exemplar of that experience. It is a joy to work with him and to welcome him once again to Washington.

Mr. President.

President Mubarak. I was very pleased to meet with President Clinton for the second time in 6 months. And our meeting today has reinforced my impression of the President as a man of courage and mutual commitment. We discussed several issues of mutual concern, and discussions revealed a great similarity of views between us. President Clinton was quite receptive and openminded.

On African matters, we agreed on the need to remain alert until apartheid is actually abolished and replaced by a democratic system of government. On Somalia, we concluded that the political solution lies in the full implementation of the resolution of Addis Ababa Conference on National Reconciliation. We are watching the situation there closely, and I am in touch with President Zenawi of Ethiopia who received a mandate to follow up the situation.

The United States and Egypt have worked together on peace in the Middle East for almost two decades. Our joint effort has been fruitful and promising. The peace process was boosted dramatically when Chairman Arafat and Prime Minister Rabin signed an historic document on the South Lawn of the White House on September 13th. That was by no means a ceremonial function. It was a living testimony to deep commitment to peace and justice. It was also a personification of the generous contribution of the U.S. to the whole process. It would have been impossible to realize this great achievement without the active American role. We thank the American people and their energetic leadership.

In the weeks ahead, we shall continue to work hard together in order to maintain a momentum and to keep the process on track. The Palestinian-Israeli Declaration of Principles should be implemented in good faith and without delay.

On the other hand, negotiations on the other tracks must be resumed with full determination to reach agreement soon. Particularly important is achievement of meaningful progress on the Syrian track promptly. I believe that the gap between the positions of the two parties can be bridged within a short period of time. The resumption of the Washington talks would present a golden opportunity for attaining this objective.

President Clinton, our discussions of bilateral relations demonstrated our shared commitment, certify our cooperation in all fields. The U.S. support for our economic reform program has enabled us to carry out this reform very successfully, indeed. Your continued support is most needed for the continuation of the program. Each and every Egyptian appreciates your support and values your friendship, Mr. President. You have been a reliable friend and partner. You can equally count on our friendship and cooperation.

I see such an opportunity to extend an invitation to President Clinton to visit Egypt at his earliest convenience. This would afford the Egyptian people an opportunity to express their appreciation and affinity to the President, to his great Nation.

Thank you.

Ukrainian Nuclear Weapons

Q. Mr. President, leaders in the Ukraine told Secretary Christopher today that they won't go along with the destruction of all of their country's long-range nuclear weapons or the signing of the Nuclear Non-Proliferation Treaty. Do you think that that stand is justified, as they say, by the instability in Russia?

President Clinton. I understand their position, but I think that it is not justified because we're making progress with Russia, too, in complying with all these agreements. And there is no evidence that any of the developments which they might conceive in their worst fears would lead to an unwillingness to cooperate in the nuclear regime.

I think they may see that as a counterweight to nonnuclear pressures they might feel in the future. But I think it's very important. We've been very clear from the beginning with Ukraine that we want to have a strong partnership with them but that we expect this work of reducing our nuclear arsenals and complying with all the relevant treaties to go forward, and we'll keep trying to do that.

Middle East Peace Process

Q. Mr. President, back on the Mideast, in your discussions with President Mubarak today, he mentioned the resumption of the Syrian track talks. What would you like to see as a concrete step forward in the peace process?

President Clinton. I think it's very important that we resume the talks between Israel and Syria. But I also think it's important that we maintain a climate in which those talks can succeed. I believe that Prime Minister Rabin and President Asad, I believe that the people of Israel and the people of Syria want to see this process go forward. But we've got to implement the Israel-PLO agreement. We need to continue to make progress on the other tracks. We need to encourage a greater receptivity in the level of contacts between Israel and the other Arab states, as has already begun. And so I want to do all of that as well. And I think that if we do all of that, I think you will see ultimately, in the not too distant future, a successful conclusion.

Could we give some—I want to give some equal time to the Egyptian journalists who are here. Go ahead.

Q. Mr. President, you have been invited to come to Egypt. Will you be visiting other Arab countries in the area? And in the meantime, would you try to resume the talks between the Israelis and the Syrians and the Lebanese before you go, and would you send Warren Christopher to the area very soon?

President Clinton. Well, I just was invited today to go, so I haven't worked out a schedule yet. I think it's fair to say that the United States and the Secretary of State will continue to be very involved in the region, and I'm very hopeful that we will have a comprehensive resumption of all the efforts in the Middle East. I think you know that that's our administration's position.

Terrorism

Q. There is extraordinary security here today for Mr. Mubarak's visit. Is this a response to a specific threat? And in general, can you tell us if you discussed any of the terrorist issues that are troubling both countries and what your discussions were on that?

President Clinton. We talked about it a little bit, and I may want the President to make a comment, or give him a chance to. I think he's made marked progress in his country in dealing with these issues. The security is at the level we thought was appropriate because of all the obvious tensions that surround the whole Middle East peace process, we think the people of all of our nations are yearning for that peace. We consider President Mubarak a valuable asset. We just wanted to go out of our way to make sure that he felt secure here in our Nation.

Q. On the terrorist issue in this country, is there a specific threat against you, sir, here——

President Mubarak. Here in the United States, you mean?

Q. Yes, that has prompted so much security?

President Mubarak. Really, I didn't hear of any of that in the United States. If you speak about in our country, we are much, far better than ever before. You may hear an incident every now and then, but it happens everywhere in the world now. But we are in a very safe country. And you could come and visit our country, walk on the streets, and so you could evaluate yourself what is the situation.

President Clinton. We have an Egyptian question in the back.

Somalia

Q. Mr. President, do you have any special role from Egypt relating to your position in Somalia? You are asking Egypt to do any special role?

President Clinton. Well, we're going to continue to discuss that over lunch after we have this press conference. But let me say this: I'm grateful for Egypt's continued involvement in Somalia, and I think that we agree, the President and I do, about what our common objectives should be there, what our hopes are. And I think we also agree that ultimately the Somalis are going to have to decide the future of their country for themselves, hopefully with the involvement of supportive Arab nations in the area.

Haiti

Q. Mr. President, on the subject of Haiti, the U.N. representative, Mr. Caputo, has suggested that former President Carter might be a useful representative, and other leaders, to try to get the process moving. Do you think that's a good idea? Would you encourage Jimmy Carter to go? And what is your assessment of whatever progress may have been made over the weekend with General Cédras?

President Clinton. Well, as I said earlier today,

it's always hazardous to be hopeful about Haiti. But I do believe that some of the signs over the weekend were hopeful, that there was some outreach, some understanding that there has to be an accommodation here, and that is hopeful to me.

Mr. Caputo has done a good job and has worked very closely with my Special Envoy there, Ambassador Pezzullo. The first I heard of this suggestion was this morning. I have discussed Haiti on several occasions with President Carter. He knows President Aristide; he did go to President Aristide's inaugural ceremony. He has been working with this administration on some other problems and some other nations. So this is not anything that we've ever discussed in a specific sense. I think that before I would make a comment on it, I'd have to see what his reaction was.

I understand Mr. Caputo mentioned Michael Manley also. What they would do under these circumstances would be up to them. But all of these things I think generally are hopeful. It means everybody is trying to reach out and bring this matter to some resolution.

Is there another Egyptian question in the back there?

U.S. Aid to Egypt

Q. Mr. President, is the American aid to Egypt going to decrease because of the peace agreement in the Middle East?

President Clinton. I wouldn't put it that way. I have continued to support strong American aid to Egypt, and I will continue to do that. And I think it's fair to say that our relationship in the future, including the aid relationship, will be a matter of close conversation between President Mubarak and me and will be whatever is appropriate to help Egypt to succeed and to lead in such a constructive manner.

Middle East Peace Process

Q. I want to follow up on your answer on Syria for a second. Do you think the political traffic in Israel right now could bear a breakthrough on the Syria-Israel front? That is, do you think Prime Minister Rabin could sell to the Israeli public Asad back on the Golan and Arafat in the West Bank in the same window of time here?

President Clinton. I don't know what the answer to that is, but I will say this: At least we can all count, and we know that if you look at the composition of the Knesset with the Shas minority party out of the coalition, temporarily at least, but not yet voting against the peace process, it is important that the Prime Minister know that there is not only a lot of popular support for what is being done but that that popular support can be translated at least into a Knesset that does not attempt to tie his hands in going forward.

Which is why the position of the United States has been, number one, that I believe Prime Minister Rabin wants a comprehensive peace in the Middle East; number two, that in order to do it he has to have the support of the people of Israel, which means we have to implement the present agreement between Israel and the PLO, we have to continue to make progress in opening up other Arab nations' attitudes toward Israel, we have to continue to make progress on the other tracks. And there has to be some time in which he can work out whatever his situation is with this parliamentary body. We don't need to have him in a position where he can't make peace.

Now, I can't offer you a definitive analysis of Israeli politics or public opinion, but I think what I'm committed to doing is to getting this thing on track. Everybody in Israel has got to know in the end there can't be a total peace in the Middle East unless there is some peace with Syria. But the timing is very important, and progress on the things that are now at hand is very important.

Is there another Egyptian question back here?

Russia

Q. Mr. President, concerning the foreign aid, are democracy and human rights records the criteria for U.S. foreign aid? If so, was your support to Yeltsin as an example or an exception for that policy?

President Clinton. Well, democracy and human rights are important, but I would argue that it's an example of that policy. Yeltsin is today the only democratically elected leader in all of Russia. He is doing his best to set up a constitution in which a Parliament will be elected democratically and it will have legitimacy, along with him. And there will be a lot of people who disagree with him in that Parliament, but they will have a legitimate base of authority under a new constitution. Also, I would say that, given the circumstances that he

confronted, he responded with real restraint, I think.

NAFTA

Q. Mr. President, can I ask a question on NAFTA?

President Clinton. Sure.

Q. You have less than a month now before the House is scheduled to vote on the North American Free Trade Agreement. How important will this vote be in terms of your Presidency? In other words, if you lose this vote and NAFTA goes down the drain, will this reflect—how seriously in terms of the big picture, in terms of your success or failure as President of the United States?

President Clinton. Well, I think the more important thing is, how important is it to the United States? I think it's very important to our country, and I'm working very hard on it. I'm going to have a series of meetings and calls today, but I've already done some work on it this morning. And then I think, beginning along toward the end of the week you will see, from then until the vote, an enormous increase in the focus of my personal efforts along with the continued full-court press of the administration.

I'm hopeful, though, I have to say. We made some good moves last week, and I think there will be some good movement this week. And from my point of view it is clearly in the interest of the United States to adopt this. It means more jobs. It means more access to more Latin markets, which means more jobs still. It means a much better climate of cooperation on drugs and immigration and a whole range of other issues with Mexico. It is a very, very important agreement.

The thing that's most important to me is I think that we're already at a point where if there were a secret ballot on NAFTA, it would carry easily. And I think that in the end, the statesmanship urges and impulses of the men and women in the House of Representatives will take over, and I think it will prevail.

Thank you very much.

NOTE: The President's 31st news conference began at 12:30 p.m. in the East Room at the White House. In his remarks, he referred to Lt. Gen. Raoul Cédras, commander of the Haitian armed forces, and Michael Manley, former Prime Minister of Jamaica.

Nomination for Ambassador to Switzerland and World Conservation Union Representative
October 25, 1993

The President announced his intention today to nominate M. Larry Lawrence to be Ambassador to Switzerland and his intention to appoint Shelia Davis Lawrence as Special U.S. Representative to the World Conservation Union, an independent scientific organization that promotes the protection and preservation of natural resources throughout the world.

"Larry and Shelia Lawrence are two of the most concerned, active, and able people that I know," said the President. "I look forward to the work that they will do for our country in Switzerland."

NOTE: Biographies were made available by the Office of the Press Secretary.

Nomination for Deputy Administrator of the Federal Aviation Administration
October 25, 1993

The President announced his intention today to nominate Linda H. Daschle to be the Deputy Administrator of the Federal Aviation Administration at the Department of Transportation.

"Linda Daschle's wide range of experience in the aviation industry, in Government, and as a consumer give her the perspective that is needed for this position," said the President. "She will be a welcome presence at the FAA."

NOTE: A biography of the nominee was made available by the Office of the Press Secretary.

Remarks Announcing Federal Procurement Reforms and Spending Cut Proposals
October 26, 1993

Ladies and gentlemen, the Presidential memorandum on electronic commerce which I have just signed is, as the Vice President said, a direct result of the work done by the National Performance Review. It will make our antiquated paper-based procurement system accessible to anybody with a personal computer. It will open up a world of possibilities to small businesses in America and drive down costs to taxpayers.

This demonstrates why the National Performance Review has been and will continue to be a success. The NPR has become a true action plan for unprecedented cost cutting and reinvention across the entire governmental process. It's dedicated to reforms that will give us a Government that actually does work better and cost less.

We want to give the taxpayer a more efficient Government, to reduce the deficit, to provide new resources so that we can also respond to urgent national needs. The proposals we announce today meet every one of those objectives. By sending to Congress a bill that produces billions in savings, we will now be able to finance an expansion of our anticrime activities at a time when the country desperately needs it. Reinventing Government is working, and I want to say a special word of thanks to the Vice President for his outstanding leadership on this project.

Today I am sending to Congress a significant package of spending cuts, totaling $10 billion, based on the National Performance Review and fulfilling a promise I made to further reduce the deficit by spending cuts in that amount— sending, excuse me, spending cuts in that amount to Congress that could be passed in this calendar year. The Government reform act phases out Federal support for wool, mohair, and honey; consolidates environmental satellite programs; streamlines the operations of the Departments of Agriculture and Housing and Urban Development; reduces costly regulation; and proposes other reforms reflecting more than 20 deficit-cutting recommendations of NPR. These cuts are part of our commitment to put our economic house in order.

With the passage of the economic plan last summer containing about $500 billion in deficit reduction, we've helped to drive down interest rates to historic low levels to keep inflation down. This has meant more private sector job growth in one year than in the previous 4; increases in housing starts; and in mid-October, we know now that auto sales have climbed by 18.4 percent, the largest amount in several years. Orders for heavy equipment continue to rise. While we have still clearly got a very long way to go and many more good-paying jobs to produce, this recovery is beginning to shift into a more promising phase. That's why our progress on continued deficit reduction is very important. We have to maintain the Government's credibility in holding down the deficit and keeping interest rates down in order to provide a stable climate for long-term growth.

We must now move to achieve real savings through procurement reform. While the private sector is becoming more flexible, more innovative, Government has become in many ways over the last 10 years even more bureaucratic. At a time when all businesses are looking for better suppliers and lower prices, the Government is too often losing suppliers and actually paying higher prices by putting up so many costly hurdles and requirements in our procurement system. Procurement waste is costing the taxpayers tens of billions of dollars, and it has to stop. We must fundamentally reform this system, saving billions of dollars and using that money in ways that meet the basic needs of the American people.

Senator Glenn and Congressman Dellums and Congressman Conyers and the other distinguished Members of Congress who have joined us here today have introduced very important procurement reform legislation which will make it easier for agencies to buy the same commercial products ordinary consumers and businesses buy off the shelf. It will cut down enormously on paperwork. It will speed deliveries. It will provide new incentives for small businesses.

At the same time, the Department of Defense has requested, with my support, immediate congressional authorization to undertake seven pilot projects to reform their own procurement processes. These projects will allow the Department to demonstrate innovative approaches to acquiring commercial jet aircraft and aircraft engines as well as items like clothing and medical supplies.

Cost-saving innovations like these are critical to our ability to meet future military needs within our budgetary limits. I might say that the Department of Defense has been so confident of these things that, after we had completed our bottoms-up review, the leaders at the Defense Department said they thought one of the ways that we could actually meet our defense needs over the next 5 years within the tough budgetary restrictions imposed would be to require these kinds of procurement reforms. And I want to thank the Department of Defense for the aggressive attitude that they have taken toward this, and we all look forward to the results they will be achieving now.

Procurement reform also will enhance national security. Procurement regulations today virtually force defense contractors to develop business practices and products that are unique only to the military. This division of industry in the United States into defense and nondefense sectors results in higher prices to the Government, less purchasing flexibility to the armed services, and too often actually denies our military state-of-the-art technologies found in the commercial marketplace. Today 5 of the top 10 U.S. semiconductor producers refuse defense business because of the burdens and special requirements the Government imposes.

Finally, procurement can work by allowing the Government to run more like a business, buying products based on price and other important considerations such as how well a supplier has performed in the past. We want the marketplace, not the bureaucracy, to determine what we buy and what we pay.

According to the NPR report, if Congress does its part in passing the legislation and we do our part in making it work, we could save more than $5 billion in the first year of this reform alone. We ought to take some of that money that your Government has been wasting all these years and use it to uphold Government's first responsibility, which is to keep our citizens safe here at home. With that money, we can make our crime bill even stronger. We can make sure we put at least 50,000 police officers on the street over the next 5 years. We can help States to build more boot camps so we can take young criminals off the street and teach them more respect for the law and give them a chance to avoid a life in prison and live a life of constructive citizenship. We can have more drug courts, like the one the Attorney General started in Florida and the one our administration is helping to launch here in DC, so we can stop sending tens of thousands of criminal addicts back onto the street every year where they'll commit more crimes if they don't get treatment first.

I want Congress to pass this crime bill and pass the savings I've asked to help pay for it. I want them to know that if these cuts aren't passed, I'm going to come back with more cuts. And if those aren't passed, I'll come back with still more. I'll keep coming back until we have the money we need to make America safer.

Procurement reform shares a common border with many of our most important goals: saving taxpayer money, reinventing Government, strengthening our military, improving our economy. But in a larger sense the steps we are taking here today are also about proving to the American people that we can honestly and seriously deal with the issues that matter most to them and that for too long too many have felt powerless to change. We can and will cut the deficit. We can and will run a Government that works better and costs less. We can and will turn those savings to helping America, including helping more Americans be safer in their homes and on their streets.

I'd like to close by introducing to you Lieutenant Colonel Brad Orton. He has a story to tell that reveals the price we continue to pay by doing nothing in this important area. During the Gulf war, the Air Force placed an emergency order for 6,000 Motorola commercial radio receivers. But because Motorola's commercial unit lacked the record-keeping systems required to show the Pentagon that it was getting the lowest available price, the deal reached an impasse. The issue was resolved in a remarkable way that Lieutenant Colonel Orton will now describe, involving the Japanese Government. This should never happen again.

Today is about taking responsibility for doing better, working together to build a better America. We can do this, Congress, the administration, the American people.

NOTE: The President spoke at 10:26 a.m. in Room 450 of the Old Executive Office Building. The memorandum is listed in Appendix D at the end of this volume.

Statement on Federal Procurement Reforms
October 26, 1993

American taxpayers have a right to expect that their Federal dollars are being put to the best possible use. The current Federal procurement system is inefficient and wasteful. It adds significant costs without providing extra value. It's time the Federal Government viewed Federal purchasing as a major source of savings by creating a more efficient and responsive Federal procurement system.

If Congress does their part and we do our part in the administration, procurement reforms in the first year alone will save enough money to fund something Americans care deeply about, fighting crime by fighting drugs and putting more police on the streets all across our country.

NOTE: The President's statement was included in a White House statement announcing procurement reforms and spending cut proposals.

Remarks and an Exchange With Reporters Prior to a Meeting With Members of Congress
October 26, 1993

NAFTA

The President. Let me say, I'll take a few questions, but I intend to have the NAFTA legislation introduced next week, and we're hoping for a vote in November right before the, well, before the recess and before I go out to Washington State to the meeting of the Pacific leaders. We're pushing right ahead on it. I feel good about that.

I did have a conversation this morning with the Prime Minister-elect of Canada. I complimented him on his stunning victory and on the remarkable similarities between his campaign and the issues that he ran on and our campaign last year. And he said, "Yes," he said, "here they accuse me of copying you, but I told them that I had been in the Parliament longer than you've been around, so I figured you copied me." [*Laughter*] We had a great talk about it. We agree that we would see each other in Seattle. I'm looking forward to that. That will probably be our first opportunity to meet.

I understand that a lot of you have questions about what impact this election means on NAFTA. From my point of view, it will have no impact at all. I see no reason to renegotiate the agreement, or any grounds or basis for it. And I think we should just go ahead, and I think that all the countries involved have a lot at stake in proceeding. So that's what we plan to do.

Q. Mr. President, did he reassure you on that issue?

Q. Does the Prime Minister want to reopen——

The President. Why don't we take one question at a time.

Q. Did he reassure you on that issue? Does he want to reopen it?

The President. We didn't have any detailed conversation about it. I think that he didn't want to talk about it this morning. He's just, after all, come from a breathtaking victory. I don't want to characterize his position. That wouldn't be fair. But we had nothing occurred in the conversation which made me have any doubt that our course of proceeding is the right course.

Health Care Reform

Q. Mr. President, the National Association of Manufacturers has again today said that the health care plan is too cumbersome, too complicated, too expensive, should be scaled back. Are you going into some real headwinds on this as you unveil it tomorrow?

The President. No. I don't know what their position is. After their position was reported last time, the next day they called and apologized.

Q. But only for leaking the letter, not for their position. They repeated the position.

The President. No, they called and said that it overstated their position. All I know is that most manufacturers are going to save money under this. And if they want to look a gift horse in the mouth, that can be their decision.

Q. But have you—scale it back?

The President. No, absolutely not. If they don't want lower premiums, they can keep higher premiums and rising costs. It's their decision. But almost all manufacturers, nearly 100 percent of them, provide health insurance. And they will be the biggest gainers in the private sector under this. Now, if they want to walk away from having their retiree burdens alleviated and having their premiums costs go way down, that's their privilege. But I think when the constituency out there, if we can get people to look at the evidence, I think that they will want to do that. I think that all they're doing is—here, this organization is like everybody else—they're going to lobby for the best deal they can get. They're going to lobby for fewer extra services so their premiums will go down even more. But keep in mind, they're already among the big winners in this thing. And I think that they're just out there staking out a negotiating position like everybody else. We've just started this, and it will go on for several months. And you'll see a lot more of it. I'm not discouraged by that at all.

Canadian Prime Minister-Elect

Q. [*Inaudible*]—Mr. President, has the stunning victory made you take the pressure off the Prime Minister-elect——

The President. I would think it would be—

1827

well, he certainly had a stunning victory. It was a real referendum in Canada. The way the press characterized it this morning, I think, is fairly accurate. People want a job-generating strategy, and they want the deficit dropped down, and those are the two things that he ran on. And obviously because he has a big parliamentary majority, he has some flexibility there. But I don't think it would be right for me to characterize, in any way, his attitude, position. It's just not the right thing to do. We had a really good conversation. Our two countries are as close probably as any two countries in the world. We have differences from time to time; we always will. But I feel very good about my conversation. And I think it's a good thing that now that he's been elected, he'll have the support he needs in the Parliament to govern. I think that's a good thing.

Spending Cuts

Q. Did you make your commitment to Senator Kerry this morning, Mr. President, with the spending cuts? Did you meet your commitment to Senator Kerry?

The President. They'll have another announcement about that. That was a whole different issue. The administration promised House Members; there weren't any Senators involved in that. There were House Members who wanted a chance to vote on at least $10 billion more in spending reductions before the end of the calendar year, without regard to what we're going to be doing next year in trying to finish the implementation of the reinventing Government report. And so, that's what we did today. And we gave them more than that because we also would like to have some cuts to fund an expansion of the crime bill to pay for more police officers and to make sure that we fully implement that.

Q. Did he ask you about——

The President. We didn't talk about that.

NOTE: The President spoke at 11:46 a.m. in the Cabinet Room at the White House. In his remarks, he referred to Prime Minister-elect Jean Chrétien of Canada. A tape was not available for verification of the content of these remarks.

Message to the Congress Transmitting a Department of Transportation Report
October 26, 1993

To the Congress of the United States:

In accordance with section 308 of Public Law 97–449 (49 U.S.C. 308(a)), I transmit herewith the Twenty-fourth Annual Report of the Department of Transportation, which covers fiscal year 1990.

WILLIAM J. CLINTON

The White House,
October 26, 1993.

Message to the Congress Transmitting a Department of Transportation Report
October 26, 1993

To the Congress of the United States:

In accordance with section 308 of Public Law 97–449 (49 U.S.C. 308(a)), I transmit herewith the Twenty-fifth Annual Report of the Department of Transportation, which covers fiscal year 1991.

WILLIAM J. CLINTON

The White House,
October 26, 1993.

Message to the Congress Transmitting the Federal Labor Relations Authority Report
October 26, 1993

To the Congress of the United States:

In accordance with section 701 of the Civil Service Reform Act of 1978 (Public Law 95–454; 5 U.S.C. 7104(e)), I have the pleasure of transmitting to you the Fourteenth Annual Report of the Federal Labor Relations Authority for Fiscal Year 1992.

WILLIAM J. CLINTON

The White House,
October 26, 1993.

Nomination for Ambassadorial and United Nations Posts
October 26, 1993

The President announced his intention today to nominate Sandra L. Vogelgesang to be Ambassador to the Kingdom of Nepal and Nelson F. Sievering, Jr., to be U.S. Representative to the International Atomic Energy Agency and his intention to appoint Arvonne S. Fraser as U.S. Representative to the United Nations Commission on the Status of Women.

"In Sandra Vogelgesang, Nelson Sievering, and Arvonne Fraser, we have three individuals who have made serious commitments to public service and to the issues they are being asked to address," said the President. "I am proud of these nominations."

NOTE: Biographies were made available by the Office of the Press Secretary.

Nomination for the National Credit Union Administration
October 26, 1993

The President announced his intention today to nominate former New Hampshire Congressman Norman E. D'Amours to the Board of Directors of the National Credit Union Administration (NCUA).

"The NCUA Board is charged with an important task, safeguarding the futures of the millions of hard-working Americans who put their savings in credit unions. I have faith in Norm D'Amours' ability to uphold that responsibility," said the President.

NOTE: A biography of the nominee was made available by the Office of the Press Secretary.

Nomination for Assistant Administrators at the Agency for International Development
October 26, 1993

The President today announced his intention to nominate Thomas A. Dine as Assistant Administrator for Europe and the Newly Independent States and Jill B. Buckley as Assistant Administrator for Legislation and Public Affairs at the Agency for International Development,

U.S. International Development Cooperation Agency.

"Thomas Dine and Jill Buckley are each experienced in their fields, and I am confident they will work hard to pursue AID's important goals," the President said.

NOTE: Biographies of the nominees were made available by the Office of the Press Secretary.

Nomination for an Assistant Secretary of Commerce
October 26, 1993

The President announced his intention today to nominate Washington, DC, lawyer Susan Esserman to be the Assistant Secretary of Commerce for Import Administration.

"Susan Esserman is an expert in international trade policy who has been widely recognized as one of the leaders in that field," said the President. "I am pleased that she has agreed to serve at the Commerce Department."

NOTE: A biography of the nominee was made available by the Office of the Press Secretary.

Remarks on Presenting Proposed Health Care Reform Legislation to the Congress
October 27, 1993

Thank you very much. Thank you, Mr. Speaker, Senator Mitchell, Senator Dole, Congressman Gephardt, Congressman Michel. To all the distinguished Members of the Congress from both Houses and both parties who are here today, I thank you for your presence and your continuing interest. I thank you for giving Hillary and me the opportunity to come here to Statuary Hall.

This has been a remarkable process. I can never remember a time in which so many Members of Congress from both parties and both Houses had so consistent and abiding commitment to finding an answer to a problem that has eluded the country and the Congress for a very long time. I want to thank the hundreds, indeed thousands, of people who have worked on this process which has led to the bill. I want to thank the literally hundreds of Members of Congress who attended the health care university recently, an astonishing act of outreach by a bipartisan majority of the United States Congress to try to just come to grips with the enormous complexity and challenge of this issue.

I believe the "Health Security Act," which I am here to deliver, holds the promise of a new era of security for every American and is an important building block in trying to restore the kind of self-confidence that our country needs to face the future, to embrace the changes of the global economy, and to turn our Nation around. A nation which does not guarantee all of its people health care security at a time when the average 18-year-old will change jobs eight times in a lifetime and when the global economy is emerging in patterns yet to be defined can hardly have the confidence it needs to proceed forward. If our Nation does that, I believe we will do as we approach the 21st century what we have always done: We will find a way to adapt to the changes of this time; we will find a way to compete and win; we will find a way to make strength out of all of our diversity.

This legislation, therefore, literally holds the key to a new era for our economy, an era in which we can get our health care costs under control, free our businesses to compete better in the global economy, and make sure that the men and women who show up for work every day are more productive because they're more secure and they feel that they can do two important jobs at once: be good members of their family, be good parents and good children, as well as good workers.

This is a test for all of us, a test of whether the leaders of this country can serve the people who sent us here and can actually take action on an issue that, as tough and complex as it is, is still absolutely central to moving us forward. And it is a test that I believe we can all pass. And so I have today just one simple request: I ask that before the Congress finishes its work next year, you pass and I sign a bill that will actually guarantee health security to every citizen of this great country of ours.

The plan that we present today, as embodied in this book as well as the bill, is very specific, it is very detailed, and it is very responsible. And though we will debate many points, and we should debate many points, let me just make clear to you the central element of this plan that is most important to me: It guarantees every single American a comprehensive package of health benefits. And that, to me, is the most important thing, a comprehensive package of health care benefits that are always there and that can never be taken away. That is the bill I want to sign. That is my bottom line. I will not support or sign a bill that does not meet that criteria. That is what we owe the American people.

Now, as we enter this debate, which I very much look forward to, I ask that we keep some things in mind. First of all, when we debate something that the administration recommends or something some of you recommend and it seems bewildering in its complexity, I ask that it be compared against what we have now, because none of us could devise a system more complex, more burdensome, more administratively costly than the one we have now. Let us all judge ourselves against, after all, what it is we are attempting to change.

Secondly, I ask that we follow the admonition that Senator Dole laid for us: Let us all ask ourselves as clearly as we can, who wins, who loses, why is the society better off, and how much does it cost or save? And if we know, let us say. And if we don't know, let us frankly admit that we may not know the answer to every question.

We have gotten in a lot of trouble as a nation, I think—and I see Senator Domenici, one of our great budget experts, nodding his head—pretending that we could know the answer to some things that we don't know the answer to. We have tried to be as conservative as we could

here in making sure that we have not overclaimed for cost savings or overestimated how small the cost of things will be. Therefore, I think we have, in our plan, put more money in than it will cost to implement this plan, but better to be wrong on that side than the other side. We have really worked hard here. And I think we must all do that.

Thirdly, I think we should all say what are the principles that animate this debate. For us, the principles are simple. They're the ones I outlined in my address to Congress, but let me briefly state them again. They are: security, over and above everything; simplicity, the system we create must be simpler than the one we have; savings, we cannot continue to spend for what we have 40 percent more than any other country and much more than that over and above what our major competitors, Germany and Japan, spend to cover fewer people; quality, we must not ask any American to give up the quality of health care; choice, people have to have choice in the private system of health care. Our plan would provide more choices to most Americans and fewer choices to none. And there must be responsibility. To pretend that we can control the costs and take this system where it ought to go without asking more Americans to assume more personal responsibility is not realistic. We have too many costs in our system that are the direct result of personal decisions made by the American people that lead to rampant inflation based on personal irresponsibility. And we have to tell the American people that and be willing to honestly and forthrightly debate it.

Now, our plan guarantees comprehensive benefits and focuses on keeping people healthy as well as treating them when they're sick by providing primary and preventive care. It reduces paperwork by simplifying the forms that have to be dealt with by doctors, by hospitals, by people with insurance. And that's important. Every one of us can agree on at least this: that the paperwork in this system costs at least a dime on the dollar more than any of our major competitors pay. We must deal with this. That's a dime on a dollar in a $900 billion health care system. We can't justify that. It has nothing to do with keeping people well or helping them when they are sick. We have to crack down on fraud. We know our system today is so complex we waste tens of billions of dollars in fraudulent medical expenses that we can change. We ought to help small and medium-sized businesses, self-employed people, and family farmers to have access to the same market power in holding their costs down that big business and Government have today.

I agree with Senator Dole or whoever it was that said this term "alliance" sounds foreboding, but an alliance is basically a group of small and medium-sized businesses and self-employed people and farmers designed to give them the same bargaining power in the health care market that only the Government and big business has today. We must do that. We cannot expect people to be at that kind of disadvantage, especially since many of them are creating most of the new jobs for the American economy.

We should, and we do, protect our cherished right to choose our doctors. Indeed, we try to increase choices for most Americans. Most workers insured in the workplace have now not very many choices about what kind of health care they receive; only about one in three have choices. Under our plan, all workers would have more choices in the kind of health care they receive without charging their employers more for the workers having the option to make that choice.

We preserve and strengthen Medicare. We give small businesses a discount on the cost of insurance. We invest more in medical research and high-quality care. We must never sacrifice that. That's something we want America to spend more on than any other country. We get something for it. It's an important part of our economy and an important part of our security. We should continue to do that.

Our plan rejects broad-based taxes but does ask everyone not paying into the system, that is still there for them when they need it, to pay in accordance with their ability to pay. Two-thirds of the funds that finance this entire system come from asking people who can access the system today, who have money but don't pay a nickel for it, to pay their fair share. And I think we ought to do that. It's not right for people to avoid their responsibility and then access the system that the rest of the American people pay for. And they pay too much because too many people don't pay anything at all.

So these are the fundamental elements of our plan, of this bill. But above all, it guarantees true health care security. It means if you lose your job, you're covered; if you move, you're covered; if you leave your job to start a small business, you're covered. It means if you or a member of your family gets sick, you're covered, even if it's a life-threatening illness. It means if you develop a long-term illness, because you will be in broad-based community rating systems, you will still be able to work. It means that the disabled community in America, full of people, millions of them, who could be in the work force today, will now be able to work and contribute and earn money and pay taxes because they will be in a health care system that will not burden their employers or put their employers at undue risk.

That's what security means. It means that we will, in other words, be able to make the most of the potential of every working American who wishes to work during the time they can work. It is a huge, huge economic benefit in that sense. Every nation with which we compete has achieved this. Only the United States has failed to do so. We are now going to be given the chance to do it. And I think we must, and I think we will.

I want to reiterate what I have said so many times. I have no pride of authorship, nor do I wish this to be a partisan endeavor or victory. We have tried to draw on the best ideas put forth over the last 60 years by both Democrats and Republicans. This bill reflects the sense of responsibility that President Roosevelt tried to put forward when he asked that the Social Security program include health care. It reflects the vision of Harry Truman, the first President to put forward a plan for national health care reform. It reflects the pragmatic approach that President Nixon took in 1972 when he asked all American employers to take responsibility for providing health care for their employees. It embodies the ideas, the commitment of generations of congressional leaders who fought to build a health care system that honors our Nation's responsibilities and who have tried to learn, too, how we might use the mechanisms of the marketplace and the competition forces that have helped us in so many other areas to work in the health care arena.

This is a uniquely American solution. It builds on the existing private sector system. It responds to market forces. It attempts to do what I think we should all be asking ourselves whether we're doing: It attempts to fix what's wrong and keep what's right. And that ought to be our guiding star, all of us, as we enter this debate.

I think by guaranteeing comprehensive benefits and high quality and allowing most people to get their coverage the way they do now, leaving important personal decisions about health care where they belong, between patients and doctors, we have done what we can to keep what is right. I think by asking people who don't pay now to be responsible, by simplifying the system, by cracking down on fraud, by making sure we minimize regulation, we are taking a long step toward doing what is necessary to fix what is wrong, to improve quality and hold down costs.

All of the alternatives that will be debated, I ask only what I have already said: Let us measure ourselves against the present system and the cost of doing nothing. Let us honestly compare our ideas with one another and ask who wins, who loses, and how much does it cost. And let us see whether we are meeting the guiding principles which ought to drive this process.

But when it is over, we must have achieved comprehensive health care security for all Americans, or the endeavor will not have been worth the effort. That is what we owe the American people. And let me say again, the most expensive thing we can do is nothing. The present system we have is the most complex, the most bureaucratic, the most mind-boggling system imposed on any people on the face of the Earth. The present system we have has the highest rate of inflation with the lowest rate of return. The present system we have is hemorrhaging, losing 100,000 people a month permanently from the health insurance system; 2 million people every month newly become uninsured, the rest of them get it back. They are never secure. The present system we have has an indefinable impact on workers in the workplace, wondering what will happen if they lose their health insurance. What does that do to their productivity, to their self-confidence, to their family life? The present system we have is eating up the wage increases that would otherwise flow to millions of American workers every year because money has to go to pay more for the same health care. The present system we have, I would remind you, my fellow Democrats and Republicans, is largely responsible for the impasse we had over the last budget and the fights we had.

Look what we did. We diminished defense as much as we should, and some of us are worried about whether we did a little more than we should. We froze domestic spending, discretionary spending, for 5 years, when all of us know we should be spending more in certain investment areas to help us convert from a defense to a domestic economy and put people back to work in our cities and our distressed urban areas. We froze it. We raised a good bit of taxes. And even though over 99 percent of the money came from people at the highest income group, nobody in this Congress wanted to raise as much money as we did. Why? Because we passed a budget after doing all of that in which Medicaid is going up at 16 percent a year next year, declining to an increase of 11 percent a year in the 5th year; Medicare is going up at 11 percent a year next year, declining to 9 percent a year in the 5th year of our budget.

That's why we did that. We could have had a bipartisan solution, lickety-split, giving the American people a plan that would have reduced the deficit and increased investment in putting the American people back to work if we were not choking on a health care system that is not working.

Now, I don't know about you, but I don't ever want us to go through that again. That is not good for the Congress; it is not good for the country; it is not good for the public interest. And the most important thing is we can't give the American people what they need. They want to be rewarded for their work. They want to know if they're asked to go back to school, if they're asked to embrace the challenges of expanded trade, if they're asked to compete and win in a global marketplace, that if they do what they're supposed to do, they'll be rewarded. They want to know that they can be good parents and good workers. They want to know if they get sick but they're still healthy enough to work, they won't have to quit because of the insurance system. They want to know if they're disabled physically or if they have had a bout with mental illness or they've dealt with any other thing that can be managed, that they can still be productive citizens. And the bizarre thing is that we could do all this and still have a system that is more efficient and wastes less than the one we've got.

So I ask you, let's start with this bill and start with this plan and give the American people what they deserve: comprehensive, universal coverage. That's what we got hired to do, to solve the problems of the people and to take this country into the 21st century.

Thank you very much.

NOTE: The President spoke at approximately 11:25 a.m. in Statuary Hall at the Capitol.

Letter to Congressional Leaders on Proposed Health Care Reform Legislation
October 27, 1993

Dear Gentlemen:

The "Health Security Act of 1993" holds the promise of a new era of security for every American—an era in which our nation finally guarantees its citizens comprehensive health care benefits that can never be taken away.

Today, America boasts the world's best health care professionals, the finest medical schools and hospitals, the most advanced research and the most sophisticated technology. No other health care system in the world exceeds ours in the level of scientific knowledge, skill and technical resources.

And yet the American health care system is badly broken. Its hallmarks are insecurity and dangerously rising costs.

For most Americans the fear of losing health benefits at some time has become very real. Our current health insurance system offers no protection for people who lose their jobs, move, decide to change jobs, get sick, or have a family member with an illness. One out of four Americans is expected to lose insurance coverage in the next two years, many never to be protected again. Altogether, more than 37 million Americans have no insurance and another 25 million have inadequate health coverage.

Rising health care costs are threatening our standard of living. The average American worker would be making $1,000 a year more today if health care accounted for the same proportion of wages and benefits as in 1975. Unless we act, health care costs will lower real wages by almost $600 per year by the end of the decade and nearly one in every five dollars Americans spend will go to health care.

Small businesses create most of the new jobs in America and while most want to cover their employees, more and more cannot. Under the current health care system, cost pressures are forcing a growing number of small business owners to scale back or drop health insurance for their employees. Small businesses spend 40 cents of every health insurance dollar for administration—eight times as much as large companies. And only one in every three companies with fewer than 500 workers today offers its employees a choice of health plan.

Our health care system frustrates those who deliver care. Doctors and nurses are drowning in paperwork, and hospitals are hiring administrators at four times the rate of health care professionals. The system places decisions that doctors should be making in the hands of distant bureaucrats. Its incentives are upside down; it focuses on treating people only after they get sick, and does not reward prevention.

Clearly, our challenges are great. This legislation is sweeping in its ambition and simple in its intent: to preserve and strengthen what is right about our health care system, and fix what is wrong.

Our needs are now urgent. A nation blessed with so much should not leave so many without health security.

This legislation draws upon history. It reflects the best ideas distilled from decades of debate and experience.

It reflects the sense of responsibility that President Franklin Roosevelt called for when he launched the Social Security program in 1933 and recommended that health care be included.

It reflects the vision of President Harry Truman, who in 1946 became the first President to introduce a plan for national health reform.

It reflects the pragmatism of President Richard Nixon, who in 1972 asked all American employers to take responsibility and contribute to their workers' health care.

And it reflects the ideas and commitment of

generations of Congressional leaders who have fought to build a health care system that honors our nation's commitments to all its citizens.

Today America stands ready for reform. For the first time, members of both parties have agreed that every American must be guaranteed health care. An opportunity has been placed before us. We must not let it pass us by.

This legislation builds on what's best about the American health care system. It maintains and strengthens America's private health care. It extends the current system of employer-based coverage that works so well for so many. It protects our cherished right to choose how we are cared for and who provides that care. It invests in improving the quality of our care.

This legislation recognizes that America cannot, and need not, adopt one model of health care reform. It allows each state to tailor health reform to its unique needs and characteristics, as long as it meets national guarantees for comprehensive benefits, affordability and quality standards. It establishes a national framework for reform, but leaves the decisions about care where they belong—between patients and the health care professionals they trust.

Under this legislation, every citizen and legal resident will receive a Health Security card that guarantees the comprehensive benefits package. People will be able to follow their doctor into a traditional fee-for-service plan, join a network of doctors and hospitals, or become members of a Health Maintenance Organization. Like today, almost everyone will be able to sign up for a health plan where they work. Unlike today, changes in employment or family status will not necessarily force a change in health coverage.

The self-employed and the unemployed will receive their health coverage through the regional health alliance, a group run by consumers and business leaders, that will contract with and pay health plans, provide information to help consumers choose plans, and collect premiums. The largest corporations—those employing 5,000 workers or more—will have the option of continuing to self-insure their employees or joining a regional alliance.

The legislation is financed by three sources: requiring every employer and individual to contribute to paying the cost of health care; raising excise taxes on tobacco and requiring small contributions from large corporations which form their own health alliance; and slowing the growth in spending on federal health care pro-

grams. Enormous efforts have been made to ensure that the financing is sound and responsible.

The Health Security Act is based upon six principles: security, simplicity, savings, quality, choice and responsibility.

Security. First and foremost, this legislation guarantees security by providing every American and legal resident with a comprehensive package of health care benefits that can never be taken away. That package of benefits, defined by law, includes a new emphasis on preventive care and offers all Americans prescription drug benefits.

Under this legislation, insurers will no longer be able to deny anyone coverage, impose lifetime limits, or charge people based on their health status or age. The legislation also limits annual increases in health care premiums, and sets maximum amounts that families will spend out-of-pocket each year, regardless of how much or how often they receive medical care.

The legislation will preserve and strengthen Medicare, adding new coverage for prescription drugs. To meet the growing needs of older Americans and people with disabilities, a new long-term care initiative will expand coverage of home and community-based care.

The legislation also provides residents of underserved rural and urban areas with better access to quality care. It also offers incentives for health professionals to practice in these areas, builds urban-rural health care networks, and protects those doctors, hospitals, clinics and others who care for people in underserved areas.

Simplicity. To relieve consumers, business and health professionals of the burdens of excess paperwork and bureaucracy, this legislation simplifies our health care system. It requires all health plans to adopt a standard claim form; creates a uniform, comprehensive benefits package; and standardizes billing and coding procedures.

Savings. The legislation promotes true competition in the health care marketplace. It increases the buying power of consumers and businesses by bringing them together in health alliances. Health plans will no longer succeed by trying to pick only healthy people to insure; they will have to compete on price and quality. This competition will be backed up by enforceable premium caps.

This legislation also criminalizes health fraud, imposing stiff penalties on those who cheat the system. And it takes steps to reduce "defensive medicine" and discourage frivolous medical malpractice lawsuits by requiring patients and doctors to try to settle disputes before they end up in court, and by limiting lawyers' fees.

Quality. The legislation empowers consumers and health care professionals by providing information on quality standards and treatment results. It calls for new investments in medical research, including heart disease, bone and joint disease, Alzheimer's disease, cancer, AIDS, birth defects, mental disorders, substance abuse and nutrition. To help keep people healthy, rather than only treating them after they get sick, the legislation pays fully for a wide range of preventive services and offers new incentives to educate primary care doctors, nurses and other family practitioners.

Choice. Through comprehensive reform, the legislation gives Americans a new level of control over their health care choices. It ensures that people can follow their doctor and his or her team into any plan they choose to join. It transfers the choice of health plan from the employer to the individual, and guarantees a choice of health plans, including at least one traditional fee-for-service plan. Doctors and health professionals may participate in multiple health plans if they wish.

Responsibility. Under this legislation, every employer and individual will be required to pay for health coverage, even if that contribution is small. It extends the current employer-based system for financing health coverage—a system that now serves nine of every ten Americans who now have health insurance. To ensure affordability, small businesses, low-wage employers and low-income individuals and families will get substantial discounts.

This legislation will strengthen our economy. Our current system is so much more costly than any other system in the world, and the American people should not be asked to pay huge new taxes in order to afford health care reform. This plan raises no new broad-based taxes, but spends our health care dollars more wisely. It levels the playing field for small businesses, making it possible for them to insure their families and employees. It eases the tremendous burden of rising health costs on big business, helping them to compete for global markets. And by bringing the explosive growth in health costs under control, it sets us in the right direction of reducing our national debt.

The legislation restores common sense to American health care. It borrows from what works today, letting us phase in change at a reasonable pace and adjust our course if needed. It builds on what works best—and makes it work for everyone. Our task now is to work together, to leave behind decades of false starts and agree on health care reform that guarantees true security. The time for action is now. I urge the prompt and favorable consideration of this legislative proposal by the Congress.

Sincerely,

BILL CLINTON

NOTE: Identical letters were sent to Thomas S. Foley, Speaker of the House of Representatives, and George J. Mitchell, majority leader of the Senate. This letter was made available by the Office of the Press Secretary on October 27 but was not issued as a White House press release.

Nomination for an Assistant Attorney General
October 27, 1993

The President announced his intention today to nominate Loretta Collins Argrett to be the Assistant Attorney General for the Tax Division at the Department of Justice.

"Enforcing the Tax Code is a challenging and important task," said the President. "Loretta Argrett is a woman with the intelligence, diligence, and expertise to get the job done well."

NOTE: A biography of the nominee was made available by the Office of the Press Secretary.

Nomination for United States District Court Judges
October 27, 1993

The President announced the nominations today of six Federal District Court judges in three States:

Harry Barnes, Western District of Arkansas
Nancy Gertner, District of Massachusetts
Reginald Lindsay, District of Massachusetts
Patti Saris, District of Massachusetts
Richard Stearns, District of Massachusetts
Allen Schwartz, Southern District of New York

"Each of these judicial nominees has had a legal career distinguished by high levels of achievement and the respect of their colleagues," said the President. "I expect great things from each of them on the Federal bench."

NOTE: Biographies of the nominees were made available by the Office of the Press Secretary.

Statement on Signing the Departments of Commerce, Justice, and State, the Judiciary, and Related Agencies Appropriations Act, 1994
October 27, 1993

Today I have signed into law H.R. 2519, the "Departments of Commerce, Justice, and State, the Judiciary, and Related Agencies Appropriations Act, 1994." This Act provides funding for the Departments of Commerce, Justice, and State, the Judiciary, and several smaller agencies.

Funding for the Department of Commerce is $3.6 billion. This funding demonstrates the importance of our efforts to promote this Nation's economic growth through high-priority investment programs in the Department of Commerce. It will help Commerce to build a stronger, more competitive private sector, able to maintain U.S. leadership in critical world markets. In particular, I am pleased that the Congress has provided increased funding for the Advanced Technology Program, the Manufacturing Extension Partnership Program, and the new "Information Highway" program. The additional funding for these programs is a critical element of my strategy to create high-wage jobs, strengthen America's technological leadership, and increase our long-run productivity and standard of living. In addition, I am pleased that the Congress provided funds for defense conversion to address the economic dislocation resulting from the end of the Cold War.

The Act also provides funding for a number of high-priority investment initiatives within the Department of Justice. For example, funds are provided for hiring new police officers. This investment will assist in putting new police officers on the streets of America in an effort to take back our neighborhoods from crime and drugs.

In addition, I am pleased that this Act provides significant additional resources to implement my Immigration Initiative, transmitted to the Congress on August 31. These funds will support efforts to provide a fair and effective immigration policy.

Finally, I am pleased the Congress has appropriated funds necessary to support many of our efforts to strengthen our security by promoting democracy abroad, such as through the National Endowment for Democracy. I am deeply concerned, however, about the reductions that were made to my request for payments to international organizations and peacekeeping activities. My Administration is committed to working with the Congress to enable the United States to meet our treaty obligations. Also, I take note of the language in the Joint Explanatory Statement of the Committee of Conference regarding congressional notification, where practicable, 15 days in advance of a U.S. vote in the U.N. Security Council to establish any new or expanded peacekeeping operation. I understand the importance of timely consultation with the Congress, but note that the notification suggested by the Congress may not always be practicable.

WILLIAM J. CLINTON

The White House,
October 27, 1993.

NOTE: H.R. 2519, approved October 27, was assigned Public Law No. 103–121. This statement was released by the Office of the Press Secretary on October 28.

Remarks and an Exchange With Reporters
October 28, 1993

California Fires and the Economy

The President. Good morning. Along with all Americans, my heart goes out to the people across southern California who have lost their homes, their possessions, and who have witnessed private property and the natural environment devastated by these terrible fires. More than 400 homes have already been consumed. And evacuations are now occurring, involving thousands of our fellow citizens.

This morning, I want to announce several specific actions that I am taking to respond to this tragedy in California. First, I have designated Los Angeles, Orange, Riverside, San Diego, and Ventura Counties as major disaster areas. This makes them available for customary Federal assistance to individuals and to State and local governments.

Second, I spoke last night with our FEMA Director, James Lee Witt, and he is proceeding to California this morning, along with the Secretary of the Interior, Bruce Babbitt, who met with Mr. McLarty this morning.

Third, I have spoken with Governor Pete Wilson and will be consulting soon with Senators Feinstein and Boxer, to receive their recommendations on how we can be more helpful to the State.

Finally, I have instructed the Chief of Staff, Mr. McLarty, to coordinate the full delivery of all appropriate Federal resources and assistance to California. We've already dispatched 20 Forest Service air tankers there and many additional Federal firefighters to the scene. I have asked Secretary Babbitt and Secretary Espy to coordinate with James Lee Witt so that we can have a full Federal response to the problems in California.

Many hundreds of people on the ground are engaged in valiant efforts to fight these fires now. Neighbors are helping neighbors. We will offer what we can to help fight the fires, to meet the needs of the victims, to stand with the people who are already doing so much.

Now, before I answer questions, I'd like to say just another word on another subject. For the past 9 months, the primary focus of this administration has been on improving the economy in ways that average Americans can actually tell were affecting their lives in a positive way. We've taken some very serious actions to reduce the deficit, to help increase the fairness of the Tax Code, to provide incentives to invest in important areas of our national economy, to try to give working families with modest incomes and children at home a better break.

Now, we're beginning to see real results, higher growth rates, lower deficits, things that over the long run will represent real progress for the American people. When our administration took office, the deficit for this year was projected to be well in excess of $300 billion. The Treasury Department and the Office of Management and Budget have confirmed today that in the end, it turned out to be substantially lower. We finished this year with a deficit of $255 billion, over $50 billion below where it was projected to be. After years of bad policies and bad estimates, when lower deficits actually went far higher, it's pleasing to me to see that a deficit came in lower than it was projected because of efforts directed to lower interest rates which had significant direct and indirect benefits to this economy.

Lower deficits and lower interest rates have sparked the beginning of a significant economic recovery. Today, we are seeing a third quarter economic growth rate reported of 2.8 percent. I might say that it would have been substantially higher but for the floods in the Middle West and the drought in the Southeast.

Although we know our economy is still not

working well enough for most Americans, these numbers make clear that the historic drop in interest rates, following the announcement of our economic plan and its ultimate passage, is sparking a sustainable recovery that is increasing investments in our future, investments in housing, in businesses, and in durable goods.

There is a lot more to do. We are, after all, as I have said now for nearly 2 years, dealing with trends that are 20 years in the making, trends of stagnant incomes, trends of exploding health care costs, trends of difficult investment decisions too long postponed in America. But we are beginning to see real progress. We are moving in the right direction, and we have to stay on this course.

I am very grateful to the people in the Congress who have supported the economic plan that has produced these low interest rates, that has led to most of the deficit reduction below the projected targets, and I think that this is clearly a good sign that we're moving in the right direction.

I also want to say that it clearly means that we have much more to do. That's why I think it's important that before the Congress goes home, we adopt NAFTA. It's important that we take this health care issue on seriously and see it through to the end. And there are a lot of other issues that we'll be dealing with at the end of this year, and especially next year, to keep this economic recovery going. But this is good news.

Q. Mr. President, on the economy, we've seen a number of false starts over the past 1½, 2 years. Are you convinced that recovery is assured now, or are you still considering some sort of stimulus package to hold in abeyance if necessary?

The President. What I believe is that we are seeing the beginning of a recovery that—you can't say it's assured, because we're in a global economy, but it is clearly sustaining itself, based on American policies and without much help from overseas because of the very slow growth to no growth in Europe and because of the economic problems in Japan.

Another reason I feel very strongly about NAFTA is that Latin America is the second fastest growing part of the world. They're actually increasing their incomes. They have a willingness and an ability, these countries do, to buy more American products. And in order to keep this recovery going and actually have it

manifest itself in more jobs and higher incomes, we are going to have to have the ability to sell our products around the world.

But yes, I think we're seeing the beginning of a very stable, long-term recovery. But keep in mind, there are many things we have to do. We are dealing in part with trends that have been 20 years in the making. And you just don't turn those around overnight.

Q. Will you travel to California?

The President. I haven't made a decision on that yet. I had a very heart-rending talk this morning with the Governor, and I tried to find the two Senators, also. I'll be talking with them, but they may be both, I think, making preparations to go on out immediately.

I did call James Lee Witt, and last night we had a long talk. And I told him I thought it was important for him to be on the ground there today, to call and to give me a report and see how we were doing.

For anybody who has ever been in that part of the State, it's very troubling. One of our administration members apparently may lose his home, has had his family evacuated in Orange County. So it's a huge fire out there, and we're going to do whatever it takes to help the people.

Q. Mr. President, can FEMA handle this after the terrible year that the administration has had with the floods? Do you have the resources to help California?

The President. Well, they did a very fine job with the floods. And I expect to get a—let me get a report from James Lee Witt when he gets out there on the scene, and we'll let you know.

This is something that we have tried to mobilize and alert the Agriculture Department and the Interior Department, not only because we have some Federal land out there that is affected but because we do have trained firefighters in those Agencies that might be able to help. So we're trying to put all that together now, and I should be able—by the middle of the afternoon, I'll know more about this.

Q. Mr. President, you've also said before that—just to follow up—that California is the weakest part of our economy. Isn't it likely that this will further drag down not only California but the rest of the country? What extra help can you give them now?

The President. Let's try to help them get the fire out first, and we'll focus on that.

David [David Lauter, Los Angeles Times].

Q. Mr. President, the last time there was a major natural disaster in California, the earthquake in the bay area, there was a lot of complaint within the State about bureaucratic redtape, bungling, what have you. I know you've tried to make improvements in FEMA during the flood period, but what sort of assurances can you offer the State that this time the job will be done right?

The President. All I can tell you is, I believe that the people who suffered in that historic flood in the Midwest believe that we did cut through the redtape, that we were on top of the situation from the beginning, and that we worked through it as best as possible. And if we do as well in California as we did there, I think the people will be satisfied.

What I want to know, in response to your question and Andrea's [Andrea Mitchell, NBC News], is what is different about this? Are there going to be different challenges? Will there be different problems? But I have every confidence that James Lee Witt will do the same job in California he did in the Middle West and, along with Mike Espy and Bruce Babbitt, we'll be on top of it. And we'll do whatever it takes to make the most of a very difficult situation.

Haiti

Q. I have a question on Haiti, Mr. President. Do you accept as fact that President Aristide won't be back in power tomorrow? And do you favor tightening sanctions?

The President. We're looking at a number of other options, and I'm also looking forward to President Aristide's speech to the United Nations, which I think he has probably concluded now. I know he was to give it this morning, but I haven't gotten a report on it. The Vice President talked with him yesterday, and we have worked very closely on this. We spent about 40 minutes on it this morning in the normal national security briefing period. We are looking at what our options are.

I think that, just from the morning press reports, if Mr. François and the others in Haiti believe that all they have to do is to wait out Aristide and everything will somehow be all right and that the international community will put up with the reestablishment of a Duvalier-like regime there, in plain violation of the overwhelming majority of the people of Haiti, I think they're just wrong.

Again, I will say, the people down there that are thwarting democracy's return have got to decide whether they want to hold on tight to a shrinking future or take a legitimate and proportionate share of an expanding future. It is their decision. But I think they are making a grave mistake, and we are looking at what our other options are.

Thank you very much.

NOTE: The President spoke at 11:12 a.m. in the Rose Garden at the White House, prior to his departure for Baltimore, MD. In his remarks, he referred to Lt. Col. Joseph Michel François, chief of the Haitian police.

Remarks to the Medical Community at Johns Hopkins University in Baltimore, Maryland
October 28, 1993

Thank you very much. You have just seen the most stunning example of one of Clinton's laws of politics, which is whenever possible be introduced by someone you've given a good position to.

I want to thank Hillary—[*applause*]—think about that. [*Laughter*] I want to thank Hillary for the absolutely wonderful work that she and the health care group have done. This has been an unprecedented effort, really, involving thousands of Americans from all walks of life. I don't know how many doctors from around America have told me it's the first time any kind of health care reform has started by asking people who are actually providing health care what they thought about it. I want to thank all the groups that were involved in it, the Nurses Association, countless groups. This group just met with 1,500 separate groups in trying to put this plan together.

And I want to say a special word of thanks to President Richardson and Dr. Block and to

Dean Johns and to Dean Gray and to Dean Sommer and all the people here at Johns Hopkins. This university has played a truly unique role in this process because so many have been involved; Hillary said over 20 faculty members, a few students, many administrators. We are very, very grateful to you. And I thank you.

You know, when a President gives a speech there's always a little meeting, a hurried little meeting that occurs beforehand, a couple of days beforehand, and the staff gets together and they say, "Well, what do we want to achieve?" And it goes something like this. "Well, you're going to Johns Hopkins. Be sure and tell them that it would be very hard for us to have done this without Ben Cardin because we can't really pass it unless he really wants to help us pass it on the Ways and Means Committee." So they say brag on Congressman Cardin, and that's in the note. So I'm doing that, and that's true. [*Laughter*] And then they say, "Here are the points you're supposed to make." And so I wrote it down. Instead of all these notes, I just wrote down, they say, "The purpose of this speech is to remind the American people that we actually have a plan, that it is written, that it is universal, that it is comprehensive, and that we actually asked people in health care to help us put it together." Now, I should just sit down. That's it. [*Laughter*]

And that is what I want to do today. I want Americans all over this country, who look to the Johns Hopkins Medical School, who know that this medical center is a shining beacon of everything that is best about our health care, to know that this plan is real; it is specific; it is concrete—within the next couple of weeks every American will be able to read it at a library, or buy it in bookstores or other places where paperback books are sold—that it is specific, that it is universal and comprehensive, and that people who actually know something about giving care to people, healing the sick and taking care of people to help them stay well, had a big role in this; that we listened and incorporated those suggestions.

And I want to talk a little bit today about what has already been said: What do we mean by keeping what's right and fixing what's wrong? But in the beginning let me say something that doesn't have anything to do with my notes because I think it's important about how we all came here. All of you came here because you had a personal history. You might wonder what

two lawyers who met in law school and got married like Hillary and me are doing, being obsessed with health care. [*Laughter*] It's an interesting and long story. My mother was a nurse anesthetist. I was permitted as a young man to go into hospital rooms, to go into emergency rooms, to go into even surgery, to watch surgery when I was a young person. And I didn't faint.

I can remember in a simpler time before there was Medicare or before there was Medicaid, when poor working people would pay my mother for performing the anesthesia in kind; when fruit pickers would come to Arkansas in the peak season and literally bring bushel baskets full of peaches to our door to pay for the service she had provided for some member of their family in the operating room.

I can remember when I met Hillary in law school, she took an extra year in law school to work with the Yale Medical School on the problems of children and the relationships of children's health and developmental problems to the law, or at that time, the relative lack of relationship of children's health and medical problems to the law.

In 1979, when I became the Governor of my State, and it was obvious we had a lot of serious problems both in terms of quality care and the availability of care, Hillary headed a task force in our State on rural health care to try to figure out what we could do to bring health care to more places in our State that didn't have it. And we set up and funded for the first time with State funds a tertiary care center at the Arkansas Children's Hospital, now the seventh largest in the country, I'm proud to say.

When I was a Governor, we went many times to the Mississippi Delta where Robbye McNair is from. And I want to thank her not only for what she's become—this is a long way from Belzoni, Mississippi, folks—but for the fact that she wants to go back there to take care of the people.

I have been in schools in the delta, which is the poorest part of America—the Mississippi Delta from Memphis to New Orleans is still America's poorest region—where as many as 30 percent of the kids have serious dental problems because even in their teen years they've never seen a dentist, they never had anybody give them any primary care advice, and where they're asked to stay in school and learn under very adverse circumstances, when they're literally in pain all day every day because they never saw a dentist.

So there are a lot of things that all sort of put these threads together that brought us to this point. And in 1990, I was asked on behalf of all the Governors to join the then Republican Governor of Delaware, now a Congressman from Delaware, Mike Castle, in trying to come up with some bipartisan Governors' approach to this because we all had millions of people who didn't have any health insurance, many others who didn't have any access to health care, and yet the Medicaid budget was breaking every State government in the country, taking money away from what we wanted to spend on education and on economic development and trying to offer opportunity to our people. So by the time I decided to run for President, I had been living with this for a very long time.

I just couldn't see how America would ever get where we needed to be by the dawn of the 21st century without dealing with the health care crisis. I didn't believe it. That's why we decided to do this. That's why we devoted so much of the last 9 months to developing this plan, to presenting it, to giving it to Congress.

And if I might, I would just like to say a couple of words about that. This is a deep human problem for every American who's ever lost health insurance, for every American who never had it, for every American who can't change jobs because someone in their family's been sick, for every nurse or doctor who tears their hair out because they spend so much time filling out useless forms, or because they have to get on the phone and call some bureaucrat and get permission to do something that anybody with a lick of sense would know they ought to do anyway.

This is a human problem. But you must understand that it has enormous ramifications for all the other aspects of your Nation's life, because as we spend more and more and more and more money on health care, and yet more and more and more people don't have access to it, and more and more others are afraid they're going to lose it, and more and more small businesses make the decision every year to get rid of their health insurance or to raise the deductible to $2,500 or $3,000 or whatever, that chips away in millions of little human stories at the collective security we need as a country to face the challenges of the present day.

We have been 20 years now when most hourly wage-earners in America are working harder for the same or lower wages, longer hours at work, less time with kids. We see a global economy full of both hope and fear; full of challenges there to be seized that offer opportunities for people and full of great pressures on people who aren't very well prepared for this global economy.

We have to face as a nation what it's going to take for us to enter that next century just a few years away now—the world's strongest country with the American dream alive and well for everybody who's willing to do what it takes to seize it. That means we have to dramatically change our economic approach, our education system, our commitment to invest and grow, the way we relate to one another. We have to make a full-scale assault on the problems that are destroying the quality of life for millions of our young people and preventing them from growing up to be what God meant them to be. And in order to have the courage to change, we're going to have to have a much higher level of certainty that if we do the right things as a people, we will at least be rewarded with the basic things of life. And it begins with the health care issue.

So I say to you that this is a very important thing on its own merits. It ought to be done. In any age in time with this set of problems and this set of opportunities in health care, somebody should be willing to act. At this time, it is critical for America to get in the shape we need to be in by the beginning of the next century so we can do what we have to do as a country.

Now, very briefly, let me say how we seek to fix what's wrong with the system and keep what's right in terms of the six principles that I laid out when I addressed Congress on this issue last month:

Number one, and most important of all, security. Some things are right with this system. A lot of people have good health insurance. Some people have health insurance that is paid for 100 percent by their employers even, that is very good, that has comprehensive benefits. We want them to be able to keep that. But we want to put a floor under what they can lose, because, keep in mind, nobody has absolute certainty today. Somebody can have a great health insurance policy, but if their company lays them off or if they decide to go try to start a small business or they change jobs, they can lose it.

So 100 percent of the people benefit from this plan, because all those with great policies now have a floor under them if this plan passes. There will be something they cannot lose. Their employer may require them to pay more than they now pay because of economic pressures, but there's a limit to how much they can be required to pay. And they can never lose coverage.

I think this is very, very important because I hear a lot of people sort of slinging their arrows over at our plan, talking about, "Well, they're going to all this trouble for the 15 percent of the people that don't have any health insurance." Well, you know, there are 15 percent that have nothing, another 100,000 a month that have nothing permanently. There are also a lot of people that have health insurance, but it doesn't amount to much. And there are people that have great policies, but they can lose it. So this puts a floor under it.

Secondly, it provides coverage for people in and out of the workplace who don't have it now in the customary way we provide it. That is, we require employers and employees who don't have any coverage now to make a contribution and provide coverage for those in the workplace. For those who are in small business and have low-wage operations, we provide discounts. For those who are the uninsured unemployed, the Government will cover them in the way we cover Medicaid patients today. So we will have security for everybody, and everybody will be more secure than they are now. No one under our plan will lose benefits from what they have now by what we do. So we keep what's good about the system, but we fix what's wrong.

Simplicity. I think when Robbye said the present system was simple, what she meant was it's good to maintain the transaction between the doctor and the patient. But make no mistake about it, when you get beyond that to the paperwork, our system is the most complex system in the world.

Somebody said, "Gosh, Clinton turned in a 1,360-page bill" or however long it is. We reckon there will be more than 10 times that much legislation repealed if our bill passes. And it's a metaphor for what's going on now. Rube Goldberg in his wildest dream could not have designed a machine that's like the American paperwork machine in medicine today.

So what do we want to do? By having a benefits package that is at least a basic comprehensive package, we will be able to have a single simple form for medical providers, a single simple form for insurers, a single simple form for people who access the system. We figure in total, maybe four or five forms, but one for each of the main aspects. That will dramatically simplify the paperwork burden.

We also will be able to devolve more decisionmaking back to the providers themselves and hold people accountable for results instead of having the Government or an insurance company try to micromanage every decision on the front end. That will drastically simplify this decisionmaking process, drastically cut down on the paperwork, and free up all across America millions and millions and millions of hours every year for people to do what they train to do, which is to take care of patients. And it is very important.

The third principle of this plan is savings; how do you keep what's right and fix what's wrong. What's right in the medical profession with regard to savings now, a lot of people are doing a good job, finally, in saving money. This institution has proved that you can provide high-quality care and still have economy. The Mayo Clinic had an inflation rate of 3.9 percent on their services last year. The Federal health insurance system has modest increases in most of its policies and decreases in some. The same is true for the California public employees system. So savings are being achieved.

How do you permit those people to continue to do what is right and fix what's wrong, which is that the overall system is still going up at 2 and 3 times the rate of inflation, that small business premiums are going up at 2 and 3 times the amount that nonsmall business premiums are? How do you effect those savings? Well, we believe the way to effect those savings, first of all, is to stop cost shifting by having everybody covered, which will save a lot of money, and secondly, to give the presently uninsured small businesses, self-employed people, and farmers the opportunity to have the same bargaining power that people in bigger units do. There's no reason that big business and Government should benefit from all the economies of scale in health care. The only reason they do today is because of the way the insurance market is organized.

So under our plan, those savings will be fairly

spread across the whole area, and we will also put Medicaid into the kind of comprehensive care delivery system that we're asking for small business, and self-employed people. So you'll have the poor, small business, and self-employed in the same sort of buying units, larger ones, that only big business and Government have today. It will produce huge savings. It will not take away the savings that others are getting. And it will fix what's wrong and keep what's right. It's high time we did it.

Three other things. Quality. How are you going to keep quality? Everybody says we've got the highest quality health care in the world, and we do. Is there something wrong there and something right? You bet there is. We always know, we know what's right, right? You're right; you're what's right about it. We know what's right about it.

What's wrong about it? First of all, too many people don't have access to health care, and too many people, when they get health care, get it when it's too late and too expensive in an emergency room. And too many people even could be covered in theory—which is what Robbye was talking about—too many people could be covered in theory by this plan and still not be covered in fact because they might have access to insurance but not access to providers.

So to fix what's wrong and keep what's right, we have tried to provide a special financial funding string for the medical research institutions, the people who do a lot of health education, for public health units in isolated urban and very sparsely populated rural areas to make sure that the access to health care as well as to insurance is there. And we have tried to emphasize primary and preventive services in this comprehensive package of benefits. Perhaps the single biggest deficiency across the board in American health care is the insufficient attention we have paid to primary and preventive services. And that is how we will improve quality and not undermine what is right.

Choice. We got a lot of letters, including from doctors saying, "You're going to make me be in an HMO, and I don't want to be." We got letters from people saying, "You're going to make me join an HMO, and I'll lose Dr. Jones, and I hate you for doing that."

So, here's the issue: How can we preserve what's right and fix what's wrong? First of all, let's be realistic about this. Americans have been

losing their choices of physicians by the millions for the last decade, right? Of all the people who are insured in the workplace, only one in three today have a choice of plans or options in what their employer has provided for them in the form of health care coverage, down from 50 percent just 7, 8 years ago.

What does our plan do? It actually gives people more choices, both providers and insured people. Insured people under our plan would have three options, at least three. Their employer's premium would be the same regardless. They might have to pay a little more depending on what option they exercised. They might have an option to be in an HMO. They might have an option to be in a PPO, where professionals got together and managed their own health plan. There's a group of 700 doctors, for example, in Nevada, that have had their premiums collectively go up, or their costs, within a range of 2 or 3 percent over 6 years now. But there's a huge range of doctor choice because there are so many doctors in the group. Or it might be strict fee-for-service medicine at the election of the person with the insurance. But at least everybody will have a choice now, which is something they don't have.

So under our plan there will be more choices. The same will be true for physicians and other health care providers—will have multiple choices about what kinds of things they can engage in because we've attempted to prohibit exclusive, mandated organized arrangements in our plans.

So we believe as a practical matter, if you look at where American medicine is today as compared with 10 years ago, our plan will actually provide more choices for both the insured and for medical providers than they now have.

And finally, responsibility. Let's be frank about this. This system lends itself to a lot of monkeying around. There's a lot of health care fraud. There is some abuse of the legal system, of malpractice. There is the ability of people to overutilize the system because there are no significant deterrences to it. Americans have a lot of habits which make us sicker and which cause us to use the health care system more, that we need to deal with. There is something to be said for the proposition that we will never really bring health care costs into line with what they ought to be until all of us are willing to assume a higher level of personal responsibility for the outcome of the health of the American people.

I want to make this last point, and I want you to think about it. Don't answer out loud, but everybody think of this in your mind. I don't know if you've thought of this, but this is the kind of thing I have to think about as President; it's my job. If I were to ask you what are the reasons that America spends 14.5 percent of its income on health care—Canada is at 10. Germany and Japan, our major competitors, are under 9; that means they spend under 9 cents on the dollar. We're spending 14.5 cents on every dollar made in America on health care. Let me just give you an idea of what some of the practical consequences of that are. Every year they spend 3 cents on a dollar more than we do investing in their infrastructure. You know what that means? That means 10 years from now, they're going to have better airports; they're going to have faster trains; they're going to have better roads. They're going to have invested in those things that may be boring but may provide a much higher quality of life and a much higher income. But they had the money. It means that they can invest in all kinds of R&D in their economy, which may give them critical advantages 10, 20 years from now because we spend this money on health care now.

So, if I ask you, why is that? How can they cover 100 percent of the people? And you can't just say they don't invest any money in medical research. It's plainly not true in Germany, one of the leading countries in the world, for example, for pharmaceutical companies. If I were to ask each of you, why is that? What's the difference in their 9 percent and our 14.5 percent? Is any of it good, from our point of view, and is some of it bad, and what can we do about it? And how much of it requires responsible decisions on the part of all of us?

Here would be my answer. This is the best I can do, and I thought about this until my brain aches for years now. I believe first of all, we spend more money on some things that we intend to keep right on spending more money on. We spend more money on medical research and more money on technology, and we don't want to give it up. And it's an important part of our economy, and we're not going to. And make no mistake about it, that also creates high-tech, high-wage jobs. When pharmaceutical companies spend a lot of money on research, they put a lot of scientists to work.

And that's a good thing for the economy.

So these are good things, and that will mean more. What's the rest, though? We have huge numbers of unnecessary procedures. We all know that. We don't do enough primary and preventive care. We all know that. We do have all kinds of fraud and abuse in this system. And we spend a dime on the dollar more in administrative costs than any other country in the world because of paperwork. That's the stuff we've got to fix.

Finally, we have certain group behaviors that we have to deal with. In the 1980's, under great financial pressures, schools all over America virtually abandoned physical education at a time when poor children needed it worse than anything. They needed not only the exercise, but they needed education in dietary habits, in personal hygiene habits, in the kinds of things that ought to be a part of a physical education curriculum. You want to lower the cost of health care? Undo that. Fix it. Go back and do something differently so that people can deal with that.

We'll never get the cost of health care down to where it is in other countries as long as we have higher rates of teen pregnancies and higher rates of low birth-weight births and higher rates of AIDS and, most important of all, higher rates of violence. We've got so many people cut up and shot in our emergency rooms, how in the world can we expect to lower our health care costs?

That's why this responsibility is so important. We begin by asking people who are taking advantage of the system to pay something into it. This business that we're going to break small business if we require all employers to pay something who don't pay anything now is not very credible.

My Small Business Administrator, Erskine Bowles, has spent 20 years creating small business. And he's perhaps the most ardent advocate for our plan. Why? Because he knows that 70 percent of the small businesses do provide some health insurance coverage. Most of them are paying too much for too little, and a lot of them are risking going broke because of the cost of the premiums. And one reason is that other people, who can access the system when they need it, don't pay anything even though they can afford to pay something. So that's the beginning of responsibility. If all of us are going to have access to this system, all of us should make a contribution in accordance with our ability to pay.

It goes way beyond that. We have certain group behaviors in this country that are imposing intolerable burdens on the health care system, which will never be remedies. And we must recognize every time another kid takes another assault weapon onto another dark street and commits another random drive-by shooting and sends another child into the Johns Hopkins emergency room, that adds to the cost of health care. It is a human tragedy. It is also the dumbest thing we can permit to continue to go on for our long-term economic health. Why do we continue to permit this to happen?

And so we need to advocate those things, too. We need to put the physical education programs back in our schools. We need to favor those, not just the Friday night contests. We need to think about the kids who need it. And we need to challenge these group behaviors. We have got to reduce the number of low birth-weight births. It's great that we can keep all of those little babies, or so many of them, alive today. But it is an unnecessary cost. We can reduce those if we work at it.

And most important of all, we have got to do something about the rising tide of violence in this country. There's a crime bill that the Congress can give you for a Christmas present that includes the Brady bill and more police officers on the street and alternatives for kids, and we ought to pass it. We ought to pass it before the Congress goes home.

Let me close with this. We are beginning now the process that will lead to a vote some-

time next year on the health care plan. It will begin with this, and the more people who know what's in this, the more people who make constructive suggestions about how it can be improved, the better off we're all going to be. So I ask you to think about this: This book will be in every library in the country. It will be available, widely available. And now that the Government Printing Office has printed it, any other publisher in the country can go out and try to print it for a lower cost. That's good. That means we'll have a little competition and these books will be everywhere. [Laughter]

I want to implore all of you to get this and read it, to get as many of your friends and neighbors as possible to read it, and to create a climate in this country where we have an honest, nonpartisan American debate to have an American solution to this issue; and that you insist that these principles be observed—that we fix what's wrong, keep what's right—and that we act on this, that we act on it before Congress goes home next year. It begins with you knowing about it. Please help us.

Thank you very much, and God bless you all.

NOTE: The President spoke at 12:20 p.m. in the Newton White Athletic Center. In his remarks, he referred to university officials William C. Richardson, president, Michael E. Johns, dean, medical faculty, Carol J. Gray, dean, School of Nursing, and Alfred Sommer, dean, School of Hygiene and Public Health; Robbye NcNair, medical student at the university; and James A. Block, president, Johns Hopkins University Hospital.

Remarks at a Rally for Mayor David Dinkins in New York City
October 28, 1993

The President. This is not one but two hard acts to follow. I am glad to be back in Queens. And I'm here because I still love New York.

I want to say that when I was waiting to come out here tonight, I listened to the choir and the music and my friend Judy Collins. And they were great, and they got me in a wonderful frame of mind. I listened to all of you cheer. I listened to my friend Gary Ackerman tell me that he grew up in a public housing unit called

Pominant near here. His mother is right over there. And I want to say right now that the first time Congressman Ackerman visited me in the White House, he looked around at the White House and he said, "Don't feel bad, Mr. President, I used to live in public housing, too."

I want to thank Tom Manton and Carolyn Maloney and Nydia Velázquez and my dear friend Floyd Flake and Gary Ackerman for being my partners in the Congress of the United

States. I want to thank Claire Shulman and Freddy Ferrer and Peter Vallone and all the other leaders of the Democratic Party here, and Tom Van Arsdale and the leaders of the House of Labor for giving us a place to meet and a cause to fight for.

I want to say a strong word for the rest of this ticket, Alan Hevesi and my friend of many years Mark Green, who will make a strong team when Mayor Dinkins is reelected on Tuesday.

And I want to say one other thing. I know I should be mindful of New York every waking minute, but once in a while, just once in a while, you slip my mind. [*Laughter*] Now, this morning I went out running, as I do every morning, and I wore a cap that I was given the other night when we showed a wonderful movie at the White House about a young man who overcomes enormous odds to fulfill his lifetime dream of playing football at Notre Dame.

Audience members. "Rudy"!

The President. The title of the movie is "Rudy." I didn't realize that when they showed it on the CNN or wherever that there might be some political connotation to that. [*Laughter*] So when I learned that there was, I remembered that there was another movie made a few months ago that I also liked very much called "Dave." So let me tell you, I liked both movies a lot, but when it comes to being Mayor, Dave's my man.

Ladies and gentlemen——

Audience member. We love you, Bill!

The President. Thank you.

Ladies and gentlemen, I have read some criticism, some of which I sort of understand, from people saying, "Well, you know, the Vice President and Mrs. Gore and the President and the First Lady, they've all been there campaigning for Mayor Dinkins. What are they doing there? They don't have a vote in New York." Well, we may not have a vote in New York, but we have a stake in New York. How can America do well if New York City or New York State don't do well? How can we be the kind of country we ought to be if the home of the Statue of Liberty is not a living example of our liberty and our triumph and the strength of our diversity?

I also know that elections always stand for things. The voters of New York, no different than the voters of any other place in America, have been through a long, tough time. For 20 years now, most hourly wage earners have been

working longer work weeks for the same or lower wages, when you take account of inflation. For 10 years, many workers have given up all their pay increases just to pay for higher health care costs. More and more when people lose their jobs, they don't get the same job back; they have to get another job. And often it doesn't pay as well or have as good benefits.

More and more, people look at the present with some sense of insecurity. All over America I've told the story of the man who worked at a hotel in Manhattan who told me that his son wanted him to support me, but if he did it, he wanted me to make his son free. And by that he meant free to walk to school without fear of being shot or attacked.

These are things that everyone in America feels. And when people are frustrated and anxiety-ridden, they naturally tend to vote to change things, whatever it is. Look at the Canadian elections. Look at what's happening in Europe, all over the world: every wealthy country having trouble creating jobs, having trouble giving people higher incomes when they work harder and smarter.

We are seeing, my fellow Americans, a lot of problems in the world and a lot of problems at home. I ran for President because I wanted to change that. But here's what I want to say to you. And this is the message I have to everyone in New York, whether like me, a Democrat born and bred, or a Republican or an independent or a member of one of the other parties here: Yes, we must change America.

Every day I get up and go to work to do that. Today we saw the deficit this year is over $50 billion less than we were told it was going to be on the day I became President. Why? Because we went after it. We brought down interest rates; we proved you could bring down the deficit. And for the first time in a long time, when you got that report the deficit was smaller, not bigger, than all the politicians said it was going to be. Yes, we need change.

Yes, we need more jobs. But in the first 9 months of this administration we have more jobs in the private sector created than in the previous 4 years. Is it enough? Of course not. But we are on the right path.

Yes, we need changes in education. Yes, we need changes so we can sell more of our products around the world. Yes, we need all kinds of changes. But here is what I want to say to you: For the people who are laboring to produce change, you should have a reward, not a punishment. If we need better education, shouldn't we reelect a Mayor—without any help in Washington, no help from Washington, found a way to keep the libraries open 6 days a week and to promote education?

If we need health care security for all, shouldn't we reelect a Mayor who's actually got a theory about how to use these public health clinics to keep people well and give primary and preventive services and keep people in a position where they can have more health care for lower costs? I think we should.

If crime is a scourge tearing at the heart of America and ripping up families and communities, shouldn't we reelect a Mayor who with no help from Washington put 6,000 more police officers on the street and, not according to his campaign literature but according to the FBI statistics, oversaw a reduction in the total number of crimes reported in all major categories from over 700,000 to over 600,000 a year? Sure, there's too much crime, but if a guy's doing right by it, why punish him? Reward him. Send a message to other people throughout America that you want change and you will reward change, and people will vote for those who have the courage to change. That's what this is about.

And tell me, you walk across to your neighboring State where Governor Florio is running for reelection, and you look here, and you see two people who said we need more cops, fewer guns, and we need to do things to give people a chance to have a better way in life; we need to give them something to say yes to, not just tell them no all the time. So we're going to prevent crime, punish crime but give people a chance to escape from a life of crime and from a fabric of destruction. When people are committed to that kind of change, no matter how frustrated, no matter how angry, no matter how hopeless people sometimes feel in their darkest moments, those are the public officials who should be rewarded. How can we make progress if the voters cannot make distinctions between those who fight for the right kind of change and those who do not? This man has earned reelection, and I hope you will give it to him on Tuesday.

The other thing I want to say to you is that it is easier to be a good President for New York City and for New York State if you have a good partner at city hall or in the statehouse. It is easier. I know we have a lot of work to

do. Today, just today, I asked Congress to act on the vision of Mayor Dinkins and Senator Moynihan so that the Federal Government can work with New York City and New York State to build a new railroad station inside the old post office on 33d Street in Manhattan. For more than half a million commuters every day, Penn Station is the gateway to New York City. We can build a beautiful new station worthy of this great future and this great city.

This is the beginning of the kinds of things we must do together. But I need your help. So what if we pass a health care plan—we've got to do that—and every one of your Members of Congress vote for it. How will it work? How will it work? We must still have the clinics in the cities where the people are isolated from care. We must still make sure the great hospitals can prosper and provide care. We must still, in short, have the kind of partnership with this city so that when we pass a bill providing health care security for all of our people, health care that is always there, health care that can never be taken away, it is really there when people show up the next day. That requires a partnership with a Mayor and a city committed to providing quality health care to all the people who live here. That is why I want you to reelect David Dinkins on Tuesday.

My fellow Americans, I believe with all my heart the decisions we make as a people in the next 4 to 5 to 6 years will shape America for 50 years. We have finally admitted as a people that we can no longer ignore the great challenges of our age: the great challenges of global economy, the great challenges of crime here at home, the challenge to make a strength out of our diversity, the challenge to educate and train our people better, the challenge to liberate our people from the scourge of fear on the streets. We know what we have to do.

We know we can no longer ignore the fact that when there is no investment in these distressed neighborhoods, whether they're in the inner cities of New York and Chicago and Detroit or back home where I come from in the Mississippi Delta, which is still the lowest income part of America, we know we can't ignore those anymore. We cannot let the fact that we know we have great problems blind us to our promise or take away our ability to distinguish between those leaders who have embraced the challenges and change and taken the steps necessary to move to the future, and those who have not.

I come here, yes, because I am a Democrat; yes, because David Dinkins is my friend; yes, because I never pass up a chance to come to Queens and New York City. Yes, I come here for all those reasons. But I'm telling you, far more important than all of that, I come here because ·I believe we need leaders who think children should have a chance to read, who think people should have a chance to live in safe neighborhoods, who believe that we have to have health care that works at the grassroots level, who have plans to put people back to work and give them jobs and hopes, who have embraced the cause of change. And I know that every day, to the best of his God-given ability,

in every way he can, David Dinkins gets up and does that. And I know when you give him 4 more years on Tuesday, he will be the best partner the President of the United States could ever have. Do it! We need you!

Thank you, and God bless you all.

NOTE: The President spoke at 6:18 p.m. at Electric Industries Hall. In his remarks, he referred to Judy Collins, entertainer; Claire Shulman, Queens Borough president; Fernando Ferrer, Bronx Borough president; Peter Vallone, speaker, New York City Council; Tom Van Arsdale, former labor leader; Alan Hevesi, candidate for New York City comptroller; and Mark Green, candidate for New York City public advocate.

Telephone Remarks to the Queens County Democratic Dinner in New York City
October 28, 1993

Hello. Thank you very much, Tom.

Ladies and gentlemen, it's great to be with you, even by telephone. I was here tonight on behalf of Mayor Dinkins, with Congressman Manton and Congressman Ackerman and Congressman Floyd Flake, Congresswoman Carolyn Maloney, and Congresswoman Nydia Velázquez. We think we did some good for Mayor Dinkins here tonight. And I know you will on election day.

I was just reminiscing with Tom about the time when I came to your meeting last year in early 1992 when I took the subway from Manhattan and I came out to Queens to the meeting, and your organization got behind me early and stayed with me through the dark days and the bright ones. And I will never forget it. And I want you to know that I am still as grateful to you today as I was on the day we won the New York primary and the day we won the general election.

I also want you to know that we're making progress on all the things that I talked about in Queens so long ago. We just got the report

today that the Government's deficit is over $50 billion less this year than we thought it was going to be; that we've got some real growth back in the economy; and that more jobs have been created in the private sector in the first 9 months of this administration than in the previous 4 years of the last one.

Now, we've still got a long way to go, and we've got a lot of work to do. I need your help to pass a comprehensive health care bill that gives health care security to all the people who live in Queens. And we've got a chance now to pass a crime bill that will put more police officers on the street, and pass the Brady bill and other bills that will keep some of these terrible guns out of the hands of kids and others who are using them in the wrong way. We've got to do that. And I need your help to do that.

But I want you to know we're moving in the right direction, and we're not going to stop until we've got this economy up and going, provided health care for all, and made our streets safer.

To do all that, I need to just remember the kind of people I met at the Queens Democratic meeting the first time I came up there. I want you to know I'll never forget you, and I'm grateful to you. I want you to stay behind your Members of Congress so they can stay behind me, and help elect the Mayor on Tuesday.

Thank you very much.

NOTE. The President spoke at 6:47 p.m. from Electric Industries Hall. In his remarks, he referred to Representative Thomas J. Manton.

Remarks at the Wall Street Journal Conference on the Americas in New York City
October 28, 1993

Thank you very much, Peter. And thank you for that wonderfully understated observation that your editorial positions don't always agree with mine. [*Laughter*]

I am delighted to be here tonight on a matter on which we both agree. I thank you for sponsoring this meeting, and I was glad to see you and my longtime acquaintance Al Hunt, who invited me. I would say "friend," but it would destroy his reputation in the circle in which we find ourselves. [*Laughter*] He invited me here only because he had been replaced by Alan Murray, and therefore he knew he could not guarantee me one line of good press for accepting this invitation. [*Laughter*] I thank you, I thank William Rhodes and Karen Elliott House and all the others who are responsible for this event.

Ladies and gentlemen, I will get right to the point. When we concluded the side agreements with Mexico and Canada in the NAFTA negotiations and actually had a proposal to take to the Congress, I really believed that the cause was so self-evidently in the interests of the United States that after a little bit of smoke and stirring around, that the votes would rather quickly line up in behalf of what was plainly in our short and long term national interests. It is no secret that that has not happened.

Since I have always prided myself on being a fairly good reader of the political tea leaves, I have pondered quite a bit about why we are engaged in a great struggle that I think is very much worth making and that I still believe we will win. But why has it been so hard? And what can all of us who believe that NAFTA ought to prevail and in a larger sense believe we need to succeed in getting a new GATT round by the end of the year and in promoting a continually more open world trading system, what is it that all of us can do to try to give new energy, new drive to this vision that we all share for the post-cold-war world?

Anyway, let's begin by why it turned out to be so hard. I think it is far more complicated than just saying that the labor movement in America and the Ross Perot-organized group had a lot of time to bash NAFTA without regard to what would ultimately be in the final agreement.

It is far more complicated than that. And it is at root a reflection of the deep ambivalence the American people now feel as they look toward the future. So that in a profound way, at this moment in time, NAFTA has become sort of the catch-all for the accumulated resentments of the past, the anxieties about the future, and the frustrations of the present. Irrelevant are the specific provisions of the agreement, which plainly make better all the specific complaints many of the people opposing NAFTA have about our relationship with Mexico.

I mean, plainly if you just read the agreement, it will cause the cost of labor and the cost of environmental compliance to go up more rapidly in Mexico. Plainly, if you just read the agreement, it reduces the requirements of domestic content for production and sale in Mexico in ways that will enable Americans to export more. Plainly, the main benefit to the Mexican people is opening the entire country in a more secure way to American investment, not for production back to the American market but to build the Mexican market, to build jobs and incomes and an infrastructure of a working market economy for more of the 90 million people who are our largest close neighbors.

So this opposition is in spite of the plain terms of the agreement. It is also in spite of the fact that plainly NAFTA could lead the way to a new partnership with Chile, with Argentina, with Colombia, with Venezuela, with a whole range of countries in Latin America who have embraced democracy and market economics. And I say this to my friends who are not from Latin America but are from other nations here tonight: We see this not as an exclusive agreement but as part of the building block of a framework of continually expanding global trade.

So this is not about the letters, the words, the phrases, the terms, or the practical impact of this agreement. That is not what is bedeviling those of us who are trying so hard to pass this agreement. This agreement has become the symbol, as I said, for the emotional frustration, anxieties, and disappointments of the American people, feelings that are shared, as we now see from the results of the recent Canadian elections and other wealthy countries, the results of the recent elections in France, manifest in the low growth rates in Europe and the low growth rates in Japan and the recent elections there.

What we are seeing is a period of global stagnation which comes at the end of several years in which global growth did not necessarily mean more jobs or higher incomes in wealthy countries. We are living in a time of great hope where there's more democracy, more adherence to market economics, when the wonders of technology are providing new areas of economic endeavor and millions of new successes every year in all continents, but where still there is so much frustration for those who cannot figure out how to make these changes friendly to them. So that in America, for example, having nothing whatever to do with NAFTA or our trade with Mexico, we are now at the end of a 20-year period when hourly wage workers have seen their incomes remain basically stagnant while their work week has lengthened; when income plus fringe benefits have gone up modestly, but mostly that's been inflation and wage costs; when for the last several years, we have seen more and more working people subject to the restructuring of industries, which means that for the first time since World War II, people who lose their jobs in America now normally don't get the same job back. They get a different job, after a longer period of time, usually with a smaller company, usually paying a lower wage with a weaker package of fringe benefits.

Now, to be sure, though, a lot of good things are happening. Manufacturing productivity in this country is growing very rapidly and has been for several years. We are recapturing part of our own automobile market, for example, this year. It's quite astonishing to see what's happened to the American manufacturers' share of the American car market. That's just one example. American productivity in the service sector is beginning to come back. And if you give me a couple of years to work with the Vice President on this reinventing Government, we'll give you more productivity in the Government sector, too, which will have a private sector impact.

But the plain fact is there are an awful lot of people in this country who feel that they are working harder, caught on a treadmill, not moving up, who feel quite insecure and uncertain.

If you look at what has happened, basically, we live in a world where money management and almost all but not all technology is mobile; where productivity and prosperity are largely a function of the skills of the work force, the level of appropriate investment and infrastructure, and in the private sector, the organization of work and the system for maintaining ever new and different skills, and the systems that support work and family, the systems that support expanding exports, and the systems that support dealing with sweeping economic change. To whatever extent any nation with a high per capita income lacks those factors, people will suffer. And there will always be some dislocation simply because of the rapid pace of change.

What happened today in America is we have a whole lot of people who have dealt with this not very well, who feel that they have worked hard and played by the rules, and who now are the seed bed of resentment welling up against NAFTA, not because of anything that's in NAFTA but because it's the flypaper that's catching all the emotion that is a part of the runoff of the last 10 or 12 years, in many cases 15 years, of experience with the global economy where the United States has not made all the investments we should have made, has not made all the changes we should have made, has not made the adjustments we should have made.

Therefore, what I have tried to do, and what I tried to do in my speech to the AFL–CIO in San Francisco recently, was to argue that we needed in America to face the future with confidence, to believe that we can compete and win, not to run away and not to pretend that these global changes had not occurred, but also to argue that we ought to have a certain base level of security in this country so we could deal with the future.

That's why I supported the family leave law, because most people who are parents also work. So we shouldn't make it impossible in America for a person to be a good parent and a good worker. I believe it adds to worker productivity even though it's a little extra cost for employers.

That's why I think we have to become the last advanced nation to provide health security to all working people, because people are going to lose their jobs in this economy. It's a dynamic economy; one that creates jobs in as many different ways as ours does will also have people losing jobs all the time. And if we want that dynamism to be there, there has to be a bedrock of security underneath it. People cannot feel, when they go home tonight to face their families, their children over the dinner table, that if they have lost their jobs, they have put their children's health in danger. So we need to build that underneath.

That's why, next year, we're going to propose radically changing the unemployment system in this country to a reemployment system where, instead of just getting benefits until they run out, you immediately begin a job search, an analysis of the jobs in the given area, the areas of job growth, and a retraining program immediately, because most people will not get their old job back. And that's what the unemployment system is premised on. It is taking taxes from employers and dragging down the economy under a false premise because it's no longer relevant to the world we live in.

What has all that got to do with NAFTA? If we had all this in place, we'd have a more secure work force, and it would be easier to argue to them we must face the future with confidence. In that connection I would like to ask those of you here who are Americans who are employers here to do one or two things tonight. Number one, I ask that you tell your own employees and publicly commit that you will support a rich, full, and adequate job retraining program for the people who will be displaced because of this agreement. This is a job winner for America. We're going to get more jobs than we lose, but some will lose.

One of the more sophisticated opponents of this agreement said to me the other day, "I

know you will create more jobs than you'll lose. But the people who get new jobs won't feel as much joy as the people who lose them will feel pain." Interesting argument. If you were on the losing end, you might agree. What do we owe those people? A far better training and retraining program than we have, a far more aggressive reemployment program than we have. You should support that so that the people who are at risk will feel that we are moving forward into the future together. It is very important.

The second thing that I ask of all of you is this, that you ask your employees who support this to contact their Members of Congress. I've had as many Republican as Democratic Members of Congress that I am lobbying say to me, "I want to hear from the people who work for the employers, not just the employers. I want to hear from people who know that their jobs will be made more secure, not less secure, if NAFTA passes." That is very important.

We have all these wavering Members of Congress now, many of them moderate Republicans and moderate to conservative Democrats, who come from districts where they have both labor union members asking them to vote against this and people who are part of the old Perot organization asking them to vote against it, and they just want some other real voters to ask them to vote for it. They just want to know there's somebody in their district who understands that this is good for America.

The last thing that I ask you to do is to lift this debate up in the last 3 weeks. I'm going to travel this country, intensify my contacts with the Congress, and try to get as many other people enlisted in this battle as possible. But we have to realize that the people of America can view this through their personal spectrum, but the Members of Congress must be statesmen and stateswomen. They have to realize what is at stake for America in this. We have to decide whether we are going to face the future with confidence and with a belief that we can compete and win, and with genuine respect for the heroic changes undertaken by our neighbors in Mexico to the south and other heroic changes being undertaken by neighbors to the south of them, and engage them in friendship and partnership, or whether we're going to turn away from all that and pretend that we can really do well in a world that we no longer try to lead.

You know, the psychological aspect of this

whole debate is absolutely fascinating to me. The element of isolationism that I see coming into some of our foreign policy debates is equally present in the NAFTA debate: "I've got to worry about myself, and I don't have time to worry about anybody else." The problem is, in the world we're living in, worrying about yourself is worrying about somebody else. We're too connected. We don't have that option. And if you think about this in more personal terms, every time an individual, a family, a State, or a nation faces a crisis brought on by change, you have only two options. You can sort of batten down the hatches, hunker down, and hope it will go away, and that works about one time in 100; or you can take a deep breath, take your licks, figure out what's happening, and embrace the future with zest. That's what America has done. That's why we're still around.

This is a real test of our character as a country, whether we believe that we can compete and win, whether we believe that partnership is good global economics and good American economics, and whether we really understand that we have to make our people see the rest of the world as an opportunity, not a threat.

So I ask all of you to think about that. To our friends here who have operations in both the United States and Mexico or other parts of Latin America, I ask you to explain to Members of Congress that nothing in this agreement makes it more attractive to invest in Mexico to sell in the American market. But this agreement does make it more attractive for Americans to invest in Mexico to help build Mexico. No longer will the *maquilladora* line be some magic line in the sand. Now you can invest in Mexico City and help to build a strong market of millions of consumers who can be even better partners with the United States. I promise you, a lot of people who will vote on this agreement and carry its fate still do not understand that elemental principle.

You need to say if you have experience in both countries that if you don't pass this agreement, everything that you don't like about the present situation will get worse. And if you do pass it, everything you like will get better.

These sound like simple things, but I tell you, I've been to so many of these meetings where all of us stand up who agree with one another, and it's like we're all preaching to the saved, as we say at home. Well, there's lots of folks out there who aren't saved yet, but they are willing to listen. And the Members of the United States Congress need to understand what the consequences of passing this are and what the consequences of not passing this are, not only in Mexico but throughout Latin America.

The changes in Mexico, political and economic, in the last several years, have been truly astonishing, of historic proportions. To continue that, they need a partner, and it ought to be us. And in the long run, even though I know some of our friends in Asia don't like this agreement now, it is in the best interest of the Asians; it is in the best interest of our friends in Europe; it is in the best interest of the world trading system for Latin America and the United States of America and Canada to grow more, to increase their wealth, diversify their activities, so that we can embrace our full share of responsibility for a new fully integrated global trading system.

I think, whether we like it or not, that NAFTA has acquired a symbolic significance, perhaps out of proportion to its narrow economic impact, not only for all those who are "agin" it but for all of us who are for it, too. We have to face the fact that it is, in our time, the debate which enables us to make a statement about what kind of country we are and what kind of partners we are going to be and what kind of future we are going to make.

And I tell you, I believe we will win in the end because I have seen Congress time and again go to the brink with the easy choice and make the hard one because they knew it was the right thing to do for America. But they need help. The two things you can most do to give that help is to say, "I am an employer. I am a taxpayer. I know that people who are disturbed by this, who are dislocated by this agreement should have access to the finest training program this country has ever provided. And I will support that. I will insist that the President and the Congress take care of the people who lose out."

And the second thing you can do is, for goodness sakes, to tell people how it works. We cannot let the legitimate grievances, the honest fears, the well-founded anxieties of people who are not doing very well in this economy stop them from doing better tomorrow. We cannot let the American people act in ways that are against their self-interest.

As I said when I was in San Francisco talking to the AFL–CIO, the truth is that this agreement will create more jobs for labor union members in the United States. We have to assert those facts, and we can prevail if we do.

Now, we have, as you know, about 2½ weeks, a little more, before the scheduled vote. That is an eternity. The Congress wants to do the right thing. I am convinced, about a week or 10 days ago we passed what I always think of as the first threshold in a big struggle in the Congress: I believe we won the secret ballot battle. That is, I think if there were no recorded votes we could ratify NAFTA tomorrow. And that is a very good sign. It is also not ignoble for people to listen to their constituents.

What we have to do now is move from winning the secret ballot battle to winning the recorded battle. We can do it. We can do it. But I ask you to remember that all those people that are hanging fire, all the undecided voters in the Congress, are carrying with them the accumulated fears, resentments, and anxieties of a lot of Americans who did the very best they could and it still didn't work out for them.

And I ask you to at least go far enough with those folks to say, "If anything happens to you, we're going to give you a chance to learn a new skill. We're going to give you a chance to change." As I tell people anyway, the average 18-year-old is going to change jobs eight times

in a lifetime anyway. We might as well get used to it. The average 60-year-old worker in America is going to have to get used to learning a new skill. They might as well learn to enjoy it. It will make life a lot more interesting.

NAFTA can be the beginning of our decision to be a secure nation in a global economy; to lead, not follow; to reach out, not hunker down. We owe it not just to our friends in Mexico and Canada and Latin America, not just to the rest of the world, we owe it to the tradition of America. And I believe we will do it. But it's going to take all hands on deck. And I came here tonight to ask for your help, as much as you can do in every way that you can, for the next 3 weeks.

Thank you very much.

NOTE: The President spoke at 8:23 p.m. in the Empire Room at the Waldorf Astoria Hotel. In his remarks, he referred to Peter R. Kann, chairman and chief executive officer, Dow Jones and Co., Inc., and publisher, the Wall Street Journal; Albert R. Hunt, executive Washington editor, and Alan Murray, Washington bureau chief, the Wall Street Journal; William R. Rhodes, vice chairman, CITIBANK; and Karen Elliott House, vice president international, Dow Jones and Co., Inc.

Statement on Signing the Departments of Veterans Affairs and Housing and Urban Development, and Independent Agencies Appropriations Act, 1994
October 28, 1993

Today I have signed into law H.R. 2491, the "Departments of Veterans Affairs and Housing and Urban Development, and Independent Agencies Appropriations Act, 1994."

The Act provides funding for the Departments of Veterans Affairs (VA) and Housing and Urban Development and independent agencies including the Environmental Protection Agency, National Aeronautics and Space Administration, and National Science Foundation. This Act will fund important activities in the space program, housing programs, environmental protection, and programs for our Nation's veterans.

I am pleased that the Act provides the funding for a number of my high-priority investment

proposals, including the National Service Initiative. The National Service Initiative will provide an opportunity for young people to obtain funding for a college education while serving the country in areas of great need such as education, environment, public safety, and human services.

The Act also provides funding for the redesigned Space Station and New Technology Investments. These programs will set a new direction for the Nation in space exploration, science, and technology.

The Act includes $6.7 billion in funding for the Environmental Protection Agency (EPA). The Act provides funds for EPA programs that protect our environment through enforcement of our environmental laws, cleanup of hazardous waste sites, and construction of needed water and waste-water treatment facilities.

The Act meets the needs of our Nation's veterans by providing $15.6 billion in VA medical care, an increase of $980 million over the FY 1993 enacted level.

The Act includes $25.4 billion in funding for the Department of Housing and Urban Development, including funding for programs such as the HOME block grants for housing, Community Development Grants, and Severely Distressed Public Housing. These programs will assist communities and individuals in revitalizing neighborhoods and increasing opportunities for home ownership.

The Act provides $3 billion in funding for the National Science Foundation, a $283 million increase over the FY 1993 enacted level. These programs will promote basic research that is vital to enabling our Nation to compete in world markets.

Regrettably, the Act does not fund all of my priority investment proposals, including the Community Investment Program and Community Development Banks. Due to tight budget constraints, the Congress has had the difficult task of balancing the competing priorities of this Act. Although I am disappointed this bill does not fund these programs and includes cuts to programs in space, science, and technology, the bill provides funding for veterans programs, housing initiatives, and environmental programs at acceptable levels. We will continue to work with the Congress to address our mutual concerns in seeking solutions to our Nation's problems.

WILLIAM J. CLINTON

The White House,
October 28, 1993.

NOTE: H.R. 2491, approved October 28, was assigned Public Law No. 103–124.

Statement on Signing the Treasury, Postal Service, and General Government Appropriations Act, 1994
October 28, 1993

Today I have signed into law H.R. 2403, the "Treasury, Postal Service, and General Government Appropriations Act, 1994."

This Act provides funding for the Department of the Treasury, the U.S. Postal Service, the General Services Administration, the Office of Personnel Management, the Executive Office of the President, and several smaller agencies. Programs within these agencies address major law enforcement activities in the United States as well as the fiscal operations and general management functions of the Federal Government.

This Act provides funding for the Internal Revenue Service (IRS) tax system modernization initiative and the tax law enforcement initiative. These initiatives are part of my investment program that was transmitted in the FY 1994 Budget. The investment in modernizing IRS will improve service to taxpayers, increase the productivity of IRS operations, and increase tax compliance. The tax law enforcement initiative will provide IRS with resources to address serious tax compliance problems and increase revenue

collections.

This Act also contains a provision that would implement, on a pilot basis, the recommendation made by the National Performance Review (NPR) that would allow up to 50 percent of an agency's unobligated funding for salaries and expenses at the end of FY 1994 to be carried forward to FY 1995. The authority is limited to agencies covered by this bill. Of the 50 percent carry-over, up to two percent of the funds may be used to finance cash awards to employees whose actions contributed to producing the savings, and up to three percent may be used for employee training programs.

As requested by the Administration, this Act eliminates a long-standing restriction on the use of Federal Employee Health Benefit program funds for eligible persons seeking abortions.

Several provisions in H.R. 2403 condition the President's authority—and the authority of certain agency officials—to use funds appropriated by this Act on the approval of congressional committees. The Administration will interpret such provisions to require notification only, since any other interpretation of such provisos would contradict the Supreme Court ruling in *INS vs. Chadha*.

The Act contains a prohibition on the implementation of the NPR recommendation to transfer the functions of the Bureau of Alcohol, Tobacco and Firearms to the Department of Justice. Because this prohibition is representative of the kind of restriction cited by the NPR as counterproductive to efficient government operations, I will work with the Congress to lift it.

WILLIAM J. CLINTON

The White House,
October 28, 1993.

NOTE: H.R. 2403, approved October 28, was assigned Public Law No. 103–123. This statement was released by the Office of the Press Secretary on October 29.

Statement on Signing the Energy and Water Development Appropriations Act, 1994
October 28, 1993

Today I have signed into law H.R. 2445, the "Energy and Water Development Appropriations Act, 1994."

This Act provides funding for the Department of Energy. In addition it provides funds for the water resources development activities of the Army Corps of Engineers and the Department of the Interior's Bureau of Reclamation. Various related independent agencies are also funded by this Act.

This Act supports a number of my high-priority investment proposals in the Department of Energy. These include cooperative research and development agreements, solar and renewable energy programs, and the Stanford Linear Accelerator Center B-Factory. The bill also supports my investment proposals for improved maintenance at Army Corps of Engineers facilities.

I am disappointed that the Congress has not provided funding in this Act for continuing construction of the Superconducting Super Collider (SSC). This project was an important element of our Nation's science program, and its termination is a serious loss for the field of high energy physics. I am glad, however, that the bill does redirect the SSC funds to be spent for orderly termination so that we can assist the affected workers and communities in Texas and elsewhere. I look forward to receiving a report from Secretary of Energy, Hazel O'Leary, on future options for the Nation's high energy physics program, now that the planned centerpiece for the field has been terminated.

I am also disappointed that, with the limited resources available, the Congress has added funds for unrequested water projects and studies. In total, this Act provides over $300 million more than I requested for such projects and studies within the Army Corps of Engineers and the Bureau of Reclamation.

I am pleased that this Act provides funding for the Dual-Axis Radiographic Hydrotest facility (DARHT). In the absence of underground nuclear weapons tests, the DARHT facility will be vital to maintaining confidence in the stockpile.

WILLIAM J. CLINTON

The White House,
October 28, 1993.

NOTE: H.R. 2445, approved October 28, was assigned Public Law No. 103–126. This statement was released by the Office of the Press Secretary on October 29.

Remarks at the Dedication of the John F. Kennedy Presidential Library Museum in Boston, Massachusetts
October 29, 1993

Thank you very much, Senator Kennedy, for those moving words and for your friendship and your leadership. Jackie and Caroline and John and all the members of the Kennedy family here assembled—Congressman Kennedy, I thank you for those fine remarks—distinguished Senators and Members of Congress and Governors here present and all of the rest of you who share a part of this historic day.

I want you to know that I felt very much at home today when I got out of the car and the Harvard band was playing the Yale song. And it reminded me of the time when President Kennedy got a degree from Yale, and he said he had the best of all worlds, a Harvard education and a Yale degree. [*Laughter*] I had the Harvard band and the Yale song. Harvard has higher standards. They haven't offered me a degree yet. But for some of us, music is more important than degrees. [*Laughter*]

The great champion of Irish mythology was the young warrior Cu Chulainn. According to legend, he was a hero without peer among mortals. One day a priest told him, "You will be splendid and renowned but short-lived." Cu Chulainn replied, "It is a wonderful thing if I am but one day and one night in the world, provided that my fame and deeds live after me."

Like Cu Chulainn's legend, John Kennedy's fleeting time among us remains a singular story in the history of our great Nation. He was our President for only a thousand days, but as has been said so eloquently by members of his family, he changed the way we think about our country, our world, and our own obligations to the future. He dared Americans to join him on an adventure he called the New Frontier. Listen now to what he said then: "The new frontier of which I speak is not a set of promises. It is a set of challenges. It sums up not what I intend to offer the American people, but what I intend to ask of them." He inspired millions of us to take a very personal responsibility for moving our country forward and for advancing the cause of freedom throughout the world. He convinced us that our efforts would be both exciting and rewarding. He reminded us that our democracy at its best is a bold and daring adventure.

Three decades have passed since President Kennedy's 3 years in office. But his legacy endures in the new frontiers we still explore. Think of his appeal for religious tolerance to the Houston Baptist ministers, and remember that just this week we passed in the Senate Senator Kennedy's religious freedom restoration act. And I thank you very much for that.

Think of the appeal he made for basic civil rights, and remember that it was just this year that we passed the motor voter act, which was the most important piece of civil rights legislation passed in a long time, and that we now have, I am proud to say, the most racially diverse administration in the history of the United States.

From his creation of the Peace Corps to the creation of the National Service Corps, which drew inspiration from City Year here in his own hometown of Boston, we see a common thread of challenging our young people to a higher calling. From his launching of the space program to the preservation and pursuit of the space station this year, we see a continued willingness of Americans, even in difficult economic time, to explore the outer reaches of our universe. From his quest for health care security for our elderly Americans to the quest for health security for all Americans embodied in the bill that the First Lady and I presented to Congress this week, we see a seamless thread of determination to finally dissolve one of the most persistent domestic problems in the history of the United States. From his pursuit of a nuclear test ban treaty to our efforts to stem the proliferation of all weapons of mass destruction, to actually dismantle much of the world's nuclear arsenal, we see a common effort for America to be leading the cause of human preservation against nuclear annihilation.

John Kennedy embodied an expansive, can-do outlook toward events beyond our shores as well as the challenges at home. He believed that billions of lives depend upon our leadership and our ideals, and in turn that our own security and prosperity are tied to reaching out to the rest of the world. That is why his picture still hangs today in homes not only in the Irish wards of Boston and Chicago but also in villages and towns from Africa to Latin America.

John Kennedy's early years were a time when most Americans did not believe we should be much engaged in the world. America turned inward after World War I, unwilling to assume the new burdens of the peace. "A return to normalcy," it was called, but in truth it was a retreat from the hard-won fields of victory. No fireman in Boston would dare turn off the hose prematurely and leave a smoldering house. But that is exactly what America did in the 1920's and the 1930's. And we paid the price in a Draconian peace and restricted trade and higher tariffs and a Great Depression and lost jobs, ruined lives, the rise of fascism abroad, and a terrible Second World War that took the lives of more American young people than any war except for our own Civil War.

Jack Kennedy came home from that Second World War with a lifelong lesson: America could not withdraw from the world. Unless we work to shape events, we will be shaped by them, often in ways that put us at great risk.

A new generation of Americans after the Second World War learned that lesson with him. Together they rebuilt Japan and Europe and contained Soviet expansionism. They founded the institutions of post-war security and prosperity. And by choosing to reach out rather than turn inward, they brought the American people a period of economic growth and security unparalleled in our history. The great middle class was built, and the American dream was born in the lives of Americans, not merely in the eyes of their parents.

Today, we stand at a similar moment of high decision. The end of the cold war has left a world of change in its wake. The Soviet empire and the Soviet Union itself are no more. Russia, once our nuclear adversary, is now our partner in reducing the nuclear threat and in expanding democracy. Ancient animosities in the Middle East are yielding to the promise of peace, a transformation made tangible to billions of people last month in a simple stunning handshake. After decades of apartheid, the Nobel Prize for Peace has gone to two leaders of different colors working for one nonracial democracy in South Africa.

These shifts have been accompanied, and in many cases pushed, by other great changes in the world, those brought about by the commu-nications revolution and the new global marketplace, entrepreneurial in spirit, intensely competitive and as fast moving as light itself. We see the consequences all around us here in America, in our workplaces, our families, our cities and towns. Some of those consequences are not at all promising. The promise of peace, freedom, and democracy is still thwarted in many places in the world. The promise of prosperity is an illusion to millions of people, not only in poor countries but increasingly in wealthy countries.

Here at home as in all other rich countries, we have had our difficulties in creating jobs and raising incomes. Technology in the moment is not leading to growth and prosperity for millions of our people. We see that in rising sets of insecurities all across America, people more insecure about their jobs, their health care, their communities, their children's education, and their very safety.

The new global economy is dominated by democracy but marred by wars and oppressions. It is expanded by new technologies and vast new horizons but limited by slow growth and stagnant jobs and incomes. Nonetheless, this new global economy is our new frontier.

Our generation must now decide, just as John Kennedy and his generation had to decide at the end of World War II, whether we will harness the galloping changes of our time in the best tradition of John Kennedy and the post-war generation, to the well-being of the American people, or withdraw from the world and recoil from our own problems as we did after World War I. Will we be the Americans of the 1920's, or will we be the Americans of the late forties and early fifties? Will we be the Americans who lifted John Kennedy to the Presidency or the Americans who turned away from the world and paid the price?

President Kennedy understood these challenges of change. He believed in opening the world's trading system. But he also believed we needed to help America's workers who did not win from the expansion of trade to adjust to the rigors of that trade and international competition.

In 1962, to help workers adjust when they lost their jobs because of trade so that they could then get jobs that would be created by an expanded global economy, John Kennedy proposed and the Congress created the Trade Adjustment Assistance Program. And he said—

listen to this—in 1962, "Economic isolation and political leadership are wholly incompatible. The United States has encouraged sweeping changes in free world economic patterns in order to strengthen the forces of freedom. But we cannot ourselves stand still. We must adapt our own economy to the imperatives of a changing world and once more assert our leadership."

Once again, we must make clear to the American people that our success at home relies on our engagement abroad, that we must face our problems at home and reach out to the world at the same time. Even more than in President Kennedy's day, the line between foreign and domestic interests is rapidly disappearing. Millions of our best jobs are tied to our ability to trade and sell our products around the world. And our ability to create millions more depends clearly on our ability to work with our friends and neighbors and partners to expand global economic opportunities. That is why we must compete and not retreat, why more than ever before a concern for what happens within our borders, down to the smallest rural town or the most thriving neighborhood in any city, depends upon a concern for what we do beyond our borders.

Over recent months, that imperative has been at the core of this administration's agenda. We've worked to support reform in Russia and the other states of the former Soviet Union. We've put our relations with Japan on a new foundation that pays more attention to the economic dynamics of the relationship between our two nations. We've pushed for a new worldwide trade accord through the GATT talks. But there is no better example of what we have tried to do to reach out to the world than our attempt to secure an agreement for a North American free trade zone with Canada and Mexico, one that can create 200,000 new jobs for this country by 1995, open a vast new market, make 90 million friends, and set a stage for moving to embrace all of Latin America, 700 million people strong, in a trading unit that will bring prosperity to them and to us.

Last night in New York I told an audience of corporate executives that if they want Americans to support free trade instead of oppose it at a time of great insecurity, they should support the Americans who will not only win but who will be temporarily dislocated; that they should support a new, more modern version of trade adjustment assistance that will work for

this time; that they had no right to ask the American people, any of them, even one of them, to sacrifice unless we were going to make a common investment so that we could grow in the spirit of common community interest in this country and with Latin America.

But today I say to you that our choice is about even more than dollars; that just as business people must take care of workers and invest in their future, Americans as a whole, without regard to their economic standing, must understand that our national destiny depends upon our continuing to reach out. That's why here in Boston, Congressman Kennedy, his predecessor Speaker O'Neill, from the congressional seat that John Kennedy once occupied, have endorsed this new expansion of America's interest. And I believe if President Kennedy were still representing that seat in Congress, he would endorse it as well.

If you remember when President Kennedy endorsed the Alliance for Progress, the Latin American countries were moving toward more accountable government and more open economies. And then a lot of reversals took place and Latin America went into a period of real upheaval, political oppression, economic devastation. It is all changing again now. Their efforts are being rewarded: more and more democracies, the second fastest growing region of the world, and a real desire to be our close friends.

President Roosevelt advocated a good neighbor policy toward Latin America. President Kennedy called it the Alliance for Progress. We know that we cannot have a bad neighbor policy. We know that we cannot have an alliance to protect ourselves at their expense. We know that the people who want to buy our products and share our future ought to have a chance to help us to solve our problems at home, even as we help them to pursue their own destiny.

Let us not send a signal by defeating this agreement that we are turning our backs on our neighbors and the rest of the world. Let us reach out to the people here in our home, throughout America, who do not support these endeavors because they have been ravaged by the economic changes of the last 15 years and they have not had their cries, their pains, their frustrations heeded by their National Government. Let us heed them. But let us not adopt a remedy for their just complaints that makes their problems worse. Let us extend ourselves in the world and invest in their future here at home. We can do that. That is the right answer.

Mr. Justice Holmes was quoted by Senator Kennedy. He once said that we must all be involved in the action and passion of our time for fear of being judged not to have lived. No one would ever level that indictment against John Kennedy.

This is our decisive moment. This is the end of the cold war. This is the dawn of the 21st century. There are many complex, frustrating problems which have very simple and profound and often painful impacts in the lives of the people that we have all struggled to serve. But in these moments, we have to reach deep into ourselves, to our deepest values, to our strongest spirit, and reach out, not shrink back. In these moments our character is tested as individuals and as a nation. The problems we share today are widely shared by other advanced nations. No one has all the answers, but we do know one thing: We will never find the answer if we don't continue on the journey. If we turn back to a proven path of failure, we will never know what we might have become in a new and different age where thankfully, hopefully, my daughter, our children, and our grandchildren will at least be free of the fear of nuclear destruction and where at least most of the competition we face will be based on what

is in our minds, not what is in our hands in the forms of weapons.

I tell you, my fellow Americans, for all the difficulties at this age, this is an age many generations of our predecessors would have prayed to live in. These are the challenges so many of our predecessors would have longed to embrace. How can we turn away from them?

What we owe John Kennedy today at this museum is to make the museum come alive not only in our memories but in our actions. Let us embrace the future with vigor. Let us say we can never expect too little of ourselves. Let us never demand too little of each other. Let us never walk away from the legacy of generations of Americans who themselves have paved the way. Let us be more like those Americans who came home after the Second World War and less like those who withdrew after the First World War.

The 21st century can be our century if we approach it with the vigor, the determination, the wisdom, and the sheer confidence and joy of life that John Kennedy brought to America in 1960.

Thank you, and God bless you all.

NOTE: The President spoke at 11:41 a.m. at the Steven E. Smith Center.

Remarks on NAFTA to Gillette Employees in Boston, Massachusetts
October 29, 1993

Thank you very much. I've had a good time here today. I'm a satisfied customer, that's true. And I rarely cut myself, and when I do, it's my fault, not yours. [*Laughter*]

Mr. Zeien and Governor Weld, Senator Kennedy, Senator Kerry, Congressman Moakley, Congressman Kennedy, and my other friends here today. This was a good experience for me for a lot of reasons. I've had a wonderful day today. We dedicated the Kennedy Museum over at the Kennedy Library. I urge you all to go and see it. It's wonderful, improved, accessible. It's terrific. And they even put a little clip of me in there talking, so I like it better. [*Laughter*]

And I spoke at the Kennedy Library about

the challenges that President Kennedy faced over 30 years ago: trying to get America to solve its problems here at home, which at that time were largely the problems of civil rights, and still to be adventuresome when looking toward the future; when he launched the space program, which we're trying to keep alive and keep going today; when he agreed to establish and push for the establishment of the Peace Corps and the Alliance for Progress in Latin America; and when he started a trade adjustment program for people who lost their jobs in trade because he knew that if we did it right, we'd always have more winners than losers, but people who lost their jobs should be retrained so they could get new and different jobs. And this is the kind of replay in some ways of that time, with a more complex and difficult set of problems.

I feel right at home here, when before—I tell people, back when I had a life, before I became President—I was the Governor of what my opponent in the last election called "a small southern State" that had 22 percent of its work force in manufacturing. And my job was essentially schools and jobs. That's what I did for a living. I was in plants all the time; I frequently worked shifts in plants. I understand a little bit about machine tools and how they work and how they're adjusted. I now know what a bam, a cam, and a pam is.

I had some plants when I was the Governor of my State that shut down and went to Mexico. And because it was a small State, I knew who they were and what they did for a living. I was quite proud of the fact that before I left office, I brought one of them back, because our people were doing a better job in productivity and product modification, just like you are.

And so I want to talk a little bit today just as briefly as I can, because Mr. Zeien has already said how this plant and this company will benefit if NAFTA passes. Everybody knows there will be some winners and some losers. But there's a lot of sort of fogginess about why this is good for America or why it's bad. And I want to go through this because I need your help. And the Congress needs your help, not his help. With all due respect to him, Members of Congress know most business people are for NAFTA, but they can figure out that if you're smart and you're running a business, you can benefit six and one-half dozen of the other. That is, you could benefit in Mexico or in the U.S. So the Members of Congress want to know that you're going to win if it passes. And you hired them; so they should want to know if you're going to win, right? They work for you, just like I do.

The first thing I want to say is, I have lived with the manufacturing changes of the last 15 years. And I would never knowingly do anything that would cost Americans jobs.

I am for this agreement for quite a few reasons. The first and big reason is this: There is no evidence whatever that a wealthy country cannot only grow wealthier but can actually create jobs and raise incomes unless it expands trade and promotes the growth of the global economy. Why? Because if you have a stagnant economy, when, as you know, you can move

money around the world in a millisecond—technology can be adapted around the world, management can be moved around the world—if you have a stagnant economy and poorer countries are growing with new manufacturing, that means that people in richer countries will work harder for less money.

That is exactly what has happened in the United States for 20 years. A lot of hourly wage earners have worked harder for lower wages. But guess what, it's happening everywhere. If you look at Europe where there's no growth today, if you look at France even when they had growth, the unemployment rate in the last 5 years never going below 9.5 percent, it is clear that a wealthy country can only grow wealthier in terms of jobs and income at a time when the global economy is growing and they are selling more of their products and services beyond their borders as well as within their borders. Nobody has ever been able to demonstrate the contrary to me in the modern world.

So therefore, one of our biggest problems in America today is no growth in Europe, no growth in Japan. One of our biggest opportunities is that Latin America, including Mexico, is the second fastest growing part of the world. And it's right here handy, and they like to buy our products.

The second thing I want to say is this: A lot of the problems people have with this NAFTA agreement they have because they believe that the present relationships we have with Mexico have encouraged people, because wages and cost of production are lower there, to go to what is called the *maquilladora* area. It's right across the American border in Mexico. If you produce there, you can send your product back into our country duty-free. We created that several years ago since we wanted to help Mexico grow. But in the 1980's when the global economy got really tough and the screws were tightened on company after company after company, a lot of people said, "Okay, we'll move down there."

Now, here's the second reason I'm for NAFTA. All the problems associated with the *maquilladora* issue will get better if we adopt it, and they won't if we don't. That is, forget about selling razor blades in Mexico. Just imagine what's going on to the plants that have moved down there. If this agreement passes, labor costs in Mexico will go up more rapidly, environmental costs will go up more rapidly.

Their requirement that products sold in Mexico be produced in Mexico will be reduced. We'll go from selling one to 50,000 or 60,000 American cars in the first year this agreement goes into effect. Their tariffs will go down.

So I understand the resentments, the fears, the insecurities of people, probably a lot of them who work within 20 miles of this plant. But we've got to read the agreement. The agreement makes those problems better, not worse. And that's the other reason I'm for it.

Finally, just let me say this: There will be some people who will be dislocated. There always are. If you have a trade agreement, just as President Kennedy recognized in 1962, there always are. I intend to ask the Congress to literally revolutionize the unemployment and the training system in this country.

You know, the average person who loses their job today does not get called back to the same company. That's the way it was for 40 years. It's not true anymore. The average person who loses a job today has to go find a job with a different company. Often it's a very different kind of job.

I agree with what Senator Kerry said: It's one thing to talk about changing work seven times in a lifetime and another thing to do it. If every one of you stays with Gillette until you retire, I'll bet you anything you'll have to change what you do. If every one of you stays with this company—some of you are quite young—for 20, 30, 40 years, you know as well as I do, 10 years from now the nature of your work will be different than it is today, even if you have the same employer. Isn't that right?

I know how different these machines are. How long ago was it when there wasn't anybody on an assembly line reading a computer? How long ago was it that you had to do all your quality checks visually and it took longer and not as well? I mean, the world is changing.

So as cruel or tough as it is, we can't pretend that it's not going to happen. You could—if we can't get all our titles straightened out, you could give us all—we could all shift and take one another's job and we couldn't repeal the changes. They're going to happen.

So we have to decide, are we going to make these changes our friend or our enemy? Or are we going to have more Gillettes or more plants close down? Are we going to find more markets so we can secure the jobs we've got, add more jobs, and so companies can afford to give pay raises to their employees, or not? That is what is at stake.

There are a lot of misconceptions about Mexico. A lot of people say, "Well, we've got a trade surplus with them now, but only because they're buying our plant and machinery so they can put up plants that 5 years from now they'll be shipping all this stuff back here, and we'll have a trade deficit." Let me tell you something: 40 percent of the dollar value of our exports in the entire world are in capital goods, that is, things that can be used in manufacturing; 60 percent in consumer products. But in Mexico, only 33 percent of their purchases of our products are in capital goods; two-thirds in consumer products, like razor blades; two-thirds—more than the global average. That country now is the second biggest purchaser of American products. There's 90 million people there, and they're handy.

And you say, "Well, what do they get out of this deal?" I'll tell you what they get out of this deal. If we adopt this deal, it will be safer and more secure and more attractive for Americans to invest in Mexico, not along the border to export to America but down in Mexico City or over in Vera Cruz or in other places to put them to work making products for themselves. And that's good for you, too. Why? Because if more of them have jobs and the more income they've got, the more products of ours they can buy.

Now, we have a trade problem in America today, but it's not with Mexico, and it's not with Latin America. Tiny Colombia has increased their purchases of American products 69 and 64 percent in the last 2 years. What's our trade problem: $49 billion trade deficit with Japan; $19 billion trade deficit with China; $9 billion trade deficit with Taiwan. We've got a $5.7 billion trade surplus with Mexico, and we're worried about them, when they want to buy more of our products?

Look, the people that are against this have legitimate fears and resentments and anger. There were a lot of workers that were thrown in the streets over the last 15 or 20 years. We have gone through two decades when a lot of hourly workers never got a pay raise. We are having a tough time creating jobs and income. But we don't want to cut off our nose to spite our face. We can't let this trade agreement become the flypaper that catches all those fears, because it will make it better not worse.

So I say, if you believe that, because you know what the experience of this company is, I want you to sit down and write a letter, not a pressure letter but a nice letter. Really, just two lines, to the Senators, to the Congressmen, or collect them all up and send them here and let them send them in. But they need to know that there's somebody out here in Massachusetts, somebody out here in south Boston, somebody in the entire United States that's going to make a living out of this deal, that understands that we're going to get more jobs and higher incomes and more opportunities if we do this. Because if we turn it away, it's really going to be a terrible thing.

You know, we actually get a trade advantage over the Japanese and the Europeans in Mexico if this passes? And if it fails and they still need the money to develop their country, what are we going to do, what's Gillette going to do in Mexico if they turn around and give that trade advantage to somebody else? If they offer this same deal to somebody else, I'll guarantee you the Japanese, the European Community would take this deal in a heartbeat. This is a good deal. It is no accident that the Ministry of Trade in Japan has come out against this deal. It is a good thing for us.

So I ask you to talk to your friends and neighbors, talk to the people who are worried about it, tell them their fears are well-founded, but they don't have anything to do with this agreement. This agreement will make it better. And meanwhile, we will keep working to build the security that Americans need.

We've already had more private sector jobs come into this economy in 9 months than in the previous 4 years. We're tackling the health care issue. We're tackling the deficit issue. Interest rates are at a 30-year low. We are moving in the right direction. But I'm telling you, nothing I do as your President within the borders of the United States can create more jobs and higher incomes unless somebody buys the stuff we produce. And that requires us to expand our market. Help us to do that by personally telling the Members of Congress you'd appreciate it if they vote for the NAFTA agreement.

Thank you, and God bless you all.

NOTE: The President spoke at 3:20 p.m. on the factory floor. In his remarks, he referred to Alfred M. Zeien, CEO, Gillette Co.

Statement on the Situation in Haiti
October 29, 1993

The military and police authorities in Haiti continue to defy the will of the Haitian people and the international community. Their persistent obstructionism has prevented democracy's return, an important United States interest. We have other interests involved as well. I am committed to ensure the safety of over 1,000 Americans living and working in Haiti. We must also give Haitians hope in their own land so they do not risk the perils of the sea to try to reach our shores.

The continued violence and intimidation by the Haitian military and police authorities have made it impossible for President Aristide to return to Haiti tomorrow, as scheduled under the Governors Island Agreement of July 3. I have called President Aristide and Prime Minister Malval today to reaffirm America's commitment to finding a negotiated solution to this crisis.

I welcome and applaud the invitation of U.N. Secretary-General Boutros-Ghali, announced by U.N./OAS Special Envoy Dante Caputo, to all parties to meet next week in Haiti to get the Governors Island process back on track. The Haitian military and police leaders must not delude themselves into thinking they have destroyed the Governors Island process. We remain firmly committed to that process and the consolidation of Haitian democracy. Next week's meeting offers the opportunity to resolve the outstanding issues between all sides. I urge all parties to act in good faith and with flexibility and with the interests of all Haitians at heart. President Aristide must be allowed to return home to the Haitian people who elected him by a landslide in 1991.

President Aristide's address to the U.N. General Assembly October 28 reaffirmed his dedication to the well-being of all his people. His emphasis on dialog and reconciliation should provide confidence that the Haitian crisis can be solved peacefully by negotiation. I urge all parties to build on that spirit at next week's meeting.

The sanctions and their enforcement are an unprecedented defense of democracy in the Americas. The U.N. and OAS sanctions and additional steps we have taken against individuals blocking a negotiated solution underscore the depth of our Nation's commitment to end this crisis. We will maintain sanctions and strictly enforce them by the U.S. Navy and Coast Guard and by ships of several allies. We will also consider the most effective ways to tighten the sanctions.

As we work for the return of President Aristide, we will maintain our policy of direct return of migrants and continue to process political asylum applications within Haiti. Mindful of the impact of sanctions on Haiti's poor, we will also continue our humanitarian assistance to assist those in need. It feeds half a million Haitian children every day and provides health services to 2 million Haitians. We will closely monitor the provision of these services and seek to ensure an adequate supply of fuel for their delivery.

The Haitian crisis challenges our country's principles and interests. We must maintain our commitment to work for its peaceful resolution. Let me say to the Haitian people: I am determined to help you restore the democracy you sacrificed so much to attain. And when it is restored, we in the international community will be by your side to help you create a future of hope.

Nomination for United States District Court Judges
October 29, 1993

The President today announced the nominations of three U.S. District Court judges from the State of Florida. The President named Henry Adams and Susan Bucklew for the Middle District of Florida and Theodore Klein for the Southern District of Florida.

With these nominations, the President has nominated 32 men and women for Federal judgeships. At the same point in their adminis-trations, President Bush had named 18; President Reagan had named 27; and President Carter had named 26 judicial nominees.

"All of these nominees have demonstrated the qualities that will make them valuable additions to the Federal bench for years to come," said the President.

NOTE: Biographies of the nominees were made available by the Office of the Press Secretary.

Teleconference Remarks on the California Fires
October 30, 1993

The President. Hello?

James Lee Witt. Good morning, Mr. President.

The President. Have we got James Lee?

Mr. Witt. Yes, sir. I have Roger Johnson with me, the Administrator of GSA, at the disaster field office here in Pasadena. Secretary Espy is also on, who is at the Oak Grove fire camp in southern California.

Secretary Espy. Hello, Mr. President.

The President. Hello, Secretary Espy. How are you?

Secretary Espy. How are you doing, sir? I'm at the Oak Grove fire camp near Altadena, California.

Mr. Witt. Also, Mr. President, we have Senator Feinstein and Senator Boxer on, and Dick Andrews, the California director of emergency service is here in the disaster field office with Roger and I.

[*At this point, Mr. Witt, Director of the Federal Emergency Management Agency, reported on conditions in California and discussed Federal, State, and private efforts to deal with the disaster.*]

The President. That's good. That's very good.

[*Mr. Andrews discussed the improvement in weather conditions, the number of fires still burning, and deployment of State and Federal resources to fight the fires. Mr. Witt then asked if the President had any questions.*]

The President. No. I want to say before I go on to Secretary Espy that I have just been terribly impressed by the work of the people who have been out there fighting the fires. I know that we have provided from the Federal Government a lot of the firefighters. And of course, there have been the folks here at the local level. But it's been really amazing to me just to watch and see how hard they've worked.

As you know, Mack McLarty, who is here with me now, has been coordinating this from our end, so I've been pretty well briefed all along. I also want to say I'm very pleased that the Insurance Association is going to have people in the disaster assistance area. That's something, as you well know, James Lee, all of us could have used for years. And that's a very, very good sign, and I thank them.

Maybe I should hear from Secretary Espy and Roger Johnson and Senator Boxer and Senator Feinstein, and maybe then I'll see if we've got any questions.

[*Secretary Espy reported to the President on the Kinneloa fire, the highest priority fire at that time, and the efforts of firefighters.*]

The President. How much Federal land have we lost out there?

Secretary Espy. Oh, gosh. We've got 150,000 or so acres already burned.

The President. But a lot of it belongs to the Federal Government, doesn't it?

Secretary Espy. Yes, sir.

The President. Twenty thousand or thirty thousand acres, something like that?

Secretary Espy. We've got two major national forests* out here, and it's under pretty good attack here. The problem in the future, of course, once the fires have receded, is revegetating and reseeding, making sure that in the Forest Service area, we can do a lot of rehabilitation. And so that's what we've got to turn our attention

once the immediate situation abates.

The President. Well, we should be able to help California with that.

Secretary Espy. Yes, sir.

The President. We know how to do that.

Secretary Espy. We are. The Soil Conservation Service will be taking the lead in the rehabilitation exercises out here.

The President. Is Jim Lyons out there with you?

Secretary Espy. Jim Lyons is here. He's been here for a couple of days. Now, he's a little bleary-eyed, he had to get up this morning to do a bunch of things, but——

The President. He used to be a firefighter, didn't he?

Secretary Espy. Yes, he said he did. We're in a place that looks like a——

The President. We just thought he ought to have a little continuing education. [*Laughter*]

Secretary Espy. That's right. We need those pale guys to get their hands dirty every now and then.

The President. I really appreciate you, Mike. Thank you.

Secretary Espy. Well, thank you. Thank you. I just can't say enough about the good work. It's very prompt, very vigorous, effective. And you know, they've been out here from day one, many without sleep, without rest, and it's just incredible to be here. It's great.

The President. Is Roger Johnson on?

Roger Johnson. He's here, Mr. President. Good morning.

The President. You saved your home, didn't you?

Mr. Johnson. Yes, sir. They saved it.

The President. Congratulations.

[*Mr. Johnson gave a brief description of the General Services Administration's disaster response and a personal view of the losses and firefighting efforts.*]

The President. That's great. How many homes were lost, 350 in Laguna alone?

Mr. Johnson. Yes. About 700 overall, I think. Jumped into an area, Emerald Bay, where we used to live. So there were a lot of our friends there, and I think the home we used to live in is gone as well.

[*Mr. Witt reported on plans for Federal and State authorities to meet with California insurance associations to provide for special needs in the application centers.*]

The President. Thank you very much.

Senator Feinstein, Senator Boxer?

Senator Feinstein. Good morning, Mr. President. How are you?

The President. I'm fine.

[*Senator Feinstein described the mobilization and organization of State firefighting strike teams and Firescope, a unified command of Federal, State, and local authorities to deal with the disaster.*]

The President. Thank you. Thank you, Senator.

James Lee, I think you and Mike——

Senator Boxer. Do you have room for one more Senator?

The President. Yes. I'm going to call in just a minute. I just wanted to say to James Lee and Mike Espy, I think you ought to make a recommendation to me on what we should do on this unified command issue after you get back.

Senator Boxer, the floor is yours.

[*Senator Boxer described the devastation, commended FEMA for its response to the disaster, and expressed her thanks to the President.*]

The President. Thank you, Senator. I want to thank both the Senators. And, Dick Andrews, I thank you, and through you Governor Wilson, you tell him that if there's anything else we can do, you just pick up the phone and call.

And, to Roger Johnson and Secretary Espy and to James Lee Witt, I thank you all for your quick response, and I can't wait to talk to you some more in person after the fire dies down some more and we make sure that we don't forget them when the fire's gone. We'll be there for the followup.

I thank you all, and I hope you have a good day and keep those winds away out there. Thank you. Goodbye.

[*At this point, the teleconference ended.*]

Q. Are you going to California?

The President. I don't know that yet. We're going to monitor the winds today. That's the big issue. I don't want to be in the way out there. They've got a lot of work to do. The thing, I think, is pretty well in hand now if they don't have a resurgence of the winds. So we're all basically going to—it's quite early there, it's still 7 a.m. in the morning. And we're just going to spend the next 4 or 5 hours waiting for the weather reports.

I've got to do the radio address, folks.

NOTE: The President spoke at 9:45 a.m. from the Oval Office at the White House. A portion of this item could not be verified because the tape was incomplete.

The President's Radio Address
October 30, 1993

Good morning. In the next few days, you'll have the chance to pick up what may be the most important book of information you'll read for yourself, your children, your parents, and others you care about. It's a book that's also very important for the future of our Nation. The book is called "Health Security: The President's Report to the American People." And while it deals with a very complex issue, the overhaul and reform of our health care system, it does so in straightforward, very human terms.

The book describes our plan to solve the Nation's health care crisis by guaranteeing every working American comprehensive health care that's always there, that can never be taken away. While many people worked hard on this book, especially the First Lady and her task force on health care reform, in many ways, the book was written by you, the American people. For a long time, since I was the Governor of my State, I've been talking with Americans who, against their will, become all too familiar with the failings of our health care system, Americans caught without insurance or with inadequate insurance when they or a loved one became ill and when they needed the coverage the most, people who had their bank accounts emptied, their trust in the system betrayed, and too often their hearts broken.

Many of you listening today know someone who has fallen through the cracks of our health care system. These cracks have become chasms that swallow hard-working Americans. More than 37 million Americans don't have health insurance at all, and 25 million more have very inadequate coverage with very high deductibles. Every month, 100,000 Americans lose their health coverage permanently.

Who are these people caught in this broken system? They are a working mother with a sick child who had to buy her own insurance and who, every month, must ask herself, "Do I pay the rent or the medical bills?"; a seventh grade teacher with breast cancer whose insurance provider disagreed with doctors over her care, the teacher had to run herself into debt to pay for her own chemotherapy; a doctor, frustrated by miles of redtape and forms that steal time he should have with his patients.

These stories are not unique. Here at the White House, Hillary and I have had over 700,000 letters about health care, and 10,000 more pour in every week. Every one of them is a cry for action. So now we have a plan for action. Our health security legislation is a detailed bill to provide comprehensive, universal coverage for our people. Of course, it's only fair to ask who pays and how much.

There's been some confusion on this, so today let me give it to you straight. Under our plan, 60 percent of all the American people will pay the same or less to get the same or better benefits. I'll repeat that: 6 out of 10 of all Americans, and even more as the reforms begin to take effect and cost increases go down, will pay the same or less for the same or better benefits.

About 25 percent of our people, people who are now underinsured or people without insurance at all who can afford to pay, will pay a little more for coverage. But many of them will actually pay less in medical bills. Right now, there are lots of people with cheap premiums, because their deductibles, their up-front costs are so high, $2,500, $3,000, even $5,000. Under our plan, their premiums may be a little higher, but their out-of-pocket costs will be lower.

Finally, about 15 percent, and only 15 percent of the American people or their employers, will pay more for the same benefits. These are the young, healthy, usually single Americans whose insurance companies gamble under the current plan that they won't get sick. Is it fair to ask them to pay a little more so we can have broad-based community rating? I believe it is. Why?

Because there are lots of young people who can't get insurance at all, because all these younger people will be older themselves someday, with children, and they'll need this fair rate. And when these young people do get sick or have an accident, or even marry someone with a preexisting health condition, well then, all bets are off. The insurance company may double their rates or drop them altogether. With our plan, their premiums may be a little higher, just a few dollars a month, but they'll be guaranteed coverage no matter what happens, and a guarantee that rates won't rise unchecked.

That's another thing I want to emphasize. Under our plan, there is a limit to what anyone can have taken away from them in health care. That's not true today. So 100 percent of the American people get something no one has today, absolute security. This plan is based on the principles of security, simplicity, savings, maintaining the quality of our health care system, maintaining and even increasing choice for consumers of health care, and insisting on more responsibility.

We focus on keeping people healthy, not just treating them after they get sick. We reduce paperwork and crack down on fraud. We protect the right to choose doctors and preserve and strengthen Medicare.

Right now I'll say again: There is no guarantee for anyone that health care will be there tomorrow. One of our citizens wrote us and said even employed insured people are one major illness away from financial disaster.

Before the end of the year, I want our lawmakers to pass a bill to guarantee health security for every American. That's the end of the congressional session next year. And I want to be clear on this. We'll debate many points of this plan, but this point must remain nonnegotiable: The health care plan must guarantee every American a comprehensive package of benefits that can never be taken away. And I will only sign a bill into law that meets that fundamental commitment to the American people. We have delayed making good on it for too long.

Our lawmakers have a big job ahead, but they won't be alone. We've seen extraordinary support from both parties to reform health care. And I promise to work with Congress every step of the way. As a responsible citizen, you have a job, too. Learn all you can about this plan. Start with a book called "Health Security," and join the debate.

Thanks for listening.

NOTE: The President spoke at 10:06 a.m. from the Roosevelt Room at the White House.

Statement on the Peace Process in Northern Ireland
October 30, 1993

I welcome the efforts of Irish Prime Minister Albert Reynolds and British Prime Minister John Major to reinvigorate the negotiations for peace in Northern Ireland. I join their condemnation of the use of violence for political ends and strongly support their commitment to restart talks among their two Governments and the four constitutional parties of Northern Ireland. Their joint statement issued yesterday in Brussels underscores their common resolve to work for peace, justice, and reconciliation in Northern Ireland. The United States stands ready to support this process in any appropriate way.

All friends of peace were outraged at the tragic and senseless IRA bombing in Belfast on October 23 and the ensuing violence. Especially in the wake of such action, we must redouble our efforts to reject violence and pursue the path of peace. As we remember the victims of the sectarian violence that has torn the region for too long, let us work together to ensure that the vision of the two Governments demonstrated in their joint statement bears lasting fruit.

Teleconference Remarks on NAFTA to the United States Chamber of Commerce
November 1, 1993

The President. Thank you very much. I'm delighted to see all of you here and to know that there are people all across the country watching this important event. I thank the chamber of commerce for organizing this and for providing the technology that makes it possible. I'm glad to see Governor Edgar of Illinois here. And I listened intently in the back room there to my former colleagues, Governor Wilson and Governor Weld, talk about NAFTA. I want to thank Dick Lesher and Ivan Gorr and Larry Bossidy for their work through USA°NAFTA and the chamber of commerce to help us pass this very important piece of legislation. And I think former Congressman Bill Frenzel, who's the cochair of our effort, is here somewhere. I want to thank him for making our bipartisan administration effort as successful as it's been.

I know that there are people all over the country here, but if you'll forgive me for a little bit of parochialism, I want to observe that there are 150 people from my home State of Arkansas listening at the Excelsior Hotel in Little Rock, where we had the economic summit last December, and one of our good employers I just shook hands with on the platform up here.

I say that to make this point: Any Governor will tell you that the job of being Governor today is the job of getting and keeping jobs and educating and training people to do them. That is the lion's share of the work, on a daily basis, of doing that job. For a dozen years, it was my job to try to deal with the pressures of global competition, the enormous economic difficulties of the 1980's. When plants closed, I knew people's names who ran the plants and worked in the plants. When people closed their plants and went to Mexico, I knew about them. And I was proud that of the three or four we lost when I was Governor, we actually brought one back before I left office. It made me feel that in part, we had squared the circle.

The point I want to make is this: Anybody who has ever dealt with these issues knows that most of the arguments being raised against NAFTA today are arguments being raised about economic forces and developments that occurred in the past. And anybody who has ever read the agreement knows that if you don't like it when people shut plants down and move to Mexico, that this agreement will actually make that less likely. And if we don't pass it, it will do nothing to stop what people who are complaining about it are complaining about.

I would never knowingly do anything that would cost an American a job. My job is to try to recover the economic vitality of this country by working in partnership with the private sector. It is important, it is imperative that we make it clear to the American people, first of all, that you ought to look at what this agreement does: It helps to alleviate the problems that led to so many jobs moving out of our manufacturing sector, either into machines or offshore, whether to Mexico or to other places.

I want to acknowledge that in Cincinnati today, Congressman David Mann is there with 130 people at the General Electric aircraft engine plant. I think if NAFTA passes we'll not only sell aircraft engines from Cincinnati, we may even sell some of that Cincinnati chili, too. In Seattle there are 100 people in attendance at the Lake Washington Technical College. One in six jobs in the State of Washington are related to trade today, and by the time most of the students at that college hit their stride, even more jobs will be dependent on trade.

I have to tell you that again I have heard all the debates on this issue. I have listened carefully to the opponents and the supporters. I have never heard anyone seriously argue that a great country with a high per capita income can expand its incomes or its jobs without expanding trade. There is simply no way to do it. There is no example anywhere now of a country that can grow more jobs without selling its products beyond its borders. And that, in the end, is the most important lesson we have to learn if we're going to make a good decision about NAFTA.

When I became President, I had a very clear set of priorities in my mind about what I thought we ought to do with this economy. I knew we had to try to bring the deficit down and get interest rates down. And it's immensely gratifying to have the lowest home mortgage rates in 25 years, the lowest 30-year rate since we've been calculating them come out in the last few months, to know that the deficit came in $55 billion less this year than we were told

it would be on January 20th. But I also know that even though there are indications that we see an increase in investment in homes, in cars, in long-term investments by businesses, in the end this economy will not grow unless we sell more of our products and services beyond our borders. We cannot simply create a healthy economy only by changes here.

The other day we announced our new export initiative, which among other things removed over $35 billion worth of high-tech equipment from export controls and opened those things to the international market, computers, supercomputers, telecommunications equipment. Someone has to buy them. In the last 2 years, Mexico has gone from purchasing 390,000 to 600,000 computers, just from one year to the next. But 600,000 in a consumer market of 90 million men, women, and children is not so many. Think what will happen when the barriers, the tariffs, go down, when there is no 20 percent tariff barrier. And think what it will be like when that tariff barrier is down for us but not for our major competitors. We've been on the opposite side of that fence a lot of times. Now we're going to be given preferential treatment in a market that we're going to help develop. It's a very, very important issue.

I want to say to all of you that if we don't approve NAFTA, it will weaken our ability to get a General Agreement on Tariffs and Trade passed by the end of the year. If we do approve NAFTA, it will not only put us in a stronger position with Mexico and with all the rest of Latin America, it will help us to say to our trading partners in Europe and in Asia what we really need is to continue to expand trade worldwide.

The real job gains in NAFTA come not just from passing NAFTA, although we are convinced it will create 200,000 new jobs by 1995. The real job gains come when we take that NAFTA agreement and we take it to Chile, we take it to Argentina, we take it to Colombia, we take it to Venezuela, we take it to the other market-oriented democracies in Latin America and enable us to create a consumer market of over 700 million people, soon to be over one billion people, early in the next century, and we use that leverage then to say to our friends in Asia and our friends in Europe that it's okay for you to have trading blocs but we need to open up trading worldwide. We need that. If we don't pass NAFTA, our leverage to get that done will be much more limited.

So I say to all of you it is important not only on its own terms, but this issue has acquired an enormous significance because of the advantage it will give us in the Mexican market over our competitors in Japan and Europe and because of the leverage that will then give us to get a worldwide trade agreement that the world desperately needs to restore global growth. Without that, we're not going to be able to sell our products; we're not going to be able to create more jobs; we're not going to be able to see our workers' incomes go up. With it, we have the prospect of having several years now of sustained, vigorous economic growth because we are getting control of our economic house; we are putting things in order; we are getting our priorities straightened out in this country; we are focusing on investment and on training. We have to have the markets.

Now let me just say one final thing about this. I think if there were a secret vote in the Congress today, we would win. Now, that's a big issue, winning the secret ballot. I say that not to criticize anyone or to put anyone down but to recognize that the pressures against NAFTA are enormous. But they reflect, as I have said many times in many places, the accumulated frustrations and grievances and insecurities people bring to this day in American history. More and more people are worried about losing their jobs. More and more people know if they lose their jobs, they won't get it back. That's true. That's true. We have an unemployment system premised on a set of conditions that no longer exist, you know, you lose your job, and then the recession's over and your old company hires you back. That only happens about one in five times now.

So there is all this uncertainty out there in America today. I understand that. And our administration has done what we could to try to alleviate the insecurities of the American working families. The family leave law was designed to say to people, "You can be a good worker and a good parent." The attempt to control health care costs and still provide health care for everyone is an attempt to say, "Yes, you may lose your job, but at least your family can be taken care of." The attempt that the Congress is making now on a bipartisan basis to pass a new crime bill is a way of saying, "We know you have to feel safer on your streets. If you work hard and play by the rules, you shouldn't worry about having your children shot going to and from school."

But with all of this, we cannot turn away from the global economy that is engulfing us. And what I want to ask all of you to do, every one of you listening to me today, is to think about what you can do between now and November 17th, either directly by contacting a Member of Congress or indirectly by getting employees or friends or others to contact Members of Congress to say, "We know America can compete and win. We are not going to turn tail and run. We have not given up on America."

The Mexican economy may have 90 million people, but today it is the size of California from Los Angeles to the Mexican border. The idea that America is just going to shrivel up if we adopt this trade agreement is ridiculous. This trade agreement is a door that opens all of Latin America to us. It is a lever that will open a broader trading system in the world to us. And we cannot run away. We've got to compete and win. You have to be, in other words, the engines of confidence in our future. And employees, people who work with you who understand this, can have a huge impact on turning what is now only a secret ballot victory on NAFTA into a public victory on November 17th.

This is a difficult time for America. And it's hard for people to have confidence when they've been battered and pushed around and worried. But we cannot turn away from the future that is there before us. I honestly believe the next 20 years could be the best 20 years this country ever had if we have the courage and the vision to take advantage of the end of the cold war, the continued efforts to reduce nuclear arms, the fact that economic competition may expand opportunity for everyone if we do it right.

When we started, NAFTA had a significance for those who were fighting against it all out of proportion, all out of proportion to the impact it could have. You saw on that film there are several unions, many major unions in this country, who are going to gain jobs if this passes. But they decided that NAFTA would be the receptacle in which all the resentments and fears and insecurities of that last 12 to 20 years of stagnant wages and economic difficulties would be poured.

It has acquired a symbolic significance for those of us who are for it, too. This is a huge diplomatic, foreign policy, and economic issue for America. You simply cannot divide domestic and foreign policy anymore, as you once could. This is a major thing for the United States. If we walk away from this, if we walk away from this and Mexico decides to pursue its development strategy, what must it do? It must make this deal with Europe or with Japan. And what would that do? That could change the purchasing habits of 90 million Mexicans and hundreds of millions of people in Latin America. It could cut us off from not only economic but political opportunities to promote democracy and freedom and stability in our hemisphere that we can now only imagine.

If we embrace it, we not only will get in the immediate future a competitive advantage in selling into the Mexican market, a way of embracing all of Latin America, but the security of knowing that America is still marching in the right direction, that we are on future's side, that we are grasping for a time when our people will be able to compete and win in a global economy that will be less protectionist, more open, more full of opportunity, and more full of peace and democracy. This is a huge issue.

So I will close with this plea to you. This is not exactly like a church service. I know I am preaching to the saved, as we say at home, but you all have to be missionaries. We only have 17 days or so. We need you to go out and make sure that your Members of Congress, every man and woman in the Congress that you can reach, is contacted by real people who say, "My life will be better." I don't know how many Members I've heard from both parties saying, "All the organized vote is against this. I'd just like to hear from a few people who will rationally tell me that their lives will be better and that our country will be better off and that our district will be better off."

Please do that. Don't miss a chance to do it. Don't wake up on the morning of November 18th and wish that you had done something to give America a brighter future; to give our hemisphere a more solid, more democratic, more market-oriented future; and to open up the future in a way that is worthy of our country and that I am convinced is absolutely essential for our long-term success. We need your help. Many of these Members, you can have more influence on them than I can, because I can only vote in one congressional district every 2 years. You can vote in all of them. We need your help.

Thank you very much.

Meryl Comer. Ladies and gentlemen, the President has agreed to take some questions. Behind you are small business owners. They all are wearing NAFTA buttons, but there's one man who's wearing an attitude button as well. Would you like to ask the President a question?

[*At this point, a participant requested the President's response to people who favor protectionism.*]

The President. I respond in two ways. Number one, most of those people believe that all managers make all decisions based on labor costs. If that were true, what you would be reading this morning about Haiti is not whether a police chief and an army guy want to make it even poorer, even though it's already the third poorest country in the world. What you would read is that Haiti had all the manufacturing jobs in America, right? I mean, if this were a case of low wages, the headlines on Haiti today would be "General Motors shuts down in Michigan," "Caterpillar leaves Illinois, goes to Port-au-Prince," right? Number one, it's not factually true that labor costs or environmental investments are the only thing involved. Germany, which has a trading system arguably more open than ours and higher labor costs, has almost one-third of its work force in manufacturing, almost twice the percentage we do. It's simply not true. How well you do in production of goods and services depends upon how productive you are, how well-organized you are, and whether you can sell.

The second thing I would say is there is this fear, because of what's happened to us, because we're going through this wrenching restructuring, that is emotional, that we can't compete and win anymore. And that's just not true either. We're going to have to be able to suit up and go out and play and win. That's the attitude issue: Do you believe that this country can win or not? I mean, we're gaining back market share in autos, American autos, shoving our foreign competitors out of the American market because of quality and price. And there are lots of other examples. Our manufacturing productivity's gone up now for a dozen years at an annual rate of over 4 percent a year. This is nuts, this idea that we can't compete and win. It is true we're having trouble creating large numbers of new jobs. That is true for every wealthy country in the world. We have to solve that problem. But no one can solve it without more markets.

Those are my answers, and I thank you.

Ms. Comer. Please raise your hand for questions. Mr. President, while I'm trying to find a question, there's a gentleman who got up at 3 this morning, milked the cows, and came because he cares about NAFTA. If you shook his hand he'd have stories to tell for years. He's right behind you in the white shirt.

The President. Where is he? I want to say this before you get to the question: That man is a dairy farmer, and sometimes I feel sorry for myself—if you think you work hard, you ought to start a dairy farm. It's a 24-hour-a-day, 7-day-a-week job. I never could figure out how any of the dairy farmers in my State even made it to their kids' high school graduation. But I thank you for coming here today.

[*Another participant asked about the economic impact if NAFTA is not passed.*]

The President. Let me say, first of all, to the opponents of NAFTA, you can't name a single solitary thing you don't like that wouldn't continue to happen at maybe a greater pace if it fails. So you don't gain anything by beating it, for the people who are against it.

In addition to that, if Mexico follows the same strategy—let's ask rationally, what do they get out of this deal? If it's such a good deal for us and we sell even more consumer products—they are already the second biggest purchaser of American products in the world, even though they're by no means a wealthy country. They buy more per person than any other country in the world except Canada. What do they get out of it? They get development capital, not to invest to export back to the American market but to build up Mexico. That's what they get.

Now, if they stay with that strategy and we turn them down, what do you think they're going to do? There's only two places they can get it. They can make the same deal with Europe or the same deal with Japan, which means they will give them preferential access to their market instead of giving us preferential access to their market. Which means that you, sir, will have to face a 20 percent disability, if you want to sell into the Mexican market, against either the European people doing more or less what you do or the Japanese business people who do. That's exactly what's going to happen.

In addition to that, we will probably see a reversal of the good feeling that now exists for the United States in Mexico and throughout Latin America and the opportunity to do this same deal with other countries—I mentioned a few, Chile, Argentina, Colombia, Venezuela; there are others—none of whom will be getting investment to export back to the American market, but all of whom will buy more American products. Those opportunities will also be lost.

So, this is a good deal for this country. And not doing it, conversely, is a very, very dangerous strategy. It's a dangerous strategy economically; it's dangerous politically. It will hurt us in the short run, and it will hurt us for 20 years. I am convinced it is a terrible, terrible mistake.

Ms. Comer. Do you have time for one more, Mr. President?

The President. Sure, I'm with you.

Ms. Comer. This gentleman flew all the way in from California. He didn't want to talk to the Governor, he wanted to talk to the President. Please go ahead.

[*The participant asked if NAFTA would increase illegal immigration.*]

The President. It won't. There's no evidence that it will. I can't even figure out that argument. I stayed up late trying to figure that one. I can't figure it out.

To be fair, let's talk about it. There is a sophisticated argument that development in Mexico increases immigration to America. And let me tell you what it is and then say why NAFTA makes it better. Most of the people who immigrate from Mexico to the United States illegally are looking for jobs. Some are looking for welfare, but most are looking for work. When we set up the *maquilladora* system along the Mexican border—which, after all, was set up by our Government to help Mexico develop, right?—the idea was you could go down there and put up a plant and then export back to the United States duty-free. So a lot of people who don't have access to other jobs in other parts of Mexico come up there, they work in the *maquilladora* plant, but they can make more money in America. Or they come looking for a job, they don't get it, so they just—it's very close to the border. So you could argue that the *maquilladora* system has perversely increased illegal immigration.

How will NAFTA reverse that? It erases the *maquilladora* line. This will permit investment to occur in Mexico City and south of there. This will permit a balanced development approach so there will not only be more jobs and higher incomes, but they'll be strewed out all over the country instead of right there on the American border, all of which will reduce illegal immigration long-term.

Also, since you said that, if NAFTA passes we will get much more cooperation from the Mexican Government in enforcing our immigration laws and our drug laws. There's no question that we'll get a higher level of cooperation on both those very important issues if this passes.

Thank you.

Ms. Comer. Was that answer worth your trip?

Q. Absolutely perfect. And I'll go home and tell——

The President. Don't you think it's right——

Q. You're absolutely right. And I'll go home and tell the story for you.

The President. Thank you.

[A participant asked why many Americans feel U.S. businesses cannot compete.]

The President. Again, you see, I don't agree with it. But we have lost a lot of manufacturing jobs in the last 20 years. We've been losing manufacturing jobs for 35 years. But the percentage of our economy devoted to manufacturing is just what it was 12 years ago. In other words, what's happening is we're doing just what happened in agriculture, going back to the beginning of this century. You've got fewer people increasing their productivity and therefore increasing their output. That doesn't mean we can't compete, it means we have to get more and more productive to compete.

Now, here's my argument to the people against NAFTA. Let's say we've got 16 percent of the American work force in manufacturing today—it is 16 to 17—producing about 20 percent of our national wealth. And let's say that 15 years ago, I can't remember, but let's say 15 years ago it was about 23 percent—I think that's about what it was—producing 20 percent of our national wealth. If you want to go back to 23 percent, what do you have to do? You have to make more things and sell them to more people.

I will say it again: Germany, a country with a shorter work week and higher labor costs but extraordinary productivity in manufacturing, has almost a third of its workers in manufacturing. Now, do they account for 20 percent of the wealth in Germany? No, they account for about 40 percent of the wealth. So if you want to

do more in manufacturing or in services or in agriculture or in anything else, you have to have somebody to sell to.

So people have missed the—they assume that when the number of manufacturing workers go down, that the production's going down because nobody's buying it. In fact, production is just where it was. It's just that more people are more productive.

So my answer to those folks is, if you want more people to work in manufacturing again, find more customers. There is no other way to do it. Find new products and more customers. This gentleman here in the environmental area, one of the things we're trying to do is to take a lot of these defense companies that are losing their defense contracts and do partnerships with the Federal Government to give them the time they need to develop new technologies. You have to find different products and more customers. There is no other way. It has nothing to do with lower wages. That's not what the problem is.

Ms. Comer. Mr. President, your friends from the Excelsior Hotel are trying to reach you.

The President. I may owe some money—[*laughter*]

Ms. Comer. They've gotten to you by fax. It's your Arkansas NAFTA coalition assembled at the Excelsior Hotel. How is that hotel?

The President. It's a very nice hotel.

Ms. Comer. Okay. All right.

The President. Also to give you—it happens to belong to some Japanese investors who employ a lot of Arkansans. I mean, I think that's the world we're living in. We can't run from it. We ought to embrace it and figure out a way to win in it.

Ms. Comer. Here is their question, Mr. President: If NAFTA fails, isn't it reasonable to expect that Japan and the European Community will step into Mexico and take much of the market away from the U.S., thereby costing U.S. jobs, not saving them?

The President. Well, I'll tell you what I would do. If I were the Prime Minister of Japan and I had a low growth rate and I had my companies going crazy because they have hidden unemployment, since they have in theory lifetime employment—so they've got about 7 percent unemployment, but it only scores at 2.5 percent, which means all those companies are carrying idle workers on their books—I would jump on this like flies on a junebug. I would be there on the next day. If Congress votes this down on the 17th of November, I would, if I were the Prime Minister of Japan, have the Finance Minister of my country in to see the President of Mexico on the 18th of November. That's what I would do. I'd say, "We've got more money than they do anyway; make the deal with us." That's what I would do. And if I were running the economic affairs of the European Community, I would do that same thing because it's a new market for them at a preferential rate, so they can actually push us out of a new market that we're already well established in. That's what I would do; that's what I think will happen. That's what you'd do, too, isn't it? If you were running——

Ms. Comer. Mr. President, you remember the budget vote?

The President. I do. As the Vice President says, whenever he votes, he always wins. [*Laughter*]

Ms. Comer. The speculation is that it's going to come down to a pretty close vote, so I was trying to see whether or not you might have the same feeling about this vote that you had about the budget vote.

The President. I'll tell you what I think will happen. I think it will pass for the same reason the budget passed. I think what will happen is people will get up to the point of decision, they will look over the abyss, Members of Congress who have been subjected to unbelievable pressure, and they will think, "Can I actually do this to my country? What are the consequences of not doing this?"

Now, you can say whatever you want to about the details of the budget, it's hard to argue with the conclusions. We've now got very stable long-term low interest rates. We've got investment going back up in the country. We've got America being complimented instead of condemned by the Europeans and the Asians for getting control of our budgetary affairs. That's what the Members of the Congress knew. So finally, they had to swap and squall and break, and everything happened, but we got enough votes to pass the thing. So, that's what I think will happen with NAFTA.

But let me say this, in order to win by a vote or two or three or four, you have to be close so that there is a magnet leading people to take the right decision. If the Members of the Congress who are under so much pressure from organized groups, whether it's the Perot crowd or the labor groups, if they sense that it's not close, they might run away from it in great numbers, which is why your efforts are so important. I honestly believe it will pass, but you need to understand, that is the dynamic that will operate in the Congress.

Let me also say that one of the things that I think is worth pointing out is we all know who's against NAFTA, but it's worth pointing out that 41 of the 50 Governors have endorsed it—and they make their living, without regard to party, they make their living creating jobs, keeping jobs—12 Nobel Prize winning economists, and every living former President. I had several of them at the White House the other day, and we were trying to figure out if there was any other issue on which all of us have ever agreed. [*Laughter*] Maybe something else equally controversial, who knows. But I think that's important.

So, that's the answer. The answer is yes, I remember the budget vote. Yes, it could be close. But in order for it to be close, you all have to push between now and then. If it's close, I think we'll win. If they perceive it's not close, then you'll see a big movement away from it just to avoid making anybody mad who's arguing to vote against it.

Ms. Comer. Thank you, Mr. President. They're here to help you. And thank you so much for your time.

The President. Thank you very much.

NOTE: The President spoke at 12:35 p.m. at the U.S. Chamber of Commerce, and his remarks were broadcast via satellite. In his remarks, he referred to Dick Lesher, chamber president; Ivan Gorr, chamber chairman and CEO and chairman, Cooper Tire and Rubber; and Larry Bossidy, chairman, USA°NAFTA, and CEO, Allied-Signal, Inc. The teleconference was moderated by Meryl Comer, chamber vice president of community development.

Remarks on Signing the Executive Order on Historically Black Colleges and Universities
November 1, 1993

Thank you very much, Mr. Vice President, Secretary Riley. Ladies and gentlemen, it's a great pleasure for me to be here today with my longtime friend chancellor Vic Hackley and with so many of the distinguished persons in the audience: Dr. Sam Myers; Dr. Joyce Payne; our longtime friend Bill Gray; Dr. James Cheek, we're glad to see you here; Dr. Art Thomas; General Alonzo Short is here, I'm glad to see you, General Short; and Mr. Emmett Paige, the Assistant Secretary of Defense for Command, Control, and Intelligence. And I also know that in addition to the Members of Congress already introduced, Congressman Bobby Scott from Virginia just came in. Somewhere he's standing; I saw him. Thank you for coming.

Now, since the Vice President was so parochial—[*laughter*]—I have four people here I want to introduce: my friends Dr. William Keaton, from Arkansas Baptist College, in the back there; Dr. Katherine Mitchell from Shorter College, I saw Katherine over here; Dr. Lawrence Davis, from the University of Arkansas at Pine Bluff; and Dr. Myer Titus from Philander Smith College, where I used to run every day in my former life.

I am so glad to see all of you here. For 130 years the institutions you represent have been beacons of hope and opportunity for Americans for whom no other options existed. You have nurtured young minds. You have built self-esteem. You've educated some of our Nation's foremost scholars and leaders. When Thurgood Marshall was refused admittance to the University of Maryland Law School because of the color of his skin, it was Howard University Law School that prepared him for the challenge, for the United States Supreme Court. Seventeen Members of the United States Congress are graduates of historically black institutions of higher education, as well as one United States Senator who is not an African-American, Senator Harris Wofford from Pennsylvania, a graduate of Howard Law School.

Martin Luther King's way to Oslo, Norway, to receive the Nobel Prize was, as the Vice President said, plainly paved by the fact that he was a Morehouse man. The rhythms of my friend Toni Morrison's writings, which garnered her this year's Nobel Prize in Literature, are rooted in her study of classics and literature at Howard University.

In seeking the best and most skilled Americans to serve here in our administration, graduates from historically black colleges and universities have been a part of our team. Energy Secretary Hazel O'Leary and the Assistant to the President for Public Liaison, Alexis Herman, are Xavier graduates. Agriculture Secretary Mike Espy and Under Secretary Bob Nash attended Howard. Our Surgeon General, Joycelyn Elders, was a graduate of Philander Smith. Sarah Summerville, my Alabama campaign coordinator and now at the Department of Defense, attended both Mississippi Industrial and Miles Colleges. And there are many more.

The Executive order I sign today and all the education initiatives that Secretary Riley discussed have to do with change, preserving educational institutions and ensuring that every young person in this country who wants to get a college education has the opportunity to do it and finding new ways to get people into college and into training programs and to help them succeed once they're there.

Since the average person will change jobs seven times in a lifetime, and the 1990 census makes it crystal clear the very harsh economic consequences of not having at least 2 years of post-high school education, we know we have much to do. This year we have begun already by reorganizing the student loan programs to cut their costs of overhead, to lower the interest rates, to change the repayment terms so that young people can now borrow money without fear of being bankrupted in paying the loans back. Now young people can borrow the money at lower interest rates and then elect to pay them back as a percentage of their incomes, without regard to the amount of the loan, so that no one will ever be discouraged from borrowing the money and, even more important perhaps, from taking a job after college which might not be a high-paying job but which might do an awful lot of good for our society, a job in our inner cities as a teacher perhaps or working in a program to help our young people. I'm very proud of the changes that we made in the student loan program, and I thank Secretary Riley for his outstanding leadership in that regard.

We have also passed the national service program which will give, over the next 3 to 4 years, up to 100,000 young Americans a chance to earn some credit against their college education and help to serve their communities at the grassroots level, to rebuild lives and to build their own minds in the process.

The Goals 2000 legislation, which Secretary Riley mentioned and to which the Vice President alluded, will forge a new partnership between our National Government and States and communities to set some meaningful national standards about what our young people should know, because we know that they're going to be competing in a global economy, and they're entitled to have a shot at the best we have to offer.

With this Executive order and working in close cooperation with Secretary Riley and Catherine LeBlanc, the Executive Director of the White House Initiative Office, we'll expand the opportunities for participation in Federal programs. Ultimately, we'll strengthen the capacity of historically black colleges and universities to provide quality education. Within the next few days, I'll announce my appointments to the Presidential Advisory Board on Historically Black Colleges and Universities and will ask my longtime friend and the former chancellor of the University of Arkansas at Pine Bluff, Vic Hackley, now at Fayetteville State University, to serve as the Chair.

I want to say a special word of thanks to the current board, which was appointed by President Bush, for their service and commitment and especially to Dr. James Cheek for his leadership. And I thank you, Dr. Cheek, for what you have done.

I'd like to close by mentioning a very disturbing article that appeared in the morning paper here. You may have seen it, about children in our Nation's Capital, not even teenagers, discussing their own funerals, planning their funerals, thinking about what they would wear and what music they hope would be played. I am profoundly concerned as we take up the debate this week on the crime bill, on the Brady bill, on the establishment of boot camps as alternatives to prison for young people, on trying to get more law enforcement officers on our streets, that we not underestimate the gravity of the task before us. Somehow we have to get those young people to you, and through you, to the world.

I know this is a difficult, frustrating, perplexing time. Every day the Vice President and I start the morning together talking about problems that have no easy solution. But I know that this ought to be a time of immense celebration and hopefulness for the American people with the end of the cold war, with the receding threat of nuclear annihilation, with the clear evidence that, for all of our problems, our economy is doing better than the other wealthy countries in creating jobs and promoting growth and that there is so much out there for us still to do.

But the truth is that we are squandering our most valuable resource, our young people, at a rate that no other nation would tolerate. We permit so many of them to grow up without the basic supports of family and community. We permit many of them to live in circumstances, frankly, more dangerous than those experienced by people we go halfway around the world to protect. And so many of them, by the time they are old enough for you to get ahold of them, aren't there for you to get hold of.

I say that not to end this on a down moment but to remind you of just how important this is, what you are doing. A lot of these kids still won't have a chance if you don't do your job well. And we have to find a way for you to reach them at an even earlier point. And if we want to make it, we've got to find a way to remind the rest of America that we are really all in this together. We cannot afford to have 11-year-olds thinking about their funerals. They need to be thinking about their children. You can do that.

Thank you very much.

NOTE: The President spoke at 1:38 p.m. in Room 450 of the Old Executive Office Building. In his remarks, he referred to Sam Myers, president, National Association for Equal Opportunity in Higher Education; Joyce Payne, director, Office for the Advancement of Public Black Colleges; William H. Gray III, CEO and president, United Negro College Fund; Art Thomas, former chairman, National Association for Equal Opportunity in Higher Education; and Lt. Gen. Alonzo E. Short, Jr., USA, Director, Defense Information Systems Agency. Following his remarks, the President signed the Executive order, which is listed in Appendix D at the end of this volume.

Statement on Signing the Rural Electrification Loan Restructuring Act of 1993
November 1, 1993

I am pleased to sign into law H.R. 3123, the "Rural Electrification Loan Restructuring Act of 1993." This Act modifies the Rural Electrification Administration (REA) direct loan programs for rural electric and telephone cooperatives. It represents the culmination of many months of long, hard work by the Congress and the Administration in our commitment to revitalize the infrastructure of rural America.

Earlier this year in my State of the Union Address, I announced my intent to reform the REA. H.R. 3123 does just that. It represents an important first step towards reforming the REA loan programs and is a good example of the Government doing more with less. This legislation will enhance our ability to provide affordable electric and telephone services in rural areas and to ensure access to the emerging telecommunications technologies that are essential for the economic strength of rural areas and the Nation as a whole. It also allows the REA for the first time to make loans for energy conservation purposes.

This Act makes much needed program adjustments to minimize budget expenditures and save over $100 million in 1994 alone. Despite this reduction in Federal assistance, rural electric and telephone consumer bills should not change substantially. By using means tests to target Federal funds and raising the maximum interest rate, H.R. 3123 allows the REA to use scarce resources more effectively. We should no longer hear about wealthy electric and telephone borrowers that receive Government loans at extremely low interest rates.

Although H.R. 3123 clearly represents a major improvement over current law, I have one concern with it. The Act places a 7 percent interest rate cap on certain REA loans, including those refinanced through the Department of the Treasury's Federal Financing Bank. Experience with Federal credit programs indicates that such statutorily fixed interest rate ceilings produce unpredictable and unintended results, including (1) inequities among borrowers using the program at different times; (2) extraordinary demands for loans when market interest rates are high; and (3) increased budget deficits. The "open-ended" character of subsidies resulting from the interest rate cap is inconsistent with the Administration's objective of managing Federal subsidies more effectively. Accordingly, my Administration will work with the Congress to remove this provision.

Nevertheless, H.R. 3123 is, overall, a solid step forward. Today I wish to congratulate the Members of Congress and friends of rural America that helped to enact this first major reform of the REA loan programs.

WILLIAM J. CLINTON

The White House,
November 1, 1993.

NOTE: H.R. 3123, approved November 1, was assigned Public Law No. 103–129.

Statement on Signing Legislation To Phase Out Wool and Mohair Subsidies
November 1, 1993

Today, in signing S. 1548, something unusual will happen: a Federal program is being abolished so that more than a half billion dollars can be saved. This is a departure from business-as-usual in Washington, where programs seem destined to live forever, and Federal dollars raised from average Americans are treated as if they were meant to be spent or squandered instead of saved. But to accomplish the change my Administration is seeking, for the economy and for our country, it is no longer adequate to conduct the business of Government bound by the old arrangements. The legislation, which phases out the wool and mohair program, eliminates an outdated program, reduces the deficit, and affirms for the American people our commitment to change.

In February of 1993, I sent to the Congress "A Vision of Change for America," the budget document accompanying my economic reform program. Among the recommendations were reforms in the wool and mohair program; subsidies provided for nearly 40 years to wool and mohair producers when materials for uniforms and gloves were deemed by the Federal Government as "strategic materials." Although the Department of Defense determined by 1960 that wool was no longer a strategic material, the subsidies continued. It would have been unthinkable to engage in an across-the-board effort to reduce the deficit—as we did in the beginning of our Administration—and not seek changes in this program.

The Congress responded well to our recommendations: first, by providing a phase-down of the subsidies in the budget reconciliation legislation I signed last August; second, in the appropriations process when the Congress provided for a moratorium for one year on wool and mohair payments. The Vice President's National Performance Review suggested that the program be terminated. This legislation does precisely that.

Since these products are no longer strategic materials; since the wealthiest producers receive the largest fraction of the payments; and since many program participants can focus their operations on other profitable sales, there is no justification for maintaining this program on the books. I therefore welcome the decision by the Congress to repeal the authority under which the program operates at the end of 1995, with payments reduced in the intervening years, so that the termination of the wool and mohair subsidy can occur in an orderly but final manner.

This legislation reduces the deficit by $514 million over fiscal years 1994 to 1998.

In February, when we first asked the Congress to reform this program, we initiated a national debate on changing the economic direction of our country. Since then, we have seen the Congress adopt nearly $500 billion in deficit reduction, and we have seen a marked and welcome change in our economic circumstances. We have seen positive changes in the deficit, and interest, inflation, and unemployment rates. Much, much more needs to be done. We need to do better in the creation of good-paying jobs. We need to make further reforms in spending by Washington, and we have proposed such reforms in the National Performance Review. We need to expand trade with adoption of the North American Free Trade Agreement. And, most of all, we must reform health care.

In the past, our citizens might well assume that Washington could not adopt this much change. But, in 1993, the American people have seen their Government fulfill its commitments on a wide variety of issues. It is my hope, as I affix my signature on S. 1548, that this additional, promised reform expands their trust for the work we must undertake in the weeks and months ahead.

WILLIAM J. CLINTON

The White House,
November 1, 1993.

NOTE: S. 1548, approved November 1, was assigned Public Law No. 103–130.

Message to the Congress Transmitting the Notice on Continuation of Iran Emergency
November 1, 1993

To the Congress of the United States:

Section 202(d) of the National Emergencies Act (50 U.S.C. 1622(d)) provides for the automatic termination of a national emergency unless, prior to the anniversary date of its declaration, the President publishes in the *Federal Register* and transmits to the Congress a notice stating that the emergency is to continue in effect beyond the anniversary date. In accordance with this provision, I have sent the enclosed notice, stating that the Iran emergency is to continue in effect beyond November 14, 1993, to the *Federal Register* for publication. Similar notices have been sent annually to the Congress and the *Federal Register* since November 12, 1980. The most recent notice appeared in the *Federal Register* on October 28, 1992.

The crisis between the United States and Iran that began in 1979 has not been fully resolved. The international tribunal established to adjudicate claims of the United States and U.S. nationals against the Iranian government and Iranian nationals against the United States continues to function, and normalization of commercial and diplomatic relations between the United States and Iran has not been achieved. In these circumstances, I have determined that it is necessary to maintain in force the broad authorities that are needed in the process of implementing the January 1981 agreements with Iran and in the eventual normalization of relations with that country.

WILLIAM J. CLINTON

The White House,
November 1, 1993.

NOTE: The notice is listed in Appendix D at the end of this volume.

Message to the Congress Reporting Budget Rescissions
November 1, 1993

To the Congress of the United States:

In accordance with the Congressional Budget and Impoundment Control Act of 1974, I herewith report 37 proposed rescissions of budget authority, totaling $1.9 billion.

These proposed rescissions affect programs of the Departments of Agriculture, Commerce, Defense, Energy, Housing and Urban Development, Interior, State, and Transportation, International Security Assistance programs, and programs of the Agency for International Development, the Army Corps of Engineers, the General Services Administration, the Small Business Administration, the State Justice Institute, and the United States Information Agency. The details of these proposed rescissions are set forth in the attached letter from the Director of the Office of Management and Budget and in the accompanying report.

Concurrent with these proposals, I am transmitting to the Congress FY 1994 supplemental appropriations language requests that would remove a variety of restrictions that impede effective functioning of the government, including certain proposals outlined in the recommendations of the National Performance Review.

Together, the supplemental language requests and the rescission proposals would result in a total budget authority reduction of $2.0 billion. My Administration is committed to working closely with the Congress to produce legislation that will achieve this level of savings.

WILLIAM J. CLINTON

The White House,
November 1, 1993.

NOTE: The report detailing the proposed rescissions was published in the *Federal Register* on November 9.

Nomination for Posts at the Department of the Air Force
November 1, 1993

The President announced today that he intends to nominate Edwin A. Deagle, Jr., to be Under Secretary of the Air Force and Clark G. Fiester to be Assistant Secretary of the Air Force for Acquisition.

"Edwin Deagle and Clark Fiester have each spent the better part of his life in watching out for our Nation's security. They are well prepared to continue that work at the Pentagon," said the President.

NOTE: Biographies of the nominees were made available by the Office of the Press Secretary.

Nomination for an Assistant Secretary of Commerce
November 1, 1993

The President announced his intention today to nominate research and international trade consultant Sue E. Eckert to be the Assistant Secretary of Commerce for Export Administration.

"Sue Eckert brings a wide range of both public and private sector experience in international trade to this position," said the President. "That experience will be invaluable as we seek to expand our country's exports to create more jobs here at home."

NOTE: A biography of the nominee was made available by the Office of the Press Secretary.

Nomination for Under Secretary of Energy
November 1, 1993

The President announced today that he intends to nominate Charles B. Curtis to be the Under Secretary of Energy. After he is confirmed, he will assume management responsibility for science and technology programs, weapons and waste cleanup programs, and energy policy matters assigned by the Secretary.

"There are few Americans who can match Charles Curtis' governmental experience or his knowledge of energy policy," said the President. "He will be an outstanding addition to Secretary O'Leary's team at the Energy Department."

NOTE: A biography of the nominee was made available by the Office of the Press Secretary.

Nomination for Ambassador to Djibouti
November 1, 1993

The President today announced his intention to nominate career Foreign Service officer Martin L. Cheshes to be the U.S. Ambassador to the Republic of Djibouti.

"Over his nearly 30-year career in the Foreign Service, Martin Cheshes has served his country well. I expect him to continue to do so during his tenure in Djibouti," said the President.

NOTE: A biography of the nominee was made available by the Office of the Press Secretary.

Exchange With Reporters Prior to a Meeting With James and Sarah Brady
November 2, 1993

Crime and Handgun Legislation

Q. Jim, is the crime bill going to pass?

The President. He asked you. Yes, it's going to pass. What do you think, Jim? He wants to know if the crime bill's going to pass and the Brady bill. That's what Terry [Terence Hunt, Associated Press] asked you.

Mr. Brady. Well, this is your house, so I'll defer to you, sir.

The President. I already said yes. You answer it.

Q. In that case, Mr. President, I'm wondering if you could tell us what the Brady bill would do in urban areas, like the District of Columbia, where the guns that kill people are not sold so much in shops but more on the street, where there's not much of a waiting——

The President. But they all do come out of regular manufacturers, and they come into the country. And what the Brady bill would do, it would make uniform the losing battle a lot of States are fighting now, because they're all alone, to at least check those people who do buy from registered gun dealers. And there are an enormous number of people who do have criminal backgrounds, who have mental health problems, who don't even meet any kind of age requirement. We would be able to check all that uniformly, nationwide. We find now that in a lot of States that have pretty strict gun laws, an enormous percentage of the guns that are confiscated by law enforcement officials every year come from other States that don't.

So we do have some evidence that these laws work, but it's not the end-all and be-all. We've got a couple hundred million guns out there. There are a lot of other problems that we need to deal with in terms of minors in possession, in terms of assault weapons, in terms of the way the permitting process works for Federal arms dealers.

But the Brady bill is the first step. And we are going to pass it this year, I believe, because the American people finally have heard the long call of Jim and Sarah Brady. They've been out here on this for years and years and years, oftentimes alone with no support. And finally, thanks to the leadership of the Members of Congress who are here and others, we're going to be able to put it over.

Q. Does it go far enough?

Q. [*Inaudible*]—enough votes——

The President. To pass it? I believe we clearly have the votes to pass it if we can get it to the floor. Mr. Schumer got it out of the House subcommittee last week, and we're hoping that the House committee will mark it up this week. Senator Biden's going to bring it up separate from the crime bill so that no one will be able to hide behind other issues in trying to find clever ways to filibuster it. And I compliment him on that. And I just believe that the time has come.

And you read all these stories, like the story that was in the Washington Post yesterday of the children planning for their funerals. I think it's going to be very difficult for the Congress to justify continued inaction on what millions of Americans believe is the number one problem in their lives.

Q. [*Inaudible*]—on the Newsday report saying that—[*inaudible*]—campaign?

The President. First of all, we did nothing improper, and I have nothing to say about it.

NOTE: The exchange began at 11:10 a.m. in the Oval Office at the White House. Former White House Press Secretary James Brady was wounded in the 1981 assassination attempt on President Ronald Reagan. His wife, Sarah, was head of Handgun Control, Inc. A tape was not available for verification of the content of this exchange.

Remarks on Endorsements of the North American Free Trade Agreement
November 2, 1993

Thank you very much, President Carter, Mr. Vice President, all the distinguished people who have spoken here today.

I would like to begin by making two observations. First of all, after hearing what has been said, I'm pretty proud to be an American today. And I think all of you should be, too. Secondly, I have been sent an extraterrestrial telegram stating, "I, too, am for NAFTA," signed Otto von Bismarck. [*Laughter*]

You know, it is something of note that every living President, Secretary of State, Secretaries of Defense, national security advisers, Secretaries of Commerce, leaders of the Federal Reserve, distinguished contributors to the American spirit like John Gardner and Father Hesburgh and other great American citizens all support this agreement, for economic reasons, for foreign policy reasons. Our own Secretary of State, Warren Christopher, is in California even as we are here, talking about the foreign policy implications of NAFTA for our Government and our country.

Why have all of us declared this issue above politics? Why have we come to agree that whatever else has divided us in the past, this will weld us together in the cause of more jobs for our people, more exports for our markets, and more democracy for our allies? Why do we all know down deep inside that this would be such a profound setback for America and the world economy and in the new global polity we are striving so honestly to create? Why are we so willing to say no to partisan politics and yes to NAFTA? I think it is because we know, as all of these have said in different ways, that NAFTA reflects this moment's expression of all the lessons we have learned in the 20th century. It reflects this moment's expression of what we learned not to do after World War I, what we learned we had to do during and after World War II. It reflects the sheer economic weight of argument that Mr. Samuelson referred to, that we have seen even more expressed just in the last few years when a higher and higher percentage of our new jobs in this country are clearly traceable directly to exports.

I see it in my own work here. For years and years and years our allies in Europe and Asia said, "Well, if America really wanted to promote global growth, you would do something about your deficit and get your interest rates down and quit taking so much money out of the global economy." And so we have tried to do that. And we have low interest rates and the deficit is coming down, and our own deficit this year was much lower, in no small measure because of those lower rates.

But we still have this great global recession. Why? Because we are not trading with one another. We are not buying and selling and investing across national lines and sparking the kind of global growth that is the only way any wealthy country, anyway, generates any new jobs.

No one attacking NAFTA has yet made a single solitary argument to refute this essential point: There is no evidence that any wealthy country—not just the United States, anyone, not one—can create new jobs and higher incomes without more global growth fueled by trade. If you strip away all the other arguments, no one has offered a single solitary shred of evidence to refute that central point.

And I know there is great insecurity and instability in all the wealthy countries in the world. You can say whatever you want about this being the first Tuesday in November; you've seen a lot of other Tuesdays come along in other nations, great political upheavals all across the world. Why? Because people feel the walls are closing in on them.

And in truth, I think when you strip all this away, we are facing a real decision about whether the psychological pressures of the moment will overcome what we know in our hearts and our minds is the right thing to do. Whether the same pressures that people in Canada feel, or France, or Japan, in a time when wealthy countries are not generating new jobs and people are working harder for stagnant wages, will those pressures make us do what is easy and perhaps popular in the moment? Or will we do what we should really do? The honorable thing to do to respond to those pressures is to take an action that may not be popular in the moment but that actually holds the promise of alleviating the pressures.

If we believe the feelings, the anxieties are

legitimate, as has been said already by other speakers, then don't we have the obligation to do what will alleviate the anxieties over the long haul, instead of play to them in the moment? That, in the end, is what this decision is all about. That is really what we mean when we say the secret ballot on this issue has already been won.

These students over here to my left are from my alma mater, Georgetown. And when I was in their place 25 years ago now, when we were studying global affairs, we came out really worrying about and thinking about the cold war and trying to debate exactly how much the pattern of the bipolar world could be manifested in every—[*inaudible*]—development, in every country in the world, in every region of the world. And sometimes we were wrong, and sometimes we were right. But at least we had a framework within which to view the world.

As Dr. Kissinger said, we are in the process now of creating a new framework. And a lot of people are complaining about how we don't have all the answers. I don't mean we, the administration, I mean we, the people. But I say to you—many of you in this room are old enough to remember, and I think I now qualify in that category—there are a lot of generations of Americans who would kill to be alive and of age in this time with this set of problems. I mean, who are we to complain about this set of problems? Very few mornings do I come to work in the Oval Office and wonder about whether some decision I make can spark a nuclear war. Very few mornings do I wonder whether, even in all the difficulties we face, we might make an economic error and a quarter of our people will be out of work, as they were during the Great Depression.

We see people in positions of responsibility going around wringing their hands about the difficulties of the moment. Yes, it's a new time. It's always difficult in a new time to see the future with clarity and to have the kind of framework you need. But none of that is an excuse to give in to the emotional pressure of the moment instead of to take steps that will alleviate the pressure. That is the dilemma before us.

You know, it's true that it's good for us economically. It's also true that what Mexico gets out of it is investment, so that if we don't take this deal somebody else probably will. And that will be bad for us economically, as has already

been said by President Carter. But the real thing that this is about is how we are going to view ourselves as we relate to the rest of the world. Keep in mind, this is not an isolated incident. This is not just a trade deal between the United States and Mexico; not even a deal that affects our relationships with the rest of Latin America, although that's where the real jobs and long-term economic benefit to us lie, perhaps; not even a deal that will help us to get the GATT agreement by the end of the year, although, I tell you, it will give enormously increased leverage to the United States to push that agreement through by the end of the year if this passes, enormous, and great incentive to other nations to support this. But over and above that, this is a decision which will demonstrate whether in this difficult moment we still have confidence in ourselves and our potential.

And I would say to all of you, anything you can do to the people at large and to the Congress in particular to instill that confidence again is very important. If we have lost our way at all in the last couple of years, it is in not having any historic memory. These are difficult problems. But for goodness sakes, give us these problems as compared with many of those our forebears faced, and give us these problems as compared to those we are about to create if we start turning away from the world that is plainly before us. Help us to give the Congress the freedom, the confidence, the courage that is inside every Member of the Congress waiting to be brought out. Help to give them the space they need to take the steps they know are right for America.

This is about whether we really have confidence in ourselves. I believe with all my heart the next 20 years can be the best we ever had. But they're going to require some tough decisions, some difficult moments, some uncertain moments. What do you do in moments like that? Do what the priests would tell you to do: Fall back on what you believe and what you know is right. What we know is right for America is to be confident, to reach out, to believe in ourselves and our potential, to believe that we can adjust to change, just as we have been doing for 200 years now.

Make three calls. Make 12 calls. Make two dozen calls. For goodness sakes, make however many you can. But remember, this is a test of our confidence. Every one of you can give confidence to someone else by the life you have lived, the experiences you have had, the things that you know. Give it now. We need it.

Thank you very much.

NOTE: The President spoke at 3:20 p.m. in the East Room at the White House. In his remarks,

he referred to John Gardner, writer and founder of Common Cause; Theodore M. Hesburgh, president emeritus, University of Notre Dame; Paul A. Samuelson, Nobel Prize-winning economist; and Henry Kissinger, former Secretary of State.

Statement on Signing Legislation on Most-Favored-Nation Trade Status for Romania
November 2, 1993

I am pleased to sign today House Joint Resolution 228, which extends most-favored-nation tariff treatment for Romania. This action, which will lower tariffs on Romanian exports to the United States, reflects Romania's significant progress thus far in rejoining the community of democratic nations. It will also assist the growth of Romania's private sector and enhance our bilateral trading relations, improving American access to one of the largest markets in Eastern Europe.

Romania's people are emerging from a long period of tyranny and Communist rule. Their road toward democracy, respect for human rights, and rule of law, and a functioning market economy is not an easy one. While important steps have been taken, more remains to be done. As Romania continues to make progress,

the United States will offer our friendship and help in tangible ways. Romania deserves recognition for its close cooperation with the United States in international organizations, particularly for its compliance with United Nations sanctions on Serbia. Romania, like the other frontline states, has made real sacrifices in this important effort, earning the appreciation of the international community.

I welcome this positive step in U.S.-Romanian relations and look forward to working with the people and leaders of Romania to promote democracy, human rights, a market economy, and prosperity.

NOTE: H.J. Res. 228, approved November 2, was assigned Public Law No. 103–133.

Nomination for Assistant Commissioners of the Patent and Trademark Office
November 2, 1993

The President announced his intention today to nominate two Assistant Commissioners of the Patent and Trademark Office in the Department of Commerce. He named Lawrence O. Goffney, Jr., to be the Assistant Commissioner for Patents and Philip G. Hampton II to be the Assistant Commissioner for Trademarks.

"Each of these men combines substantial legal

experience with a solid background in engineering," said the President. "I have great confidence in their ability to maintain the highest standards at the Patent and Trademark Commission."

NOTE: Biographies of the nominees were made available by the Office of the Press Secretary.

Remarks on Signing the Message Transmitting Proposed NAFTA Legislation to the Congress and an Exchange With Reporters
November 3, 1993

The President. Ladies and gentlemen, today I am sending to Congress the implementing legislation for NAFTA. This will create the world's largest tariff-free zone, from the Canadian arc to the Mexican tropics, with more than 370 million consumers and over $6.5 trillion of production. It will clearly benefit America's workers. Mexican tariffs today are 2½ times United States tariffs. As the walls come down, we estimate that another 200,000 American jobs will be created by 1995.

NAFTA will also enable us to operate in an unprecedented manner in other areas. It will improve environmental conditions on the U.S.-Mexican border, something that all Americans know we need to do and something that all Mexicans know we need to do. It will be the stimulus for economic growth beyond Mexico, enabling us to go into the rest of Latin America with similar agreements. And perhaps most important in the short run, it will give the United States access to the Mexican markets on terms more favorable than those available to many of our competitors who have also rapidly been expanding their sales into Mexico, whether from Europe or Japan or the rest of Asia.

If we turn away from NAFTA, we risk losing the natural trade advantage that should come to the United States as Mexico and the rest of Latin America build market economies and stronger democracies. If we embrace NAFTA, it is one strong step to take this country into the 21st century with a revitalized economy. That is clearly in the forefront of the minds of all Americans, and that is why we are all pursuing it here in this bipartisan fashion.

I want to thank the Democratic and the Republican leaders of the Congress who are here with me today, thank them for their tireless efforts, along with our administration, Ambassador Kantor, Mr. Daley, Mr. Frenzel, and others. We are working hard. We are making progress, and I hope when we send this bill up to the Congress today that it will reaffirm the clear interest of the United States in adopting this agreement.

I'd like to sign it now, and then we'll take a couple of questions.

[At this point, the President signed the message transmitting the proposed legislation to implement the North American Free Trade Agreement.]

Q. Mr. President?
The President. I have to sign two, there being two Houses. [*Laughter*]

Election Results

Q. Mr. President, it's a year after your election and the Democrats have now lost two Senate seats, two Governors, the mayors of—[*inaudible*]—the largest cities in the country. Do you view it in any way as a judgment on your policies in the Democratic Party?

The President. No. When Governor Robb was elected Governor of Virginia in 1981, I didn't think it was a repudiation of President Reagan. We also won a lot of mayors' races last night, including a lot of people who were early supporters of mine and very instrumental in the campaign. And we won the special elections for the House of Representatives that had come up that we had before. I don't think you can draw too much conclusion from this. I think what you can say is, the American people want change, and they want results. The point I want to make is that I believe every Member of Congress, without regard for party, who votes for this agreement will be rewarded for it, because it represents change and the creation of more economic opportunity. I think it represents change and results. That's the way incumbents are going to survive, by providing the kind of changes that the voters want.

Q. So you don't think it's any reflection on you, or any referendum on you or your programs?

The President. Let me say this: I was elected Governor of my State five times. Once I was elected in 1984 when Ronald Reagan got 59 percent of the vote in my State, and I got 63 percent. Voters are extremely discriminating. They make their own judgments for their own reasons. I think it is a manifestation that the voters are not yet happy with the pace of economic renewal, social reunification in this country. They're worried about crime. They're worried about all of these other social problems we've got. And I think it's also a sense they have that Government's not yet working for them.

And all that is right. There's nothing wrong about that. And I think that all people who are in, if they want to stay in, are going to have to work together until we produce economic results, a country that's coming together instead of coming apart, and political reform. But that's why I will say again, it's certainly not a message to run and hide from the tough issues; that is not what it is. And that's why I think, again, I think NAFTA is symbolic of the kinds of things that people ought to be doing across party lines, because it will create economic opportunity. And that will lower voter anxiety. When people won't have to worry about whether the economy is growing or not, they'll be much more secure, and we'll be able to deal with a whole lot of these other issues that we've got. That's why I think this is a very important, symbolic issue.

NAFTA

Q. Do you have the votes?

The President. Do we have the votes? We don't have them today, but we're getting there. Really, I think all of these people would admit, thanks to all of them, we're making rapid progress. And we had a real movement in the last 10 days or so, and I think you'll see more and more progress in the next few days.

Q. Are you going to win?

The President. Yes. We're going to win it.

Q. Are you cutting too many deals? The big sugar deal, is this just——

The President. No.

Q. Isn't that protectionist, the sugar concessions for the Louisiana Members?

The President. I think the Ambassador is going to have a—you're going to have a press conference this afternoon to talk about that, aren't you?

Ambassador Kantor. Yes.

The President. We haven't done anything that's not consistent with what we said we'd try to do from the beginning on this agreement. And Mickey's going to talk about it today.

NOTE: The President spoke at 10:25 a.m. in the Oval Office at the White House.

Remarks to the Community in Ambridge, Pennsylvania
November 3, 1993

Thank you very much. It is wonderful to be back in Pennsylvania, wonderful to be here in western Pennsylvania with so many of my friends and so many of the people who helped to make one year ago today, the day that I was elected President, a wonderful day for me. I thank you for that.

I thank Congressman Klink for coming here today and hosting us here today in his district. He's done a terrific job being your advocate. He has, on occasion, chewed my ear off about the interests of the people in this area, and I know you can be proud of him for what he has done. I thank Senator Specter for coming here today and for being willing to work across party lines to solve this problem that has affected him and every other American and every other American family. I thank my good friend, Senator Wofford—I want to say a little more about him in a moment—for coming here and

for nourishing this issue long before it was popular. I want to thank you, Mayor Panek, for having us here today. And I thank Congressman Murphy for coming up with us. And I thank my friends from Allegheny County: Commissioner Tom Forrester and the outgoing Mayor of Pittsburgh who's serving the end of her term, Mayor Sophie Masloff. We're glad to see you, Sophie. [*Applause*] Thank you.

I want to thank your superintendent, Dr. DePaul, and your principal, David Perry, for having us here. And let me say, as an old band boy, I congratulate the band on your achievement, and I wish you well.

I wanted to come here to Pennsylvania today to put this book in the library here in your wonderful hometown, in that beautiful library, to symbolize the placement of the health care plan in 1,600 Federal depository libraries all across America today and in hundreds of others who will ask for and receive copies of the book. Soon it will not only be in your libraries but it will be on your bookstands. I ask every one of you to get this book and read it.

It deals with a system that is central to our personal health, our family's health, our community's health, and the economic strength and well-being of our Nation. For that reason alone it may contain the most important information of any book you could read this year. What we want the American people to do, as has already been said, is to read this book, to get familiar with the dynamics of the problem: Why is it that our health care system costs more than any other nation's, about 40 percent more of our income, and still is the only major health care system in the world that doesn't provide health insurance to everyone? Why is it that it's so expensive and yet 100,000 Americans a month lose their health insurance permanently? Why is it that it's so costly and yet we still don't have the primary and preventive services that help to keep people well? What could we do to provide coverage to people with long-term diseases or people with disabilities who could be more independent, who could make more of a contribution to our national life if only they could get better health insurance themselves?

Some of the American citizens who deal with their disabilities every year are in this audience today. I thank them for their courage in coming here. And I say to you, you and your families will be among those most advanced by this effort, but so will we all be helped. There are untold numbers of people on public assistance today who would not be there if only they had access to preventive, primary, and comprehensive health care. You should ask and answer these questions.

Two years ago when Pennsylvania elected Harris Wofford in a stunning upset on the health care issue, you fired a shot heard 'round America. You said something to the people making public policy that had not been heard before. You said, "I know this is a complicated problem. I know there are lot of interests on all sides. I know this gives people a headache. I know there's always something you can say to object to any reform. But I still expect you to deal with it because it is eating the heart out of America. There is too much insecurity. There is too much cost. There is too little health care. Do something to make it better." And

we got the message.

One year ago when I crossed this country, I had already spent over 2 years as a Governor trying to come to grips with a health care system that was threatening to bankrupt the State governments of the country with higher and higher costs for Medicaid programs for the poor, both elderly and nonelderly; with working people in my State who worked hard and played by the rules and wondered why they were working because their children didn't have health insurance; with elderly people who were not quite poor enough to be on Medicaid, so every month they were making a decision about whether to buy food or the medicine they needed to stay out of the hospital and save the rest of us even more money, as well as keeping themselves healthier; and on and on and on.

Hillary and I have personal friends, friends from our childhood, who have told us the most heart-wrenching stories. A friend of ours who runs a small business and has only four employees because he had one employee with one child who had Down syndrome. And because this young man couldn't change his job and because that family couldn't be let go, their premiums went up so much in that small business that they had to go to a $2,500 deductible for the families, which as many of you know, depending on what your income is, is like not having any insurance at all. And many people are on even higher ones.

I say that to make this point. This book is a specific, detailed reflection of years of common effort, months of effort in which thousands of people were involved: doctors, nurses, other health care providers, consumers, business people—small, medium, and large—people in the insurance industry, people in all aspects of health care. And it attempts to do something no one has yet done, except for this product, which is to say here is specifically how we would propose to change it.

And when those come forward—who should come forward—who disagree with us, I ask only that they be held to the same standard. Where is their book? What are their answers? Who pays for theirs? Where are the costs in theirs? What is their answer? Hold them to the same standard.

The bottom line, my fellow Americans, is this: We have to create a system of comprehensive benefits that are always there that can never be taken away. You know here in this river valley as well as any group of Americans—look back over the last 20 years—you know we are living in a churning economy that sometimes helps us and sometimes hurts us. You know how few guarantees there are in life anymore. You know how many people have been hurt by the insecurity and the uncertainties of the sweeping global economic changes that we have. We have to be able to say to the American people, if you're willing to work hard and play by the rules, if you're a good taxpaying citizen, if you're poor and you have children, no matter what happens to you, you will always have basic health care. And we know we can do it, because every other country besides us has already done it.

We can do it. We're tired of making excuses for why we spend 10 cents on the dollar more on paperwork, regulation, and insurance premiums than any country in the world and we can't figure out how to get health care to real people. We are tired of making excuses, and we are ready to solve the problem.

When I look at all these young people here and I think about what their future is going to hold and I realize we are so close to the 21st century and you see the kids on either side of all of us adults who are sitting in the middle—although there are some young people in the middle, too; young is defined by whoever is a day younger than you are—[*laughter*]—I think about what I know in my heart are the challenges of this country. We basically have three huge challenges as we move toward the 21st century. One is economic stagnation. We're not creating enough jobs, and too many people are working harder without ever getting a raise. Right? [*Applause*] Two is, we are not dealing with the social problems we have. We are coming apart when we ought to be coming together. We have seen communities and families under stress. There are too many children who are subject to violence on our streets and in our schools. We have too many human problems that are not being faced. And the third problem is that the political system has too much talk and too little action on the real problems. It is too dominated by vested interest and fears.

Now, in our way we have tried to address all these things in the last 10 months since I have been your President. The budget plan we adopted brought interest rates to their lowest point and mortgages to their lowest point in 25 years. And we now have more private sector

jobs which have come into America in the last 10 months than in the previous 4 years. Is it enough? Of course not, but it's a darned good beginning. We're moving in the right direction.

The second thing—and we talked about this on the plane coming up here—to try to put the American family back together. We have passed the family leave law so you can get some time off without losing your job with a sick child or a sick parent. On April 15th this year, when taxes are due, over 15 million American working families will get a tax break because they have children and because they are working hard and they're still below the Federal poverty line. They will be lifted above it. It's the biggest incentive to get off welfare we've ever had, to reward the working people who make modest incomes and have children.

To all the students, I say this Congress lowered the cost of college loans, made the terms of repayment easier, and will give thousands of young people a chance to work their way through college by serving their communities in national service.

The last thing I want to say is we are also, between now and Thanksgiving, determined to do something that gives communities a chance to fight crime more, with more police officers on the street, with alternatives for correction, and by passing the Brady bill. To make the political system work better, this Congress has before it today a campaign finance reform bill, a bill to limit the influence of lobbyists, a bill to require Congress to live under the same laws that it requires private employers to live under, and a bill to give the President the power to make specific line-item vetoes in unnecessary spending. All of those are before the Congress today.

But there is no issue which combines all three of these things like health care. Health care is important to the economy. Why? Because we're spending 40 percent more of our income than any other nation on health care; we're getting less for it. That means if you want our cars to sell at home and overseas, they're having to pay a nickel on the dollar more than the Germans and the Japanese are for health care for every dollar in every automobile. It's important to our economy that we do something to stop health care costs from going up at 3 times the rate of inflation.

It's important to our social fabric. Why? Because how can you tell America's families that they ought to get a good education and they ought to be willing to be retrained all through their lives and they ought to play by the rules, when they know if one bad thing happens to them they'll have to go home at night and look at their children, and they won't even be able to provide health care. How can we hold this country together?

And it is important for making the political system work. Why? Because there will never be an issue, never, at least in my tenure, where so many special interests have so much to gain or lose based on the decisions made by Congress.

You know, my wife had a little argument with the Health Insurance Association about a television ad they're running. So they're going to come out, they're going to run another ad and tell you they've got a better idea, except we're all still waiting for it.

Let me tell you what the issue is. You need to know what's behind those ads. This is the only country in the world that has 1,500 separate companies writing thousands and thousands and thousands of different policies designed to divide people up into smaller and smaller and smaller groups, so that some of you are in insurance groups so small that 40 percent of your premium goes to overhead, profit, and administrative costs. It is because of that that hospital after hospital after hospital tells us that their doctors, their nurses, their administrators are spending millions of dollars a year in time filling out unnecessary forms because people have to keep up with all these insurance policies.

It is because of that that a doctor I grew up with told me the other day that it was bad enough that he and his partner in a two-doctor firm—clinic—had to hire a lot of people to do administrative work. He now had to hire one woman to do nothing but stay on the phone all day to call these hundreds of different insurance companies, to pound on them to pay what they already owed. You pay for that when they hire somebody else to do that. That is what is going on here.

Now, look, there are a lot of good people who do this work. They're entitled to work, too. But you've got to make up your mind. Do you want to spend one dime on every dollar for health care when we're already spending 14.5 percent of our income—no other nation over a dime, 10 percent of their income; Germany and Japan at 9 percent of their income—do

you want to keep paying 10 cents on every dollar to pay for profit and paperwork and bureaucracy that no other people anywhere in the world pay, money that could go to cover the uninsured, money that could go to give primary and preventive care, money that could go to give mammograms to women, to give cholesterol tests to men, to give dental help to children, to give drugs to the elderly who are above the poverty line but still don't have enough money to pay their drug bill?

To me it is an easy answer. But you need to know what is fueling those television ads you see from a lot of these special interest groups. There's a lot of money in this health care system that doesn't have a rip to do with your health care. And we want to develop it in a way that can be devoted to your health care.

They say, "What are you going to do when the money runs out?" You know, our plan proposes to raise public spending at twice the rate of inflation for the next 5 years instead of 3 times the rate of inflation. Nobody's cutting anything. We are going to have to have some discipline in this system like every other system we have. You are not going to run out of health care, but we are going to limit the extent to which you can be gouged in a system over which you now have no control. I think that is what you want. We have to have some discipline in this system, as in every other system of our life. If we need discipline for our kids in the schools, discipline on our streets, and enforcement of the law, we ought to have discipline in how our health care system operates. It shouldn't be able to run crazy.

So I say to you, my fellow Americans, under this plan no insurance company can take away your coverage. There is a limit to how much it can increase. What we are trying to do over the long run is to bring ourselves into a position where we increase health care costs at the rate of inflation plus the rate of population growth, utilization of the system every year.

There will have to be special provisions, as we make them, for new technologies, for medical research, for all those things that give us the best health care in the world to the people who can access it. But I tell you, we did not put this plan together without talking to literally hundreds of doctors and nurses and other health care providers. We heard them.* They are screaming, literally screaming, for relief from the over complicated, burdensome, bureaucratic paperwork decisions that are driving the costs of this system through the roof.

And I ask you to remember that when you hear the million-dollar campaign ads of those who are going to tell you that we cannot have health security and comprehensive benefits for all at a price that will not break the American economy. I refuse to believe we can't do something everybody else has done. I think America can still do things that no one else has done. We can certainly do things that everybody else has done.

Let me say a special word about senior citizens. Our plan does not change Medicare at all. It preserves the benefits of Medicare and the integrity of the system. But our plan does cover prescription medicine for the elderly as well as for the nonelderly.

Now, let me tell you why that's important. If you look at the United States as compared with Germany, for example—two countries that have great pharmaceutical systems—we don't use as many prescription drugs as the Germans do. Why? Because they're not covered in our health care plans. Because they're not covered for elderly people on Medicare who aren't on Medicaid. What does that mean? It means people don't get the medicine they need. Eventually, they get sicker. They go to the hospital, and it costs more money. It is very important for the elderly, also important for a lot of these young people who might have asthma or some other condition that would require medication. Our plan covers it, and I think America should have it.

Under this plan we also move to cover long-term care for elderly people who aren't in nursing homes. This is a big deal, folks. The fastest growing group of Americans are people over 80. And more and more of our elderly people are going to need some help but want to maintain as much independence as possible. Our plan, over a period of time, as we can afford it, gives our older citizens the chance to maintain that independence. Nobody else does it. That's another good reason to support it, and I hope you will.

Finally, let me say to the students here, you will be more affected by this than any of the rest of us. You will live your whole life in an American economy hurtling toward the 21st century that will or won't escape economic stagnation, that will or won't bring us together as a family again and promote the values that made this community great, that will or won't have a political system that works through problems instead of just talks about them. The test of that, in large measure, will be this.

I say, this may not be perfect, but it is the only comprehensive plan that gives security to all Americans. It is the only one. I challenge the others to come forward with their ideas, send you their books, stand on their ideas. And I urge all of you to read this, ask the questions, and push ahead. America needs it. The next generation needs it. And you need it right here in this wonderful town.

Thank you, and God bless you all.

NOTE: The President spoke at 2:21 p.m. in the gymnasium at Ambridge Area High School. In his remarks, he referred to Mayor Walter Panek of Ambridge and Samuel A. DePaul, superintendent of schools, Ambridge Area School District.

Remarks on the California Fires
November 3, 1993

Good evening. For just a few moments, I want to speak to you good people in southern California who are enduring in an agonizing tragedy with the spread of the wildfires. Whenever natural disasters like this strike one region of our Nation, all the rest of us try to pull together as one community, a family, to help those in need. That's what Americans do. And that's why the prayers and good wishes of all the citizens of our Nation are with the people of California. We're facing those fires together.

This has to be a terrifying experience for children awakened at night by their parents and carried away from their homes before they're lost; for property owners, some of whom have faced down a wall of fire with nothing more than a garden hose in their hands and a prayer in their hearts; and especially, for the gallant, heroic men and women who are fighting these fires and risking their lives to save people and property from being consumed by the blaze.

I'm especially grateful for the work of the pilots, many of whom have flown after dark into strong winds to drop water on the fires to contain their fury. Their actions and the work of countless others define the word "courage," and we can never repay them for what they have done and what they are still prepared to do.

In the fires which struck the southland, we've moved quickly to speed Federal resources and a strong Federal response to those places where it could do the most good in helping the State and local efforts. After designating several counties as major disaster areas, we dispatched Forest Service air tankers and Federal firefighters to the scene. At my direction, Mr. McLarty, the White House Chief of Staff, has coordinated the Federal response. The Director of the Federal Emergency Management Agency, James Lee Witt, traveled immediately to the scene of the fires, along with Agriculture Secretary Mike Espy and our General Services Administrator, from Orange County, Roger Johnson. We worked with Governor Wilson and his emergency director, Dick Andrews, as well as the leaders in your congressional delegation, especially your Senators Boxer and Feinstein.

And until these fires are out, those in the inland empire, and the new ones tearing through the Santa Monica mountains, our work will continue, and we won't rest either. For these new fires, the Federal response has already begun. We're providing 37 air tankers, 100 fire crews amounting to 2,000 Federal firefighters, 86 fire engines, and 22 helicopters.

I've just spoken with FEMA Director Witt, and he assures me that the Federal efforts are well coordinated with the extraordinary work being done by private citizens and State and local government. I talked with Governor Wilson, and he said the same thing. Just a few moments ago, Director Witt announced my decision to provide $15 million to the California

Office of Emergency Services to help pay for the State and local firefighting costs. This advance will be supplemented as further costs are identified in the coming weeks.

I know this is a big burden for California with all your other troubles, and we ought to do what we can to help. I know, too, from dealing with natural disasters in my home State of Arkansas that these problems put unbearable strains on the budgets of State and local government as well as on private citizens. We're going to try to help communities shoulder their extraordinary expenses that they're facing through no fault of their own. As we provide this help, we'll monitor the situation closely so that we can do more when more is needed to be done.

I know there are people who suffered losses who are upset and frightened about the future. I know there are families concerned about leaving their homes in the fire's path and moving to safety, perhaps spending the night in a shelter. I know there are public safety officers and firefighters who are exhausted from their exertions. And I know there are children who are frightened.

For them especially, but for all of you, I know words alone will not heal your hurt or make you whole. But I hope you will take some solace in knowing that your country is concerned about you and that I am closely following the work being done to protect you. I hope you are sustained by the knowledge that communities in California are pulling together and neighbors are helping each other. This is what our great country is all about.

Have faith, and take heart. Soon the tragedy will pass, and the recovery will begin. And as this happens, and you know that it will, you will be in the prayers and hearts of your fellow citizens. You are not facing these fires alone.

Thank you, and God bless you.

NOTE: The President spoke via satellite at 8:45 p.m. from Room 459 of the Old Executive Office Building to the southern California community.

Statement by the Press Secretary on Drug Control Policy
November 3, 1993

The President today signed a decision directive that provides a policy framework for U.S. international drug control efforts as part of the Administration's overall counterdrug policy. The President designated Director Lee Brown of the Office of National Drug Control Policy as responsible for oversight and direction for all counterdrug policies, in coordination with the National Security Council.

In his directive to Agencies involved in the fight against illicit drugs in the hemisphere, the President said that the scourge of illegal narcotics is severely damaging the social fabric of the United States and other countries. He said that the operation of international criminal narcotics syndicates is a national security threat requiring an extraordinary and coordinated response by civilian and military agencies, both unilaterally and by mobilizing international cooperation with other nations and international organizations such as the U.N., OAS, and international financial institutions.

The President's directive, the result of an exhaustive 8-month review of U.S. international policies and strategies, instructed Federal Agencies to change the emphasis in U.S. international drug programs from the past concentration largely on stopping narcotics shipments to a more evenly distributed effort across three programs:

—assisting source countries in addressing the root causes of narcotics production and trafficking through assistance for sustainable development, strengthening democratic institutions and cooperative programs to counter narcotics traffickers, money laundering, and supply of chemical precursors;

—combating international narco-trafficking organizations;

—emphasizing more selective and flexible interdiction programs near the U.S. border, in the transit zone, and in source countries.

He directed that a working group chaired by the State Department manage implementation of the international strategy, reporting its activities to Director Brown.

The President stressed the need for American leadership in the fight against international drug trafficking. He pledged to work with the Congress to ensure adequate funding for international counterdrug programs.

Message to the Congress Transmitting Proposed Legislation To Implement the North American Free Trade Agreement
November 3, 1993

To the Congress of the United States:

I am pleased to transmit today legislation to implement the North American Free Trade Agreement, an agreement vital to the national interest and to our ability to compete in the global economy. I also am transmitting a number of related documents required for the implementation of NAFTA.

For decades, the United States has enjoyed a bipartisan consensus on behalf of a free and open trading system. Administrations of both parties have negotiated, and Congresses have approved, agreements that lower tariffs and expand opportunities for American workers and American firms to export their products overseas. The result has been bigger profits and more jobs here at home.

Our commitment to more free and more fair world trade has encouraged democracy and human rights in nations that trade with us. With the end of the Cold War, and the growing significance of the global economy, trade agreements that lower barriers to American exports rise in importance.

The North American Free Trade Agreement is the first trade expansion measure of this new era, and it is in the national interest that the Congress vote its approval.

Not only will passage of NAFTA reduce tariff barriers to American goods, but it also will operate in an unprecedented manner—to improve environmental conditions on the shared border between the United States and Mexico, to raise the wages and living standards of Mexican workers, and to protect our workers from the effects of unexpected surges in Mexican imports into the United States.

This pro-growth, pro-jobs, pro-exports agreement—if adopted by the Congress—will vastly improve the status quo with regard to trade, the environment, labor rights, and the creation and protection of American jobs.

Without NAFTA, American business will continue to face high tariff rates and restrictive nontariff barriers that inhibit their ability to export to Mexico. Without NAFTA, incentives will continue to encourage American firms to relocate their operations and take American jobs to Mexico. Without NAFTA, we face continued degradation of the natural environment with no strategy for clean-up. Most of all, without NAFTA, Mexico will have every incentive to make arrangements with Europe and Japan that operate to our disadvantage.

Today, Mexican tariffs are two and a half times greater than U.S. tariffs. This agreement will create the world's largest tariff-free zone, from the Canadian Arctic to the Mexican tropics—more than 370 million consumers and over $6.5 trillion of production, led by the United States. As tariff walls come down and exports go up, the United States will create 200,000 new jobs by 1995. American goods will enter this market at lower tariff rates than goods made by our competitors.

Mexico is a rapidly growing country with a rapidly expanding middle class and a large pent-up demand for goods—especially American goods. Key U.S. companies are poised to take advantage of this market of 90 million people. NAFTA ensures that Mexico's reforms will take root, and then flower.

Moreover, NAFTA is a critical step toward building a new post-Cold War community of free markets and free nations throughout the Western Hemisphere. Our neighbors—not just in Mexico but throughout Latin America—are waiting to see whether the United States will lead the way toward a more open, hopeful, and prosperous future or will instead hunker down

behind protective, but self-defeating walls. This Nation—and this Congress—has never turned away from the challenge of international leadership. This is no time to start.

The North American Free Trade Agreement is accompanied by supplemental agreements, which will help ensure that increased trade does not come at the cost of our workers or the border environment. Never before has a trade agreement provided for such comprehensive arrangements to raise the living standards of workers or to improve the environmental quality of an entire region. This makes NAFTA not only a stimulus for economic growth, but a force for social good.

Finally, NAFTA will also provide strong incentives for cooperation on illegal immigration and drug interdiction.

The implementing legislation for NAFTA I forward to the Congress today completes a process that has been accomplished in the best spirit of bipartisan teamwork. NAFTA was negotiated by two Presidents of both parties and is supported by all living former Presidents of the United States as well as by distinguished Americans from many walks of life—government, civil rights, and business.

They recognize what trade expanding agreements have meant for America's economic greatness in the past, and what this agreement will mean for America's economic and international leadership in the years to come. The North American Free Trade Agreement is an essential part of the economic strategy of this country: expanding markets abroad and providing a level playing field for American workers to compete and win in the global economy.

America is a Nation built on hope and renewal. If the Congress honors this tradition and approves this agreement, it will help lead our country into the new era of prosperity and leadership that awaits us.

WILLIAM J. CLINTON

The White House,
November 3, 1993.

NOTE: This message was released by the Office of the Press Secretary on November 4.

Message to the Congress Transmitting NAFTA Supplemental Agreements
November 4, 1993

To the Congress of the United States:

By separate message, I have transmitted to the Congress a bill to approve and implement the North American Free Trade Agreement (NAFTA). In fulfillment of legal requirements of our trade laws, that message also transmitted a statement of administrative action, the NAFTA itself, and certain supporting information required by law.

Beyond the legally required documents conveyed with that message, I want to provide you with the following important documents:

- The supplemental agreements on labor, the environment, and import surges;
- Agreements concluded with Mexico relating to citrus products and to sugar and sweeteners;
- The border funding agreement with Mexico;
- Letters agreeing to further negotiations to accelerate duty reductions;
- An environmental report on the NAFTA and side agreements;
- A list of more technical letters related to

NAFTA that have previously been provided to the Congress and that are already on file with relevant congressional committees.

These additional documents are not subject to formal congressional approval under fast-track procedures. However, the additional agreements provide significant benefits for the United States that will be obtained only if the Congress approves the NAFTA. In that sense, these additional agreements, as well as the other documents conveyed, warrant the careful consideration of each Member of Congress. The documents I have transmitted in these two messages constitute the entire NAFTA package.

I strongly believe that the NAFTA and the other agreements will mark a significant step forward for our country, our economy, our environment, and our relations with our neighbors on this continent. I urge the Congress to seize this historic opportunity by approving the legislation I have transmitted.

WILLIAM J. CLINTON

The White House,
November 4, 1993.

Exchange With Reporters in Lexington, Kentucky
November 4, 1993

Elections and NAFTA

Q. Mr. President, isn't it going to be a lot tougher to get NAFTA votes from Democrats after the election results?

The President. No.

Q. Why not?

The President. What in the world would that have to do with anything?

Q. Well, Members are going to say that you can't get the numbers.

The President. That's ludicrous. That's just a Washington story. That's ridiculous. What about all the mayors that walked in with no opposition that were active in my campaign in the primaries? That's ridiculous. I'm proud of the showing that those two guys had, Florio and

Dinkins. They came back from the dead. Everybody wrote them off. Besides that, NAFTA wasn't an issue in any of those races. I just think it's ridiculous. The only thing they need—[*inaudible*]—is doing the right thing for America. And I think they will.

The real evidence is that if people think you're for change you get elected, and if they think you're for the status quo that's not working, you're—[*inaudible*]—and the proper change this time is to support NAFTA.

NOTE: The exchange began at approximately 1:30 p.m. at Lexmark International, Inc. A tape was not available for verification of the content of this exchange.

Remarks on NAFTA to Employees of Lexmark International in Lexington
November 4, 1993

The President. Thank you very much. You know, Roberta was nervous as a cat, but she did a good job, didn't she? Let's give her a hand. She did great. [*Applause*]

I want to thank Marvin Mann for his remarks and for hosting us here today; my longtime friend and former colleague Governor Jones for his support and his kind remarks; your fine Congressman, Scotty Baesler, for his support of NAFTA. And I want to thank also—there are people here from at least four other operations, business operations, in this area I know of. Raise your hand if you're here so I'll know whether I've got it right. There are people here from Texas Instruments, I think. Where are you? Over here. From Monarch Tool and Manufacturing, from Rand McNally, and from DataBeam. Gosh, I can't believe they roped you off over here. They're afraid you'll pick up some trade secrets, I think. [*Laughter*]

I wanted to come here to Kentucky and to this plant and to you folks today to talk about the North American Free Trade Agreement. I also asked to come to a place where I could spend some time with real American workers, men and women whose lives are on the line every day and whose children have a stake in the decisions that I must make and the Congress must make for you and for our economy.

I came here mostly to answer questions. And I'm going to take some time answering questions when I finish my remarks, so I hope you'll be thinking of them, questions about this North American Free Trade Agreement, about our economy, about how they fit together. And if you have some hard questions just give them to me with the bark off. I'm used to it. One of the things that dealing with the distinguished Washington press corps back there does is to sort of harden you to the questions of daily life, and now I look forward to them every day.

I also want to say to you this: Before I became President I was Governor of a State not all that much unlike Kentucky. My job was to try to create jobs and keep jobs. It was to try to educate people so they could do the jobs of today and tomorrow. For most of the time I was Governor, our unemployment rate was above the national average, but we kept working

to export, to increase investment, both domestic and foreign, to improve our education and training programs. And in my last year in office, in every month we were first or second in the country in job growth after a long dry spell. We had plants shut down and move to Mexico when I was Governor of my State, at least three that I know of. I'm proud to say that we got one of them to come back, because our people were more productive and they were good at changing the product line on a quick basis when the demand required it.

I say that to make this point, first and foremost: I spent most of the last 20 years around hard-working people who were struggling to survive and sometimes to get ahead in a tough global economy. I ran for President because I was worried about the future of our country and my own child's future moving toward the 20th century, because I thought we had three great problems: economic stagnation, a society that was coming apart with violence and other problems when it ought to be coming together, and a political system that was not facing up to the problems, where there was a huge gap between what people in public office said and what they did. And ever since I have been in Washington, I have been trying to change that. We've tried to give the economy some help by bringing the deficit down, getting interest rates down, getting the economy going again. We've had more private sector jobs come into this economy in the last 9 months than in the previous 4 years. We're beginning to turn it around.

But I came here to talk about this trade agreement today for one simple reason: Every wealthy country in the world, including the United States, is having trouble creating jobs. Every wealthy country in the world in the last 10 years saw an increase in inequality. That is, middle class people's wages didn't keep up with inflation, while people who were particularly able to triumph in the global economy had their incomes go way up. So what had happened in America from World War II until about 10 or 15 years ago—which was we all got richer but we came together, the country was growing together—began to change, and we began to grow apart, so that a majority of our people were working a longer work week for the same or lower wages to pay more for the basics in life, health care, housing, education. And I was concerned about that.

We can bring the deficit down; we can get interest rates down; we can get investment back up. But there is nobody anywhere in the world who has come forward with a good argument for any way to create more jobs and raise the incomes of working people without expanding trade. You've got to have more people to buy more products if you want to have the benefits of all the increasing productivity.

When we were coming here today, Mr. Mann said, "You know, we're producing a new product, and the workers really figured out how to produce it. We have a new way of dealing with defects, and they figured out how to do that. We now have all this empty space in this factory because they figured out how to do more in less space and increase productivity." Well, if you want the benefits of that, you've got to have more people to buy the things that you're producing, because productivity is the same person producing more in less time, right? No wealthy country can create more jobs and increase incomes, I will say again, without expanding world trade and global economic growth. Nobody has explained how that gets done. And nobody fighting this trade agreement has made an argument about how that gets done. It cannot be done.

About a half of the growth of our economy in the last 5 years has come from exports. Jobs that are tied to exports, on average, pay about 17 percent more than jobs that have nothing to do with exports. We do have trade problems in America, but they aren't with Mexico. Five years ago we had a $5.6 billion trade deficit with Mexico. This year we're going to have a $5.5 billion trade surplus with Mexico. The Mexican people collectively bought over $40 billion worth of American products last year. We have a big trade deficit with our trading partners in Asia, and I'm working hard to do something about that. I'm going out to Washington State to meet with the leaders of all the Asian countries later this month. But we need to know that right here at home, on our border, there are people who like American products who are dying to buy them.

Let me just give you one example: This company produces components that go into personal computers. Three years ago Mexico bought

120,000 computers from us, last year 390,000, this year 600,000. There are 90 million people there. This trade agreement, NAFTA, takes the tariff on computers and for software from 20 percent to zero. In other words, instead of 600,000 computers, we can be selling millions there. That's just one example. It will create jobs for us. Exports from Kentucky alone have grown 350 percent to Mexico over the last 5 years because they've been bringing their tariffs down.

Now, if this trade agreement passes, NAFTA, we estimate America will add another 200,000 jobs by 1995 alone. Why? For the following reasons: Number one, our tariffs today on Mexican products are much lower than their tariffs on ours, so when they take theirs down we'll gain more. Number two, they have a lot of domestic content requirements, especially on automobiles. In other words, they say, "If you want to sell them in the Mexican market you've got to make this stuff here." That alone, that change alone, we estimate will enable our autoworkers here in America to go from selling only 1,000 cars in Mexico to 50,000 to 60,000 cars in Mexico next year alone. This is a big deal.

Now, the people who are against this, what do they say? They say, "You don't want to have a trade agreement with Mexico because look at all the jobs that went to Mexico in the 1980's because they had low wages and lax environmental enforcement. And all this will do is to make that happen everywhere in the country. It will be a disaster."

That one fellow talks about the giant sucking sound. Let me tell you something, folks. I know a little about this. I was a Governor of a State that lost plants to Mexico. My State was small enough that if somebody shut a plant down and moved it to Mexico, there was a good chance I knew who they were, the people that ran the plants, the people that worked in the plants. I used to go stand at plants on the last day they were open and shake hands with people when they walked off the job for the last time. I know something about that. And I want you to understand this very clearly from somebody who's lived through this: This agreement will make that less likely, not more likely. If we beat this NAFTA agreement, anybody who wants to go down to Mexico, right across the line, for low wages, for lax environmental enforcement, can go right on doing it and can make products there and put it back into the

American market with zero tariff as long as they're close enough to the border, if we beat it.

If we adopt it, their tariffs will go down on our products; their requirements that we produce in their country to sell in their country will go down: less incentive to move factories there. They will get factories all over their country, not to import stuff to America but to produce for the Mexican market. That's what they get out of this.

The short of it is everything bad that everybody tells you about with this agreement can go right on happening if we don't adopt it. If we do adopt it, it will get better. Why? Because wages will go up faster in Mexico if they adopt it, because they'll have more growth and because the trade agreement requires them to observe their own labor code, and the President has committed to raise the minimum wage every time economic growth goes up every year. Number two, for the first time their own environmental codes, which are pretty good on the books, will have to be enforced because they're in this trade agreement. This has never happened in the whole history of world trade where one country has said, you can put our environmental laws in the trade agreement and enforce them. We'll be able to do that.

The third thing I want to say to you is that you know this here in Kentucky because you trade so much. Wage rates are not the only thing that determine where smart people put their plants. Otherwise there would be no plants at all in Kentucky, and Haiti would have no unemployment rate. Right? I mean, you don't even have to take the Americans' word for it. Look at where Toyota is. Pretty close to here, right? BMW, where are they? South Carolina. Mercedes just made a decision; where did they go? To Mexico? No, to Alabama. Why? Because a study recently concluded on the auto industry shows that you can manufacture a car in America and put it in an American showroom for over $400 less than you can manufacture it in Mexico and put it in an American showroom, because our workers are more than 5 times more productive, and the transportation cost is less, even though the labor costs are higher.

We can compete and win. People talk all the time about the apparel industry because we phased out some of the protections on apparel and textiles. Do you know that we exported to Mexico $1.6 billion of textiles and apparels last year? We sent to them. They wanted to buy our stuff. Even there, we can compete when given the chance.

Now, will some people be dislocated? Yes, they will. Some people will be dislocated if we do nothing. Every year, Americans lose their jobs. And one of the tough parts of the world economy we're living in is that now, unlike it was 10 or 20 years ago, when people lose their jobs, they don't normally get back the same job they lost. They normally have to find a new job. That means that we owe you, those of us who are in Washington, we owe you a system of education and training and investment incentives that will help people to find new jobs. We have to do that, and we are going to do that.

The whole unemployment system today is a joke for the economy we're facing today. I know that, and I know we have to fix it. But that has to be done without regard to NAFTA. NAFTA creates jobs. NAFTA makes the problems we've got in our trade and investment with Mexico go down, not go up. NAFTA enables us—and this is the last point I want to make— NAFTA enables us to take this trade agreement with Mexico and extend it to other countries in Latin America who are democracies and believe in free market economics. And that's where the real jobs come in, when you've got a whole trading bloc from Canada all the way to the southern tip of Latin America, when you've got over 700 million people working together and trading together. And we know those people like Americans, like American products, and want to be a part of our future.

It is our insurance policy. We hope that we will have a new trade agreement by the end of the year when all nations, from Asia to Europe and all around, lower their barriers to our products. We hope that. But we know the people in Latin America like our people, like our culture, like our products, will buy them if they get a chance, and are dying to do it. And they are going to look at Congress and how we vote on this NAFTA legislation, and they're going to decide whether America is going to be a trustworthy, reliable leader and partner in the years ahead to make this world what it ought to be.

I have worked my heart out for this because I think it's good for your jobs and good for your children's future. And I don't think we can afford to cut and run. We cannot turn away from the world. If I thought for a minute that we could run off from this agreement and all the others and build a wall around this country and make jobs stable again and raise incomes, well then I would certainly do it because it would be in your interest. But it won't happen. You cannot run and hide from the world we are living in. So we better just rear back and do exactly what this company's doing: We're going to have to compete and win. I think we can do it. This is a big vote.

I compliment your Congressman for having the courage to be for this agreement. I hope you'll ask the other Members of the Kentucky delegation and the Senators to vote for it, because it will determine in large measure where we go as an economy over the next 10 years and whether we can escape this terrible trap that is gripping Japan and Europe and the United States of not being able to create enough jobs and not being able to raise people's incomes every year. We've got to turn it around. This is the first step, and I ask you to help us get it done.

Thank you very much.

We've got some microphones in the back. Who has the mikes? Raise your hands. Anybody have a question about this? There are some. Just go through and find people, and I'll go from mike to mike. Go ahead.

[*A participant asked if Mexico had similar tariffs on trade with the European Community and Asia and if Mexico might sign trade agreements with Europe and Asia if NAFTA did not pass.*]

The President. The answer to both questions is yes. And let me explain that. Let's just take computers because that's an easy example. If you take computers, there's a 20 percent tariff on all computers made outside of Mexico for sale in Mexico, on our products, on European products, on Japanese products. If this agreement goes through, the tariffs will be phased out on American products; they will maintain the same tariffs on Japanese and European products. So we will get a trade advantage over them in the Mexican market, in return for which they will get more access to American investment throughout their country.

If we don't do it, what will happen? They'll go get the money from Japan or Europe, and they'll give them the same deal. And they won't be nearly as concerned as we have been at what effect this has on American wages and on the environment, because they don't live next door to Mexico. I mean, what would you do? If I were the Finance Minister of Japan, on the day after Congress voted down the North American Free Trade Agreement, I'd get on an airplane and go to Mexico City and cut a deal. That's what I would do. And the risk of that is very high.

That's one reason why, in addition to these others—I should have said this in my talk— every living former President, every living former Secretary of State, every living former Secretary of the Treasury, every living Nobel Prize-winning economist, and 41 of the 50 Governors have endorsed this. You know, these economists, they disagree on more stuff than all the living former Presidents do. You might think any one of us would do something wrong to you, but surely not all of us would at the same time, right? [*Laughter*] And that's one reason.

Next question.

Q. Can NAFTA help improve exports to Japan and the European Community as well?

The President. It can indirectly, and let me tell you why. That's a very good question, and it's important. Let me explain, first of all, from the point of view of these other nations that have basically caught up to the United States since World War II. That's not all bad; that's enabled them to buy more of our products. But in Asia, most nations have developed by willfully keeping their wages down, getting very high savings rates, plowing back the savings into new plant and equipment and new products all the time. That's what they've done. When you do that, you don't have enough money to buy other people's products.

So Japan has a big trade surplus with us. They've been very good about investing in our country and putting our people to work, but they still don't buy as many of our products. This year, for the first time, we're selling some rice to them, for example, which is at least popular back where I come from. China has a $19 billion trade surplus with us—we buy 38 percent of all the exports of China, all of us do—Taiwan this year about $9 billion, although it goes up and down. Europe will have a trade deficit or a trade surplus with us. Sometimes they buy a lot more from us than they sell us, but they have to be growing to do it. Now their economies are flat.

Here's what I think will happen. I can't promise you this, but here's what I think will happen. If we adopt NAFTA, the rest of the world, Europe and Japan will see, "Well, America might have a whole trading bloc, from Canada down to the southern tip of South America, and we could be really at a disadvantage there. So we better adopt this new worldwide trading agreement they wanted, lower our tariffs, lower our barriers, let them sell into our markets so we'll have at least some access to the rest of the markets."

So I think NAFTA will be a huge indirect incentive for Japan and for Europe to reach an agreement on a new world trading system by the end of the year that I've been pushing for hard and that we've been working for, for years and years. If that happens, you will see a very large increase in the number of manufacturing jobs in America in a short time, just because Europe and Japan have so much more money than Mexico does. I mean, there's more of them, and they've got more money. So I think that would really be a godsend, and I think there's a good chance that it will happen.

[*A participant asked about programs to help displaced American workers.*]

The President. He said there's a big difference of opinion about what will happen in the long and the short run. Even if it's good for us in the long run, will we lose some jobs in the short run? What did we do for people who lost their jobs when I was in Arkansas? And what have we proposed to do with this NAFTA agreement? All good questions.

First, let me say what I think will happen in the long and short run, then let me answer the other two questions. And this is a complicated thing. There will still be people from the United States who will vest in factories in Mexico if this agreement goes through. But today when people invest in factories in Mexico, they invest along the American border in factories for the purpose of producing there and selling here. What the Mexicans want is to, in effect, erase that borderline and get investments in Mexico City to put people to work there to produce for the Mexican market, not for the American market. That's what they get out of this deal. And obviously, the more investment they get down there and the more jobs that are created and the more they sell to themselves, the higher their incomes will be and the more they'll be able to spend money on foreign

products, too.

Today—this is an astonishing thing—Mexico buys more American products per capita than any country in the world except Canada, even though it's still a poor country. That's because 70 percent of all the money they have to spend on foreign products gets spent on American products. So what I think will happen is, there will be more investment by Americans in Mexico, but instead of being along the border to make products to sell back here, it will be down in the country to make products to sell in the country. That will put more people to work. It will stabilize the population. Over the long run it will reduce illegal immigration and will increase their ability to buy our products.

Now, will some people be dislocated? Probably, because nearly every trade agreement that creates jobs costs some. When that happened at home, what we did was several things. First of all, we'd go into a community if it had high unemployment and actually offer to invest money at the State level to help attract new industries to that town. Then we would offer to share the cost of training the workers. And if it was a distressed community, we would also give them an enterprise zone that would give extra tax incentives to invest there.

What we're doing at the national level is to provide much more money for job retraining, number one. Number two, we're going to set up a development bank to try to get funds for indigenous businesses to start in areas that have been hurt by this, which I think is very important. And number three, we're going to have something we now—we don't call them enterprise zones, we call them empowerment zones at the Federal level—that we're going to locate in some of the most distressed communities in this country that will give huge incentives for people in the private sector to put Americans back to work in high unemployment areas. There is not enough Government money to fix all these problems. You've got to get the private sector to invest and put people back to work. So those are the three things we're working on doing now. That's a very good question.

Q. Since this is basically an extension of the U.S.-Canada trade agreement, what numerical benefits has the U.S. gained from the U.S.-Canadian trade agreement?

The President. Well, the trade agreement we have with Canada is—it is an extension of it, but what we did with Canada was to basically take more and more of our trade and put it into a free trade zone, that is, we took quotas off, we lowered tariffs. But Canada and the United States are both quite well-developed countries. So the main benefit that we got out of the Canada-U.S. trade agreement is we got to sell more of the things that we were really good at producing or had a low cost advantage in, they got to sell more of what they were good at producing or had a low cost advantage in, so that we essentially got to play to our strengths. And the volume in trade in both countries went way up.

Our trade with Canada is more or less in balance. But even when trade is in balance, it can be a great benefit to both countries if, by putting it in balance, it grows faster than your economy would have grown otherwise. In other words, if we added more economic growth and they added more economic growth, we both came out ahead. And that's been the primary benefit there.

In the case of Mexico, because they're at a different point in their development, in all probability we will continue to have a trade surplus with them, and they will get an investment advantage from us in the rest of their country. So I do think that the two countries are not too analogous now. I think 30 years from now they will be. But I think in the meanwhile—let me just say, the people in Mexico who are not for this deal, and there are people in Mexico who are not for it, they're not for it because they think that they're giving us a permanent trade surplus with them in return for having access to our capital, because Mexicans like American products so much.

So there will be a difference there. In other words, they can't possibly quite enter into the same relationship with us that Canada did because they're not capable, their economy's not big enough or diverse enough yet. The Mexican economy, even though 90 million people live there, is about the size of the California economy from Los Angeles to the Mexican border. That's about how big it is, about one-twentieth the American economy.

Q. Good afternoon, Mr. President. Thank you for coming to Lexmark. We certainly appreciate it. I'd like to take us into the future, say, maybe 1996, the month October, Hillary is ahead by maybe five points in the—no, I understand that you'll be running for reelection; hopefully, Congressman Baesler will be right there with you.

The President. I don't know; this has turned out to be a hard job. [*Laughter*] Go ahead.

[*The participant then asked about possible legislation to help displaced workers.*]

The President. The people who are specifically displaced, there are only three things you can do for them in my opinion, that I can think of, anyway. And I've been working at this now for the better part of 20 years, on and off. One is, they should have access to a system of training and education that is much more effective than the one we have today. The Federal Government's got 150 different employment training programs. The unemployment system, as all of you know, still works like it used to: You get an unemployment check, and you're supposed to basically check around and see if you can find a new job. But the idea is, people wait until the benefits run out, hoping their old employer will call them back. That used to happen; it doesn't happen much anymore. What we're going to do is to construct a system that will give anybody who loses their job because of a trade-related dislocation access to a much better training program, much more quickly, tied to identifying those areas where the jobs are growing in number anywhere within driving distance of them, first thing.

Secondly, we're going to have a development bank, a North American development bank which will concentrate its activities in areas where there have been substantial job losses to try to start new job enterprises there.

The third thing we're going to do is to develop special investment incentives targeted to those areas where the jobs have been lost. Those are the only things that I can think of that we can do, except to give you a healthy economy that's producing more jobs.

One of the things that makes this so frightening to people is that it used to be—I mean, when I was a kid, when somebody lost their job, when the country had a 3 percent unemployment rate, that was like having zero unemployment, because there were 3 percent of the people who were moving around all the time. Now when people lose their jobs, they're afraid they'll never get another one or they'll never get another one paying as much as the one that they just lost. So we have a much heavier responsibility.

The answer to your question is that you should be able to see these specific programs on the books not by October of '96 but by the end of the budget cycle in '94; we should have passed these programs and put them in place for those folks, because that's when you'll begin to see it. In other words, when we adopt the trade agreement the end of this year, we have $90 million set aside right now for extra training investment for those folks in the short run, to buy us a year and a half to enact a new training program and investment strategy. But we should be able to get it done by the end of '94 when Congress goes home; that's our goal. And if I could plug my wife a bit, if we provide health care security to all of them, that'll also be a huge incentive, because then at least they won't lose that for their children.

Q. Welcome to Lexmark, Mr. President. My question is, do you have any concerns, if there are any concerns, about Canada's recent leadership change being—and it is an anti-NAFTA leadership change. Are you concerned about that?

The President. Basically, no. We've had a lot of conversations with the new leader of Canada and the new party. He raised a lot of the same questions about NAFTA that I did. And when I called him—I mean, what I wanted to do with this trade agreement, and I guess I ought to tell you that, I wanted to have three things added to the agreement, which have been added. One is, I wanted to know that there would be some device by which we could make sure the Mexicans were moving to enforce their own labor code so that we would raise labor standards on both sides of the border. We have that now.

Secondly, I wanted to know that they would enforce their environmental laws, because they weren't now. Their environmental code is actually pretty good, but it's not being enforced. So we set up a mechanism for doing that and a financing mechanism to get the money to do it.

The third thing I wanted was a provision that would take account of unintended consequences. And that really goes to something that two or three of you have asked about. That is, suppose all these brilliant people who have been negotiating this turn out to be wrong about something, not just for us but for them, too? I mean, suppose within a year after this deal takes effect, there's some small but not insignificant part of their economy or ours that seems to be on the verge of just vanishing like that, something no

one foresaw? This agreement has a provision to put the brakes on that and to reinstitute the former system as it applies to that sector of the economy for a period of 3 years while we work it out. So there's a protection against unintended consequences.

And the last thing I guess I ought to say is, suppose any party becomes convinced that the others are proceeding in bad faith; you can pull out with 6 months notice. That's another thing most Americans don't know. This is not the enemy. In other words, if somebody turns out to be lying or some development turns out to be unanticipated, there are ways to correct this.

Now, to go back to your specific question, Canada likes what we did on the environmental agreement, on the labor agreement; they wanted that done. They now have substantially, to the best of my knowledge, no more problems with Mexico. They have some outstanding problems with us in trade, which we are negotiating through now. We do not believe that it will be in any way necessary to reopen the agreement to resolve those problems, and we're working hard on them and we have been this week. So I feel pretty optimistic that it'll be okay.

Let's get over here. Give equal time to the other folks here.

Q. Mr. President, many Americans and American companies are concerned with intellectual property rights, and particularly in the Mexican market. Has there been any provision in NAFTA to address that?

The President. Yes. The NAFTA agreement offers protections for intellectual property rights and for investment, which I think are quite important. You know, the intellectual property rights may sound esoteric to some of you, may sound like somebody wants to write a book and not have it copied, and that's part of it. But it's also part of the software business and part of anything that comes out of people's creative skills. It's a big part of America's economic advantage in the world is that we develop all these ideas.

And I've just been working to try to open other markets for a lot of our products that were closed during the cold war because we were worried about letting other people get our technology or our ideas. And we've just taken the wraps off $37 billion a year worth of computers, supercomputers, and telecommunications equipment. And we're looking at some others, some software and things like that. And one of the problems is protecting the intellectual property rights of our people around the world. But I think you will find that the provisions there on intellectual property substantially improve what happens now there.

Q. Mr. President, I haven't seen too many things in my life that Republicans and Democrats have agreed on. You may have noticed some of that in Washington. Doesn't it scare you when your opponents suddenly become friendly? And also, are there some human rights demands in this thing?

The President. He's worried about the agreement because the Republicans and Democrats agree on it, right?

Let me just say, first of all, back when I was a Governor I had much less partisanship to contend with than I do in Washington. It seems to be a disease that grips the water up there. But I think what happens, I think all these people who have served as President, when they get out and they have no other personal agenda really, by and large, and they look on their country and they look at the rest of the world, and most people, after they've been President and they can't run for anything else or do much else in terms of their personal ambition or politically, I think that they really are saying what they honestly believe to be in the best interests of the country.

Now, there are a lot of people who have criticized the NAFTA agreement, coming out of the labor movement, particularly, on the grounds that there are violations of human rights in Mexico or the Mexican system is not as democratic as ours is. It is different from ours and not as open and democratic as ours. But it is becoming more democratic. Again, I think if we shut them off from us, it is likely to become less democratic.

We do a lot of trade with a lot of other countries that are not as close to us politically as they are. I mean, we've had a lot of political problems, for example, with China after Tiananmen Square. But we keep buying a lot of products from them, and most American business interests have asked us to continue to do it. And many American labor interests have asked us to continue to do it because we're beginning to invest over there and get some markets over there.

I think we have to be mindful of that. And if we think that there are abuses of human rights

anywhere, we should stand up to them. And I've tried to do that. But I don't think, given the dramatic improvements in the people who, on that score, who are operating in Mexico in the last several years, I don't think that that's a good argument to run away from this trade agreement.

That is, to me, the Salinas government and the man who was there before him started a move away from their anti-American, single-party, hunker-down, isolate-from-the-world, operate-in-ways-that-we-don't-consider-acceptable system, to one that's more pro-American, more open, and more democratic. I think they are moving in our direction. I think if we reject them, they will develop a different strategy, and it'll make it less likely that they will grow in human rights and democracy observance.

Q. It's been estimated that this is going to require $2.4 billion in funding over the next 5 years. How do your propose that we generate that funding?

The President. I don't think it will. What will it require the money for? What's the money going to be spent on? They keep throwing these dollars around. What money will be required?

Q. The lack of tariffs, what we're charging on tariffs now, funding for the programs that would be for the displaced jobs, et cetera.

The President. Over the next 5 years, I'll tell you what I think it will cost. The tariffs are a tax, essentially, and we're going to reduce the tariffs; that costs $2.5 billion over 5 years. The package that we sent up to the Congress will replace those tariffs by having a temporary fee of $1.50 on foreign travel, air travel coming into the United States, and by changing some of the ways we collect customs and things of that kind. They will make up the $2.5 billion.

Then, we think that the training programs will cost about $90 million in the first year, and then thereafter more. But they will be funded next year in the budget cycle, in the ordinary course of planning the Federal budget, not massive amounts.

On the environmental cost, we've now got an agreement with the World Bank to finance through appropriate loans several billion dollars' worth of environmental cleanup in Mexico which will be paid back presumably by the polluters themselves in Mexico; they have to work out the repayment terms.

Now, that will be the lion's share of it. There may be some environmental obligations on us that are not yet fully paid for, but they won't get up to anywhere near the figure you mentioned. And we have a border commission with some money in the till there, a few hundred million dollars, and some other bonding options that we have to fund the environmental costs. So we've covered the loss of tariffs in the bill now before the Congress, the training programs will be covered as part of the training initiative I present to the Congress next year, and the only other issue we have to worry about is whatever comes up over the next 5 years in environmental costs that we have to pay for in America; that is usually done by asking the people who do the pollution to pay the lion's share of cleaning it up through making bond payments. So I think we're going to be okay on that.

A lot of the costs have been way overstated, in my view, based on what we know.

Marvin Mann. I hesitate to interrupt this important discussion, but we here at Lexmark have a serious problem.

The President. You've got to go back to work? [*Laughter*]

Mr. Mann. Our laser printers are so hot in the marketplace that people want more of them than we can build. And so these people are going to be mad at me. They're going to be upset at me if I don't let them get back to work soon. [*Laughter*] So please take one more question, and then we probably ought to close.

Q. It's my understanding that some tariffs will still be in place after the agreement comes into effect. My question is what percentage of goods going each way will still have tariffs on them immediately after, and then after 5 years?

The President. Most of them will be all gone after 5 years. I can't answer that, but I'll get you an answer. If you give me your address, I'll sent you a specific answer to it.

Let me tell you, this was a part of the negotiation, but some of the particularly sensitive items that were clearly felt by one side or the other to need a longer period of time to get to where they could fully compete were given more time. There are a few things where the phaseout goes all the way to 7 years or 10 years. But by and large, there are substantial reductions in the tariffs immediately, and almost all the reductions occur within the first 3 years.

And let me just back up and say, while the products that we've mentioned here, and I think all the products that are produced by any of these folks at these five companies that could

be sold into Mexico, have a 20 percent tariff, some Mexican products are less. And the average Mexican tariff is just a little over 10 percent. But a lot of the stuff where we've got real hot opportunities, that's a 20 percent tariff. So that's why I've been so interested in them. Our average tariff on their products is 4 percent.

Where there is a longer phaseout period, it's normally because we have something called a nontariff barrier, that is, an absolute limit on how much can come in. That's normally on textiles and apparel. So there's a longer period of phaseout there to make sure that there's more of an opportunity to adjust to whatever the competitive developments are, so that we don't just throw cold water on them.

I wish I could stay all day. You guys have been great. I hope you will support this. It means more jobs for this country.

And also, don't forget, one of the things I want to emphasize again, it didn't come up in the questions. When I was at the United Nations a few weeks ago, I had a reception for the leaders of all the other Latin American countries who were there. And I can tell you that Argentina and Chile and Venezuela and Colombia and Bolivia and a lot of other countries that are struggling to maintain democracy want to open up markets with us, and they want to buy our products. Tiny Colombia, in the last 2 years, has increased their purchase of American products by 69 to 64 percent a year. This is a big deal. But if we don't do NAFTA, they'll wonder whether we're really serious about embracing all of Latin America.

Again, I say I hope you will support it. I do believe that it will give us in the short term a competitive advantage over the Europeans and the Japanese. But the most important thing is it will pressure them to adopt a new worldwide trade agreement. American workers are now the most productive in the world. You've got to believe in yourselves. We can do this. We can compete. We can win if we have access to the markets. That's what this gives us.

Thank you very much. We need your help.

NOTE: The President spoke at 1:45 p.m. on the production floor. He was introduced by employee Roberta Canady. In his remarks, he referred to Marvin L. Mann, president and chief executive officer, Lexmark International, Inc. A portion of the question-and-answer session could not be verified because the tape was incomplete.

Announcement of Senior Executive Service Appointments
November 4, 1993

The President today approved seven men and women for Senior Executive Service posts at the Department of Housing and Urban Development, the Department of Labor, and the Agency for International Development, U.S. International Development Cooperation Agency.

"I am pleased to announce the addition of these hard-working men and women to my administration," the President said.

Department of Housing and Urban Development

Jeanne K. Engel, General Deputy Assistant Secretary for Housing, Federal Housing Commissioner

Art Agnos, Regional Administrator, Region IX

Margery Austin Turner, Deputy Assistant Secretary for Research, Evaluation, and Monitoring, Office of Policy Development and Research

Department of Labor

Edmundo A. Gonzales, Deputy Assistant Secretary, Office of the American Workplace

Oliver B. Quinn, Deputy Solicitor of Labor, Office of the Solicitor

U.S. International Development Cooperation Agency

Nan Borton, Director, Office of Foreign Disaster Assistance, Bureau for Food & Humanitarian Assistance, Agency for International Development

Ramon E. Daubon, Deputy Assistant Administrator, Bureau of Latin America and the Caribbean, Agency for International Development

NOTE: Biographies of the appointees were made available by the Office of the Press Secretary.

Remarks on Establishing the Bipartisan Commission on Entitlement Reform and an Exchange With Reporters
November 5, 1993

The President. First of all, I want to thank the leaders of Congress who are here and make a couple of comments, if I might. I am delighted that now both Houses have acted on the crime legislation. I congratulate the House and the Senate, and I look forward to working with them on getting the strongest possible crime bill out we can and hopefully meeting that goal that I have had for a long time now of putting another 100,000 police officers on the street, which I am convinced will do more in less time to lower the crime rate than anything else. I also hope that we can now move forward to a debate in the Senate and the House on the Brady bill. I hope that it will pass before the Senate goes home and the House goes home.

Finally, let me make one other preliminary comment. During all the debates on the budget, many of which were acrimonious and partisan, there was virtually 100 percent understanding on the part of every Member of Congress that, over the long run, our ability to bring our budg-

et closer to balance and to free up money for needed investments required us to take a hard look at the entitlements part of our budget.

The budget that we have just adopted has been very successful in many ways. It's helped to bring interest rates to historically low levels. We've got investment coming back into the country. We have more jobs coming back in. But we don't have the money to invest in new ventures that might be important to our national defense or to our economic growth and that's because we had to adopt steep defense cuts and a hard freeze on domestic spending for 5 years while the entitlement growth continued unchecked.

As a result of that, today I am establishing by Executive order a bipartisan commission to look into the issue of entitlements of our Government, how it works and what's the impact on the budget long-term, as well as into the general tax structure of the Federal Government. I want to acknowledge and thank the leaders, Republican and Democrat, of the House and the Senate for agreeing to support this Commission and name members to it. Two-thirds of the members will be appointed by the congressional leadership on a strictly bipartisan basis. I will appoint a third.

And then I want to give special attention to two Members of the Congress who have worked on this very hard. One is Senator Kerrey, who had the idea for this Commission, and I intend to name him the Chair. The other is Senator Danforth of Missouri, who is in his last term but has been interested in the entitlement issue for a very long time, and I have asked him to serve as the Vice Chair. We will be naming the rest of the Commission in the fairly near future. But I'm hopeful that this Commission, by next spring, will be able to do some work which will chart a future for the Congress and for the country, which will enable us to do the people's business up here and keep the country moving forward into the 21st century.

So I thank all the leadership for their willingness to support this. And I'm going to sign the Executive order and then we'll answer a few questions and get on with our meeting, because there's a vote in the Senate.

[At this point, the President signed the Executive order.]

NAFTA Television Debate

Q. Mr. President, why are you putting the Vice President up against the king of the one-liners? Aren't you sacrificing a political career here?

The President. Let me say this, I certainly appreciate the way you characterized it. If we get an honest discussion of the issues, the Vice President will do just fine because he's an accomplished debater and, more importantly, because he's got the evidence on his side. I understand why Mr. Perot wanted to have a rally packed with people that he could get there who already had their minds made up against NAFTA. But I think the Vice President's issued the challenge to show up in Florida and have Larry King moderate the debate. And if we get a genuine discussion of the issues, I'm very confident that he'll do fine. It was his idea; I've got to compliment him. It wasn't mine. Wasn't it?

The Vice President. Absolutely——

Q. Why do you feel it's necessary to take on Ross Perot to do what many people would consider sinking to his level?

The President. Why are you sinking to his level, Mr. Vice President? *[Laughter]* Why did you want to do that?

The Vice President. I think the country does this from a discussion of the facts about NAFTA. What we're finding is that a whole lot of people in the Congress say, "We agree with you on the facts, but we're getting a lot of political pressure on the other side. Is there any way that you can get the facts out to a wider audience?" And I think the discussion of what NAFTA really does—it creates new jobs in America. The volume of our products being shipped to Mexico has been increasing twice as fast as the volume of their goods being shipped here. The more discussion of the facts, the better.

Q. Are you going to do one debate or three, Mr. Vice President?

The Vice President. Well, I've contacted Larry King and said that—first of all, I issued this challenge; he accepted and proposed Florida. I said I'll be there on Sunday. I contacted Larry King. And we want a neutral format and a neutral place. I don't want to go to a rally filled with 20,000 people on one side of the issue. He was generous to say that he would buy the television time. Well, let's let Larry King provide the television time.

Senator Mitchell. Why don't you pay for the television time?

The Vice President. I considered that—*[laughter]*—I considered just picking up the tab.

Q. Mr. President, aren't you the slightest bit concerned, not the least bit worried?

The President. No. We're making progress on NAFTA. I feel good about it. And what we find is that if people—I went yesterday, when he was having a press conference saying I wouldn't answer questions from ordinary workers. I was with a thousand ordinary working people in Kentucky answering their questions. They were good questions, good, firm, hard questions. But I just believe that this is one of those issues where the truth will set you free. I think the more people know, the more they'll be for it.

We have confidence. The Vice President, actually, when he went on David Letterman, .I knew that he could stick up Ross Perot on one-liners, right? So, that's it.

Thank you very much.

NOTE: The President spoke at 10:44 a.m. in the Cabinet Room at the White House. The Executive order is listed in Appendix D at the end of this volume.

Teleconference on NAFTA With Midwest Farmers, Ranchers, and Agricultural Broadcasters and an Exchange With Reporters
November 5, 1993

The President. Hello?

Q. Hello, Mr. President.

The President. How are you?

Q. Well, pretty good today, sir. How are you?

The President. I'm great. Thank you for taking this time to visit with us.

Q. Thank you for affording us the opportunity.

The President. I know that all of you have some questions, but I'd like to make just a brief opening statement, if I might. As all of you know, I think, before I took this job I was a Governor of an agricultural State, and I learned very early that the future of agriculture in America is in exports. We've got over 700,000 agriculture jobs in America today that are export-related. And if NAFTA passes, that number will continue to rise, meaning more jobs for people in our farm communities.

I know now that a big part of my job as President is going to be to continue to raise more and more opportunities for exports in America, and I'm doing that and the negotiations we have going on with Japan now, we even have some hopes that we're going to be able to sell some rice in Japan before too long, which is a big issue for farmers in my part of the country.

We're working hard across the board to get a new GATT agreement that will open agricultural markets for our farmers. And NAFTA is a part of our comprehensive strategy to boost farm income.

Since 1986, our agricultural exports to Mexico have nearly tripled. Mexico is now our fastest growing major export market. In 1992 we exported almost $4 billion worth of products to Mexico, 40 percent higher than 1990. And the Agriculture Department—and Secretary Espy is here with me today as you know—estimates that we will export $2.6 billion more with NAFTA

than without it by the end of the transition period in the agreement.

So I think this is a good deal for our farmers. It's an even better deal this week than it was last week because of some of the agreements made by the Mexican Government affecting sugar and citrus and, to a lesser extent, vegetables. But it is clearly a good thing for America's farmers. That's why most of the major farm groups have endorsed it. And I'm looking forward to discussing it with the farmers today and with the people from the ag radio networks. So maybe we ought to get right into your questions and go forward.

I think Howard Hardecke is first. Is that right?

Q. That is correct, Mr. President.

The President. I remember when I was at your school.

Q. You're kidding.

The President. [*Inaudible*]—it was a great night.

Q. Yes, it was.

The President. My second grade teacher was there. I hadn't seen her since she left Arkansas. She was my second and third grade teacher. I really enjoyed that.

[*At this point, Mr. Hardecke asked if other cattle-producing countries could import cattle duty-free through Mexico under NAFTA.*]

The President. That's a good question. And believe it or not, it's a question that applies not only to agriculture but to some of our manufacturing. We have strict rules of origin that apply to our agriculture as you know already——

Q. Yes.

The President. ——and there is nothing in the NAFTA agreement which changes that, so that the rules of origin that apply to Australian beef coming here directly would apply to them with equal force after NAFTA passes if they pass through Mexico. In other words, there's no loophole in the agreement to escape our rules of origin. So you'll be all right with that.

Q. Okay, appreciate it.

The President. Thank you. Terry Baer, are you next?

Q. Yes, sir.

The President. Howard, did you have another question? I want to make sure I've got this right, now.

Q. We were told we had one question, so——

The President. Okay. Well, go ahead, Terry.

Q. Okay. Greetings, Mr. President, from central Illinois. I live near Edelstein, Illinois, which is near Peoria in central Illinois, and I have a grain production operation, consisting of corn and soybeans, and then I also work at Caterpillar, Inc., in Peoria.

The President. Good for you. I've been there.

Q. Yes well, I personally met you there when you were campaigning.

The President. It's a great company.

Q. Yes it is, and I'm glad they're as close to my farm as they are. It works out real well.

The President. It cuts the transportation cost of the equipment, too, doesn't it?

Q. It sure does. So, Mr. President, I have a question on NAFTA for you. And that is, if NAFTA does not pass, what efforts do you see of Mexico forming treaties with other countries who also compete for the same markets as our U.S. farmers, and what effect might that have on our future farm economy and foreign competition for our U.S. products?

The President. I think it'll make it a lot tougher on us. Keep in mind Mexico has been opening its economy, its purchases of foreign products have been going up across the board. They want to give us some special opportunities to export into the Mexican market in return for being able to attract more investment to their country. So they will have to pursue their strategy of getting more investment and opening their markets to get it somewhere else if we don't take advantage of this. And, therefore, it could be an enormous setback for us. It would just give our competitors a big leg up in one of the fastest growing markets in the world.

And of course, depending on whom they reached out to, it could really hurt the farmers. If the European Community, for example, decided that they would try to replace the United States in NAFTA, it could really foreclose a lot of farm markets. You know all the troubles we've been through just trying to get a new GATT agreement. I'm very, very concerned about it.

I would also point out to all the farmers who are listening that we believe if we do NAFTA, and Mexico as the example will lead us to the same opportunities in other Latin American countries with big possibilities for agricultural exports of all kinds. So I think it's a big plus if we do it, but frankly I think we have to face the fact that Mexico has got to have a plan B. And if we turn out to be unreliable, if we can't see through this trade agreement, they will be forced to turn elsewhere to try to get capital and in return for that will almost certainly be willing to give the same kind of extra access to their market that the United States now has just for the asking if we'll go ahead and adopt this agreement.

Q. Well, I agree with you if they do seek treaties with other countries and we fail to ratify NAFTA, it will put us at a big disadvantage. And so you feel that Mexico is aggressively seeking agreements whether it's with us or whether it's with our competitors.

The President. Right now they've aggressively sought it with us. But they've made it clear, and they've been very much willing to let us put some things in this trade agreement, I might add, that have never been in any other trade agreement. I mean, they've agreed with us to invest more money in cleaning up the environment and to subject their own environmental code to the trade controls of this agreement. They've agreed to do the same thing with their labor code. No other country's ever done that in a trade agreement. So they very much want to deal with the United States. Mexican people like American products of all kinds. They are now the second biggest per capita purchasers of American products, even though their incomes aren't very high. We sell over $40 billion worth of stuff down there every year. Seventy cents of every dollar the Mexicans spend on foreign products are spent on American products. And we have a chance to dramatically increase that or run the risk of shutting it down. And I think it would be a terrible mistake to turn away from it.

Q. Yeah, I agree, and rest assured that I will do all I can to help you get this passed. I would hate to think that our U.S. Congress would pass up a chance at free trade.

The President. Also good for Caterpillar, you know. Caterpillar's one of the greatest exporting companies in the whole United States.

Q. Yeah, I realize that.

The President. One of the few companies that's been able to really triumph in the Japanese market. And the more per capita income goes up in Mexico, the better that company will do, too. I appreciate that. Thank you very much.

Q. Thank you.

Secretary Espy. Mr. President, could I just jump right in one second just to agree with you.

The President. Sure.

[*Secretary Espy stated that Mexico is interested in expanding the trade relationship with the United States but would quickly look elsewhere should NAFTA fail.*]

The President. Is Bill Wheeler on the phone?

Q. Hello, Mr. President. Hello, Secretary Espy.

The President. You calling us from Montana?

Q. Yes sir, from Missoula, Montana. That's the western part of the State.

The President. I've been there. I know it well.

Q. Well, we hope that you see fit to come again. We would extend the invitation certainly.

The President. Thank you.

[*Mr. Wheeler described the regional impact on grain producers of Canadian grains crossing the border under the Canada-United States Free Trade Agreement and asked if NAFTA would rectify that situation.*]

The President. Well, let me first of all say that the agreement itself won't rectify it, but it will make it somewhat better, and by opening other markets it'll make a big difference. Let me make three or four comments. First of all, for all the others that are listening, there's been a special problem with a lot of our farmers in the northern part—[*inaudible*]—especially the wheat farmers, because of exports from Canada and because the support of the prices in Canada comes primarily in transportation supports, something that were not covered. Those supports were not covered when the United States negotiated its agreement with Canada several years ago.

Now, under this agreement, there will be certain provisions which should help to address the problem a little bit, such as end use certificates for Canadian imports that will help improve it. [*Inaudible*]—no, in an attempt to offset the impact of the Canadian imports, I approved export enhancement supports for American wheat to Mexico recently.

Thirdly, I've asked the Secretary of Agriculture, now that there's been a Canadian election and there's a new Canadian Agriculture Minister ready to take office, to go to Canada and to sit down and meet with him about this issue, because it is not covered by the agreement, to see what we can do to go forward.

The last thing I'd like to say is, I think that the prices are going to go up here in America if we adopt the NAFTA agreement, because the primary thing NAFTA does is to give us access to sell more of our wheat and other grain crops to Mexico so that we'll have access to that market, and that will help to not only provide more sales but, as you know, increase the price.

So I think it will be better, but it does not specifically address the provision you don't like from the Canadian agreement that was made several years ago. We're going to try to do that in these negotiations the Secretary of Agriculture is going to undertake. And I think we sent a signal to the Canadians that we're concerned about it when we use the export enhancement program to try to sell some of our wheat to Mexico to offset what had happened to the farmers.

Q. Well, Mr. President, if Congress approves NAFTA, when will NAFTA go into effect, and will all parties involved sign simultaneously?

The President. The answer is, it'll go into effect everywhere at the same time. But the different provisions are phased in over several years.

Mike, were you going to say something?

[*Secretary Espy acknowledged several weak points in the Canada-United States Free Trade Agreement and indicated that NAFTA did not have those weak points.*]

The President. But to go back to your question, if we can pass it now, it will go into effect starting the first of 1994, at the beginning of the next year. But there are some provisions that are phased in. We will get the lion's share of the benefits from the tariff reductions almost immediately, and we'll see a big increase in American exports in 1994 if it goes in. But there are some things—for example, some of our markets phase out their protection over a period of 7 or 8 years.

Q. Thank you, Mr. President.

The President. Thanks.

Now, Murray Corriher? Is that right?

Q. China Grove, North Carolina.

The President. Where is that?

[*Mr. Corriher briefly described economic conditions working against farmers and asked if NAFTA would increase prices enough to allow them to stay in business.*]

The President. The answer to that is, it should. Having lived on a farm and having been a Governor of a farm State for many years, I've learned never to say that something will increase farm prices. But the answer is that it should for this reason: There's no question that American exports will increase in the aggregate if NAFTA passes, and that Mexico is our fastest growing farm export market. Normally, when there's an increased demand for products abroad, that has an impact in increasing prices at home. That is, unless there is something that happens here at home that dramatically reduces domestic consumption, increasing demand abroad will increase the prices, because the aggregate supply and demand relationship will change. So it should happen.

Secondly, farmers should have their prices rise because they'll recover some of the monies that now go to tariffs in their trade. And we know that that will have some positive impact.

So for those reasons, I certainly would be real surprised if there was not an increase in the price and an increase in farm profits. You know, most Americans don't know this, but when the cost of production goes up 5 times as fast as the price of the product, the only way the farmers or any farmers are still in business in America is that we have the most productive farmers in the world. But there is a limit to how much you can do, and one of the things I like about NAFTA is, by giving the tariff relief and by increasing the total volume of agricultural sales, we should be able to have a positive impact on the price.

Q. I certainly hope so.

The President. I do, too. I wouldn't be for this if I didn't think it was going to help you, and I think it will.

Q. I wouldn't be for it, either, if I didn't think it would help.

The President. Thank you, Murray.

Q. Thank you.

The President. I think we're supposed to turn to the broadcasters now, and I think we're staying in North Carolina.

Bill Ray?

Q. Yes, Mr. President.

The President. You're from Elizabeth City, North Carolina?

Q. That's true. We sure are. The question that I had for you, Mr. President, this afternoon is, how do you think NAFTA will affect U.S. positions of negotiations at the GATT? What happens if this thing doesn't pass?

The President. It weakens our ability to get a GATT agreement by the end of the year because—well, let me back up and say I think most farmers know we're worked real hard to open up more European markets and other ag markets. As I said earlier, we're working hard to make some progress in the Asian markets, in Japan, especially, with some of our products. The GATT agreement is critical to that. If we beat NAFTA, then other countries who are reluctant to support GATT will say, "Well, look at America. They're becoming more protectionist. Why shouldn't we?" On the other hand, if we pass NAFTA, it will dramatically increase our credibility in the GATT negotiations. And it will reinforce our commitment and, I think, give a lot of courage to people in the European countries who want to do the same thing. The truth is that we've had so many hard economic years that nearly everybody thinks we're in a sort of a win-lose situation, that there's no such thing as a win-win trade agreement. But no wealthy country, whether it's the United States or the European countries or Japan and Asia, can grow and increase incomes unless you increase the volume of world trade. That's the only way we can do it today.

So we need the GATT agreement. It will help us in the short run, in terms of jobs, even more than NAFTA because it involves so many more people. Over the long run, NAFTA's going to help us because it will bring in all of Latin America. But if we don't adopt NAFTA in November, it's going to be hard to get the GATT done in December. And I can't promise that every country is going to agree in December, regardless. But we will have a much, much better chance to pass that GATT deal if Congress will adopt NAFTA. And that's a huge thing for America's jobs and incomes.

Q. Mr. President, it looks like it would be

really tough on Mickey Kantor if he has to go back to Brussels without a NAFTA deal.

The President. It will be tough on him. Right after the NAFTA vote, I'm going out to Washington State to meet with the leaders of many of the Pacific countries, trying to convince them to buy more of our products and trying to work out a new trade relationship there. And again, if NAFTA passes, I'll have a lot of leverage in dealing with that. If it doesn't pass, it will make it more difficult for me to argue that the United States is trying to lead a big, broad-based coalition of trading nations. And after all that we've been through in the 1980's with our industries changing and restructuring, we now in agriculture and in industry are the most productive country in the world. We can sell anywhere. We can do well even in the countries with wages much lower than ours if we just have access to the markets.

So this GATT thing is a big deal. And if we pass NAFTA, I'll have a lot better chance of bringing home that bacon along with Ambassador Kantor.

The next person is, I think, Max Armstrong in Chicago.

Q. Hi, Mr. President.

The President. How you doing?

[*Mr. Armstrong asked if Mexican producers would be held to the same standard as American producers in areas such as pesticides and food safety requirements.*]

The President. Yes. Absolutely. And I might say a related thing, since you're calling me from Chicago and we've got a lot of teamsters in the upper Middle West and a lot of trucking enterprises: If a Mexican truck driver under this agreement stays with a load of produce, agricultural produce, or an industrial product or anything else, crossing from Mexico into the United States, then that truck driver must meet all the same standards that an American driver would have to meet on an American highway.

Our standards control, whether it's on the safety of food or on the safety on our highways. And that's very important. That's one of the things that we worked hard—and the flip side is true, too. We have to comply with their standards when operating in their country or when selling food into their country. And one of the biggest problems we had, one of the reasons that I insisted on these side agreements before I would agree to present this trade agreement

to Congress is that Mexico, historically, has had some good laws on the books that weren't vigorously enforced. And so what we wanted to make sure of was that, not only would our laws be observed on food coming into our country but that they would observe their own laws, just as we have to observe ours.

So I think that, overall, the quality of all of these operations will go up if we honor that.

Q. So there should be no concern among U.S. consumers about quality?

The President. Absolutely not. No. We are not going to permit food to be sold here which does not meet the standards that American food has to meet.

And, by the way, we import other food from a lot of other countries now, and it's the same thing there. We didn't change that at all, and we wouldn't think of it.

Q. Thank you, Mr. President.

The President. Is Taylor Brown next?

Q. Yes, Mr. President, thank you.

The President. And you're from Billings, Montana?

Q. Sure am. I'm a long way from Bill Wheeler, but we're in the same State.

The President. You sure are. I've been to Billings, too. It's the third biggest State, isn't it?

[*Mr. Brown asked about planned action on the issue of Canadian grain imports.*]

The President. Let me tell you what I think I should do first. And let me remind you, when I came into office, I raised this issue. I acknowledged it. Our Trade Representative embraced it. To send a signal to the Canadians that we were serious about this, we used the export enhancement program to give our own wheat an advantage down in Mexico. We also did it with barley. So I know this is a problem, and I've tried to send a clear signal to the Canadians that we intend to see it addressed.

If you've been following this in the last few days, you know they've got some issues that they want to discuss with us, also, that don't have anything to do with the NAFTA agreement, but two-way trade agreement between the United States and Canada. So I have asked the Secretary of Agriculture to go up there, and before we take any further action, at least sit down face to face with the new government, hear them out, and have them hear us out.

The reason I want to do that is because we do have, still, a significant trade surplus in agriculture with Canada through bread, pasta, and other processed foods, including products that contain American wheat. I've always followed the policy that before I put another person I'm dealing with in a position of retaliating, at least they have to know where we're coming from and why. So I want the Secretary of Agriculture to go up there and sit down and try to work through this.

But there is no question that when the last agreement was made several years ago with Canada, we did not reach to the subsidies that relate to their transportation and to the unique way in which the Canadian Wheat Board operates, which every wheat farmer in America now understands and which puts our folks in a difficult position.

I will say again, on the NAFTA agreement, whatever you think about that, this is a net advantage to an American wheat farmer because it opens more products, more markets to American wheat. And so it'll certainly help, and it'll help to get the price up.

Mike, do you want to say anything else about what you're going to do?

[*Secretary Espy said he would continue to work on those problems.*]

The President. Is George Lawson on the phone?

Q. Yes, Mr. President.

The President. Are you calling from Wichita?

Q. Yes, sir. Can you hear me okay?

The President. I can hear you fine.

Q. Mrs. Clinton and Vice President Gore were in Wichita during the campaign. I hope you'll get a chance to visit our all-American city at some point.

The President. I'd like to. I was there a couple of years ago, and I really enjoyed it. It's a beautiful town.

Q. Can you explain for us how NAFTA will be able to add jobs to the U.S. agriculture sector?

The President. Yes, and let me say since you're in Wichita, I might just mention we talked a lot about wheat and grains and how the markets will grow there as the tariffs go down. But I also think, given where you are and the people that listen in mid-America AgNet, I ought to emphasize that Mexico is also one of the fastest growing markets for American wheat—I mean American meat, especially processed meat products. And all these

exports will increase with NAFTA because the tariff on beef will be phased out to zero.

Mexico already accounts for about a quarter of U.S. pork exports, and as the tariffs go down, incomes go up, we'll expand those exports to Mexico. Poultry exports have increased from $16 million in 1987 to over $153 million in 1992, and that demand is just growing like wildfire. And interestingly enough, it's a nice compliment to the American consumption habits, because of the preference for different kinds of meat. So, I think you're going to see obviously more grains, just pure and simple, because the tariffs are coming down and because we've got access to the market and we can get the grain there in a hurry and efficiently. But I also want to emphasize there's going to be a big increase in meat exports, too.

[*Secretary Espy added that increased exports to Mexico would lead to the creation of jobs in the United States.*]

The President. Is Rodney Peeples—Roddy Peeples?

Q. That's correct, Mr. President.

The President. San Angelo, Texas?

[*Mr. Peeples expressed his concern that the President has turned over the NAFTA debate with Ross Perot to the Vice President.*]

The President. I thought I elevated the debate by allowing the Vice President to debate with him. I don't consider Ross—first of all, in the Congress Ross Perot is not the primary problem we've got. The primary problem we've got in the Congress is the united, intense, and sometimes vociferous endorsement—efforts of the labor movement to beat this and to convince Republicans that they basically like, they'll get them opponents, and Democrats, if they like, they'll never give them money again. So that's the big problem we've got.

Mr. Perot's arguments have been largely discredited when he's been questioned on them and when the evidence has been examined. But it was the Vice President's idea all along to challenge him to a debate. So I debated him three times last year, and the more we got to talk about the issues, the better it got. So I think the Vice President will do just fine. I've got a lot of confidence in him.

Q. And the follow-up question to that one, sir—and this one's probably a minor point except for those who are affected by it—watermelon producers in Texas. Can you take a watermelon question?

The President. Yes. You know I was born in a town that grows big watermelons, so I can do that.

Q. [*Inaudible*]—and under the yoke of a lot of labor and wage and environmental regulations that Mexican producers do not have.

The President. Yes.

Q. The question is, is there any chance that the phaseout period for the present 20 percent tariff on imported watermelons could be extended from the proposed 10 years to 15 years, since the phaseout on the tariffs on some of the other crops I'm told are going to be that long?

The President. I don't think so. We think it's enough for our folks to be okay under it. Keep in mind, one of the things that's going to happen—and I want to emphasize this very strongly because—and this relates to another question that was raised earlier—one of the things that's plainly going to happen in this trade with agriculture, even though the agreement streamlines customs and inspection procedures, is that we're going to have a very vigilant oversight of safety standards and quality. And I believe what you're going to see, when you've got a 10-year phaseout period with Mexican incomes rising more rapidly across the board because of this trade, is that you are not going to see the kind of economic disadvantage at the end of this phaseout period to a lot of the agricultural products that some fear now because the cost of production in Mexico, in terms of sheer labor, is lower. I mean, I really believe that we're going to do a lot better on some of these things than we think. Now we have in the agreement— I want to emphasize this—there is a provision in the agreement that allows us to slow anything down if there is a so-called surge, that is, if there is a totally unforeseeable development that threatens to take out some sector of our economy.

By the way, the Mexicans have the same thing if we do that to them, if there's some totally unpredictable or unforeseen economically adverse development here in the term of—in the businesses—the surge—that there is provision in this agreement to slow that down and take another look at it. So there is sort of a safety hatch here. And I think that, plus the fact that we're going to be quite vigilant in making sure that the safety standards are going to be ob-

served for the production and the delivery of our food, will provide the protection that we need.

The Secretary of Agriculture just passed me a note and reminded me, too, that just last— we are this week, we got an agreement from the Mexicans to do a yearly review of the impact of this trade agreement on all vegetables. So there may be an argument about what a watermelon is, but it's included in the agreement.

Secretary Espy. Yeah, Mr. President, as you said, we are conscious of impact on commodities across the board, and we've made improvements when it comes to sugar and citrus, but also when it comes to fruits and vegetables. There will be a yearly review of impact on fruits and vegetables, and if we think that there is deleterious and a huge negative impact on American vegetable industry then these agreements allow for consideration of a snapback.

Q. Thank you very much, Mr. President and Secretary Espy.

The President. Thank you. I want to thank all the farmers and all the broadcasters for their questions today and for listening. And for those of you who support this agreement, I want to tell you I'm very grateful. I think it's a very, very important part of our attempt to open America to the rest of the world, to take advantage of the high productivity of our farmers and our manufacturing workers, our service industries, and to build bridges to the rest of Latin America and to get this GATT agreement done. And I know that every active farmer in this country understands what it could mean to us if we can pass this GATT agreement by the end of the year. I believe that passing NAFTA is a big first step to getting that done. It will plainly put America on the side of expanded trade and give us some leverage as we go down the road.

So I hope you'll do whatever you can to tell your Members of Congress, without regard to party, that you're for this, that this is good for America. And meanwhile the Secretary of Agriculture and I will keep working on the problems that all of you outlined today. We won't forget them. We've taken the steps that we thought we could to date. And the Secretary is going up to Canada soon.

Mike, would you like to say anything before we get off the phone?

Secretary Espy. No, sir, I think you've said it all. Thank you.

The President. Thank you for your hard work. Thanks, appreciate it, fellas.

[*At this point, the teleconference ended, and the President took questions from reporters.*]

Interest Rates

Q. Mr. President, are you concerned about interest rates creeping up?

The President. No. I mean, what's happened is, the economy's getting much healthier. And you've had huge increases in home sales. We've had big increases in other economic activity. And when that happens, when the economy really begins to show signs of recovery, it's hard to keep interest rates at a 25- or 30-year low.

Because there is no inflation apparent in this economy, I don't expect a big increase in the rates. And we're going to watch it very closely obviously. But we've had an awfully good run with low interest rates, and a lot of people have taken advantage of them. From the time we announced the intention to have a serious effort to reduce the deficit, until I introduced my economic plan, until it passed, the interest rates dropped dramatically. And they've stayed down.

I was on a plane the other day coming back from one of my NAFTA meetings, and two of the people riding with me told me they've refinanced their homes this year. And one was saving just under $300 a month, the other was saving about $500 a month on the refinancing. These things have happened to millions of people around the country, and there's still good opportunities there for home mortgages, both for new ones and for refinancing.

But if the economy really picks up, there will have to be some movement in the interest rates. I don't think there will be a lot because—as long as we can keep inflation down. And I wouldn't be surprised, by the way, to see, as one of the experts reported in the press today, I wouldn't be surprised to see them drop again. I was kind of concerned when we had this big surge in housing and big surge in new investments that there might be a little pickup in it. But I'm not alarmed by it right now.

NAFTA Television Debate

Q. Mr. President, Ross Perot says he doesn't like the idea of the debate forum that the Vice President suggested. He says the Vice President ought to bring you and some of your spin doctors to his event. Is there any chance you'd agree to that?

The President. No, what Ross Perot wants, as always, is a show, not a debate. I mean, he basically wants Al Gore to show up at a rally that he's paid for with a crowd full of people that don't like NAFTA in the first place so they can shout at Al Gore, and in the hope that the shouting will obscure the arguments and the evidence and the facts. And that's not a debate or a discussion. What we suggested, and what Al did—it was all his idea—was that he call Larry King, Larry King host an honest and quiet and straightforward discussion that the American people could watch in their living rooms, one that would shed light and not heat. And I could understand why that's not Mr. Perot's preferred format. I mean, he'd rather have a rally where he's paid for it, has organized all these people to come, they're all against it anyway, and they shout at Al Gore. I don't blame him, but no sensible American would expect that to substitute for a debate. I mean, I think everybody can pretty well figure out——

Q. Do you think he's trying to wimp out?

The President. Win what?

Q. Wimp out of a head-on-head debate?

The President. You know, you all get into that name-calling character. I'm not going to do that. I think he's trying to negotiate the best possible position for himself. But it wouldn't be a credible debate for us to show up at his rally.

NOTE: The teleconference began at 1:23 p.m. in the Oval Office at the White House.

Letter to Congressional Leaders Reporting on the Cyprus Conflict
November 5, 1993

Dear Mr. Speaker: (*Dear Mr. Chairman:*)
In accordance with Public Law 95–384 (22 U.S.C. 2373(c)), I am submitting to you this report on progress toward a negotiated settle-

ment of the Cyprus question. The previous report covered progress from the remainder of February, through July 15, 1993. The current report covers the remainder of July through September 15, 1993.

Shortly after the visit of U.S. Special Cyprus Coordinator Maresca, Special U.N. Representative for Cyprus Joe Clark visited Ankara July 21–22, where he met with Turkish Prime Minister Ciller, Deputy Prime Minister Inonu, Foreign Minister Cetin, and Ministry of Foreign Affairs Cyprus Expert Ambassador Ulucevik. Like Maresca, Clark stressed the need for public Turkish support for the confidence-building measures (CBMs) and was reassured by the Turkish side of its commitment to support the package.

Also on July 22 Mr. Clark met with U.S. Ambassador to Turkey Richard Barkley. Ambassador Barkley welcomed Mr. Clark's visit to Ankara, and noted the continuing high-level U.S. support for his mission. Both Mr. Clark and Ambassador Barkley welcomed the fact that there is now a more open and informed debate within Turkey about the Cyprus issue.

On July 26 in Nicosia, the U.N. Secretary General's Deputy Special Representative for Cyprus, Mr. Gustave Feissel, met with President Clerides of Cyprus. This was followed by a meeting on July 27, also in Nicosia, between Mr. Feissel and Turkish Cypriot leader Mr. Rauf Denktash. At both meetings, Mr. Feissel stressed the importance of overcoming the lack of information on the CBMs among the Turkish Cypriots.

U.S. Ambassador to Cyprus, Robert Lamb, met with Mr. Denktash on July 30 and reiterated the U.S. position that the CBMs offer the one feasible route toward cooperation. Mr. Denktash stated that he was preparing a list of technical questions on the CBMs, but saw no prospect of movement on the U.N. process, including the CBMs, until after the Turkish-Cypriot elections scheduled for November 28.

Although it was expected that Mr. Denktash would present his technical questions at his meetings with Mr. Feissel on August 6 and 7, he failed to do so. At those meetings, he told Mr. Feissel that any movement would have to wait for the scheduled elections to take place in the north.

On Friday August 13, Assistant Secretary of State for European and Canadian Affairs Stephen Oxman met with Turkish Foreign Minister

Cetin in Washington. Mr. Oxman reminded the Foreign Minister that the United States attaches great importance to a resolution of the situation in Cyprus. While noting that the Turkish Cypriots are in the midst of their election process, he stressed that it is of the utmost importance to maintain the momentum on the CBMs. Mr. Oxman said that the Turkish Cypriots now face the choice of either moving toward the CBMs package or being further isolated. Mr. Oxman also used this opportunity to urge the Turkish Foreign Minister to use Turkey's considerable influence with the Turkish Cypriots to move the process along—specifically, by publicly announcing Turkish support for the CBMs package, by encouraging early elections, and by urging the Turkish Cypriots to communicate promptly with the United Nations with regard to outstanding questions on the CBMs package.

Turkish Ministry of Foreign Affairs Under Secretary Ulucevik travelled to northern Cyprus August 24–26. While there he met with Turkish Cypriot leaders and privately relayed Turkey's support for the CBMs.

Mr. Clark visited Washington on August 26 and met at the National Security Council with National Security Advisor Anthony Lake, and at the State Department with Under Secretary Peter Tarnoff, European and Canadian Affairs Acting Assistant Secretary Alexander Vershbow, and U.S. Special Cyprus Coordinator Ambassador Maresca. In all three meetings, Mr. Clark expressed appreciation for U.S. initiatives in Cyprus and urged continued U.S. support to maintain progress on the CBMs. Mr. Clark emphasized that the status quo cannot continue and was costly to all involved. He also requested that the United States discuss with the Turkish government the need for the Turks to reiterate their support for the U.N. "set of ideas." Under Secretary Tarnoff reiterated the United States unwavering support for the CBMs and for Mr. Clark's role in promoting them. Ambassador Maresca agreed with Mr. Clark that we had to press for the promised list of specific Turkish-Cypriot questions about the CBMs package.

On August 26, Ambassador Maresca met with Mr. Sahinbas, Deputy Chief of Mission at the Turkish Embassy in Washington. Ambassador Maresca told Mr. Sahinbas that it was important that all interested parties work to maintain the viability of the CBMs package past the election period in northern Cyprus. Ambassador Maresca and Mr. Sahinbas agreed that progress would be difficult until after the elections of November 28.

The final meeting during the period covered by this report was Ambassador Maresca's meeting with Under Secretary Ulucevik in Ankara on September 2. Ambassador Ulucevik spoke highly of the work of Mr. Clark and looked forward to presenting Turkish views to Mr. Clark in late September. Ambassador Maresca stressed the need to make positive progress on the CBMs package and supported Mr. Clark's efforts to develop understanding and sympathy for the package in the Turkish-Cypriot community.

Finally on September 14, the Secretary General issued his "Report on his Mission of Good Offices in Cyprus." The Secretary General noted that the President of Cyprus, Mr. Clerides, had reaffirmed his community's willingness to move forward with the provisions in the CBMs package proposed for Varosha and for Nicosia International Airport. The Secretary General also noted that the Turkish Cypriot leader, Mr. Denktash, continued his criticism of the package. The report stated that inaccurate and incomplete information had been presented on the impact of the Varosha/Airport provisions, thus causing confusion for the Turkish Cypriots. In addition, it said that the Turkish Cypriots looked to Turkey for guidance, but the Turkish government had not yet sufficiently conveyed its support for the package to the Turkish Cypriots. In the report, the Secretary General also proposed to send a team of senior experts to Cyprus in early October to address questions, which have been raised concerning the effects of the CBMs package.

The Secretary General's report ended on a cautionary note. He stated that it is not possible to continue the current effort indefinitely. He stressed that it is essential that he receive the full cooperation and support of the Turkish Cypriots. If the current efforts do not succeed soon, he continued, he would have to invite the members of the Security Council to consider alternate ways to promote the effective implementation of the United Nations many resolutions on Cyprus.

Despite the lack of progress during the period this report covers, we are still working for the approval of the CBMs. As I stated in my August 12 letter to Prime Minister Ciller, the United States seeks Turkey's support in helping to achieve a settlement. The Turkish-Cypriot community must recognize that if it rejects this proposal, which is viewed by the rest of the world as fair and constructive, it risks even greater isolation than it presently faces. I hope that this can be avoided. In the meantime, I will continue to lend full support to the U.N. efforts.

I will continue to use all my energies in assisting in finding a solution to the Cyprus problem and look forward to your support in this effort.

Sincerely,

WILLIAM J. CLINTON

NOTE: Identical letters were sent to Thomas S. Foley, Speaker of the House of Representatives, and Claiborne Pell, Chairman of the Senate Committee on Foreign Relations.

Message to the Congress Transmitting the Republic of Korea-United States Fishery Agreement
November 5, 1993

To the Congress of the United States:

In accordance with the Magnuson Fishery Conservation and Management Act of 1976 (Public Law 94–256; 16 U.S.C. 1801 *et seq.*), I transmit herewith an Agreement Between the Government of the United States of America and the Government of the Republic of Korea Extending the Agreement of July 26, 1982, Concerning Fisheries off the Coasts of the United States, as extended and amended. The agreement, which was effected by an exchange of notes at Washington on June 11, 1993, and October 13, 1993, extends the 1982 agreement to December 31, 1995. The exchange of notes together with the 1982 agreement constitute a governing international fishery agreement within the requirements of section 201(c) of the Act.

In light of the importance of our fisheries

relationship with the Republic of Korea, I urge that the Congress give favorable consideration to this agreement at an early date.

WILLIAM J. CLINTON

The White House,
November 5, 1993.

Letter to Congressional Leaders on the Proposed Balanced Budget Amendment
November 5, 1993

Dear Mr. Speaker: (*Dear Mr. Leader:*)

I write to express my firm opposition to the proposed balanced budget amendment to the Constitution of the United States (S.J. Res. 41 and H.J. Res. 103). While I am deeply committed to bringing down our Nation's deficit, this proposed balanced budget amendment would not serve that end. It would promote political gridlock and would endanger our economic recovery.

The Administration fought hard to pass a historic deficit reduction plan because we believe that deficit reduction is an essential component of a national economic growth strategy. As you know, I worked tirelessly with the Congress to gain passage of the largest deficit reduction package in the Nation's history. This legislation includes a "hard freeze" on all discretionary spending, a virtually unprecedented constraint on Federal spending. Through the National Performance Review, a new rescission package, and a major proposal to limit the growth of Medicare and Medicaid through comprehensive health care reform, we are taking continuing steps to keep the deficit on a downward path. I have also long supported such procedural innovations as enhanced rescission authority or a line-item veto and would consider workable budget proposals that distinguish between consumption and investment. The Bipartisan Commission on Entitlement Reform will come forward with suggestions on controlling entitlement costs and other serious budget reforms. Thoughtful, specific reforms are better policy than a rigid Constitutional amendment.

The balanced budget amendment is, in the first place, bad economics. As you know, the Federal deficit depends not just on Congressional decisions, but also on the state of the economy. In particular, the deficit increases automatically whenever the economy weakens.

If we try to break this automatic linkage by a Constitutional amendment, we will have to raise taxes and cut expenditures whenever the economy is weak. That not only risks turning minor downturns into serious recessions, but would make recovery from recession far more difficult. Let's be clear: This is not a matter of abstract economic theory. Contractionary fiscal policy in the 1930s helped turn an economic slowdown into a Great Depression. A balanced budget amendment could threaten the livelihoods of millions of Americans. I cannot put them in such peril.

Moreover, at presently anticipated growth rates, the deficit reduction required by this amendment could be harmful to average hardworking American families. Supporters of this amendment must be straight with the American people. Given the current outlook for the FY 1999 budget, the amendment would require some combination of the following: huge increases in taxes on working families; massive reductions in Social Security benefits for middle class Americans; and major cuts in Medicare and Medicaid that would make it impossible to pass meaningful health reform legislation. This latter result would be particularly ironic and counterproductive because comprehensive health reform is our best hope not only for providing health security for all Americans, but also for bringing down the long-term structural deficit. The fact that these consequences will not be clear to most Americans for a few years does not relieve us of the responsibility of facing them today.

We must reject the temptation to use any budget gimmicks to hide from the specific choices that are needed for long-term economic renewal. The amendment by itself would not reduce the deficit by a single penny. The only way we can continue to make progress on bringing down the deficit while investing more in our future is to continue the process of making tough and specific policy choices. If we avoid such straightforward debate now, the likely outcome will be accounting subterfuge and gimmicks when the easy promise of a balanced budget amendment runs up against difficult political realities. A gridlocked Congress would encourage members to look for an easy way out— for example, by moving more Federal programs off budget or by imposing more unfunded mandates on the States. Ironically, the amendment might encourage less rather than more fiscal responsibility.

The amendment's potential impact on our constitutional system is as troublesome as its effect on the economy. The proposed amendments are so vague and complex that budgets quickly could be thrown into the courts to be written by appointed judges with life tenure, rather than the people's elected officials in the Congress. Surely, we can do better than this.

Finally, I believe that economic and budgetary decisions should distinguish between investment and consumption. Those who manage a family budget know that there is a fundamental difference between spending money on a lavish meal, and paying the mortgage on a home that is an investment in one's future economic security. Under this balanced budget amendment,

there is no distinction between cutting a dollar in waste and a dollar in a valuable investment in technology that could make us a richer and more competitive Nation in the future. That is unacceptable to me. We need to find ways to reduce the deficit and increase investment in ways that enhance not undermine the economic security and potential of our people and their communities. We must bring down the budget deficit at the same time we make progress on bringing down the investment deficit through investments in those who helped us win the cold war, through more resources to fight drugs and crime, and by giving all Americans the opportunity for quality education and training throughout their lifetimes.

I remain firmly committed to the goal of deficit reduction. But I am just as firmly opposed to this balanced budget amendment, because it would simply delay honest debate over the hard choices needed for long-term economic growth and could imperil the economic stability of the Nation and our fledgling recovery.

Sincerely,

BILL CLINTON

NOTE: Identical letters were sent to Thomas S. Foley, Speaker of the House of Representatives, and George J. Mitchell, Senate majority leader.

Announcement of Senior Executive Service Appointments
November 5, 1993

The President today named 22 men and women to Senior Executive Service positions in a number of Federal Agencies and Departments, including the National Aeronautics and Space Administration, the Environmental Protection Agency, the Overseas Private Investment Corporation, the Office of Personnel Management, the Peace Corps, and the Departments of State, Transportation, Education, and Justice.

"This group of talented men and women will provide solid support for our Cabinet Secretaries and agency heads who have taken on the challenge of making our Federal Government work better for the American people," the President said.

National Aeronautics and Space Administration

Alan Ladwig, Senior Policy Analyst

Department of State

Toni Grant Verstandig, Deputy Assistant Secretary, Near Eastern Affairs

Department of Transportation

Eugene A. Conti, Jr., Deputy Assistant Secretary, Budget and Programs

Environmental Protection Agency

Felicia A. Marcus, Regional Administrator, Region IX

Peace Corps

Frederick M. O'Regan, Regional Director,

Eurasia Middle East Region

Margaret Goodman, Regional Director, Asia Pacific Region

Victor C. Johnson, Regional Director, Inter-America Region

John P. Hogan, Associate Director of International Operations, International Operations

Judy Harrington, Associate Director for Volunteer Support, Volunteer Support

U.S. International Development Cooperation Agency

Charles D. Toy, Vice President/General Counsel, Overseas Private Investment Corporation

Office of Personnel Management

Valerie Lau, Director of Policy, Office of the Director

Lorraine Pratte Lewis, General Counsel, Office of the General Counsel

Department of Education

Linda G. Roberts, Special Adviser on Education Technology, Office of the Deputy

Secretary

Jamienne S. Studley, Deputy General Counsel, Regulations and Legislation Service

Department of Justice

Diane P. Wood, Deputy Assistant Attorney General, Antitrust Division

Lois J. Schiffer, Deputy Assistant Attorney General, Environment and Natural Resources

John A. Rogovin, Deputy Assistant Attorney General, Civil Division

Mark I. Levy, Deputy Assistant Attorney General, Civil Division

Irvin B. Nathan, Principal Associate Deputy Attorney General

Merrick B. Garland, Deputy Assistant Attorney General, Criminal Division

Eva M. Plaza, Deputy Assistant Attorney General, Civil Division

Nancy E. McFadden, Deputy Associate Attorney General, Office of the Associate Attorney General

NOTE: Biographies of the appointees were made available by the Office of the Press Secretary.

The President's Radio Address
November 6, 1993

Good morning. This week I spoke with American workers and farmers who are succeeding in our competitive global economy. On Thursday, I went to Lexington, Kentucky, and visited the Lexmark factory, where they make computers, printers, and keyboards for sale all over the world. Anybody who thinks our American workers can't compete and win should have gone there with me. Yesterday I spoke with farmers from Illinois, Missouri, Montana, and North Carolina. They produce corn, soybeans, timber, and wheat, and they raise cattle. Just like the workers in Lexington, these farmers are eager to export more products all across the world, including to our neighbors in Mexico. The folks I spoke with on Thursday and Friday understand what's at stake in the debate about the North American Free Trade Agreement, or NAFTA for short. For them the debate is simple; it's about paychecks, not politics.

In Lexington, I also met with workers from Monarch Tool and Manufacturing. Their sales in Mexico have grown dramatically over the last 3 years. Teddie Rae True, who works at Monarch, told me she supports NAFTA because, she said, "Without it, I might not have a job." A lot of what we do depends on foreign trade. Roberta Canady has worked at Lexmark for 16 years. She said she still wants more facts about NAFTA, but she knows that, and I quote her, "The bottom line is whether it will promote more jobs for the people of the United States." Let me assure Roberta Canady and all of you: NAFTA means more exports, and more exports means more jobs for Americans.

There's been so much fog surrounding this issue that it's time to shed some light. NAFTA is good for us because it will cut the tariffs on trade between the United States and Mexico. Tariffs are taxes that countries put on products from other countries. NAFTA will eventually cut these taxes down to zero. It will also reduce Mexican laws which now require some products sold in Mexico to actually be made there.

Now, that makes a much bigger difference for the United States than for Mexican products that would be sold here. Let me tell you why. Right now, Mexico's tariffs on our products are 2½ times higher than our tariffs on theirs. NAFTA will remove those barriers, opening up a growing market for our goods and services and creating hundreds of thousands of new jobs for our people.

The fact is that today Mexican consumers are already buying over $40 billion worth of American products. And if NAFTA passes, they'll buy even more. Seventy cents of every dollar that Mexico spends on foreign products are spent right here in the United States. And when Mexico takes down its tariff barriers, that means more sales and more jobs for our industries, from cars to computers.

Right now, Mexico puts a 20 percent tariff on cars and virtually requires that cars sold in Mexico be made there. With NAFTA, those barriers will be lowered. That's why the big three auto companies predict that in just the first year after NAFTA, they could go from selling only 1,000 cars in Mexico to selling 60,000.

It's the same with computers, which also face a 20 percent tariff. Three years ago, by one estimate, Mexico bought 120,000 computers from us. Last year they bought 390,000. This year it's estimated they'll buy 600,000. And that's with a 20 percent tariff. When NAFTA lowers the tariff barrier, the United States will gain a 20 percent advantage over our competitors from Europe and Japan. And Mexico, with a population of nearly 90 million, could buy millions more of our computers, creating tens of thousands of new jobs here in our country.

For our country, for every wealthy country, the only way to create new jobs and to raise incomes is to export more products. For the past 5 years about half the growth in our economy has come from exports. And jobs related to exports pay 17 percent more than other jobs in the American economy. That's why NAFTA is part of my overall strategy to sell our products all over the world at a time when our leading rivals are also expanding their own markets in their own backyard. Western Europe is becoming a giant trading bloc. Japan is expanding its investment and trade in much of Asia. And now

with NAFTA we can create the biggest trading bloc in the world, starting with Canada and Mexico and then expanding to the rest of Latin America. Many of the Latin American countries really want to buy more American products, to be a part of our trading bloc. They're just waiting to be asked, and they're waiting to answer, depending on what happens to NAFTA.

Given a fair chance, I know American workers can compete and win in our own hemisphere and throughout the world. Those who believe otherwise underestimate the American people. We still have the most productive workers in the world, and they've gotten more productive in the last 15 or 20 years.

On Tuesday night, Vice President Gore will debate a leading critic of NAFTA. The debate will be facts against fear, the fear that low wages and lower costs of production in Mexico will lead to a massive flight of jobs down there. Well, if we don't pass NAFTA, that could still be true. The lower wages and the lower cost of production will still be there. But if we do pass it, it means dramatically increased sales of American products made right here in America. It reduces the incentive to move to Mexico to sell in the Mexican market. And remember, the tariffs that we put on their products are already low.

So we have to face the choice of facts versus fear. When Americans have faced that choice in the past, they've always chosen honesty and hope. Ultimately, this debate is a test of not only our purpose in the world but our own confidence in ourselves. I know the last several years have been tough on hard-working middle class Americans. I ran for President to change that, to give people health care security and security in their education and training and security as family members and workers. But I also promised to challenge you to embrace the world economy, because we can't run away from these change. Will we hunker down and say, "My goodness, we're going to be overcome by a trade agreement with Mexico," a country with an economy only 5 percent as big as ours, or are we going to reach out to the rest of the world and say we can compete and win again?

My visit to Lexington, Kentucky, and my talk with those farmers on the phone yesterday reminded me that Americans are hopeful and hard working. When the moment of decision comes, I believe ordinary working Americans will agree with every living President, every living Secretary of State, every living Secretary of the Treasury, every living Nobel Prize-winning economist, and over 40 of the 50 Governors that NAFTA means expanding markets. And we have to have expanding markets, not shrinking hori-

zons. Our jobs and our children's jobs depend on it.

Thanks for listening.

NOTE: The President spoke at 10:06 a.m. from the Oval Office at the White House.

Interview With Timothy Russert and Tom Brokaw on "Meet the Press" November 7, 1993

Mr. Russert. Welcome again to "Meet the Press," today a special edition live from the White House. I'm with my colleague, Tom Brokaw.

Mr. President, this is our 46th birthday. You're 47. You strike me as the kind of guy who maybe watched the first program from your cradle. [*Laughter*]

The President. I wish I could. I didn't have a television then. I was 1 when you started, but I was 9, I think, when we got our first television in 1956. So I couldn't start, but I did watch it often after that.

NAFTA

Mr. Russert. Well, it's great to have you here. Let's start—we'll have to talk about it today— let's start with NAFTA, the North American Free Trade Agreement. Your closest supporters say that if the vote were held today, you're still 30 votes short. True?

The President. I don't think we're quite that short, but we're 30 votes short of having explicit expressed commitments. I think we'll make it, however.

Mr. Russert. What role has Ross Perot played in this debate?

The President. I think he's kept things stirred up. That's what he likes to do. But I think, frankly, the vociferous organized opposition of most of the unions, telling these Members in private they'll never give them any money again, they'll get them opponents in the primary, the real roughshod, muscle-bound tactics, plus the fact that a lot of the business supporters of NAFTA have not gotten their employees and rank-and-file people to call and say they're for it. In any issue like this, the intensity is always with people who are against it. Those things are difficult.

But again I will say I have been quite heart-

ened by the responses of the last 10 days, more and more of these Members of Congress, men and women who want to do right by their country, don't want to hurt the United States, and understand that NAFTA means more jobs, not just in Mexico but throughout Latin America, a huge trading bloc of people helping to take us to the 21st century.

NAFTA Television Debate

Mr. Russert. Bob Dole mentioned last night that you were elevating Ross Perot. Are you concerned that you're going to recreate a monster?

The President. No, Ross Perot has got enough money to elevate himself. He can buy his way on national television and buy his own exposure and have very little accountability, except when he makes the mistake of coming on this program with you.

Mr. Russert. Without his charts. [*Laughter*]

The President. Yes. The same mistake I made today. [*Laughter*] I think the Vice President will do well. Ross Perot is the master of the one-liner and the emotional retort, but I believe that the Vice President has an unusual command of the facts and a real commitment, a profound commitment to this issue. And the American people who watch Larry King will see that it's no accident that all the Presidents, living Presidents, and all the living Nobel Prize-winning economists and 41 of the 50 Governors are for this. It's good for the American economy.

Mr. Russert. Are you trying to demonstrate to the undecided Democratic Congressmen, listen, this is a choice between Clinton-Gore and Perot?

The President. Absolutely not. He is a visible spokesperson for this. As I said to you, at least for the undecided Democrats, our big problem is the raw muscle, the sort of naked pressure that the labor forces have put on.

Mr. Russert. Are you afraid the Democratic Congressmen are in the pocket of labor?

The President. No, I didn't say that. But I said that a lot of them are saying, "Well, I'm not hearing from these business people who are for it; their employees are not telling me they're for it. And I'm hearing from all these people either pleading with me based on friendship or threatening me based on money and work in the campaign. And I don't hear it."

So I think what we want to do and what the Vice President's trying to do here, and this was his idea, is to let the American people listen. Yes, Ross Perot is against it. Yes, a number of other people, Pat Buchanan and others, are against it. But if all the Presidents are for it, all the Secretaries of State, all the Nobel Prize-winning economists, who've never agreed on anything the rest of their lives probably, and virtually all of the Governors are for it, it must be good for the American economy.

Mr. Russert. We have, in fact, lost jobs to Mexico. And their concern is we'll lose more, and also the depressed wages. There's a clause in the treaty which, with 6 months' notice, any side can void it. Would you say to the American people that if the treaty passes, you'll monitor it? And if, say, in 2 years you are convinced there is a sucking of jobs and a depression of wages, you would move to abrogate the treaty?

The President. If I thought the treaty were bad for the American economy, of course, I would do that. But let me tell you, there's another provision of the treaty that we negotiated that I also want to emphasize because it goes more to the heart of what many Americans are worried about. It deals with the so-called surge problem. That's a term of art which in common language means, well, what if this is a good deal for America and a good deal for Mexico, but some part of our economy, or theirs, to be fair, has an overwhelmingly negative impact? If something that nobody ever dreamed happened, there's also a provision that allows us to slow the agreement down as it applies to that.

So there's no question that we have the protections we need. We can get out in 6 months if it's bad for us, and we can stop anything horrible and unforeseen. This treaty is going to make the problems with Mexico of the last 15 years better. It will raise labor costs in Mexico; it will raise the environmental investments in Mexico; it will reduce the trade barriers to our selling products in Mexico. It means more sales and more jobs.

And also keep in mind, Mexico is just 5 percent of the American economy. It will improve our relationships with our biggest neighbor and thereby help us to take this kind of deal to the rest of Latin America so that we can establish a 700-million-person trading bloc. That's real jobs for America.

APEC Meeting and NAFTA

Mr. Russert. The day after the vote November 17th, the next day, on the 18th, you leave for Seattle to meet with 14 other nations, China, Japan. If you go there having lost NAFTA, what does it do to your standing?

The President. Well, I'd say I'd sure rather not do it. Let me give you the flip side. If I go there and NAFTA passes in the House, it will be a clear statement to Asia, number one, that the United States is not withdrawing from the world, that we are determined to be the world's leading economic power by competing and winning, not from running away. Number two, I will be able to say what I have been saying to the Asians: Asia is important to us, but we want free trade, we want access to your markets.

They will see us developing the NAFTA market, which is not just Mexico, it's Latin America, Canada, the whole 9 yards. And that will be enormous pressure on them to conclude these world trade agreements, these GATT talks by the end of the year. It will also help us with Europe to do that.

So I can't tell you how important I think it will be. If we go out there without this agreement, they may say, "Well, President Clinton wants to have an open door to Asia, but is he really going to be a tough competitor? They ran away from Latin America, their best friends and best consumers. And can he deliver? Will the Congress run away from him even if he tries to expand trade?" My ability to get done what is plainly in the economic interest of this country will be weakened.

Now, that's very important, because almost all these people who are against NAFTA are still for the GATT talks, for the big treaty on world trade. They all know it will create hundreds of thousands of manufacturing jobs for America. They should consider how much harder it's going to be to get GATT if the House votes NAFTA down and how much easier it will be to get GATT if the House adopts NAFTA.

Health Care Reform

Mr. Brokaw. Mr. President, let's talk about health care. There's been a lot of confusion about the numbers coming out of the White House. Mrs. Clinton went to the Hill and said that if the Clinton plan passes, costs will go up for about 35 percent to 37 percent of those now covered. Then Donna Shalala, Secretary of Health and Human Services, said 40 percent. Last week, Leon Panetta said 30 percent. Even your strongest advocates, like Jay Rockefeller, were holding their heads, in effect, in anguish. Another Democrat said, "We've got to prove that Democrats can count." Hasn't your credibility been hurt on the whole cost issue?

The President. Maybe, but what I would like to emphasize is we're the only people who have a plan. It's very easy for everybody else to sit up in the peanut gallery. This is a very complex thing. And keep in mind, you're talking about small amounts of money, is this person going to pay $6 more a month or $60 less a month, trying to calculate how it would go if this plan would be passed just as it is.

Now, let me say what was wrong with the early figures, where they said 40 percent of the people with insurance would pay more. Here's what was wrong with them, why they were too high. Of the people who have insurance today, we now think that 70 percent will pay the same or less for the same or better benefits. Why did they say 60 before? Because they neglected to calculate this: A lot of people who have insurance don't really have it. That is, they have $5,000 deductibles, so they're paying every year. They just may not be paying it in their insurance premium. So they went back and calculated based on what we now know about how much out-of-pocket people pay. You have $2,500, $3,000, $5,000 deductible. That is something they neglected to think about.

So now who will pay more under this, who has insurance already? People who have essentially catastrophic policies, that have very limited benefits, and young, single workers will pay more because if they pay more it will enable us to have what's called community rating, so that if a working family—middle-aged working family—with a sick child can still get insurance at an affordable cost. And all young workers

who don't have insurance will be brought into the insurance system, and even they will get something for it. That is, what they get for it is knowing their insurance can ever be taken away. There will be a floor.

Finally, let me say this: If you look at the experience of the last 12 years when health costs really started to take off, and then you think about what it will be like 5 years from now, 100 percent of the American people will pay more 5 years from now than the rate of inflation if we don't do something. In other words, at least what we're trying to do will lower the rate of increase for all the American people. So within 5 years everybody will be better off, I believe.

Mr. Brokaw. Mr. President, no one disagrees with the idea that you have engaged the country in a debate about health care which is long overdue. But the fact is that you want to add 37 million people to the insurance pool. There are new technologies coming on board all the time that cost a lot more money. You're willing to pick up the early retirement benefits for corporations. You've added mental health and free prescriptions. It seems to a lot of folks that you ought to be going slower and that you ought to accept kind of phased-in universal health care coverage in 5 years. Would that be acceptable to you?

The President. But the problem is—we are phasing it in over 3 years, through all of '90. We're anticipating passing this program in '94 and then letting people have '95, '96, and '97. But let me emphasize, Tom, the people who make that argument assume something that we assume all the time in America, that we just can't do things that other people can do. We tolerate conditions in America that are intolerable in other countries.

Now, the condition we tolerate by not having everybody insured is higher health care costs. That is, you've got folks in medicine in your family, you know this, not insuring everybody raises health care costs because all those people without insurance, if they need health care, will get it. They'll get it when it's too late, too expensive, and someone else will pay for it. And that rifles the cost. So by accelerating the moment of universal coverage, you not only do the morally right thing by finally letting America join the ranks of all these other advanced countries in giving everybody health security, you immediately begin to lower the rate at which costs increase.

So you can argue about all these other things, but it seems to me delaying the time of universal coverage will aggravate the price battle, not make it better. We assume that universal coverage will cost more when every other country that has universal coverage is paying much less than we are and having less inflation.

Living Will

Mr. Brokaw. Would you sign a living will publicly? About one-third of our health care costs in America go to the last year of life. Mrs. Clinton has talked about you doing that. Are you prepared to do that?

The President. I certainly would sign one. I don't know if I would do it in public, but I'd be glad to tell you what's in it. I don't know, I've never thought about a public demonstration of a private act like that. But we've given a lot of thought to it because of the experience I had with my stepfather when he died, when Hillary's dad died earlier this year. I think families should think about living wills and should have them. It's not something that Government should impose on them. But we do have a lot of extra costs that most people believe are unnecessary in the system, and that's one way to weed some of them out.

Health Care Reform

Mr. Brokaw. And ultimately, are we going to have to come to health rationing in America, especially those heroic procedures that are long on odds and very expensive, take that money and spend it on prenatal care and other procedures that might extend life at the beginning, not at the end?

The President. Well, let me say before we make that decision, we should acknowledge two things. One is, we're rationing health care right now. There's a huge rationing going on now. It's just a roll of the dice whether you have it or not and what you get.

What we do know is that if our plan passes and we put more emphasis on primary and preventive health care and primary physicians getting out there and taking care of people and stopping bad things from happening, we'll have less need for those extreme procedures.

I do not believe we want America to pull back from the technological advances that we all treasure. I do not believe we want to tell people they can't have procedures that have a

realistic chance of saving their lives or returning them to normal. So I suspect they'll always be willing to pay a little more than any other country in the world to do that. But if we do more on the primary side, we'll be better off.

Mr. Russert. Mr. President, you're still confident we'll get a health care bill by next year?

The President. Oh, I think we will, absolutely.

Mr. Russert. We have to take a break. We'll be back with more from President Bill Clinton in the Oval Office. We'll talk a little bit about foreign policy.

[*At this point, the television stations took a commercial break.*]

North Korea

Mr. Russert. We're back live from the Oval Office.

Mr. President, a lot of growing concern about North Korea, a country that we fought some 40 years ago. Will you allow North Korea to build a nuclear bomb?

The President. North Korea cannot be allowed to develop a nuclear bomb. We have to be very firm about it. This is a difficult moment in our relationship with them and, I think, a difficult moment for them. They're one of the most, perhaps the most isolated country in the world, with enormous economic problems, trying to decide what direction to take now, sometimes seeming to reach out to South Korea, sometimes seeming to draw back.

I spend a lot of time on this issue. It's a very, very major issue. We have got to stop the proliferation of nuclear weapons, and particularly North Korea needs to stay in the control regime. They don't need to withdraw. Now, there is a lot of disagreement about what we should do now. I just want to assure you and the American people that we are doing everything we possibly can to make the best decisions, to be firm in this. We are consulting with our allies in South Korea and Japan. They are most immediately affected by what we do and how we do it. And we have worked with the Chinese who, despite our other differences, have helped us to try to work through this.

Mr. Russert. Would one of the options be a preemptive strike, the way the Israelis took out the Iraqi nuclear reactor?

The President. I don't think I should discuss any specific options today. All I can tell you is that I tried to issue the sternest, clearest possible statement about this when I was in Korea. Nothing has changed since then. I think you asked me a question about it one time also, Tom. This is a very grave issue for the United States.

Mr. Russert. There are 800,000 North Korean troops amassed on the South Korean border. If the North Koreans invaded South Korea, would that, in effect, be an attack on the United States?

The President. Absolutely. We have our soldiers there. They know that. We still have people stationed near the Bridge of No Return. I was up there on the bridge; I was in those bunkers with our young Americans. They know that any attack on South Korea is an attack on the United States.

Russia

Mr. Brokaw. President Yeltsin of Russia has said over the weekend that he wants to now delay the Presidential election until 1996. That is a full term for him, but he had said publicly that he would do it in the spring of next year. You had endorsed that. Now for him to pull back from that public commitment to elections next spring, is that a mistake on his part?

The President. I have not spoken with him directly, because I didn't—late yesterday evening I was made aware of his comments, so I'm not sure exactly what he said and exactly what he meant. His comments are subject to more than one interpretation. I do think the following things. I think he had always assumed he would run for reelection, and his comments seem to indicate that he may not want to do that and he may want to simply finish his term. As long as he is promoting democracy, as long as he is promoting human rights, as long as he is promoting reform, I think the United States should support him. He has been brave and consistent. I think on this issue, we'll have to see how it plays out. I'm sure after the elections of the Parliament in December, they will have something to say about it.

One of the things that Boris Yeltsin has really understood is that it's not good if he's the only source of legitimate democratic power in Russia. And he is now. He's been elected twice by the Russian people in the last couple of years. After December, we'll have another major player, sort of like the President and the Congress here. And as we know, there will be a different source of legitimate democratic power, and we'll

see how it works out.

China

Mr. Brokaw. Let me ask you about China. You said during the course of the campaign that President Bush coddles China despite a continuing crackdown on democratic reformers, the brutal subjugation of Tibet, the irresponsible exportation of military and nuclear technology. Your administration now is demonstrably warming up toward China. Have conditions changed there?

The President. Well first of all, let's talk about what we've done. The Chinese have complained because they think we've been so much firmer and colder. We imposed sanctions because of weapons technology transfers that the Chinese engaged in that we opposed. So we have taken steps there that were not taken previously.

But we also have had a consistent economic relationship with them. The United States this year will purchase 38 percent of China's exports—little-known fact. The American people, not the American business community that wants to invest there. American people have been very good to the Chinese people in supporting their economic advances. We believe their movement toward market reform and decentralization will promote more democracy in China and better policies.

I want to engage President Jiang on that, and I think we can do so. But we also have to be very firm on these issues of proliferation of weapons of mass destruction and human rights. But I think we have to pursue both courses at once. I don't think you can isolate a country as big as China, as important to the world's future as China, but neither can you simply turn away from things that you cannot abide. And that's what we've tried to do. We've tried to strike the right balance, and I think we have.

United Nations Peacekeeping Efforts

Mr. Brokaw. Even some of your partisans on Capitol Hill believe that you've not shown a strong enough hand on foreign policy. After your experience in Somalia, will you be as eager to get involved with the United Nations in operations of that kind in the future?

The President. I think what we have to do is to recognize that the United Nations peacekeeping function is still very important and sometimes works very, very well. What they've done in Cambodia, with our financial support but with no Americans there, is truly remarkable. Will it transform Cambodia? Who knows? Maybe it will all go back to the way it was, but at least the United Nations has given Cambodia a chance. That is what we are doing for Somalia. Will they be able to overcome their historic, deeply embedded clan warfare? I'm not sure. But at least we're giving them a chance.

What's wrong with the United Nations peacekeeping operations is that it's too much of an ad hoc thing: Some work, some don't, and a lot of the command and control operations, a lot of the training details, a lot of the simple organizational things that are important have not been worked through. So the United States favors a substantial restructuring and upgrading of the peacekeeping operations in ways that would permit us to participate in the future with a much higher level of confidence.

Somalia

Mr. Russert. Let's turn to Somalia, Mr. President. The reports yesterday that the United States troops will take again a very visible role. What does that mean?

The President. Well, when I announced that we would pursue the political objective a few weeks ago, I also said we would stay there and complete our mission. Our mission there is to deliver the humanitarian supplies and to keep the lines of communications open. We stood down from patrolling the roads when the voluntary cease-fire was announced in Somalia, to try to let things calm down and to try to get the political process going. Now that there is a political process, as always there is, there's also a lot of maneuvering in a quasi-military sort of way. We cannot allow that to undermine the humanitarian mission, and our people cannot be expected, our young soldiers there cannot be expected to just sort of hunker down and stay behind walls. It almost puts them at greater risk. So we have to go out now and make sure the ordinary conditions of the U.N. peacekeeping mission are continued even in Mogadishu. And that's what we're doing.

Mr. Russert. The Secretary-General of the U.N., Boutros Boutros-Ghali, said that unless you disarm the warlords and the clans and put together and fashion a political settlement before you leave, the mission will have been a failure.

The President. I disagree with that. First of all, that's the argument he made to the Bush administration. President Bush's administration simply refused to get involved in disarmament. Arguably, it would have been easier then, at the moment when we came in, when everybody was starving and we were at our moment of maximum popularity and leverage, but I'm not sure that decision is wrong.

In the end, the international community will have to broker political resolutions within countries. But our ability to stop people within national boundaries from killing each other is somewhat limited and will be for the foreseeable future. I mean, they are going to have to make up their mind. I think the better course is to get these African nations, to get Ethiopia, to get Eritrea, to get their neighbors involved in trying to work out a political solution.

Those people now remember what it was like before we came there. We're going to do everything we can in the next several months to get this political solution going. But for us to go in and disarm would run the risk of our becoming, in effect, combatants on one side or the other, particularly if some said, yes, we'll disarm, and others said no.

Mr. Russert. In retrospect then, it was a mistake for you to send the Rangers to try to capture Mr. Aideed?

The President. No, that was a different issue. The mistake was—and I want to clarify this, because I am proud of what those Rangers did. The ones who gave their lives did not die in vain. The ones who gave their lives and were wounded in the last instance did it because of the tradition of the Rangers of never leaving anybody behind, even someone who has been killed. And I feel terrible about what happened.

But what they were doing is trying to enforce the law. Their mission was to try to arrest people who were suspected of murdering the Pakistani U.N. soldiers. The mistake was not that they were trying to do that. The mistake was that we were out doing that, and while we were doing that the political dialog shut down, so that the people that were associated with Aideed thought we, the U.N., not we, the U.S., but we, the U.N., were trying to cut them out of Somalia's future. And what we had tried to do is to lower our profile on the military police side so that the political dialog can start again. Now that that's going on, we're going to do the U.N. mandate.

Mr. Russert. And all troops will be out by

March 31st?

The President. Yes.

Mr. Russert. Quickly on Haiti.

The President. If I can go back to my statement. They'll be out by March 31st, except for a couple of hundred support personnel who may be there to do just logistical things that——

Mr. Russert. Which is what you said before.

The President. That's right.

Haiti

Mr. Russert. Haiti. The military leaders have refused to meet. Your policy, the United States policy is to reinstate Mr. Aristide. Is it now time to broaden the embargo from just fuel to everything?

The President. We have to strengthen the embargo. There are two options. We can, in effect, have a total embargo and try to shut the country down. That will be more painful in the near term to the average Haitians who are already suffering. We can also try to do something that will target those people that are causing this problem, which is to get all of the other nations in the world to side with us in freezing the assets of the wealthy Haitians who are plundering that country, keeping democracy from taking root, and supporting the police chief and the military. I would prefer to do that, but I'm not going to rule out the other things. And we're following this on a daily basis, spending a lot of time with it.

Mr. Russert. So we could have a complete embargo on all goods?

The President. That is an option, but I also hope that the other wealthy nations of the world that have assets deposited from these Haitian interests who are keeping democracy from returning will join us in freezing those assets. That would really help. That would do more in less time to change the political climate than anything.

Mr. Russert. President Bush invaded Panama to remove Noriega. Would you consider invading Haiti to reinstate Aristide?

The President. I don't want to rule anything in or out. But let me just say that there's a difference here, though. He went to Panama not only to remove Noriega for the Panamanians but because Noriega, himself, was wanted for violating American law as a drugrunner.

Prime Minister Malval and President Aristide have both not called for us to do that. In fact, one of the problems we had with the Governors Island Agreement is that neither they nor the other side wanted the United States or the U.N. there in a police function. That is, those folks we were trying to land there the other day were supposed to train the army to be the army corps of engineers, to rebuild the country. Neither side has wanted that and they had these bad memories of invasion. Last time the Americans went there in 1915, we stayed nearly 20 years. So they have not asked for that. But I don't think we should rule anything in or out.

Mr. Russert. Your stated policy of the United States is to reinstate Mr. Aristide. The CIA has gone around this town saying that Aristide is mentally unstable. Can you as Commander in Chief tolerate that insubordination by the CIA?

The President. Well, I think you have to ask yourself whether it's insubordination or not. And let me tell you what I mean by that. The CIA is duty-bound to tell the Congress what it knows. That's the law. Just like the Joint Chiefs of Staff are duty-bound to go, when asked, express their personal opinion if they have an opinion different than the President, even though they work for me.

In secret hearings the CIA told the Senate what they told me before, which is that they thought they had some evidence which questioned Mr. Aristide's ability to be President of Haiti. All I can tell you is—and I'm glad in a way that it came out, since it had been whispered around—that based on my personal experience, the Vice President's repeated contacts with him, the willingness of Aristide to work with our people, he has done everything he said he would do. And more importantly, he agreed to put in Mr. Malval, who is a respected businessman, to give some balance.

Aristide may not be like you and me; he's had a very different life. But two-thirds of the Haitians voted for him, and he has shown a willingness to reach out and broaden his base. So I just disagree with—and I also disagree that the old CIA reports are conclusive in their evidence. But they had a legal responsibility to tell the Senate. If I had put the thumb on them, you'd be asking me, "Why are you gagging the CIA from giving American intelligence to the Senate Intelligence Committee?"

Mr. Russert. I might ask you that.

The President. You would.

Foreign Policy Team

Mr. Russert. Finally in this round, a lot of

calls or suggestions that Secretary of Defense Aspin, Secretary of State Christopher resign. Are they secure in their positions?

The President. I don't think that the President should even discuss that sort of thing, those personnel things. Let me say this: I think they deserve credit for doing well on many big things. This administration has secured the interest of America in dealing with Russia, in dealing with the Middle East, in raising economic issues to a new high, in conducting a thorough security bottoms-up review of the Pentagon and our military operations, and in many other areas.

We found three problems that we inherited here, when we got in, that are very difficult problems, in Bosnia, Somalia, and Haiti. And every day you can pick up the newspaper and see opinions on both sides about what we should do or a myriad of sides. We're doing the best we can on those. And we're going to do it, and we're going to do it with the team we've got, as long as we're all working together. I think that they have worked very hard, and I think that some of the attacks on them have been quite unfair.

Mr. Russert. Mr. President, we have to take a break. We'll be back with more from the Oval Office and talk about crime and kids in America.

[*The television stations took a commercial break.*]

Mr. Russert. We're back on "Meet the Press." I'm with my colleague, Tom Brokaw, talking to the President of the United States in the Oval Office.

Decline of the American Family

Mr. President, in recent months on "Meet the Press," we've talked to Senator Pat Moynihan, Washington Post columnist William Raspberry, the Reverend Jesse Jackson about the problem of kids and crime. And they are in agreement that the breakup of the traditional family as we know it—two out of every three black kids born this year will be born out of wedlock, two out of five white children born out of wedlock—is the breakup of the traditional family unit a national crisis?

The President. Absolutely. It is absolutely a crisis.

Mr. Russert. And what can you do about it as President?

The President. I think that as President I have to do two things. One is to speak about it and

to focus the attention of the Nation on it. I went to the University of North Carolina recently and spoke to the 200th anniversary there of the university and gave a major speech trying to deal with the combined impact of the breakdown of the family and the rise in violence and the rise in drugs and the lack of economic opportunity and——

Mr. Russert. Is there a correlation between crime and drugs and breakdown of the family?

The President. Absolutely. Let me back up and say I think America has two big challenges. One is to change in ways that will permit us to go into the 21st century winning as a country and as individuals. The second is to provide security in the face of all these changes so that people can have a coherent life and that we can't do that with economic stagnation or with social disintegration, and we're fighting with both. I mean, today in the Washington Post, there's a story of four people killed over the weekend, nine people wounded. A guy picks up a 1-year-old daughter—maybe his daughter—a 1-year-old child, drives away, and people drive after him, shoot him in the head, and the bullet then goes through the girl's body and blows her shoe off. You know, 3 or 4 days ago, an 11-year-old girl planning her own funeral, I mean, these things are terrible.

Let me just say, I've called the Attorney General last night; we talked for 30 minutes about this on the phone. We have got to use this administration to awaken in all Americans an understanding of this and to get everyone to ask what their personal responsibility is to try to help rebuild the family and the conditions of community. Then we have to follow policies which will do that.

Mr. Brokaw. Mr. President, do you think that there has been enough dialog within the black community about this whole issue, families without fathers? Jesse Jackson recently has started a campaign on black-on-black violence. But there really—among the activists in the black community, there hasn't been much public dialog. Has that disappointed you?

The President. Well, let me say this. I think there should be more. And I think that we should all be willing to face up to all the reasons why this has occurred. The famous African-American sociologist—at least he's famous in our circles—William Julius Wilson at the University of Chicago wrote a little book a few years ago called "The Truly Disadvantaged." It's only about 180 pages long, but it graphically shows you what has happened to black families in the inner cities and how the decline of the black family is associated not simply with the rise of welfare but with the evaporation of jobs for black males in those areas.

So I think, first, we ought to pass our crime bill here and put another 100,000 police on the street and do it right in community policing. But we also have to get work back into the lives of people. You know, you can't have generation after generation not knowing work and expect there to be structure and order in people's lives. That's one of the things that Colin Powell—retired as Chairman of the Joint Chiefs of Staff—he talked about maybe he could be a role model for people outside of the military who have none of the structure that's what makes the military go in this country.

Mr. Brokaw. So much of this is driven by drugs. Your administration has kind of taken drugs off the radar screen. Do you think you're going to have to take a harder line on drugs?

The President. Well, first of all, I don't think that's a fair characterization. The administration has had to subject the drug budget to the same ruthless discipline that nearly every other budget has been subject to. So that while we have increased some drug funding, like in the block grant program, some of the rest of it has not been increased. What I have tried to do is to get people to see the drug problem, first of all, in terms of stopping the major sources, and then here at home, focusing on drugs in terms of treatment and education and integrating it with our overall strategy on law enforcement and violence.

I think this country needs a community strategy which deals with the crises of drugs, violence, crime, the family, and work. And we need to go not only nationally, but at the grassroots level. And we need to understand that there's some basic things we have to do. If you want families to stay together, you've got to make it possible for people to be successful workers and successful parents.

If I could just briefly tell this one story: A couple of Sundays ago, we had a family in here taking a tour, a man, a wife, three daughters. One of these children was in a wheelchair. She was in this Make-A-Wish program, you know, a sick child wants to go see the President. I say hello. We have a picture. On the way out, the man says, "Mr. President, just in case you

think that one person doesn't make a difference," he said, "you signed the family leave bill, which gives me the right to spend time with my sick child and not lose my job. If you hadn't done that, if Congress hadn't passed it, I would have had to choose between spending this precious time with my daughter, who's probably not going to live, or keeping my job for my other two daughters and my wife. And I don't have to choose now. Don't ever think that what you do doesn't make a difference."

A few days later that little girl died. But that man knows that he was a good parent and a good worker. That's just one example of the kind of things we have to do that have moral content even though they may be public policies.

But no matter what we do, there has to be a reawakening of responsibility in every community. That goes back to your other question: Should the black community be debating this? They should. Should the white community be debating this? We should.

Racial Tension in Urban Areas

Mr. Brokaw. All of this, it seems to me, is fueling greater racial tensions, especially in the urban areas. Do you think that the racial tension and the racial climate in urban America now is better or worse than it was, say, 10 years ago?

The President. I think for middle class people it's much better. I think the level of comfort among people of different races is much higher. I think the appreciation for diversity is greater. I think for people who are outside the economic mainstream, it is much, much worse.

My God, we've got kids planning their funerals, 11-year-old kids. But the crying shame is, those people also want to be a part of mainstream America. I mean, look at these children. When they make these plans for their funerals, are they out there breaking the law? And one thing I'd like to say to the rest of America is, you read these horrible stories about how many people get killed on the weekends—most of the people that lived in all of those neighborhoods never break the law, work for a living for modest wages, pay their taxes, trying to do right by their kids. I mean, this country is falling apart because we have allowed a whole group of us to drift away. It's not an under class anymore, it's an outer class.

Mr. Russert. Mr. President, can we talk about

this in direct terms without a cloud of political correctness hovering over the subject?

The President. I think we have to. I think we've got to. I think Jesse Jackson, frankly, has performed a good service by going out and starting this debate again when the American people are willing to listen. We've got to be able to sit down and tell people what we think. I think that the American people are willing to put aside political correctness. But if we want to say tough things about the breakdown of the family and the responsibility of people who live in these communities, we also have to say tough things to the rest of America about how you can't just ignore these people until you have to read about how they're having children, children having children, and nobody's married and they're having babies and these kids are dying. You've got to have some structure in these communities and some opportunity. If you want to preach the American dream to them, there's got to be something there at the end of the road. So there's something for all of us to do here.

Mr. Russert. Mr. President, we have to take another break. We'll be back in just a moment to talk about Bill Clinton's first year in office.

[*The television stations took a commercial break.*]

President's Approval Rating

Mr. Russert. We're back with the President of the United States in the Oval Office.

Mr. President, your poll numbers are low, but the one that's most striking to me is that since you've been President, the number of people who think the country is on the wrong track has doubled. What happened?

The President. Well, they may not know what's going on. And I think we should all ask ourselves what responsibility that has. Let's look at the facts. Let's just look at the facts. Since I became President, we have lowered the deficit, lowered interest rates, kept inflation down. This economy has produced more private sector jobs in the first 9 months than in the previous 4 years. Jobs are up and investment is up. We have shown discipline and direction in the budget. It was a remarkable achievement. Not only that, in that budget we did something that has not been done for 20 years, we tried to reverse the inequality of incomes. We asked the wealthy to pay more, and we gave over 15 million work-

ing families, comprising about 50 million Americans, a tax cut because they're working hard and still hovering around the poverty line. Most Americans don't know that.

Mr. Russert. So it's just a communications problem?

The President. Well, let me finish.

Mr. Russert. Please.

The President. In that program, one of the things I promised the American people to do to try to add more security to their lives was to open the doors of college education to everybody. We reformed the college loan program; we lowered the interest rates; we strung out the repayments. Most Americans don't know that. We passed the family leave law, which I just spoke about. We have a major health care proposal on the table. We have opened any number of economic avenues of opportunity that everyone agrees with. We've got $37 billion more in high-tech equipment up for exports now, created hundreds of thousands of jobs.

So the economic record of this administration in only 9 months is very good. The educational record of this administration is good. What we're doing on health care is unprecedented in our lifetime. The foreign policy record on the issues that really affect our national security is good.

There are the problems that nobody's figured out how to resolve; I concede that. I do not know what the answer to this is. But I know this: I believe that when historians look at this first year, they will be hard pressed to find many first years of Presidencies that equal ours. The Congressional Quarterly said the other day that only President Eisenhower had had a higher success rate in Congress than I have. If you go out and ask the average American, they think I hardly ever get anything passed.

Mr. Russert. But the voters——

The President. Now, that may be—that's right, that may be my fault, it may be somebody else's fault. But the reality is, the economy is going in the right direction, I'm keeping the commitments of the campaign to empower people through education and through health care initiatives and through all these other things. Why don't they know that? I don't know. I gave a speech the other day to 250 people from my home town, my home State who were up here, and I just went through these specific things. And they said, "There must have been a conspiracy to keep this a secret; we didn't know any of this."

Mr. Russert. But in six States since you've been President, Senate seats in Texas and Georgia, Governorships in Virginia, New Jersey, mayoralties in New York and Los Angeles have all gone Republican. There must be some small message in there for you.

The President. Well, I think the message is people still want change. But you know, you're from Buffalo. Don't you believe that all politics is local? I was a Governor for 12 years, and I can honestly say, with 150 Governors I served with I never heard one say, not one, that he or she won or lost an election because of the President.

Now, what are these things saying? They say people are still upset at crime, they're upset at the lack of jobs, they're upset when they're paying more taxes and think they're not getting something else for it. But we are addressing each of those things. Whether it's in the economic program, the health care program, the reinventing program, expanding trade, we are addressing those things.

I think that what I have to do is to do a better job of getting out there and getting the record there. But what happens here is every day is just a new battle. I don't know anybody who's out there who believes that all these elections are any more than a referendum on what people want for their mayors and their Governors.

Media Coverage

Mr. Brokaw. Mr. President, Jimmy Carter used to complain that the White House press was here simply to play "gotcha." Are you saying, in effect, that the press coverage has failed you and failed the country?

The President. No. Well, I think it may have failed the country some, but I don't take it personally, and I don't think it's a "gotcha" thing. I think, in a way it may be my fault. I go from one thing to another, so we have one moment on national service, for example—a signature idea of my campaign, something we know the American people care about—and it happens, but it happens in the middle of all these other things so nobody knows it happened. I think that's the big problem.

Mr. Brokaw. Let me ask you about 1996. You had a meeting in the White House the other day with Colin Powell; he endorsed NAFTA. Do you think Colin Powell is a Democrat or a Republican? And do you think he'll run for office in '96?

The President. You'll have to ask him that. I don't think I should speak for him.

Mr. Brokaw. Well, what's your instinct?

The President. I don't have an instinct. Let me just say this: What I have determined to do is to get up every day and do what I think is right and try to move this country forward and keep the commitments I made to the American people and follow it through with real conviction and just let everything else happen. I can't control a lot of the events. But I do think it is astonishing to me, and I take this on myself maybe more than you, but that—is to go back to Al Gore's line in the campaign, "What should be up is up; what should be down is down." We're moving in the right direction, and people should know that. And if they don't, then I have to examine why they don't. But perhaps you do, too.

Mr. Russert. Mr. President, we have to take a break. We'll be right back after this break.

[*The television stations took a commercial break.*]

Mr. Russert. We're back with the President. Tom Brokaw, you have a question.

President's Health

Mr. Brokaw. Even in the Oval Office, you can hear the local protest outside about firefighters or something in Washington, DC. You know that it is like living in a fishbowl here. Comedians have had a lot of fun with the fact that you run every day, but you don't seem to lose any weight. In fact, what can you tell us about your personal health? Have you lost weight?

The President. A little bit.

Mr. Brokaw. And have you changed your eating habits?

The President. Yes, quite a bit since I've been here. I have lost weight. I gained a lot of weight in the campaign. I'm now almost back to where I was 2 years ago. I've lost weight, and lost, I don't know, 2 or 3 inches off my waist. But I run 6 days a week, and I just try to—it's like everything else, I think you just have to get up, sort of show up every day, and try to make a little progress. I think that's what you do in life.

The Presidency

Mr. Russert. Mr. President, a friend of yours

told me that you jokingly sometimes refer to life in the White House as "the crown jewel of the Federal penitentiary system."

The President. That's right.

Mr. Russert. How confining has it been?

The President. Well, it's pretty confining. I always say I don't know whether it's the finest public housing in America or the crown jewel of the prison system. It's a very isolating life. And one of the things that frustrates me is that I get more easily out of touch and maybe even out of harmony with the American people—that's the question you asked me earlier. I also know that every little word I say can be sort of twisted, you know. And again, I don't fault anybody, but I just have to be careful.

Mr. Russert. We have just a few seconds.

The President. Did you see what Gergen just did? He brought in this thing saying that the headline is now that Clinton accused labor of roughshod tactics. I mean, those guys are my friends. I just don't agree with them on NAFTA. We're going to all work together——

Mr. Russert. We have just a few seconds. Is there one thing that, a year ago, you were absolutely certain of that you're not quite sure about now?

The President. Yes. I was absolutely certain a year ago that I could pursue this aggressive agenda of change and that every step along the way I'd be able to tell the American people what I was doing and convince them that we're going right. We are pursuing it, we're making in a way a little more progress than I thought we would, but there's a big gap between what we've done and what I've been able to tell the people about. I've got to do a better job.

Mr. Russert. Thank you for letting us join you in the Oval Office today. I take it this is the room you'll invite the Buffalo Bills after they win the Super Bowl?

The President. That's right. The Buffalo Bills will be here if they win the Super Bowl this year.

Mr. Russert. Mr. President, thank you very much.

Mr. Brokaw. You'll be in office a long time if that's the case. [*Laughter*]

NOTE: The interview began at 9 a.m. in the Oval Office at the White House.

Message to the Congress on Rhinoceros and Tiger Trade by China and Taiwan
November 8, 1993

To the Congress of the United States:

On September 7, 1993, the Secretary of the Interior certified that the People's Republic of China (PRC) and Taiwan are engaging in trade of rhinoceros and tiger parts and products that diminishes the effectiveness of the Convention on International Trade in Endangered Species of Wild Fauna and Flora (CITES). Five rhinoceros species and the tiger are listed in Appendix I of CITES, which means that the species are threatened with extinction and no trade for primarily commercial purposes is allowed. Although recent actions by the PRC and Taiwan show that some progress has been made in addressing their rhinoceros and tiger trade, the record demonstrates that they still fall short of the international conservation standards of CITES. This letter constitutes my report to the Congress pursuant to section 8(b) of the Fisherman's Protective Act of 1967, as amended (Pelly Amendment) (22 U.S.C. 1978(b)).

The population of the world's rhinoceros has declined 90 percent within the last 23 years to the present level of less than 10,000 animals, and the tiger population has declined 95 percent within this century to the present level of about 5,000. Neither the PRC nor Taiwan has fully implemented the international standards established by CITES for controlling the trade in these species, and the poaching of rhinoceroses and tigers continues in their native ranges fueled in part by the market demand in the PRC and Taiwan. These populations will likely be extinct in the next 2 to 5 years if the trade in their parts and products is not eliminated.

To protect the rhinoceros and tiger from extinction, all countries and entities that currently consume their parts and products must implement adequate legislative measures and provide for enforcement that effectively eliminates the trade, including taking actions to comply with the criteria set down by CITES in September 1993 and fully cooperating with all CITES delegations. The PRC and Taiwan have made good faith efforts to stop the trade in rhinoceros and tiger parts and products, and have, since the announcement of Pelly certification, undertaken some positive legislative and administrative steps in this regard. These efforts, however, have yet to yield effective reductions in trade.

I wish to support and build on these good faith efforts undertaken by the PRC and Taiwan. At the same time, I would like to make clear the U.S. position that only effective reductions in the destructive trade in these species will prevent the rhinoceros and tiger from becoming extinct. Accordingly, I have established an Interagency Task Force to coordinate the provision of U.S. technical assistance to the PRC and Taiwan to help them eliminate their illegal wildlife trade. I have also instructed the Department of the Interior, in coordination with the Department of State and the American Institute in Taiwan, to enter immediately into dialogue with the PRC and Taiwan regarding specific U.S. offers of trade and law enforcement assistance.

Actions by the PRC and Taiwan that would demonstrate their commitment to the elimination of trade in rhinoceros and tiger parts and products could include: at a minimum, consolidation and control of stockpiles; formation of a permanent wildlife or conservation law enforcement unit with specialized training; development and implementation of a comprehensive law enforcement and education action plan; increased enforcement penalties; prompt termination of amnesty periods for illegal holding and commercialization; and establishment of regional law enforcement arrangements. I would expect that in taking these actions, the PRC and Taiwan would take account of the recommendations by the CITES Standing Committee and other CITES subsidiary bodies. In that regard, I am pleased to announce that the United States will participate in a delegation to the PRC and Taiwan organized by CITES to evaluate their progress between now and the March 1994 CITES Standing Committee meeting.

At its last meeting, the CITES Standing Committee unanimously recommended that parties consider implementing "stricter domestic measures up to and including prohibition in trade in wildlife species now" against the PRC and Taiwan for their trade in rhinoceros and tiger parts and products. The United States is prepared, through close dialogue and technical aid, to assist the PRC and Taiwan. I hope that both will demonstrate measurable, verifiable, and substantial progress by March 1994. Otherwise, import prohibitions will be necessary, as recommended by the CITES Standing Committee.

WILLIAM J. CLINTON

The White House,
November 8, 1993.

Statement on the Resignation of the Deputy Secretary of State
November 8, 1993

I accept with regret the resignation offered today by Clifton Wharton, who has served our country honorably as Deputy Secretary of State. My administration has benefited greatly from his dignified presence, and it will be diminished by his departure.

Clifton Wharton's service as Deputy Secretary has been outstanding. Over the past 10 months, he has made many important contributions to our Nation's foreign policy. Through his leadership on reform of AID and other foreign assistance programs and his important work on the reorganization of the State Department, as well as through his successful mission to Southeast Asia and his prodigious efforts in Latin America, he has distinguished himself at every turn. Every aspect of his service has demonstrated the same drive and talent that marked his earlier successes in the worlds of business and education.

I know that Cliff is dedicated to our country's service. I continue to need and value his insights and counsel, and I hope to be able to continue calling on him for specific assignments in the days ahead. He and his family have my fondest wishes for a successful future.

Nomination for the Commodity Futures Trading Commission
November 8, 1993

The President today announced his intention to nominate John E. Tull, Jr., as a member of the Commodity Futures Trading Commission.

"As a farmer who has dedicated years of service to State commodity boards, John Tull has the experience to serve as an informed and effective member of the CFTC," the President said. "I am pleased to name him to this important board."

NOTE: A biography of the nominee was made available by the Office of the Press Secretary.

Nomination for Posts at the United States Information Agency
November 8, 1993

The President announced today that he intends to nominate John P. "Jack" Loiello to be the Associate Director of the U.S. Information Agency for Education and Cultural Affairs, and that he has appointed Charles Fox to be the Director of USIA's WORLDNET TV and Film Service.

"Jack Loiello's long experience in promoting international goodwill makes him an outstanding choice for this position," said the President. "Likewise, Charles Fox brings a distinguished record in academia, the media, government, and business to this post at WORLDNET."

NOTE: Biographies were made available by the Office of the Press Secretary.

Nomination for Ambassador to Angola
November 8, 1993

The President announced today that he intends to nominate career Foreign Service officer Edmund T. DeJarnette, Jr., to be Ambassador to the Republic of Angola.

"I am very pleased to be making this announcement today," said the President. "Edmund DeJarnette's extensive experience in Africa makes him an outstanding choice for this post."

NOTE: A biography of the nominee was made available by the Office of the Press Secretary.

Remarks on Endorsements of the North American Free Trade Agreement
November 9, 1993

The President. Thank you. Thank you very much for being here. After what David and Kathleen said, I'm not sure there's much left for me to say. I thought they were terrific, and

I thank them for coming, for what they said, and for putting this issue squarely where it ought to be: on the questions of jobs and opportunity for the American people.

We asked you to come here today in the hope that together you would help us to pass the NAFTA legislation through Congress, and that if you have questions about this you could ask them. So I want to basically spend this time to open the floor to questions to you. But I would like to make just a few remarks if I might by way of introduction.

First of all, it's important to put this NAFTA agreement into the larger context of our Nation's economic strategy. And it's important that I at least tell you from my point of view how it fits. Our Nation is a churning cauldron of economic activity now, with a lot of opportunity being created and a lot of hardship being developed at the same time. The world is changing very rapidly. The American economy is changing very rapidly. For 20 years the wages of the bottom 60 percent of our work force, more or less, have been stagnant as people work harder for the same or lower wages. We know that over the last 20 years, as we've become more and more enmeshed in the global economy, the jobs have been changing more rapidly. We know now that when a person loses a job, for example, usually a person will find another job, but it's not the same old job. It used to be the normal course of events was you'd have a lay-off, but you wouldn't just lose a job. Those things are all changing now.

We know that through the discipline of the market economy our productivity now is the highest in the world again in manufacturing and in many other areas. But we also know that there's been a whole lot of reduction of employment in many areas to get that higher productivity, with fewer people producing more output. So this is a time of enormous opportunity and enormous insecurity. We have to have a full-court-press, comprehensive economic strategy to achieve what should be the objective of every American, more jobs and higher growth rates.

In our administration, we began with trying to get the deficit down, trying to drive interest rates down, and trying to keep inflation down. Those historically low interest rates have led to literally millions and millions of people refinancing their home mortgages, refinancing their business debt, increasing investment in our country. The result has been that even though

we don't have as many jobs as we'd like, the private sector has produced more jobs in the last 10 months than in the previous 4 years. And if we can keep interest rates and inflation down and investment up, we're going to have more and more and more growth. That's encouraging.

The last budget bill provided special tax incentives for people to invest in new and small enterprises where most of the new jobs are being created. Extended research and development tax credits provided for extra incentives to convert from these defense technologies to domestic technologies. We recently took $37 billion worth of high-tech equipment off the restriction list for export so we could put American products into play in the global economy.

But with all of that, no one has shown how a wealthy country can grow wealthier and create more jobs unless there is global economic growth through trade. There is simply no evidence that you can do it any other way. About half America's growth in the last 7 years has come from trade growth. And the jobs that are tied to trade, on average, pay about 17 percent more than jobs which are totally within the American economy, so that it is impossible for all these other strategies to succeed—if by success you mean creating more jobs, more growth, and higher incomes—unless there is a level of global economic growth financed through expanded trade that Americans can take advantage of. We can't get there.

So that brings us to NAFTA, and how does it fit, and why should we do it. This agreement will, as all of you know, lower American tariffs but will lower Mexican tariffs and trade barriers more than American tariffs, because ours are lower anyway. This agreement will help us to gain access to a market of 90 million people, which has shown a preference for American products unprecedented in all the world. Seventy percent of all the purchases by Mexican consumers of foreign products go to American products. This agreement will unite Canada, Mexico, and the United States in a huge trading bloc which will enable us to grow and move together.

This agreement will also—and this is very important—produce most of its jobs by enabling us to use the Mexican precedent to go into the whole rest of Latin America, to have a trading bloc of well over 700 million people, and will also—and I see some of you in this audience I know who are interested in this—this agreement, if adopted by the Congress, will increase the leverage that I, as your President, will have to get an agreement on the world trade round, the GATT round, this year with Europe and with Japan and with the other nations involved because they will see, "Well, we want access to that big Latin American market, and the way to do it is to adopt a world trade agreement. We don't want America to have an overwhelming preferential treatment in Mexico and other countries, so we'll have to give them more access to our markets in Europe and Asia."

It will also make a statement that America intends to go charging into the 21st century still believing we can compete and win and that we intend to lead the world in expanding horizons, not in hunkering down. And believe you me, no one knows quite which way it will go. This is why the NAFTA agreement has acquired a symbolic and larger significance even than the terms of the agreement, because we know that if the United States turns away from open markets and more trade and competition, how can we then say to the Europeans and the Japanese they must open their markets to us, they must continue to expand? So the stakes here are very large indeed.

Now, let's deal with the arguments against NAFTA. The people who are against it say that if this agreement passes, more irresponsible American companies will shut their doors in America and open doors in Mexico because the costs are cheaper and this agreement allows them to do that all over the country. To that I answer the following: Number one, I was the Governor of a State for 12 years that had almost 22 percent of its work force in manufacturing. I saw plants close and go to Mexico, brought one back before I left office. I know why they did it. I know how they did it. I understand the pressures, particularly on the lower wage companies with low margins of profit.

But my answer to you is, there is the *maquilladora* system now in practice in Mexico. If anybody wants to go down there to produce for the American market, they can do that now. And if we defeat NAFTA, they can continue to do that, and it will be more likely that they will do that. Why? This is the nub of the argument: Because clearly, with the agreements we have on labor committing Mexico to enforce its own labor code and make that a part of

an international commission on the environment, clearly, we're going to raise the cost of production in Mexico. Clearly, when Mexico lowers its domestic content requirement on automobiles, for example, we'll be able to go from 1,000 to 60,000 American-made cars sold in Mexico next year. There will be less incentive to go to Mexico to produce for the American market, less incentive, not more.

What does Mexico get out of this then? What they get out of it is they have 90 million people there now producing for themselves. What they want is American investment in Mexico to hire Mexicans to produce goods and services for Mexicans so they can grow their economy from within. Is that bad for us? No, that's good for us. Why? Because the more people down there who have jobs and the better the jobs are, the more they can buy American products and the less they will feel a compulsion to become part of America's large immigration problem today. So that is good for us.

This is very important. I would never knowingly do anything to hurt the job market in America. I have spent my entire life, public life, trying to deal with the economic problems of ordinary people. I ran for this job to alleviate the insecurity, the anxiety, the anger, the frustration of ordinary Americans.

Tonight there will be a debate that a few people will watch on television in which, with a lot of rhetoric, the attempt will be made to characterize this administration as representing elite corporate interests and our opponent as representing the ordinary working people. Let me tell you something, this lady, I wish she were going to be on the debate against Mr. Perot tonight. He wouldn't have much of a shot against her because she so obviously disproves the argument. This is a debate about what is best for ordinary Americans.

Look around this room. The rest of us are going to do fine, aren't we? Let's not kid ourselves. If this thing were to go down, everybody in this room would figure out some way to be all right. That's true, isn't it? I mean, most of you are here as influence centers in your congressional district because you'll figure out a way to land on your feet. Unless the whole country goes down the tubes, most of you will figure out a way to be innovative and work around whatever the rules are. We are doing this because it allows our country as a whole to expand, to grow, to broaden its horizons, the people who can't be here.

You know, it's an amazing thing. Again I will say, the resentments, the hurts, the anxieties, the fears that have been poured into this debate are real and legitimate and deserve a response. And we should all recognize that. You just think how people feel when they've worked for 20 years and they get a pink slip, and they're just treated like a disposable can of soda pop. I mean, this is a tough deal. Think about the Members of Congress that are being asked to vote for this agreement when they've got 15 percent, 20 percent unemployment in their districts and they represent these big inner-city neighborhoods or these big, distressed rural areas where there's no investment going into their areas. There are legitimate problems out there.

What is wrong is that they have made NAFTA the receptacle of their resentment instead of seeing it as one step toward alleviating the problem. And that is my point, not that there's anything wrong with the worries and the fears and the hurts that are brought to this table but that this country has never, never run from competition, except one time, and it helped to bring on the Great Depression. And with every evolutionary stage of the global economy in this century, we have always led the effort to broaden opportunity and always welcomed the rigor of competition and felt that we could do it. And we have got to do that again.

So I ask you as earnestly as I can to remember that you are speaking for the very people who may think they're arguing against this. This is about what's going to happen to our country. There is no evidence, I will say again, there is no evidence anywhere in the world that you can create jobs, raise income, and promote growth in an already wealthy country unless there is global growth, financed and fueled through expanded trade. There is simply no evidence for it.

I want to go out to meet with the President of China and the Prime Minister of Japan and the heads of all of those Asian countries and tell them we're happy to buy their products, they ought to buy more of ours, and they need to stimulate their economy. I want to go to the Europeans and say, "Okay, give us the world trade agreement. You don't have to hunker down and close up. You can expand, and we'll do it together." But if we don't do this with our closest neighbor, it's going to be hard for

us to have the credibility to make the case for the world.

Thank you very much.

Q. Mr. President, one of the concerns of the United States, as you're well aware, concerns the potential for job loss. We've all heard how the passage of NAFTA will create job loss in the United States. I'd like to share with you a different view, and that is that the passage of NAFTA will actually create jobs. I'm with the World Trade Center Association, and we're actually inundated by requests from our Pacific rim members, asking us to identify locations in the United States where, after NAFTA is passed, they can come in and build industry to protect their market share in the United States. They see NAFTA as taking jobs away from the Pacific basin, and they want to be able to counter that by coming over to the United States and actually building industry to satisfy this market share.

The President. That's a good point. You all heard what he said, didn't you? He just said that he's with the World Trade Center, and he gets a lot of requests for information about sites in the United States where people in Asia would look at putting up operations to protect their share of the American market if NAFTA passes.

Let me give you another example, more indirect, something I think you'll see a lot of. Mattel toy factory announced that they would in all probability move an operation from China to Mexico and buy all their products of plastic from the United States instead of from Asia. So there will be an indirect job benefit there. But there are millions of these things; it's incalculable. That's what always happens if you decide you're going to expand opportunity and growth and then let the ingenuity of the marketplace work for the interest of ordinary people.

Let me just say one thing about that. Every major study but one has predicted a job gain for NAFTA in the United States. And the major study that predicted a job loss predicted it in large measure because they estimated that there would be fewer immigrants coming into this country and taking jobs here as a result of it. So that still may not be a net increase in unemployment. All the others estimated net job gains.

Now, there obviously will be people who lose their jobs, as there are today. We're talking net. When somebody says there's a net job gain of 200,000, you say, "Well, if you gain 210 and lose 10, the 10 who lose feel more pain than the 210 who gain, arguably." What does that mean? That means that this administration has an obligation, and the Congress, I want to emphasize has an obligation and the business community has an obligation to support a legitimate strategy for retraining all these workers at a high level of quality in a relevant way and developing a strategy for investment across this country. That is what we're working on. That's what we're going to give the working people.

The other point that needs to be made is there is no power to protect the people of this country from the changes sweeping through the global economy. I mean, the average 18-year-old is going to change work eight times in a lifetime anyway, whatever we do. But we do have an obligation to help them, those who are in difficulty, and we will meet that obligation.

Q. Thank you, Mr. President. As an African-American, I have a basic question. As you know, historically, African-Americans have experienced high unemployment, lower pay. In fact, we created the phrase, "Last hired, first fired." I would further suggest to you that we're probably the most vulnerable members of this society. Given those set of facts, I would like to hear your response to why African-Americans, in general, and African-American politicians should support NAFTA.

The President. African-Americans, in general, and African-American politicians should support NAFTA, first of all, because it means more jobs. Secondly, as we found when we had our products fair here, it means opportunities for a lot of small businesses. As Ms. Kaminiski said, there will be tens of thousands of small businesses who will be—and minority entrepreneurs, by and large, are smaller businesses. They should support it because anything that increases the job base of America will help; and finally because, even though this gentleman is from Utah, most of the big service industries that will expand their job base in America because of the opportunities in Mexico are located in larger cities and have a substantial percentage of their hires coming from the minority community.

And having said that, let me make one other point. That will not solve all the problems. We've got a crime bill. We've got to have a family strategy. We've got to have a whole economic strategy for the distressed areas of this country. We have to have a reemployment system instead of the unemployment system we've

got. It will not answer all of the problems. But it is not an argument to vote against NAFTA that it doesn't solve every problem. In other words, that's what the other side's done. They've loaded all of the problems of the 1980's onto this NAFTA vote, which actually makes them better. We don't want to get in a position of overclaiming for it. This doesn't solve all of the problems of the American economy, but it does solve substantial ones that ought to be addressed.

Q. Mr. President, I'm from Texas, and I'm very concerned about the environment on the border. How will NAFTA affect the borders?

The President. It will improve the environment on the border. That's why we've gotten so many environmental organizations to endorse this. Not all the environmental groups are for it, but most of the environmental groups that are against it are against it for something that often happens to progressives: They're making the perfect, the enemy of the good. That is, they think it ought to be better, but it's very good.

This agreement, first of all, requires every nation to enforce its own environmental laws and can make the failure to do so the subject of a complaint through the trade system. Secondly, to support this agreement, the World Bank has committed about $2 billion in financing, and we have agreed to set up a North American development bank to have $2 to $3 billion worth of infrastructure projects in the beginning on both sides of the border.

So there are substantial environmental problems associated with *maquilladora* operations, substantial. They are significant; they are real. They affect Mexicans; they affect Americans. If this trade agreement passes, this will be the most sweeping environmental protection ever to be part of a trade agreement, and it will make the environment better, not worse. And by the way, it will create jobs for a lot of people on both sides of the border in cleaning up the environment, jobs that won't happen and environmental clean-up that won't happen if we vote it down.

Q. Mr. President, I'm a manufacturer from the great State of Arkansas. Is there anything in the agreement that's going to keep China from putting in a factory and importing into Mexico and then turning the goods right straight back to us?

The President. There is nothing in the agreement that will prohibit other countries from actually hiring people, but there are rules of origin. What we do have protection against, and what we are actually strengthening now, is using Mexico as a way station to get around, like, the multifiber agreement, which provides a lot of protection to our apparel manufacturers. All the agriculture people are concerned about it, too. Everybody is concerned about the fact that if—well, let me back up, and for the benefit of everybody else, let me say this: Most of the trade restrictions that Mexico has and most of the restrictions we have on them are in the form of tariffs. Our tariffs don't amount to much; they're 4 percent. Mexican tariffs run between 10 to 20, by and large. They amount to much more. So we get a huge break on the tariff thing.

In the case of apparels and one or two other things, including some agricultural products, there are nontariff restrictions, like the multifiber agreement, that will give Mexico some greater access to the American market in apparels. The real problem there would be—but it's done over a 10-year period, as you know, it's phased in gradually over a 10-year period. The real legitimate problem would be, is if Mexico becomes a transshipment point for either beef, for jackets, for anything. And I want to be candid here: One of our big challenges is going to be to make sure that we have enough customs officials to stop the abuses that might happen in transshipment in agricultural and in the manufacturing sectors of our economy that are protected by things other than tariffs. We are working right now on setting up a special customs department section to do nothing but that. And I think we'll be able to satisfy the American people about it.

Let me make one other comment about that. There is a big incentive for Mexico not to let its country become a transshipment point, which is that under this agreement anybody who wants to can withdraw from it with 6 months notice. There's another big incentive in this agreement that almost no one has talked about. The term of art is called "surge." But basically what it means is, under this agreement, if there is an unanticipated adverse impact, bad impact on some sector of our economy or the Mexican economy, either side can raise that and say, "Listen, we talked this through, nobody anticipated this happening; this is terrible." And that portion of the economy can, in effect, be shield-ed for a period of 3 years while we work that out.

So there are some good protections built in here from both our side and from their side against adverse reactions. Again, fairly unique things, but we owe you a good customs section, and we're doing our best to set it up.

Q. Mr. President, I'll try not to make this sound like a speech, but we've been weaving fabrics in central Pennsylvania since 1896. We have fifth-generation employees. I have been courted by the State of Mississippi to move there for years, but we're not going to; we're staying in Pennsylvania. My people have suffered job loss because of flawed trade policy for many, many years. They understand that NAFTA is the first trade policy that opens markets for us. They understand the security that that brings. And I've committed to them to bring back some of those jobs we lost when Congress approves NAFTA on the 17th or whenever they make up their minds to do so. So thank you.

The President. Good for you. Thank you.

Let me just say, I want to emphasize this. The evidence is, the evidence is clear: We have seen a productivity increase in the American manufacturing sector at 4 and 5 percent a year for more than a decade now. You'd have to look real hard to see any example like that of economic improvement of performance.

Now, why didn't it manifest itself in economic growth? Because one way we got more productive was we used more machines and fewer people, we used more technology, and it takes time for those kinds of changes to manifest themselves in economic opportunity. But you just heard him make the point: The only way you can be both productive and expand your employment base is if you got more people to buy your stuff, which means you either have to raise the incomes of the jobs of the people in your own country. And even when you do that, if you're a wealthy country, it's not enough, you have to have global markets.

I really appreciate what you said, sir.

I can take one more, I think.

Q. Mr. President, will NAFTA allow for labor organizations to—[*inaudible*]—its support, or help labor organizations move into Mexico and bring the standard of the Mexican labor up?

The President. Well, let me tell you, let me answer the question this way: NAFTA requires Mexico and the United States and Canada to follow their own labor laws. Mexico has a very good labor code on the book. But President Salinas would be the first one to tell you, it has been widely ignored. The Salinas government has also promised, in addition—but let me just explain what this means. It means that if there is evidence that they are violating their own labor laws, that that can be the subject of a trade complaint and can be worked through the trade system just like putting up a trade barrier.

There is no precedent; no trade agreement has ever done this before. I know a lot of my friends in labor say, "Well, it ought to be stronger. It ought to have this, that, and that other thing." There has never been a country ever willing to subject its labor code to trade sanctions before, never happened. So I think it's a pretty good first step.

The other thing they've agreed to do is to raise their minimum wage on at least an annual basis as their economy grows. And their wage structure works just like ours: When you raise the minimum wage, it bumps up through the whole system. And their wages have been growing rather rapidly.

Right now all the basic analyses show—and this is ultimately the best hope that I think will happen in the apparel industry over the next 10 years—is that our productivity edge is slightly greater than their wage edge. And if we can keep growing at a normal rate in terms of productivity—that is, our productivity is roughly a little over 5 times greater than theirs and our wage levels on average are about 5 times higher than theirs. But if our productivity continues to grow, their wages are rising much more rapidly than ours, as they would because they're on such a low base. I think over the next 10 years what their objective is, is to grow into a full partner, like Canada, where the cost of living is about the same, the trade is more or less in balance, but the volume is huge. I mean, that's really what our objective ought to be. Canada has the biggest two-way trade relationship with the United States of any country in the world. And it benefits both countries because both of us have about the same cost of living.

And what we've tried to do is to get this thing worked out right, including putting the labor code in there, so that Mexico can't do what so many Latin American countries have done before to kill their economic programs and their political programs. They've given up on democracy, and they haven't had the courage to develop a middle class. This government is committed, I believe, down there to developing a middle class, and they've certainly done more than any government in history to do it. And they can't do it without observing their labor code.

Q. [*Inaudible*]—to support strikes and labor actions?

The President. Yes. That's what the labor code requires. Their labor code permits that. And they'll have to honor that now or just be constantly caught up in all these trade actions. And again I say, I know our friends and my friends in the labor movement wanted Mexico to agree to put the average manufacturing wage into the trade agreement. But you have to understand, they have allowed us to have a trade agreement that gets into their internal politics more than any country in history on the environmental policy and on labor policy. Also, I will say again, we can compete with these folks. We can do it. And I need your help to convince the Congress. Thank you.

Before I go, let me ask you one more time: Please personally contact the Members of Congress about this, whether Republican or Democrat. This is not a partisan issue, this is an American issue. I had a little trouble when I got here, but I'm determined by the time I leave that we will see economic policy as a part of our national security and we will have a bipartisan economic policy, the way we had to have a bipartisan foreign policy in the cold war. We have got to do it, and expanding trade has got to be a part of it.

Thank you.

NOTE: The President spoke at 11:55 a.m. in Room 450 of the Old Executive Office Building. In his remarks, he referred to David Boyles, senior vice president of operations and systems, American Express Travelers Check Group, Salt Lake City, UT; and Kathleen Kaminiski, co-owner, Triseal Corp., Chicago, IL.

Message to the Congress Reporting on Panamanian Government Assets
November 9, 1993

To the Congress of the United States:

I hereby report to the Congress on developments since the last Presidential report on April 21, 1993, concerning the continued blocking of Panamanian government assets. This report is submitted pursuant to section 207(d) of the International Emergency Economic Powers Act, 50 U.S.C. 1706(d).

On April 5, 1990, President Bush issued Executive Order No. 12710, terminating the national emergency declared on April 8, 1988, with respect to Panama. While this order terminated the sanctions imposed pursuant to that declaration, the blocking of Panamanian government assets in the United States was continued in order to permit completion of the orderly unblocking and transfer of funds that the President directed on December 20, 1989, and to foster the resolution of claims of U.S. creditors involving Panama, pursuant to 50 U.S.C. 1706(a). The termination of the national emergency did not affect the continuation of compliance audits and enforcement actions with respect to activities taking place during the sanctions period, pursuant to 50 U.S.C. 1622(a).

Since the last report, $400,000 has been unblocked by specific license. Of the approximately $5.9 million remaining blocked at this time, some $5.3 million is held in escrow by the Federal Reserve Bank of New York at the request of the Government of Panama. Additionally, approximately $600,000 is held in commercial bank accounts for which the Government of Panama has not requested unblocking. A small residual in blocked reserve accounts established under section 565.509 of the Panamanian Transactions Regulations, 31 CFR 565.509, remains on the books of U.S. firms pending the final reconciliation of accounting records involving claims and counterclaims between the firms and the Government of Panama.

I will continue to report periodically to the Congress on the exercise of authorities to prohibit transactions involving property in which the Government of Panama has an interest, pursuant to 50 U.S.C. 1706(d).

WILLIAM J. CLINTON

The White House,
November 9, 1993.

Nomination for the Communications Satellite Corporation
November 9, 1993

The President announced today that he intends to nominate Peter S. Knight, a former top aide to Vice President Gore, to serve on the Board of Directors of the Communications Satellite Corporation.

"Peter Knight, through his many years of work for the Vice President and his private sector accomplishments, has established himself as an expert on communications matters with a solid grasp of business management," said the President. "I think he will be an outstanding addition to COMSAT's board."

NOTE: A biography of the nominee was made available by the Office of the Press Secretary.

Remarks in a Telephone Conversation With the Vice President on the NAFTA Television Debate
November 10, 1993

The President. Hey, how are you?

The Vice President. I'm doing great, thank you.

The President. Well, you were great last night.

The Vice President. Well, I appreciate that.

The President. It was really wonderful. I was so proud not only of what you said but of how you said it, kind of appealing to people's hopes instead of their fears. It was terrific, and of course all the results today show that you really can make these arguments to the American people and tell the truth and prevail. I'm just elated.

The Vice President. Well, thank you, Mr. President. We've got a few days left now, as you well know, and your voice is being heard by hundreds of people here at Storage Technology who have been working in behalf of NAFTA because they're trying to sell products into Mexico, and they have a 20 percent tariff they have to overcome now, which would go down to zero if NAFTA passes. It's already zero coming in the opposite direction, and if NAFTA doesn't pass, these folks have to worry about a Japanese company coming in to locate in Mexico to serve that growing market and then use it as an export platform to compete right here in the United States. They want to base these jobs here in the United States instead. So you're talking to the right audience here, Mr. President. We're trying to get the message out all over the country. So thank you so much for your call.

The President. Well, I want to say to all the people who are there, first, thank you for receiving the Vice President and Tim Wirth today, and thank you for your support of this. I urge you to do what you can in the next few days to communicate your feelings to as many Members of Congress as you can reach, because there is a lot of justifiable fear and anxiety and insecurity in this country about the changing economy. And we have to show the Members of Congress that Americans can compete and win in this global economy if we're given half a chance and that this agreement is the beginning of our reach for the rest of the world in a way that will create jobs.

There is no evidence that the United States or any other rich country can create a lot of new jobs without expanding trade. NAFTA is a big first step for us, and you know that very well. And if you know it and you believe it, I ask you not only to cheer for the Vice President today—he deserves it, he was terrific last night—but help us to win this fight next week. Tell the Members of Congress that this means American jobs and a better and brighter future for our country. We need your help. We need your help. We've got to have hope win out over fear next week in this NAFTA vote. We can do it with people like you. I thank you, and I thank you, Vice President Gore.

The Vice President. Thank you, Mr. President.

The President. See you when you get home.

The Vice President. See you back in the office tomorrow.

The President. Bye-bye. Thanks.

[*At this point, the telephone conversation ended, and the President took questions from reporters.*]

Q. Mr. President, what was Perot's big mistake?

The President. Well, I just think that the Vice President appealed to the hopes of the American people and also talked about the facts and also cited specific examples. He called the names of people who worked in factories, who were in small businesses, who would specifically benefit from this expansion of trade. And he also appealed to the Members of the Congress to do what was right for the country and to make this straightforward argument to the people.

Mr. Perot basically said anybody that didn't agree with him, no matter how deep their conscience was, they were going to try to get rid of them out of the Congress. One appealed to hope and reasoning, the other appealed to fear and threat. And I think you can see what the results were in the public opinion polls. The American people said, "This makes sense to us." And I think the more people who hear it, the more sense it will make.

NOTE: The President spoke at 1:08 p.m. in the Oval Office at the White House. In his remarks, he referred to Tim Wirth, Under Secretary of State for Global Affairs. The exchange portion of this item could not be verified because the tape was incomplete.

Remarks at a Ceremony for the Vietnam Women's Memorial Project
November 10, 1993

The President. I want to welcome Diane Evans and all the members of the Vietnam Women's Memorial Project who are here to do an unveiling of a model of the statue which will be formally commemorated tomorrow on Veteran's Day. I have a few other remarks I want to make in a moment, but let me just say that the people who have worked on this project deserve the thanks of the Nation. They have worked for years and years, and today and tomorrow are very big days for them.

I wanted to give them the opportunity to be seen today by the United States in bringing this model to the White House, where it will be on permanent display. And I want to introduce Diane now to say whatever she'd like to say and then do the unveiling.

[*At this point, Ms. Evans, chair, Vietnam Woman's Memorial Project, thanked the President and presented him with a replica of the statue to honor the women who served in the Vietnam war. Sculptor Glenna Goodacre then made brief remarks.*]

The President. This is wonderful.

Secretary Babbitt, Mr. Brown, do you want to say anything?

[*Secretary of the Interior Bruce Babbitt and Secretary of Veterans Affairs Jesse Brown praised the symbolism of the memorial.*]

The President. These documents, first of all, are witnesses that I am going to sign attesting the conveyance of the memorial to the Department of the Interior. This is a proclamation which names the National Women's Veterans Recognition Week, that on this year is Veterans Day, to recognize the special importance of that. So I am going to sign these with all these pens so that all the people here can have——

[*At this point, the President signed the memorandum of understanding and the proclamation, and Ms. Evans presented him with a commemorative program.*]

The President. Thank you. Thank you all very much.

NAFTA Television Debate

Q. Mr. President, we know you're happy with the performance of the Vice President. Is there going to be any effect on Capitol Hill?

The President. I think so. We'll talk more about it in the press conference in a few minutes.

NOTE: The President spoke at 1:17 p.m. in the Oval Office at the White House. A tape was not available for verification of the content of these remarks. The proclamation is listed in Appendix D at the end of this volume.

The President's News Conference
November 10, 1993

The President. Good afternoon, ladies and gentlemen. As we approach the end of this congressional session, just before Thanksgiving, it's important that our people know that here in Washington we are finally tackling issues that are central to the lives of all Americans, replacing gridlock and inaction with progress in the pursuit of the common good.

In the last few months, we passed the largest deficit reduction package in history. Interest rates and inflation have remained at historic lows. Millions of Americans have been able to refinance their homes. Investment is up, and more new jobs have come into our economy in the last 10 months than in the previous 4 years. There's been a real effort to improve security for America's working families with the dramatic expansion in the earned-income tax credit, to help working Americans with children who live on modest incomes to do better through tax reductions. We've opened more of our products in high-tech areas to exports. We've passed the family leave law. We've expanded opportunities for people to invest in new businesses in this country. And we've presented a comprehensive plan that will put real health care security within reach of every American. We're working on reinventing our Government to do more with less, and I am proud to say that the Congress is clearly signaling today its determination to move on reforming campaign finance laws. A bill passed the Senate several months ago. Today the House committee is voting out a bill which I believe the House of Representatives will pass.

This is a record of real achievement. But in the next few weeks before we go home, Congress will be challenged to take even greater strides in protecting the personal security of Americans and in creating more opportunities for us to compete and win in the global environment.

The Senate is completing work now on our crime bill, legislation that will fulfill the campaign promise I made to put 100,000 additional police officers on the street, to keep felons behind bars, to take criminals off the street, to provide boot camps and alternative service for first-time youthful offenders, and to remove guns from the hands of people who should not have them. We have a real shot now to pass the Brady bill. After years, 12 years, of heroic activism by Jim and Sarah Brady, Congress is finally determined, I believe, to stand up to the interests against the Brady bill and to take action on crime, which is the number one personal security issue for most Americans.

A week from today, Congress will decide whether to expand exports and jobs by passing the North American Free Trade Agreement. The case for NAFTA could not have been made more forcefully or eloquently than it was by Vice President Gore last night in his debate with Mr. Perot. Last night the Vice President showed that just stating the facts about NAFTA and showing our concern for the interests of working Americans can overcome the fears, the distortions that have been leveled against this agreement. NAFTA means exports; exports means jobs. No wealthy country in the world is growing more jobs without expanding exports.

When the American people hear that case, they showed last night they are willing to listen and willing to join not only millions of other Americans like those the Vice President called by name last night but every living former President, former Secretary of State, Nobel Prize-winning economists, and over 80 percent of the

sitting Governors.

The contrast we saw last night was clear. Mr. Perot warned Members of the House of Representatives that they would face awful retaliation if they voted their conscience on NAFTA. The Vice President urged the Members of the House to vote for hope against fear; to vote for the proposition that Americans can compete and win in the global economy; to vote their conscience and tell the constituents back home why they were voting as they were. And if the preliminary results on the debate last night are any indication, the Members of the House of Representatives can trust the American people with the facts and with their own convictions.

This vote comes at a defining moment for our Nation. We have been through a very tough period. For 20 years—20 years—60 percent of the American people have been working harder for the same or less wages. We have had great difficulty in increasing the productivity that is absolutely essential to creating jobs and raising incomes. But we have now done it. This country is now the most productive country in the world across a broad spectrum of manufacturing and service activities in this economy. We can win. And we have to decide, beginning next week, whether we're going to reach out to compete and win or try to withdraw.

I will say again one point I want to make about NAFTA, before I open the floor to questions, that was not emphasized last night simply because it didn't come up as much. This agreement means more jobs, but the real job growth for America will come when two other steps are taken. It will come when all the other Latin democracies and free market economies also join in a great trade group with Mexico, Canada, and the United States. And it will come because once this happens, we will have enormously increased influence in the world community to argue that we ought to adopt a worldwide trade agreement before the end of the year, to get that new GATT agreement. That will influence Asia, it will influence Europe, if the House votes for NAFTA. The stakes for this country, therefore, are quite high. I believe the House will do the right thing.

I want to say, too, that I am grateful that today Congressman Hoagland, Congressman Kreidler, Congressman Dicks, Congressman Valentine, and Senator Nunn announced their support for NAFTA. I think that we will see more coming in the days ahead, and I think by the time we get to vote counting, we'll have enough to win.

Thank you.

Helen [Helen Thomas, United Press International]?

Foreign Policy Team

Q. Mr. President, U.S. foreign policy endeavors have been less than successful in Somalia, Haiti, Bosnia. And on Sunday on "Meet the Press" you seemed to be lukewarm about your foreign policy team. Is Secretary Wharton being made your sacrificial lamb? And are you planning a shakeup of your foreign policy team? I mean, is that the signal?

The President. No to both questions. First of all, I did not mean to be lukewarm. I have always followed a policy as long as I've been a chief executive of not discussing a lot of personnel issues. But I will say again what I said on Sunday. This team has worked hard on a lot of difficult issues. I think they deserve high marks for dealing with the central, large, strategic issues of this time, dealing with the former Soviet Union, working on bringing down the nuclear threat, working on stemming nuclear proliferation, working on peace in the Middle East, working on putting economics at the forefront of our foreign policy.

Secondly, Mr. Wharton is not being made a scapegoat in any way, shape, or form. What he worked on at the State Department, in my judgment, he did a good job on. He worked on reorganization; he worked on the aid programs; he worked on a number of issues that have nothing to do with the controversies which were thorny when I got here and are still thorny today in Somalia, Haiti, and Bosnia. It would be a great mistake for anyone to misinterpret what happened. I think you have to take his remarks on their own terms. But believe me, his departure has nothing to do with scapegoating. I have the highest regard for him. And I am grateful for the service he rendered.

Israel

Q. Mr. President, there's a growing expectation that Israel and Jordan are going to sign a peace treaty when Prime Minister Rabin visits the White House on Friday. Could you tell us what's the likelihood of that? And also on Mr. Rabin, Israeli radio says that he's written you a letter asking you to cut the prison sentence of convicted spy Jonathan Pollard to 10 years.

Are you going to do that?

The President. First of all, I am delighted by the reports of progress in the relationships between Israel and Jordan. And as you know, we are talking with both of them. And we've been involved with that. But I don't think anything will happen Friday on that. I would be pleased if it did. But the truth is, we have no reason to believe that anything will be happening Friday.

On the Pollard case, it is true that the Prime Minister has written me about Jonathan Pollard. I have asked the Justice Department to review his case, as I do in every request for executive clemency. I have not received a report from them yet. And I will not make a decision on the Pollard case until I get some sort of indication from them.

Yes, Wolf [Wolf Blitzer, CNN]?

Ross Perot

Q. Mr. President, there are some who suggest that you deliberately wanted to have the Vice President debate Mr. Perot in order to elevate Mr. Perot as a potential threat to Republicans down the road more than Democrats. Did you have those kinds of interests in mind?

The President. I wish I were that Machiavellian. It never occurred to me. I wanted the Vice President to debate Mr. Perot because I believed—and I know that the conventional wisdom around here was that it was a mistake—but first, I want to give credit where credit's due. The Vice President, not the President, the Vice President had the idea that maybe this was the time to have a debate and to do it on Larry King.

My immediate response, however, was very positive, because I believe the American people—first of all, we know they're hungry for debate. They know we have to change, and they're deeply skeptical of people in politics. So the more direct access people have to this issue, one that affects their lives, the more feeling they get for the facts and the arguments as well as for the conviction of the parties involved, I just think it's better. So there was no ulterior motive in that whatever.

Q. Mr. President, the polls indicate that Vice President Gore did do well in the debate last night and that Mr. Perot did not do so well. You clearly believe he was wounded on the issue of NAFTA. Do you think that carries over into his role in politics in general? Does it hurt his standing as a political force in this country in the future?

The President. Well, I don't have any idea. I don't know about that. I will say this: I think there are a lot of people out there who are alienated from the political system for good reasons. One of the greatest frustrations I have as President is that it is often difficult for me to cut through the din of daily events here to keep speaking to those people and to try to keep them involved.

I think that they will feel more supportive of not only this administration but of the American political system, if we can produce sustained economic growth, greater security for people who work hard and play by the rules; if we can produce a genuine effort to fight crime and to deal with the problems of the breakdown of the society and family in many of the troubled areas of our country; and if we can produce political reform, if we can produce campaign finance reform and lobby reform, and if the Congress sometime in the next few weeks passes a law that says they'll live under the laws that they pass and impose on the private sector.

These are the things that you keep hearing from people who voted in the last election for Mr. Perot. I think what we should focus on, those of us who are here, is addressing the concerns, the hopes, and the fears of those people. And the rest of it will take care of itself. We'll just have to see what happens.

NAFTA

Q. Mr. President, the White House has complained and Mr. Gore has scored some points about Mr. Perot's exaggerations and exaggerations of the anti-NAFTA forces. But last night the Vice President said that 22 out of 23 studies have shown job increases. He cited a figure of 400,000. The Joint Economic Committee, a bipartisan committee of Congress, said that's not true. Doesn't it hurt your arguments for NAFTA when——

The President. What did they say was not true?

Q. Well, they said that the studies were being double counted and that he did not cite the job losses so he wasn't giving a net figure and that actually in the overall size of the economy, that those really are not that significant, or can't be properly counted.

The President. Let me just respond to that on the specific allegations—I have always tried to couch NAFTA as a job winner, a net job winner. That is, I think that the evidence is clear that not just in the long run but in the near run, we'll have more job gains than job losses out of this. There will plainly be some job losses. But the point I have tried to make always is, we have a lot of job losses every year in America we can't prevent. So when we have an opportunity to create more jobs, we are almost morally bound to do it, when we can have a net job gain.

I don't think the Vice President willfully misstated that, because we've had this conversation a long time—many times. But a lot of the extreme claims on both sides ignore the fact that Mexico itself, on its own terms, only comprises 4 to 5 percent of the size of the American economy. The size of the Mexican economy today is about the size of California's economy from the Los Angeles County line, the north line, down to the Mexican border. And therefore, the ability of the Mexicans in the near term to hurt the American economy, or to totally inflate it, is somewhat limited.

As you know, we said that we thought we would gain 200,000 jobs over the next 2 years. Well, last month our economy produced 177,000 jobs. Let me reiterate what I said in my opening remarks. The thing that's important about this is that it makes a statement that we're reaching out to expand trade. It really will; 200,000 jobs is nothing to sneeze at. And almost all of our people believe that the net will be well above 150,000. That is, that's nothing to sneeze at in 2 years, especially since they will be higher paying jobs.

But the important thing is that by showing we can have this relationship with Mexico, we will rapidly be able to move to conclude similar agreements with other market-oriented democracies, with Chile, with Argentina, with a whole range of other countries in Latin America. And this then will give us the psychological leverage—just as for the anti-NAFTA people this has become the repository of all their resentments, for us that are for it it's become the symbol of where we want to go in the world. This will give me enormous leverage when I get on the airplane the day after the NAFTA vote and go out to meet with the General Secretary of the People's Republic of China, when I go out to meet with the Prime Minister of Japan and all the other leaders of Asia, when I try to convince the Europeans that it's time for a worldwide trade agreement.

And nearly everyone who has analyzed what we agreed to about the time of the G–7 on the GATT round, the new trade agreement, concludes that it will add hundreds of thousands of jobs, significant jobs near-term, to the American economy. So I say that, on balance, this is a huge deal for America, but both sides need to be very careful not to make extreme claims. This is a job winner for our country, more jobs with Latin America, even more jobs when we have a new world trade agreement. It all begins with NAFTA.

Q. Mr. President, do you have any regrets about your comments about labor during the Sunday television interview, your comment about the naked pressure that they've exerted on Members of Congress on NAFTA? And what are you going to do to kiss and make up with them?

The President. I sent a little note to Mr. Kirkland the other day and said I hoped my comments Sunday morning didn't ruin his Sunday afternoon. And I told him basically what I said before. I have enormous respect for many of the people who are fighting us on this. I just think they're wrong. But specifically, I don't think a Congressman who has been a friend of the labor movement for 20 years should be told that he or she will get an opponent in the next election or never get any more help on this one vote. I just disagree with that.

If you go back and look at the interview, I was trying to make the point that I thought in the Congress the labor movement was a bigger force in keeping this from passing than the Perot folks were. I didn't mean to hurt their feelings, but I can't retract what I said because I don't think it's right for people to be told, "If you vote your conscience on this vote we're through with you forever, no matter what you've done with us before." I think that's bad and it's not conducive to good government.

Q. We seem to be heading for one of those cliffhangers next week in the House, kind of high political drama that Washington enjoys. I can't imagine, though, sir, that perhaps you enjoy it quite as much. And I wonder as you look back on this if you feel that this issue could perhaps have been managed differently, perhaps an earlier start that would have enabled you to make what you seem to feel is a very strong case a bit more easily?

The President. I think the only way we could

have started earlier is if we'd been able to conclude the side agreements sooner; because keep in mind, first of all, I ran for this job with a commitment to support NAFTA if I could get the right side agreements. This thing was dead in the water in January when I became President. It was gone. There was no support among the Democrats in the House. There were Republicans who thought they weren't going to be able to vote for it. Yes, the opposition then got geared up and made a lot of charges against it. But the only thing we had to hold out was the promise that we could conclude side agreements that would improve the environmental issues and that would deal with the labor issues and that would give us some leverage for people to move forward. If we had been able to conclude those agreements more quickly, then we could have started the campaign more quickly.

Q. You don't think these side agreements added credence to the idea that it was a flawed agreement and perhaps hurt politically?

The President. No, I don't think so. But I don't know. Anybody can always second-guess. But what I always tried to say about NAFTA was that the concept was sound and that we needed an agreement with Mexico. One of the things we haven't talked about very much is it means a lot to the United States to have a neighbor with 90 million people that is moving toward democracy, that is moving toward an open economy, and that is moving toward greater friendship with us. I mean, this is a big deal. If you want cooperation in the immigration problem, the drug problem, this means a lot to us.

I always felt that we would get there, but in dealing with at least the people in our party, we had to be able to have something to show that would indicate we were making progress in these areas. So that's all I can say. We may be able to be second-guessed, but the thing simply wasn't ready, and I didn't have anything to argue with.

Q. Mr. President, a moment ago you stated that your leverage would be increased in Seattle if you get a NAFTA victory. Could you come at it from the other side? If you have a NAFTA defeat on Wednesday, would that in any way diminish your prestige in Seattle or your ability to conduct foreign policy?

The President. I don't think it would diminish my ability to conduct foreign policy except in the economic area. I think it would limit my ability to argue that the Asians should open their markets more. And after all, our trade problem, in terms of open markets—if you look at it, where is our trade deficit: $49 billion with Japan, $19 billion with China, $9 billion with Taiwan. We have a $5.4 billion trade surplus with Mexico. So I think my ability to argue that case forcefully that "You ought to open your markets; look at what we're doing," will be undermined. And I think, more importantly, my ability to argue that the Asians and the Europeans should join with me and push hard, hard to get a world trade agreement through the GATT round by the end of the year will be more limited. There's no question about it.

Look, the anxieties that we have here, the same thing is going on in Japan, where they're not generating jobs and they've got staggering income. Same thing in Europe; it's been years since the European economy as a whole has generated new jobs. So in each of these great power centers of the world there are these debates every day just like the one that went on last night between the Vice President and Mr. Perot. They're debating it: Are they going to be more open or more closed? Which way are they going to go? And so I think that my ability to tip the scales in that debate in the right direction for history and for the American people will be limited significantly in the short run if we lose NAFTA. It will not be good for the United States.

Anticrime Efforts

Q. Mr. President, beyond signing a crime bill, if and when one hits your desk, what else can you do? What else will you do about crime and violence?

The President. Well, I think that there's a lot more we have to do. I think the administration has got to examine everything we can do to try to put together an approach that will challenge every community in this country and every organization in this country and every individual in this country to make a contribution with us in restoring the conditions in which civilized life can go on.

I think that the crime bill is very important. I don't want to minimize that. I know some disagree that it is. It really will make a difference if you put another 100,000 police out there. We're losing the ratio of police to crime. We have been for 30 years. This is an important issue. It matters whether we get these police

out there, if they're properly trained and properly deployed in community policing.

But we have to rebuild families and communities in this country. We've got to take more responsibility for these little kids before they grow up and start shooting each other. We have to find ways to offer hope and to reconnect people. When children start shooting children the way they're doing now, and little kids go around planning their own funerals, what that means is that there are a whole lot of people, millions of people in this country, who literally are not even playing by the same set of rules that all the rest of us take for granted. And we have learned in this country to accept many things that are unacceptable. And I think the President has a pulpit, Teddy Roosevelt's bully pulpit, that I have to use and work hard on and try to live by, to try to help rebuild the conditions of family and community and education and opportunity.

And I'll just say one last thing about that. What a lot of these folks that are in such desperate trouble need is a unique combination of both structure and order and discipline on the one hand and genuine caring on the other. It is impossible to structure life in a society like ours where there is no family or at least no supervising, caring adult on the one hand, and on the other hand where there is no work. If you go generation after generation after generation and people don't get to work—you think about your lives, think about what you're going to do today, what you did this morning when you got up, what you'll do tonight when you go home. If you think about the extent to which work organizes life in America and reinforces our values, our rules, and the way we relate to one another and the way we raise our children, and then you imagine what it must be like where there is no work—I know the budget is tight. I know there are all kinds of tough problems. I know that people with private capital, even with our empowerment zones, may not want to invest in inner cities and decimated rural areas, but I'm telling you, we have to deal with family, community, education, and you have to have work; there has to be work there.

Q. Mr. President, on the issue of crime, could you explain a little bit more about how the White House, how your administration is going to accomplish some of those things?

The President. Yes. First of all, the Attorney General and Secretary Cisneros and a number of other people are now working in our administration on how we can develop a comprehensive approach to the whole issue of violence in our society and how we can merge that with what we want to do in terms of community empowerment and how it will fit with all the things that we are now doing. And I think what you will see from us over the next several months is a sustained, organized, disciplined approach so that we don't just respond to the horror we all feel when a little kid gets shot after being picked up off the street, like happened here last weekend, or when these children plan their funerals. I want to put this right at the center of what we're doing.

I have spent years going to neighborhoods and talking to people and dealing with issues that most politicians in National Government have not talked a lot about. I care a great deal about this. There is a lot of knowledge in this town about it. Senator Moynihan wrote a very powerful article just a couple of weeks ago on how we have defined deviancy down. I think there's an enormous bipartisan willingness to face this. What I think I have to do is to mobilize every person in my Government to do what can be done to address these problems. And you will see that coming out after the Congress goes home and in my address to the people next year when the Congress begins.

Q. Mr. President, you mentioned Senator Moynihan. He's proposed a Federal tax on bullets that would make certain kind of bullets, particularly cop-killer bullets, prohibitively expensive. Do you support the general idea of an ammunition tax? And would you like to see it to be part of the financing for your health care package, as Senator Moynihan has proposed?

The President. Well, Senator Moynihan has been very candid in saying that what he really wants to do is to try to use this to deal with the problem of gun violence in America. I think the health care plan that I put forward will finance itself in the way that we have, and I think we should proceed with that. I think that this idea of his, however, deserves a lot of consideration.

But one of the things that I question in my own mind is if some of these bullets are being manufactured solely for the purpose of having a devastating effect on someone's body if they hit someone's body, whether we ought not just to get rid of those bullets. Because if you look

at the money that can be raised as a practical matter, in the context of this Federal budget or the health care budget, it's limited. I agree with the Treasury Secretary. Secretary Bentsen stated our position. We think the Senator has given us an interesting idea. We're looking at it. We're seeing what the objectives are. But some of that ammunition, it would seem to me, there might be a consensus that we ought not to make it at all in this country.

New Jersey Election

Q. Mr. President, it turns out that your friend Jim Florio in New Jersey may have lost the election by a narrow margin because of an approach dreamed up by the Republican strategists which depressed the black voter turnout. What do you think about that tactic?

The President. First, I think we should all acknowledge that people have died in this country, given their lives to give other Americans, especially African-Americans, the right to vote. And this allegation, if it is true—and I say if it is true—I don't know what the facts are, but if it is true, then it was terribly wrong for anyone to give money to anybody else not to vote or to depress voter turnout. And it was terribly wrong for anyone to accept that money to render that nonservice to this country.

NAFTA

Q. Can you give us a count right now of how many votes you have in the House on NAFTA?

The President. No, because it's changing every day. But we're getting a lot closer. I honestly believe we're going to win it now, and that's not just political puff. I think we'll make it. I'll be surprised if we don't win now.

Q. [*Inaudible*]—what is going to happen to Latin America if NAFTA is not passed. What would be the impact in the United States, not in you but in the people of the United States if NAFTA is not approved?

The President. Well, if it's not passed, we'll lose a lot of opportunities to sell our products. We will not do one single thing to discourage people from moving to Mexico to set up plants to get low wages to sell back in here. We will depress the environmental and labor costs more than they otherwise would be depressed in Mexico, which will make it harder for us to compete. It'll be bad for America if we do it.

Haiti and Bosnia

Q. Mr. President, so far you haven't talked about Haiti and Bosnia. The situation in those two countries seems to have gotten worse in the year since you've been elected. Right now, what can you tell us you're doing to reverse the situation in the short term, or do you fear that this is going to go on all winter long in Bosnia as well as in Haiti?

The President. Well, the problem or the conditions in Bosnia at least seem to be that none of the parties now, including the government, at least at the moment we speak, based on what I knew this morning, are of a mind to make peace on any terms that the others will accept, because there are different military results being achieved on the ground there in different places in ways that make all the parties feel that they shouldn't agree now. Under those conditions, all we can do is to try to make sure that we minimize the human loss coming on for this winter, that we try to get the United Nations to agree to let the NATO position that the United States put together on the availability of air power in the event that Sarajevo is seriously shelled be an actual live option and not just something on the books, and that we make sure our humanitarian program works.

I will say this—I want to emphasize this—the airlift to Bosnia, which this Nation has spearheaded, has now gone on longer than the Berlin airlift. And it's one of the most comprehensive humanitarian aid efforts in history. And we'll have to keep doing it.

In Haiti, I'd like to say a word or two about that. First of all, it's important that the people of Haiti understand that the people who brought this embargo on were Mr. François and General Cédras, because they didn't go through with the Governors Island Agreement.

Now, I believe that Mr. Malval and President Aristide are willing to talk in good faith and try to reach an accommodation that would enable us to get back on the path to democracy and to implementing that agreement. I grieve for the people of Haiti. We feed almost 700,000 people a day in Haiti. We participate actively, the United States does. I don't want anybody else to be hurt down there. But I think it's very important that the people of Haiti understand that the people that brought this embargo on them were François and Cédras in breaking the agreement that was agreed to by all parties there. And we have to try to reach another agreement so that the country can go back to normal.

NAFTA

Q. The financial community has been worried about Mexico's policy of gradually devaluing the peso and saying that this would underscore the low-wage environment there. What would you foresee under a NAFTA pact that was approved as far as the relationship between the dollar and the peso? And would we end up finding the Federal Reserve having to support the peso because of our tighter economic relationship?

The President. Actually, I would think that—I want to be careful how I say this because I don't want anything I say now to have an impact in the Mexican financial markets today, but I believe that you have to just say that the peso would become stronger if NAFTA passes because it would strengthen the Mexican economy. And normally, when you've got a strong economy that's growing, the value of the currency will rise.

Khanh Pham

Let me say, I know we've got—no, no, no, I'm sorry. I want to introduce someone before we go, because I think I would be remiss, here at a press conference with all of you, not to do this. I'd like to ask Khanh Pham to stand. Would you stand up?

I want to tell you a little bit about this young woman. She's here today with a program that puts role models and young people together. And she said that her role model was Dee Dee Myers, so she wanted to come here and be here. But let me tell you about her. Maybe she should be our role model.

When she was 2½ years old, she was cradled in her 5-year-old brother's arms as her mother made a desperate run for freedom from Vietnam. They forced their way onto an overcrowded small wooden boat after giving away their life savings for those spots. They endured heavy seas, were separated on the boat for a period of time. They watched people die before being picked up by a U.S. naval ship, the U.S.S. *Warden.*

After coming here, because of language barriers, her mother could only get jobs in manual labor. She also baked Vietnamese pastries to sell. She held two or three jobs at a time. Sometimes she didn't have enough money to wash the clothes so the family would have to wash them in their tub, while Khanh and her brother would try to teach their mother English.

A couple of years ago, she missed several months of school while she single handedly worked with all the agencies and authorities here to get her two sisters back from Vietnam into the United States. Finally, they were reunited a year and a half ago, and they now live with Khanh and her mother. She is 17, a senior at Reston High School in Virginia. She holds an office with her student government, and she's a student representative elected to the board of governors, a city office in Reston.

And as I said, she's spending the day here today. She's interested in being in the press today, but one day she hopes to be America's Ambassador to Vietnam.

Thank you for coming here.

Thank you, ladies and gentlemen.

NOTE: The President's 32d news conference began at 3:05 p.m. in the East Room at the White House. In his remarks, he referred to Col. Joseph Michel François, chief of the Haitian police; Lt. Gen. Raoul Cédras, commander of the Haitian armed forces; and Haitian Prime Minister Robert Malval.

Message to the Congress Reporting on the National Emergency With Respect to Iran
November 10, 1993

To the Congress of the United States:

I hereby report to the Congress on developments since the last Presidential report on May 14, 1993, concerning the national emergency with respect to Iran that was declared in Executive Order No. 12170 of November 14, 1979, and matters relating to Executive Order No. 12613 of October 29, 1987. This report is submitted pursuant to section 204(c) of the International Emergency Economic Powers Act, 50 U.S.C. 1703(c), and section 505(c) of the International Security and Development Cooperation Act of 1985, 22 U.S.C. 2349aa–9(c). This report covers events through October 1, 1993. The last report, dated May 14, 1993, covered events through March 31, 1993.

1. There have been no amendments to the Iranian Transactions Regulations, 31 CFR Part 560, or to the Iranian Assets Control Regulations, 31 CFR Part 535, since the last report.

2. The Office of Foreign Assets Control (FAC) of the Department of the Treasury continues to process applications for import licenses under the Iranian Transactions Regulations.

During the reporting period, the U.S. Customs Service has continued to effect numerous seizures of Iranian-origin merchandise, primarily carpets, for violation of the import prohibitions of the Iranian Transactions Regulations. Office of Foreign Assets Control and Customs Service investigations of these violations have resulted in forfeiture actions and the imposition of civil monetary penalties. Additional forfeiture and civil penalty actions are under review.

3. The Iran-United States Claims Tribunal (the "Tribunal"), established at The Hague pursuant to the Algiers Accords, continues to make progress in arbitrating the claims before it. Since my last report, the Tribunal has rendered two awards, both in favor of U.S. claimants. Including these decisions, the total number of awards has reached 547, of which 369 have been awards in favor of American claimants. Two hundred twenty-two of these were awards on agreed terms, authorizing and approving payment of settlements negotiated by the parties, and 147 were decisions adjudicated on the merits. The Tribunal has issued 36 decisions dismissing claims on the merits and 83 decisions dismissing claims for jurisdictional reasons. Of the 59 remaining awards, 3 approved the withdrawal of cases and 56 were in favor of Iranian claimants. As of September 30, 1993, the value of awards to successful American claimants from the Security Account held by the NV Settlement Bank stood at $2,351,986,709.40.

The Security Account has fallen below the required balance of $500 million almost 50 times. Iran has periodically replenished the account, as required by the Algiers Accords, by transferring funds from the separate account held by the NV Settlement Bank in which interest on the Security Account is deposited. The aggregate amount that has been transferred from the Interest Account to the Security Account is $874,472,986.47. Iran has also replenished the account with the proceeds from the sale of Iranian-origin oil imported into the United States, pursuant to transactions licensed on a case-by-case basis by FAC. Iran has not, however, replenished the account since the last oil sale deposit on October 8, 1992, although the balance fell below $500 million on November 5, 1992. As of September 28, 1993, the total amount in the Security Account was $213,507,574.15 and the total amount in the Interest Account was $5,647,476.98.

Iran also failed to make scheduled payments for Tribunal expenses on April 13 and July 15, 1993. The United States filed a new case (designated A/28) before the Tribunal on September 29, 1993, asking that the Tribunal order Iran to make its payment for Tribunal expenses and to replenish the Security Account.

4. The Department of State continues to present other United States Government claims against Iran, in coordination with concerned Government agencies, and to respond to claims brought against the United States by Iran. In June and August of this year, the United States filed 2 briefs and more than 350 volumes of supporting evidence in Case B/1 (claims 1 and 2), Iran's claim against the United States for damages relating to the U.S. Foreign Military Sales Program. On September 29, the United States submitted a brief for filing in all three Chambers of the Tribunal concerning the Tribunal's jurisdiction over the claims of dual nationals who have demonstrated dominant and effective U.S. nationality. In addition, the Tribunal issued an order accepting the U.S. view that Iran has to support all aspects of its claim in Case A/11, in which Iran claims the United States has breached its obligations under the Algiers Accords, rather than to ask the Tribunal to first decide "interpretative issues" separate

from the merits of its case. In another case, the Tribunal declined Iran's request that it stay a case against Iran in U.S. courts for an alleged post-January 1981 expropriation, where the plaintiffs' case at the Tribunal had been dismissed.

5. As reported in November 1992, Jose Maria Ruda, President of the Tribunal, tendered his resignation on October 2, 1992. No successor has yet been named. Judge Ruda's resignation will take effect as soon as a successor becomes available to take up his duties.

6. As anticipated by the May 13, 1990, agreement settling the claims of U.S. nationals for less than $250,000.00, the Foreign Claims Settlement Commission (FCSC) has continued its review of 3,112 claims. The FCSC has issued decisions in 1,568 claims, for total awards of more than $28 million. The FCSC expects to complete its adjudication of the remaining claims in early 1994.

7. The situation reviewed above continues to implicate important diplomatic, financial, and legal interests of the United States and its nationals and presents an unusual challenge to the national security and foreign policy of the United States. The Iranian Assets Control Regulations issued pursuant to Executive Order No. 12170 continue to play an important role in structuring our relationship with Iran and in enabling the United States to implement properly the Algiers Accords. Similarly, the Iranian Transactions Regulations issued pursuant to Executive Order No. 12613 continue to advance important objectives in combatting international terrorism. I shall continue to exercise the powers at my disposal to deal with these problems and will continue to report periodically to the Congress on significant developments.

WILLIAM J. CLINTON

The White House,
November 10, 1993.

Nomination for a United States District Court Judge
November 10, 1993

The President today nominated Judge Daniel Hurley to serve as a U.S. District Court judge

for the Southern District of Florida.

"Daniel Hurley has distinguished himself in

close to 20 years on the bench as a judge of outstanding capability," said the President. "I expect him to meet that same high standard

as a Federal District Court judge."

NOTE: A biography of the nominee was made available by the Office of the Press Secretary.

Letter to Attorney General Janet Reno on Child Pornography
November 10, 1993

Dear Madam Attorney General:

A dispute recently has arisen over the scope of the current federal child pornography law. This dispute impelled the Senate to adopt a "sense of the Senate" resolution expressing its view that the law reaches broadly. I fully agree with the Senate about what the proper scope of the child pornography law should be.

I find all forms of child pornography offensive and harmful, as I know you do, and I want the federal government to lead aggressively in the attack against the scourge of child pornography. It represents an unacceptable exploitation of children and contributes to the degradation of our national life and to a societal climate that appears to condone child abuse.

This Administration supports the broadest possible protections against child pornography and exploitation. I understand that the Justice Department recently filed a brief in which the Department concluded that the current child pornography law is not as broad as it could be. Accordingly, the Justice Department should promptly prepare and submit any necessary legislation to ensure that federal law reaches all forms of child pornography, including the kinds of child pornography at issue in the Senate resolution.

Sincerely,

BILL CLINTON

NOTE: This letter was released by the Office of the Press Secretary on November 11.

Remarks at a Veterans Day Breakfast
November 11, 1993

Good morning. Please be seated.

Hillary and I and Secretary Aspin, Secretary Brown are delighted to have you here. We wanted to begin this Veterans Day with the leaders of our veterans organizations, with the officials of the Veterans Administration, with many of our men and women in uniform today, especially those who distinguished themselves in the very difficult firefight in Somalia on October 3d. Some of those brave soldiers are here with us today, and I know you've met them, but I'd like to begin by just asking them to stand and be recognized and asking all of us to thank them. [*Applause*] Thank you very much. Our Nation is very proud of them and their comrades for the bravery they showed on that day and for the work they continue to do.

This is an important Veterans Day. This is the 75th anniversary of the end of World War I, a defining war for our Nation, when our forebears decided that we could no longer be a totally isolated or isolationist country.

Later this morning, during ceremonies at Arlington Cemetery, I will present a commemorative medal to Mr. Stanley Coolbaugh, a veteran of the First World War who will accept it on behalf of the 30,000 living veterans of World War I. He was born in another century in a relatively young nation protected by vast oceans. He was forced as a young man, along with our Nation, to answer a profound question which we still have to ask and answer today: To what extent must America engage with the rest of the world; to what extent can we just stay home and mind our own business? Sometimes that answer is easy, as it was when we were attacked at Pearl Harbor and entered the Second World War and as it became clear at the end of the Second World War when we had to try to contain the expansion of communism and engage in the cold war, an effort which ultimately led to perhaps the greatest peacetime victory in the world, the collapse of the Soviet empire.

Now today we have to ask some of the hard questions again, about how much we should engage and whether we can withdraw. Some of those difficult questions are being answered by our men and women in uniform all around the world. Some of them have to be answered by those of us here in Washington on nonmilitary matters. I want to say a special word of thanks in that regard to the American Legion for endorsing the North American Free Trade Agreement. I said the other day to Admiral Crowe, who is here, that I was amazed that there were so many senior military officers who had spontaneously come up to me and said that they favor this treaty. And he and others observed, "Well, if you've ever been in uniform and been around the world, you know what it means to have the opportunity to live in peace with your two biggest neighbors and to have commerce and friendly cooperation and competition and what it means to live and grow together." So I thank you all for that.

This is a day when the United States has to reaffirm its commitment to our veterans. On Memorial Day we thank those veterans who have given their lives for our country and their families. Today we thank those veterans who have given their service to our country and who are still here among us and for whom we feel not only great affection but a profound sense of obligation.

On Memorial Day, I pledged that our Government would declassify virtually all the documents related to all individuals held as prisoners of war or missing in action, to help answer questions that have haunted too many families for too long. Some of those questions may never be answered, but we have to try. And I can tell you that as of last night, in keeping with my commitment on Memorial Day to finish this job by Veterans Day, we have done that. We have declassified all the relevant documents that we can to answer the questions about the MIA's and the POW's.

Secondly, I had the opportunity yesterday to sign a proclamation to honor our women veter-

ans in National Women Veterans Recognition Week, and to welcome to the office that I hold now Diane Evans and the board of the Vietnam Women's Memorial Project. They presented me with this wonderful replica of the statue being dedicated today to recognize the sacrifices of all the veterans of the Vietnam War and to further the process of healing and reconciliation. It is a magnificent work of art, gripping in so many ways. And I know that today's ceremony will grab the attention and the emotions and the convictions of the American people.

Third, I am about to sign into law an increase in the cost of living allowance for our disabled veterans. With the leadership of the relevant chairmen in our Congress, Senator Jay Rockefeller and Congressman Sonny Montgomery, this new law will help 2.5 million American veterans and their families to keep pace with the rising cost of living.

And finally, as you know, with the leadership of the First Lady and many others, we are doing our best to provide health security to all American people in a way that will improve the access and quality of veterans' health care in America. Of all the plans that have been addressed to deal with the health care problem, ours is the only one that has made a serious effort to address the concerns of our veterans. I'm very proud of that, and I thank all of you who had anything to do with it.

With these actions on this Veterans Day, we continue a contract we can never fulfill to defend our Nation's security, to defend the security in the interest of those who have served our Nation and made it secure. I know that your service can never be repaid in full, but it can always be honored and must never be forgotten. So today, as I sign this law, let me tell you on behalf of a grateful Nation, we honor you, we will not forget you, and we are grateful for the security that you provide for all of us.

Thank you very much.

NOTE: The President spoke at 9 a.m. in the East Room at the White House. In his remarks, he referred to Adm. William J. Crowe, Jr., USN (Ret.), Chairman of the President's Foreign Intelligence Advisory Board. S. 616, the Veterans' Compensation Rates Amendments of 1993, approved November 11, was assigned Public Law No. 103–140.

Remarks at the Veterans Day Ceremony at Arlington National Cemetery, Virginia
November 11, 1993

Thank you very much, Secretary Brown, General Brady, distinguished leaders of our veterans' organizations, Secretary Aspin and General Shalikashvili and the leaders of our Department of Defense and our military services, and to all of you, my fellow Americans.

Today we gather to honor those who have rendered the highest service any American can offer to this Nation, those who have fought for our freedom and stood sentry over our security. On this hillside of solemn remembrance and at gravesites and in veterans' halls and in proud parades all across America, today we join as one people to appreciate a debt we can never fully repay.

Every American who ever put on this Nation's uniform in war or peace has assumed risks and made sacrifices on our common behalf. Each of the 1.6 million men and women now in our forces today bears our common burden. This day belongs to all of them, to all who have protected our land we love over all the decades and now, over two centuries of our existence. From the minutemen who won our independence to the warriors who turned back aggression in Operation Desert Storm, it belongs to those who fell in battle and those who stood ready to do so, to those who were wounded and those who treated their wounds, to those who returned from the service to friends and families and to the far too many who remain missing.

We honor our veterans on this day because it marks the end of the First World War. On the 11th hour of the 11th day of the 11th month there crept an eerie silence across the battlefields of Europe, and 4 years of unbelievable destruction then came to an end. Today on the 75th anniversary of that Great War, it is fitting for us to recall and salute those from every service who contributed to the allied victory, embodied today by the fine figure of Mr. Coolbaugh who stood here and received this medal.

Our victory in that "war to end all wars" was a great test of whether our Nation then could reach out and become involved in the rest of the world. Many of the soldiers who fought in that war, including the men whom we honored here today, were born in another century, a time in which America felt secure on this great and vast continent protected by two oceans.

We entered World War I knowing that we could no longer run from the rest of the world. But in the end, while that war proved our strength, it did not prove our wisdom, for within the span of a short generation after it, we neglected during a careless peace what had been so dearly won in a relentless war. We turned our backs on the rest of the world. We ignored new signs of danger. We let our troops and arms fall out of readiness. We neglected opportunities for collective security in our own national interest. We succumbed to the siren's song of protectionism and erected walls against peaceful commerce with other nations. Soon we had a Great Depression, and soon that depression led to aggression and then to another world war, one that would claim a half million American lives.

Now, once more we stand at the end of a great conflict. The cold war is over. The lesson America won in the Second World War led us to contain communism in the cold war and led to the greatest peacetime victory the world has ever known, the collapse of the communist system and the Soviet empire. Our long and twilight struggle against that expansionist adversary has ended. And even as the world marvels at this achievement, once again history is about to take the measure of our wisdom.

Our generation is being asked now to decide whether we will preserve freedom's gains and learn freedom's lessons. We are being asked to decide whether we will maintain the high state of readiness that stood behind our victory or fritter away the seed corn of our security, asked whether we will swell the global tide of freedom by promoting democracy and open world markets or neglect the duty of our leadership and in the process and, in the withdrawal, diminish hope and prosperity not only for our own people but for billions of others throughout the world who look to us.

One of the greatest honors we can pay to our veterans on this Veterans Day is to act with the sufficient wisdom necessary to preserve the gains they have won through their hard service and great sacrifice. To honor those who served in Europe and Korea and Vietnam and the Persian Gulf, in scores of posts at home and abroad, let us today resolve we will not shrink from the responsibilities necessary to keep our Nation secure and our people prosperous.

We also honor our veterans today by noting the outstanding service being rendered around the world at this moment by the most talented and the best prepared group of men and women who have ever worn our Nation's uniforms. This morning I had the privilege and the honor to host for breakfast not only the leaders of our Nation's veterans' organizations but also 17 of the Army Rangers, Special Operations forces and infantrymen who recently returned from our mission in Somalia. Afterwards, I invited them and their commanders into the Oval Office where we sat and had a visit. I was profoundly impressed by them and by their service.

Not enough of our fellow Americans know the real story of what happened during the terribly difficult firefight in Mogadishu on October 3d, a fight in which they demonstrated great ability, success, and unbelievable valor. During that raid, a Blackhawk helicopter was downed. Despite this setback, the Special Operations forces conducted their raid with precision, apprehending 20 people suspected of involvement in the murder of United Nations peacekeepers in the Somali mission. At that point, they could have pulled back to safety, confident in the success of their mission. After all, what they had come to do was over. But they share an ethic that says they can never leave a fallen comrade behind. So some 90 of them formed a parameter around the downed aircraft in an attempt to retrieve the wounded and the dead. They found they could not dislodge the body of one pilot, but they refused to leave him behind. They braved hours and hours of the fiercest enemy fire. Eighteen of them ultimately perished; over 70 were wounded. They exacted a terrible toll on their adversaries, casualties 10 times as great, fatalities 20 times as great.

I want to note their presence with us here today. I want to thank them, and I want you to let them know that we know they did their mission well and that we are proud of them. Please stand up. Here they are. Please stand up. [*Applause*] We owe it to them and to their colleagues to ensure that our forces remain the best trained, the best equipped, the best prepared in the world. And we will do that. We also owe those who serve in our Nation's military the assurance that what they have done for us will not be forgotten. We owe to our veterans a health care system that is there for them when they need it and provides high quality and compassionate care. We owe to our veterans a measure of the security they have provided to us. And that is why, earlier today, I was proud to sign a bill which helps to increase the retirement benefits of our disabled veterans.

And as we remember all of those whom we see today and those whom we can imagine who are serving for us or who have served, we must never forget those who were never accounted for. That obligation never dies until we know the whole truth. Just this month, we secured an agreement from the Chinese to return the remains of three American aviators whose cargo plane crashed there in the Himalayas in 1943. Our Nation has a particular responsibility to pursue the fate of our missing from the war in Vietnam. On Memorial Day, I pledged here that our Government would declassify and make available virtually all documents related to those who never returned from that war and that I would do it by this day, Veterans Day. I can tell you that last evening, the Secretary of Defense completed that task. That promise has been fulfilled. I know that our Government, our Nation together have a solemn obligation to the families of those who still are missing to do all we can to help them find answers and peace of mind.

Every year, our humble words on Veterans Day can never do justice to the sacrifices made by our veterans, by those who returned and those who did not, by those who live among us today and those who live only in our memories. We know we can never repay the debt, but still we try because we know their sacrifices should be in our hearts every day.

So on this day let us simply repeat to America's veterans what is inscribed on the medals that have been awarded to thousands of those who served in World War I: A grateful nation remembers.

Thank you very much.

NOTE: The President spoke at 11:35 a.m. at a wreath-laying ceremony at the Tomb of the Unknowns.

Remarks at the Veterans Affairs Medical Center in Martinsburg, West Virginia
November 11, 1993

Thank you very much. I want to say a special word of thanks to Tom Weaver and to all the people on the staff here at this wonderful, wonderful health facility for making me feel so welcome today and for taking me around at least one of the floors and giving me a feel for the kind of care that's provided. I really thank them.

I'd also like to thank Senator Rockefeller for flying down here with me today on the helicopter—I hope the helicopter didn't bother you too much when it landed—and my good friend Congressman Wise and Governor Caperton. All three of them in different ways have worked hard to try to provide quality health care for the veterans of our country and for all Americans. And as I'm sure all of you know, that's a big struggle that we're involved in now in Washington, and it's nice to have three allies from West Virginia.

I told Jay Rockefeller today that we wouldn't be up there fighting for national health care if it hadn't been for him fighting for it a long time before someone could run and win a Presidential race on that issue, and I thank Jay for that. I also want to encourage you, Governor Caperton; this health care is a complicated issue. You just have to keep fighting. It's like pushing a rock up a hill, but eventually we get to the top, don't we?

I want to also say to all of you here in West Virginia, I'm especially glad to be here on Veterans Day. This whole area of the country has the look and feel of my home State of Arkansas. And one of the men I met today when touring the hospital, a man named Overman, was actually born in Arkansas. So I sat on his bed and looked out the window and thought I was home. He didn't have an accent. [Laughter]

We're here today to honor all the Americans who have worn our Nation's uniform, those who have contributed in war and those who have stood in peace, people who have protected our security and people for whom we now have a moral obligation to protect their security. I wanted to come here to this hospital today to drive that point home. I know we can never fully repay the debt that we owe as a country to our veterans. But we can honor that debt and partially repay it by making sure that we have quality, secure, and comprehensive health care for all the veterans of the United States.

This morning I had the honor of hosting a breakfast at the White House for the leaders of our veterans groups and for several of the brave young soldiers who have been serving our country in Somalia and who were involved in the ferocious firefight on October the 3d. And this morning I was also pleased to sign into law a bill, which Senator Rockefeller was the leading sponsor, which increases the cost of living allowance to our disabled veterans, which goes into effect on December 1st. Even though this is late in the year, thanks to the leadership of Senator Rockefeller who's the chairman of the Senate Veterans' Affairs committee and his counterpart in the House, my neighbor, Sonny Montgomery from Mississippi, this will be paid on time beginning in January of 1994.

Again, let me say how much I appreciate the leadership that Senator Rockefeller has exhibited, not only on the issue of health care for all Americans but on the special needs of our Nation's veterans. We stand together, along with Congressman Wise, in our determination to make sure that we do something about the health care issue to provide real and genuine and comprehensive security to all the people of this country before the Congress goes home next year. We have to do that.

The Veterans Administration today operates the Nation's largest health care system. And as I said today, I saw a health care facility here that any American, any American, would be proud to be a part of, to work in or to be a patient in. Under the leadership of Secretary of Veterans Affairs Jesse Brown and the Deputy Secretary, Hershel Gober, who's here with me today somewhere—Hershel where are you? He's not up here on this stage because he's heard this speech before, he said. We're going to continue to work for that.

When I was out in the crowd outside shaking hands, I was pleased to see that one lady had already purchased a paperback copy of the administration's proposed health plan that was put together by the group that the First Lady headed. One of the things that I want to encourage all of you to do is to get a copy of that plan and read it. I'm very proud of the fact that the health care reform plan proposed by our administration is the only one that embraces the VA as a real resource for high-quality, affordable health care for our people. Under our plan, all veterans would be eligible to receive their comprehensive national health care benefit package through the VA system. Veterans with service-connected disabilities and low-income veterans who choose VA would receive this care with no copayments or deductibles. And no veteran in need of health care would ever be turned away from a VA hospital if our plan became law.

This Veterans Day is a special one. It marks the 75th anniversary of the armistice which ended World War I. And as all of you know, that was the occasion for commemorating Veterans Day. We are fortunate today that there are about 31,000 living veterans from World War I, and four of them are with us. I want to acknowledge them today and to tell you that today we'll be giving them this medal commemorating their service in World War I and a certificate. The medal says: 75th Anniversary, World War I. And then on the back, it has two great slogans: A grateful Nation remembers, and They came on wings of eagles.

Now, let me introduce them to you: Mr. Benjamin Valentine. Where are you? There's Mr. Valentine. He's right there. I want to tell you a little bit about him. He served in the Army from May 1918 through May 1919. He was assigned to the Quartermaster Corps and embarkation depot at Charleston, South Carolina. In his civilian life he worked in a brickyard, and his favorite leisure activities were hunting and fishing.

The next honoree is Mr. Ernest Deetjen. Where is he? Mr. Deetjen. Let me tell you a little about him. He served in the Army as a cook with the 331st Supply Company. He enlisted in June 1918 and served in France from October of 1918 until October of 1919. In his civilian life, he opened the first A&P in Hagerstown, Maryland—good for him—and later opened his own store. And since we're here in this outstanding health facility, I should also mention that his uncle helped discover the X-ray process and brought the procedure to the Johns Hopkins Hospital in Baltimore. I also learned today that this fine gentleman actually

once met President Woodrow Wilson. I think in France, I believe, in Versailles in France, he met President Wilson. Now, let me tell you why that's important. Not only was President Wilson a member of the same political party as I am, but every year there's a new President, a famous American shoe company, Johnson and Murphy from Nashville, Tennessee, writes the President a letter and offers the President a pair of shoes and tells you what every other President's ordered since 1856. So when I got my shoes, they said, "Dear Mr. President, you have the biggest feet in the White House since Woodrow Wilson." [*Laughter*] So, Mr. Deetjen, we're glad to see you.

Mr. Robert Hannah. Where is he? Let's recognize him. Here he is. Mr. Hannah served as a courier in the 317th Infantry from September of 1917 through June of 1919. He worked as a logger. He helped to build the Cass Railroad in West Virginia. He worked in an aircraft plant. His last job was with Bethlehem Steel in Sparrows Point, Maryland. He's certainly earned his way through life. Let's give him a hand. [*Applause*]

And our last honoree is Mr. Milton Garland from Waynesboro, Pennsylvania. Stand up, Mr. Garland. This man has an amazing story. He served in the first division of the Navy from July of 1918 through September of 1921. At the age of 98, he is still known as "Mr. Refrigeration" because, at his age, he still teaches refrigeration classes in Waynesboro for the Frick Refrigeration Company. He has designed ice rinks, food refrigeration units, and petrochemical controls, and he's still working at his chosen profession. Let's give him a hand. [*Applause*]

I close by asking you to remember that the service that these fine people rendered is being replicated today all around the world by the men and women who wear our uniforms. Today they are the best-trained, best-equipped, ablest people who have ever worn the uniform of the United States of America. They would not be able to do that today, had it not been for the contributions of people like these four men we honor. So I ask you to remember what this says: A grateful Nation remembers. Thank you all very much.

NOTE: The President spoke at 2:04 p.m. in the Domiciliary. In his remarks, he referred to Thomas Weaver, director of the Veterans Medical Center.

Statement on Signing the Department of the Interior and Related Agencies Appropriations Act, 1994
November 11, 1993

Today I have signed into law, H.R. 2520, the "Department of the Interior and Related Agencies Appropriations Act, 1994."

H.R. 2520 provides funds for various programs of the Department of the Interior and Energy, the Forest Service (Department of Agriculture), and the Indian Health Service (Department of Health and Human Services). Funding for various independent agencies such as the Smithsonian Institution and the National Foundation on the Arts and the Humanities is also included.

The Act provides funding to further the protection and rehabilitation of America's inventory of natural and cultural assets, including our national parks and forests.

I am pleased that the Act includes funding in support of the Forest Plan for the Pacific Northwest, which will help both to begin implementation of ecosystem management and to offset economic disruptions to forest communities in Washington, Oregon, and Northern California.

The Act provides funding for my proposal to establish a National Biological Survey. This new bureau within the Department of the Interior will facilitate improvement in the quality of biological research. Better science will result in improved decision-making in the management of the Nation's federally managed lands and will enable Federal land managers to avoid future contentious actions under the Endangered Species Act.

The Act provides funding for a number of my investment proposals for energy conservation and fossil energy research and development. These investments are important for our Nation's energy future.

WILLIAM J. CLINTON

The White House,
November 11, 1993.

NOTE: H.R. 2520, approved November 11, was assigned Public Law No. 103–138.

Statement on Signing the Department of Defense Appropriations Act, 1994
November 11, 1993

Today I have signed into law, H.R. 3116, the "Department of Defense Appropriations Act, 1994." H.R. 3116 supports the Administration's major defense priorities and reflects a spirit of cooperation between the Administration and the Congress to provide for a strong national defense. I am very pleased that the Congress has addressed budget issues in such a way that provides balanced support for my number one priority, the readiness of our forces. I also appreciate the support that the Congress has given to key investment and modernization proposals, especially my efforts to create a strong defense reinvestment program.

However, I do have serious reservations about a provision in section 8151 of this Act. I construe section 8151(b)(2)(ii) as not restricting my constitutional responsibility and authority as Commander In Chief, including my ability to place U.S. combat forces under the temporary tactical control of a foreign commander where to do otherwise would jeopardize the safety of U.S. combat forces in support of UNOSOM II. Such U.S. combat forces shall, however, remain under the operational command and control of U.S. commanders at all times.

WILLIAM J. CLINTON

The White House,
November 11, 1993.

NOTE: H.R. 3116, approved November 11, was assigned Public Law No. 103–139.

Remarks in a Telephone Conversation With Representative Ed Pastor on NAFTA
November 12, 1993

Representative Pastor. Good morning.

The President. Hello, Ed.

Representative Pastor. Yes, good morning, Mr. President.

The President. How are you?

Representative Pastor. I'm doing well, sir, beautiful weather here in Arizona.

The President. It's beautiful here, too.

Representative Pastor. The reason I called you was to let you know that November 17, we'll be supporting you on the free-trade agreement.

The President. Thank you very much. We need your help.

Representative Pastor. And I give a lot of credit to this to Congressman Esteban Torres. As you know, he worked very hard to get that NAD bank. And I know that with it we can do some things along the border.

I had a conversation yesterday with the EPA Administrator, and we talked about the resources that will be available. That was one of my concerns. So I look forward to working with her and with you to help the border communities along our Mexican-U.S. border.

The President. Thank you very much, Ed. As you well know, these environmental difficulties are going to get a lot better if NAFTA passes now that we've got the development bank there. And it also means more jobs along the border on both sides working on environmental cleanup. So I'm very encouraged.

I also want you to know that since you've been gone we've had a pretty good run in picking up some folks. Congresswoman Anna Eshoo from California came out yesterday, and we got five Congressmen from the Rust Belt. David Mann from Ohio became the first Democrat in Ohio to come out for NAFTA along with Congressman Hobson and Congressman Kasich. And then we got two Republicans from Michigan and two Members of Congress in the last week switched from no to yes, Marilyn Lloyd and Rick Lehman.

Representative Pastor. Well, Mr. President, you're doing very well.

The President. Well, we're making progress anyway. And we got Gerry Studds and Steny Hoyer when they came out last week. I think that was a good sign because they'll work hard and try to help us pass this thing. So I'm feeling much better than I did a few days ago. But I'm glad to have this phone call from you, and I just want to encourage you to try to sway every vote you can. And let's keep working until we bring it in.

Representative Pastor. Well, I'm going to be working with Members of the Hispanic Caucus. I know that some are still undecided, so we'll be working with them.

The President. We've got about four outstanding that I think we can still get if we all work hard.

Representative Pastor. Well, we're all going to work hard for you and, hopefully, at the final count we'll be past the 218 that we need. But I'm very happy to join you in this effort and at this time would like to ask you to consider coming to Arizona one of these days.

The President. I'd like to come back. You know it's been a while since I was there. I was there during the campaign, and the State was actually very good to me. I was amazed as we came so close to victory there. And I'm anxious to come back, and I want to be your guest.

Representative Pastor. Well, you have a standing tee time, so let me know when you—and we've got a lot of mulligans. [*Laughter*] Let me know when you want to come out.

The President. Thanks. I've played golf in Arizona, and it was a good round for me; so I have wonderful memories of that. I'll do that. Thank you.

Representative Pastor. Okay. Thank you Mr. President.

The President. Bye.

Representative Pastor. Have a good day.

[*At this point, the telephone conversation ended, and the President took questions from reporters.*]

Q. Where does this put you, roughly, in terms of the number of votes you need now? Sunday you said you needed about 30.

The President. Oh, no, we're much closer now. I think we'll get what we think we have to get on the Democratic side, and I'm working with the Republicans. I see all this stuff about their difficulties, but I don't buy that. I think that they've got some of the same problems our folks do.

I think it's clear to everybody now—let me say this again, if there were a secret ballot, this would pass by 50 votes or more. And I think everyone knows that. So now it's a question of getting the people who are in there harder for NAFTA and who know it's good for American jobs and who know it's an important part of our foreign policy for the future, that it will develop America by reaching out to the world, that it will lead to a trade pact with all of Latin America, that it will help us with the Pacific and Europe. It's a matter of sort of bringing that conviction to the fore.

And I will say again, I think that from the point of view of the Congress, the number one virtue of the debate between the Vice President and Mr. Perot is that Al Gore showed that if

you are on the right side of an issue and if you believe it, you can convince your constituents that you're right and that it's in their interest. And so I'm still very upbeat about this. But I think there will be clouds around this issue right to the last.

Q. Well, just in a ballpark idea, I mean, is it fair to say less than 20 votes away or——

The President. It's fair to say that I've got a list that makes me think we can do what we always thought we'd have to do. In fast track, I think the Democrats only had—when they voted for the fast track negotiations here, I think they only had 95 votes. But I've always thought we could do our part and we could get 218 votes on Wednesday, and I still believe we're going to.

NOTE: The President spoke at 9:19 a.m. in the Oval Office at the White House.

Exchange With Reporters Prior to Discussions With Prime Minister Yitzhak Rabin of Israel
November 12, 1993

Middle East Peace Process

Q. Mr. President, are you considering a stop in the Middle East during your Europe trip in January to help the momentum of the Middle East peace process?

The President. The Prime Minister and I are going to talk about what we can do to keep this going, but that's not one of the things that's been raised so far by anyone.

[*At this point, one group of reporters left the room, and another group entered.*]

Q. President Clinton, is King Hussein strong enough to make peace with Israel before President Asad?

The President. I think he's in a good position to proceed now. And of course, we all have come out for a process that will lead to comprehensive peace in the Middle East. But I think King Hussein obviously wants peace, and the recent elections must surely encourage him.

I think the people of Jordan want peace.

Q. Do you think there's a chance to reach any progress with the Syrians?

The President. I hope so. We're going to discuss that today and a number of other issues. Over the long run, I think we'll have to make progress with everyone.

PLO Terrorism

Q. Mr. Prime Minister, what's your comment on the involvement of PLO people in the kidnaping and killing of an Israeli?

Prime Minister Rabin. We consider it as a great and dangerous violation of the commitment of the PLO. In the letter that was signed by the Chairman of the PLO to me, he committed himself to renounce and reject terrorism. Keeping commitments is the basis for the advancement towards peace. We'll keep our commitments; we demand them to keep their commitments and to come up openly in renouncing and taking the disciplined measures to which he is committed, as it is written in the letter that he signed and sent to me.

NOTE: The exchange began at 10:41 a.m. in the Oval Office at the White House. A tape was not available for verification of the content of this exchange.

The President's News Conference With Prime Minister Yitzhak Rabin of Israel
November 12, 1993

The President. Good afternoon, ladies and gentlemen. It's a great pleasure for me once again to have the opportunity to host my friend Prime Minister Rabin. I first welcomed him to the White House last March. At that time, he stated with great conviction that he felt the time had come to make peace and that he was ready to make the necessary steps and to take the necessary risks for peace. I told him that if that were to be the case, it was the job of the United States to minimize those risks. We both committed to make 1993 a year of breakthrough for peace in the Middle East.

On September 13, that commitment was transformed into history through the simple handshake on the South Lawn of the White House. Israel's historic effort with the Palestinians was due, in large measure, to the courageous statesmanship of Prime Minister Rabin.

Shortly thereafter, the United States convened a donors' conference to help provide the funds necessary to speed and facilitate the reconciliation. Yet there is still much work to be done to turn the promise of September 13th into a comprehensive and lasting peace. The Prime Minister and I have agreed it must be a peace that secures Israel's existence and one that endures for generations. We agreed on the need for prompt and effective implementation of the Palestinian-Israel accord. We must not allow the opponents of that agreement to derail the new progress that this year has brought. And leaders who seek peace must speak out in a loud and clear voice against those who would destroy those aspirations for peace.

The Prime Minister and I discussed the next step toward our common objectives. We agreed that peace between Israel and Syria is essential to achieving that objective of comprehensive peace. I told the Prime Minister that I have been delighted by the progress Israel has made

with Jordan following the historic meeting between Crown Prince Hassan and Foreign Minister Peres, which I hosted a few weeks ago. We discussed how the United States and Israel, working together, can achieve a peace agreement with Jordan and Israel in the near future. Morocco, Tunisia, Indonesia, and other Arab and Muslim states have also taken encouraging steps to respond to Israel's peace commitments.

I told the Prime Minister that I believe even more needs to be done to reinforce the progress already made by the PLO and Jordan. In particular, I think the time has come to end the Arab boycott of Israel, a relic of past animosity that simply has no place in the architecture of peaceful relations we are all working to build in the Middle East.

During our talks we discussed what the United States can do to enhance Israel's security as it comes to grips with the very real risks it is taking to achieve this peace.

I reaffirmed my commitment to work with the Congress, to maintain our present levels of assistance, and to consult with Congress to consider how we can use loan guarantees and other forms of assistance to Israel to help Israel defray the cost of peace.

We also discussed ways the United States can help Israel defend itself from its adversaries and long-term threats to its security. And I renewed America's unshakable pledge to maintain and enhance Israel's qualitative security edge.

Mr. Prime Minister, as you go home, I hope you will tell your people that as they turn their energies and talents to the hard and daring work of building that comprehensive peace, the American people will stand by them.

Prime Minister Rabin. Mr. President, the Vice President, Secretary of State, Secretary of Defense, ladies and gentlemen. A few weeks ago we took part in the historical moment of signing of the Declaration of Principles between Israel and the PLO.

Mr. President, we appreciate and are thankful for the role that you have played in bringing the Declaration of Principles to its conclusion. We hoped and we continue to hope that this significant step will bring an end to 100 years of terrorism and bloodshed.

Today we are in the midst of negotiations to implement the Declaration of Principles signed here on the lawn of the White House on September 13th. I told you, Mr. President, that these are complicated negotiations, and in the process of reaching an agreement there will be ups and downs. But I am quite sure that we and the Palestinians have passed the point of no return in our efforts to implement the agreement.

This is why the PLO must condemn vigorously, openly, and immediately any action that is in flagrant violation of the commitment to renounce terrorism. The basis for our advance and progress in the implementation of the agreement is that each side must keep its commitments.

The signing of the DOP has created a new hope and opened many opportunities in our negotiations with other Arab parties to the Washington negotiations for peace. We hope and expect that with your assistance, Mr. President, that these talks will be continued as soon as possible.

We have found that direct and quiet contacts between Israel and its partners in the effort to achieve a comprehensive peace is the best way to overcome prejudices of the past. The less the talks are exposed to the limelight of the media, the better are the chances to achieve agreements.

We believe that you, Mr. President, and the Secretary of State can assist in facilitating this particular mode of negotiations. We are therefore ready to continue with your assistance the negotiation with Syria, Jordan, and Lebanon. We believe that the substantial common agenda concluded with Jordan and further efforts made since can serve as a basis towards a major development on the road to the treaty of peace.

We also look forward to achieve results in the negotiation with Syria and Lebanon, recognizing the importance of making progress in these areas. The positive conclusion of negotiations with the Arab neighbors will bring about a real comprehensive peace and will open the road to stability and prosperity for all the peoples and states in the region.

Mr. President, in a letter that I wrote to you at the beginning of this year, I expressed Israel's readiness to take risks for the sake of peace. I was more than thankful, Mr. President, for your statement in which you declared your readiness to minimize the risk that Israel is willing to take for peace. Indeed, Mr. President, you have taken effective steps in this spirit.

In our talks today, we discussed the ways and the methods by which we should proceed in the peace negotiations and also to find additional means to strengthen Israel in view of the threats to the security of the state and to provide safety to its population. Mr. President, peace and stability in the Middle East are threatened daily by yet another danger, the offensive mounted by the forces of radicalism and extremism. The offensive is twofold, against any Arab moderate, pragmatic regimes as such, and against the peace process. Our discussions today also dwelt on this issue, and we agreed to initiate on ongoing dialog between us as well as with the other concerned parties.

Mr. President, we all appreciate the firm position that you have taken against the Arab boycott. The boycott can never be accepted and certainly not when the peace process is being advanced. For the people of Israel to support the government's peace policy, they must feel that the attitudes and the atmosphere have actually changed after September 13th. We feel that our goodwill is yet to be matched.

On the plane that brought me to the United States, there came two parents, the Katz family, whose son, Yehuda, has been missing in action since 1982. We are investing serious efforts to bring back Yehuda and all the other MIA's and prisoners. Your government and other friendly nations have helped in this humanitarian mission. We trust that you will continue in this sacred task.

Today, you have gracefully told me and all the Israelis of your decision to strengthen the security of Israel. More specifically, your decision to continue the level of security assistance, to maintain our qualitative edge through the supply of advanced aircraft, the lifting of technological barriers, especially in the field of computers, and your decision to beef up our capacity to defend ourselves against missiles is most significant.

Mr. President, I return home stronger in

many aspects, more confident in our ability to reach peace, and reassured that thousands of miles away from Israel, we have a true friend in the White House that we can rely on.

On this occasion I would like in very simple words to say to you and to you, to the Vice President, the Secretaries of State and Defense, your administration, and the American people, thank you, and God bless you.

Middle East Peace Process

Q. Mr. President, you said the peace between Israel and Syria is essential for reaching a comprehensive peace in the region. What does the administration intend to do to advance peace talks between Israel and Syria? And did you hear anything from the Prime Minister that would encourage you to either send Secretary Christopher back to the region or facilitate some sort of back-channel, behind-the-scenes talks to get those talks moving?

The President. You can see by the question, Mr. Prime Minister, it's hard for the United States to facilitate talks out of the press. [*Laughter*]

We discussed the whole question of the relationship between Israel and Syria, what the United States could do. The Prime Minister reaffirmed his belief that peace in the Middle East would require progress on all the tracks, including the tracks with Syria and Lebanon. And we discussed some specific things that we will be exploring, the United States, over the next several weeks. Beyond that, I think I shouldn't go. But I feel confident that we'll be able to continue to pursue this.

Yes, ma'am?

PLO Terrorism

Q. Mr. President, we heard Mr. Rabin condemn the PLO for the recent attack on a Jewish settler 2 weeks ago. Do you share the view that it's a violation of the PLO-Israeli agreement? And were you just urging Chairman Arafat to renounce it?

The President. I agree with what the Prime Minister said. I think that Chairman Arafat now, under the terms of the agreement, is dutybound at a minimum to condemn it. I think we all recognize that he may not have total control over everyone who acts in the name of Fatah, but he is now bound by the terms, the clear terms of the agreement, to condemn it.

Is anyone here from the Israeli press we could acknowledge?

Jonathan Pollard

Q. Mr. President, are you considering the release of Jonathan Pollard? And Mr. Prime Minister, did you raise this issue with the President?

The President. Perhaps I could answer both questions. The Prime Minister did raise the issue with me. We discussed it, and I explained that under our procedures here, I cannot make a decision on the Pollard case until the Justice Department makes a recommendation to me. Under the United States Constitution, I do not have to follow the recommendation of the Justice Department, but under our procedures I have to get one. And when I get one—it won't be too long in the future—I will then review it and make a decision.

Rita [Rita Braver, CBS News].

Technological Support to Israel

Q. Mr. President, from Prime Minister Rabin's remarks it sounded like you have decided to sell Israel or make available to Israel, the F–15E fighter jet. Is that true? And can you tell us a little bit more about the technological and weaponry support that you're going to give the Israelis?

The President. Well, we are working on an agreement to make available a number of planes to the Israelis. The Prime Minister is going to meet with Secretary Aspin on Monday, and they are going to try to work through the details. And I think I should wait until they have done that, and we'll be able to make an announcement I think shortly after that. But there will be a number of planes being made available to Israel as part of this ongoing effort between us.

Someone else from the Israeli press.

Israel-Jordan Relations

Q. Mr. President, can we expect a new three-way handshake, I mean, this time with maybe King Hussein within the duration of the Prime Minister's visit in America?

The President. Not on this visit. But nothing would please me more than to have another visit where that would occur. But I think not on this visit.

NAFTA and Health Care Reform

Q. Mr. President, on the subject of NAFTA,

a number of Congressmen from tobacco States, such as Congressman Steve Neal, have suggested that if the tobacco tax that has been proposed for health care were reduced from 75 cents to 40 cents, that they might bring along 6 or 10 votes. Is that something that you would consider if you were short of votes, or is that something that you would completely, categorically rule out?

The President. That issue has not been brought up to me, but I can tell you this: There were a lot of people who urged that we ought to have a $2-a-pack tobacco tax, if you remember. I asked for the 75 cents because that's what our searching effort, our agonizing effort to determine what the cost of this program would be turned up as what is needed. And therefore, I cannot foresee circumstances under which I would be willing to change that position, because it would imperil the whole health care program. So there has been no—I didn't want to raise any money from anybody to do anything other than to pay for the health care program, although I think that higher tobacco taxes discourage use, and that's a good thing. But that wasn't what was behind it. So——

Q. ——votes at the end of the game?

The President. I have no reason to believe that that will ever come into play. If it changes, I'll be glad to tell you, but I have no reason to believe that that will happen.

Someone from the Israeli press?

Middle East Peace Process

Q. Mr. President, I have two questions actually. Are you going to send Secretary Christopher to the Middle East to activate the Syrian-Israeli track and to mount active support for the Palestinian agreement, or do you prefer to wait until Mr. Rabin gives you the green light to express desire to deal with Syria?

The second one for Rabin. Mr. Rabin, are you ready to go for the—are you going to fight as—are you going to fight——

Prime Minister Rabin. We are talking about peace, not the resumption of fighting.

Q. No, I mean, in a domestic battle. Are you going to fight a domestic battle for an agreement with Syria right now, or do you still think that the Israeli public is not ready for it yet?

The President. The answer to the first question is that we have not made a specific decision about when the Secretary will return to the

Middle East. But we have ongoing contacts with Syria. You may know that I received the Foreign Minister of Syria here in the White House not very long ago. I have conversations from time to time with President Asad, and we will continue our dialog with them in working toward peace.

Prime Minister Rabin. Israel has a long tradition of keeping its commitments. Whatever we take upon ourselves, every agreement that we sign, we will carry out. We expect those who sign with us agreements to keep, to fully keep, their commitments as we do. There is no need to fight. It's true, in Israel there is an opposition to the position that the government has taken, to the agreement that has been signed, to the ways to carry it out. But we are a democratic country and once the decision is taken, it is carried out.

Q. Mr. President, both you and the Prime Minister mentioned the Arab boycott of Israel. You suggested in the past that should now be lifted. But so far, a number of America's closest friends in the Arab world have refused to take that step. Have you received any indications from the Saudis perhaps or from other Arab states that have been close to America that they're now prepared to take that step? And what can you do to try to get them to do that?

The President. Let me answer you in this way: I have received some indications that the enforcement of the boycott is not as vigorous as it once was, but that some of the countries involved are reluctant to explicitly lift it. I wanted to raise the issue again today publicly because I believe that a big key toward achieving peace is maintaining support within the State of Israel for the peace process and for the risks that it entails.

Perhaps the most important benefit of the ceremony here on September 13th, even though it thrilled billions of people around the world, is that it clearly enhanced the willingness of the people of Israel to support the peace process.

So I intend to continue to work on that. And I have some ideas about how I should do it, but I would rather wait until we have achieved more concrete results before talking about it.

Someone else from Israel?

Q. If Arafat doesn't condemn terror, should Israel suspend the talks with the PLO?

The President. That will be a decision for Israel to make.

Q. Could the Prime Minister——

Prime Minister Rabin. I believe that we have to stick to our commitments. I expect another side to keep its commitment. I will not answer on a hypothetical situation.

The President. Mr. Friedman [Thomas L. Friedman, New York Times].

Q. Arafat has been rather slow in getting the PLO organized to fulfill these negotiations. We've seen that on both the political and security front. I wondered if you could elaborate on (a) are you satisfied with the PLO's performance up to now in the negotiations, and (b) what will you do if the PLO does not condemn these actions?

The President. On the second question, I don't think I can give a better answer than the Prime Minister did. I used to give that response. I should return to it more often, I think. But let me go back to the first question, which I think is quite important.

I wish that the pace had been more rapid. But I think it is important to recognize that the PLO itself, by its very nature, by the nature of its organization and its activities over the last many, many years has never had the responsibility of going through the mechanics that have to be discussed in this agreement: How do the lights get turned on in the morning; how is the food distributed; how are the houses built? How are these things done? So I think, in fairness, I would be quite concerned if I thought that the fact that we're a little bit slow in the pace here was the result of some sort of deliberate desire to undermine an accord they had just signed off on.

At the present moment, I really believe it is more a function of the whole organization not being organized for or experienced in the work in which they must now engage. And so the Prime Minister and I talked about this quite a bit, and we still have high hopes that if the timetable is not met, at least it can be nearly met for the conclusion of these specific and concrete things. I think it is more a function of this is sort of an alien role for them, and I think they're working into it. But I'm hopeful now that there is a level of engagement which will permit us to push it through to success.

Press Secretary Myers. Last question.

Q. I would like to ask you a question concerning the agreement, the peace agreements. There was a discussion that what was needed was economic development. There were a number of projects on the Gaza concerning water, canals, energy resources, et cetera. I'd like to ask, what is your estimate of the magnitude of funding needed in order to get these projects into motion? And also, what are the consequences if these projects are not realized within a certain amount of time in the Gaza? And perhaps the Prime Minister would like to answer that question, too.

Prime Minister Rabin. As of today, Israel supplies all the electricity needs of the Gaza and the West Bank. There is no shortage of electricity there. The question, what will be the projects that will be built there, how much the consumption of energy and other items including water—we continue also to add to the water supplies of Gaza by a pipeline that supplies them water. We need to negotiate all this before we negotiate to tall figures. It will not be a serious statement.

The President. But let me respond, though, to that. When we had the donors' conference here, working both individually and multilaterally, we have commitments over the next few years for several billion dollars and a few hundred million dollars right off the bat. We think that's enough to make a big difference.

I have asked our people to identify some specific high return, quick investment infrastructure projects that could be instituted and effected quickly that would have a significant economic benefit to the people in the affected areas that we could proceed with just as quickly as the agreements make that possible. So I think there's money there to do what needs to be done in the near term once there is a system which guarantees that the investments, whether they be in infrastructure or new economic development, will have the result that we want.

Brit [Brit Hume, ABC News].

Q. Thank you, Mr. President. I'd like to ask the Prime Minister, if I could, something about what you said to Mr. Clinton today about the Pollard case and why the matter continues to be such a priority with you, sir.

Prime Minister Rabin. I don't believe it would be advisable to me to add on this issue to what the President said.

The President. One last question from the Israeli press.

Q. I'd like to ask you, in the near future will you send a new ambassador to Tel Aviv? When do you think the time will come to move your Embassy to Jerusalem?

The President. I think from the question you ask you know what my long-standing position on that issue has been. But I have to resort to the position that I have taken on this ever since these talks began, and that is that the United States should not at this time make any statement which in any way injects the United States into a peace process that must be carried out by the parties themselves. And for me to say anything about that one way or the other at this moment in my judgment would run the risk of throwing the process out of kilter. There will be time to discuss that and to make statements about that later on down the road at a more ripe occasion.

Thank you.

NOTE: The President's 33d news conference began at 12:11 p.m. in the East Room at the White House. In his remarks, he referred to Jonathan Pollard, U.S. Navy employee convicted of selling national security information to Israel.

Media Roundtable Interview on NAFTA
November 12, 1993

The President. We're having a good couple of days. Yesterday we had 10 or 11 Members endorse NAFTA.

Q. Could you speak up a little bit, sir?

The President. Yesterday we had 10 or 11 people endorse the treaty, both Republicans and Democrats, including three Members from Ohio, a Rust Belt State where we hadn't had any endorsements before; two from Michigan. Today we have five or six—we have six confirmed, and we have five who've already announced their endorsement today for NAFTA, all Democrats, all six of them. So we're making some progress.

Perhaps the most remarkable thing that has happened today is something I just saw. The president of the Massachusetts Building Trades Council endorsed NAFTA with this letter. It's a real profile in courage. He said—this quote—he said, "No longer can nations afford to build invisible walls at their borders because there are no national borders to free trade." And he basically said at the end of his letter that "President Clinton is trying to improve on the status quo. His opponents, perhaps without knowing it, are defending the status quo." Leo Purcell, a pretty brave guy. I hope he's still got his job tomorrow.

Q. Can we get a copy of that letter?

The President. Oh, sure.

Q. I have one question that sort of follows up on what you just said. In Springfield, Zenith moved its television manufacturing plant to Mexico a couple of years ago. How do you address blue-collar concerns from people who have seen that happen and they hear Perot and they just naturally fear that the same thing's going to happen?

The President. Well, first of all, let me make this statement at the outset. One of the things that our administration has never denied is the fears of middle class Americans about the loss of their jobs or the loss of their incomes. About 60 percent of our work force has suffered from stagnant wages or worse for almost two decades. So my answer to them is not that their fears are unfounded—they have legitimate fears and experience to base that on—but that this agreement will improve their conditions, not make it worse. And let me explain why.

I think this is at the nub of at least the negative side of the argument. First, let me say by way of background that I was the Governor of a State for 12 years that had plants close and move to Mexico. And I worked very, very hard to try to restructure my State's economy, to maintain a manufacturing base, and to rebuild from the hard, hard years we had in the early eighties. And my State did not have an unemployment rate below the national average in any year I was Governor until last year, when we ranked first or second in the country in job growth. But it was a long, painful process of rebuilding. I know a lot about this. We lost jobs to Mexico.

Now, the point I want to make about this is, number one, Mexico had a very small role in the decline of manufacturing jobs in America in the last 15 years. They declined because of foreign competition from rich countries as well as poor countries. If you look at just the manufacturing trade advantage, you will find that obviously the biggest trade deficit we have is with Japan, a rich country.

Number two, a lot of this happened in every advanced country because of productivity increases that came because of mechanization. Just the improvements in technology meant that we could produce more things with fewer people. That's what rise in productivity means. So manufacturing has been going through something of the same thing that agriculture went through. When I was born, in my home State, an enormous percentage of our people worked on the farm. Now it's down to probably 4 percent, even though Arkansas is a big farm State. So a lot of these things are big long-term developments.

Number three, the device which made Mexico particularly attractive for plant was the so-called *maquilladora* system, which basically identifies an area along the Mexican-American border in which plants can locate and produce for the American market and send it back in here without paying tariffs, taking advantage of the low wages in Mexico and the other lower costs of production.

Now, if you look at that and you look at what NAFTA does, it's easy to see how NAFTA will make it less likely, not impossible—I'm not saying none of this will ever happen—but it will be less likely than it is now that we'll have significant movement of manufacturing facilities to Mexico for low wages. Why is that? For one thing, NAFTA will give bigger markets to American manufacturers here at home by lowering the tariff barriers and by doing something else which is quite important: It reduces the domestic content requirements that Mexico imposes on American manufacturers, which means that—domestic content basically says you've got to make this stuff here if you want to sell it here. So that the auto industry, for example, estimates that they'll go from selling 1,000 to 50,000, 60,000 cars, made in America, in Mexico in one year. So we'll have more access to the market.

Secondly, what Mexico gets out of this is not more plants to produce for the American market. If NAFTA passes, under the terms of the side agreement our administration negotiated, there is no question that environmental costs will go up in Mexico because of the environmental side agreement. There is no question that labor costs will go up more rapidly in Mex-

ico because Mexico is the first country ever to put its labor code, which it admits has regularly been violated, and now they put their labor code into this trade agreement. So that if they violate their labor code, we can bring a trade action against them.

And furthermore, President Salinas has said that he will raise the minimum wage on an annual basis as the economy of the country grows. So if NAFTA passes, wage rates will go up more rapidly, costs of production from environmental protection will go up more rapidly, trade barriers to American products will go down more, the requirements to produce in Mexico if you want to sell in Mexico will go down more. Therefore, the conditions which people are worried about, which are legitimate conditions, will be improved if NAFTA passes, not aggravated.

Now, that's a long answer, but that's the nub of the negative argument against this. And I think it's important to get it out.

Q. Mr. President, that's an economic argument, and a good one. Congressman Sawyer from northeast Ohio makes that same argument but says he hasn't been able to overcome the emotional objections to it, and the perception that it won't do the things you said it would do seem impossible to overcome. Why should a Member who can't overcome this perception in his district be willing to vote for it, and what can you do to help such a Member overcome any political backlash to him or her if this happens?

The President. Well, first, let me say I have enormous respect for him, for Sawyer. If you look at the way that other votes have lined up in Ohio and if you look at his district, I think the fact that he's been willing to have a very honest and open and candid conversation about this with all of the people of his district about this is very much to his credit. But he lives in a place that has lost a lot of high-wage, high-dollar manufacturing jobs.

My response is the debate between Vice President Gore and Ross Perot. That is, the most important lesson that any Congressman should take out of that debate is not that Al Gore defeated Ross Perot on a night in October—or November. The most important lesson is that if you believe it's the right thing to do, and you make the arguments to your people, you can do that. In other words, if Congressman Sawyer's representatives believe that he is doing this because he thinks it will get them more jobs and make America stronger economically, then the evidence of the public reaction to the Gore-Perot debate is that you can do that and survive, that people will support you, that they will stay with you. And that's what I believe. In other words, I told a group of business executives who were in here the other day lobbying for this, I said, you need to go out and tell people you're doing this for middle class America. I said, you look around this room. Every one of us is going to be all right whether NAFTA passes or not, whether GATT passes or not. We'll figure out some way to do okay in the system. But the country as a whole will not grow as much. No rich country can grow richer, can increase incomes, can increase jobs unless you expand the base to which you sell. That's the whole theory of trade. It built a massive middle class in America after the Second World War. It rebuilt Europe and Japan, and now it can revitalize Latin America.

I also think it's important, by the way, for the Tom Sawyers of the world, let me say this, and for all the others, that we not overstate, just as I think the opponents of NAFTA have grossly overstated the negative effects. I mean Mexico, after all, is less than 5 percent of—[*inaudible*]. The idea that we're trying to convince people that they sort of snookered the United States in a trade negotiation, and we're going to collapse the American economy, it really shows you how anxiety-ridden a lot of Americans are, that many people believe that.

On the other hand, it's important not to overestimate the number of jobs that can be created. That is, Mexico has gone from a $5.7 billion trade deficit 5 years ago to a $5.4 billion trade surplus last year. Most of the smart money in Mexico is that the trade deficit for them will get bigger. That is, we'll sell more near-term because they'll get more investment to develop their own economy in the long term.

But the real job generator for us in NAFTA is going to be not only for the specific industries that will sell more in Mexico, but that will open Chile, Argentina, all of Latin America. And we will then be able to say—when I go out there the day after the House votes, if I win, it will be a lot easier for me to look the Japanese, the Chinese, the heads of the other 13 Asian countries in the eye and say, "We want to grow with you. Asia's growing very rapidly. We want to buy your products, but you have to buy ours.

And we need to adopt a new world trade agreement." So that's what I would say to Tom Sawyer.

Q. Along that same line, could you analyze for us what is at stake for you and for the country in this and how it feels having this fate in the hands of your opposition party, particularly Newt Gingrich, who is a man who has been your opponent in most cases and is asking you for something very specific now, some kind of written protection for Republicans? Are you willing to give that? I know that's three questions.

The President. Let me start at the back and come forward. [*Inaudible*] First of all, I volunteered even before Newt asked, but I agree with him, that if a Republican votes for NAFTA and is opposed in the congressional races next year by a Democrat who attacks the Republican for voting for NAFTA, then I will say, for whatever it is worth, in any given district that I think that the attack is unfair, that the vote was not a partisan vote, and that it was in the national interest. And I do not believe any Member of Congress should be defeated for voting for NAFTA. That's all they've asked me for. In other words, they haven't asked me to prefer Republicans over Democrats. But they want me to say——

Q. In writing.

The President. Well, I'll give it to them in writing, I'll give it to them in public statements. I do not believe any Member of Congress should be defeated for doing what is plainly in the national interest.

Now, what was your other question?

Q. How does it feel having Republicans——

The President. Well, I don't mind it. I wish we had more bipartisan efforts for change. If you look at the fact that 41 Governors at least have come out for this and only 2 have come out explicitly against it, I think we ought to have more common economic efforts.

I thought the Republicans made a mistake. They may have hurt me politically by simply refusing to work with us on the economic program. But I think over the long run, we're going to come out ahead because it's produced deficit reduction, low interest rates, low inflation, and more jobs in 10 months than were created in the previous 4 years. So I think they made a mistake. The national security issues of the nineties by and large, are going to be economic issues, by and large. And to whatever extent we can pursue the national security in a bipartisan fashion, we're better off doing so.

Also, a lot of the divisions that have ripped the Congress today do not break down into any traditional liberal or conservative terms, or Republican and Democratic terms. They're more like who's pro-change and who's against it, who's willing to go beyond the status quo in the debate and who's not. And it's amazing how it shifts from issue to issue, not only among Republicans and Democrats but among people who would otherwise define themselves as liberals and conservatives. So I'm not concerned about that. I think Newt Gingrich is doing the best he can with Mr. Michel to produce the votes that they think they can produce. And he sure knows I'm doing the best I can to produce the votes I can produce.

The first question is, what's at stake. What's at stake, in my judgment, is something more than the sheer terms of this economic debate. I think, first, what's at stake is the strategy and the attitude and the conviction America will take in moving toward the 21st century economically. Are we going to try to do it by reaching out to the rest of the world, by saying we can compete and win, by building on the enormous productivity gains in the private sector of the United States over the last several years to do what is the time-tested way for a wealthy country to grow, to create jobs and incomes, and promote peace, that is, by reaching out, involving—[*inaudible*]—in trade. Or are we going to say we just don't think we can compete and win anymore with anybody until they pay their workers as much as we pay ours and until everything else is equal on every last scale. So even though here's a country that we've got a trade surplus with, that's buying more from us than we're buying from them, we're just not going to do it, I think, because we're just hurting too bad. Now, the hurts are legitimate. But you cannot do that. So I think that this will define our country's attitude for some time.

Secondly, I think the second thing that's at stake is we may lose the chance to have a stable, good, strong, growing economic relationship with our neighbor in the south and lose the chance to build that sort of partnership with all of Latin America. I hope it is not so if we don't—[*inaudible*]—but it could happen.

The third thing is it could cost us getting a new world trade agreement in the GATT round by the end of the year, because the

French, for example, will be able to say, "Well, you say we shouldn't be protectionist, you say we shouldn't protect our agriculture, you want us to get into a world trade agreement that will bring America hundreds of thousands of jobs, and yet you walked away from a no-brainer on your southern border." So I think that America's abilities to forge a globally competitive but cooperative world in the 21st century in which we can compete and win, whether it is with Asia or with Europe or with Latin America, I think will be significantly undermined if we defeat this. It is far bigger than just the terms of this agreement.

First, this agreement took on abnormal symbolic significance for those who were against it. They poured into the agreement all the accumulated resentments of the 1980's. Tom Sawyer's right about that; they did. I mean, a lot of the people who are against this, it's very moving to listen to them, to watch them. They almost shake when they talk about it. And it's real and honest the way they feel. But then, because of that, and because it became clear that the Congress might actually not adopt it, which is unheard of for the Congress to walk away from a trade agreement, it then took on a much greater symbolic significance for those of us who are for it. So it is about jobs and growth and opportunity for Americans by its own terms. And it is much better than letting the status quo go on. But it has bigger stakes as well.

Q. Congressman Tom Andrews, a Democrat from Maine, has criticized the way in which labor groups and your administration has gone about trying to win over his support. And I quote from Andrews: "I've been asked in so many ways, 'What do you need? What will it take?' We do a great disservice to this country when we make this a matter of pork-barrel auctioneering or we make it an issue of what threats we will respond to." What's your response to Andrews' concern?

The President. I agree with him. I think, first of all, a lot of the people who are fighting this are good friends of mine. I've been close to and worked with the labor movement, and I believe in a much higher level of partnerships between management and labor and Government, and I am not trying to create a low-wage economy. But I think it is wrong for people who are on the other side of this issue to tell Members of Congress who have voted with labor for years that they're never going to give them a contribution and they're never going to support them again, or get them an opponent even—some of them, they've said, well, they'd get opponents in primaries.

I agree with him that neither should we get into a bartering situation. I have to tell you that Members of Congress with whom I have talked—I can only speak for the ones with whom I have talked—the ones who have talked to me about things they wanted me to do if they voted for this were within the realm of what I would call legitimate concerns for their constituents. Let me just give you, if I might, one, the thing that I was most active in that I'm very proud of, because I believe in it anyway, and that was the desire of Congressman Esteban Torres from California and a number of the other Hispanics and Members of Congress who live along the border to develop this North American development bank as a way of financing infrastructure improvements to clean the environment up on both sides of the Rio Grande River. That creates jobs. It's in the public policy interest. It ameliorates the harsh impacts of the past.

When Lucille Roybal-Allard came out for this, who comes from one of the lowest, poorest districts in America, has workers that may be adversely affected by this, she wanted to know that in January we were really going to have the kind of comprehensive job retraining program dovetailed into the unemployment system that we should have had 15 years ago. She didn't ask me for a highway or a bridge or anything. She wanted me to try to take care of her folks. So that, I think, is legitimate.

Now, when other people come up to you, though, and say, "Look, I've been threatened, I may lose my seat, and will you help me do thus and so," if we can do it and there's nothing wrong with it, then we're trying to do it because we're trying to win. I think it's very much in America's interest. But I believe Tom Andrews is right. This issue should be resolved insofar as possible based on what's in the national interest.

Q. Mr. President, this morning when we put a notice in the paper asking people to call in with questions for you, here's one from Charlotte. He says, "I'd like to know, if the President's opinion is that NAFTA is so good for the United States, why is there so much opposition against it by people in the country?"

The President. Everyone knows that Mexico is a country that has a lower per capita income than the United States. And everyone knows that American business interests have moved plants to Mexico to produce for the American market. That's very different from investing in Mexico to hire Mexicans to produce for the Mexican market. That's a good thing. We should support that because the more Mexicans who have good jobs, the more they can buy American products. That symbolizes, those plants along the Rio Grande River symbolize the loss of America's industrial base to many people and the fact that literally millions of Americans, over half of American wage earners have worked harder for the same or lower wages for more than a decade. So NAFTA, the reason that so many people are against it is it's the symbol for so many people of their accumulated resentments of the last 10 to 15 years. Now, that's why there are so many people against it. And then there are a lot of people who say, "Well, I don't like this, that, or the other thing." There's no such thing as a perfect agreement that satisfies 100 percent of everybody's concerns.

But again, I would say, what I've found and what I thought Al Gore did so well in his television appearance—you have to be able to say to people, "Look, you can't vote on your emotions alone. You also have to vote on your head; you have to think through this. Look at what this agreement does. This makes the problems of the last 12 to 15 years better, not worse."

But I understand those fears. I mean, I have never questioned the integrity of anybody's anxiety. I got elected President because most people were working harder for less. That's the only reason I won the election and because people thought the society was coming apart and because there was no clear sense of where we were going. And when I ran for President, I said I like NAFTA, but I want to try to have a side agreement on the environment, side agreement on labor standards, and protection. This is another issue I want to emphasize: protection for unforeseen consequences. And there are two protections in there that I want to mention.

One is that we can, either of us, anybody can get out in 6 months notice. So if it turns out we're wrong, we can walk away from it. And if I thought it were hurting America, I would do so. It would be my duty to do so, and I would do so. The second thing deals with the more likely problem, which is suppose this turns out to be basically a good thing for us and basically a good thing for them, but there's some totally unforeseen consequence in one sector of the economy. We wouldn't want to withdraw, because it's basically a good thing. There is also a provision in here, the so-called surge provision, which allows us to identify some sector that's being decimated—it gives the Mexicans the same right, as it should—that no one ever thought about and to put the brakes on this agreement for 3 years while we try to work it out as it applies to that specific sector. So those are two protections that I would say to your friend in Charlotte.

Q. Mr. President, Congressman David Mann from Cincinnati, he voted against you on your budget and tax package, and now he's come out on your side on this one. Part one, do you forgive him now for the budget vote, now that he is supporting you on this? Part two, is there anything you've agreed to do for Mann to help him? And thirdly, he, like a lot of these other Congressmen we've been talking about, is going to have to run in a very heavy labor district next spring and face another potentially very tough primary. What would you suggest to him in terms of campaigning over this issue, and how should he defend himself on it?

The President. First of all, the only thing that David Mann asked me to do was to be supportive of the decision that he has made. And I told him that I would, I'd be very happy to help him deal with it. Remember, I went to the AFL–CIO convention in San Francisco to defend my position. I don't want to run away from labor. I want the working people of this country to stay with the Democratic Party. I want the small business people to come back to the Democratic Party. I believe this is in their interest. So I will certainly stand with him, foursquare.

In terms of the other thing, there's nothing for me to forgive. I think that the Members who voted for the economic program, including Tom Sawyer, have been proved right. And I think next April when people get their tax bills and you see somewhere between 15 and 18 million working families get a tax cut because they're working for modest wages with children, and see less than 2 percent of the American people get a tax increase, I think that April 15th is our friend. And all the rhetoric that

people heard about, it will go away, will vanish, and people will see that we did ask wealthy Americans to pay more of the load, and we did reduce the deficit, and we did bring interest rates and inflation down, and we did begin the process of creating jobs. So I think that time is on my side.

Q. But Mann voted——

The President. I know he did, but let me go back to what I said before. There are also a lot of people working against NAFTA who voted for me last time. What I have got to do is to try to develop a majority for change in the Congress.

It's funny, I think the American people—I see the Wall Street Journal said the other day that 70 percent of the people thought there was just as much gridlock now as there had been, and that's plainly not true. It's not true. What they're doing is, we're making hard decisions by narrow margins. That's very different than not taking up hard questions because there's gridlock. So when people read about all this contentiousness, they shouldn't be deterred by that. These are tough issues. If they were easy issues, they'd have been handled years ago. But making hard decisions by narrow margins is breaking gridlock. I've just got to keep working with David Mann on one hand or my friend David Bonior on the other hand and with the Republicans who are going to vote with us on this. We've got to create a majority for responsible change. That's what we've got to do.

Q. Mr. President, did you discuss this letter with Joe Moakley, and has it had any effect on his position?

The President. No, I just got it right before I came in here. I went with Joe to the Gillette factory, you know, when I was there for the dedication of the Kennedy Museum. And I know this is a tough vote for him in a large measure because Joe Moakley is a very loyal guy, and the guys that have been with him all these years are against this. I hope this will affect him. When Gerry Studds came out for NAFTA, I had the feeling that we might be on the verge of making some real breakthrough in Massachusetts, and we're working hard on it. Joe Kennedy came out earlier, as you know. So I'm hoping that we'll get some more in Massachusetts. It can make a big difference for us.

Q. One other followup, if I may, on a slightly more general question. Are you concerned that the issue has become one of race baiting and ethnic division with the language of what the——

The President. I think it is for some people, but not for others. I don't want to inject it into this. I thought what Mr. Perot said was very unfortunate. I'm sure you saw perhaps in the New York Times or the Washington Post yesterday, one of the papers carried a story about intense negative reaction in Mexico over his rhetoric. But much as I want to win this fight, I don't want to be unfair to my opponents. I don't think that that is nearly as big a factor as the sheer fear of middle class people that the system is out of control, that the middle class is going to work hard and get the shaft, that business executives cannot be trusted to put their workers or their interests high on their list of priorities, that the Government cannot be trusted to protect the interests of average working people, and that the system is working against them and even if they can't stop it, they ought to just try to put their thumb in the dike one more time. I think that is a much bigger deal.

Now, let me say this, I think a lot of people are less sensitive than they should be to how many people there are in Mexico who are sophisticated, well-educated, productive people of good will who want to build a kind of democratic partnership with our country and want to build a big middle class in their country. That is, I don't think, in other words, there's racism involved so much as I think that many of the opponents of NAFTA have dismissed the real talent and energy and capacity of the Mexican people to be good partners with us. That's not racism, it's because their own fears have overtaken them.

Q. Mr. President, in New Jersey, every House Democrat except Bob Torricelli has come out against this. Why do you think it's such a tough sell in New Jersey, and do you think you can get Mr. Torricelli's vote?

The President. I hope we can get his vote because he's been a real leader on issues in this hemisphere. I think to be fair to all concerned, Bob Torricelli has more personal experience and knowledge of this. And the voters in his district would be more likely to understand it because he does know so much about it, because he's been a leader on all these issues in the Caribbean and in Latin America. He has lived these issues, and I think he has a real feel for it.

I think what happened in New Jersey was that the Democrats reacted to the fact that New Jersey's had a very tough economy. There's a lot of anxiety. That's what I think. But I wish I could get some of them back between now and voting day, because I've had any number of Members of Congress come to me just since the debate and say, "I know this is the right thing to do; I just don't know how to get there." Ultimately, the very sad thing is that if this issue were being decided by secret ballot, we'd have a 50-vote victory, at least.

Q. What does that show? What does that indicate?

The President. It doesn't show a lack of courage. I don't want to say that; I don't think that's fair. It shows the extent to which the organized efforts and the crying anxieties of people are combining to pull Congressmen back. I just hope that we can overcome it by Wednesday. I think we can.

Q. Mr. President, in Florida, Mickey Kantor seems to have delivered an agreement on citrus, sugar, and winter vegetables. There are two concerns still out there, it seems. And one I know that Bob Graham has discussed with you personally; that's parity for the Caribbean Basin countries. The other one might be part of what's got Torricelli hanging out there yet, concern among Cuban-Americans that Mexico still has pretty good relationships with Cuba and is supporting Castro. Can you address those?

The President. First, I think Congressman Johnston came out for it, for NAFTA yesterday. And I hope we'll get a lot of the other Florida Democrats and the Republicans. They could turn the tide, actually. Florida is one of the keys in what happens to NAFTA. They have a huge number of votes that are not firmly declared.

Now, on the two issues you raised, I have talked to Senator Graham twice at great length about the Caribbean Basin Initiative issue, and I think he has some legitimate concerns which I want to work with him on. But here is the problem: I think that their concerns—I think we can solve this. That is, what the Members of the Florida delegation who have real concerns about these Caribbean countries and want them to do well and not be hurt, that is, they don't want production shifted from Caribbean nations to Mexico, I think we can work that out. And I think we can work that out with the support of the Mexicans. But that is a matter that it requires a greater attention to detail, in effect creating a new set of understandings, than solving the citrus problem or the sugar problem or the winter vegetable problem. So that if we were to just up and say, well, this is something we've fixed or agreed to now or the Mexicans were to agree to, we'd be asking them to do something now that they wouldn't be able to fully assess the implications of. And I think there is every indication that we could lose as many votes as we could gain from doing that. That's the real problem there.

I think we can work this out. But if I promise parity with all the implications that could make now, there's a chance that we could lose as many or more votes as we could gain because we simply don't have time to sit down and work out the level of detail on the Caribbean Basin Initiative that I want. I think that the principle is sound; I think that the objective is sound; I think we can get there. But if the vote hinges on that, I just don't think we can do it.

And I feel the same way on the Cuban issue. Colombia—take another example—Colombia has increased their purchases of American products 69 and 64 percent in the last 2 years. It has also had some greater contact with the Castro regime. Should we tell them we don't want them to buy our products anymore?

The French—every time I see President Mitterrand, he tells me how wrong I am about Cuba. I think we're right about Cuba and they're wrong. But I think that we have to recognize that our embargo has been quite successful, that we have hurt the economy significantly, that it is contributing to, it is hastening the day when the outdated Communist system will collapse and Cuba will have to open. I don't think there's any question that these gestures of openness that have come out of the Castro regime in the last several months have been the direct result of our policy of pressure and firmness.

So I believe in our policy. But I don't think that we can rationally expect that we can leverage anybody right now to go along with it who doesn't agree with it. I mean, Mexico does have a history of dealing with Cuba. There's nothing I can do about it. I very much regret, after all the support that I have given to the Cuban Democracy Act, to Radio and TV Marti—no Democrat in my lifetime, in the White House at least, has come close to taking the strong position I have on this, agreeing with the Cuban

American community. And I'm sorry that Congressman Menendez in New Jersey and Congresswoman Ros-Lehtinen, Congressman Diaz-Balart feel the way they do. But there's nothing I can do about it. I think the interest of the United States in dealing with Mexico, the border they share with us, the 90 million people they have, getting cooperation on immigration and drug issues, and—[*inaudible*]—jobs and growth outweigh the others. And I have to pursue the agreement.

Haiti

Q. Following up on a regional question, are you at all concerned about these reports coming out of Haiti that the embargo is causing the deaths of children? Has that raised any question in your mind about the policy?

The President. Well, yes. If you read the whole report, it's very interesting what it says. It says that the accumulation of the policies and the politics of the country are increasing the death rate of children every month. And I am very concerned about it. We feed over 650,000 people a week in Haiti. When I read the story, the thing that I was really concerned about—we could increase that if we need to. That is, if malnutrition is a problem, we can increase the delivery and the distribution of food.

I was particularly concerned when I saw the story—and we had a meeting on it, the national security people, the next morning—about the people saying that they were supposed to get medicine and they couldn't, because we thought when we did the embargo that we had taken care of that. So I asked our people to go back immediately and see what we could do to improve the delivery to the country and the distribution of medical supplies and medical care. And I would like to be given at least a while to try to see if we can't deal with that issue. I was very concerned about the report.

On the other hand, the people of Haiti need to know that the reason this embargo occurred is because of the police chief, Mr. François, and because of General Cédras and because they welshed on the Governors Island Agreement. The United States was willing to insist on full compliance of the Governors Island Agreement, including the amnesty provisions from President Aristide and from the Malval government, and they were willing to go along with it.

Has everybody asked a question?

NAFTA

Q. In a couple of years from now, what if, despite their protestations to the contrary, you find that a Procter and Gamble-type corporation or a Ford Motor Company or the Cincinnati—[*inaudible*]—companies like that, what if you find that they are indeed moving plants to Mexico, moving manufacturing operations to Mexico, which they said they wouldn't do? What would you tell the chief executives of those corporations?

The President. First of all, if they continue to move high-wage—those good plants to Mexico for the purpose—in other words—there's a difference. I want to make a clear distinction here, because I don't want to mislead anybody. If an American corporation wants to invest in Mexico City, to hire Mexicans to produce for the Mexican market, I don't think we should be against that. I think we should support that because that would create more middle-class Mexicans that will buy more American products. That's what the Mexicans get out of this deal. A lot of Americans say to me all the time, they say, "Mr. President, if this is such a hot deal for us, why do the Mexicans want it? What do they get out of it?" Of course, the whole idea of trade is that both sides win, that there are win-win agreements in this world. What they get out of it is investment in their country to develop their country to produce products and services for their people. Now, they will, in turn, buy more of our services.

To go back to your point, if I ever become convinced this is a bad deal for America, I'll just give notice and leave, if it's a bad deal for America. If certain companies are clearly abusing this agreement—well, let me back up and say there is no possibility they could do that. Let me tell you why. Put yourself in their position. This agreement does not prohibit what has been not only permitted but encouraged for years by our Government, which is setting up plants along the Mexican border with the United States to sell back into America. Now, if that continues unabated in a way that's bad for America, I think we ought to take note who's doing it, try to jawbone them out of it, and ask also if there's something we can do to help keep these companies operating in America, just the way I did when I was the Governor in my State. I think we'll be able to keep more

jobs here if this passes than if it doesn't.

On the other hand, let me pitch it to you another way: If NAFTA doesn't pass, what possible leverage do I have over these folks? I lose a lot of leverage. Now, again, I'm not saying nobody will ever do this, but the point that we have to drive home to the American people is that the present system makes it relatively more attractive to do this than Mexico after NAFTA will.

There was a man here last week from a fifth-generation Philadelphia, Pennsylvania-based furniture manufacturer, who talked about how he said, "They tried to get me to move to the South for years. Then the people tried to get me to move to Mexico. I wouldn't move anywhere; I'm staying in Pennsylvania. But I am going to sell more products and hire more people if you pass this deal." I think there will be more examples of that than there will be people who shut down and move. I think the President, however, should discourage and jawbone people from doing it, regardless.

Q. Thank you very much. Thank you, sir.

Q. Would you lose any leverage domestically if this thing goes down?

The President. Well, perhaps for a time. There's always a drag in politics. I don't think that would be permanent. I'm far more concerned—the effect on me is irrelevant. It's impossible to calculate what the twists and turns in the next 6 months or 2 years or 3 years will be. That doesn't matter. What matters is this is good for the American people, so it will be bad for them if it goes down. And it would clearly be bad for the United States in terms of our leadership to promote more growth, more economic partnerships, in terms of our leverage to get those Asian markets open.

Keep in mind, if we get a new GATT agreement, we'll get more access to the Asian markets. Our trade problem is not with Mexico. Here's a country that's with a much lower income than we have, spending 70 percent of all their money on foreign purchases, on American products, buying stuff hand over fist. Our trade problem is not with them. Our trade problem is $49 billion with Japan, $19 billion with China, $9 billion with Taiwan, because those countries are growing very fast with their high savings, low cost, heavy export, minimum import strategy. We need that.

Our other big trade problem is a stagnant Europe. In other words, Europe is pretty open to our stuff, except for agriculture. They've been pretty open toward us. But when there's no growth, they have no money to buy anything new. So the thing that I'm most worried about is that it will put America on the wrong side of history and it will take us in a direction that

is just where we don't want to go as we move toward the 21st century. That overwhelms every other concern.

NOTE: The President spoke at 2:30 p.m. in the Roosevelt Room at the White House.

Statement on the Massachusetts Building Trades Council Endorsement of NAFTA
November 12, 1993

Today, we saw a profile in courage. Leo Purcell, president of the Massachusetts Building Trades Council, endorsed NAFTA in a letter to fellow union workers.

In addition to saying, as I have, that this is a choice between change and status quo, Purcell wrote, "No longer can nations afford to build

invisible walls at their borders because there are no longer national borders to free trade."

I applaud Mr. Purcell for his leadership, courage, and vision and for his strong confidence in the American worker.

NOTE: A copy of Mr. Purcell's letter was made available by the Office of the Press Secretary.

Letter to Congressional Leaders Transmitting the Notice on Continuation of Emergency Regarding Chemical and Biological Weapons Proliferation
November 12, 1993

Dear Mr. Speaker: (Dear Mr. President:)

On November 16, 1990, in light of the dangers of the proliferation of chemical and biological weapons, President Bush issued Executive Order No. 12735 and declared a national emergency under the International Emergency Economic Powers Act (50 U.S.C. 1701 *et seq.*). Under section 202(d) of the National Emergencies Act (50 U.S.C. 1622(d)), the national emergency terminates on the anniversary date of its declaration unless the President publishes in the *Federal Register* and transmits to the Congress a notice of its continuation.

The proliferation of chemical and biological weapons continues to pose an unusual and extraordinary threat to the national security and foreign policy of the United States. Therefore, I am hereby advising the Congress that the national emergency declared on November 16, 1990, must continue in effect beyond November 16, 1993. Accordingly, I have extended the national emergency declared in Executive Order

No. 12735 and have sent a notice of extension to the *Federal Register* for publication.

Section 204 of the International Emergency Economic Powers Act and section 401(c) of the National Emergencies Act contain periodic reporting requirements regarding activities taken and money spent pursuant to an emergency declaration. The following report is made pursuant to these provisions. Additional information on chemical and biological weapons proliferation is contained in the report to the Congress provided pursuant to the Chemical and Biological Weapons Control and Warfare Elimination Act of 1991.

The three export control regulations issued under the Enhanced Proliferation Control Initiative are fully in force and have been used to control the export of items with potential use in chemical or biological weapons or unmanned delivery systems for weapons of mass destruction.

During the last 6 months, the United States

has continued to address actively in its international diplomatic efforts the problem of the proliferation and use of chemical and biological weapons.

More than 150 nations have signed the Chemical Weapons Convention (CWC) and a number already have ratified it. In my speech to the United Nations General Assembly on September 27, I called upon all countries, including my own, to ratify the Convention quickly so that it may enter into force on January 13, 1995. The United States is also playing a leading role in the work of the CWC Preparatory Commission, which is meeting in The Hague to work out the procedural and administrative details for implementing the Convention.

The United States participated in the Ad Hoc Group of Government Experts convened by the Third Biological Weapons Convention (BWC) Review Conference to identify and examine potential verification measures. The consensus final report of the Group is expected to provide the basis for further consideration of this issue at a special conference of BWC states parties. As part of my new nonproliferation policy, I have decided that the United States will promote new measures that provide increased transparency of activities that could have biological weapons applications to help deter violations of the Convention.

The membership of the Australia Group (AG)

of countries cooperating against chemical and biological weapons (CBW) proliferation stands at 25. At the June 1993 meeting, members agreed to honor each other's export license denials for AG-proscribed items (the "no-undercut" policy), thus enhancing the effectiveness of the Group's common export controls. At the same meeting, the AG finalized its package of comprehensive export controls on biological agents and related production equipment and agreed to promote broad contacts with nonmembers following all future Australia Group meetings. Members also resolved to expand their dialogue about CBW issues with non-member countries with a view to encouraging the introduction and implementation of effective CBW nonproliferation measures worldwide.

Pursuant to section 401(c) of the National Emergencies Act, there were no additional expenses directly attributable to the exercise of authorities conferred by the declaration of the national emergency.

Sincerely,

WILLIAM J. CLINTON

NOTE: Identical letters were sent to Thomas S. Foley, Speaker of the House of Representatives, and Albert Gore, Jr., President of the Senate. The notice is listed in Appendix D at the end of this volume.

Appointment of Regional Representatives for the Department of Education
November 12, 1993

The President appointed five regional representatives for the Department of Education today. The five will serve as liaisons to State, local, and private education organizations and as advocates for the administration's education policies. They are:

Brenda Dann-Messier, Region I, Boston (serves Connecticut, Maine, Massachusetts, New Hampshire, Rhode Island, and Vermont)

W. Wilson Goode, Region III, Philadelphia (serves Delaware, District of Columbia, Maryland, Pennsylvania, Virginia, and West Virginia)

Sally H. Cain, Region VI, Dallas (serves Arkansas, Louisiana, New Mexico, Oklahoma, and Texas)

Lynn Osborn Simons, Region VIII, Denver (serves Colorado, Montana, North Dakota, South Dakota, Utah, and Wyoming)

Carla Nuxoll, Region X, Seattle (serves Alaska, Idaho, Oregon, and Washington)

"As former Governors who spent years trying to improve our States' education systems, Secretary Riley and I are committed to an Education Department that is responsive to the needs of States and communities," the President said in making the announcement. "The people who will serve as the Department's regional representatives share that commitment and will work hard to fulfill it. I am very proud of these choices."

NOTE: Biographies of the appointees were made available by the Office of the Press Secretary.

Appointment for the J. William Fulbright Foreign Scholarship Board
November 12, 1993

The President appointed four members today to the J. William Fulbright Foreign Scholarship Board, which selects students, scholars, teachers, and trainees to participate in educational exchanges as Fulbright scholars. It also finances educational activities for Americans abroad and for foreign citizens in the United States and promotes American studies in foreign countries and foreign language training and area training in the United States. The Board is comprised of 12 members, appointed by the President. The new members appointed today are Victoria Murphy of Maine, Hoyt Purvis of Arkansas, Robert Rose of Connecticut, and Lee Williams of Arkansas.

"Like many Arkansans, I have long regarded Senator William Fulbright as both a role model and a mentor," said the President. "The Fulbright scholarships are his most lasting achievement. I trust that these four Board members, two of whom served on his staff, will work to preserve his legacy."

NOTE: Biographies of the appointees were made available by the Office of the Press Secretary. The Office of the Press Secretary also issued a clarification which stated that the appointment of Hoyt Purvis would take effect on January 1, 1994, while the other appointments were effective immediately.

Exchange With Reporters Prior to Departure for Memphis, Tennessee
November 13, 1993

Middle East Peace Process

Q. Mr. President, PLO Chairman Arafat seems to have condemned the murder of an Israeli at the end of October. Do you think this is in response to your request and Mr. Rabin's request?

The President. Well, perhaps, but regardless I think it's a very positive sign. I've only received limited reports this morning, but from what I've heard it's a very positive sign. It's the sort of thing that will enable them to work together and to implement the accord.

Q. Were there any direct contacts between you and Arafat in order to get him to condemn the murder?

The President. We had no direct contacts, the White House did not, but we made it very clear what our position was, and I think that the Israelis—they have direct contact of course with the PLO now because of the implementation of the accord. And I think perhaps again I would say we maybe ought to give most of the credit to that. I hope the meeting yesterday highlighted it and our position is clear. But they need to keep their word to each other, that's the most important thing.

NAFTA

Q. What about NAFTA, how do you feel about NAFTA today?

The President. Feel a little better. We had a good day yesterday; you know we've had three big days. I think we've had 27 people come out, and I think we're going to have another good day today. We'll have several of those who are declared down in Memphis with us, and we're making some pretty good inroads now in places where I didn't know we could get some votes. So it's going to be a hard weekend, but I think we'll make it.

Q. [Inaudible]

The President. What I have always said is if they're opposed on the grounds of NAFTA next year, I'd be happy to say in any district in America or to any district in America that I think NAFTA is in the public interest, it's in the national interest, and it should not be the basis on which any Member of Congress, without regard to party, is voted out. Thanks.

NOTE: The exchange began at approximately 8:25 a.m. on the South Lawn at the White House. A tape was not available for verification of the content of this exchange.

The President's Radio Address
November 13, 1993

Good morning. This week, Americans celebrated Veterans Day, the day we set aside to thank those who served, kept us secure, and helped preserve the freedoms each of us cherish.

On Thursday, after paying my respects to the veterans at Arlington Cemetery, I met with two groups of patriots who span the generations: some of the remaining veterans of World War I and active duty personnel who served with such distinction in Somalia. These brave Americans are linked across the years to each other and to history by the valor with which they served our Nation. None of them shrunk from danger or challenge. In troubled times, they reached beyond our borders to protect our interests.

And as the world undergoes the most profound changes in the last 50 years, today we can draw a very powerful lesson from their courage and their vision. Just as we never protected our country by shrinking from a military threat, we cannot protect our prosperity by shrinking from our economic challenges.

Since I became President, our administration has been dedicated to restoring the American economy, to making work pay for all Americans again, to creating the conditions that will allow our private sector to create more jobs and higher incomes and more opportunity for everyone.

This economic program is beginning to work. We've lowered the deficit, kept inflation down, pushed interest rates down to record lows. Millions of Americans have refinanced their homes and businesses. And even though we still don't have as many jobs as we'd like, the private sector has produced more jobs in the last 10 months than in the previous 4 years.

Ultimately, however, the only way a wealthy nation can grow and create jobs and lift incomes is to lower trade barriers and expand trade in a growing global economy. There simply is no other way that any rich country in the world can create jobs and raise incomes than to find other customers for their goods and services. America is no exception. We have a chance to do this in a few days when Congress considers the trade agreement called NAFTA.

The North American Free Trade Agreement will lower Mexico's barriers to American exports. When these barriers come down, we'll sell another 55,000 more American-made cars in Mexico next year alone. We'll sell hundreds of thousands more computers and create 200,000 new high-paying jobs in the next 2 years. NAFTA is a real good deal for America. And if we don't open up Mexico for our products, you can be sure that the Europeans and the Japanese will open up Mexico for theirs.

You see, if NAFTA passes, we'll have a competitive advantage over the Japanese and the Europeans in the Mexican market. If it fails, and Japan or Europe takes up the challenge that we walked away from, then they'll have an advantage over us.

Why then do some of our fellow citizens fear NAFTA so much? Because in the last 20 years their world has changed a lot and often not for the better. Technology can now go anywhere in the world. Money and information travel the globe in a millisecond. Skills we once had alone, others now share.

This new global economy has created an awful lot of opportunity, but it's also created a lot of hardship. We have to do many things to adjust. We're working now to devise a completely new system to replace our outdated unemployment system called reemployment. So that anyone who loses a job, for whatever reason, will immediately receive the education and training and job placement help they need. We passed the family leave law so that you can't lose your job when you take some time off for a newborn baby or a sick parent; so that people can be good workers and good family members at the same time. We've got to have health care reform, and we've presented a plan that will provide, for the first time in our history, health care security to all Americans, even if they lose their jobs. And we're determined to fight crime with more police on the beat, more boot camps for youthful offenders, more jail cells for people who need that, too. That's what the crime bill, now moving through the Congress, will do.

So in education, in health care, in family leave, in crime, we're working hard to give the American people the security all of us need to face the changes we confront. But we cannot make the world the way it was. We simply cannot protect our workers, their jobs, and their incomes from the winds of global competition by trying to build walls. The only way to provide economic security and expanded opportunity for the middle class in this country is to take this new world head on, to compete and to win. And we can win. The American worker is now the most productive worker in the world again. We can out-compete and out-perform anyone anywhere. We will be number one again for a long time if we reach out to the world to compete. That's why American workers have nothing to fear from NAFTA and why American workers should be very concerned if we vote NAFTA down, walk away from Mexico and the rest of Latin America and the opportunities they present.

The day after Congress votes on NAFTA, I'm going to Seattle to meet with the leaders from Asian countries, including China and Japan, to ask them to open up their markets to our products, too. By the end of this year I'm going to try very hard to conclude an even bigger worldwide trade agreement that will bring down trade barriers to our products in Europe and the world over. Together with other nations, we can literally reignite growth in the world's economy and create millions of new jobs and export opportunities for all Americans. But we must begin this week by passing NAFTA. NAFTA is not only a trade agreement with Mexico, it has become a symbol of our commitment to growth and to trade throughout the world. And believe me, whichever way the Congress votes, it will send a signal to every nation in the world about our intentions. Are we going to maintain our lead in the global economy and push others to open their markets to our products and services and to everyone else's, or are we going to retreat into a shell of protectionism?

If we pass NAFTA, it can put us at the center of the largest trading bloc in the world with Canada and Mexico, one that will quickly grow larger as we bring in the rest of Latin America. If we don't, we'll be stuck while someone else takes advantage of the opportunity. You know, this vote will tell us a lot about who we are as Americans in 1993. Great nations are defined not by how they act when the rules are clear and the future is set and the times are easy but by the choices they make during periods of great change when the future is not clear, the times are tough, and people have to forge their own future.

This is a defining moment for America. Will we seize the moment? Will we vote for hope over fear? The history of America's greatness says we will, for we've always triumphed when our Nation has engaged the world and great challenges it offers. By passing NAFTA, Congress can demonstrate that we intend to compete and win in a thriving global economy. We took the lead in creating it, now we have to make it again for the 21st century. We can build a future we'll be proud to leave our children, and the future begins on Wednesday with a positive vote for the North American Free Trade Agreement.

Thanks for listening.

NOTE: The address was recorded at approximately 3:40 p.m. on November 12 in the Oval Office at the White House for broadcast at 10:06 a.m. on November 13.

Remarks on Arrival in Memphis
November 13, 1993

Thank you very much for coming out here in the wind and rain and braving the elements. It's kind of like what we have to do to get things done in Washington. I'm glad to see you here.

I want to thank my good friend Governor McWherter, Mayor Morris, Mayor Herenton. Thank you all for being here today. I want to thank these fine Members of Congress who are here. Harold Ford made a great statement in support of the North American Free Trade Agreement. I'm very grateful to him and to Bob Clement and to Jim Cooper for their support. I also want to introduce some other Members of Congress who are here: first of all, from our neighboring State of Louisiana, two Members who have expressed their support today, Representative Bill Jefferson and Representative Jimmy Hayes. I want to thank your Congresswoman Marilyn Lloyd for her support for NAFTA. And I want to introduce two Members of my congressional delegation from Arkansas, Blanche Lambert and Ray Thornton, and thank them for their support.

Let me ask you something. Were you proud of Al Gore the other night in his debate? I mean, was he great or what? I want to tell you something, folks. This vote over the North American Free Trade Agreement has brought out a lot of feelings and emotions in this country that I think probably need to be brought out. We've seen in the opposition to NAFTA a lot of the legitimate fears that the American people have developed because so many hard-working Americans have worked and worked and worked, and they've still lost their jobs. Or they worked harder year-in and year-out, and they never got a pay raise. And the global economy has been pretty tough on a lot of people in the States represented here today, on people in Tennessee and Louisiana and Arkansas, and all of us know that.

Let me tell you, when I was Governor of my State, I saw plants shut down and move to Mexico or just disappear altogether or move production all the way to Asia. I understand that very well. I want you to know that there's not a person on this platform today, including the President, who would be supporting this agreement if we weren't convinced that it will bring more jobs to Tennessee and Louisiana and Arkansas. That's why we're for it.

I came here today to make a point. I'm wearing a tie that was made in Little Rock, Arkansas, and shoes that were made in Nashville, Tennessee. I believe we can compete and win in the global economy. You heard the Governor say that since 1987, exports to Mexico from Tennessee have increased by 300 percent. That's 10,000 jobs due to exports for Mexico. In our State, exports have also tripled in the same time period. We have 5,000 jobs now based on exports to Mexico. In Louisiana, exports have doubled since 1987. Louisiana will be a big winner if all those trade barriers come down because of the increased activity around the Port of New Orleans. We know that this will mean more jobs for this country. Why? Because when the trade barriers come down—their trade barriers are 2½ times as high as ours—as they earn more money and make more money, they'll spend more money on American products. Seventy cents of every dollar Mexico spends on foreign products is spent on American products.

Why will it also make a difference? Because if we make this agreement with Mexico, we'll be able to use it as a basis for similar agreements with all the other Latin American countries. Someday we'll have a trade bloc going from Canada to the United States to Mexico to the rest of Latin America, over 700 million people buying from each other, selling to each other, helping each other to grow.

My fellow Americans, I worked my heart out in this country right here for the last 12 years to bring more jobs to the people of my State. And one thing I know: You cannot put more people to work at a time when productivity is increasing—which means that fewer people can produce more things—you can't put more people to work unless you've got more people who will buy your products and services. Without expanding your customer base, there is no way to create more jobs. It cannot be done. And we have got to learn that in America. We cannot let other people outtrade us. We can outwork anybody in the world. We still have the most productive workers in the world. We've learned a lot of hard lessons in the last 12 years, but we've got to have more customers. And that's what this is about.

So I ask all of you, all of you, to support the members of the Tennessee congressional delegation that have come out for NAFTA, to support the members of the delegations from Arkansas and Louisiana and from the other States that are supporting this, to give our country a chance to compete and win.

On the day after Congress votes on this agreement, I have to fly out to Washington State to meet with the President of China, the world's largest country; with the Prime Minister of Japan, the country that had the largest growth rate in the 1980's; with 13 other leaders of Asian nations. That's the fastest growing part of the world. I'm going to say to them, "We want to be your partner. We will buy your products, but we'd like for you to buy ours." If we adopt NAFTA, it will be a lot easier for me to make that case.

I want the American people to be confident about the future. I want them to believe we can do better. In the last 10 months we've seen interest rates come down, inflation down, the deficit's come down. Millions and millions of Americans have refinanced their homes and their businesses, and this economy has produced more jobs in the last 10 months than in the previous 4 years. But I'm telling you, you and I know there are not near enough jobs, and incomes are not going up near enough. And the reason is we don't yet have enough people who will buy our products and services.

We need more growth in the world economy, and we need more customers. And Wednesday we're going to take a big first step with NAFTA, thanks to the people of Tennessee, your Vice President, your congressional delegation, and the other Members who are here.

Thank you very much.

NOTE: The President spoke at 10 a.m. at the Air National Guard Ramp, Memphis International Airport. In his remarks, the President referred to Mayor William N. Morris, Jr., of Shelby County and Mayor W.W. Herenton of Memphis.

Remarks to the Convocation of the Church of God in Christ in Memphis
November 13, 1993

Thank you. Please sit down. Bishop Ford, Mrs. Mason, Bishop Owens, and Bishop Anderson; my bishops, Bishop Walker and Bishop Lindsey. Now, if you haven't had Bishop Lindsey's barbecue, you haven't had barbecue. And if you haven't heard Bishop Walker attack one of my opponents, you have never heard a political speech. [*Laughter*]

I am glad to be here. You have touched my heart. You've brought tears to my eyes and joy to my spirit. Last year I was with you over at the convention center. Two years ago your bishops came to Arkansas, and we laid a plaque at the point in Little Rock, Arkansas, at 8th and Gaines, where Bishop Mason received the inspiration for the name of this great church. Bishop Brooks said from his pulpit that I would be elected President when most people thought I wouldn't survive. I thank him, and I thank your faith, and I thank your works, for without you I would not be here today as your President.

Many have spoken eloquently and well, and many have been introduced. I want to thank my good friend Governor McWherter and my friend Mayor Herenton for being with me today; my friend Congressman Harold Ford, we are glad to be in his congressional district. I would like to, if I might, introduce just three other people who are Members of the Congress. They have come here with me, and without them it's hard for me to do much for you. The President proposes and the Congress disposes. Sometimes they dispose of what I propose, but I'm happy to say that according to a recent report in Washington, notwithstanding what you may have heard, this Congress has given me a higher percentage of my proposals than any first-year President since President Eisenhower. And I thank them for that. Let me introduce my good friend, a visitor to Tennessee, Congressman Bill Jefferson from New Orleans, Louisiana—please stand up; and an early supporter of my campaign, Congressman Bob Clement from Tennessee, known to many of you; and a young man who's going to be coming back to the people of Tennessee and asking them to give him a promotion next year, Congressman Jim Cooper from Tennessee, and a good friend. Please welcome him.

You know, in the last 10 months, I've been called a lot of things, but nobody's called me a bishop yet. [*Laughter*] When I was about 9 years old, my beloved and now departed grandmother, who was a very wise woman, looked at me and she said, "You know, I believe you could be a preacher if you were just a little better boy." [*Laughter*]

Proverbs says, "A happy heart doeth good like medicine, but a broken spirit dryeth the bone." This is a happy place, and I'm happy to be here. I thank you for your spirit.

By the grace of God and your help, last year I was elected President of this great country. I never dreamed that I would ever have a chance to come to this hallowed place where Martin Luther King gave his last sermon. I ask you to think today about the purpose for which I ran and the purpose for which so many of you worked to put me in this great office. I have worked hard to keep faith with our common efforts: to restore the economy, to reverse the politics of helping only those at the top of our totem pole and not the hard-working middle class or the poor; to bring our people together across racial and regional and political lines, to make a strength out of our diversity instead of letting it tear us apart; to reward work and family and community and try to move us forward into the 21st century. I have tried to keep faith.

Thirteen percent of all my Presidential appointments are African-Americans, and there are five African-Americans in the Cabinet of the United States, 2½ times as many as have ever served in the history of this great land. I have sought to advance the right to vote with the motor voter bill, supported so strongly by all the churches in our country. And next week it will be my great honor to sign the restoration of religious freedoms act, a bill supported widely by people across all religions and political philosophies to put back the real meaning of the Constitution, to give you and every other American the freedom to do what is most important in your life, to worship God as your spirit leads you.

I say to you, my fellow Americans, we have made a good beginning. Inflation is down. Interest rates are down. The deficit is down. Investment is up. Millions of Americans, including, I bet, some people in this room, have refinanced their homes or their business loans just in the last year. And in the last 10 months, this economy has produced more jobs in the private sector than in the previous 4 years.

We have passed a law called the family leave law, which says you can't be fired if you take a little time off when a baby is born or a parent is sick. We know that most Americans have to work, but you ought not to have to give up being a good parent just to take a job. If you can't succeed as a worker and a parent, this country can't make it.

We have radically reformed the college loan program, as I promised, to lower the cost of college loans and broaden the availability of it and make the repayment terms easier. And we have passed the national service law that will give in 3 years, 3 years from now, 100,000 young Americans the chance to serve their communities at home, to repair the frayed bonds of community, to build up the needs of people at the grassroots, and at the same time, earn some money to pay for a college education. It is a wonderful idea.

On April 15th when people pay their taxes, somewhere between 15 million and 18 million working families on modest incomes, families with children and incomes of under $23,000, will get a tax cut, not a tax increase, in the most important effort to ensure that we reward work and family in the last 20 years. Fifty million American parents and their children will be advantaged by putting the Tax Code back on the side of working American parents for a change.

Under the leadership of the First Lady, we have produced a comprehensive plan to guarantee health care security to all Americans. How can we expect the American people to work and to live with all the changes in a global economy, where the average 18-year-old will change work seven times in a lifetime, unless we can simply say we have joined the ranks of all the other advanced countries in the world; you can have decent health care that's always there, that can never be taken away? It is time we did that, long past time. I ask you to help us achieve that.

But we have so much more to do. You and I know that most people are still working harder for the same or lower wages, that many people are afraid that their job will go away. We have to provide the education and training our people need, not just for our children but for our adults, too. If we cannot close this country up to the forces of change sweeping throughout the world, we have to at least guarantee people the security of being employable. They have to be able to get a new job if they're going to have to get a new job. We don't do that today, and we must, and we intend to proceed until that is done.

We have a guarantee that there will be some investment in those areas of our country, in the inner cities and in the destitute rural areas in the Mississippi Delta, of my home State and this State and Louisiana and Mississippi and other places like it throughout America. It's all very well to train people, but if they don't have a job, they can be trained for nothing. We must get investment into those places where the people are dying for work.

And finally, let me say, we must find people who will buy what we have to produce. We are the most productive people on Earth. That makes us proud. But what that means is that every year one person can produce more in the same amount of time. Now, if fewer and fewer people can produce more and more things, and yet you want to create more jobs and raise people's incomes, you have to have more customers for what it is you're making. And that is why I have worked so hard to sell more American products around the world; why I have asked that we be able to sell billions of dollars of computers we used not to sell to foreign countries and foreign interests, to put our people to work; why next week I am going all the way to Washington State to meet with the President of China and the Prime Minister of Japan and the heads of 13 other Asian countries, the fastest growing part of the world, to say, "We want to be your partners. We will buy your goods, but we want you to buy ours, too, if you please." That is why.

That is why I have worked so hard for this North American trade agreement that Congressman Ford endorsed today and Congressman Jefferson endorsed and Congressman Cooper and Congressman Clement, because we know that Americans can compete and win only if people will buy what it is we have to sell. There are 90 million people in Mexico. Seventy cents of every dollar they spend on foreign goods, they spend on American goods.

People worry fairly about people shutting down plants in America and going not just to Mexico but to any place where the labor is cheap. It has happened. What I want to say to you, my fellow Americans, is nothing in this agreement makes that more likely. That has happened already. It may happen again. What we need to do is keep the jobs here by finding customers there. That's what this agreement does. It gives us a chance to create opportunity for people. I have friends in this audience, people who are ministers from my State, fathers and sons, people—I've looked out all over this vast crowd and I see people I've known for years. They know I spent my whole life working to create jobs. I would never knowingly do anything that would take a job away from the American people. This agreement will make more jobs. Now, we can also leave it if it doesn't work in 6 months. But if we don't take it, we'll lose it forever. We need to take it, because we have to do better.

But I guess what I really want to say to you today, my fellow Americans, is that we can do all of this and still fail unless we meet the great crisis of the spirit that is gripping America today.

When I leave you, Congressman Ford and I are going to a Baptist church near here to a town meeting he's having on health care and violence. I tell you, unless we do something about crime and violence and drugs that is ravaging the community, we will not be able to repair this country.

If Martin Luther King, who said, "Like Moses, I am on the mountaintop, and I can see the promised land, but I'm not going to be able to get there with you, but we will get there"—if he were to reappear by my side today and give us a report card on the last 25 years, what would he say? You did a good job, he would say, voting and electing people who formerly were not electable because of the color of their skin. You have more political power, and that is good. You did a good job, he would say, letting people who have the ability to do so live wherever they want to live, go wherever they want to go in this great country. You did a good job, he would say, elevating people of color into the ranks of the United States Armed Forces to the very top or into the very top of our Government. You did a very good job, he would say. He would say, you did a good job creating a black middle class of people who really are doing well, and the middle class is growing more among African-Americans than among non-African-Americans. You did a good job; you did a good job in opening opportunity.

But he would say, I did not live and die to see the American family destroyed. I did not live and die to see 13-year-old boys get automatic weapons and gun down 9-year-olds just for the kick of it. I did not live and die to see young people destroy their own lives with drugs and then build fortunes destroying the lives of others. That is not what I came here to do. I fought for freedom, he would say, but not for the freedom of people to kill each other with reckless abandon, not for the freedom of children to have children and the fathers of the children walk away from them and abandon them as if they don't amount to anything. I fought for people to have the right to work but not to have whole communities and people abandoned. This is not what I lived and died for.

My fellow Americans, he would say, I fought to stop white people from being so filled with hate that they would wreak violence on black people. I did not fight for the right of black people to murder other black people with reckless abandon.

The other day the Mayor of Baltimore, a dear friend of mine, told me a story of visiting the family of a young man who had been killed—18 years old—on Halloween. He always went out with little bitty kids so they could trick-or-treat safely. And across the street from where they were walking on Halloween, a 14-year-old boy gave a 13-year-old boy a gun and dared him to shoot the 18-year-old boy, and he shot him dead. And the Mayor had to visit the family.

In Washington, DC, where I live, your Nation's Capital, the symbol of freedom throughout the world, look how that freedom is being exercised. The other night a man came along the street and grabbed a 1-year-old child and put the child in his car. The child may have been the child of the man. And two people were after him, and they chased him in the car, and they just kept shooting with reckless abandon, knowing that baby was in the car. And they shot the man dead, and a bullet went through his body into the baby's body, and blew the little bootie off the child's foot.

The other day on the front page of our paper, the Nation's Capital, are we talking about world peace or world conflict? No, big article on the front page of the Washington Post about an 11-year-old child planning her funeral: "These are the hymns I want sung. This is the dress I want to wear. I know I'm not going to live very long." That is not the freedom, the freedom to die before you're a teenager is not what Martin Luther King lived and died for.

More than 37,000 people die from gunshot wounds in this country every year. Gunfire is the leading cause of death in young men. And now that we've all gotten so cool that everybody can get a semiautomatic weapon, a person shot now is 3 times more likely to die than 15 years ago, because they're likely to have three bullets in them. A hundred and sixty thousand children stay home from school every day because they are scared they will be hurt in their schools.

The other day I was in California at a town meeting, and a handsome young man stood up and said, "Mr. President, my brother and I, we don't belong to gangs. We don't have guns. We don't do drugs. We want to go to school. We want to be professionals. We want to work hard. We want to do well. We want to have families. And we changed our school because the school we were in was so dangerous. So when we stowed up to the new school to register, my brother and I were standing in line and somebody ran into the school and started shooting a gun. My brother was shot down standing right in front of me at the safer school." The freedom to do that kind of thing is not what Martin Luther King lived and died for, not what people gathered in this hallowed church for the night before he was assassinated in April of 1968. If you had told anybody who was here in that church on that night that we would abuse our freedom in that way, they would have found it hard to believe. And I tell you, it is our moral duty to turn it around.

And now I think finally we have a chance. Finally, I think, we have a chance. We have a pastor here from New Haven, Connecticut. I was in his church with Reverend Jackson when I was running for President on a snowy day in Connecticut to mourn the death of children who had been killed in that city. And afterward we walked down the street for more than a mile in the snow. Then, the American people were not ready. People would say, "Oh, this is a terrible thing, but what can we do about it?"

Now when we read that foreign visitors come to our shores and are killed at random in our fine State of Florida, when we see our children planning their funerals, when the American people are finally coming to grips with the accumulated weight of crime and violence and the breakdown of family and community and the increase in drugs and the decrease in jobs, I think finally we may be ready to do something about it.

And there is something for each of us to do. There are changes we can make from the outside in; that's the job of the President and the Congress and the Governors and the mayors and the social service agencies. And then there's some changes we're going to have to make from the inside out, or the others won't matter. That's what that magnificent song was about, isn't it? Sometimes there are no answers from the outside in; sometimes all the answers have to come from the values and the stirrings and the voices that speak to us from within.

So we are beginning. We are trying to pass a bill to make our people safer, to put another 100,000 police officers on the street, to provide boot camps instead of prisons for young people who can still be rescued, to provide more safety in our schools, to restrict the availability of these awful assault weapons, to pass the Brady bill and at least require people to have their criminal background checked before they get a gun, and to say, if you're not old enough to vote and you're not old enough to go to war, you ought not to own a handgun, and you ought not to use one unless you're on a target range.

We want to pass a health care bill that will make drug treatment available for everyone. And we also have to do it, we have to have drug treatment and education available to everyone and especially those who are in prison who are coming out. We have a drug czar now in Lee Brown, who was the police chief of Atlanta, of Houston, of New York, who understands these things. And when the Congress comes back next year, we will be moving forward on that.

We need this crime bill now. We ought to give it to the American people for Christmas. And we need to move forward on all these other fronts. But I say to you, my fellow Americans, we need some other things as well. I do not believe we can repair the basic fabric of society until people who are willing to work have work. Work organizes life. It gives structure and discipline to life. It gives meaning and self-esteem to people who are parents. It gives a role model to children.

The famous African-American sociologist William Julius Wilson has written a stunning book called "The Truly Disadvantaged" in which he chronicles in breathtaking terms how the inner cities of our country have crumbled as work has disappeared. And we must find a way, through public and private sources, to enhance the attractiveness of the American people who live there to get investment there. We cannot, I submit to you, repair the American community and restore the American family until we provide the structure, the values, the discipline, and the reward that work gives.

I read a wonderful speech the other day given at Howard University in a lecture series funded by Bill and Camille Cosby, in which the speaker said, "I grew up in Anacostia years ago. Even then it was all black, and it was a very poor neighborhood. But you know, when I was a child in Anacostia, a 100 percent African-American neighborhood, a very poor neighborhood, we had a crime rate that was lower than the average of the crime rate of our city. Why? Because we had coherent families. We had coherent communities. The people who filled the church on Sunday lived in the same place they went to church. The guy that owned the drugstore lived down the street. The person that owned the grocery store lived in our community. We were whole." And I say to you, we have to make our people whole again.

This church has stood for that. Why do you think you have 5 million members in this country? Because people know you are filled with the spirit of God to do the right thing in this life by them. So I say to you, we have to make a partnership, all the Government agencies, all the business folks; but where there are no families, where there is no order, where there is no hope, where we are reducing the size of our armed services because we have won the cold war, who will be there to give structure, discipline, and love to these children? You must do that. And we must help you. Scripture says, you are the salt of the Earth and the light of the world, that if your light shines before men they will give glory to the Father in heaven. That is what we must do.

That is what we must do. How would we explain it to Martin Luther King if he showed up today and said, yes, we won the cold war. Yes, the biggest threat that all of us grew up under, communism and nuclear war, communism gone, nuclear war receding. Yes, we developed all these miraculous technologies. Yes, we all have got a VCR in our home; it's interesting. Yes, we get 50 channels on the cable. Yes, without regard to race, if you work hard and play by the rules, you can get into a service academy or a good college, you'll do just great. How would we explain to him all these kids getting killed and killing each other? How would we justify the things that we permit that no other country in the world would permit? How could we explain that we gave people the freedom to succeed, and we created conditions in which millions abuse that freedom to destroy the things that make life worth living and life itself? We cannot.

And so I say to you today, my fellow Americans, you gave me this job, and we're making progress on the things you hired me to do. But unless we deal with the ravages of crime and drugs and violence and unless we recognize that it's due to the breakdown of the family, the community, and the disappearance of jobs, and unless we say some of this cannot be done by Government, because we have to reach deep inside to the values, the spirit, the soul, and the truth of human nature, none of the other things we seek to do will ever take us where

we need to go.

So in this pulpit, on this day, let me ask all of you in your heart to say: We will honor the life and the work of Martin Luther King. We will honor the meaning of our church. We will, somehow, by God's grace, we will turn this around. We will give these children a future. We will take away their guns and give them books. We will take away their despair and give them hope. We will rebuild the families and the neighborhoods and the communities. We won't make all the work that has gone on here benefit just a few. We will do it together by the grace of God.

Thank you.

NOTE: The President spoke at 11:51 a.m. at the Mason Temple Church of God in Christ. In his remarks, he referred to Elsie Mason, widow of Charles Harrison Mason, founder, Church of God in Christ; denomination officers Louis Henry Ford, presiding bishop, Chandler David Owens, first assistant presiding bishop, Cleveland L. Anderson, second assistant presiding bishop, L.T. Walker and Donnie Lindsey, Arkansas jurisdictional bishops, and Philip A. Brooks, general board member, Detroit, MI; and Mayor Kurt Schmoke of Baltimore, MD.

Remarks to the Community in Memphis
November 13, 1993

Thank you for that wonderful welcome. Thank you for your sign about NAFTA. I didn't give it to her, I promise. [*Laughter*] Reverend Whalum, it's wonderful to be in your church, and I thank you for hosting this townhall meeting. Last year Reverend Whalum accepted my invitation to come to Arkansas to the Governor's mansion and to meet with me about a number of the problems you'll be discussing today. And it's good to see him again. He came to my house, and I'm in his house now.

I want to thank my good friend Harold Ford who started helping me in my quest to become President early and, long before that, worked with me to help reform the welfare laws to give people both the obligation to work and the opportunity to grow and thrive. And the two things go together, and I thank Harold Ford

for that. I'm glad to be here with Congressman Clement and with Congressman Jim Cooper. I'm glad to see them both up here talking. I was especially glad to see Jim talking because he's going to come back and ask you for a promotion next year, and he needed to get warmed up here, and I like that. I'm glad our good friend Congressman Jefferson came all the way from New Orleans to be with us today. That was good. Mayor Morris, it's good to see you. And I saw Mayor Herenton earlier today.

And I want to say a special word of thanks to my good friend Governor McWherter. I think he's one of the finest Governors in the country, and a person could never ask for a better friend. And I thank you. We were out in the wind at the airport announcing the support of several Members of Congress for the North American

Free Trade Agreement. And Congressman Jefferson from New Orleans, who didn't know Governor McWherter very well, looked at him and he said, "You were probably a better Governor than Bill Clinton, and you're certainly a better windbreaker than he was." [*Laughter*]

Let me say, too, you know, this town hall meeting was scheduled before I announced that I was coming here to speak to the annual convention of the Church of God in Christ. And Congressman Ford invited me to come by; I wanted to come. The leader of our office of drug policy and a member of my Cabinet, Lee Brown, is here, and he'll be speaking after I leave. I'm going to introduce him as I go. Lee was the police chief in Atlanta, in Houston, and in New York and really pioneered the development of community policing in our country and proved that if you not only had enough police officers but if you deployed them in the right way, you could actually prevent crime from occurring as well as catch criminals more quickly, and in preventing crime from occurring, you could build bridges in neighborhoods and put lives back together and put communities back together.

So I want to implore you not to turn this into just a speechmaking event. This is a discussion of crime and violence as a public health issue. It affects you and your lives and the lives of your children. So when I go, you stay. Will you do that? I want you to be a part of this. This is important.

I want you to know why this is such a big issue to me as an American, a husband, a father, as well as President. I got elected President on some very basic commitments. I said that I would try to get the economy going again. I said I would try to restore the middle class and give hope to the poor by rewarding work and supporting families. I said that I would try to bring the country together again, across the lines of region and income and race, so that we could work together to ensure a better future for everyone.

Now, in the last 10 months we've worked hard largely on the economy, to get the deficit down, to keep inflation down, to get interest rates down. That means investment's up. I don't know, but I bet there are a lot of people in this room even who were able to refinance a home in the last year. Millions of Americans have done that and lowered their monthly payments. In the last 10 months the economy has

produced more jobs in the private sector than in the previous 4 years.

But we all know that's not enough, we have to do more. I came here to support the North American Free Trade Agreement today for a simple reason, and that is that our workers are becoming more productive and more competitive; they have to to survive in the world. But productivity means that the same person can produce more in the same or less time, right? So if fewer people are producing more stuff, the only way you can create more jobs and higher incomes is if you have more customers for the things you're producing.

So that's very important; this trade agreement's important to me. But when you get through all of that, you have to come back to the fact that this country is going to have a very hard time making it unless we do something about this wave of crime and violence that's tearing the heart out of America. And it affects everybody who thinks they're not affected by it. It affects you in many ways by forcing you as taxpayers to pay a lot more money to put people in the penitentiary than you otherwise would. You know, this country now has a higher percentage of people in prison than any other country in the world. Do you know that? That's something we're number one in. And we know in spite of that, a lot of people get out before they should.

It means that you pay more in health care. Why? Because this really is a public health problem. I have spent years studying the American health care system and trying to figure out why we spend 40 or 50 percent more than anybody else on health care and we still can't figure out how to give health care to everybody. And I'll tell you one reason. One reason is that on any given night, our emergency rooms are filled with people who are cut up and shot, who don't have any health insurance, and the rest of us pay for it.

Now, that's not the number one—we ought to be concerned about them and others; I don't mean that on a human level. But you just need to know that if you say to me 4 years from now, "Mr. President, why haven't you brought our health care costs more in line with everybody else's and given health care to everybody?"—if you want the costs brought into line, we're going to have to stop shooting and cutting each other up so much. It's a big health care issue. You can't blame the doctors, and you can't blame the hospitals, and you can't blame—even though I get crossways with them from time to time, this is not the insurance companies' fault. This is society. When people show up bleeding and shot, there they are. Right? So this is a huge public health problem.

But more importantly, it's doing something just awful to our country. The other day I met with my good friend the Mayor of Baltimore, when I was up at Johns Hopkins Medical Center talking to them about our health care plan. And he told me that the night before he had had to visit a home of an 18-year-old boy who was a fine young man who went out every Halloween for years with real young kids so they could go trick-or-treating safely in the neighborhood. And they were walking down the street and crossed the street. There was a 14-year-old boy with a gun and a 13-year-old boy without one. And the 14-year-old handed the 13-year-old the gun and dared him to shoot across the street at the 18-year-old. And he did, and he killed him.

That kind of stuff happens all the time. In our Nation's Capital the other day a man came along the street and grabbed up a little 1-year-old girl, put her in a seat beside him, and sped off in a car. And some people who were after him ran after him, started shooting. They shot him dead. The bullet went through his body and hit the little girl, went down through her foot, and blew her little bootie off. A 1-year-old child.

In the Washington Post in our Nation's Capital the other day there was an article about children so convinced they would never grow up that at the age of 11, they were planning their funerals. Little girl saying, "Well, now, if I have a funeral, play these hymns at the church," and another one saying, "If I have a funeral, put me in this dress."

Now, it's going to be hard for me or any other President or any Member of Congress to organize this country with the private sector to compete and win in the global economy if we have the kind of public pathology we have today, where children are shooting children with weapons more advanced than the police have.

I come from across the river in Arkansas where we're about to start or maybe they have already started deer season. And some towns, we shut the schools and the factories down at the opening of deer season because nobody shows up anyway. [*Laughter*] I understand all

about the right to keep and bear arms, and I was in the woods when I was barely old enough to walk. But I'm telling you, no sane society would allow teenagers to have semiautomatic weapons and go on the streets and be better armed than the police officers. It is crazy. And nobody else does. Only we do. We have to ask ourselves, what are we going to do about this? How did this happen? And I think, frankly, if we're going to find the answers, we're going to have to all check a lot of our baggage at the door. We've got to check our partisan political baggage; we've got to check our racial identities; we've got to check everything at the door. We've just got to be honest children of God and honest Americans and try to analyze how did we get in the fix we're in in this country and what are we going to do about it.

And I have to tell you, I've spent time, I've talked to a lot of young people who were and some who are in gangs. I once had someone go down to the penitentiary and interview every teenager who was there doing a life sentence for murder. Long before I ever thought of running for President I went to south central Los Angeles—which later became famous when it burned down—a couple of years before I ever thought of even getting in this race, just sat in church basements and places like that and talked to people about what was going on. And as nearly as I can determine, what has happened is a combination of the following: Number one, too many of these kids are growing up without family supports, without the structure and value and support they need.

Number two, too many of those kids also have no substitute for the family that's positive. The word "gang" has a bad connotation now. The truth is we all want to be in gangs, if a gang is a group of people that think like you do and do like you do. I mean, what's the difference in the Baptist Church and the Church of God in Christ? They're two different gangs who still want to get to heaven when they die. Right? I mean, really, you think about that. What's the difference in the Democrats and the Republicans? They're two different gangs, and they obey the law, and they vote on election day, and they've got different ideas about how to solve problems. This is very important to understand. We all want to be part of groups. And we get meaning out of our lives from being part of groups, you know?

When Tennessee beat Arkansas so bad this

year in football, and the Vice President rubbed it in because we beat them last year, we were members of two different gangs. It was competition and friendly and wholesome and good. This is very important to understand. So if you take the family supports away from these kids, and then there is nothing where they live that puts them in a good gang, that's why they get in gangs that are bad. It's very important to understand that.

The third thing that has happened that is different from what happened 30 years ago when people were poor is that you not only have a worse family situation and no other community supports—I mean, 30 years ago, even when kids didn't grow up in intact families in poor neighborhoods, they still lived in places where on every block there was a role model. The person who owned the drugstore lived in the neighborhood. The person that owned the grocery store lived in the neighborhood. The people that filled the churches on Sunday lived in the neighborhoods where they went to church. Now, the third thing that's happened is, weekend drunks have been substituted by permanent drug addicts and drug salesmen. Abuse of alcohol has been replaced by a drug culture that makes some people money destroying other people's lives. It's different. And it is not simple or easy, what to do about it. Mr. Brown's going to talk more about that in a minute.

The fourth thing that has happened is that the central organizing principle of any advanced society has been evaporated, and that is work. Forget about work in and of itself, to earn money and contribute to the rest of our wealth. If you don't have work in neighborhoods and in communities, it is hard for people to organize their lives. It is hard for parents to feel self-esteem. It is hard for them to feel confident giving their kids rules to live by. It is hard for the relationship between the parent and the child to work just right. It is hard for the child to look out and imagine that by working hard things will work out all right.

Now, there are lots of other problems. But I'm convinced that those are the four biggest ones: the breakdown of the family, the breakdown of other community supports, the rise of drugs—it's not just in terms of drug abuse but in terms of a way to get rich—and the absence of work.

And I believe that in order to deal with this,

we're going to have to all work together in a whole new national contract. But I believe this is an economic issue. I think it's a public health issue. I think it's a national security issue. And besides that, I'm just tired of trying to explain to myself when I go to bed at night why so many American kids aren't going to make it when they ought to.

So there are things for the Federal Government to do, the President, and the Congress. There are things for the States to do, things for the local folks to do. There are things the private sector has to do. And there are certainly things for the churches to do. But I want to submit to you that there are things that every American citizen's going to have to do.

This family breakdown problem has developed over 30 years. It didn't just happen overnight. The community erosion developed over a long period of time. We cannot rebuild all these institutions overnight, but we can start saving these kids, in the words of a good friend of mine, the same way we lost them, one at a time, which means that there's something for all of us to do here. There is something for all of us to do. And we need both love and discipline. We need both investment in these kids and our future, and we need rules by which people live. We need both. It's not an either/or thing.

That's why I say that I think if we really work at it, we can get beyond the Republican, Democrat; who's a liberal, who's a conservative; who's black, Hispanic, or white. This is a huge human problem for America. And we have to face it. I believe that my daughter's future is limited every time another child gets shot in any community in this country. That's what I believe. Every time a kid in Memphis is deprived of a future, I think it limits all the rest of us. That's what I believe. If we believe that, I think we can get there. And let me just suggest where I think we have to start nationally.

The first thing we have to do is to try to make people more secure. Until people are physically secure, it is difficult to get them to change and to do other things. We have a crime bill now moving through the Congress, which would, among other things, put another 100,000 police officers on the street. It's important not only to put them on the street but to have them trained and to have them properly deployed. As Lee Brown will tell you, if you do it right, you can reduce the crime rate and you can prevent crime and repair lives even as you are catching criminals more quickly. We should start there.

I think we ought to pass the crime bill because it offers boot camps instead of penitentiaries for first-time offenders. I think we need to do something to increase the safety of our schools; 160,000 children stay home every day because they're afraid of school. One in five children goes to school every day armed with a knife, a gun, or a club, every day. We've got to change that.

I think we have to provide as much as we can an environment in which the police have a chance to do their job and in which kids are not encouraged to kill each other. There are three bills now being considered in the Congress as a part of this crime bill that I favor. One says that if you're not old enough to go to war or vote, you ought not to be old enough to have a handgun legally, and protects the right to hunt and practice by saying that young people under the supervision of their parents or other appropriate adults can do that. The other bill is the Brady bill, which says that we ought to have a waiting period and check out people's criminal history and mental health history before we just sell them a gun. And the third bill basically says that people ought not to buy in ordinary commerce automatic and semiautomatic weapons, the only purpose of which is to kill other people. Now, no other country would permit that to happen., I think those things should pass. This crime bill is working its way through the Senate, has passed the House, could be given to the American people for Christmas; and I think we ought to do it. That's where we need to start.

Then we need to recognize, as we did in our health care bill, that you have got to have drug education and drug treatment on demand without delay. And we ought not be putting people out of the penitentiary unless they get drug treatment when they need it. And we ought not to let this country go forward. There are many American families that are not poor, that are not in the inner cities that have been touched by the problems of drug abuse. But I can tell you, and there is no simple, easy answer to this, and nothing works for everybody, but good drug treatment does work more than half the time. And we don't provide it. And we're all paying for it. So we need to work on that. And we have an obligation there at the national level.

We also have got to find a way to work with the private sector, even though we are in serious trouble in terms of having enough money to do anything in this country, we have got to find useful work for people who live in dangerous, distressed, dysfunctional areas. We have got to give structure, order, and discipline to lives again through work. We have got to do it.

The last thing I would say to you is that we can do these things at the national level. But we have to give these kids hope again. We have to give their families hope again. We have to give their parents who are trying hope again. I stopped in that housing project, like Harold said. It may be one of the poorest places in this town, but I know that most people who live in that housing project do not break the law, do not abuse drugs, and are doing the best they can. And a lot of people forget that. A lot of people forget that. So that's something you're going to have to do. That's your job.

I live in Washington; you live in Memphis. You've got to do that here. You've got to do that. You've got to do it through the churches, through the businesses, through the community groups. You've got to help slowly but surely get this society back to a point where families can be reconstituted, where there can be supports for kids that don't have families so they're in a good gang, not a bad gang. We can do this, folks.

And you know, people have been talking about this for years, but this is the first time in my memory that I think the American people are about fed up, up to their ears in it, scared to death about what's happening to our children and their future, and understand that it affects all the rest of us. We can do this. We can do this.

I'll make this pledge to you: If you'll work on it here, I'll work on it there. I can no longer justify knowing that there's something I can do to make people safer on the streets and our not doing it. I can no longer justify knowing there are things we can do that work to reduce the drug problem and not doing it. I can no longer justify going to bed at night thinking about these children killing other children, thinking about these little kids planning their funerals and not doing something about it. We can do this. And keep in mind, you're working with the same material that's inside you. These are people we're talking about. We can turn this country around if we'll check our divisions at the door, rely on what unites us, and go to work.

Thank you very much, and God bless you.

Now, before I go, I want to introduce the man who is affectionately called the drug czar. It makes him sound like he sells drugs instead of stops them, doesn't it? [*Laughter*] Dr. Lee Brown grew up in California. As I said, he was the police chief in Atlanta, Houston, and New York. He instituted a program of community policing in New York City, where the police went back on the beat, started walking in the neighborhoods. And despite all the preconceptions, according to the FBI statistics in the last 2 years the crime rate in New York City went down in all seven major FBI categories, because they started giving the police force back to the neighborhoods and the people and working with friends and neighbors to try to stop bad things from happening and catch people who do them when they do. That is a remarkable thing.

I asked him to come onto my administration, and I pledged to him that I would make the Drug Policy Director a member of the President's Cabinet and that we would get every last department of the Federal Government working on the drug problem because I thought he had a comprehensive view. I thought he understood how you can't just divide drugs from all these other issues, that we had to deal with all this together, we had to start at the grassroots level, and that we could really get something done if we had creative, good people working hard. He's a remarkable man. I am deeply honored that he's in our Cabinet. I hope you will welcome him here today and stay here and participate. Remember, you've got to do your part, too. He's here to help you.

Thank you very much. Dr. Lee Brown.

NOTE: The President spoke at 1:20 p.m. at the Olivet Baptist Church. In his remarks, he referred to Kenneth Twigg Whalum, pastor of the church.

Letter to Congressional Leaders on Haiti
November 13, 1993

Dear Mr. Speaker: (*Dear Mr. President:*)

1. In December 1990, the Haitian people elected Jean-Bertrand Aristide as their President by an overwhelming margin in a free and fair election. The United States praised Haiti's success in peacefully implementing its democratic constitutional system and provided significant political and economic support to the new government. The Haitian military abruptly interrupted the consolidation of Haiti's new democracy when in September 1991, it illegally and violently ousted President Aristide from office and drove him into exile.

2. The United States, on its own and with the Organization of American States (OAS), immediately imposed sanctions against the illegal regime. The United States has also actively supported the efforts of the OAS and the United Nations to restore democracy to Haiti and bring about President Aristide's return by facilitating negotiations between the Haitian parties. The United States and the international community also offered material assistance within the context of an eventual negotiated settlement of the

Haitian crisis to support the return to democracy, build constitutional structures, and foster economic well-being.

3. My last report detailed asset freezes and entry prohibitions that I ordered be imposed against individuals associated with the illegal regime on June 4. That report also described the imposition of mandatory oil, arms, and financial sanctions by the United Nations Security Council on June 23 and the tightening of the OAS trade embargo in the same period.

4. Since those events my Administration has intensively supported the negotiating process, using the international community's determination as expressed in the sanctions to bring about the restoration of democracy and return of President Aristide. Our efforts bore fruit in the July 3 Governors Island Agreement between President Aristide and Haitian military Commander in Chief General Cedras. That agreement establishes a comprehensive framework for achievement of our policy objectives in Haiti. Progress in implementing its provisions permitted the suspension of the United Nations,

OAS, and our own targeted sanctions at the end of August.

5. However, as the date for fulfillment of the final terms of the Governors Island Agreement including the return of President Aristide neared, violence in Haiti increased and, on October 11, the Haitian military and police failed to maintain order necessary for the deployment of U.S. and other forces participating in the United Nations Mission in Haiti. This Haitian military intransigence led to the reimposition of U.N. and OAS sanctions on October 18. That same day, I ordered the reimposition of our targeted asset freeze and entry prohibition, the scope and reach of which were at the same time significantly enhanced.

6. This report details the measures we have instituted and enforced pursuant to the requirements of the International Emergency Economic Powers Act. Military refusal to honor obligations incurred in the Governors Island Agreement persists to this date. However, I remain committed to the restoration of democracy in Haiti and I am confident that the application of the measures described in this report will significantly buttress our efforts to achieve that outcome.

7. As noted in my previous report, on June 30, 1993, I issued Executive Order No. 12853 to implement in the United States petroleum, arms, and financial sanctions mandated by United Nations Security Council Resolution No. 841 of June 16, 1993. The order broadened U.S. authority to block all property of the *de facto* regime in Haiti that is in the United States or in the possession or control of U.S. persons, prohibiting transactions involving Haitian nationals providing substantial financial or material contributions to, or doing substantial business with, the *de facto* regime in Haiti. Executive Order No. 12853 also prohibited the sale or supply from the United States of petroleum, petroleum products, arms, or related materiel of all types. Finally, the order also prohibited the carriage on U.S.-registered vessels of petroleum or petroleum products, or arms and related materiel, with entry into, or with the intent to enter, the territory or territorial waters of Haiti.

Apparent steady progress toward achieving my firm goal of restoring democracy in Haiti permitted the United States and the world community to suspend economic sanctions against Haiti in August. With our strong support, the United Nations Security Council adopted Resolution No. 861 on August 27, 1993, calling on Member States to suspend the petroleum, arms, and financial sanctions imposed under United Nations Security Council Resolution No. 841. Resolution No. 861 noted with approval the Governors Island Agreement signed in New York on July 3 between the President of the Republic of Haiti, Jean-Bertrand Aristide, and the Commander in Chief of the Armed Forces of Haiti, Lieutenant General Raoul Cedras. Similarly, the Secretary General of the OAS announced on August 27 that the OAS was urging Member States to suspend their trade embargoes.

As a result of these U.N. and OAS actions and the anticipated swearing-in of Prime Minister Robert Malval, the Department of the Treasury, in consultation with the Department of State, suspended U.S. trade and financial restrictions against Haiti, effective at 9:35 a.m. e.d.t. on August 31, 1993. The suspension permitted new trade transactions with Haiti and authorized new financial and other transactions involving property in which the Government of Haiti has an interest. Property of the Government of Haiti that was blocked before August 31 would be unblocked gradually and when requested by that government. However, property of blocked individuals of the *de facto* regime in Haiti was unblocked as of August 31, 1993.

The Haitian military betrayed its commitments, first by the acceleration of violence in Haiti that it sponsored or tolerated, and then on October 11 when armed "attachés," with military and police support, obstructed deployment to Haiti of U.S. military trainers and engineers as part of the United Nations Mission in Haiti. On October 13, 1993, the U.N. Security Council issued Resolution No. 873 that terminated the suspension of sanctions, effective October 18, 1993. Therefore, we have taken three steps to bring the sanctions to bear once again on those who are obstructing the restoration of democracy and return of President Aristide by blocking fulfillment of the Governors Island Agreement and implementation of the relevant U.N. Security Council resolutions.

First, effective at 11:59 p.m. e.d.t., October 18, 1993, I issued Executive Order No. 12872, authorizing the Department of the Treasury to block assets of persons who have: (1) contributed to the obstruction of U.N. resolutions 841 and 843, the Governors Island Agreement, or the activities of the United Nations Mission in

Haiti; (2) perpetuated or contributed to the violence in Haiti; or (3) materially or financially supported either the obstruction or the violence referred to above. This authority is in addition to the blocking authority provided for in the original sanctions and in Executive Order No. 12853 of June 30, 1993, and ensures adequate scope to reach U.S.-connected assets of senior military and police officials, civilian "attachés," and their financial patrons. A list of 41 such individuals was published on November 1, 1993, by the Office of Foreign Assets Control of the Department of the Treasury (58 *Fed. Reg.* 58482). A copy of the notice is attached.

Second, also effective at 11:59 p.m. e.d.t., October 18, 1993, the Department of the Treasury revoked the suspension of its sanctions, so that the full scope of prior prohibitions has been reinstated. The reinstated sanctions again prohibit most unlicensed trade with Haiti and block the assets of those entities and persons covered by the broadened authority granted in Executive Order No. 12853 of June 16, 1993. Restrictions on the entry into U.S. ports of vessels whose Haitian calls would violate U.S. or OAS sanctions if they had been made by U.S. persons are also reinstated.

Third, on October 18, I ordered the deployment of six U.S. Navy vessels off Haiti's shore to enforce strictly the U.N. sanctions and our regulations implementing the OAS embargo. Our ships have been, or will shortly be, joined by vessels from the navies of Canada, France, Argentina, the Netherlands, and the United Kingdom.

8. Economic sanctions against the *de facto* regime in Haiti were first imposed in October 1991. On October 4, 1991, in Executive Order No. 12775, President Bush declared a national emergency to deal with the threat to the national security, foreign policy, and economy of the United States caused by events that had occurred in Haiti to disrupt the legitimate exercise of power by the democratically elected government of that country (56 *Fed. Reg.* 50641). In that order, the President ordered the immediate blocking of all property and interests in property of the Government of Haiti (including the Banque de la Republique d'Haiti) then or thereafter located in the United States or within the possession or control of a U.S. person, including its overseas branches. The Executive order also prohibited any direct or indirect payments or transfers to the *de facto* regime in

Haiti of funds or other financial or investment assets or credits by any U.S. person, including its overseas branches, or by any entity organized under the laws of Haiti and owned or controlled by a U.S. person.

Subsequently, on October 28, 1991, President Bush issued Executive Order No. 12779, adding trade sanctions against Haiti to the sanctions imposed on October 4 (56 *Fed. Reg.* 55975). This order prohibited exportation from the United States of goods, technology, and services and importation into the United States of Haitian-originated goods and services, after November 5, 1991, with certain limited exceptions. The order exempted trade in publications and other informational materials from the import, export, and payment prohibitions and permitted the exportation to Haiti of donations to relieve human suffering as well as commercial sales of five food commodities: rice, beans, sugar, wheat flour, and cooking oil. In order to permit the return to the United States of goods being prepared for U.S. customers by Haiti's substantial "assembly sector," the order also permitted, through December 5, 1991, the importation into the United States of goods assembled or processed in Haiti that contained parts or materials previously exported to Haiti from the United States. On February 5, 1992, it was announced that specific licenses could be applied for on a case-by-case basis by U.S. persons wishing to resume a pre-embargo import/export relationship with the assembly sector in Haiti.

9. The declaration of the national emergency on October 4, 1991, was made pursuant to the authority vested in the President by the Constitution and laws of the United States, including the International Emergency Economic Powers Act (IEEPA) (50 U.S.C. 1701 *et seq.*), the National Emergencies Act (50 U.S.C. 1601 *et seq.*), and section 301 of title 3 of the United States Code. The emergency declaration was reported to the Congress on October 4, 1991, pursuant to section 204(b) of IEEPA (50 U.S.C. 1703(b)). The additional sanctions set forth in the Executive order of October 28, 1991, were imposed pursuant to the authority vested in the President by the Constitution and laws of the United States, including the statutes cited above, and represent the response by the United States to Resolution MRE/RES. 2/91, adopted by the Ad Hoc Meeting of Ministers of Foreign Affairs of the OAS on October 8, 1991, which called on Member States to impose a trade embargo

on Haiti and to freeze Government of Haiti assets. The current report is submitted pursuant to 50 U.S.C. 1641(c) and 1703(c), and discusses Administration actions and expenses since the last report that are directly related to the national emergency with respect to Haiti declared in Executive Order No. 12775, as implemented pursuant to that order and Executive Order No. 12779.

10. Since my report of July 12, 1993, the Office of Foreign Assets Control of the Department of the Treasury (FAC), in consultation with the Department of State and other Federal agencies, has issued three amendments to the Haitian Transactions Regulations (the "Regulations"), 31 C.F.R. Part 580. First, as previously reported, on June 4, 1993, FAC issued General Notice No. 1 (Haiti), entitled "Notification of Specially Designated Nationals of the *de facto* Regime in Haiti." This Notice listed persons identified as (1) having seized power illegally from the democratically elected government of President Aristide on September 30, 1991; (2) being substantially owned or controlled by the *de facto* regime in Haiti; or (3) having, since 12:23 p.m. e.d.t., October 4, 1991, acted or purported to act directly or indirectly on behalf of the *de facto* regime in Haiti on under the asserted authority thereof. The effect of the Notice was (1) to block within the United States or within the possession or control of U.S. persons all property and interests in property of the blocked individuals and entities and (2) to prohibit transfers or payments to them by U.S. persons. The Regulations were amended on July 27, 1993, to incorporate as Appendix A the list of persons and entities identified in General Notice No. 1 (58 *Fed. Reg.* 40043). A copy of the amendment is attached to this report.

Second, consistent with United Nations Security Council Resolution No. 861 of August 27, 1993, and the August 27, 1993, announcement of the Secretary General of the OAS, the Regulations were amended on August 31, 1993, (58 *Fed. Reg.* 46540) to suspend sanctions against Haiti. A copy of the amendment is attached to this report. The amendment, new section 580.518, prospectively suspended trade restrictions against Haiti and authorized new financial and other transactions with the Government of Haiti. The effect of this amendment was to authorize transactions involving property interests of the Government of Haiti that came within the United States or within the possession or

control of U.S. persons after 9:35 a.m. e.d.t., August 31, 1993, or in which the interest of the Government of Haiti arose thereafter. Newly authorized transactions included, but were not limited to, otherwise lawful exportations and importations from Haiti, brokering transactions, and transfers of funds to the Government of Haiti for obligations due and payable after 9:35 a.m. e.d.t., August 31, 1993.

The amendment did not unblock property of the Government of Haiti that was blocked as of 9:35 a.m. e.d.t., August 31, 1993, nor did it affect enforcement actions involving prior violations of the Regulations, which would continue to be vigorously prosecuted. Blocked property of the Government of Haiti was to be unblocked by specific license on a case-by-case basis in consultations with that government. However, the amendment unblocked all blocked property of the Banque de l'Union Haitienne and of all individuals previously listed in Section I of Appendix A to the Regulations.

Third, as noted previously, consistent with United Nations Security Council Resolution No. 873 of October 13, 1993, and Executive Order No. 12872 (58 *Fed. Reg.* 54029, October 20, 1993), the Regulations were amended effective 11:59 p.m. e.d.t., October 18, 1993 (58 *Fed. Reg.* 54024); to reimpose sanctions against Haiti. A copy of the Executive order and of the amendment are attached to this report. The amendment removes section 580.518, discussed above.

11. In implementing the Haitian sanctions program, FAC has made extensive use of its authority to specifically license transactions with respect to Haiti in an effort to mitigate the effects of the sanctions on the legitimate Government of Haiti and on the livelihood of Haitian workers employed by Haiti's export assembly sector, and to ensure the availability of necessary medicines and medical supplies and the undisrupted flow of humanitarian donations to Haiti's poor. For example, specific licenses were issued (1) permitting expenditures from blocked assets for the operations of the legitimate Government of Haiti; (2) permitting U.S. firms with pre-embargo relationships with product assembly operations in Haiti to resume those relationships in order to continue employment for their workers or, if they choose to withdraw from Haiti, to return to the United States assembly equipment, machinery, and parts and materials previously exported to Haiti; (3) permitting U.S.

companies operating in Haiti to establish, under specified circumstances, interest-bearing blocked reserve accounts in commercial or investment banking institutions in the United States for deposit of amounts owed the *de facto* regime; (4) permitting the continued material support of U.S. and international religious, charitable, public health, and other humanitarian organizations and projects operating in Haiti; (5) authorizing commercial sales of agricultural inputs such as fertilizer and foodcrop seeds; and (6) in order to combat deforestation, permitting the importation of agricultural products grown on trees.

12. During this reporting period, U.S.-led OAS initiatives resulted in even greater intensification and coordination of enforcement activities. The U.S. Coast Guard, whose cutters had been patrolling just beyond Haiti's territorial waters, significantly increased vessel boardings, identification of suspected embargo violators, and referrals for investigation. Continued close coordination with the U.S. Customs Service in Miami sharply reduced the number of attempted exports of unmanifested, unauthorized merchandise.

Since the last report, 16 penalties, totaling approximately $65,000, have been collected from U.S. businesses and individuals for violations of the Regulations. Seven violations involved unlicensed import- and export-related activity. As of September 21, 1993, payments of penalties assessed against the masters of vessels for unauthorized trade transactions or violations of entry restrictions totalled approximately $45,000. Total collections for the fiscal year have exceeded $210,000.

13. The expenses incurred by the Federal Government in the 6-month period from April 4, 1993, through October 3, 1993, that are directly attributable to the authorities conferred by the declaration of a national emergency with respect to Haiti are estimated at approximately $3.1 million, most of which represent wage and salary costs for Federal personnel. Personnel costs were largely centered in the Department of the Treasury (particularly in FAC, the U.S. Customs Service, and the Office of the General Counsel), the Department of State, the U.S. Coast Guard, and the Department of Commerce.

I am committed to the restoration of democracy in Haiti and determined to see that Haiti and the Haitian people resume their rightful place in our hemispheric community of democracies. Active U.S. support for U.N./OAS efforts to resolve the Haitian crisis has led to the reimposition of sweeping economic sanctions. I call on all of Haiti's leaders to recall the solemn undertakings in the Governors Island Agreement and to adhere to those pledges, so that the sanctions can be lifted and the process of rebuilding their beleaguered country can begin. The United States will continue to play a leadership role in the international community's program of support and assistance for democracy in Haiti.

I will continue to report periodically to the Congress on significant developments pursuant to 50 U.S.C. 1703(c).

Sincerely,

WILLIAM J. CLINTON

NOTE: Identical letters were sent to Thomas S. Foley, Speaker of the House of Representatives, and Albert Gore, Jr., President of the Senate. This letter was released by the Office of the Press Secretary on November 15.

Remarks on NAFTA to Small Business Leaders
November 15, 1993

The President. Thank you very much. When Manny and Rick were talking I leaned over to Bill Daley, and I said, "You know, these guys are really good. We need to put them on the stump."

I want to thank you all for being here today. And before I make any more remarks, there are a couple of people I would like to introduce who have not yet been introduced. First of all, I think all of America has seen that our administration has pursued the ratification of this agreement in the Congress on a strictly bipartisan basis on the theory that it was in the best interest of America and the American economy and that after all that we've been through in the last 15 or 20 years, adjusting to the global economy, all the ups and downs, it's an important part of our national security to have a sensible global economic policy.

When we organized this campaign I asked Bill Daley to come in from Chicago. And then we were very fortunate to have the services of his Republican counterpart, the former leader of the Republican Party in the House of Representatives on the issue of trade, Congressman Bill Frenzel from Minnesota. And he's over here, so I wanted to introduce him. Thank you.

I also want to introduce another person who is a longtime friend of mine and in more ways than one responsible for my being here today, with this introduction. If you look at the opposition to NAFTA, much of it is coming from people who are involved in the manufacturing sector of our economy, who justifiably note that the percentage of our work force in manufacturing has declined and that wages have been more or less stagnant for a long time. Some say that the answer to that is to keep the barriers high here and not worry about lowering the barriers elsewhere. That has never worked for any country ever in the entire history of global economics. The State in this country that has the highest percentage of its work force in manufacturing by far is North Carolina. And the Governor of North Carolina is here today with us and a strong supporter of NAFTA, my friend Governor Jim Hunt. Please welcome him.

We wanted to meet here today in this marvelous museum not to focus on the past but to make a point about our past. If you look around at all these different displays, all the exhibits, you see that the one constant in American economic history has been change. The reason we have been able to build a dominant economy is that we have been at the forefront of innovation in new products, new services, new technologies, new production techniques, new management techniques, new sales techniques.

We know now that a lot of what we have seen in the last 20 years in terms of competition from around the world is the direct result of our success in, first, winning the Second World War; secondly, rebuilding our former foes in Germany and Japan; thirdly, supporting a global trading system so that everybody could have the benefit of capitalism and free enterprise; and fourthly, the fact that there are a lot of other

people in the world who are smart and work hard and do things well, too, so that the arena of competition has gotten much bigger.

In that connection, however, it cannot be denied that for all of the difficulties we've had in the last several years, we've had astonishing growth in productivity in many sectors of our economy. Every single analysis still says we have the most productive workers in the world. And it is clear that if we can expand our customer base, we'll be able to solidify job gains and income increases. There is no way any wealthy country in this world can increase jobs and incomes without increasing the number of people who buy that nation's products and services. There is simply no other way to do it, just like there's no way you can increase your business unless people buy more of whatever it is you're selling. It is the same for a nation.

I understand well why there are so many people in this country today who are skeptical about any change because they feel so burned by the economic problems of the last 10 to 15 years. I understand that. But if ever a group of Americans understood the risk of competition and change, it is the small business community. If there is one sector of our economy that sort of lays it on the line every day, it is the small business community. If you look at the incredible churning of the number of small businesses in America today, the number that are created and the number that don't make it, if any group of Americans could come to the Nation's Capital and say, hey, we can't stand any more insecurity, it would be you, right?

Audience members. Right!

The President. So why is the small business community in America overwhelmingly in support of NAFTA? Because you understand also the only way to sell more is to have more customers, and the only way to succeed is to compete and win. And you know something that everyone in America has to learn: that we cannot run from the forces of competition. We have to face them and overcome them and continue to change and grow.

That is what America has always done. That is the meaning of this exhibit. If you look around, you see in this exhibit the history of the accumulated lives of innovative, creative entrepreneurs, the people who paved the way for all of you to be here today. And on Wednesday, we are going to see the United States Congress pass a vote which will either be in the great tradition of all those who put their products in this museum and all you who come to this Nation's Capital, or will be the exception to the rule but one for which there is some evidence that maybe we just will turn away one more time.

Every time we have done that, this country has gotten burned. Every time. And all the people who are against it say, "Well, there's something different about this. This is worse, or this is different, or whatever." I say to them, if we don't adopt this we will never know how good it can be. If all the naysayers turn out to be wrong, the treaty gives us a right to withdraw in 6 months. Why don't we just wait and see whether we're right or they're right?

You know we're right. You know it because it is consistent with your own life experience. And the argument that is being made here, that we shouldn't even try, we should give up before we engage, is really very, very bad for our country and ignores the enormous productivity gains that have been achieved by Americans in the last several years. We are now in a position to take advantage of our productivity gains. But all of you know what productivity is, it's the same number of people producing more, or fewer people producing more. So now, if you want to have more jobs and more incomes, we have to have more people to sell to. It is clear and self-evident.

I want you to contact these Members of Congress in the next 2 days and make the case I just made about insecurity. If any group of people in America understands how change can take you away overnight, it is the small business community. You are for this because you know you cannot repeal the laws of change, you can-

not run away from them. And the competitive system in America with winners and losers has produced far more winners than losers over the last 200 years, far more winners than losers. And this will produce more winners than losers. This is the way to grow the American economy. You understand it, and we need you.

One of our Nation's strongest advocates for small business, also from North Carolina, is the Director of the Small Business Administration, Erskine Bowles. And I predict he will go down in history as one of the most popular members of our administration because he's the first SBA Director in a long time who's made a living creating small businesses. That's what he's done for 20 years, helped people start small businesses, helped them expand, helped them sell their products overseas, helped them pierce foreign markets in the private sector. And he is a terrific advocate for NAFTA.

We were talking the other day about this and it's how I obviously, as you might imagine, since I'm now on my fourth or fifth or sixth conversation with some of these Members of Congress about this issue, I keep trying to think of the argument that can be made. So I implore you again, I don't want to sound like a broken record, but talk to the Members of Congress. Tell them you know all about insecurity, but you know that we can compete and win if we have enough customers to sell to.

Thank you, and God bless you.

NOTE: The President spoke at 10:20 a.m. at the Smithsonian Museum of American History. In his remarks, he referred to Manuel Silva, founder, Pan American Engineering, and Richard Harris, president, Pulsair, Inc.

Statement on the Outcome of the Puerto Rican Referendum
November 15, 1993

I fully support the determination of the citizens of Puerto Rico to continue their commonwealth status.

I am especially gratified by the high level of participation in Sunday's referendum, and I look forward to maintaining the relationship of friendship and mutual respect that the United States enjoys with the people of Puerto Rico.

Appointment for the Federal Council on the Aging
November 15, 1993

The President announced today that he will appoint four new members to the Federal Council on the Aging, a 15-member panel that advises and assists the President on matters relating to the special needs of older Americans. The President appoints one-third of the Council's members, three of whom must be more than 60 years of age.

"The senior citizen community, our parents and grandparents, is one of our great resources," said the President. "It is important that we ensure that Government policies are helpful to them and that we make sure to seek their wisdom as we decide on those policies."

The members appointed today are Alice B. Bulos, William B. Cashin, Olivia P. Maynard, and Myrtle B. Pickering.

NOTE: Biographies of the appointees were made available by the Office of the Press Secretary.

Letter to House Republican Leader Robert H. Michel on NAFTA
November 15, 1993

Dear Mr. Leader:

On more than one occasion I have been asked whether the North American Free Trade Agreement (NAFTA) might become a divisive issue in the 1994 Congressional elections. Each time I have been asked this question I have expressed the hope that this issue would continue to be viewed in a spirit of bipartisan cooperation befitting an issue of such historical importance.

Since I have sought the support of all members of the House of Representatives for the NAFTA implementing legislation as a matter of compelling national interest, I hope to discourage NAFTA opponents from using this issue against pro-NAFTA members, regardless of party, in the coming election.

After our shared success later this week, when I will have the pleasure of sending thank you letters to at least 218 House members, I will reaffirm my position on the inappropriateness of fighting NAFTA again in the 1994 election.

As always, you have my respect and appreciation.

Sincerely,

BILL CLINTON

NOTE: This letter was made available by the Office of the Press Secretary on November 16 but was not issued as a White House press release.

Letter to Congressional Leaders on NAFTA
November 15, 1993

Dear Mr. Speaker: (Dear Mr. Leader:)

As we approach the end of an intense debate over the North American Free Trade Agreement (NAFTA), I want to share with you my reasons for believing Congressional approval of NAFTA is essential to our national interest.

We share a commitment to ensuring that our country has the world's strongest and most competitive economy, to maintaining and creating jobs for our workers, and to making sure that opportunities are there for our children as they join the workforce of the future. That is why I am fighting for the approval of NAFTA. I am convinced that it will help strengthen our economy—in the near term and in the long run.

Our nation's prosperity depends on our ability to compete and win in the global economy. It is an illusion to believe that we can prosper by retreating behind protectionist walls. We will succeed only by ensuring that we have the world's most competitive companies, productive workers, and open markets in which to sell our manufactured goods, services, and agricultural products.

I understand that NAFTA is, for many, a reminder of the economic hardships and insecurities that have grown over the past 20 years. Obviously, NAFTA did not cause those problems. In fact, it is part of the solution. We are world-class producers of everything from computers and automobiles to financial services and soybeans. We can compete anywhere, but we need to ensure that markets around the world are open to our products.

Mexico represents an enormous opportunity for our businesses, our workers, and our farmers. Exports there have already soared since 1986, when Mexico began to open its market and lower trade barriers. But the status quo in the trading relationship—in which Mexico's trade barriers are far higher than ours—is still unacceptable. NAFTA represents both free and fair trade. It changes the status quo by wiping away the Mexican barriers.

NAFTA provides us preferential access to the Mexican market: 90 million people, in one of the most dynamic growing economies in the world, who look to us for consumer goods, agricultural products and the infrastructure needed to build a modern economy. It is the gateway to the fast growing markets of Latin America, which are also opening, where we have a natural advantage over Japan and the European Community. Turning away from this opportunity would be a serious self-inflicted wound to our economy. It would cost us jobs—in the short and long term.

Many opponents of NAFTA say that they don't oppose a trade agreement with Mexico. They say they just oppose this NAFTA, and suggest that it be renegotiated. We should be under no illusions. This is a far-reaching and fair agreement. It was negotiated painstakingly over three years with input from a broad array of groups, and it is in the best interest of the United States, Mexico and Canada. It represents an unprecedented effort to include in a trade agreement provisions to enhance environmental protection and workers rights. It was negotiated by a Republican President, and endorsed and strengthened by a Democratic President. If it were defeated, no government of Mexico could return, or would return, to the negotiating table for years to come. Mexico would turn to others, like Japan and the European Community, for help in building a modern state—and American workers, farmers, and businesses would be the losers.

Of course, NAFTA is not a magic bullet for all our economic problems. But there is no question that NAFTA will benefit every region of our country. It is no accident that NAFTA has the support of more than two-thirds of the nation's governors and Members of Congress from every part of the nation. They understand the benefits that will flow to their states, regardless of region.

My main reason for supporting NAFTA is that it will be good for the competitive U.S. economy that we are trying to build. But there is another critical issue that I ask you to consider. After World War I, the United States chose the path of isolation and protectionism. That path led directly to the Depression, and helped set the world on the path to World War II. After World War II, we chose to engage with the world, through collective security and expanded trade. We helped our allies rebuild, ushered in a period of unprecedented global economic growth, and prevailed over communism.

Now we face another defining moment. The rejection of NAFTA would set back our relationship with Mexico, and Latin American beyond, for years to come. It would send a signal that the world's leading power has chosen the path of pessimism and protectionism. It would gravely undermine our ability to convince other countries to join us in completing the Uruguay Round, which is essential to expand trade and enhance global growth.

Rejecting NAFTA would, quite simply, put us on the wrong side of history. That is not our destiny. I ask the House of Representatives to join me in choosing the path of expanded trade, to make the decision to compete in the world, rather than to retreat behind our borders. We are a great country, and we cannot shrink from this test.

Sincerely,

BILL CLINTON

NOTE: Identical letters were sent to Thomas S. Foley, Speaker of the House of Representatives, and Robert H. Michel, House Republican leader. This letter was made available by the Office of the Press Secretary on November 16 but was not issued as a White House press release.

Remarks on Signing the Religious Freedom Restoration Act of 1993
November 16, 1993

Thank you very much, Mr. Vice President, for those fine remarks and to the Members of Congress, the chaplains of the House and the Senate, and to all of you who worked so hard to help this day become a reality. Let me especially thank the Coalition for the Free Exercise of Religion for the central role they played in drafting this legislation and working so hard for its passage.

It is interesting to note, as the Vice President said, what a broad coalition of Americans came together to make this bill a reality; interesting to note that that coalition produced a 97-to-3 vote in the United States Senate and a bill that had such broad support it was adopted on a voice vote in the House. I'm told that, as many of the people in the coalition worked together across ideological and religious lines, some new friendships were formed and some new trust was established, which shows, I suppose, that the power of God is such that even in the legislative process miracles can happen. [*Laughter*]

We all have a shared desire here to protect perhaps the most precious of all American liberties, religious freedom. Usually the signing of legislation by a President is a ministerial act, often a quiet ending to a turbulent legislative process. Today this event assumes a more majestic quality because of our ability together to affirm the historic role that people of faith have played in the history of this country and the constitutional protections those who profess and express their faith have always demanded and cherished.

The power to reverse legislation by legislation, a decision of the United States Supreme Court, is a power that is rightly hesitantly and infrequently exercised by the United States Congress. But this is an issue in which that extraordinary measure was clearly called for. As the Vice President said, this act reverses the Supreme Court's decision Employment Division against Smith and reestablishes a standard that better protects all Americans of all faiths in the exercise of their religion in a way that I am convinced is far more consistent with the intent of the Founders of this Nation than the Supreme Court decision.

More than 50 cases have been decided against individuals making religious claims against Government action since that decision was handed down. This act will help to reverse that trend by honoring the principle that our laws and institutions should not impede or hinder but rather should protect and preserve fundamental religious liberties.

The free exercise of religion has been called the first freedom, that which originally sparked the development of the full range of the Bill of Rights. Our Founders cared a lot about religion. And one of the reasons they worked so hard to get the first amendment into the Bill of Rights at the head of the class is that they well understood what could happen to this country, how both religion and Government could be perverted if there were not some space created and some protection provided. They knew that religion helps to give our people the character without which a democracy cannot survive. They knew that there needed to be a space of freedom between Government and people of faith that otherwise Government might usurp.

They have seen now, all of us, that religion

and religious institutions have brought forth faith and discipline, community and responsibility over two centuries for ourselves and enabled us to live together in ways that I believe would not have been possible. We are, after all, the oldest democracy now in history and probably the most truly multiethnic society on the face of the Earth. And I am convinced that neither one of those things would be true today had it not been for the importance of the first amendment and the fact that we have kept faith with it for 200 years.

What this law basically says is that the Government should be held to a very high level of proof before it interferes with someone's free exercise of religion. This judgment is shared by the people of the United States as well as by the Congress. We believe strongly that we can never, we can never be too vigilant in this work.

Let me make one other comment if I might before I close and sit down and sign this bill. There is a great debate now abroad in the land which finds itself injected into several political races about the extent to which people of faith can seek to do God's will as political actors. I would like to come down on the side of encouraging everybody to act on what they believe is the right thing to do. There are many people in this country who strenuously disagree with me on what they believe are the strongest grounds of their faiths. I encourage them to speak out. I encourage all Americans to reach deep inside to try to determine what it is that drives their lives most deeply.

As many of you know, I have been quite moved by Stephen Carter's book, "The Culture of Disbelief." He makes a compelling case that today Americans of all political persuasions and all regions have created a climate in this country in which some people believe that they are embarrassed to say that they advocate a course of action simply because they believe it is the right thing to do, because they believe it is

dictated by their faith, by what they discern to be, with their best efforts, the will of God.

I submit to you today, my fellow Americans, that we can stand that kind of debate in this country. We are living in a country where the most central institution of our society, the family, has been under assault for 30 years. We are living in a country in which 160,000 schoolchildren don't go to school every day because they're afraid someone will shoot them or beat them up or knife them. We are living in a country now where gunshots are the single leading cause of death among teenage boys. We are living in a country where people can find themselves shot in the crossfire of teenagers who are often better armed than the police who are trying to protect other people from illegal conduct. It is high time we had an open and honest reaffirmation of the role of American citizens of faith, not so that we can agree but so that we can argue and discourse and seek the truth and seek to heal this troubled land.

So today I ask you to also think of that. We are a people of faith. We have been so secure in that faith that we have enshrined in our Constitution protection for people who profess no faith. And good for us for doing so. That is what the first amendment is all about. But let us never believe that the freedom of religion imposes on any of us some responsibility to run from our convictions. Let us instead respect one another's faiths, fight to the death to preserve the right of every American to practice whatever convictions he or she has, but bring our values back to the table of American discourse to heal our troubled land.

Thank you very much.

NOTE: The President spoke at 9:15 a.m. on the South Lawn at the White House. H.R. 1308, approved November 16, was assigned Public Law No. 103–141.

Remarks on Governors' Endorsements of NAFTA and an Exchange With Reporters
November 16, 1993

The President. Thank you very much. Thank you, Mr. Vice President, and thank you to all

the Governors who are here and to the many Governors who are not here who have helped us in this battle to pass NAFTA.

I think I should say by way of sort of a parenthesis at the outset of my remarks, in reaction to Governor Thompson's eloquent comments about the Rose Bowl, that in view of the wisdom of the voters in Michigan, Ohio, and Wisconsin in the last election, this administration has no position on that football game. [*Laughter*]

You know, I looked at the Governors who are here with me, and I had to think—I actually counted. We are about equally divided back here between Democrats and Republicans. And I think it is an interesting statement that these who have come here and those who are not here who have also endorsed this agreement are more or less equally divided in about the ratio the parties hold of gubernatorial offices. And the reason for that is that if you're a Governor today, a big part of your job is keeping the job base you have, trying to find more jobs, and when you lose jobs, trying to replace them as quickly as possible.

It's not unusual to see a Governor who actually knows huge numbers of employers by name, who's been in, in my case, literally hundreds of manufacturing facilities and different small businesses and who understands how businesses rise and fall and how they fit within the economy of the State, the Nation, and the globe. The job of Governors is to create jobs, to keep jobs, to enhance the economic base and the economic security of our people.

Any of these Governors will tell you that it is difficult to hold onto this job if your voters don't believe you have a clear economic program and that your State is moving in the right direction against all the odds. Many of us have served in very difficult economic times, with high unemployment rates caused by all kinds of factors. But we always found that the people of our State wanted us to have a theory about how the economy works and how we were going to get more jobs. That is what these folks do for a living.

So I am especially honored to have these Governors here and to have their support because they understand on a bipartisan basis that a big part of America's national security involves the ability to create economic security for our people. They further understand that the only way to have economic security is to compete and win in the global economy.

As I have said many times and I want to say here on the eve of this great vote, every wealthy country in the world today is having trouble creating new jobs. Productivity increases, which are necessary to compete in the global economy, in the short run sometimes cause difficulty in creating jobs because a more productive worker means fewer people can produce more products and services. Therefore, if you want more jobs at higher wages in this world, you have to have more customers. There is no way around that.

No one has seriously advanced the proposition that the United States can grow jobs and raise incomes, our most urgent economic priority, without having more customers for our products and services. The Governors understand that. That is why they do not seek to run away from change or to shield their people from change but instead to embrace it, to compete and win. That is the great message that must be carried to the Congress over the next 24 hours as the Members prepare for this vote.

This really is a vote about whether we're going to try to hold onto yesterday's economy or embrace tomorrow's economy. It's about the past and the future. You know, if I could wave a magic wand and return every American to absolute job security with no competition at all, I might do that although I'm not sure our country would be better off. At least more and more people think that that is a possibility as you hear this NAFTA vote. And I'm telling you folks, these Governors understand that is not a possibility.

Governors have stood at the doors of plants when they closed. I have stood by plants and shaken hands with workers, hundreds of them, when they walked off the job for the last time. If I thought that this was going to cost the American people jobs, I would not be for this agreement and neither would these Governors. Our work is putting Americans to work.

Now, in the last 10 months, with the deficit down, with inflation down, with interest rates down, this economy has produced more jobs in the private sector than in the previous 4 years. And every American can tell you that's very fine, but it's nowhere near enough. We cannot get more jobs in this economy until we have more customers for our products and our services.

Tomorrow the Congress has simply got to vote for hope over fear, for the future over the past, they've got to vote for confidence in the ability of the American people to compete and win. These Governors are closer to their workers than any other public officials in the country. They know we can compete and win. So do I. And tomorrow I think the House of Representatives will say the same thing.

Thank you very much.

NAFTA

Q. Mr. President, you have stressed bipartisanship here. But Lane Kirkland says that you have really abdicated the leadership of the Democratic Party with your all-out campaign.

The President. My job is to try to lead the United States and to try to help this country move forward and to do what I think is right to get that done. I do not believe we can grow this economy without expanding our trade. I'm doing the job that the people elected me to do, to try to expand the economy.

Q. Can you explain about the political cover, as it's been described, that you're offering Members of Congress, Republicans and Democrats, in terms of NAFTA not being a legitimate political issue in the 1994 campaign?

The President. I have told all Members of Congress who vote for this that I will do everything I can to defend this vote and to say that a vote for this agreement should not be the basis for defeating any Member of Congress without regard to party. And I believe that.

Q. Mr. President, Ross Perot has accused you of giving away billions of dollars in taxpayers' monies to buy votes in favor of NAFTA. And he says that what you're doing makes the scandal in New Jersey look like peanuts. What do you say about that?

The President. I say that the Vice President, first of all, disposed of most of Mr. Perot's arguments pretty well the other night. The Members of Congress who come to me and ask me for things have asked me to help their people. The people that I've talked to in Congress have been nobly motivated. Most of them have taken great risks and, as you heard, were threatened on national television with their very political life by Mr. Perot the other night to vote for this. When they come to see me, they want to know things like: Is this job training package going to be really adequate? How do I know the members of my district are going to have access to job training programs? What are you going to do to ensure that the environmental standards will be kept? And how quickly will we see in-

vestments in cleaning up the environment along the border?

Those are the kinds of substantive questions that we've been asked to hammer out and work through and give assurances on. I think that is the job of a Member of Congress. I don't feel badly about that at all.

Q. Mr. President——

Q. Mr. President—sorry.

The President. Go ahead. Both of you. [*Laughter*]

Q. Isn't there a danger, Mr. President, these kind of side deals you've had to make on sugar, citrus, wheat can end up undermining the very thing you tried to do with the trade agreement?

The President. No.

Q. Why not?

The President. Well, the side agreements we made on agriculture were just like the side agreements we made on the environment and on the labor standards. They don't undermine the fundamental things in the agreement. The Mexican tariffs come down. The barriers to trade go down. The Mexicans have access to nationwide investment in their country. We win; they win. The big things in the agreement are still wholly intact, and as a matter of fact, I think it's a much better deal than it was a year ago.

Q. How do you feel about this bipartisan coalition? There was an extraordinary joint whips committee meeting yesterday. When all the votes are being counted in the middle of the rollcall, do you really trust Newt Gingrich with what may be the future of your Presidency?

The President. First of all, I wouldn't even characterize it that way. I believe that Newt Gingrich believes in NAFTA just like I do. And I believe he wants it to pass. And do I trust him to do everything he can to deliver every vote he can? You bet I do.

And let me say that, you know, we can't win for losing around here. I mean, when we were voting on the budget, you were asking me wasn't it terrible we didn't have any Republicans voting with us. I like the idea of people in the two parties working together when they agree. I do not like the idea that any party's, either party's discipline would prevent people who agree with one another from working together toward the national good. I think that's what the American people want us to do. I think they want us to disagree when we disagree, to agree when we agree, but not to let our labels keep us from working together.

So this has been an immensely rewarding thing for me to work with the Republicans who agree with us on this issue. Mr. Bonior has worked very hard with the Republicans who agree with him on the issue, and I would like to see more of it in America. I think that our country would work better if we could work out agreements and work together in a constructive way, particularly on issues that affect our national security.

When I was a boy, looking at Washington from afar, growing up, the normal thing was for the Republicans and Democrats to work together on foreign policy because everyone understood that was our national security. Well frankly, folks, a lot of these economic issues are our national security today. And I hope we'll see a lot more of this bipartisanship.

Q. Do you have the votes?

The President. We're getting there. I never say that until they're counted, you know, but I feel good today. We're getting there.

Q. Mr. President, a lot of people have characterized this as a test of your Presidency. And the stakes seem to have been ratcheted up, particularly in the last few days, to the point where one Senator was quoted as saying your political future is at stake and, at the very least, the future of any political programs you want to enact. Do you think that is an exaggeration, or are the stakes really that high?

The President. I think the stakes for our country are high. What happens to me is not nearly as important as what happens to the country. Thursday morning I'll wake up, and I'll get on that plane and go to the APEC meeting and do the best I can for America. A month from now people may be concerned about something else. But what I want to emphasize is the importance of this to our country.

I want to make, in closing, since this is my last shot, one argument that none of us have made yet again this morning. And that is that NAFTA is the gateway to all of Latin America, to 700 million people. It is an insurance policy against protectionism in the rest of the world. And it is an enormous lever for us to convince our friends in the Pacific region and our friends in Europe to complete the worldwide trade agreement, the GATT round, by the end of the year so we can continue to expand the global economy.

Yes, sir.

Q. Mr. President, your opponents on this issue, Mr. Gephardt, for instance, say that if NAFTA fails they will immediately offer to renegotiate it with you, to revive it. If NAFTA does not pass tomorrow night, is it dead, or are you going to immediately try to work with them to renegotiate it?

The President. They're missing the point. They can renegotiate with me all they want. They can't renegotiate it with the Mexicans. I think the Government of Mexico has made it quite clear that this trade agreement includes environmental concessions and labor concessions on their part, which I think are good for them, by the way, but never before put into a trade agreement by any nation ever. I think it is clear what they will do is to look to other nations to make other deals. You see, even the Canadians said today that if we voted it down, they'd try to make a separate agreement with Mexico. I feel quite sure that other nations will as well.

Q. Mr. President, what are you learning from this intensive campaign? Are there a lot of disappointments? And do you have any unusual surprises?

The President. There haven't been any disappointments. Actually, what I'm learning from this campaign is that an awful lot of people really love this country and many Members of Congress are literally willing to put their political careers on the line tomorrow night to do what they think is right, even though they're not quite sure their voters agree with them yet. Every Member we get who's in a difficult district, who's voting for this is doing it because he or she believes that it's in the interest of their constituents even if they haven't quite persuaded them yet. And it's been a deeply moving thing for me.

I also would tell you all that we've had a lot of close votes up here, but we're moving the ball forward in this country. It is hard to do hard things. And sometimes hard things win by narrow margins. But America is going through a period of real change and ferment at a time of great difficulty for millions of our citizens. So the fact that this is tough, it should be exhilarating to all of us who are carrying forward. It's just our responsibility to take the tough fight and go forward.

North Korea

Q. Mr. President, on one other topic, are you willing to give up military exercises in South

Korea in exchange for nuclear inspections in North Korea?

The President. I'm not at liberty even to comment on that now. The negotiations are going on, and I don't think I should comment. I'll have more to say about that, I hope, in the next few days.

One last question. Go ahead.

Canadian Agricultural Subsidies

Q. Have you decided to ask Canada to change its grain pricing policies? And are you prepared to seek tariffs or quotas, if they don't, on durum wheat?

The President. First of all, I don't think I should prefigure my conversation with the Prime Minister of Canada. I'm going to have my first meeting with him in just a couple of days, and we're going to discuss some of the issues outstanding between us, including the differences both of us have with each other's definition of what constitutes fair trade in agriculture. The Prime Minister has made an interesting suggestion, which is that we ought to try to reach agreement on what does or doesn't constitute a subsidy, something which was not done before our agreement with Canada was developed. And that is what led to a lot of this misunderstanding because they have things that our farmers consider to be significant subsidies that are indirect. So we're going to meet and visit about that when we get out to the Pacific. Right now, we've got to pass NAFTA.

Thank you very much.

NOTE: The President spoke at 11:05 a.m. at the North Portico to the West Wing at the White House. In his remarks, he referred to Gov. Tommy G. Thompson of Wisconsin.

Remarks on the House of Representatives Action on the North American Free Trade Agreement and an Exchange With Reporters
November 17, 1993

The President. Thank you very much. Just a few minutes ago the House of Representatives voted to approve the North American Free Trade Agreement. NAFTA will expand our exports, create new jobs, and help us reassert America's leadership in the global economy. This agreement is in the deep self-interest of the United States. It will help make working Americans, the world's most productive workers, winners in the world economy.

I want to thank the lawmakers of both parties who gave their support to NAFTA. Many of them, as everyone knows, showed real courage in voting their consciences and what they knew to be in the best interest for their Nation. I want to thank all the citizens who worked so hard for this, the business leaders, especially the small business leaders, the spokespersons for the NAFTA fight, including Lee Iacocca who's here with us tonight.

I want to say a special word of thanks to the members of the Cabinet who labored so hard and long, especially Mickey Kantor, our Trade Ambassador, for his tireless effort on the side agreements and to lobby this through, and the Secretary of the Treasury, who is a native of south Texas and who understands so clearly why this is in our interests. And I want to say a special word of thanks to Vice President Gore for bringing home the message to the American people in his superb debate performance.

Tonight's vote is a defining moment for our Nation. At a time when many of our people are hurting from the strains of this tough global economy, we chose to compete, not to retreat, to lead a new world economy, to lead as America has done so often in the past. The debate over NAFTA has been contentious. Men and women of good will raised strong arguments for and against this agreement. But every participant in this debate wanted the same things: more jobs, more security, more opportunity for every American. And so do I.

I thank those who worked with us. I thank especially the people who organized the grassroots effort in our behalf, Bill Daley and former Congressman Bill Frenzel. I also thank the passionate defenders of the working people who oppose NAFTA for exercising their right to speak out. And they were right to speak out against economic conditions which have produced too few jobs and stagnant incomes, as well as inadequate strategies for retraining our workers and investing in our people and our places that need them. They fought hard, and they have my respect.

But in an economy where competition is global and change is the only constant, we simply cannot advance the security of American workers by building walls of protection around our economy or by pretending that global competition isn't there. Our only choice is to take this new world head on, to compete, and to win. That's why it's so important that we pass NAFTA, and I hope the Senate will complete the process in the next few days.

By eliminating Mexico's tariffs and restrictive rules we'll be able to export more cars, more computers, and other products and keep more American workers on the job here at home. NAFTA will raise environmental and labor standards in Mexico. And I want to ask tonight labor and management to work together with our administration to ensure that the labor and environmental provisions of NAFTA are honored. We must make sure that this pact works to America's advantage.

NAFTA is a big step, but just the first step in our effort to expand trade and spark an economic revival here and around the world. One legitimate point that the opponents of NAFTA made is that we will do even better in the global economy if we have a training system and a retraining system and a job placement system for our workers worthy of the challenges they face. We simply must guarantee our workers the training and education they need to compete in the global marketplace. And I call on the coalition that passed NAFTA to help me early next year present to the Congress and pass a world-class reemployment system that will give our working people the security of knowing that they'll be able always to get the training they need as economic conditions change.

We must also provide our citizens with other things, with health care that can never be taken away, with increased investment in people and places and jobs. And we must continue the fight to lower foreign trade barriers which slow economic growth here in the United States and around the world.

Tomorrow I go to Seattle to meet with the leaders of 15 Asian Pacific economies. I will ask them to work toward more open markets

for our products. When I return, I'll reach out to the other market-oriented democracies of Latin America, to ask them to join in this great American pact that I believe offers so much hope to our future. And next month we will urge our European and Asian competitors to complete work on the worldwide trade agreement that can literally create hundreds of thousands of jobs here in the United States as we open markets all across the globe.

We've faced choices before like the one we faced tonight, whether to turn inward or turn outward. After World War I, the United States turned inward and built walls of protection around our economy. The result was a depression and ultimately another world war. After the Second World War, we made a very different choice. We turned outward. We built a system of expanded trade and collective security. We rebuilt the economies of our former foes and in the process created the great American middle class.

Tonight, with the cold war over, our Nation is facing that choice again. And tonight I am proud to say, we have not flinched. Tonight the leaders of both parties found common ground in supporting the common good. We voted for the future tonight. We once again showed our strength. We once again showed our self-confidence, even in this difficult time. Our people are winners. And I believe we showed tonight we are ready together to compete and win and to shape the world of the 21st century.

Thank you very much.

Q. Mr. President, how are you going to make up with the Democratic leaders who fought this trade agreement so vociferously?

The President. Well, I thought what they all said tonight was a very good signal. At the end of that debate I was deeply moved by the efforts that people on both sides of the issue made to reach out to each other and to say that we have to make this work now, we have to go forward now, we have to build our economy. And I think you will see that happening. I think you will see a greater sense of unity and commitment to have the kind of job training programs we need, to have the kind of investment strategies we need to keep forcing these trade barriers down abroad.

And I must say, too, I hope we'll see in the future some more of this bipartisan effort to build economic security for Americans, because a lot of our national security in the future is going to be involved with rebuilding our economic strength from the grassroots up. And that's a very hopeful part of this debate.

Q. What about the relationship with organized labor, sir?

The President. Well, one of the things I learned, again, in this fight is that they have an enormous amount of energy and ability to organize and ability to channel the passions and feelings of their workers. You know, when you think about it, we had the White House, the leaders of both parties, an enormous amount of support, and we had to come from a long

way back to win this fight because of the work they did largely. And what I want to do is to ask them to join me now, as I said tonight, in making sure that the labor and environmental agreements are honored, in going on to the health care battle, in going on to other economic battles, and in making sure we give our working people the kind of education and training programs they need to compete in this different and very competitive global economy.

Thank you.

NOTE: The President spoke at 11:03 p.m. in the Grand Foyer at the White House.

Nomination for Chair of the Federal Deposit Insurance Corporation
November 17, 1993

The President announced his intention today to nominate Ricki Rhodarmer Tigert to be Chair of the Federal Deposit Insurance Corporation. If confirmed by the Senate, Tigert would be the first woman to head a Federal banking agency.

"Ricki Tigert is highly qualified for this position, with broad-based experience in both the executive and legislative branches of the Federal

Government, as well as at the Federal Reserve," said the President. "Her 15 years of private and public sector experience in banking and financial issues have prepared her well for the important task of safeguarding the savings of millions of American bank depositors."

NOTE: A biography of the nominee was made available by the Office of the Press Secretary.

Nomination for Appeals Court and District Court Judges
November 17, 1993

The President today nominated Judith Rogers, currently chief judge of the DC Court of Appeals, to be U.S. Court of Appeals judge for the District of Columbia Circuit. He also nominated attorney Thomas Vanaskie to be a U.S. District Court judge for the Middle District of Pennsylvania.

"I am particularly proud to be making these appointments today. Judith Rogers' career has been one of historic firsts, and she will be only the second African-American woman ever to

serve on a U.S. Court of Appeals. I am confident that she will continue the outstanding work she has done on Washington's highest court," said the President. "Likewise, I firmly believe that Thomas Vanaskie will exhibit all the qualities of an outstanding jurist on the District Court."

NOTE: Biographies of the nominees were made available by the Office of the Press Secretary.

Remarks on Departure for Seattle, Washington
November 18, 1993

Thank you very much. Thank you, ladies and gentlemen. Thank you, Mr. Vice President.

Let me just say that I have never been involved in an effort in which there were so many diverse people working so hard with so little concern for who got the credit after the battle was over.

I thank all those who were mentioned last night and were mentioned today by the Vice President. I will say again that I believe that his stunning performance in the debate on the Larry King show played a major role in our victory.

Now that the House has voted for the North American Free Trade Agreement, voted for America to continue to compete and win in the global economy, I want to say again how grateful I am to the Members who voted with us and how deeply I respect the opinions and convictions of those who did not and those who supported them.

It is for us now to make sure that this agreement is speedily passed by the United States Senate and then implemented as it was intended to be implemented, with the cooperation of both labor and management to make sure that it works to the benefit of the United States and to all the working people of our country. It is also our responsibility to press on until we have the kind of education and training programs we need.

And finally, it is our responsibility to make sure that we make the most of this effort in terms of our relationships with our neighbor to the south, Mexico, the rest of Latin America, and hopefully with nations all across the world who are committed to open and free trade, to lowering the barriers that they have to our products and services and to working together for more global opportunity, jobs, and growth.

Last night I called President Salinas, and I told him that the Vice President and Chief of Staff McLarty would be available to go to Mexico City when NAFTA is ratified by both nations, to meet with him and his government for indepth discussions about how best to launch this great new era in North American relations. The President gracefully welcomed this suggestion and invited the Vice President to travel to Mexico as soon as NAFTA is approved by the United States Senate and by the Mexican Senate, which is expected to be this Tuesday.

Now I am leaving for the first ever Asian and Pacific Economic Cooperation forum in Seattle with the strength in hand to fight for open markets throughout the world. The 15 Asian-Pacific economic partners that I will meet are dynamic and powerful traders and competitors. From the creative tension between their nations and ours can come an economic expansion that will sustain us for years to come. The fastest growing part of the world economy is in Asia.

One thing is clear, by taking the courageous step of opening trade in our own hemisphere we have the economic, the political, and the moral standing to make the case that that ought to be done throughout the world, that America is serious about lowering trade barriers and promoting growth in our country and throughout the globe.

I look forward to this trip and to continuing the fight. I will remind you again, as I have said so many times in the past, there is simply no evidence that the United States or any other wealthy country can grow jobs and increase incomes unless the world economy is growing and unless we have more customers for our goods and services. We took a long step in the right direction last night, and I intend to take more steps on that course in the next few days in the Pacific Northwest.

Thank you very much.

NOTE: The President spoke at 11:28 a.m. on the South Lawn at the White House. A tape was not available for verification of the content of these remarks.

Remarks on Arrival in Seattle
November 18, 1993

Thank you very much. Thank you very much, Governor Lowry and Mayor Rice, Chairman Shrontz, ladies and gentlemen. I thought I ought to bring Air Force One home. And I'm glad to be back here myself, and I do love this town. Seattle has been wonderful to me. The State of Washington has been good to me. Without your support I would not have been able to take office as President and to work every day to keep the commitments I made to the American people to try to change this country for the better.

I want to thank you especially today for all the work that you in this city have done and all the work people throughout this State have done to help this Asian-Pacific Economic Cooperation meeting come off as well as it has. Everyone says you've been a wonderful host. I thank you, and your Nation thanks you.

Frank noted that a number of my Cabinet members came here with me today, along with Congressman Norm Dicks and Heather Foley, the wife of House Speaker Tom Foley. I wanted to say also that Senator Patty Murray had planned to come home with me today. I invited her here. And I want you to know why she's not here. She's not here because she is in Washington fighting to pass a crime bill that keeps in the ban on assault weapons to make our streets safer. I'm proud of her for doing that.

You know, I've been to this wonderful city for many reasons. I came here as a Governor to a Governors' Conference. I've been here on vacation. I came here many times asking your help to become President. Today I come on a truly historic mission, for this is the first meeting ever of the leaders of the nations of the Asian-Pacific Economic Cooperation group. I'll have a chance to meet with the Prime Minister of Japan, the President of China, the leaders of the other nations in this group. We'll be able to talk about regional economics and political developments. We'll be focusing on what we can do to help our own people.

Make no mistake about it: Ultimately, this meeting is about the jobs, the incomes, and the futures of the American people; about exerting American leadership in a world where there isn't a lot of growth now, so jobs are not secure,

incomes are stagnant in every wealthy country on Earth. The only way we can turn this around now is to have more growth not only in America but throughout the world.

With all of the difficulties we have today, our economy is growing more than Europe's economy. It is growing faster today than Japan's economy. Our problem in America today and Boeing's problem today is that there's not enough growth in the world economy, so people don't have enough money to buy these airplanes. And we're going to change that, beginning at this meeting for the Pacific region. I know we can do that.

America's workers are still the world's most productive. America can compete and win all over the world in all markets, if only given a fair chance and if there are sensible partnerships to promote growth. People cannot spend money they do not have.

So we come here today, hoping to drive down trade barriers, open up trade opportunities, and promote more growth. Seattle has long seen itself as the portal of the Pacific. Today, it is the portal to the Asian-Pacific region, the world's fastest growing economy, the largest region in our world in terms of population, with enormous potential for American prosperity and new partnerships for peace and freedom and democracy.

Washington exports more per person than any other State in our Nation. And over 80 percent of those exports go to the Asian-Pacific region. You know that. You know also that Boeing is America's largest exporter, and that no company in the world better exemplifies the potential of worldwide economic partnerships to create opportunity for people right here at home in America.

I'm proud that I've worked with the Transportation Secretary and the Commerce Secretary and others in my administration to see that your aircraft get full and fair consideration in the global market. Someone sort of made fun of me the other day. They said, "You know, President Clinton is almost like a rug merchant out there selling American products." Well, I'm not ashamed that I've asked other countries to buy Boeing, and I'll do it again if given half the chance.

I was so pleased this week that Boeing reached an agreement with Gulf Air, based in Bahrain, to sell six of your new 777 wide-body planes with an option to purchase another six, an agreement that could be worth $2 billion. I was pleased to read in the paper today of Boeing's agreement with Southwest Airlines. I think you all know we're working on other sales in the Middle East. And I'm also proud to say that I am delighted that Boeing was selected as the prime contractor for America's space station, something I worked hard to save from the budget ax in the last session of Congress. That's another global partnership because now we're going to develop that space station in partnership with the Russians in further pursuit of peace and global economic prosperity.

And finally, I want to say a special word of thanks to Congressman Norm Dicks for his initiative in getting Congress to initiate a new airlift initiative to supplement our present airlift capacity and replace some of our old planes by buying off-the-shelf commercial airlines, like the 747. I commend Norm Dicks for that initiative. It can save the Defense Department money and put people in Washington State to work.

I ask you here to continue your resolve in the face of adversity, to be an example to the rest of our Nation that we can compete and win in this global economy.

As Frank said, and as Governor Lowry and Mayor Rice noted, we've just come through a tough fight in the Congress where good people on both sides argued about what was best for the working families of America. I did everything I could for 12 years to advance the cause of working people as a Governor. I ran for President because I thought we could expand the horizons of young people and preserve the American dream and make a strength out of our diversity in the Nation as you have done in Seattle. That's why I ran.

This debate over NAFTA was very profitable, very productive, but sometimes very painful because some of the best friends I ever had were on the other side of that debate. And they were on the other side because they were tired of seeing Americans work harder for lower wages to pay higher prices for health care, housing, and education to have less security in their basic lives. That was a genuine fear that should be honored by every person in public life today. Those are the fears we have to answer.

I disagreed on the solution because I believe that the only way a rich country can grow richer is to find more customers for its products and services. In the absence of that we cannot continue to grow.

We are getting more and more productive, as we have to do to compete. But what does that mean? That means fewer people can produce more things. If fewer people produce more things and you still want more jobs at higher incomes, there must be more customers. There is no alternative.

But make no mistake about it, my fellow Americans, the fight over NAFTA shows us the best of both sides. The winning side was right. We ought to expand our trade. We've got to bring down trade barriers. We have to reach out to the rest of the world. We need a partnership, not only with Mexico but with all of Latin America, 700 million people plus, in a giant trading cooperative partnership. We need that. But we also need to guarantee every American working family the education and training they need, the investment in their communities they need, the security of health care that can never be taken away, and an economic policy dedicated to growing jobs and raising incomes and benefiting the ordinary citizens of this country. That is what we have to do.

Our economic strategy is simple, direct, and I think correct: Put our own economic house in order, enable our people to compete and win in the global economy, and find more markets for our products and services. Just in the last 10 months the United States Congress has enacted an historic economic plan that has brought interest rates down to record lows, kept inflation down, increased investment, permitted millions of Americans to refinance their homes, and created more jobs in the private sector in the last 10 months than in the previous 4 years. It is not nearly enough, but it's a darn good beginning, and we're glad to have it.

We must now move on to invest in education and training and new technologies, and helping us to win from downsizing defense by converting to domestic technologies and opening the world to those markets. We can do it, and that's what this meeting is all about. So I say to you, again, you have helped America to make history here in Seattle.

The meeting of the leaders of the Asian-Pacific region, if we make wise decisions and if we begin a long-term, disciplined partnership for growth and opportunity, can create jobs here and jobs across the Pacific, can raise incomes here and give hope to people who never had it all across the largest ocean on the globe. We can do this. And when we do, I hope you will always take pride in knowing that it began here in Washington, America's trading State, America's model for the future, in a town that's been awfully good to me and is now a wonderful example for the entire United States.

Thank you very much, and God bless you all.

NOTE: The President spoke at 2:50 p.m. at Boeing Field. In his remarks, he referred to Mayor Norman B. Rice of Seattle and Frank A. Shrontz, chairman and chief executive officer, Boeing Co.

Message to the Congress Transmitting a Report on United States Activities in the United Nations
November 18, 1993

To the Congress of the United States:

I am pleased to transmit herewith a report of the activities of the United States Government in the United Nations and its affiliated agencies during the calendar year 1992. The report is required by the United Nations Participa-tion Act (Public Law 264, 79th Congress; 22 U.S.C. 287b).

WILLIAM J. CLINTON

The White House,
November 18, 1993.

Statement by the Press Secretary on the President's Message on NAFTA to Latin American Heads of State
November 18, 1993

Following passage of the NAFTA implement-ing legislation by the House of Representatives on November 17 the President sent the follow-ing message to heads of state and government of Paraguay, Uruguay, Brazil, Chile, Argentina, Ecuador, Venezuela, Peru, Colombia, Suriname, Guyana, Bolivia, Costa Rica, Panama, Honduras, El Salvador, Dominican Republic, Belize, Gua-temala, Nicaragua, Haiti, Barbados, The Baha-mas, St. Lucia, St. Vincent and The Grenadines, St. Kitts and Nevis, Antigua and Barbuda, Ja-maica, Dominica, Trinidad and Tobago, and Grenada:

"I am pleased to inform you that the imple-menting legislation for the North American Free Trade Agreement was passed on November 17 by the United States House of Representatives. This represents the first critical step on the road to U.S. implementation of the Agreement. I hope to win approval of the implementing legis-lation next week by the United States Senate. The other signatory parties, Canada and Mexico, are completing their ratification procedures.

"This is an historic occasion. The NAFTA will benefit all the people of our hemisphere. It manifests the confidence and optimism with which the United States and our immediate neighbors face the future. It epitomizes our dedication to the development of a cooperative and prosperous post-Cold War world based on open and dynamic economies, a clean environ-ment, protection of workers' rights and expan-sion of democracy.

"The NAFTA will capitalize on the tremen-dous opportunities which reforms in Mexico and elsewhere in the Americas have given us to open the way to trade liberalization throughout the hemisphere. As we link our economies we not only will increase the efficiency of production in each country but also will create new, better quality jobs and improve the entire hemisphere's competitiveness in the global marketplace. The NAFTA will set the stage for freer trade and sustainable, more equitable economic development throughout Latin America and the Caribbean for the benefit of our combined populations of 700 million. It will also give an enormous boost to our efforts to complete the GATT Uruguay Round so we can continue to expand the global economy.

"I am grateful for the hemisphere-wide backing the NAFTA enjoys. Your expressions of support, both individual and issued collectively through the Organization of American States,

the Rio Group, the Caribbean Community and the Meeting of Central American Presidents have helped me convey to the people of the United States the commitment of Latin American and Caribbean nations to opening their markets so that freer trade may benefit all. I am proud to have your support in this historic endeavor and I look forward to working with you to make freer trade throughout this hemisphere a reality."

Nomination for the Export-Import Bank of the United States
November 18, 1993

The President announced his intention today to nominate Maria Luisa M. Haley to be a member of the Board of Directors of the Export-Import Bank of the United States.

"I have been very impressed with Maria Haley's work over the years, as an aide to me here at the White House, and working for our

Industrial Development Commission in Arkansas," said the President. "I expect that she will continue to do well on the Export-Import Bank Board."

NOTE: A biography of the nominee was made available by the Office of the Press Secretary.

Nomination for United States District Court Judges
November 18, 1993

The President today nominated two U.S. district court judges for Louisiana: Tucker Melancon for the Western District, and Helen "Ginger" Berrigan for the Eastern District.

"I have pledged to the American people that I would appoint Federal judges committed to

public service," said the President. "In Tucker Melancon and Ginger Berrigan, the people of Louisiana will have just that."

NOTE: Biographies of the nominees were made available by the Office of the Press Secretary.

Exchange With Reporters Following Discussions With Prime Minister Jean Chrétien of Canada in Seattle
November 18, 1993

NAFTA

Q. [*Inaudible*]—resolve your differences on NAFTA?

The President. Well, I wouldn't say we resolved them all, but we had a very good meeting, and we agreed that our respective trade representatives would get together, Mr.

MacLaren and Ambassador Kantor, and try to work through the issues in a timely fashion. And I feel comfortable that we've set up a good process. We've identified what the points of concern are, and I think we've got a good shot to work it out.

Q. Mr. Prime Minister, can you resolve the issues now without completely reopening

NAFTA?

Prime Minister Chrétien. That debate is going on at this time. We've discussed the nature of the problem and we tried to find a way to solve the problem. I guess we could, but I'm not sure. That's why, you know, we'll have to reflect on the nature of the problem, and we have only a few weeks to make a final decision because proclamation is for the first of January. But I'm confident that they seem to understand our position and understand the American position, too. So, yes, I'm optimistic that we can find a solution. The technique is something to be worked on, and we'll find a solution. There is always a solution to a problem.

Q. What are the—problems?

Prime Minister Chrétien. For us, we talk about a clear definition of what is subsidy and what is dumping and counterbidding. We want to have rules on that; it's extremely important for us. So we're debating that at this moment, how can we find the process to solve this problem and discuss other issues like water and so on. We hope to find the proper solution in the weeks to come.

Trade With Japan and China

Q. Mr. President can you coax China and Japan to open their markets to U.S. products?

The President. We hope so. That's one of the things we're working on here. And in a larger sense, both Canada and the United States being the sort of Western partners in this Asian-Pacific economic group, we want very much to continue to buy from those Asian countries, and we want them to buy our products. We want to build a free trading relationship that will support the growth of Asia and support jobs in our nations. Both of us are very excited about it. We're happy to have this meeting here being hosted in North America.

Prime Minister Chrétien. We want to reassure them, too, that what is happening in North America at this moment, it's not a bloc that will become protectionist. It's very important that they understand that now we want to expand trade with the other nations in the Pacific, because there will be more wealth around the world, more jobs for the people who are seeking jobs—United States and Canada.

NOTE: The exchange began at approximately 9:15 p.m. at the Westin Hotel. This exchange was released by the Office of the Press Secretary on November 19. A tape was not available for verification of the content of this exchange.

Remarks to the Seattle APEC Host Committee
November 19, 1993

Thank you so much for that warm welcome, and thank you, all of you, for everything you have done to make this conference of the Asian-Pacific economic council a success. I want to thank your Governor for his leadership in coming all the way to Washington, DC, to help me pass the NAFTA agreement and for speaking up for it and as the leader of the State which leads America in per capita trade. I want to thank my good friend Mayor Rice, who heads this wonderful city which has been voted the best city in America in which to do business, in no small measure because of your Mayor.

I'm glad to see my friend and former colleague Governor Roberts out there. I must say I sort of jumped when Governor Lowry introduced her as his neighbor to the south. I never thought of Oregon in the south before. That's a lesson for this whole conference: Perspective is very important. [*Laughter*]

I have one member of your delegation here, Congressman Norm Dicks, who came back with me yesterday; and Speaker Foley is on the way. But I'm glad to see him here. The Washington delegation has been enormously supportive of this administration in the cause of economic expansion, and I am very grateful for that.

Senator Murray wanted to come back with me also, but she's on the floor of the Senate even as I speak here, debating the crime bill and trying to pass it with 100,000 new police officers and the Brady bill and an historic ban on assault weapons, which she's working hard to keep in the bill. For my part, I hope it stays in there.

I love Seattle. I always love to come here.

I called home last night, and both my wife and my daughter had chewed me out because I was here, and they weren't. We've had some wonderful days here. This morning I got up, and I went running in Green Lake Park. And I didn't turn green, but I nearly did. It was a vigorous run.

I am delighted that so many members of our administration came with me: The Secretary of Commerce, Ron Brown, my Chief of Staff, Mack McLarty, and our National Economic Adviser, Bob Rubin, are over here to my right, but we also have the Trade Ambassador, Mickey Kantor, here and the Secretary of State, Warren Christopher. They've all come here to make it clear how important we believe this wonderful meeting is to our future interests, as I know you do. I'm glad to see so many of my friends here from other States in the West and, indeed, from all across America.

This organization, APEC, has historically had 15 members that together account for more than half the world's output: Australia, Brunei, Canada, China, Indonesia, Japan, Hong Kong, Malaysia, New Zealand, the Philippines, Singapore, South Korea, Chinese Taipei, Thailand, and the United States. At this meeting, we are adding Mexico and Papua New Guinea. This will be the first time that the leaders of all of these economies have gathered together. APEC reflects the Asian-Pacific values of harmony and consensus building. Our goal this week will be to do some of both.

This city is the appropriate place to have this meeting. Not only is Washington State the most trade-oriented State in the Union, but as I learned from the Governor on the way up the stairs when I asked him, 80 percent of your trade is tied to the Asian-Pacific region, and 90 percent of the imports to this port in Seattle come from Asia. Over half of Boeing's planes, Microsoft's computer programs, and Washington's wheat are sold abroad.

Today I want to talk with you who have done so much to make this meeting a reality about why APEC and the Asian-Pacific region will play a vital role in our American quest to create jobs and opportunity and security. And I want to begin by talking about what I believe our broader purposes as a nation must be as we near the end of this tumultuous century.

Once in a great while, nations arrive at moments of choice that define their course and their character for years to come. These moments are always hard, because change is always hard, because they are steeped in controversy, because they are often full of risk. We know and regret the moments when our Nation has chosen unwisely in the past, such as when we turned the world toward protectionism and isolationism after World War I or when we failed for so long to face up to the awful consequences of slavery. We celebrate the chapters of American history in which we chose boldly: the Declaration of Independence, the Louisiana Purchase, the containment of communism, the embrace of the civil rights movement.

Now we have arrived again at such a moment. Change is upon us. We can do nothing about that. The pole stars that guided our affairs in the past years have disappeared. The Soviet Union is gone. Communist expansionism has ended. At the same time, a new global economy of constant innovation and instant communication is cutting through our world like a new river, providing both power and disruption to the people and nations who live along its course.

Given the disappearance of the Soviet threat and the persistence of problems at home, from layoffs and stagnant incomes to crime rates, many Americans are tempted to pull back and to turn away from the world.

This morning, I ran with some of my friends from Seattle, and we were talking about the irony that some of us felt being so excited about this meeting and all of its promise and prosperity. And one of my friends who is a judge here was going to court to deal with candidates for parole and talking to me about all the young children who are in trouble, even in this, one of our most vibrant cities. In times like this, it is easy to just turn away. Our people have a right to feel troubled. The challenge of the global economy and our inadequate response to it for years is shaking the moorings of middle class security. So are the destructive social developments here at home and our inadequate response to them. But we simply cannot let our national worries blind us to our national interests. We cannot find security in a policy of withdrawal guided by fear. We must, we must pursue a strategy of involvement grounded in confidence in our ability to do well in the future.

Our security in this new era clearly requires us to reorder our military forces and to refine our force structure for the coming years. But our national security also depends upon enlarging the world's community of market democracies because democracies make more peaceful and constructive partners. That's why we're leading an ambitious effort to support democratic and market reforms in all the nations of the former Soviet Union.

And more than ever, our security is tied to economics. Military threats remain, and they require our vigilance and resolve. But increasingly, our place in the world will be determined as much by the skills of our workers as by the strength of our weapons, as much by our ability to pull down foreign trade barriers as our ability to breach distant ramparts.

As President I've worked to put these economic concerns of our people at the heart of our domestic and our foreign policy. We cannot remain strong abroad unless we are strong at home. Stagnant nations eventually lose the ability to finance military readiness, to afford an activist foreign policy, or to inspire allies by their examples. You have only to look at what happened to the former Soviet Union to see that lesson writ large. It collapsed from the inside out, not from the outside in.

At the same time, creating jobs and opportunities for our people at home requires us to be engaged abroad, so that we can open foreign markets to our exports and our businesses. Today exports are the life blood of our economic growth. Since the mid-1980's, half our increases in incomes and almost all the expansion in manufacturing jobs in the United States have been tied to exports. This trend will continue. All wealthy nations—and many more than we—are having difficulty creating jobs and raising incomes even when there is economic growth. Why is that? Because workers in advanced countries must become ever more productive to deal with competition from low-wage countries on the one hand, and high-skilled, high-tech countries on the other. Being more productive simply means that fewer and fewer people can produce more and more goods.

In an environment like that, if you want to increase jobs and raise incomes, the only way to do it is to find more customers for each country's product. There is no alternative. No one has yet made any convincing case that any wealthy country can lower unemployment and raise incomes by closing up its borders. The only way to do it is to expand global growth and to expand each country's fair share of global trade. This country must do both.

To prosper, therefore, we have to try to get all nations to pursue a strategy of growth. I have worked hard on that. For 10 years, I watched America go to these G–7 meetings and be hammered on by other nations to reduce our deficit, to stop taking money out of the global pool of investment capital, to help to contribute to global growth by showing some discipline here at home. Well, we've done that. We've done that. And now we must get our partners in Europe and Japan to also follow strategies that will promote global growth.

Much of our trade deficit problems today are the result directly of slow economic growth abroad. And this Nation now is growing more rapidly than all of our wealthiest competitors. We must do that. But we must also compete, not retreat. We cannot confuse our objectives with our problems. We have no alternative, even in a time of slow global economic growth, to taking the steps to expand world trade.

We are pursuing a new global trade agreement under GATT by the end of this year. In July, we negotiated a market opening agreement at the G–7 to help advance the GATT process. That market opening agreement offers the prospect of hundreds of thousands of new jobs in the American economy.

We have placed our vital relationship with Japan on a new foundation that will allow our workers and our businesses greater access to Japanese markets when we complete the process. We have established a new dialog for economic cooperation with Korea aimed at improving trade and the regulatory environment for the United States and other foreign businesses in that nation.

Now, after a long and difficult national debate, we're about to secure something I have fought for tooth and nail, as the previous speakers discussed, the North American Free Trade act. I fought for NAFTA because I believe it will create American jobs and a lot of them and because I believe it will improve the quality of our life and because I know it will lead us to similar agreements with the rest of the market democracies in Latin America and because I believe that it sends a message that our hemisphere wanted to hear and that the world needs to hear: The cold war may be over, but the United States is not about to pull up its stakes and go home. We will remain engaged in the world.

This, after all, is the real significance of

NAFTA. It does not create a trading bloc; it is a building block in our efforts to expand world economic opportunity and global growth and, in the process, to promote jobs and opportunity for Americans.

Wednesday's vote for NAFTA enables me to begin this APEC meeting bolstered by a bold expression of America's intent to remain involved in the world. And the NAFTA vote combined with this APEC conference greatly strengthens our push for an even bigger potential breakthrough, a new GATT agreement.

I want to be clear about this. This Nation will not accept a flawed agreement, but if we can achieve one that meets our standards, the benefits to our people could be enormous. Over the first 10 years, a good GATT agreement could create 1.4 million American jobs and boost the average American family income by $1,700 a year. Over a decade, it could expand the world's economy by $5 trillion. This, my fellow Americans, is the answer to 20 years of stagnant wages for the hard-working middle class.

Our willingness to fight for these initiatives, for NAFTA, for an invigorated APEC, for a good new GATT agreement, should make it clear to the world that America will lead the charge against global recession and the pressures for retrenchment it has created, not just here in our country but in all the advanced nations of the world. Years from today, Americans will look back on these months as a moment when our Nation looked squarely at a new economic era and did not flinch from its challenges.

As we exert our leadership in the global economy, we have to pursue a three-part strategy. We must first continue to make our economy and our people more competitive. Second, we must focus our global initiatives on the fastest growing regions. Third, we must create new arrangements for international relations so the forces of this new era benefit our people as well as our partners.

Our first challenge involves actions here at home. After years of neglect we're putting our economic house in order so that we can compete and win abroad. We've enacted a sweeping deficit reduction measure that points the way back to solvency. The deficit this year was cut about $50 billion below where it was estimated to be on the day that I took office, largely because of plummeting interest rates that are directly resultant from the deficit reduction efforts.

We're investing in education and training and the knowledge and skills of our people and the technologies of the future. We're working to ensure that we have the means to adjust to a dynamic world economy. We created some special bridge programs for any workers displaced by NAFTA. And early next year, I will propose a plan to transform America's unemployment system into a reemployment system of lifetime education and training and job placement services for workers who have to change jobs many times. Particularly as we enact NAFTA, we must recognize that we have a solemn obligation to make our involvement in international trade serve the interest of our people. That means they have to be able to adjust to change.

And if I might just add a parenthesis here to all of you who are very much future oriented, this country today is really being limited in what we can do because so many of our systems, economic and social, are organized for conditions that no longer exist. We are not organized to make the changes we all want to make.

The unemployment system is simply an example of that. The unemployment system was created at a time when the average length of unemployment was shorter than it is today and when the average unemployed person when called back to work went back to his or her former employer, which is not the case today. So unemployment could literally be a more passive system. You could draw money out of it. Your wage would go down for awhile, but you knew you'd be called back to your old employer. That's fine for a static economy. It doesn't work for a dynamic economy where the average 18-year-old must change jobs seven times in a lifetime, where the average unemployed person is unemployed for longer, and when most people don't get called back to the same job they gave up.

The unemployment system, in short, is now an unfair tax on employers because it doesn't function and a rip-off for employees because it doesn't help them. Why? Because the system was organized for a reality that isn't there anymore. So what the Labor Secretary is trying to do is to set up a system where people who lose their jobs immediately—and even before they lose their jobs, if possible—begin training programs, begin job placement programs, begin thinking about what the future really holds, instead of living with a system that was yesterday's reality and is today's sham.

Time here does not permit this, but there are a lot of creative people in this room, and I cannot resist this opportunity to say, if you will look at the operative systems in the courts, in the juvenile system, in all the social systems in this country, in the education and training systems, and in the economic arrangements of this country, you will find example after example after example after example where good, bright, creative people, who know what the problems are, are struggling with organizations which thwart their ability to deal with the world as it is. This is one of our great challenges, my fellow Americans, and we must face it.

With the end of the cold war, we're trying to open billions of dollars' worth of formerly restricted high-tech goods to export markets. We're working to speed the conversion of companies, of workers, of communities from defense to commercially successful economies. With the Vice President's leadership, we're reinventing Government, reducing bureaucracy. We're about to reform our health care system in ways that will relieve businesses burdened by unfairly rising costs and provide security for families terrorized by uncertain coverage.

All these steps to make our people and our Nation better prepared to thrive in this competitive economy are important. The beginning steps, while limited, are beginning to pay off. The deficit has declined. Interest rates have been at historic lows. Inflation rate remains low while investment is increasing. Housing starts have climbed for 3 straight months. Employment is increasing. In the first 10 months there has been more private sector job increase than in the previous 4 years. To be sure, there is still much to do, but this is a good beginning.

The second part of this strategy must be to expand the sweep of our engagement. For decades, our foreign policy focused on containment of communism, a cause led by the United States and our European allies. I want to emphasize this here today: Europe remains at the core of our alliances. It is a central partner for the United States in security, in foreign policy, and in commerce. But as our concern shifts to economic challenges that are genuinely global, we must look across the Pacific as well as the Atlantic. We must engage the world's fastest growing economies.

Our support for NAFTA is a recognition not only that Mexico is our closest big neighbor and a very important part of our future but that Latin America is the second fastest growing part of the world and a part of the world increasingly embracing both democracy and free market economics, two things that have eluded that continent for too long.

The fastest growing region, of course, is the Asian Pacific, a region that has to be vital for our future, as it has been for our past. A lot of people forget that we began our existence as a nation as a Pacific power. By the time of George Washington's Inauguration, American ships were already visiting China. In this century, we fought three major wars in the Pacific. Thousands of our people still remain stationed in the region to provide stability and security in the armed services. And our cultural bonds are profoundly strong. There are now 7 million American citizens of Asian descent.

The Asian Pacific has taken on an even greater importance as its economy has exploded. It's a diverse region spanning 16 time zones, having at least 20 different major languages and hundreds of dialects. This is a region where many rice farmers still harvest their crops by hand, and yet it is the home to the world's fastest growing cities. Yet amid this great diversity a distinct economy has emerged, built upon ancient cultures connected through decentralized business networks, linked by modern communications, and joined by common denominators of high investment, hard work, and creative entrepreneurship.

What has happened to Asia in the past half-century is amazing and unprecedented. Just three decades ago, Asia had only 8 percent of the world's GDP. Today it exceeds 25 percent. These economies are growing at 3 times the rate of the established industrial nations. In a short time, many of these economies have gone from being dominoes to dynamos; from minor powers racked by turmoil—[*applause*]—yes, you can clap for them. It's true.

The press will ask me at the end of this speech who gave me that phrase. It came from Win Lord, our Assistant Secretary of State for Far Eastern Affairs. He also gives me good ideas, as well as good phrases. [*Laughter*]

This is a hopeful time. For the first time, for the first time in this century, no great military rivalry divides the Asia-Pacific region. Active hostilities have yielded to possibilities for cooperation and gain. Of course, the region still has problems and dangers. Tens of millions of

Asians still live on less than a dollar a day. There are territorial disputes, ethnic tensions, and weapons proliferation. This sudden growth has led to serious environmental strains from smoke-choked cities to toxic dumping. And there are human rights abuses and repression which continue to affect millions of people throughout the region.

The economic explosion has been a source of anxiety for many Americans. Our workers are concerned that their jobs, their markets are being lost to Asia. Of the nations that are represented here, I believe we have a trade deficit with all but one. These trade imbalances with Japan and China alone account for more than two-thirds of our total trade deficit. And we do have a trade deficit, as I said, with virtually every one of the nations.

Yet, ultimately the growth of Asia can and should benefit our Nation. Over the past 5 years, our exports to every one of these nations has increased by at least 50 percent. Much of what Asia needs to continue on its growth pattern are goods and services in which we are strong: aircraft, financial services, telecommunications, infrastructure, and others. Already, Asia is our largest trading partner. Exports account for 2.5 million jobs here in America, to Asia. Increasing our share of that market by one percent would add 300,000 jobs to the American economy. This is an effort worth making.

Of course, we must continue to press the nations to be more open to our products as we are to them. We've made a good start with the economic framework agreement with Japan, and I look forward to discussing the elements of that and the progress we can make with Prime Minister Hosokawa later today.

We're also determined to work with China to eliminate its trade barriers and to raise the issue of our continuing concerns over human rights and weapons sales. I look forward to doing all that when I meet with President Jiang today, in an effort to put our relationship with China on a more constructive path but still one that deals with all of these issues that are important to the United States.

We do not intend to bear the cost of our military presence in Asia and the burdens of regional leadership only to be shut out of the benefits of growth that that stability brings. It is not right. It's not in the long-term interest of our Asian friends. And ultimately, it is a trade relationship that is simply not sustainable. So

we must use every means available in the Pacific, as elsewhere, to promote a more open world economy through global agreements, regional efforts, and negotiations with individual countries.

As we make these efforts, United States business must do more to reach out across the Pacific. I know Seattle's business community understands the potential that lies in the Asian-Pacific region. But millions of our businesses do not. We cannot have customers where we are not there to make the sale. I want American businesses to see the opportunities, to hear the success stories not only here but all across the Nation. I want more American businesses to follow the examples of firms like H.F. Henderson Industries in West Caldwell, New Jersey, which manufactures automatic weighing systems. This small firm's sales to China, South Korea, Australia, Singapore, and Hong Kong have added over two dozen jobs to its payroll of 150. You think about that. If every company in America with 150 employees could add two dozen jobs by exports to Asia, we would have a much smaller unemployment problem in a very short time. We have to do a better job of piercing those markets even as we press for them to be open.

In July, I made my first trip overseas as President to Asia. During that trip, I proposed this leaders meeting and described a vision of a new Pacific community. To underscore the importance we place on working for shared prosperity, for security, and for democracy, as I said earlier, the Secretary of State, the Secretary of Commerce, our Trade Representative, they've all come to Seattle, all going to give major speeches here, all going to make our presence felt. We want to be a partner with all of the other nations that are here in making this Pacific community.

But as I said earlier about our problems here at home with the unemployment system, you could also say the same thing about the international system. We have to develop new institutional arrangements that support our national economic and security interests internationally.

If you look at the end of World War II and the success that flowed from it, that didn't happen by accident. Visionaries like Harry Truman and George Marshall, George Kennan, Dean Acheson, Averell Harriman worked with other nations to build institutions like NATO, the IMF, the World Bank, the GATT process. We take it for granted now. But it took them a few years to put this together. And it wasn't self-evident at the time that it had to be done. And a lot of people thought it was a waste of time or effort, and others thought that it would never work, and others thought that it wasn't even a good idea. But these people had the vision to see that collective security, expanded trade, and growth around the world were in the interest of the ordinary American citizen.

We now have to bring the same level of vision to this time of change. We've done that through our vote for NAFTA. We will do so again at the NATO summit this January, where I will recommend a new partnership for peace to draw Central and Eastern Europe toward our community of security. And we're working to build a prosperous and peaceful Asian-Pacific region through our work here with APEC.

This is still a young organization. I want to salute those who had the vision to establish it, such as former Australian Prime Minister Robert Hawke and others, including President Bush and those in his administration who wanted to host this regional leaders meeting in Washington State. But I want to say also that we now must imagine what this organization should be in the 21st century.

Over time, there is a lot we may be able to do through this organization that no one ever thought about before. It could become a forum for considering development priorities in Asia, for working with the Asian Development Bank to assure that all can share in the region's economic growth. It could help to focus attention on barriers to trade and growth. It could evolve into a forum for dispute resolution on economic matters.

The mission of this organization is not to create a bureaucracy that can frustrate economic growth but to help build connections among economies to promote economic growth. Although we are still only formulating APEC's agenda, we can speculate what some of those connections might be.

This organization, for example, could help to set up common telecommunication standards so firms don't need to have a different product design for each separate country. It could help us to move toward an open skies agreement that could lower fares for airline passengers and cargo and provide greater consumer choices over routes. It could promote solutions to the environmental problems of this populous and

energy-devouring region, problems that are truly staggering today, so that we could guarantee that a polluted quality of life does not undermine a rising standard of living.

Protecting the Pacific environment also can be a particular source of American business opportunities. Asia's purchases of environmental equipment likely will rise by $40 billion by the end of this decade. And our Nation, which has pioneered many of those technologies, should be there to claim the large share of that market.

APEC can complement our Nation's other efforts to open world trade. It can provide a counterbalance to our bilateral and our global efforts. If we encounter obstacles in a bilateral negotiation, we should be able to appeal to other APEC members to help us to resolve the disputes. If our efforts to secure global trade agreements falter, then APEC still offers us a way to expand markets within this, the fastest growing region of the globe.

I expect this first meeting of APEC leaders to focus on getting acquainted and on sharing perspectives. Whatever we do must be done in a spirit of genuine partnership and mutual respect in the interest of all of the nations involved. This cannot be a United States show. This has got to be an Asian-Pacific combined partnership.

Nonetheless, I believe it is our obligation to propose some tangible steps to move forward. We will propose that Secretary Bentsen organize a meeting of the APEC's finance ministers to advance our dialog on the broad issues affecting economic growth. We will propose the formation of an Asia-Pacific business roundtable to promote greater discussion within the region's private sectors. We will ask the leaders to endorse the establishment of an Asia-Pacific education foundation to promote understanding and a sense of community among our region's young people. These first steps are small. But we should not understate or underestimate the scope of the journey that they could begin.

Today we take for granted the importance of many institutions that seemed unlikely when they were first created. For example, we can't imagine now how we could have weathered the cold war without NATO. In the same way, future generations may look back and say they can't imagine how the Asian-Pacific region could have thrived in such a spirit of harmony without the existence of APEC. Even though this organization is in its infancy and its first leaders meeting is not intended to make decisions, we should not hesitate to think boldly about where such efforts could lead.

For this organization, these meetings and these relationships we are forging today can lead our members toward shared expectations about our common responsibilities and our common future. Even now we can begin to imagine what a new Pacific community might look like by the end of this decade, and that's not very far away.

Imagine an Asian-Pacific region in which robust and open economic competition is a source of jobs and opportunity without becoming a source of hostility and instability, a sense of resentment or unfairness. Imagine a region in which the diversity of our economies remains a source of dynamism and enrichment, just as the diversity of our own people in America make our Nation more vibrant and resilient. Imagine this region in which newly emerging economic freedoms are matched by greater individual freedoms, political freedoms, and human rights; a region in which all nations, all nations, enjoy those human rights and free elections.

In such a future we could see Japan fast becoming a model of political reform as well as an economic colossus, pursuing policies that enable our economic relations to be a source of greater mutual benefit and mutual satisfaction to our peoples. We could see China expressing the greatness and power of its people and its culture by playing a constructive regional and global leadership role while moving toward greater internal liberalization. We could see Vietnam more integrated into the region's economic and political life after providing the fullest possible accounting of those Americans who did not return from the war there.

We could even see a Korean Peninsula that no longer braces for war but that lives in peace and security because its people, both north and south, have decided on the terms of reunification. We could see a region where weapons of mass destruction are not among the exports and where security and stability are assured by mutual strength, respect, and cooperation, a region in which diverse cultures and economies show their common wisdom and humanity by joining to preserve the glory of the Pacific environment for future generations.

Such goals extend beyond tomorrow's agenda. But they must not lie beyond our vision. This week our Nation has proved a willingness to reach out in the face of change to further the cause of progress. Now we must do so again. We must reach out to the economies of the Pacific. We must work with them to build a better future for our people and for theirs. At this moment in history, that is our solemn responsibility and our great opportunity.

Thank you very much.

NOTE: The President spoke at 9:42 a.m. in the Spanish Ballroom at the Four Seasons Hotel.

Exchange With Reporters Prior to Discussions With Prime Minister Morihiro Hosokawa of Japan in Seattle
November 19, 1993

China

Q. Mr. President, having accused the Bush administration of "coddle China," what is your response to those who are upset about the computer sale and other initiatives which you are making to the Chinese?

The President. That we haven't changed our policy. Our policy is to try to engage China but to be very firm with the human rights issues, to be very firm on the weapons proliferation issues. But there are 1.2 billion people in China, and we don't believe we can achieve our objectives within the context of complete isolation. And in this case, the computer sale for their weather service is something that they could get elsewhere if they didn't get it from the United States. I think it is an important indication that we are willing to work with them if they will reciprocate across a whole broad range of issues involving human rights, proliferation, and trade. And of course, in my next meeting I'll have a chance to talk about that.

Japan

Q. And sir, what do you expect from the Japanese now? It's been a few months since Tokyo——

The President. Well, first of all, let me say it has been a few months, but it's been a remarkable few months for Japan. I want to applaud the Prime Minister on his successes in promoting political reform. We had a very good meeting already today, and we have many more things to discuss.

I have invited him to the United States, and he has accepted to come in early February to continue our discussions on our bilateral economic relationships and what we can do to improve them, to deal with the trade deficit, and to do a number of other things that we're trying to do. And so we're going to have another meeting in early February, and we'll have more to say about that then.

But I've been very impressed, I must say, with the changes that he's making in Japan and with so much on his plate with the political issue that they still—this government has opened its construction market more to us, something that I very much appreciate. And it's an indication that we'll be able to make more progress in the months ahead.

Asian-Pacific Security

Q. Sir, when you spoke of APEC promoting security for Asia-Pacific nations, what did you have in mind? Anything along the lines of what NATO does for European security?

The President. What I meant by that is I think that we all have to work together, as we are now, on the issues of concern to us. As you know, the United States is very concerned that North Korea not become a nuclear power and adhere to the missile technology control regime, I mean, the nonproliferation of nuclear weapons issue. And we have worked very hard to try to get our inspectors in there through IAEA. And the Japanese and the Chinese, I might add, have been very cooperative with us and tried very hard to give us good advice, and we consulted together. That's the kind of thing I think we have to do more of.

Japan

Q. Can we ask the Prime Minister a question, please? Mr. Prime Minister, now that you've won your political reforms, do you think it will be possible to open up, including the rice market perhaps?

Prime Minister Hosokawa. First of all, let me say that I haven't succeeded in completing my political reform. In the Japanese House of Counselors, the situation is more difficult. And let me give you an idea. It is something like the difficulty which was faced by the U.S. Congress recently with regard to the NAFTA issue. The same level of difficulty is facing me in trying to pass political reform in the Japanese House of Counselors.

Now, with regard to the rice issue that you raised, let me point out that this is a very serious issue in Japan, and one has to be very careful in not getting this rice issue in the way of political reform.

Now, let me also say that, of course, Japan is ready to make its utmost effort to bring about the successful conclusion of the Uruguay round. But having said all of this, I will have to continue to make and exert my best efforts in order to successfully complete Japanese political reform.

[At this point, one group of reporters left the room, and another group entered.]

APEC and Japan

Q. Mr. President, do you agree with the Prime Minister on the concept of the Asian-Pacific community?

The President. We have some more talks to hold, but I believe we are generally in agreement that we should attempt to use this forum to broaden trade and deepen understanding and perhaps to accelerate the pace at which we can increase trade and economic growth in the region.

I must say, this is, I believe, my first opportunity to talk to the Japanese press since my United Nations speech. I have been very impressed with the work the Prime Minister and the new government have done in passing political reform—I know it's not over yet, but it's making good progress—and in reaching out to the United States on a number of issues. So I'm pleased with the way things are going now and very appreciative of the work the Prime Minister is doing.

Q. Mr. President, is there any difference of the atmosphere of this meeting and the former meeting in September with Prime Minister Hosokawa?

The President. With the meeting last September?

Q. Yes.

The President. I don't know how to describe it. That was also, I thought, a very good meeting. But I have an intense interest in the changes that are going on in Japan now, and I am watching them with great admiration. As you know, I think, based on what I said when I was in Japan for the G–7 meeting, I strongly feel that both our nations have a lot of changes to make. And it's always difficult to make change. So I think this meeting—there's a lot of feeling that we share a certain destiny here—the Prime Minister working on his political reform measures, and I've been working on trying to open the trading systems through NAFTA. I really very much respect what is going on in Japan.

NOTE: The President spoke at 12:14 p.m. in the North Kirkland Cutter Room at the Rainier Club. A tape was not available for verification of the content of this exchange.

Remarks and an Exchange With Reporters Following Discussions With President Jiang Zemin of China in Seattle
November 19, 1993

The President. Good afternoon. I have just completed a meeting with President Jiang of China which I believe was very productive. It was an important meeting for the people of China and the people of the United States. China, after all, is home to one of every five people who live on this planet and is the world's fastest growing major economy. We have to work together on a wide range of issues of regional significance and of global significance.

President Jiang said to me in a letter that we need to talk to each other not because we have no differences but because we do have differences and need to resolve them. Today I tried to be as forthright and clear as I could about our common interests and about our clear differences.

We agreed on the need to work on improving our relationship. We know that what we do affects not only our own people but all the people in the world. When we work together we're a powerful force for security and economic progress. As fellow members of the U.N. Security Council, we have worked side by side on many things, including Cambodia and Haiti.

In our meeting I reaffirmed the United States support for the three joint communiques as the bedrock of our one China policy. We agreed on the need to preserve the peace and stability of the Korean Peninsula and to work together to ensure that North Korea resolves the world's concerns over its nuclear problems.

We also discussed very frankly areas of dis-agreement. I emphasized to President Jiang the need for early, concrete progress on aspects of China policy and practice that are of deep concern to the American people: human rights, including Tibet; trade practices; and nonproliferation. Over the past few months we have had a number of bilateral meetings in Beijing and Washington to explore the possibilities for progress in these key areas. Our meeting today is a part of that ongoing process. I hope it can lead to substantial advances.

In our meeting today I especially stressed our concerns in the area of human rights. Last May I put forward key human rights conditions that must be met if most-favored-nation status to China is to be renewed next spring. I told President Jiang that I welcome our dialog on human rights. I hope we can make significant progress on these issues very soon. I mentioned in particular the need for prison access by the ICRC, the question of releasing political prisoners, especially those who are sick. I particularly mentioned the case of Wang Jontao. I asked for a dialog on Tibet with the Dalai Lama or his representatives. And I discussed the question of prison labor and the need for our customs officials to visit other facilities as already called for in our memorandum of understanding.

In other words, on the question of human rights, I attempted to be quite specific, not implying that the United States could dictate to China or that China could dictate to the United States the general conditions or institutions of our society, but clearly recognizing that there are human rights issues that are a barrier to the full resolution of normal and complete and constructive relations between our two nations.

I also emphasized the need for progress on our trade imbalance. We discussed the needs for greater market access and for the protection of intellectual property rights. I think our trade relationships alone indicate that the United States has not attempted to isolate China but instead has attempted to assist its movement into the global economy. After all, this year we will purchase about a third of the total Chinese exports, and we must do a better job of selling our products and services into that market.

I also stressed that we look to China to participate fully in international efforts to stem weapons proliferation. We continue to have differences on these issues. But we agreed that we should seek to resolve them through dialog and negotiation. This is clearly in the interest of both nations.

As we approach the 21st century, the relationship between our two countries will be one of the most important in the world. I believe that my meeting today with President Jiang established our determination to build on the positive aspects of our existing relations and to address far more candidly and personally than we have in the past the problems that remain between our two nations. I look forward to continuing that dialog during tomorrow's APEC leaders meeting and in other ways in the coming months.

I believe we have made a good beginning. I always believe the best beginning in a challenging situation is to be as frank and forthright as possible. And I think that I did that, and I believe that he did that.

Let me make just one other comment about a domestic issue; then I'll answer a couple of questions. I'd like to compliment the United States Senate in passing the crime bill today. It is absolutely imperative that we now resolve the differences between the Senate and the House bill, that we move ahead to get 100,000 police on the street as quickly as we can. It will still take several months even after the bill is signed to train the police and put them out there. It is a terribly important issue.

There are other matters in the bills, especially the boot camps, that I think are important. But I am distressed at the Senate filibuster of the Brady bill. I know they're going to vote one

more time tonight, and before they leave, I would urge the Senate to pass the Brady bill. It has been delayed far too long. And the attack against it, that it will not solve all the gun violence in the United States, ignores the fact that it will solve some of our problems by actually permitting us to do a weapons check of the criminal and mental health backgrounds of people who want to buy handguns. It will, it will turn up people who should not be able to buy guns, many of whom will have criminal records, some of whom may have outstanding warrants.

This is an important issue for our country. I understand that some people think the politics are still difficult. But clearly, it is the right thing to do. And I hope the Senate will reconsider its filibuster and permit the majority to rule. There's plainly a heavy majority for the Brady bill. That majority should be able to carry the day.

China-U.S. Relations

Q. Mr. President, in the photo opportunity prior to your meeting with President Jiang, he sounded reluctant to even discuss in any great detail the questions of human rights and weapons proliferation. What was his response to your concerns about those issues? And since you appear so reluctant to push China into any sort of isolation, just what do you have at your disposal to bring China around? What's your leverage there?

The President. Well, first of all, I think anybody should be reluctant to isolate a country as big as China with the potential China has for good, not only good for the 1.2 billion people of China who are enjoying this unprecedented economic growth but good in the region and good throughout the world. So our reluctance to isolate them is the right reluctance.

On the other hand, I laid down a human rights policy and a policy on trade and nonproliferation that we are going to pursue: the human rights policy in the context of MFN renewal next year and the trade and nonproliferation policies, in the proper context, that we are already pursuing. And I think that the leverage is not insignificant. After all, we are their major purchaser of products and services. We have been their commercial friend, as we should have been. I do not begrudge that. But we have got to have progress on these three fronts.

I would remind you these two countries have been somewhat estranged ever since Tiananmen

Square. And the very fact that we talked today I think is a positive sign that both of us are interested in trying to resolve our respective problems. I don't think you ever lose anything by talking with someone as long as you're honest. And I don't think there was any doubt about where the United States stands on these issues today.

Q. And his response, Mr. President?

The President. Well, he did engage and discuss a number of those things. I think, given the nature of the political environment in China and their historic reluctance to discuss these issues in public, the press statement that he made was consistent with their historic pattern. But I thought we began a dialog, and that's all I think I should say today.

North Korea

Q. Mr. President, in your meeting with Prime Minister Hosokawa and also as you mentioned in your meeting with President Jiang, you discussed the subject of North Korea. What can you tell us about your sense of how that situation is developing, whether we're moving toward a situation in which you're going to be faced with a deadline because of the IAEA's inability to eventually continue to monitor? And what sort of assurances have you gotten from the Chinese on cooperation on that issue?

The President. Well, first of all, that's precisely what we want to avoid. We want to avoid the situation where the IAEA can no longer certify that North Korea is nonnuclear. So you're in the worst of both worlds; you don't know whether it is, but you can't say that it isn't. That is what we're trying to avoid.

Secondly, you should understand that perhaps next only to South Korea, both China and Japan are deeply interested in the same objective. They do not wish to have a nuclear North Korea. And so they support the policy of trying to prevent that from happening. All three of those countries have a great deal of sensitivity about what is most likely to bring about that result. They are worried about whether sanctions would backfire. And we have discussed with them some other options, perhaps taking a more comprehensive approach to all the differences between us in an attempt to demonstrate again to North Korea that they have nothing to be afraid of from an honest dialog with the South and from allowing the inspectors to come back in.

So we are looking at what some other options are now. But this is a very important issue, and the United States, I think, clearly has the responsibility to lead on this issue. And we are doing our best to do it. We are on top of it. And I know there are those who think we should have taken a different course, who think, well, maybe we just haven't been involved in this. But I would remind you that South Korea, Japan, and China are intimately interested and personally affected by those developments. And we have consulted extensively with all three of them all along the way, and we are pursuing the policy we think has the best chance of success.

Japan

Q. Mr. President, in advance of this meeting, one journalist described Japan's historic posture toward the United States as one of obsequious arrogance, namely the endless stonewalling of various trade issues. It took us no less than 22 years to get Washington apples into Japanese markets. What is your sense of the posture of the new Japanese Government toward moving things on so we will not have to wait 22 years, for instance, to get American rice into that market?

The President. This is a different government and a different time with different objectives for the internal economy of Japan. I think that the present policy is not sustainable. On the other hand, this government was elected and this Prime Minister was elected to deal with a wide range of issues. They are working on their political reform agenda now, and I think they will conclude it soon.

The United States supports those efforts at political reform and believes that they should be encouraged. It's part of the change that is sweeping the world. After that, I believe that Prime Minister Hosokawa will move seriously on the two great economic issues that we share in common: One is what should be done to make sure that at times like this when there's a global recession, the United States, Japan, and Europe follow policies that will promote higher rates of global growth, because we can't grow unless there's a global economic growth pattern. Secondly is, what can we do to follow up on our framework agreement in which we identified some very specific areas in which we expect mutually to work together to get real results? My vision, as I said to Prime Minister

Hosokawa, for Japan is that as we move toward the 21st century, Japan will become like other great powers in terms of its openness to investment and to trade and that together we will help to create a world of far more sustained and sustainable growth and opportunity for our own people and, in the process for the developing nations as well.

Taiwan

Q. Mr. President, you just mentioned three communiques and one China policy. Does that mean somebody raised the issue of Taiwan in the bilateral meeting? And secondly, since you've visited Taiwan four times and most knowledgeable of the Taiwan issue, what you want to do in deal with U.S.-Taiwan relations?

The President. I have been there many times. I've been there five times, actually. And I have been very impressed with the remarkable transformation of the country as it has gotten more prosperous and more democratic and impressed also by the amount of investment from Taiwan into China. So that it seems that the two countries are getting along on a commercial basis, even as the rest of us are confronted with political dilemmas from time to time.

We did not really discuss that today in any detail whatever. The policy of the United States on one China is the right policy for the United States. It does not preclude us from following the Taiwan Relations Act, nor does it preclude us from the strong economic relationship we enjoy with Taiwan. There's a representative, as you know, here at this meeting. So I feel good about where we are on that. But I don't think that will be a major stumbling block in our relationship with China. I think we can work through these other things, that the practical ingenuity of the Chinese people themselves seems to be at least on a course to resolve that in some form or fashion in the years ahead.

Thank you very much.

NOTE: The President spoke at 3:15 p.m. at the Rainier Club.

Remarks at a Dinner for the APEC Forum and Business Leaders in Seattle
November 19, 1993

To my fellow leaders of the APEC nations and distinguished guests, we gather here tonight in Washington State at an historic moment. At least two other times during this century a great global struggle has ended and a new era has dawned. That has happened again today. It falls to each of us, as it fell to leaders then, to imagine and to build a new future for our people. I deeply appreciate the willingness that each of you has shown to make the long trip here to be together today.

I want to express my appreciation for the warm hospitality of the people and the elected officials of this beautiful city of Seattle in the Evergreen State of Washington. All of us in the Asian Pacific live as neighbors in a region that has long been characterized by both its commerce and its conflicts. The question for our future is whether we can reap the bounty of the Pacific without bringing its storms. There are vast differences among our economies and our people; yet these can be a great source of enrichment.

I hear the complex music of our many differing languages, and I know that in each of them our words for work, for opportunity, for children, for hope carry the same meaning. I see the roots of our many ancient civilizations, whether Confucian or Islamic or Judeo-Christian. I know there is much we can learn from each other's rich and proud cultures. Above all, I look at the perpetual motion of this region's ports, its factories, its shipping lanes, its inventors, its workers, its consumers, and I know we are all united in a desire to convert that restless energy into better lives for our people.

Tomorrow all of us will go for a day of discussion on beautiful Blake Island. I believe that discussion can help to foster among us a sense of community, not a community of formal, legal economic integration as in Europe but a community such as neighbors create when they sit down together over coffee or tea to talk about house repairs or their children's schools, the kind of community that families and friends create when they gather on holidays to rejoice in their common blessings. Such gatherings are not driven by charters or bylaws but by shared interests and aspirations, bonds that are often more powerful, enduring than those which are written down.

So it is with this community I hope we can create together. We have common concerns about the conditions in our neighborhood, about regional trade barriers, about our shared environment. We have common aspirations: good jobs for our workers, rising standards of living for our children, and peace among our nations. And now we have a common forum for pursuing our common goals. Tonight and tomorrow let us continue developing a shared sense of purpose as expansive as the ocean that unites our lands.

Our great novelist Herman Melville once wrote this about the Pacific Ocean. He said it rolls the midmost waters of the world, the Indian Ocean and the Atlantic being but its arms. Thus this mysterious, divine Pacific zones the world's whole bulk about, makes all coasts bay to it, seams the tide beating of the Earth.

Working as partners we have an historic opportunity to harness the tides of the Pacific so that they may lift all our people to a better future.

Tonight I ask each and every one of you here to join me in a toast to the Pacific community, a region at peace, prosperous, and free. Hear, hear.

Thank you.

NOTE: The President spoke at 8:30 p.m. in the Spanish Ballroom at the Four Seasons Hotel.

Letter to the Speaker of the House of Representatives on the Penny-Kasich Deficit Reduction Proposal
November 19, 1993

Dear Mr. Speaker:

I write to express my strong opposition to the Penny-Kasich amendment to H.R. 3400.

Over the past year, we have taken bold and serious steps to bring down the federal budget deficit and regain control of our economic destiny. We can be proud of the $500 billion in deficit reduction—including $255 billion in spending cuts—that we accomplished for fiscal years 1994 through 1998. The hard freeze on discretionary budget authority and outlays is the most significant step that has ever been taken to control discretionary spending. Likewise, my executive order establishing targets for mandatory spending (along with the specific mandatory savings contained in the reconciliation bill) is the first real step that has been taken to control unforeseen increases in entitlement programs. Furthermore, we have introduced the most detailed plan ever to provide universal health coverage and control the rise in health care spending—which is the main culprit in driving up the budget deficit.

With specific regard to fiscal year 1994, we have already achieved, in the budget and appropriations process, savings of some $12 billion from the 1994 cap on budget authority. That is a major accomplishment. I have also sent to the Congress a 6-year $9 billion package of additional spending reductions and a $2 billion fiscal year 1994 rescission bill. I am also supporting efforts to increase these savings as contained in H.R. 3400. The primary changes will be: (1) increasing the rescission proposal to $2.6 billion in fiscal year 1994; and (2) a specific requirement to implement the National Performance Review (NPR) proposal to eliminate 252,000 positions from the federal work force. These and other actions will bring the total savings in the package to $25-$30 billion, as likely to be scored by the Congressional Budget Office.

In addition to these spending cuts, my Administration is working with the Congress on major reforms in the procurement process to be based on the principles established in the Vice President's NPR. If the legislation follows those principles, we anticipate that the procurement measure will save another $22 billion over 6 years on top of the $25 billion—$30 billion in spending cuts described above.

The Penny-Kasich amendment to this savings package includes many meritorious spending cuts. Indeed, many of them have been proposed by my Administration to finance health care reform and meet the unprecedented spending caps in the recently passed economic plan. As they have included several of our cuts in their package, we will include several of these cuts in either our package or our FY 1995 budget proposal. Yet, despite these areas of common ground, I strongly believe that the amendment should not be passed for the reasons set forth below:

Health Care Reform. In the aftermath of the $500 billion deficit reduction plan, the largest trouble spot in the federal budget is the spiraling cost of health care. The best single hope for reducing the long-term structural deficit is passage of fundamental health care reform to bring these costs under control. Yet, Penny-Kasich claims over $40 billion of the potential Medicare savings needed for *any* serious health care plan. Therefore, it hurts, not helps, our effort to bring the federal deficit down. Denying these savings to health care reform would reduce the flexibility needed for any plan, and fracture the growing consensus for universal coverage and cost containment. The fact that the authors have chosen to modify their proposal by *increasing* the magnitude of the health care cuts is particularly disturbing.

A Substantial Budget Gap Will Be Created: Our economic plan already requires an unprecedented 5-year "hard" freeze on discretionary spending that will require serious cuts in nearly every part of the budget. This strict spending constraint already puts severe limits on spending, and will require serious cuts in nearly every part of the budget. Indeed, we already need to find over $50 billion in additional discretionary savings to meet our deficit reduction targets and protect needed investments in fighting crime, defense conversion, infrastructure, training and education and other investments that most Americans believe are essential to economic growth. The original Penny-Kasich proposal would mandate an *additional* $53 billion reduction of the discretionary spending caps. Because at least $20 billion of its specific spending cuts are already included in my plan, Penny-Kasich leaves a *$70 billion gap* between the deficit reduction mandate and the savings that are specified. Efforts to close this gap could harm important national priorities.

Defense. We are already undertaking a measured reduction in defense spending, carefully designed to protect our security needs. As defense makes up roughly half of total discre-

tionary spending, the need to close a $70 billion discretionary spending gap would create pressure for arbitrary defense cuts in force structure, force modernization, training and readiness, base cleanup, and defense conversion that could threaten our national security. Secretary of Defense Aspin and General John Shalikashvilli, the Chairman of the Joint Chiefs of Staff, believe that the amendment "duplicates DoD reductions already taken to the current budget levels . . . [and] would require cuts to personnel strength that would seriously degrade the support necessary to maintain readiness." In their letter to Congress, the Secretary and General went on to state, that the amendment and that while "[w]e appreciate the enormous pressures that deficit reduction goals have placed on federal spending, . . . we do not believe this Congress is willing to allow our military forces to become the hollow shells that existed in the late 1970s."

Bipartisan Commission on Entitlement Reform. As you know, I have issued an executive order establishing a bipartisan commission to consider further entitlement reform. I believe that such detailed and deliberate consideration is the better way to address the difficult issues in our complex entitlement programs.

Economic Growth and the Timing of Deficit Reduction. We have already enacted the largest deficit reduction package in our nation's history. While our economy still has a long way to go, the benefits of all of our actions are beginning to show. In the first 9 months of our Administration, the economy has created 200,000 more private sector jobs than were created over the last 4 years. The economic plan has led to historic lows in interest rates and mortgage rates, which are fueling an investment-led recovery while allowing millions of American families to refinance their homes or find better opportunities to buy their first home. Over 90 percent of small businesses are already eligible for new or additional tax cuts due to our economic plan. And starting January 1, 1994, over 15 million American households with full-time workers will receive new or additional tax cuts so that those who work full-time will not have to live in poverty.

While we still must do more to get our economy working for all Americans, recent economic indicators suggest—and my Secretary of the Treasury and Chair of the Council of Economic Advisers agree—that our plan provided the right dose of deficit reduction. We should give that plan time to work and not take risks with our now fledgling recovery.

Together, we have made major strides in bringing down the deficit while still taking the steps we need to ensure national security and economic growth. Many of the ideas contained in the Penny-Kasich legislation can help move us in that direction, but for the reasons listed above, the amendment as a whole is flawed and must be rejected.

Sincerely,

BILL CLINTON

NOTE: This letter was made available by the Office of the Press Secretary but was not issued as a White House press release.

Message to the Congress Transmitting the Russia-U.S. Fishery Agreement
November 19, 1993

To the Congress of the United States:

In accordance with the Magnuson Fishery Conservation and Management Act of 1976 (Public Law 94–265; 16 U.S.C. 1801 *et seq.*), I transmit herewith an Agreement Between the Government of the United States of America and the Government of the Russian Federation Amending and Extending the Agreement on Mutual Fisheries Relations of May 31, 1988. The agreement, which was effected by an exchange of notes at Washington on March 11 and September 15, 1993, extends the 1988 agreement through December 31, 1998. This agreement also amends the 1988 agreement by simplifying the provisions relating to the issuance of licenses by each Party to vessels of the other Party that wish to conduct operations in its 200-mile zone and by adding the requirement that the Parties exchange data relating to such fishing operations. The exchange of notes to-gether with the present agreement constitute a governing international fishery agreement within the meaning of section 201(c) of the Act.

The agreement provides opportunities for nationals and vessels from each country to continue to conduct fisheries activities on a reciprocal basis in the other country's waters. The agreement also continues a framework for cooperation between the two countries on other fisheries issues of mutual concern. Since the 1988 agreement expired October 28, 1993, and U.S. fishermen are conducting operations in Russian waters, I strongly recommend that the Congress consider issuance of a joint resolution to bring this agreement into force at an early date.

WILLIAM J. CLINTON

The White House,
November 19, 1993.

Message to the Congress Reporting Budget Deferrals
November 19, 1993

To the Congress of the United States:

In accordance with the Congressional Budget and Impoundment Control Act of 1974, I herewith report four new and two revised deferrals of budget authority, totaling $7.8 billion.

These deferrals affect International Security Assistance programs as well as programs of the Agency for International Development, the Department of State, and the General Services Ad-ministration. The details of these deferrals are contained in the attached report.

WILLIAM J. CLINTON

The White House,
November 19, 1993.

NOTE: The report detailing the deferrals was published in the *Federal Register* on November 30.

Message to the Congress Transmitting the Convention on Biological Diversity
November 19, 1993

To the Senate of the United States:

I transmit herewith, for the advice and consent of the Senate to ratification, the Convention on Biological Diversity, with Annexes, done at Rio de Janeiro, June 5, 1992, and signed by the United States in New York on June 4, 1993. The report of the Department of State is also enclosed for the information of the Senate.

The final text of the Convention was adopted in Nairobi by the Intergovernmental Negotiating Committee for a Convention on Biological Diversity (INC) on May 22, 1992. The INC was preceded by three technical meetings of an Ad Hoc Working Group of Experts on Biological Diversity and two meetings of an Ad Hoc Working Group of Legal and Technical Experts. Five sessions of the INC were held, from June 1991 to May 1992. The Convention was opened for signature at the United Nations Conference on Environment and Development in Rio de Janeiro on June 5, 1992.

The Convention is a comprehensive agreement, addressing the many facets of biological diversity. It will play a major role in stemming the loss of the earth's species, their habitats, and ecosystems through the Convention's obligations to conserve biodiversity and sustainably use its components as well as its provisions that facilitate access to genetic resources and access to and transfer of technology so crucial to long-term sustainable development of the earth's biological resources. The Convention will also create a much needed forum for focusing international activities and setting global priorities on biological diversity.

The objectives of the Convention as set forth therein are the conservation of biological diversity, the sustainable use of its components, and the fair and equitable sharing of benefits arising out of the utilization of genetic resources. These objectives are implemented through specific provisions that address, *inter alia*, identification and monitoring, *in situ* and *ex situ* conservation, sustainable use, research and training, public education and awareness, impact assessment, access to genetic resources, access to and transfer of technology, technical and scientific cooperation, handling of biotechnology and distribution of its benefits, and financing.

Economic incentives will help all Parties achieve the environmental benefits of conservation and sustainable use of biological diversity. The Administration thus supports the concept that benefits stemming from the use of genetic resources should flow back to those nations that act to conserve biological diversity and provide access to their genetic resources. We will strive to realize this objective of the Convention. As recognized in the Convention, the adequate and effective protection of intellectual property rights is another important economic incentive that encourages the development of innovative technologies, improving all Parties' ability to conserve and sustainably use biological resources. The Administration will therefore strongly resist any actions taken by Parties to the Convention that lead to inadequate levels of protection of intellectual property rights, and will continue to pursue a vigorous policy with respect to the adequate and effective protection of intellectual property rights in negotiations on bilateral and multilateral trade agreements. In this regard, the report of the Department of State provides a detailed statement of the Administration's position on those provisions of the Convention that relate to intellectual property rights.

Biological diversity conservation in the United States is addressed through a tightly woven partnership of Federal, State, and private sector programs in management of our lands and waters and their resident and migratory species. There are hundreds of State and Federal laws and programs and an extensive system of Federal and State wildlife refuges, marine sanctuaries, wildlife management areas, recreation areas, parks, and forests. These existing programs and authorities are considered sufficient to enable any activities necessary to effectively implement our responsibilities under the Convention. The Administration does not intend to disrupt the existing balance of Federal and State authorities through this Convention. Indeed, the Administration is committed to expanding and strengthening these relationships. We look forward to continued cooperation in conserving biological diversity and in promoting the sustainable use of its components.

The Convention will enter into force on December 29, 1993. Prompt ratification will demonstrate the United States commitment to the conservation and sustainable use of biological diversity and will encourage other countries to do likewise. Furthermore, in light of the rapid entry into force of the Convention, early ratification will best allow the United States to fully

represent its national interest at the first Conference of the Parties.

I recommend that the Senate give early and favorable consideration to this Convention and give its advice and consent to ratification, subject to the understandings described in the accompanying report of the Secretary of State.

WILLIAM J. CLINTON

The White House,
November 19, 1993.

Nomination for United States District Court Judges
November 19, 1993

The President nominated eleven individuals to be U.S. district court judges. They are:

Fred Biery, Western District of Texas
W. Royal Furgeson, Western District of Texas
Orlando Garcia, Western District of Texas
John Hannah, Eastern District of Texas
Janis Graham Jack, Southern District of Texas
Franklin D. Burgess, Western District of Washington
Michael J. Davis, District of Minnesota
Ancer Haggerty, District of Oregon
Michael A. Ponsor, District of Massachusetts
Marjorie O. Rendell, Eastern District of Pennsylvania
Lesley Brooks Wells, Northern District of

Ohio

"As the Senate completes its work for this session, I am very pleased at the progress we have made in filling judicial vacancies," said the President. "We have nominated more Federal judges by Thanksgiving than any of my recent predecessors and have appointed judges who are marked by both their excellence and commitment to public service. I intend to continue on this course when the Congress returns next year."

NOTE: Biographies of the nominees were made available by the Office of the Press Secretary.

The President's Radio Address
November 20, 1993

Good morning. This week at a time when many Americans are hurting from the strains of the tough global economy, our country chose courageously to compete and not to retreat. With its vote Wednesday night for the North American Free Trade Agreement, the House of Representatives sent a message to the world: Yes, the cold war is over, but America's leadership for prosperity, security, and freedom continues.

The morning after the NAFTA vote I came to Seattle to convene an historic meeting of the leaders of the Asia-Pacific Economic Co-

operation forum. Passage of NAFTA strengthened my hand with the leaders of the Asian-Pacific economies as I worked to make their markets as open to our products and services as our market is to theirs.

The only way to achieve lasting prosperity and real economic security for our people is for America to expand our exports by reaching out to the world, not retreating from it. In plain language, we've got to have more customers for our products and services. But after two decades when good paying jobs have been lost and incomes of working people have stagnated and

Government has done too little to prepare our people for the global economy, it's understandable that many middle class Americans are anxious about change.

Three decades after the Presidency of John F. Kennedy, we must again embrace his vision of an America that seeks to open markets abroad while investing in the skills of our workers and the strength of our communities here at home. Our Nation has a solemn obligation to our working men and women to make sure that they share in the opportunities that expanded trade will produce. That's why we're investing in education and training and technology, the competitive edge for our working men and women, and why we must do more.

That's why I propose changing our unemployment system into a reemployment system so that our working people will have the security of knowing they'll always get the training they need as economic conditions change. You know, it used to be that when people lost their job, they stayed unemployed for a few weeks, and then they were called back to the same old job. Now people are unemployed for longer periods of time and usually don't get the same job back. That's why we've got to change this unemployment system, and we must give people a lifetime right to education and training.

It's also why we're fighting to provide every American with the security of comprehensive health care benefits that can never be taken away, so that they can face the fact that even with changing jobs, they'll be able to survive and their family's health care will be taken care of.

Our efforts to invest in the strength and skills of our people and to expand world trade are part of a coordinated strategy to increase American exports, create American jobs, and raise American incomes. American workers are the most productive, the best in the world.

Given a fair chance and a level playing field, we can outinnovate, outproduce, and outcompete any people. That's why I support NAFTA. It reduces Mexican tariffs on our products, which are currently 2½ times higher than our tariffs on theirs. It eases Mexico's requirements that many of the products sold there, particularly cars and trucks, must be made there. These are some of the reasons why in just 2 years NAFTA will create an estimated 200,000 high-wage jobs for workers here at home.

NAFTA is more than a trading block. It's a building block in our efforts to assert America's global leadership on behalf of American jobs and opportunity. This week in meetings with the leaders from the Asian-Pacific area, I'm striving to expand America's access to some of the largest and the fastest growing markets in the world. The stakes are very high. Asian economies have been growing at 3 times the rate of the established industrialized nations. Much of what Asia needs to continue its growth are goods and services in which our country has a strong competitive position: aircraft, financial services, telecommunications, and construction. Already Asia is our largest trading partner, and our exports to Asia account for 2.5 million American jobs.

Increasing our share of this market by just 1 percent would translate into some 300,000 new American jobs. And it's my job to help create more of those jobs for our working men and women. That's why I'm working to put our economic relationship with Japan on a more equitable basis and why I'm determined to see China eliminate many of its trade barriers to our products and services, as well as expressing our concern over human rights and weapons sales.

Our progress this week is part of our efforts for an even more important breakthrough: a worldwide trade agreement by year's end that would open more markets for American products and services in over 100 nations throughout the world. If we achieve an agreement that meets our standards, the benefits for the American people will be immense. Over 10 years the agreement will create hundreds of thousands of American jobs and substantially increase the average family's income.

As we enter this season of hope, let us remember that we live at a historic moment. Now that the cold war is over, we must do what America did at the end of World War II, invest in ourselves and lead the world toward peace and prosperity. Just as we did a half century ago, Americans can find common ground in supporting the common good.

When it comes to preparing our work force for global competition and building an American economy that exports our products and not our jobs, we must all work together, business and labor, Democrats and Republicans, those who have supported NAFTA and those who have opposed it.

Soon our families will be gathering together

for Thanksgiving to offer our gratitude to God for life's blessings. For all our difficulties, we live in a moment of peace and promise that would have gladdened the hearts of generations that came before us and justified their faith in the future. The challenges we face today, providing our people with the skills and security they need to prevail in peaceful competition with citizens all over the world, is one our pred-

ecessors would have longed to embrace. After this week, I'm even more confident that we will embrace that challenge, not evade it.

Thanks for listening, and a happy Thanksgiving to you and your families.

NOTE: The address was recorded at 10:10 a.m. on November 18 in the Cabinet Room at the White House for broadcast at 10:06 a.m. on November 20.

Remarks and an Exchange With Reporters Following Discussions With APEC Leaders in Seattle
November 20, 1993

The President. Good afternoon, ladies and gentlemen. As we approach the end of a week of APEC activities, we've just completed 3 hours of meetings among 14 APEC economic leaders. It's been a pleasure for me and an honor for the United States to host this week's events and to convene this historic meeting on this beautiful island.

The Asian-Pacific region will provide an increasingly vital role for our Nation and the world. The region is home to 40 percent of the world's people, includes the world's fastest growing economies, and the leaders standing here represent half the world's economic output.

This week's events have been a success for all the region's peoples. We've laid a foundation for regional efforts to create jobs, raise incomes, expand business opportunities, and foster regional harmony. This week we took several tangible steps toward these goals.

On Monday and Tuesday over 1,500 business people engaged in trade came together to focus on the region's potential to benefit their bottom lines. Later in the week, our ministers agreed to a package of market-opening measures designed to help bring the Uruguay round to the GATT to a successful conclusion by December 15th. And the ministerial meeting agreed to develop an action plan in the near future to reduce barriers to business throughout our region, such as differing product standards.

The capstone of this week's activities has been this first-ever leaders meeting. Our discussions this morning, which will continue in the afternoon, give us a chance to become better ac-

quainted and to compare our visions for our own nations and for our diverse and dynamic region. By meeting and talking we've been able to forge a stronger regional identity and a stronger purpose. That purpose is captured in the vision statement we just released.

The statement sets forth our shared view of a regional economy characterized by openness, cooperation, dynamic growth, expanded trade, improved transportation and communications, and high-skilled, high-paying jobs. We've welcomed the challenge of the eminent persons group to achieve free trade in the Asian-Pacific region, advance global trade liberalization, and launch concrete specific programs to move us toward these long-term goals.

In our discussions last evening and today, I've been struck by how many priorities we share: strong, sustainable economic growth; more open markets; better jobs, working conditions, and living standards for our own people; better education for our children and our adults; and protection of the region's unique environment. Of course, we will not always agree on how to achieve those goals. But at least now, for the first time, our region has a means to hold serious policy discussions on such questions as how to remove trade barriers or how to sustain robust growth.

If you ask me to summarize in a sentence what we've agreed, it is this: We've agreed that the Asian-Pacific region should be a united one, not divided. We've agreed that our economic policies should be opened, not closed. We've agreed to begin to express that conviction by doing everything we possibly can to get a good GATT agreement by December 15th.

With today's meeting, we're helping the Asian-Pacific to become a genuine community, not a formal, legal structure but rather a community of shared interests, shared goals, and shared commitment to mutually beneficial cooperation.

The development of that community is certainly in the interest of the American people and all the people of this region. We should be pleased with the progress we've made. And let me say again how honored I am on behalf of the United States to have had the opportunity to host all these leaders.

Thank you very much.

Economic Cooperation

Q. Mr. President, there was no sign of any flexibility from China in the area of—or with Japan on the trade imbalances. Can you say, were any minds or attitudes changed during the course of this meeting?

The President. You're referring to meetings that I had yesterday and discussions we had. Today I'm the host of the meeting where we discussed economic issues, and I frankly believe by—I'll make you a prediction on the economic issues: By next June or July, certainly by a year from now, I believe that the responsibilities of the United States and Japan to do more to promote global economic growth will have been, in large measure, advanced. And I think you will see that we've done some of the things that we should, both of us. So today we focused on what we could do together economically, and I think that's what I ought to respond to today.

China-Taiwan Relations

Q. Mr. President, the fact that—representatives from Taiwan and China to join you to discuss about the issues—I wonder, how do you find your respective vision for these areas? And in your opinion, how does this meeting affect the relationship between Taiwan and China?

The President. Well, that's something for them to determine. I invited, as the host, all the members of this organization, which was the appropriate thing to do. Actually, I'm struck by how much common investment and common activity there is now, and by the common strategies of high savings and investment, hard work and entrepreneurism that are sweeping that part of the world. It is immensely impressive, I think,

to anyone who has observed it.

Malaysia

Q. Mr. President, what do you think about Malaysia's absence from this meeting? And what do you think about the EAEP, the East Asia economic party?

The President. Well, first of all, I'm in favor of anything which increases regional economic cooperation and advances the economic interests of people as long as it doesn't close off economic opportunities for others. And I wish Mr. Mahathir were here, and I look forward to meeting him someday.

North Korea

Q. Mr. President, how serious is the situation in North Korea as a threat to this whole region? And is that something that you discussed today at the meeting?

The President. We didn't discuss it today, but it was discussed yesterday. And I look forward to meeting with President Kim in Washington. He's going back to Washington, and we'll be meeting there and talking about it. It is a source of concern to us, but one that we believe we can find solutions to. And we're going to be taking some initiatives in that area in the not-too-distant future.

New Zealand

Q. Mr. President, is New Zealand now figuratively out of the cold, if not literally? Have you now restored the political relationship with New Zealand?

The President. Actually, we're out in the cold today. [*Laughter*]

The Prime Minister and I had a good talk about that, and we agreed that we would at least take a good look at our relationship and see what else might be done. We have an awful lot in common and a lot of natural instincts toward friendship and cooperation. And I think both of us are uncomfortable with what has become of our relationship over the last several years. So we'll take another look at it; we may have something to say about it, but not today and not tomorrow.

Economic Cooperation

Q. Mr. President, when you were talking about NAFTA you mentioned several times Taiwan, Japan, and China are the three major obstacles when you're dealing with U.S. trade deficit. A lot of people think that was not very helpful when you're trying to cooperate with Asian countries. I was wondering, after this meeting——

The President. Wait, wait, wait. You can ask the question, but let me restate what I said.

What I said to the American people was simply the fact that the people who were against NAFTA acted as if Mexico essentially was going to displace the entire industrial production of the United States or significant portions of it. And I pointed out the fact that we have a trade surplus with Mexico and that our largest operating trade deficits are with Japan, China, and Taiwan. That's simply a fact. That's not an act of hostility, it's just a stated fact. So, go ahead, ask the question.

Q. The question is, after this meeting, will you think that in the future that United States is willing to use cooperation instead of Article 301 type of trade retaliation threat to deal with these problems?

The President. Well, I think, first of all, we've used Article 301 rather sparingly. And secondly, we do seek cooperation. That's the whole purpose of this meeting. That's one of the reasons that I wanted all the leaders to come here, because I think that we have so much in common in terms of our shared views about what the economy of the 21st century ought to look like and what our roles ought to be in it, that I think we can do a lot through cooperation. And we're working very hard to do that.

In the end, if we're going to develop the right kind of free market system, it is going to have to be a cooperative one. But it's going to have to be one that is plainly in the interest of all the people involved in the system. That is, everyone has to be going forward together.

Multilateral Trade Negotiations

Q. Mr. President, how hard and fast is the December 15th deadline for successful completion of the GATT round? It's slipped a couple of times previously. Would you be prepared to extend it if you don't have agreement by then?

The President. Well, it's not entirely up to me, and of course, we have certain legislative authority in America, as you know, that controls that.

All I can tell you is that I think we want to take this moment of opportunity that, frankly, the House of Representatives, and I hope today that the Senate, will give impetus to through NAFTA, and that we are trying to give energy to through our meeting here and through our clear statement again that we want the Asian-Pacific region to be united, not divided, economically; open, not closed; and committed to GATT. We want to seize this moment to try to get it done now. And I've always found that when you're working on an objective, you shouldn't discuss what you'll do if you don't get there until after you don't get there. We still think we can be there, and we're going to try.

Thank you very much.

NOTE: The President spoke at 12:45 p.m. on Blake Island. In his remarks, he referred to Prime Minister Mahathir bin Mohamad of Malaysia. A tape was not available for verification of the content of these remarks.

Remarks and an Exchange With Reporters Prior to a Luncheon With APEC Leaders in Seattle
November 20, 1993

Deficit Reduction Proposal

The President. Ladies and gentlemen, as you know I'm supposed to be hosting a lunch in there, so I can't stay long. But there's one thing going on back in Washington I wanted to comment on today, and that is the debate over further budget reduction measures and specifically the Penny-Kasich amendment. I want to make

a couple of points.

First of all, we have not only passed the biggest deficit reduction program in history, which has produced very low interest rates and stable growth, we have presented the Congress with another package of cuts that includes a procurement reform bill that could save us up to $20 billion. I have started the process of appointing an entitlement commission which could look at the entitlements of this country where the real growth in Federal spending is. We are going to offer an amendment which will strengthen our own budget reduction measure to take it up to $30 billion. And that's what I think we ought to do, we ought to focus on those things.

The Penny-Kasich amendment has a number of problems, but let me just emphasize two. First of all, it clearly would take cuts in Medicare and Medicaid that we have allocated for health care reform in a way that would make national health reform impossible this year. It would take away the possibility of getting a comprehensive national health reform bill. And secondly, it would run the risk of having further cuts in the defense budget that, in my judgment, has already been cut certainly as much as it possibly can be, if not a little beyond.

So because it would cut defense and because it would remove the possibility of health care reform and because we have gotten interest rates down very low with what we have already done and there is an alternative the Congress can embrace—the further cuts we've recommended, the procurement reform, and the entitlement commission—I hope that that amendment will be defeated and that our approach will be embraced. I think it is a far more disciplined approach, far more likely to produce good economic results and to leave open the possibility of health care reform and to be far more responsible in terms of national defense. So that's what I hope will happen today.

Handgun Control Legislation

Q. Mr. President, in addition, back in Washington there's also been—[*inaudible*]—on the Brady bill. Could you tell us what is your understanding of where the Brady bill stands this evening? And would you be willing to accept the compromise, the latest compromise that's put forth by the Republicans?

The President. Well, I'm having an analysis sent to me. I think that the Republicans must be very uncomfortable with having once again thwarted the will of the majority of the Senate and now over 80 percent of the American people. Actually, I'm just surprised. So I want to see what changes they want to make. I'm not for watering down the Brady bill. The Brady bill is important. Perhaps they have some change that is procedural that from their point of view makes it less onerous, that doesn't change the substance of it. But I would want to see it and have a chance to have it evaluated before I made any comment.

I think that the American people would think a lot more of the Congress if the Brady bill passed both Houses before they left. I am genuinely surprised. I can't believe that the Republicans in the Senate really want to filibuster this bill to death. I think that surely that won't happen. So we'll just have to wait and see.

Q. So you don't think it's dead?

The President. Oh, no, no. Not dead for this session, this session meaning early next year, too? You mean between now and when they go out? I think it depends on when they go out and what else can be offered. They may be prepared to hold up the bill over Christmas until early next year. I don't know. I'm surprised by this. I have to say I am surprised. I thought after the bill passed the House, especially by such a healthy margin, that the majority rule would prevail in the Senate. And we'll just have to see. We've still got a few hours, and let's just see whether something can be broken. We're working on it.

Thank you.

NOTE: The President spoke at 1:10 p.m. on Blake Island.

Exchange With Reporters Following Discussions With APEC Leaders in Seattle
November 20, 1993

Q. Mr. Clinton, are you pleased at the outcome of today's meeting?

The President. Yes, and we agreed to meet again next year in Indonesia.

Q. When you look back on this how will you——

The President. I think 10 years from now people will look back on this meeting as a very historic meeting because we agreed to meet and then we agreed to meet again next year to work on a number of issues of mutual concern to our people. I think this is really the assurance that the people need that our region will remain unified and committed to an open economy.

Q. Standing here with leaders of the Pacific Rim, what's your message to the European Community?

The President. That we want them to be part of an open economy, too; this is not an exclusive operation. We want the Asia-Pacific community to be united but not closed, united but open. And what we want to say to Europe is we're committed to doing everything we can to get a good GATT agreement between now and December 15th; we want your help, let's do it.

Q. What about us? [*Laughter*]

The President. I thought it was the pool——

Q. No, no——

The President. [*Inaudible*]—in Indonesia. President Soeharto has invited us to meet in Indonesia next year. We decided to do it. We agreed on a number of very specific things that we would work on over the coming year. And the message again is that we want this community to be united, not divided, and open, not closed.

I was asked a question over there, "What's the message to Europe?" The message to Europe is we want this to be a united but open community and we want Europe to work with us to get a good GATT agreement by the end of the year. That's the message we want to send to our European friends. We don't want an exclusive trading bloc, we want them to join us in a new world trading system.

Q. Do you feel these countries are all as open to the United States as you'd like them

to be?

The President. Well, we talked about that. That's one of the reasons that we're meeting here so that we can do more business with each other. And we talked about some specific things we might do to work toward that: the development of some nonbinding but agreed-upon principles for investment and access, the development of some technology transfer programs that could really help the United States in working with other countries with severe environmental problems, for example.

So we have made the commitments that I think we need to make at this meeting to move to a position where this community will be an even better thing for the United States to be a part of on terms that everyone can win on. So we're very hopeful. But the first thing we hope we can do is get a new world trade agreement by the end of the year.

Q. So will this be an annual event, the leaders of the APEC——

The President. Well, no, it's going to happen twice. You'll see us next year. We'll see if we'll decide to do it again. Now we're all going to Jakarta. This will be—for the Americans it will be interesting. Sign up for the trip now. [*Laughter*]

Q. [*Inaudible*]—difficult for you to communicate from various areas of Asia-Pacific area—is it difficult for you to communicate to us naturally or a very comfortable situation?

The President. Oh, I think it's like all other human relations, the more we're together the more natural it is. It got better as it went along—like life.

NOTE: The exchange began at 3:05 p.m. on Blake Island. A tape was not available for verification of the content of this exchange.

Remarks to the United States Coast Guard in Seattle
November 20, 1993

Thank you very much. This is a warm reception in more ways than one. And after a cold day on the boat, it's a wonderful thing to behold.

I want to thank Admiral Lockwood and Captain Murray and all the men and women of

the Coast Guard for the wonderful assistance that I have received today and that our Nation receives every day.

The Blake Island meeting I think was a great success. Indeed, these have been a good few days for the United States. We had the leaders of 14 of the Asian-Pacific nations here in Seattle for a couple of days. We represent 40 percent of the world's people, half the world's economy, the fastest growing economies in the world. And I can tell you that the spirit of this meeting was incredibly positive, people believing that we had to reach out even more to one another, we had to lower our barriers, we had to make it possible for all of us to grow in peace and harmony and prosperity. It's the sort of thing that people join the Coast Guard of the United States to make sure happens. And you should feel very good about it.

And of course, when the Congress—the House of Representatives passed the North American Free Trade Agreement the other night—you say, "That's about Mexico and Canada. What does that have to do with all these other countries?" The Prime Minister of Singapore got up in our meeting, and he said, "I don't know what would have happened if Congress had voted that treaty down because the rest of us would have thought that America was going to turn away from the world. We would have said that you weren't going to be there."

Instead you had the President of Korea, the President of the Philippines, you had the President of Indonesia, the Prime Minister of Thailand, all these people saying, "We want you to be involved in our future. We want the future of Pacific to be a united Pacific, not a divided Pacific. We want it to be an open future, not a closed future. We want our diversity to be a source of strength."

Even in our differences, we found a way to talk. As you know, the discussion I had with the President of China was the first discussion that the leader of the United States has had with the leader of the world's most populous country and the fastest growing economy on the Earth since the unfortunate incidents at Tiananmen Square. So we began at least to have a conversation about our differences as well as what we have in common. This was a remarkable meeting.

To have the Prime Minister of Japan, a genuine reformer, a person who is committed to changing his country and the way it relates to the rest of the world, including the United States, in positive ways, come here and sit for a whole day today and listen, as did I, to the other leaders and talk about what kind of common ground we could find, it was very moving.

And then when we got off the boat tonight, they told me, Congressman McDermott, that the Senate passed NAFTA a few minutes ago and then passed the Brady bill. So it's been a good day for the United States. So I would say that the 200 years that the Coast Guard has been there for America and her people have been well rewarded by the work that has been done for America in these last few days.

I would say, Captain Murray, your obvious and genuine heartfelt emotion at this moment is justified by what a wonderful country this is and what great people we have in the United States Coast Guard. I know you were there to help the victims of Hurricane Andrew; to assist those who were washed away by the flooding in the Midwest, the worst flood in well over 100 years; to work with the Red Cross and the people of California to help to fight the deadly wildfires.

On any day, the Coast Guard, on average, will save the lives of 16 people and help 360 others in distress. That's a pretty good record. In a place like Seattle, people understand the importance of your work. I hope by my coming here today and the publicity that this visit will generate, that Americans everywhere will understand how much they owe to the United States Coast Guard.

A lot of Americans don't know about your efforts to stem the flow of illegal drugs, but it helps to make every community safer. And I want to tell you that we're looking for new and innovative ways to do more of that and ways that are more effective. Your work in tracking foreign fishing fleets helps protect the important American industry and strengthens our economy. Your work in responding to some 8,000 oil and chemical spills a year helps protect the environment that all Americans cherish and enjoy. Your support for scientific work, such as with your icebreakers in the Arctic, adds to the entire Nation's research base at a time when we need desperately to invest more in research and development for our future economy as well as for our environmental security. Your efforts in monitoring the seas for the growing influx of illegal immigrants also serves our national interests in a difficult area. And in times of war, you and the entire Coast Guard stand ready to protect our Nation in the most fundamental ways. The Coast Guard has long helped to augment our naval forces through work like antisubmarine and surface warfare. For all of these efforts, your Nation and your President are in your debt.

Your work underscores a crucial point: In order to make life better for people within our borders, we often need to take actions beyond our borders. As modern transportation and communications make the world smaller and smaller, we must engage abroad to succeed at home. And that was the whole point of this meeting we had on Blake Island.

I spent the better part of a year and a half campaigning to the American people in the race for President. And everywhere I went I said that we had reached a time when there was no longer an easy dividing line between foreign policy and domestic policy, between defense policy and economic policy, that clearly we could not be strong abroad if we were not strong at home but that it was no longer possible for a wealthy country to have a strong economy at home without being involved abroad and succeeding and winning in the global competitive economy.

Clearly, our Nation could not be secure without a strong defense, but in these tough economic times we could not pay for a strong defense without a strong economy. And so, every day and especially during the budgetary season, I will be required to make some very difficult decisions. Some of the calls will be right, and occasionally I will doubtless make some of them wrong. But I want you to know that every call will be determined on the basis of what I honestly believe is best for the long-term security and prosperity of the American people, based on those simple ideas.

There is no longer a simple dividing line between defense policy and economic policy, no longer a clear line between foreign policy and domestic policy. America, like it or not, is part of a world that is increasingly more interdependent, a world in which we are rewarded when we are productive and aggressive in selling our products and services, and in which we are punished if we refuse to compete.

There are those who long for a world in which the American people could be more secure and more immune from change. I, at least, long for a world in which we are more secure. But we cannot do it by trying to immunize ourselves from change. No free society is immune from the winds blowing through the world today. We have to find a way to make these changes our friend and not our enemy. We have

to find a way to train every American as well as the men and women of the Coast Guard are trained to do their job. We have to find a way to give people the sense that they will have access to learning and relearning for a lifetime. We have to find a way to invest in those things which will give the promise of real hope and opportunity. And I say to you as Americans, we have got to find a way to give structure, order, discipline, hope, and love back to those millions of American children who do not have the daily supports that you take for granted if you're a member of the United States Coast Guard, but without which life is very difficult to live on successful terms.

I hope today as we look out on these beautiful waters and remember that our history and our heritage are rooted to the sea, that most of our Americans came across the oceans to get here to become Americans, that we must, just like we did in the beginning, be a nation that reaches out across the seas to new markets and new opportunities and new horizons.

To those of our friends and neighbors in the Pacific and elsewhere, we're going through a difficult and challenging time. Not all our roads are easy. But this is a time which we should be grateful to live in, for after all, the cold war is over; the threat of nuclear destruction recedes. The hopes of people really have a chance to be realized in a peaceful environment. And many of the problems we have are problems of our own making that we can unmake if we have the discipline and will and vision and sheer persistence to face them and work them through.

Therefore, I say to you that I value your service and your sacrifice, your talent and your dedication, not only because you help to make our Nation stronger but because I hope that every time an American citizen sees you in this uniform, that that will help us to remember what kind of people we are and where we need to go.

Thank you, and God bless you all.

NOTE: The President spoke at 4:59 p.m. at the Seattle Coast Guard Support Center gymnasium at Pier 36. In his remarks, he referred to Rear Adm. Joseph W. Lockwood, USCG, 13th district commander, and Capt. Charles W. Murray, USCG, commanding officer, Seattle Coast Guard Support Center. A tape was not available for verification of the content of these remarks.

Remarks at a Reception Honoring Senator Dianne Feinstein in San Francisco, California
November 20, 1993

Thank you very much, William Lewis Brown, Junior. [*Laughter*] I love San Francisco. Willie Brown gets called by his full name, and Clarence Clemmons replaces the Marine Band.

You know, I once told Dianne Feinstein I would do anything legal I could for California. It turned out that that included replacing her at her own fundraiser. You wonder how I get those one-vote margins—no chore is too large or small for the President to perform. [*Laughter*] Dianne throws a party for 750 people, Dick doesn't even come to the airport to meet me, and I show up here to speak anyway. [*Laughter*]

It reminds me, you know, the last time I was in California a few weeks ago, I went down to L.A., and I had been through an interesting period of humbling, as I periodically experience. I mean, first, Al Gore goes on the Letterman show and is a smash hit, smashing his little ashtray and proving that we're going to reinvent Government, and he becomes a media star. I get beat up in the news; he has fun on Letterman. [*Laughter*] Then Hillary goes before the Senate and answers questions for 5 days without notes, and there's a poll in USA Today saying that 40 percent of the American people think she's smarter than I am. They asked me what I thought about it. I said what I thought was I couldn't understand how the other 60 percent missed it. [*Laughter*]

But then they told me I had a trip to California. I have such a wonderful time when I come out here. And I thought, well, I'll go out there, and they'll make me feel like a real President again. So I went to L.A., and they said I was going to stay in the Beverly Hilton Hotel." And Merv Griffin owns it, and I said, "It will be great. I'll bet Merv Griffin will be there to meet me there, and I'll feel really important. And they'll give me a nice room, and I'll have a great view of that beautiful golf course that's across the street from the hotel." That all happened. But here's what else happened—so help me, this is not made up. I get there, and I'm spruced up, because there's Merv Griffin all dolled up, and shakes hands, says, "How are you? I'm glad you're here at my hotel. I got you a wonderful suite upstairs. There is one

permanent resident on the floor where you'll be staying, and I thought it was appropriate for you to be there with him." I mean, it's Los Angeles; I was thrilled; my mind was going crazy, right? I get on the elevator; I get up to the umpty-dump floor, whatever it was; the elevator opens, and there holding a dozen roses for me is Rodney Dangerfield. It's true. He gives me a dozen of something called jungle roses with "a little respect" on the card. [*Laughter*]

Well, I am glad to be back. Senator Feinstein really is coming home. They worked late, hard, and well tonight in the United State Senate, not only passing 2 days early the trade agreement but also passing at long last the Brady bill.

I've found a lot of things to like and admire about Dianne Feinstein, even when she's wearing me out. That's one of the things I admire about her. I called her one night, and I said, "Nobody wears me out as effectively as you do." She's always got a new idea about something that will help this State. But I was never more proud of her than I was the other day when she called and she said, "You're for that assault weapons ban, aren't you?" And I said, "You know I am." She said, "Well, we've got to try to put it on the bill, and I want you to help me, and here's who I want you to call." So I said, "Okay, I'll do it." And she said, "If you call one person, it will be all over the Senate, and they'll know that you're not kidding about it." So then she got into this interchange which you probably remember with a Senator of the other party that said that—the implication was if she weren't a woman and if she weren't from California, she might know something about handguns. And she blistered him about what she knew about handguns and weapons generally. I want to tell you, it was a sweet moment in a town full of sanctimony to see another hot air balloon burst. [*Laughter*]

Sometimes I feel like I'm in a time warp. We live in a wonderful country, but there are a lot of kids in trouble. And you've got streets where the gang members are better armed than the policemen, and innocent people are getting shot in the crossfire. And the time before last when I was out here in California, I was in Sacramento, as I remember, to do a town meeting. And there were people connected in towns all over the State. And this one young man said he was changing the school he was in because he and his brother didn't want to be in gangs; they didn't want to own guns; they didn't want to be in trouble; they didn't want to do drugs. They just wanted to get a good education; they wanted to go to college; they wanted to make a good life for themselves. So they changed schools to go to a safer school. And he and his brother were standing in line registering, and his brother got shot down in the line registering for school, in the school building.

And that could happen everywhere. And yet, you listen to these debates on the crime bill, the kind of things we're trying to do, and it sounds like some people are just literally in another world. Well, I've got to give the Senate and the House credit: They passed the Brady bill. They passed a crime bill that will give the cities of our country the actual means to reduce the crime rate. Don't let anybody kid you that more police officers properly deployed won't reduce the crime rate, not just catch criminals but reduce the crime rate. There is no question that it will work.

My friend Bob Lanier, the Governor of Houston, Texas, just got reelected with 91 percent of the vote because he told the people if they'd vote for him he would, through new people and overtime, put the equivalent of another 655 police officers on the street, he would deploy them properly, they'd have community policing, and the crime rate would go down. He did it, and the crime rate went down 17 percent in one year. And the people sent him back to the Mayor's office.

This will make a difference, this crime bill. But it makes a difference also that there are boot camps as opposed to prisons for youthful offenders, to give them a chance to do something constructive with their lives. And it makes a difference that the Brady bill passed. And it makes a difference that Dianne's amendment got on the Senate version of the bill. And when it goes to conference, I hope to goodness we can keep it the whole way.

I want you to know that because you have two highly unusual, very gifted first-year United States Senators in Dianne Feinstein and Barbara Boxer, who have both made a profound impact on the politics of this country, and I am in their debt because, as Willie said, you know, I've had a few votes up there that weren't landslides. [*Laughter*] Every time Al Gore and I are together, he sits up and looks at a crowd and says, "You know what the difference in me and other people in the Federal Government are? When I vote in the United States Senate, I'm always on the winning side." You have to think about that. When he said that, I knew he could beat Ross Perot in that debate. [*Laughter*]

It has been, as Willie said, an eventful 10 months. And with the help of the person you're here to honor tonight, we made a good beginning at turning the conditions around that have caused our country and this State so much grief. The United States Congress passed the largest deficit reduction package in history that gave us historically low interest rates, kept inflation down, enabled literally millions and millions of Americans to refinance their homes, and helped to produce more jobs in the private sector in the first 10 months of this administration than in the previous 4 years. Do we need more jobs? You bet we do, but that's a pretty good beginning.

That budget bill had an expanded earned-income tax credit—which is a long phrase now unfamiliar to Americans, but on April 15th it will become much more familiar—which does the most important job that we have done in our Tax Code in 20 years in rewarding work. For it says to all those lower income working people who have been working harder for less for two decades and who have children in their homes, we will reward your work. If you are at or near the poverty line, we will lift you up if you are willing to work and raise your children. We will not punish you for the decision to labor on and make the best you can of your life. It is profoundly significant and the biggest incentive for people to move from welfare to work that has been adopted in my lifetime. It will affect 14 million working families and almost 50 million Americans in those families when it becomes law, when the next tax returns are filed.

This tax bill also gave the high-tech community in northern California and throughout the country what they have been asking for for years: a capital gains treatment for long-term investments in new and small business; an expansion of the research and development tax credit; and by the way, a radical—yes, you can clap for that, that's all right. [*Applause*] And something that almost nobody knows, it also radically reorganized the student loan program to keep one of the real commitments I made in the Presidential campaign of 1992, to open the doors of college education to all Americans. Because now, under this law, the interest rates on college loans will be lowered. The terms for repayment will be lengthened. Young people who choose to be public school teachers or do other public service work will be able to pay those loans back no matter how much they borrow as a percentage of their income. It will be tougher for people to evade repaying the loans, but they'll be much, much easier to repay.

The Congress also passed a national service law which 3 years from now will permit 100,000 young Americans—8 times as many as ever served in one year in the Peace Corps—100,000 to work in a domestic peace corps to rebuild this country from the grassroots up and earn credit against a college education for doing it.

This Congress also passed and I signed the family and medical leave law, which gives people the right to have time off from their jobs. You know, sometimes when you're in Washington, you're always answering questions about process and who's up and who's down and who's in and who's out, what does this vote mean, and what do you have to say about what this politician said about you. And sometimes you just forget all about the human impact of what you do or don't do.

About a month ago, on Sunday morning I came in from my morning jog, and I looked in the ground floor of the White House, and one of my young staffers was taking a family around on a tour, which is very unusual on Sunday morning. There was a man and his wife and three children. One of the children was in a wheelchair. And it was one of these Make-A-Wish Foundation families, you know; the child was very ill, and her wish was to come to the White House and see the President. So I went over and shook hands with them and asked if they would excuse me. I told them I'd go up and get cleaned up and try to look like the President again, and we'd take a picture. And I came down in a few minutes, and we took the picture. And I was going about my business, and the man grabbed me by the arm and turned around, and he said, "Let me tell you something, Mr. President, just in case you think what you do here doesn't matter. My little girl is really sick, and she's probably not going to make it. And because of that family leave law, I've been able to take some time off from my job and spend some time with my child. It's the most important time I've ever had in my life. And if that law hadn't passed, I would have had to choose between spending this time with this child or staying at my job and supporting the two children who are going to make it in my family. And I didn't have to make that choice. Don't you ever think what you do up here doesn't make a difference."

I tell you that because sometimes when you come to dinners like this, it is easy to forget. You say, "Well, my friends are doing this, and I like Dianne, and I'm here for this." You are also here for larger purposes. And we have established together a record we can be proud of. But there is still much to be done. Still in process but not resolved are the crime bill, the Brady bill—because the House and the Senate passed two different versions, they have to be resolved—the campaign finance reform bill, the lobby reform bill, and the legislation to finally, at long last, provide health care security to all Americans. We have a lot to do, and it matters whether this Senator is reelected to the United States Senate.

I also want you to know it matters because of what we are trying to do for this country that specifically affects California. As I said, Senator Feinstein and Senator Boxer constantly are giving me their laundry lists of things that they think that this Government can do to help this State. And almost always it's also very, very good for the whole country.

We have removed from export controls $35 billion worth of high-tech equipment, computers, supercomputers, telecommunications equipment, thanks to the relentless work of the Secretary of Commerce, Ron Brown, who is here with me tonight. And California will benefit from that. [*Applause*] Stand up.

We've transferred 200 acres, or I have directed it—we have to work out the details—from Alameda Air Station to the Port of Oakland. We are cutting through redtape so that the dredging of the port can start 8 months earlier than it otherwise would have. And the most exciting thing to me is our technology reinvestment project where we're putting up for competition limited Federal dollars to match with private funds for defense contractors to come up with things that can be done in a post-cold-war economy to create the high-tech jobs of the future.

In the last round, the first of three rounds of projects, California got almost 25 percent of the projects fair and square through a completely competitive bidding process. And why not? That's why your unemployment rate is so high now, because you had such a high percentage of reliance on defense. You should have a high percentage of reward for conversion from a defense to a domestic economy. And we're going to do more of those things—[*applause*]—the Congress believes it.

Ultimately, however, the economy of this State cannot recover unless the economy of America recovers and moves toward a high-tech, high-wage, highly competitive future and one in which all of our children are taken along instead of so many being left behind.

I ran for President because I thought there were two great problems in this country we had to address: One was to try to bring the economy back. The other was to try to bring the American people together, to make a strength out of our diversity, and to stop leaving so many of our children behind. We have made a good beginning on that.

One of the reasons I fought so hard for the highly controversial trade agreement with Mexico and Canada is that I have studied relentlessly for years the job-creating figures and the unemployment figures of every State in this country and every major advanced industrial nation in the world. Every rich country is having trouble creating jobs. Productivity, which is important to compete, is not leading to the creation of new jobs in much of the world today because productivity means fewer people can produce more things. And therefore, if fewer people produce more things, unemployment will stay high and wages will stay flat unless there are more customers for those things, which means we must have higher rates of growth in the world economy, and the United States must have more customers. There is no other way for us ultimately to grow this economy. We have to have a higher rate of growth and more customers. The trade agreement means more customers. The meeting I had today with the leaders of those 13 other Pacific nations means higher rates of growth and more customers if we do what we're supposed to do. That is what

we must be about.

But that also will not work unless we are willing, my fellow Americans, to take up the hard work of healing the wounds of the last 10 and 20 and 30 years here at home. The whole practice of rearing children has been under assault for three decades in America. Middle class wages have been under assault for two decades here in this country, and more and more working people are actually poor. And for a very long time we have followed an economic theory that said if we made our country more unequal and ran the debt up, somehow it would all work out, regardless if whether we invested in the growth of this economy or not.

It is time to address those things. The crime bill is a beginning. The earned-income tax credit is a beginning. We are making beginnings. Trying to deal with health care and giving Americans health care security, whether they've got a job or not, whether they've been sick or not, is a beginning. Every disabled person in America, every person who is now HIV positive but healthy enough to work in America, every person in this country with a small business will be advantaged if we can finally join the ranks of every other country in the world and give affordable health care to all of our people. It is also positive economics.

I met just this week, as you know, with the Prime Minister of Japan, with the Prime Minister of Canada, with the leaders of a lot of other countries. And they said, "How much money do you spend on health care?" I said, "Fifteen percent of our income." They said, "What? And how many people do you have insured?" I said, "Thirty-seven million." They said, "What?" And I said, "You know what, nobody believes we can fix it. Every time I say we're going to fix it by doing what other people have done that worked, they say, 'Oh, it's going to cost more money.'" And they say, "What?" [*Laughter*]

I'm telling you, folks, we have got to fix this. We can't go on spending a dime on the dollar more than any other country in the world does on paperwork in our health care system and expect to do anything but be punished for it economically and in human terms.

But beyond all that, we have got to recognize that we cannot be what we're supposed to be if children are shot with reckless abandon in our streets, if children grow up without a future, and if people go around bemoaning it but don't want to do anything about it. And the President of the United States and the United States Congress can only do so much. Some of this will have to be done community by community, neighborhood by neighborhood, family by family, block by block.

But we can do it. If you leave here tonight believing anything, I want you to believe our country is on the move again. I'm telling you, those leaders of those Asian countries were exhilarated when we passed that trade agreement because they thought we were going to turn away from the world and walk away. And they know now we're not. But I'll tell you something else: Everyone of them admitted that the opposition to NAFTA deserved to be honored because of the rampant insecurity of working people in every advanced country in the world. The story I had to tell here was the same story that I heard from Canada, from Australia, from New Zealand, increasingly true in all of Europe,

and even now coming to be true in Japan. We have got to find a way to reward people who work hard and who are competitive. And we have got to find a way to bring all of our people along.

This administration is pursuing that direction as vigorously as we know how. We are on the move. And we are going to get there if you in California, who have the largest stake in our future success, will make sure that in Washington the President has partners like Senator Dianne Feinstein.

Thank you very much.

NOTE: The President spoke at 9 p.m. in the Grand Ballroom at the Fairmont Hotel. In his remarks, he referred to William L. Brown, Jr., California State Assembly speaker; Clarence Clemmons, saxophonist; and Richard C. Blum, the Senator's husband.

Remarks at Our Lady Help of Christians School in Los Angeles
November 21, 1993

Thank you so much. It's wonderful to see all of you here today. I want to thank everyone who has made my visit here so wonderful so far, especially all the people in the courtyard behind us who took me through "Christmas in other Lands," gave me something to eat from every land represented. I thank you, Cardinal Mahony, for being here. I thank you, Father Santillan, for the wonderful work that you and others do at this parish and at this wonderful school. I thank you, Gloria Molina, for being my friend and the national cochair of my campaign last year. And I want to thank all the members of the various elected groups who are here today, the State officials, the local officials who care about you and your future, for joining me here today.

There are three people I want to mention who aren't here today because they're back in Washington, and I hope the Cardinal will forgive them, but the Congress is actually meeting on Sunday, only because they're trying to be home for Thanksgiving. But the Members of Congress from this area, Xavier Becerra, Lucille Roybal-Allard, and Esteban Torres, all asked me to give

you their love and best wishes. I thank them for their support of our administration and for their support of you.

I started out this morning in Pasadena meeting with about two dozen people who lost their homes or whose family members lost their homes in the fire. And I got this interesting little button—I don't know if you can see it— it looks almost like a stone pin from where you are, but it's actually just a button that was burned up in the fire. And a man who saved two other homes but who lost his own, found 50 of these pins. And he and his wife had them on. And from a distance I said, where did you get those pins? And he told me what they were, and he gave me one. This is just a charred reminder of the courage and the heroism of the people of this area who struggled through those terrible fires. I thank them for what they did, and I hope that their decency and courage in an emergency will inspire all the rest of us to do better everyday of our lives. I wish all of you could have been there with me at the Presbyterian church in Pasadena today to see them.

I wanted to come here today because I came here to this community during my campaign for President. I walked the streets of this community. I talked to children and adults. I talked to working people. I talked to people who didn't have work but wanted it. I talked to people who are worried about the violence and the crime, about the pressures on the families and the dangers to the children. And I want you to know that every night when I go to bed in the White House I think of the children of this country, of their future, of the dangers and the problems, of the hopes and the dreams.

We are working now in Washington to pass a bill which will make a big step toward making our streets safer, something that Mayor Riordan ran on when he ran for mayor. If the bill passes, the crime bill, which has now passed both Houses of the Congress, we may be able to give our cities and this country up to 100,000 more law enforcement officers to protect people, to keep crime from occurring in the first place.

Thanks to your Senator Dianne Feinstein, the Senate passed a bill which will ban assault weapons and which bill ban the possession of handguns by young people. And both Houses have passed a version of what we call the Brady bill, which would make people wait 5 days before they get a handgun so we can check their criminal background, their age, their mental health history.

All these things will help. All these things will help, but in the end, my fellow Americans, we have to take our communities back community by community, neighborhood by neighborhood, block by block, family by family, child by child.

Our disregard for life in this country is seen coast to coast. This morning I got up and read the Los Angeles Times and saw that a 2-year-old child was killed last night because her mother took her on an expedition in which the gang her mother was associated with got in a fight with another gang, and random shooting into their car felled no adult, just a 2-year-old innocent child. In Pasadena, which used to have a very different sort of image, they are gripped, haunted by the thought that three children were killed on Halloween—teenagers. Across the country in Baltimore, the Mayor of Baltimore told me a heart-rending story of going to the home of an 18-year-old child who made it his practice every Halloween to take little children

out so that they could go trick-or-treating safely. And they were walking down a street, and across the street a 14-year-old boy and a 13-year-old boy were standing. And the 14-year-old had a gun and dared the 13-year-old to shoot across the street. And so he did and killed an older child whose only offense was that he wanted little children to be able to go out and trick-or-treat safely on Halloween.

What we want America to look like is what we see here today: the faces of these children safe and secure, learning and whole, looking toward the future, believing in their lives, living by their values. That's what we want America to look like.

And so I tell you, we are doing everything we can to try to give you the tools you need to make your community safer. But we have to make up our mind that we will no longer tolerate children killing children, children having guns and being better armed than police officers, neighborhoods unsafe. We can do better. And we're going to have to do it for all of our people without regard to race or income or region. You deserve as much, and we have to do it.

Father Santillan mentioned Cesar Chavez. Think how horrified he would be, God rest his soul, if he were still here today to pick up the paper and read about the 2-year-old child being killed. He was a devotee of nonviolence and self-sacrifice, not violence and self-indulgence.

Tomorrow we celebrate with regret the 30th anniversary of the assassination of our Nation's only Roman Catholic President, John Kennedy. Think how he would feel, after having spent his time as President reaching out to Latin America in the Alliance for Progress, reaching here at home to get our young people into the Peace Corps, trying to help improve opportunities for Americans, to think of all the horrible things that are happening to our young people in this country.

Think of how Robert Kennedy, who flew to California and helped Chavez break a 26-day fast, would feel here today. Hands bleeding from the clutches of an adoring mob at the end of this fast, Robert Kennedy said this to the farm workers those long years ago: "When your children and grandchildren take their place in America, going to high school and college and taking good jobs at good pay, when you look at them you will say"—he said to the farm workers—"'I did this. I was there at the point of difficulty and danger.' And though you may be old and bent with labor, no man will stand taller than you when you say, 'I marched with Cesar.'" They marched so that these children could have opportunity, not danger. And we have to give it to them.

But let me also say to you, my fellow Americans, I am well aware that we cannot repair the troubled wounds of this country simply by making ourselves safer on our streets. We must also give our young people more to say yes to. I have worked as hard as I could to turn this economy around, to bring jobs to this country, to bring jobs to this troubled part of our Nation. Southern California now has a higher unemployment rate than any other State. We have got to do better. I know and you know that not only faith and family but work, work is required to organize society, to keep it safe and whole and strong and marching forward.

And so we have made a good beginning. In 10 months more new jobs have come into the private sector than in the previous 4 years but nowhere near enough to put all the people of east Los Angeles to work who want their jobs. We must do better, and we will.

I fought hard and without apology for the North American Free Trade Agreement because I know Mexico is our partner in the future, whether anyone likes it or not, and we have to grow together in strength together. And because I know that no wealthy country on the face of this Earth can create more jobs for its people or higher incomes for people who work harder and smarter unless there are more customers for the products and services the people produce, we have to have those customers. We will find some of them in Mexico and in Chile and in Venezuela and in Colombia and in Argentina and all over Latin America, because we are reaching out to our friends south of our borders again for a great new partnership, for opportunity there and opportunity here in east Los Angeles. It is important.

And you may have seen that I had the leaders of 14 Asian-Pacific nations together in Washington State for the last 2 days. One of them, the President of the Philippines, came to Los Angeles today to go to church with Filipino-Americans in this county. We know that that is the fastest growing part of the world, and they, too, will be our partners in providing jobs for our people. But in the end, we must take care of our own better.

The reason so many working people, the reason so many Hispanic-Americans oppose the North American Free Trade Agreement is that they had seen too many times when the working people of this country worked harder and harder for less and less security. And so I say to you, we have to have good, decent education not just for these children but for adults throughout their lives so they can always get new jobs. We have to have health care not just for those who can afford it or who are lucky enough to have jobs where it's covered but health care that can never be taken away. Every other advanced country has it. And we must have it here, too.

And we have to have an investment strategy that will help our people everywhere, everywhere, to find the jobs that they deserve. Since I became President, the Secretary of Commerce Ron Brown, who is here with me today, has made over a dozen trips to California. I have been here seven times. We are working hard to turn this economy around, not because of some abstract unemployment number but because the faces in this crowd are willing to make America a model of what every society in the world ought to be in the 21st century, where diversity is strength, where diversity is richness and laughter and fullness and hope. Because everybody who works hard, everybody who learns well, everyone who lives by the values that are cherished in this parish has a chance to be rewarded. That, I believe, is God's will for all of us on this Earth, and we must work for it.

Thank you all, and God bless you.

NOTE: The President spoke at 1:38 p.m. on the school playground. In his remarks, he referred to Roger Cardinal Mahony, Archbishop of Los Angeles; Father Juan Santillan, parish priest; and Gloria Molina, Los Angeles County commissioner.

Exchange With Reporters Prior to Discussions With President Fidel Ramos of the Philippines
November 22, 1993

American Airlines Strike

Q. Mr. President, are you willing to intervene in the American Airlines strike?

The President. Well, I'm concerned about it. I've asked the Secretary of Transportation and the Secretary of Labor to look at the situation, and we're looking into it now. But I don't want to raise any false signals. We're looking into it, we're examining it, and we're looking at all the options. No decision has been made.

Congressional Priorities

Q. Mr. President, what are your priorities now if Congress wraps up before they head home?

The President. Well, as they head home here, I hope the House will pass campaign finance reform today. And I still have a little hope that they can work out their differences over the Brady bill and give it to the American people for a Thanksgiving present. I would like that very much.

Deficit Reduction Proposal

Q. What about the Penny-Kasich——

The President. Well, as you know, I think that's a mistake. I think if it were to pass, if it were to actually become law, it would imperil health care. It would raise the prospect of further defense cuts, which are very unwise. It also sort of heads off the disciplined approach we had planned for next year with the entitlements commission and with the further budget cuts that are scheduled anyway that we still have to make. So I think it would be a mistake.

Q. Were you surprised——

North Korea

Q. Have you ruled out a preemptive strike in North Korea?

The President. I have nothing to say other than what I said at the APEC meeting about that. We're working hard on that issue, and I've consulted with the South Koreans and with the Japanese and with the Chinese at the APEC meeting extensively about that issue.

Handgun Control Legislation

Q. Were you surprised that the Brady bill got a new lease on life? And you thought it would happen?

The President. I mean, I think that those who were filibustering it really considered where they were and where the American people were, and they were out of harmony with the American people. The American people want us to act on crime. They want us to do something about violence. They want us to move forward. And the Brady bill is symbolic of the serious effort to move forward. And so I was very pleased. I appreciate the fact that the filibuster was abandoned.

[*At this point, one group of reporters left the room, and another group entered.*]

Philippines

Q. Mr. President, what in the Philippines interests you?

The President. Well, just about everything that goes on in the Philippines interests me. Our country and the Philippines have a long and deep friendship that goes back many decades. And I was very impressed with the leadership that President Ramos showed at the APEC meeting in Seattle and the vision he demonstrated about the importance of our remaining partners in the Asian-Pacific region in the years ahead. So I'm looking forward to having the chance today to talk to him about what the two of us can do together to strengthen our partnership.

NOTE: The exchange began at 1:15 p.m. in the Oval Office at the White House. A tape was not available for verification of the content of this exchange.

The President's News Conference With President Fidel Ramos of the Philippines
November 22, 1993

President Clinton. Good afternoon, ladies and gentlemen. I want to read this statement about the meeting I have just concluded with President Ramos, and then we'll have remarks by the President. And then I want to make a statement about the airlines issue, after which we will both answer questions.

First, let me say it's a great pleasure for me to welcome President Fidel Ramos of the Philippines to Washington. We had a very good discussion at the historic APEC leaders' meeting in Seattle, and I'm delighted that he accepted my invitation to come to the White House for further talks.

Our two nations have enjoyed warm relations for almost a century now. Our soldiers have fought side by side. President Ramos knows the value of our cooperation first hand, having himself served in combat in Korea. I'd also like to congratulate him as a graduate of West Point for the award he recently received from the United States Military Academy as one of their outstanding graduates.

Throughout the cold war, the Philippines hosted two of our key military bases in the Pacific. And now with the cold war over, the Philippines remains one of our Nation's most vital friends and allies in the Asian-Pacific region.

The Philippines also helped lead the march toward democracy over the past decade. We all recall the impressive courage of the Philippine people in 1986 as their prodemocratic struggle inspired freedom-loving people everywhere in the world. President Ramos played an important role in that drama. And it is fitting, as I said, that he has been honored by West Point and recognized by people all across America for his devotion not only to democracy but to the cause of human rights.

In our discussions today, President Ramos and I covered a range of bilateral, regional, and global issues. We reviewed the results of last week's APEC meetings and agreed to work jointly to advance the spirit of community in our region. We share the goal of achieving open trade and investment, prosperity, and increasing regional economic integration. We agreed that Congress' approval of NAFTA this past week will bolster our regional efforts to reduce trade barriers and may improve our chances of securing an acceptable new GATT agreement.

I told the President that I very much admire his own efforts toward economic liberalization. I'm impressed by his steps to free foreign exchange and liberalize trade and investment and by his ongoing efforts to achieve reform in banking, taxation, and customs.

Our bilateral relations with the Philippines have witnessed a transformation in recent years. The end of the cold war and the closure of our bases there, however, have not changed the basis for continuing cooperation between our two nations. We've now begun a renewed partnership, based on our long historical association, our shared values, our expanding trade and investment links, our bilateral security cooperation, and our common dedication to democracy and human rights.

We took several steps today to enhance our partnership, agreeing among other things to negotiate a bilateral extradition treaty which will help us to combat global crime, terrorism, and narcotics trade. We agreed to pursue a mutual legal assistance treaty to facilitate evidence exchanges in criminal matters and again to strengthen our cooperation in narcotics control. I want to thank President Ramos for his action to ensure the renewal of our close security cooperation. Those efforts have enabled a successful visit of the U.S.S. *O'Brien* to Manila in a joint military exercise on Philippine territory.

We look forward to continuing cooperation with the Philippines, in APEC, the ASEAN regional forum, the United Nations, and on global issues ranging from nonproliferation to environmental protection, something that President Ramos referred to over and over again at the APEC meeting just a few days ago.

President Ramos has been a strong friend of the American people, and I look forward to working closely with him and the Philippine people in the days ahead.

Let me say in introducing him, also, that there's been a great deal of discussion over the last couple of years, and certainly in recent days, about whether the basic cause of human rights is somehow a product of the Western cultural tradition. If you look at the Philippines, the Philippine version of human rights shows that human rights can take root anywhere and be appreciated, revered, and respected anywhere, thanks in no small measure to President Ramos.

The floor is yours, sir.

President Ramos. Thank you, Bill.

Ladies and gentlemen, today President Clinton and I set a new orientation for Philippine-American relations. These relations have a long history behind them. But the fundamentally altered political and economic environment in the world and in our region and the changed requirements of both our peoples have made it necessary and desirable for both of us to embark on a new partnership.

This new partnership we affirm shall be based on the values that both Americans and Filipinos cherish deeply: the sanctity of human rights, the value of democracy, and the efficacy of the free market. President Clinton strongly supports our commitment to these values, something which we find encouraging and for which we are grateful.

Our partnership, we agreed, shall also be anchored more firmly than ever before on the benefits that both our countries derive from our economic relationship. I deeply appreciate the support which President Clinton expressed for our program of economic reform and economic development, and I value the confidence that he manifested in the program's success.

I also thank President Clinton for the steps that this administration intends to take to encourage more American investments in the Philippines. At the same time, I raised with him the question of improved access for Philippine exports to the American market. And in the context of our economic partnership, President Clinton and I resolved to work even more closely together for the punctual and successful conclusion of the Uruguay round and in general the further liberalization of the world economy, even as we recognize the special requirements of the developing countries.

Security cooperation, particularly within the framework of the Philippine-U.S. Mutual Defense Treaty of 1951 remains a vital element in Philippine-American relations. President Clinton and I agreed that our cooperation in security matters must be strengthened despite the changes in the global and regional security situation which no longer requires the permanent stationing of American forces in the Philippines.

The mutual defense treaty continues to be valuable to the security of East Asia. We welcome and appreciate, as do others in the region, the continuing American commitment to regional security which President Clinton reaffirmed today, including America's determination to oppose any resort to the use of force in the Kalayaan or Spratly area.

A human link in our relation with the United States is the community of over 2 million Filipinos in this country. I appreciate President Clinton's recognition of their contribution to American society. And in order to be able to assist each other better in the enforcement of the law, President Clinton and I agreed that our officials should begin work on an extradition treaty between our two countries.

I also raised to President Clinton two matters that are close to my heart. The first is the old issue of the rights of the Filipino veterans of World War II. The other is the so-called Amerasian children issue.

Finally, my delegation and I thank President Clinton and his delegation for the warmth and cordiality with which we conducted our discussions. Those discussions, I am sure, will lead to a new and a strong partnership for the benefit of both Americans and Filipinos.

Thank you, Mr. President.

American Airlines Strike

President Clinton. Thank you, Mr. President.

I would like now to read a statement on the airline strike, and then we'll take some questions from both the American and the Filipino press here.

I am pleased to announce that I have spoken with both parties involved in the American Airlines strike and that both have agreed in principle to end the strike and to return to the bargaining table immediately. They've also agreed to resolve all matters under dispute through binding arbitration. All American Airlines flight attendants will be reinstated.

I believe this agreement represents an important step forward for all Americans, including families that will be able to reunite over the holidays, the flight attendants themselves, all of whom will now be able to return to their jobs, and American Airlines which can now return to serving the traveling public. I hope this is the beginning of a happy holiday season for all of us.

I want to encourage all the people involved in the American Airlines family to now return to work together without any bitterness and with a spirit of mutual respect as they attempt to work through these issues through binding arbitration. This company and its employees are a very important part of the American economy, a very important part of the airline sector that has been troubled for the last couple of years and that is a very important part of our high-tech future.

I am very pleased by the agreement which has been reached. And I now ask all parties involved to approach it in good faith and with good spirits. I also want to say that I have spoken with the Secretary of Transportation and the Secretary of Labor, along with members of the National Mediation Board, and I want to thank them for the work that all of them did to help to bring matters to this point today. I am very pleased by this development, and again I want to thank the representatives of both sides, the attendants and the company, for making this important statement. And I look forward to the ultimate resolution of the issues.

Helen [Helen Thomas, United Press International].

North Korea and Japan

Q. Mr. President, is it true that the United States is prepared to sweeten the pot, give aid, recognition, call off Team Spirit, if North Korea agrees to nuclear inspection? And with the Japanese access to plutonium, don't you worry about Japan building the bomb?

President Clinton. Well, how many questions was that?

Q. Three. [*Laughter*]

President Clinton. Good for you.

Q. [*Inaudible*]

President Clinton. I'm glad to know you were keeping score. [*Laughter*]

As you know, President Kim of South Korea will be here tomorrow. And our administration has been working on a new approach to deal with this issue. I want to discuss it with him tomorrow, and then I expect to have an announcement on it.

I think it's fair to say that Japan does not wish to become a nuclear power and that in my talks with Prime Minister Hosokawa and with President Jiang of China, it was obvious to me that no one in the region wants North Korea to become a nuclear power. So we're going to do everything we can in close consultation with the countries most affected in the region to try to find a resolution to this. I also discussed this with President Ramos today because the Philippines has important membership on the IAEA, and he gave me his thoughts on it. We are working on it. I want to consult with President Kim tomorrow, and then I expect to have another announcement.

American Airlines Strike

Q. Mr. President, can you tell us, how did this American Airlines settlement come about? What role did you play in it? You said that you talked to both sides today. Did you put pressure on either side to accept this?

President Clinton. No, I don't think that would be a fair characterization of it. We were contacted—and our staff can give you some more background later after the press conference—and the White House has been actively involved all morning trying to bring the parties to this point. But to be fair, they were willing to be brought to this point. They were interested in trying to figure out what procedures we might follow so that we could get the strike over with, bring the flight attendants back, start the planes flying again. So I have to give them a large share of the credit. But they were willing to have us try to work out this arrangement, and I am grateful for that.

Bruce Lindsey had a lot to do with it this morning, talking to representatives of the two sides on the phone and talking to the Labor Department, the Transportation Department about what had been done to date and kind of getting a sense of where we were. And it all fell into place about an hour ago. And then I had to call them both, and we had to go over it all one more time to make sure that we were all singing out of the same hymnal about how the process would work and what rules would apply and things of that kind. And I feel quite good about it.

Is there anyone from the Korean press who has a—I mean, Filipino press?

Q. Philippine press, Mr. President.

President Clinton. Go ahead.

The Philippines

Q. Both you and President Ramos, have you discussed any details concerning the United States commitment to the multilateral aid initiative to the Philippines? And will you please expand on your talks concerning the vets, the veterans issue, as well as the Amerasians?

President Ramos. To the first of the three questions, let me say that we hardly discussed aid at all, but the main focus of our discussion was economic cooperation, which would result in more investment and trade in the Philippines and within Asia and the Pacific. In regard to the veterans problem, President Clinton and I agreed that we will continue looking at ways and means to make it right for the Filipino veterans of World War II. Of course, we both realize that there is legislative action involved, and the solution of the problem is not entirely within the hands of the Executive. Regarding the problem of the so-called Amerasian children, we agreed to work on this matter as well as to encourage the nongovernment organizations to do their part. I informed President Clinton that there is an NGO that is very active in the Philippines representing the concerned people of the United States, called the Pearl Buck Foundation, that has been in this kind of work for a long, long time now and with which we intend to establish close linkages on the part of the Philippine Government and also our Philippine NGO's.

Presidential Security

Q. Mr. President, on this 30th anniversary of President Kennedy's assassination, do you personally feel that the case is closed, that Lee Harvey Oswald did act alone without any assistance? And secondly, as you travel around, are you concerned about your own personal security as you wade into crowds and go around and talk to people?

President Clinton. I am satisfied with the finding that Lee Harvey Oswald acted alone. I'm also very satisfied with the work done by the Secret Service in my behalf. Most of the crowds that I see now have been through some sort of screening process, particularly if there's been a lot of advance notice of my coming. But it's impossible for a democratic leader in a free world, I think, to live in a shell. One of the greatest things a President has to guard against all the time is just becoming isolated from the feelings, the concerns, the conditions of daily life that all other Americans have to confront. And so there's always going to be a tension, if you lead a free country and you're accountable to all the citizens of that country, between the legitimate desire of the security forces to protect

you and the desire that I have not to lose touch and get totally out of sync with the lives of all the people whom I must represent.

Anyone else from the Filipino press? Yes.

Extradition Treaty

Q. Yes, President Clinton, an extradition treaty has been tried before between the Philippines and the United States. What issues remain from the point of view of the United States before such a treaty can be concluded?

President Clinton. Well, let me say we did not even discuss the outstanding issues today. We want to leave that to our negotiators. I think what President Ramos wanted to know was whether I was willing to do it. And the answer is I am very much willing to do it, and I believe that we will succeed.

Handgun Control Legislation

Q. Mr. President, the Brady bill has come so close before and failed with the end of a congressional session. Is there anything that you can do or that Democratic leaders can do to try to save it from an obstacle in the conference committee and to try to get the Senate to agree to the conference before Congress goes home?

President Clinton. Well, we might have just a shred of a chance of that. You know, the Senate was anxious to leave, and they've worked hard this year. The Congress has worked very hard. The House just passed overwhelmingly a comprehensive campaign finance reform, so that's another issue that the House and the Senate have acted on they'll have to conference. There may be some small chance it can be done now. But I don't want to hold out false hope. I would like it if it can be done. I would love it if the Congress could give the Brady bill to the American people for Thanksgiving. But I do believe that the size of the vote in the Senate and the marked shift almost overnight in the position of those who were promoting the filibuster shows an awareness that we have to lead on this crime and personal security issue and an understanding that the American people want something done at the national level and they want something done at the local level. And they want people to roll up their sleeves and go to work, not get in the way. So I believe that even if we fail to secure it at this 11th hour, that it'll pass when the Congress comes back and fairly quickly. I wish that it could be done now. I don't know if it can be done now.

Q. So why should people wait another few months?

President Clinton. I don't think they——

Q. They won't be back until——

President Clinton. I don't think they should. I think it should pass now. But I don't know if I can get it done. If it were up to me, it would be done right this minute; it would have been done months ago. But I can just tell you, we are working on it. We are exploring all possible options. I don't know if it can be done.

Extradition Treaty

Q. As a loyal member of the Philippine press, I'm quite disturbed about the extradition treaty. Are you planning to make provisions to protect the interests of political asylum, from the Philippines and vice versa, Mr. President?

President Ramos. The details are being worked out by our respective legal staffs. But I think you will appreciate the fact that the two governments have finally undertaken this effort on a joint basis.

During the Marcos period when the regime was very repressive and a lot of Filipinos came over to the United States to seek asylum, naturally there was no agreement on extradition because the United States wanted to protect those that had sought political asylum in this country. But we shall be concerned here with really extradition in the strictly criminal sense, as applying to violators of the revised Penal Code of the Philippines.

Environmental Issues

Q. Can I just follow up, sir, very important, on the environmental issue. I know you have talks on extradition and Amerasian and veterans. I think environment is a very important issue and is a concern not only of Asian countries but all countries in this world. Have you discussed anything on how to protect the environment for the Philippine side?

President Ramos. I brought it up at the APEC meeting itself as a concern of developing countries as well as of countries in the Asia-Pacific region. I discussed this extensively with Vice President Gore during our meeting, and I repeated it in our meeting with President Clinton.

The Philippines must be recognized as one of the first, if not the first, Asian countries that created the mechanism to implement the guidelines agreed to by most countries in the Earth summit in Rio in June 1992. And we're proud that we have this kind of a record in the international community. And we are very thankful to the United States Government for supporting many efforts on our part to improve our own Philippine environmental situation.

President Clinton. Let me just give you one specific example that President Ramos suggested, not now but in Seattle, that we look at establishing within the APEC region a technology transfer center that would accelerate the movement of technology for environmental protection and cleanup from the countries that have it to those that need to acquire it. So I think you can look forward to a time when we will really press this forward. It's very much in the interest of the United States, both environmentally and economically to do. And I really appreciate the fact that of all the APEC leaders, President Ramos was the one most insistent that we make progress on this.

Crime and the Community

Q. Mr. President, you've been talking a lot lately about children killing children. And a number of sociologists are now suggesting that not enough focus has been put on the parents who fail to supervise these children. Do you agree with that? And what can be done about it?

President Clinton. Absolutely, I agree with that. I think that the conditions you see today in a lot of the most desperate areas of our country are the result of a confluence of forces, one of which is plainly the breakdown of order within the family and the kind of direction and support that traditionally has been the province of parenthood. That's one reason, one thing.

Secondly, there has been a simultaneous breakdown of a lot of the community supports and alternatives to parental guidance that used to exist in a lot of communities. After all, there have always been children in trouble. There have always been children who had parents who were neglectful of them, even abusive of them. But in times past, there have been more alternative community supports than there are now. And one of the reasons that my speech to the Church of God in Christ got such a warm reception from the folks there is that many of them feel that they're holding back an even worse deluge, that the churches are almost the only community supports left in a lot of these neighborhoods.

The third thing, obviously, is the decline of available employment in a lot of these neighborhoods, so that a lot of the role models who would have been there, people who would have been there either in the home or in the neighborhood, are not there.

And then the fourth thing are the rise of drugs, not only as an instrument of personal abuse but also as an alternative economic system.

And then, finally, the ready availability of weapons, especially handguns and assault weapons, to reinforce an alternative economic and social order; all these things are working together. But clearly, we're going to have to have more efforts by people at the grassroots level, the churches, the community organizations, the local folks, to reinforce a sense of parental responsibility and accountability in whatever way we can.

Thank you. We have to go.

NOTE: The President's 34th news conference began at 2:30 p.m. in the East Room at the White House. In his remarks, he referred to Bruce Lindsey, Assistant to the President and Senior Adviser.

Remarks at the National Democratic Institute Dinner
November 22, 1993

Thank you very much, Ken. And thank you, ladies and gentlemen, for that warm welcome and for the work you do. It's a real honor for me to be here tonight among so many friends and colleagues who have worked so hard to promote democracy throughout the world. The work of NDI is well-known and highly prized, from Russia and the Baltics to Mexico, Paraguay to the African Continent and many other places where you are working to breathe life into the idea of democracy. I salute you for that work.

I think the knowledge that so many Americans have of your work and the credibility it has gained in the Congress is one reason that I was able to secure, with the help of some of the people here present, a substantial increase in funding for the National Endowment for Democracy at a time when we were cutting more than half the items in the domestic and the foreign budget.

I would also like to thank you for Brian Atwood and for the fine job he's done at AID.

I am delighted that tonight you're honoring two extraordinary leaders, Korean President Kim Yong-sam and Senator George Mitchell. Their lives have given meaning to the ideals which have inspired so many millions of people around the world who struggle for democracy.

President Kim's valiant efforts since his service as a young assemblyman to bring democracy to Korea are a model to aspiring democrats everywhere. He has certainly paid a price for his devotion to freedom and democracy. And all of us and all freedom-loving people everywhere in the world should honor the personal price he paid, and then the fact that, once given the chance to govern his country, he lived in office by the ideals he expressed out of office. More should do the same.

I also want to thank the NDI for honoring my good friend Senator George Mitchell, whose contributions to democracy, whose work for responsive Government here at home, and whose personal integrity prove once again that politics can be an honorable profession. When I went to the meeting of the Asian-Pacific leaders in Seattle, on the heels of the remarkable vote for the NAFTA treaty in the House of Representatives and its following overwhelming support in the Senate—something which, I add, I am convinced is good for democracy in Mexico and throughout Latin America—George Mitchell made sure that I did not forget that one of my missions was to espouse the cause of human rights in all the countries of the world who seek to be our full partners in moving toward the 21st century, and I thank him for that.

Not long before I came over here tonight, and after I finished the day's work, I went home to be with my daughter for a few moments. And she had a friend from school over, and they're studying for an examination around the kitchen table, the way I did so many times when I was her age. And we turned on the evening news because I wanted to see what was on about the airline strike which was settled today, and I thank the parties involved for doing that. And there was a special on, as you might imagine, about John Kennedy, since this is the 30th anniversary of his death. And it showed a lot of predictable footage, but I enjoyed watching it all the same. And the people who were commenting on the channels I watched all pointed out that everyone who was old enough to remember could tell you exactly where he or she was at that moment on that fateful Friday 30 years ago.

But the thing that I was most moved by was the comment that, at that time, 30 years ago, the American people believed in their Government and believed in their President and believed in the promise of democracy to improve the lot of the people of this country and people throughout the world. And of course, the commentator went on to point out how much more difficult it is today, not only in our country but throughout the world because of economic stagnation, because of the pressures from the middle class, because of the continuing inability of democracy to deliver on some of the deepest hopes and dreams of humankind.

I say to you tonight that if we had more people in public life like George Mitchell and President Kim, the confidence of the people of the world in democracy would go up, and the confidence of the people of the United States in who we are, what we believe in, and what we're capable of doing would increase. And so I ask you tonight, as you honor them on this fateful anniversary, to ask also of yourselves, what can we do together to make people really believe in the cause for which these men and so many others have given so much.

Thank you, and good night.

NOTE: The President spoke at 8 p.m. at the Washington Hilton Hotel. In his remarks, he referred to Ken Wollack, president of the institute.

Message to the Congress Transmitting the Railroad Retirement Board Report
November 22, 1993

To the Congress of the United States:

I hereby submit to the Congress the Annual Report of the Railroad Retirement Board for Fiscal Year 1992, pursuant to the provisions of section 7(b)(6) of the Railroad Retirement Act and section 12(1) of the Railroad Unemployment Insurance Act.

WILLIAM J. CLINTON

The White House,
November 22, 1993.

Statement on House of Representatives Action on Campaign Finance Reform
November 22, 1993

Today, the House of Representatives overwhelmingly passed comprehensive campaign finance reform legislation based on my proposal earlier this year.

The public has made clear that it expects change in the way Washington works and politics is conducted. This legislation is a major step toward ensuring that Government serves the national interest and not narrow interests. It sets up a system of spending limits; it opens up the airwaves to debate; it curbs the role of PAC's; and it bans the use of soft money in Federal elections.

I congratulate the House leadership for their energetic effort to pass this difficult legislation, and I look forward to signing the strongest possible bill when it reaches my desk in its final form. All in all, this is a breakthrough for political reform and a sign that we have heard the American people.

Appointment for Deputy Counsel to the President
November 22, 1993

The President announced today that he has appointed Washington attorney Joel Klein to be Deputy Counsel to the President. The appointment is effective December 1, 1993.

"With a long and distinguished record of achievement and public service, Joel Klein has proven himself one of the finest lawyers in Washington. His wisdom has been invaluable to me on a number of occasions already, and I expect that he will be an important advisor to me as Deputy Counsel," said the President.

NOTE: A biography of the appointee was made available by the Office of the Press Secretary.

Nomination for Treasurer of the United States
November 22, 1993

The President announced today that he has nominated Ohio treasurer Mary Ellen Withrow to be the Treasurer of the United States. The position is subject to Senate confirmation.

"Mary Ellen Withrow is an outstanding public servant who has been widely recognized for her innovative and efficient management of the people of Ohio's money," said the President. "As U.S. Treasurer she will play an important role in our efforts to cut waste and improve the management of public money in the Federal Government."

NOTE: A biography of the nominee was made available by the Office of the Press Secretary.

Remarks and an Exchange With Reporters Prior to a Meeting With Congressional Leaders
November 23, 1993

The President. I want to make a brief statement; then I'll answer a question or two.

The primary purpose of this meeting is for me to have a chance to thank the bipartisan congressional leadership for their cooperation and for our good working relationship here in this first year. I first met with this group on January 26th. We've met many times since then. I've been to Capitol Hill, I think, 15 times. This is only the second time in 60 years when there's been no Presidential veto in a year. Sometimes the major initiatives that were passed were passed with partisan votes but many times with bipartisan votes. And this was a remarkable year.

We passed the big deficit reduction package, which has kept interest rates down and inflation down and has contributed to a major increase in investment and job growth in the country. We passed with bipartisan support national service, NAFTA, the family and medical leave bill, major flood relief for people in the Middle West; both Houses have passed the campaign finance bill, a crime bill, the Brady bill. Health care reform has been introduced. This has been a very productive year, and I am extremely grateful to the leadership of both Houses for working so closely with the White House.

I also want to just thank the Members of Congress for working so hard. By my count they spent about 40 percent more hours in session than is normal for this year. And I appreciate that, and I wish them a good Thanksgiving.

The last point I would like to make is, as most of you know, the person who handled my congressional relations, Howard Paster, will be leaving the White House at the end of the year. And I want to publicly thank him for the work he did with both Houses, in both parties, and representing me so effectively. I think he's done a wonderful job, and he's going to be hard to replace.

Representatives Bonior and Gephardt

Q. You don't think that Bonior and Gephardt did you any favors this year, do you?

The President. They did me a lot of favors. If they hadn't voted for the budget and helped me pass it, we would have never gotten it enacted.

Handgun Control Legislation

Q. Mr. President, what's your reaction to Senator Dole's latest attempt to hold up the Brady bill? And what do you think you can do about it?

The President. Wait a minute. We're working on that. And I think—they're not as far apart as you think, at least Senator Dole. I still have—you know me, I believe in miracles. I believe that we may still get this worked out.

Senator Dole. He called me—when I came

in. [*Laughter*]

Q. Is Senator Mitchell going to call the Senate back if they don't pass it today?

The President. Well, that's up to Senator Mitchell. But let us work today. Let's see what we can do today. We're working on something today, and let's let today pass, and then we'll be able to talk about it.

Q. Well, what does Senator Mitchell say?

Senator Mitchell. It's very nice of you to come here and wish us a happy Thanksgiving.

No, the answer is that if we don't work it out and pass it today, we will be back next week.

Q. Senator Dole, what will it take for you to throw your support behind the Brady bill now?

Senator Dole. I think we can talk to you later. [*Laughter*]

The President. We're trying to get this worked out. Give us a chance. We're trying to get this worked out.

Assistant to the President for Legislative Affairs

Q. And who's replacing Howard?

The President. I haven't made a decision. Are you interested in the job, Jim [Jim Miklaszewski, NBC News]?

Q. No, thank you. I've seen what he had to go through this past year.

The President. Lower pay and longer hours, it's the kind of thing——

NOTE: The President spoke at 9:35 a.m. in the Cabinet Room at the White House. A tape was not available for verification of the content of these remarks.

Exchange With Reporters Prior to Discussions With President Kim Yong-sam of South Korea
November 23, 1993

North Korea

Q. We'll ask about Korea this time. Are you both on board with the same package for North Korea to permit international inspection of its nuclear sites?

President Clinton. Well, we'll have a statement about that later. We just started our meet-

ing. So I think we have to have the meeting before we can make a statement.

Q. But it appears that President Kim seems to have a deviation in the policy.

President Clinton. We haven't had our meeting yet. Give us a chance to talk about it, and then we'll be glad to comment about it.

Q. Are your options limited since China and

Japan don't want you to proceed with sanctions?

President Clinton. I think I'd like to comment on all that in the—we'll have a press statement, and then I'll answer questions about it. But I really would like to speak with President Kim first.

Q. Do you know if North Korea has a nuclear weapon at this point?

President Clinton. I want to have this meeting first and then I'll——

Q. What else can we ask you about?

Q. Nothing ventured——

Philadelphia State Senate Campaign

Q. Are you going to ask the Attorney General to look into the Philadelphia State senate race? One of the——

Q. Gingrich said you would.

Q. Are you going to do that, do you think?

President Clinton. The first I even knew about it was this morning. I don't know enough about it to give an answer. I'll have to look into it. I had not heard anything about it until this morning. I knew nothing about it until he mentioned it this morning.

President Kim's Visit

Q. How come you didn't jog together today?

President Clinton. Tomorrow. I don't know if he'll run with me tomorrow, but I'd like him to.

Q. It depends on how late your dinner is.

[*At this point, one group of reporters left the room and another group came in.*]

President Kim. My impression is that most of the journalists would like to raise interest by describing the subject as a very difficult issue. In fact, sometimes they're very simple ones, in a way unnecessarily complicates—[*inaudible*]

I think that this time we had a very sizable amount of journalist delegation this time. More than 100 people, I think, accompanied me on my visit in the U.S. this time.

President Clinton. They all got to go first to Seattle, and then here?

President Kim. Yes.

NOTE: The exchange began at 11:08 a.m. in the Oval Office at the White House. A tape was not available for verification of the content of this exchange.

The President's News Conference With President Kim Yong-sam of South Korea
November 23, 1993

President Clinton. Good afternoon. It is a great pleasure and an honor for me to welcome President Kim Yong-sam to Washington today. During my visit to Seoul in July, I had the opportunity to visit with President Kim at the Blue House, which is Korea's Presidential residence. I am honored to return his gracious hospitality today by welcoming him to our White House.

I have a great deal of admiration for President Kim, who for decades has worked tirelessly to broaden Korea's democracy at great personal cost to himself. His democratic passage to the Presidency is an inspiring measure of Korea's progress, proof that freedom knows no regional bounds. I'm delighted his contributions to Korean democracy were acknowledged when he received the Averell Harriman award from the National Democratic Institute last evening.

The discussions President Kim and I held today were far ranging and highly productive. We continued our conversation from the APEC leaders meeting in Seattle and expressed our mutual support for APEC's ideal of an Asian-Pacific region even more closely integrated through open markets and open societies.

Today we discussed the actions President Kim is taking to advance that vision in his nation. He's taken a number of encouraging steps to remove barriers to foreign investment, open financial markets, and strengthen intellectual property rights. I'm also very encouraged by the good start of the U.S.-Korea dialog on economic cooperation. We must work now to implement the proposals raised in that dialog. Our economic cooperation will be especially vital as both our nations seek to achieve a new GATT agreement in the next few weeks. Like the United

States, Korea has both a crucial role and a substantial stake in bringing the Uruguay round to a successful conclusion.

The most important piece of our discussions centered on North Korea. We are both concerned by North Korea's concentration of forces near the Demilitarized Zone and by its refusal to grant international inspectors full access to its nuclear sites.

In recent weeks, my administration has been working with the Congress, South Korea, Japan, our partners in the United Nations Security Council and others to address North Korea's nuclear program in a firm manner. Today I reaffirmed to President Kim America's unyielding commitment to South Korea's security. My administration has made it clear to North Korea that it now faces a simple choice. If it abandons its nuclear option and honors its international nonproliferation commitments, the door will be open on a wide range of issues not only with the United States but with the rest of the world. If it does not, it risks facing the increased opposition of the entire international community.

Our goals in this matter are clear: a nonnuclear peninsula and a strong international nonproliferation regime. To these ends, we are prepared to discuss with North Korea a thorough, broad approach to the issues that divide us, and once and for all to resolve the nuclear issue. But we cannot do that in the absence of a dialog between North and South Korea and while there is still growing doubt about the continuity of IAEA safeguards.

North Korea's nuclear program and its continuing military threat pose serious challenges to both South Korea and America. Our two nations have worked together to overcome these challenges before. Our friendship was forged in the heat of war as our forces fought shoulder to shoulder to turn back aggression. Our friendship has continued over four decades since that war ended as the people of Korea have transformed their country into an economic and democratic model for the entire region.

I've enjoyed working with President Kim to deepen the historic friendship between our two nations. And I look forward to working with him and with the Korean people in the days to come, on economic issues and on important issues of security.

Mr. President.

President Kim. Ladies and gentlemen, first of all I would like to thank President Clinton for his welcome extended to me at the White House today. Having met with President Clinton in Seoul in July and Seattle last week and here in Washington, DC, today, I feel like I'm meeting an old friend.

President Clinton has aptly summarized what was discussed in our meeting this morning, so I would like to add only a few points to what he has mentioned. President Clinton reaffirmed the strong commitment of the United States to the security of Korea and made it clear that there would not be an additional reduction of U.S. troops stationed in Korea until the North Korean nuclear issue has been resolved.

President Clinton and I agreed to continue our close working relationship to ensure peace on the Korean Peninsula as well as its regional stability. In particular, I welcomed and supported President Clinton's policy of continuing to maintain the strategy of forward deployment by the United States in the Asia-Pacific region, including the Korean Peninsula.

As for the North Korean nuclear issue, President Clinton and I reaffirmed our shared belief that the resolution of this issue should not be delayed any longer, as it poses great threats not only to the security of Korea but also to the global nonproliferation regime. In particular, we agreed to make thorough and broad efforts to bring about a final solution, bearing in mind the grave concern the international community has demonstrated over this issue. Both of us expressed satisfaction over the close cooperation between our two governments on this issue. And we once again agreed that the maintaining a close working relationship is essential to the complete resolution of this issue.

President Clinton and I shared our mutual satisfaction over the success thus far of the dialog for economic cooperation, a mechanism that we had agreed to establish in our meeting in July. We hope that our two countries will be able to draw up a long-term plan to expand our mutually beneficial economic cooperation.

I also explained to President Clinton that the internationalization of the Korean economy, along with the liberalization and deregulation were major goals of the new economic policy that my government has actively pursued, and that the new economic policy would help broaden the scope of the Korea-U.S. economic partnership.

During our discussion, I congratulated the

President Clinton, the success of the APEC leaders economic conference that was held in Seattle last week. And I would like to pay high tribute to the President for his outstanding leadership which helped to make the meeting a resounding success. We are convinced that this meeting will be recorded as an important milestone that heralds the coming era of a new Asia-Pacific partnership. Based upon the continued development of APEC, President Clinton and I reaffirmed our resolve to work closely together to build a new Pacific community.

I'm entirely satisfied with today's meeting. I'm confident that our meeting will help Korea-U.S. relations to evolve to an even higher dimension of partnership.

Finally, I again would like to express my gratitude to President Clinton for the warm welcome and hospitality.

Thank you.

North Korea

Q. Mr. President, you've spoken of a new approach to get North Korea to open up its nuclear program to inspection. Did the two of you agree today on a new approach, and does that represent any relaxation in the U.S. stand? And if so, why wouldn't that be rewarding North Korea for its intransigence?

President Clinton. We did not agree to relax anything. What we agreed was that the two of us, based on our own security needs, would reexamine what our policies are if the North Koreans are willing to allow IAEA inspectors and resume the serious dialog with the Republic of Korea; that we needed to make it clear that all of our security decisions would be made in light of that context. And I don't consider that weakening our position or changing it or rewarding aggression. In fact, what we want to do is to diminish the military tensions in the area. That has to begin by a willingness on the part of North Korea to allow the inspections and to resume the dialog.

Yes, Helen [Helen Thomas, United Press International]?

Q. Mr. President, it doesn't sound like you two are in sync on what to do about North Korea. And also, do you think that North Korea will accept our approach of more concessions?

President Clinton. Well, we're asking them to make two concessions that they're already committed to do. And we're committing then that the two of us will reexamine our security ap-

proach in light of that. But we're not divided at all. We reached agreement. We, indeed, have reconciled the precise language that would be used by each of us in this statement today. So there is no division between the two countries on our position.

Q. Will you call off the military maneuvers?

President Clinton. That is something that would have to be decided by both of us at a later date, depending on what would be done or not done by North Korea. We've made no decision on that and no commitment on that, and we couldn't now.

Q. Mr. President, I have two questions, one for President Kim and one for President Clinton. President Kim, it might be a little general question, however, you have denied several times that—the concept of the absorption unification; so that statement can be construed to the effect that you are giving up your constitutional authority to—[*inaudible*]—North Korea in the case of the self-destruction of the Kim Il-song regime and followed by the big anarchial situation like East Germany. And—[*inaudible*]—also give some clear statement for the North Korean people who are waiting for the new morning, as you said yesterday, for democracy and hope.

And for Mr. Clinton, North Korea has managed a lot to wage a war if U.N. sanctions will be imposed on North Korea. And also on report, actually—[*inaudible*]—quoting a Pentagon classified material, Korea and the United States is losing if war broke out again in the peninsula. So that kind of information is giving some warning more and more to the general innocent people in both North Korea and South Korea. So what is the clear and maybe present remarks concerning that matter, the menace of the possible Korean war again?

Thank you.

President Kim. I would like to respond to your question first. It is our basic policy that we will not try to absorb North Korea. And I mentioned this to the Chinese leader, Mr. Jiang Zemin, when I met him in Seattle and also asked him to convey this message towards North Korea, because we know that North Korean regime is very concerned about the possibility of such an absorption be happening. And the Chinese President promised that he will do so, that is, to convey the message towards North Korea.

Of course, it is very difficult to predict what

will happen in North Korea in the future. But I doubt the report that North Korea can launch a successful attack on South Korea and win the war. I very much doubt it. The reason is that South Korean Armed Forces has grown very strong, and in fact after the launching of the new government in Korea, we have replaced all those politicized military generals and established a professional military who will respond very effectively to any provocations or any attempt from North Korea. So combined forces of the United States and Republic of Korea, very stable, decisive, and very strong.

As President Clinton mentioned when he visited Korea, we very much believe in the policy of the United States, the new government's policy, that as long as Korean people want the U.S. forces to be stationed in Korea, then there will be no reduction, no pullout of the U.S. troops.

So I would like to once again reassure you that our defense capability and defense posture remains unchanged. And we are in a position that can deal with North Korea in a position of strength.

President Clinton. With regard to the two questions you asked me, let me say that neither President Kim nor I are eager to go to the United Nations and ask for sanctions against North Korea. We had discussed with the leaders of Japan and China at the recent APEC meeting the fact that that is not a particularly attractive option. We have offered as clearly as we could to North Korea the opportunity to reassess our relationships, at least in terms of our security requirements, if they will simply follow their own commitments and honor them on the IAEA inspections and on resuming the dialog with the Republic of Korea.

Now, as to your second question, I can only reiterate what I said when I was in Korea. I know of no one who seriously believes that the United States and the Republic of Korea would be defeated in a war of aggression by North Korea if they were to attack. And I made it as clear as I could that if they were to do that, they would pay a price so great that the nation would probably not survive as it is known today.

Q. Mr. President?

The President. Yes, Wolf [Wolf Blitzer, Cable News Network].

Q. The International Atomic Energy Agency has suggested that there is a time sensitivity

to going back into North Korea and inspecting the two nuclear facilities, a month or 2 months maximum. After that, they couldn't guarantee that North Korea was, in fact, abandoning some sort of nuclear weapons program. Is that, in fact, the case? Is there a month or two that you have now in order to resolve this issue?

And a question to President Kim: Do you support this notion that if the North Koreans do accept some sort of inspection and resume a dialog with you, that the United States and South Korea should cancel the joint military exercises, Team Spirit, next year?

President Clinton. First of all, there is some time sensitivity on this, based on what we hear from the IAEA inspectors. And that's the reason that we're coming forward now and trying to make another good faith effort to reach out and reason with North Korea.

President Kim. With regard to the issue of inspection of the nuclear facilities in North Korea, President Clinton and I share opinion that still inter-Korean mutual inspection is very important. North Korea and South Korea seem to have different position with regard to the meaning of the exchange of special envoy. I think that North Korea is more interested in holding an inter-Korean summit meeting through this exchange of special envoys, whereas our side, Republic of Korea, is more concerned about removing the suspicions regarding the nuclear facilities, that is, mutual inspection by both Koreas of those facilities.

There is a speculation that if North Korea accepts International Atomic Energy Agency inspection and resumes dialog with South Korea, then there will be concessions to be given to North Korea in return.

I think this matter of suspending Team Spirit exercise should be dealt in its own. And of course, the United States and Republic of Korea will consult very closely about how to deal with the problem caused by North Korea's nuclear development. And in that sense, we are in full accordance with each other.

Q. I'd like to ask a question, addressing the question to President Kim. You've said you cannot wait indefinitely, and when is the limit in time? How are you going to decide that is the limit? For President Clinton, you say thorough and broad approaches you would apply, and in Seattle during your press conference, you used the term "comprehensive approach." Comprehensive approach, is it the same term that

North Koreans are talking about with regard to nuclear issues and other issues involved? And is there any difference between the——

President Kim. I'll respond to your question first. The fact that I said we will not wait endlessly doesn't mean that we will necessarily set a certain deadline. And I don't think it is appropriate for me to specifically mention the possibility of setting a deadline. And perhaps I will make no more comments about that.

With regards to your referring to the terminology of whether it will be comprehensive approach or whether it will be package deals, I see the possibility of these different terminologies creating confusion and misleading. Therefore, what we have agreed today between President Clinton and I—and I would very much want you to pay attention to the phrases that we have used today—is that we will make thorough and broad efforts to bring the issue to the final conclusion. And that stands on its own. And please make sure that you pay attention to these new phrases.

Q. Mr. President, I'm a little confused by what you and the Korean President have offered today. Why after so many months do you believe that review of your security possibilities and talk-

ing to the Koreans about potential concessions in the future will cause them to change their minds when they have not at this point, so far, and when it appeared that there was some sort of actual concessions that you were getting ready to make?

President Clinton. Well, any concessions—first of all, concessions is the wrong word. Any gesture we make, any move we make based on our—must be based on our appreciation of what the security situation is. And they are the ones, after all, who are out of line with the international law and their own commitments. So, we can't make any decisions about what we would do until we see what they do. That's all we're saying today. But we have clearly broadened the dialog on this, or given them, rather, the more specific thing would—we've given them a chance to broaden the dialog. We'll just have to see if they take us up on it.

Thank you very much.

NOTE: The President's 35th news conference began at 1:07 p.m. in the East Room at the White House. President Kim spoke in Korean, and his remarks were translated by an interpreter.

Remarks on Signing the South African Democratic Transition Support Act of 1993
November 23, 1993

Thank you all for joining us this afternoon. It's a great honor to have so many people in the White House to celebrate the signing of legislation that marks the realization of a great dream, the transition of South Africa to a nonracial democracy and the end of apartheid.

So many of you have contributed mightily to the realization of that dream, and I thank you all for being here. But I want to especially recognize the presence here of the family of Amy Biehl, who herself did so much to further that cause. Thank you so much for coming.

For generations the people of South Africa lived under the crushing burden of an immoral system which exacted a terrible toll and ultimately could not endure. Over many years, you and many others have shown courage and determination in joining with South Africa's op-

pressed majority to hasten apartheid's demise. This ceremony is, in large measure, a salute to the work you have done.

In 1986, after years of effort and despite a Presidential veto, Congress imposed strict economic sanctions on South Africa. Our Nation vowed those sanctions would be lifted only on the day when South Africa was irreversibly on the road to a nonracial democracy. Last week that day for which millions have worked and prayed and suffered finally arrived. Nelson Mandela, F.W. de Klerk and other leaders formally endorsed the transitional constitution, a bill of rights, and other agreements achieved during nearly 2 years of hard negotiations. And this April, the people of South Africa, all races together, will go to the polls for the first time in three centuries. We urge those who are not participating in this historic process to do so.

This is a moment of great hope for South Africa and its supporters around the world but also a moment of great uncertainty. Decades of institutionalized segregation in South Africa have left a bitter legacy of division, of poverty, of illiteracy, of unemployment. For South Africa's democratic transition to succeed, the first post-apartheid government will need the resources to combat those conditions. The South African people have declared their determination to confront the challenge of change in order to pursue a better future. I am determined that our Nation will stand by them as they face the difficult challenges ahead. The bill I'm about to sign will help to ensure that those resources are available. It lifts our remaining economic sanctions and gives South Africa access to the resources of the international financial institutions. It urges all our State and local governments and private entities to end their economic restrictions on South Africa as well.

Through these and other steps, this bill will help South Africa expand the prosperity of its entire population, but removing sanctions will not be enough. Americans who have been so active in toppling the pillars of apartheid must remain committed to building South Africa's nonracial market democracy.

For this reason, I've asked Secretary of Commerce Ron Brown to lead a mission to South Africa to explore trade and investment opportunities, particularly with South Africa's black private sector. I am pleased that Ruth Harkin, our President and CEO of the Overseas Private Investment Corporation, along with many private sector leaders, will be going as a part of the delegation. I deeply appreciate the bipartisan support this bill received, and I appreciate Congress' cooperation in passing it so quickly so that Secretary Brown and the delegation could carry the message of hope and commitment as they travel to Johannesburg, Soweto, Cape Town, and Durban.

And now, with great pleasure, I sign into law this act celebrating the triumph of the human spirit, the perseverance of the South African people, the dream of freedom's new dawn, and the commitment of the American people to see that dream come true. *Nkosi Sikelel, i' Afrika.* God bless Africa, and God bless America.

NOTE: The President spoke at 2:18 p.m. in the Roosevelt Room at the White House. In his remarks, he referred to Amy Biehl, American Fulbright scholar slain in South Africa in August; South African President Frederik Willem de Klerk; and African National Congress President Nelson Mandela. H.R. 3225, approved November 23, was assigned Public Law No. 103–149.

Message to the Congress Transmitting the Chemical Weapons Convention
November 23, 1993

To the Senate of the United States:

I transmit herewith, for the advice and consent of the Senate to ratification, the Convention on the Prohibition of the Development, Production, Stockpiling and Use of Chemical Weapons and on Their Destruction (the "Chemical Weapons Convention" or CWC). The Convention includes the following documents, which are integral parts thereof: the Annex on Chemicals, the Annex on Implementation and Verification, and the Annex on the Protection of Confidential Information. The Convention was opened for signature and was signed by the United States at Paris on January 13, 1993. I transmit also, for the information of the Senate, the Report of the Department of State on the Convention.

In addition, I transmit herewith, for the information of the Senate, two documents relevant to, but not part of, the Convention: the Resolution Establishing the Preparatory Commission for the Organization for the Prohibition of Chemical Weapons and the Text on the Establishment of a Preparatory Commission (with three Annexes), adopted by acclamation by Signatory States at Paris on January 13, 1993. These documents provide the basis for the Preparatory Commission for the Organization for the Prohibition of Chemical Weapons (Preparatory Commission), which is responsible for preparing detailed procedures for implementing the Convention and for laying the foundation for the international organization created by the Convention. In addition, the recommended legislation necessary to implement the Chemical Weapons Convention, environmental documentation related to the Convention, and an analysis of the verifiability of the Convention consistent with Section 37 of the Arms Control and Disarmament Act, as amended, will be submitted separately to the Senate for its information.

The Chemical Weapons Convention is unprecedented in its scope. The Convention will require States Parties to destroy their chemical weapons and chemical weapons production facilities under the observation of international inspectors; subject States Parties' citizens and businesses and other nongovernmental entities to its obligations; subject States Parties' chemical industry to declarations and routine inspection; and subject any facility or location in the territory or any other place under the jurisdiction or control of a State Party to international inspection to address other States Parties' compliance concerns.

The Chemical Weapons Convention is also unique in the number of countries involved in its development and committed from the outset to its nonproliferation objectives. This major arms control treaty was negotiated by the 39 countries in the Geneva-based Conference on Disarmament, with contributions from an equal number of observer countries, representing all areas of the world. To date, more than 150 countries have signed the Convention since it was opened for signature in January of this year.

The complexities of negotiating a universally applicable treaty were immense. Difficult issues such as the need to balance an adequate degree of intrusiveness, to address compliance concerns, with the need to protect sensitive nonchemical weapons related information and constitutional rights, were painstakingly negotiated. The international chemical industry, and U.S. chemical industry representatives, in particular, played a crucial role in the elaboration of landmark provisions for the protection of sensitive commercial and national security information.

The implementation of the Convention will be conducted by the Organization for the Prohibition of Chemical Weapons (OPCW). The OPCW will consist of the Conference of the States Parties, which will be the overall governing body composed of all States Parties, the 41-member Executive Council, and the Technical Secretariat, an international body responsible for conducting verification activities, including on-site inspections. The OPCW will provide a forum in and through which members can build regional and global stability and play a more responsible role in the international community.

The Convention will enter into force 180 days after the deposit of the 65th instrument of ratification, but not earlier than 2 years after it was opened for signature. Thus, the Convention can enter into force on January 13, 1995, if 65 countries have deposited their instruments of ratification with the depositary for the Convention (the Secretary General of the United Nations) by July 1994. The 2-year delay before the earliest possible entry into force of the Convention was intended to allow Signatory States time to undertake the necessary national legislative and procedural preparations and to provide time for the Preparatory Commission to prepare for implementation of the Convention.

The Convention is designed to exclude the possibility of the use or threat of use of chemical weapons, thus reflecting a significant step forward in reducing the threat of chemical warfare. To this end, the Convention prohibits the development, production, acquisition, stockpiling, retention, and, direct or indirect, transfer to anyone of chemical weapons; the use of chemical weapons against anyone, including retaliatory use; the engagement in any military preparations to use chemical weapons; and the assistance, encouragement, or inducement of anyone to engage in activities prohibited to States Parties. The Convention also requires all chemical weapons to be declared, declarations to be internationally confirmed, and all chemical weapons to be completely eliminated within 10 years after its entry into force (15 years in extraordinary cases), with storage and destruction monitored through on-site international inspection. The Convention further requires all chemical weapons production to cease within 30 days of the entry into force of the Convention for a State Party and all chemical weapons production facilities to be eliminated (or in exceptional cases of compelling need, and with the permission of the Conference of the States Parties, converted to peaceful purposes). Cessation of production, and destruction within 10 years after the entry into force of the Convention (or conversion and peaceful production), will be internationally monitored through on-site inspection.

In addition, the Convention prohibits the use of riot control agents as a method of warfare, reaffirms the prohibition in international law on the use of herbicides as a method of warfare, and provides for the possibility for protection against and assistance in the event of use or threat of use of chemical weapons against a State Party. The Administration is reviewing the impact of the Convention's prohibition on the use of riot control agents as a method of warfare on Executive Order No. 11850, which specifies the current policy of the United States with regard to the use of riot control agents in war. The results of the review will be submitted separately to the Senate.

The Convention contains a number of provisions that make a major contribution to our nonproliferation objectives. In addition to verification of the destruction of chemical weapons, the Convention provides a regime for monitoring relevant civilian chemical industry facilities through declaration and inspection requirements. States Parties are also prohibited from providing any assistance to anyone to engage in activities, such as the acquisition of chemical weapons, prohibited by the Convention. Exports to non-States Parties of chemicals listed in the Convention are prohibited in some instances and subject to end-user assurances in others. Imports of some chemicals from non-States Parties are also banned. These restrictions will also serve to provide an incentive for countries to become parties as soon as possible. Finally, each State Party is required to pass penal legislation prohibiting individuals and businesses and other nongovernmental entities from engaging in activities on its territory or any other place under its jurisdiction that are prohibited to States Parties. Such penal legislation must also apply to the activities of each State Party's citizens, wherever the activities occur. Through these provisions, the Convention furthers the important goal of preventing the proliferation of chemical weapons, while holding out the promise of their eventual worldwide elimination.

The Convention contains two verification regimes to enhance the security of States Parties to the Convention and limit the possibility of clandestine chemical weapons production, storage, and use. The first regime provides for a routine monitoring regime involving declarations, initial visits, systematic inspections of declared chemical weapons storage, production and destruction facilities, and routine inspections of the relevant civilian chemical industry facilities. The second regime, challenge inspections, allows a State Party to have an international inspection conducted of any facility or location in the territory or any other place under the jurisdiction or control of another State Party in order to clarify and resolve questions of possible noncompliance. The Convention obligates the challenged State Party to accept the inspection and to make every reasonable effort to satisfy the compliance concern. At the same time, the Convention provides a system for the inspected State Party to manage access to a challenged site in a manner that allows for protection in its national security, proprietary, and constitutional concerns. In addition, the Convention contains requirements for the protection of confidential information obtained by the OPCW.

The Convention prohibits reservations to the Articles. However, the CWC allows reservations to the Annexes so long as they are compatible with the object and purpose of the Convention. This structure prevents States Parties from modifying their fundamental obligations, as some countries, including the United States, did with regard to the Geneva Protocol of 1925 when they attached reservations preserving the right to retaliate with chemical weapons. At the same time, it allows States Parties some flexibility with regard to the specifics of their implementation of the Convention.

Beyond the elimination of chemical weapons, the Chemical Weapons Convention is of major importance in providing a foundation for enhancing regional and global stability, a forum for promoting international cooperation and responsibility, and a system for resolution of national concerns.

I believe that the Chemical Weapons Convention is in the best interests of the United States. Its provisions will significantly strengthen United States, allied and international security, and enhance global and regional stability. Therefore, I urge the Senate to give early and favorable consideration to the Convention, and to give advice and consent to its ratification as soon as possible in 1994.

WILLIAM J. CLINTON

The White House,
November 23, 1993.

Nomination for Posts at the Department of Defense
November 23, 1993

The President announced today that he has nominated Richard F. Keevey to be the Chief Financial Officer of the Department of Defense and Stephen M. Ryan to be the Department's Inspector General.

"We must ensure that our Nation's defense dollars are spent frugally, and that the vast operations of the Pentagon are managed in the most efficient manner possible," said the President. "Under Secretary Aspin's leadership, great strides have been taken towards eliminating waste and fraud, and ensuring the most cost-effective procurement and management processes possible. With a seasoned manager like Richard Keevey and an experienced investigator like Stephen Ryan on board, those efforts will progress even further."

NOTE: Biographies of the nominees were made available by the Office of the Press Secretary.

Remarks at the State Dinner for President Kim Yong-sam of South Korea
November 23, 1993

Mr. President, Mrs. Kim, distinguished guests, 4 months ago the First Lady and I were deeply honored by the warm hospitality that the President and Mrs. Kim extended to us during our visit to Korea, including a memorable state dinner at Korea's Blue House. Tonight it is our pleasure to welcome President and Mrs. Kim to the first state dinner we've held here at the White House.

Mr. President, your leadership for democracy and your great personal sacrifice in the cause of democracy in Korea has been an inspiration to freedom-loving people around the world. And you have provided leadership, as well, for your country's remarkable economic performance which has made Korea a model for other nations. Terrain that once was bomb-scarred and war-ravaged today supports modern factories and new skyscrapers. In just 33 years, Korea's output has increased an astounding 100-fold.

The optimism and perseverance that have made South Korea great can also be found in abundance here in our Korean-American community. Over 1 million Korean-Americans today are contributing greatly to the dynamism of our American life. They are building bonds of cooperation across an ocean of opportunity, bonds that will serve our two nations well as we meet the many challenges that face us both in the years ahead.

For 43 years, Mr. President, America and Korea have stood shoulder to shoulder to preserve security on the peninsula. Today, new challenges such as North Korea's nuclear program continue to demand our vigilance and our determined effort. But they also demand that we demonstrate vision. You and I share a vision, Mr. President, a vision of a Korea at peace and one day reunited on terms acceptable to the Korean people.

During my visit to Korea in July, I was moved not only by the beauty of the "Land of the Morning Calm" but also by the spirit of the people. When I visited Seoul, I gained a better appreciation of the scope of Korea's economic success, the miracle on the Han. When I stood on the somber bridge at the Point of No Return, I gained a deeper appreciation for Korea's continuing security challenges. When I spoke to the National Assembly, I gained an inspiring appreciation of Korea's commitment to democracy. And when I went jogging with President Kim, I gained a fresh appreciation for the warmth, the vigor, and the endurance of Korea's leader.

President Kim, it is with great admiration for you and for the people of Korea that I invite everyone here to join me in a toast to you and to the Republic of Korea. May democracy continue to flourish there, and may the dream of peaceful reunification on the Korean Penin-

sula soon become a reality.

To President and Mrs. Kim and the people of the Republic of Korea. Hear, hear.

NOTE: The President spoke at 8:38 p.m. in the State Dining Room at the White House.

Remarks and an Exchange With Reporters at the Thanksgiving Turkey Presentation Ceremony
November 24, 1993

The President. Good morning, ladies and gentlemen and boys and girls. It's good to see you here. I want to especially thank Congresswoman Leslie Byrne for joining us, along with Stuart Proctor, the National Turkey Federation president, and the turkey, clapping for the president—[*laughter*]—Thomas Bross, the chairman of the federation and a turkey farmer from Pennsylvania who raised this year's Thanksgiving turkey, and the National Turkey Federation staff. Finally, I want to welcome the fourth-grade students who are here from Springfield Estates Elementary School in Springfield, Virginia. Welcome to all of you. I'm glad you're here for Thanksgiving.

As President, this is my first year to have the honor of accepting the annual Thanksgiving turkey and granting the turkey the annual Presidential pardon. [*Laughter*] After this ceremony, this turkey will retire to a 1930's working farm replica in Northern Virginia.

We've come together today to have a little fun but also to express our gratitude in this Thanksgiving season for God's many blessings, a time to impress upon younger people the heritage of our Nation and the commitment we all have to justice and freedom and peace.

It's also a time to reach out in service to others not as fortunate as we are. In a few hours, Hillary and I will visit the new Covenant Baptist Church here in Washington where church members and homeless families are coming together to prepare a Thanksgiving dinner. Thanksgiving, when we all bask in the generosity and hospitality of our own family and friends, reminds us that we also belong to a larger community full of people who often are not as fortunate as we are.

It's a time to value those things and to re-

member how strong we are when we come together to overcome adversity. In the last few months I've had a chance to spend a lot of time in the Middle West, dealing with the floods and their aftermath, and then last Sunday I went to church in California with two dozen people who went through the horrible trauma of the wildfires in the West. And I saw again what people can do when they pull together and remember that we are all in this together.

Tomorrow, I'll have the great good fortune of celebrating Thanksgiving with my family, reflecting on the past year and looking to the future. I'll have the chance to say a prayer of thanks for the many blessings that I have enjoyed. I ask all of you to do that. I wish you well on this Thanksgiving and to remember also our continuing obligations for our fellow Americans who don't have many of the things we take for granted. Together we can make this country stronger and have even more to be thankful for next Thanksgiving.

Thank you very much. [*Applause*] And thank you for the applause.

Somebody pointed out this morning that this may not be the only turkey I've had in my administration, but this is one I will certainly set free. [*Laughter*]

[*At this point, the President spoke with the children.*]

Turkey Presentation

The President. I'm experienced in this. I come from the fourth largest turkey-growing State in the country .

Q. Is this your first Presidential pardon?

The President. It is my first Presidential pardon.

Q. You're going into great detail over this—

[*inaudible*]

The President. Yes, we were talking to the kids about the turkey. This is a very well behaved turkey.

Q. We were hoping for something better, actually.

The President. I asked the gentleman who raised him, you know, if they went to any trouble, any extra effort to raise him, and he said that they had spent a lot of time handling him, so he's more comfortable around people.

Q. Were you concerned at all about this, because this has some ridiculous aspects for a President——

The President. So many of my predecessors have participated in this—[*inaudible*]. I actually didn't mind it. I think it's kind of funny, and it's an annual ritual. As I said, it's a little easier for me because I've been around turkeys all my life. I didn't mean it like that—[*laughter*]— and I come from a State that grows a lot of turkeys. We also have a huge wild turkey population at home, too, so it's not as alien an experience for me as it would be for some people.

Q. Do you think the Founding Fathers made the right choice not choosing a turkey as the national bird?

Q. You know Franklin proposed it. He really did.

The President. Yes, he did. Well, actually, let me tell you—but what Franklin meant—wild turkeys, and they're quite beautiful, if you've ever seen them. They're bottom heavy, like a regular turkey, but they're quite beautiful. And they can go from zero to 35 miles an hour in no time, something most people don't know, an amazing creature to see operate in the woods. And being out there in the woods on an early November or December morning, listening to the turkeys, actually, in our State, it's turkey season earlier.

Q. Does this remind you of any of the Members of Congress you've been dealing with in the last—[*laughter*]—

Q. Speaking of that, what's the latest——

Handgun Control Legislation

Q. What's the latest on the Brady bill?

The President. I don't know. Senator Mitchell has put a very, I think, good offer on the table. He has offered, with my strong support, to put in a separate bill as soon as they come back, several provisions of the Brady bill that we don't think would weaken the bill that Senator Dole wanted, one of which deals with the automation of records and when that could supplant the waiting period, when the records are automated, that 67 Senators voted for before, including Senator Dole. One deals with giving them what they wanted, which was a 4-year instead of 5-year time period, with an extra year it could be extended at the Attorney General's discretion. And I think there's another change in there. Senator Mitchell has gone the extra mile, and I have authorized him to say that I will strongly support the legislation so that it would permit the Senate Republicans to give up on the filibuster and send the Brady bill to us now and we could give it to the American people for Thanksgiving. That's what I think they ought to do, but we'll just have to see. I certainly hope they——

Q. Why do you think the Republicans are so adamant?

The President. I don't know. I think they're just—[*inaudible*]. I don't know. People who don't want the bill are holding it hostage. We should have done this long ago. It's an important first step in trying to get ahold of gun violence in this country and make our streets safer and enable our police officers to do their jobs better. And we now have the support of 80 percent of the American people and a big majority in the Senate. We know we have over 60 Senators prepared to vote for this bill, but the political gridlock is holding one more than 40 of them. In the filibuster system, you know, 41 percent of the Senate can prevent a bill from coming to a vote. I think it's a terrible mistake, and I hope we can break out of it today.

Q. What kind of a political price are the Republicans going to pay for this, after citing the statistics they used——

The President. Well, I think the American people want us to act. I think they do not want this to be a partisan political issue. I think the safety of our streets has become also a national security issue. I think the American people want us to act. And I don't want to make it a partisan issue. I have bent over backwards not to. I want to work with the Republicans on the crime bill. I want to put another 100,000 police officers on the street. I want that assault weapons ban. I don't think it ought to be a partisan issue. But their partisan filibuster is making it a partisan issue, and I think that it's a mistake for them to do it. But we're going to keep working as hard as we can. I still think we've got a chance to get it done, and I hope that the American people will be supportive. I know they are; that's what they're hearing out there. We've just got to keep on plugging.

Q. Hasn't it become personal, also, Mr. President? Senator Dole thinks he was sandbagged by the Democrats.

The President. Well, I know he thinks that, and I don't want to get into this, because I can't—I mean, he says that, but this has nothing to do with the underlying merits. This is either a good bill or not a good bill, number one. Number two, the Republicans on the conference committee were not even on the regular committee, and they were people who had no intention of voting for the Brady bill if all the changes they wanted were adopted. So the Democrats argued that they felt that they didn't know what they were supposed to talk about with people who weren't going to vote for it regardless and who weren't even on the committee that had jurisdiction of the Brady bill. So you can hear arguments on both sides about that, but that's irrelevant, that's irrelevant.

This is a good thing for the American people. It's a good first step. It's the right thing to do. If you stay around these battles now, and you've been through all of the stuff we've been through just in the last year, all of us—if you go around letting your personal feelings get in the way of doing the public interest, we'd never get anything done around here.

NOTE: The President spoke at 10:36 a.m. in the Rose Garden at the White House.

Remarks at the Covenant Baptist Church
November 24, 1993

The President. Thank you. First of all, let me say to you, Pastor, and to the whole staff and family of Covenant Baptist Church, I thank you for taking us in here and letting us be a part of what Hillary and I have always done at Thanksgiving, being a part of some ministry to take Thanksgiving to people who would otherwise not have it. I want to also thank the Coalition for the Homeless that's working with you for the work that they have done to try to turn homelessness into a temporary condition by moving people through shelters into having the skills and the strength and the power to take control of their own lives.

I think it's important that the people of America know, all the people of America know, that in our cities where people have many problems, most of the people who live there are good, God-fearing, law-abiding, hard-working people who are doing things like this to help their friends and neighbors and who want things to work better.

So my commitment to you is to do what I can as President to help you succeed here, in your church and on your streets. And I hope that all Americans on this Thanksgiving, including many Americans like me and Hillary and our family who have more than they could ever have asked for, will take some time out to work, as you are working, so that other people who don't have so much can also have something to be thankful for on Thanksgiving and throughout the year.

Thank you, and God bless you all.

[At this point, the President and Hillary Clinton were presented with T-shirts.]

The President. Let me say one other thing, Reverend Wiley. I like this church also because you've got a husband and wife team here who are both pastors, both pastors of this church, and making this thing work as a family, along with your distinguished father who preceded you in the pulpit. Reverend Wiley, it's good to see you. And we like to see people working together like this and all of you doing that. I appreciate it and respect it very much. Thank you for your service and your ministry. I'll wear this jogging. Thank you.

Handgun Control Legislation

Q. Mr. President, did you get a deal on the Brady bill?

The President. It looks like the Brady bill is going to be passed any minute, and I am very happy. Right before I left to come over here, it appeared that an agreement could be reached between Senator Mitchell and Senator Dole to end the Republican filibuster of the Brady bill. I am elated. It is a wonderful Thanksgiving present for the American people. It will enable us nationwide for the first time in history to check people who are trying to buy handguns for their age, for their mental health history, for their criminal history. It will be a beginning in what must be a long and relentless assault on the problems of crime and violence in this country. And we are beginning. It's a great Thanksgiving present, and next year

I look forward to passing the crime bill and to continuing to do this work for as long as I'm in this job. It's very important.

We're going to rebuild the families, the neighborhoods, the communities, the schools, and safety and security, from the grassroots up. This is the first step. I am very happy. Thank you very much.

NOTE: The President spoke at 1:46 p.m. In his remarks, he referred to Dennis and Christine Wiley, pastors, Covenant Baptist Church.

Teleconference on the Passage of Handgun Control Legislation and an Exchange With Reporters
November 24, 1993

Q. How soon do you think for the signing, Mr. President?

The President. Early next week, I hope. We're working on it.

Q. And what about the compromise? Are you satisfied with the kind of compromise the Republicans want to bring to a vote?

The President. They asked for the right to bring it to a vote and to know that it wouldn't be vetoed if they could pass it. We all agreed, all of us together, that that was acceptable.

Q. Do you think the Republicans were afraid to go home to their districts this weekend without reaching some kind of agreement?

The President. I think the American people would have been real disappointed if Congress had gone home without this bill. And I think they'll be very happy now. It's a great Thanksgiving present.

[*At this point, the telephone conversation began.*]

The President. Hello, Senator Mitchell, how are you doing? Mr. Speaker?

Senator Mitchell. [*Inaudible*]

The President. You sure are. I told you last night, see.

Senator Mitchell. [*Inaudible*]

The President. Well, we are delighted. I am here with the Vice President, Attorney General Reno, and Jim and Sarah Brady in the Oval Office, and we're all happy as can be. And we thank you very much for a wonderful session of Congress and a wonderful ending.

Senator Mitchell. [*Inaudible*]—back to health care next year.

Speaker Foley. A lot of work to be done next year, Mr. President, we're going to look forward to working with you on.

The President. And we're ready to roll, and we're very grateful to you. You have a good Thanksgiving and a good Christmas.

Speaker Foley. I'd like to put on Bob Michel here just to say a word to you.

Senator Mitchell. And Bob Dole as well——

The President. Please do.

Senator Mitchell. ——without whose cooperation we could not have achieved this result today.

Representative Michel. Hi, Mr. President, this is Bob Michel speaking.

The President. Hello, Bob.

Senator Dole. Bob Dole——

The President. Hi, Bob. Thank you both very much.

Senator Dole. Well, we think it was kind of a capstone of the whole session to get the Brady bill behind us. As I indicated yesterday, I thought we could do it if we just hung in there.

The President. Well, it worked out, and all of us are very pleased and very grateful. And I'm especially glad that we're ending this session on two measures where there was substantial bipartisan support for the progress that we're making. And I'm very appreciative of it, grateful to both of you. I hope you have a good holiday.

Senator Dole. Same to you, Mr. President.

Representative Michel. Yeah, thank you very much, Mr. President.

The President. Take care of that shoulder, Bob.

Representative Michel. [*Inaudible*]—I would have to agree with the assessment. It got confrontational at times, but it's nice to leave in an amicable mood when we're talking the same language. We'll be back next year.

The President. Can't wait to see you.

Representative Michel. Happy Thanksgiving to both you and Mrs. Clinton.

The President. Thank you.

Speaker Foley. Goodbye, sir.

The President. Goodbye, Mr. Speaker.

Senator Mitchell. Okay, thank you again, Mr. President. Have a good Thanksgiving.

The President. Thank you, Senator Mitchell.

Senator Mitchell. Talk to you soon.

The President. Bless you. Bye-bye.

[*At this point, the telephone conversation ended.*]

The President. I would just like to say before we leave, on behalf of the Vice President and the Attorney General and myself, that we believe very passionately in the Brady bill. As all of you who were involved in the campaign know, I spoke about it at every campaign stop and every country crossroads in this country. But none of this would have ever happened if it hadn't been for the courage and dedication and constancy of Jim and Sarah Brady. They worked for 7 years for this day. This is their victory, and I'm glad to be a small part of it.

And I hope that it means what I believe it does, which is that the American people are serious about our doing something about mindless violence, about the terrible conditions under which our young people are laboring, where so many of the children are being shot, weapons of mass destruction that they shouldn't even have in the cities or anywhere else in this country. And I hope this is the beginning of our effort to rebuild the fabric of this country from the grassroots up.

Our administration is dedicated to that. The Attorney General has spent her life working on it. And if this is the beginning of what I think it is, then the entire Nation owes Jim and Sarah Brady even more than for the Brady bill; they have changed the focus of our Nation. It's high time. It took them too many years to do it. What a wonderful Thanksgiving for them. And we are thankful for them. Thank you very much.

James Brady. Thank you, Mr. President.

NOTE: The President spoke at 2:50 p.m. in the Oval Office at the White House. In his remarks, he referred to former White House Press Secretary James Brady, who was wounded in the 1981 assassination attempt on President Ronald Reagan, and his wife, Sarah, head of Handgun Control, Inc.

Statement on the Nomination for Commander in Chief of the United States Southern Command
November 24, 1993

I am pleased to announce that I have nominated Lt. Gen. Barry R. McCaffrey to succeed Gen. George A. Joulwan as Commander in Chief of U.S. Southern Command and for promotion to the rank of General, United States Army.

Lieutenant General McCaffrey has had a long and brilliant career spanning nearly three decades. He has served our Nation proudly in four combat tours and in seven foreign nations. As commanding general of the 24th Infantry Division, he deployed the division to Saudi Arabia and led it on combat missions essential to the success of Operation Desert Storm. In addition, his performance in sensitive and demanding staff positions in Washington, including his current role as Director for Strategic Plans and Policy, Joint Staff, has distinguished him as one of our Nation's foremost military analysts and strategists. He has fully demonstrated both the military expertise and political acumen needed to fill one of our most strategically important postings.

I have asked Lieutenant General McCaffrey to apply his considerable talents to enhancing the important security relationships we have developed with our neighbors in the region, to refining the role of the U.S. Southern Command in hemispheric affairs, and to continuing the outstanding work done by General Joulwan.

I have the utmost trust and confidence in his ability to do so.

Statement on the Technology Reinvestment Project
November 24, 1993

We're putting the people and expertise that helped America win the cold war to work on restoring America's industrial competitiveness. We are bringing together private industry, State and local governments, and community colleges to form technology deployment alliances. Together they will see to it that small manufacturers have access to the latest and best information, techniques, equipment, and know-how.

The TRP's industrial outreach program is designed to promote the best in American manufacturing practices and expertise. We mean to recreate in industrial America the same success that the agricultural extension programs had in making America number one in agriculture. The States have pioneered programs to apply technology to industrial needs. With a Federal partner, these programs can help smaller defense firms adjust and compete in commercial markets. The goal is a simple one: more jobs for American workers.

NOTE: This statement was included in a White House announcement of the second group of awards in the technology reinvestment project.

Statement on Signing the Unemployment Compensation Amendments of 1993
November 24, 1993

Today I am pleased to sign into law H.R. 3167, the "Unemployment Compensation Amendments of 1993." This legislation will provide the unemployed and their families with important assistance by extending eligibility for the Emergency Unemployment Compensation (EUC) program to individuals exhausting their regular unemployment benefits. EUC benefits would be extended from last October 2 through February 5 of next year. In addition, the legislation will accelerate the reemployment of workers by requiring the establishment of a worker profiling system in each State to link workers most likely to experience long-term unemployment with effective job search assistance.

There are some important signs that the economy continues to improve and that a job recovery is underway. In the first 9 months of my Administration, our economy has created 1.3 million private sector jobs, which is more than were created in the previous 4 years combined.

With the solid foundation provided by the enactment of the economic program this summer, I believe the economy will continue to grow and create more new jobs.

However, the improvement in the economy is not yet solid enough to justify discontinuing the EUC program. It is therefore appropriate that we extend EUC to provide support to help unemployed workers pay their grocery bills and other living expenses while they seek new employment.

Just providing income support to the unemployed is not enough. The Administration is committed to moving from the present system that simply buffers the pain of unemployment toward a new system that speeds displaced workers into reemployment. The critical first step in this transformation is the requirement in this Act that States establish a worker profiling system.

Under these systems, workers filing for unemployment benefits who have permanently lost their jobs and are likely to need reemployment services would be identified early in their period of unemployment. These workers would then be referred to, and offered, job search assistance. There is strong evidence from demonstration projects in New Jersey and other States that such systems reduce the period of unemployment experienced by these workers as well as the associated costs and pain of such unemployment. In short, the workers benefit through earlier reemployment, the Federal Government benefits through reduced unemployment insurance costs and increased tax receipts, and the economy benefits through increased productivity.

I believe these worker profiling systems will make a real difference and provide new oppor-

tunities for unemployed workers. We will build upon this approach in proposing a comprehensive reemployment program early next year that will provide displaced workers with greatly enhanced access to early, effective, and comprehensive services.

In combining the requirement for worker profiling systems with the extension of EUC, H.R. 3167 makes a significant down payment on systemic reform and contributes to enhancing the economic security of American workers.

WILLIAM J. CLINTON

The White House,
November 24, 1993.

NOTE: H.R. 3167, approved November 24, was assigned Public Law No. 103–152.

Message to the Congress Transmitting the Report on the Caribbean Basin Initiative
November 24, 1993

To the Congress of the United States:
I transmit herewith the first report of the operation of the Caribbean Basin Initiative. This report is prepared pursuant to the requirements of section 214 of the Caribbean Basin Economic

Recovery Expansion Act of 1990 (19 U.S.C. 2702(f)).

WILLIAM J. CLINTON

The White House,
November 24, 1993.

The President's Radio Address
November 27, 1993

Good morning. This week my family celebrated Thanksgiving as most American families did. We gathered around a table filled with the bounty of our great country, and we thanked the Lord for all we have and all we can hope for.

No holiday tradition is more American than Thanksgiving. Indeed, no people have better reasons to give thanks, because no people have been more blessed. This holiday also signals the beginning of the end of the year, a time that many of us will use to take stock and to reflect. By any measure this has been an eventful year for our Nation.

On the road and in letters from my fellow Americans, I've been touched and buoyed by the words of support for the changes we have put in place and the progress we've made. It's been a good beginning: Inflation is down; interest rates are down to historic lows; the deficit is down; investment is up. Many of you listening today are among the millions of Americans who've refinanced your homes or your businesses in just the last year because of the drop in interest rates. And in the last 10 months, the economy has produced more private sector jobs than in the previous 4 years. And now that Congress has approved the North American

Free Trade Agreement and I have gone to Seattle to meet with the leaders of all the Asian-Pacific economies, I know we can stimulate our jobs machine even more with increased exports.

There's so much else that we've been able to do to help our workers and our families. Congress also passed and I signed into law the family and medical leave law. Now workers have a right to take some time off to take care of a sick family member or newborn child without losing their jobs. It will help to make America a place where you can be a successful worker and a successful parent.

We've also moved to help our students by reforming the college loan law so that loans are easier to get, with lower interest rates and better repayment terms and stiffer requirements to pay the loan back.

We signed into law the National Service Act, which 3 years from now will allow 100,000 young Americans to earn some money against their college education while rebuilding their communities from the grassroots up.

We won passage of our reforms in each House in campaign finance. And when the Congress comes back, if the House and Senate can agree, we can do a lot more to take special interest politics out of our congressional elections and therefore our decisionmaking process.

We passed an economic program, which will give a real tax break to working families with children to try to make sure that everybody who works 40 hours a week in this country with a child in the home will be lifted well above the poverty line. But there's still a lot to do.

Under the leadership of the First Lady, we've now got a health security proposal. And it's my fond hope that before the end of next year, Congress will pass a plan that will give every American comprehensive health care that can never be taken away.

The crime bill has been passed in both Houses. It will put more police officers on the street, up to 100,000 of them, build more prisons, establish boot camps for young first-time offenders, it will ban assault weapons. But we have to resolve those two differences and pass that crime bill early next year.

We're making progress in the fight against crime. Just before the Congress left, it adopted legislation requiring a 5-day waiting period before anyone can purchase a handgun, so there can be a check for someone's age, mental health history, and criminal record. This action was a

national victory in the fight against crime and violence and a very personal victory for Jim and Sarah Brady, a family touched by violence who turned tragedy into triumph by fighting for 7 long years to pass this important legislation to protect the rest of us from individuals who shouldn't be permitted to possess or use handguns. We've waited a long time to pass the Brady bill, but it's just the latest example of how we brought to Washington the change we promised in the last campaign.

In 10 months we've broken the gridlock. We've won much of what I set out to do in my first year. Much of the change that I talked about when I ran for President is beginning to be accomplished now. The fact is, according to the highly respected Congressional Quarterly, this administration, working with both parties, has had more of its major legislation adopted in this first year than any other administration in the last 40 years.

Every one of these changes, every step we take, has to be measured in a job that a mother or father finds or an opportunity a child gains or in better prospects for a business owner or in safer streets and a more secure future. Every step forward, if it helps to invigorate our economy, our community, our families, is a step worth taking. But ultimately these steps will be steady only if we begin together to do more to fix America from the inside out.

We have to be concerned with the number of families that have totally broken down, the number of young women giving birth to children out of wedlock. It's sweeping the country upward and offward—upward and all across racial lines. We have to be concerned that without the structure, the discipline, the love of families, too many children face a future stripped of hope. Too many kids now live without enough hope or enough love or enough discipline.

We have to be concerned that in both our cities and our rural areas, the value of life has been cheapened. Too many children are killing children with weapons of destruction that are even more efficient and sophisticated than the police, who are supposed to protect the people, have.

For our part, we're working hard to provide economic security, health care security, and safety in community and in this way to remove some of the stress that hurts our families. We're working hard to open opportunities to make the changes sweeping the world friendly to the

American working family. It's been said that the family is the test of freedom. It tests our freedom and our sense of responsibility. And that's the best reason to try to preserve families and to try to alleviate some of the terrible, terrible burdens that have aggravated the strains on family life for nearly 30 years now.

So, my fellow Americans, on this most treasured of holiday weekends, as we give thanks for what we have, let's remember what so many millions of Americans don't have. Let's remem-

ber how much both work and family mean to civilized life. We can restore and repair the basic fabric of our society only if we build up both: work and family. Together, I believe we can do that.

Thanks for listening.

NOTE: The address was recorded at 12:15 p.m. on November 24 in the Oval Office at the White House for broadcast at 10:06 a.m. on November 27.

Letter to Congressional Leaders Reporting on Iraq's Compliance With United Nations Security Council Resolutions
November 29, 1993

Dear Mr. Speaker: *(Dear Mr. President:)*

Consistent with the Authorization for Use of Military Force Against Iraq Resolution (Public Law 102–1), and as part of my effort to keep the Congress fully informed, I am reporting on the status of efforts to obtain Iraq's compliance with the resolutions adopted by the U.N. Security Council.

Inspections and sanctions have significantly debilitated Iraq's ability to reconstitute its weapons of mass destruction (WMD) programs in the near future. The U.N. Special Commission on Iraq (UNSCOM) and the International Atomic Energy Agency (IAEA) have effectively put the Iraqi nuclear weapons program out of business in the near term. The United Nations has destroyed Iraqi missile launchers, support facilities, and a good deal of Iraq's indigenous capability to manufacture prohibited missiles. It has reduced Iraq's ability to produce chemical weapons; UNSCOM teams continue to inventory and destroy chemical munitions. The United Nations has inspected, and will monitor, several facilities identified by Iraq as capable of supporting a biological weapons program.

Continued vigilance is necessary, however, because we believe that Saddam Hussein is committed to rebuilding his WMD capability, especially nuclear weapons, and is most likely continuing to conceal weapons-related activities from the U.N. It is therefore extremely important that the international community maintain current sanctions and continue its efforts to establish the long-term monitoring regime re-

quired by U.N. Security Council Resolution 715. Although Iraq has said that it is ready to comply with that Resolution, it still must take significant steps, including the provision of new data about the suppliers of its WMD program. Rolf Ekeus, the Chairman of UNSCOM, has told Iraq that it must establish a clear track record of compliance before he can report favorably to the Security Council. We strongly endorse this approach.

The "no-fly zones" over northern and southern Iraq permit the monitoring of Iraq's compliance with Security Council Resolutions 687 and 688. Over the last two years, the northern no-fly zone has deterred Iraq from a major military offensive in the region. Since the no-fly zone was established in southern Iraq, Iraq's use of aircraft against its population in the region has stopped.

The United States is working closely with the United Nations and other organizations to provide humanitarian relief to the people of northern Iraq, in the face of Iraqi Government efforts to disrupt this assistance. We have provided temporary generators and spare parts to preserve supplies of electricity in the region since the Iraqi Government cut off power on August 5, 1993. We continue to support U.N. efforts to mount a relief program for persons in Baghdad and the South and to ensure that supplies are not diverted by the Iraqi Government. We are continuing to work toward the placement of human rights monitors for Iraq as proposed by Max van der Stoel, Special Rapporteur of the U.N. Human Rights Commission, and to work for the establishment of a U.N. Commission to investigate and publicize Iraqi war crimes and other violations of international humanitarian law.

On September 20, after a review of Iraqi compliance with Security Council resolutions, the President of the Security Council issued a statement noting that there was no consensus to modify the existing sanctions regime. That regime exempts medicine and, in the case of foodstuffs, requires only that the U.N. Sanctions Committee be notified of food shipments. The Sanctions Committee also continues to consider and, when appropriate, approve requests to send to Iraq materials and supplies for essential civilian needs. The Iraqi Government, in contrast, has maintained a full embargo against its northern provinces and has acted to distribute humanitarian supplies only to its supporters and to the military.

The Iraqi Government has so far refused to sell $1.6 billion in oil as previously authorized by the Security Council in Resolutions 706 and 712. Talks between Iraq and the United Nations on implementing these resolutions have ended unsuccessfully. Iraq could use proceeds from such sales to purchase foodstuffs, medicines, materials, and supplies for essential civilian needs of its population, subject to U.N. monitoring of sales and the equitable distribution of humanitarian supplies (including to its northern provinces). Iraqi authorities bear full responsibility for any suffering in Iraq that results from their refusal to implement Resolutions 706 and 712.

Proceeds from oil sales also would be used to compensate persons injured by Iraq's unlawful invasion and occupation of Kuwait. The U.N. Compensation Commission has received about two million claims so far, with another 500,000 expected. The U.S. Government is preparing to file a sixth set of individual claims with the Commission, bringing U.S. claims filed to roughly 3,000. At its most recent session September 27–29, the Commission's Governing Council discussed how to allocate funds among different claimants but did not make decisions.

Security Council Resolution 778 permits use of a portion of frozen Iraqi oil assets to fund crucial U.N. activities concerning Iraq, including humanitarian relief, UNSCOM, and the Compensation Commission. (The funds will be repaid, with interest, from Iraqi oil revenues as soon as Iraqi oil exports resume.) The United States is prepared to transfer up to $200 million in frozen Iraqi oil assets held in U.S. financial institutions, provided that U.S. contributions do not exceed 50 percent of the total amount contributed. We have arranged a total of over $100 million in such matching contributions thus far.

Iraq still has not met its obligations concerning Kuwaitis and third-country nationals it detained during the war. Iraq has taken no substantive steps to cooperate fully with the International Committee of the Red Cross (ICRC), as required by Security Council Resolution 687, although it has received over 600 files on missing individuals. We continue to work for Iraqi compliance.

Although the Iraq-Kuwait border has been demarcated, incidents continue. On November 15, Iraq released Mr. Kenneth Beaty, a U.S. citizen, who had been detained by Iraq since he crossed the border accidentally in April 1993. Also on November 2, a small group of Iraqi police in uniform entered Kuwaiti territory and, with their guns drawn, stopped Kuwaiti citizens in two vehicles. Three Iraqis were wounded in an ensuing fight. Iraq admitted that its police had crossed into Kuwait. The U.N. Iraq-Kuwait Observer Mission (UNIKOM) continues to monitor the border.

Iraq can rejoin the community of civilized nations only through democratic processes, respect for human rights, equal treatment of its people, and adherence to basic norms of international behavior. Iraq's government should represent all Iraq's people and be committed to the territorial integrity and unity of Iraq. The Iraqi National Congress (INC) espouses these goals, the fulfillment of which would make Iraq a stabilizing force in the Gulf region.

I am grateful for the support by the Congress of our efforts.

Sincerely,

BILL CLINTON

NOTE: Identical letters were sent to Thomas S. Foley, Speaker of the House of Representatives, and Robert C. Byrd, President pro tempore of the Senate.

The President's News Conference With President Ramiro De Leon of Guatemala
November 30, 1993

President Clinton. Good morning. This morning it was my great honor to welcome seven outstanding Central American leaders to the White House: President Cristiani of El Salvador, President Endara of Panama, President Callejas of Honduras, President Calderon of Costa Rica, President Chamorro of Nicaragua, President De Leon of Guatemala, and Prime Minister Esquivel of Belize.

These leaders have made an historic contribution to our hemisphere by helping to build democracy and peace in a region that until very recently was riven by civil strife. I'm grateful that they were able to break away from the Miami conference on the Caribbean, which they are attending with leaders from the private sector, from throughout the Caribbean Basin, to discuss ways to advance regional prosperity.

President De Leon has struggled heroically on behalf of democracy and human rights in Guatemala. And he's just achieved an important political accord that will bring more accountable government to his nation. President Cristiani played a central role in ending El Salvador's civil war and has been critical to the success of the peace accords. President Chamorro has worked hard to bring reconciliation and democracy to Nicaragua. I want to acknowledge President Callejas for his leadership in consolidating democracy in Honduras and President Calderon for advancing Costa Rica's traditions of social justice and the rule of law. President Endara has safeguarded Panama's return to democracy. And Prime Minister Esquivel has earned praise for his government's sound economic policies and his own personal integrity.

For years, few regions of our world endured more suffering than Central America. But today, few regions are better poised to reap the benefits of the end of the cold war. This is the first time in the 20th century that all of these nations have come here to the White House to meet the President of the United States, every one of them being headed by democratically elected leaders. It is an historic and very important moment.

The people of Central America are clearly dedicated to the harvest of reconstruction and renewal. They're healing divided societies, reviving stalled economies, and working toward closer integration among themselves and their other neighbors. My message today to these distinguished leaders and to the millions whom they represent is simple: The United States will be there as your partner to help. We will not make the mistake of abandoning this region when its dramatic recovery is not yet complete. We will remain engaged to help Central America attain peace, consolidate democracy, protect human rights, and achieve sustainable development. Our Nation has a direct stake in Central America's stability and prosperity. The United States exports $6 billion in goods to these countries, supporting over 100,000 American jobs.

Today we discussed steps that Central America's nations can take to strengthen our economic ties, including further trade liberalization and better protection of worker rights, intellectual property, and the environment. We also discussed the impact of the North American Free Trade Agreement, which all of these leaders strongly supported. The Vice President is leaving this afternoon for Mexico where he will deliver a major address on American engagement in Latin America. This morning we agreed that NAFTA's historic passage can serve as a catalyst for the expansion of free trade to other market democracies throughout the hemisphere, something I have long supported. And we shared concerns about NAFTA's potential short-term effects on the flow of trade and investment to Central America. I pledged that my administration will work with Congress and Central American governments to design affirmative strategies to stimulate regional trade.

As our economic relationship evolves, so must the nature of the United States support for economic development in Central America. We will continue bilateral aid programs. At the same time, the region's rising creditworthiness has allowed international financial institutions to increase their role, and we strongly support that. We will work to develop a new, more mature economic partnership with Central America based on trade expansion, multilateral support for economic reforms, and better coordination of bilateral and multilateral aid programs.

These leaders today have told us that they seek to work together to become a model region for sustainable development. And we are prepared to work with them in that enterprise. I can think of no more important common endeavor.

With the elections of the last several years, democracy has taken root in Central America's rugged terrain. Now the challenge facing this region is to build democratic institutions that endure, that are honest, that are responsive, that are effective. We are prepared to work closely with Central America to promote reform in the judiciary, the civil service, education, and health care. Good governance will advance our mutual objectives to bolster democracy, promote social opportunity, and clear the path for freer trade.

Just a few years ago, this morning's meeting would have been literally unthinkable. Now, in the midst of this great progress, it would be unthinkable for us not to meet. The prosperity and security of this hemisphere which we share depends more than ever on our continued cooperation.

It is now my honor to introduce President De Leon, who will also speak for his fellow Central American leaders.

Mr. President.

President De Leon. Thank you very much. Good morning. At this time of great and transcendental changes in the world order, in Central America, in the United States, and especially in our reciprocal relations, today we just had a Presidential meeting which we consider not only a very pleasant one but an extremely constructive one. We were able to exchange with President Clinton, whom we would like to thank for his invitation, our points of view on issues and problems of great importance having to do with our bilateral relationship as well as recent events in Central America on the one hand and in the United States on the other hand.

I would like to summarize what we have discussed as follows. As far as democracy and governance, first of all we underscored the efforts made in our region for the consolidation of pluralistic and participatory systems, giving special priority to respect for individual, civil, and political human rights, which has allowed great progress in the recent years in the solution of the great conflicts we have.

We showed that we Central American countries continue to work to achieve true participatory democracy involving growth with social justice and without confrontation and that solidarity and dialog are essential principles to which we are giving priority as the underpinnings of the strengthening of our democracies.

As to economic and social development and the fight against poverty, on these points we said to President Clinton that the magnitude of the problem of poverty in our countries is of great importance. It is a problem which will have to be solved with political will and solidarity. The fight against poverty, we said, is not just a matter of supporting social welfare investment, but it is a matter of supporting productive investment through private investment, supporting the productive sector, and supporting the insertion of our economies into the world market. We have to fight the scourge of poverty through consistent management of our economic and our social policies. We told the President that we are emerging with great difficulty and with degrees of difference from one country to the other, emerging from a deep and prolonged recession which punished those least able to defend themselves especially, badly. I am talking here about the poorest of the poor.

As far as economic adjustment is concerned, with great optimism we said to the President that we Central Americans are now looking toward the future with a positive vision. We are transforming antiquated schemes. And now the societies realize that they have to assume costs but in an attitude of solidarity in order to achieve peace, development, democracy, and especially the respect for human rights, both individual and economic, social and cultural rights.

We emphasize that governments must become more efficient as administrators and public servants, allowing the state to act where it must and generate conditions so that the private sector can act in a more decentralized and participatory manner. Regarding self-effort and external assistance, we discussed how happy we Central Americans are to be making our own efforts and advancing toward positive results, a demonstration of which is the recent signing of the protocol to the Treaty of Central American Economic Integration. At the same time though, we recalled that these internal efforts must be supported as they have been by external cooperation. And here the support offered by the United States has had, has, and will continue to have great importance. We also said to President Clinton that we feel that this particular historic moment is the very worst one to be cutting back on cooperation, external cooperation. It is the best time to maintain it and increase it, convinced that democracy is more than the simple and mere holding of regular elections.

Finally, on the NAFTA and the Caribbean Basin Initiative, the Central American Presidents said in this Presidential summit meeting, that our bilateral agenda with the United States is going to be very strongly influenced not only by the changes in Central America but also by the historic decision of Canada, the United States, and Mexico to form an expanded free trade area. We said that we applaud this decision, which marks a fundamental and positive change in inter-American relations, and that we feel that this does constitute a creative answer to the emerging international reordering. We also considered, we said, that NAFTA implies the need for the Central American region to redouble its efforts and to become stronger so that we can expand to serve more competitive markets.

We made two proposals to President Clinton. First of all, we expressed to him our great interest in initiating consultations to incorporate the Central American countries into the North American Free Trade Agreement and, at the same time, that the real possibilities be considered to make the CBI benefits be equal to the NAFTA benefits. We said that we felt that this should be done within the framework of respect for the environment. And we had a very favorable response to our suggestion that Central America should become a model area of sustainable development in the environmental framework. We have taken the political decision to suggest this, and President Clinton has decided to give this idea his backing.

We also said that we would be very appreciative for any support and backing that the U.S. Government could give to the negotiations within the framework of the Uruguay round to expand liberalization of world trade for products of interest to us. We are grateful for the efforts that the United States has made to increase our access to the European Common Market, and we are hoping that there will be a negotiated solution with the EC.

Finally, and given the welcome and the interest which was so emphatically shown by President Clinton to the regional proposals we made,

the Presidents of the Central American region wish to repeat here our satisfaction at the fruitfulness and constructive nature of this meeting. And we have decided to set up a high-level commission among us to follow up the process of incorporation of Central America into the North American Free Trade Agreement. This constitutes a very important way to combat poverty in Central America and thus achieve peace and consolidate democracy and development with social equity for the entire Central American isthmus.

Thank you.

Nicaragua and El Salvador

Q. Could you discuss the loosening aid to Nicaragua? And also did you discuss the emergence of death squads in El Salvador?

President Clinton. We discussed the aid to Nicaragua issue very briefly. I have decided just in the last couple of days to approve the release of the aid from FY '93 because of the significant progress made in Nicaragua in asserting civilian control over the military and in trying to resolve some American property claims and on a number of other issues there. So I feel good about that.

With regard to El Salvador, what we basically discussed was the continuation of the democratic process and the upcoming elections and the hope that the recent violence there would not in any way interrupt that. And I feel comfortable that they are proceeding along that path.

What I'd like to do is to try to alternate questions and take a question from people representing Central American press and then go back to the American press and go back and forth, if I could.

Yes, in the back.

Central America and NAFTA

Q. Mr. President, as the President of Guatemala has said Central American countries are interested in having that parity with NAFTA because they feel that they are going to start feeling the impact of NAFTA in about 5 years. What was your response? Are you willing to give them that parity?

President Clinton. Let me say specifically what we talked—we talked about two different issues. One is the question of involving Central America in the process that produced NAFTA, that is, an expansion of a free trade area to the rest of Latin America. That's something, as

I think all of you know, I have long been interested in and have talked about it when I was running for President. And I told him that I had asked Ambassador Kantor to basically, when we conclude our GATT efforts—we're preoccupied, as you know, with the GATT agreement now—after we conclude our GATT agreements and if NAFTA goes through with the proclamation of Canada which has to be done by the first of the year, shortly after the first of the year, to begin a study and come up with a recommendation to me about how to proceed with reference to the rest of Latin America in the free trade process.

Now secondly, the other issue we discussed was a narrower one, and that is, how can we make sure that the NAFTA agreement, as it begins to be implemented, does not hurt the Caribbean countries who are in the Caribbean Basin Initiative? That is, neither Mexico nor the United States and certainly not Canada ever intended for there to be a transfer of investment from the Caribbean to Mexico, just a simple shift. That would defeat the whole purpose of what we're trying to do here in growing the area. So we are looking into now what we can do on a shorter term basis to just make sure that doesn't happen. As I said, that was never any part of Mexico's strategy or interest, never any part of the United States. So I think we'll have a more near-term recommendation on that regard.

Salman Rushdie

Q. Mr. President, many Muslims, including some who support the United States, are upset about your meeting with author Salman Rushdie. Was there any advice from the State Department or others that there were risks involved in this meeting? And do you think that it might undercut support for the Middle East peace process?

President Clinton. To be frank, there was some division among our people about whether I should see Mr. Rushdie when he was here. He met with Mr. Lake, and then I was over in the Old Executive Office Building, and Mr. Lake brought him over there so I could see him and shake hands with him. We visited probably for a couple of minutes. And there was some—because our view of the first amendment and free speech is different from that held by many Muslims throughout the world, including many who are our friends. I understand that.

I did it to make the point not that I agree with the attacks on Islam in the book that Mr. Rushdie wrote but that in our country and in the countries who respect freedom of speech, freedom of speech includes especially the willingness to respect without threatening the life of or the rights of people who write things that we do not agree with. Indeed, for a Westerner, I have tried for more than 20 years now to study and have an appreciation of Islam. And I respect the religion, and I respect the culture enormously. So I mean no disrespect to the people who have that religious faith. But I do think it's important that here in the United States we reaffirm our commitment to protect the physical well-being and the right to speak of those with whom we may intensely disagree. That's what our Constitution does. So I hope that I will not be misunderstood. I believe I made the right decision.

Yes, ma'am.

Aid to Central America

Q. Mr. President, you mentioned that one of the programs will include multilateral aid to Central America. However, the AID budget has been substantially cut and will continue to be cut in the future. What has been your commitment in this regard to the nations of Central America?

President Clinton. First of all, let's discuss that. The AID budget was cut in the last budget cycle. And we are basically in a 5-year period now where we've committed not to increase Federal discretionary spending even for inflation. So there will be a cut of all spending relative to inflation, which means if we want to increase one area of our spending, we have to cut something else proportionately. And I'm going now into a series of meetings—I had my first one yesterday—on next year's budget, which will require us to make some difficult decisions.

What I said to the leaders was I would do my best to maintain some level of bilateral assistance but that the United States would try to make sure that the multilateral aid offset whatever cuts we had in bilateral assistance, number one, and number two, that I would do my best to strengthen the economic relationship between the United States and these nations in the hope that increasing trade and investment would do far more than bilateral aid ever could anyway to strengthen the long-term economic well-being of the two nations.

Thank you very much.

Trade, Development, and Democracy

[*At this point, a question was asked in Spanish, and a translation was not provided.*]

President De Leon. As I said, in addition to being a very pleasant meeting, it was an extremely fruitful one. Our proposals were welcomed very forthrightly by the U.S. side. And we had the hope, because of the interest that President Clinton showed in our presentations, that we would be able to do something concrete on two areas in particular: one, in connection with a free trade expansion to Central America, and secondly, that we could get the same benefits as NAFTA for the CBI countries.

In addition to that, we had the suggestion which was accepted vis-a-vis the environmental pilot projects. We think that it would be wonderful if that pilot project for sustainable development should be carried forward in Central America. This would be great not just for Central America but for the entire world.

For President Clinton regarding democratization of the region and with respect for human rights to achieve greater cooperation with the United States Government, I would say that we ourselves, we the Central American countries, we are giving signals of this advance and progress, difficult in some cases, fragile in others, but we are going toward true democracy. We have the case of El Salvador, Honduras, Panama; democracy has come later in some cases, sooner in others. I never mention Costa Rica when we talk about this, because Costa Rica has always been a democracy and an example for the entire world and the case of Belize,

which has also been a democracy.

Guatemala has had the worst problems, and 5 months ago we had another break of our institutional and constitutional order. But we showed the world that we have begun to mature in our society. In Guatemala we've begun to learn what the democratic society is and means. This has been done incredibly peacefully, and I say "incredibly" because of the antecedents in our country. And we have been able to get out of a political crisis, which was very difficult, between the three branches of Government, with an agreement which was the best one possible for our people, because the constitutional changes for the first time have taken place without a coup d'etat. The interruption of the constitutional mandate of the Congress and the supreme court is going to be corrected by the purest expression of democracy, that is, a popular election. Therefore, I gave the example of Guatemala, excuse me for that, but I think our problems are the worst. And I think that the rest of the region also has given signs of consolidating the democratic system.

So there was no conditionality; quite the opposite. What we had was total backing of a proposal and a desire for the United States to continue helping us consolidate our democracies, fragile in some cases, more consolidated in other cases, but continue to work for the sake of consolidating peace.

President Clinton. Thank you.

NOTE: The President's 36th news conference began at 11:22 a.m. in the East Room at the White House. In his remarks, he referred to Anthony Lake, Assistant to the President for National Security Affairs. President De Leon spoke in Spanish, and his remarks were translated by an interpreter.

Remarks on Signing Handgun Control Legislation
November 30, 1993

Thank you very much, Sarah and Jim and General Reno, Mr. Vice President, Mrs. Musick. Thank you for your wonderful remarks.

There were two Members of Congress who inadvertently were not introduced. I want to recognize them because they've played a major role in this: one of our Democratic leaders in the House, Steny Hoyer, and Senator Herb Kohl from Wisconsin, who also sponsored the bill to make it illegal for minors to possess handguns, and I thank you for that, sir.

Senator Metzenbaum, Congressman Schumer, Senator Mitchell; and others who gave birth to this great effort; to all the law enforcement representatives, the Governors, the mayors, the folks from Handgun Control who are here; to the families whose lives would have been changed for the better if the Brady bill had been law; Mrs. Musick and my friend Cathy Gould and her children, Lindsey and Christopher who lost a husband and father who would be here today if the Brady bill had been law, I am honored to have all of you here in the White House. I also want to say a special word of thanks to the Members of Congress who were out there early on this, when there was some considerable political risk either attached to it or thought to be attached. The Brady bill was first introduced almost 7 years ago by Congressman Ed Feighan of Ohio on February 4th, 1987. I can't resist saying a special word of thanks to the Members who come from difficult districts who voted for this bill. My good friend and Congressman, Beryl Anthony from Arkansas, lost a tough race in 1992, and part of the reason was that he voted for the Brady bill. And the NRA came after him in an unusual election. He said to me on the way in here, he said, "If it cost my seat, it was worth it."

Everything that should be said about this has already been said by people whose lives are more profoundly imbued with this issue than mine. But there are some things I think we need to think about that we learned from this endeavor as we look ahead to what still needs to be done.

Since Jim and Sarah began this crusade, more than 150,000 Americans, men, women, teenagers, children, even infants, have been killed with handguns. And many more have been wounded—150,000 people from all walks of life who should have been here to share Christmas with us. This couple saw through a fight that really never should have had to occur, because still, when people are confronted with issues of clear common sense and overwhelming evidence, too often we are prevented from doing what we know we ought to do by our collective fears, whatever they may be.

The Brady bill has finally become law in a fundamental sense not because of any of us but because grassroots America changed its mind and demanded that this Congress not leave here without doing something about this. And all the rest of us—even Jim and Sarah—did was to somehow light that spark that swept across the people of this country and proved

once again that democracy can work. America won this battle. Americans are finally fed up with violence that cuts down another citizen with gunfire every 20 minutes.

And we know that this bill will make a difference. As Sarah said, the Washington Post pointed out that about 50,000 people have been denied the right to buy a handgun in just four States since 1989. Don't let anybody tell you that this won't work. I got a friend back home who sold a gun years ago to a guy who had escaped from a mental hospital, that he hadn't seen in 10 years. And he pulled out that old form from the 1968 act and said, "Have you ever been convicted of a crime? Have you ever been in a mental hospital?" The guy said, no, no and put the form back in the drawer. And 12 hours later six people were dead, and my friend is not over it to this day. Don't tell me this bill will not make a difference. That is not true. It is not true.

But we all know there is more to be done. The crime bill not only has 100,000 new police officers who, properly trained and deployed, will lower the crime rate by preventing crime, not just by catching criminals. It also has a ban on several assault weapons, long overdue; a ban on handgun ownership and restrictions on possession of handguns by minors; the beginning of reform of our Federal firearms licensing systems; and an effort to make our schools safer. This is a good beginning. And there will be more to be done after that.

But I ask you to think about what this means and what we can all do to keep this going. We cannot stop here. I'm so proud of what others are doing. I'm proud of the work that Reverend Jesse Jackson has been doing, going back now to the streets and talking to the kids and telling them to stop shooting each other and cutting each other up, and to turn away from violence. I'm proud of people like David Plaza, not so well-known, a former gang member who has turned his life around and now coordinates a program called gang alternative programs in Norwalk, California, telling gang members they have to take personal responsibility for their actions and turn away from violence; Reverend William Moore, who organized parents and educators and other clergy in north Philadelphia to provide safety corridors for kids going to and from school—160,000 children stay home every day because they're scared to go to school in this country—and all the police officers on the street who have restored confidence in their neighborhoods, becoming involved in ways that often are way beyond the call of duty, people like Officer Anthony Fuedo of Boston, who took a tough section of east Boston and transformed it from a neighborhood full of fear to one which elderly people now feel safe sitting on benches again.

We can do this but only if we do it together. And I ask you to think about this: I come from a State where half the folks have hunting and fishing licenses. I can still remember the first day when I was a little boy out in the country putting a can on top of a fencepost and shooting a .22 at it. I can still remember the first time I pulled a trigger on a .410 shotgun because I was too little to hold a .12 gauge. I can remember these things. This is part of the culture of a big part of America. But people have taken that culture—we just started deer season—I live in a place where we still close schools and plants on the first day of deer season, nobody is going to show up anyway. [*Laughter*] We just started deer season at home and a lot of other places. We have taken this important part of the life of millions of Americans and turned it into an instrument of maintaining madness. It is crazy. Would I let anybody change that life in America? Not on your life. Has that got anything to do with the Brady bill or assault weapons or whether the police have to go out on the street confronting teenagers who are better armed than they are? Of course not.

This is the beginning of something truly wonderful in this country if we have learned to separate out all this stuff we've been hearing all these years, trying to make the American people afraid that somehow their quality of life is going to be undermined by doing stuff that people of common sense and good will would clearly want to do and every law enforcement official in America telling us to do it.

So, I plead with all of you today, when you leave here to be reinvigorated by this, to be exhilarated by the triumph of Jim and Sarah Brady and all these other folks who didn't let their personal losses defeat them but instead used it to come out here and push us to do better.

And each of you in turn, take your opportunity not to let people ever again in this country use a legitimate part of our American heritage in ways that blinds us to our obligation to the present and the future. If we have broken that, then there is nothing we cannot do. And when I go and sign this bill in a minute, it will be step one in taking our streets back, taking our children back, reclaiming our families and our future.

Thank you.

NOTE: The President spoke at 1 p.m. in the East Room at the White House. In his remarks, he referred to former White House Press Secretary James Brady, who was wounded in the 1981 assassination attempt on President Ronald Reagan; his wife, Sarah, head of Hand Gun Control, Inc.; and Melanie Musick, who became a supporter of the Brady bill after her husband was shot and killed in 1990. H.R. 1025, "To provide for a waiting period before the purchase of a handgun, and for the establishment of a national instant criminal background check system to be contacted by firearms dealers before the transfer of any firearm," approved November 30, was assigned Public Law No. 103–159.

Remarks on Presenting the Presidential Medals of Freedom
November 30, 1993

Thank you very much, ladies and gentlemen, distinguished guests, all. We have Members of Congress here, members and former members of the United States Supreme Court, and a number of distinguished Americans who share in common a friendship with one or more of our distinguished honorees today. I welcome you all here.

One of the greatest pleasures of being President is the authority to choose recipients of the Presidential Medal of Freedom, the highest honor given to civilians by the United States. And so today it is my honor to award the Medal of Freedom to five great reformers of the 20th century who changed America for the better: Mrs. Marjory Stoneman Douglas, the late Joseph

Rauh, Judge John Minor Wisdom, the late Justice Thurgood Marshall, and Justice William Brennan.

Today they join a distinguished list of citizens in a process initiated by my great predecessor Harry Truman in 1945. Like Harry Truman, all five of them rank among our Nation's great champions of the underdog. Indeed, most of their lives are stories of underdogs themselves. Two of them are sons of immigrants. Justice Brennan's parents came here from Ireland near the time that Mr. Rauh's father and grandfather came here from Germany. One, Justice Marshall, was the great-grandson of slaves. And one, Mrs. Douglas, is descended from a founder of the Underground Railroad. America gave them the freedom to be their best, and they honored our country by becoming five legendary defenders of our freedoms in return.

When this medal was created at the end of World War II, America had great decisions to make about what kind of nation we wanted to be. The postwar years were those which unlocked great forces that would transform our society profoundly and permanently. A baby boom and a development boom brought Americans more mobility and more economic opportunity than they had ever enjoyed before. But this new mobility also opened our eyes to problems we had been previously unwilling to acknowledge: the legal barriers set up to prevent black Americans and working people from sharing in the opportunities afforded to others; the growth that devoured the value of our disappearing regional identities and fragile natural landscapes.

It was during this time in 1947 that Marjory Stoneman Douglas published her best-selling book, "The Everglades: River of Grass," a monumental work on Florida's unique ecosystem, one of our Nation's greatest natural resources. The next year, 1948, gave us the Democratic National Convention that nominated Harry Truman, where Hubert Humphrey delivered one of the earliest and most impassioned speeches on behalf of civil rights ever given from a national platform. There Joseph Rauh, Jr., won his fight to make civil rights a part of the National Democratic Party platform and an indelible part of our national agenda.

In 1954 Thurgood Marshall won a case before the United States Supreme Court called *Brown* v. *Board of Education*, the decisive blow against legal segregation, a decision that would have more impact on civil rights in America than any other single action since President Lincoln signed the Emancipation Proclamation just upstairs in this White House.

In 1955, Joe Rauh and others celebrated victory over McCarthyism, whose abuses of freedom they had fought so fearlessly.

In 1956, President Eisenhower named New Jersey Supreme Court Justice William Brennan to the United States Supreme Court, launching one of the most influential careers in the Court's entire history. And the following year, in 1957, Eisenhower named John Minor Wisdom to the U.S. Court of Appeals, where he and his colleagues pioneered our Nation's landmark decisions on civil rights. He made a lot of good appointments, Mr. Eisenhower.

We honor these people not for any private success, not for any personal pursuit of glory but for their selfless devotion to the public interest and their tireless lifetime of achievement in the public arena. Because of what they did, our Nation is a better place, and our lives, all of us, are richer. I'd like to briefly review that before the official citations are read.

Marjory Stoneman Douglas, all of 103 years old, has always been ahead of her time. She was born in Minneapolis on April 7th, 1890, raised in Massachusetts, graduated from Wellesley College in 1912, and moved to Florida. She was one of the pioneering women in journalism when she joined the staff of the Miami Herald in 1914. She served the Red Cross in Europe during World War II and returned to the United States to wage a campaign for the passage of the women's suffrage amendment—I said World War II; I meant World War I—and to continue a career writing about the distinctive regional character of southern Florida.

Her advocacy on behalf of the Everglades in Florida long before there was ever an Earth Day is legendary. It has been an inspiration to generations of conservationists, environmentalists, and preservationists throughout our Nation and especially to my administration, in the work of Vice President Gore and the Administrator of the EPA, another woman from Florida, Carol Browner. She is much admired by the Attorney General who shares her south Florida roots, and I am glad to see her here today, also.

Beyond Florida, Marjory Stoneman Douglas is a mentor for all who desire to preserve what we southerners affectionately call "a sense of place." And Mrs. Douglas, the next time I hear someone mention the timeless wonders and powers of Mother Nature, I'll be thinking about you.

Joseph Rauh grew up in an immigrant family to become America's leading labor lawyer and advocate of civil liberties. He studied under Felix Frankfurter, clerked for Supreme Court Justice Benjamin Cardozo and then Frankfurter when he was named Cardozo's successor by President Franklin Roosevelt. He was a champion of working people and labor movement reforms. Among his clients were Walter Reuther's United Auto Workers, A. Philip Randolph's Brotherhood of Sleeping Car Porters, and Joseph Yablonski's wing of the United Mine Workers.

When he returned from the Army after the Second World War, he founded Americans for Democratic Action to help stem the influence of communism in the United States, and he was elected its vice chairman, a post once held by Vice President Humphrey, Arthur Schlesinger, and the theologian Reinhold Niebuhr.

Later, as the group's chairman, he called the ADA a group of independent-minded people grappling with the old line machines of both parties on behalf of good government, not a bad slogan. He represented playwright Arthur Miller against the Government intrusion of the McCarthy committee and was an outspoken champion of civil liberties until his death last year. He may have left us with the most appropriate quotation for this ceremony when he said, "What our generation has done is bring equality into law. The next generation has to bring equality in fact."

John Minor Wisdom, a senior judge on the U.S. Court of Appeals at 88½ years old, still handles a caseload as large as any active judge on the bench. But he stands out among his peers as a truly first-class legal scholar who writes brilliant opinions, including his landmark opinion on voting rights in *United States* v. *State of Louisiana* in 1963, and his historic opinions to open the University of Mississippi to black students in *Meredith* v. *Fair* in 1962. He is a son of the old South who became an architect of the new South. His father attended Washington College in Virginia when its students marched in the funeral of its president, Robert E. Lee. His background makes his progressive decisions all the more remarkable, because I don't think the South could have made it

through those trying times without leaders like Judge Wisdom.

He may be the only medal recipient today who was once a member of the Republican National Committee. He became the father of the modern Republican Party in Louisiana when he moved it away from reactionary isolationism to the moderation of President Eisenhower. His outspoken calls for reform in government and public education and civil rights are something of which all southerners and members of both political parties can justly be proud.

None of our advances in civil rights would have been possible without the indefatigable energy of the late Thurgood Marshall. As an attorney and later as Solicitor General of the United States under President Johnson, he presented the most monumental arguments before the Supreme Court since Daniel Webster in the early years of our Republic, more than a century earlier. If President Kennedy had not named him an appeals court judge in 1961 or President Johnson had not named him the first black Justice on the United States Supreme Court in 1967, his mark on America would still loom very, very large today.

He gave his career to defend black people from violence carried out by mobs in the name of justice. As founder and chief counsel of the NAACP's Legal Defense and Education Fund, he waged systematic war against laws that kept black people out of voting booths and their children out of publicly funded schools. He did more to make Martin Luther King's dream of equality real in the lives of our people than anyone in our time. Together, he and Justice Brennan became the twin pillars of liberty and equality on the Court.

Justice Marshall's son, Thurgood, Jr., who coordinates legislative affairs in the office of the Vice President, said his father would have been most proud of this award by being honored alongside Justice Brennan, his close friend and colleague through so many years of battles.

Justice Brennan is the author of the most enduring constitutional decisions of our last decades, including *Baker* v. *Carr* on one person, one vote, and *Times* v. *Sullivan* which brought the free speech doctrine into the latter half of the 20th century. He's already been acknowledged by friends as well as foes as one of the most pivotal giants in the history of the Court, perhaps its staunchest defender of freedom of the individual against Government intrusions. As he once told Bill Moyers, the role of the Constitution is, and I quote, "the protection of the dignity of the human being and the recognition that every individual has fundamental rights which Government cannot deny."

Justice Brennan served longer than any Justice in this century but two, and his impact and legacy have changed the Court in our country for all time.

For all these people here, it must be a great sense of honor to be joined by so many distinguished Americans, members of the Cabinet, former members of the Cabinet, members of the Supreme Court, former members of the Supreme Court, and Members of the Congress. I thank all of you for being here. But I think we should all recognize that the people who should really be grateful to all of them are ordinary Americans, many of whom may not even know their names but whose lives have been forever changed by their labors.

I'd like now to ask my military aide to read the citations.

[*At this point, Maj. Leo Mercado, Jr., USMC, Marine Corps aide to the President, read the citations.*]

My fellow Americans, we often pay our debts, by acknowledging it, to our Founders. In the beginning of this country, Thomas Jefferson told us something we dare never forget, which is that we must also pay our debts to our reformers, for all the Founders did was to give us something that has to be recreated in every age and time. Today we have acknowledged that debt to five great reformers. We can only repay it if we follow in their footsteps.

Thank you very much.

NOTE: The President spoke at 3:48 p.m. in the East Room at the White House.

Nomination for the Federal Deposit Insurance Corporation
November 30, 1993

The President announced today that he has nominated Anne L. Hall to be a member of the Board of Directors of the Federal Deposit Insurance Corporation, and he has re-nominated Andrew C. Hove to be a Board member and Vice Chair.

"With their banking expertise and demonstrable commitments to public service, Anne Hall and Andrew Hove are outstanding choices for the FDIC Board," said the President. "They will work hard to ensure that the American people's savings are secure."

NOTE: Biographies of the nominees were made available by the Office of the Press Secretary.

Remarks to the Advisory Commission on Intergovernmental Relations
December 1, 1993

Thank you very much. First, Governor Winter and to all the other members of the Commission, let me thank you for your willingness to serve. I very much believe in the potential of this group, both because of the quality of the individuals on it and because of the way it's constituted, with representatives from the Federal, the State, and the local government and with both Democrats and Republicans here. I also want to say a special word of thanks to my friend, Bill Winter, for being willing to serve as Chair. He is one of my closest personal as well as political friends. When he was willing to do this, because I knew that he had spent years thinking about a lot of these issues, I felt that we had a chance to make this group succeed.

When we began to talk 2 years ago, more than two years ago now, about whether I would run for President, he and I agreed that one of the things that we needed to do was to somehow restore the integrity, the strength, the vitality of the relationships between the various levels of government.

One of the biggest problems we've got in this country today is that everybody knows that there are a lot of things that the government has to be involved in at some level, but there is a great skepticism about the ability of government to do its job, particularly here in Washington, a skepticism not without foundation, I might add.

There was a wonderful article in the Wall Street Journal the other day, talking about the attitudes of people in a town in Illinois about the health care issue. And one of the people who was quoted in the article had a one-sentence quote that I thought summarized in a way the dilemma that we all face, at least those of us who go to work here in Washington every day. The man said, "I believe in government, but I'm not sure I trust it." You know, in other words, I believe in the idea; I know that there are some things a government has to do that can't be done without the government, but I'm not sure they get done right, either because people will not do the right thing or because it won't be confidently done.

Because I served a dozen years as a Governor and worked on these federalism issues from another perspective and because I worked in a, I think, considerably less partisan atmosphere—it's just the nature of State and local government to be more problem-focused and somewhat less ideologically oriented—I think I've got a pretty good sense about what the potential is of this group to try to help us in our efforts to redefine what we should be doing here in Washington and how we can be working with you better.

The first thing I want to tell you is that I'm very serious about these issues and that I want to pursue them vigorously, thoroughly, consistently, and with the appropriate level of visibility. I'm glad to see my good friend Secretary Riley here, who also has shared the experience with Bill Winter and I—we were Governors together for a long time—and who has a good feel for these things, too.

Carolyn Lukensmeyer is here to report to you on the federalism suggestions that came out of the National Performance Review, the Vice President's reinventing Government report. He wanted to be here personally, but I asked him to go to Mexico today to deliver an important

speech in the aftermath of the passage of the North American Free Trade Agreement legislation last week, and that's why he's there today and not here. But there are some important recommendations in the National Performance Review that I hope (a) will be endorsed by this group, (b) may be amplified on it, and (c) that you may have some ideas about how we can actually implement them. We get a lot of wonderful ideas up here, but there's a lot of slips between the cup and the lip. So we need your help on that.

Secondly, there are a whole series of empowerment initiatives that we have tried to take to enable State and local governments to do their jobs better by creating a different environment. The empowerment zone legislation is one. If these empowerment zones work to actually get private sector investment and public-private partnerships at the local level going in otherwise economically distressed areas of our country, then I think you will see them sweep the country. I think the Congress will be more than willing to vote more of the empowerment zones if we can prove it works. Well, that requires a level of partnership and followthrough that the Federal Government alone can certainly not provide.

The community enterprise board we've set up, designed to see what we can do to sort of push down more decisionmaking at the governmental level and to require more partnerships to build from the grassroots up, is an important thing.

I issued an Executive order on unfunded mandates which a lot of you were involved in helping me put together. Our administration has been quite vigorous in granting waivers to States for welfare reform experiments and for some health care reform experiments. I want to continue to do that, and I want you to explore with me what we can do to help you do your jobs better.

Perhaps the most important recommendation of the reinventing Government commission was that we consolidate a lot of these grants and let you fashion your own use for the Federal money that's been set aside in too many little discrete pieces for the benefit of people at the local level. So there are a whole lot of issues we can deal with.

The main point I want to leave you with today is that I haven't forgotten what it was like to be on the other end of this relationship, first. Secondly, my appointment of Bill Winter and the quality of this Commission demands that we take your work seriously. Thirdly, we actually need for you to think about what specific steps ought to be pursued in defining what the Federal role ought to be.

And let me just say one thing in closing out of respect to the Members of Congress who are here. There's been a lot of discussion in this town which will give way to reality as we move into the first budget year and as we move into next year's budget about how much we did or didn't cut spending. I asked yesterday Leon Panetta to tell me how many Federal accounts there are, you know, separate lines in the appropriations bill, where there's actually less money this year to be spent than there was last year. And the answer is 356 specific Federal accounts will have less money in this fiscal year than they did in the last year. Notwithstanding that, in the coming budget year, under the budget plan we now have, we're going to have to have significant other budget cuts in various areas.

Now, what I'm interested in doing is figuring out—and what the Members of Congress will have to help do—is to figure out within a Government Department and then across departmental lines, what is it that the Federal Government should be doing, and if not doing, what should the Federal Government be funding for you to do? And what things are we doing that may be nice but are relatively inessential at a time when we clearly have—the biggest dilemma for the Congress is this: almost every person in the Congress, without regard to whether they're a liberal or a conservative or a Democrat or a Republican, believes that we have to continue to reduce the deficit. We know that the serious efforts we've made have produced low interest rates, higher investment, housing starts, the biggest in 14 years; the beginning of this lumbering big economy coming back. On the other hand, virtually every Member of the Congress, including the most conservative Republicans, believe we are not investing enough in certain areas that prevent bad things from happening, that develop the capacity of people, and most importantly of all, help us to make this transition from a defense to a domestic commercial economy.

The great gaps in structural unemployment from California to New York and Connecticut, occasioned by the big cutbacks in defense spending, have made most everybody in the Congress quite sensitive to what kinds of investments we ought to have at the national level to generate jobs and high wage jobs.

So in order to achieve both those objectives, we have to be much more disciplined about what our job is and what your job is; about which of our programs really make a difference and which are nice but don't make that much of a difference; about how we can shift Federal spending to more investment and relatively less consumption, to make it more forward-thinking. And there is a real willingness, I think, in the Congress, to listen to and learn from the shared experiences of people in State and local government as we are forced to make these decisions. And believe me, whatever targets we do or don't adopt next time, if we just stay with the budget we've got, there is going to be an extremely rigorous and difficult budgetary process beginning here early next year. Anyone who's really studied the numbers knows that when you get beyond the rhetoric to the reality, there are a whole lot more reductions that are going to have to be made.

So on the other hand, everybody wants to increase funding in some areas. To whatever extent we are in sync with that and we are building the kind of partnership we ought to be, this country's going to be much better off. And to whatever extent you feel that the Government in Washington is doing the right thing, given its difficulties, and you can communicate that, we will collectively begin to rebuild the confidence of the American people that we're doing the best we can with the tax money they give us and in operating the Government in a more efficient and effective way.

I personally believe the consolidation of a lot of these discrete programs is very important. But if we do it, we have to find a way, and I hope that there will be candid conversations about this. I hope the Members of Congress will be candid with the State and local governmental representatives about this.

There are reasons why these programs get created in the way they do—where you have 150 separate training programs; we shouldn't, but we do—why we have all these other programs in little pieces, when it would be better if they were in one big piece and you had a laundry list of permissible things that could be done with this money. And then you would design what's best for your city, your county, or your State. And I hope we can get into exploring that, because I'm convinced, with the amount of money fairly fixed and with the demands on the money and with the differences, the drastic differences in economics from place to place, you need a lot more flexibility than you've got. But we need to be candid here about why the laws are the way they are, what the problems have been in the past, and what kind of new arrangements we can make if we're going to have any hope of implementing the reinventing Government recommendations on consolidating the grants.

So that, in short, Mr. Chairman, are some of the things that I wanted to say. I believe in the potential of this group. I want to work with you. I want to help to make sure that

you have both consistent support and the appropriate level of visibility so that we send the message out to the country that we are trying to work through these things and give the American people a Government that they can not only believe in but also trust.

Thank you very much.

NOTE: The President spoke at 10:01 a.m. in the Indian Treaty Room of the Old Executive Office Building. In his remarks, he referred to Carolyn Lukensmeyer, deputy project director for management, National Performance Review. The Executive order of October 26 on enhancing the intergovernmental partnership is listed in Appendix D at the end of this volume.

Remarks on the Observance of World AIDS Day
December 1, 1993

Now, there's a guy I'd like to vote for. [*Laughter*]

Thank you so much, Alexander, for what you said and the way you said it and for the power of your example. Father O'Donovan, Dr. Griffith, Kristine Gebbie, ladies and gentlemen, I'm delighted to see all of you here. I thank my friend Representative Eleanor Holmes Norton for coming.

I want to especially thank all of you here who are devoting your time and indeed your lives for the quest for a better way to deal with AIDS and, of course we hope, ultimately a cure. I want to thank especially the people who are living with AIDS who met with me today in their hospital rooms and who walked the corridors of the hospital with me. I won't mention them all, but I met a remarkable man named Larry Singletary upstairs who was a real inspiration to me. And I met his grandmother who was a real inspiration to both of us. And a beautiful young woman named Jenny Dorr who walked the halls with me, who came down with me. Stand up, Jenny. I think my goal ought to be to see that Jenny Dorr gets to live to a ripe old age.

Today I think just about every American who's ever been touched by AIDS will think of people they know who have died or who

have suffered family loss. I don't know if it was by accident or design, but I want to thank whoever put this part of the quilt up here with a picture of my good friend Dan Bradley, who for many years was the national leader of the Legal Services Corporation. I have a friend who lost her mother and another friend who lost his wife to AIDS because of tainted blood transfusions, and many others.

But I want to say a special word of appreciation today for the people who are infected with HIV and the people who are living with AIDS who are committed to living, to those who work in the White House and those who work in the administration and those who, around the country, have given support to me and helped me to give some support to them. Some of them are here today, and I thank them for the power of their example and for their commitment to life.

In a funny way this whole disease is bringing out the best and the worst in America, isn't it? I mean, it's exposing some of our prejudice in ways that are self-defeating since every family and every child is now at risk. And yet it's also showing us the courage, the self-determination, the incredible capacity of the American people to give and to love. We see our legendary refusal to adopt organized and disciplined solutions to big social problems. And yet we also see, as I will document in a moment, a remarkable willingness on the part of people who can make a difference to try to do more.

On Monday I met with several religious leaders who are responding in their own way to the AIDS crisis, people who are largely involved in caring for people with AIDS, many of whom are also involved, courageously for them, in trying to educate our children in the schools to prevent AIDS.

And I was impressed with the wide variety of religious perspectives. We had conservative evangelicals around the breakfast table with the liberal rabbi, mainstream Protestant ministers, and Catholic clergy. Every one of them, however, agreed on at least two things: One is that it is the moral high ground for people of faith to care for people with AIDS and the moral low ground to run away from it. And the second thing, and perhaps even more important over the long run, is that it is not only ethical conduct but an ethical obligation to speak openly with people, especially young people, about what they must do and not do in order to avoid becoming infected.

There was a Methodist bishop, Fritz Mutti, Topeka, Kansas, who lost two of his sons to AIDS—two—who spoke about these obligations. He talked about how he and his wife had worked against their own fear and loneliness to bring out their personal experience in a way that would give power to their efforts to deal with the crisis before us.

I met Reverend Steve Pieters, who has been living with AIDS for more than a decade now, one of America's longest survivors, explaining how he stays alive through hope and through his own faith.

For nearly every American with eyes and ears open, the face of AIDS is no longer the face of a stranger. Millions and millions of us have now stood at the bedside of a dying friend and grieved. Millions and millions of us now know people who have had AIDS and who have died of it who are both gay and heterosexual—both. Millions and millions of us are now forced to admit that this is a problem which has diminished the life of every American.

And as I enter this battle next year to try to provide for the first time in this history of this country affordable and quality health benefits for all Americans, millions and millions of us know that one of the reasons we have such

an expensive health care system, even though it doesn't do as much in terms of coverage as any other major country's health care system, is that we pay a terrible price for the rate of AIDS that we have in this country and the costs that it imposes because we don't do more on the front end.

On Sunday, the cover story in the New York Times Sunday Magazine was written by a journalist named Jeffrey Schmalz, who lived and just a couple of weeks ago died with AIDS. He was a remarkable man who interviewed me in a very piercing way when I was running for President. I was impressed then with the totally frank, almost brutal, and unsentimental nature of the interview in which we engaged and with the quality of his mind and spirit and the precision of his questions.

If you saw the article or you heard about it, you know that basically what the article said was AIDS is sort of receding in the public consciousness as a thing to be passionate about, that it was true not only in our administration but in the community at large and even in the gay community. That was the theory of the article. And I think he was saying that people were just frustrated dealing with what they considered to be a perpetually uphill battle, not that it was politically unacceptable anymore to talk about AIDS or deal with it but that there just seemed to be no pay-off. And so he challenged us all with these words in the article, "I am dying. Why doesn't someone help us?"

I have to say to you that I think that is a good question and a good challenge. I do believe that all of us, each in our own way, sometimes just want to go on to other things. Even some of my friends who are infected just want to go on to other things—maybe especially them. They just get sick of talking about it and thinking about it and focusing on it.

The purpose of this day is to remind us that our attitudes, behavior, and passion should be revved up in the other 364 days of the year.

[*At this point, an audience member interrupted the President's remarks.*]

It's okay. It's all right. It's all right.

Let me change the subject a minute and get back to it. Last night I went to see "Schindler's List." We had a special showing of it for the Holocaust Museum. And it's not going to be a highly advertised movie, and it's coming out around Christmas time. It will be tough for people to see this. I implore every one of you to go see it. It is an astonishing thing. "Schindler's List," it's about a non-Jew who, as a member of the Nazi Party, saved over 1,000 Jews by his personal efforts in World War II from the Holocaust.

The reason I say that is this: Part of my job is to be a lightning rod. Part of my job is to lift the hopes and aspirations of the American people, knowing that as long as you're trying to lift hopes and lift aspirations you can never fully close the gap between what you're reaching for and what you're actually doing, and knowing for sure that there's no way I can now keep everybody alive who already has AIDS. So the fact that he's in here expressing his frustration to me means at least that they expect me to do something, which is a step forward. I don't take it personally.

The reason I ask you to go see the movie is you will see portrait after portrait after portrait of the painful difference between people who have no hope and have no rage left and people who still have hope and still have rage. I'd rather that man be in here screaming at me than having given up altogether, much rather.

So let me go forward and tell you what we're trying to do, and let me then invite you to tell me what else we should do, because that's really what I came here to do today, to say here's what we have done in a year and to invite you to tell me what else we should do.

I think, first of all, it's clear that this administration has made a significant financial effort, as the Schmalz article pointed out in the New York Times. We've increased programs for prevention by $45 million, a very substantial increase. What we still need to do is to convince people who do the preventing that they ought to do it where the people are who need the information. We must, we must, we must convince more people to reach the children where the children are in the schools and where the adults are in the workplace.

I have directed every Federal office to provide its employees with education about AIDS prevention. We asked the 3 million Federal employees to take the information home to their families and to their communities. I have challenged every business to take similar action, but not every business and certainly not every school is doing it. We can deny the reality that every family is at risk until we know someone who

is, but we do so at great peril to ourselves.

We've increased the research funding for AIDS by over 20 percent, and we increased funding in the Ryan White health care act for care by 66 percent. And I want to remind you that this was at a time when overall domestic spending was held absolutely flat and when over 350 items in the Federal budget this year are smaller than they were last year. Where there was an absolute cut, we got substantial increases. Why? Because again, I say this shows the best and the worst about the country, a reluctance to deal with the problem, the absence of a systematic approach at every community level, but the understanding in Congress that even though we've got to slash a lot of the funding we have for various programs to reduce the deficit, we had to do more here. And I frankly think the Congress deserves a lot of credit for doing it at a very difficult time when many people said that the politically smart thing was to cut everything no matter what and no matter what the consequences. So I feel good about that. And I think you should feel good about that.

We do have a National AIDS Policy Coordinator. We do have an effort going now that we announced yesterday to see what we can do to slash the rules and the regulations and the bureaucracy to move drugs to people more quickly, to see what will work and what will help. And that is terribly important. We are marshaling more resources and making more efforts. But there must be other things we can do.

The theme of the World AIDS Day is "Time To Act." The argument that Jeffrey Schmalz made in his article was that we also ought to talk more. And for those of us in positions of leadership, talking is acting. I have to tell you that one of the things that I underestimated when I became President was the actual power of the words coming from the bully pulpit of the White House to move the country. I overestimated my capacity to get things done in a hurry in the Congress, but when I read the other day in the Los Angeles Times that I had the best record of any President in 40 years, I said, "Pity the others." I'm an impatient person. I'm a victim of my own impatience. But I do think sometimes all of us underestimate the power of our words to change the attitudes and the range of behavior of other people, not just me but you, too.

And it is clear to me that no matter how

much we put into research, no matter how much we put into treatment, no matter how much we put into education, someone besides the politicians will do the research, the treatment, and the education. And it has to be a daily thing.

The next thing I'd like to say is, I think the best thing we can do for people who are living with HIV and living with AIDS is to pass a comprehensive health care plan so that people do not lose their benefits. That is important, and let me say that is important for two reasons. One is obvious. One is what I saw in the hospital rooms up there when I asked people, you know, or they had already prepared to tell me: How is your care being paid for? Where do you live? Do you still have a place to live? Do you have a job to go back to if you get well enough to go back? What is the circumstance of your life? The first thing is just simply having the security of knowing that there will be a payment stream to cover quality care.

But the second thing, I think, is also important. And that is the point I began this talk with, which is that we have to affirm the lives of people who are infected and the living. And if you know that you have health insurance that can never be taken away and that the cost of it will not vary because you will be insured in a big community pool with people who are not infected and therefore whose real costs are lower, then there is never an incentive for someone to fire you or not to hire you. That is important. That's a big part of therapy in any kind of problem, being able to live to the fullest of your God-given capacities, to work, to go, to do.

And it would be good for the economy, by the way, to know that nobody had to be put off to the side or there were no incentives not to maximize the capacity of every person who lives in the country. So that this health care issue, the providing the security, is not just important for having the funding stream for the health care, it's also important to make sure that we are liberating the potential of people who want to work and contribute for as long as they can. It is a huge deal.

And I hope when we begin this debate in earnest next year that those of you who work in this area, either in the care of people with AIDS or those of you who are part of the activist community, will make sure that both those points get made to the United States Congress.

We have too many people in this country with a contribution to make to the rest of us and to the whole, dying to make it, who can't because of the crazy-quilt health system we've got. And I think we should do it.

Finally, let me just say that there is a lot of talk always, and I have been part of this, talking about how each of us has to take personal responsibility for our own conduct. And I believe that. But if you want children to do that, they have to be educated as to the consequences of their conduct, which means someone else has to do it. And it is also true that since literally every American can be affected in some way by this, all the rest of us have personal responsibilities, too.

And so again I say to you, I think we have done a good job in the first year of this administration if you measure "good job" in terms of organizing ourselves properly, funding the effort more adequately, identifying some of the major problems in the bureaucracy and going after them.

But Jeffrey Schmalz, in his last article, issued a rebuke to me. He said, "You cannot let this slide as an issue until it is over." And he was right. But he also issued a rebuke to everyone else in the country, everyone else. If you just look at the sheer numbers, if you look at what is happening in some African countries, if you look at what is happening in other nations around the world, if you had no other concern in your own country but the cold-blooded one of how your own country was going to pay for its collective health care needs and deal with its economic crises, if that was your only concern, if you never had a heartbeat of compassion, you would have to be nearly obsessed with this problem.

And so I say to you, my fellow Americans, tonight when I go home, I will see the face of Alexander. And I will wish that someday he will be able to give that speech on his own behalf. He deserves that chance. I will see the face of Jenny, and I will want her to live to a ripe old age. And all of us, all of us have something we can do. I invite you to tell me what else you think I can do and to ask yourselves what else you can do.

Thank you very much.

NOTE: The President spoke at 11:50 a.m. in the Pre-Clinic Science Building at Georgetown University Medical Center. In his remarks, he referred to Alexander Robinson, president, DC Care Coalition; Father Leo J. O'Donovan, president, Georgetown University; Dr. John F. Griffith, director, Georgetown University Medical Center; Kristine Gebbie, National AIDS Policy Coordinator; and Larry Singletary and Jenny Dorr, AIDS patients at the medical center. The related proclamation of November 30 is listed in Appendix D at the end of this volume.

Exchange With Reporters Prior to Discussions With Prime Minister Carl Bildt of Sweden
December 1, 1993

North Korea

Q. Mr. President, what do you make of what North Korea has publicly said following your statements last week?

The President. I don't know what to make of it yet. I wouldn't overreact to it. We're just going to have to see. The one thing I've learned here over the last year in dealing with North Korea is that it's important not to overreact, either positively or negatively, to something that they say which may not mean the same thing to them that it does to us the first time we hear it. And I mean that on the upside as well as the downside. We're just going to have to see and kind of work through this and see what happens.

Q. Is it still possible they'll come around and allow international inspections?

The President. I think it is. I hope it is, and I think it is.

Q. Do you agree with Director Woolsey, who said that he believes that they might be willing to go to war rather than let you hold inspections?

The President. I've tried to review his remarks, and I'm not sure I would characterize it quite in that way. I think, like all of us, he's very concerned about it, and he's studied it very closely. And all I can tell you is we have a strategy; we're going to pursue it, and we're going to keep going.

[At this point, one group of reporters left the room, and another group entered.]

Sweden

Q. Mr. President—Swedish press—why did you decide to meet with Mr. Bildt?

The President. Well, we haven't met yet. And I admire him, and I'm jealous of him because he's 3 years younger than I am. And so I wanted to see about this man who's taken Europe by storm and who's so much younger than me. We have a lot in common. And Sweden, you know, coming into the EC has—the end of the cold war has enabled us to cooperate on a whole range of things. We agree on a lot of issues, and I've really been interested, just kind of looking for an opportunity to meet with the Prime Minister. And this is a nice day for him to be here in Washington because after this we're going to have a chance to go over and meet with our Nobel Prize winners this year.

Q. Mr. President, what role would you like to see Sweden play in the new environment in Europe after the cold war?

The President. I think that's a decision that the Swedes will have to make for themselves. But let me say, I'm very, very impressed with the role that Sweden has been playing in trying to work through to a constructive solution to some of the problems in Europe and working its way into the security framework of Europe as well as the economic partnership of Europe. I think that your nation is in a position to really exercise a leadership role.

NOTE: The exchange began at 3:30 p.m. in the Oval Office at the White House. A tape was not available for verification of the content of this exchange.

Nomination for Assistant Secretaries of the Army and Navy
December 1, 1993

The President announced today that he intends to nominate Robert M. (Mike) Walker to be Assistant Secretary of the Army for Installations, Logistics, and Environment, and Robert B. Pirie, Jr., to be Assistant Secretary of the Navy for Installations and Environment.

"With their long years of experience in military policy, Mike Walker and Robert Pirie are well qualified for these positions," said the President. "I am looking forward to their service at the Pentagon."

NOTE: Biographies of the nominees were made available by the Office of the Press Secretary.

Statement on Implementation of the North American Free Trade Agreement
December 2, 1993

I am delighted that, as a result of discussions following up on our meeting in Seattle, Canadian Prime Minister Chrétien has announced his intention to proclaim the NAFTA by January 1, 1994. We look forward to the smooth and effective implementation of this historic agreement on January 1, so that all three countries can begin to reap the benefits of expanded trade, economic growth, and job creation in North America with the largest free trade area in the world.

NOTE: The proclamation of December 15 and the Executive order of December 27 on implementation of NAFTA are listed in Appendix D at the end of this volume.

Message to President César Gaviria of Colombia on the Death of Pablo Escobar
December 2, 1993

Dear Mr. President:

I just learned of the success of your long struggle to bring Pablo Escobar to justice. I want to offer my congratulations to you and the Colombian security forces for your courageous and effective work in this case. Hundreds of Colombians, brave police officers and innocent people, lost their lives as a result of Escobar's terrorism. Your work honors the memory of all of these victims. We are proud of the firm stand you have taken, and I pledge to you our continued cooperation in our joint efforts to combat drug trafficking.

Sincerely,

BILL CLINTON

NOTE: An original was not available for verification of the content of this message.

Letter to Congressional Leaders Transmitting the Notice on Continuation of Libyan Emergency
December 2, 1993

Dear Mr. Speaker: (*Dear Mr. President:*)

Section 202(d) of the National Emergencies Act (50 U.S.C. 1622(d)) provides for the automatic termination of a national emergency unless, prior to the anniversary date of its declaration, the President publishes in the *Federal Register* and transmits to the Congress a notice stating that the emergency is to continue in effect beyond the anniversary date. In accordance with this provision, I have sent the enclosed notice, stating that the Libyan emergency is to continue in effect beyond January 7, 1994, to the *Federal Register* for publication.

The crisis between the United States and Libya that led to the declaration on January 7, 1986, of a national emergency has not been resolved, and Libya continues to use and support international terrorism. Such Libyan actions and policies pose a continuing unusual and extraordinary threat to the national security and vital foreign policy interests of the United States. For these reasons, I have determined that it is necessary to maintain in force the broad authorities necessary to apply economic pressure to the Government of Libya to reduce its ability to support international terrorism.

Sincerely,

WILLIAM J. CLINTON

NOTE: Identical letters were sent to Thomas S. Foley, Speaker of the House of Representatives, and Albert Gore, Jr., President of the Senate. The notice is listed in Appendix D at the end of this volume.

Statement on Signing the International Parental Kidnapping Crime Act of 1993
December 2, 1993

Today I have signed into law H.R. 3378, the "International Parental Kidnapping Crime Act of 1993." This legislation underscores the seriousness with which the United States regards international child abduction. It makes this crime, for the first time, a Federal felony offense.

H.R. 3378 recognizes that the international community has created a mechanism to promote the resolution of international parental kidnapping by civil means. This mechanism is the Hague Convention on the Civil Aspects of International Child Abduction. H.R. 3378 reflects the Congress' awareness that the Hague Convention has resulted in the return of many children and the Congress' desire to ensure that the creation of a Federal child abduction felony offense does not and should not interfere with the Convention's continued successful operation.

This Act expresses the sense of the Congress that proceedings under the Hague Convention, where available, should be the "option of first choice" for the left-behind parent. H.R. 3378 should be read and used in a manner consistent with the Congress' strong expressed preference for resolving these difficult cases, if at all possible, through civil remedies.

WILLIAM J. CLINTON

The White House,
December 2, 1993.

NOTE: H.R. 3378, approved December 2, was assigned Public Law No. 103–173. This statement was released by the Office of the Press Secretary on December 3.

Remarks to the Democratic Leadership Council
December 3, 1993

Thank you very much. Thank you very much, Senator Breaux, and ladies and gentlemen, thank you for that warm welcome. It's wonderful to be back here. I want to thank John Breaux for his leadership of the DLC, his constancy, and his friendship and support to me in this last challenging year. I want to congratulate Dave McCurdy, who has been one of our most faithful members for a long time, on his upcoming leadership of the DLC.

I want to say how wonderful it is for me to see so many of you, my friends from all across America here, particularly some of my friends from New Hampshire I see in the audience. Hillary spent yesterday in New Hampshire and came home gloating that she had been there and I hadn't. Thank you very much.

What's Bruno doing over here? Are you segregating him?

I have given a lot of thought to what I ought to say here today. It was 8 or 9 years ago now that—well, almost 9 years ago—after the Democrats had lost yet another Presidential election, that a group of Democrats gathered to try to sharply define what we stood for and where we wanted our party to go. It was clear that we needed an infusion of new ideas and new energy, a new direction and reinvigoration into the party that most of us belong to by heritage, instinct, and conviction.

My wife used to tell me—I repeated often on the campaign trail—that insanity was doing the same thing over and over again and expecting a different result. But we decided we would try some new things and see if we could produce some different results, because we knew that our country needed a new direction. After all, in the previous 12 years we had seen the quadrupling of the deficit, the stagnation of wages, profound economic and social problems in this country going unaddressed, and middle class Americans continuing to stay with our opponents in the other party largely because they felt we could not be trusted to promote their economic interests or their values and our policies here at home, to promote our national interests abroad or to give them a Government that gave them honest value for the hard-earned dollars they put into it in taxes.

In the Democratic Leadership Council we always understood that for our politics and our policies to move this Nation, we had to express the basic values of mainstream America and promote those economic interests. The heart and soul of the American experiment has always been a personally secure and growing middle class, challenged to achieve new opportunities, challenged to be part of a larger community, challenged ever more to assume the new responsibilities of each new age.

The American dream that we were all raised on is a simple but powerful one: If you work hard and play by the rules, you should be given a chance to go as far as your God-given ability will take you. Throughout our history our party has been the fulcrum that allowed working people to lift themselves up into the middle class. And we know that if we're to be true to our historic mission we must be the party of the values and the interests of the middle class and, more importantly, the values and the interests of those who want to become part of the growing middle class and the American dream. We must fight their fight. We must give voice to their concerns. We must give them the chance to build security while embracing change. And above all, we must honor those basic values of opportunity, responsibility, and community, of work and family and faith. This is what it means, in my view, to be a new Democrat. I was proud to campaign as one, I'm proud to govern as one.

Because we are Democrats we believe in our party's historic values of opportunity, social justice, and an unshakable commitment to the interests of working men and women and their children. Because we are new Democrats we promote those old values in new ways. We believe in expanding opportunity, not Government. We believe in empowerment, not entitlement. We believe in leading the world, not retreating from it. We believe that the line between domestic and foreign policy is becoming increasingly blurred as the interests and the future of every American and every city and hamlet in this country is increasingly caught up with events that happen beyond our borders. And most of all, we believe in individual responsibility and mutual obligation, that Government must offer opportunity to all and expect something from all, and that whether we like it or not, we are all in this battle for the future together.

With that vision and those values, I believe that these ideas are beginning to change our Nation. When I was preparing this speech last night, I came across a talk I gave back in March of 1990 when I became the chairman of the DLC, and I found a few words I wanted to repeat today.

I said that everyone hopes that the 1990's will see a political renaissance for the National Democratic Party. Every one of us knows we can't realize all our goals until we elect a Democratic President, but I believe that in the end any resurgence for the Democrats depends upon the intellectual resurgence of our party. That's another way of saying that ideas matter.

If you look at the elections in the last several months, it seems to me the real message of them has been lost in the argument about party labels, and we don't win 100 percent of them. People say, "Well, they should have won the ones they won. What about the ones they lost?" Look what the message was in Dennis Archer's victory in Detroit—one of our strong DLC members who will be here later—or in my friend Bob Lanier's 91 percent victory in Houston. He said, "Elect me. I will stop spending money on this, and I will instead spend money on police, and I will deploy them properly and the crime rate will go down." And sure enough, it did, and 91 percent of the people reelected him. Look at the common threads that run through all these elections and you will see the ideas that we have been working to espouse in the Democratic Leadership Council for years and years.

I believe that we have achieved a victory of new ideas. I come here to say more than anything else, however, that when you produce policies that embody these values of opportunity and responsibility and community in a democratic society—small d—that elects people to Congress and that requires the President to work with the Congress, that requires the accommodation of various interests all across the country in the private sector and requires a partnership with people at the State and local level, having the best ideas in the world does not free you of the obligation to make difficult decisions.

I further come here to say that we don't want to be in the position that some of our predecessors were in the other party where they were willing, from time to time, to exalt political rhetoric over reality and where they were willing, from time to time, to let the perfect become the enemy of the good.

Our obligation is to do good things to move this country forward that embody our ideas and our philosophies. That does not relieve us of the obligation to make the hard decisions. It imposes that obligation on us, and that is what we are trying to do.

As we approach the end of the year it is time to take stock of how far we have come, and I want to start, again, by paying my debts to this organization. Seven Cabinet members of this administration were DLC members—seven.

My Chief of Staff, Mack McLarty, who came with me today, was an early and strong supporter of the DLC. We have Elaine Kamarck who was one of yours who did such a brilliant job on our reinventing Government program. And Bruce Reed and Bill Galston are the intellectual firepower behind what we're doing in welfare reform and crime and family preservation. Jeremy Rosner wrote the wonderful words that I was privileged to speak at the Middle East peace signing, one of the best speeches I have had the opportunity to give as the President. I know it was a pretty good subject, but I had a pretty good speech writer, too, thanks to his growth, and I think you had a lot to do with that. There are so many others, Doug Ross, Jim Blanchard, and others, who are active in the DLC, who are now part of our administration.

I also want to thank those who are here today from my administration to talk about national service, welfare reform, and other things, including Donna Shalala and Eli Segal and Roger Altman. Let's look at what we've done together. And let me begin by again thanking the DLC members and the Congress, many of whom are here behind me, and without whom none of this would have happened.

The first thing we did was to move beyond the failed economic policies of the past, beyond tax-and-spend and beyond trickle-down. Our economic plan is imbued with ideas the DLC has been advocating for years. We had the largest deficit reduction plan in history, fueled in part by more than 350 specific spending cuts that I have now signed entirely into law. And I want to remove some of the veil of rhetoric about that. I'm not talking about smaller increases than were in the last Bush budget. I'm talking about 350 accounts in the Federal budget where we are spending less money this year than we did last year. Real spending cuts.

We did ask the wealthiest Americans to pay their fair share, and overwhelmingly, most of them told me as I was campaigning around the country, "I will do that if you'll bring the deficit down and give me value for money in what you spend the money on." This was not a question of class warfare; it was a question of fundamental fairness trying to reverse the situation in which the middle class found itself for the last 12 years of paying higher taxes on lower income.

In addition to that, for working families with less than $180,000 a year in income, there will be no tax increase. Let me read you from a review of the new tax law written by the Kiplinger personal finance magazine, hardly an arm of the Democratic Party. I quote from Kiplinger—where were these people when I needed them, when we were debating this in Congress? I quote, "About 110 million Americans will file individual tax returns next spring. On 108 million of them taxes will take a smaller bite than they did this year." That's right, smaller. The fact is, Kiplinger says, "More than 98 percent of us are not affected by the higher income tax rates which reach back to the first of the year. Our tax bills will go down a bit on the same income because taxes are indexed for inflation." If you are part of the forgotten middle class, don't forget that.

In addition, in this economic plan there are progrowth DLC ideas, investment incentives. Small business expensing is dramatically increased so that 90 percent of the small businesses in this country, because of the increase in the expensing, will pay lower Federal income taxes this year than they did last year, 90 percent. There is a venture capital gains tax here for small businesses and new businesses where the investment is held for 5 years or longer, tax rate cut by 50 percent. There are expansions in the resource and development tax credit and other things designed specifically to spur high technology growth in areas where we need it and where we have great opportunities moving toward the 21st century.

There are pro-work, pro-family welfare reform ideas in this economic plan, including the earned-income tax credit, about which I will speak more later, I think the most significant pro-work, pro-family economic reform we have enacted in 20 years. There are reinventing Government DLC ideas in this economic plan, including a major overhaul of the college loan program in which we save billions in administrative costs and put it into providing lower interest loans to college students who can pay them back on easier terms as a percentage of their income. But we toughen the collection terms so we make sure they can't beat the bill. These things were all in that economic plan, and because of that, what really matters is the result.

And let me say here, a cautionary note, this country is dealing with structural economic challenges of 20-year duration. We are dealing with social challenges that have been building for 30 years. We are reversing economic policies that were in place for 12 years. We will not be able to turn this around overnight. The average American has not yet felt a significant change in his or her economic circumstances. But look at the direction we are going in. We have historically low interest rates. Inflation is down to very low levels, 20-year low levels. Investment is up. Housing sales last month were at a 14-year high. The unemployment rate drop this month was the best drop in 10 years.

We've had 1.6-plus million new jobs come into this economy since January. The private sector jobs since January are about 50 percent more, almost 50 percent more than were created by the private sector in the previous 4 years. One of the ironies is that under this administration for the next 4 years, Government jobs won't grow as much as they did in the past 4 years. The private sector jobs will grow more.

Now we have a long way to go. We still are dealing with stagnant incomes. We are still dealing with the fact that more and more people who lost their jobs lose them permanently and have to find new and different jobs. And that imposes new obligations on us. But we have unemployment down, investment up, no inflation, and low interest rates. We are moving in the right direction.

The decision to go after the deficit and to do it in a progressive, fair way with new ideas was the right decision. And the rhetoric is now being wiped away by the reality. The Kiplinger report will be found now by ordinary people when they get their tax forms in April. And a lot of the blows that this administration and this party suffered unfairly and wrongly in the last year happened because people put out bogus rhetoric that could not be overcome by the reality. Now when you see the Kiplinger report and the tax forms come out, and people don't pay more taxes, they pay less and we've got low inflation, high investment, more jobs, and lower unemployment, the truth will out just like it always does.

Again I will say, all the good ideas in the world does not relieve you of the obligation to make the hard decisions and to do it in a way that permits us to go forward. That is, somebody has to decide, and we have to move, and we have to act, and it all has to count up to a majority so you can go forward. That's what democracies do.

But it won't be enough. This on its own terms will not be enough to expand incomes and create jobs sufficient to restore the interest of middle class America. Why? Because you have to have a growing economy in a global context. With productivity going up, a lot of big companies are downsizing. They are going to become more profitable. But what does productivity increase mean? It means the same person can produce more, right? Sometimes it means fewer people can produce more. We've had utterly astonishing growth in productivity in the manufacturing section in America, now coming into the service sector and into the Government sector, as we use more and more new technology. What does that mean? That means fewer people do more work. That means higher unemployment, and since you got all these unemployed people out here, it means pressure to keep wages down.

So if you want incomes to go up and jobs to increase, what must you do? You must have more customers. There have to be more customers for America's goods and services. There is no other way to increase incomes and to increase jobs in this country.

That is why we have pursued another course, long advocated by the DLC, trying to broaden the opportunity for Americans to sell their goods and services. That is why last summer I met with the G–7 and got those countries to agree to expanding market access for manufacturing products. That is why I have started trying to build a new and very different relationship with Japan. It is simply unsustainable over the long run for these two great economies to have the kind of imbalance in our economic relationship that we have. That is why I fought so hard

along with the DLC for the North American Free Trade Agreement. And that is why our Trade Ambassador, Mickey Kantor, has hardly slept for the last 48 hours as we try to work out an agreement with Europe that's good for us and good for them on the GATT rounds, so that we can try to get a new worldwide trade agreement by the end of the year.

I want to say a special word of thanks to all of you who were involved in the NAFTA struggle. It was not an easy one. The Speaker of the House called it a Lazarus project: It came back from the dead. But I particularly appreciate the courageous stance taken by those who had to disagree with their friends honestly and openly because none of us could figure out how to grow this economy and grow more jobs unless we have more customers in an environment in which the global economy is growing. That's why I went out to meet with the APEC ministers.

Someday the whole story of this great struggle will be known, but I do want to say I am very grateful to the people in the Congress who did the work, and to Mr. McLarty who kept in close touch with the President's office in Mexico, and to all the people on my staff and all the people who have made this happen, people like my good friend Steny Hoyer, who really stuck his neck out on this and took a big risk for it.

It is a simple, elemental principle that we must grow the global economy if a rich country, whether it's America, Japan, or the European Community, is going to be able to maintain higher incomes and more jobs.

Now, the second thing we've got to do is to enable people to succeed in this economy. In other words, we have to enable people in America—if we have good economic policies and if we can get global economic growth, we have to enable more Americans to succeed. It must be possible in our country, in other words, to be a successful worker and a successful parent, since most workers are parents and most parents have to work. That's why I supported and signed the Family and Medical Leave Act, something you would support. That's why I fought so hard in the economic plan for the earned-income tax credit.

That phrase is totally Greek to most people. They don't understand it. But what it means is that on April 15th between 15 and 16 million working families in this country, representing over 40 million American citizens who worked this year for incomes of $23,000 a year or less—going up to $26,000 in a couple of years—will get an income tax reduction. Why? Because even though they work 40 hours a week and they have children in the home, they are at, just below, or just hovering above the Federal poverty line. This is the most important thing we can do in welfare reform, to make a simple statement that if you have kids and you work 40 hours a week, you will not be in poverty; we will reward your work. The tax system will keep you out of poverty.

It was a very, very difficult thing to do because it costs money, and it complicated the politics of passing the budget. But it was the right thing to do because unless we can reward work and family at the same time, we are not going to get where we need to go. And it matters. We cannot ask the American people to be in the position every year—and for many of them, every week and every day—of choosing between being a good parent and a good worker. You have to be able to succeed at both in the world in which we are living. And I think it was terribly important.

The next thing I want to say is we've got to train a whole generation to think about work in a different way, and we have to reorganize our systems. We literally have to reinvent our systems for dealing with how people deal with work, the loss of it, and the acquisition of new jobs. There are lots of things involved in that, but one of them plainly is opening the doors of college education to all Americans. I mentioned earlier that we have reformed the student loan law. We also passed one of the DLC's most cherished ideas, the national service act, into law, thanks to, literally, the parenting work of Eli Segal in developing the legislation, getting it through, setting up the organization, and maintaining the confidence of large numbers of Republicans as well as Democrats in the United States Congress.

And I know he's going to talk about that in a moment, but 3 years from now, 100,000 young people will be able to earn some money for further education while rebuilding their communities from the grassroots up. This idea has the potential to totally reshape the way Americans think about their country and to bring a dramatic change in this country on a whole range of social problems from the grassroots up. And Senator Nunn and Congressman McCurdy and any number of other people in the DLC

were out there pounding on this idea for years and years and years. And I thank you for that, and I hope you are proud of the fact that it is a law of the land.

The last thing I want to say about what we've tried to do already is that we recognized in this organization a long time ago that if people didn't feel a certain level of basic security, it was very difficult for them to make the changes we need to make. If you want to challenge people to seize opportunities and to assume more responsibility, if you want people to be able to live with, basically, the chaotic nature of the world in which we find ourselves—a very exciting world if you can figure out how to win in it—there has to be some sense that the basic fabric of society is being maintained, that there is some order, some security, some discipline which we need to observe.

That is why this crime and violence issue is so important: huge increases in violent crime in many communities in this country; police at an increasingly disadvantageous position—now over three violent crimes for every police officer in the country, where it used to be the reverse, three police officers for every crime just 30 years ago; and all the stories you know about children killing children, or young teenagers being better armed than police officers.

We know there are some things that work. We know—the DLC does, we've been advocating this for years—that community policing works. Mayor Lanier in Houston just proved it in the ultimate way, by getting over 90 percent of the vote. I was trying to think of who else could get 90 percent of the vote for anything. It tells you how passionately people care about this public safety issue.

We are trying our best in these difficult budget times to get a crime bill out that will produce 100,000 new police officers. But they must be properly trained and properly deployed. That is a challenge for you in the DLC; it is a challenge for us as Americans to make sure not only that we pass a bill in Congress that provides the police officers but that when they get down to whatever town or city they're in, that they are properly trained and properly deployed. Community policing works. You can lower crime, not just by catching more criminals but because it actually helps to prevent crime from occurring in the first place. It really matters.

There are some other things we ought to do in that crime bill, too, and I'll just mention two. We need to provide alternative punishments for youthful offenders so that we can use the prison space we have to keep people who shouldn't get out for as long as they should stay in. The boot camp proposals are in this crime bill, another DLC idea that we have advocated for years and years, something that I tried to do at home when I was a Governor. And it's an important part of the bill.

There are two other things in the bill. Senator Kohl, from Wisconsin, has put an amendment in to ban the ownership of handguns by young people under 18 and to limit access to them to properly controlled circumstances by minors. And it passed overwhelmingly.

Then there was an amendment by Senator Feinstein to ban several assault weapons and to specify a number of hunting weapons that cannot be restricted at all because they're hunting rifles and they are things that people use for sporting purposes. I think it is a good, balanced amendment, and I hope it will be in the final provision of the crime bill.

Lastly, let me say that I was elated earlier this week, on Tuesday, to sign the Brady bill into law, and I thank the DLC for its longstanding support of the Brady bill.

I also want to say that it is perfectly clear to me that one of the biggest problems we face as Democrats is that we know that the Government has a role to play in dealing with a lot of these problems. But we also know that in America there is a historic distrust of Government that is healthy. And in the more recent years that distrust has risen to record levels which is not healthy, and we have to do something about it. But the only way we can do anything about it is by giving people better value for their Government. And I want to really say a special word of thanks for the work that David Osborne and Elaine Kamarck have done in helping the Vice President on this reinventing Government project.

I want you to know that this is not just a report. The report recommends that we do what most companies have been doing for years to eliminate unnecessary layers of management and empower front-line workers to become more responsive to customers to constantly improve our services. We are moving to implement that report. The House voted right before they left to implement our recommendation to reduce by 252,000 by attrition, not by laying people off, the Federal work force over a 5-year period.

The Senate voted to pay for the crime bill by doing that. But both have agreed that we ought to do it.

The question now is whether we will be given the tools to do it in a humane and responsible way, in a way that is good for the Federal employees, good for the Federal work force, good for the taxpayers of the country. But it is a very important thing. We can only make this Government work if we have the tools to do it. We have, for example, clear evidence that the Pentagon can meet a lot more of our national security needs if we have procurement reform, that we are still wasting billions of dollars in the way we buy things.

When I was in Alameda the other day on the U.S. carrier *Carl Vincent* having lunch with some career Navy personnel, an enlisted man with 19 years of service told me that he had just—because he was on a ship he had access to emergency procurement, sort of an escape hatch from the procurement clause—he said, "I went down to a computer store and I bought a personal computer for this ship for something we needed that cost one-half as much and had twice the capacity of the computer required to be bought in the procurement regulations of the Federal Government." That is still going on.

We have a procurement reform bill pending in the Congress. If we are going to do what you want us to do on reinventing Government we have got to be given the legal authority to manage this Government with the same sort of flexibility and common sense that people in the private sector have.

And you know, I've got my longtime friend and former colleague and your former chairman, Chuck Robb, behind me. I mean, he's been preaching this stuff for years, and when he was a Governor, he worked on it. And I can just tell you that there are things we can do to save billions of dollars and still increase investment where we need it, but we have to be given the tools to do it.

So I ask the DLC to urge the Congress to pass the structural reforms we need to have the kind of budgeting, procurement, and personnel practices that will permit us to save money and increase investment in our future at the same time.

Now, next year we have a lot of challenges ahead of us: health care, welfare reform, redoing the system of education and job training and unemployment, to mention the three biggest, perhaps. And I would like to say just a word about each of them in terms of the ideas of the DLC.

First, we have to provide our workers and businesses the security they need to know that they will not be bankrupted by an illness or paralyzed by the constant fear of the loss of coverage. Almost nobody in America today really knows for sure that they will never lose their health care coverage—for sure, no matter what happens to them or what happens to their business.

I want you to know what this budget really looks like, and the only reason the deficit is a continuing problem. I wish I had a graph here. If I had a graph here and this were zero on spending—this is zero, zero increases. Here is where defense is going, down; domestic spending, flat. That means every time we put more money into Head Start we have cut that much money somewhere else. Interest on the debt is going up some because even though interest rates are low, the corpus of the debt is getting bigger. Then our revenues are going up like this, about 8 percent next year, retirement going up because of the cost-of-living that everybody gets who is on Social Security or any kind of retirement. But the big numbers are Medicare, 11 percent, one year. This is at 3½ percent inflation max, right? One percent growth in the Medicare rolls, 2 percent growth in the Medicaid rolls. Medicare going up 11 percent, Medicaid going up 16 percent. That is it. At a time when the most conservative Republicans in the Congress would say we should be spending more on new high-technology ventures and in defense conversion and in trying to help us adjust from a defense to a domestic economy, that's what we're spending our money on.

And I talked to executive after executive facing the same thing. But there is good news. The Federal health insurance program, which is big and has bargaining power, has actually had many of its policies lower this year than they were last year. The State of California, which is in terrible financial shape—so everybody knows they don't have a lot of money and which has huge bargaining power—has negotiated a cost increase in its premiums less than the rate of inflation.

So what do we have to do with health care? Again, to avoid the stale debate of right and left—one side says, well, the present system is just going to cure itself, and another is saying that the Government ought to take it over and operate it—what can we do?

If you go back to what you wrote in "Mandate for Change"—when Jeremy Rosner was back in domestic policy instead of foreign policy—you say we should be able to change the rules of the private health care market to produce universal coverage and lower cost, better quality care. I agree with that.

We have to offer the American people a new choice, that is, guaranteed private insurance. I think there have to be two changes in the existing system. First of all, you have to provide health insurance that you can never lose, whether you are in or out of work, and no matter what kind of job you are in, because a lot of people are going to go from big companies that have big benefits to smaller companies in the inevitable restructuring of the economy.

And you have to give greater consumer power, market power, to small businesses and to self-employed people. And in order to do it you have to go to a broad-based community rating scheme, in my judgment, so that there is no disincentive for little companies to hire people who have had somebody in their family who has been sick, who has had a preexisting condition.

Now, every other country in the world with which we compete, including those that are doing quite well, has figured out how to do this. We're the only people who haven't figured out how to do it. I just refuse to believe that we can't figure out how to give health care security to everybody in this country and to give equal bargaining power, market power, in the marketplace to small businesses and self-employed people. I just refuse to believe that. I think we can.

We can disagree about a lot of things, but I think everybody would admit we ought to have a system in which there is a good comprehensive benefit package, including primary and preventive care that is given to every family, and that people have to assume some personal responsibility for it and ought to be prepared to pay something for it, but that we ought to do that.

If we don't, you're going to continue to see your Federal Government faced with insolvency. We're going to continue to have to cut all of our spending from domestic investments, many of which 80 percent of the people in this room think we ought to be making. We're going to continue to see massive cost shifting from the Government to the private sector and within the private sector from some companies to others, and often the companies with the most generous health care benefits are the ones that are the most vulnerable in global competition.

This is a nutty system, and we have to fix it. And we have to fix it without messing up what is wonderful about it, the quality of care, the availability of emerging technologies. The things that people do today in this health care system that are very good—we can fix what's wrong without messing that up. And there are a lot of options we can pursue to get there, but I would just urge you to stick with what was in the "Mandate for Change." Do not give up on universal coverage. And do not give up on the proposition that there has to be a competitive capacity for all, all employers, including small businesses and the self-employed. If you will stay with that, then we can reach an agreement next year which will be the most historic domestic achievement for this country in a generation. And we have to do that.

With regard to welfare reform, let me just say very briefly—I want to say again how much I appreciate the work that Bruce Reed has done, the work that Bill Galston has done. We are moving toward making welfare a second chance, not a way of life. We have made this debate an interesting one in which there is now a Republican counterproposal. I don't agree with all of it, but there are some very good ideas in it. It really gives me the cause to believe that we might be able to make a bipartisan coalition here with a big majority, to try to give people who are trapped in poverty and unemployable in present circumstances a chance to be successful parents and successful workers. And I am very, very encouraged by that. I think you will be too.

Finally, just let me say this. We have terrible problems today in America because a lot of people who want to work are not employable or can't ever get a job where their wages will go up because they don't have the skills. Let me just mention two or three things that we are trying to do.

The Secretary of Education, one of the former DLC members, has his education reform bill which will pass early when the Congress comes back, the Goals 2000 bill, that does what we've been advocating for years. It puts the Federal Government—instead of trying to micromanage the schools, we're going to provide the schools with the money that the teachers and the principals need at the grassroots level to figure out how to meet the national education goals. And we will measure schools by their results, not by overregulating their influence. And we will give them some standards by which they will be able to tell whether they are measuring up to global standards or not. And we will focus more on trying to give them the tools and the information they need to follow strategies that work.

I'm telling you, every problem in American education has been solved by somebody somewhere, including people under the most adverse circumstances. What we need to do is to have the Federal Government help to spread that instead of getting in the way. And we are changing the whole approach to that, thanks to Secretary Riley and the support we have received all across the education community, from the NEA, from the AFT, from the administrators, from the school boards, from people who are really committed to changing the nature of the Federal role in public education. There is also in this bill explicit provision for the kind of reforms the DLC has advocated in terms of supporting local districts who want to have charter schools, who want to have public school choice, who want to do the kinds of things that many districts have wanted to do where the Federal Government has essentially taken no position in the past. That can be a part of this reform.

The other thing that we are doing is to try to work out with the Secretary of Education and the Secretary of Labor a national system of apprenticeships to move people from school to work who aren't going to 4-year colleges. Everybody who doesn't go to a 4-year college and get the degree at least needs 2 years of further education and training. And our school-to-work program makes a good beginning on that.

The final thing we're trying to do is to deal with the terrible problem of the unemployment system. Today, if you are an employer and you pay the unemployment tax, you are paying for a system that is dysfunctional. You are basically paying for a lot of workers to draw a reduced income until it's obvious that the unemployment runs out and they are not being called back to their old jobs. The unemployment system was developed in a time when people were called back to their old jobs.

What we need to do is to develop an immediate system of reemployment so that the minute someone knows they are going to be unemployed, they are immediately eligible for retraining, for job placement, for the kind of services that will give people the chance to make a quick start back in life and to use that unemployment stream to get continuous retraining. I hope that we can get the employer community, the labor community together in this country to do this. Secretary Reich's most important contribution to this entire administration may be changing people's understanding of the way the institution we have here has nothing to do with the nature of unemployment for most Americans anymore. That is our big reinventing Government challenge for next year.

Now, let me say finally that the reports say that this administration had the best year in terms of congressional success of any in the last 40 years. You heard Senator Breaux say—and I've called Senator Lieberman in the middle of the night enough to know—that the Congress worked 40 percent more this year, spent 40 percent more hours on the job than last year, 40 percent more. We made a difference. If we can do health care, welfare reform and reform the education and training system next year, we'll make more of a difference. If we can keep growing this economy with stable, secure policies, it will begin to be felt in the lives of middle class Americans.

But I will end where I began. The Democratic Party has got to be a grassroots party. It has got to reflect not only the economic interests but the basic values of most American people. And there are a lot of things that we have to do in this country that deal with crime and violence and restoring the family and restoring communities that cannot be done, not now, not ever, by the President and the Congress alone

that require private sector initiatives, that require people at the State and local level to act.

The most important thing we ever said in the DLC was that in the end there can be no successful opportunity without responsibility, and you can't run a country unless everybody recognizes that we are in a community in which we have responsibilities to one another and in which we go up or down together. That was the most important thing we ever said.

So I ask you as you leave here, I hope you will go home and talk about how the ideas that you have fought for are being brought to life in this administration. But more important than that, I hope you will go home and remember that no matter who the President of the United States is, until the American people are prepared to take responsibility for their futures and until we are prepared to recognize again not just in our rhetoric but in our lives that this is one country and we have got to find a way to make a strength out of our diversity, we have got to stop wasting so many kids, we have got to stop permitting the incredible level of social disintegration that we have permitted, we will never become what we ought to.

And when we become the party that is the grassroots, bottom-up, personal responsibility, community-oriented party committed not only to saying to the President and the Congress, "This is what we want you to do for America," but to proclaiming every day, "Here is what we are doing for America," we will not be where we all set out to go. I think we're well on the way.

Thank you very much, and God bless you.

NOTE: The President spoke at 10:31 a.m. at the Sheraton Washington Hotel. In his remarks, he referred to George Bruno, DLC New Hampshire State chapter organizer, and David Osborne, consultant with the National Performance Review.

Exchange With Reporters
December 3, 1993

Personal Security and Responsibility

Q. [*Inaudible*]—as far about what you meant by personal security when you talked about that

theme and also about values?

The President. Personal security means, among other things, that people who are out there struggling in this country to work for a living and raise their kids should be safe on the streets and should have access to health care and should have access to a decent education for the course of their lifetimes.

Q. But you also mentioned personal responsibility along with that. What responsibility do they have?

The President. Well first of all, the Government cannot create success. The people have responsibilities in the area of work to make sure they're educated and trained. They're going to have responsibilities in the welfare reform area to take education, training and move from welfare to work. They're going to have responsibilities in the health care area, those who don't have health insurance, to pay for some of their own health care.

And in a larger sense, in every community in this country we can put 100,000 more police officers out there. We can train them right. But people are going to have to start recovering these families and these neighborhoods community by community. The private sector is going to have to invest in these neighborhoods. We've got these empowerment zones which give people tax incentives to invest in poor neighborhoods, but people who live in those cities are going to have to invest in them.

Q. Are you going to start talking to people about maybe not having children they can't afford to take care of? Is this something that you're worried about?

The President. Well, I talked about this a lot in the last couple of days. We've got to bring down the number of children who are born out of wedlock; that's what we've got to do. And people are going to have to think more about their future, more about their children's future, and when they do have children both parents are going to have to take more responsibility for them. We're going to have to crack down on identification of paternity, on child support enforcement. We're going to have to demand that people take more responsibility for the consequences of their action, including taking care of their children.

Q. Are you going to be talking about that more in the future? Is this something we're going to hear about?

The President. Absolutely. One of the reasons I asked Dr. Elders to be the Surgeon General is because we have been involved in an effort for years to try to drive down this teen pregnancy rate. I think that the out-of-wedlock teen pregnancy rate is threatening the whole family structure of communities in this country and undermining our ability to recover as a people.

Democratic Leadership Council

Q. Have you made up with the DLC?

The President. I don't think there's anything to make up about. Breaux saved my budget.

Q. He didn't vote for the Brady bill.

The President. He saved the budget. But the DLC—well, there's no political correctness test here. Nobody can agree on every issue. But the DLC endorsed the Brady bill early. The DLC was an early supporter of the Brady bill, an early supporter of family medical leave, and——

Q. You haven't been critical about them, so they've been a little critical of you.

The President. Yes, but that's why I—they said some things about the budget earlier on that I thought were not accurate. But Breaux didn't; he stayed with us on it and helped us pass it. So did Lieberman. So did Steny. So did most of the leaders. But I think they were wrong, and I said that.

On the health care thing, if you go back and read the DLC's health care package, which was written by Jeremy Rosner who now works in the White House, I think we're much closer on health care than you think. I think that a lot of this stuff has been overblown. Every time one of them or one of us says, "Here's what the difference is between our two health care plans," somebody says, "Oh, they're dumping on each other again." I think that it's just an honest discussion. I predict that you will see an accommodation that will cause a health care plan to pass next year that has universal coverage and good benefits, and that's what I want.

Thank you.

NOTE: The exchange began at 11:37 a.m. at the Sheraton Washington Hotel. A tape was not available for verification of the content of this exchange.

Remarks and a Question-and-Answer Session on Health Care in Bernalillo, New Mexico
December 3, 1993

The President. Thank you very much. He did a good job, didn't he? For a fellow that's not used to doing this, he did a great job.

Well, first of all, Doctor, I want to thank you and all your colleagues for welcoming me into the clinic today. I enjoyed the tour. I enjoyed listening to you talk about what you've done. And I have to tell you that I saw something in that clinic today that no law can ever compensate for or require, and that is a level of constant commitment to the people of this area. That must be a priceless treasure, just the idea that you've committed your life here. And I thank you for that.

I'd also like to thank Mayor Aguilar and Mrs. Aguilar for welcoming me here and—with their grandson back there. I enjoyed it, meeting them. And I appreciate the little—I'm about to fall in the hole here. This would make millions of people happy if I fell over—[*laughter*] I think I'm pretty well set now. They gave me a wonderful little proclamation declaring this day Bill Clinton Day in Bernalillo, which I am grateful for, and this wonderful piece of art. Thank you.

I brought a number of people out here with me. But I want to recognize some of them because they will have a major say in what we ultimately do as a nation on the health care issue. First, members of your congressional delegation: Senator Bingaman and his wife, Anne, who's in our administration in the Justice Department. Senator Domenici, thank you for coming, sir. My good friend Congressman Richardson, who fought so hard for NAFTA, and his wife, Barbara, thank you for being here. Congressman Steve Schiff and Congressman Joe Skeen are here. Thank you for coming. We have a lot of State officials, but I do want to introduce my good friend Governor Bruce King here and his wife, Alice. Thank you, Bruce. Alice, are you there? Thank you, Alice. And your Lieutenant Governor, Casey Luna, flew back with me. Is he here in the audience somewhere? He wrote me a good letter endorsing our efforts in health care, which I really appreciated, as a Lieutenant Governor and as a small business person.

I want to talk just a few moments today about what we're trying to do with this health reform effort, how the plan that I have presented to Congress would, in my view, help things for this doctor and this clinic and all of you who are served here and, perhaps more importantly, how it would help to provide these kind of services to other people in New Mexico and throughout the United States.

Let me begin by saying that I think most of you know that before I became President, I was for 12 years the Governor of Arkansas, and there are thousands of people from my State now living in New Mexico. I see them every time I come out here. It is also a very rural State. I spent a lot of time as a boy in communities that make this place look like a thriving large metropolis, in little small towns in country crossroads. All my mother's people come from a place that now only has about 50 people in it. I spent a lot of time as Governor trying to keep open rural health clinics, keep open rural hospitals, develop clinic services or primary care or emergency services for people who live in isolated rural areas. So I have a certain familiarity with a lot of the kinds of problems that you have. I've also seen a lot of those problems get worse and some get better over the last 15 years. And Doctor, I think you've been here 17 years, is that right? So about the same timeframe of your service, I have been involved in public service dealing with health care in another way.

I came here today to listen, to learn, and to try to explain what we're trying to do. Let me just briefly summarize how this health care plan would affect you and your families and your community.

First of all, it would provide for the first time in our history a system of universal coverage. Every family and every person in every family would have a comprehensive package of benefits which would include primary care, the kind of care you get here, and preventive care services that you would always have even if you changed jobs, even if you lost a job, even if someone in your family got sick so you had what the insurance companies now call a preexisting condition.

In addition to that, it would recognize that in rural areas there are 21 million Americans today who don't have access to primary care physicians or have inadequate access to primary care physicians. So that even if you gave an American family a health insurance card and there was no doctor to see, you would have coverage that would be meaningless. So this plan makes a real effort to increase people's access to health care in rural areas by doing two or three things: first of all, by guaranteeing funding to rural health clinics that are publicly funded; by increasing the funding stream to clinics like this one—rural doctors are the most likely to have to do uncompensated care—to make sure there will be some payment coming in for all the people who get care within any clinic; by taking steps to remedy the doctor shortage. You heard the doctor say that he didn't leave here in part because there was no national health corps facility or physician to come in behind him. Today, we're only providing funds for about 1,100 doctors a year in the National Health Service Corps. Under our plan, we go from 1,100 to 3,000 doctors a year by just after the turn of the decade and the century. So we would be, in other words, every year providing enough extra doctors to serve another couple of million patients in America at a reasonable ratio of doctors to patients. So that would make a huge difference in the quality of rural health care.

Now, there are a lot of things we do to try to get doctors to come to rural areas. But the National Health Service Corps is one, providing more scholarship funds; providing more access to partnerships with people in health care centers like the ones that you mentioned is another. The other thing I want to emphasize is that a lot of people who have health insurance policies, in rural areas especially, tend to be underinsured. And one of the things that we've learned is: As Americans, we spend a huge amount of money on health care that we wouldn't spend if people had primary and preventive health care and if people had access to adequate medication. There are a lot of people who have all kinds of physical problems that could be adequately treated and their conditions could be maintained if they had adequate medication. A lot of people who have mental health problems that could be better managed and treated if they had access to a steady amount of appropriate medication.

So one of the good things about our health care plan is that under the bill we presented, in the comprehensive benefit coverage, all families, whether they get care from the Medicare or Medicaid programs or through private health care programs, would have access to prescription drugs. There would be a copay, you'd have to put some money up front in it, but everybody would have access to those drugs. We believe that will lower the incidence of hospitalization and, over the long run, really lower the cost of health care by helping people to stay healthy and to maintain their own health conditions.

How do we pay for this? The program would be paid for by a combination of sources. First of all we would require employers who don't cover their employees at all to cover their employees. And if their employees are not covered at all now, the employees would have to pay up to 20 percent of the premium themselves. The employer's contribution would be capped at 7.9 percent of payroll. But small businesses, which dominate rural areas, would be eligible for discounts on their guaranteed private insurance plan, which would dramatically lower in many cases the percent of payroll they would have to pay.

Is this fair? I think it is. In every other country with which we compete, everybody makes a contribution directly or indirectly to the health care system. Today, everybody gets health care, but often when it's emergency care, when it's too late, and then their costs are paid by somebody else. They're either shifted back to the taxpayers or shifted onto other employers through higher insurance premiums. But by giving discounts to people who are smaller employers, we think that's a fair thing to do.

How will the discounts be paid for, and how will the extra services be paid for that the Government's going to provide? By lowering the rate at which we're seeing medical inflation explode Medicare and Medicaid programs. Today the Government programs are increasing at 3 times the rate of inflation. Under our system, which would put more people on Medicare and Medicaid in the larger competitive bidding blocks with self-employed people and small businesses and others, we think we can cut the rate of increase in these costs at least to twice the rate of inflation and take the difference that we've already budgeted to pay for some of these other programs.

There are no general taxes in this program.

We do seek to raise the cigarette tax. And we ask the biggest companies, that can opt out of our system to provide their own health care plan—they will get a huge drop in their premiums as a result of our system—we ask them to make a modest contribution, trying to help pay for those that are uninsured and may need subsidies. That's how we pay for it. And we think it will work.

There will also be a lot more competition in the system than there is now. That will drive costs down. But we don't take that into account in figuring out what it costs. So we think the system will not cost even as much as we say it will, once you take account of the increased competition.

If you're a small business person or a self-employed person, the best thing about this program is that you'll be able to have access to a better health insurance policy at a lower price because for the first time, small business people and self-employed people will be able to have access to less costly premiums and will have the same sort of bargaining power in health care, particularly those who live in the bigger areas, that only big businesses and governments do today. Small business and individuals are at a terrible disadvantage today.

So that's how the system works briefly. There are a lot of other specific questions I'm sure you'll want to ask me. I'm here, and I also brought a couple of my staff folks here who helped to work on putting this program together and especially spent a lot of time on rural health care. I personally spent one full day in the White House talking about rural health care to make sure that before we sent this plan up to Congress we would have a program that was very sensitive to the needs of rural health care, to the needs of Native Americans, to the needs of people that are underinsured as well as those that are uninsured.

So, we'll try to answer your questions, but now I'd like to hear from the folks you brought here, Doctor, and to thank you very much for that.

[*At this point, clinic physician Alan Firestone read a list of participating community members, patients, and clinic employees. He then introduced participant Miranda Sapien.*]

The President. Let me just say, if you can hear, these mikes aren't too strong, so you have to speak right into them so everybody can hear.

Pretend you're singing to it. [*Laughter*]

[*Ms. Sapien began speaking but was interrupted by the noise of a passing train.*]

The President. At least it's not in the middle of the night, right?

[*Ms. Sapien then discussed caring for her elderly parents in her home and the need for affordable home health care and respite care for the elderly, especially in rural areas.*]

The President. No, as a matter of fact, this is a big problem everywhere in America, and the fastest growing group of our population in America are people over 80 years of age. And in general, I think we want to encourage families to stay together. The way the system works today, if you spend yourself into poverty you become eligible for Medicaid, and then you can go to a nursing home. There aren't very many Medicare certified nursing homes in the U.S. The older people are Medicare-eligible. So one of the things that our plan seeks to do, although I don't want to mislead anybody, we don't know how much it would cost. We can't know precisely how much it would cost if we started tomorrow covering everybody with this kind of long-term care. A lot of us believe that over the long run it would save money because more people would stay at home if there was some provision for in-home care and for respite care so that the families could have a break. But we do phase in long-term coverage over a period of several years as a part of this plan.

And one of the things that we're also trying to do is to encourage some of the State reform efforts that are going on now where many States are looking at whether they can set aside some of the money that is presently allocated to nursing home care to also cover in-home care. I applaud you for doing it. I think since we know that the percentage of people who are quite old is going to increase and more and more people will be quite alert and will be able to function at a fairly high level but there may be some care needed and more as time goes on, I think it's quite important that we keep this long-term care part of our program, even though it's going to take us several years to get it fully phased-in.

Lynn Mathes. Lynn was—I'll let her tell us. But I think—were you fully employed? And she was injured.

Turn it on, will you, whoever's got the mike.

It worked great for her.

[*Ms. Mathes explained that she had been injured while employed as a horse trainer and her former employer would no longer pay for her therapy. She did not receive any help from insurance companies but was able to pay some of her expenses through her work as an artist.*]

The President. Unfortunately, the story you just told is all too typical. The reason I laughed is the doctor has a work of art on his wall inside that another artist gave him as an in-kind payment. And I can remember when my mother was a nurse anesthetist, I can remember when people, in the appropriate season, used to go pick fruit and pay her in return for her services. That works for a few people. I don't think it's a very good way to run a country.

Let me just say, the way our system would work if we reformed the insurance system is that that simply would not happen because everybody would be covered, there would be a clear package of benefits, there would be a single form, you would just turn it in. And your employer would never—I'm glad your employer tried to get it covered, at least. A lot of small employers are terrified of a serious thing like this because they know that their insurance is already so much more expensive than larger employers or than Government insurance, and they're afraid they'll be priced right out of the market. Under our system, everybody would be able to buy insurance on equal terms, and the coverage would be uniform and consistent. So you wouldn't ever be putting an employer in a bind just because it was a small employer. Or if you were a self-employed artist and that was your only job, you'd have access to a really affordable policy.

But you have to understand, this is the only country in the world with 1,500 separate health insurance companies writing thousands and thousands of different policies. And if they delay paying on you, then that in effect gives them time to earn interest on that money. So eventually, even if they pay, they've made a good deal out of it if they can delay payment for 2 or 3 or 4 or 5 or 6 months. But it may impair your ability to get certain care. This happens everywhere.

You just heard what the doctor said. At the time when his caseload is doubled here—patientload—they have increased the number of people who devoted themselves to paperwork by sixfold. That's because this is the only country in the world that has literally 1,500 different companies writing thousands and thousands of different policies, where the doctors in the clinics have to hire people, trying to get payment when they're entitled anyway, and where the coverages are so complicated and different, when you put that with all the rules and regulations that the Government has, that you spend enormous amounts of time just trying to work out the transaction who's going to pay when. One of the primary benefits—perhaps the best benefit to doctors and clinics—of our plan is that we'd actually be able to have a single form for insurers, a single form for clinics, a single form for patients. And it would cut out a lot of this incredible paperwork and administrative cost.

We spend about 10 cents on the dollar—let me tell you how much money that is. We're going to spend $900 billion on health care this year. So 10 cents on the dollar is $90 billion dollars a year. That's a lot of money. That's 1½ percent of our gross domestic product. We spend about that much more on administrative costs than any other country in the world spends on their health care system. That's how bad it is. And you get caught in it, in the delay.

[*Dr. Firestone mentioned the concerns of a small business owner about the cost of providing health insurance and workers' compensation for her employees.*]

The President. The health care cost of workers' comp would be folded into the health care plan, which would save a lot of small business people a ton of money. Slightly more than half of the workers' comp premium is health care costs, that would be folded in. And that's a huge concern to small business people and also to people in certain targeted industries, like in my home State, the loggers and the people in the wood products industry. They have huge workers' comp bills. So that would really help.

Again, I would have to know exactly how many employees the lady has and what the average income is of the employees, but they would be eligible for a discount rate. I can just tell from what you said to me, she would not pay the 7.9 percent. She would pay some lesser percentage of the payroll. But having been on the other side of it, she can understand what it's like if there is none.

Let me say, there are a lot of part-time workers in our country today and probably will be more. Under the way the bill has been presented to Congress, if you work 30 hours a week or more, you would be insured as a full-time worker and your employer would have to pay the full cost of the premium and you would have to pay your 20 percent match. If you're under that, down to 10 hours a week, the employer could pay a proportionate amount of that, a smaller percentage, and therefore your premium would be less. And if you outran that in using the health care system because you're a part-time worker, and that would be eligible for the public subsidy. So we try not to bankrupt people who have part-time employees or discourage people from hiring part-time employees. But we think they ought to pay at least a portion of their benefits.

[Dr. Firestone introduced Dr. Jack Vick, who discussed the difficulties of providing quality health care in rural areas but stated that he will continue his rural practice.]

The President. I'm just glad you're going back. Let me just mention a couple of things you mentioned, because there are answers to some of them, and there aren't answers to some of them—at least if there are answers to some of them, I don't know what they are. But one of the best things, I think, from the point of view of the benefits package that we tried to do in this plan is to provide more coverage for primary and preventive services, pap smears, mammograms, cholesterol tests, important things that are early warning signals that may head off far more severe health care problems and actually save the system money.

Secondly, I think part of the answer to the problems of doctor exhaustion and overcommitment, simply increasing the number of doctors in rural areas and trying to tie them more into partnerships with urban medical centers and with university health centers. Without going into all the details, I think we've got some good systems to do that.

We also are working on one aspect of malpractice reform that will encourage more family practitioners to do things like deliver babies or set simple fractures where they are in rural areas. Based on an experiment that started in the State of Maine, where basically if you're a family practice doctor and you do these procedures out where people live, because you need to do it there, and you can prove that you've

followed a set of guidelines approved not by the Government but by your national professional group, that raises a presumption that you were not negligent and sort of gets you out of this whole malpractice bind.

Now, what I don't have an answer for, and I don't think there is one right now, is what you do with the problem pregnancy. I think if you think you've got a problem case, you still have to send it—whatever discomfort there is—to a place where you think the care will be appropriate. If there's an answer to that one, I don't know what it is. But I do think that we want more family doctors, and we want more family doctors out there in the rural areas doing things they know they can do but they're still afraid not to do because of the malpractice problem. And being able to prove that there's a set of nationally accepted guidelines for this kind of procedure in a rural area and that you've followed them, it seems to me will do a lot to alleviate both the cost of the malpractice insurance and the fear of the lawsuit.

[Dr. Vick asked about coverage for mental illness.]

The President. Well, we think the basic benefits package should include mental health benefits, pretty comprehensive mental health benefits, as well as medication for treatment of mental illness. I know this is a particular interest of Senator Domenici and a number of other Members of the Congress. But let me say this has been a big fight in our administration, essentially with the bookkeeping of health care. That is, we can't ask the Congress to pass, and the Congress cannot pass, any bill that they don't think they have a pretty good feel for how much it will cost and how it will be paid for.

So, we have been through a lot of very tough sessions with the actuaries for health care, people who are supposed to be experts in health care costs, to figure out how much the mental health benefit will cost and how we have to phase it in over time. Right now we phase in mental health benefits, comprehensive mental health benefits, between now and the year 2000, although other health care costs would be covered by the beginning of 1997, the end of 1996, in all the States.

So, I'm glad you said that. I'm glad you said it here in this rural setting because, again, as you know much better than I, there are a lot of mental health problems that can be treated, that can be managed, that can allow people to be productive members of society, and that can therefore be a very cost-effective thing to do, as well as the humane thing to do. And we have to get these benefits in.

Again, I believe that our actuaries have overestimated the cost and underestimated the benefits of including comprehensive mental health benefits. But nonetheless, we can't—again, I don't want to mislead the American people. I don't want to overpromise. And I don't want to pass a bill that breaks the bank. So right now we provide for the phasing-in of the mental health benefits, with the benefits to trigger in about the year 2000 to do what you say we should do.

[*Dr. Firestone introduced Cel Gachupin, who discussed health care concerns of Native Americans and then shared the tragic story of his son's death from asthma.*]

The President. Thank you for sharing it, and thank you for having the courage to share it. I don't know if I can give you an answer to the policy questions you raised. Thank you very much for what you said.

The first thing you said was you often had to drive your son past hospitals to get to the Indian Health Service. Under our plan, if it passes the way we have presented it, American Indians will be able to get health care either through the Indian Health Service or through another network of health care at their own choice. So that if people, because of where they happen to live, have much better access to some other health care provider, they will be, at their own choice, they will be able to choose to use those facilities.

But we feel that the United States has a solemn obligation to maintain the Indian Health Service. And as you probably know, the funding has dropped over years as the number of people using it has dropped. So one of the things that— after the leaders of tribes from all over America came to see us in Washington about this, one of the things we did was to go back and amend the plan to try to strengthen the financial support for the health care service so they would be able to provide particularly the kind of serv-

ices to people who are out-patients like your son was. So I think in this case, we will give the American Indians more personal choice than many now have. You won't be forced to the health care service. You'll have the option of using something else. But if you do use it, it should be better funded than it now is.

[*At this point, Dr. Firestone asked about benefits for children with multiple disabilities and chronic illnesses and presented the President with a letter regarding their needs. He then thanked the President for visiting the clinic.*]

The President. I can't answer the question you just asked me. But I'll get an answer, and I'll get back to this lady who wrote you the letter—or to me—the letter. I'll do it.

Let me just say before we close, and then I want to say hello to all of you and then go back around and see the kids who have been waiting so patiently, if they're still there. I don't know if they are. I hear some people chanting in the background.

When the new year comes and the Congress comes back into session, there will be a few months of really intense debate on this. Just think about this town and the size of this town and the diversity of the things we've heard about already today, as well as all the things we haven't heard about. This is a very complicated matter. But in the end it comes down to something very simple. We are spending a much bigger percentage of our income on health care than any other country in the world, and yet we are the only major country who doesn't provide everybody health care coverage that is always there, that can never be taken away.

And we have permitted a system to develop so that now, coming out of medical school, only about one in seven doctors are committed to do what this doctor has done and this doctor wishes to do. So we have to change that. And it is perfectly clear that it will not happen unless the Congress is prepared to go through the incredibly rigorous process of reviewing the bill that I presented, listening to anybody else's alternatives and hearing the human voices that we have heard today, and coming to grips with this problem and actually acting on it.

This is something we should have done a generation ago when we could have saved untold billions of dollars and no telling how many lives. But we can do it now, and we have to do it. And I would just implore you to work with us, make sure we don't make any mistakes we can possibly avoid, but give the Members of Congress from your State the courage to face this problem that our Nation has neglected for too long.

Thank you very much.

NOTE: The President spoke at 4:04 p.m. at the El Pueblo Health Services Clinic.

Statement on Signing the Hazard Mitigation and Relocation Assistance Act of 1993
December 3, 1993

Today I am pleased to sign into law S. 1670, the "Hazard Mitigation and Relocation Assistance Act of 1993."

The flooding that occurred in the Midwest this past summer was unprecedented in our history in scope, magnitude, and duration. The sheer number of victims, flooded homes, farms, and businesses, and the extent of damage to public facilities called for an unprecedented response from the nine affected States, local governments, volunteers, and the Federal Government—and respond they did.

Now that most of the flood waters have receded, it is time to reestablish lives disrupted by the weeks and months of rain and flooding and to rebuild property damaged by those waters. For many, rebuilding in the same place will be out of the question. And for many who want to move, relocating off the flood plain may not be possible without help.

With this legislation, my Administration and the Congress have taken an important step toward providing the help needed. This Act authorizes a greater Federal contribution toward acquiring and relocating structures damaged by floods than was available before. It provides higher ceilings on the amounts of Federal disaster funds that can be available to help flood victims move out of harm's way. And in assisting in the relocation of homes and other structures, it provides greater assurance than perhaps any other measure that the people helped will not have to suffer such damage and disruption from flooding again. It will be less costly to help the flood victims move now and reestablish their lives than to bear the expense of repeated flooding.

I congratulate and thank the many Members of the House and Senate in both parties who worked so diligently to pass this legislation. I especially commend the leadership of Representatives Volkmer and Gephardt, Senators Harkin and Danforth, and other Members of the congressional delegations of the Midwestern States, as well as the prompt action of the leaders of the House Committee on Public Works and Transportation and the Senate Committee on Environment and Public Works.

WILLIAM J. CLINTON

The White House,
December 3, 1993.

NOTE: S. 1670, approved December 3, was assigned Public Law No. 103–181.

Statement on the Technology Reinvestment Project
December 3, 1993

To win in the new global economy and safeguard our national security, America must invest in new technologies with both commercial and military applications. This program will help give us the edge that will keep America strong and create new jobs at the same time.

This program is designed to keep American manufacturing workers, from the engineers to the machine operators, at the top of their fields. Efficient, high-quality production using a skilled, well-equipped work force will put American products on shelves throughout the world and put Americans to work in high-paying jobs here at home.

NOTE: This statement was included in a White House announcement of the third group of awards in the technology reinvestment project.

Appointment for Environmental Protection Agency Regional Administrators
December 3, 1993

The President today approved John H. Hankinson, Jr., as Regional Administrator, Region IV, and Jane N. Saginaw as Regional Administrator, Region VI, at the Environmental Protection Agency.

"I am pleased today to name these two hard-working individuals to our team at EPA," the President said.

NOTE: Biographies of the appointees were made available by the Office of the Press Secretary. This item was not received in time for publication in the appropriate issue.

Nomination for National Highway Traffic Safety Administrator
December 3, 1993

The President today announced his intention to nominate Ricardo Martinez, M.D., to be Administrator of the National Highway Traffic Safety Administration with the Department of Transportation.

"Ricardo Martinez has dedicated his career to improving trauma care and curtailing car accident deaths," the President said. "As a firsthand witness to the tragedy accidents can inflict on individuals, families, and communities, he will work hard to ensure the National Highway Traffic Safety Administration uses all of its resources to make our roads safer."

NOTE: A biography of the nominee was made available by the Office of the Press Secretary. This item was not received in time for publication in the appropriate issue.

Remarks at the "Celebration '94" Reception in Albuquerque, New Mexico
December 3, 1993

The President. You know, when Bruce said to Alice, "Just give the President whatever it is you have," I said, "Heck, Bruce, I want the ranch." [*Laughter*] I like the Stetson, but I mean, if I really get a choice—[*Laughter*]

Ladies and gentlemen, I am glad to be here. Glad to be back in New Mexico. How many of you were here—I just got off the phone with Hillary. She was working in New Hampshire yesterday, so she's home tonight. I just got off the phone with her. How many of you were here when we were here the night of the election—all night—remember that? The press has a way of finding out everything about you if you become President. President Reagan loved jelly beans, and President Bush didn't like broccoli and last week the Wall Street Journal reported our dark secret that Hillary and I are addicted to salsa. [*Laughter*] And it all happened because of you, because we stayed up all night living on that before the election.

I am so glad to be back in New Mexico. I'm glad to be here with Ray Powell and with you, Mr. Speaker. Thank you for being such a good emcee. I want to thank my longtime friend Bruce King. I don't know if you remember what he said. There are only three living Americans who served as Governors in the seventies, the eighties, and the nineties: Cecil Andrus of Idaho, Bruce King, and me. It was the longest time before any of us could get a promotion. We had a lottery, and in the beginning we thought I won, but sometimes in the last year I wasn't sure I didn't lose. [*Laughter*] I love Bruce King. The first time I ever met Bruce and Alice and Bruce laid all that, you know, that "Aw, shucks," stuff on me—[*laughter*]—"Aw, shucks," you know, I checked three times to make sure I still had my billfold in my pocket. Aw, shucks. [*Laughter*] I appreciate the fact that Bruce is missing the start of the annual Lobo Classic Basketball Tournament tonight. I know what a sacrifice it is. He did it for the money, not me. [*Laughter*] But I'm glad he's here anyway. You can tell we're friends; you can't make fun of your enemies. [*Laughter*]

I want to say, too, how glad I am to be here with Bill and Barbara Richardson. Bill Richardson was the national cochair of the Adelante Con Clinton movement. Thank you for bringing your posters; there's two there. But he never did anything more important for America than in his leadership in the fight for the passage of NAFTA. I can tell you, on September 14th, the day after we had the signing of the peace agreement between Israel and the PLO, we formally kicked off the NAFTA fight after all the side agreements on labor and the environment were done. And we had the endorsement of all the living former Presidents. We had four Presidents and former Presidents there, President Ford, President Carter, President Bush, and myself. We were 100 votes behind. We were maybe that close—[*laughter*]—100 in the House of Representatives. And Bill Richardson soldiered on when others were saying, "Well, they ought to give up." And some of my friends who were on the other side of the issue even suggested maybe we ought not have a vote because they didn't want us embarrassed. And Richardson and I were too dumb to know we were beat—[*laughter*]—so we just kept on going. It worked out all right, and the Nation

is in his debt. And New Mexico will benefit enormously because of the astonishing national leadership he provided on that issue.

I gave—what did you say?

Audience members. [*Inaudible*]

The President. I need a vitamin pill tonight. [*Laughter*] I also want to say that Jeff Bingaman likes me because I brought Anne here tonight. I gave her the day off at the Justice Department. Sometimes being President is just like being a school principal, you give people an excused absence. [*Laughter*]

And I want to say Bill mentioned the technology reinvestment projects, but I want to, if I might, just take a minute to talk about Jeff Bingaman and what he did, not only for New Mexico but for the country there. In 1992, when I was running for President, the United States Congress under the leadership of Senator Bingaman provided for the expenditure of a few hundred million dollars to help America make the conversion, the painful conversion from a high-tech, defense-based economy to a high-tech commercial economy. And there were a number of things in the bill that they passed. And as a candidate for President, I strongly supported the bill. And it passed before I could be elected President. And guess what? And I thought, well, here I am cutting off my nose to spite my face. I'm out there asking Congress to pass this bill, which will put a few hundred million dollars into the hands of the President I was running against to put the American people back to work in the way I've been saying we should do for the last 5 years. And guess what? They wouldn't spend any money because they didn't believe in it.

And so when I became President, we went to work on trying to give life to Jeff Bingaman's idea that a little bit of public money in the context of the hundreds of billions of dollars we've been spending on defense should be offered to the private sector in matching funds for people who would come up with ideas that could be used to take defense technologies and turn it into domestic jobs and American high-tech opportunities for the 21st century. So earlier this year, we released the first round of grants, and in the whole year we wound up with over $400 million worth of funds. Congress was so astonished by the success of the program that they have come back and voted to spend even more money on it in the year we're now involved in, in fiscal year '94.

Now, I want you to understand how important this is. In the first round of applications, when we put up $400 million, we had almost 3,000 projects submitted for funding that, with public and private money together, would require $8.5 billion. That's how hungry American entrepreneurs, universities, laboratories, and big companies are to be part of this defense conversion effort, to find ways to create the jobs of the 21st century out of all the work we've put into defense research over the last 40 years. It is a very important thing. And none of this would have happened if Jeff Bingaman of New Mexico hadn't been the catalyzing influence, the energy behind this idea.

I also want to say it is true that in the first three rounds of grants that we're now completing today, New Mexico got a total, I think, of nine big projects. And on a per capita basis, you almost certainly led the country in grants. But you did it on the merits—not just the labs but the universities.

So I'm honored to be here tonight with all these friends of mine on this stage and all of you out there to thank you for voting for Bill Clinton and Al Gore in 1992, to thank you for providing leadership like Bill Richardson and Jeff Bingaman and Bruce King, to ask you to keep them in and keep them strong, and to ask you to keep supporting the direction our country is taking.

When I became President, we had had the 4 worst years of job creation since the Great Depression. We had had 12 years in which our national debt had quadrupled, while our investment in our people had gone down. We had had 20 years of the global economy requiring American middle class people to work longer hours every week for the same or lower wages. We had out-of-control health care costs with 100,000 Americans a month losing their health coverage. So we were paying more for less. And almost everybody in this country thought things were going in the wrong direction. I said until I was blue in the face, even to those who were most enthusiastic about our campaign, that we couldn't expect immediate overnight results, but we could turn the country around. And what I want you to know, my friends, is after the first year, we have turned the country around. We are moving in the right direction.

The economic plan which the Congress adopted reduced the deficit, had over 356 separate— over 350, 356 to be exact—separate spending cuts. Now, that's not Government language for "We're cutting the rate of increase in the previous budget." There's 356 accounts that have less money this year to spend than they did last year; increased investments in things like defense conversion and new technologies and worker training and Head Start, things that build our country over the long run; raised taxes on fewer than 2 percent of the American people earning the largest amounts of money whose taxes had been lowered while their incomes went up in the eighties; gave an enormous, an enormous boost to the ideas of family and work by providing tax cuts to over 15 million working families whose incomes were $23,000 a year or less, because we wanted to say to people, "We know you've got kids in your home; we know you're working hard for modest incomes. We want the tax system to lift you out of poverty, not drive you into it. We want you to be successful as parents and successful as workers." That will affect over 40 million Americans who are either the workers, the spouses, or the children of the families who will get tax relief under this economic plan in April.

And what are the results? What are the results? Historically low interest rates; very low inflation; increased investment; a 14-year high in housing sales last month; a 10-year drop in unemployment this month, that is, it dropped more from month to month than in any time in 10 years; almost 50 percent more private sector jobs created in the first 11 months of this year than in the previous 4 years. Has it affected most Americans yet? No. Are we moving in the right direction? You bet we are. We have to keep going until we do see the benefits go to every American family. But we are moving in the right direction.

This Congress not only passed the motor voter bill, which Bill Richardson mentioned, it also passed the Family and Medical Leave Act, which gives people the right to take a little time off without losing their jobs when there's a baby born or a sick parent. This Congress passed the national service bill, which 3 years from now will give 100,000 young Americans the chance to earn some money against further education after high school by working in community service projects to rebuild the fabric of our country from the grassroots up. This Congress passed the Brady bill, which will require a waiting period for handguns. And both Houses of Congress have passed campaign finance reform—they just have to reconcile the two bills—and a crime bill which will enable us to put another 100,000 police officers on the streets, have boot camps for first-time youthful offenders, and do other things to make the American people safer in their homes and their schools and on their streets and in their neighborhoods.

Bill Richardson was generous in what he said, that no one knows that this was the most successful legislative session in history, since we've only been keeping score like this for 40 years. But it's not bad since they've been keeping score.

I say to you, this is a good beginning. But it is just the beginning. NAFTA was important, but we need to keep going until we've got all of Latin America committed to democracy, free-market economics, and an economic partnership with the United States. That's good, but we also need a new global trading agreement. I spent a good deal of time today working trying to get the nations of the world to conclude this so-called GATT agreement by December 15, our deadline, because it is estimated that that will add over one million jobs to the American economy within the next decade if we can successfully conclude it.

Why is this important? Why was it important enough for people like Jeff Bingaman and Bruce King and Bill Richardson and Bill Clinton even to argue with some of our friends over? It is this simple, it is this simple: We can't keep any of our businesses in America today unless we become more productive. But being more productive means the same person can produce more goods or more services; maybe even fewer people can produce more goods and more services. Well, if there's no more demand for the goods and services and fewer people produce them, what happens? Unemployment goes up, and you don't have to raise wages because there are all these people who are out there unemployed who are more than happy to work for less. So if you want productivity—which you have to have to compete with other countries—to lead to higher wages and more jobs, you must have more customers for American products and American services. That's what these trade agreements are all about.

We have got to expand the rate of growth in the world to find more customers for what we do well. And that will enable us not only to have more jobs but to change the job mix to get the higher wage jobs in there, to raise people's incomes for the first time in 20 years. It's going to be hard to turn this around. But for 20 years most Americans have been working harder for less. We have got to try to do better than that. And the only way to do it is to provide more customers.

The second thing we have to recognize is that a lot of our people are still not able to compete in that global economy, which means we have to have a better system for training our young high schoolers who don't go on to college, a better system for giving our working people lifetime education and training opportunities, a better system for recognizing that the unemployment now is not like it used to be where people would go on unemployment and then a couple of weeks later they would get called back to their old company. Most people who are unemployed now have to find a new job with a new employer. That means that this coming year we're going to have to totally revise the entire unemployment system and make it a reemployment system, immediately give people education and training and job placement. I challenge all the people who supported us in NAFTA, who wanted America to have more customers, to make sure Americans can take advantage of that instead of be punished by it, by retraining the American work force for the 21st century. That is our great challenge.

That's why the welfare reform program that we're going to deal with next year is so important. You have a lot of people out there who had children when they were children, who have never been in the work force, who have no education. They cannot command a living wage in a global economy. We owe it to ourselves, as well as to them, to set up a system where we favor work over idleness but where we give people a chance to succeed in a highly competitive economy. We are all going to have to face the fact that we have new challenges. If we want our people to succeed as workers, we have to let them succeed as parents too, because most working people have children, and most people with children have to work. That means family leave is important, that means a tax system that doesn't punish low-wage workers is important, and that means that it is important to have welfare reform and lifetime training.

The last thing I want to say is I came here, before I was here tonight, to go out to a wonderful little community near here to talk about health care. If we don't control health care costs and provide health care security to all of our people, we will not have the underpinning of social security we need to have the courage to make the changes that the global economy imposes on us.

Next year we are going to do health care, welfare reform, and revise the education and training program. Then they'll say, "Well, that's a better year than they had last year." And it will be for America. We can do it together. Thank you, and God bless you all.

NOTE: The President spoke at 8:35 p.m. at the Albuquerque Convention Center. In his remarks, he referred to Gov. Bruce King of New Mexico and his wife, Alice; Ray Powell, State chairman, Democratic Party of New Mexico; Representative Bill Richardson and his wife, Barbara; and Senator Jeff Bingaman and his wife, Anne.

The President's Radio Address
December 4, 1993

Good morning. Today I'm in Los Angeles to hold a meeting on the economy and its impact on southern California. A year ago this month, I hosted a national economic summit to get the best ideas from all across America on how to implement the economic strategy I ran for President to implement, a strategy to regain control of our economic destiny; to put confidence back into our people; to strengthen our families; a strategy to rebuild the American dream by restoring middle class values of opportunity, responsibility, and community, rewarding work and family and faith.

For too long the Government in Washington ignored roadblocks that stood in the way of an economic recovery: our investment deficit that hurts workers caught in changing times and communities plagued by crime, a budget deficit that drains money from our economy, a trade deficit that keeps us from selling our products and services around the world. All these roadblocks have kept America from moving and have hurt California especially, because California had so many high-tech employees in the defense industry, which as all of us know has been cut back a lot since 1987 and the end of the cold war in 1989. And now California, like the rest of America, is paying the price but even more so, not only because it's our biggest State but because one in five jobs lost permanently in our economy in the last few years has been lost in the southern part of this State.

But during the time I've been President, we've tried to take these roadblocks head-on for all America. Let me say how. First, the strength of our economy and the security of our jobs is now tied to our ability to sell our products abroad. More and more Americans are becoming more productive. That means fewer people can produce more goods and services. That's a good thing to compete in the global economy, but only if we have more customers to buy those goods and services. That's the only way we can grow our economy, increase jobs, and increase incomes of working people.

That's why we just passed the North American Free Trade Agreement. With NAFTA we'll sell more products stamped "Made in the USA." We're also working hard on a world trade agreement between now and December 15th in the GATT talks. And we've established better trade relations with Japan specifically and with the Asian countries in general.

California is our strategic link to the economies in Latin America and to the Pacific rim. This State exports more than any other State. One in every 10 jobs out here is now tied to exports. We've launched our country's first national export strategy. It will benefit all the States in America. We've cut back Government export controls on $37 billion worth of high-tech communications products. It's good for trade. It's good for workers in high-tech industries in places like California, New York, and many States in between.

Just yesterday we announced the third round of grants in our technology reinvestment project. This plan helps defense firms to make the transition to a commercial economy. It takes military technologies developed with American tax dollars during the cold war and puts them to use in the civilian economy. It will create thousands and thousands of jobs in the years ahead all across our Nation. It's just part of a national defense conversion plan that totals $20 billion in new investment over 5 years.

We've taken other steps to strengthen the value of work, our families, and the communities we live in. For all of you who work and raise children and still live near the poverty line, we've expanded your earned-income tax credit. About 20 million of you will pay lower income taxes next April 15th. For American families, this is a signal that we value work over welfare. We've also passed the family and medical leave law so that people can care for a sick parent or a new baby without fear of losing their jobs. We've redesigned dramatically the student loan program, lowering interest rates and making it easier for more of you to get student loans and to pay them back on better terms. And we've also made it much simpler and easier for people to get small business loans.

Our economic plan has brought the deficit down. Interest rates are down. Inflation is down, and people are beginning to benefit. People are beginning to buy their first homes, and over 5 million Americans have refinanced their home mortgages. Single family housing starts are at their highest level in 6 years, and existing home sales are at a 14-year high.

Maybe you've borrowed money to expand your business. Economic indicators from durable goods to business spending on equipment to auto sales show manufacturing and consumer confidence picking up. Personal income is up. And more jobs have been created in the first 11 months in this administration than in the entire 4 years of the previous administration in the private sector, about 50 percent more now.

Now, all that is encouraging news. But frankly, it hasn't reached everyone yet. It hasn't reached into every family with economic benefits. And way too many people still lack good jobs. As I said earlier, of all the jobs lost nationally since 1990, one in five are right here in southern California.

This afternoon I'm going to Canoga Park in the western part of the San Fernando Valley for a meeting on the economy with business and community leaders. We'll meet face to face in an informal setting to go over their ideas, to see what's working, and to identify what we could all be doing to create more jobs and more opportunity.

But our goal in California is the same as our goal nationwide: to build an economic recovery that will carry us through the changes in our economy and put us on the road to lasting economic growth in a global climate that is very tough and highly competitive. For our Nation to stay strong, every American must have a chance to compete and win. We've still got a lot of work ahead of us, but we're working hard. And all of you will have to work hard, too.

None of what we do in our economic session today will matter if people aren't ready to seize opportunities, take responsibility to rebuild their communities. This simply cannot be done by Government alone, certainly not just at the national level. Leaders can't protect the economic interest of our middle class if our people aren't living and working by middle class values, rebuilding our communities from the ground up, home by home, street by street, and block by block. I need all of you to help me so that we can do this together.

In times of change, we've always sought the new opportunities, the new opportunities for ourselves, our families, and our neighbors. That expansive, forward-looking spirit is what brought people out here to California in the first place, across wagon trails and over highways on the open road. Well, times have changed; they always do. But we're trying to put America on the right road to reach a better tomorrow. Unemployment is down, and jobs are up. We're moving in the right direction. But there is so much more to do. To move forward we have to go down the road together.

Thanks for listening.

NOTE: The President spoke at 10:06 a.m. from the Beverly Hills Hotel in Los Angeles, CA.

Remarks in a Roundtable Discussion on the California Economy in Canoga Park, California
December 4, 1993

Thank you very much, Mayor, and thank you, Secretary Brown. I want to say a few words and then introduce your State's two Senators, after which we will begin the program. First, let me thank all of you who are here today, those of you around the table and those of you who are out in the audience.

I wanted to do this in California, this meeting, as a necessary followup to what many of us have been doing here in the last year and also because I thought it would be useful to do this in light of the economic conference we had in Little Rock one year ago this month, that some of you here in this room attended. I held that conference in an attempt to get the best ideas I could from all kinds of people all over the country about how to implement the economic strategy that I had run for President to put into effect. I wanted to get our country moving again. I wanted to try to restore jobs and incomes, to make us more competitive as we move toward the 21st century, and to give people who were outside the mainstream of economic life a chance to get in it.

As Secretary Brown has said, we have been convinced all along, just looking at the numbers, that we couldn't restore the American economy without restoring the California economy. Most of this year, the unemployment rate here has been roughly 3 percent above the national average and has been aggravated into two areas which are causing us the most trouble nationwide, that is, the huge numbers of poor people in inner cities who can't get jobs at all and the very large number of middle class workers who have lost jobs who can't get new jobs or can't get jobs as good as the ones that they lost. Those two problems together are bearing down on the Nation and are certainly a big problem here.

We've learned some things in the last year. We've learned that there is no silver bullet, that the problems are complex and require a broad-base approach. We've learned that you can make real progress, especially if you're willing to be disciplined and pay the price of time. We've learned that national action is not sufficient, that there has to be a partnership that is public and

private and that is State and local and sometimes community based as well as a national effort. And we've learned that you can't really leave any stone unturned. I want to refer in a minute to a point the mayor made.

I'd like to briefly summarize what's happened in the last year that's affected California in terms of our national policies and some California-specific efforts. First of all, the deficit reduction part of our economic plan that went into effect on October 1st actually has real reductions in spending in 356 separate accounts in the Federal budget. That's not lesser increases, that's actual reductions this year over what we spent last year.

We did raise income taxes on something less than 2 percent of the American people, but we also lowered taxes for 90 percent of the small businesses in the country, passed the venture capital gains tax that the venture capitalists heavily concentrated in California have been asking for for years, passed some passive-loss rules that the real estate folks in California have been pleading for for years, expanded the research and development tax credit which is very important to this State.

Over the last 10½ months, you see a remarkable thing in a world economy that's in recession. In America, interest rates have stayed down at historic levels; inflation has been at historically low levels; investment is up; personal income is up; more private sector jobs, almost 50 percent more private sector jobs now in the first 10½ months of this year than in the previous 4 years; over 5 million Americans have refinanced their homes. And we see the beginning of a national economic recovery that is quite impressive. So that part of the economic strategy—keep inflation down, keep interest rates down, get investment up—is working.

The second part of our strategy was to have more sales, more markets, and more products. We sought more sales through removing controls on exports that had previously been controlled during the cold war, $37 billion in computers and telecommunications equipment alone. About one-third of that market comes out of the State of California. So in the years ahead that will create tens of thousands of new jobs in this State, just by a national economic policy that was clearly in the interests of our country. Now, the Secretary has already mentioned the national export strategy.

With regard to markets, we pursued NAFTA; we pursued a new relationship with Japan; we have reached out to the other countries in Asia. We are doing our best in the remaining 11 days to reach a world trade agreement with GATT. I don't know if we're going to get there, but it won't be for lack of effort.

I want to say since we are in southern California, I want to say that I think that Mickey Kantor has done an absolutely brilliant job as our Trade Ambassador, fighting for the economic interests of this country and still trying to promote an expanded system of global trade. If we get a good agreement, the manufacturing opportunities there and the opportunities for the audiovisual folks that are heavily concentrated in both California and New York, our first and second largest States with the second and third highest unemployment rates in the country, are absolutely astounding. So we're working very, very hard on that.

With regard to more products, we've got an unprecedented partnership with the Big Three auto makers to produce a clean car, a whole strategy with environmental products in general, and the technology reinvestment project, which all of you know about and which California has done very well in, indeed, getting about 15 percent of the grants but 30 percent of the money that's come out of our effort to work in partnership with the private sector to take defense technologies to create jobs for the commercial economy at home and abroad.

The next part of our strategy has been to invest more in people and communities. The Mayor mentioned our family preservation strategy. There have been many other things. We changed the education formulas in ways that have benefited California. We have provided hundreds of millions of dollars of more money to help deal with the burden of immigration here in health care and in education. We have supported the Community Development Bank, the empowerment zones, and increasing infrastructure in the Red Line extension here. These things are all very necessary. And I want to come back to that in a minute as I sort of leave you with the questions that I have.

The last point I want to make in terms of looking toward the future is that we've got to do something about crime and violence if we want the whole California economy to recover. Look at the cover of Business Week here: "Rampant crime is costing America $425 billion a year. What can be done?" Plenty. Now, if you assume this number is right, let me just give you some feel for what $425 billion a year is. Our annual deficit is $255 billion this year. It was about $50 billion less than it was supposed to be when we took office; $425 billion is considerably more than that. If we had $425 billion to invest in this country, we could lower the unemployment rate by 3 percent in California within a year, just if we had it to invest in the whole country. This is a very serious thing. It says, "What can be done?" Plenty. And Business Week sort of advocated the administration's and the mayor's crime prevention, crime reduction strategy. More police reduces crime; it doesn't just help you catch criminals. If you deploy police in community settings, it reduces crime. It reduces the incidence of crime.

Focus on punishment. Do the right things by the juveniles, have boot camps, have alternative systems that give people hope that haven't done things so serious that you have to lock them up for long periods of time. Do more on drug treatment and drug rehabilitation and drug testing. Do more on job training and reinvestment and neighborhood safety. And do more to get the huge volume of guns out of the hands of teenagers and others who should not have them. That's what this says. And it's a money issue that is directly affecting the capacity of southern California to recover economically—don't ever think it's not for a minute—and every other urban area in this country.

So, having said that, we will have more investments as we can. Let me just leave you with the problems from my perspective at the national level, if I might. Number one, we've got to be willing to pay the price of time. Middle class wages have been stagnant or declining for 20 years under the pressure of the global economy. We have huge increases in productivity now in the manufacturing and in the service sector. That's the good news. But what that means is fewer people can produce more things. So we've got to have a lot more customers. We've got to have a lot more customers around the world. That's why trade's so important.

We've had social decline in this country for 30 years. A lot of the problems that we're dealing with now are the tail end of a 30-year downward spiral that all of us bear some responsibility for not addressing earlier and more vigorously. We can turn it around. We absolutely can, but it's going to take some time.

Number two is the changing nature of jobless people. It used to be people would lose their jobs; they'd be called back to their old jobs after a certain period of unemployment. Now it's much more structural, and people are not likely to get their same old job back. We have to revolutionize our approach to unemployed people. We need to scrap the present unemployment system and convert it into a reemployment system to move people through this economy more quickly. It's very, very important, especially when you go through the same kind of restructuring you're going through here.

Number three is, we're still not making, in my judgment, enough investment in the areas—and this is not just California—but enough investment in the areas that have been disproportionately hurt by either defense cuts or by disinvestment in our urban areas.

And finally, our problem is, at the national level, we have a real conflict that the American people have imposed on the Congress and on me that can't—we don't need to glaze it over. We know we need to invest more money all across the country, pure investments, things that create jobs. At the same time, the American people are telling the Congress to adopt a balanced budget amendment. And we have already adopted a 5-year budget which cuts defense, holds domestic spending flat, and is increasing only in retirement and health care costs. So

every time I spend more money as the President or the Congress appropriates more money to invest in defense conversion, we have to cut something else out of the domestic budget right now. And all those people who said we haven't made any cuts, you just wait until we show up in January and I put that new budget on.

So all I'm saying is we have to keep bringing this deficit down. But we need the support of thoughtful people in the business community, in the labor community, and community leaders to work through these things with us. We also have to keep investing. This mayor and this city need the police officers on the street. We need investment, and we need partnerships in areas hit by defense conversion and in areas of the inner cities where there's been total disinvestment.

So we can do these things together but not if the political pressures force us to overlook the economic realities. And we're going to have to have really thoughtful support from the private sector if we're going to make the right kind of decisions, and it needs to be as nonpartisan or bipartisan as possible. We need to try to make our economic policies a matter of our national security. Those are the problems from my perspective. I'd like to now call on Senator Feinstein and Senator Boxer to talk.

Thank you.

NOTE: The President spoke at 10:20 a.m. at the space shuttle main engine final assembly area, Rockwell International/Rocketdyne Division. In his remarks, he referred to Mayor Dick Riordan of Los Angeles.

Remarks to Employees at Rockwell International in Canoga Park
December 4, 1993

Thank you very much, Mr. Beall, Mr. Paster, ladies and gentlemen of Rockwell and Rocketdyne. I am very glad to be here. I want to thank all of you for coming, the workers in this great facility. And some of my workers in the last campaign from the Inland Empire I know came here. They're here somewhere over there. I thank you for coming.

I also want you to know that we're all a little embarrassed to be so late here, but if you got

to watch the meeting that just occurred, you know that there were so many people with so many ideas about what we could do together to rebuild the California economy. Having asked them there, I could hardly walk away and not listen to them. I was so moved by the people who came and what they said and how very specific they were. It made me really have greater faith than ever before that together we can turn this economy around and get things going again for California and for the entire country.

I also want to say a special word of thanks to you for the sign that I walked under coming out here that said, "Thank you, Mr. President, for the space station." We worked hard to save it. We're going to work hard to keep it. It's an important part of our future, and so are you.

I ran for President, my fellow Americans, because I thought this country had two great problems: I thought we had to restore the American economy so that it worked again for middle class Americans and gave all Americans a chance to work their way into the middle class, and I thought we had to pull this country together again and make a strength out of our diversity, so that we can go into the 21st century as the greatest country in the world and so that every person can live up to the fullest of their ability.

[*At this point, the President was interrupted by a noise in the factory.*]

What is that? That's not my hot air for a change. [*Laughter*] If you can hear me, I'll talk over it unless we're in some kind of danger.

When I came to the White House in January, I had an economic strategy that I wanted to implement for all the country. And I knew there was a special problem here in California, the State that is not only our biggest State with our strongest economy but the State that by January was the most economically hurt because of a combination of factors: the decline in defense spending, the collapse of real estate, the stagnation of the economies to the East, which trade with California and which were not buying as many of our exports. All these problems combined at once to give terrible, terrible burdens to the people of California, much higher than average unemployment rates and an attitude that was dragging the whole country down. And it became clear to me that unless we could turn the economy of California around, we would never fully be able to lift the economy of America.

I came here today, a year after I held a national economic summit in my home State to get the best ideas I could about implementing our national economic strategy, to have an economic meeting here in California to assess what we have done in the last year and what we need to do in the years ahead.

I want to tell you first that I am convinced that this economy can recover for four reasons:

first, because the national economy is now experiencing clear and consistent signs of recovery; second, because many of the things that we have done for the national economy will have a particular impact in California; third, because we are targeting resources to this State in programs that will help the economy, not by hurting other States but by giving California its fair consideration; and finally, fourthly, and most importantly of all for all of you, because we have committed ourselves in this administration to fight for a 5-year, $20 billion program of defense conversion so that we don't leave the people who won the cold war out in the cold, we invest in technologies for a commercial peacetime economy that can create jobs in California and jobs in this company.

Let me take these issues one by one. When I became President, I committed to bring the deficit down, to get interest rates down, to keep inflation down, to get investment up, and to give people incentives to invest in this economy. The Congress after a lot of struggling, adopted an economic plan, which I had pushed very hard. And here's what the plan does. It does raise taxes on somewhat less than 2 percent of our people, the wealthiest Americans whose incomes went up while their taxes went down in the 1980's. It also cuts taxes on 15 to 16 million working families who work 40 hours a week, have kids in their house, and are barely above the poverty line, so they'll be working and not on welfare. It gives the potential of a tax break to 90 percent of the small businesses in this country if they'll invest more money in their businesses. It increases the research and development tax credit to help companies like this one. It changes the rules to help people restore the real estate economy in States like California.

And in a year, look what's happened, look what's happened. We have historically low interest rates. Over 5 million Americans have refinanced their homes. We have low inflation rates. We have investment up. Housing sales were at a 14-year high last month. And we've had more jobs come in the private sector in the last 10 months than in the previous 4 years. We are moving in the right direction. Most Americans have not felt it yet, but you can't ignore the facts. The direction of the economy is good, not bad. We are coming back, and that will benefit the State of California and the people who live here.

The second thing I want to say is, there are a lot of things we're doing that will really help California just because of how the economy is organized here. We are focusing on new markets. We are focusing on new products. We are focusing on new opportunities for the American economy. Not very long ago, we removed from export controls $37 billion worth of high-tech products and computers and telecommunications, one-third of which are manufactured in this State. That will create tens of thousands of new jobs by permitting us to sell things abroad that we couldn't sell during the cold war. It will make a huge difference.

We're helping to build a national information superhighway to computerize all kinds of information to facilitate economic transfers. California is in a remarkable position to take advantage of that. We have a whole new technology initiative that will enable us to do things that will benefit this State disproportionately.

And finally, let me say, I know this is one of the more controversial things I've been involved in, but I have strongly supported efforts to increase trade, like NAFTA, because you can't keep and generate more high-tech jobs unless you have more customers. You know in this plant, don't you, that the American worker, under all the economic pressures of the 1980's, the American worker once again has become by far the most productive worker in the world. Now, we all know that.

But what else do we know? You know it here. What does productivity mean? That means fewer people can produce more goods and services. That means you have to have more customers for your goods and services if you want more jobs and higher incomes. So productivity is good. It is a precondition of having a strong economy. But it is not enough. It is not enough unless the world economy is growing. Unless we are experiencing an opportunity to increase the sales of our products and services, we can't have more jobs and higher incomes, not in California, not in the United States. So, you betcha, I want to sell more to Mexico and the rest of Latin America. I want to sell more to Asia. That's why I invited the heads of 15 Asian nations to come to the United States to meet with me. I want to sell more around the world. That's why we're working hard to reach agreement by December 15th on a new worldwide trade agreement, because I know that's the only way in the long run I can protect good jobs

and high incomes and create more jobs. And I hope you'll support that.

We've also really tried to invest money in this economy. The most important thing we've done is to give American companies the chance to be partners with the United States Government in converting from a defense to a domestic economy in the technology reinvestment project, which this year alone awarded over $420 million in grants for new technologies for the future. Yes, the things we've done specifically for California are important, $300 million more to deal with the problems of education caused by the influx of immigration, another $500 million to help offset the health care costs of the State because of immigration, a $1.3 billion for an infrastructure project to extend that Red Line and create new jobs. Those things are important.

But you know as well as I do, most of the new jobs in this country have to be created by people like you in the private sector. That's why the most important thing we can do is to help build new partnerships to take advantage of this wonderful technological wizardry that came out of all our defense investment and put it to work in the domestic economy, building a 21st century economy on high-tech commercial purposes based on the investments we've made in the cold war technology instead of letting them go to waste. We let that happen for too long. We started cutting defense in 1987. We didn't start rebuilding our economic base until 1993, but we're not going to let another year go by without doing it. I know that you know as part of this technology reinvestment project, Rocketdyne received an award for several million dollars to design and develop a portable environmental monitor to identify low concentrations of hazardous chemicals.

This is a big deal. We will be able to assess the impact of toxic spills and auto emissions, chemical warfare agents on the battlefield. We'll be able to do something that is good for defense and something that is good for our domestic economy. We'll be able to do something we have all known for years we ought to be able to do, which is to create an enormous number of high-wage, high-tech jobs by cleaning up the environment and developing technologies we can then sell to other countries to create jobs in America cleaning up their environment.

Rockwell also led two other winning teams, announced yesterday, one to improve the fuel efficiency of automobiles and heavy construction equipment, at a potential fuel savings—listen to this—by as much as a billion dollars a year by the year 2000, another to allow medical personnel to monitor and diagnose trauma patients remotely, whether they're in rural clinics or far-off battlefields. Again, this is a huge deal. In America, rural health care is confronted with certain inevitable limits, whether it's in California or my home State of Arkansas or anywhere else. You cannot put all the high-tech equipment in the world in every rural area, but accidents occur there. If technology that has been developed to help people on the battlefields deal with the wounded, when only a medic is there and they need some high-tech connection, can be applied to rural health situations in America, it means again more jobs for Rockwell, a stronger economy for America, and a better quality of life. That is the sort of thing that this National Government should be doing to rebuild the economy of California and the United States and to move us forward.

Let me just say in closing, I know it gets frustrating to see how long it takes to make these changes be felt in your lives. I know that, but just remember, just remember if you look at our two biggest problems—the economy, working Americans have been working harder for stagnant wages for 20 years now. We cannot turn it around overnight, but we can turn it around. If you look at what's happening to our society, the rising rate of crime, the continued breakdown of the family unit, the increasing number of children being born to children out of wedlock, all these things that are disintegrating our society, that has been going on for 30 years. It did not start overnight. We can turn it around if we begin now. It won't happen overnight, but we can do it.

I just ask you to remember what can happen in a year. One year ago, the deficit was going up, not down, and interest rates were not dropping as they are now. A year ago, we didn't have the kind of bipartisan coalition passing bills like the Brady bill and a crime bill to put 100,000 police on the street. This Congress, in a bill almost nobody knows about, revolutionized the student loan problem to lower interest rates on college loans, make the repayment terms easier. And they passed the national service bill which will enable 20,000 people this year and 100,000 people 3 years from now to serve their community at the grassroots level solving problems and to earn their way through college.

These are big changes that didn't happen a year ago.

A year ago, we did not have a strategy to increase the exports of this country. We did not have the North American Free Trade Agreement, a new dialog with Japan, a real, intense effort to turn this whole trading situation around. If we can pass, by December 15th, if we can get the trading nations of the world to agree on a dramatic reduction of tariffs everywhere, what that means is that American manufacturing products will lead to creation of over a million new jobs in this country in the next 10 years. We did not have that, and I hope we can get it in the next 10 days. That is the kind of difference you can make in just a year. And it's just the beginning.

These grants that were just announced to Rockwell—the idea was approved by the Congress a year ago, but there was opposition in the Pentagon and in the previous administration. They did not believe this Government had an obligation to help you convert from a defense to a domestic economy. I know we do, and I believe this money—10 years from now, 20 years from now you will look back on this and say this is the best money we ever spent. And next year there will be more of it. We are just getting warmed up. You are our partners in building an America for the 21st century.

A lot of this may sound real detailed and complicated, but to me it's very simple. I think my job, as your President, is to get this country into the next century as the strongest nation in the world. I think my job, as your President, is to do everything I can to see that you have the opportunity and are challenged to assume the responsibility to build a community in this country that will enable every man and woman, every boy and girl to live to the fullest of their God-given capacities. That's my job. To do it, we're going to have to compete and win the global economy; we're going to have to educate and train our people; we're going to have to invest in those things that will produce jobs and incomes and opportunities; and we're going to have to take our streets, our communities, our families, and our neighborhoods back and do something about the terrible ravages of crime and violence that are consuming this country. But we can do it. We can do it.

I ask you always to be impatient with me and with this country. Push us to do better. Push us to keep making progress. But also recognize we got in the fix we're in—20 years in the decline of wages, 12 years in the explosion of the deficit, 30 years in the social problems we've got. We can turn it around. It won't happen in a day. But if we work together and we work hard, every year we can see progress. We can see progress. And we will look ahead to the 21st century as the best years our country ever had because we did our job now to rebuild America.

Thank you for what you're doing. I'll stay with you. God bless you.

NOTE: The President spoke at 1:50 p.m. on the main factory floor. In his remarks, he referred to Donald Beall, chairman, Rockwell International, and Robert Paster, president, Rocketdyne Division.

Remarks at the Creative Artists Agency Reception in Beverly Hills, California
December 4, 1993

I want to thank you, Michael, for that wonderful introduction. Even more I want to thank you and Judy for meeting me at the door with your three children, which reminded me what my job is all about. Are they great looking kids or what? [*Applause*] I want to thank you and Bill and Ron for hosting us all here. It's good to be back in this gorgeous building. And I'm delighted to be here with my good friend David Wilhelm and Secretary Ron Brown, who has been to California more than a dozen times in this first year of our administration trying to put together an approach that will help our Government to help you recover economically. I thank Kathleen Brown and Gray Davis and especially my good friend Senator Dianne Feinstein for being here with us. I hope you will send her back to the Senate. I also want to say a special word of thanks to so many of you in this audience who worked for me in the last election, who made appearances for me, who helped to raise funds and helped to make arguments and who stood up for me in the face of some pretty wilting criticism.

I appreciated what Michael said about the fullback Presidency. One of my predecessors, Woodrow Wilson, who interestingly enough I learned had the biggest feet of any President until I came along—[*laughter*]—Woodrow Wilson was a great scholar, and he wrote a book, a much criticized book, about George Washington. But he said that the most important thing about George Washington when this country was getting off the ground was he never knew when he had been defeated in battle. He did not have enough sense to know when he was beat,

so he just kept on going.

Well, there's something to be said for that. We measure out our lives too many times in short durations. And we measure defeat in the moment instead of over the long run. I did not run for this office for so long and under such difficult circumstances either to squander the opportunity to change this country by not trying to or by giving up in the face of opposition or even my own mistakes. For it is clearly true that in a time of great change with unprecedented challenges, if you try to do a lot of things, every now and then you won't do the right thing. But I think if your ears and eyes are open and your heart's in the right place, better to make a mistake and correct it than to sit on the sidelines and not try to change the country.

I came to California today to meet for a period of what turned out to be about 3½ hours, which is why we're a little late tonight, with a lot of community leaders from all walks of life to talk about what we had done together in the last year and what we could do in the year ahead to help to rebuild this economy and to rebuild hope and opportunity and community here. And afterward I went into the plant where we were at Rockwell and talked to a lot of folks who were working in the plant and gave an account of this last year. I don't want to do that tonight except to say that when I was upstairs meeting some of you, it was interesting to me what was mentioned going through the line. Some people said, "I'm really glad you fought so hard for NAFTA and passed it." Others said, "I'm glad you're trying to get a new world trade agreement through GATT, but I'm glad you're fighting for the interest of the entertainment industry while you're doing it." Many said, "Thank you for the Brady bill." And some talked about the speech and encounter that I experienced on World AIDS Day.

But everybody who talked to me at least had a sense of possibility, a possibility of change, a possibility of improvement, a possibility that we were really doing things again. I ran for President because I thought this country had two great problems. I thought we were going in the wrong direction economically and otherwise, and I thought we were coming apart when we ought to be coming together. I ran because I wanted this country to go into the 21st century still the greatest country in human history and because I want every person who lives in this country to have a chance to live up to their God-given potential, something most of us in this room have had to such an extreme degree that we almost take it for granted that it's there for everyone.

And in the last year we have made a good beginning. Michael was kind enough to read the list of most of the important initiatives. This economic program to bring the deficit down and keep interest rates down and inflation down is very important. We've had a 14-year high in home sales. We've got the unemployment rate going down. We've got more private sector jobs in 10 months than in the previous 4 years. We are moving in the right direction even though, to be candid, most Americans haven't felt it yet, especially here in California. Plainly the direction is the right one.

We've tried to help families put their lives together and help people who are working and who have children succeed as parents and as workers, one of the biggest challenges in America today, one we all face, many of us. But since most parents have to work and most workers are parents, we can't go where we need to go unless we are committed to the proposition that people ought to be able to succeed in both roles. That's why the family leave law was so important.

Perhaps the most moving experience I've had inside the White House occurred a couple of Sundays ago, maybe about six now or eight. I came in from my morning run, and there was a family there, a father, a mother, three children. And I noticed the middle child was in the wheelchair. And I went over and shook hands with them. It's very unusual for people to be touring the White House on Sunday morning, but this little girl was part of the Make-A-Wish Foundation. And she was desperately ill, and she wanted to see the White House and meet the President, so they brought her in there. And I shook hands with them, and I was a little embarrassed to be in my jogging outfit so I went up and got cleaned up, and I came down looking like a real President— [*laughter*]—and stood there to shake hands with the family and to take a picture. So we took a proper picture. And I was walking off, and the father grabbed me by the arm really strong. And I turned around, and he said, "Just in case you think what you do doesn't matter around here," he said, "my little girl is probably not going to make it. But I have been able to take time off from my job to spend time with her. It's the most important time I've ever spent in my life, especially if she doesn't make it. And because of that family leave bill, I could take that time off without fear of losing my job and hurting my wife and my other two children. Nobody should ever have to make that decision, and now we don't. Don't you ever think what you do here does not have an impact on people where they live."

I say that to make this point: In the end, the true test of our endeavors is whether they enrich the meaning of the lives of the people who live in this country. In the end, all the statistics and numbers and did you pass more bills than anybody else and all that sort of stuff—really matters that were they the right bills, and did they affect people, and are they moving people both forward and together.

And I came here tonight really to ask for your help for this reason: I believe that we can move this economy in the right direction, even though the decisions are unbelievably difficult when you're trying to reduce the deficit and increase investment where you need to increase it at the same time. I believe we can get a good set of trade agreements to expand global trade. I believe we can have a good technology policy. I believe we can redo the unemployment system and have a good training system in this country again. I believe, in short, that we can make the kinds of changes, public changes we need to make to move this country forward.

But we have to face the fact that millions and millions and millions of our fellow Americans are caught not only in an economic under class but almost in an outer class totally apart from the life that the rest of us take for granted. And it is because they are the ones who have been hardest hit by the combined force of a loss of economic opportunity, the destruction of community support, and the erosion of family itself. And the vacuum that is created has been filled for all too many of them by organized violence, organized around guns and gangs and drugs, with no offsetting forces.

And as Michael implied, some of that has been aggravated by the fact that there are not sustaining forces in our culture which tend to offset that. As I told the ministers in Memphis a few weeks ago at the Church of God in Christ convention, when they invited me into the pulpit where Martin Luther King gave his last sermon, there are problems this Nation has that cannot be fixed by the passage of a law or by an official decree from the President of the United States. They require us to change from the inside out and to change family by family, community by community.

I have a good friend with whom I grew up at home who wrote me of a conversation she had with some other people who were bemoaning the fate of all these kids in trouble, and this person said, "Well, how in the world are we going to save these kids?" And my friend said, "We're going to save them the same way we lost them, one at a time." If you think of that, society is largely organized around work and family. We have too many people today living in this world without either. And nature—and to be sure, they represent nature—abhors a vacuum. And that vacuum is being filled by all kinds of forces which are fundamentally destructive of those people ever becoming what they ought to be.

Now, we are trying to deal with that as much as we can through public policy, through the Brady bill and through Senator Feinstein's effort to ban assault weapons and through—[*applause*]—that's worth an applause—I met your distinguished police chief for the first time tonight, even though I've been bragging on him for years now—through the effort to provide another 100,000 police officers in properly trained, properly deployed in community policing settings throughout the country, because that will actually diminish crime and provide alternative role models for young people.

There are a lot of other things we are trying to do. But I am telling you, the fact is it is awfully hard to put lives back together in an environment in which there are no lives organized fundamentally by work, by family, and by other community organizations that shape values and behavior; when impulses govern the lives of young people who cannot even fully understand the implications of what it means, often, to pick up a gun and pull the trigger; and when madly we permit many of these children, who themselves were never even given the fundamental basics of self-esteem and self-control and respect for others, weapons that make them better armed than the police who are supposed to be patrolling their streets.

But the fundamental problem is what has happened to all of them inside and what does not happen to them day by day. One hundred and sixty thousand kids in this country stay home from school every day because they are afraid of being shot or knifed on the way to school or in the schoolhouse.

Now, what's all that got to do with you? First of all, you have the capacity to do good, culturally, to help to change the way we behave, the way we think of ourselves. You have clearly, many of you, reinforced the awareness of our obligations to our environment, and we have begun to change in fundamental ways. Look at the way we changed our ideas about smoking in recent years, culturally, not because laws made us do it but because as a people we just decided to move in a different direction. You've helped to battle world hunger and make people more realistic as well as caring about AIDS, and you've promoted world peace. And through the people at MTV and others who have promoted the motor voter bill, you've really advanced the civil rights cause by opening up a franchise to young people and to many who would otherwise not have registered and voted.

Now what we have are people who are vulnerable to cultural forces that the rest of us find entertaining, that are not in and of themselves bad when made part of a culture that is organized by work, by family, and by other institutions. I love television. I saw two or three of you tonight and quoted about some time I'd seen you on television recently. I love that. I am a movie-goer almost to the point of compulsion, have been since I was a small boy.

But you think of it, all of us who love that. How is our life organized? We spend most of our time working. We spend a lot of our free time, most of us, with our families. We have other ties to a community which shape our values, our conduct, our priorities, what we do with our money, how we think about our obligations. But what might be entertaining to us— a violent, thrilling movie or television program, a torrid but fundamentally amoral use and manipulation of people in what may be for us just an entertaining 30 minutes or an hour—if it's 10 or 11 hours a day of relentless exposure into the minds of people who have never been taught to understand the consequences of their action, never had any kind of internal structure motivated and driven by seeing their parents go to work every day and having a regular relationship with family and having other institutions, then these things can unintentionally set forth a chain reaction of even more impulsive behavior, even more inability to deal with conflict in nonviolent ways and to pass up the aggressive influences and impulses that all of us feel but most of us learn at some point in our lives not to act on. And it all gets worse if the void left by the loss of family and work and other institutions is filled by gangs and guns and drugs.

So, what I ask you for tonight is not to wear a hair shirt and say, "Mea culpa, I wish I hadn't done this, that, or the other thing," but to recognize that what may be one person's moment of entertainment, even exhilaration, the taking your mind off the pressures of the day, can, when multiplied by 1,000, have a cumulative impact that at the very least does not help to bring a whole generation of people back from the brink. I'm telling you, if we don't find a way to deal with this, the rest of these endeavors ultimately will fail. We will not be able to make a strength out of our diversity. We will not be able to restore the ladder from poverty to the middle class that can be climbed through work and education. We will not be able to put our people back together again and use our money on education and opportunity instead of crime and jail.

So what I ask you to do is to join a partnership with me, not to stop entertaining or even titillating, not to stop frightening or thrilling the American public, but to examine what together you might do to simply face the reality that so many of our young people live with and help us as we seek to rebuild the frayed bonds of this community, as we seek to give children nonviolent ways to resolve their own frustrations, as we seek to restore some structure and some

hope and some essential dignity and purpose to lives that have been dominated by chaos or worse.

We must do this. Make no mistake about it. No society, no society can prosper allowing huge pockets of people to go on forever without the opportunity to work, allowing huge pockets of children to go on without the opportunity to get a decent education, allowing huge sections of cities to be no man's lands, where the law of the automatic assault weapon controls. We cannot do well if we permit that to happen. We need every last dollar we can to invest in growth and opportunity and positive good things. And we have to use every means at our command.

There are few things more powerful in any time and place than culture. The ability of culture to elevate or debase is profound. You know it, and you sense it in the power you have when you do something you're really proud of. Does that mean we should never have any violent movies? Of course not. I think, to mention one, "Boyz N the Hood" was a great movie because it showed the truth about what happens when chaos is replaced with destruction. I know the young man who made the movie is here tonight. But I ask you to think about this. We have got to do this for our country. Together, so many of you have more influence over different kinds of people that you will never meet, that you're not aware of, than a President's speech can bring to bear.

For 30 years the American family has been under assault. The assault attacked black families first because they were most vulnerable economically. The same thing is now happening to other families. More and more children are born out of wedlock; more and more children are being born without parents; more and more children being abandoned; more and more kids growing up in violent neighborhoods. The racial differences were largely determined by who got hit first because of economic vulnerability. But now it is happening to everybody. So 30 years of family assault, 20 years where most working people had stagnant wages, 20 years of developing huge pockets where no one had a job— there have always been poor people in this country, but most of them have always been able to work—12 years in which we exploded public debt by consuming in the present instead of investing more in the future, these things happened over a long period of time.

Meanwhile, we want more and more entertainment, more and more instantaneously, as Michael said. We want more and more news, more and more instantaneously. Just give us the thing and let us focus on something else. For all of us who have highly structured, successful lives where our attention is diverted to the big fundamental things in our life, this works fine. For people living in chaos, it is a disaster.

And so I ask you, while you entertain the rest of us, let us together do something to rebuild the bonds of community, to restore the spirit of these children, to give people a chance to build whole lives around solid values so that they, too, will have internal structures that will permit them the luxury of the diversion some of us call entertainment.

We must rebuild this country fundamentally. And we have to have the support of people who can shape our culture to do it. It is our job, and if we do it, we will be proud we did.

Thank you, and God bless you all.

NOTE: The President spoke at 6:48 p.m. at the Creative Artists Agency (CAA). In his remarks, he referred to CAA chairman Michael Ovitz and his wife, Judy; Bill Haber and Ron Meyer, CAA partners; David Wilhelm, chairman, Democratic National Committee; Kathleen Brown, California State treasurer; and Gray Davis, California State comptroller.

Exchange With Reporters Prior to Discussions With Prime Minister Felipe Gonzalez of Spain
December 6, 1993

North Korea

Q. Mr. President, the IAEA has apparently rejected the North Korean response. Do you agree with that rejection?

The President. Well, what the IAEA has said is that they didn't think it was entirely adequate. But we have to go back and respond to them and we—at least they came forward, they reacted to our initiative. And we're consulting with the South Koreans now. We'll have a conversation with them and see what happens.

Q. Was it inadequate in your eyes——

The President. Well, obviously they didn't say, "We liked everything the United States said," and yes. So we were hoping that we could move more quickly, but I'm not entirely discouraged. We're talking to the South Koreans, and then we'll go back to the——

Multilateral Trade Negotiations

Q. Do you think the GATT agreement will be reached today in Brussels, Mr. President?

The President. I don't know. I just spoke with Ambassador Kantor right before the Prime Minister came in, and they've made some more progress. There are still a couple of sticking issues. We'll just see.

Q. On agriculture?

The President. I think they're doing quite well on agriculture. We'll have to see.

[*At this point, one group of reporters left the room, and another group entered.*]

Meeting With Haitian Leaders

Q. Mr. President, are you going to be meeting with President Aristide and Prime Minister Malval today? And what will you want to be discussing with them?

The President. I don't think we'll have a final decision on that until sometime after noon. So I can't say yet. But we'll let you know as soon as we know for sure.

Spain

Q. Do you forecast many differences between the social security system between Spain and the United States?

The President. Are there many differences?

Q. Yeah.

The President. Well, there are some, but I'm really looking forward to my conversation with the Prime Minister about it. All the countries, in Europe, Japan, and the United States, we're all having many of the same troubles. We're having troubles creating new jobs and growing the economy.

I think Spain clearly would benefit from any initiative we can all take to increase economic growth throughout the world. It's hard for any of us to grow unless the overall world economy is growing. And I really admire the reforms the Prime Minister has pursued, and I'm going to do what I can to support a high rate of growth in the world which would drive the unemployment rate in Spain down. I think it's very important.

Cuba

Q. Mr. President, the embargo?

Q. Do you bring that to your hand—something about the Cuban embargo?

The President. I'm sure we'll talk about Cuba.

Q. The end of the embargo, maybe?

The President. Not today, no.

NOTE: The exchange began at 11:37 a.m. in the Oval Office at the White House. A tape was not available for verification of the content of this exchange.

The President's News Conference With Prime Minister Felipe Gonzalez of Spain
December 6, 1993

The President. Good afternoon, ladies and gentlemen. In April, I had the honor and the pleasure of welcoming King Juan Carlos and Queen Sofia of Spain to the White House. Today, on the 15th anniversary of Spain's constitutions, I'm delighted to welcome Prime Minister Gonzalez.

When Spain hosted the Olympics last year, the world reveled in the modern bustle of Barcelona and the timeless beauty of the Iberian countryside. Spain's vibrant example inspires those around the world who are working to release market forces and political freedom from the shackles of the past. And few countries share as many rich cultural and historical ties to Spain as does America. The land on which I was born was once a part of the Spanish empire.

Our two countries are friends and allies. For over a decade, Prime Minister Gonzalez has led Spain with vision and with purpose. In our discussions today, I praised the Prime Minister for Spain's achievements at home during his years in office and for the increasingly important role Spain has come to play in the international community. As a strong NATO ally, vigorous proponent of European integration, current member of the U.N. Security Council, and significant trading nation, Spain has earned and exercised positions of true global leadership. Spain is serving the cause of humanitarian relief through its admirable participation in the U.N. protective force in Bosnia. We were all deeply saddened to learn about the death of a Spanish officer and the wounding of another there over the

weekend. In Central America, Spain continues to provide important support for the development of peaceful and prosperous democracies. And the Madrid Conference, organized by Spain in 1991, helped make possible a fundamental shift in the dynamics of the Middle East.

Today, the seeds planted in the Madrid are beginning to bear fruit as the Middle East moves closer to a just and lasting peace. Spain and the United States share a strong interest in expanding global economic growth and job creation. We discussed today the recent enactment of NAFTA and its potential as a building block for free trade, not only throughout Latin America but around the world. And we agreed on the critical importance of a successful conclusion to the GATT Uruguay round. All trading nations must now redouble their efforts in these last few days to secure a good GATT agreement.

The Prime Minister and I also discussed preparations underway for the NATO summit meeting in January. We both want to use that occasion to reaffirm the strength and the durability of the transatlantic relationship. We want to make concrete progress in adapting NATO, one of the most successful military alliances in all history, to the new realities and opportunities it faces.

Five centuries ago, Spain reached across the Atlantic to discover a new world. Today as partners, Spain and America set sail for a new century. And in that spirit, I am proud and honored to welcome Prime Minister Gonzalez and to extend to him and to the Spanish people a warm greeting from all Americans.

Mr. Prime Minister.

Prime Minister Gonzalez. Thank you very much, Mr. President. Let me simply add to what President Clinton has said that it's been a great pleasure for me to make this official visit to the United States of America. This has been important to me. I have been following very closely the electoral program that led to the President's triumph and what he has been doing with them since then. And I think the Spanish press will understand quite a bit that when we talk about education, infrastructure, health reform, that we hear that talked about in the United States and we understand it; we feel it in our heart, too, because it's something we are doing.

I'd like to thank President Clinton. This visit to Washington has allowed us to cordially exchange points of view in depth on our bilateral relations, European relations, the evolutions and changes taking place in Latin America, and certain different shared objectives we have in that part of the world. And it has allowed us to talk about the NATO summit in January, as the President mentioned. There are many problems, many challenges that we face after the Eastern bloc and the Iron Curtain fell. And obviously we face new challenges that NATO must meet. I think it's also worthy to mention that the GATT conversations may lead to success in the short term.

As I said when I congratulated the President for the approval of NAFTA, I wasn't simply being courteous and diplomatic. I said that because I think that NAFTA has great importance for the U.S., for its relations with Mexico, and moreover, I think it's an axis for future developments with all of Latin America, in spite of the fact that it will be necessary to adapt to that new reality.

So I think this has been an especially interesting visit. It's a very intense visit, I would add, and I think this is a good prolog. I have invited the President to visit Spain. I think he liked the idea, and I certainly hope that he gets a chance to do so.

And I've mentioned that my government is especially interested to see him in Spain. We know that he has visited Spain in the past, that he has taken contact with our country, and I'm sure that would make it easier to explain our country to him now. And I'm sure he's interested. So I certainly hope to see Mr. Clinton,

President Clinton, in Spain in the future.

Thank you.

North Korea

Q. You mentioned today that the IAEA said that North Korea's proposal for nuclear inspections was not entirely adequate. What's the United States view of that? Do we accept it in part, in full, or not at all?

The President. Well, as I said earlier, obviously we're not entirely satisfied with the response of the North Koreans to the proposal we put forward, but we're going to meet about it later today, and then we're going to consult with the South Koreans and our other allies in the area and formulate our next move. I think it's important for me to have the opportunity to meet and discuss this, and I will be doing so this afternoon. And then it's equally important for us to get back to the South Koreans and others, so I'll probably have more to say about it in the next day or two. But I think that, in fairness, I need to wait until I talk to my principal advisers and also talk to our allies.

Q. Is there any part about it you like?

The President. Well, what I liked most about it was there was some indication on their part that they understood that we needed to both start inspections and the dialog again between the South and the North; that was clear. And so it's like all these things in international diplomacy, the devil's in the details. But I'm hopeful that we can work something out, and I don't want to say more until I have a chance to meet with my advisers and also to talk to our allies.

Global Economy

Q. Would you share, for both of you, any ideas or differences about how to push the economy in the world?

The President. Actually we did. I'd let the Prime Minister answer that, but we've talked a lot about how the United States, Japan, and Europe all have obligations to try to get the growth rate up and what each of us needs to do. And we talked about how that plus a system of expanded trade could reward Spain for all the changes that you have made and generate more jobs.

Actually, the Spanish experience has been quite impressive in the growth you've had until the global recession of the last couple of years. So we've got to get out of that, and we have to do that, it seems to me, with a coordinated economic strategy.

Mr. Prime Minister.

Prime Minister Gonzalez. Well, first of all, let me stress that we fully agree on the need for coordination, coordination of the developed world, the countries of the developed world, in order to overcome an economic crisis and promote growth and create jobs. Coordination is even more important if you take into account that the economy is becoming globalized, so we need coordination.

We agree that successful GATT negotiations leading to agreement will be positive, and I think we agree on certain specific current policies such as coordination for lowering interest rates in Europe in order to spur investment and thus contribute to restarting the European economy. I think we are well aware that growth, growth even in powerful, large countries like the U.S., if it isn't carried out in coordination and collaboration with other countries such as Europe and Japan, will encounter greater obstacles than it would with good coordination. So, that is quite clear, and I think that's the way out of a recession.

Somalia

Q. In Somalia last week, Americans saw the extraordinary scene of General Mohamed Farah Aideed being escorted out of Mogadishu in an American armored personnel carrier and flown to Ethiopia in an Army jet. How would you explain that to the families of those whose soldiers were killed in Somalia just 2 months ago?

The President. I would tell them that they were over there fighting ultimately for a peace to take place. And as I have said many times before, that action was fundamentally successful. They achieved their objective. They arrested a lot of people. We still have under custody the people who we think are the most likely to have been seriously involved in the murder of the Pakistani soldiers and to have caused difficulties for the Americans. We have started the process of having an independent commission look into that.

I said back in August that we were in the business of trying to solve this thing politically. Everyone thought it was important that General Aideed go to that peace conference. And Ambassador Oakley, who had to make this decision on the spur of the moment without much time to consider whether there were any other op-

tions, knew that the only other conceivable option was not going to be accepted and that he had to get the peace conference going. And so he thought it was the right thing to do. And I will stand behind his decision.

Summit of the Americas

Q. I would like to ask Mr. Gonzalez whether he has any comments on the U.S. initiative regarding the Summit of the Americas next year in this country.

Prime Minister Gonzalez. If you allow a comment before that, first of all, we ourselves don't have troops in Somalia, but we do in the ex-Yugoslavia. If the President will allow me, let me say that when one is involved oneself, it's harder to say. But let me say that in regard to the presence, the U.S. presence and other presence in Somalia has its cost. It has its human cost. But it has saved tens of thousands of lives, of innocent lives. It saved them from a death by hunger. Now, that isn't as visible. It's not stated as often in the media, but in honor of truth, let us say that it isn't a worthless sacrifice that has been made. Tens of thousands of people are reaping benefits from the sacrifice of those lives.

Secondly, I have been able to tell both the President and the Vice President when they mentioned this initiative to me about the summit meeting of heads of states of Latin America: When you look at the history of Latin America from the Second World War up until the present, I think there isn't a more timely, a better time, then, to bring the heads of state from all of the Americas together at one time and in one place. All of us want to see greater democracy, the elimination of violent alternatives, and a greater economic opening throughout the area, and we don't want to see any kind of return to the temptation of supernationalism that has caused so much damage to the Americas in the past. So I think that initiative will find—[*inaudible*]—a very positive reception.

North Korea

Q. I wonder, sir, if I could get back to Korea for a moment, if you could characterize the near-term urgency of the situation over there, why it's so important now to settle this as quickly as possible.

The President. In Korea?

Q. Yes, sir.

The President. The near-term urgency is basically a function of what the IAEA has said. The longer they go on without adequate inspections, the more difficult it is for them to be able to certify the actual condition of the North Korean nuclear program and that's what the issue is. That's why we're trying to work it through as quickly as we can so we won't finally and completely break the chain that enables the IAEA to make certain representations to the rest of the world about where they are on that.

Someone else from Spain? Yes, ma'am.

Cuba

Q. Yes. I have a question for you. I would like to know if there is any sign of change, economic and political opening, in Cuba. Will you be able to take a moderate view and lessen the economic pressures being brought to bear on Cuba in the future?

The President. Well, as you know, the United States believes that the pressures we have brought to bear on Cuba are responsible, in some measure, for the very modest openings that we've seen coming out of Cuba with regard to travel and assets and a few other things. I see no indication that the nation or that the leadership, the Castro government, is willing to make the kind of changes that we would expect before we would change our policy.

Missile Targeting

Q. Mr. President, are you going to aim our long-range nuclear missiles away from Russia?

The President. Well, as I said back in April, around the summit with President Yeltsin, that's something we have under consideration, and we're working it through now. We're working very hard with the Russians to continue the denuclearization and to make them and ourselves and others feel more secure with that move. So that's one of the things we've had under consideration, but no final decision has been made.

Cuba

Q. I guess Cuba was an issue today. Did you learn anything from the Prime Minister's experience on Cuban issues? President, Prime Minister, do you think it would be better to have Cuba attend meetings of international organization? Would that lead to greater democracy in Cuba? Or should Cuba be not allowed to partake in these international organizations until they're a democracy?

The President. Yes, I learned something from talking to the Prime Minister. I found it very interesting. We've not had any contact with Cuba for a good long while now. So I asked him a number of questions, and I listened very closely to what he said.

Prime Minister Gonzalez. I think everyone can understand that we agree on what our common goals are for Cuba. In other words, I think we all want to see Cuba to join in with the rest of the Latin American countries in moving towards greater democracy and open economy. I think we agree on what we want Cuba to become. We have had some Ibero-American meetings, and in those meetings we did not exclude anyone. But I can understand that if we're talking about a meeting of all the democratic-elected leaders of the hemisphere, there would be exceptions and not just Cuba. I imagine Haiti would not be invited. If all the democratically elected leaders were meeting, Haiti wouldn't be there, either.

Health Care Reform

Q. Mr. President, right now the American Medical Association is meeting in New Orleans, and it seems like there is a big question about whether or not they are going to support your health program. How important is that to you, and what do you say to them about the obvious disagreement that's going on there?

The President. Well, first of all, I have been, frankly, pleased by the constructive response that the leadership of the AMA has taken to this point. As you know, it is a very different response than has been taken to any other health care initiative in the 20th century, different than their response to Medicaid or Medicare or to previous efforts at universal coverage. And I would hope they would do what the leadership has been doing, which is to explain what they want and where they differ and to keep working with us.

Let me say that I'm also very impressed and gratified by the response that a number of the other physicians' groups have had, the family practitioners, the pediatricians, and others who have been much more uniformly supportive.

There are a couple of things that I would expect are driving the debate at their meeting. First of all, there are some groups of specialists who disagree with our proposal to shift the Federal investment in medical schools to encourage more family practitioners. But I don't see how anyone rationally could object to that since we are only turning out about 15 percent of our graduates in family practice, and we need more than twice that, looking ahead.

Then there are those who feel so strongly that fee-for-service is the right way for doctors to be reimbursed that they object to the fact that our plan would require a fee-for-service option to be given to everybody who doesn't have insurance now but would also require other options as well. To that, I would respond that those folks don't have any health insurance at all now and this will make it possible for them to get some, and some will choose fee-for-service.

Moreover, among those who do have insurance, every year fewer and fewer and fewer of them have that option. So, we're not accelerating a process that's not already well underway. We're simply trying to cover everyone on more or less equal terms, and we're going to at least give people the option to choose fee-for-service, which is something many people who are already covered don't have. So, I would hope they would consider those things and continue the dialog.

Q. Do you need them to get—[inaudible]

The President. I don't know about that. The more support we have, the easier it will be to pass. That's like anything else.

Angola

Q. On the role of fostering new democracies in the world that you both referred, I would like to hear your comments, both of you, on the situation in Angola, the lack of visible progress on the ground, and if you envisage any wider exercise that, in this case, that we see in Somalia these days, for restoring peace in Angola.

The President. It's a different situation than Somalia was when we went in there and much more hazardous. I don't foresee that. We have named a special emissary there. We are working

hard on it, and I'm very disturbed by it. You know, the loss of life has been very severe. The number of children maimed by land mines there, I believe, is now the largest number in any conflict that we know about. I hope we can make some progress. I discuss it with our people at least once a week, sometimes more often. And we sometimes feel we are making progress, and then it slips back. So, I wish I had a more hopeful scenario. I can tell you the United States is involved in it, that we are keeping up very closely with events, and we are doing our best to try to bring the conflict to a peaceful conclusion.

Prime Minister Gonzalez. I was in Angola just before the last elections, and it would seem that the international community has taken a firm decision to move forward respecting the results of any truly free and fair elections. The international community recognized that those elections were free and fair and that the results should thus be respected.

However, one of the parties in Angola did not respect the elections and were probably one of the bloodiest—[inaudible]—of the civil war that ever existed. So internationally, I think we need a high degree of coordination to try to get both parties to simply stop and try to help the country get back on the track of economic development. It's a country with tremendous resources and has tremendous economic potential. We haven't talked about that today, but I think all of us in the international community agree that we have to try to get those who ignored the rules of democracy in the past to respect the electoral results.

Thank you.

NOTE: The President's 37th news conference began at 2:01 p.m. at Blair House. In his remarks, he referred to Somali warlord Mohamed Farah Aideed. Prime Minister Gonzalez spoke in Spanish, and his remarks were translated by an interpreter.

Remarks to Senior Citizens
December 6, 1993

Today we will have between 7,000 and 8,000 senior citizens going through the White

House—just today—seeing and getting the tour and everything. So I'm glad you did it, and

Hillary and I just wanted to comment and say hello to you and ask you just to take a few minutes and visit with us about this year and what we're going to be doing next year on the health care issue, because our efforts to change the health care system affect senior citizens about as much as any group in the country.

And the most important things that I wanted to emphasize about what we're trying to do is first, we don't mess up what's all right now. We leave Medicare alone, the way it is, except that we add for senior citizens as well as for working people a prescription drug benefit for the first time. When I ran for President—and I spent so much time in the New Hampshire area when I was running and I went to countless little meetings like this—the number one thing that people would tell me who were on Medicare is that they wanted a prescription drug benefit, that it was a terrible burden. So the way that this benefit will work is that every year there will be a $250 deductible after which everyone's Medicare policy will cover the drugs that they are prescribed plus a modest copay, a small one.

The other thing that this does that I think is so important is to provide some options under long-term care. Today, there are a couple of problems with long-term care. One is that oftentimes people can't get it unless they spend themselves from Medicare down into the Medicaid eligibility, and then often the only option they have is a nursing home. So, what we want to do is to keep the nursing home option but to add in-home care, to add community-based— like boarding home—care to the nursing home option. And we will phase that in over a few years as we achieve savings from the other

changes in the program. But those are the things that I think are very, very important to our country.

The fastest growing group of Americans are people over 80. And we know that with proper medication people of all ages actually are more likely to stay out of hospitals, more likely to stay healthy, more likely to have lower health care costs over the long run. But that's especially true of senior citizens. We also know that with the fastest growing group of people being over 80, not everybody will be in the same condition. And more and more people will want to have the option to stay at home or maybe to leave for a few hours a day and be in some sort of community-based care system. So, we think it's really important to move away from an undue bias on nursing homes to let people have broader options. So, that's basically what this health care plan does.

And we're going to do our best to try to pass it next year and bring about some real security for people who are—for younger people who don't have Medicare, the most important thing about it is it will give them a package of health care benefits that they can never lose. That's the biggest problem for people who are insured in the system today: they can lose their benefits. And about 100,000 Americans a month lose it permanently. A lot of Americans are insured at work, but their children aren't insured. There are all these problems, and those will be fixed. But for senior citizens, the number one benefit will be the prescription drugs and the change in the coverage of long-term care.

NOTE: The President spoke at 3:25 p.m. in the Oval Office at the White House.

Remarks Prior to Discussions With President Jean-Bertrand Aristide and Prime Minister Robert Malval of Haiti and an Exchange With Reporters
December 6, 1993

The President. I would like to make a statement first. I want to welcome President Aristide back to the White House and also welcome Prime Minister Malval here for the first time and the other people associated with the effort to bring democracy back to Haiti.

I want to reaffirm the support of the United

States for the democratic impulses of Haiti and for the return of President Aristide. I'd also like to compliment Prime Minister Malval on his announcement today of his intention to remain on after December 15th as Acting Prime Minister and to try to revitalize and broaden the talks in Haiti within the framework of the

Governors Island Agreement. The United States will support this Haitian initiative and seek the support of the U.N. and the OAS. We have no reason to believe that they will not also be supportive, and so we are looking forward to discussing that. They just got here, and we're going to have discussion about that.

Haiti

Q. Besides the sanctions, what steps are you willing to take to help restore democracy to Haiti?

The President. Well, let's wait until we have a meeting here. We're going to have a discussion about all those things, and there will be more to say about that.

North Korea

Q. How about North Korea then, Mr. President? Did you come to any decision in your meeting today?

The President. We worked through the problem, and at the end of the meeting I authorized our folks to go back to the South Koreans and our allies, and I expect to have a talk with President Kim sometime in the next 24 hours. We'll talk a little more about it then. I want to talk to them before I say more.

NOTE: The President spoke at 6:45 p.m. in the Oval Office at the White House. A tape was not available for verification of the content of these remarks.

Letter to Congressional Leaders Reporting on Sanctions Against the Federal Republic of Yugoslavia (Serbia and Montenegro)
December 6, 1993

Dear Mr. Speaker: (Dear Mr. President:)

On May 30, 1992, in Executive Order No. 12808, President Bush declared a national emergency to deal with the threat to the national security, foreign policy, and economy of the United States arising from actions and policies of the Governments of Serbia and Montenegro, acting under the name of the Socialist Federal Republic of Yugoslavia or the Federal Republic of Yugoslavia, in their involvement in and support for groups attempting to seize territory in Croatia and Bosnia-Herzegovina by force and violence utilizing, in part, the forces of the so-called Yugoslav National Army (57 *FR* 23299, June 2, 1992). The present report is submitted pursuant to 50 U.S.C. 1641(c) and 1703(c). It discusses Administration actions and expenses directly related to the exercise of powers and authorities conferred by the declaration of a national emergency in Executive Order No. 12808 and to expanded sanctions against the Federal Republic of Yugoslavia (Serbia and Montenegro) (the "FRY (S/M)" contained in Executive Order No. 12810 of June 5, 1992 (57 *FR* 24347, June 9, 1992), Executive Order No. 12831 of January 15, 1993 (58 *FR* 5253, January 21, 1993), and Executive Order No. 12846 of April 26, 1993 (58 *FR* 25771, April 27, 1993).

1. Executive Order No. 12808 blocked all property and interests in property of the Governments of Serbia and Montenegro, or held in the name of the former Government of the Socialist Federal Republic of Yugoslavia or the Government of the Federal Republic of Yugoslavia, then or thereafter located in the United States or within the possession or control of U.S. persons, including their overseas branches.

Subsequently, Executive Order No. 12810 expanded U.S. actions to implement in the United States the U.N. sanctions against the FRY (S/M) adopted in United Nations Security Council Resolution No. 757 of May 30, 1992. In addition to reaffirming the blocking of FRY (S/M) Government property, this order prohibits transactions with respect to the FRY (S/M) involving imports, exports, dealing in FRY-origin property, air and sea transportation, contract performance, funds transfers, activity promoting importation or exportation or dealings in property, and official sports, scientific, technical, or other cultural representation of, or sponsorship by, the FRY (S/M) in the United States.

Executive Order No. 12810 exempted from trade restrictions (1) transshipments through the FRY (S/M), and (2) activities related to the United Nations Protection Force (UNPROFOR), the Conference on Yugoslavia, or the European Community Monitor Mission.

On January 15, 1993, President Bush issued Executive Order No. 12831 to implement new sanctions contained in United Nations Security Council Resolution No. 787 of November 16, 1992. The order revoked the exemption for transshipments through the FRY (S/M) contained in Executive Order No. 12810, prohibited transactions within the United States or by a U.S. person relating to FRY (S/M) vessels and vessels in which a majority or controlling interest is held by a person or entity in, or operating from, the FRY (S/M), and stated that all such vessels shall be considered as vessels of the FRY (S/M), regardless of the flag under which they sail.

On April 26, 1993, I issued Executive Order No. 12846 to implement in the United States the sanctions adopted in United Nations Security Council Resolution No. 820 of April 17, 1993. That resolution called on the Bosnian Serbs to accept the Vance-Owen peace plan for Bosnia-Herzegovina and, if they failed to do so by April 26, called on member states to take additional measures to tighten the embargo against the FRY (S/M) and Serbian-controlled areas of Bosnia-Herzegovina and the United Nations Protected Areas in Croatia. Effective April 26, 1993, the order blocks all property and interests in property of commercial, industrial, or public utility undertakings or entities organized or located in the FRY (S/M), including property and interests in property of entities (wherever organized or located) owned or controlled by such undertakings or entities, that are or thereafter come within the possession or control of U.S. persons.

2. The declaration of the national emergency on May 30, 1992, was made pursuant to the authority vested in the President by the Constitution and laws of the United States, including the International Emergency Economic Powers Act (50 U.S.C. 1701 *et seq.*), the National Emergencies Act (50 U.S.C. 1601 *et seq.*), and section 301 of title 3 of the United States Code. The emergency declaration was reported to the Congress on May 30, 1992, pursuant to section 204(b) of the International Emergency Economic Powers Act (50 U.S.C. 1703(b)). The additional sanctions set forth in Executive Orders No. 12810, No. 12831, and No. 12846 were imposed pursuant to the authority vested in the President by the Constitution and laws of the United States, including the statutes cited above, section 1114 of the Federal Aviation Act (49

U.S.C. App. 1514), and section 5 of the United Nations Participation Act of 1945, as amended (22 U.S.C. 287c).

3. Since the last report, the Office of Foreign Assets Control (FAC) of the Department of the Treasury, in consultation with the State Department and other Federal agencies, has amended the Federal Republic of Yugoslavia (Serbia and Montenegro) Sanctions Regulations, 31 CFR Part 585 (58 FR 35828, July 1, 1993), to implement Executive Order No. 12846. A copy of the amendment is enclosed with this report.

Effective 12:01 a.m. e.d.t., April 26, 1993, Executive Order No. 12846 blocks all property and interests in property of all commercial, industrial, or public utility undertakings or entities organized or located in the FRY (S/M), including the property and interest in property of entities (wherever organized or located) owned or controlled by such undertakings and entities, that are or thereafter come within the United States or the possession or control of U.S. persons (amended section 585.201). Section 1(a) of Executive Order No. 12846 expressly blocks property subject to U.S. jurisdiction of many entities, both U.S. and foreign, heretofore blocked pursuant to the regulatory presumption of FAC that all entities organized or located in the FRY (S/M), as well as entities owned or controlled by them, are controlled directly or indirectly by the Government of the FRY (S/M).

New section 585.215 implements section 1(c) of Executive Order No. 12846 to provide that, except as otherwise authorized, conveyances and/or cargo that comes within the United States and is not otherwise subject to blocking, but is suspected of a violation of United Nations Security Council resolutions imposing sanctions against the FRY (S/M), shall be detained pending investigation and, upon a determination by the Secretary of the Treasury or his delegate that a violation has occurred, shall be blocked. New section 585.216 of the Regulations implements section 1(b) of Executive Order No. 12846 to provide that, except as otherwise authorized, all expenses incident to the blocking and maintenance of property blocked pursuant to the Regulations shall be charged to the owners or operators of such property. Section 585.216 also provides for the discretionary liquidation of property blocked under these sections, with net proceeds placed in a blocked account in the name of the property's owner.

New section 585.217 provides that no vessel registered in the United States or owned or controlled by U.S. persons, other than U.S. naval vessels, may enter the territorial waters of the FRY (S/M) without specific authorization (Executive Order No. 12846, section 1(d)). New section 585.218 prohibits, unless specifically authorized pursuant to the statement of licensing policy in new section 585.524, any dealing by a U.S. person relating to the unauthorized importation from, exportation to, or transshipment through the United Nations Protected Areas in the Republic of Croatia and those areas of the Republic of Bosnia-Herzegovina under the control of Bosnian Serb forces, and activities promoting such trade (Executive Order No. 12846, section 1(e)).

The prohibitions of Executive Order No. 12846 apply notwithstanding any prior contracts, international agreements, licenses or authorizations, but may be modified by regulation, order, or license. New section 585.419 states that Executive Order No. 12846 does not invalidate existing authorizations and licenses issued pursuant to Executive orders with respect to the FRY (S/M), unless terminated, suspended, or modified by FAC.

In addition to implementing the provisions of Executive Order No. 12846, the amended Regulations expand the general license in section 585.509 to permit certain "Qualified Transactions," in the form of debt-for-equity or debt-for-debt swaps in rescheduled commercial debt of the former Yugoslavia, where the Yugoslav debt being swapped was originally incurred by an entity in Bosnia-Herzegovina, Croatia, Macedonia, or Slovenia. These transactions are pursuant to the New Financing Agreement for Yugoslavia of September 20, 1988.

As part of the international effort to tighten economic sanctions against Yugoslavia, FAC has issued a series of General Notices listing "Blocked Federal Republic of Yugoslavia (Serbia and Montenegro) Entities and Specially Designated Nationals (SDNs)." Three additional General Notices have been issued by FAC since my last report. General Notices No. 4, No. 5, and No. 6 announced the names of 349 additional entities and five individuals determined by the Department of the Treasury to be Blocked Entities or SDNs of the FRY (S/M). General Notices No. 4, No. 5, and No. 6 supplement the listings of General Notice No. 1 (57 *FR* 32051, July 20, 1992), General Notice No.

2 (January 15, 1993), and General Notice No. 3 (March 8, 1993), and bring the current total of Blocked Entities and SDNs of the FRY (S/M) to 850. Copies of General Notices No. 4, No. 5, and No. 6 are attached.

Of the two court cases in which the blocking authority was challenged as applied to FRY (S/M) subsidiaries and vessels in the United States, the Government's position in the case involving the blocked vessels was upheld by the Fifth Circuit Court of Appeals. Supreme Court review has been requested. The case involving a blocked subsidiary remains to be resolved.

4. Over the past 6 months, the Departments of State and Treasury have worked closely with European Community (the "EC") member states and other U.N. member nations to coordinate implementation of the sanctions against the FRY (S/M). This has included visits by assessment teams formed under the auspices of the United States, the EC, and the Conference for Security and Cooperation in Europe (the "CSCE") to states bordering on Serbia and Montenegro; deployment of CSCE sanctions assistance missions (SAMs) to Albania, Bulgaria, Croatia, the Former Yugoslav Republic of Macedonia, Hungary, Romania, and Ukraine to assist in monitoring land and Danube River traffic; bilateral contacts between the United States and other countries for the purpose of tightening financial and trade restrictions on the FRY (S/M); and establishment of a mechanism to coordinate enforcement efforts and to exchange technical information.

5. In accordance with licensing policy and the Regulations, FAC has exercised its authority to license certain specific transactions with respect to the FRY (S/M) that are consistent with the Security Council sanctions. During the reporting period, FAC has issued 137 specific licenses regarding transactions pertaining to the FRY (S/M) or assets it owns or controls, bringing the total as of October 15, 1993, to 563. Specific licenses have been issued (1) for payment to U.S. or third-country secured creditors, under certain narrowly defined circumstances, for pre-embargo import and export transactions; (2) for legal representation or advice to the Government of the FRY (S/M) or FRY (S/M)-controlled clients; (3) for the liquidation or protection of tangible assets of subsidiaries of FRY (S/M)-controlled firms located in the United States; (4) for limited FRY (S/M) diplomatic representation in Washington and New York; (5) for pat-

ent, trademark, and copyright protection and maintenance transactions in the FRY (S/M) not involving payment to the FRY (S/M) Government; (6) for certain communications, news media, and travel-related transactions; (7) for the payment of crews' wages and vessel maintenance of FRY (S/M)-controlled ships blocked in the United States; (8) for the removal from the FRY (S/M) of certain property owned and controlled by U.S. entities; and (9) to assist the United Nations in its relief operations and the activities of the U.N. Protection Forces. Pursuant to regulations implementing United Nations Security Council Resolution No. 757, specific licenses have also been issued to authorize exportation of food, medicine, and supplies intended for humanitarian purposes in the FRY (S/M).

During the past 6 months, FAC has continued to oversee the liquidation of tangible assets of the 15 U.S. subsidiaries of entities organized in the FRY (S/M). Subsequent to the issuance of Executive Order No. 12846, all operating licenses issued for these U.S.-located Serbian or Montenegrin subsidiaries or joint ventures were revoked, and the net proceeds of the liquidation of their assets placed in blocked accounts.

The Board of Governors of the Federal Reserve Board and the New York State Banking Department again worked closely with FAC with regard to two Serbian banking institutions in New York that were closed on June 1, 1992. The banks had been issued licenses to maintain a limited staff and full-time bank examiners had been posted in their offices to ensure that banking records are appropriately safeguarded. Subsequent to the issuance of Executive Order No. 12846, all licenses previously issued were revoked. FAC is currently working with the Federal Reserve Board and the New York State Banking Department to resolve outstanding issues regarding the banks.

During the past 6 months, U.S. financial institutions have continued to block funds transfers in which there is an interest of the Government of the FRY (S/M) or an entity or undertaking located in or controlled from the FRY (S/M). Such transfers have accounted for $36.6 million in Yugoslav assets blocked since the issuance of Executive Order No. 12808.

To ensure compliance with the terms of the licenses that have been issued under the program, stringent reporting requirements are imposed. Nearly 500 submissions were reviewed since the last report and more than 180 compliance cases are currently open. In addition, licensed bank accounts are regularly audited by FAC compliance personnel and by cooperating auditors from other regulatory agencies.

6. Since the issuance of Executive Order No. 12810, FAC has worked closely with the U.S. Customs Service to ensure both that prohibited imports and exports (including those in which the Government of the FRY (S/M) has an interest) are identified and interdicted, and that permitted imports and exports move to their intended destination without undue delay. Violations and suspected violations of the embargo are being investigated and appropriate enforcement actions are being taken. There are currently 42 cases under active investigation. Civil penalties collected from financial institutions for violations involving transfers of funds in which the Government of the FRY (S/M) has an interest have totaled more than $21,000 to date.

7. The expenses incurred by the Federal Government in the 6 month period from May 31, 1993, through November 29, 1993, that are directly attributable to the authorities conferred by the declaration of a national emergency with respect to the FRY (S/M) are estimated at more than $3.9 million, most of which represent wage and salary costs for Federal personnel. Personnel costs were largely centered in the Department of the Treasury (particularly in FAC and its Chief Counsel's Office, and the U.S. Customs Service), the Department of State, the National Security Council, the U.S. Coast Guard, and the Department of Commerce.

8. The actions and policies of the Government of the FRY (S/M), in its involvement in and support for groups attempting to seize and hold territory in Croatia and Bosnia-Herzegovina by force and violence, continue to pose an unusual and extraordinary threat to the national security, foreign policy, and economy of the United States. The United States remains committed to a multilateral resolution of this crisis through its actions implementing the binding resolutions of the United Nations Security Council with respect to the FRY (S/M).

I shall continue to exercise the powers at my disposal to apply economic sanctions against the FRY (S/M) as long as these measures are appropriate, and will continue to report periodically to the Congress on significant developments pursuant to 50 U.S.C. 1703(c).

Sincerely,

WILLIAM J. CLINTON

NOTE: Identical letters were sent to Thomas S. Foley, Speaker of the House of Representatives, and Albert Gore, Jr., President of the Senate.

Message on the Observance of Hanukkah, 1993
December 7, 1993

I am pleased to send my warmest greetings to all who are celebrating Hanukkah.

The Festival of Lights, a joyous holiday that commemorates a miracle, is a fitting time to give thanks for the blessings of the past year. One of those great blessings was the historic handshake between the Prime Minister of Israel and the Chairman of the Palestine Liberation Organization—something that surely would have seemed a miracle just a short time ago. Hanukkah serves as a reminder that faith and perseverance can sustain us against the most difficult odds.

We live in a world weary of violence and determined to take steps to advance the cause of peace. We live in a nation that has made a renewed commitment to improving our communities and using our rich ethnic heritage to unite us, rather than to divide us. The strong beliefs and confidence that brought victory to the Maccabees and eight days of light to the Temple can guide us as we face the momentous challenges of our times. The eternal lesson of Hanukkah—that faith gives us the strength to work miracles and find light in times of darkness—inspires all of us to strive toward a brighter future.

In this holiday season, let us rededicate ourselves to creating a more peaceful world for all.

BILL CLINTON

NOTE: This message was released by the Office of the Press Secretary on December 7.

Statement on the Tentative Agreement To End the Coal Strike
December 7, 1993

I would like to commend the United Mine Workers of America and the Bituminous Coal Operations Association for coming together and producing a tentative agreement in this contentious strike.

This agreement represents good news for the coal industry, good news for its workers, and more good news for the economy as we approach the holiday season.

I applaud Mine Workers President Rich Trumka and BCOA Chief Bobby Brown for their dedication and commitment to an outcome that will support a strong and productive mining industry in America.

And I extend special thanks to former Secretary of Labor Bill Usery who was brought into this challenging mediation process at the request of Secretary of Labor Bob Reich. Bob assured me that Bill's history of stepping into and resolving tough disputes would prove to be invaluable to the negotiations. He was right.

Statement on Appointment of Assistant to the President and Deputy Chief of Staff
December 7, 1993

I've known Phil for a long time and believe that his integrity, personal qualities, and record of management success will be a genuine asset to the White House.

NOTE: This statement was included in a White House announcement naming Office of Management and Budget Deputy Director for Management Philip Lader as Assistant to the President and Deputy Chief of Staff.

Appointment for the John F. Kennedy Center for the Performing Arts
December 7, 1993

The President announced today that he intends to appoint Lew R. Wasserman to the Board of Trustees of the John F. Kennedy Center for the Performing Arts, Smithsonian Institution. The Kennedy Center's 30-member Board of Trustees is responsible for the Center's maintenance and administration, including oversight of its $75 million annual budget.

"Lew Wasserman's long and distinguished career in the entertainment industry has been truly remarkable," said the President. "Just as impressive is his commitment to public service. The Kennedy Center, one of our country's greatest artistic institutions, will benefit from his trusteeship."

NOTE: A biography of the appointee was made available by the Office of the Press Secretary.

Remarks on Signing the North American Free Trade Agreement Implementation Act
December 8, 1993

Thank you very much. I'm delighted to see all of you here. I thank Speaker Foley and the Republican leader, Bob Michel, for joining us today. There are so many people to thank, and the Vice President did a marvelous job. I do want to mention, if I might, just three others: Laura Tyson, the Chair of the Council of Economic Advisers; Bob Rubin, head of my national economic team; and one Republican Member of the House that wasn't mentioned, Congressman David Dreier, who went with me on a rainy day to Louisiana to campaign for NAFTA. There are many others that I might mention, but I thank all of you for what you have done.

I also can't help but note that in spite of all the rest of our efforts, there was that magic moment on Larry King, which made a lot of difference. And I thank the Vice President for

that and for so much else. In the campaign, when we decided to come out for NAFTA, he was a strong supporter of that position in our personal meetings, long before we knew whether we would even be here or not.

I also would be remiss if I did not personally thank both Mickey Kantor and Mack McLarty for the work they did, especially in the closing days with the Mexican trade representatives and the Mexican Government. I'd also like to welcome here the representatives from Mexico and Canada and tell them they are, in fact, welcome here. They are our partners in the future that we are trying to make together.

I want to say a special word of thanks to the Cabinet because we have tried to do something that I have not always seen in the past. And we try to get all of our Departments and all of our Cabinet leaders to work together on all the things that we all care about. And a lot of them, therefore, had to take a lot of personal time and business time away from their very busy schedules to do this. I thank the former leaders of our Government that were mentioned and our military. I can't help but noting, since General Powell is here, that every senior military officer with whom I spoke about NAFTA was perhaps—they were as a group perhaps the most intensely supportive of any group I spoke with. And I think it is because they have in their bones the experience of the world of the last several decades. And they knew we could not afford to turn away from our leadership responsibilities and our constructive involvement in the world. And many of them, of course, still in uniform, were not permitted to say that in public and should not have been. But I think I can say that today I was profoundly personally moved by the remarks that they made.

I do want to say, also, a special word of thanks to all the citizens who helped us, the business leaders, the labor folks, the environmental people who came out and worked through this—many of them at great criticism, particularly in the environmental movement—and some of the working people who helped it. And a group that was quite pivotal to our success that I want to acknowledge specifically are the small business people, many of whom got themselves organized and came forward and tried to help us. They made a real difference.

And they've been mentioned, but I couldn't let this moment go by without thanking my good friend Bill Daley and Congressman Bill Frenzel for their work in helping to mobilize this effort. Congressman Frenzel wrote me a great letter the other day and sent me one of his famous doodles that he doodled around the NAFTA legislation, which I am now having framed. But they sort of represented the bipartisan spirit that encaptured the Congress, encaptured the country in the cause to change. I hope that we can have more than that in the days and months and years ahead. It was a very fine thing.

This whole issue turned out to be a defining moment for our Nation. I spoke with one of the folks who was in the reception just a few moments ago who told me that he was in China watching the vote on international television when it was taken. And he said you would have had to be there to understand how important this was to the rest of the world, not because

of the terms of NAFTA, which basically is a trade agreement between the United States, Mexico, and Canada, but because it became a symbolic struggle for the spirit of our country and for how we would approach this very difficult and rapidly changing world dealing with our own considerable challenges here at home.

I believe we have made a decision now that will permit us to create an economic order in the world that will promote more growth, more equality, better preservation of the environment, and a greater possibility of world peace. We are on the verge of a global economic expansion that is sparked by the fact that the United States at this critical moment decided that we would compete, not retreat.

In a few moments, I will sign the North American free trade act into law. NAFTA will tear down trade barriers between our three nations. It will create the world's largest trade zone and create 200,000 jobs in this country by 1995 alone. The environmental and labor side agreements negotiated by our administration will make this agreement a force for social progress as well as economic growth. Already the confidence we've displayed by ratifying NAFTA has begun to bear fruit. We are now making real progress toward a worldwide trade agreement so significant that it could make the material gains of NAFTA for our country look small by comparison.

Today we have the chance to do what our parents did before us. We have the opportunity to remake the world. For this new era, our national security we now know will be determined as much by our ability to pull down foreign trade barriers as by our ability to breach distant ramparts. Once again, we are leading. And in so doing, we are rediscovering a fundamental truth about ourselves: When we lead, we build security, we build prosperity for our own people.

We've learned this lesson the hard way. Twice before in this century, we have been forced to define our role in the world. After World War I we turned inward, building walls of protectionism around our Nation. The result was a Great Depression and ultimately another horrible World War. After the Second World War, we took a different course: We reached outward. Gifted leaders of both political parties built a new order based on collective security and expanded trade. They created a foundation of stability and created in the process the conditions which led to the explosion of the great American middle class, one of the true economic miracles in the whole history of civilization. Their statecraft stands to this day: the IMF and the World Bank, GATT, and NATO.

In this very auditorium in 1949, President Harry Truman signed one of the charter documents of this golden era of American leadership, the North Atlantic Treaty that created NATO. "In this pact we hope to create a shield against aggression and the fear of aggression," Truman told his audience, "a bulwark which will permit us to get on with the real business of Government and society, the business of achieving a fuller and happier life for our citizens."

Now, the institutions built by Truman and Acheson, by Marshall and Vandenberg, have accomplished their task. The cold war is over. The grim certitude of the contest with communism has been replaced by the exuberant uncertainty of international economic competition. And the great question of this day is how to ensure security for our people at a time when change is the only constant.

Make no mistake, the global economy with all of its promise and perils is now the central fact of life for hard-working Americans. It has enriched the lives of millions of Americans. But for too many those same winds of change have worn away at the basis of their security. For two decades, most people have worked harder for less. Seemingly secure jobs have been lost. And while America once again is the most productive nation on Earth, this productivity itself holds the seeds of further insecurity. After all, productivity means the same people can produce more or, very often, that fewer people can produce more. This is the world we face.

We cannot stop global change. We cannot repeal the international economic competition that is everywhere. We can only harness the energy to our benefit. Now we must recognize that the only way for a wealthy nation to grow richer is to export, to simply find new customers for the products and services it makes. That, my fellow Americans, is the decision the Congress made when they voted to ratify NAFTA.

I am gratified with the work that Congress has done this year, bringing the deficit down and keeping interest rates down, getting housing starts and new jobs going upward. But we know that over the long run, our ability to have our internal economic policies work for the benefit of our people requires us to have external economic policies that permit productivity to find expression not simply in higher incomes for our businesses but in more jobs and higher incomes for our people. That means more customers. There is no other way, not for the United States or for Europe or for Japan or for any other wealthy nation in the world.

That is why I am gratified that we had such a good meeting after the NAFTA vote in the House with the Asian-Pacific leaders in Washington. I am gratified that, as Vice President Gore and Chief of Staff Mack McLarty announced 2 weeks ago when they met with President Salinas, next year the nations of this hemisphere will gather in an economic summit that will plan how to extend the benefits of trade to the emerging market democracies of all the Americas.

And now I am pleased that we have the opportunity to secure the biggest breakthrough of all. Negotiators from 112 nations are seeking to conclude negotiations on a new round of the General Agreement on Tariffs and Trade; a historic worldwide trade pact, one that would spur a global economic boon, is now within our grasp. Let me be clear. We cannot, nor should we, settle for a bad GATT agreement. But we will not flag in our efforts to secure a good one in these closing days. We are prepared to make our contributions to the success of this negotiation, but we insist that other nations do their part as well. We must not squander this opportunity. I call on all the nations of the world to seize this moment and close the deal on a strong GATT agreement within the next week.

I say to everyone, even to our negotiators: Don't rest. Don't sleep. Close the deal. I told Mickey Kantor the other day that we rewarded his laborious effort on NAFTA with a vacation at the GATT talks. [*Laughter*]

My fellow Americans, bit by bit all these things are creating the conditions of a sustained global expansion. As significant as they are, our goals must be more ambitious. The United States must seek nothing less than a new trading system that benefits all nations through robust commerce but that protects our middle class and gives other nations a chance to grow one, that lifts workers and the environment up without dragging people down, that seeks to ensure that our policies reflect our values.

Our agenda must, therefore, be far reaching. We are determining that dynamic trade cannot lead to environmental despoliation. We will seek new institutional arrangements to ensure that trade leaves the world cleaner than before. We will press for workers in all countries to secure rights that we now take for granted, to organize and earn a decent living. We will insist that expanded trade be fair to our businesses and to our regions. No country should use cartels, subsidies, or rules of entry to keep our products off its shelves. And we must see to it that our citizens have the personal security to confidently participate in this new era. Every worker must receive the education and training he or she needs to reap the rewards of international competition rather than to bear its burdens.

Next year, our administration will propose comprehensive legislation to transform our unemployment system into a reemployment and job retraining system for the 21st century. And above all, I say to you we must seek to reconstruct the broad-based political coalition for expanded trade. For decades, working men and women and their representatives supported policies that brought us prosperity and security. That was because we recognized that expanded trade benefited all of us but that we have an obligation to protect those workers who do bear the brunt of competition by giving them a chance to be retrained and to go on to a new and different and, ultimately, more secure and more rewarding way of work. In recent years, this social contract has been sundered. It cannot continue.

When I affix my signature to the NAFTA legislation a few moments from now, I do so with this pledge: To the men and women of our country who were afraid of these changes and found in their opposition to NAFTA an expression of that fear—what I thought was a wrong expression and what I know was a wrong expression but nonetheless represented legiti-mate fears—the gains from this agreement will be your gains, too.

I ask those who opposed NAFTA to work with us to guarantee that the labor and side agreements are enforced, and I call on all of us who believe in NAFTA to join with me to urge the Congress to create the world's best worker training and retraining system. We owe it to the business community as well as to the working men and women of this country. It means greater productivity, lower unemployment, greater worker efficiency, and higher wages and greater security for our people. We have to do that.

We seek a new and more open global trading system not for its own sake but for our own sake. Good jobs, rewarding careers, broadened horizons for the middle class Americans can only be secured by expanding exports and global growth. For too long our step has been unsteady as the ground has shifted beneath our feet. Today, as I sign the North American Free Trade Agreement into law and call for further progress on GATT, I believe we have found our footing. And I ask all of you to be steady, to recognize that there is no turning back from the world of today and tomorrow. We must face the challenges, embrace them with confidence, deal with the problems honestly and openly, and make this world work for all of us. America is where it should be, in the lead, setting the pace, showing the confidence that all of us need to face tomorrow. We are ready to compete, and we can win.

Thank you very much.

NOTE: The President spoke at 10:37 a.m. in the Mellon Auditorium. H.R. 3450, approved December 8, was assigned Public Law No. 103–182.

Exchange With Reporters
December 8, 1993

Violent Crime

Q. Give us your reaction, sir, to the shootings on Long Island—[*inaudible*]—in the shootings.

The President. First of all, it's a terrible human tragedy, and my sympathies go out to all the families involved.

I will say, I think we have to note that the gun that was used contained, apparently, two 15-round clips that were expended while this man in a manic state was walking down the subway aisle. And one of the reasons we ought to pass the crime bill is that Senator Feinstein's amendment to limit assault weapons would make those 15-round clips illegal. They're not necessary for hunting or sports purposes, and it simply allows you to shoot and wound more people more quickly. So I hope that this will give some more impetus to the need to act urgently, to deal with the unnecessary problems of gun violence in the country.

The second thing I would say is that while no one believes that there is anything we can ever do to solve every problem of someone who snaps mentally and does something terrible like this, and we have to acknowledge that honestly, there are a lot of things that we're going to have to do in this country to get violence under control that relate to rebuilding our communities and healing across racial lines and economic lines. But we need to start with public safety. Put those 100,000 police officers on the street. Pass this ban on assault weapons and these multiround clips. And let's get about the business of making the country safer.

Q. [*Inaudible*]—requirement for licensing and testing to purchase a gun?

The President. Well, that was recommended to me, as you know, by the Mayor-elect of New York and the Mayor of Los Angeles, and I've asked the Attorney General to review it and make a recommendation to me on it. I think I should wait to hear from her on it. It is interesting how we regularly have requirements, for example, for getting and driving cars that don't apply to the use of guns. When I was a boy and first started to hunt, you know, one of the first things I was told was you have to learn how to use a gun safely and responsibly. And it's something I think we ought to look at. But I want to ask the Attorney General for an opinion before I discuss it further.

Lobbyists

Q. Sir, Roy Neel and Howard Paster are getting very lucrative jobs in PR and lobbying. Doesn't that, at the very least, give the impression of a revolving door that you spoke against?

The President. What I spoke of was not that citizens should go back to their private lives from Government and not that they shouldn't be able to use the knowledge and experience they have, but they shouldn't be able to abuse it.

What we did was to erect bigger walls against abuse. Neither one of them can ever lobby for a foreign interest and neither one of them can lobby the Executive Office of the President for 5 years on any matter even though the law only requires one year. So we've raised the wall higher, which is exactly what I promised to do.

Now if, in addition to that, the House will follow the Senate's lead and pass the lobby bill, lobby restriction bill, which will put restrictions on the activities of lobbyists and disclose more of them, and if the House and Senate will agree to a good campaign finance reform bill and the Congress will agree to live under the laws it imposes on private employers—if they'll do all that, which is on our agenda, then I think the public confidence will be much, much higher.

Surgeon General Joycelyn Elders

Q. Dr. Elders, obviously, has said a lot of things that have created a controversy, but unless I'm mistaken, this is the first time I can remember her making a comment that was a fundamental disagreement with you and that a member of your administration talked about reining her in—that she needs to only speak for the administration.

The President. I just don't agree with that position. When you have someone as outspoken and energetic as she is, there's going to be times when she'll be outspoken and energetic in a way that I don't necessarily agree with.

Q. Is she allowed to disagree with you?

The President. But I certainly stand behind her foursquare as Surgeon General. I think she's done a good job, and she's beginning to really focus the country on a lot of these public health problems. So, she needs to make it very clear that—and I think she did, to be fair—that I just disagree with that. I have thought about it a lot, and I think the cost of legalizing drugs would far outweigh the benefits. But I think the fact that everybody in America feels overwhelmed and determined to do something about crime and violence and drugs and gangs is a very positive thing. So we'll just go from here.

President's Health

Q. Mr. President, how's your back?

The President. Much better, thank you. It just happens every couple of years. I wait for it to heal up, and I go back to running. It's fine.

NOTE: The exchange began at 2:11 p.m. at Blair House. During the exchange, the President referred to a December 7 incident in which a gunman on the Long Island Rail Road in Garden City, New York, killed 5 persons and wounded 20 before he was subdued by 3 other passengers. A tape was not available for verification of the content of this exchange.

Remarks to Mayors and Chiefs of Police on Violent Crime
December 9, 1993

Thank you, Mayor Abramson, and thank all of the rest of you for coming here. I have looked forward to this meeting and to receiving this plan ever since the first discussion we held.

I believe that this Nation is really prepared in a way that it has not been before, at least in my experience, to do something about violent crime, to do something about all of its causes, and to try to come together across the lines of region and party and the size of the units in which we live to deal with these things that are tearing the heart out of our country. I think the rapid change of opinion and movement on the Brady bill at the end of the last session is an example of that. I think the size of the margin by which Senator Feinstein's amendment was added to the crime bill in the Senate to ban 35 kinds of assault weapons was evidence of that. And so I think we are prepared to begin.

I would just like to make a couple of points, and then I came here, I'm sure along with the Attorney General and FBI Director and Dr. Brown, our Director of Drug Control Policy, as much to listen as to talk. I want to listen to you. But I would like to just put a few things on the table.

The first thing is that it is important that we get a good crime bill out early when the Congress comes back. And we'd like your help in defining what that is. The Senate and the House versions are different. The most clearly manifest difference is that the Senate version has more money in it and therefore would enable us to fund in this crime bill the full 100,000 extra police officers that I have supported since I began running for President.

As you point out in your report, it will take some time to train and deploy those people, but I know that it makes a difference. I think the margin of Mayor Lanier's reelection is evidence that people know that if you properly deploy trained personnel, it just doesn't serve to catch criminals quicker, but because of the relationships they develop in the community and their visibility, it actually reduces crime. I think there should be some alternative punishment for youthful offenders, boot camps and perhaps other things. I think that is very important.

Beyond that, we ought to talk about what else we do and where we go. But I want to emphasize that even with intense commitment in this city, you have to do the things that are before you. You have to get done what you can do at the moment and then move on to what's next on the agenda. So I think it is imperative that we move on the crime bill and the 100,000 police officers in the street and the boot camps as soon as we can when the Congress comes back.

I also think we ought to recognize that we don't have all the money in the world, and we don't want to spend a lot of money on things that will be of marginal significance. I was glad to see you advocating in this paper—I've just been skimming it over—that we ought to give attention to drug treatment as well as drug enforcement, that we needed to deal with supply and demand in an evenhanded way. We need some more investment to do that.

The last point I want to make is that this is the first step, but only the first step we have to take in restoring the conditions of civilized life to a lot of our cities. The reason a lot of these things are happening is that there has been a simultaneous decline of work, family, and community, the things that really organize life for all the rest of us. And we are going to have to rebuild them all. And it is not going to happen overnight, because these deteriorations have happened over a period of decades. But people can sense whether you are going in the right direction or the wrong direction, and I think we have to work together to change the direction. I am confident that we can. There are also maybe some things we can do administratively. And you have the people here who want to hear from you about that, and we want to go forward with that.

And finally let me say I think we ought to set up an ongoing relationship so that you can continue to work with us, get input, and help us to work through some of the difficult decisions that are always required when you move from the level of speaking to doing. And so we'd like very much to have, Mayor, some sort of ongoing mechanism that this administration can relate to from the membership of this group.

Lastly, let me say that I'm grateful for the participation here not just of the mayors but of the several police chiefs. It's good to see all of you here. I think we can do something.

I think the American people are tired of hurting and tired of feeling insecure and tired of the violence, and it makes such a huge gap between what we say and what we do and how we want to live and how we are forced to live. And it's affected now so many more people beyond the immediate victims of crime. It's changing everyone's life in ways that are quite destructive. We have to move. And I think we're prepared to move. And I think with this document, you've given us a good basis to begin.

I thank you very much.

NOTE: The President spoke at 10:41 a.m. in the Indian Treaty Room of the Old Executive Office Building. In his remarks, he referred to Mayor Jerry Abramson of Louisville, KY, president, U.S. Conference of Mayors, and Mayor Bob Lanier of Houston, TX.

Remarks on the Federal Fleet Conversion to Alternative Fuel Vehicles
December 9, 1993

Thank you very much. Please be seated. Thank you, Mr. Vice President and Secretary O'Leary and my longtime friend Garry Mauro.

I want to thank this task force for a job well done. I'd be remiss if I didn't ask the members of the task force who are here just to stand so we can be recognized. If you served on the task force, please stand up. [*Applause*] Thank you.

I also know that we had about 250 others, many of whom are in this room, who worked on the various subgroups of this task force. And I thank all of you. I thank Garry Mauro, the Texas land commissioner who has been my friend for more than 20 years, for his backbreaking work on this. I also want to thank the staff director, Tom Henderson, who is over here, who worked so hard on it. Thank you, Tom, for your work. Stand up. [*Applause*] Thank you. I thank Susan Tierney. And I want to say a special word of thanks to Hazel O'Leary for the statement she just made. One of my better predecessors, Harry Truman, once said that his job consisted largely of trying to talk people into doing what they ought to do without his having to ask them in the first place. [*Laughter*] So I didn't even have to ask her to comply. She

has removed a major part of my job. But I thank her for that.

Today I am directing the White House Office on Environmental Policy, headed by Katie McGinty, to cooperate with the Department of Energy in their ongoing programs to put these recommendations into action. These recommendations point the way to using the purchasing power of our National Government to promote vehicles that run on clean, domestic fuels, including natural gas, ethanol, methanol, propane, and electric power. The Federal Government is one of the Nation's leading purchasers of cars and vans and trucks and other vehicles. We buy tens of thousands of them each year, and even with the Vice President's reinventing Government report, we'll have to keep buying a few. Your recommendations show how we can make the best use of that purchasing power by buying alternative fuel vehicles in cities where air pollution is most severe, where Federal fleets are largest, where alternative fuels are available, where our efforts will be reinforced by State and local governments and private companies also committed to these goals.

The task force has identified cities where the

Federal investment will produce the biggest markets when linked with State, local, and private efforts. Some of these cities are already converting their fleets, their buses, their service vehicles, their regular cars. By linking with these local efforts, a modest Federal investment can help jumpstart locally and regionally significant programs.

Americans don't want Federal bureaucrats deciding what's best on the local levels. And in this case, especially, one size does not necessarily fit all. But our efforts do serve three very important goals. First, we protect the environment. Second, we create new jobs by promoting the use of fuels that are produced in the United States and by encouraging American companies to build vehicles that use those fuels. Third, we reduce our reliance on foreign oil. Americans want a clean environment, secure jobs, and a more independent country, and these alternative fuels help us to achieve those objectives.

We build on the successful experience at State and national levels in government and in business. Garry Mauro has already converted the Texas State government's fleet of vehicles to clean domestic fuels. And you just heard Secretary O'Leary manifest her commitment to doing the same with the Federal fleet. Many members of this task force have started to convert their companies' fleets of vehicles. Very often I preach to the converted; today, I'm preaching to the converters, I think. [*Laughter*] I can't believe I said that. It's been a long week. [*Laughter*]

I do want to say, seriously, that this effort is very important to me and has been from the beginning because it manifests two things that I believe very deeply and I believe all Americans must come to believe if we're going to really take this country where we have to go.

The first is that protecting the environment goes hand in hand with economic growth as we move toward the 21st century. If you look at what's happening in this country and around the world, at the crying need to increase the rate of growth and at the same time to protect this planet, it is apparent that the future will be what we desire only if we can achieve both great levels of environmental protection and higher rates of growth. If we fail at either one, and if we fail to reconcile the two, we do so at our peril and at the peril for the whole planet.

The second is that in a complicated, fast-changing world, Government can best lead by example, not by bureaucratic fiat. I believe that very strongly. We have to try to create environments, incentives, conditions in which the objectives we desire will be more likely to occur. And the recommendations of this task force achieve that objective very, very well.

So for all of that, I thank you all, those of you who contributed to this report. The best I can do is to do my very best to implement the recommendations of the task force. And I pledge to you that the Vice President and I and the Office of the White House, with the Office of Environmental Policy and with the Chief of Staff's well-known historic bias for natural gas, somehow we will find the way to make these task force recommendations come alive in the Federal Government and in the lives of the American people. Thank you very much.

NOTE: The President spoke at 11:47 a.m. in Room 450 of the Old Executive Office Building.

Remarks on Lighting the National Christmas Tree
December 9, 1993

Ladies and gentlemen, I'd like to begin my remarks by asking that we recognize the years of devotion that Joe Riley has given to this Pageant of Peace. Let's give him a big hand. [*Applause*]

This has been a wonderful night for Hillary and for Chelsea and for me. I thank Sandy Duncan for doing such a wonderful job in her tennis shoes; I think she looked sort of graceful limping out there. The DC Choral Kaleidoscope was wonderful. And I think Willard Scott is a perfect Santa Claus. You know, he will take any excuse to wear hair. [*Laughter*] But he looked beautiful. I'm especially glad to see my friends

Charley Pride and Phil Driscoll. I thank them for being here. I thought they were terrific, as was the Air Force Band that I'm proud of as the President very, very much. Thank you all so much for what you've done.

In this Pageant of Peace we come together in the spirit of our better selves, wishing that somehow, some way, we could feel the way we feel tonight and in this Christmas season, every day, all year long. We are joined by simple and universal convictions: a shared faith, a shared joy, a shared commitment now to follow the directions of our faith, to love our neighbors as ourselves, to be grateful for what we have, to wish that others had it, and to take some time to give more of ourselves to others.

I ask tonight that all of us, each in our own way, express our gratitude to the men and women of our Armed Forces who are overseas in this Christmas season, to all those who serve us here in the United States, to our families and friends, and to all those to whom we could give a little something extra.

But most of all, because of all the difficulties we have had in the United States in these last couple of years, with violence in our own land affecting not only adults but more and more of our children, I ask tonight, at this Pageant of Peace, that we pray in this Christmas season that we be given the wisdom and the courage, the heart, the renewed sense of common humanity, to do what we can to bring more peace to the streets, the homes, and the hearts of our own people and especially our children. That is something that would be perfectly consistent with the faith and the life we celebrate tonight, something we could take out of this Christmas season that would be the greatest gift we could ever give to ourselves, to our children, and to our beloved land.

Thank you. God bless you all. And now I'd like to ask my family to come up and help me to light the Christmas tree.

NOTE: The President spoke at 5:50 p.m. on the Ellipse. In his remarks, he referred to entertainers Sandy Duncan, Willard Scott, Charley Pride, and Phil Driscoll.

Remarks in a Telephone Conversation With the Space Shuttle *Endeavour* Astronauts and an Exchange With Reporters
December 10, 1993

The President. Hello?

Col. Richard O. Covey. Hello, sir.

The President. Can you hear us?

Col. Covey. Yes, sir, I can hear you loud and clear.

The President. Well, the Vice President and I wanted to call you and congratulate you on one of the most spectacular space missions in our history. We're all so proud of you, and we've been able to see you do all those things. It's just been wonderful, and I want to thank each and every one of you for what you've done. You made it look easy.

Col. Covey. Well, we appreciate the thanks and congratulations, sir. That's nice, particularly coming from you. As you know, great adventures are once-in-a-lifetime opportunities, and the seven of us were lucky to be able to be part of this great adventure.

The President. I know that you know this, but you have really both educated and inspired people all over the world. I don't think any of us will ever forget the image of K.T. lifting the damaged solar panel over her head and then letting it go. That was a moment of high drama. Maybe you should come down here and help us stage our events on Earth. [*Laughter*]

Mission Specialist Kathryn C. Thornton. I think it's easier to throw away solar panels. [*Laughter*]

The President. I'm glad the press corps heard you say that. [*Laughter*]

[*At this point, the Vice President congratulated the astronauts and the National Aeronautics and Space Administration.*]

Dr. F. Story Musgrave. I'm Story Musgrave, sir. I'm one of the EVA group members. As you can see now, we've got some different colors here. The magenta, I guess you call it, are the space walkers, and the ones up front there in navy blue, they're the ones that took care of us and launched us, took care of us during the space walks, and will bring us back home.

What it took was incredible attention to detail and an incredible amount of energy to identify what surprises might come up and try to assure that we would get the job done, an immense amount of training. But I think it did, and the challenge was a very, very ambitious mission to restore Hubble, to fix the spherical aberration, to restore Hubble so it will be good for many, many more years of science. A very ambitious mission, but it did take the kind of stuff that we have, and it's mostly attention to detail, identifying surprises, turn over every stone, and give it all of the energy we've got.

The President. It also took at least one person who is making his fifth journey into space. You can't imagine what a wonderful picture you are there. You and the two men behind you proved that you can walk in space with or without facial hair. [*Laughter*] I tell you—Yes, well—and he's both.

Another thing that you did, I believe, to follow up on what the Vice President was saying, I think you gave an immense boost to the space program in general and to America's continuing venture in space. In this last session of Congress, we had quite a struggle to preserve the space station and an adequate ongoing budget for NASA because we were cutting so much else. I'm really gratified that we were able to do it, and I hope that this stunning example of what can be accomplished will really reinforce the support for America in space, both in the Congress and in the country. I think it will. All of you were just absolutely wonderful.

[*The Vice President welcomed the crewmember from Switzerland and noted the international nature of the space program.*]

Mission Specialist Claude Nicollier. Well, I feel very privileged to have been selected for this mission as a representative of the European Space Agency. As you know, the European nations participated in this program, in the design and the manufacture and the exploitation of the scientific results, and I feel really very privileged and happy to have been selected as a crewmember, as the foreign crewmember of this mission.

The President. Let's see, who have we not heard from? The rest of you have to talk. There's somebody back home looking for you.

Col. Covey. Well, I was a little bit remiss,

sir, and I didn't introduce all of the crew. You just heard from Claude Nicollier, the other member of the orbiter crew who did a lot of the mechanical arm flying. Along with Claude was my copilot, Ken Bowersox on my right here. And the other EVA crew members, besides K.T. and Story are Tom Akers on my far left and Jeff Hoffman behind me. I'm sure they would all like to make a statement, then I'll let Sox start off.

Comdr. Kenneth D. Bowersox. Yes, sir, I just wanted to say I'm proud to be from a country that supports efforts like this. I think space exploration reflects the continuing pioneering spirit of the American people, and I think it's something we can all be proud of.

Mission Specialist Jeffrey A. Hoffman. Hello, Mr. President. Thanks for your congratulations. Of course, for every one of us seven up here, there are literally hundreds of people on the ground, on the ground team who have put just as much effort and energy and talent into this mission to make it a success as we have. And they not only deserve the credit for it, but we sure wish they could be up here with us.

Dr. Musgrave. Mr. President, I think that this mission is unique in another way, and that is that it has really combined two aspects of space exploration. It has joined the use in space for scientific exploration—which the Hubble telescope is so exciting, and everyone in the astronomical community and all over the world is waiting to see the results now of the newly refurbished Hubble—and it's joined that with the human space program. And this is very exciting, and I think it is only the first part of showing what people and machines and scientific exploration and human ingenuity can do in the environment of space.

The President. Well, thank you all. Let me just say again that we are all so proud of you, and I appreciate what each and every one of you have said. It's a real clear message about not only your incredible abilities and your courage and the support you got from all of those hundreds of people helping you back down here but of the profound importance of our country continuing its adventures in space. We depend on it down here for so much scientific knowledge, and we're going to do what we can do to support you and to support NASA and to support the space program. And you have taken an enormous step forward for building that kind of support, not just in the minds but in the hearts and the spirits of the American people. And you've done it with great good humor. And we thank you so much.

The Vice President. Thank you, a wonderful, inspiring success story.

Col. Covey. Well, we truly appreciate those words, and we thank you for taking the time to talk with us now and also for taking the time to be supportive of our Nation's space programs. It's very important to us, and I can't tell you how proud we are to be able to represent those programs and to be able to help bring NASA back to new heights if we can do that.

The President. You already have. Thanks.

Astronauts. Thank you.

The President. Good luck.

[*At this point, the telephone conversation ended, and the President took questions from reporters.*]

Space Program

Q. Mr. President, do you believe that this flight was a make-or-break effort for NASA?

The President. I don't know about that. I think that this flight's success will plainly illustrate the importance of NASA's many missions and reinforce the understanding of that importance in the American people and the support for it.

The Vice President. It's just the pressurization. [*Laughter*]

The President. I thought it was someone hissing at my response. [*Laughter*]

Q. Is it a new lease on life for the space program?

The President. Well, I think the space program got a new lease on life in this last session of Congress after the completion of the Best report and the redesign of the space station and Congress reaffirming the support for the space station. And then the support we've achieved, at least from the leadership, the appropriate committees in Congress, for the Russian participation in the whole continuing vision of the space station, I think that was very important. But this probably will galvanize the public's imagination and support again in a way that nothing we could have ever done in this town would have accomplished.

Gun Control

Q. Sir, on a more down-to-earth issue, are you ready to fully endorse this idea of gun ownership licensing and registration?

The President. Well, as I said, there are a whole lot of different ideas that have been advanced in this whole area, including a much better oversight of people who actually sell weapons in the country and a whole series of things on that. That's a question of Federal registration, as well as some State and local registration, too, at least for over-the-counter sales. And there are any number of other issues.

Keep in mind, I keep saying we have to do these things one at a time. The crime bill with the amendment by Senator Feinstein which passed the Senate has not yet passed the House. That's a very important step because that will be a measure of the willingness of the Congress to move forward here in banning some of these assault weapons. But another big step will be getting the Federal Government, the Treasury Department, ATF, the capacity to define identical assault weapons that may not be mentioned by name in the law but that are the same thing with just some minor modification to try to get around the law. In other words, there are a whole set of issues here that I believe we have to look at and make decisions on and then set up a set of priorities based on how much we can get done how quickly.

On the issue of the registration of either the guns themselves or the people who own them, you know, in the question of automobiles we have both people registered, you know, people have an automobile license, and the cars themselves are registered. And that's all done at the State level, but a lot of the information is in national computers for law enforcement purposes. For example, if someone steals your car today and drives it to another State and leaves it in the parking lot of a shopping center and it's found, the license number could be fed back into the computer, and you could be told within a matter of a few seconds, normally, that your car's been turned up and where it is. So what I am doing now is to ask the Justice Department to work with our staff to analyze all these proposals both on the merits, if it's right or wrong, and secondly, for the details, how could it be done, and thirdly, what should we do in what order. And that's what I'm looking at now.

The main thing I can tell you is that we are committed to going further. The Brady bill was a good first step. It will save some lives, especially for people who have established records of mental problems or clear criminal records. But it is nowhere near enough. It is the beginning, and we have got to move forward.

Q. [Inaudible]

The President. I'm not ruling it out at all, I mean, I—[*inaudible*]—but you heard my answer. I just think it is very important that we know exactly what we're talking about: How would it be done? What are the mechanics? How does it rank in order of priority with these other things we have to do, both in terms of what's most urgent, number one, and number two, what can we most likely get done quickest?

And let me just emphasize, if you look, there was a study in one of the papers just in the last 10 days on the deaths of young people by gunshot in one of our major cities which concluded that the increase in the death rate was attributable over a brief period of time, like over the last 5 years—we're not talking about 20 but over the last 5 years—entirely to the dramatic increase in the use of semiautomatic assault weapons as opposed to single-shot guns. That single thing had raised the death rate in the last 4 or 5 years more than any other thing.

So, there are lots of issues here. We're going to try to deal with them all in an aggressive and forthright way, but we have to figure out exactly what to do and in what order. The possibility of movement here has just opened up, and the American people need to keep the pressure on, and we'll keep moving.

North Korea

Q. Mr. President, the North Koreans seemed pretty inflexible yesterday in their statement about their offer being "take it or leave it." Is there more flexibility in private than they're showing in public?

The President. Well, let me just say we have some hope for the continuing discussions. When negotiations are going on, I'm always reluctant to characterize them one way or the other, whether it's GATT or with North Korea. I just don't want to do that. But if you've asked me, have I given up on the discussions, the answer to that is no. We're aggressively pursuing them.

NOTE: The President spoke at 8:37 a.m. in the Oval Office at the White House.

Interview on "The Home Show"
December 10, 1993

Gary Collins. The President of the United States, ladies and gentlemen.

The President. Gary.

Sarah Purcell. Hello, Mr. President, how are you?

The President. How are you? Glad to see you.

Ms. Purcell. Pleasure to meet you.

The President. Thank you.

Ms. Purcell. Thank you. Welcome to your own home.

The President. Here we are.

Mr. Collins. By the way, have you done all your shopping yet?

The President. No, I haven't even started.

Mr. Collins. Oh, yes, we know what you're going to get, though.

The President. You do?

Mr. Collins. Well, it's bigger than a breadbox but smaller than a bus.

Hillary Clinton. Now, don't give it away.

Mr. Collins. Oh, I'm sorry.

Ms. Purcell. You know how these men are——

Mr. Collins. That's good—[*inaudible*]—what are you getting——

The President. I accept.

Hillary Clinton. He seems very happy.

The President. Hi, Socks.

Ms. Purcell. Can you give us any hints about what your plans are for a gift for——

The President. No, I wouldn't do that.

Ms. Purcell. We saw your last year's gifts.

The President. I have made a decision. Do you like that?

Mr. Collins. Well, somebody told us that you shop Christmas Eve, is that correct? Do you like that?

The President. I do two things actually, though. At least in the past I have. When we lived in Arkansas, I had a little closet that was just mine, and I shopped all year long for everybody that I knew, just a little bit here and there. And I'd travel around, and I'd buy something, and I shoved it all in the closet. And then about 10 days before Christmas, I'd take it out and organize it. And then I would find out what I hadn't done, and then I'd go out the day before Christmas and shop.

Ms. Purcell. Now, who did your wrapping, or did you do the wrapping?

The President. Well, the people who worked at the Governor's mansion did some of it, and then I did some of it. I did a lot of it myself.

Ms. Purcell. Are you pretty good?

The President. Chelsea and I would do a lot at the end. I'm pretty good actually.

Ms. Purcell. Yes.

The President. I'm not bad.

Mr. Collins. I just hate it. I would walk a mile rather than wrap a package.

The President. Well, you know, at the end of the—the last 2 or 3 days I get in the Christmas spirit in a big way, and I do a lot of that stuff.

Mr. Collins. Is that starting to build for you now? I mean, first Christmas in the White House as President.

The President. But really, I become like a little boy again around Christmastime. I don't want to sleep. I just want to, you know, do things.

Mr. Collins. This has really been a year for you folks, hasn't it? I mean, all the things that have been going on, the health reform, NAFTA, the Brady bill. I mean, the list goes on and on, and it just seems you're just getting started. And the polls seem to reflect kind of a turnaround in the feelings about the White House and what the effort is here. It must give you a tremendous sense of pleasure.

The President. Well, when we took office, you know, there was so much to be done and such a huge wall of cynicism that we had to pierce. And you know, when you start really changing things, there are going to be a lot of broken things around and about. So we knew it would be tough, but it was really gratifying to come to the end of the year and to see these ratings come out saying that I had more success than any President in the last 40 years in the first year and things like that. I think people are beginning to see, well, the economy's getting better and the country's moving. I'm very, very grateful for it.

Mr. Collins. So it's going to be a great message this Christmas.

The President. It's going to be a happy Christmas at our place.

Mr. Collins. What do you like about it most? I mean, what's the highlight of Christmas for you—if you had to pick one thing?

The President. If I had to pick one thing, it would be our family's sort of renewed sense of togetherness. It happens every year. Just the sense of gratitude we feel, it really kind of comes together, we feel. We try to remember what Christmas is really a celebration of, and it brings us closer together.

Ms. Purcell. You come from a single-parent family, and I know that Christmas probably is a lot different for you now. How do you feel about those changes in your life? And how does it mean——

The President. Well, I'm just—I'm very grateful. I'm extremely grateful to my mother, who was widowed three times in her life, a very brave lady. And she did a good job for me and for my brother. We're grateful to her. And I think it's real important, as Hillary and I go across the country and try to get more families to stay together and more intact families and support more responsibility for fathers, to point out that there are an awful lot of single parents out there—mostly women but some men—who have done a superb job, who've been fanatically loyal to their children, who've made great sacrifices for their children. You know, if every parent in this country, whether there was a two-parent family or single-parent family, had the internal fortitude and the external skills to put their children first in their lives, the problems in this Nation would drop dramatically in a decade. Ten years from now you wouldn't recognize this country.

Ms. Purcell. I absolutely agree.

Mr. Collins. If we could just keep the spirit of Christmas going a little bit beyond New Year's, we'd have remarkable results.

We talked about earlier tradition. We talked about the food that you're going to share on Christmas Day and so forth. And we waited for you to arrive because I understand, and we have a good source here, that on Christmas Eve part of the fun is doing carols and acting out roles. We heard that you're awfully good.

Hillary Clinton. He's a good singer, too.

Mr. Collins. Is he?

Ms. Purcell. Is he a good singer?

The President. I love Christmas carols.

Ms. Purcell. And you act out the parts in the carols, from what I understand. Somebody's Rudolph and someone's——

Mr. Collins. What's one of his big hits?

Hillary Clinton. Well, "The Twelve Days of Christmas," you have 12 different things to do. So, that's a special thing.

The President. I'm a very good partridge in a pear tree. [*Laughter*]

Mr. Collins. Can you give us an example?

Hillary Clinton. We've never known quite how to act that out, so it's different every year.

The President. Maids a-milking, you know. Swans swimming. [*Laughter*]

Mr. Collins. We'll be back with the Twelve Days of Christmas.

Hillary Clinton. What is it, nine lords a-leaping?

The President. I can't believe I did—yes——

Ms. Purcell. We'll take a break and be right back as soon as we can remember them all.

[*At this point, the network took a commercial break.*]

Ms. Purcell. [*Inaudible*]—but they actually have, and then you had something that you wanted to present them with, didn't you?

Carol Duvall. Well, I do feel a bit like it's bringing coals to Newcastle to bring you a Christmas ornament after looking at all these gorgeous, gorgeous trees. But we did know that you have an official White House heart ornament that a lot of the quilters around the country had made. Well, we wanted to get into the act, but I know that a lot of our ladies don't all sew, they don't all quilt. So, I tried to copy the idea with a nonsewing one. And this is our little ornament for you.

Mr. Collins. That's a little ornament. Take a look at it. All right, there it is, and here we go.

Ms. Duvall. Now, you're supposed to turn it around to the other side.

Mr. Collins. Turn it around.

Hillary Clinton. Oh!

The President. That's great.

Mr. Collins. Oh, I remember that.

Hillary Clinton. That's so neat.

Mr. Collins. Mr. President, if you can hold that real close over your shoulder, we'll get a——

Ms. Duvall. They've got a shot of it. I'll have to tell you that was before this meeting, so I had to cut that out of a magazine. But it was a nice picture of you.

Hillary Clinton. Oh, thank you. We'll put that on our personal tree.

The President. We've been collecting these ornaments, you know, for a very long time now.

Ms. Purcell. And I know that the two of you have been giving a lot of thought to this being your first year in the White House, your first Christmas in the White House. And I know you must have some special thoughts of things you might wish for the Nation for the New Year and for the holidays. Would you like to start, Mrs. Clinton?

Hillary Clinton. Well, I just wish that the feeling of Christmas and the meaning of Christmas could find a place in the heart of everyone in the country and that it wouldn't be just seasonal, but it would go on and on and help change the way we treat each other and live together.

The President. My hope is that we will achieve more peace on Earth next year, peace in the Middle East, relief of tensions in other places in the world, but mostly that the American people will find a way to bring peace to our own streets, our own homes, our own communities. Our Nation is too violent. It makes a mockery of all the things we say we believe. It is turning the joy of childhood into a tragedy for too many millions of children. And I'm going to work real hard next year to have more peace on this piece of Earth that we inhabit in the United States.

Mr. Collins. Well, I don't know how you can work any harder than you've worked this year.

Ms. Purcell. Absolutely.

Mr. Collins. With the surge in popularity, the people turning to the Government to say, "please help us; it looks like we can't do this ourselves," are you going to feel much more bolder next year in terms of your campaigns and——

The President. Well, I don't know if we can get any more done than we did this year, but I think we can. I think we can move forward on health care, on crime and violence, and on reform of the welfare system to move more people into permanent jobs, which I think will strengthen families. Those are the three things we're going to be——

Ms. Purcell. Two enormous jobs to tackle, but thank you so much for sharing this with us. We really appreciate here at "The Home Show"——

Mr. Collins. We wish you the very, very best holiday.

Ms. Purcell. And thank you for sharing it with us.

The President. Thank you.

NOTE: The interview began at 11:49 a.m. in the Diplomatic Reception Room at the White House.

Appointment for the General Services Administration
December 10, 1993

The President announced today that he has appointed Maine businessman Robert J. Dunfey, Jr. to be the Deputy Regional Administrator of the General Services Administration for Regions I and II, covering the Northeastern part of the country.

"This appointment reaffirms the commitment that I have made, along with Administrator Roger Johnson, to bringing people with sound management experience into the GSA," said the President.

NOTE: A biography of the appointee was made available by the Office of the Press Secretary.

Appointment for the Federal Home Loan Mortgage Corporation
December 10, 1993

The President announced today that he intends to appoint three individuals, Jerry MacArthur Hultin, Raymond J. McClendon, and James B. Nutter, to the Board of Directors of the Federal Home Loan Mortgage Corporation (Freddie Mac), a stockholder-owned corporation chartered by Congress in 1970 which supports home ownership and rental housing through the creation and development of a secondary market for residential mortgages.

"Jerry Hultin, Raymond McClendon, and James Nutter all bring years of financial management experience to the task of overseeing the important work of Freddie Mac," said the President. "I appreciate their willingness to serve."

NOTE: Biographies of the appointees were made available by the Office of the Press Secretary.

Nomination for Army, Navy, and Air Force Assistant Secretaries
December 10, 1993

The President today announced his intention to nominate Deborah P. Christie to be Assistant Secretary of the Navy for Financial Management; Rodney A. Coleman to be Assistant Secretary of the Air Force for Manpower, Reserve Affairs, Installations, and Environment; and Helen T. McCoy to be Assistant Secretary of the Army for Financial Management.

"Secretary Aspin is putting together strong management teams in every branch of the service," said the President. "These three nominees are prime examples of that effort."

NOTE: Biographies of the nominees were made available by the Office of the Press Secretary.

The President's Radio Address
December 11, 1993

Good morning. This morning I want to talk to you about crime and violence and what we can all do about it.

On Tuesday evening in Garden City, New York, a gunman shot and killed 5 rush-hour commuters on the Long Island Rail Road and wounded 20 others. On Thursday night in California, there was a memorial service for 12-year-old Polly Klaas. She'd been kidnaped from her bedroom 2 months ago. Her little body was found last Saturday.

These tragedies are part of the epidemic of violence that has left Americans insecure on our streets, in our schools, even in our homes. The crime rate has hit every American community from our oldest cities to our smallest towns to our newest suburbs. As a suburban California woman, the mother of a 10-year-old girl, said a few days ago, "There's no safe place to go. There's no place that's safe."

If our Nation is to find any meaning in these tragedies, we must join together to end this epidemic of violent crime and restore the fabric of civilized life in every community. There is now some hope amidst the horror because decent people are fighting back against crime.

Just before Thanksgiving I signed the Brady bill into law. It requires a 5-day waiting period before anyone can purchase a handgun so there can be a check of someone's age, mental health, and criminal record. The Brady bill became law because you, the American people, were stronger than the gun lobby.

On Thursday, together with Attorney General Janet Reno, FBI Director Louis Freeh, and Drug Policy Coordinator Lee Brown, I met with mayors and police chiefs from 35 cities. They told me they need more police on the streets, a ban on assault weapons, and action to keep drugs and guns away from vulnerable young people. And I intend to give the folks on the front lines the resources and the support they need to win the fight against crime.

I call upon Congress when they return in January to pass promptly a strong crime bill that will put 100,000 more police officers on the street, prohibit assault weapons, and provide fundings for more boot camps for first-time offenders.

I want to put 100,000 new police officers on the streets of our communities so they can walk their beats and work with neighborhood people. Putting more police on the streets will do more to reduce crime than anything else we can do.

The ban on assault weapons and the restrictions on semiautomatics are important because they'll stop criminal gangs from being better armed than the police. And these restrictions would have prevented the gunman on the Long Island Rail Road from having two 15-round clips of ammunition that enabled him to maim and kill so many people with such deadly speed. Assault weapons and 15-round clips have nothing to do with hunting or sports. They just let criminals shoot people more quickly. A recent study in one of our major cities showed that the increasing death rate among young people hit with gunshots was due almost entirely to the fact that the weapons themselves were more likely to be semiautomatic and therefore more deadly.

Boot camps have been endorsed by every major law enforcement organization in America. They give first offenders a second chance to learn some discipline. And they open more space in the prisons for hardened, violent criminals.

Now that Congress is home for the holidays, tell your Senators and Representatives to pass a strong crime bill so your family can be safer. You know, the new year begins just 3 weeks from today. I'd like to suggest a New Year's resolution for every Senator and every Representative: Let's pass the crime bill as soon as you return.

There's so much more we're doing and more we need to do. Under the leadership of Dr. Lee Brown, our Drug Policy Director and the father of community policing, we're strengthening enforcement and prevention. We're increasing the focus on hardcore users who fuel the crime and violence and the tragic waste of human lives.

Next summer in our national service program, AmeriCorps, thousands of young people will help with community policing, escort older people, and board up abandoned buildings so they can't be turned into crack houses. The young people in the Summer of Safety will be an inspiring example for Americans of all ages to work together to make our streets safer by acting on our finest values.

Let's face it, drugs and guns and violence fill a vacuum where the values of civilized life used to be. Work and family and community are the principles, the institutions, upon which the great majority of Americans are building their lives. We need to restore them and the sense of hope and discipline that will give every man and woman, every boy and girl the opportunity to become the people God intended them to be.

In recent weeks, I've spoken to leaders from the religious community and the entertainment community about the obligation we all share to fight violence with values. Last week I was proud to hear that the Inner City Broadcasting Corporation of New York, which owns five radio stations throughout the country, will no longer play songs that advocate violence or show contempt for women. And I understand that two stations in Los Angeles, KACE, owned by former Green Bay Packer Willie Davis, and KJLH, owned by Stevie Wonder, have also adopted this policy. Whether we're ministers or moviemakers, business people or broadcasters, teachers or parents, we can all set our sons and daughters on a better path in life so they can learn and love and lead decent and productive lives.

In this holiday season, as we rejoice in the love of our families and hold our children a little closer, we should also strengthen the bonds of community. We can make our neighborhoods and our nations places of shared responsibility, not random violence. The tragedies of this week remind us that there is no place to hide. The lessons of our history remind us that Americans can accomplish anything when we work together for a common purpose.

As we begin this season of celebration and rededication, let's remember the words of Theodore Roosevelt, a great President who was once a police commissioner too: "This country will not be a good place for any of us to live in, unless we make it a good place for all of us to live in."

Thanks for listening, and God bless you all.

NOTE: The President spoke at 10:06 a.m. from the Oval Office at the White House.

Statement on Organized Crime in the United States and Italy
December 12, 1993

In the ongoing struggle against the Mafia and other international crime syndicates, the United States renews its pledge of solidarity with and support for the Government and people of Italy. Organized crime is a scourge that has exacted a terrible toll in both our nations, a toll in lives ravaged by narcotics, brutalized by violence, destroyed by murder.

The Government of the United States, like the Government of Italy, is committed to fighting back, to reclaiming our streets, and to punishing those whose criminal conduct tears at the fabric of our societies and threatens the lives of our citizens. Accordingly, I am directing the Department of Justice and the Department of the Treasury to do all they can to strengthen the cooperation between American and Italian law enforcement.

As evidence of our resolve, Louis Freeh, Director of the Federal Bureau of Investigation, and Ronald K. Noble, Assistant Secretary for Enforcement in the Department of the Treasury, are in Italy this weekend for high-level meetings with Italian authorities to discuss new steps we can take to combat organized crime. Director Freeh and Assistant Secretary Noble are speaking today in Palermo on these joint law enforcement efforts. They will underscore the debt that we and all nations owe to Judge Giovanni Falcone, the courageous jurist murdered while leading the fight against the Italian Mafia, and to the scores of other brave Italians who put their lives on the line every day in the battle against organized crime.

The United States Government was pleased that we were able to assist Italy in the search for Judge Falcone's murderers. FBI laboratory experts facilitated the processing of DNA evidence at the crime scene in Sicily. Their help proved to be a crucial factor leading to the recent filing of charges against a large number of suspects.

Director Freeh is also carrying our message

of commitment and cooperation to Italian law enforcement officials. Their sustained and determined assistance has helped American law enforcement officials make real and tangible progress against the Mafia in the United States.

Letter to Congressional Leaders on Trade With Kyrgyzstan
December 9, 1993

Dear Mr. Speaker: (Dear Mr. President:)

I am writing to inform you of my intent to add Kyrgyzstan to the list of beneficiary developing countries under the Generalized System of Preferences (GSP). The GSP program offers duty-free access to the U.S. market and is authorized by the Trade Act of 1974.

I have carefully considered the criteria identified in sections 501 and 502 of the Trade Act of 1974. In light of these criteria, and particularly Kyrgyzstan's level of development and initiation of economic reforms, I have determined that it is appropriate to extend GSP benefits

to Kyrgyzstan.

This notice is submitted in accordance with section 502(a)(1) of the Trade Act of 1974.

Sincerely,

WILLIAM J. CLINTON

NOTE: Identical letters were sent to Thomas S. Foley, Speaker of the House of Representatives, and Albert Gore, Jr., President of the Senate. This letter was released by the Office of the Press Secretary on December 13. The related proclamation of December 9 is listed in Appendix D at the end of this volume.

Remarks at a Conference on Entitlements in Bryn Mawr, Pennsylvania
December 13, 1993

Thank you very much. Ladies and gentlemen, it's a pleasure for me to be here. I have looked forward to this conference with great anticipation for some time. I want to thank Congresswoman Margolies-Mezvinsky for getting this together and for inviting me here. I thank President McPherson and this wonderful institution for hosting us. I'm delighted that Speaker Foley and Congressman Penny are here from the Congress, and Senator Kerrey and Senator Wofford, your own Senator, are here to talk about these important issues. I want to also thank all the people who helped to put this conference together and to all the people in our administration who were invited and are here participating. We pretty much shut the town down in Washington today and just sort of came up here to Pennsylvania to talk about entitlements.

This is a very serious subject, worthy of the kind of thoughtful attention that it will be given today. I hope there will be a great national

discussion of the issues that we discuss today, and I hope that this will be the beginning of a debate that will carry through for the next several years.

I ran for President because I thought our Nation was going in the wrong direction economically and that our society was coming apart when it ought to be coming together. I wanted to work hard to create jobs and raise incomes for the vast mass of Americans and to try to bring our country back together by restoring the bonds of family and civility and community, without which we cannot hope to pass the American dream on to the students who are here at Bryn Mawr or the students who will come behind.

To do this, we must all, without regard to party or philosophy, at least agree to face the real problems of this country: 20 years of stagnant wages; 30 years of family decline, concentrated heavily among the poor; 12 years in which our debt has quadrupled, but investment in our future has lagged, leaving us with twin deficits, a massive budget deficit and a less publicized investment deficit, the gap between what we need to invest to compete and win and what we are receiving in terms of new skills and new opportunities. These things are linked. Creating jobs in growth requires that we bring down both the budget deficit and the investment deficit. High Government deficits keep interest rates high; they crowd out private demands for capital; they take more Government money to service the debt. All this tends to reduce investment, productivity, jobs, and ultimately, living standards.

The deficit increased so dramatically over the last 12 years because of things that happened on the spending side and on the revenue side. Defense increased dramatically until 1987, but it's been coming down since then quite sharply. However, the place of defense, as we'll see later, has been more than overtaken by an explosion in health care costs going up for the Government at roughly 3 times the rate of inflation. Interest on the debt is obviously increased more when interest rates were high than now, but always when the accumulated national debt goes up. And the larger number of poor people in our country has inevitably led to greater spending on programs that are targeted to the poor.

On the revenue side, the tax cut of 1981 wound up being roughly twice the percentage of our income that was originally proposed by President Reagan as the President and the Congress entered into a bidding war. And then in 1986 we adopted indexing, a principle that is clearly fair but reduced the rate of growth of Federal revenues by adjusting people's taxes downward as inflation pushed their incomes upward. And finally, a prolonged period of very slow growth has clearly reduced Government revenues and added to the deficit.

If you look at this chart, you will see that we inherited a deficit that was projected to be actually—when I took office, for the fiscal year that ended at the end of September—above $300 billion. And it was headed upward. The blue line here is what I found when I became President. It was clear that something had to be done. I asked the Congress to pass the largest deficit reduction package in history. It had $255 billion in real enforceable spending reductions from hundreds of programs. Now, let's make it clear what you mean.

When you hear the word spending "reductions" or "cuts" in Washington terms, it can mean two things. One is a reduction in the rate of increase in Government spending from the previous 5-year budget, which is still an increase in spending but not as much as it would have been had the new reduction not taken place. The second thing it might mean is what you mean when you say "cut," which is you spend less than you did before you used the word. [*Laughter*] And it is important to know which one you're talking about. However, both are good in terms of reducing the deficit over a 5-year period. We not only reduced the rate of increase but actually adopted hundreds of cuts this year. The budget year that started on October 1st has less spending than the previous year in 342 separate accounts of the Federal budget. Adjusted for inflation, this means a discretionary spending cut of 12 percent over the next 5 years, more than was done under the previous two administrations. If this continues, according to the Wall Street Journal, then by 1998, discretionary spending—that is the nonentitlement spending and discounting interest on the debt, the things that we make decisions on every year—will be less than 7 percent of our annual income, about half the level it was in the 1960's.

In addition to the discretionary spending cuts, our budget did reduce entitlements, making reductions in agricultural subsidies, asking upper income recipients of Social Security to pay more tax on their income, lowering reimbursements to Medicare providers, making other adjustments in Medicaid and in veterans' benefits. Now, all these cuts are already on the books. We are also cutting, with the help of the Vice President's National Performance Review, over 250,000 positions from the Federal payrolls, largely by attrition and early retirement over the next 5 years. We're finally attempting to reform the system in ways that will permit us to save billions of more dollars in discretionary spending through reform of personnel budgeting and, most importantly, procurement systems, if the Congress will authorize all three of those systematic reforms.

We also passed some taxes: a modest 4.3 cents-a-gallon gas tax, which so far has been barely felt because we have the lowest price in oil in many, many years, so the price of gasoline has actually dropped since the gas tax was put on. We also asked the top 1.2 percent of Americans to pay higher income taxes because their incomes went up the most, and their taxes dropped the most in the previous 12 years. The corporate income tax on corporations with incomes above $10 million a year was raised. Middle class families will pay slightly less taxes because, again, of the adjustments for inflation. And taxes were cut for 15 million families who worked for very modest wages as a dramatic incentive to get them to continue to choose work over welfare.

When Congresswoman Mezvinsky and her colleagues voted for this economic plan, they voted for your economic future, for lower deficits, higher growth, and for better jobs. They did vote to cut spending. They did not vote to raise taxes on the middle class. And frankly, the kinds of radio ads that have been—this is the only political thing I'm going to say today—but the kind of radio ads that have been run against her in this district do not serve the public interest because they do not tell the truth. If somebody wants to say that we should not have raised income taxes on the top 1.2 percent of the American people, let them advertise that on the radio. If someone wants to say that the corporate income taxes above $10 million a year in income should not have been raised, let them advertise that on the radio. If someone wants to say that the gas tax was unfair, let them advertise that on the radio. But do not try to tell the American people there were no budget cuts and they paid all the tax increases, because that is simply not true. And we have a lot of work to do in this country and a lot of honest disagreements to have; we need not expend our energy on other things.

And if you don't believe that, read the front page of the Wall Street Journal this morning. That is hardly the house organ of my administration. [*Laughter*] Read the front page of the Wall Street Journal this morning talking about the unprecedented cuts that this budget made. It does not do anybody any good to continue to assert things about that economic plan that are not true. The markets had it figured out. That's why interest rates are down and investment is up. That's why inflation is down and more jobs have come into this economy in the last 10 months than in the previous 4 years. The markets figured it out. All the smoke and mirrors and radio ads in the world couldn't confuse the people that had to make investment decisions and read the fine print.

That's the good news. Now let's talk about the continuing problems, the real problems. The economic plan which the Congress adopted represents the red line. That's how much less the deficit will be. And the aggregate amount between these two lines is how much less our total debt will be by 1998. The yellow line represents where we can go, by conservative estimates, if the health care plan is adopted. You still have an operating deficit, and the national debt will still increase by this amount, but not by that amount.

So we are clearly better off with the economic plan. We will have to make further cuts, by the way, to meet this red line. We're not done with that. We will be better off still if we do something about health care—I'll say more about that in a minute—but there is still more to be done. The debt of this country now is over $4 billion. That means our accumulated debt is more than two-thirds our annual income. It is important that the debt, as a percentage of our annual income, go down. It is way too high, much higher than it has been outside of wartime. It is important that the annual deficit, as a percentage of our income, go down. It will go down under this plan, but we can do more to try to reduce the aggregate debt and the deficit as a percentage of our income. Both of them are too high.

Now, let's look at the next chart here. I think you all have it out in the audience. This chart just basically shows where your money goes. When you pay Federal taxes or when the Government, on your behalf, borrows money, in debt, we spend 47.4 percent in entitlements—that is what we're here to talk about today—about 21 percent on defense, it's going down, as you'll see in a minute; about 18 percent on nondefense discretionary, which is being held constant; and about 14 percent in interest on the national debt.

Let's look at the next chart now. This chart gives you an idea of which spending categories are headed in which direction. Average annual real growth—now, I want to tell you what this means. I haven't lived in Washington very long so I still use ordinary meanings for words. So I'm not very good—[*laughter*] When you see "real" on a Government chart, that means adjusted for inflation. You'll never find that in a dictionary, but that is what it means. In other words, these are the numbers adjusted for inflation at a projected inflation growth of more or less 3½ percent a year. If you look at that, you see defense is going down. Frankly, we're reducing it as much as I think we responsibly can and, in fact, more than we responsibly can unless Congress will pass the procurement reform so the Defense Department can buy what it needs for our national defense at more efficient prices. But I hope that will happen. Other entitlements—we'll come to that in a minute, what those other entitlements are—they're also going down relative to inflation. That is basically the entitlements for the poor and the veterans' benefits and agriculture benefits.

Nondefense discretionary is a little under zero, as you see. That's all the investments for education, for training, for technology, for defense conversion, for you-name-it, anything for infrastructure, for roads, anything we spend money on that we have an option not to spend money on that—we'll come back to that—is going down relative to inflation. If there were no inflation numbers here, it would actually be just a tiny bit above the line, but it is functionally zero. For all practical purposes, if I want to increase the amount of money, for example, we spend on Head Start in Pennsylvania by a million dollars, we have to cut something else by a million dollars. We are not increasing the aggregate amount of this kind of discretionary spending. Net interests will go up, and again, this is adjusted for inflation, so it is continuing to rise because the amount of the debt is continuing to rise.

Social Security will go up, again, adjusted for inflation. This is the population increase, effectively, in Social Security. There aren't new benefits being added, so there will be a couple of percent growth in population between now and 1998. So it will go up by the amount of increasing numbers of people on Social Security.

And look what happens to health entitlement. It's going up more than twice as much as Social Security, more than 3 times as much as net interest, and everything else is going down. Now that's what's happening. Let's go on to the next chart.

As the chart shows here, this is the new revenues we're getting in this year. Now, the new revenues include the tax increases that we just talked about. They're about 40 percent of that revenue growth. The rest of it's just ordinary increases in tax revenues to the Government coming from increasing employment or increasing incomes. So every year we get some revenue

growth. This revenue chart is about 60 percent ordinary revenue growth, 40 percent new taxes. As you can see, the whole thing goes to deficit reduction, interest increases, and entitlement increases. That's where the money went.

Eighty percent of the new revenues, including taxes and revenue growth, went to deficit reduction and interest increases; 20 percent of it went to entitlement increases. As you can see, that does not leave a great deal of room for any kind of future investments. This is something that presumably both Senator Kerrey and Congressman Penny will talk about today. But there is, I think it's fair to say, a broad consensus in the Congress among Republicans and Democrats, among liberals and conservatives, that there are some things on which we are not spending enough money to get us to the 21st century. We have put ourselves in a box after the last—trying to work our way out of this deficit business so that we do not have the flexibility to make those kind of growth-oriented investments in the public sector. That is a dilemma. So we have two continuing dilemmas, if you will: one, we've still got a deficit and a debt problem; two, there are things which literally over 80 percent of the Congress, both parties, would agree we should invest more in that we simply cannot invest more in because of the problem we have with the budget. Could we go on now to the next chart? Let's go on to the next chart.

Now, this gives you a picture of entitlement spending. And I know Alice Rivlin talked about this a little before, and she knows a lot more about it than I ever will, but I think it's worth going back over because this is an entitlements conference. So it's worth focusing on what an entitlement is and, when you hear people use that term, what they are.

So look at this. These entitlement programs are programs that provide benefits for people that have certain characteristics. People who meet the test of eligibility for the program get it, notwithstanding some previously budgeted amount for that program. That's why they're called entitlements. For example, someone who has paid into the Social Security Trust Fund along with his or her employer who is 65 becomes entitled to Social Security. You just go to the Social Security office with the documents that prove you're eligible, and you're going to get the check no matter how many other people qualify for Social Security. Since it's hard to know in advance exactly how many people will apply for benefits, Congress doesn't set aside a specific amount of money as it does for the discretionary spending programs. Instead, it simply directs to Treasury to make payments to everybody who applies and qualifies for the benefits under the laws.

There are two main kinds of entitlements. And you can just see by looking up here what they are. They are the contributory entitlements, that is, you're entitled to something because you paid into it. It's contract oriented. Social Security is a contributory entitlement. Medicare is a contributory entitlement. Federal retirement is a contributory entitlement. You did the work; you put the money aside; you get it back.

Then there are the entitlements for those in need or entitlements that are in a special category because you can't predict how much is going to be needed every year. The entitlements for those in need would include AFDC, supplemental security income, the Medicaid program, medical care for the poor. Agriculture is in a separate category. It has been treated as an entitlement partly because it's so caught up in the global economy, it's impossible to predict from year to year how much of the support subsidies will be needed.

Now, the contributory retirements are sometimes called middle class entitlements because they benefit everybody, the middle class or, Mr. Peterson will tell you in a few minutes, the upper middle class or the wealthy. If you pay in, you get it back plus a cost of living increase. Now, the poor people's entitlement, I said, are mostly in the category of like AFDC and food stamps and Medicaid. But let me show you something about these entitlements, because most people, I think, don't know this: Social Security is 43 percent of the total; Medicare is 18 percent; Medicaid is 11 percent; Federal retirement is 8 percent; unemployment is 5 percent, obviously it goes up or down, depending on what the unemployment rate is and how long people are unemployed; food stamps are 4 percent; "other" is 11 percent. In the other, you have agriculture, veterans, supplemental security income, which is for lower income elderly people, and AFDC. The welfare program of this 11 percent is 2 percent. The average monthly welfare benefit in America is actually lower today, adjusted for inflation, than it was 20 years ago. The program is more expensive because there are more poor people. But I think it's

quite interesting to point that out. Most people are surprised to know that the welfare budget is about 2 percent of the entitlements or about 1 percent of the overall Federal budget.

Now, the entitlement programs for the needy, as you can see, make up about 12 percent of the whole budget or about a quarter of the entitlement spending. The biggest entitlements are Social Security and Medicare. They are about 61 percent of the total. When you add Federal civilian retirement and military retirement, you've got over two-thirds of the entitlements there.

Now, I think it's important to point out, just in passing, that behind every one of these entitlements there's a person. That's why it's so controversial when they're debated in Congress. It's not just organized interest groups. There are people who believe they are literally entitled to receive something back that they paid into. It is the middle class entitlements, that have united us and brought us together, that also have the strongest constituencies and provoke the biggest controversies when we get into dealing with this. And these programs are also very important in human terms.

I just might mention, too, if you look at Medicare, before Medicare, there was a good chance that Americans, when they got older, would need charity care, would simply do without health care. Today nearly 34 million people go to see a doctor or get medical care because of the Medicare program. Social Security has changed, literally, what it means to be old. In the beginning of 1985, for the first time in our history, the percentage of our elderly people who were above the poverty line was better than the percentage of the population as a whole. In other words, the poverty rate for the elderly was lower than the poverty rate of the general population.

It is very difficult to say that this was a bad thing. That was, I argue, a good thing. We should not view this whole program, in other words, as welfare. It is not a welfare program. Does that mean that there should be no changes in it? No, it just means that we should be very sensitive about the fact that this is something that has worked. Because of these programs, we are a healthier people. We are a more unified country. We treat our elderly with greater dignity by having allowed them to earn a decent retirement and to maintain a middle class standard of living, independent of whatever their children are required to do and to make them more independent over the long run. This is a huge deal in a country where the fastest growing group of people, in percentage terms, are people over 80 years of age. This is a big deal.

Now, I recommended exposing more of the incomes of the top 10 or 12 percent of Social Security recipients, somewhere in that range, to taxation, and Congress adopted a modified version of that plan. That was an entitlements move. I thought it was an appropriate thing to do because a lot of people in upper income levels, by definition, have other sources of income, too, and will get back what they paid into Social Security plus reasonable interest growth in a reasonably short period of time. So I thought it was fair to do that.

We recommended upper income people pay more for Medicare benefits. I think that is reasonable to do because the Medicare payment itself only covers a small percentage of the total cost of Medicare. Where I think we should draw the line, however, is in trying to have happen to the elderly middle class what is happening to the nonelderly middle class. All over the world today, and certainly in all the advanced countries of the world, the middle class is under assault. Earnings inequality has increased in the last 12 years. It is becoming very difficult for working people to sustain a middle class way of life. We are going to have to all change. We've got to change our Government policies. People are going to have to acquire much higher levels of skill and be committed to training for a lifetime. There are a lot of things that have to be done. But the general policy point, I think, is valid. We do not want to deal with a problem like the deficit which is aggravated because middle class people's incomes have stagnated by having the same sort of income stagnation for the middle class elderly.

So I think there are things we can do to deal with this. They will be discussed later. We did some things to deal with the entitlements in the last budget. But let us not say that it was a bad thing to dramatically reduce poverty among elderly people or that it is a bad thing for our consumer economy to maintain a large number of middle class people in their retirement years. That means that we have to have honest, specific, and clear discussions of this, as unencumbered as possible by these sort of rhetorical bombs flying in the air from the left and the right, just talking it through and listen-

ing to each other and asking ourselves: What will be the practical impact of proposed change A, B, or C, and will we all be more secure? Will our children and our grandchildren be better off? Will this help to stabilize and increase the middle class ballast of our society? And I think we are on the verge perhaps of having that discussion in no small measure because of this kind of conference.

Now, let's go on, and let's look at what I think the real problem in the entitlements is, is clearly the danger signal for the long run. Let's look at the next chart. As you can see, 20 years ago, health spending and entitlements, Medicare and Medicaid, 13 percent of the total; 1983, 19 percent of the total; 1993, 30 percent of the total; 2003, 43 percent of the total. Keep in mind—and this is with the number of elderly people going up like crazy, so the population of people drawing Social Security is going way up, right? And still, look at that. So clearly, that is the portion of Government spending that is out of control. That is the portion of entitlement spending that is out of control. Now let me just illustrate it by a couple more charts real quickly.

Let's go to the next one. Nondefense discretionary outlays are going down as a percent of our income. Social Security outlays as a percentage of our income is solid, stable here. It could go up some in the next century, is projected to, when all the baby boomers go in. I heard Ms. Rivlin refer to that as the President's generation. I am the oldest of the baby boomers. But still, you see, it's stable as a percentage of the gross national product. And the Congress, in 1983, after the bipartisan commission on Social Security made recommendations for fixing Social Security, attempted to keep this number stable by gradually raising the retirement from 65 to 67, by about a month a year over a prolonged period of time starting just in the next century.

Now let's go on to the last one. This chart shows you that unlike Social Security and discretionary spending, medical spending is going up like a rocket. Medicare and Medicaid have tripled since 1982. Medicare and Medicaid will soon cost more than Social Security. And next year for the first time—in large measure because Medicaid is a State-Federal matching program, so that every State has to put in money along with the Federal Government—next year, for the first time, States will spend more money on health care than education. And since I supported this—I see other present and former Governors around this table. In the 1980's we said to the National Government, "You've got a problem with the deficit. We'll spend more on education; you do what you have to do to deal with your other problems." This is a very serious danger signal. If you want the States to spend more educating people, getting children to the point where they can compete, training the work force—to have the States all of a sudden spending more on health care than education is a very serious danger signal for the distribution of responsibilities between the State and the Federal Government.

Now, we have some options. If we want to control Medicare and Medicaid spending, basically we have some options. And to be fair, again I want to say, during the 1980's under the Reagan and Bush administration, the two administrations and the United States Congress did try to cooperate on several things to control Medicare and Medicaid spending. They took total pricing controls away from hospitals and doctors. They tried to do a number of things. But what happened? If you control the price of a given product in this environment, what happens? Providers can provide more products, I mean, more of the same product, right? You increase the volume if you lower the price, and the money still goes up. That's one problem.

Secondly, poverty increased in the eighties and is continuing to increase among the poor, both the idle and the working poor, and that drives the Medicaid budget up. So controlling unit prices didn't work. The other thing you could argue that we could do is to try to control the categories within Medicare and Medicaid, basically, just spend less. In other words, even though they're entitlements, just say we are going to spend less on certain categories by both controlling volume and price. Is there a problem with that? Yes there is. What is it? Any doctor or hospital will tell you that there has been a lot of cost shifting in this health care system, and it's one of the causes of rising prices and inefficiency. Cost shifting largely occurs in two ways: when hospitals have to care for people who don't have any insurance or when they provide Government funded health care at less than their cost of providing the service, they shift the cost onto the private sector.

So we could bring this deficit down, we could do this—I want to—let's 'fess up, we could do this. We could just cut how much we're going to spend on Medicare and Medicaid, even though it's an entitlement, in terms of price per unit and volume. We can just take 'er down. But if we do that, what will happen? Those costs will be shifted by the health care providers to the people who already are providing insurance with the impact that it will be a hidden tax increase on businesses and on employees. Employees will probably see it in not getting pay raises they otherwise would have gotten. Businesses will see it in spending more on health insurance premiums and having less to reinvest in the business or to take in profits. I don't think it is a fair thing to do. That is why our administration has argued that if you really want to solve this problem, you have to go back and have comprehensive health care reform.

This is the only country in the world that doesn't find a way to solve that issue—the only advanced nation, that is, that doesn't give basic health care to all its citizens within a framework that controls costs in the public and private sector. We're spending 14.5 percent of our income on health care. Nobody else is over 10; Germany and Japan are at 9. The health outcomes of other countries are roughly similar to ours. We can't get down to where they are because we spend more on technology and more on basically costly treatments than other countries do and more on medical research. And that's fine. And we can't get down to where they do because we have more violence and higher rates of AIDS and other very expensive diseases than other countries. But we could do better. And unless we do better in an overall way, in my judgment, we are going to be in trouble.

Now, we had a nonpartisan analysis by the respected firm of Lewin-VHI last week about our health care plan. This company does research on the economics of health care for businesses, unions, consumer groups. It includes people who served in the Reagan and Bush administrations as budget and health officials. They say that our plan will reduce the deficit. We think it will reduce it even more than they will. I won't get into the details of that today. We're here to talk about entitlements. The point I want to make is I believe you don't get entitlement control, you don't get ultimate deficit control unless you do something about Medicare and Medicaid. I believe you don't get that done just by cutting Medicare and Medicaid unless you want to hurt the private sector. Therefore, I think we have to have some sort of health reform. That's what I believe. You have to decide if you believe that, but I think it's important.

Let me just close with this. This is the lead editorial in this morning's Washington Post. It says—on the entitlements mess—and it says as follows: "Nor have all the entitlements been badly behaved in recent years in terms of costs. The health care programs are the budget busters. By contrast Social Security costs have risen in stately fashion with population and inflation. And the costs of all the other entitlements taken together, including those that support the poor, has declined in real terms." Remember what "real" means in Washington, less than the rate of inflation. "The real Federal budget problem"—that's the normal word "real"; here they mean real like you do—"the real Federal budget problem isn't entitlements, it's health care."

So I say to you we can talk about these other entitlements, and we should. As we talk about them, let us not make our middle class squeeze problem worse than it is already. That's one of the profound problems that is driving this country. One of the reasons that Senator Wofford is in the Senate today is because of the anxieties of middle class workers in Pennsylvania.

Let us continue to work on this deficit. Let us realize the deficit is too big and the debt is much too large as a percentage of our gross national product. Let us realize that there are two problems with it. One is the deficit, and the other is we aren't investing enough. But on the entitlements issue, I would argue the real culprit is health care costs, and we can only address it if we have comprehensive health care reform.

And let me close by saying one more time, if Marge Mezvinsky hadn't voted for that budget, we wouldn't be here celebrating economic progress or talking about entitlements. We'd still be back in Washington throwing mudballs at each other. And I respect her for that, and I'm glad to be here today.

NOTE: The President spoke at 10:45 a.m. at Bryn Mawr College. In his remarks, he referred to Mary Patterson McPherson, president of the college; Alice M. Rivlin, Deputy Director of the Office of Management and Budget; and Peter G. Peterson, former Secretary of Commerce and president of the Concord Coalition.

Remarks on the Russian Elections and an Exchange With Reporters in Bryn Mawr
December 13, 1993

The President. I'd like to, first of all, congratulate the Russian people on having their first parliamentary election—it was a clear democratic exercise throughout the country—and to say how very pleased I am that the new constitution was adopted because this now lays a foundation for a long-term—a legitimacy for democracy and for the expression of popular will that will not be just solely dependent upon the occasional election for President. So I think that is also very, very good.

In terms of the results of the parliamentary elections themselves, I am informed by our people there that we don't yet really know what the results are going to be because a lot of the votes and a lot of the major areas have not been counted yet and it's not clear what the final distribution will be.

I will say this, I'm not particularly surprised by the showing of the ultranationalist party, because the Russian people have suffered a lot in the last few years. And you saw the same sort of thing happening in Poland, where there had been a lot of economic adversity. It's hard for people to go through these changes and not have a certain percentage of them vote for candidates which articulate protests most forcefully. So I wasn't particularly surprised.

I do think that it will be possible for a majority of people who favor democracy and don't favor a dramatic change of course in foreign policy for Russia to put together a coalition in the Parliament who can work with the President and go forward. So I'm quite hopeful.

But I think in any country where ordinary people are having a hard time you're going to have some significant protest vote, including the United States.

Russia

Q. Mr. President, do you anticipate any change in your policy, American policy toward Russia in terms of aid, in terms of galvanizing the allies to somehow address this protest movement and try to diffuse it?

The President. Well, let me answer you this way. First of all, we need to wait in terms of— I anticipate no change in my policy in general terms towards Russia. I think we ought to wait and see how the votes come in, what the distribution of seats in the Parliament will be and how it all shakes out. It will be quite some time before you have a real feel for what's going to happen.

But I do think that the vote in Poland and this vote send a signal about how difficult it is to convert from that old Communist system to a market economy at a time of global recession, when the ability of any other nation or group of nations to give a big infusion of capital to provide temporary security is not there. If you look even in East Germany in the recent votes, where they've gotten a massive amount of money from West Germany, still just the transition process is extremely painful. And keep in mind all these changes, these economic and political changes, are playing out in the former Soviet Union and in Eastern Europe, the former Warsaw Pact countries, at a time of global recession when there is deep frustration and alienation among middle class voters in the wealthiest countries.

So this should not be too surprising. I think what it means is that we have to think through our approach to these nations and remember that there has to be a lot of sensitivity to the ability of ordinary working people to navigate their way through all these tough changes and at least be able to imagine how they're going to come out on top at the end. And I think that there will be a little more sensitivity to that, hopefully not just in the United States and Europe and Japan but also in the international organizations themselves.

Multilateral Trade Negotiations

Q. One of the things that people have been looking for is a way of breaking through the global recession or the GATT talks. What is your sense of where that stands now? Have they cleared away enough barriers to get an agreement by Wednesday, or are they still hung up on the audiovisual——

The President. Well, I've not received a final report today. As you know, I did quite a bit of work on it yesterday. I had a talk with Prime Minister Balladur and Prime Minister Major and Chancellor Kohl, and our folks, they're all working very hard. And the United States, I think, has certainly bent over backwards on all the issues outstanding that required us to show some flexibility. We have shown some, including in the audiovisual area and certainly in the agricultural area and some other areas.

I think it would give a big boost of confidence if we could get it done, but it's important that it be a good agreement. And I'm hopeful, but I don't know much more than I did yesterday afternoon real late. I'm hopeful, but I can't say for sure.

Russia

Q. Will the election affect, at all, your scheduled trip to Russia next month? For example, will you meet with Mr. Zhirinovsky during your visit to Moscow?

The President. I've made no decisions. I haven't even had a chance to talk about that. I had always assumed that when I went there after the parliamentary election that there would be some opportunity for me to relate to the parliamentarians as well as to the President. That's something we had always assumed. But in terms of who and how and what the specifics are, there have been absolutely no discussions of that. They haven't had time yet. They've just had the election.

Thank you.

NOTE: The President spoke at 2:21 p.m. at Bryn Mawr College. During the exchange, a reporter referred to Vladimir Zhirinovsky, leader of the Liberal Democratic Party in Russia.

Message to President Arpad Goncz of Hungary on the Death of Prime Minister Jozsef Antall
December 13, 1993

Dear Mr. President:

Please accept and convey to the Hungarian people my sincere condolences on the sad occasion of Prime Minister Antall's death. The Prime Minister's passing is a loss not only for Hungary but also for democratic nations around the world.

As Hungary's first post-Communist Prime Minister, Mr. Antall will be remembered for his strong leadership and commitment to freedom during these historic times. He was a friend to the United States and an active partner in the international effort to deepen and secure democracy, stability and economic reform in Central and Eastern Europe. His loss will be greatly felt in Europe and here in the United States.

Our thoughts and prayers are with Prime Minister Antall's family and the people of Hungary at this difficult time.

Sincerely,

WILLIAM J. CLINTON

NOTE: An original was not available for verification of the content of this message.

Remarks at a Fundraiser for Senator Daniel Patrick Moynihan in New York City
December 13, 1993

Thank you. Thank you very much, Senator Moynihan and Liz.

You know, before I met Pat Moynihan, I actually thought I knew something about government. Now I just feel like I'm getting a grade every time I talk in front of him. [*Laughter*] It's not always a good one.

I am honored to be here with Liz and with Pat, honored by the partnership that they have kept and the faith they have kept with the American people as well as with their own family for 40 years, deeply honored to have the chance to serve as your President while Senator Moynihan is the chairman of that committee which makes a quorum if he's there and I, his messenger, are there—I'm his messenger, I think. [*Laughter*]

A few months ago, when the fate of our economic plan was hanging in the balance and we didn't have a vote to spare, there were people in Washington who said, and I quote, "The very survival of this President now rests squarely on the shoulders of Daniel Patrick Moynihan, chairman of the Senate Finance Committee." Thank God he didn't shake me off. [*Laughter*] We made it here tonight.

And tonight, if this were a normal time, I would come and talk about the things that we often talk about: about the new GATT round that Senator Moynihan mentioned, about the fact that the economic program we passed which was so controversial has now been largely shorn of its false myths, the front page of the Wall Street Journal today saying that they said there were no spending cuts in it, but guess what? They cut a lot of spending, they cut a lot of entitlements, they cut and cut and cut. That's the Wall Street Journal, hardly the house organ of my administration—[*laughter*]—saying that. And of course, the markets have largely spoken with lower interest rates and inflation and higher rates of investments and a 19-year low in late home mortgage payments, millions of Americans refinancing their homes, more jobs in the private sector in 10 months than in the previous 4 years. I'd like to talk all about that. I do believe that by and large our country is going back in the right direction economically. And with all of our difficulties, and Lord knows they're plenty, we are now the envy of the other advanced industrial countries. In Europe and Japan they're having far worse troubles than we are at this moment. Not that I wish that on them; if they were doing better we would be, too.

I'd like to talk about how the image I had of Senator Moynihan—and even after working with him a little bit, but before I became President—was different than reality, something I'm very sympathetic with. You know, I thought, "Well, Moynihan has got an IQ of 300; he can't be bothered with the dirty details of practical politics. But if I hang around long enough I'll get four or five things that we can move the world with." And then he started wearing me out about Penn Station and New York's Medicaid match rate, and Lord knows, there is nobody who works me worse in an old-fashioned way for his constituents than Daniel Patrick Moynihan and does a better job of it. So I could give a speech about that, you know. But tonight we have to talk about what Mr. Chairman mentioned. The Washington Monthly once described Pat Moynihan's career as one long and exhilarating assault on conventional wisdom. He told us more than a decade ago what would happen if we kept increasing spending and cutting revenues at the same time. And sure enough, we quadrupled our debt in 12 years.

A decade before its collapse, Senator Moynihan said the Soviet Union was doomed. He also wrote a very powerful prediction and later turned it into a book called "Pandemonium," about what would happen when you strip the veneer of communism off those troubled lands.

But long before I ever ran for President on my platform of opportunity and personal responsibility and renewing the bonds of community in this country, he had been warning us, as you heard tonight, reading from that stirring article now 28 years old, which could have been written last week. He has been for a generation the champion of the American family, not one of those politicians who use slogans like "family values" to divide us but who really tried to live out those values and to find ways to vote for programs and push ideas and change actions that would help ordinary people in this State and this Nation to keep their own families together and to raise their children and to be rewarded if they worked hard and played by the rules.

I have read over and over and over again that wonderful passage which Senator Moynihan quoted to you tonight. I can tell you what most of you already know. One of the things that impresses me about it, coming as I do from the kind of family I come from, is that that passage was written 28 years ago not by a trust fund baby telling people on food stamps how to live but by a son of Hell's Kitchen, a onetime longshoreman, a person who knows what it means to see chaos and difficulty and adversity firsthand.

Here's what I think we're up against today. I believe that in every traditional way I could do a good job as your President, and the Congress could continue to support me. And notwithstanding the press reports to the contrary, it has now apparently been established that they have supported me more faithfully than they have any President in his first year in 40 years, since they've been keeping these statistics. I'm very grateful for that. We can work on increasing the growth rate. We can work on bringing the deficit down. We can work on rebuilding the training systems of our country. We can pass a new health care program, and Lord knows we need to. We can do these things. But unless, unless we face the fact that year in and year out we are losing an enormous percentage of our people to our common future and that they, in turn, are making the rest of us much more miserable and less free and less hopeful in our own lives, this country will not become what it ought to be.

I look into these places that break our collective heart, and I see the collapse of economic opportunity, the collapse of families, and the loss of supporting community institutions that used to bind up the wounds of so many individual kids in trouble in every community that had them when I was a boy. I wonder which came first. I don't think it's relevant anymore to know what was the chicken and what was the egg. I do know that back in April Senator Moynihan said that, in talking about the differences here between 1993 and 50 years before, he said, and I quote, "In 1943 the illegitimacy rate in New York City was 3 percent. Last year it was 45 percent—a lot of poor people here in 1943."

When Pat Moynihan wrote the article that he just quoted from a few moments ago, the illegitimacy rate among white Americans was 1 in 20, among African-Americans, was 1 in 5. Since that time, in 28 years, the rate among black Americans has tripled, the rate among white Americans has quadrupled, most all of it concentrated among people who are very poor, not very well educated, and in what I have come to call an increasingly outer class, estranged from the rest of us. If we keep going at this rate, within a decade more than half the children born in this country will not be born into a family where there is or has been a marriage.

Now, he's been talking about this for 28 years. What else has happened in 28 years? Well, for 20 years, because of the pressures of the global economy and because of our inadequate response to them, the wages of middle class Americans have more or less been stagnant. But every year there are more and more people who are poor, people who are not working, and people who are working and still poor. And that's what I meant when I said, you take the most troubled neighborhoods in this country, most people who live in them work hard for a living, don't break the law, doing the best they can, and in some ways, are the real heroes in this country because most of them are working hard and still just barely getting by. And they deserve our honor and our respect.

But the economic opportunities that once beckoned people to our cities have long gone for many middle class people who didn't have a lot of education. When you lose both family and work, the two things that most of us organize our lives around, you create a vacuum in any society. And, as with any other vacuum, nature abhors it; it will be filled. People cannot live in total chaos. Some alternative organizations will take root. And what has happened in our country is that in places which we have permitted to be without family and work, where the community organizations have folded up tent and left behind them, where very often only the churches are there standing alone against the deluge, and the people in the social services overpowered, and the police outmanned, what happens is that gangs take root as a form of social organization and drugs take root not just as a form of self-destruction but as an economic endeavor. And then, as an enforcement mechanism, violence comes along in even greater amounts.

And now, because we have permitted, by a flight of, in my view, collective insanity, even teenagers to be better armed than police in most of our big cities, you see a dramatic increase just in the last decade in the death rate of young people who are shot. Why is that? Because they're more likely to be shot by assault weapons like the kind that was used on the Long Island Rail Road a few days ago. A study came out right after that horrible incident,

chronicling one of our biggest cities in the Middle West, saying that 100 percent of the increase in the death rate from gunshot wounds among teenage boys was due to the use of assault weapons with rapid cartridges, so they had more bullets in their bodies. It wasn't very complicated.

So I would argue to you we have, first of all, seen a vacuum develop. It happened over a generation, and anybody that tells you it can be turned around with a lot of words or even good actions in a moment is wrong. There are good people out there now standing against the tide, doing their best. I call to your attention the article on the cover of the New York Times Sunday Magazine yesterday about that brave policeman. Gosh, I'd like to meet that guy. If you haven't read it, you ought to go read it, talking about how one person still can make a difference in restoring some sanity and safety and reinforcing values in people's lives.

And so we come, those of us who are in Washington running your business, Senator Conrad and Senator Lautenberg, Chairman Moynihan and I, we come to work every day knowing that we almost have two tasks. We've got these rational challenges: get the deficit down, get investment up, train the work force better, expand trade, do things that will work. And for most of us it will really work. But knowing that underneath that there is this erosion taking place where a lot of people are just being lost, to themselves and to the rest of us. Those kids that were singing to us up there tonight, they sang "God Bless America," they sang the national anthem, and they deserve for it to be true. They deserve for it to be true.

I don't want to get into a lot of programs tonight. We got the Brady bill done. We've got the crime bill coming up. It really does make a difference how many police are on the street if they are well trained. We have to do more on the drug front. We have to deal with health care, in part because this crime and violence is a public health problem. But I don't want to talk so much about programs. It is just to ask you to leave here tonight, if you are really going to give your money to reelect this man, which you must do because he is a national treasure, you should leave here tonight determined to do what you can to create a political constituency to make it possible for him to make the ideas that have been popping in his mind for a generation real in the lives of our people.

In other words, what I'm asking you to do

tonight is you don't have to agree that whatever we decide to do on the assault weapons ban is right around the edges, or whatever. But you should leave here tonight far more intolerant than you came here of some of the conditions which obtain in this country. Last winter Senator Moynihan wrote, and I quote, "We have been redefining deviancy so as to exempt much conduct previously stigmatized." We have been, quote, to use his phrase, "defining deviancy down," below the threshold of acceptability. Then he said in more blunt language, "We're getting used to a lot of behavior that is not good for us."

Now, just today there was a Justice Department study that says 20 percent of the students surveyed in certain schools in high crime areas carried guns to school on a regular basis, and 83 percent of juvenile offenders have used or carried guns prior to their arrest. That is just one example. We tolerate all kinds of things nobody else would put up with. Why, if we are so smart, would we tolerate, for example, having the only advanced country in the world with a health care system that spends 40 percent more than everybody else and covers fewer people and instead of spending it on pharmaceuticals or doctors or nurses, spends more and more of it on paperwork than anybody else? Why would we do that? Why do we put up with that? Why aren't we free enough to know that we have got to invest in policies that will promote work over welfare and family over solitude and community over division? We know better than this. And we have just become so callous because, basically, this country has worked pretty well for the rest of us. But I'm telling you, it's coming back on the rest of us.

Tonight before I came down here, I called and asked if those three men who had the guts to go subdue the man who did the shooting on the Long Island Rail Road would come up and see me before I came down to the dinner. I just wanted to see them and talk to them and ask them how they were feeling and figure out, why did these guys do this, take responsibility? Suppose the guy had gotten the clip in the gun quicker. You know, it looks now like they couldn't have been hurt. Do you think they knew that then? In the flash of an eye were they all that certain that they couldn't have been shot? I don't think so. They did something. They took responsibility. And they came from fine families. One has four children; one has three

children; the other, a younger man, brought his parents and his brother and sister. They had a lot to lose. They acted. They took responsibility. They saved lives. We ought to be proud of them.

So they started talking about how each one of them made the decision, almost simultaneously and not together, to do this. And finally they just knew it was insane not to act. And so they took some chance, and they acted. And all three of them said to me, as they looked around at their families, that they now realized how fragile this country was and how no one was safe from violence but how they all had to have an interest in what happened to everybody else. And they volunteered; they said, "You know, Mr. President, if you're going to really try to do something about crime and violence, you think there's something we can do, call us. We'd like to help." In the moment of that encounter they all of a sudden realized that by a simple act of heroism, they had also come to an understanding which now imposed responsibilities on them they didn't feel before they did it.

And that's what I ask of you. Do you really like Senator Moynihan? Do you really admire him? If you really agree with all of the things that he's written, if you think the time has come to stop worrying about what you feel is politically correct and just say what you believe and try to get this country back together again and start saving these children again, then you must become more intolerant of things that we take for granted. We cannot permit this country to continue to waste the lives of a whole generation of children.

I just want to make one more point. I ran for President because I thought the country was going in the wrong direction economically and because I thought we were coming apart when we ought to be coming together. I think we've done a good job of beginning to change economically. And I can't make us come back together all by myself. This has got to be a deal we do together. I am not giving you a bunch of negative talk. I am a congenital optimist. But I don't believe public officials serve the public interest by giving happy talk when hard news is called for or by using tough facts to divide people instead of unite them.

So in the intolerance I ask for, I ask for your intolerance of conditions, not of people. Remember those kids you heard singing tonight when you go home. There's just millions of them out there, and they're bright and good. They can do anything that they have to do to take this country into the 21st century, if we can simply do what we have to do to stop some of the crazy things that we have permitted. Don't expect it to happen overnight. This family degeneration has happened over 30 years. The wages have been stagnant for 20 years. The deficit has been exploding, and investment in productive things have been declining for 12 years.

We do not have to do it overnight. But we must become intolerant in a consistent way, in a compassionate way, and we must believe that what worked for so many of us will work for tomorrow's children, too. If we believe that and we act on it, then our intolerance can give our country a new birth.

Thank you, and God bless you all.

NOTE: The President spoke at 9 p.m. at the Waldorf Astoria Hotel. In his remarks, he referred to Elizabeth Moynihan, the Senator's wife.

Remarks on Presenting the Malcolm Baldrige National Quality Awards
December 14, 1993

Thank you very much. Secretary Brown and former Secretaries of Commerce, Members of Congress, members of the Baldrige family, and the honorees and all their supporters waving the flags and the signs in the back. It's kind of nice, after all of the speeches I've given and all the crowds I have to see, those kinds of signs waved at me when I speak.

Before I present the Baldrige Award today I would like to talk just a moment about the progress of the GATT negotiations which Secretary Brown mentioned. Today the United States negotiators have achieved a breakthrough in the talks to conclude a new round in the General Agreement on Tariffs and Trade. We are now on the verge of an historic victory in our efforts to open foreign markets to American products.

I do want to make it clear, however, that the negotiations are not concluded yet. Thorny issues remained, and I have instructed our negotiators to push very hard for our objectives as they conclude the remaining details. I've made it clear that I will not accept a bad GATT but that we will not spare any effort to fight for a good one. Now the United States and the European Community are in a position to work shoulder to shoulder to push for concessions from other nations in the final hours.

The stakes are immense. This would be the single largest trade agreement ever. It writes new rules of the road for world trade well into the next century. It would cut other countries' tariffs for our goods, on average, by more than

one-third. When fully phased in, it could add as much as $100 billion to $200 billion to the United States economy every year. It opens foreign markets to our manufacturing and agricultural products and for the first time covers services. It does all of this while preserving our sovereignty and especially our ability to retaliate against unfair foreign trade practices.

With NAFTA, our Nation chose to take the new world economy head on, to compete and win and not retreat. Our willingness to lead set the pace for other nations of the world. Americans have reason to be proud; we're on the way to making this world change in a way that works for us. I know that all of you join me in wishing our negotiators well and hoping that we can conclude a successful agreement. We have another day.

I'm delighted to be here in this wonderful auditorium again, the same place where we signed the historic NAFTA legislation just a few days ago. A lot of people thought that that fight would end up in defeat. But I felt if we stuck by it, if we just kept arguing that a wealthy country can only create jobs and raise incomes by increasing the number of its customers for goods and services, in the end we would prevail. And we did, thanks in large measure to an enormous bipartisan coalition of people from all over America and to the efforts of Secretary Ron Brown who worked very hard on it as well as Mickey Kantor and so many others. I'm honored to be with you again for this happy occasion because, like NAFTA, the Malcolm Baldrige

Quality Award is an important part of our effort to change the way America thinks about doing its business.

In the months since I have been in office, we've been taking all the specific actions we can to try to help our Nation adapt to the changing world we find, working to create a climate in which private enterprise can grow and prosper and put Americans back to work. From the deficit reduction program to NAFTA to addressing the credit crunch to the deregulation of high-tech exports to the successful meetings with the G-7 nations and the Asian-Pacific nations, the goal is the same: to make our people more secure in the shifting economic environment at home and abroad by allowing us to compete and to win.

With the reduction in the deficit and the other actions, we see inflation down, interest rates down, job creation up, personal income up. We see things moving in the right direction. Consumer confidence rose 18 percent in November. We've had 7 months of increased retail sales. Last month, people who were delinquent in their home mortgages were at their lowest level in 19 years. Over 5 million Americans have refinanced their homes. Millions of others have refinanced other debt. Manufacturing is expanding.

We are trying, in other words, to take care of our business in the Government so you can take care of your business: increasing productivity, creating jobs and incomes for the American people. When both of us do our part, the Government and the private sector, we're on our way to long-lasting economic growth.

Six years ago, the United States Government, in a previous administration, exercised the wisdom of establishing the Baldrige Award. In no time, because of the astounding success of its winners in taking care of their business, the award became a symbol of excellence and an inspiration for the rebirth of American competitiveness. For that, we owe a good deal to the legacy of the award's namesake. Until his untimely and tragic death in 1987, Commerce Secretary Malcolm Baldrige was a voice in urging Americans to focus on quality. His cause lives on through this award named for him. And we are honored very much to have his family here with us today.

The idea of quality took hold as American companies become more and more aware of the intense and growing competition from overseas and more and more clear in this country of ours, we could never hope to compete in America by lowering our cost of doing business, and particularly our labor costs, to the level of the poorest nations of the world. The challenge is clear: How do we learn from our competitors? How do we meet them head on? How do we learn from each other in every workplace in America? All these success stories have a common theme: Companies that listen to the needs of their customers and the ideas of their workers, companies that streamline their operations and adopt the idea of continuous improvement in products and services. It's management from the top down and from the bottom up, better known now as quality management.

Through the Baldrige Award and the principles of quality management it embraces, countless businesses have found new and stronger life. Beyond manufacturing, these principles are now beginning to be applied in fields like health care, education, and yes, believe it or not, even Government. By giving both employees and customers a say in how businesses are run, these businesses have built pride and productivity while improving management and product and services. Quality management is clearly a win-win formula. It helps businesses to do well, it beefs up our competitiveness around the world, and it helps to create jobs and to stabilize and increase incomes for our working people. This year's winners are outstanding examples of that.

I got my schooling in total quality management and what it can do when I was the Governor of my home State of Arkansas. That's when I got to know the people at Eastman Chemical Company. On several occasions I visited their plant in Batesville, Arkansas, and I used to tell a story on the campaign trail at home, walking into a room, seeing a guy—this plant is sort of out in the country—and seeing a guy working a computer wearing cowboy boots and one of those big rodeo championship belt buckles. If you're not from the rodeo country, you've never seen one, but if you've never seen one, the first time you see one, it looks like a silver dish you might give as a wedding present to someone. [*Laughter*] Anyway, I walked into this room, and this guy had his jeans and his boots on and his big rodeo belt buckle on, listening to country music, working a computer. And he launched into a much more eloquent speech than I had ever given about the importance of raising the skills of American workers so we could provide for our families and our children and their future.

I also traveled to the headquarters of Eastman Chemical in Kingsport, Tennessee, for a closeup look at the progress they were making there. They were always a big help to me in implementing what I was trying to do at home. Indeed, Eastman Chemical loaned me one of their executives, Asa Whitaker, who worked to set up the Arkansas quality management program, which was the first State governmentwide program of its kind in the entire United States of America. Today that company is justifiably the large manufacturing winner of the Malcolm Baldrige National Quality Award for 1993.

It's a $4 billion company with almost 18,000 employees in the manufacture of chemicals, fibers, and plastics for customers around the world. Under Ernest Davenport's leadership, the company has concentrated on teamwork aimed at quality management and a relentless effort to exceed customers' expectations. It's a strategy that works. For the last 4 years, more than 70 percent of its 7,000 customers have ranked Eastman as their number one supplier.

I say, also, that my experience with this company and the quality management work we did is one of the reasons that we decided to undertake the National Performance Review of the Federal Government, under the Vice President's leadership. And in that connection, I ask all of you to help us to achieve some of the systematic reforms that we are searching for that require some approval from the Congress, especially the reform of the personnel, the budgeting, and most importantly, the procurement systems of the Government. We could save a lot more money and increase our productivity if we were free to do that.

Chuck Roberts, the vice president of Ames Rubber Corporation of Hamburg, New Jersey, said there are probably more people in this auditorium today than all the people who work at Ames. Now, when I read this, I found myself up here when Ron Brown was speaking trying to count the number of people in the auditorium. [*Laughter*] Four hundred and fifty people work at Ames, and I think there are at least 100 more than that here today. But it's quality and not quantity that's being measured. Still, even with 450 employees, Ames is the largest manufacturer in the world of rollers for mid- to large-size copiers. It's the small business win-

ner of this year's Baldrige Award. At Ames, it's not unusual to find second- and third-generation employees with the company. The atmosphere is like family and like a team. Workers even call each other teammates. Every worker belongs to at least one of 40 company groups dedicated to quality improvement. The impact of these groups collectively has been dramatic. Since 1989, it's increased productivity by 48 percent. And in the last 5 years, teammate ideas have saved the company and its customers more than $3 million. As a small producer in a large industry, Ames president and chief executive officer Joel Marvil, has made his company a model in applying quality management.

One thing that distinguishes these two companies is that both have expanded the idea of partnership between companies and suppliers, between workers and managers, even partnership with the environment. Both these companies have been industry leaders in environmental safety, and their success has further proved that the choice between growth and the environment is a false one. In the end, we must find a way to have both.

In our Nation, we know we have the brightest managers, the best workers, and the most advanced technologies. But we also have to prove that we can all put it together in ways that lead to increasing productivity, increasing jobs, and increasing incomes. I couldn't help thinking as I was reviewing the history of those of you who are winning this award today that if more American companies operated like you do, there would be much less anxiety when we have to make changes, like we did when we had to decide what to do about NAFTA, because a lot of opposition to NAFTA really had nothing to do with the terms of the agreement but instead had to do with the incredible anxiety that working people felt that their jobs and their incomes and their families weren't really all that important to their employers and that if there was some sort of short-term advantage to be gained by a company, even if it led to the long-term damage to their families, that the advantage would be chosen over the family.

When you look at the long-term productivity of the kinds of companies that are really proving that you can make good money in America by using new partnerships with your workers, you see a level of security and trust and almost fanatic devotion to the cause of the enterprise, that if we had it everywhere, it would be much easier for America to take the steps we need to broaden our horizons, to reach out to other countries, to increase trade. So I thank you for that, and I hope other companies will follow your example because we need more people at work, happy, secure, and supporting the objectives that you have supported.

Make no mistake about it, the winners of the Baldrige Award have done a great service for America, and they have done a service that only the private sector can provide in this great capitalist economy. This is a free enterprise system. Government has responsibilities to set a framework, to promote growth policy, to do those things which cannot be done in the private sector. But in the end we rise or fall economically based on whether our system is working for the benefit of the people that labor in it day in and day out. And given the fact that so much of our security today and in the future is a question of our economic security and our ability to compete and win, I think it is nowhere near an overstatement to say that these two companies, Ames Rubber and Eastman Chemical, have done a great service not just to themselves, their employees, and their customers but to the United States. And we congratulate them today.

Thank you very much.

NOTE: The President spoke at 10:35 a.m. at the Mellon Auditorium.

Exchange With Reporters
December 14, 1993

Multilateral Trade Negotiations

Q. Mr. President, are you disappointed about audiovisuals in the GATT?

The President. Well, I'm disappointed we didn't get it resolved, but I sure wanted it out of there once I realized—I didn't want to settle for a bad deal. So we took it out, and now it will be subject to the ordinary trade rules. I think it's far better than accepting what was offered. And no one I knew, including the people in the audiovisual industry, thought it was worth bringing the whole thing down over. They just didn't want to get stuck with a bad deal. In other words, if we could get it out, which we did, as Americans, they want our country to benefit from these overall big reductions in tariffs. But they just didn't want to get trapped into something that wasn't good. So I think we're in pretty good shape.

Russia

Q. Mr. President, now that you have had another day to think about the Russian election results——

The President. Well, obviously—no, I haven't talked to anybody about my trip to Russia— any of our people. So I don't know what I'm going to do there. I think that it is—I'll say just what I said yesterday—I think it was probably largely a protest vote. I think that when people are having a tough time and they have a tough time over a long period of years, they often look for simple answers. It's not unique to Russia. You can see that in many other democracies throughout the world and throughout history. It's not all that unusual. I don't think any of us expect to be giving up Alaska any time soon. But I think, there must be a lot of people in Russia who are extremely frustrated and have a high level of anger because they've been through a lot of tough times.

And the people running the multinational institutions that are trying to help these countries convert from old-line Communist, top-down, command-and-control economies to market economies need to be very sensitive to that. I think we need to ask ourselves not so much about him right now, but about what this means for democracy in Russia, in Poland, and in other republics of the former Soviet Union and the other countries of Eastern Europe. And I'll have more to say about that as we go along.

Q. Would you rule out——

The President. Look, I have talked to nobody about anything. I can't even comment on that. I have not discussed my trip. We have not— except in general terms with my own staff. We've been working on other things. I have not had time to even think about it.

NOTE: The exchange began at approximately 11 a.m. at the Mellon Auditorium. A tape was not available for verification of the content of this exchange.

Appointment for Chair of the Commission on Immigration Reform
December 14, 1993

The President today appointed former Texas Congresswoman Barbara Jordan to chair the Commission on Immigration Reform. The nine-member Commission was created by Congress in 1990 to evaluate the impact of the recent changes in immigration policy and to recommend further changes that might be necessary by September 30, 1994, and again by September 30, 1997.

"I have chosen Barbara Jordan, one of the most well respected people in America, to chair this Commission because immigration is one of the most important and complex issues facing our country today," said the President. "I am confident that Congresswoman Jordan will use her prodigious talents to thoughtfully address the challenges posed by immigration reform, balance the variety of competing interests, and recommend policies that will be in our country's best interests."

NOTE: A biography of the appointee was made available by the Office of the Press Secretary.

Appointment for Special Assistant to the President and Deputy Press Secretary
December 14, 1993

The President announced today that he has appointed Ginny Terzano to be Special Assistant to the President and Deputy White House Press Secretary. The appointment is effective January 1.

"The perspective that comes with Ginny's experience in the media and as a spokeswoman will make her a strong addition to our communications team," said the President. "I look forward to her joining us here at the White House."

NOTE: A biography of the appointee was made available by the Office of the Press Secretary.

The President's News Conference
December 15, 1993

Multilateral Trade Negotiations

The President. With that introduction, ladies and gentlemen, I am pleased to announce that the United States today, as you know, concluded negotiations with over 110 other nations on the most comprehensive trade agreement in history. This agreement eliminates barriers to United States goods and services around the world. It means new opportunities, more jobs, and higher incomes. And it cements our position of leadership in the new global economy.

This GATT agreement advances the vision of economic renewal that I set out when I took the oath of office. The first task in pursuing that vision was to get our economic house in order. The economic plan which passed earlier this year has resulted in lower interest rates, lower inflation, booming home construction, and the creation of more private sector jobs in this year than in the previous 4 years, and the highest level of consumer confidence now in 17 years.

But our renewal also depends on engaging actively with other nations to boost worldwide economic growth and to open markets to our goods and services. No wealthy country in the world today can hope to increase jobs and raise incomes unless there are more customers for its goods and services. Just since the Fourth of July, our administration has taken several major steps toward that goal. First, at the Tokyo G–7 summit we secured a market opening agreement among the major economies that breathed new life into these world trade talks. In November the Congress passed the North American Free Trade Agreement, which creates the world's largest free trade area. In the first-ever meeting of the Asia Pacific economic leaders in Seattle, we strengthened our ties to the world's fastest growing region. Now, after negotiations that have spanned 7 years and three U.S. administrations, we have secured a new GATT agreement. I have said repeatedly that I would not accept a bad agreement simply for the sake of getting one. I made clear that the final product had to serve our Nation's interests.

This agreement did not accomplish everything we wanted. That has been well documented. And we must continue to fight for more open markets for entertainment, for insurance, for banking, and for other industries. But today's GATT accord does meet the test of a good agreement for three reasons.

First, this new agreement will foster more jobs and more incomes in America by fostering an export boom. At its core, it simply cuts tariffs, the taxes charged by foreign nations on American products in 8,000 different areas, on average by one-third. By sparking global growth, it is estimated that this agreement can add as much as $100 to $200 billion per year to our economy once it is fully phased in. It will create hundreds of thousands of good-paying American jobs.

Second, this agreement sharpens our competitive edge in areas of United States strength. Under this agreement, free and fair rules of trade will apply for the first time not only to goods but to trade in services and intellectual property. This will help us to stop other nations from discriminating against world-class American businesses in such industries as computer services, construction, engineering, and architecture. And it will crack down on piracy against the fruits of American innovation, which today is costing United States firms $60 billion a year, about one percent of our total gross domestic products.

Finally, it does these things while preserving our ability to retaliate against unfair trade practices and our right to set strong environmental and consumer protection standards for economic activity here in the United States. That's why I believe this new GATT is good for America.

Over the coming years, we have a solemn obligation to ensure that its benefits are broadly shared among all the American people. We must ensure that working men and women have the skills, the training, the education to compete and win under these new rules. Our Nation's gains must be their gains. Next year we will be working harder on that.

Because this agreement will benefit our people and because it meets our standards of success, I've decided to notify the Congress today of my intention to sign this agreement. I look forward to consulting closely with Congress and the American people about how best to put its provisions into effect.

I want to congratulate all our trade negotiators, many of whom have hardly slept in the last several days, and especially Ambassador Mickey Kantor for this historic breakthrough. The American people should know that they were well represented by people I personally observed to be tough and tireless and genuine advocates for our interests and our ideals.

All of us can be proud that at this critical moment when many nations are facing economic troubles that have caused them to turn inward, the United States has once again reached outward and has made global economic growth our cause. This year we've worked hard to put the economic interest of America's broad middle class back at the center of our foreign policy as well as our domestic policy. Not since the end of World War II has the United States pushed to completion trade agreements of such significance as NAFTA and GATT. We've shown leadership by example. We've set forth a vision for a thriving global economy. And our trading partners to their credit have also rallied to that cause.

Today's agreement caps a year of economic renewal for our Nation. It should give us added reason for confidence as we enter the new year. But it should also reinforce our determination to do better in the new year.

Helen [Helen Thomas, United Press International].

Russia

Q. Mr. President, are you concerned, as many seem to be, over the rise of ultranationalism in Russia? And do you have any bulwark against a replay of the thirties if this happens to Russia, if there is this kind of closing out and rise of what's being considered fascist——

The President. Well, let me say, of course I am concerned about some of the comments that have been made by the leader of the so-called Liberal Democratic Party in Russia. I think no American, indeed, no citizen of the world who read such comments could fail to be concerned.

On the other hand, I think it's important to recognize that we don't have any evidence at this time that the people who voted for that party were embracing all those comments, or indeed, may have even known about them. And we don't yet know what direction the new Parliament will try to take. Am I concerned about that? Yes, I am. Do I think that this means there will be a big new dangerous direction in Russian policy? I don't think there's any evidence to support that.

Q. How about your policy?

The President. Well, because I don't know that there will be any change in Russian policy, I don't see any basis for a change in our policy at this time. On the other hand, it's something that we'll have to watch and work with. I think it calls on all of us to redouble our efforts to support the process of reform in Russia in a way that the ordinary citizens can understand will redound to their benefit.

I believe this was clearly a protest vote, fueled by people who have been in, many of them, in virtual economic free fall and who have also suffered the kind of psychological damage that comes to people when they work harder for less money or when they lose their jobs or when they don't see any better day at the end of all the change. It is a more extreme example of what you have seen in our Nation and in other nations throughout the world. Thankfully, in the West where you've seen protest votes

or votes against the established order of things, they've been within much more normal channels of debate. But I think plainly we have to assume that this is primarily a protest vote. We have to watch it. We have to stand up for what we believe in. But I think we should continue to support reform in Russia.

Rita [Rita Braver, CBS News].

Q. Sir, even if it is a protest vote, what can the U.S. do, if anything, to reverse this tide? And what's to say that it isn't going to keep going in the direction of fascism?

The President. Well, first of all, some of it's being done already. I mean, I think the wide publicity being given to all the comments and statements will give you some indication before too long about whether people in the street in Russia embrace the stated print positions on all the things that have been said or whether it was a protest vote.

But again let me say, keep in mind, this is the first popularly elected Parliament under a legitimate system of elections, to the best of my knowledge, that Russia has ever had. There are now two centers of democratic legitimacy in Russia, the President and the Parliament. And they will interface with one another in ways that are some predictable and some that are unpredictable. You can tell that from our experience here.

I think it's important at this moment not to overreact. I don't mean to say we shouldn't be sensitive, but I just think let's wait and see who the people are who take their seats in the Parliament and what they do and what they say.

Q. Mr. President, is Yeltsin under increasing pressure to hold the elections now before 1996? And if so, do you think he should?

The President. I don't know about that. I don't have an opinion about that. I think that's a decision for them to make.

Jim [Jim Miklaszewski, NBC News].

President's Approval Ratings

Q. Mr. President, in recent opinion polls, your personal and job approval ratings have been on a steady and some might say significant rise, while Ross Perot's have been pretty much plummeting. I mean, what's going on here? Can you tell us?

Q. And he has a followup. [*Laughter*]

Q. [*Inaudible*]

Q. [*Inaudible*] Thank you very much.

The President. Either you guys are going to

be really mad at him for asking the question or he has some check that I have bounced that he has a picture of. [*Laughter*]

Q. Can't wait for the kicker.

The President. What I think is happening is, first of all, the American people are beginning to feel—just beginning, there's a long way to go—beginning to feel some benefit of the economic changes brought on by the lower interest rates and the higher investment. I mean, when you have, like we had last month, a 19-year low in the number of people who are late paying their home mortgages and when millions of people refinance their homes in a year, when you have the job rate picking up, those things are bound to have an effect.

Then I think we had a series of highly publicized struggles for change in the Congress that came out in favor of the position that our administration had taken. And the most visible ones lately, obviously, were NAFTA and the Brady bill. So I think those were the two reasons why. I think the American people want results and they also want an administration that will take on the tough problems and try to see them through.

Q. And Mr. Perot?

The President. I can't comment on that. You ought to ask the Vice President about that. [*Laughter*]

Middle East Peace Process

Q. On the Middle East, Mr. President, on the Middle East, do you think there's still hope? The date has passed——

The President. Absolutely. Absolutely.

Q. Have you talked to any of the parties?

The President. No, but I met with the Secretary of State this morning, and we talked about it. I asked him to talk to me about it, and we are still planning on going forward with our initiatives next year. It will be a major part of what we're going to do.

Thank you very much.

Health Care Reform

Q. Mr. President, on health care, a quick question on health care?

The President. One more. All right, one more, one more. [*Laughter*] It's Christmas, guys.

Q. It seems as if a lot of Republicans seem to be really going after the health care reform proposal as you initially advanced it, and they're saying now they don't want to compromise. Jack

Kemp says that it may have started off as an iceberg; it's going to wind up ice cubes. And Cheney is now saying he's totally opposed to it. Gingrich is saying there's no room for compromising on many of the aspects of the health care reform package. How far are you willing to go in making this health care package palatable to Republicans so it won't simply be a Democratic initiative?

The President. Well, I told you what my principles were. My principles are two: universal coverage, without which you will never slow the rate of cost increase and stop the cost shifting; and a package of comprehensive benefits. I don't want to go through the whole catastrophic insurance fight that Congress had a few years ago. You all remember what happened there.

Beyond that, I'm willing to talk to them about it. But I would just point out that today the questions really should be directed to them: What is your position? We now know that there are another 2.3 million people without insurance, that number of uninsured going up steadily. How do you justify leaving in place a system that costs 40 percent more of our income than any other system in the world and does much less? What is your justification for the status quo? It is the most bureaucratic system that exists anywhere in the world, and it has not worked.

So their rhetoric, you know, I realize you can lob rhetoric that sounds very good, but I don't think that the rhetoric corresponds to the reality of the proposal. The proposal we made leaves in place the choice of doctors, gives more consumer choice to the American people than they have today, and will simplify lives for America's physicians if it passes.

So I would have to say again, I welcome this debate, and it's fine to have a debate over principles on this issue. I want to. I told you what my two were. So when they say that they want to fight us, my question back is, what's your answer to the fact that the number of uninsured Americans is going up every single day? It's going in the wrong direction. Our plan would take it in the right direction.

Thank you.

NOTE: The President's 38th news conference began at 2:10 p.m. in the Briefing Room at the White House. In his remarks, he referred to Vladimir Zhirinovsky, leader of the Liberal Democratic Party in Russia.

Remarks on the Resignation of Les Aspin as Secretary of Defense
December 15, 1993

Ladies and gentlemen, it is with real sadness that today I accept Secretary Aspin's request to be relieved of his duties as Secretary of Defense for personal reasons. I am very grateful that he's agreed to remain at his post until January 20th, and beyond if necessary, so that we can plan together for the coming year and effect a smooth transition at the Pentagon.

Les has been a close adviser and a friend of mine for a long time. I have valued his wise counsel as a key member of our national security team. And I have told him that after he takes the break he's requested, I very much hope he will consider other assignments for this administration.

During a lifetime of public service in Congress, with our transition, and at the Pentagon, Les Aspin has made invaluable contributions to this Nation's defense and security. None of them have been more significant than his service as Secretary of Defense. Along with the Joint Chiefs of Staff, he has provided solid leadership for our uniformed and civilian defense personnel during a period of transition that is historic and has at times been unsettling.

He helped launch creative policy responses to the fundamental changes of this era, from the dissolution of the Soviet empire to the growing challenges of ethnic conflict and weapons proliferation. And through it all, he has led with character, with intelligence, with wisdom, and the unflappable good humor that is both his trademark and his secret weapon.

One of his most important contributions in this past year has been his efforts to help our administration relate our defense strategy in this new era and our defense spending. Under his leadership, the Pentagon conducted the first comprehensive review of our forces since the end of the cold war. This now well-known, bottom-up review has provided our Nation with a profile of this era's threats and a vision of our force structure that will guide our Nation's military for many years to come.

He's provided steady leadership for the entire defense community as it has confronted the inevitable downsizing that accompanied the end of the cold war. He acted on the recommendations of the base closure commission in a way that demonstrated equity, responsibility, and a great concern for the communities and the families that were hit hard by the closure of our military facilities. And as we've reduced our force levels, he's been the first to voice concerns for the men and women in uniform who shoulder the burden of our national security.

His leadership has also been invaluable in helping our country to adapt to our military social changes. He led the way in our efforts to open the doors for women to serve our Nation in combat roles and helped to ensure more equitable rules toward homosexuals in our military. He's provided creative leadership as he's mobilized the Pentagon to develop new and stronger responses to the many security challenges of this new era, such as his new counterproliferation initiative. And on a range of tough decisions and tough challenges abroad, from Bosnia to Korea, he has called them as he saw them, bringing to bear a lifetime of experience and dedication and a razor-sharp mind to our Nation's security interest.

Above all, Secretary Aspin has provided deep strategic thinking and leadership at a time of profound change in this world. As a result, when our citizens go to bed tonight, we can do so secure in the knowledge that our Nation is building the right forces and acquiring the right capabilities for this new era.

I will always appreciate the thoughtful and dedicated and ultimately selfless service that Les Aspin provided to me and to this Nation over this last year. I asked a lot of him, tough times and tough problems. He gave even more to me, to our military, and to our country than was asked, and I will always be very, very grateful.

Thank you.

NOTE: The President spoke at 5:21 p.m. in the Oval Office at the White House.

Letter Accepting the Resignation of Les Aspin as Secretary of Defense
December 15, 1993

Dear Les:

It is with deep sadness that I accept your request that, for personal reasons, you be relieved of your duties after your years of intense, unselfish and extraordinarily effective service to our nation and its security. I am grateful that you are prepared to remain at your post through January 20, or beyond if necessary, as we work through the immediate issues before us and as we manage a smooth transition to your successor.

I hope that after you have taken the break you have requested, you will consider other important assignments that you would find challenging and personally rewarding.

I am proud of your accomplishments over the past year, and you should be, as well. In the Congress, in the campaign and as Secretary of Defense, you have been an effective leader in efforts to harness together our defense strategy and defense resources, culminating in this year's Bottom Up Review. Together with the Joint Chiefs of Staff, you skillfully managed difficult issues—such as the military service of homosexuals and women in combat—that could have proved both deeply divisive and damaging to our military effectiveness and readiness. You helped conduct the first review of our nuclear posture since the end of the Cold War and advanced a new counter proliferation strategy. And you helped in the distinguished appointment of a new Chairman of the Joint Chiefs of Staff, General John Shalikashvili.

All of this took skill and hard work, and all Americans are in your debt for it.

I look forward to urging you once again to bring your great skills and deep devotion to your country's service.

With admiration,

BILL CLINTON

Dear Mr. President,

It has been one year since you asked me to serve as your Secretary of Defense. It has been an honor for me to work with you as we have reshaped our country's military to protect Americans in a vastly changed world.

I am proud of the progress we have made in dealing with these changes. We now have a clear strategic sense of the new dangers we now face. After a year's work we will be able to secure our country against these new dangers with a Bottom Up Force. By strategically defining the strengths we need and honestly projecting how much this force will cost, we have also built a new consensus to invest what is necessary to underwrite this Bottom Up Force. As a result we have moved for the first time in fifteen years away from the polarizing debates about how much we should spend on defense and worked together to build the military strengths we know we need. This has helped end the gridlock that for years kept us from governing and from concentrating on our agenda at home.

We have also worked together with our uniformed military leadership to find common ground on some difficult social issues that were avoided in the past and which could have divided our military. So we can now ensure that we will have a ready to fight force without the continuing distractions of these controversies.

As you know, dealing with these changes have made it a tough year for us all—tough issues, tough calls.

I share your pride in the progress we have made. But now, as we have discussed on previous occasions, I ask you to relieve me of the duty as your Secretary of Defense on January 20. I ask this for quite personal reasons. I have been working continually for over two decades to help build a strong American military. It's time now for me to take a break and undertake a new kind of work.

Of course, I pledge my every effort to support you and my successor in a smooth and orderly transition. You can continue to draw on one of the strongest and most talented senior management teams the Department of Defense has ever seen. Bill Perry and General Shali will give you a continuity of leadership as my successor works with the Senate to assume office.

Finally, I want to thank you for the honor of serving you and our country. You are a great Commander-In-Chief. I know that while you are our President our country will grow in all of its strengths, Americans will continue to be secure, our men and women in uniform will always be honored, and we will be true to our best values as a people.

Sincerely,

LES ASPIN

NOTE: These letters were made available by the Office of the Press Secretary on December 15 but were not issued as White House press releases.

Statement on the Peace Process in Northern Ireland
December 15, 1993

I warmly welcome today's joint declaration of Prime Ministers Albert Reynolds and John Major proposing a framework for peaceful resolution of the situation in Northern Ireland. I have followed with intense interest the British and Irish Prime Ministers' courageous search for peace. Their flexibility has led London and Dublin, for the first time, to acknowledge the other's deepest aspirations. The joint declaration reflects the yearning for peace that is shared by all traditions in Ireland and creates an historic opportunity to end the tragic cycle of bloodshed.

Difficult issues still remain to be resolved, including questions at the heart of national and cultural identity and majority and minority rights. But as Prime Minister Reynolds said, the framework recognizes that differences can be fully and satisfactorily addressed and solved through the political process on the basis of fundamental principles of agreement and consent. It reflects the belief of both Governments that the way forward lies through dialog and cooperation, without compromising the beliefs of either tradition. I am especially heartened that, in the words of Prime Minister Major, the framework "closes no doors, except the door to violence." We hope that all parties will be inspired by the vision Mr. Reynolds and Mr. Major have shown.

I reaffirm the readiness of the United States to contribute in any appropriate way to the new opportunities which lie ahead in Northern Ireland. Our support for renewed political dialog remains steadfast.

In this season of hope, the call for peace on Earth has a special resonance in Northern Ireland. No side which claims a legitimate stake in the future of Northern Ireland can justify continued violence on any grounds. I call on those who would still seek to embrace or justify violence to heed the words of Paul and "cast off the works of darkness, and . . . put on the armor of light."

Letter on the Swearing-In of John D. Holum as Director of the United States Arms Control and Disarmament Agency
December 15, 1993

Dear John:

I am delighted to extend my congratulations as you are sworn in as the Director of the Arms Control and Disarmament Agency.

There are few challenges more pressing today than arms control and nonproliferation. Already we have taken several steps to address these challenges. In the past year, we have submitted the Chemical Weapons Treaty to the Senate. We have ratified the Open Skies Treaty. We have advanced new proposals on a comprehensive test ban and the ABM Treaty, and have made substantial progress in the denuclearization of the States of the Former Soviet Union. We have elevated nonproliferation on the national agenda and with your leadership will be pursuing a range of measures such as focused regional strategies and comprehensive approaches to the dangers posed by fissile materials. These steps and others we will take together can make our people safer and our nation more secure.

Much remains to be done to meet these challenges. Under your guidance, ACDA will play a crucial role in advancing the full range of our arms control and nonproliferation agenda. I look forward to having the benefit of your counsel, your expertise and your leadership skills as we work together to ensure a safer world for generations to come.

Sincerely,

BILL CLINTON

NOTE: This letter was released by the Office of the Press Secretary on December 16.

Letter to Congressional Leaders on the General Agreement on Tariffs and Trade
December 15, 1993

Dear Mr. Speaker: *(Dear Mr. President:)*

I believe that we have created a unique opportunity to build an international trading system that will ensure the orderly and equitable expansion of world trade and contribute to the prosperity of the United States in coming generations. After seven long years the conclusion of the Uruguay Round of multilateral trade negotiations is at hand. The Round will result in the largest, most comprehensive set of trade agreements in history. With the conclusion of the Round, we will have successfully achieved the objectives that Congress set for the United States in the negotiations.

In accordance with section 1103(a)(1) of the Omnibus Trade and Competitiveness Act of 1988, as amended ("Act"), I am pleased to notify the House of Representatives and the Senate of my intent to enter into the trade agreements resulting from the Uruguay Round of multilateral trade negotiations under the auspices of the General Agreement on Tariffs and Trade. These agreements are listed and identified below and are more fully described in an attachment to this letter.

The United States can and must compete in the global economy. In many areas of economic activity we are already world leaders and we are taking measures at home to strengthen further our ability to compete. In section 1101 of the Act the Congress set as the first overall U.S. negotiating objectives for the Uruguay Round more open, equitable and reciprocal market access. I am particularly pleased to advise you that the Uruguay Round results will provide an unprecedented level of new *market access* opportunities for U.S. goods and services exports. In the attachment to this letter is a summary description of the agreements on market access for goods and services that we have achieved in the Round. Of special note are the number of areas where we and our major trading partners have each agreed to reduce tariffs on goods to zero. The schedules of commitments reflecting market access in services cover a wide range of service sectors that are of great interest to our exporting community.

The *Agreement on Agriculture* will achieve, as Congress directed, more open and fair conditions of trade in agricultural commodities by establishing specific commitments to reduce foreign export subsidies, tariffs and non-tariff barriers and internal supports.

The *Agreement on Textiles and Clothing* provides for trade in textiles and apparel to be fully integrated into the GATT for the first time. As a result, trade in textiles will be subject to the same disciplines as other sectors. This transition will take place gradually over an extended period. At the same time, the agreement provides an improved safeguards mechanism. It also requires apparel exporting countries to lower specific tariff and non-tariff barriers, providing new market opportunities for U.S. exporters of textile and apparel goods. The agreement contributes to the achievement of the U.S. negotiating objectives of expanding the coverage of the GATT while getting developing countries to provide reciprocal benefits.

In fulfillment of the second overall U.S. negotiating objective, the reduction or elimination of barriers and other trade-distorting policies and practices, the Uruguay Round package includes a number of agreements to reduce or eliminate non-tariff barriers to trade. These agreements, which are described in the attachment, address *Safeguards, Antidumping, Subsidies and Countervailing Measures, Trade-Related Investment Measures, Import Licensing Procedures, Customs Valuation, Preshipment Inspection, Rules of Origin, Technical Barriers to Trade,* and *Sanitary and Phytosanitary Measures.* The agreements strengthen existing GATT rules and, for the first time in the GATT, discipline non-tariff barriers in the areas of investment, rules of origin and preshipment inspection. The agreements preserve the ability of the United States to impose measures necessary to protect the health and safety of our citizens and our environment and to enforce vigorously our laws on unfair trade practices.

The *Agreement on Government Procurement* will provide new opportunities for U.S. exporters as a result of the decision to expand the coverage of the agreement to government procurement of services and construction; we will, however, only extend the full benefits of the agreement to those countries that provide satisfactory coverage of their own procurement. Negotiations on improvements in the *Agreement on Trade in Civil Aircraft* and on a *Multilateral Steel Agreement* are continuing. These agreements should provide for more effective disciplines and reduce or eliminate trade-distorting policies and practices in two industries of importance to our economy. I will fully consult with the Congress throughout these negotiations, and plan to enter into these agreements if the negotiations produce results that are acceptable to the United States.

As a result of the *Agreement on Trade-Related Intellectual Property Rights (TRIPS)* and the *General Agreement on Trade in Services (GATS),* we will now have for the first time internationally agreed rules covering areas of trade of enormous importance to the United States. These agreements represent a major step forward in establishing a more effective system of international trading disciplines and procedures. GATS contains legally enforceable provisions dealing with both cross-border trade and investment in services and sectoral annexes on financial services, labor movement, telecommunications and aviation services. More than 50 countries have submitted schedules of commitments on market access for services. The

TRIPS agreement provides for the establishment of standards for the protection of a full range of intellectual property rights and for the enforcement of those standards both internationally and at the border.

The Uruguay Round has produced a number of other agreements that will create a more effective system of international trading disciplines and procedures.

The *Understanding on Rules and Procedures Governing the Settlement of Disputes* will provide for a more effective and expeditious dispute resolution mechanism and procedures which will enable better enforcement of United States rights. Congress identified the establishment of such a system as the first principal U.S. trade negotiating objective for the Round. The procedures complement U.S. laws for dealing with foreign unfair trade practices such as section 301 of the Trade Act of 1974.

The *Agreement Establishing the World Trade Organization* will facilitate the implementation of the trade agreements reached in the Uruguay Round by bringing them under one institutional umbrella, requiring full participation of all countries in the new trading system and providing a permanent forum to address new issues facing the international trading system. The WTO text recognizes the importance of protecting the environment while expanding world trade; negotiators have also agreed to develop a work program on trade and the environment and will recommend an appropriate institutional structure to carry out this work program. Creation of the WTO will contribute to the achievement of the second principal U.S. negotiating objective of improving the operation of the GATT and multilateral trade agreements.

The U.S. objective of improving the operation of the GATT is also furthered by a number of understandings, decisions and declarations regarding the GATT and its operations. The *Trade Policy Review Mechanism* will enhance surveillance of members' trade policies. The *Understandings Concerning Interpretation of Specific Articles of the General Agreement on Tariffs and Trade 1994 (GATT 1994)* concern the Interpretation of Articles II:1(b), XVII, XXIV, XXVIII and XXXV, and Balance-of-Payments Provisions. There is also an *Understanding in Respect of Waivers of Obligations Under the General Agreement on Tariffs and Trade 1994.*

The *Ministerial Decisions and Declarations* state the views and objectives of Uruguay Round participants on a number of issues relating to the operation of the global trading system, provide for the continuation of the improvements to the dispute settlement system that became effective in 1989 and deal with other matters concerning the dispute settlement system. The Ministerial Decisions and Declarations that are now proposed for adoption are described in the attachment. At this time, implementing legislation does not appear to be necessary for these instruments.

I will continue to consult closely with the Congress as we conclude the Round. There are a few areas of significance that we were unable to resolve at this time. In order to ensure more open, equitable and reciprocal market access, in certain agreements we have made U.S. obligations contingent on receiving satisfactory commitments from other countries, and we will continue to work to ensure that the best possible agreement for the United States is achieved. I will not enter into any agreement unless I am satisfied that U.S. interest are protected. With regard to entertainment issues, we were unable to overcome our differences with our major trading partners, and we agreed to disagree. We will continue to negotiate, however,

and until we reach a satisfactory agreement, we think we can best advance the interests of our entertainment industry by reserving all our legal rights to respond to policies that discriminate in these areas.

In accordance with the procedures in the Act, the United States will not enter into the agreements outlined above until April 15, 1994. After the agreements have been signed, they will be submitted for Congressional approval, together with whatever legislation and administrative actions may be necessary or appropriate to implement the agreements in the United States. The agreements will not take effect with respect to the United States, and will have no domestic legal force, until the Congress has approved them and enacted any appropriate implementing legislation.

Sincerely,

WILLIAM J. CLINTON

NOTE: Identical letters were sent to Thomas S. Foley, Speaker of the House of Representatives, and Albert Gore, Jr., President of the Senate. This letter was released by the Office of the Press Secretary on December 16.

Remarks to Physicians Supporting the Health Security Plan
December 16, 1993

Thank you very much, ladies and gentlemen, all of you, for being here. And I want to say a special word of thanks to the physicians who have joined us here today; to Secretary Shalala and to Ira Magaziner and to the First Lady for all the work they have done. I thank especially my longtime friend and one of our family's physicians in the past, Dr. Betty Lowe, and I thank Dr. Bill Coleman for the remarks that they made.

You know, I can't help but note right here at the outset that, I think it was just yesterday or the day before, one of the congressional opponents of our approach said that it was socialist. When I heard that Alabama accent and that Arkansas accent—we've got a doctor from rural Mississippi here and another one from North Carolina—I thought, "These people do not look like a bunch of socialists to me." [*Laughter*]

I'll tell you what they do know. They know that it's not easy to be a doctor in the world today. They still know what it's like to deliver a baby in the middle of the night or to get a call at daybreak from a mother whose child has a 102 fever or to care for an asthmatic patient for whom every breath is a struggle. They know what it's like to really make people's lives better, to save people's lives, and to maintain in a very personal way the quality of American medicine as the finest in the world. And I'm convinced that they would not do anything to weaken that quality and are here because they want to work with us to improve it and make it available to all Americans.

More than anything, these leaders and the physicians whom they represent, many of whom are in the audience today, understand the problems of a health care system in which millions live in fear of losing their coverage while costs keep rising, in which last year over 2 million Americans did lose their coverage so that at the latest count we are up to nearly 39 million Americans without health insurance. They know that we have to fix what's wrong with this system without messing up what's right.

Our plan strengthens and restores what is best about our medicine and places the doctor-patient relationship back at the heart of the American health care system. It protects the American people's cherished right to choose their doctors. Indeed, it enhances that right by making it clear that people not now insured cannot be put into plans where they have no choice of doctors, something which is happening increasingly to Americans already under the present system and will continue to increase if we do nothing.

Under our plan, individuals, not their employers, have the freedom to choose the health plan that best meets their needs and desires. That means they can stay with their family doctors. Our plan also guarantees much greater freedom for the patient-doctor relationship, guaranteeing that the doctor, who knows what is best for the patient, and not some insurance or Government bureaucrat will make the decisions about care.

And finally, of course, as has been said, this plan supported by these doctors guarantees universal coverage through the requirement of private insurance mandated in each employment unit with a system of discounts for small businesses and businesses that have a lot of low-wage employees. Now, I think that is very, very important to emphasize. These physicians here represent over 300,000 American physicians. They know that if we're ever going to control the cost of health care and provide quality health care to everyone, we simply have to have universal coverage. It is not only an ethical imperative; it is a practical necessity.

They also are in the best position to judge the importance of a universal coverage requirement that has comprehensive benefits, including primary and preventive care coverage. We have spent ourselves a fortune of money in America by not taking care of primary and preventive health care in health insurance policies. It has been a big mistake, and we have paid for it.

I appreciate their support for holding down the cost increases. I certainly appreciate their support, as you would expect, for the proposition

that the significant amount of taxpayer money that goes into medical education should be now used to encourage more primary and family practitioners in a country in which we are now, frankly, graduating a disastrously low number of family doctors from our medical schools.

I am most grateful, however, again, because the presence of these physicians here debunks the notion that the plan we have presented is some sort of big Government, bureaucratic plan that erodes the doctor-patient relationship and reestablishes its basic principle. Every other advanced country in the world has figured out how to cover their citizens but us. And we're spending 50 percent more of our income on health care than most countries. And too much of it is going to people who are not doctors, who are not nurses, who are not providing hospital or clinical care, but who are just shuffling papers in a maze that is the most bureaucratic, complicated system on the face of the Earth today.

Now, I also want to say that this morning I received a letter, an interesting letter from the American Medical Association, which represents fewer than 300,000 doctors, but still a substantial number—just not as many as are represented on this stage, but still a large number—reaffirming, reaffirming the support of the AMA for universal coverage and clarifying the position taken by the house of delegates recently, in which Dr. Todd says that they are still for universal coverage, that they are not opposed to an employer mandate, but that they think other options for achieving universal coverage in addition to an employer mandate should be considered. And I appreciate that, and I think we all should.

I do not wish this debate in this coming year to become unduly partisan, both within the medical community or the American political community. The truth is that all Americans have a common interest in universal coverage, primary and preventive care, slowing the rate of medical inflation, and reducing the incredible bureaucracy and regulatory intrusion into the health care system. All Americans have a common interest in that. They have an economic interest; they have a human interest, every family.

As I have said many times, there are very few families in this country that are not at risk of losing their health care. Most of them just don't know it until they lose it, their coverage.

So we all have a common interest. And at this holiday season I would hope that we could do away with the destructive and counterproductive labels. I would hope we'll all get a laugh when we think about this eminent panel of Socialists up here on the platform—*[laughter]*—and learn to laugh about that and in this holiday season remind ourselves that perhaps the greatest gift we can give to our country in common is a greater sense of community and security, a major portion of which is universal health care.

Thank you very much.

NOTE: The President spoke at 11:55 a.m. in Room 450 of the Old Executive Office Building. In his remarks, he referred to Dr. Betty Lowe, president, American Academy of Pediatrics; Dr. William Coleman, president, American Academy of Family Physicians; and Dr. James Todd, executive vice president, American Medical Association.

Remarks Announcing the Nomination of Admiral Bobby R. Inman To Be Secretary of Defense
December 16, 1993

Ladies and gentlemen, yesterday I announced that Secretary Aspin would be stepping down as Secretary of Defense next month after a year of devoted service. I want to stress again how deeply grateful I am on behalf of all Americans for his hard work and his many unique contributions to the Pentagon and to our national defense.

To ensure the greatest possible continuity, I wanted to announce a successor as soon as possible. So today, I am very pleased to announce my intent to nominate Admiral Bob Inman as the next Secretary of Defense.

Admiral Inman was one of our Nation's highest ranking and most respected military officers. He was a four-star admiral whose career in the Navy and in our intelligence community and in private business has won him praise from both Democrats and Republicans who admire his intellect, his integrity, and his leadership ability.

The Admiral's experience in serving our Nation is truly impressive. He personally briefed Presidents Eisenhower and Kennedy. He held senior positions under Presidents Ford, Carter, Reagan, and Bush. Former Secretary of Defense James Schlesinger called Admiral Inman "a national asset." And I know he will be a national asset as Secretary of Defense.

He brings to this job the kind of character all Americans respect. The son of a gas station owner in a small east Texas town, he rose to distinction and success on the basis of his brains, his talent, and his hard work. He finished high school at 15, graduated from college at 19, joined the Naval Reserve at 20, and then launched an impressive 31-year career in the Navy. He served on an aircraft carrier, two cruisers, and a destroyer as well as on onshore assignments as an analyst for naval intelligence. In 1976, at the age of 45, he became the youngest vice admiral in peacetime history. Bob Inman's stellar intelligence work caught the attention of many military and civilian leaders and prompted his elevation to several high posts in the intelligence community. He served as Vice Director of the Defense Intelligence Agency, Director of the National Security Agency, and Deputy Director of the Central Intelligence Agency. Because of his outstanding service, he was awarded the National Security Medal by President Carter.

Over the past decade since Admiral Inman left Government, he served in a wide range of private sector positions, including CEO of two private sector electronics firms, Chairman of the Federal Reserve Bank of Dallas, and a teacher at his alma mater, the University of Texas. He's also served on 11 not-for-profit corporate boards. And in all these roles, Admiral Inman has established a reputation for penetrating analysis, strong leadership, and a rock-solid commitment to this Nation's security. Those qualities will serve our Nation well as the Admiral becomes our next Secretary of Defense.

This is a time of great change in our world. We must build on the work Les Aspin began with a bottom-up review to ensure that we have the right forces and strategy for this new era. We must ensure that, even as we reduce force levels, our military remains ready to fight and win on a moment's notice. We must ensure that our men and women in uniform remain the best trained, the best equipped, the best prepared fighting force on Earth. And we must maintain and build strong bipartisan support in the Congress and in the country for the foreign policy and national defense interests of our Nation.

I am confident that Admiral Inman is the right leader to meet these demanding challenges. I am grateful that he's agreed to make the personal sacrifices necessary to return to full-time Government service and to accept this important assignment at this pivotal time in world events. I'm delighted that he will be joining our national security team, and I thank him for his service to the Nation.

NOTE: The President spoke at 1:33 p.m. in the Rose Garden at the White House.

Statement on Signing the Preventive Health Amendments of 1993
December 16, 1993

Since the beginning of my Administration, we have worked with the Congress on ways to strengthen the Nation's health care system. This partnership for the personal security of America's families moved forward when I signed into law H.R. 2202, the Preventive Health Amendments of 1993.

The primary purpose of this new law is to extend the early detection and disease prevention activities of the Centers for Disease Control and Prevention (CDC), especially by strengthening our efforts for the early detection of breast cancer. While it contains a number of excellent provisions, I am especially pleased to advance the Nation's agenda as it relates to women's health concerns.

Among the provisions of H.R. 2202 are new funds authorized for appropriations in the form of grants by the CDC to States for the detection and treatment of women's reproductive and breast cancers. This program addresses an important national need.

Over 2.5 million women in the United States have breast cancer, and about 182,000 additional cancers are expected to have been detected this year. Once every 12 minutes, a woman dies from breast cancer in the United States, often leaving behind a grieving husband, desolate children, and anguished friends. While mammography is by no means a cure, in many instances, it does detect cancer and leads to reductions in the death rates from the illness among women when appropriate follow-up treatment occurs. Though we don't know what causes breast cancer, how to prevent it or cure it, we do know that broader access to mammograms will make an important medical, personal, and economic difference due to increased early detection.

The legislation expands our efforts not only in breast and cervical cancer prevention but also in areas such as injury control, violence prevention, tuberculosis prevention and research, and trauma care. It is an excellent example of how a bipartisan approach to improving the health care available to Americans can provide needed benefits to so many people.

Much more can and must be done. Health care reform is going to change fundamentally and for the better the manner in which we deal with women's health, especially breast cancer. We know we can reduce deaths from breast cancer by insuring that all women see their health care provider on a regular basis and have access to the tests they need, including mammography when appropriate. Under my Health Security Act, no woman who needs a mammogram will ever be denied one because she cannot pay for it.

WILLIAM J. CLINTON

The White House,
December 16, 1993.

NOTE: H.R. 2202, approved December 14, was assigned Public Law No. 103–183. This statement was released by the Office of the Press Secretary on December 17.

Remarks Announcing the Annenberg Foundation Education Challenge Grants
December 17, 1993

Thank you very much, Secretary Riley and Secretary and Mrs. Bentsen, Deputy Secretary of Education Madeleine Kunin. I want to mention some of the people who are here. I'm glad to see Senator Kennedy, Senator Pell, and Congressman Reed here, and my former colleagues and friends Governor Romer and Governor Edgar, Dr. Gregorian and David Kearns and Ted Sizer and Frank Newman and so many people that I've worked with over the years. When Walter Annenberg was giving his very brief statement, it reminded me of a comment that the President with the best developed mind, Thomas Jefferson, once said. He said, "You know, if I had more time I could write shorter letters." [*Laughter*] So I think he said all that needed to be said.

Walter and Leonore Annenberg have done a remarkable and truly wonderful thing on this day in giving the largest private gift in American history to the future of America's children. It could not have come at a better time. In a moment all of you will repair to another place and discuss in greater detail exactly what this gift will do and how it will be done. But since I spent the better part of my life in public service laboring to improve public education, I want the press and the American people to know that there are two things that are important about this gift: its size and the way the money is going to be spent.

It could not come at a better time, 10 years after the issuance of "A Nation At Risk" report and on the eve, we all earnestly hope, of the passage of our "Goals 2000 Act," which attempts to put into law a mechanism by which the United States can achieve the national education goals adopted by the Governors and by the Bush administration jointly in 1989.

In our legislation, we attempt to set high academic standards, to give our country world-class schools, to give our children a way to fulfill their dreams instead of their nightmares, along with the other things we've tried to do: reforming the student loan program; opening the doors of college to everyone; trying to develop a national system of moving from school to work for those who don't go to college; pushing a

safe schools act so that we don't have 160,000 kids stay home every day because they're afraid to go to school; establishing a system of lifetime learning. These things make a real difference. But if I have learned one thing in all the years, in all the countless hours that Hillary and I have spent in public schools all across this country, it is that the true magic of education in the end occurs between teachers and students and principals and parents and those who care about what happens in the classroom and outside the classroom.

And one of the things that has plagued me all these years is seeing all the successes, because, I tell you, I have tried to focus the American people in the last several weeks on the crime and violence that is consuming so many millions of our young people. But what is important for America to know is that there is another reality out there. There are two realities that are at war, one with the other. There is the reality that we all see: too many guns and too much violence in schools that don't function. There is another reality: In the most difficult circumstances you can find anywhere in this country, there are children and parents who obey the law, who love their country, who believe in the future, and who are in schools working with teachers who are succeeding by any standard of international excellence against all the odds.

Therefore, it is clear that the most pressing need in this country today, the most pressing need, is to have a standard of excellence by which all of us can judge our collective efforts, down to the smallest schoolroom in the smallest community in America, and then to have a system to somehow take what is working against all the odds and make it work everywhere.

All these people who are in this room who have devoted their lives to education are constantly plagued by the fact that nearly every problem has been solved by somebody somewhere, and yet we can't seem to replicate it everywhere else. Anybody who has spent a serious amount of time thinking and looking about this knows that that is the central challenge of this age in education.

That's why Ted Sizer has devoted his career to establishing a system which can be recreated and adapted to the facts of every school. That's why David Kearns left a brilliantly successful career in business and wrote a book about what works in reinventing schools. That's why my friend Frank Newman stopped being a university president and went to the Education Commission of the States and every year hounded Governors like me to help him, because we knew that there were examples that work, and nobody has unraveled this mystery. That's why people often run for Governor and stay Governors of States, believing that we can somehow have the alternative reality that is out there prevail in the end.

And the way this money is going to be allocated is just as important as how much money is being offered, because Walter Annenberg has challenged the rest of us to match his efforts today and in a way is challenging America to realize that there are millions of good kids and good teachers and good efforts being made out there. And the time has come for us to say, here are the national standards, here is a way of measuring whether we're meeting them, and here's a way of recognizing that in reality all these things have to happen school by school, neighborhood by neighborhood, student by student. And what is our excuse, when we can give you a hundred examples of where it's working, for not having thousands and thousands and thousands examples of where it's working?

That is the magic of what is being done. This is a very, very important day for American education and for America's future. And the people in the United States will forever be in the debt of these two fine people.

Thank you very much.

NOTE: The President spoke at 10:34 a.m. in the Roosevelt Room at the White House. In his remarks, he referred to Gov. Jim Edgar of Illinois; Gov. Roy Romer of Colorado; Vartan Gregorian, president, Brown University; David Kearns, president, New American Schools Development Corp.; Theodore R. Sizer, chairman, Coalition for Essential Schools; and Frank Newman, president, Education Commission of the States.

Statement on Signing the Government Securities Act Amendments of 1993
December 17, 1993

Today I have signed into law S. 422, the "Government Securities Act Amendments of 1993." S. 422 permanently reauthorizes the Treasury Department's rulemaking authority under the Government Securities Act and extends important investor protections to the Government securities market. It also provides important new surveillance tools to the Department of the Treasury and the Securities and Exchange Commission. This legislation will help maintain the confidence of investors in the integrity of the Government securities market. It will thus ensure that the Treasury has access to an efficient and liquid market, which is vital to selling the Government's debt at the lowest possible cost.

I am pleased that the legislative process achieved compromises acceptable to the many interested participants. I thank all involved for their hard work culminating in the enactment of this comprehensive and needed legislation. As a result of their efforts, the Federal Government now has the tools necessary to ensure the continuing integrity, efficiency, and liquidity of the Government securities market.

WILLIAM J. CLINTON

The White House,
December 17, 1993.

NOTE: S. 422, approved December 17, was assigned Public Law No. 103–202.

Statement on Signing the Resolution Trust Corporation Completion Act
December 17, 1993

Today I am pleased to sign into law S. 714, the "Resolution Trust Corporation Completion Act." This legislation enables the Federal Government to honor its pledge to protect the nearly 3 million depositors in the thrifts controlled by the Resolution Trust Corporation (RTC) that await final resolution. It represents a decisive step toward bringing the savings and loan debacle to a conclusion.

The Act removes the April 1, 1992, expiration date on $18.3 billion that the Congress appropriated in 1991, thereby making the money available to protect depositors. This amount should enable the RTC to complete all pending and anticipated resolution activities.

The Act codifies the RTC management reforms Treasury Secretary Lloyd Bentsen an-

nounced in March, many of which have already been implemented. It also reaffirms the Administration's commitment to provide additional opportunities for women- and minority-owned businesses to participate in the RTC's contracting activities.

This legislation will bring to a close a costly episode in our Nation's financial history. I appreciate the efforts of all those who have worked to make its enactment possible.

WILLIAM J. CLINTON

The White House,
December 17, 1993.

NOTE: S. 714, approved December 17, was assigned Public Law No. 103–204.

The President's Radio Address
December 18, 1993

Good morning. On this last Saturday before Christmas I want to thank you for listening before you go shopping. And on behalf of America's retailers, I promise I won't keep you long today.

I'd like to talk a little bit about our economic future. I don't mean next week's sales, as strong as I hope they'll be. I mean the future that you and your children will enjoy as families and as workers in the global economy that is taking shape around us.

When I entered office, I pledged that economic renewal would be my highest mission. Our first order of business was to get our own economy in competitive trim. That's why we enacted an economic plan that reduces our deficit by half a trillion dollars over the next 5 years while making targeted investments in technology, education and training, and defense conversion to help those industries and people who have been hurt by defense cutbacks.

Already, that plan is helping to earn important dividends. Interest rates are at historic lows. Inflation is down. We've had 4 straight months of rising housing starts, and last month there

was a 19-year low in the number of people who were late in their home mortgage payments. Millions of people have refinanced their homes and businesses, and the country's created more private sector jobs this year alone than in the previous 4 years combined. Consumer confidence is up dramatically. Ordinary Americans are finally beginning to feel the impact of this recovery. But there is a lot more to do.

First, while renewal must begin here at home, we also have to reach beyond our borders if we are to prosper over the long run. That's one message I have to leave with you today. We're in a time of enormous economic change. Old Communist economies are giving way to market forces. Information, ideas, and money speed around the planet at the speed of light. The new global economy is generating incredible prosperity but also an awful lot of uncertainty and dislocation.

Americans are worried, rightly, about the security of their jobs, about the ability of their companies to stay afloat, about the flight of factories abroad and whether the people running their companies really care about them, about the opportunities all our children will have. It's understandable that so many Americans view the global economy as a threat. But we have to resist the impulse to withdraw behind our trade barriers. From the founding of our Republic to the settling of our broad prairies, it's always been in the American character to reach out and shape our own destiny. We must draw on that spirit for our Nation to thrive in this new age.

Our workers in today's economy are more productive than ever. Fewer people are producing more and more goods and services. But in an environment like that, the only way to create more jobs and to raise incomes is to have more customers. And that means more exports. That's why, in this global economy, America must compete and not retreat.

Since this summer, our administration has taken several important steps to do that. First, at a July summit in Tokyo, we reached agreement with our major trading partners in Europe, Japan, and Canada to open their markets in a number of sectors to our products. We also struck a new agreement with Japan that can begin to correct our unacceptable trade imbalance with them.

Second, in November we secured congressional approval of the North American Free Trade Agreement. NAFTA creates the world's largest free trade area. For America, that means we can find new customers in Mexico, and that in turn means more jobs here at home. And NAFTA can lead to similar arrangements with emerging free market economies all across the Latin American area.

Just after we passed NAFTA, I convened a first-ever meeting in Seattle with leaders from the Asian-Pacific region, the fastest growing economy in the world. I made it clear that our Nation intends to share in the rising tide of Pacific prosperity.

And just this week, we concluded the GATT world trade talks that began 7 years ago. This is a good, solid deal for our workers and our businesses. It cuts foreign tariffs on U.S. products in 8,000 different product areas by an average of a third. Once it's fully in place, it will add as much as $100 billion to $200 billion to our economy every year, and create hundreds of thousands of new and good-paying American jobs.

When you put that with the fact that we have removed export controls from over $35 billion in high-tech computers and telecommunications equipment, I'm proud of the strides our country has made toward opening our economy, generating more jobs from trade and renewal this year.

Not since the end of World War II has the United States secured so many historic trade expansion agreements in so short a period. These efforts are making the world's economic changes work to our advantage, and they're reestablishing our leadership in global affairs. But none of this would have been possible without the work that you do every day to make our Nation stronger, to make our communities more vibrant, and our families more secure.

This year, we've worked hard to help you in those daily strivings. We've put the economic interests of America's broad middle class back at the center of our policies at home with a fairer Tax Code, with a tax break to 15 million lower wage working families to encourage them to keep working and raising their children and to stay off welfare with passage of the family and medical leave law.

And during the coming year, my administration will continue to work so that all Americans can benefit from this new global economy. That means we have to pass a dramatic retraining program, pass our school-to-work program to help with apprenticeships for non-college-bound young people, pass the safe schools act and our safe streets initiative to put 100,000 more police officers on your streets, and pass universal health care reform so that health care will be a security for American families and always be there.

As we celebrate our blessings during this holiday season, let's remember that Americans have never cowered from change; we have always mastered it. That is something to be grateful for. And together, we're going to do it once again.

Thanks for listening.

NOTE: The President spoke at 10:06 a.m. from the Oval Office at the White House.

Teleconference Remarks on Community Policing Grants and an Exchange With Reporters
December 20, 1993

The President. It's nice to hear all of you. I'm here with the Vice President and Attorney General Reno and our Drug Director, Lee Brown, to congratulate all of you for working so hard to help make your communities and, of course, our country safer again. Today I'm proud to announce that the six of you on this phone, along with the leaders of 68 other cities and towns all across the country, will receive the first grants to put more police on the street and expand community policing.

The Justice Department received applications from more than 1,000 communities across our Nation, and the proposals we got for community policing from your police departments were truly outstanding. I know these grants are simply a downpayment on our pledge to put 100,000 new police officers on the streets. It's just the beginning. As soon as Congress comes back in 1994, I want them to send me a crime bill that finishes that job and puts 100,000 more police on the street, expands boot camps and drug courts like the one the Attorney General started in Miami, gets handguns out of the hands of minors, and bans assault weapons.

Earlier this month, as all of you know, I signed the Brady bill which broke 7 years of gridlock on this issue. And we just can't afford to wait any longer for the crime bill. In the meanwhile I'm excited about what you're doing because we know community policing works. It worked for our Drug Director, Lee Brown, in Houston and New York, and it's working all across the country.

So I want to just thank all of you very much and say that I wish I could be there with you today. I wish I could see your police officers. And I hope you'll tell them all that help is on the way, and we'll do our best to be there for you, to be good partners with you. And I know I'm speaking for the Vice President, the Attorney General, and Lee Brown in saying we'll stay after this until the job is done.

[*At this point, the President introduced Mayor Richard Riordan of Los Angeles, CA, Mayor James Griffin of Buffalo, NY, Mayor Paul Tauer of Aurora, CO, Mayor Sharpe James of Newark, NJ, Mayor Nelson Wolff of San Antonio, TX,* and Mayor Gary Loster of Saginaw, MI, and each made brief remarks.]

The President. Thank you very much, Mayor.

I want to ask the Attorney General now to say a word, because the Justice Department, as you know, managed the process by which your cities were selected. I think they did a very good job, and so I'd like to call on her and let her say a few words.

Attorney General Reno. Mayors, I just want to thank you. Your applications were so impressive. They indicate just what can be done with community policing, how it can both prevent crime and identify the real bad guys who need to be put away. And this is the first round; there are more to come. And we look forward to working with you in a real, true partnership. Merry Christmas.

The President. I'm going to let Lee Brown say a word to you now. You know, he started a community policing program in New York City. And I don't know if you saw it, but last week there was a wonderful cover story in the New York Times Sunday Magazine about a police officer named Kevin Jett who works eight square blocks in one of the toughest neighborhoods in New York. And the story pointed out that he not only arrests criminals but he also prevents a lot of crimes from occurring in the first place. And I think that's the emphasis we ought to have here. This is not simply a question of catching people who break the law in a violent fashion; it's preventing crime.

So I want Lee to say a word.

Mr. Brown. Let me congratulate the mayors and certainly the police chiefs for being selected. I've experienced community policing in Houston and New York; New York, for example, after one year we saw crime go down in every major category for the first time in 36 years. I see it as not only a better but a smarter and certainly more cost-effective way of using police resources.

So congratulations to all of you, and Merry Christmas.

The President. In closing, let me say, I know that from Los Angeles to Michigan, we've Members of Congress who are actually there today, as well as in Buffalo and perhaps in some other places. And I really thank all of you for your support. Somebody told me that Mayor Riordan had the whole southern California delegation there, and if he does, I bet he's talking about more than law enforcement. I hear all of the movement in the background. I wish you all a happy holiday, and I thank you. You know, when you're taking these kind of affirmative actions, the President can't do it alone. We've got to have the support of Congress. And I really appreciate their presence there.

And thank you all so much. And congratulations to you and to the 68 other cities and towns who are in the vanguard of this move to bring community policing to our entire Nation.

Thank you very much.

Anticrime Legislation

Q. Do you think you're going to get that bill through?

The President. Oh, I do, yes.

Q. The atmosphere has changed, hasn't it?

The President. It has changed. You know, there may be some differences between us and the House on the amount of the bill or exactly how it should be spent, but I think there is now a clear bipartisan commitment in both Houses for the 100,000 police officers on the street, for the drug courts, and for some of the other innovations. And so we're very, very hopeful that we can do it.

I think having the mayors, again, out there in small towns as well as the big cities, the Democrats and the Republicans marching arm in arm, it's changed the dynamic of this issue in America in a way that I think will be very good in helping us to make our people safer.

Q. Do you think Congress is getting the message at home while they're at home?

The President. Big time. That's our sense, that they're really hearing from the people that they just have to have more security on the streets, in their schools and communities.

The Economy

Q. Mr. President, are you taking too much credit for the growth of the economy? There have been stories suggesting that it may not be all your doing.

The President. Well, I saw those stories. I got tickled this morning. I took a poll around the staff. We just had a 2-hour meeting on the budget, and I said, if the economy were bad who do you think would be blamed? *[Laughter]*

I'm not so concerned about who gets the credit really. The American people get the credit, if they go back to work, if they're becoming more competitive, if they're investing their money.

I do know this: Even going back after the election, from the time we announced our deficit reduction plan to the time it was presented, to the time it was enacted, to the present day, the steady, disciplined drop in interest rates has played a major, major role in helping millions of people to refinance their homes and businesses—last year we had a 19-year low in delinquencies in home mortgages—and getting all this investment for new jobs.

So I believe our economic policies are stabilizing this country and contributing to this recovery. I think a lot of Americans have been working for years and years and years to be competitive in the global economy, and I think that is to their credit. I mean, we have a private sector economy. No person in public life can take credit for it. But if we hadn't done what we have done on the economic plan to drive interest rates down and to spur reinvestment, I don't think we'd be where we are on the economy.

Q. But every day we read about thousands being laid off.

The President. Well, it's still a terrible problem. That's why I always say we've got a lot more to do.

The problem that all rich countries are facing now is that productivity, which has always been a good thing in the economy—that is, fewer people produce more goods and services increases their ability to earn more income—that's a problem unless you can sell all the goods and services you're producing. If you don't, it keeps unemployment higher than it should be, and it depresses wages.

So that will be our challenge next year. That's why I wanted to get NAFTA this year; that's why I wanted to get that GATT trade agreement this year; that's why I wanted to try to start a new relationship with Japan and the Far East this year, so we would have more customers for our goods and services, so we can grow this economy.

Q. Are you going to have the flexibility to deal with the job training issues and retraining, given the budget situation?

The President. Well, I've already spent 2 hours on that today, and I expect I'll spend a couple more hours on it. I certainly——

Q. Can you wrap it up now the budget's over?

The President. Well, we're not done yet, but we worked hard on that today. We're going to keep working. We have a few more days. But the retraining issue is important because there have been a lot of news stories lately—many of you perhaps have run them—showing that people that either have high skill levels or are capable of getting them in a hurry have much shorter periods of unemployment and are much more likely to get good-paying jobs.

We still don't have the kind of retraining system we need. So that's going to be a big part of next year's initiative.

Haiti

Q. Prime Minister Malval is criticizing President Aristide openly for being an obstacle to some sort of reconciliation. Are you on board with Prime Minister Malval or President Aristide? Where are you trying to throw your support?

The President. I wouldn't say it's an either-or thing. Let me say, we have been working with this Friends of Haiti group, with our friends in Canada and France and Venezuela, to try to come up with a new approach that would restore democracy, would create the conditions where President Aristide could return, and would meet the fundamental objective we tried to meet in the Governors Island accord: to guarantee the security and the human rights and safety of all the parties in the previous disputes.

So we're going to take another run at it and see if we can do something on it. And it's going to require some flexibility on all sides. It just is. And we'll just have to see if we can get there. We're going to try, hard.

Q. Thank you.

The President. Thank you all very much.

NOTE: The President spoke at 11 a.m. in the Oval Office at the White House. The exchange portion of this item could not be verified because the tape was incomplete.

Remarks on Signing the National Child Protection Act of 1993
December 20, 1993

I'm delighted to see all of you here. And I want to especially recognize Secretary Shalala and my good friend Marian Wright Edelman. Senator Biden, thank you for being here, sir; Congresswoman Schroeder; Congressman Edwards; and my former colleague and longtime friend Governor Jim Thompson from Illinois; Oprah Winfrey; Lynn Swann; and Andrew Vachss. Thank you all very much for helping this day to come to pass.

The holiday season is a time for sharing the warmth of human contact with families and friends. And making this a joyous and safe time for children everywhere is important. That makes this legislation, the National Child Protection Act, especially significant. With it we can give a great gift, a much improved system for protecting our children from being abused or harmed by those to whom we have entrusted them.

Not unlike the Brady bill, this law creates a national data base network. This one can be used by any child care provider in America to conduct a background check to determine if a job applicant can be trusted with our children, and if not, to prevent that person from ever working with children.

For the first time, we'll have a system in place to protect the many millions of American children who receive care and supervision in formal day care and in other settings from other organizations. This law will give us the tools we need to safeguard children from those who have perpetrated crimes of child abuse or sex abuse or drug use or those who have been convicted of felonies. It's very important that we give working parents peace of mind about child care.

A majority of mothers with young children now work outside the home. Six million children are placed in formal day care settings every day. Balancing work and family is hard, and parents are worried about their personal security and the security of their children in an increasingly violent world.

Like the Brady bill and the crime bill, which I hope and believe will pass soon, this act will help us to take our streets, our neighborhoods, the institutions we rely on, back for American values and American children. There is nothing more important that our Government could be doing now.

Like all change, passing this important law has not been easy. And there are many to thank. First of all, I thank you, Oprah, for a lifetime of being committed to the well-being of our children and for giving child abuse issues such wonderful coverage on your show. You wrote the original blueprint for this law, and we're grateful, becoming a tireless advocate for its passage, lobbying Members of Congress of both parties for more than 2 years, and lobbying the President—people occasionally do that, too. All of us, but especially our children, owe you their gratitude.

Now we can help to prevent child abuse with this measure, not just to catch people who do it. It's a great cause and a remarkable achievement, and I want to thank all the rest of you

who were involved in it.

Finally, let me say, especially for the benefit of the Members of Congress here, this is the last piece of legislation I will sign from this session of Congress. It wraps up a very productive session, a session that dealt with family leave and motor voter and a new economic plan that brought low interest rates and recovery, with the national service bill that I think will galvanize the imagination of a whole generation of young people, with new trade legislation, and with the Brady bill. But this is a good bill to end on, a bill that ends where all of us should begin, by putting our children first.

Thank you very much. I'd like to invite you all to come up here for the signing.

NOTE: The President spoke at 11:54 a.m. in the Roosevelt Room at the White House. In his remarks, he referred to Marian Wright Edelman, president and executive director, Children's Defense Fund; Oprah Winfrey and Lynn Swann, television hosts; and Andrew Vachss, originator of the concept of the legislation. H.R. 1237, approved December 20, was assigned Public Law No. 103–209.

Statement on Signing Persian Gulf War Veterans Health Care Legislation
December 20, 1993

I am deeply concerned about the reports of health problems afflicting a number of our Persian Gulf veterans. The legislation I am signing today, H.R. 2535, addresses those problems by authorizing the Department of Veterans Affairs (VA) to treat them for any disease that may have resulted from their exposure to toxic substances or environmental hazards in the Gulf.

Since our troops returned home over 2 years ago, we have heard from many who are experiencing serious health problems for which modern medicine is having difficulty establishing a cause or a diagnosis.

With parades and a national outpouring of gratitude, we showed those brave men and women our appreciation for the sacrifices they made for all of us. Now we must stand by those who are suffering.

The symptoms these veterans experience have

included, among other things, fatigue, painful muscles and joints, bleeding gums, skin rashes, short-term memory loss, and hair loss. With this legislation, the VA will have the authority to provide to these veterans both inpatient and outpatient care on a priority basis. Thus, we can help make certain that these veterans' health care needs are met as fully as possible while important research into their problems goes forward.

This legislation also provides for reimbursement to these veterans for any copayments they may have made to the VA for care that might have been necessary because of their exposures in the Persian Gulf.

In addition, this legislation extends the VAs authority to:

- furnish Vietnam veterans with care that may be related to their exposure to agent orange;

- furnish veterans who participated in nuclear weapons tests or in the occupation of Hiroshima or Nagasaki with care that may be related to their exposure to ionizing radiation;
- provide women veterans with sexual trauma counseling; and,
- maintain its regional office in the Philippines.

Over 650,000 service men and women from United States forces valiantly forced Sadam Hussein's armies from Kuwait, and earned the respect and admiration of people around the globe. They also earned our Nation's undying gratitude and support.

WILLIAM J. CLINTON

The White House,
December 20, 1993.

NOTE: H.R. 2535, approved December 20, was assigned Public Law No. 103–210.

Statement on Establishment of the United Nations High Commissioner for Human Rights
December 20, 1993

I welcome the decision today by the United Nations General Assembly to establish a High Commissioner for Human Rights. Since Eleanor Roosevelt first fought for the Universal Declaration of Human Rights in 1948, the United States has led the way to ensure that the United Nations is a strong force for human dignity and respect for basic civil and political rights. The High Commissioner will be an influential and persuasive advocate for human rights around the world.

The High Commissioner's mandate to promote human rights worldwide will include coordinating human rights activities within the United Nations system, providing advisory services and technical assistance to governments and regional human rights organizations, and engaging in dialog with governments on promotion of human rights.

Today's action achieves one of my key goals for this year's U.N. General Assembly and advances an enduring goal of American foreign policy. The United States will lend its full support to the High Commissioner's efforts to ensure that the citizens of the world are able to live free from repression and fear.

Appointment for Assistant to the President for Congressional Affairs
December 20, 1993

The President announced today that he has appointed Pat Griffin to be the Assistant to the President for Congressional Affairs. Mr. Griffin, an experienced professional with experience in academia, government, and the private sector, will begin work at the White House in mid-January.

"I am very glad to have someone of Pat Griffin's skill and experience leading my legislative team here at the White House," said the President. "We have an ambitious agenda on the Hill for the next year, with difficult challenges like health care, crime, and welfare reform to be addressed. I am counting on Pat to work closely with Members on both sides of the aisle to move those issues forward."

NOTE: A biography of the appointee was made available by the Office of the Press Secretary.

Nomination for an Assistant Secretary of Education
December 20, 1993

The President announced today that he intends to nominate Rodney A. McCowan to be the Assistant Secretary of Education for the Office of Human Resources and Administration. Mr. McCowan has been serving as Chief of Staff to Deputy Secretary of Education Madeleine Kunin. As Assistant Secretary, he will oversee the Department's administrative functions, including human resources, information systems, Government reinvention initiatives, and labor-management relations.

"Rodney McCowan is an experienced manager who has done an excellent job at the Department of Education since the beginning of this administration," said the President. "I hope that he will continue to do well in his new capacity."

NOTE: A biography of the nominee was made available by the Office of the Press Secretary.

Remarks at the Groundbreaking Ceremony for the Pan Am Flight 103 Memorial in Arlington, Virginia
December 21, 1993

Thank you very much. Thank you. I believe, ladies and gentlemen, before you sit we should give a standing ovation to Jane for all the work that she has done here. [*Applause*] Thank you very much, Senator and Mrs. Kennedy, Senator Lautenberg, General Reno, and most importantly, the families, friends, and supporters of Pan Am 103.

On this day, 5 years ago, Pan American flight 103 was torn from the sky over the hills of Lockerbie, Scotland. Today we assemble in solemn remembrance to dedicate a simple monument to the victims of a savage act of terrorism. Here there will soon stand a cairn, the traditional Scottish marker for the resting place of the dead, built of 270 stones to memorialize 259 passengers and crew and the 11 villagers below whose lives were stolen without warning. Each tells the story of a life wrongfully cut short. Like so many of you here today, these granite stones have traveled a long way, carved from a quarry in Lockerbie and donated to the families of those who were murdered. These rose-red stones are now given to the Nation to stand here among so many silent markers of our Nation's sacrifice.

There were on that day 189 Americans, including 25 members of our Armed Forces, aboard Pan Am 103. We honor them. This memorial will serve as lasting testament to the innocent who died, to the grieving who survive them, to the brave who found in tragedy the strength and the persistence to ensure that their children, their parents, their brothers and sisters would not be forgotten.

I know this season must be especially difficult for all of you. I know you still see their faces and hear their voices and feel their absence, and nothing the rest of us can do can erase that loss. But I say to you today that our Nation will never stop pursuing justice against those who caused it, for the attack on Pan Am 103 was an attack not only on the individuals from 21 nations who were aboard the aircraft, it was an attack on America.

Our creed of freedom and opportunity is not a mere abstraction and neither are its enemies. Indeed, the states that sponsor terrorism know that the American idea is a mortal threat to their illegitimate and repressive authority. They know, too, that history, the rising tide of democracy seen everywhere in the world, is turning against them. And so with terrorism and any other means at their disposal, they lash back. We saw it in Pan Am 103. We saw it at the World Trade Center. We saw it in an attempt to assassinate former President Bush. These outlaws seek to legitimize their voice through violence, to advance their agenda through threats, to cripple our daily lives through fear. My friends, you and the efforts you have made are proof that they fundamentally misunderstand the character of America.

Just a few moments ago, I had the opportunity to meet with some representatives of the families of Pan Am 103. It was clear to me as never before that the brutality of their crime only fortified your determination, and I can tell you it only fortifies the determination of your Nation and its Government. That is why we remain determined to see that those who murdered those who were aboard Pan Am 103 are brought to justice, why we have demanded the surrender of the two Libyans indicted for this vicious offense, why we have pushed for and secured tougher international sanctions against Libya, and why we will not rest until the case is closed.

As we break ground, let us vow again that we will do all we can to protect our people. And let us draw renewed strength from the lives of the individuals in whose memories we come to honor.

I want to read to you in closing the words of Georgia Nucci, who lost her son over Lockerbie and later assembled an extraordinary book about the lives of each of the victims. As she returned from Scotland, she wrote the following: "Out of the ashes of this disaster came a torrent of love and friendship and help freely given from a whole community that was itself a victim."

Today is the shortest day of the year. But the winter solstice is also a turning point from which the light begins to return. While this season and this day for you and for all Americans are blackened by the agony of senseless loss, I pray that each of your lives will be brightened in some measure by the monument we dedicate here.

Let us grieve for those who fell from the firmament, and those who lay below, on that winter day still frozen so clearly in your memory. The Bible says: "Blessed are they that mourn, for they shall be comforted." As each stone is set in this cairn, may your wounds set and heal as well. And as long as this monument shall stand, may you find comfort in the knowledge that your Nation stands behind you.

I ask you now to join me in a moment of silent prayer.

I'd like now to ask Constable George Esson and Eleanor and Nicky Bright to join Jane Schultz down here for the groundbreaking ceremony.

NOTE: The President spoke at 10:23 a.m. at Arlington National Cemetery. In his remarks, he referred to Jane Schultz, executive vice president, Victims of Pan Am Flight 103; Chief Constable George Esson of Dumfries, Scotland; and Eleanor and Nicky Bright, family members of a Pan Am flight 103 victim. The proclamation of December 17 on the fifth anniversary day of remembrance is listed in Appendix D at the end of this volume.

Remarks Honoring UNICEF Health Heroes
December 21, 1993

Thank you. Thank you very much, Jim. Hillary and I are delighted to have you and so many of your friends from around America here today for the presentation of this report. We especially appreciate the presence here—I see Senator Leahy, Senator Sarbanes, and Congressman Obey. I don't know if Senator Dole and Congressman Porter are here, but I think they were coming. I'm delighted to see, from the administration, Tim Wirth from the State Department; Secretary Shalala from HHS; our United Nations Ambassador, Madeleine Albright; our AID Administrator, Brian Atwood; and the Surgeon General, Dr. Joycelyn Elders. There are many other distinguished people here, but most of all I'm glad to see the children here. For after all, we're here to celebrate a season filled with the joy of children and to remind ourselves of much of the work still to be done.

James Agee once wrote, "In every child who is born under no matter what circumstances, the potentiality of the human race is born again, and in him, too, our terrific responsibility toward human life, toward the utmost idea of goodness, the horror of error, and of God." We are here in part to note the outstanding work of the fine man who just spoke.

Jim Grant and UNICEF are among the best

friends any child could have. UNICEF was the driving force behind the historic world summit for children 3 years ago when leaders of 150 nations met to define the goals for improving health and welfare of our children by the year 2000. Jim and UNICEF continue to see that all the rest of us do our part to make progress toward those goals.

Today, with the annual State of the World's Children Report, UNICEF lays down another marker for the rest of us. The U.S. Agency for International Development also releases its own report on child survival. And these impressive reports both mark the progress that has been made as well as outlining what still we must do. They document, for example, that over the past decade the international community has reduced the instances of some of the world's worst childhood diseases: measles, polio, and neo-natal tetanus, by over half. Yet we have still so much to do. Around the world, children suffer more than anyone else from poverty, malnutrition, disease, environmental decay, and even armed conflict. Today and every day in villages and neighborhoods around the globe, 30,000 children will die from malnutrition and preventable disease. As Jim has noted, behind each of these statistics there's a face, a family, a set of hopes and dreams, and a future that now will never be.

And while the plight of children abroad is especially acute, we must never forget that poverty, hunger, and disease are not strangers to our children here in the United States. One of every five of our children lives in poverty. By the time they're 15 years old, nearly one-third of our children in inner cities will have known someone who has died violently. One of my highest goals is to see that the next generation of our children grows up with more health, more security, more safety, and more hope than those of this generation. That's one of the reasons why we worked so hard for the Family and Medical Leave Act, for the new crime bill, for the Brady bill, and perhaps most importantly, for universal health care coverage for all of our people.

The First Lady and Secretary Shalala and others are working on a health care reform plan that, when enacted, will provide complete preventive care and health security for over 8 million American children that today are uninsured. We're working to boost the immunization rate of our 2-year-olds to 90 percent; striving to en-

sure adequate nutrition for all of our children, including full funding for the women, infants and children's feeding program; fighting the plague of violence against our children; and committed also to improving the lives of children in other lands, not out of simple charity but also out of prudence, because investing in the children of the world can be the most cost-effective way not only to relieve suffering but to advance economies, to promote self-sufficiency, to promote democracy, and to avert future conflicts.

There have been times when the fight for the world's children seemed to be a losing one. But the children's summit and related events have transformed that frustration into hope. Our own Nation can take pride in decades of our leadership, with bipartisan support here at home on behalf of worldwide efforts to improve children's health.

The continuing leadership of this Nation is revealed in the work of the six health heroes we will honor here today and countless others like them. Building on their contributions and concentrating on the most cost-effective way of helping children, we're making great strides in areas like immunization and child nutrition. We're determined to build on this progress.

Under the direction of AID Director Brian Atwood, we proposed an overhaul of our foreign assistance programs to reflect new times and new priorities. At the heart of this is a vision for sustainable development centered on human development, a vision that will help us to make progress in child health, population, and environmental protection, a cause the Vice President has done so much to advance. Working with UNICEF and other governmental and nongovernmental organizations, we want to make those goals at the children's summit come true. That's the best Christmas present we could give to the world.

So today I call on Americans in private and public life to join with leaders in developing nations to help ensure that we do make tangible progress, especially in three key areas. First, by the year 2000, we ought to set our sights on getting 90 percent of the world's children vaccinated for measles and on virtually eradicating polio, as surely as the world eradicated smallpox decades ago. Second, we should strive to give at least 80 percent of the world's children access to lifesaving treatment for the world's two biggest childhood killers, diarrhea and pneumonia.

Third, on nutrition, the world can make enormous improvements through simple steps such as eliminating Vitamin A deficiency, which can be deadly, and by promoting more breast feeding for infants.

These are simple low-cost strategies. They don't require space-age technology. They rely on basic medicines, inexpensive vaccines, drinkable water, access to family planning, and expanded educational opportunities, especially for women and girls. And we can afford to do our part in this effort because the financial burden will be shared among many nations.

If we let the world's children suffer, we know that in time we'll reap a bitter harvest of despair and desperation and violence. We know that when children grow up healthy and nurtured, they're more likely to do better by their own children, they're more likely to become citizens and contributors, more likely to add to the global marketplace. This is how free societies and open markets evolve, how global progress happens, how future friends of the United States and these children will be created.

We still call this, I think instructively, the post-cold-war era. The problem with that designation is it tells us where we've been but not where we're going. We have to chart a new path, channeling the remarkable forces at work in this era with a bold vision of what might be. Let us today commit that our children and the world's children will figure large in that vision, that the post-cold-war era will instead be the world's era of peace and prosperity and humanity in which our minds and hearts work together to give all children a better life.

Now I'd like to ask our six health heroes to step forward and to be recognized for the outstanding work they've done. First, Dr. Gretchen Berggren, being recognized for her lifelong commitment to the health of the world's children as a medical missionary and an innovator in community-based nutrition and primary health care; next, Dr. William Foege, for his long commitment to the health of the world's children through his global leadership on immunization goals and the eradication of smallpox; Dr. Norbert Hirschorn, for his distinguished career in public health and his leadership in demonstrating the value of oral rehydration therapy to change children's lives all around the world; Dr. Donald Hopkins, for his leadership in the global effort to eradicate Guinea worm and other diseases and to assure safe water and better sanitation to support children's health around the world; Patrice Jeliffe, for her lifetime commitment to the world's children as a public health expert, promoting breast feeding and appropriate weaning foods and practices in the developing world; Dr. Carl E. Taylor, for his sustained work around the world, from India to Beijing, which has demonstrated key linkages among nutrition, family size, and other efforts on child survival.

Thank you.

NOTE: The President spoke at 2:28 p.m. in the East Room at the White House. In his remarks, he referred to Jim Grant, American Executive Director, United Nations Children's Fund (UNICEF).

Statement on House Majority Leader Richard Gephardt's Support for Legislation on the General Agreement on Tariffs and Trade
December 21, 1993

I welcome Majority Leader Richard Gephardt's support for the implementation of the Uruguay round agreement. His statement reflects the fact that we have a strong agreement that promises important benefits for U.S. industry, services, and agriculture. The majority leader's support will help make it possible to imple-ment the agreement expeditiously, with a strong base of congressional support.

The overriding commitment of this administration in trade policy has been to open markets and expand trade—multilaterally where possible, and bilaterally where necessary—and to enforce trade laws against unfair trade practices by other trading nations. The successful Uruguay round result strengthens our hand in doing so, and I look forward to working with the majority leader and others in Congress on the implementing legislation.

Nomination for an Assistant Secretary of Commerce
December 21, 1993

The President announced today that he intends to nominate Thomas R. Bloom to be Chief Financial Officer and Assistant Secretary for Administration at the Department of Commerce. Upon confirmation by the Senate, Mr. Bloom will supervise the overall administration and budget of the Commerce Department.

"In this time of constrained budgets, we need people with the financial and management expertise of Thomas Bloom to ensure that the taxpayers' money is effectively managed," said the President. "I welcome his service at the Commerce Department."

NOTE: A biography of the nominee was made available by the Office of the Press Secretary.

Nomination for Vice Chairman of the Joint Chiefs of Staff
December 21, 1993

The President announced his intention today to nominate Adm. William A. Owens, USN, to be Vice Chairman of the Joint Chiefs of Staff, Department of Defense. Admiral Owens will succeed Adm. David E. Jeremiah, USN, who is retiring.

"Admiral Owens has served his country proudly and with distinction for 35 years. He has held a number of challenging assignments and demonstrated strong leadership ability," said the President. "I am certain that he will perform up to the high standards set by his predecessor, Admiral Jeremiah, in this key post."

NOTE: A biography of the nominee was made available by the Office of the Press Secretary.

Nomination for Chief Counsel at the Small Business Administration
December 21, 1993

The President announced his intention today to nominate Jere W. Glover, the founder of several small businesses, to be the Small Business Administration's Chief Counsel for Advocacy. The Chief Counsel acts as a spokesman for small business interests throughout the Government, as well as being an adviser to the SBA Administrator and overseeing the development of research and economic analysis projects on behalf of the small business community.

"Jere Glover knows what it takes to make a small business successful, and he knows how Government works. As the SBA's Chief Counsel, he will work to make every part of the Federal Government responsive to small businesses' needs."

NOTE: A biography of the nominee was made available by the Office of the Press Secretary.

Appointment for Posts at the United States Office of Consumer Affairs
December 21, 1993

The President announced today that he will appoint Polly B. Baca to be Director and Paul Steven Miller to be Deputy Director of the Department of Health and Human Services U.S. Office of Consumer Affairs. The Office of Consumer Affairs is the primary Agency in the Federal Government for consumer affairs and has responsibility to both the White House and the Department of Health and Human Services on this issue.

"We have a responsibility to the American people to ensure that they are treated fairly in the consumer marketplace," said the President. "I am counting on Polly Baca and Paul Miller to run this important office and to represent the needs of consumers throughout the Federal Government."

NOTE: Biographies of the appointees were made available by the Office of the Press Secretary.

Remarks Announcing Grants for Programs for the Homeless
December 22, 1993

Thank you, Reverend Steinbruck. He was so good I kind of hate to spoil the occasion. [*Laughter*] I want to thank all of you for being here, those of you who work in the field of homelessness. I want to thank Senator Riegle and Congressman Vento and Congressman Frank and Congressman Kildee for their support in the Congress. I want to say how good it is to see my friend Mayor Schmoke here who's done so much in the housing area. And I want to thank, too, Secretary Cisneros and Assistant Secretary Cuomo for the leadership they have shown.

I want to try to explain why, 3 days before Christmas, this is an important event not just because of the money involved but because this represents a different approach to what has become our most painful and, as a country, I think one of our most embarrassing social problems.

We have tried to look beyond the issue of temporary shelters to the question of permanent relief from the condition of homelessness. And I congratulate Assistant Secretary Cuomo and all the people at HUD, who worked with a lot of you who labor in housing and have for years for the homeless, a lot of you who've worked with the mentally ill, with people who have other problems, in coming up with an approach that at least gives us a chance to try to go beyond the symptoms to the cause, to try to deal with this problem on a long-term basis.

For years, our Nation's attention has been properly focused on the emergency needs of the homeless and the efforts just to find people a place to stay on a cold night. That's an important thing. Nearly every day when I go out running I run by a group of homeless men who sleep on the grates within two blocks of my back door. And we've developed a kind of a friendly relationship. They say hello to me. I say hello to them. I wish to goodness on the days that are cold and windy, when I find it difficult to find the courage to run, they at least didn't have to spend the night there. But I also know that there are other factors at work inside the minds and hearts of those people which make some of them reluctant to come in and which make it impossible for them to stay in.

So we have tried to ask some other questions with this proposal: What kind of skills and assistance do homeless people need to really move from the streets to places of their own? How do we help maintain their housing in more permanent and stable ways when lives themselves have often never been permanent or stable in any traditional sense?

For some of the homeless we may never find the answers. For whatever sad reason, some people do drift beyond the outer realm of society and never come back. But a lot of others, especially the parents and their children, can be lifted out of their helplessness and hopelessness if we relate to them in the right way.

You heard the Secretary say that yesterday the United States Conference of Mayors said that as much as 43 percent of the homeless population may now be parents and children. The mayors' press conference yesterday was the first one ever attended by an administration official since the mayors formed their task force on homelessness 10 years ago. And I want to thank again the leadership at HUD, starting with the Secretary, for bringing new energy and attention to this.

I didn't have much to do with it except to ask that simple question when my longtime friend Henry Cisneros and I talked about this. I just said, "Will we ever be able to show the American people that there aren't so many people on the streets?"

On Sunday there was a wonderful piece in the New York Times Sunday Magazine about a woman who has transformed an old stereotype of single-room occupancy hotels and replaced it with a new model to help meet the long-term needs we're discussing. She's reinvented this single-room occupancy housing to create well-kept places and integrate services for people with special needs and disabilities. And in so doing, she's helping people regain control over their lives.

None of the initiatives of this administration—strengthening work and family and community—can be done without forming a partnership with people on the front-lines, like that lady and like so many of you in this room, the people who give of themselves not just on Christmas Day but every day. But as Christmas approaches, I hope the American people will, in all their Christmas prayers, save room for a simple one,

that all of us somehow might realize the humility to know how blessed we are to be in this country, and still to remember those who are not blessed, though they are among our midst.

This Christmas all many of them wish for is a place to spend the night. But what we know is, if they're going to have a place to spend the night, they have to have a place where they can live and grow and deal with the demons that bedevil so many of us in this country.

I have a list—I won't read it to you but I was—that Henry gave me that kind of is representative of the kinds of people who are getting these grants. Sometimes I think we make them more inaccessible to ordinary Americans by talking about things like support services and transition services and this, that, the other thing. But in plain English, what we're trying to do is take people who are battered and bruised and broken, but who still have a lot of God's grace left in them, and find a way to bring all that back to the surface and put their own lives back more in their control.

I hope this new approach works. If it does, it will be because of a lot of you out there on the front-lines who are making it work, like this fine and funny man of the cloth. If it does, we will have given the American people a good Christmas present.

Thank you very much.

NOTE: The President spoke at 2:55 p.m. in the Roosevelt Room at the White House. In his remarks, he referred to Rev. John Steinbruck, pastor, Luther Place Memorial Church.

Message on the Observance of Christmas
December 22, 1993

Warmest greetings to all who are celebrating Christmas in this season of hope.

Each year at this time, we gather together with our loved ones. We teach our children to believe that, with faith and hard work, their dreams can come true. We reach out to each other in caring and fellowship. We look to the future with hope and always with the most earnest of mankind's prayers—the prayer for peace.

Thankfully, at this Christmastime, we can joyously celebrate the results of our prayers.

Around the world, people are embracing the promise of the post-Cold War era, throwing off the shackles of tyranny and committing themselves to the ideals of democracy. Old enemies who met for centuries on the battlefield are now meeting on common ground to discuss peace. In our own country, many citizens are rededicating themselves to improving their communities and to ending the crime and violence that still threaten us. This has indeed been a year worthy of the Prince of Peace.

I have always believed that the Christmas spirit of giving and caring joins children and parents across the country and around the world. This year, let us listen to the dreams of our children and gain strength from their idealism. On this holiday, let us reach out to the people around us and work for a world at peace.

Hillary joins me in extending best wishes to all for a very merry Christmas.

BILL CLINTON

Statement by the Press Secretary on the President's Telephone Conversation With President Boris Yeltsin of Russia
December 22, 1993

The President telephoned Russian President Yeltsin in Moscow this morning. The two leaders spoke for 30 minutes.

The President offered his congratulations to President Yeltsin and the Russian people on the recent free and fair elections held in Russia and on the adoption of a new constitution. President Yeltsin said that he and the Russian Government intended to work well and constructively with the new Parliament.

The two leaders discussed preparations for their January meetings in Moscow, agreeing that part of the agenda would include a review of U.S.-Russian economic cooperation to date. In this connection the President reaffirmed strong U.S. support for economic reform and democracy in Russia. President Yeltsin confirmed his intention to continue a firm course of economic reform in Russia.

The two Presidents also discussed foreign policy issues that will be on the agenda for their January meetings. They agreed on the need to continue the cooperative tripartite dialog with Ukraine, with the aim of resolving the complex set of nuclear issues. President Yeltsin affirmed that Russia had no intention of interfering in the affairs of its neighbors. The President reiterated the U.S. hope for concrete movement on the question of the withdrawal of Russian troops from Latvia and Estonia.

Nomination for Deputy Commissioner of Patents and Trademarks
December 22, 1993

The President announced today that he will nominate Michael K. Kirk to be the Deputy Commissioner of Patents and Trademarks at the Department of Commerce.

"Michael Kirk has a long record of public service at the Patent and Trademark Office. I am confident that he will do well as Deputy Commissioner."

NOTE: A biography of the nominee was made available by the Office of the Press Secretary.

Nomination for Director of the United States Mint
December 22, 1993

The President announced today that he intends to nominate Phillip N. Diehl, until recently the Chief of Staff at the Department of the Treasury, to be the Director of the U.S.

Mint.

"As a senior member of Secretary Bentsen's staff, both in the Senate and at the Treasury, and during his service in Texas' State Government, Phil Diehl has distinguished himself as a public servant of high quality," said the Presi-

dent. "He has the skills and experience that it takes to be an effective manager of the U.S. Mint."

NOTE: A biography of the nominee was made available by the Office of the Press Secretary.

Appointment for Assistant to the President and Deputy Chief of Staff
December 22, 1993

The President and Chief of Staff Thomas F. "Mack" McLarty today announced the appointment of Harold Ickes to be Assistant to the President and Deputy Chief of Staff, reporting to Mr. McLarty. In that capacity, Ickes will have major responsibility for efforts to enact the health security act next year.

The President made the following statement:
"I am pleased that my good friend Harold Ickes will be joining our team. Harold combines a savvy political sense, honed by years of experience in national politics, with a deep commitment to improving the lives of average citizens. I admire his insight and his sharp wit."

Appointment for the Small Business Administration
December 23, 1993

The President today appointed Maine small businessman Patrick K. McGowan to be the Small Business Administration's Regional Director for Region I, covering all of New England.

"I am very proud to make this appointment today," said the President. "Patrick McGowan

knows what small businesses need and will do everything that he can to help New England small business."

NOTE: A biography of the appointee was made available by the Office of the Press Secretary.

Nomination for Chief Financial Officer of the National Aeronautics and Space Administration
December 23, 1993

The President today announced his intention to nominate Arnold G. Holz, assistant comptroller and director of general accounting for the State of Maryland, to be Chief Financial Officer at the National Aeronautics and Space Administration.

"The depth of experience that Arnold Holz has acquired in 34 years of complex accounting, auditing, and financial reporting activities is a

welcomed addition to the Nation's space exploration program as it enters a new era of international cooperation to build a space station and prepares for sustained human exploration of the solar system," the President said.

NOTE: A biography of the nominee was made available by the Office of the Press Secretary.

Christmas Greeting to the Nation
December 25, 1993

The President. On this Christmas Day all over our Nation, Americans are gathering in celebration of faith and family and tradition.

Hillary Clinton. This season has a special magic. It may be cold outside, but we all feel an inner warmth. We are renewed with every kindness we give and receive. The celebration is as big as the world, and yet, it is as private as every Christmas wish that a child of any age has ever dreamed.

The President. So on this day, our greatest gift is the one within, the emergence and the sharing of our better selves. Our Christmas prayer is that each of us be given the strength to bring peace and good will to every community and to every American, especially to every child.

Peace for them is our greatest wish.

We are especially grateful to the men and women of our Armed Forces who are overseas this holiday away from their own families, preserving the freedoms that the rest of us cherish. We wish all Americans a joyous and blessed holiday.

Merry Christmas.

Hillary Clinton. And a happy New Year.

NOTE: The greeting was videotaped at 12:40 p.m. on December 16 in the Diplomatic Reception Room at the White House for broadcast on December 25. A tape was not available for verification of the content of these remarks.

The President's Radio Address
December 25, 1993

Good morning. On this Christmas morning, I won't keep you very long because I know many of you may still have presents under your trees waiting to be opened. But I do want to send my warmest Christmas greetings to all Americans.

For Hillary, Chelsea, and me, this is our first Christmas in Washington. We've taken great joy in decorating the White House with trees and ornaments and decorating our own Christmas tree upstairs in the residence. We've taken even greater joy in seeing our fellow Americans share in the beauty and the history of their house, the people's house, here in our Nation's Capital, as tens of thousands have come through to see the White House at Christmastime.

Like so many of you, we've been joined by relatives and friends. We've been reminded of all we have to be thankful for. For this holiday season is a time to remember what we value and what gives our lives meaning. Today Christians celebrate God's love for humanity made real in the birth of Christ in a manger almost 2,000 years ago. The humble circumstances of His birth, the example of His life, the power of His teachings inspire us to love and to care

for our fellow men and women.

On this day we should be especially grateful that here in America we all have the freedom to worship God in our own way, for our faith is purest when it is the offering of a free and joyous spirit. We are a nation of many faiths and beliefs, united in a sense of mutual respect, shared values, and common purpose. Each of our faiths teaches that none of us can live alone, for we all belong to something larger than ourselves. Each teaches that we can see the image of God reflected in our fellow men and women, whatever their creed or color. Each teaches that our responsibilities to God are reflected in our responsibilities to each other. "If I am not for myself, who will be for me?" the Rabbi Hillel asked. "But if I am only for myself, who am I?"

Part of the miracle of this season is that each of us can hear what Abraham Lincoln called "the better angels of our nature." As we gather with our families, our friends; as we hear stories of our parents and grandparents; as we delight in the laughter of our own children and grandchildren, we're reminded again that we are part of a great sea of humanity including those who came before us and those who will live long afterward. That sense of connection is part of the joy of this season, part of the reason why, no matter how cold it gets, our hearts remain warm.

As we rejoice in the best of what life can be, we ask ourselves how we can act in the spirit of the season not just on this day but on every day. As we look into the eyes of our children filled with life and laughter and promise, we're reminded of our most sacred obligation: nurturing the next generation. Every father and mother must do whatever we can to help our children live decent and responsible lives so they can be the people God intended them to be. And as the National Conference of Catholic Bishops declared in a pastoral letter, "No government can love a child, no policy can substitute for a family's care. The undeniable fact is that our children's future is shaped both by the values of their parents and the policies of our Nation." So we must act as parents, and we must also act as citizens.

On this day of all days, we are reminded of our obligations to every child, not just our own. As long as there are children whose parents can't afford to take them to the doctor, as long as there are young people who live in fear that they will die before their time from gang violence and random gunfire, then each of us is diminished. If each of us could find the wisdom, the courage, and the commitment to help bring peace to all our own streets and peace of mind to our own families here in America, we could give a wonderful gift to our-selves, to our children, and our beloved country.

For most of us, this is a day of well-earned rest. But it's also a day when we remember that along with family and community, work gives purpose and structure to our lives. In this country, everyone who is able to work should be able to find work. And everyone who works should be able to support a family. When we restore dignity and security of work for all people, we'll go a long way toward restoring the fabric of life in all our communities. I'm glad that more Americans are working today than there were last year, but I know we've got a long way to go.

I also want to say a special word of thanks to all those who are working today who may wish they weren't working on this day, from those who care for the sick in our hospitals to those who patrol the streets of our communities. Most of all, we honor the service men and women who stand sentry for our freedom every day of the year. Because of their vigilance on this Christmas Day, our Nation is at peace. And although they may be thousands of miles away, they are close to us today.

To all those who hear me now, wherever this Christmas morning finds you, I wish you the best of holiday seasons, and may God bless you and your family.

NOTE: The address was recorded at 9:55 a.m. on December 22 in the Roosevelt Room at the White House for broadcast at 10:06 a.m. on December 25.

Statement on the Death of Norman Vincent Peale
December 25, 1993

The name of Dr. Norman Vincent Peale will forever be associated with the wondrously American values of optimism and service. Dr. Peale was an optimist who believed that whatever the antagonisms and complexities of modern life brought us, that anyone could prevail by approaching life with a simple sense of faith. And he served us by instilling that optimism in every Christian and every other person who came in contact with his writings or his hopeful soul.

In a productive and giving life that spanned the 20th century, Dr. Peale lifted the spirits of millions and millions of people who were nourished and sustained by his example, his teaching, and his giving. While the Clinton family and all Americans mourn his loss, there is some poetry in his passing on a day when the world celebrates the birth of Christ, an idea that was central to Dr. Peale's message and Dr. Peale's work. He will be missed.

Memorandum on Implementation of NAFTA
December 27, 1993

*Memorandum for the Secretary of State,
the United States Trade Representative*

Subject: Proposed North American Free Trade
Agreement

Having considered the relevant measures
taken by Canada and Mexico, together with the
recommendation of the United States Trade
Representative, I have determined that Canada
and Mexico have implemented the statutory
changes necessary to bring those countries into
compliance with their obligations under the
North American Free Trade Agreement and that
they have made provision to implement the Uniform Regulations provided for under Article 511
of the Agreement regarding the interpretation,
application, and administration of the rules of
origin. The United States has completed nec-

essary legal procedures in accordance with Article 2203 of the Agreement.

Pursuant to section 101(b) of the North
American Free Trade Agreement Implementation Act (Public Law 103–182), I hereby direct
the Secretary of State to exchange notes with
the Government of Canada and the Government
of Mexico providing for the entry into force,
on January 1, 1994, of the Agreement, in accordance with Article 2203 thereof.

WILLIAM J. CLINTON

NOTE: This memorandum was released by the Office of the Press Secretary on December 28. The
proclamation of December 15 and the Executive
order of December 27 on implementation of
NAFTA are listed in Appendix D at the end of
this volume.

Letter to Congressional Leaders Transmitting a Report on Implementation of NAFTA
December 27, 1993

Dear Mr. Speaker: (Dear Mr. President:)
Pursuant to Section 101(b)(1)(B) of the North
American Free Trade Agreement Implementa-
tion Act, I am pleased to submit the attached
report regarding the implementation of the
North American Free Trade Agreement.

Sincerely,

WILLIAM J. CLINTON

NOTE: Identical letters were sent to Thomas S.
Foley, Speaker of the House of Representatives,
and Albert Gore, Jr., President of the Senate. This
letter was released by the Office of the Press Secretary on December 28.

Statement on the Nomination of Strobe Talbott To Be Deputy Secretary of State
December 28, 1993

I am delighted by the decision of Secretary
of State Warren Christopher to nominate Ambassador Strobe Talbott to become Deputy Secretary of State. I have known and respected
Ambassador Talbott for over 25 years and have
always found him to be a man of great ability,

intellect, and vision. He has performed superbly
in his current role as Ambassador at Large for
the former Soviet Republics, and I have full
confidence in his ability to perform equally well
in this new capacity at the Department of State.

Message on the Observance of Kwanzaa
December 29, 1993

I take great pleasure in extending warm greetings to all who are observing the festival of Kwanzaa during this holiday season.

While Kwanzaa has only been celebrated for a quarter century in our country, it has grown steadily each year, inviting more people to embrace their African heritage. Today, millions of people of African descent gather together with loved ones to enjoy this special holiday based on the rich cultural traditions of Africa.

At a time when we are seeking ways to revitalize our neighborhoods and empower those who have been powerless for too long, Kwanzaa encourages us to rebuild and gives us the opportunity to celebrate the strengths of the African American community. The seven principles of Kwanzaa—unity, self-determination, collective work and responsibility, cooperative economics, purpose, creativity, and faith—provide young people with the pride, direction, and inner strength to work for a brighter future.

On each of the seven days, from Umoja to Imani, I wish all those who are commemorating Kwanzaa a wonderful holiday season of hope and joy.

BILL CLINTON

NOTE: This message was made available by the Office of the Press Secretary on December 29 but was not issued as White House press release.

Appendix A—Digest of Other White House Announcements

*The following list includes the President's public sched-
ule and other items of general interest announced by
the Office of the Press Secretary and not included
elsewhere in this book.*

August 3

In the morning, the President went jogging with
Democratic National Committee "Break the Gridlock"
student volunteers. In the late afternoon, the President
met with Oklahoma State leaders. In the evening,
he attended a dinner honoring Representative Jack
Brooks at the Hyatt Regency Hotel on Capitol Hill.

The President announced his intention to nominate
Robert Fossum to be Assistant Secretary of the Air
Force for Space Policy and Ernest DuBester to be
a member of the National Mediation Board. He also
announced that he has designated Jessica L. Parks
as Vice Chair of the Merit Systems Protection Board.

August 6

The President extended his condolences to Queen
Fabiola and the people of Belgium on the death of
King Baudouin I. The White House announced that
former President Gerald Ford will lead the delegation
to the funeral on August 7 in Brussels.

The President announced his intention to nominate
Edna Fairbanks-Williams and Ernestine P. Watlington
to be members of the Board of Directors of the Legal
Services Corporation.

August 9

In the morning, the President traveled to Charleston, WV, and he returned to Washington, DC, in
the afternoon.

August 10

The President appointed Richard Schifter to serve
on the National Security Council staff as Special Assistant to the President and Counselor.

August 12

In the morning, the President traveled with Hillary
and Chelsea Clinton to St. Louis, MO, where he attended a reception honoring heroes of the Midwest
floods at the Ramada Henry VIII Hotel. In the afternoon, they traveled to Denver, CO. In the evening,
the President traveled to Oakland, CA.

August 13

In the morning, the President met with the East
Bay Conversion and Reinvestment Commission and
toured a community development site at the Oakland
Naval Supply Center.

In the afternoon, the President returned to Denver,
CO. There he joined Hillary and Chelsea Clinton,
and they traveled to Vail for the weekend.

August 16

In the early morning, the President and Hillary
and Chelsea Clinton traveled from Vail, CO, to Tulsa,
OK. In the afternoon, they traveled to Springdale,
AR.

August 17

The President announced his intention to nominate
the following persons to the positions indicated:

Luis Sequeira, Assistant Secretary of Agriculture for
  Science and Education;
Anthony A. Williams, Chief Financial Officer, De-
  partment of Agriculture;
Michael DiMario, Public Printer of the United
  States;
Margaret A. Browning, member, National Labor
  Relations Board;
Magdalena Jacobsen, member, National Mediation
  Board; and
Anthony P. Carnevale, Chairman, National Commis-
  sion for Employment Policy.

The White House announced the President has in-
vited the following Caribbean leaders to the White
House for a working luncheon on August 30:
—Prime Minister Hubert Ingraham of the Bahamas;
—President Cheddi Jagan of Guyana;
—Prime Minister Patrick Manning of Trinidad and
  Tobago;
—Prime Minister P.J. Patterson of Jamaica;
—Prime Minister Erskine Sandiford of Barbados.

August 18

In the late afternoon, the President and Hillary
and Chelsea Clinton returned to Washington, DC.

In the evening, the President had a telephone conversation with Prime Minister Morihiro Hosokawa of
Japan to congratulate him on his recent assumption
of the post.

August 19

In the afternoon, the President and Hillary and
Chelsea Clinton traveled to Martha's Vineyard, MA,
for a vacation.

August 29

In the late evening, the President and Hillary and
Chelsea Clinton returned to Washington, DC.

August 31

The White House announced that the President has invited Prime Minister Carlo Azeglio Ciampi of Italy to the White House for a working lunch on September 17.

The White House announced that the President sent to the Congress fiscal year 1994 budget amendments for the Department of Justice to support the immigration initiative announced on July 27.

September 3

In the morning, the President traveled to Dover, DE, where he toured the Opportunity Skyway school-to-work program at the Sussex County Airport. He then returned to Washington, DC, in the early afternoon.

In the late afternoon, in a ceremony on the State Floor, the President received diplomatic credentials from Ambassadors Tuiloma Neroni Slade of Western Samoa, Carlo Jagmetti of Switzerland, Koumbairia Laoumaye Mekonyo of Chad, Toomas Hendrik Ilves of Estonia, Peter P. Chkheidze the Republic of Georgia, Loucas Tsilas of Greece, Paul Boundoukou-Latha of Gabon, Marc Michael Marengo of Seychelles, Raul C. Rabe of the Philippines, and Odeen Ishmael of Guyana.

The White House announced that the President will host Prime Minister Paul Keating of Australia at the White House on September 13.

September 5

In the morning, the President and Hillary Clinton traveled to Miami, FL.

September 6

In the morning, the President and Hillary Clinton went to Florida City, FL, where they toured the reconstruction of buildings and homes damaged during Hurricane Andrew. Later in the morning, they went to Homestead, FL, where they surveyed hurricane damage to the Homestead Senior Community Center and met with community members. In the afternoon, the President and Hillary Clinton went to Cutler Ridge, FL, and they returned to Washington, DC, in the early evening.

September 7

In the morning, the President hosted a breakfast for business leaders.

September 8

In the afternoon, the President had lunch with business leaders.

The White House announced that the President sent to the Congress amendments to the fiscal year 1994 appropriations request for the Department of Energy.

September 9

In the morning, the President traveled to Cleveland, OH, and he returned to Washington, DC, in the afternoon.

In the evening, the President and Hillary Clinton hosted a reception at the White House in honor of the 22d anniversary of the John F. Kennedy Center for the Performing Arts.

September 10

In the morning, the President traveled to Sunnyvale, CA. Following his arrival in the afternoon, he toured the North Valley Job Training Partnership program (NOVA) at ILC Technology, Inc., and later met with representatives of the NOVA program at the Sunnyvale Community Center.

In the early evening, the President traveled to Houston, TX.

September 11

In the afternoon, the President returned to Washington, DC.

September 13

In the morning, the President met with President George Bush and President Jimmy Carter in the Oval Office. In the afternoon, the President had lunch with Prime Minister Yitzhak Rabin of Israel.

September 14

In the morning, the President had breakfast with President Bush, President Carter, and President Gerald Ford.

September 15

In the morning, the President traveled to New Orleans, LA, and he returned to Washington, DC, in the afternoon.

September 16

In the afternoon, the President met with the National Conference of Black Mayors.

September 21

In the afternoon, the President and Hillary Clinton hosted a luncheon for columnists.

September 22

In the afternoon, the President met with:
—United Kingdom Foreign Minister Douglas Hurd;
—recipients of the Boys and Girls Club Youth Service award;
—Chief of Staff Thomas F. McLarty.

September 23

In the afternoon, the President met with former Chrysler Corp. chairman Lee Iacocca.

In the early evening, the President and Hillary Clinton traveled to Tampa, FL, where they attended a reception at the Tampa Performing Arts Center. Later in the evening, they went to St. Petersburg, FL.

September 24

In the afternoon, the President and Hillary Clinton returned to Washington, DC.

The President announced his intention to nominate the following persons to be Representatives and Alternate Representatives of the U.S. to the 48th session of the General Assembly of the United Nations:

Representatives:

Madeleine Korbel Albright, of the District of Columbia

Esther Peterson, of the District of Columbia

Sam Gejdenson, U.S. Representative from the State of Connecticut

William F. Goodling, U.S. Representative from the State of Pennsylvania

Alternate Representatives:

Edward S. Walker, Jr., of Maryland

Victor Marrero, of New York

Karl Frederick Inderfurth, of North Carolina

Stuart George Moldaw, of California

September 26

In the morning, the President traveled to New York City, where he attended a Latin American reception at the Waldorf Astoria Hotel.

September 27

In the morning, the President had meetings with U.N. Secretary-General Boutros Boutros-Ghali and U.N. General Assembly President Samuel Rudolph Insanally at the United Nations Building. Later in the morning, the President met with members of the U.S. mission staff at the U.S. Mission Building.

After returning to the Waldorf Astoria Hotel in the late afternoon, the President met with:

—President Cesar Gaviria of Colombia;

—Prime Minister Rafiq al-Hariri of Lebanon;

—President Joaquim Alberto Chissano of Mozambique.

In the evening, the President hosted a reception for heads of delegations at the Waldorf Astoria Hotel. Following the reception, he returned to Washington, DC.

September 29

In the afternoon, the President had lunch with business leaders.

September 30

In the afternoon, the President had lunch with the Vice President.

The President appointed 11 members to the President's Foreign Intelligence Advisory Board. They will join the Board's Chairman, Adm. William J. Crowe, Jr., USN (Ret.), who was appointed in January. The new members are:

Gen. Lew Allen, Jr., USAF (Ret.)

Zoe Baird

Ann Z. Caracristi

Sidney D. Drell

Thomas F. Eagleton

Anthony S. Harrington

Robert J. Hermann

Harold W. Pote

Lois D. Rice

Warren B. Rudman

Maurice Sonneberg

October 1

In the morning, the President attended the investiture of Justice Ruth Bader Ginsburg at the U.S. Supreme Court.

In the afternoon, the President received diplomatic credentials from Ambassadors Raul Enrique Granillo Ocampo of Argentina, Hagos Ghebrehiwet of Eritrea, Gabriel Silva of Colombia, Ahmed Suliman of Sudan, Donald Eric Russell of Australia, Anund Priyay Neewoor of Mauritius, Dean Russell Lindo of Belize, Serguei Nikolayevich Martynov of Belarus, Arifin Mohamad Siregar of Indonesia, and Andreas J. Jacovides of Cyprus.

October 3

In the morning, the President and Hillary Clinton attended the 41st annual Red Mass at St. Matthew's Cathedral with members of the Supreme Court.

In the afternoon, the President traveled to Sacramento, CA, and in the evening, to San Francisco.

October 4

In the afternoon, the President traveled to Los Angeles, CA. In the evening, he attended the Democratic Congressional Campaign Committee dinner at the Beverly Hilton Hotel.

The White House announced that the President appointed two officials to the Department of Commerce: Michael J. Copps as Deputy Assistant Secretary for Basic Industries and Rolland Schmitten as Assistant Administrator of the National Marine Fisheries Service in the National Oceanic and Atmospheric Administration.

October 5

In the evening, after returning from Los Angeles, CA, to Washington, DC, the President attended the Democratic Senatorial Campaign Committee dinner at the Washington Hilton Hotel.

October 6

In the morning, the President met with Members of Congress on NAFTA. Later in the morning, he met with NATO Secretary General Manfred Woerner.

October 7

In the morning, the President met with Members of Congress on the situation in Somalia. Later in the morning, he met with Members of Congress on NAFTA. Following the meetings, he had lunch with the Vice President.

In the afternoon, the President met with Foreign Minister Farouk al-Shara of Syria.

October 8
In the early afternoon, the President traveled to New Brunswick, NJ, and he returned to Washington, DC, in the evening.

October 9
In the morning, the President and Hillary and Chelsea Clinton traveled to New Haven, CT, where they met with Special Olympics participants and Clinton Avenue School fourth graders in Woolsey Hall at Yale University. In the evening, they returned to Washington, DC.

October 12
In the afternoon, the President traveled to Raleigh-Durham, NC. He then went to the University of North Carolina at Chapel Hill for the opening ceremony of the university's bicentennial commemoration and then attended a reception at George Watts Hill Alumni Center. He returned to Washington, DC, in the late evening.

October 13
In the evening, the President and Hillary Clinton hosted a Hispanic Heritage Month reception.

October 14
In the morning, the President met with Members of Congress on NAFTA.

In the afternoon, the President had a telephone conversation with Chief Warrant Officer Michael Durant in Mogadishu, Somalia.

October 15
The President announced his intention to nominate George W. Haley to be a Commissioner of the Postal Rate Commission. Mr. Haley recently completed a term as the Commission's Chairman.

October 18
The White House announced that the President will host an informal meeting with the economic leaders of 15 Organization for Asian-Pacific Economic Cooperation (APEC) members in Seattle, WA, on November 19–20.

The President congratulated the winners of the 1993 Malcolm Baldrige National Quality Award for excellence in quality management, Eastman Chemical Co. of Kingsport, TN, in the manufacturing category and Ames Rubber Corp. of Hamburg, NJ, in the small business category.

October 19
The President announced his intention to nominate Jesse L. White to be Cochair of the Appalachian Regional Commission.

The White House announced that the President has approved the recommendation of the Secretary of Defense that U.S. Army Special Operations Com-

mand elements (Rangers) be returned to the United States from Somalia within the next few days.

October 20
The President announced his appointment of the following individuals to be members of Emergency Board No. 223, to investigate and make recommendations for settlement of a railroad labor dispute:

Bonnie Weinstock, of Melville, NY, Chair;
M. David Vaughn, of Gaithersburg, MD, member; and
Charlotte Gold, of Palm Beach Gardens, FL, member.

October 22
In the afternoon, the President had a working luncheon with Cabinet members at Blair House.

The White House announced that Ambassador Paul J. Hare has been named the U.S. Special Representative to the Angolan peace process.

The White House announced that President Clinton has invited President Kim Yong-sam of Korea to visit the White House on November 23.

October 24
In the morning, the President met with patients at the Walter Reed Army Medical Center.

October 26
The President announced the following Senior Executive Service appointments:

Robert E. Litan as Deputy Assistant Attorney General, Antitrust Division;
Kelly H. Carnes as Deputy Assistant Secretary of Commerce for Technology Policy; and
Dr. Melville "Jo Ivey" Boufford as the Principal Deputy Assistant Secretary of Health and Human Services.

October 27
In the afternoon, the President and Hillary Clinton had lunch with Members of Congress in the Mansfield Room at the Capitol.

October 28
In the morning, the President and Hillary Clinton traveled to Baltimore, MD. In the afternoon, the President traveled to New York City, and in the evening, to Boston, MA.

October 29
In the afternoon, the President toured the Gillette Building in south Boston. In the evening, he returned to Washington, DC.

October 30
In the evening, the President and Hillary Clinton attended the Presidential gala at Ford's Theatre.

The White House announced that the President has invited President Fidel V. Ramos of the Philippines to the White House on November 22.

November 1

The White House announced that the President sent to the Congress a package of $2 billion in fiscal year 1994 spending cuts and reform measures.

November 2

The White House announced that the President has invited Prime Minister Yitzhak Rabin of Israel to the White House on November 12.

The White House announced that the President awarded the Presidential Medal of Freedom to entertainer and humanitarian Martha Raye.

November 3

In the late morning, the President and Hillary Clinton traveled to Ambridge, PA, where they presented a copy of "Health Security: The President's Report to the American People" to Laughlin Memorial Library. In the early evening, they returned to Washington, DC.

The White House announced that the President has signed the United States instrument of ratification of the Treaty on Open Skies.

November 4

In the morning, the President met with Members of Congress on NAFTA. Following the meeting, he traveled to Lexington, KY, where he toured the laser printer manufacturing facilities at Lexmark International, Inc. In the early evening, he returned to Washington, DC.

November 5

In the afternoon, the President met with Gen. Colin L. Powell, USA, Ret.

The President announced his intention to nominate four individuals for administration positions:

Greg Farmer, Under Secretary of Commerce for Travel and Tourism;

Henry F. Graff, member, Assassination Records Review Board;

Mary Lucille Jordan, member, Federal Mine Safety and Health Review Commission; and

T.R. Lakshmanan, Director, Bureau of Transportation Statistics, Department of Transportation.

November 8

In the morning, the President met with Members of Congress on NAFTA.

In the evening, the President hosted a dinner for Members of Congress at the White House.

November 9

In the morning, the President met with Members of Congress on NAFTA. In the afternoon, he held an interview with Connie Chung for the news program "Eye to Eye."

The President announced that he has appointed the following senior officials of his administration to serve on special boards or commissions:

Secretary of the Interior Bruce Babbitt to the Martin Luther King, Jr., Federal Holiday Commission;

National Security Adviser Anthony Lake to the Board of Trustees of the Woodrow Wilson International Center for Scholars; and

Jack Quinn, Chief of Staff to the Vice President; Sally Katzen, Administrator of Information and Regulatory Affairs, Office of Management and Budget; and John Podesta, White House Staff Secretary, to the Council of the Administrative Conference of the United States.

November 10

In the morning, the President met with Members of Congress on NAFTA.

The President announced that $130 million in Federal funds have been made available to assist the homeless and needy in local communities through the Federal Emergency Management Agency's Emergency Food and Shelter National Board Program.

November 11

In the afternoon, the President traveled to Martinsburg, WV, where he visited patients at the Martinsburg VA Medical Center. In the late afternoon, he returned to Washington, DC.

November 13

In the morning, the President traveled to Memphis, TN, and he returned to Washington, DC, in the evening.

November 16

In the morning, the President met with Richard Spring, Deputy Prime Minister and Foreign Minister of Ireland. In the afternoon, the President met with Mieko and Masaichi Hattori, parents of Japanese exchange student Yoshihiro Hattori, who was killed in Louisiana in October 1992.

The President announced the following Senior Executive Service appointments:

Department of Labor
T. Michael Kerr, Director, Executive Secretariat
Meridith Miller, Deputy Assistant Secretary, Pension and Welfare Benefits Administration
Robert M. Portman, Deputy Assistant Secretary, Office of the American Workplace
Robert A. Rodriguez, Deputy Assistant Secretary, Office of Policy
Michael A. Silverstein, Director of Policy, Occupational Safety and Health Administration

Department of Energy
Agnes P. Dover, Deputy General Counsel for Legal Services

November 17

The President made available fiscal year 1993 emergency appropriations for the Department of Agriculture to be used for watershed protection systems damaged by flooding along the Mississippi River and its tributaries and to continue implementation of the new emergency wetlands program that allows the voluntary conversion of certain cropland to wetlands.

November 18

In the late morning, the President traveled to Seattle, WA. In the afternoon, he met with Prime Minister Chuan Likphai of Thailand at the Westin Hotel.

November 19

In the afternoon, the President greeted APEC leaders in the Main Dining Room at the Rainier Club. He then attended a reception given by the Seattle APEC Host Committee at the Seattle Art Museum.

The President announced that he has appointed 10 members to the National Partnership Council:

James B. King, Director of the Office of Personnel Management;

Thomas Glynn, Deputy Secretary of Labor;

Philip Lader, Deputy Director for Management, Office of Management and Budget;

Jean McKee, Chairman, Federal Labor Relations Authority;

John Calhoun Wells, Federal Mediation and Conciliation Director;

George Munoz, Chief Financial Officer, Department of the Treasury;

Edwin Dorn, Assistant Secretary of Defense;

Robert M. Tobias, president, National Treasury Employees Union;

John N. Sturdivant, president, American Federation of Government Employees, AFL–CIO;

Robert S. Keener, president, National Federation of Federal Employees; and

John F. Leydon, secretary-treasurer, Public Employees Department, AFL–CIO.

The President announced the following Senior Executive Service appointments:

Department of Agriculture

Deborah A. Dawson, Executive Assistant to the Administrator, Agricultural Stabilization and Conservation Service

Paul Scott Shearer, Deputy Assistant Secretary for Congressional Relations

Department of the Treasury

Glen Arlen Kohl, Tax Legislative Counsel

Eric J. Toder, Deputy Assistant Secretary for Tax Analysis

Jacqueline J. Wong, Senior Adviser to the Assistant Secretary for Tax Policy

November 20

In the morning, the President attended meetings with APEC leaders at the Tillicum Village Lodge on Blake Island in Seattle, WA. Following a working lunch hosted by the President, they resumed their meetings until the late afternoon.

In the early evening, the President traveled to San Francisco, CA, and in the late evening, to Pasadena.

November 21

In the morning, the President met at the Pasadena Presbyterian Church with congregation members and neighbors to discuss their experiences in the fires that occurred in October. Following the meeting, he attended church services and the Alternative Christmas Festival.

In the afternoon, the President traveled to Los Angeles, and he returned to Washington, DC, in the late evening.

November 24

In the morning, the President went jogging with President Kim Yong-sam of South Korea. In the afternoon, he met with British novelist Salman Rushdie in the Old Executive Office Building.

In the late afternoon, the President and Hillary and Chelsea Clinton went to Camp David, MD, for the holiday weekend.

November 26

The White House announced that the President has invited seven Central American leaders to a breakfast meeting at the White House on November 30.

November 28

In the evening, the President and Hillary and Chelsea Clinton returned to the White House from Camp David, MD.

November 29

In the morning, the President hosted a breakfast meeting for religious leaders active in the AIDS community. Following the breakfast, the President had telephone conversations with Chancellor Helmut Kohl of Germany and President Leonid Kravchuk of Ukraine.

In the evening, the President and Hillary Clinton attended the taping of a performance in the PBS "In Concert at the White House" series.

November 30

In the evening, the President and Hillary Clinton attended a private screening of the movie "Schindler's List" at the Cineplex Odeon.

December 1

In the morning, the President met with AIDS patients at Georgetown University Medical Center.

In the afternoon, the President attended a tea hosted by the First Lady for the five American Nobel laureates of 1993.

The President declared a major disaster existed in Missouri and ordered Federal aid to supplement State and local recovery efforts, following severe storms, tornadoes, and flooding from November 13–19.

The President announced he intends to nominate the following new members of the U.S. Enrichment Corporation:

William J. Rainer;
Margaret Hornbeck Greene;
Kneeland C. Youngblood;
Frank G. Zarb; and
Greta Joy Dicus.

The President appointed Minnesota Governor Arne Carlson to be a member of the Advisory Commission on Intergovernmental Relations.

December 2

The President announced the following Senior Executive Service appointments:

Denise Marie Michel, Senior Policy Adviser to the Secretary of the Treasury;

William E. Mounts, Director of Commercial Items and International Systems Acquisition, Department of Defense;

Linton Wells II, Director of Policy Support, Department of Defense;

Cynthia Gibson Beerbower, International Tax Counsel, Office of Tax Policy, Department of the Treasury;

Jeffrey A. Meeks, Chief of Staff, U.S. Customs Service, Department of the Treasury;

Carol A. Dortch, Region IV Director, General Services Administration;

Parks D. Shackelford, Deputy Administrator for State and County Operations, Agricultural Stabilization and Conservation Service, Department of Agriculture;

Ann Terry Pincus, Director, Office of Research, U.S. Information Agency;

Dawn Johnsen, Deputy Assistant Attorney General, Office of Legal Counsel, Department of Justice;

Ilene J. Leff, Assistant Secretary for Finance and Management, Office of Administration, Department of Housing and Urban Development;

Mark Bohannon, Chief Counsel, Technology Administration, Department of Commerce;

Sally Susman, Deputy Assistant Secretary of Commerce, Office of Legislative/Intergovernmental Affairs;

Lewis S. Alexander, Chief Economist and Adviser to the Secretary of Commerce;

David Satcher, Director, Centers for Disease Control, Department of Health and Human Services;

William F. Benson, Deputy Assistant Secretary of Health and Human Services, Administration on Aging;

Grantland Johnson, Department of Health and Human Services Regional Director, Region IX, California;

Wandra Gail Mitchell, General Counsel, Agency for International Development, U.S. International Development Cooperation Agency;

Robert Kent Boyer, Deputy Assistant Administrator, Bureau of Legislative Affairs, Agency for International Development, U.S. International Development Cooperation Agency.

December 3

In the afternoon, the President traveled to Albuquerque, NM, where he toured the El Pueblo Health Services Clinic. In the evening, he traveled to Los Angeles, CA.

December 5

In the early morning, the President returned to Washington, DC.

In the evening, the President and Hillary Clinton hosted a reception for the 1993 Kennedy Center honorees. Following the reception, they attended the Kennedy Center Honors program at the John F. Kennedy Center for the Performing Arts.

December 7

In the morning, the President had a telephone conversation with President Kim Yong-sam of South Korea. In the late morning, he met with Mayor-elect Rudolph Giuliani of New York City and then had lunch with business leaders. In the late afternoon, he met with a group of Buffalo Soldiers.

In the evening, the President and Hillary Clinton hosted a congressional holiday ball.

December 8

In the afternoon, the President had lunch with Godfrey Sperling Group columnists at Blair House. Later in the afternoon, he met with children from the Washington, DC, Jewish Community Center's afterschool program to celebrate the first night of Hanukkah.

The President announced his intention to nominate Ronald B. Lewis to be Chair of the Administrative Conference of the United States.

December 9

In the afternoon, the President received diplomatic credentials from Ambassadors Einar Benediktsson of Iceland, Pierre Damien Boussoukou-Boumba of the Congo, Gaetan Rimwanguiya Ouedraogo of Burkina Faso, Mamadou Mansour Seck of Senegal, Jose Goncalves Martins Patricio of Angola, Andres Petricevic Raznatovic of Bolivia, Paulo Tarso Flecha de Lima of Brazil, Dato Paduka Awang Haji Jaya bin Abdul Latif of Brunei Darussalam, Alfonsas Eidintas of Lithuania, Jacques Bacamurwanko of Burundi, Nicolae A. Tau of Moldova, and Lublin Hasan Dilja of Albania.

The President had a telephone conversation with Jacques Delors, President of the European Commission, to discuss GATT agreements.

The White House announced that the President and President Hafiz al-Asad of Syria have agreed to meet in Geneva, Switzerland, in January 1994.

The President announced that he intends to appoint Cathryn Buford Slater to be Chair of the Advisory

Council on Historic Preservation. He also appointed GSA Administrator Roger Johnson, Transportation Secretary Federico Peña, and EPA Administrator Carol Browner to be members of the Council.

December 10

The President announced that he intends to nominate Edward J. Gleiman to be a Commissioner of the Postal Rate Commission, and to designate him as the Commission's Chair pending his confirmation by the Senate.

The President announced his intention to appoint Peter Y. Chiu and Alan Craig Kessler to the Risk Assessment and Management Commission.

The President made available $60 million in previously appropriated funds to the Corps of Engineers for the repair of levees damaged in the Midwest floods.

The President made available to the Departments of Transportation and Commerce $31.4 million in emergency funding for highway repair in the flood-ravaged Midwest and for other disaster recovery efforts.

The President appointed the following individuals to Senior Executive Service positions:

Department of Agriculture
Kenneth Ackerman, Manager, Federal Crop Insurance Corporation
Neal Flieger, Deputy Administrator, IGA and Disaster Assistance, Food and Nutrition Service

Department of Commerce
Sally C. Ericsson, Associate Deputy Under Secretary, Economics and Statistics Administration
Susan Fruchter, Counselor to the Under Secretary, National Oceanic and Atmospheric Administration
C. Howie Hodges II, Assistant Director for Program Development, Minority Business Development Agency

Department of Education
Naomi Katherine Karp, Special Adviser to the Assistant Secretary, Office of Education Research and Improvement

Department of Housing and Urban Development
Kevin Marchman, Deputy Assistant Secretary, Distressed and Troubled Housing, Office of Public and Indian Housing

Department of the Interior
E. Thomas Tuchmann, Special Assistant to the Secretary

Department of Justice
Paul Bender, Principal Deputy Solicitor General
Kevin V. Di Gregory, Deputy Assistant Attorney General, Criminal Division
John M. Hogan, Assistant to the Attorney General
H. Jefferson Powell, Deputy Assistant Attorney General, Office of Legal Counsel

Laurie Overby Robinson, Associate Deputy Attorney General

Department of State
Johannes Albert Binnendijk, Principal Deputy Director, Policy Planning Staff

Department of Transportation
Gloria Jeff, Associate Administrator for Policy, Federal Highway Administration
George Reagle, Associate Administrator for Motor Carriers, Federal Highway Administration

December 11

In the evening, the President and Hillary Clinton attended a Washington Ballet performance of "The Nutcracker" at the Warner Theatre.

December 12

In the afternoon, the President had telephone conversations with Prime Minister Edouard Balladur of France, Prime Minister John Major of Great Britain, and Chancellor Helmut Kohl of Germany on the GATT multilateral trade negotiations.

In the evening, the President and Hillary and Chelsea Clinton attended the "Christmas in Washington" program at the National Building Museum.

December 13

In the morning, the President traveled to Bryn Mawr, PA, where he attended a luncheon at Bryn Mawr College. In the afternoon, he traveled to New York City, where he met with the three men who helped apprehend the Long Island Rail Road gunman on December 7. He returned to Washington, DC, in the late evening.

December 14

The President announced that he intends to nominate David Birenbaum to be Deputy Permanent Representative to the United Nations for Management and U.N. Reform, with the rank of Ambassador.

December 16

The President announced that he has made the following appointments:

LaVarne Addison Burton, Senior Adviser to the Assistant Secretary for Management and Budget, Department of Health and Human Services;
Mary Lou Crane, Regional Administrator, Region I, Department of Housing and Urban Development;
Vonya Beatrice McCann, Deputy Assistant Secretary of State, Telecommunications;
Donald M. Itzkoff, Deputy Administrator, Federal Railroad Administration;
Wushow (Bill) Chou, Deputy Assistant Secretary of the Treasury, Information Systems;
Michael J. Armstrong, Regional Director, Region VIII, Federal Emergency Management Agency;
Rita A. Calvan, Regional Director, Region III, Federal Emergency Management Agency;

Karen R. Adler, Regional Administrator, Region II, General Services Administration; and

Leslie R. Jin, General Counsel, U.S. Information Agency.

December 17

In the afternoon, the President hosted a Christmas celebration for children in the State Dining Room.

The President announced that he is designating Gail McDonald, who has been serving as Acting Chair of the Interstate Commerce Commission, to be Chair of the ICC and that he intends to nominate Linda J. Morgan as a Commission member.

December 20

In the afternoon, the President met with Marc Klaas, father of Polly Klaas, a 12-year-old girl who was abducted from her home in Petaluma, CA, and murdered.

December 23

The White House announced that the President has invited Prime Minister Ruud Lubbers of The Netherlands to meet with him at the White House on January 4.

December 27

In the morning, the President traveled to Cambridge, MD, where he went duck hunting at Tieder Farm. He returned to Washington, DC, in the afternoon.

In the late afternoon, the President and Hillary and Chelsea Clinton traveled to Hot Springs, AR.

The White House announced that the President declared a major disaster existed in the Commonwealth of Virginia and that he ordered Federal aid to supplement State and local recovery efforts in the area struck by severe storms and tornadoes on August 6.

The White House announced that the President will make a state visit to Moscow on January 12–15, 1994, at the invitation of President Boris Yeltsin of Russia.

December 28

In the morning, the President joined Hillary and Chelsea Clinton in Little Rock, AR. Following a shopping trip in the afternoon, the President and Hillary Clinton attended a private reception at the Old State House.

In the evening, the President and Hillary and Chelsea Clinton went to Fayetteville, AR, where they attended a University of Arkansas Razorbacks basketball game at Bud Walton Arena.

December 29

In the late morning, the President and Hillary and Chelsea Clinton traveled to Hilton Head, SC, where they attended the 1994 Renaissance Weekend.

Appendix B—Nominations Submitted to the Senate

The following list does not include promotions of members of the Uniformed Services, nominations to the Service Academies, or nominations of Foreign Service officers.

Submitted August 2

William Green Miller,
of Virginia, to be Ambassador Extraordinary and Plenipotentiary of the United States of America to Ukraine.

Submitted August 4

Reginald Bartholomew,
of the District of Columbia, a career member of the Senior Foreign Service, class of Career Minister, to be Ambassador Extraordinary and Plenipotentiary of the United States of America to Italy.

Roger R. Gamble,
of Virginia, a career member of the Senior Foreign Service, class of Minister-Counselor, to be Ambassador Extraordinary and Plenipotentiary of the United States of America to the Republic of Suriname.

Mark Gregory Hambley,
of California, a career member of the Senior Foreign Service, class of Counselor, to be Ambassador Extraordinary and Plenipotentiary of the United States of America to the Republic of Lebanon.

William Dale Montgomery,
of Pennsylvania, a career member of the Senior Foreign Service, class of Counselor, to be Ambassador Extraordinary and Plenipotentiary of the United States of America to the Republic of Bulgaria.

John Roggen Schmidt,
of Illinois, for the rank of Ambassador during his tenure of service as the Chief U.S. Negotiator to the Uruguay round.

John J. Hamre,
of South Dakota, to be Comptroller of the Department of Defense, vice Sean Charles O'Keefe, resigned.

Reed E. Hundt,
of Maryland, to be a member of the Federal Communications Commission for a term of 5 years from July 1, 1993, vice Alfred C. Sikes, resigned.

Jean C. Nelson,
of Tennessee, to be an Assistant Administrator of the Environmental Protection Agency, vice E. Donald Elliott, resigned.

Nora Slatkin,
of Maryland, to be an Assistant Secretary of the Navy, vice Gerald A. Cann, resigned.

Submitted August 6

Pierre N. Leval,
of New York, to be U.S. Circuit Judge for the Second Circuit, vice George C. Pratt, retired.

M. Blane Michael,
of West Virginia, to be U.S. Circuit Judge for the Fourth Circuit, vice James M. Sprouse, retired.

Martha Craig Daughtrey,
of Tennessee, to be U.S. Circuit Judge for the Sixth Circuit (new position).

Leonie M. Brinkema,
of Virginia, to be U.S. District Judge for the Eastern District of Virginia, vice Albert V. Bryan, Jr., retired.

Deborah K. Chasanow,
of Maryland, to be U.S. District Judge for the District of Maryland, vice Alexander Harvey II, retired.

Jennifer B. Coffman,
of Kentucky, to be U.S. District Judge for the Eastern and Western Districts of Kentucky, vice Eugene E. Siler, Jr., elevated.

Peter J. Messitte,
of Maryland, to be U.S. District Judge for the District of Maryland, vice Joseph Howard, retired.

Lawrence L. Piersol,
of South Dakota, to be U.S. District Judge for the District of South Dakota, vice Donald J. Porter, retired.

Thomas M. Shanahan,
of Nebraska, to be U.S. District Judge for the District of Nebraska (new position).

David G. Trager,
of New York, to be U.S. District Judge for the Eastern District of New York (new position).

Martha A. Vazquez,
of New Mexico, to be U.S. District Judge for the District of New Mexico, vice Santiago E. Campos, retired.

Alexander Williams, Jr.,
of Maryland, to be U.S. District Judge for the District of Maryland, vice Norman P. Ramsey, retired.

William Roy Wilson, Jr.,
of Arkansas, to be U.S. District Judge for the Eastern District of Arkansas, vice G. Thomas Eisele, retired.

David P. Rawson,
of Michigan, a career member of the Senior Foreign Service, class of Counselor, to be Ambassador Extraordinary and Plenipotentiary of the United States of America to the Republic of Rwanda.

Daniel Collins,
of Ohio, to be a member of the Board of Directors of the National Railroad Passenger Corporation for a term of 4 years, vice Charles Luna, term expired.

Richard A. Boucher,
of Maryland, a career member of the Senior Foreign Service, class of Counselor, to be Ambassador Extraordinary and Plenipotentiary of the United States of America to the Republic of Cyprus.

Diane Blair,
of Arkansas, to be a member of the Board of Directors of the Corporation for Public Broadcasting for a term expiring January 31, 1998, vice Sharon Percy Rockefeller, term expired.

The following named persons to be, members of the Board of Directors of the Legal Services Corporation for the terms indicated:

For terms expiring July 13, 1995:
Hulett Hall Askew, of Georgia, vice William Lee Kirk, Jr.
Laveeda Morgan Battle, of Alabama, vice J. Blakeley Hall.
John G. Brooks, of Massachusetts, vice Guy V. Molinari.
Nancy Hardin Rogers, of Ohio, vice Jo Betts Love.

For terms expiring July 13, 1996:
Douglas S. Eakeley, of New Jersey, vice Basile J. Uddo.
F. William McCalpin, of Missouri, vice Penny L. Pullen.
Maria Luisa Mercado, of Texas, vice Thomas D. Rath.
Thomas F. Smegal, Jr., of California, vice Norman D. Shumway.
John T. Broderick, Jr., of New Hampshire, vice Howard H. Dana, Jr.

William B. Gould IV,
of California, to be a member of the National Labor Relations Board for the remainder of the term expiring August 27, 1993, vice Clifford R. Oviatt, Jr., resigned.

William B. Gould IV,
of California, to be a member of the National Labor Relations Board for the term of 5 years expiring August 27, 1998 (reappointment).

Leslie M. Alexander,
of Florida, a career member of the Senior Foreign Service, class of Counselor, to be Ambassador Extraordinary and Plenipotentiary of the United States of America to Mauritius, and to serve concurrently and without additional compensation as Ambassador Extraordinary and Plenipotentiary of the United States of America to the Federal and Islamic Republic of the Comoros.

Einar V. Dyhrkopp,
of Illinois, to be a Governor of the United States Postal Service for the term expiring December 8, 2001.

Lynne Ann Battaglia,
of Maryland, to be U.S. Attorney for the District of Maryland for the term of 4 years, vice Richard D. Bennett, resigned.

Paula Jean Casey,
of Arkansas, to be U.S. Attorney for the Eastern District of Arkansas for the term of 4 years, vice Charles A. Banks, resigned.

Paul Edward Coggins,
of Texas, to be U.S. Attorney for the Northern District of Texas for the term of 4 years, vice Marvin Collins, resigned.

Paul Kinloch Holmes III,
of Arkansas, to be U.S. Attorney for the Western District of Arkansas for the term of 4 years, vice J. Michael Fitzhugh.

Scott M. Matheson, Jr.,
of Utah, to be U.S. Attorney for the District of Utah for the term of 4 years, vice David J. Jordan, resigned.

Joseph Preston Strom, Jr.,
of South Carolina, to be U.S. Attorney for the District of South Carolina for the term of 4 years, vice John S. Simmons, resigned.

Jane Alexander,
of New York, to be Chairperson of the National Endowment for the Arts for a term of 4 years, vice John E. Frohnmayer, resigned.

John D. Negroponte,
of New York, a career member of the Senior Foreign Service, class of Career Minister, to be Ambassador Extraordinary and Plenipotentiary of the United States of America to the Republic of the Philippines.

Richard N. Gardner,
of New York, to be Ambassador Extraordinary and Plenipotentiary of the United States of America to Spain.

Peter F. Romero,
of Florida, a career member of the Senior Foreign Service, class of Counselor, to be Ambassador Extraordinary and Plenipotentiary of the United States of America to the Republic of Ecuador.

Morton H. Halperin,
of the District of Columbia, to be an Assistant Secretary of Defense, vice David J. Gribbin III, resigned.

Frederick F.Y. Pang,
of Hawaii, to be an Assistant Secretary of the Navy, vice Barbara Spyridon Pope, resigned.

Katharine G. Abraham,
of Iowa, to be Commissioner of Labor Statistics, U.S. Department of Labor, for a term of 4 years, vice Janet L. Norwood, term expired.

Robert P. Crouch, Jr.,
of Virginia, to be U.S. Attorney for the Western District of Virginia for the term of 4 years, vice E. Montgomery Tucker, resigned.

John Despres,
of the District of Columbia, to be an Assistant Secretary of Commerce, vice Quincy Mellon Krosby.

Joseph Swerdzewski,
of Colorado, to be General Counsel of the Federal Labor Relations Authority for a term of 5 years, vice Alan Robert Swendiman, resigned.

Submitted September 7

David J. Barram,
of California, to be Deputy Secretary of Commerce, vice Rockwell Anthony Schnabel, resigned.

Carol Bellamy,
of New York, to be Director of the Peace Corps, vice Elaine L. Chao, resigned.

Marian C. Bennett,
of the District of Columbia, to be Inspector General, United States Information Agency, vice George F. Murphy, Jr., resigned.

Alan John Blinken,
of New York, to be Ambassador Extraordinary and Plenipotentiary of the United States of America to Belgium.

Parker W. Borg,
of Minnesota, a career member of the Senior Foreign Service, class of Minister-Counselor, to be Ambassador Extraordinary and Plenipotentiary of the United States of America to the Republic of Iceland.

Eugene A. Brickhouse,
of Virginia, to be an Assistant Secretary of Veterans Affairs (Human Resources and Administration), vice Ronald E. Ray, resigned.

Margaret V. W. Carpenter,
of California, to be an Assistant Administrator of the Agency for International Development, vice Reginald J. Brown, resigned.

Herbert L. Chabot,
of Maryland, to be a Judge of the United States Tax Court for a term expiring 15 years after he takes office (reappointment).

The following named persons to be Assistant Secretaries of Labor:

Joseph A. Dear, of Washington, vice Gerard F. Scannell, resigned.
Martin John Manley, of California, vice Robert Michael Guttman, resigned.

Edward P. Djerejian,
of Maryland, a career member of the Senior Foreign Service, class of Career Minister, to be Ambassador Extraordinary and Plenipotentiary of the United States of America to Israel.

Daniel A. Dreyfus,
of Virginia, to be Director of the Office of Civilian Radioactive Waste Management, Department of Energy, vice John Wesley Bartlett, resigned.

The following named persons to be members of the Board of Directors of the Legal Services Corporation for the terms indicated:

Edna Fairbanks-Williams, of Vermont, for the term expiring July 13, 1995, vice Jeanine E. Wolbeck.
Ernestine P. Watlington, of Pennsylvania, for the term expiring July 13, 1996, vice George W. Wittgraf.

Toby Trister Gati,
of New York, to be an Assistant Secretary of State, vice Douglas P. Mulholland, resigned.

Gordon D. Giffin,
of Georgia, to be a member of the Board of Directors of the Overseas Private Investment Corporation for a term expiring December 17, 1993, vice Evan Griffith Galbraith, term expired.

Gordon D. Giffin,
of Georgia, to be a member of the Board of Directors of the Overseas Private Investment Corporation for a term expiring December 17, 1996 (reappointment).

William J. Gilmartin,
of Pennsylvania, to be an Assistant Secretary of Housing and Urban Development, vice Russell K. Paul, resigned.

Eduardo Gonzalez,
of Florida, to be Director of the United States Marshals Service, vice Henry Edward Hudson, resigned.

The following named persons to be members of the Assassination Records Review Board:

Kermit L. Hall, of Oklahoma (new position).
John R. Tunheim, of Minnesota (new position).

Jo Ann Harris,
of New York, to be an Assistant Attorney General, vice Robert S. Mueller III, resigned.

Swanee Grace Hunt,
of Colorado, to be Ambassador Extraordinary and Plenipotentiary of the United States of America to the Republic of Austria.

Carol J. Lancaster,
of the District of Columbia, to be Deputy Administrator of the Agency for International Development, vice Mark L. Edelman, resigned.

Neal F. Lane,
of Oklahoma, to be Director of the National Science Foundation for a term of 6 years, vice Walter E. Massey, resigned.

Thomas A. Loftus,
of Wisconsin, to be Ambassador Extraordinary and Plenipotentiary of the United States of America to Norway.

R. Noel Longuemare, Jr.,
of Maryland, to be Deputy Under Secretary of Defense for Acquisition, vice Donald C. Fraser, resigned.

Thomas Michael Tolliver Niles,
of Kentucky, a career member of the Senior Foreign Service, class of Career Minister, to be Ambassador Extraordinary and Plenipotentiary of the United States of America to Greece.

Steven O. Palmer,
of Michigan, to be an Assistant Secretary of Transportation, vice Michael James Toohey.

Edward Joseph Perkins,
of Oregon, a career member of the Senior Foreign Service, class of Career Minister, to be Ambassador Extraordinary and Plenipotentiary of the United States of America to Australia.

William Lacy Swing,
of North Carolina, a career member of the Senior Foreign Service, class of Career Minister, to be Ambassador Extraordinary and Plenipotentiary of the United States of America to the Republic of Haiti.

Richard W. Teare,
of Ohio, a career member of the Senior Foreign Service, class of Minister-Counselor, to be Ambassador Extraordinary and Plenipotentiary of the United States of America to Papua New Guinea and to serve concurrently and without additional compensation as Ambassador Extraordinary and Plenipotentiary of the United States of America to Solomon Islands and Ambassador Extraordinary and Plenipotentiary of the United States of America to the Republic of Vanuatu.

Donald Richard Wurtz,
of California, to be Chief Financial Officer, Department of Education, vice William Dean Hansen, resigned.

Linda Tsao Yang,
of California, to be U.S. Director of the Asian Development Bank, with the rank of Ambassador, vice Victor H. Frank, Jr., resigned.

David M. Barasch,
of Pennsylvania, to be U.S. Attorney for the Middle District of Pennsylvania for the term of 4 years, vice David Dart Queen, resigned.

Veronica Freeman Coleman,
of Tennessee, to be U.S. Attorney for the Western District of Tennessee for the term of 4 years, vice Edward G. Bryant, resigned.

Edward L. Dowd, Jr.,
of Missouri, to be U.S. Attorney for the Eastern District of Missouri for the term of 4 years, vice Stephen B. Higgins.

Helen Frances Fahey,
of Virginia, to be U.S. Attorney for the Eastern District of Virginia for the term of 4 years, vice Richard Cullen, resigned.

Claude Harris, Jr.,
of Alabama, to be U.S. Attorney for the Northern District of Alabama for the term of 4 years, vice Jack W. Selden.

Kathryn E. Landreth,
of Nevada, to be U.S. Attorney for the District of Nevada for the term of 4 years, vice William A. Maddox, resigned.

Jay Patrick McCloskey,
of Maine, to be U.S. Attorney for the District of Maine for the term of 4 years, vice Richard S. Cohen, resigned.

Betty Hansen Richardson,
of Idaho, to be U.S. Attorney for the District of Idaho for the term of 4 years, vice Maurice O. Ellsworth.

Edmund A. Sargus, Jr.,
of Ohio, to be U.S. Attorney for the Southern District of Ohio for the term of 4 years, vice D. Michael Crites, resigned.

Henry Lawrence Solano,
of Colorado, to be U.S. Attorney for the District of Colorado for the term of 4 years, vice Michael J. Norton, resigned.

Doris Meissner,
of Maryland, to be Commissioner of Immigration and Naturalization, vice Gene McNary, resigned.

Submitted September 14

Daniel L. Spiegel,
of Virginia, to be the Representative of the United States of America to the European Office of the United Nations, with the rank of Ambassador.

Submitted September 15

Shirley Sears Chater,
of Texas, to be Commissioner of Social Security, vice Gwendolyn S. King, resigned.

The following named persons to be the Representative and Alternate Representatives of the United States of America to the 37th Session of the General Conference of the International Atomic Energy Agency:

Representative:
   Hazel Rollins O'Leary, of Minnesota

Alternate Representatives:
   Ivan Selin, of the District of Columbia
   Jane E. Becker, of the District of Columbia

Submitted September 16

Kathy Elena Jurado,
of Florida, to be an Assistant Secretary of Veterans Affairs (Public and Intergovernmental Affairs), vice Edward T. Timperlake, resigned.

Robert W. Perciasepe,
of Maryland, to be an Assistant Administrator of the Environmental Protection Agency, vice LaJuana Sue Wilcher, resigned.

John Calhoun Wells,
of Texas, to be Federal Mediation and Conciliation Director, vice Bernard E. DeLury, resigned.

Lauri Fitz-Pegado,
of Maryland, to be Assistant Secretary of Commerce and Director General of the United States and Foreign Commercial Service, vice Susan Carol Schwab, resigned.

Elliott Pearson Laws,
of Virginia, to be Assistant Administrator, Office of Solid Waste, Environmental Protection Agency, vice Don R. Clay, resigned.

Lynn R. Goldman,
of California, to be Assistant Administrator for Toxic Substances of the Environmental Protection Agency, vice Linda J. Fisher, resigned.

Submitted September 17

Theresa Anne Tull,
of New Jersey, a career member of the Senior Foreign Service, class of Minister-Counselor, to be Ambassador Extraordinary and Plenipotentiary of the United States of America to Brunei Darussalam.

Corlis Smith Moody,
of Minnesota, to be Director of the Office of Minority Economic Impact, Department of Energy, vice Melva G. Wray, resigned.

Jon Ernest DeGuilio,
of Indiana, to be U.S. Attorney for the Northern District of Indiana for the term of 4 years, vice John F. Hoehner, resigned.

Christopher Droney,
of Connecticut, to be U.S. Attorney for the District of Connecticut for the term of 4 years, vice Stanley A. Twardy, Jr., resigned.

Peggy A. Lautenschlager,
of Wisconsin, to be U.S. Attorney for the Western District of Wisconsin for the term of 4 years, vice Kevin C. Potter, resigned.

Thomas Paul Schneider,
of Wisconsin, to be U.S. Attorney for the Eastern District of Wisconsin for the term of 4 years, vice John E. Fryatt, resigned.

Emily Margaret Sweeney,
of Ohio, to be U.S. Attorney for the Northern District of Ohio for the term of 4 years, vice Joyce J. George, resigned.

Submitted September 23

Victor L. Tomseth,
of Oregon, a career member of the Senior Foreign Service, class of Minister-Counselor, to be Ambassador Extraordinary and Plenipotentiary of the United States of America to the Lao People's Democratic Republic.

Jennifer Anne Hillman,
of the District of Columbia, for the rank of Ambassador during her tenure of service as Chief Textile Negotiator.

Gilbert F. Casellas,
of Pennsylvania, to be General Counsel of the Department of the Air Force, vice Ann Christine Petersen, resigned.

Submitted September 24

Cassandra M. Pulley,
of the District of Columbia, to be Deputy Administrator of the Small Business Administration, vice Paul H. Cooksey, resigned.

Ginger Ehn Lew,
of California, to be General Counsel of the Department of Commerce, vice Wendell Lewis Willkie II, resigned.

John Chrystal,
of Iowa, to be a member of the Board of Directors of the Overseas Private Investment Corporation for a term expiring December 17, 1994, vice H. Douglas Barclay, term expired.

Ernest W. DuBester,
of New Jersey, to be a member of the National Mediation Board for a term expiring July 1, 1995, vice Joshua M. Javits, term expired.

Jonathan Z. Cannon,
of Virginia, to be an Assistant Administrator of the Environmental Protection Agency, vice Christian R. Holmes IV, resigned.

Jonathan Z. Cannon,
of Virginia, to be Chief Financial Officer, Environmental Protection Agency, vice Christian R. Holmes IV, resigned.

Rosemary Barkett,
of Florida, to be U.S. Circuit Judge for the Eleventh Circuit, vice Paul H. Roney, retired.

Raymond A. Jackson,
of Virginia, to be U.S. District Judge for the Eastern District of Virginia, vice Richard L. Williams, retired.

Joanna Seybert,
of New York, to be U.S. District Judge for the Eastern District of New York (new position).

John Joseph Kelly,
of New Mexico, to be U.S. Attorney for the District of New Mexico for the term of 4 years, vice Don J. Svet.

Carl Kimmel Kirkpatrick,
of Tennessee, to be U.S. Attorney for the Eastern District of Tennessee for the term of 4 years, vice Jerry G. Cunningham, resigned.

Michael Rankin Stiles,
of Pennsylvania, to be U.S. Attorney for the Eastern District of Pennsylvania for the term of 4 years, vice Edward S.G. Dennis, Jr., resigned.

Submitted September 30

Larry E. Byrne,
of Virginia, to be Associate Administrator of the Agency for International Development, vice Scott M. Spangler, resigned.

Submitted October 1

Diane B. Frankel,
of California, to be Director of the Institute of Museum Services, vice Susannah Simpson Kent, resigned.

Henry Allen Holmes,
of the District of Columbia, to be an Assistant Secretary of Defense, vice James R. Locher III, resigned.

Theodore E. Russell,
of Virginia, a career member of the Senior Foreign Service, class of Minister-Counselor, to be Ambassador Extraordinary and Plenipotentiary of the United States of America to the Slovak Republic.

Richard H. Stallings,
of Idaho, to be Nuclear Waste Negotiator, vice David H. Leroy, resigned.

Gerald Mann Stern,
of California, to be Special Counsel, Financial Institutions Fraud Unit, Department of Justice, vice Ira H. Raphaelson, resigned.

Submitted October 5

Robert S. Gelbard,
of Washington, a career member of the Senior Foreign Service, class of Minister-Counselor, to be Assistant Secretary of State for International Narcotics Matters, vice Melvyn Levitsky, resigned.

Submitted October 7

Nicholas Andrew Rey,
of New York, to be Ambassador Extraordinary and Plenipotentiary of the United States of America to the Republic of Poland.

David W. Hagen,
of Nevada, to be U.S. District Judge for the District of Nevada, vice Edward C. Reed, Jr., retired.

Claudia Wilken,
of California, to be U.S. District Judge for the Northern District of California (new position).

Mary Dolores Nichols,
of California, to be an Assistant Administrator of the Environmental Protection Agency, vice William G. Rosenberg, resigned.

Submitted October 13

Kendall Brindley Coffey,
of Florida, to be U.S. Attorney for the Southern District of Florida for the term of 4 years, vice Leon B. Kellner, resigned.

Frances Cuthbert Hulin,
of Illinois, to be U.S. Attorney for the Central District of Illinois for the term of 4 years, vice J. William Roberts, resigned.

Nora Margaret Manella,
of California, to be U.S. Attorney for the Central District of California for the term of 4 years, vice Lourdes G. Baird, resigned.

Sherry Scheel Matteucci,
of Montana, to be U.S. Attorney for the District of Montana for the term of 4 years, vice Doris Swords Poppler, resigned.

Submitted October 14

John David Holum,
of South Dakota, to be Director of the United States Arms Control and Disarmament Agency, vice Ronald Frank Lehman II, resigned.

Michael F. DiMario,
of Maryland, to be Public Printer, vice Robert William Houk, resigned.

Bernard E. Anderson,
of Pennsylvania, to be an Assistant Secretary of Labor, vice Cari M. Dominguez, resigned.

K. Terry Dornbush,
of Georgia, to be Ambassador Extraordinary and Plenipotentiary of the United States of America to the Kingdom of the Netherlands.

Edward Elliott Elson,
of Georgia, to be Ambassador Extraordinary and Plenipotentiary of the United States of America to Denmark.

Marc Charles Ginsberg,
of Maryland, to be Ambassador Extraordinary and Plenipotentiary of the United States of America to the Kingdom of Morocco.

Thomas L. Siebert,
of Maryland, to be Ambassador Extraordinary and Plenipotentiary of the United States of America to Sweden.

Sidney Williams,
of California, to be Ambassador Extraordinary and Plenipotentiary of the United States of America to the Commonwealth of the Bahamas.

J. Davitt McAteer,
of West Virginia, to be Assistant Secretary of Labor for Mine Safety and Health, vice William James Tattersall, resigned.

Submitted October 19

Mark L. Schneider,
of California, to be an Assistant Administrator of the Agency for International Development, vice James Henry Michel, resigned.

Submitted October 20

Olivia A. Golden,
of the District of Columbia, to be Commissioner on Children, Youth, and Families, Department of Health and Human Services (new position).

Jane M. Wales,
of New York, to be an Associate Director of the Office of Science and Technology Policy, vice J. Thomas Ratchford, resigned.

Submitted October 21

Martha Anne Krebs,
of California, to be Director of the Office of Energy Research, Department of Energy, vice William Happer, resigned.

Mary Rita Cooke Greenwood,
of California, to be an Associate Director of the Office of Science and Technology Policy, vice Karl A. Erb, resigned.

Alan D. Bersin,
of California, to be U.S. Attorney for the Southern District of California for the term of 4 years, vice William Braniff, resigned.

James Burton Burns,
of Illinois, to be U.S. Attorney for the Northern District of Illinois for the term of 4 years, vice Fred L. Foreman, resigned.

Joseph Leslie Famularo,
of Kentucky, to be U.S. Attorney for the Eastern District of Kentucky for the term of 4 years, vice Karen K. Caldwell.

Walter Charles Grace,
of Illinois, to be U.S. Attorney for the Southern District of Illinois for the term of 4 years, vice Frederick J. Hess, resigned.

Michael David Skinner,
of Louisiana, to be U.S. Attorney for the Western District of Louisiana for the term of 4 years, vice Joseph S. Cage, Jr., resigned.

Submitted October 25

Gary L. Lancaster,
of Pennsylvania, to be U.S. District Judge for the Western District of Pennsylvania, vice Timothy K. Lewis, elevated.

Donetta W. Ambrose,
of Pennsylvania, to be U.S. District Judge for the Western District of Pennsylvania, vice Gerald J. Weber, retired.

Wilkie D. Ferguson, Jr.,
of Florida, to be U.S. District Judge for the Southern District of Florida, vice William M. Hoeveler, retired.

Charles A. Shaw,
of Missouri, to be U.S. District Judge for the Eastern District of Missouri (new position).

Sandra Louise Vogelgesang,
of Ohio, a career member of the Senior Foreign Service, class of Minister-Counselor, to be Ambassador Extraordinary and Plenipotentiary of the United States of America to the Kingdom of Nepal.

John F. Hicks, Sr.,
of North Carolina, to be an Assistant Administrator of the Agency for International Development, vice Allison Podell Rosenberg, resigned.

Anthony A. Williams,
of Connecticut, to be Chief Financial Officer, Department of Agriculture, vice Charles R. Hilty, resigned.

Preston M. Taylor, Jr.,
of New Jersey, to be Assistant Secretary of Labor for Veterans' Employment and Training, vice Thomas E. Collins III.

Margaret A. Browning,
of Pennsylvania, to be a member of the National Labor Relations Board for the term of 5 years expiring August 27, 1996, vice Mary Cracraft, term expired.

Magdalena G. Jacobsen,
of Oregon, to be a member of the National Mediation Board for the term expiring July 1, 1996, vice Kimberly A. Madigan, term expired.

George J. Kourpias,
of Maryland, to be a member of the Board of Directors of the Overseas Private Investment Corporation for a term expiring December 17, 1994, vice James Thomas Grady, term expired.

M. Larry Lawrence,
of California, to be Ambassador Extraordinary and Plenipotentiary of the United States of America to Switzerland.

Norman E. D'Amours,
of New Hampshire, to be a member of the National Credit Union Administration Board for the term of 6 years expiring August 2, 1999, vice Roger William Jepsen, term expired.

The following named persons to be members of the Assassination Records Review Board:

William L. Joyce, of New Jersey (new position).
Anna K. Nelson, of the District of Columbia (new position).

Submitted October 27

Loretta Collins Argrett,
of Maryland, to be an Assistant Attorney General, vice Shirley D. Peterson, resigned.

Harry F. Barnes,
of Arkansas, to be U.S. District Judge for the Western District of Arkansas, vice Morris S. Arnold, elevated.

Nancy Gertner,
of Massachusetts, to be U.S. District Judge for the District of Massachusetts, vice A. David Mazzone, retired.

Reginald C. Lindsay,
of Massachusetts, to be U.S. District Judge for the District of Massachusetts, vice David Sutherland Nelson, retired.

Patti B. Saris,
of Massachusetts, to be U.S. District Judge for the District of Massachusetts, vice Walter Jay Skinner, retired.

Allen G. Schwartz,
of New York, to be U.S. District Judge for the Southern District of New York, vice Vincent L. Broderick, retired.

Richard G. Stearns,
of Massachusetts, to be U.S. District Judge for the District of Massachusetts, vice John Joseph McNaught, retired.

Lottie Lee Shackelford,
of Arkansas, to be a member of the Board of Directors of the Overseas Private Investment Corporation for a term expiring December 17, 1995, vice J. Carter Beese, Jr., resigned.

Submitted October 29

Martin L. Cheshes,
of Georgia, a career member of the Senior Foreign Service, class of Minister-Counselor, to be Ambassador Extraordinary and Plenipotentiary of the United States of America to the Republic of Djibouti.

Henry Lee Adams, Jr.,
of Florida, to be U.S. District Judge for the Middle District of Florida, vice Susan H. Black, elevated.

Susan C. Bucklew,
of Florida, to be U.S. District Judge for the Middle District of Florida, vice William J. Castagna, retired.

Theodore Klein,
of Florida, to be U.S. District Judge for the Southern District of Florida, vice James W. Kehoe, retired.

Patrick Michael Patterson,
of Florida, to be U.S. Attorney for the Northern District of Florida for the term of 4 years, vice Kenneth W. Sukhia, resigned.

Katrina Campbell Pflaumer,
of Washington, to be U.S. Attorney for the Western District of Washington for the term of 4 years, vice Michael D. McKay, resigned.

Charles Joseph Stevens,
of California, to be U.S. Attorney for the Eastern District of California for the term of 4 years, vice George L. O'Connell, resigned.

Margaret A. Browning,
of Pennsylvania, to be a member of the National Labor Relations Board for the remainder of the term expiring December 16, 1997, vice John N. Raudabaugh.

Brian J. Donnelly,
of Massachusetts, to be an Alternate Representative of the United States of America to the 48th Session of the General Assembly of the United Nations.

Sue E. Eckert,
of Rhode Island, to be an Assistant Secretary of Commerce, vice Michael Paul Galvin, resigned.

Martin A. Kamarck,
of Massachusetts, to be First Vice President of the Export-Import Bank of the United States for a term of 4 years expiring January 20, 1997, vice Eugene Kistler Lawson, term expired.

Steven Kelman,
of Massachusetts, to be Administrator for Federal Procurement Policy, vice Allan V. Burman, resigned.

Dwight P. Robinson,
of Michigan, to be President, Government National Mortgage Association, vice Raoul Lord Carroll, resigned.

L. Ronald Scheman,
of the District of Columbia, to be U.S. Executive Director of the Inter-American Development Bank for a term of 3 years, vice Larry K. Mellinger, resigned.

Nelson F. Sievering, Jr.,
of Maryland, to be the Representative of the United States of America to the International Atomic Energy Agency, with the rank of Ambassador.

M. Douglas Stafford,
of New York, to be an Assistant Administrator of the Agency for International Development, vice Andrew S. Natsios, resigned.

Withdrawn October 29

Margaret A. Browning,
of Pennsylvania, to be a member of the National Labor Relations Board for the term of 5 years expiring August 27, 1996, vice Mary Cracraft, term expired, which was sent to the Senate on October 25, 1993.

Submitted November 2

James J. Molinari,
of California, to be U.S. Marshal for the Northern District of California for the term of 4 years, vice Glen E. Robinson.

Joe Russell Mullins,
of Kentucky, to be U.S. Marshal for the Eastern District of Kentucky for the term of 4 years, vice Sherman L. Hansford.

John Patrick McCaffrey,
of New York, to be U.S. Marshal for the Western District of New York for the term of 4 years, vice Daniel B. Wright.

Phylliss Jeanette Henry,
of Iowa, to be U.S. Marshal for the Southern District of Iowa for the term of 4 years, vice Warren D. Stump.

Charles M. Adkins,
of West Virginia, to be U.S. Marshal for the Southern District of West Virginia for the term of 4 years, vice James P. Hickman.

Submitted November 5

Edmund T. DeJarnette, Jr.,
of Virginia, a career member of the Senior Foreign Service, class of Minister-Counselor, to be Ambassador Extraordinary and Plenipotentiary of the United States of America to the Republic of Angola.

Don Carlos Nickerson,
of Iowa, to be U.S. Attorney for the Southern District of Iowa for the term of 4 years, vice Gene W. Shepard, resigned.

Stephen John Rapp,
of Iowa, to be U.S. Attorney for the Northern District of Iowa for the term of 4 years, vice Charles W. Larson, resigned.

Donald Kenneth Stern,
of Massachusetts, to be U.S. Attorney for the District
of Massachusetts for the term of 4 years, vice Wayne
A. Budd, resigned.

G. Ronald Dashiell,
of Washington, to be U.S. Marshal for the Eastern
District of Washington for the term of 4 years, vice
Paul R. Nolan.

Nancy J. McGillivray-Shaffer,
of Massachusetts, to be U.S. Marshal for the District
of Massachusetts for the term of 4 years, vice Robert
T. Guiney.

Donald R. Moreland,
of Florida, to be U.S. Marshal for the Middle District
of Florida for the term of 4 years, vice Richard L.
Cox, resigned.

Togo Dennis West, Jr.,
of the District of Columbia, to be Secretary of the
Army, vice Michael P.W. Stone, resigned.

Joe Robert Reeder,
of Texas, to be Under Secretary of the Army, vice
John W. Shannon, resigned.

Richard Danzig,
of the District of Columbia, to be Under Secretary
of the Navy, vice J. Daniel Howard, resigned.

John E. Tull, Jr.,
of Arkansas, to be a Commissioner of the Commodity
Futures Trading Commission for the term expiring
April 13, 1998, vice William P. Albrecht, resigned.

Submitted November 8

Wally B. Beyer,
of North Dakota, to be Administrator of the Rural
Electrification Administration for a term of 10 years,
vice James B. Huff, Sr.

Christine Ervin,
of Oregon, to be an Assistant Secretary of Energy
(Energy Efficiency and Renewable Energy), vice J.
Michael Davis, resigned.

Barbara Pedersen Holum,
of Maryland, to be a Commissioner of the Commodity
Futures Trading Commission for the term expiring
April 13, 1997, vice Fowler C. West, resigned.

Stuart George Moldaw,
of California, to be an Alternate Representative of
the U.S. to the 48th Session of the General Assembly
of the United Nations.

Submitted November 9

Charles R. Baquet III,
of Maryland, to be Deputy Director of the Peace
Corps, vice Barbara Zartman, resigned.

Submitted November 10

Melvyn Levitsky,
of Maryland, a career member of the Senior Foreign
Service, class of Career Minister, to be Ambassador
Extraordinary and Plenipotentiary of the United States
of America to the Federative Republic of Brazil.

David Nathan Merrill,
of Maryland, a career member of the Senior Foreign
Service, class of Career Minister, to be Ambassador
Extraordinary and Plenipotentiary of the United States
of America to the People's Republic of Bangladesh.

Brian C. Berg,
of North Dakota, to be U.S. Marshal for the District
of North Dakota for the term of 4 years, vice Errol
Lee Wood.

Daniel T.K. Hurley,
of Florida, to be U.S. District Judge for the Southern
District of Florida, vice James C. Paine, retired.

Floyd A. Kimbrough,
of Missouri, to be U.S. Marshal for the Eastern District of Missouri for the term of 4 years, vice Willie
Greason, Jr.

Charles William Logsdon,
of Kentucky, to be U.S. Marshal for the Western
District of Kentucky for the term of 4 years, vice
Ralph A. Boling.

Submitted November 16

Michael V. Dunn,
of Iowa, to be Administrator of the Farmers Home
Administration, vice La Verne G. Ausman, resigned.

Submitted November 17

Jeanette W. Hyde,
of North Carolina, to be Ambassador Extraordinary
and Plenipotentiary of the United States of America
to Barbados, and to serve concurrently and without
additional compensation as Ambassador Extraordinary
and Plenipotentiary of the United States of America
to the Commonwealth of Dominica, Ambassador Extraordinary and Plenipotentiary of the United States
of America to St. Lucia, and Ambassador Extraordinary and Plenipotentiary of the United States of
America to St. Vincent and the Grenadines.

Judith W. Rogers,
of the District of Columbia, to be U.S. Circuit Judge
for the District of Columbia Circuit, vice Clarence
Thomas.

Thomas I. Vanaskie,
of Pennsylvania, to be U.S. District Judge for the Middle District of Pennsylvania (new position).

Submitted November 18

Maria Luisa Mabilangan Haley,
of Arkansas, to be a member of the Board of Directors of the Export-Import Bank of the United States for the remainder of the term expiring January 20, 1995, vice Constance Bastine Harriman.

Frederick Gilbert Slabach,
of Mississippi, to be an Assistant Secretary of Agriculture, vice Franklin Eugene Bailey, resigned.

James H. Scheuer,
of New York, to be U.S. Director of the European Bank for Reconstruction and Development, vice William G. Curran, Jr.

Helen G. Berrigan,
of Louisiana, to be U.S. District Judge for the Eastern District of Louisiana, vice Patrick E. Carr, retired.

Tucker L. Melancon,
of Louisiana, to be U.S. District Judge for the Western District of Louisiana, vice Thomas E. Stagg, Jr., retired.

Robert Dale Ecoffey,
of South Dakota, to be U.S. Marshal for the District of South Dakota for the term of 4 years, vice Gene G. Abdallah.

Rosa Maria Melendez,
of Washington, to be U.S. Marshal for the Western District of Washington for the term of 4 years, vice Noreen T. Skagen.

Robert James Moore,
of Alabama, to be U.S. Marshal for the Southern District of Alabama for the term of 4 years, vice Howard V. Adair.

James Robert Oakes,
of Louisiana, to be U.S. Marshal for the Western District of Louisiana for the term of 4 years, vice Brian P. Joffrion.

Cleveland Vaughn,
of Nebraska, to be U.S. Marshal for the District of Nebraska for the term of 4 years, vice Thomas A. O'Hara, Jr.

Richard Rand Rock II,
of Kansas, to be U.S. Marshal for the District of Kansas for the term of 4 years, vice Kenneth L. Pekarek.

William D. Hathaway,
of Maine, to be a Federal Maritime Commissioner for the term expiring June 30, 1998 (reappointment).

Hugh Dinsmore Black, Jr.,
of Arkansas, to be U.S. Marshal for the Western District of Arkansas for the term of 4 years, vice James C. Patterson.

John B. Ritch III,
of the District of Columbia, to be the Representative of the United States of America to the Vienna Office of the United Nations and Deputy Representative of the United States of America to the International Atomic Energy Agency, with the rank of Ambassador.

Submitted November 19

Linda Hall Daschle,
of South Dakota, to be Deputy Administrator of the Federal Aviation Administration, vice Barry Lambert Harris, resigned.

Rebecca Aline Betts,
of West Virginia, to be U.S. Attorney for the Southern District of West Virginia for the term of 4 years, vice Michael W. Carey, resigned.

Robert Charles Bundy,
of Alaska, to be U.S. Attorney for the District of Alaska for the term of 4 years, vice Michael R. Spaan, resigned.

Larry Herbert Colleton,
of Florida, to be U.S. Attorney for the Middle District of Florida for the term of 4 years, vice Robert W. Genzman, resigned.

Harry Donival Dixon, Jr.,
of Georgia, to be U.S. Attorney for the Southern District of Georgia for the term of 4 years, vice Hinton R. Pierce, resigned.

Lezin Joseph Hymel, Jr.,
of Louisiana, to be U.S. Attorney for the Middle District of Louisiana for the term of 4 years, vice Paul Raymond Lamonica.

David Lee Lillehaug,
of Minnesota, to be U.S. Attorney for the District of Minnesota for the term of 4 years, vice Thomas B. Heffelfinger, resigned.

Kenneth Ray Oden,
of Texas, to be U.S. Attorney for the Western District of Texas for the term of 4 years, vice Ronald F. Ederer, resigned.

Daniel J. Horgan,
of Florida, to be U.S. Marshal for the Southern District of Florida for the term of 4 years (reappointment).

Patrick J. Wilkerson,
of Oklahoma, to be U.S. Marshal for the Western District of Oklahoma for the term of 4 years, vice Stuart E. Earnest.

Shirley Sachi Sagawa,
of Virginia, to be a Managing Director of the Corporation for National and Community Service (new position).

George W. Haley,
of Maryland, to be a Commissioner of the Postal Rate Commission for the term expiring October 14, 1998 (reappointment).

Peter S. Knight,
of the District of Columbia, to be a member of the Board of Directors of the Communications Satellite Corporation until the date of the annual meeting of the Corporation in 1996, vice James B. Edwards.

Appendix C—Checklist of White House Press Releases

The following list contains releases of the Office of the Press Secretary which are not included in this book.

Released August 2

Transcript of a press briefing by Press Secretary Dee Dee Myers

Statement by Press Secretary Dee Dee Myers on the NATO decision on air strikes on Bosnian Serbs

List of participants in meeting with Congressional Progressive Caucus members

Released August 3

Transcript of a press briefing by Press Secretary Dee Dee Myers

White House statement on administration action on timber sales

Transcript of a press briefing on the economic program by Secretary of the Treasury Lloyd Bentsen and Director of the Office of Management and Budget Leon Panetta

Released August 4

Transcript of a press briefing on the Executive orders on budget control and the deficit reduction fund by Director of the Office of Management and Budget Leon Panetta

Transcript of a press briefing by Director of Communications Mark Gearan

White House statement on the Executive order on Federal compliance with right-to-know laws and pollution prevention requirements

Released August 5

Transcript of a press briefing by Press Secretary Dee Dee Myers

Released August 6

Transcript of a press briefing on employment and the economic program by Deputy Secretary of the Treasury Roger Altman and Chair of the Council of Economic Advisers Laura D'Andrea Tyson

Transcript of a press briefing by Press Secretary Dee Dee Myers

Announcement of nomination for members of the Board of Directors of the Legal Services Corporation

Announcement of nomination for seven U.S. attorneys

White House statement on the President's meeting with Mario Chanes de Armas

Released August 7

Statement by Press Secretary Dee Dee Myers on Senate ratification of the Open Skies Treaty

Released August 8

Statement by Press Secretary Dee Dee Myers on the attack on U.N. forces in Mogadishu

Released August 9

Statement by Press Secretary Dee Dee Myers congratulating Prime Minister Morihiro Hosokawa of Japan

Released August 10

Transcript of a press briefing by Director of Communications Mark Gearan

Statement by Press Secretary Dee Dee Myers on the appointment of Richard Schifter to the National Security Council as Special Assistant to the President and Counselor

Released August 11

Transcript of a press briefing by Director of Communications Mark Gearan

Transcript of a press briefing by Deputy Attorney General Phil Heymann and Deputy Assistant to the President for Domestic Affairs Bruce Reed

Transcript of a press briefing by Secretary of Defense Les Aspin and Deputy National Security Adviser Sandy Berger

White House statement on the plan to expand community policing and reduce gun violence

Released August 12

Statement by Press Secretary Dee Dee Myers on the technology reinvestment project

White House statement on funds in the flood relief legislation

Transcript of a press briefing on the President's meeting with Pope John Paul II by Ambassador to the Holy See Raymond L. Flynn in Denver, CO

Released August 17

Statement by Press Secretary Dee Dee Myers on the upcoming visit of five Caribbean leaders on August 30

Released August 19

Announcement of appointment for the White House Office of Communications

Released August 20

Transcript of a press briefing by Press Secretary Dee Dee Myers

Statement by Press Secretary Dee Dee Myers on the President's telephone conversation with Japanese Prime Minister Morihiro Hosokawa

Released August 25

Transcript of a press briefing by Press Secretary Dee Dee Myers

Released August 26

Transcript of a press briefing by Press Secretary Dee Dee Myers

Released August 27

Transcript of a press briefing by Ricki L. Seidman, Assistant to the President and Counselor to the Chief of Staff

Statement by Acting Press Secretary Ricki L. Seidman on suspension of economic sanctions against Haiti

Released August 31

White House statement on the fiscal year 1994 budget amendments for the Department of Justice to support the immigration initiative announced on July 27

Released September 1

Transcript of a press briefing on the midsession budget review by Director of the Office of Management and Budget Leon Panetta, Chair of the Council of Economic Advisers Laura D'Andrea Tyson, and OMB Deputy Director Alice Rivlin

Transcript of a press briefing by Press Secretary Dee Dee Myers

Released September 2

Transcript of a press briefing by Press Secretary Dee Dee Myers

Statement by Press Secretary Dee Dee Myers on Nigeria

Statement by Press Secretary Dee Dee Myers on Nicaragua

Announcement of appointment for Special Adviser to the President for NAFTA

Released September 3

Statement by Press Secretary Dee Dee Myers on the President's upcoming meeting with Prime Minister Paul Keating of Australia

White House statement on the Oval Office restoration

Released September 7

Transcript of a press briefing on reinventing Government by National Performance Review consultants David Osborne and John Sharp

Statement by Press Secretary Dee Dee Myers on the President's planned meeting with President Alija Izetbegovic of Bosnia

Released September 8

Transcript of a press briefing by Press Secretary Dee Dee Myers

Announcement of nomination for 10 U.S. attorneys

Released September 9

Statement by Press Secretary Dee Dee Myers on plans to announce health care reforms

Released September 12

Transcript of a press briefing on health care reform by Senior Adviser for Policy Development Ira Magaziner and members of the President's Task Force on National Health Care Reform

Released September 13

White House statement on the renewal of the Trading With the Enemy Act and U.S. policy toward Vietnam

Transcript of a press briefing on the Middle East peace process by Ambassador Dennis Ross, State Department Special Coordinator, and Martin Indyk, Special Assistant to the President for Near East Affairs

Released September 14

Statement by Press Secretary Dee Dee Myers on the violence in Haiti

Announcement of nomination for U.S. Permanent Representative to the European Office of the United Nations

Released September 16

Transcript of a press briefing by Press Secretary Dee Dee Myers

Transcript of a press briefing on health care reform by Small Business Administrator Erskine Bowles and Deputy Assistant Secretary of Health and Human Services Ken Thorpe

White House statement on Senator David Pryor's pharmaceutical restraint agreements

Statement by Dr. Arthur Flemming, former Secretary of Health, Education, and Welfare, on the President's health care reform proposal

Released September 17

Transcript of a press briefing on health care reform by Tim Hill, chair, Administrative Simplification Group, President's Task Force on National Health Care Reform; John Silva, practicing physician specializing in information technology, Department of Defense; Rick Kronick, senior health analyst, and Lynn Margherio, senior policy analyst, President's Task Force on National Health Care Reform

Released September 18

Announcement of nomination for five U.S. attorneys

Released September 20

Transcript of a press briefing by Press Secretary Dee Dee Myers

Released September 21

Transcript of a press briefing on Russia and health care reform financing by Director of Communications Mark Gearan, Assistant to the President for Economic Policy Robert Rubin, Director of the Office of Management and Budget Leon Panetta, Deputy Secretary of the Treasury Roger Altman, and Chair of the Council of Economic Advisers Laura D'Andrea Tyson

White House statement announcing an address by National Security Adviser Anthony Lake on U.S. foreign policy

Released September 22

Transcript of a press briefing by Press Secretary Dee Dee Myers

White House statement announcing U.S. attorneys confirmed by the Senate

Released September 23

Statement by Press Secretary Dee Dee Myers on the Transitional Executive Council in South Africa

List of 55 radio talk show hosts invited to broadcast live from the White House lawn

List of attendees of the health care rally on the South Lawn and letters of support for the President's health care plan

Released September 24

Transcript of a press briefing on the North American Free Trade Agreement (NAFTA) by U.S. Trade Representative Mickey Kantor, Environmental Protection Agency Administrator Carol Browner, Associate Attorney General Webb Hubbell, Under Secretary of State for Global Affairs Tim Worth, Special Counselor to

the President for NAFTA William Daley, and Special Adviser to the President for NAFTA William Frenzel

Released September 27

Fact sheet on nonproliferation and export policy

Responses by Press Secretary Dee Dee Myers to questions on U.S. arrearages for U.N. budget and peacekeeping assessments

Released September 28

Transcript of a press briefing by Press Secretary Dee Dee Myers

Statement by Press Secretary Dee Dee Myers on replacement of U.S. troops participating in UNOSOM II in Somalia

Released September 29

Fact sheet entitled "Toward a National Export Strategy: A Report of the Trade Promotion Coordinating Committee"

White House statement on partnership with auto makers for increased fuel efficiency

Released September 30

Transcript of a press briefing by Director of Communications Mark Gearan

List of winners of the National Medal of Science and the National Medal of Technology

Transcript of a press briefing on regulatory reform by Director of the Office of Management and Budget Leon Panetta, Chief of Staff for the Vice President Jack Quinn, and Office of Information and Regulatory Affairs Administrator Sally Katzen

Advance text of citation for the Presidential Medal of Freedom presentation to Colin L. Powell

Released October 1

Transcript of a press briefing by Press Secretary Dee Dee Myers

List of Members of Congress meeting with President on NAFTA

White House statement on emergency assistance to earthquake victims in India

Released October 4

White House statement announcing a ceremony to honor 18 artists and scholars

Fact sheet on announcement of the preferred site for the B-Factory

White House statement announcing the President's request to Congress for funds to rebuild the Cypress Freeway

Released October 5

Transcript of a press briefing by Press Secretary Dee Dee Myers in Culver City, CA

Released October 6

Transcript of a press briefing on health care reform and the economy by Assistant to the President for Economic Policy Robert Rubin, Chair of the Council of Economic Advisers Laura D'Andrea Tyson, Secretary of the Treasury Lloyd Bentsen, Secretary of Labor Robert Reich, and Small Business Administrator Erskine Bowles

List of Members of Congress meeting with the President on NAFTA

Released October 7

List of Members of Congress meeting with the President on NAFTA

List of Members of Congress meeting with the President on Somalia

Transcript of a press briefing on Somalia by Secretary of State Warren Christopher, Secretary of Defense Les Aspin, and Adm. David Jeremiah

Released October 8

Statement by Senior Adviser for Policy Development Ira Magaziner on cost estimates in the President's health care reform proposal

White House statement containing excerpts of letters from business leaders supporting the President's health care reform plan

Released October 12

Transcript of a press briefing by Press Secretary Dee Dee Myers

Statement by Press Secretary Dee Dee Myers on Haiti

White House statement on the availability of emergency funds under the Emergency Supplemental Appropriations Act

List of Members of Congress meeting with the President on NAFTA

Released October 13

Transcript of a press briefing by Press Secretary Dee Dee Myers

Statement by Press Secretary Dee Dee Myers on legislation signed by the President

Statement by Vice President Albert Gore, Jr., on the Bell Atlantic-TCI merger announcement

Announcement of nomination for Ambassadors to The Netherlands and Denmark

White House statement announcing the withdrawal of Shirley Chisholm's nomination to be Ambassador to Jamaica

Released October 14

List of Members of Congress meeting with the President on NAFTA

Statement by Press Secretary Dee Dee Myers on the President's telephone conversation with Chief Warrant Officer Michael Durant

Released October 15

Statement by Director of Communications Mark Gearan on the Vice President's telephone conversation with President Jean-Bertrand Aristide of Haiti

Released October 16

Statement by Director of Communications Mark Gearan on United Nations Security Council action to adopt sanctions on Haiti

Released October 18

Transcript of a press briefing by Press Secretary Dee Dee Myers

Statement by Press Secretary Dee Dee Myers on the 1993 Malcolm Baldrige National Quality Awards recipients

Statement by Press Secretary Dee Dee Myers on Haiti

Statement by Press Secretary Dee Dee Myers on the decision of Pakistan to provide 1,500 additional troops for the U.N. mission in Somalia

White House statement announcing the upcoming informal meeting of Organization for Asian-Pacific Economic Cooperation (APEC) members in Seattle, WA

Released October 19

Transcript of a press briefing by Press Secretary Dee Dee Myers

Statement by Press Secretary Dee Dee Myers on deployment of forces in Somalia

Transcript of a press briefing on reduction of greenhouse gases by Director of the White House Office of Environmental Policy Kathleen McGinty, Secretary of Energy Hazel O'Leary, Secretary of Transportation Federico Peña, and Environmental Protection Agency Administrator Carol Browner

List of Members of Congress meeting with the President on NAFTA

White House statement announcing the climate change action plan

Announcement of nomination for a Cochair of the Appalachian Regional Commission

Released October 20

Transcript of a press briefing by Press Secretary Dee Dee Myers

Statement by Press Secretary Dee Dee Myers on Haiti

White House statement announcing the signing of the Executive order on Federal acquisition, recycling, and waste prevention

White House statement announcing the establishment of Presidential Emergency Board No. 223

Released October 21

Text of a letter to the President from Jerry Jansinowski, president, National Association of Manufacturers, on health care reform

Statement by Press Secretary Dee Dee Myers on legislation signed by the President

Statement by AIDS Policy Coordinator Kristine Gebbie on effective HIV prevention in adolescents

White House statement announcing the resignation of Marla Romash as Communications Director for the Vice President

Released October 22

Transcript of a press briefing by Press Secretary Dee Dee Myers

Statement by Press Secretary Dee Dee Myers on the designation of Ambassador Paul J. Hare as U.S. Special Representative to the Angola peace process

Announcement of nomination for four U.S. attorneys

List of Members of Congress meeting with the President on NAFTA

White House statement announcing technology reinvestment project early award selections

Joint Turkey-U.S. statement

Released October 26

Transcript of a press briefing by Director of the Office of Management and Budget Leon Panetta on reinventing Government

Transcript of a press briefing on health care reform by Senior Adviser for Policy Development Ira Magaziner and Director of the Office of Management and Budget Leon Panetta

List of Members of Congress meeting with the President on NAFTA

Announcement of three Senior Executive Service appointments

White House statement on the initiative to overhaul Government buying

Released October 27

Statement by Press Secretary Dee Dee Myers on correction of the table of contents of the "Health Security Act of 1993"

Statement by Press Secretary Dee Dee Myers on legislation signed by the President

Transcript of a press briefing by Deputy Secretary of the Treasury Roger Altman on health care reform

Released November 1

Transcript of a press briefing by Press Secretary Dee Dee Myers

Announcement of nomination for three U.S. attorneys

Statement by Press Secretary Dee Dee Myers on transmittal to the Congress of $2 billion in spending cuts and reform measures for fiscal year 1994

Released November 2

Statement by Press Secretary Dee Dee Myers releasing statements by former Presidents George Bush, Ronald Reagan, and Gerald Ford endorsing NAFTA

White House statement on the award of the Presidential Medal of Freedom to Martha Raye

Released November 3

Statement by Press Secretary Dee Dee Myers on the administration's intent to seek an international legal prohibition of ocean disposal of low-level radioactive waste

Announcement of nomination for five U.S. marshals

Statement by Press Secretary Dee Dee Myers on the President's signing of the instrument of ratification of the Treaty on Open Skies

Released November 4

White House statement on the upcoming meeting of Organization of Asian Pacific Economic Cooperation (APEC) leaders in Seattle, WA

Released November 5

Fact sheet on the Bipartisan Commission on Entitlement Reform

Text of a letter from Jack Quinn, Chief of Staff to the Vice President, to broadcast journalist Larry King regarding arrangements for a debate on NAFTA between the Vice President and Ross Perot

Statement by Press Secretary Dee Dee Myers on release of unclassified and declassified documents relating to Salvadoran human rights cases

Announcement of nomination for three U.S. attorneys and three U.S. marshals

Released November 8

Transcript of a press briefing by Press Secretary Dee Dee Myers

Transcript of a press briefing by Secretary of the Treasury Lloyd Bentsen on the economy

Released November 9

Transcript of a press briefing by Press Secretary Dee Dee Myers

Released November 10

Statement by Press Secretary Dee Dee Myers on declassification of documents relating to the Vietnam war and American POW/MIA's in Southeast Asia

Released November 11

Statement by Press Secretary Dee Dee Myers on sanctions by the United Nations Security Council against Libya

White House statement on the presentation of commemorative medals to four World War I veterans

Released November 15

Transcript of a press briefing by Press Secretary Dee Dee Myers

Released November 16

Transcript of a press briefing by Press Secretary Dee Dee Myers

Statement by Press Secretary Dee Dee Myers on the President's meeting with Deputy Prime Minister Richard Spring of Ireland

Text of a letter endorsing NAFTA from five former Presidents to Members of Congress

Fact sheet on the Religious Freedom Restoration Act of 1993

Announcement of nomination for eight U.S. marshals

Released November 17

Transcript of a press briefing by Press Secretary Dee Dee Myers

Transcript of a press briefing by Secretary of the Treasury Lloyd Bentsen on the economy and NAFTA

White House statement announcing the availability of emergency funds for use on damaged watershed protection systems along the Mississippi River and its tributaries

Released November 18

Announcement of nomination for six U.S. marshals

Released November 19

Transcript of a press briefing on the Penny-Kasich deficit reduction amendment to H.R. 3400 by Director

of the Office of Management and Budget Leon Panetta and Secretary of Defense Les Aspin

Released November 22

Memorandum on the "Health Security Act of 1993"

Released November 23

Transcript of a press briefing by Director of Communications Mark Gearan and Assistant to the President for Legislative Affairs Howard Paster

Statement by Press Secretary Dee Dee Myers on the 1993 congressional session

Statement by Press Secretary Dee Dee Myers on White House restoration

Announcement of nomination for six U.S. marshals

List of Members of Congress meeting with the President

Released November 24

Transcript of a press briefing on the technology reinvestment project awards by Secretary of Commerce Ron Brown and Deputy Secretary of Defense William Perry

Statement by Press Secretary Dee Dee Myers on the Chemical Weapons Convention

Fact sheet on the Chemical Weapons Convention

White House statement on the President's planned Thanksgiving holiday at Camp David, MD

Fact sheet on the national Thanksgiving turkey

White House statement announcing the second group of awards in the technology reinvestment project

Released November 29

Transcript of a press briefing by Press Secretary Dee Dee Myers

Statement by Press Secretary Dee Dee Myers correcting a reference made in the afternoon briefing

List of religious leaders attending a breakfast meeting with the President

Released November 30

Transcript of a press briefing by U.S. Trade Representative Mickey Kantor on GATT

White House statement announcing the President's signing of H.R. 2401 and H.R. 3341

List of participants attending the Brady bill signing ceremony

List and biographies of Presidential Medal of Freedom recipients

Released December 1

Statement by Press Secretary Dee Dee Myers on the President's meeting with Prime Minister Carl Bildt of Sweden

List of Advisory Council on Intergovernmental Relations members meeting with the President

List of Nobel laureates meeting with the President

Transcript of a press briefing on the Penny-Kasich amendment to H.R. 3400 by Director of the Office of Management and Budget Leon Panetta and Secretary of Defense Les Aspin

Announcement of nomination for five members of the U.S. Enrichment Corporation

Announcement of appointment for a member of the Advisory Commission on Intergovernmental Relations

Released December 2

Transcript of a press briefing by Press Secretary Dee Dee Myers

Statement by Press Secretary Dee Dee Myers on the President's plans to travel to Europe

Announcement of nomination for U.S. Marshal for Western Arkansas

Released December 3

Transcript of a press briefing by Chair of the Council of Economic Advisers Laura D'Andrea Tyson on the economy

Statement by Press Secretary Dee Dee Myers on legislation signed by the President

Statement by Press Secretary Dee Dee Myers announcing the upcoming visit of Prime Minister Gonzalez of Spain

Statement by Press Secretary Dee Dee Myers on the President's telephone conversation with Prime Minister Edouard Balladur of France on GATT negotiations

Statement by Press Secretary Dee Dee Myers on the President's meeting with President Ketumile Masire of Botswana

Statement by Press Secretary Dee Dee Myers on sanctions against Libya

White House statement announcing the third group of awards in the technology reinvestment project

Released December 4

Fact sheet on the urban revitalization demonstration program

Background on the California economic roundtable

Released December 6

Statement by Press Secretary Dee Dee Myers on the Presidential elections in Venezuela

Released December 7

Transcript of a press briefing by Press Secretary Dee Dee Myers

Statement by Press Secretary Dee Dee Myers on the death of President Felix Houphouet-Boigny of Cote d' Ivoire

Released December 8

Transcript of a press briefing by Press Secretary Dee Dee Myers

Transcript of a press briefing on reform of the Community Reinvestment Act by Secretary of the Treasury Lloyd Bentsen, Assistant to the President for Economic Policy Robert Rubin, and Comptroller of the Currency Eugene Ludwig

List of children attending the celebration of the first night of Hanukkah with the President

Released December 9

Transcript of a press briefing on health care financing by Secretary of the Treasury Lloyd Bentsen and Director of the Office of Management and Budget Leon Panetta

Transcript of a press briefing by Press Secretary Dee Dee Myers

List of mayors and police chiefs meeting with the President and the Attorney General for a discussion on crime

Statement by Press Secretary Dee Dee Myers announcing the President's planned meeting with President Hafiz al-Asad of Syria in Geneva, Switzerland

Released December 10

Transcript of a press briefing by Press Secretary Dee Dee Myers

Transcript of a press briefing by U.S. Trade Representative Mickey Kantor on the General Agreement on Tariffs and Trade

Statement by Press Secretary Dee Dee Myers on the Human Rights Day, Bill of Rights Day, and Human Rights Week, 1993, proclamation signing ceremony

Released December 12

Statement by Press Secretary Dee Dee Myers on the President's telephone conversations with Prime Minister Edouard Balladur of France, Prime Minister John Major of Great Britain, and Chancellor Helmut Kohl of Germany on GATT

Released December 13

Statement by Press Secretary Dee Dee Myers on the elections in Russia

Released December 14

Transcript of a press briefing by Press Secretary Dee Dee Myers

Transcript of a press briefing on GATT by Assistant to the President for Economic Policy Robert Rubin, Chair of the Council of Economic Advisers Laura D'Andrea Tyson, Deputy National Security Adviser Sandy Berger, Deputy Assistant to the President for Economic Policy Bowman Cutter, and Special Assistant to the President for Economic Policy Robert Kyle

Transcript of a press briefing by the Council of Economic Advisers

Released December 16

Statement by Press Secretary Dee Dee Myers on legislation signed by the President

Biography of Bobby Ray Inman

Text of a letter from Senior Adviser for Policy Development Ira Magaziner to the American Medical Association

Released December 17

Transcript of a press briefing on the Annenberg Foundation education challenge grants by Secretary of Education Dick Riley, New American Schools Development Corporation President David Kearns, Coalition for Essential Schools Chairman Ted Sizer, Illinois Governor Jim Edgar, and Colorado Governor Roy Romer

Statement by Press Secretary Dee Dee Myers on legislation signed by the President

Statement by Press Secretary Dee Dee Myers on the Emergency Board proposed framework to settle the Long Island Rail Road contract impasse

Released December 20

Fact sheet on the National Child Protection Act of 1993

Transcript of a press briefing on administration economic accomplishments by Secretary of the Treasury Lloyd Bentsen, Assistant to the President for Economic Policy Robert Rubin, and Chair of the Council of Economic Advisers Laura D'Andrea Tyson

Statement by Press Secretary Dee Dee Myers on Social Security and related tax withholding for an employee of Adm. Bobby R. Inman

Statement by Director of Communications Mark Gearan on the distribution of Vincent Foster's files

Released December 21

Fact sheet on the groundbreaking for the Pan Am 103 Memorial

Transcript of a press briefing on the UNICEF report on children by Secretary of Health and Human Services Donna Shalala, UNICEF Executive Director Jim Grant, and Agency for International Development Director Brian Atwood

Released December 22

Transcript of a press briefing by Chief of Staff Thomas F. (Mack) McLarty and Director of the Office of Management and Budget Leon Panetta

Transcript of a press briefing on homeless program grants by Secretary of Housing and Urban Development Henry Cisneros and Assistant Secretary of Housing and Urban Development Andrew Cuomo

Fact sheet on homeless program grants

Released December 23

Statement by Press Secretary Dee Dee Myers on the upcoming visit of Prime Minister Ruud Lubbers of The Netherlands

Statement by Director of Communications Mark Gearan on the President's instructions to make available to the Justice Department all documents relating to the Whitewater Development Corporation

Released December 27

Statement by Press Secretary Dee Dee Myers on the President's upcoming visit to Russia

Appendix D—Presidential Documents Published in the Federal Register

This appendix lists Presidential documents released by the Office of the Press Secretary and published in the Federal Register. The texts of the documents are printed in the Federal Register (F.R.) at the citations listed below. The documents are also printed in title 3 of the Code of Federal Regulations and in the Weekly Compilation of Presidential Documents.

PROCLAMATIONS

Proc. No.	Date 1993	Subject	58 F.R. Page
6584	Aug. 1	Helsinki Human Rights Day, 1993	41621
6585	Aug. 11	To Designate Peru as a Beneficiary Country for Purposes of the Andean Trade Preference Act	43239
6586	Aug. 18	Women's Equality Day, 1993	44433
6587	Sept. 3	National POW/MIA Recognition Day, 1993	47199
6588	Sept. 9	National D.A.R.E. Day, 1993 and 1994	47981
6589	Sept. 13	Commodore John Barry Day, 1993	48585
6590	Sept. 13	Gold Star Mother's Day	48587
6591	Sept. 13	Minority Enterprise Development Week, 1993	48589
6592	Sept. 15	National Hispanic Heritage Month, 1993	48771
6593	Sept. 17	Citizenship Day and Constitution Week, 1993	49173
6594	Sept. 21	National Historically Black Colleges and Universities Week, 1993	49901
6595	Sept. 21	National Farm Safety and Health Week, 1993	49903
6596	Sept. 22	National Rehabilitation Week, 1993 and 1994	50243
6597	Sept. 22	Energy Awareness Month, 1993	50245
6598	Sept. 30	Death of General James H. Doolittle	51559
6599	Sept. 30	To Amend the Generalized System of Preferences	51561
6600	Sept. 30	National Breast Cancer Awareness Month, 1993	51721
6601	Sept. 30	Fire Prevention Week, 1993	51723
6602	Oct. 4	Child Health Day, 1993	52205
6603	Oct. 5	Mental Illness Awareness Week, 1993	52387
6604	Oct. 5	German-American Day, 1993	52389
6605	Oct. 6	National Disability Employment Awareness Month, 1993	52627
6606	Oct. 7	Country Music Month, 1993	52875
6607	Oct. 8	Leif Erikson Day, 1993	53097
6608	Oct. 8	Columbus Day, 1993	53099
6609	Oct. 8	National School Lunch Week, 1993	53101
6610	Oct. 9	General Pulaski Memorial Day, 1993	53103
6611	Oct. 14	National Down Syndrome Awareness Month, 1993	53831
6612	Oct. 15	White Cane Safety Day, 1993	53833
6613	Oct. 16	World Food Day, 1993 and 1994	54025
6614	Oct. 16	National Forest Products Week, 1993	54027
6615	Oct. 18	National Mammography Day, 1993	54269
6616	Oct. 20	National Biomedical Research Day, 1993	54909
6617	Oct. 21	National Consumers Week, 1993	57535
6618	Oct. 23	United Nations Day, 1993	57715
6619	Oct. 28	National Domestic Violence Awareness Month, 1993 and 1994	58255
6620	Nov. 3	National Health Information Management Week, 1993	59157
6621	Nov. 5	Veterans Day, 1993	59637
6622	Nov. 10	National Women Veterans Recognition Week, 1993	60359
6623	Nov. 14	Geography Awareness Week, 1993 and 1994	60769
6624	Nov. 16	National Farm-City Week, 1993	61607
6625	Nov. 17	Thanksgiving Day, 1993	61609
6626	Nov. 18	National Children's Day, 1993	61797
6627	Nov. 18	National Military Families Recognition Day, 1993	61799
6628	Nov. 22	National Family Week, 1993 and 1994	62257
6629	Nov. 24	National Adoption Week, 1993 and 1994	63021
6630	Nov. 29	National Hospice Month, 1993 and 1994	63277

PROCLAMATIONS—Continued

Proc. No.	Date 1993	Subject	58 F.R. Page
6631	Nov. 29	National Home Care Week, 1993 and 1994	63279
6632	Nov. 30	World AIDS Day, 1993	63883
6633	Dec. 3	National Drunk and Drugged Driving Prevention Month, 1993	64363
6634	Dec. 6	International Year of the Family, 1994	64667
6635	Dec. 9	To Amend the Generalized System of Preferences	65279
6636	Dec. 10	Suspension of Entry as Immigrants and Nonimmigrants of Persons Who Formulate, Implement, or Benefit From Policies That Are Impeding the Transition to Democracy in Nigeria	65525
6637	Dec. 10	Human Rights Day, Bill of Rights Day, and Human Rights Week, 1993	65527
6638	Dec. 10	Wright Brothers Day, 1993	65529
6639	Dec. 14	National Firefighters Day, 1993	65865
6640	Dec. 15	Modification of Import Limitations on Certain Dairy Products	65867
6641	Dec. 15	To Implement the North American Free Trade Agreement, and for Other Purposes	66867
6642	Dec. 17	Fifth Anniversary Day of Remembrance for the Victims of the Bombing of Pan Am Flight 103	67625
6643	Dec. 21	National Law Enforcement Training Week, 1994	68289

EXECUTIVE ORDERS

E.O. No.	Date 1993	Subject	58 F.R. Page
12856	Aug. 3	Federal Compliance With Right-To-Know Laws and Pollution Prevention Requirements	41981
12857	Aug. 4	Budget Control	42181
12858	Aug. 4	Deficit Reduction Fund	42185
12859	Aug. 16	Establishment of the Domestic Policy Council	44101
12860	Sept. 3	Adding Members to the Committee on Foreign Investment in the United States	47201
12861	Sept. 11	Elimination of One-Half of Executive Branch Internal Regulations	48255
12862	Sept. 11	Setting Customer Service Standards	48257
12863	Sept. 13	President's Foreign Intelligence Advisory Board	48441
12864	Sept. 15	United States Advisory Council on the National Information Infrastructure	48773
12865	Sept. 26	Prohibiting Certain Transactions Involving UNITA	51005
12866	Sept. 30	Regulatory Planning and Review	51735
12867	Sept. 30	Termination of Emergency Authority for Certain Export Controls	51747
12868	Sept. 30	Measures To Restrict the Participation by United States Persons in Weapons Proliferation Activities	51749
12869	Sept. 30	Continuance of Certain Federal Advisory Committees	51751
12870	Sept. 30	Trade Promotion Coordinating Committee	51753
12871	Oct. 1	Labor-Management Partnerships	52201
12872	Oct. 18	Blocking Property of Persons Obstructing Democratization in Haiti	54029
12873	Oct. 20	Federal Acquisition, Recycling, and Waste Prevention	54911
12874	Oct. 20	Establishing an Emergency Board To Investigate a Dispute Between The Long Island Rail Road and Certain of Its Employees Represented by the United Transportation Union	54921
12875	Oct. 26	Enhancing the Intergovernmental Partnership	58093
12876	Nov. 1	Historically Black Colleges and Universities	58735
12877	Nov. 3	Amendment to Executive Order No. 12569	59159
12878	Nov. 5	Bipartisan Commission on Entitlement Reform	59343
12879	Nov. 8	Order of Succession of Officers To Act as Secretary of the Navy	59929
12880	Nov. 16	National Drug Control Program	60989
12881	Nov. 23	Establishment of the National Science and Technology Council	62491
12882	Nov. 23	President's Committee of Advisors on Science and Technology	62493
12883	Nov. 29	Delegating a Federal Pay Administration Authority	63281

EXECUTIVE ORDERS—Continued

E.O. No.	Date 1993	Subject	58 F.R. Page
12884	Dec. 1	Delegation of Functions Under the Freedom Support Act and Related Provisions of the Foreign Operations, Export Financing and Related Programs Appropriations Act	64099
12885	Dec. 14	Amendment to Executive Order No. 12829	65863
12886	Dec. 23	Adjustments of Rates of Pay and Allowances for the Uniformed Services	68708
12887	Dec. 23	Amending Executive Order No. 12878	68713
12888	Dec. 23	Amendments to the Manual for Courts-Martial, United States, 1984	69153
12889	Dec. 27	Implementation of the North American Free Trade Agreement	69681

			59 F.R.
12890	Dec. 30	Amendment to Executive Order No. 12864	499

OTHER PRESIDENTIAL DOCUMENTS

Doc. No.	Date 1993	Subject	58 F.R. Page
	Aug. 11	Memorandum: Importation of Assault Pistols	50831
	Aug. 11	Memorandum: Gun Dealer Licensing	50833
93–33	Aug. 19	Presidential Determination: Assistance to African refugees	45777
93–34	Aug. 19	Presidential Determination: Assistance to Mozambican refugees	45779
	Sept. 11	Memorandum: Streamlining the bureaucracy	48583
93–38	Sept. 13	Presidential Determination: Extension of the exercise of certain authorities under the Trading With the Enemy Act	51209
93–40	Sept. 28	Presidential Determination: Assistance to Mexico	51975
93–41	Sept. 29	Presidential Determination: Funding for peacekeeping in Liberia	51977
	Sept. 30	Notice: Continuation of Haitian emergency	51563
	Sept. 30	Memorandum: Negotiated rulemaking	52391
93–43	Sept. 30	Presidential Determination: Assistance to the United Nations to support the reestablishment of police forces in Somalia	52207
94–1	Oct. 1	Presidential Determination: Refugee admissions	52213
	Oct. 26	Memorandum: Streamlining procurement through electronic commerce	38095
94–3	Oct. 29	Presidential Determination: Delegation of authority concerning trade action taken against Japan	58637
	Nov. 1	Notice: Continuation of Iran emergency	58639
	Nov. 12	Notice: Continuation of emergency regarding chemical and biological weapons proliferation	60361
	Dec. 2	Notice: Continuation of Libyan emergency	64361

Subject Index

AARP. *See* Retired Persons, American Association of
ABC News "Nightline"—1568
Abortion—1546, 1581-1583, 1663, 1855
Acquired immune deficiency syndrome (AIDS). *See* Health and medical care
Administrative Conference of the U.S.—2213, 2215
Advisory. *See* other part of subject
Aeronautics and Space Administration, National—1854, 1917, 2148, 2203
Aerospace industry. *See* Aviation industry
AFL-CIO. *See* Labor & Congress of Industrial Organizations, American Federation of
Africa. *See* specific country
Agency. *See* other part of subject
Aging, Administration on. *See* Health and Human Services, Department of
Aging, Federal Council on the—1998
Aging, White House Conference on—1808
Agricultural Marketing Service. *See* Agriculture, Department of
Agricultural Stabilization and Conservation Service. *See* Agriculture, Department of
Agriculture
    Disaster assistance—1367, 1368
    Exports—1906
    International government subsidies—1494, 1910, 1911, 2005
    Trade negotiations and agreements. *See* Commerce, international
    Wool and mohair subsidies—1878
Agriculture, Department of
    Agricultural Marketing Service—1438
    Agricultural Stabilization and Conservation Service—1369, 1438, 2214, 2215
    Assistant Secretaries—1720, 2209
    Budget—1799
    Chief Financial Officer—2209
    Commodity Credit Corporation—1368, 1370
    Crop Insurance Corporation, Federal—2216
    Deputy Assistant Secretaries—1438, 2214
    Deputy General Counsel—1438
    Emergency funding for flood damage and wetlands—2213
    Farmers Home Administration—1425, 1438
    Food and Nutrition Service—2216
    Forest Service—1838, 1865, 1891, 1958
    Rural Development Administration—1438
    Rural Electrification Administration—1720, 1877
    Secretary—1329, 1366-1368, 1424, 1446, 1461, 1838, 1865, 1891, 1908, 1910-1912
    Soil Conservation Service—1865
    Special Supplemental Food Program for Women, Infants and Children (WIC)—1799
AID. *See* Development Cooperation Agency, U.S. International

AIDS. *See* Health and medical care
AIDS Policy Coordinator, Office of the National—1641, 2089
Air Force, Department of the
    See also Armed Forces, U.S.
    Assistant Secretaries—1880, 2153, 2209
    Deputy General Counsel—1686
    Under Secretary—1880
Air traffic controllers. *See* Professional Air Traffic Controllers Organization
Airline Industry, National Commission to Ensure a Strong Competitive—1392
Airline industry. *See* Aviation industry
Albania, Ambassador to U.S.—2215
Alcohol, Tobacco and Firearms, Bureau of. *See* Treasury, Department of the
All-American Cities Award—1515
Ambassadors. *See* specific country
American. *See* other part of subject
AmeriCorps—1545
Ames Rubber Corp.—2171, 2212
Angola
    Ambassador to U.S.—2215
    Civil conflict—2132
    Peace process, U.S. Special Representative—2212
    U.S. Ambassador—1933
    U.S. national emergency—1611
Angola, National Union for the Total Independence of—1611
Annenberg Foundation—2186
APEC. *See* Asia-Pacific Economic Cooperation forum
Appalachian Regional Commission—2212
Appeals, U.S. Court of—1349, 1596, 2007
Arab news media—1477
Argentina, Ambassador to U.S.—2211
Arkansas, President's visits—2209, 2217
Armed Forces, U.S.
    See also specific military department; Defense and national security
    Ban on homosexuals in the military—1657
    Base closings—1373
    International role
        See also specific country or region
        Deployment authority—1763, 1768, 1770, 1958
    National Guard—1800
    POW's/MIA's—1953, 1955
    Supreme Allied Commander, Europe—1683
Armenia, investment treaty with U.S.—1449
Arms and munitions
    See also Defense and national security; Nuclear weapons
    Arms control negotiations and agreements—1615, 1616, 1976, 2061
    Assault weapons, importation—1362
    Chemical and biological weapons—1397, 1587, 1615, 1639, 1975, 2061, 2073

Arms and munitions—Continued
Export controls—1616, 1630
Missile systems—1615
Nonproliferation—1615, 1630, 1639
Restriction of sales to Angola—1611
Arms Control and Disarmament Agency, U.S.—1699, 2179
Army, Department of the
See also Armed Forces, U.S.
Assistant Secretaries—2092, 2153
Corps of Engineers—1369, 1374, 1856, 2216
Secretary—1533
Special Operations Command (Rangers)—1955, 2212
Under Secretary—1533
Walter Reed Medical Center—2212
Arts and the Humanities, National Foundation on the
Arts, National Endowment for the—1350
Budget—1958
Museum Services, Institute of—1360
Arts, National Endowment for the. See Arts and the Humanities, National Foundation on the
Arts, National Medal of the—1693, 1699, 1706
Asia-Pacific Economic Cooperation forum—1491, 1495, 1921, 2008, 2009, 2014, 2019, 2025, 2030, 2032, 2034-2036, 2045-2047, 2056, 2212, 2214
Asia-Pacific region
See also specific country
Defense and security—1491, 2021
Economic growth—2017
Trade with U.S.—2014, 2018
Asian Development Bank—1426, 2019
Assassination Records Review Board—1438, 2213
Association. See other part of subject
Atomic Energy Agency, International. See United Nations
Australia
Ambassador to U.S.—2211
Prime Minister—1490, 1491, 2210
Austria, U.S. Ambassador—1456
Automobile industry—1627
Aviation Administration, Federal. See Transportation, Department of
Aviation industry
Growth and competitiveness—1392, 2009
Labor disputes—2048, 2049
Aviation, Treaty on Open Skies—2213
Awards. See other part of subject

B-Factory. See Science and technology, electron/positron collider
Bahamas
Prime Minister—1407, 2209
U.S. Ambassador—1748
Banking—1367, 1378, 1855, 2188
Barbados, Prime Minister—1407, 2209
Belarus, Ambassador to U.S.—2211
Belgium
King—2209
U.S. Ambassador—1456
Belize
Ambassador to U.S.—2211
Prime Minister—2075
Biological weapons. See Arms and munitions

Bituminous Coal Operations Association—2138
Black Mayors, National Conference of—2210
B'nai B'rith—1813
Board. See other part of subject
Bolivia, Ambassador to U.S.—2215
Bosnia-Herzegovina
Arms embargo—1430
Conflict resolution—1297, 1311, 1410, 1430, 1455, 1532, 1616, 1620, 1622, 1632, 1764, 1770, 1781, 1949, 2136
Humanitarian assistance—1949
No-fly zone—1740
President—1455
United Nations Security Council resolutions—1740
U.S. military, potential role—1781
Boys and Girls Clubs of America, youth service award—2210
Brady bill. See Law enforcement and crime, gun control
Brazil, Ambassador to U.S.—2215
Breast Cancer Coalition, National—1761
Brunei
Ambassador to U.S.—2215
U.S. Ambassador—1533
Btu tax. See Taxation, energy tax
Budget, Federal
See also specific agency; Economy, national; Taxation
Congressional votes—1343, 1346, 1349, 1355
Defense spending—2027, 2035, 2159
Deficit—1302, 1304, 1317, 1322, 1327, 1330, 1333, 1335, 1338, 1339, 1344, 1347, 1351, 1356, 1381, 1825, 1838, 1878, 1916, 2026, 2034, 2046, 2157, 2158
Entitlement spending—1333, 1904, 2027, 2156-2163
Fiscal year 1994—1355, 1641, 1642, 1799, 1800, 1837, 1854-1856, 1958, 2213
Penny-Kasich proposal—2026, 2034, 2046
Proposed constitutional amendment—1916
Rescissions and deferrals—1740, 1879, 2028
Spending cuts—1299, 1300, 1303, 1316, 1327, 1335, 1338, 1351, 1356, 1824, 1828, 2026, 2157
Supplemental appropriations, fiscal year 1993—1365-1368
Buffalo Soldiers—2215
Building Sciences, National Institute of—1698
Bureau. See other part of subject
Burkina Faso, Ambassador to U.S.—2215
Burundi, Ambassador to U.S.—2215
Business and industry
See also specific company or industry
Credit availability—1378
Enterprise zones. See Enterprise zones
Industry conversion and job retraining—1374, 1659, 1673, 1679, 1801, 1805
Job training—1434, 1467
Manufacturing—1873
Private sector partnership with Government—1627
Productivity and competitiveness—1445, 1627, 1851, 1996, 2114, 2170
Research and development—1627, 1649, 1673

Business and industry—Continued
  Small and minority business—1299, 1307, 1352, 1356, 1378, 1504, 1551, 1560, 1574, 1579, 1603, 1688, 1834, 1845, 1995
  Taxes and deductions. *See* Taxation
Business for Social Responsibility—1783

California
  Cypress Freeway reconstruction—1680, 1683
  Democratic Party event—2039
  Economic conditions—1466, 1649, 1678, 2117, 2120
  Fires—1838, 1864, 1890
  Governor—1838, 1891
  President's visits—1372, 1466, 1648, 1652, 1667, 1677, 1686, 2039, 2043, 2115, 2117, 2119, 2123, 2209-2211, 2214
  Private school voucher initiative—1672
Cambodia, U.S. recognition—1616
Canada
  Agriculture Minister—1908
  Free trade with Mexico and U.S.—2092
  International Trade Minister—2012
  Prime Minister—1827, 1828, 1901, 2005, 2012, 2092
  Trade with U.S.—1354, 1899, 1908, 1910, 2012, 2206
  U.S. Ambassador—1354
Capitol, U.S.—1813
Caribbean Basin Initiative—2071
Caribbean Community and Common Market—1410
Caribbean region
  See also specific country
  Economic growth—1972, 2077
  Trade with U.S.—1407, 1410
CARICOM. *See* Caribbean Community and Common Market
CBS News—2213
Centers for Disease Control and Prevention. *See* Health and Human Services, Department of
Central America. *See* specific country; Latin America
Central Intelligence Agency—1809, 1926, 2091
Chad, Ambassador to U.S.—2210
Chamber of Commerce, U.S.—1868
Charles Frankel Prize—1693, 1699, 1706
Chemical Weapons, Organization for the Prohibition of—2062
Chemical weapons. *See* Arms and munitions
Child Protection Act of 1993, National—2192
Children and Families, Administration for. *See* Health and Human Services, Department of
Children and youth
  See also specific subject
  Child care providers, background check system—2192
  Child pornography laws—1952
  Juvenile crime—1422
  Parental kidnapping, international—2093
Children's National Medical Center—1523
China
  Human rights—2022, 2023
  Nuclear testing—1531, 1694
  President—2022, 2037
  Rhinoceros and tiger trade—1931

China—Continued
  Trade with U.S.—1493, 1924, 2018, 2020, 2023
Christmas—2146, 2201, 2204, 2216, 2217
Chrysler Corp.—2210
Church of God in Christ—1981
CIA. *See* Central Intelligence Agency
Cities
  See also State and local governments
  Enterprise zones. *See* Enterprise zones
  Private sector investment in inner city areas—1660
Citizens Medal, Presidential—1703
Civil rights
  See also specific subject
  Discrimination—1328, 1359, 1402, 1536
  Religious freedom—2000
Civil Rights, Commission on—1532, 1623
Coal industry, labor disputes—2138
Coast Guard, U.S. *See* Transportation, Department of
Colleges and universities. *See* specific institution; Education
Colombia
  Ambassador to U.S.—2211
  Drug trafficking—2092
  President—1779, 2092, 2211
Colorado
  Governor—1592
  President's visits—1370, 1371, 1376, 2209
  Wilderness preservation legislation—1376, 1377
Colorado Wilderness Act of 1993—1376, 1377
Combined Federal Campaign. *See* Government agencies and employees
Commendation, Presidential Certificate of—1365
Commerce, Department of
  Assistant Deputy Secretary—1426
  Assistant Secretaries—1522, 1772, 1830, 1880, 2199
  Budget—1776, 1837
  Chief Counsel for Technology Administration—2215
  Chief Economist—2215
  Chief Financial Officer—2199
  Deputy Assistant Secretaries—1426, 2211, 2212, 2215
  Deputy Secretary—1467
  Deputy Under Secretary—1426
  Disaster assistance funding—2216
  Economic Development Administration—1369, 1776
  Economics and Statistics Administration—2216
  Minority Business Development Administration—2216
  Oceanic and Atmospheric Administration, National—1369, 1426, 2211, 2216
  Patent and Trademark Office—1884, 2202
  Secretary—1372, 1393, 1461, 1467, 1595, 1631, 1639, 1678, 1684, 1758, 1776, 2018, 2045, 2061, 2117, 2123, 2169
  Space Commerce Director—1426
  Standards and Technology, National Institute of—1776
  Telecommunications and Information Administration, National—1426, 1776
  Trade Administration, International—1426
  Under Secretary—2213

Commerce, international
See also specific country or subject; Economy, international
Boycott of companies doing business with Israel—1644, 1961, 1964
Export controls. See Arms and munitions
Exports, U.S.—1629, 1649, 1659, 1675, 1680, 1759, 1778, 1807, 2180
General Agreement on Tariffs and Trade (GATT)—1375, 1449, 1491, 1680, 1748, 1850, 1869, 1883, 1906, 1909, 1912, 1921, 1935, 1969, 1974, 2012, 2015, 2031, 2034, 2097, 2141, 2164, 2169, 2172, 2173, 2180, 2189, 2198
Generalized System of Preferences (GSP)—1640, 2156
Group of Seven nations (G-7)—1527, 2015
Intellectual property rights—1901, 2181
Investment treaties—1449-1451, 1468
Military exports. See Arms and munitions
North American Free Trade Agreement (NAFTA)—1375, 1376, 1381, 1389-1391, 1401, 1406, 1407, 1410, 1436, 1470, 1485, 1490, 1492, 1494, 1496, 1521, 1592, 1593, 1625, 1629, 1642, 1656, 1658, 1680, 1738, 1759, 1772, 1773, 1777, 1793, 1800, 1823, 1827, 1839, 1850-1854, 1859, 1860, 1868, 1882, 1885, 1892, 1894, 1895, 1905, 1906, 1918, 1920, 1933, 1940, 1943, 1945, 1946, 1948, 1949, 1959, 1966, 1975, 1977, 1978, 1980, 1987, 1995, 1998, 2001, 2005, 2008, 2010-2012, 2016, 2030, 2037, 2045, 2075, 2077, 2092, 2097, 2139, 2206
Protectionism—1871
Trade negotiations and agreements—1345, 1491, 1527, 1908, 2180
Commission. See other part of subject
Committee. See other part of subject
Commodity Credit Corporation. See Agriculture, Department of
Commodity Futures Trading Commission—1933
Communications
News media. See specific State or news organization
Telecommunications—1630
Communications Satellite Corporation—1940
Community development. See Banking
Community Enterprise Board, President's—1459, 1460
Community Service Trust Act of 1993, National and—1543
Conference. See other part of subject
Congo, Ambassador to U.S.—2215
Congress
See also specific subject
Armed forces command, role—1763, 1768, 1770
Black Caucus—1535
Budget votes—1343, 1346, 1349, 1355
Campaign finance reform. See Elections
Hispanic Caucus—1518
House Republican leader, retirement—1684
Lobby reform—2143
Members, meetings with President—1642, 1738, 1772, 1800, 1827, 2054
North American Free Trade Agreement vote—2005, 2008
Progressive Caucus—1297

Congress—Continued
United Nations peacekeeping operations, notification—1837
Congressional Black Caucus Foundation—1535
Congressional Hispanic Caucus Institute—1518
Connecticut, President's visit—1722, 1729, 2212
Conservation
See also Environment
Forest preservation—1325
Wilderness and wildlife preservation—1376, 1377, 1931, 2029
Consumer Product Safety Commission—1808
Corporation. See other part of subject
Corps of Engineers. See Army, Department of the
Costa Rica, President—2075
Council. See other part of subject
Court. See other part of subject
Covenant Baptist Church—2067
Creative Artists Agency—2123
Credit Union Administration, National—1829
Crime. See Law enforcement and crime
Crop Insurance Corporation, Federal. See Agriculture, Department of
CSCE. See Security and Cooperation in Europe, Conference on
Cuba
Democracy and freedom—1347, 1410
Economic sanctions—1412, 1973, 2131
Customs Service, U.S. See Treasury, Department of the
Cyprus
Ambassador to U.S.—2211
Conflict resolution—1393, 1754, 1913
President Clerides—1393, 1394, 1914, 1915
President Vassiliou—1393
Turkish Cypriot leader—1394-1396, 1914, 1915
U.S. Ambassador—1395, 1914
U.S. Special Coordinator—1393-1396, 1914
Czech Republic, taxation convention with U.S.—1798

Defense and national security
See also Arms and munitions; Nuclear weapons
Laws and practices relating to former Soviet Union—1430
Military strength and deterrence—1375, 1802, 1807
U.S. military, use in international operations—1763, 1770
Defense conversion. See Business and industry; Science and technology
Defense, Department of
See also specific military department; Armed Forces, U.S.
Assistant Deputy Under Secretaries—1426, 1686
Assistant Secretaries—1425, 1685
Budget—1763, 1770, 1958, 2027, 2035
Chief Financial Officer—2064
Chief of Protocol—1686
Commercial Items and International Systems Acquisition Director—2215
Deputy Assistant Secretaries—1426, 1685, 1686
Deputy Assistant to Assistant Secretary—1685
Deputy General Counsel—1686
Deputy Under Secretary—1686

Defense, Department of—Continued
  Employer Support of the Guard and Reserve, National Committee for—1426
  European Command, Commander in Chief—1683
  Inspector General—2064
  Joint Chiefs of Staff—1363, 1412, 1637, 2027, 2199
  Outreach America Director—1686
  Peace Enforcement Director—1686
  Policy Support Director—2215
  Principal Assistant Deputy Under Secretary—1686
  Principal Deputy Assistant Secretary—1686
  Procurement practices—1825
  Reinvestment Assistance Task Force—1426, 1685
  Secretary—1412, 1677, 1715, 1955, 1963, 2027, 2153, 2177, 2178, 2212
  Secretary nominee—2184
  Southern Command, Commander in Chief—2069
  Special Adviser—1686
  Special Assistant to Assistant Secretary—1685
  Special Assistant to Secretary—1686
Deficit, Federal. *See* Budget, Federal
Delaware, President's visit—1432, 2210
Democracy, National Endowment for—1837, 2052
Democratic Institute, National—2052
Democratic Leadership Council—2094, 2103
Democratic National Committee—1707, 1794, 2209
Democratic Party
  Democratic Congressional Campaign Committee—2211
  Democratic Senatorial Campaign Committee—2211
  Health care campaign, national—1392
  State party organizations, fundraisers, etc. *See* specific State
Department. *See* other part of subject
Deposit Insurance Corporation, Federal—2007, 2084
Depository Institutions Disaster Relief Act of 1993—1367
Development, Agency for International. *See* Development Cooperation Agency, U.S. International
Development Cooperation Agency, U.S. International
  Development, Agency for International (AID)—1344, 1425, 1427, 1829, 1904, 2078, 2197, 2215
  Overseas Private Investment Corporation (OPIC)—1462, 1918, 2061
Disabled persons—1577
Disaster assistance
  Agriculture—1366, 1368
  California Cypress Freeway reconstruction—1680, 1683
  California fires—1838, 1864, 1890
  Flooding, relocation assistance—2110
  Hurricane Andrew—1424, 1441, 1442
  Midwest flooding—1365-1368, 1405, 1424, 1565, 2110, 2213, 2216
  Missouri flooding—2214
  Virginia storms and tornadoes—2217
District Court, U.S.—1349, 1596, 1809, 1837, 1864, 1951, 2007, 2012, 2030
District of Columbia
  Budget—1485
  National Guard, use in anticrime efforts—1800
  Superior Court—1772
Djibouti, U.S. Ambassador—1880

Drug abuse and trafficking
  See also Law enforcement and crime
  Capture of Pablo Escobar—2092
  International cooperation—1892
  Treatment programs—1661, 1985, 1990
Drug Control Policy, Office of National—1380, 1461, 1660, 1812, 1892, 1985, 1991, 2154, 2190

East Bay Conversion and Reinvestment Commission—2209
Eastman Chemical Co.—2170, 2212
EC. *See* European Community
Economic Advisers, Council of—1392
Economic Council, National—1631
Economic Development Administration. *See* Commerce, Department of
Economics and Statistics Administration. *See* Commerce, Department of
Economy, international
  See also specific country; Commerce, international
  Growth—1527, 1531, 1614, 1668, 1802, 1851, 1861, 1882, 2015, 2024, 2097, 2127, 2129
Economy, national
  See also Banking; Budget, Federal; Commerce, international
  Environmental policies, impact—1318, 1773
  Growth—1629, 1759, 1869, 1934, 2015, 2096, 2170
  Inflation and interest rates—1300, 1337, 1838, 1913, 2191
Ecuador, investment treaty with U.S.—1468
Education
  College loans—1369, 1579, 1654, 1671, 1875, 2041
  Cultural diversity—1418
  Goals, national—1342, 1418, 1654, 1671, 1735, 1747, 1799, 2101, 2186
  Historically black colleges and universities—1875
  Learning, methods and theories—1417
  National service program—1312, 1315, 1412, 1456, 1543, 1580, 1665, 1854, 2041
  Post-secondary and job training—1432, 1434, 1467, 1654, 1658, 1659, 1672, 1799, 2101
  Private sector grants—2186
  Safe schools initiative—1655
  Teachers—1340, 1419, 1665
  Vouchers—1672
Education, Department of
  Assistant Secretary—2195
  Bilingual Education and Minority Languages Affairs Director—1426
  Budget—1799
  Deputy General Counsel—1918
  Education Research and Improvement, Office of—2216
  Regional representatives—1976
  Rehabilitation Services Administration—1440
  Secretary—1342, 1433, 1461, 1654, 1875, 1876, 1976, 2101
  Special Adviser—1918
  Special Assistant to Communications Director—1426
  Special Education Programs Director—1426
Egypt, President—1818, 1819
El Salvador, President—2075

Elections
  Congressional campaign financing—2053
  State and local. *See* specific State
Emergency Management Agency, Federal—1365-
  1367, 1369, 1370, 1405, 1565, 1838-1840, 1864,
  1865, 1891, 2213, 2216
Employment and unemployment
  Family leave—1343, 1600, 1670
  Job creation—1374, 1388, 1390, 1433, 1486, 1489,
    1531, 1576, 1658, 1659, 1669, 1673, 1760, 1778,
    1802, 1859, 1868, 1896, 1936, 1945, 1968, 2002,
    2015, 2042, 2121
  Job training and reemployment—1434, 1467, 1488,
    1538, 1658-1660, 1669, 1711, 1852, 1900, 2016,
    2070, 2101, 2114
  Rates—1434
  Unemployment benefits—2070
  Workers' compensation—1385, 1579, 2107
Employment Policy, National Commission for—2209
Empowerment zones. *See* Enterprise zones
Endeavour. See Space program, shuttle
Energy
  See also specific industry
  Alternative fuels—2145
  Conservation—1415
  Fuel-efficient automobiles—1627
  Oil, supplies—1706
Energy, Department of
  Assistant Secretaries—1429, 1777
  Budget—1856, 1958, 2210
  Deputy General Counsel—2213
  Secretary—1679, 1856, 2145
  Under Secretary—1880
Enrichment Corporation, U.S.—2215
Enterprise zones—1423, 1461, 1678
Entitlement Reform, Bipartisan Commission on—
  1904, 2027
Environment
  See also Conservation
  Air quality—1626
  Biological diversity, convention—2029
  Economic growth, impact—1318, 1773
  Global climate change—1773
  Hazardous materials and waste—1340
  International cooperation—1617
  Pollution prevention—1340
  Recycling—1781
  Solid waste—1781
Environmental Policy, White House Office on—2145
Environmental Protection Agency—1318, 1370, 1374,
  1461, 1649, 1854, 1917, 2111
Eritrea, Ambassador to U.S.—2211
Estonia
  Ambassador to U.S.—2210
  President—1623
Ethiopia, President—1729
European Bank for Reconstruction and Develop-
  ment—1426
European Community—1771, 2215
Executive Leadership Council—1792
Executive Office of the President
  See also specific office or council
  Budget—1855

Export-Import Bank of the U.S.—1631, 2012

Family and Medical Leave Act of 1993—1343, 1670
Family leave. *See* Employment and unemployment
Farmers Home Administration. *See* Agriculture, De-
  partment of
FBI. *See* Justice, Department of
Federal. *See* other part of subject
Federation. *See* other part of subject
FEMA. *See* Emergency Management Agency, Federal
Fish and Wildlife Service, U.S. *See* Interior, Depart-
  ment of the
Fishing. *See* Maritime affairs
Flooding. *See* Disaster assistance
Florida
  Hurricane Andrew—1424, 1441, 1442, 2210
  President's visits—1441, 1442, 1568, 1588, 2210
Food and Drug Administration. *See* Health and
  Human Services, Department of
Food and Nutrition Service. *See* Agriculture, Depart-
  ment of
Foreign Assets Control, Office of. *See* Treasury, De-
  partment of the
Foreign Claims Settlement Commission of the U.S.
  See Justice, Department of
Foreign Intelligence Advisory Board, President's—
  2211
Foreign operations, export financing, and related ap-
  propriations legislation—1641
Foreign policy, U.S. *See* specific country, region, or
  subject
Forest Service. *See* Agriculture, Department of
France
  President—1973
  Prime Minister—2164, 2216
Freedom of Information Act—1685
Freedom, Presidential Medal of—2081, 2213
Fulbright Foreign Scholarship Board, J. William—
  1977

G-7. *See* Commerce, international
Gabon, Ambassador to U.S.—2210
Gay and lesbian rights. *See* Civil rights, discrimination
General Agreement on Tariffs and Trade (GATT). *See*
  Commerce, international
General Services Administration—1426, 1452, 1855,
  1865, 1891, 2153, 2215, 2217
Generalized System of Preferences (GSP). *See* Com-
  merce, international
Geological Survey, U.S. *See* Interior, Department of
  the
Georgetown University Medical Center—2214
Georgia, Republic of, Ambassador to U.S.—2210
Germany
  Chancellor—1448, 1556, 2164, 2214, 2216
  Ratification of Maastricht Treaty—1771
Gillette Co.—1860, 2212
Government agencies and employees
  See also specific agency
  AIDS in the workplace, policies and programs—
    1641
  Alternative fueled vehicle use—2145
  Budgets, carry-over of funds—1855
  Combined Federal Campaign—1393

Government agencies and employees—Continued
Cooperation with State and local governments—
2085
Customer service standards—1471
Freedom of Information Act implementation—1685
Hazardous waste and pollution prevention—1340
Information, electronic access—1824
Internal regulation reduction—1472
Labor-management relations—1670, 1671
Personnel reductions—1472
Political activities—1695, 1696
Procurement practices—1452, 1824, 1826
Recycling and recycled products use—1781
Reform—1310, 1382, 1444, 1452, 1458, 1460, 1469,
1824, 2085, 2099, 2157
Regulatory review and reform—1627, 1633, 1635,
1636
Senior Executive Service—1426, 1438, 1904, 1917,
2212-2214, 2216
Solid waste prevention and reduction—1781
Government National Mortgage Association. *See*
Housing and Urban Development, Department of
Government Performance and Results Act of 1993—
1310
Government Printing Office—2209
Government Securities Act Amendments of 1993—
2187
Governors' Association, National—1381
Greece
Ambassador to U.S.—2210
Cyprus conflict. *See* Cyprus
Group of Seven nations (G-7). *See* Commerce, inter-
national
Guatemala, President—2075, 2076
Gun control. *See* Law enforcement and crime
Guyana
Ambassador to U.S.—2210
President—1407, 2209

Habitat for Humanity—1421
Haiti
Assassination of Justice Minister—1749, 1755
Civil conflict—1730, 1743-1745, 1755, 1764, 1766,
1769, 1770, 1782, 1810, 1840, 1863, 1926, 1973,
1991, 2133, 2192
Economic sanctions—1640, 1730, 1731, 1747, 1755,
1756, 1764, 1769, 1782, 1801, 1810, 1864, 1926,
1949, 1973, 1991-1994
President—1407, 1536, 1730, 1731, 1744, 1746,
1749, 1755, 1756, 1764, 1767, 1809, 1819, 1822,
1840, 1863, 1926, 1949, 1991, 2133, 2192
Prime Minister—1407, 1745, 1746, 1755-1757,
1764, 1767, 1810, 1819, 1863, 1926, 1949, 1992,
2133
Refugees—1810
United Nations Security Council resolutions—1769,
1782, 1992
U.S. Ambassador—1456, 1757
U.S. national emergency—1640
U.S. Special Envoy—1757, 1809, 1822

Haiti—Continued
U.S. training assistance—1730, 1731, 1744, 1755-
1757
Hanukkah—2138, 2215
Hatch Act Reform Amendments of 1993—1694, 1696
Hazard Mitigation and Relocation Assistance Act of
1993—2110
Head Start. *See* Health and Human Services, Depart-
ment of
Health and Human Services, Department of
Aging, Administration on—2215
Budget—1799
Centers for Disease Control and Prevention—2185,
2215
Children and Families, Administration for—1426
Consumer Affairs, U.S. Office of—2200
Deputy General Counsel—1426
Food and Drug Administration—1799
Head Start—1799
Health Care Financing Administration—1426
Health, National Institutes of—1325, 1799
Indian Health Service—1425, 1958, 2109
Medicare and Medicaid—1298, 1383, 1385, 1387,
1430, 1514, 1523, 1534, 1542, 1547, 1558, 1560,
1571, 1577, 1578, 1581-1583, 1602, 1605-1607,
1656, 1676, 1687, 1689, 1690, 1714, 1765, 1788,
1790, 1833, 1835, 1890, 2027, 2035, 2100, 2105,
2106, 2133, 2160-2162
Principal Deputy Assistant Secretary—2212
Public Health Service—1448, 2103, 2143
Regional Directors—2215
Secretary—1461, 1489, 1761
Senior Adviser to Assistant Secretary—2216
Social Security Administration—1325, 1799
Health and medical care
Abortion. *See* Abortion
Acquired immune deficiency syndrome (AIDS)—
1572, 1641, 1799, 2087, 2214
Alzheimer's disease—1690
Cancer—1761, 2185
Dental benefits—1580
Drug abuse, treatment programs. *See* Drug abuse
and trafficking
Drugs, prescription—1559, 1578, 1605, 1687, 1689,
1835, 1890, 2133
Experimental procedures and treatments—1604,
1654
Health care reform—1298, 1307, 1331, 1335, 1353,
1375, 1383-1388, 1392, 1398, 1401, 1414, 1420,
1429, 1432, 1437, 1500, 1504, 1520, 1523, 1529,
1534, 1538, 1539, 1546, 1549, 1553, 1555, 1556,
1566, 1568, 1589, 1594, 1596, 1599, 1646, 1650,
1653, 1656, 1657, 1662, 1675, 1686, 1713, 1717,
1727, 1736, 1761, 1764, 1785, 1791, 1827, 1830,
1834, 1841, 1866, 1887, 1922, 1923, 1957, 2027,
2035, 2042, 2100, 2104, 2131, 2133, 2162, 2182
Health security card—1558, 1664, 1675
Health security plan, proposed legislation—1830,
1834, 1841, 1866, 1886, 2104, 2131, 2162, 2176,
2182
Immunization programs—1414, 1799

Health and medical care—Continued
Insurance—1298, 1384, 1501, 1505-1512, 1524, 1540, 1546, 1550, 1552, 1558-1563, 1569, 1572-1574, 1576, 1577, 1579-1581, 1584, 1585, 1597, 1601-1607, 1651, 1656, 1657, 1675, 1691, 1714, 1717, 1787, 1827, 1831, 1834, 1842, 1866, 1889, 1922, 2104, 2107
Long-term care—1570, 1687, 1690, 2106, 2133
Medical malpractice—1552, 1580
Mental health—1570, 2108
Physicians—1540, 1541, 1551, 1580, 1585, 1662, 2105, 2108, 2182
Preventive services—1558
Quality—1561, 1572, 1578
Universal coverage and guaranteed benefits—1558, 1571, 1596, 1600, 1646, 1831, 1835, 2176, 2183
Veterans health care. *See* Veterans Affairs, Department of
Workers' compensation—1385, 1579, 2107
Health Care Financing Administration. *See* Health and Human Services, Department of
Health Care Reform, President's Task Force on National—1401, 1557, 1600, 1692, 1866
Health, National Institutes of. *See* Health and Human Services, Department of
Highway Administration, Federal. *See* Transportation, Department of
Highway Traffic Safety Administration, National. *See* Transportation, Department of
Hispanic Heritage Month, National—2212
Historic Preservation, Advisory Council on—2216
Historically Black Colleges and Universities, President's Board of Advisors on—1876
Holy See, Head, Roman Catholic Church—1370, 1371
Home Loan Mortgage Corporation, Federal—1442, 2153
"Home Show, The"—2150
Homeless persons—2200, 2213
Honduras, President—2075
Housing
Federal programs and grants—1416, 1421, 1442, 1679, 1855, 2200
Homeownership—1416, 1421
Housing and Urban Development, Department of
Administration, Office of—2215
Budget—1854, 1855
Deputy Assistant Secretaries—1441, 1904, 2216
General Deputy Assistant Secretary—1904
Government National Mortgage Association—1345
Housing programs and grants—1416, 1421, 1442, 1679, 1855, 2200
Regional Administrators—1904, 2216
Secretary—1416, 1424, 1441, 1445, 1461, 1517, 1536, 1680, 1947, 2201
Housing Partnership, National—1698
Housing Partnerships, National Corporation for—1698
Human rights. *See* specific country
Hungary
President—2165
Prime Minister—2165
Hurricanes. *See* Disaster assistance

IAEA. *See* United Nations, Atomic Energy Agency, International
Iceland, Ambassador to U.S.—2215
IMF. *See* Monetary Fund, International
Immigration and naturalization
See also specific country
Border control—1656, 1664, 1805
Federal policy—1319, 1837
Legislation—1319
Immigration and Naturalization Service. *See* Justice, Department of
Immigration Reform, Commission on Legal—2173
India, humanitarian assistance—1646
Indian Affairs, Bureau of. *See* Interior, Department of the
Indian Health Service. *See* Health and Human Services, Department of
Indonesia
Ambassador to U.S.—2211
President—1493, 2036
Information Agency, U.S.—1427, 1730, 1933, 2215, 2217
Information and Regulatory Affairs, Office of. *See* Management and Budget, Office of
Institute. *See* other part of subject
Intergovernmental Relations, Advisory Commission on—1771, 2084, 2215
Interior, Department of the
Associate Solicitors—1426
Budget—1958
Deputy Assistant Secretary—1426
Fish and Wildlife Service, U.S.—1370
Geological Survey, U.S.—1370
Indian Affairs, Bureau of—1370
Minerals Management Service—1426
Park Service, National—1370
Reclamation, Bureau of—1856
Secretary—1318, 1461, 1838, 1931, 1942, 2213
Special Assistant to Secretary—2216
Internal Revenue Service. *See* Treasury, Department of the
International. *See* other part of subject
Interstate Commerce Commission—2217
Investigation, Federal Bureau of. *See* Justice, Department of
Iran, U.S. national emergency—1879, 1950
Iraq
Economic sanctions—1308, 1587, 2074
Human rights—1587, 2073
Humanitarian assistance—1587, 2073
Iraq National Congress—1588
No-fly zones—1587, 2073
Nuclear weapons development—1586, 2073
President—1310, 1587, 2073
United Nations Security Council resolutions—1586, 2073
U.S. national emergency—1307
Ireland
Deputy Prime Minister—2213
Foreign Minister—2213
Prime Minister—1868, 2179
Ireland, Northern. *See* Northern Ireland
Israel
Agreement with Jordan—1643

Israel—Continued
Agreement with Palestine Liberation Organization—
1457, 1463, 1475, 1483, 1820, 1961
Defense and security—1481
Economic boycott. *See* Commerce, international
Foreign Minister—1457, 1476, 1481, 1490, 1493,
1643, 1961
News media—1480
Prime Minister—1457, 1464, 1476, 1477, 1480,
1481, 1490, 1493, 1794, 1795, 1821, 1823, 1960,
1961, 2210, 2213
Taxation convention with U.S.—1775
Italian-American Foundation, National—1816
Italy
Organized crime—2155
Prime Minister—1526, 2210
U.S. Ambassador—1527

Jamaica
Prime Minister—1407, 2209
U.S. Ambassador nominee—1742
Japan
Foreign Minister—1477
Prime Minister—1619, 2020, 2024, 2037, 2209
Trade with U.S.—1620, 2018, 2024
Johns Hopkins University—1840
Joint Chiefs of Staff. *See* Defense, Department of
Jordan
Agreement with Israel—1643
Crown Prince—1643, 1961
King—1960
Judiciary. *See* specific court
Justice, Department of
Assistant Attorney General—1836
Assistant to Attorney General—2216
Associate Deputy Attorney General—2216
Attorney General—1329, 1362, 1380, 1446, 1461,
1536, 1571, 1590, 1661, 1685, 1812, 1927, 1947,
1952, 2143, 2190
Budget—1837, 2210
Deputy Assistant Attorneys General—1918, 2212,
2215, 2216
Deputy Associate Attorney General—1918
Foreign Claims Settlement Commission of the
U.S.—1951
Immigration and Naturalization Service—1663
Investigation, Federal Bureau of (FBI)—1312, 1328,
1380, 1427, 1661, 1812, 2155
Principal Associate Deputy Attorney General—1918
Principal Deputy Solicitor General—2216
Special Counsel—1699

Kazakhstan, investment treaty with U.S.—1450
Kennedy Center. *See* Smithsonian Institution
Kennedy Presidential Library, John F.—1857
Kentucky, President's visit—1894, 1895, 2213
KFMB-TV—1806
KGTV—1804
KNSD-TV—1805
Korea, North, nuclear weapons development—1923,
2024, 2049, 2057-2059, 2127, 2129, 2131
Korea, South
Fishery agreement with U.S.—1915

Korea, South—Continued
President—2049, 2052, 2055, 2056, 2064, 2134,
2212, 2214, 2215
Kwanzaa—2207
Kyrgyzstan
Investment treaty with U.S.—1450
Trade with U.S.—2156

Labor & Congress of Industrial Organizations, Amer-
ican Federation of—1442, 1667
Labor Day—1437, 1439
Labor, Department of
Apprenticeship programs—1442
Assistant Secretaries—1425
Budget—1799
Deputy Assistant Secretaries—1904, 2213
Deputy Solicitor—1904
Executive Secretariat Director—2213
Inspector General—1360
Mine Safety and Health Administration—1425
Occupational Safety and Health Administration—
1670, 2213
Secretary—1369, 1433, 1446, 1461, 1467, 1494,
1517, 1670, 1671, 2016, 2046, 2049, 2101, 2102,
2138
Veterans Employment and Training Service—1425
Labor issues
See also specific industry
Union opposition to North American Free Trade
Agreement—1920, 1946
Labor Relations Authority, Federal—1829
Labor Relations Board, National—1670, 2209
Latin America
See also specific country
Trade with U.S.—1779, 1851, 1869, 1903, 2011,
2077
Latvia, President—1623
Law enforcement and crime
See also Drug abuse and trafficking
Anticrime legislation—1360, 1379, 1593, 1655, 1719,
1721, 1812, 1826, 1947, 1985, 1989, 2023, 2040,
2044, 2098, 2142, 2144, 2154, 2191
Capital punishment—1380
Child care provider background check system—2192
Child pornography—1952
Crime prevention efforts—1590
Federal funding—1361, 1380, 1719, 1837, 2190
Gun control—1332, 1361, 1362, 1380, 1513, 1538,
1591, 1593, 1655, 1666, 1712, 1718, 1719, 1721,
1737, 1767, 1812, 1881, 1948, 1985, 1988, 1990,
2023, 2035, 2040, 2044, 2046, 2050, 2066-2068,
2079, 2099, 2143, 2144, 2149, 2154
Juvenile crime—1422
National Guard, use in anticrime efforts—1800
Organized crime—2155
Parental kidnapping, international—2093
Prisons—1473
Safe schools initiative—1655
Lebanon, Prime Minister—1645, 2211
Legal Services Corporation—1370, 2209
Lexmark International, Inc.—1895, 2213
Libya
Pan Am Flight 103 bombing, role—2196
U.S. national emergency—2093

Lithuania
  Ambassador to U.S.—2215
  President—1623
  Withdrawal of Russian troops—1448
Louisiana
  News media—1334
  President's visit—1496

Malaysia, Prime Minister—2033
Malcolm Baldrige National Quality Awards—2169, 2212
Management and Budget, Office of—1631, 1634-1636, 1879, 2159, 2213
March on Washington for Jobs and Freedom, 30th anniversary—1400, 1402
Maritime affairs
  Fish imports to U.S.—1758
  Fishery agreements—1797, 1915, 2028
  Whale conservation—1684
Martin Luther King, Jr., Federal Holiday Commission—2213
Maryland
  Governor—1420
  President's visits—1412, 1840, 2217
Maryland, University of—1413
Massachusetts, President's visits—1402, 1857, 1860, 2209, 2212
Massachusetts Building Trades Council—1975
Mauritius, Ambassador to U.S.—2211
Medal. *See* other part of subject
Mediation Board, National—2209, 2049
Medical Association, American—2183
Medicare and Medicaid. *See* Health and Human Services, Department of
"Meet the Press"—1920
Merit Systems Protection Board—2209
Mexico
  Illegal immigration to U.S.—1656, 1780, 1805, 1872
  Labor laws—1938
  President—1967, 2008
  Trade with U.S.—1389, 1391, 1406, 1487, 1497, 1630, 1658, 1673, 1680, 1760, 1778, 1793, 1850, 1853, 1861, 1869, 1885, 1896, 1900, 1906, 1907, 1911, 1918, 1921, 1934, 1967, 1968, 1978, 1980, 1999, 2003, 2006, 2206
MIA's. *See* Armed Forces, U.S.
Middle East
  See also specific country
  Economic assistance—1642, 1643, 1965
  Peace efforts—1406, 1431, 1457, 1463, 1475, 1477, 1480-1484, 1642, 1643, 1794, 1815, 1820, 1821, 1823, 1961, 1963, 1964
Military, U.S. *See* Armed Forces, U.S.
Mine Safety and Health Administration. *See* Labor, Department of
Mine Safety and Health Review Commission, Federal—2213
Minerals Management Service. *See* Interior, Department of the
Mining, mine safety and health—1554
Minority business. *See* Business and industry
Minority Business Development Administration. *See* Commerce, Department of

Mint, U.S. *See* Treasury, Department of the
Missouri
  Flooding—2214
  President's visits—1365, 2209
Moldova
  Ambassador to U.S.—2215
  Investment treaty with U.S.—1451
Monetary Fund, International—1586, 1595, 1682
Montenegro
  Economic sanctions—2134
  Government assets held by U.S.—2134
  United Nations Security Council resolutions—2134, 2135
  U.S. national emergency—2134
Morocco
  King—1490, 1493
  U.S. Ambassador—1748
Mortgage Association, Federal National—1442, 1759
Mozambique, President—2211
MTV—1546
Museum Services, Institute of. *See* Arts and the Humanities, National Foundation on the

NAFTA. *See* Commerce, international
NASA. *See* Aeronautics and Space Administration, National
National. *See* other part of subject
Native Americans. *See* Indians, American
NATO. *See* North Atlantic Treaty Organization
Navy, Department of the
  See also Armed Forces, U.S.
  Assistant Secretaries—2092, 2153
  Under Secretary—1685
Nepal, U.S. Ambassador—1829
Netherlands
  Prime Minister—2217
  Taxation convention with U.S.—1807
Nevada, news media—1315
New Jersey
  Governor—1716
  Gubernatorial election—1948
  President's visit—1716
New Mexico, President's visit—2104, 2111, 2215
New York
  Democratic Party events—1608, 1846, 1849, 2165
  New York City mayoral election—1608, 1846
  President's visits—1599, 1608, 1612, 1618, 1619, 1846, 1849, 1850, 2165, 2211, 2216
New Zealand, Prime Minister—2033
News media. *See* specific State or news organization
Nicaragua
  Economic assistance—2077
  President—2075
Nobel Prizes—1431, 1758
North American Free Trade Agreement (NAFTA). *See* Commerce, international
North American Free Trade Agreement Implementation Act—2139
North American Free Trade Agreement, Task Force on the—1389, 1391
North Atlantic Treaty Organization—1364, 1455, 1622, 1683, 1741, 1746, 1763, 1764, 1770, 2019
North Carolina, President's visit—1732, 2212
North Carolina, University of—1732, 2212
Northern Ireland, conflict resolution—1868, 2179

Norway
  Middle East peace efforts, role—1465, 1482
  U.S. Ambassador—1400
  Whaling activities—1684
Nuclear weapons
  See also Arms and munitions; Defense and national
    security
  Arms control negotiations and agreements—1448,
    1615, 1694, 1821
  Nonproliferation—1587, 1615, 1639, 2057
  Testing—1318, 1319, 1531, 1615, 1694, 1856

OAS. *See* States, Organization of American
Occupational Safety and Health Administration. *See*
  Labor, Department of
Oceanic and Atmospheric Administration, National.
  See Commerce, Department of
Office. *See* other part of subject
Ohio, President's visit—1457, 1458
Oil. *See* Energy
Oklahoma, President's visit—1381
Omnibus Budget Reconciliation Act of 1993—1355
Organization. *See* other part of subject
Our Lady Help of Christians School—2043
Overseas Private Investment Corporation (OPIC). *See*
  Development Cooperation Agency, U.S. Inter-
  national

Palestine Liberation Organization—1457, 1463, 1475-
  1477, 1480, 1481, 1483, 1794, 1795, 1820, 1961,
  1963, 1965, 1977
Palestinians, self-government—1476-1478, 1481, 1643
Pan Am Flight 103, memorial—2195
Panama
  Government assets held by U.S.—1940
  President—2075
  Trade with U.S.—1758
Papua New Guinea, U.S. Ambassador—1456
Parental Kidnapping Crime Act of 1993, Inter-
  national—2093
Park Service, National. *See* Interior, Department of
  the
Partnership Council, National—1671, 2214
PATCO. *See* Professional Air Traffic Controllers Orga-
  nization
Patent and Trademark Office. *See* Commerce, Depart-
  ment of
Peace Corps—1426, 1522, 1545, 1917
Pennsylvania, President's visits—1886, 2156, 2163,
  2216
Performance Review, National. *See* Government agen-
  cies and employees, reform
Personnel Management, Office of—1641, 1855, 1918
Peru, trade with U.S.—1364
Philippines
  Ambassador to U.S.—2210
  Extradition treaty with U.S.—2050, 2051
  Human rights—2048
  President—2045-2047, 2212
Poland
  Fishery agreement with U.S.—1797
  U.S. Ambassador—1625
Pollution. *See* Environment
Postal Rate Commission—2212, 2216

Postal Service, U.S.—1855
POW's. *See* Armed Forces, U.S.
Presidential. *See* other part of subject
President's. *See* other part of subject
Prevailing Rate Advisory Committee, Federal—1776
Preventive Health Amendments of 1993—2185
Professional Air Traffic Controllers Organization—
  1670
Public Broadcasting, Corporation for—1799
Puerto Rico, commonwealth status, referendum—1997

Railroad Administration, Federal. *See* Transportation,
  Department of
Railroad industry, labor disputes—2212
Railroad Retirement Board—2053
Reclamation, Bureau of. *See* Interior, Department of
  the
Recycling. *See* Environment
Red Cross, American—1782
Refugees. *See* specific country or region
Reinventing Government. *See* Government agencies
  and employees, reform
Religion
  See also Civil rights
  President's views—1403
Religious Freedom Restoration Act of 1993—2000
Research and development. *See* Business and industry;
  Science and technology
Reserve System, Federal—1300
Resolution Trust Corporation—2188
Retired Persons, American Association of—1686
Risk Assessment and Management Commission—2216
Robert Wood Johnson Hospital—1716
Rockwell International—2119
Romania, trade with U.S.—1884
Rosh Hashana—1462
Rural areas, development—1799
Rural Development Administration. *See* Agriculture,
  Department of
Rural Electrification Administration. *See* Agriculture,
  Department of
Russia
  Civil conflict—1553, 1556, 1632, 1633, 1647, 1653,
    1668, 1677, 1682, 1693
  Economic assistance—1641, 1694
  Energy and Space, U.S.-Russian Joint Commission
    on—1429, 1448
  Fishery agreement with U.S.—2028
  Foreign Minister—1476, 1632, 1633
  Parliamentary elections—2163, 2172, 2175
  President—1429, 1448, 1553, 1556, 1632, 1633,
    1648, 1653, 1668, 1677, 1682, 1693, 1754, 1766,
    1823, 1924, 2202, 2217
  Prime Minister—1429, 1448
  Trade with U.S.—1640
  Troop withdrawals—1448, 1623
  U.S. laws relating to former Soviet Union—1430

Saint Lawrence Seaway Development Corporation. *See*
  Transportation, Department of
Saudi Arabia, King—1478
Schools. *See* specific institution; Education
Science and technology
  Communications. *See* Communications

Science and technology—Continued
   Computers—1630, 1649, 1659, 1675, 1680, 1807
   Electron/positron collider—1679, 1856
   Military and defense technology, civilian uses—
      1374, 1628, 1649, 1659, 1673, 1679, 1712, 1801,
      1804-1806
   Research and development—1627, 1649, 1673
   Space program. *See* Space program
   Super collider—1305, 1856
   Technology reinvestment programs and grants—
      1801, 1804-1806, 2070, 2110, 2112, 2115, 2121
Science and Technology, National Medals of—1636
Science and Technology Policy, Office of—1354
Science Foundation, National—1554, 1855
Secret Service, U.S. *See* Treasury, Department of the
Securities and Exchange Commission—2187
Security and Cooperation in Europe, Conference on—
   1527, 2136
Security Council, National
   Assistant to President for National Security Affairs—
      1914, 2213
   Special Assistant to President for National Security
      Affairs—2209
Senegal, Ambassador to U.S.—2215
Senior Executive Service. *See* Government agencies
   and employees
Serbia
   Economic sanctions—2134
   Government assets held by U.S.—2134
   United Nations Security Council resolutions—2134,
      2135
   U.S. national emergency—2134
Service, Corporation for National and Community—
   1456
Service program, national. *See* AmeriCorps; Education
Seychelles, Ambassador to U.S.—2210
Shipbuilding industry—1645, 1649
Singapore, Prime Minister—2037
Slovak Republic, taxation convention with U.S.—1798
Small business. *See* Business and industry
Small Business Administration—1360, 1369, 1378,
   1426, 1461, 1506, 1507, 1509, 1510, 1512, 1574,
   1845, 1997, 2199, 2203
Small Business Commission, White House Conference
   on—1475
Small Business Guaranteed Credit Enhancement Act
   of 1993—1378
Small Business, White House Conference on—1379
Smithsonian Institution
   Budget—1958
   John F. Kennedy Center for the Performing Arts—
      2139, 2210, 2215
Social Security—1336, 1514, 1666, 2159, 2161
Social Security Administration. *See* Health and Human
   Services, Department of
Soil Conservation Service. *See* Agriculture, Depart-
   ment of
Solomon Islands, U.S. Ambassador—1456
Somalia
   Attack on United Nations forces—1598, 1743, 1745,
      1753

Somalia—Continued
   Civil disorder—1410, 1411, 1526, 1528, 1529, 1531,
      1624, 1668, 1681, 1704, 1716, 1729, 1739, 1742,
      1743, 1745, 1773, 1925, 2130
   Humanitarian assistance—1598, 1616, 1621, 1622,
      1624, 1694, 1704, 1739, 1753, 1925
   U.S. military, role—1411, 1529, 1598, 1621, 1624,
      1668, 1677, 1681, 1694, 1703, 1716, 1729, 1734,
      1739, 1742, 1751, 1752, 1772, 1955, 2212
   U.S. Special Envoy—1705, 1729, 1742, 2130
South Africa
   African National Congress—1456, 1593, 1594, 1758
   Economic sanctions—1594, 2060
   President—1456, 1593, 1758
   Transition to democracy—1456, 1594, 2060
South America. *See* specific country; Latin America
South Carolina, President's visit—2217
Soviet Union, former. *See* specific country
Space program
   Shuttle—2147
   Space station—1305, 1854, 2010, 2149
Spain
   Prime Minister—2127, 2128
   U.S. Ambassador—1359
Special Olympics—2212
Sports, basketball—1698
Standards and Technology, National Institute of. *See*
   Commerce, Department of
State and local governments
   See also specific State or subject; Cities
   Community programs and services—1515
   Cooperation with Federal Government—2085
   Federal block grants—1458-1460, 2085
   Health and medical care—1383-1385, 1387, 1388
State, Department of
   Ambassadors. *See* specific country
   Assistant Secretaries—1914
   Budget—1837
   Deputy Assistant Secretaries—1426, 1917, 2216
   Deputy Secretary—1932, 1944, 2206
   International organizations and peacekeeping activi-
      ties, funding—1837
   Legal Adviser, Office of the—1427
   Policy Planning Principal Deputy Director—2216
   Secretary—1345, 1393-1395, 1457, 1463, 1464,
      1476-1479, 1617, 1639, 1644, 1694, 1769, 1821,
      2018, 2176, 2206
   Treaties and conventions, reports—1345, 1449-1451,
      1468, 1775, 2029, 2061
   Under Secretary—1914
States, Organization of American—1991
Sudan, Ambassador to U.S.—2211
Super collider. *See* Science and technology
Supreme Court of the U.S.—1312, 1314, 1358, 2000,
   2211
Surgeon General of the Public Health Service. *See*
   Health and Human Services, Department of
Sweden
   Prime Minister—2091
   U.S. Ambassador—1748
Switzerland
   Ambassador to U.S.—2210
   U.S. Ambassador—1824

Syria
 Foreign Minister—1964, 2212
 President—1479, 1645, 1821, 1964, 2215

Taiwan, rhinoceros and tiger trade—1931
Task force. *See* other part of subject
Tax Court, U.S.—1462
Taxation
 See also Budget, Federal; Economy, national
 Capital gains—2040
 Earned-income credit—1320, 1331, 1337, 1352,
  1356, 1420, 1443, 1512, 1538, 1600, 1671, 2040,
  2097
 Energy tax—1316, 1320, 1338
 Health insurance deduction—1385, 1577
 International agreements—1775, 1798, 1807
 Legislation—1311, 1322, 1327, 1330, 1335, 1336,
  1338, 1347, 1351, 1356, 2157
 Low-income housing credit—1416
 Self-insured business tax—1563, 1573, 1575, 1790,
  1835, 2106
 Small business investment deduction—1330, 1337,
  1352, 1356, 1512
 Tobacco tax—1563, 1573, 1575, 1790, 1835, 1964,
  2106
Teachers Hall of Fame, National—1340
Technology. *See* Science and technology
Telecommunications and Information Administration,
 National. *See* Commerce, Department of
Tennessee, President's visit—1980, 1981, 1986
Texas
 Governor—1473
 President's visit—1468, 1469
Textile industry—2180
Thailand, Prime Minister—2214
Thanksgiving Day—2065, 2067
Thrift Depositor Protection Oversight Board—1427
Timber industry—1325
Trade. *See* specific country; Commerce, international
Trade Administration, International. *See* Commerce,
 Department of
Trade Promotion Coordinating Committee—1631
Trade Representative, Office of the U.S.—1365, 1381,
 1389, 1391, 1407, 1748, 1910, 2012, 2018, 2078,
 2097, 2174, 2206
Transportation, Department of
 Annual reports—1828
 Aviation Administration, Federal—1824
 Civil Rights Director—1438
 Coast Guard, U.S.—1369, 2036
 Commercial Space Transportation Director—1438
 Deputy Assistant Secretary—1917
 Disaster assistance funding—2216
 Highway Administration, Federal—2216
 Highway and motor vehicle safety, reports—1776
 Highway Traffic Safety Administration, National—
  2111
 Railroad Administration, Federal—2216
 Saint Lawrence Seaway Development Corporation—
  1554
 Secretary—1369, 1392, 1461, 2046, 2049
 Transportation Statistics, Bureau of—2213
Transportation. *See* specific industry

Treasury, Department of the
 Alcohol, Tobacco and Firearms, Bureau of—1856,
  2149
 Assistant Secretaries—1543, 2155
 Budget—1855
 Customs Service, U.S.—1427, 1664, 1950, 1995,
  2137, 2215
 Deputy Assistant Secretaries—1543, 2214, 2216
 Foreign Assets Control, Office of—1308, 1950,
  1994, 1995, 2135-2137
 Government securities, rulemaking authority—2187
 Internal Revenue Service—1367, 1855
 International Tax Counsel—2215
 Mint, U.S.—2202
 Secret Service, U.S.—2050
 Secretary—1461, 1612, 1769, 1948, 2019, 2135,
  2188
 Senior Adviser to Assistant Secretary—2214
 Senior Policy Adviser—2215
 Senior Tax Adviser—1427
 Tax Legislative Counsel—2214
 Treasurer of the U.S.—2054
Treaties and conventions. *See* specific country, region,
 or subject; State, Department of
Trinidad and Tobago, Prime Minister—1407, 2209
Turkey
 Cyprus conflict. *See* Cyprus
 Deputy Prime Minister—1914
 Economic Commission, U.S.-Turkish Joint—1750
 Economic losses in Persian Gulf conflict—2078
 Foreign Minister—1395, 1396, 1914
 Kurdish Communist party (PKK), terrorist acts—
  1752
 President—1395
 Prime Minister—1749, 1914, 1915
 U.S. Ambassador—1914

Ukraine
 Arms control negotiations and agreements—1448,
  1821
 President—1448, 2214
Unemployment Compensation Amendments of 1993—
 2070
UNICEF. *See* United Nations
UNITA. *See* Angola, National Union for the Total
 Independence of
United Kingdom
 Foreign Minister—2210
 Northern Ireland. *See* Northern Ireland
 Prime Minister—1556, 1868, 2164, 2179, 2216
United Mine Workers of America—2138
United Nations
 Administrative reforms—1617
 Atomic Energy Agency, International—1587, 1615,
  1829, 2024, 2058, 2059, 2073, 2127, 2129, 2131
 Children's Emergency Fund, International
  (UNICEF)—1618, 2196
 Commission on the Status of Women—1829
 Environment and Development, Conference on—
  2029
 General Assembly—1612, 2211
 High Commissioner for Human Rights—2194
 Human Rights Commission—1808

United Nations—Continued
    Peacekeeping, role—1616, 1622, 1746, 1924
    Regional conflicts. *See* specific country or region
    Secretary-General—1393-1397, 1616, 1668, 1729, 1730, 1863, 1915, 2062, 2211
    Security Council—1394-1396, 1622, 1755, 1837
    Trade law convention, international—1345
    U.S. assessments and arrears—1617
    U.S. Government activities, report—2011
    U.S. Representatives—1394, 1396, 1617, 1808, 1829, 2211, 2216
    U.S. *See* other part of subject
Universities and colleges. *See* specific institution; Education
University. *See* other part of subject
Urban League, National—1328

Vanuatu, U.S. Ambassador—1456
Vatican. *See* Holy See
Veterans Affairs, Department of
    Assistant Secretary—1425
    Budget—1854
    Persian Gulf war veterans, health care legislation—2193
    Secretary—1942
    Under Secretary—1633
    Veterans Health Administration—1956
Veterans Day—1952, 1954, 1956
Veterans Employment and Training Service. *See* Labor, Department of
Vice President
    Community Enterprise Board, President's, Chair—1460
    Energy and Space, U.S.-Russian Joint Commission on, role—1429, 1448
    Federal Government reform, role—1444, 1452, 1469
    North American Free Trade Agreement debate—1905, 1940
    Regulatory process, role—1634
Vietnam Women's Memorial Project—1942
Virginia
    President's visits—1452, 1954
    Storms and tornadoes—2217
Voluntarism—1412, 1543

Wall Street Journal—1850
Washington, President's visit—2009, 2012, 2013, 2020, 2022, 2025, 2032, 2034-2036, 2214
Weapons. *See* Arms and munitions; Nuclear weapons

Welfare system, reform—1420, 2101
West Virginia, President's visits—1350, 1956, 2213
Western Samoa, Ambassador to U.S.—2210
White House fellows—1697
White House Fellowships, President's Commission on—1697
White House Initiative Office—1876
White House Office
    Assistants to President
        Communications, Director—1749
        Congressional Affairs—2194
        Deputy Chiefs of Staff—2139, 2203
        Domestic Policy—1460
        Economic Policy—1460
        Intergovernmental Affairs—1349
        Legislative Affairs—2055
        National Security Affairs—1914, 2213
        Scheduling and Advance, Director—1595
        Science and Technology—1679
        Senior Adviser—2049
        Staff Secretary—2213
    Chief of Staff—1838, 1865, 1891, 2210
    Deputy Assistant to President and Press Secretary—1448, 1456, 1598, 1693, 1694, 1892, 2011, 2202
    Deputy Assistants to President
        Intergovernmental Affairs—1449
        Political Affairs, Deputy Director—1449
    Deputy Counsel to President—2054
    Special Adviser to President for North American Free Trade Agreement—1436
    Special Assistant to President and Deputy Press Secretary—2173
    Special Assistant to President for National Security Affairs and Counselor—2209
    Staff reduction and reorganization—1634
WIC. *See* Agriculture, Department of
Woodrow Wilson International Center for Scholars—2213
World AIDS Day—2087
World Conservation Union—1824
World War I, 75th anniversary—1957
World Youth Day—1372

Yale University—1722
Yom Kippur—1595
Yugoslavia
    Montenegro. *See* Montenegro
    Serbia. *See* Serbia

Name Index

Abbas, Mahmoud—1476
Abraham, Katherine G.—2221
Abshire, Sheryl—1340
Ackerman, Gary L.—1609
Ackerman, Kenneth—2216
Adams, Henry Lee, Jr.—1864, 2227
Adkins, Charles—2227
Adler, Karen R.—2217
Agnos, Art—1904
Aideed, Mohamed Farah—1411, 1531, 1624, 1677, 1729, 1743, 1745, 1772, 2130
Albright, Madeleine K.—1394, 2211
Alegria, Ricardo E.—1693, 1702
Alexander, Jane—1350, 1700, 2220
Alexander, Leslie M.—2220
Alexander, Lewis S.—2215
Alfiero, Anna—1341
Allen, Lew, Jr.—2211
Altman, Roger—1300, 1346
Ambrose, Donetta W.—1809, 2226
Anderson, Bernard E.—2225
Anderson, Michael J.—1426
Andrews, Dick—1865, 1891
Andrews, Thomas H.—1969, 1970
Angevine, Josephine—1603
Annenberg, Leonore—1693, 1700, 2186
Annenberg, Walter—1693, 1700, 2186
Antall, Jozsef—2165
Anthony, Beryl, Jr.—2080
Aponte, Priscilla—1544
Arafat, Yasser—1457, 1463, 1464, 1476-1481, 1795, 1963, 1977
Argrett, Loretta Collins—1836, 2226
Aristide, Jean-Bertrand—1536, 1730-1732, 1744, 1746, 1755, 1756, 1764, 1767, 1801, 1809, 1810, 1819, 1822, 1840, 1863, 1926, 1949, 1973, 1991, 1992, 1994, 2133, 2192
Armstrong, Max—1910
Armstrong, Michael J.—2216
Asad, Hafiz al- —1477-1479, 1645, 1821, 1964, 2215
Askew, Hulett Hall—2220
Askew, Stacey—1500
Aspin, Les—1412, 1677, 1715, 1757, 1782, 1927, 1955, 1963, 2027, 2177, 2178, 2184
Atakol, Kenan—1396
Atkinson, Stan—1653
Atwood, J. Brian—2052, 2197

Babbitt, Bruce—1318, 1838, 1840, 1942, 2213
Baca, Polly B.—2200
Bacamurwanko, Jacques—2215
Bachula, Gary—1426
Baer, Terry—1907
Baggiano, Faye—1426
Baird, Zoe—2211

Baker, James A., III—1484
Baliles, Gerald L.—1392
Balladur, Edouard—1556, 2164, 2216
Baquet, Charles R., III—1522, 2228
Barakat, Russell G.—1759
Barasch, David M.—2222
Barbano, Jo—1689
Barkett, Rosemary—1596, 2224
Barkley, Richard—1914
Barnes, Harry F.—1837, 2226
Barram, David J.—2221
Bartholomew, Reginald—2219
Battaglia, Lynne Ann—2220
Battle, Laveeda Morgan—2220
Bayer, Robert—1686
Beard, Lillian—1559
Beaty, Kenneth—2074
Becker, Gary—1431, 1432
Becker, Jane E.—2223
Becraft, Carolyn—1686
Beerbower, Cynthia Gibson—2215
Bellamy, Carol—1545, 2221
Bender, Paul—2216
Benediktsson, Einar—2215
Bennett, Marian C.—2221
Benson, William F.—2215
Bentsen, Lloyd—1305, 1346, 1389, 1391, 1948, 2005, 2019, 2027, 2188
Berardo, Susan—1604
Berg, Brian C.—2228
Berger, Joseph—1686
Berggren, Gretchen—2198
Bernath, Cliff—1685
Berrigan, Helen (Ginger)—2012, 2229
Berry, Mary Frances—1532
Bersin, Alan D.—2225
Betts, Rebecca Aline—2229
Beyer, Wally B.—1720, 2228
Biden, Joseph R., Jr.—1359, 1362, 1433, 1763, 1881
Bieber, Owen—1626
Biehl, Amy—2060
Biery, Fred—2030
Bilbray, James H.—1317
Bildt, Carl—2091
Bingaman, Jeff—2112
Binnendijk, Johannes Albert—2216
Bir, Cevik—1746, 1751
Birenbaum, David—2216
Black, Hugh Dinsmore, Jr.—2229
Black, Leslie—1341
Blair, Diane—2220
Blancato, Robert B.—1808, 1817
Blanchard, James J.—1354
Bland, Carol—1653

Blinken, Alan John—1456, 2221
Bloom, Thomas R.—2199
Bogdanoff, Stewart R.—1341
Boggs, Lindy—1498
Bohannon, Mark—2215
Bolger, James—2033
Bonior, David E.—1390, 1391, 1406, 1484, 1971, 2004, 2055
Boren, David L.—1298, 1301, 1304, 1306, 1313
Borg, Parker W.—2221
Borton, Nan—1904
Bossidy, Larry—1868
Boucher, Richard A.—2220
Boufford, Melville—2212
Boundoukou-Latha, Paul—2210
Boussoukou-Boumba, Pierre Damien—2215
Boutros-Ghali, Boutros—1393-1397, 1617, 1668, 1729, 1730, 1863, 1915, 1925, 2211
Bowen, Cheryl P.—1426
Bowersox, Kenneth D.—2148
Bowles, Erskine B.—1506, 1507, 1509, 1510, 1512, 1574, 1845, 1997
Boxer, Barbara—1664, 1678, 1838, 1866, 1891, 2040, 2041
Boyer, Robert Kent—2215
Bradbury, Darcy—1543
Bradley, Bill—1333
Bradley, Dan—2087
Brady, James S.—1812, 1881, 2068, 2069, 2080
Brady, Sarah—1812, 1881, 2068, 2069, 2080
Bratton, William—1362
Brazauskas, Algirdas—1623
Breaux, John B.—1337, 2102, 2103
Brennan, William—2082, 2083
Brickhouse, Eugene A.—2221
Brinkema, Leonie M.—2219
Brinson, J. Ron—1500
Broadfoot, Elma—1516
Broderick, John T., Jr.—2220
Brody, Kenneth D.—1631, 1782
Brokaw, Tom—1920
Brook, Robert—1572
Brooks, Jack—1362, 2209
Brooks, John G.—2220
Brothers, Floyd—1516
Brown, Ann Winkelman—1808
Brown, Bobby—2138
Brown, Dion—1655
Brown, Hank—1376
Brown, Jesse—1942, 1956
Brown, Judy—1689
Brown, Lee Patrick—1361, 1380, 1428, 1660, 1812, 1892, 1987, 1991, 2154, 2190
Brown, Ronald H.—1372, 1391, 1393, 1467, 1595, 1631, 1678, 1684, 1776, 2009, 2018, 2041, 2045, 2061, 2169
Brown, Taylor—1910
Browner, Carol M.—1318, 1374, 1389, 1391, 1771, 2216
Browning, Margaret A.—1670, 2209, 2226, 2227
Bryan, Richard H.—1317, 1626

Bucklew, Susan C.—1864, 2227
Buckley, Jill—1829
Bulos, Alice B.—1998
Bundy, Robert Charles—2229
Buntrock, Grant B.—1438
Burdine, Brigitte—1501
Burgess, Franklin D.—2030
Burns, James Burton—2225
Burton, LaVarne Addison—2216
Busch, Daniel—1734
Bush, George—1475, 1484, 1485, 1489, 1533, 1621, 1704, 1738, 1751, 1768, 2210
Byrd, Robert C.—1739, 1751
Byrne, Larry E.—2224

Cain, Sally H.—1976
Calderon, Rafael Angel—2075
Calendar, Marcia—1601
Calhoun-Senghor, Keith—1426
Califa, Antonio—1438
Callejas, Rafael Leonardo—2075
Calloway, Cab—1693, 1700
Calvan, Rita A.—2216
Camilion, Oscar—1393, 1394
Campbell, Ben Nighthorse—1376
Campbell, Carroll A., Jr.—1387
Canady, Roberta—1918
Cannon, Jonathan Z.—2224
Caputo, Dante—1755, 1822, 1863
Caracristi, Ann Z.—2211
Cardin, Benjamin L.—1841
Carlson, Arne H.—2215
Carnes, Kelly H.—2212
Carnevale, Anthony P.—2209
Carpenter, Margaret V.W.—2221
Carter, Jimmy—1475, 1484, 1485, 1489, 1533, 1738, 1745, 1822, 2210
Carter, Stephen—1403, 2001
Case, Helen—1341
Casellas, Gilbert F.—2223
Casey, Paula Jean—2220
Cashin, William B.—1998
Castle, Michael N.—1386, 1842
Castos, Marie—1602
Caviaiola, Larry—1686
Cédras, Raoul—1730, 1731, 1757, 1822, 1949, 1973, 1991, 1992
Celeste, Richard—1392
Cermak, Shelly—1503
Cetin, Hikmet—1395, 1396, 1914
Chabot, Herbert L.—1462, 2221
Chafee, John H.—1767
Chambers, Merle Catherine—1475
Chamorro, Violeta—2075
Charles, Ray—1693, 1701
Chasanow, Deborah K.—2219
Chater, Shirley Sears—1325, 2223
Cheek, James—1876
Chernomyrdin, Viktor—1429, 1448
Cheshes, Martin L.—1880, 2226
Cheston, Sheila—1686
Chisholm, Shirley—1742

Chissano, Joaquim Alberto—2211
Chiu, Peter Y.—2216
Chkheidze, Peter P.—2210
Chou, Wushow (Bill)—2216
Chrétien, Jean—1827, 1828, 1901, 2005, 2012, 2092
Christiani, Alfredo—2075
Christie, Deborah P.—2153
Christopher, Warren M.—1393-1395, 1457, 1464, 1476-1479, 1484, 1644, 1694, 1757, 1766, 1782, 1821, 1882, 1927, 1964, 2018, 2206
Chrystal, John—1462, 2224
Chuan Likphai—2037, 2214
Chung, Connie—2213
Ciampi, Carlo Azeglio—1526, 2210
Ciller, Tansu—1749, 1914, 1915
Cisneros, Henry G.—1383, 1416, 1424, 1441, 1445, 1517, 1536, 1680, 1947, 2201
Clark, Joseph—1395, 1396, 1914, 1915
Clark, Stephen—1804
Clay, William—1694
Clement, Bob—1980
Clerides, Glafcos—1393, 1394, 1914, 1915
Clinger, William F., Jr.—1310
Clinton, Chelsea—1518, 1568
Clinton, Hillary Rodham—1384, 1403, 1501, 1504, 1543, 1557, 1568, 1646, 1647, 1840, 1866, 2150, 2204, 2214
Coffey, Kendall Brindley—2225
Coffman, Jennifer B.—2219
Coggins, Paul Edward—2220
Coleman, Rodney A.—2153
Coleman, Veronica Freeman—2222
Colleton, Larry Herbert—2229
Collins, Daniel—2220
Collins, Gary—2150
Comer, Meryl—1871
Conti, Eugene A., Jr.—1917
Conyers, John, Jr.—1310, 1825
Cook, Ed—1516
Coolbaugh, Stanley—1952
Cooper, Jim—1980
Copps, Michael J.—2211
Corriher, Murray—1909
Covey, Richard O.—2147
Crane, Mary Lou—2216
Crouch, Robert P., Jr.—2221
Crowe, William J., Jr.—1953, 2211
Crown Prince Hassan—1643-1645, 1961
Culea, John—1806
Cuomo, Andrew M.—2200
Cuomo, Mario M.—1608
Cuomo, Matilda—1817
Curtis, Charles B.—1880

Dalai Lama—2022
Daley, William M.—1389, 1391, 1406, 1436, 1759, 1800, 1885, 1996, 2005, 2140
Dalpino, Cathy Elizabeth—1426
D'Amato, Alfonse—1359
D'Amours, Norman E.—1829, 2226
Danforth, John C.—1905, 2110
Dann-Messier, Brenda—1976

Danzig, Richard—1685, 2228
Dark, Ida Daniel—1341
Daschle, Linda H.—1824, 2229
Dashiell, G. Ronald—2228
Daubon, Ramon E.—1904
Daughtrey, Martha Craig—1349, 2219
Davenport, Ernest—2171
Davis, Michael J.—2030
Davis, Willie—2155
Davison, Robert P.—1426
Dawson, Deborah A.—2214
de Armas, Mario Chanes—1347
de Klerk, Frederik Willem—1456, 1758, 2060
De Leon, Ramiro—2075
de Passe, Suzanne—1792
Deagle, Edwin A., Jr.—1880
Dean, Howard—1771
Dear, Joseph A.—1670, 2221
DeConcini, Dennis—1323, 1333, 1334
Deetjen, Ernest—1957
DeGuilio, Jon Ernest—2223
DeJarnette, Edmund T., Jr.—1933, 2227
Dellums, Ronald V.—1374, 1516, 1678, 1825
Delors, Jacques—2215
Demirel, Suleyman—1395
Denktash, Rauf—1394-1396, 1914, 1915
Despiwa, Delores—1368
Despres, John—2221
DeVito, Danny—1817
Di Gregory, Kevin V.—2216
Diaz, Rafael—1772
Diaz-Balart, Lincoln—1973
Dicks, Norman D.—1943, 2010
Dicus, Greta Joy—2215
Diehl, Phillip N.—2202
Dilja, Lublin Hasan—2215
DiMario, Michael F.—2209, 2225
Dine, Thomas A.—1829
Dinkins, David—1599, 1608, 1846, 1849, 1894
Dion, Judy—1503
Dixon, Harry Donival, Jr.—2229
Djerejian, Edward P.—2221
Dole, Bob—1327, 1338, 1751, 1831, 2055, 2066-2068
Domenici, Pete V.—1776, 2108
Donnelly, Brian J.—2227
Doolittle, James H.—1625
Dorn, Edwin—2214
Dornbush, K. Terry—2225
Dornsife, N. Cinnamon—1426
Dorr, Jenny—2087
Dortch, Carol A.—2215
Douglas, Marjory Stoneman—2082
Dover, Agnes P.—2213
Dowd, Edward L., Jr.—2222
Drell, Sidney D.—2211
Dreyfus, Daniel A.—2221
Drier, David—2139
Droney, Christopher—2223
DuBester, Ernest W.—2209, 2224
Dunfey, Robert J., Jr.—2153
Dunlap, John—1671

Dunn, Michael V.—1425, 2228
Durant, Michael—1729, 1739, 1742, 1760, 2212
Duvall, Carol—2152
Dyhrkopp, Einar V.—2220

Eagleburger, Lawrence S.—1484
Eagleton, Thomas F.—2211
Eakeley, Douglas S.—2220
Eaton, Robert J.—1626
Eckert, Sue E.—1880, 2227
Ecoffey, Robert Dale—2229
Edwards, Edwin W.—1500
Eidintas, Alfonsas—2215
Ekeus, Rolf—1586, 2073
Elders, M. Joycelyn—1448, 1513, 1536, 2103, 2143
Elizondo, Rita—1518
Elson, Edward Elliott—2225
Endara, Guillermo—2075
Engel, Jeanne K.—1904
Ericsson, Sally C.—2216
Ervin, Christine—1777, 2228
Escobar, Pablo—2092
Eshoo, Anna G.—1959
Espy, Mike—1366-1368, 1424, 1446, 1838, 1840, 1864, 1891, 1908, 1910-1912
Esquivel, Manuel—2075
Esserman, Susan—1830
Estrada, Rudolph I.—1475
Evans, Diane—1942, 1953

Fahey, Helen Frances—2222
Fairbanks-Williams, Edna—2209, 2221
Famularo, Joseph Leslie—2225
Farmer, Greg—2213
Farquhar, Michele C.—1426
Fawbush, Wayne H.—1438
Fazio, Vic—1649
Feighan, Edward F.—2080
Feingold, Russell D.—1333
Feinstein, Dianne—1664, 1678, 1838, 1866, 1891, 2039, 2044, 2099, 2142, 2144
Feissel, Gustave—1393-1396, 1914
Ferguson, Wilkie D., Jr.—1809, 2226
Ferraro, Geraldine—1808, 1817
Fiester, Clark G.—1880
Fillmore, Earl—1734
Filner, Bob—1806
Firestone, Alan—2106
Fish, Mark—1604
Fisher, Edmond—1431
Fisher, Peggy Zone—1475
Fitz-Pegado, Lauri—1522, 2223
Flamm, Kenneth—1686
Flecha de Lima, Paulo Tarso—2215
Flieger, Neal—2216
Florio, Jim—1592, 1717, 1894
Flynn, Raymond Leo—1646
Flyte, Mary Catherine—1501
Foege, William—2198
Foley, Thomas S.—1326, 1357, 2026, 2068
Forbeck, Helen—1685
Ford, Dietra L.—1427

Ford, Gerald R.—1484, 1485, 1489, 1534, 1738, 2209, 2210
Ford, Harold E.—1980, 1983, 1986
Ford, Wendell H.—1484
Ford, William D.—1747
Forsythe, Dell—1576
Fossum, Robert—2209
Fox, Charles—1933
François, Joseph Michel—1730, 1757, 1840, 1949, 1973
Frank, Barney—2200
Frankel, Diane B.—1360, 2224
Franklin, John Hope—1693, 1702
Fraser, Arvonne S.—1829
Freeh, Louis J.—1312, 1328, 1380, 1427, 1812, 2154, 2155
Freeman, Bennett—1426
Freiberg, Debbie—1559
Frenzel, Bill—1436, 1800, 1868, 1885, 1996, 2005, 2140
Friedman, C. Hough—1475
Fruchter, Susan—2216
Fuedo, Anthony—2081
Fulbright, J. William—1977
Fuller, Linda—1421
Fuller, Millard—1421
Furgeson, W. Royal—2030

Gachupin, Cel—2109
Galston, William A.—2095, 2101
Gamble, Roger R.—2219
Garamendi, John—1651
Garamendi, Patricia Wilkerson—1426
Garcia, Eugene E.—1426
Garcia, Orlando—2030
Gardner, Booth—1748
Gardner, John—1882
Gardner, Richard N.—1359, 2221
Garland, Merrick B.—1918
Garland, Milton—1957
Gati, Toby T.—2221
Gaviria, Cesar—1779, 2092, 2211
Gejdenson, Sam—2211
Gelbard, Robert S.—2224
Gephardt, Richard A.—1357, 1391, 1484, 2055, 2110, 2198
Gertner, Nancy—1837, 2226
Ghebrehiwet, Hagos—2211
Gibbons, John Howard—1679
Giffin, Gordon D.—1462, 2221
Gillies, Ewen—1605
Gilmartin, William J.—2221
Gingrich, Newt—1484, 1800, 1968, 1969, 2003
Ginsberg, Marc Charles—1748, 2225
Ginsburg, Marty—1359
Ginsburg, Ruth Bader—1312, 1314, 1321, 1358, 1663, 2211
Giuliani, Rudolph W.—2143, 2215
Gleiman, Edward J.—2216
Glenn, John—1310, 1458, 1694, 1825
Glennen, Robert—1342
Glover, Jere W.—2199

Glynn, Thomas P.—2214
Gober, Hershel—1956
Goffney, Lawrence O., Jr.—1884
Goh Chok Tong—2037
Gold, Charlotte—2212
Golden, Olivia A.—2225
Goldman, Lynn R.—2223
Goncz, Arpad—2165
Gonzales, Edmundo A.—1904
Gonzalez, Eduardo—2222
Gonzalez, Felipe—2127, 2128
Goodacre, Glenna—1942
Goode, W. Wilson—1976
Goodling, William F.—1747, 2211
Goodman, John—1686
Goodman, Margaret—1918
Gordon, Gary—1734
Gore, Albert, Jr.—1310, 1312, 1346, 1382, 1390, 1429,
    1444-1448, 1454, 1467, 1469, 1472-1474, 1504,
    1559, 1568, 1629, 1663, 1670, 1694, 1756, 1773,
    1824, 1840, 1876, 1905, 1911, 1913, 1920, 1940,
    1943-1945, 2003, 2005, 2008, 2068, 2147
Gore, Tipper—1501, 1504
Gorr, Ivan—1868
Gotbaum, Joshua—1685
Gottfried, Derek—1544
Gould, William B., IV—1670, 2220
Goulding, Marrack—1394
Grace, Walter Charles—2225
Graff, Henry F.—2213
Graham, Bob—1972
Granger, Kay—1516
Granillo Ocampo, Raul Enrique—2211
Grant, Jim—2196
Grasso, Richard—1817
Gray, Hanna Holborn—1693, 1702
Green, Mark—1847
Greene, Margaret Hornbeck—2215
Greenspan, Alan—1300
Greenspun, Brian Lee—1475
Greenwood, Marci—1354
Greenwood, Mary Rita Cooke—2225
Griffin, James—2190
Griffin, Pat—2194
Grizzard, Michael B.—1523
Gunderson, Steve—1747

Hackley, Vic—1876
Hackney, Sheldon—1700
Haftel, Linda—1601
Hagen, David W.—2224
Haggerty, Ancer—2030
Hale, Marcia L.—1349, 1771
Haley, George W.—2212, 2230
Haley, Maria Luisa M.—2012, 2229
Hall, Anne L.—2084
Hall, Kermit L.—1438, 2222
Halperin, Morton H.—2221
Hambley, Mark Gregory—2219
Hamilton, Arthur M.—1771
Hammond, Jeffrey—1719
Hampton, Philip G., II—1884

Hamre, John J.—2219
Hankinson, John H., Jr.—2111
Hannah, John—2030
Hannah, Robert—1957
Harawi, Ilyas—1478
Hardecke, Howard—1906
Hare, Paul J.—2212
Hariri, Rifiq al-—1645, 2211
Harkin, Ruth R.—2061
Harkin, Tom—2110
Harrington, Anthony S.—2211
Harrington, Judy—1918
Harris, Claude, Jr.—2222
Harris, Elihu—1516
Harris, Jo Ann—2222
Hart, Gary—1376
Harvey, Mary Ellen—1686
Hata, Tsutomu—1477
Hatamiya, Lon Shoso—1438
Hatch, Orrin G.—1359
Hathaway, William D.—2229
Hattori, Masaichi—2213
Hattori, Meiko—2213
Hattori, Yoshihiro—2213
Hawes, Bess Lomax—1693, 1701
Hayes, James A.—1980
Hedien, Wayne—1517
Heffernan, James—1504, 1524
Hehir, Thomas—1426
Heiskell, Andrew—1693, 1703
Helling, Roberta—1516
Helm, Sheila—1686
Henderson, Tom—2145
Henry, Phylliss Jeanette—2227
Herman, Alexis—1792
Hermann, Robert J.—2211
Hernandez, Richard—1426
Hesburgh, Theodore M.—1882
Hevesi, Alan—1847
Hiatt, Arnold—1789
Hickox, Amy—1686
Hicks, John F.—1344, 2226
Hillman, Jennifer Anne—2223
Hirschorn, Norbert—2198
Hoagland, Peter—1943
Hoar, Joseph P.—1746
Hobson, David L.—1959
Hodges, C. Howie, II—2216
Hoffman, Jeffrey A.—2148
Hogan, John M.—2216
Hogan, John P.—1918
Holladay, Wallace—1794
Holladay, Wilhelmina—1794
Holley, Nelda—1500
Hollings, Ernest F.—1776
Holmes, Henry Allen—1425, 2224
Holmes, Paul Kinloch, III—2220
Holum, Barbara Pedersen—2228
Holum, John David—1699, 2179, 2225
Holz, Arnold G.—2203
Hopkins, Donald—2198

Horan, Michael J.—1588
Horgan, Daniel J.—2229
Horn, Joan Kelly—1426
Hosokawa, Morihiro—1619, 1936, 2018, 2020, 2024, 2037, 2049, 2209
Hove, Andrew C.—2084
Howard, Henry, Jr.—1730
Hoyer, Steny H.—1414, 1959, 2079, 2097, 2103
Huang, Josephine S.—1426
Hulin, Frances Cuthbert—2225
Hultin, Jerry MacArthur—2153
Hundt, Reed E.—2219
Hunt, Jim, Jr.—1735, 1996
Hunt, Swanee Grace—1456, 2222
Hurd, Douglas—2210
Hurley, Daniel T.K.—1951, 2228
Hussein, Saddam—1587, 1749, 2073
Hyde, Jeanette W.—2228
Hymel, Lezin Joseph, Jr.—2229

Iacocca, Lee—1800, 2210
Ickes, Harold—2203
Ilves, Toomas Hendrik—2210
Inderfurth, Karl Frederick—2211
Ingraham, Hubert—1407, 1409, 2209
Inman, Bobby R.—2184
Inonu, Erdal—1914
Insanally, Samuel Rudolph—2211
Ishimaru, Stuart J.—1623
Ishmael, Odeen—2210
Itzkoff, Donald M.—2216

Jack, Janis Graham—2030
Jackson, Anne—1689
Jackson, James K., Sr.—1341
Jackson, Jesse—1929, 2080
Jackson, Lee—1426
Jackson, Raymond—1596, 2224
Jacobsen, Magdalena—2209, 2226
Jacovides, Andreas J.—2211
Jagan, Cheddi—1407, 2209
Jagmetti, Carlo—2210
James, Sharpe—2190
Jaya bin Abdul Latif—2215
Jeff, Gloria—2216
Jefferson, William J.—1980
Jeffords, James M.—1646, 1692
Jeliffe, Patrice—2198
Jensen, Patrica A.—1438
Jeremiah, D.E.—1757, 2199
Jett, Kevin—2190
Jiang Zemin—1924, 1936, 2018, 2022, 2037, 2049
Jin, Leslie R.—2217
Johnsen, Dawn—2215
Johnson, Frank—1427
Johnson, Grantland—2215
Johnson, Roger W.—1453, 1865, 1891, 2216
Johnson, Victor C.—1918
Johnston, Harry—1972
Johnston, J. Bennett—1306, 1335
Jones, Clark—1475
Jordan, Barbara—2173

Jordan, Mary Lucille—2213
Jordan, Michael—1698
Joseph, Stephen C.—1685
Joulwan, George A.—1683
Joyce, William L.—1438, 2226
Jurado, Kathy Elena—1425, 2223

Kaczmareck, Jean—1501
Kamarck, Elaine Ciulla—2095, 2099
Kamarck, Martin A.—2227
Kantor, Michael (Mickey)—1381, 1391, 1410, 1437, 1800, 1885, 1886, 1910, 2005, 2012, 2018, 2078, 2097, 2118, 2127, 2139, 2169, 2174
Karp, Naomi Katherine—2216
Kasich, John R.—1959
Katzen, Sally—2213
Kearns, David—2187
Keating, Paul—1490, 1491
Keener, Robert S.—2214
Keevey, Richard F.—2064
Kelly, John Joseph—2224
Kelly, Mary Francis—1475
Kelly, Sharon Pratt—1801
Kelman, Steven—2227
Kennedy, Edward M.—1315, 1448
Kennedy, John F.—1857, 2050
Kennedy, Joseph P., II—1744, 1859, 1971
Kennedy, Kerry—1557
Kerr, T. Michael—2213
Kerrey, J. Robert—1342, 1905
Kessler, Alan Craig—2216
Khanh Pham—1949
Khasbulatov, Ruslan—1653
Kildee, Dale E.—1747, 2200
Kim Yong-sam—2033, 2037, 2049, 2052, 2055, 2056, 2064, 2134, 2212, 2214, 2215
Kimball, Katherine W.—1426
Kimbrough, Floyd A.—2228
King Baudouin I—2209
King Fahd—1478
King Hassan II—1490, 1493
King Hussein I—1477, 1960, 1963
King, James B.—2214
King, Larry—1905
King, Martin Luther, Jr.—1400
Kirk, Michael K.—2202
Kirkland, Joseph Lane—1946
Kirkpatrick, Carl Kimmel—2224
Kissinger, Henry A.—1484, 1769
Klaas, Marc—2217
Klaas, Polly—2217
Klein, Joel—2054
Klein, Theodore—1864, 2227
Knight, Peter S.—1940, 2230
Kohl, Glen Arlen—2214
Kohl, Helmut—1448, 1556, 2164, 2214, 2216
Kohl, Herb—1297, 1767, 2079, 2099
Kohlenberg, Sherry—1761
Koop, C. Everett—1542, 1549, 1551, 1561
Kopp, Wendy—1665
Koppel, Ted—1568
Koumbairia, Laoumaye Mekonyo—2210

Kourpias, George J.—1462, 2226
Kozyrev, Andrey—1476, 1632
Kravchuk, Leonid—1448, 2214
Krebs, Edwin—1431
Krebs, Martha Anne—2225
Kregor, Karl—1502
Kreidler, Mike—1943
Kunitz, Stanley—1693, 1701

Lader, Philip—2139, 2214
Ladwig, Alan—2217
Lake, Anthony—1914, 2078, 2213
Lakshmanan, T.R.—2213
Lamb, Robert—1395, 1914
Lambert, Blanche M.—1980
Lancaster, Carol J.—2222
Lancaster, Gary L.—1809, 2226
Landreth, Kathryn E.—2222
Lane, Neal F.—2222
Lanier, Bob—1470, 1713, 2040, 2098
Lau, Valerie—1918
Lautenschlager, Peggy A.—2223
Lawrence, M. Larry—1824, 2226
Lawrence, Shelia Davis—1824
Laws, Elliot Pearson—2223
Lawson, George—1911
Leavitt, Michael—1771
LeBlanc, Catherine—1876
Leff, Ilene J.—2215
Lehman, Richard H.—1959
Leonard, Thomas A.—1759
Lesher, Dick—1868
Leval, Pierre N.—1349, 2219
Levine, Marty—1656
Levitsky, Melvyn—2228
Levy, Mark I.—1918
Lew, Ginger Ehn—2224
Lewis, Lorraine Pratte—1918
Lewis, Ronald B.—2215
Leydon, John F.—2214
Lieberman, Joseph I.—2102, 2103
Lillehaug, David Lee—2229
Limon, Lavinia—1426
Lindo, Dean Russell—2211
Lindsay, Reginald C.—1837, 2226
Lindsey, Bruce—2049
Lissakers, Karen—1586
Litan, Robert E.—2212
Lloyd, Marilyn—1763, 1959, 1980
Loftus, Thomas A.—1400, 2222
Logsdon, Charles William—2228
Logue-Kinder, Joan—1543
Loiello, John P.—1933
Longuemare, R. Noel, Jr.—2222
Lord, Winston—2017
Loster, Gary—2190
Love, Susan—1762
Lubbers, Ruud—2217
Luken, Bonnie—1438
Lukensmeyer, Carolyn—2085
Luna, Casey—2104
Lungren-Maddalone, Christine—1342

Lynch, Thomas—1516
Lyons, James—1865

MacLaren, Roy—2012
Magaziner, Ira—1384, 1530, 1692
Mahan, Michelle—1523
Mahathir bin Mohamad—2033
Mahdesian, Michael—1427
Major, John—1556, 1868, 2164, 2179, 2216
Malary, Guy—1749, 1755
Malval, Robert—1745, 1755-1757, 1764, 1767, 1810, 1819, 1863, 1926, 1949, 1973, 1992, 2133, 2192
Mandela, Nelson—1456, 1593, 1594, 1758, 2060
Manella, Nora Margaret—2225
Manley, Martin John—2221
Manley, Michael—1822
Mann, David—1869, 1959, 1971
Mann, Marvin—1896, 1903
Manning, Patrick—1407, 1408, 2209
Manton, Thomas J.—1609
Marchman, Kevin—2216
Marcus, Felicia A.—1917
Marcus, Rudolph—1431
Marengo, Marc Michael—2210
Maresca, John J.—1393-1396, 1914, 1915
Margolies-Mezvinsky, Marjorie—1353, 2158
Marrero, Victor—2211
Marshall, Thurgood—2082, 2083
Martin, Timothy—1734
Martinez, Ricardo—2111
Martynov, Serguei Nikolayevich—2211
Marvil, Joel—2171
Mason, Keith—1449
Masten, Charles C.—1360
Mathes, Lynn—2106
Matheson, Scott M., Jr.—2220
Matteucci, Sherry Scheel—2225
Mauro, Garry—2145, 2146
Maynard, Olivia P.—1998
McAteer, J. Davitt—1425, 2225
McCaffrey, Barry R.—2069
McCaffrey, John Patrick—2227
McCalpin, F. William—2220
McCann, Vonya Beatrice—2216
McCauley, Mildred—1690
McClendon, Raymond J.—2153
McCloskey, Jay Patrick—2222
McColl, Hugh—1332
McCowan, Rodney A.—2195
McCoy, Helen T.—2153
McCurdy, Dave—2098
McDonald, Gail C.—2217
McFadden, Nancy E.—1918
McGillivray-Shaffer, Nancy J.—2228
McGinty, Kathleen A.—2145
McGowan, Patrick K.—2203
McKee, Jean—2214
McLarty, Thomas F. (Mack)—1346, 1449, 1838, 1865, 1891, 2008, 2097, 2139
McNair, Robbye—1841
Meeks, Jeffrey A.—2215
Meissner, Charles—1522

Meissner, Doris—1664, 2223
Melancon, Tucker L.—2012, 2229
Melendez, Rosa Maria—2229
Meles, Zenawi—1729
Menendez, Robert—1973
Mercado, Leo, Jr.—2084
Mercado, Maria Luisa—2220
Meri, Lennart—1623
Merrill, David Nathan—2228
Merrill, Robert—1693, 1701
Messitte, Peter J.—2219
Metzenbaum, Howard M.—2079
Metzler, Cynthia A.—1426
Mfume, Kweisi—1536
Michael, M. Blane—1349, 2219
Michel, Denise Marie—2215
Michel, Robert H.—1800, 1969, 1998, 2068
Mickelson, George S.—1384
Mikulski, Barbara A.—1414
Miller, Arthur—1693, 1701
Miller, Bob—1318, 1771
Miller, Joyce—1670
Miller, Meridith—2213
Miller, Paul Steven—2200
Miller, William Green—2219
Mitchell, George J.—1306, 1346, 1357, 1751, 1763, 1905, 2052, 2055, 2066, 2068, 2079
Mitchell, Graham R.—1772
Mitchell, Wandra Gail—2215
Mitterrand, François—1556, 1973
Miyazawa, Kiichi—1621
Moakley, John Joseph—1971
Moldaw, Stuart George—2211, 2228
Molina, Gloria—1771
Molinari, James J.—2227
Montgomery, G.V. (Sonny)—1953, 1956
Montgomery, Thomas—1746
Montgomery, William Dale—2219
Montoya, Regina—1349
Moody, Corlis Smith—2223
Moore, Mike—1362
Moore, Robert James—2229
Moore, William—2080
Moreland, Donald R.—2228
Morgan, Linda J.—2217
Morrison, Toni—1703
Mounts, William E.—2215
Moyer, Paul—1655
Moynihan, Daniel Patrick—1357, 1359, 1543, 1547, 1590, 1599, 1605, 1608, 1848, 1948, 2165
Mubarak, Hosni—1818, 1819
Mullins, Joe Russell—2227
Munoz, George—2214
Murdock, Clark A.—1426
Murphy, Victoria—1977
Murray, Patty—2009
Musgrave, F. Story—2147
Mutti, Fritz—2088
Myers, Dee Dee—1489, 1949

Nangle, Karen—1501
Naples, Shirley Cunningham—1341

Nathan, Irvin B.—1918
Natori, Josie—1475
Neel, Roy M.—2143
Neewoor, Anund Priyay—2211
Negroponte, John D.—2220
Nelson, Anna K.—1438, 2226
Nelson, Jean C.—2219
Newman, Frank—2187
Nichols, Mary Dolores—2224
Nickerson, Don Carlos—2227
Nicollier, Claude—2148
Niles, M.T.—2222
Nixon, Richard M.—1647
Noble, Ronald K.—2155
Nucci, Georgia—2196
Nunn, Sam—1306, 1682, 1752, 1943, 2098
Nussbaum, Karen Beth—1670
Nutter, James B.—2153
Nuxoll, Carla—1976

Oakes, James Robert—2229
Oakley, Robert B.—1705, 1729, 1742, 1743
Ochmanek, David—1426
Ochoa, Ellen—1518
Oden, Kenneth Ray—2229
Oedegeest, Carol—1504
O'Leary, Hazel Rollins—1678, 1679, 1792, 1856, 2145, 2146, 2223
O'Malley, William—1362
O'Neill, Thomas P., Jr. (Tip)—1859
O'Regan, Frederick M.—1917
Orton, Brad—1826
Osborne, David—2099
Oswald, Lee Harvey—2050
Otero, Jack—1670
Ouedraogo, Gaetan Rimwanguiya—2215
Owens, William A.—2199
Oxman, Stephen A.—1914
Ozal, Turgut—1394

Packwood, Bob—1647
Padilla, Jose R.—1427
Palacios, Alejandro J.—1427
Palmer, Steven O.—2222
Panetta, Leon E.—1346, 2086
Pang, Frederick F.Y.—2221
Parks, Jessica L.—2209
Paster, Howard G.—1346, 2055, 2143
Pastor, Ed—1959
Patricio, Jose Goncalves—2215
Patricof, Alan—1474
Patterson, P.J.—1407, 1409, 1411, 2209
Patterson, Patrick Michael—2227
Peale, Norman Vincent—2205
Peeples, Roddy—1911
Peer, Wilbur T.—1438
Peña, Federico—1392, 2009, 2046, 2049, 2216
Perciasepe, Robert W.—2223
Peres, Shimon—1457, 1476, 1481, 1490, 1493, 1643-1645, 1961
Perkins, Edward Joseph—2222
Perot, Ross—1303, 1490, 1905, 1911, 1913, 1920, 1941, 1943, 1944, 1972, 2003

Peterson, Esther—2211
Petricevic Raznatovic, Andres—2215
Pezzullo, Lawrence—1757, 1809, 1822
Pflaumer, Katrina Campbell—2227
Pickering, Myrtle B.—1998
Piersol, Lawrence L.—2219
Pieters, Steve—2088
Piley, Mabel—1502, 1534
Pincus, Ann Terry—2215
Pirie, Robert B., Jr.—2092
Pitts, Otis, Jr.—1441
Plaza, David—2080
Plaza, Eva M.—1918
Podesta, John—2213
Polas, Jerry—1670
Poling, Harold A.—1626
Pollard, Jonathan—1944, 1963
Ponsor, Michael A.—2030
Pope John Paul II—1362, 1370, 1371
Portman, Robert M.—2213
Pote, Harold W.—2211
Powell, Alma—1638
Powell, Colin L.—1364, 1637, 1704, 1715, 1928, 2213
Powell, H. Jefferson—2216
Prewitt, Jana Sawyer—1426
Pulley, Cassandra M.—2224
Purcell, Leo—1966, 1975
Purcell, Sarah—2150
Purvis, Hoyt—1977

Quarterman, Cynthia L.—1426
Quinn, Jack—2213
Quinn, Oliver B.—1904

Rabe, Raul C.—2210
Rabin, Yitzhak—1457, 1463, 1464, 1476-1478, 1480,
   1481, 1490, 1493, 1645, 1794, 1795, 1821, 1823,
   1944, 1960, 1961, 1977, 2210, 2213
Rahall, Nick J., II—1351
Rainer, William J.—2215
Ramirez, Sol—1516
Ramos, Fidel—2037, 2046, 2047, 2212
Rangel, Charles B.—1536
Ransom, David—1394
Rapp, Stephen John—2227
Rauh, Joseph, Jr.—2082, 2083
Rauschenberg, Robert—1693, 1701
Rawson, David P.—2220
Ray, Bill—1909
Raye, Martha—2213
Reagan, Ronald—1317
Reagle, George—2216
Reed, Bruce—2095, 2101
Reeder, Joe Robert—1533, 2228
Reich, Robert B.—1389, 1391, 1433, 1446, 1467,
   1494, 1517, 1670-1672, 1725, 1747, 2016, 2046,
   2049, 2101, 2102, 2138
Reid, Harry—1317
Rendell, Marjorie O.—2030
Reno, Janet—1328, 1362, 1380, 1390, 1428, 1446,
   1536, 1571, 1590, 1591, 1685, 1767, 1812, 1927,
   1947, 1952, 2068, 2143, 2154, 2190

Resnik, Joel—1685
Rey, Nicholas Andrew—1625, 2224
Reynolds, Albert—1868, 2179
Reynoso, Cruz—1623
Ricchetti, Steven—1346
Rice, Lois D.—2211
Richards, Ann W.—1445
Richards, Lloyd—1693, 1702
Richardson, Betty Hansen—2222
Richardson, Bill—2112
Richardson, Sally R.—1426
Ricks, Gregg—1414
Riegle, Donald W., Jr.—2200
Rierson, Matthew—1734
Riggins, Reshard—1544
Riley, Joseph H.—2146
Riley, Richard W.—1342, 1433, 1654, 1671, 1735,
   1747, 1771, 1782, 1876, 2101
Riordan, Richard—2044, 2143, 2190, 2191
Ritch, John B., III—2229
Rizzuto, Phil—1817
Robb, Charles S.—2099
Roberts, Chuck—2171
Roberts, Linda G.—1918
Robinson, Cassandra Pulley—1360
Robinson, Dwight P.—1345, 2227
Robinson, Laurie Overby—2216
Rock, Richard Rand, II—2229
Rockefeller, John D., IV—1351-1353, 1953, 1956
Rodriguez, Robert A.—2213
Rogers, Harold—1777
Rogers, John—1685
Rogers, Judith W.—2007, 2228
Rogers, Nancy Hardin—2220
Rogovin, John A.—1918
Romer, Roy—1592
Romero, Peter F.—2221
Ros-Lehtinen, Ileana—1973
Rose, Robert—1977
Rosenberg, Paul L.—1426
Rosner, Jeremy D.—2095, 2100, 2103
Rostenkowski, Dan—1357
Roth, William V., Jr.—1310
Roybal, Lucille Becerra—1518
Roybal-Allard, Lucille—1970
Rubin, Robert E.—1346, 2139
Ruda, Jose Maria—1951
Rudman, Warren B.—2211
Rushdie, Salman—2078, 2214
Russell, Donald Eric—2211
Russell, Theodore E.—2224
Russert, Timothy—1920
Rutskoy, Aleksandr—1653
Ryan, Stephen M.—2064

Sabo, Martin Olav—1357
Sagawa, Shirley Sachi—2230
Saginaw, Jane N.—2111
Sahinbas, Aydin—1914
Salinas, Carlos—1487, 1656, 1967, 2008
Samuelson, Paul A.—1882
Sandiford, Erskine—1407, 1408, 2209

Sapien, Miranda—2106
Sargus, Edmund A., Jr.—2222
Saris, Patti B.—1837, 2226
Sasser, Jim—1357
Sasso, John R.—1759
Satcher, David—2215
Sawyer, Thomas C.—1967, 1968, 1971
Scheman, L. Ronald—2227
Schenk, Lynn—1807
Scheuer, James H.—2229
Schiffer, Lois J.—1918
Schiffer, Robert L.—1427
Schifter, Richard—2209
Schmalz, Jeffrey—2088
Schmidt, John Roggen—2219
Schmitten, Rolland—2211
Schmoke, Kurt—2200
Schneider, Mark L.—1425, 2225
Schneider, Thomas Paul—2223
Scholz, Chuck—1367
Schroeder, Patricia—1376
Schugan, Randall—1734
Schumer, Charles E.—1881, 2079
Schwartz, Allen G.—1837, 2226
Seck, Mamadou Mansour—2215
Segal, Eli J.—1421, 1544, 1795, 1814, 2098
Seidman, Ricki—1595
Selin, Ivan—2223
Sequeira, Luis—2209
Seybert, Joanna—1596, 2224
Shackelford, Lottie Lee—1462, 2226
Shackelford, Parks D.—2215
Shalala, Donna E.—1366, 1489, 1540, 1761, 1762, 1782
Shalikashvili, John M.—1363, 1757, 1782, 2027
Shanahan, Thomas M.—2219
Shanker, Albert—1671
Shara, Farouk al- —1964, 2212
Sharp, John—1445, 1469, 1471
Shaw, Charles A.—1809, 2226
Shaw, Larry—1475
Shays, Christopher—1414
Shearer, Paul Scott—2214
Sheppard, Audrey—1686
Shriver, Robert Sargent, Jr.—1545
Shulman, Claire—1609
Shultz, George P.—1484, 1769
Siebert, Thomas L.—1748, 2225
Siegler, Mark—1584
Sievering, Nelson F., Jr.—1829, 2227
Silva, Gabriel—2211
Silver, Jonathan M.—1426
Silverman, Margie—1500, 1534
Silverstein, Michael A.—2213
Simons, Lynn Osborn—1976
Simpson, Alan K.—1484
Simpson, Bobby Charles—1440
Singletary, Larry—2087
Siregar, Arifin Mohamad—2211
Sizer, Theodore R.—2187
Skaggs, David E.—1376

Skinner, Michael David—2225
Slabach, Frederick Gilbert—1720, 2229
Slade, Tuiloma Neroni—2210
Slater, Cathryn Buford—2215
Slatkin, Nora—2219
Smegal, Thomas F., Jr.—2220
Smith, John F., Jr.—1626
Smith, Launice—1721
Smith, Marie—1691
Smith, Neal—1777
Smith, Rolland—1805
Soeharto—1493, 2036, 2037
Solano, Henry Lawrence—2223
Somers, Suzy—1501
Sonneberg, Maurice—2211
Soren, Tabitha—1546
Speer, Daniel—1516
Spiegel, Daniel L.—2223
Spotila, John T.—1426
Spring, Richard—2213
Stafford, M. Douglas—2227
Stallings, Richard H.—2224
Stark, Fortney Pete—1678
Stearns, Richard G.—1837, 2226
Stegner, Wallace—1377
Steinberg, Mark R.—1426
Stenholm, Charles W.—1336
Stephens, Darrel—1591
Stern, Donald Kenneth—2228
Stern, Gerald Mann—1699, 2224
Stevens, Charles Joseph—2227
Stiles, Michael Rankin—2224
Strauss, Richard—1552
Stroger, John—1771
Strom, Joseph Preston, Jr.—2220
Strong, Jermone—1500
Studds, Gerry E.—1959, 1971
Studley, Jamienne S.—1918
Sturdivant, John M.—1671, 2214
Styron, William—1693, 1702
Suliman, Ahmed—2211
Sullivan, Leon—1792
Susman, Sally—2215
Sweeney, Emily Margaret—2223
Swerdzewski, Joseph—2221
Swing, William Lacy—1456, 1757, 2222
Sykes, Donald—1426

Talbott, Strobe—2206
Tarnoff, Peter—1914
Tau, Nicolae A.—2215
Tauer, Paul—2190
Taylor, Carl E.—2198
Taylor, Paul—1693, 1702
Taylor, Preston M., Jr.—1425, 2226
Teare, Richard W.—1456, 2222
Terzano, Ginny—2173
Thornton, Kathryn C.—2147
Thornton, Ray—1980
Tierney, Susan F.—2145
Tigert, Ricki Rhodarmer—2007
Tobias, Robert M.—2214

Todd, James—2183
Toder, Eric J.—2214
Tomseth, Victor L.—2223
Torres, Esteban Edward—1970
Torricelli, Robert G.—1972
Townsend, Jean—1602
Toy, Charles D.—1918
Trager, David G.—2219
True, Teddie Rae—1918
Trujillo, Michael—1425
Trumka, Rich—2138
Tsilas, Loucas—2210
Tuchmann, E. Thomas—2216
Tucker, Bil—1429
Tucker, Jim Guy—1384
Tull, John E., Jr.—1933, 2228
Tull, Theresa Anne—1533, 2223
Tunheim, John R.—1438, 2222
Turner, Margery Austin—1904
Tyson, Laura D'Andrea—1392, 2027, 2139

Ulmanis, Guntis—1623
Ulrich, Laurel T.—1693, 1703
Ulucevik, Tugay—1393, 1914, 1915
Usery, W.J., Jr.—2138

Valentine, Benjamin—1957
Valentine, Tim—1943
van der Stoel, Max—1587, 2073
Van Wick, Mary Jane—1602
Vanaskie, Thomas I.—2007, 2229
Vance, Cyrus—1484
Varmus, Harold—1325
Vassiliou, George—1393
Vaughn, Cleveland—2229
Vaughn, M. David—2212
Vazquez, Martha A.—2219
Velasquez, Joe—1449
Vento, Bruce F.—2200
Vershbow, Alexander—1914
Verstandig, Toni Grant—1917
Vick, Jack—2108
Vickery, Raymond E., Jr.—1522
Villarreal, Jose—1759
Vogel, Raymond John—1633
Vogelgesang, Sandra Louise—1829, 2226
Volkmer, Harold L.—2110

Wagner, Mark—1685
Wald, Michael S.—1426
Wales, Jane M.—1354, 2225
Walker, Edward S., Jr.—1396, 2211
Walker, Robert M.—2092
Wang Jontao—2022
Warner, John W.—1752
Wasserman, Lew R.—2139
Watlington, Ernestine P.—2209, 2221
Weaver, Frank—1438
Weinstock, Bonnie—2212

Wells, John Calhoun—2214, 2223
Wells, Lesley Brooks—2030
Wells, Linton, II—2215
West, Togo Dennis, Jr.—1533, 2228
Wharton, Clifton R., Jr.—1932, 1944
Wheeler, Bill—1908
Whitaker, Asa—2171
White, Jesse L.—2212
White, John—1578
White, Michael D.—1516
Wilder, Billy—1693, 1702
Wiley, Christine—2067
Wiley, Dennis—2067
Wilhelm, David—1392, 1711
Wilken, Claudia—2224
Wilkerson, Patrick J.—2230
Williams, Alexander, Jr.—2220
Williams, Anthony A.—2209, 2226
Williams, Floyd L., III—1427
Williams, John—1515
Williams, Lee—1977
Williams, Lindsey—1498
Williams, Robert—1426
Williams, Sidney—1748, 2225
Willis, Roy—1686
Wilson, Charles—1336
Wilson, Pete—1654, 1838, 1839, 1891
Wilson, William Julius—1985
Wilson, William Roy, Jr.—2220
Winfrey, Oprah—2193
Winter, William F.—1771, 2084, 2086
Wirth, Tim—1377
Wisdom, John Minor—2082, 2083
Wise, Robert E., Jr.—1351
Withrow, Mary Ellen—2054
Witt, James Lee—1365, 1366, 1405, 1782, 1838, 1839, 1864, 1891
Woerner, Manfred—2211
Wofford, Harris—1887
Wolf, Frank R.—1635
Wolff, Nelson—2190
Wonder, Stevie—2155
Wong, Jacqueline J.—2214
Wood, Diane P.—1918
Woodbury, Gary M.—1475
Woolsey, R. James—2091
Wurtz, Donald Richard—2222

Yang, Linda Tao—2222
Yates, Sidney R.—1703
Yeltsin, Boris—1429, 1448, 1549, 1553, 1556, 1593, 1632, 1633, 1648, 1653, 1668, 1677, 1693, 1709, 1754, 1766, 1823, 1924, 2163, 2164, 2202, 2217
York, Joseph—1341
Youngblood, Kneeland C.—2215

Zarb, Frank G.—2215

Document Categories List

Addresses to the Nation

Economic program—1321
Joint session of Congress on health care reform—1556
Somalia, U.S. military involvement—1703

Addresses and Remarks

See also Addresses to the Nation; Bill Signings; Interviews With the News Media; Meetings With Foreign Leaders and International Officials
Advisory Commission on Intergovernmental Relations—2084
AFL-CIO, San Francisco, CA—1667
Alameda, CA—1372
All-American Cities Award recipients—1515
Ambridge, PA—1886
American Airlines strike—2047
American Association of Retired Persons, Culver City, CA—1686
Annenberg Foundation Education Challenge Grants, announcement—2186
Anticrime initiative, announcement—1360
Arlington National Cemetery, wreath-laying ceremony—1954
Arts and humanities awards
    Dinner—1706
    Presentation ceremony—1699
Asia-Pacific Economic Cooperation forum, Seattle, WA
    Dinner—2025
    Host Committee—2013
    Luncheon—2034
    Meetings with APEC leaders—2032
Bipartisan Commission on Entitlement Reform, Executive order signing ceremony—1904
B'nai B'rith, 150th anniversary—1813
Brady bill, Senate approval—2068
Budget control and deficit reduction, Executive order signing ceremony—1333
Business for Social Responsibility, conference—1783
California fires—1838, 1864, 1890
Canada, U.S. Ambassador, swearing-in ceremony—1354
Canoga Park, CA, roundtable discussion on State economy—2117
"Celebration '94", reception in Albuquerque, NM—2111
Charleston, WV—1350
Children's National Medical Center—1523
Christmas
    Greeting to the Nation—2204
    National Christmas tree lighting—2146
Church of God in Christ, Memphis, TN—1981
Clean car initiative, announcement—1626

Addresses and Remarks—Continued
Cleveland, OH—1458
Community policing grants, teleconference—2190
Congressional Black Caucus Foundation, dinner—1535
Congressional cooperation—1555, 2054
Congressional Hispanic Caucus Institute, dinner—1518
Covenant Baptist Church—2067
Creative Artists Agency, reception in Beverly Hills, CA—2123
Cutler Ridge, FL—1441
Defense Department
    Joint Chiefs of Staff, Chairman
        Nomination announcement—1363
        Retirement ceremony in Arlington, VA—1637
    Secretary
        Nomination announcement—2184
        Resignation—2177
Democratic Leadership Council—2094
Democratic National Committee
    Breakfast—1707
    Fundraising dinner—1794
Departure for Seattle, WA—2008
Dinkins, Mayor David
    Fundraising dinner in New York City—1608
    Rally in New York City—1846
Dinner honoring former Presidents—1484
Economic program—1326, 1343, 1346
Economic recovery—1838
Entitlements conference in Bryn Mawr, PA—2156
Executive Leadership Council, dinner—1792
Federal Bureau of Investigation Director, swearing-in ceremony—1427
Federal fleet, conversion to alternative fuel vehicles—2145
Federal procurement reforms and spending cut proposals—1824
Feinstein, Senator Dianne, reception in San Francisco, CA—2039
General Services Administration employees, Franconia, VA—1452
Gillette Co. employees, Boston, MA—1860
Haiti—1809
Health care reform
    Legislation, presentation to Congress—1830
    Physicians and supporters—1539, 2182
    Question-and-answer session in Bernalillo, NM—2104
    Rally—1565
    Remarks in New York City—1599
    Response to letters—1500, 1599
    Small business leaders—1504
    Town meeting in Tampa, FL—1568
Historically black colleges and universities, Executive order signing ceremony—1875

Addresses and Remarks—Continued

Homelessness, Housing and Urban Development Department grants announcement—2200

Homestead, FL—1441

Israel-Palestine Liberation Organization agreement
Remarks—1457, 1463, 1483
Signing ceremony—1475

John F. Kennedy Presidential Library, Boston, MA—1857

Johns Hopkins University, Baltimore, MD—1840

Lexmark International, Inc., employees, Lexington, KY—1895

Malcolm Baldrige National Quality Awards, presentation ceremony—2169

Martha's Vineyard, MA—1402

Mayors and chiefs of police—2144

Memphis, TN
Arrival at Memphis International Airport—1980
Community—1986

Middle East peace process—1643

Midwest flooding
Federal aid—1365
Tribute to community heroes in St. Louis, MO—1365

Moynihan, Senator Daniel Patrick, fundraiser in New York City—2165

National Breast Cancer Coalition—1761

National Democratic Institute—2052

National export strategy, announcement—1629

National Governors' Association, Tulsa, OK—1381

National Italian-American Foundation, dinner—1816

National Medals of Science and Technology, presentation ceremony—1636

National Performance Review
Remarks in Houston, TX—1469
Report announcement—1444

National Urban League—1328

Nobel Prize, 1992 recipients—1431

North American Free Trade Agreement
Debate—1940
Endorsements—1882, 1933, 2001
Environmental impact—1592
House of Representatives approval—2005
Jobs and Products Day trade fair—1777
Legislation, transmittal signing ceremony—1885
Meetings with Members of Congress—1738, 1772, 1800, 1827
Midwest agricultural community, teleconference—1906
Remarks in New Orleans, LA—1496
Small business leaders—1995
Special Adviser to President, announcement—1436
Supplemental agreements, signing ceremony—1485
Task Force Chairman, announcement—1389
Telephone conversation with Representative Pastor—1959

North Valley Job Training Partnership, Sunnyvale, CA—1466

Opportunity Skyway school-to-work program in Georgetown, DE—1432

Addresses and Remarks—Continued

Our Lady Help of Christians School, Los Angeles, CA—2043

Pan Am Flight 103 memorial, groundbreaking ceremony in Arlington, VA—2195

Presidential Medal of Freedom, presentation ceremony—2081

Queens County Democrats, New York City—1849

Radio addresses—1347, 1379, 1398, 1400, 1439, 1468, 1533, 1596, 1646, 1721, 1759, 1811, 1866, 1918, 1978, 2030, 2071, 2115, 2154, 2188, 2204

Regulatory planning and review, Executive order signing ceremony—1633

Robert Wood Johnson Hospital, New Brunswick, NJ—1716

Rockwell International employees, Canoga Park, CA—2119

Russia—1647, 2163

Sacramento, CA, arrival at McClellan Air Force Base—1648

St. Petersburg, FL—1588

San Francisco, CA—1677

Seattle, WA, arrival at Boeing Field—2009

Senior citizens—2132

Space shuttle *Endeavour* astronauts—2147

Summer of Service forum in College Park, MD—1412

Supreme Court of the U.S., Associate Justice
Confirmation—1312
Swearing-in ceremony—1358

Teachers Hall of Fame inductees—1340

Technology reinvestment project—1801

Thanksgiving turkey, presentation ceremony—2065

Town meetings
Health care reform on ABC News "Nightline" in Tampa, FL—1568
Sacramento, CA—1652

UNICEF health heroes—2196

United Nations
General Assembly, New York City—1612
Luncheon in New York City—1618

U.S. Capitol, 200th anniversary—1813

U.S. Chamber of Commerce—1868

U.S. Coast Guard, Seattle, WA—2036

University of North Carolina, Chapel Hill, NC—1732

Veterans Affairs Medical Center, Martinsburg, WV—1956

Veterans Day, breakfast—1952

Vietnam Women's Memorial Project—1942

Wall Street Journal Conference on the Americas in New York City—1850

White House Conference on Climate Change—1773

White House fellows—1697

White House interfaith breakfast—1403

World AIDS Day—2087

Yale University, New Haven, CT—1722

Appointments and Nominations

See also Digest (Appendix A); Nominations Submitted (Appendix B); Checklist (Appendix C)

Appointments and Nominations—Continued
  Agriculture Department
    Assistant Secretary (Congressional Relations)—1720
    Farmers Home Administration, Administrator—1425
    Rural Electrification Administration, Administrator—1720
  Air Force Department
    Assistant Secretaries
      Acquisition—1880
      Manpower, Reserve Affairs, Installations, and Environment—2153
    Under Secretary—1880
  American Red Cross, Board of Governors, members—1782
  Army Department
    Assistant Secretaries
      Financial Management—2153
      Installations, Logistics and Environment—2092
    Secretary—1533
    Under Secretary—1533
  Assassination Records Review Board, members—1438
  Civil Rights Commission
    Chair—1532
    Staff Director—1623
    Vice Chair—1623
  Commerce Department
    Assistant Secretaries
      Administration—2199
      Export Administration—1880
      Import Administration—1830
      International Economic Policy—1522
      Technology Policy—1772
      Trade Development—1522
      U.S. and Foreign Commercial Service, Director General—1522
    Chief Financial Officer—2199
    Patent and Trademark Office
      Assistant Commissioners
        Patents—1884
        Trademarks—1884
      Deputy Commissioner—2202
  Commodity Futures Trading Commission, Commissioner—1933
  Communications Satellite Corporation, Board of Directors, member—1940
  Consumer Product Safety Commission, Chairman—1808
  Defense Department
    Assistant Secretaries
      Economic Security—1685
      Health Affairs—1685
      Special Operations and Low-Intensity Conflict—1425
    Chief Financial Officer—2064
    European Command, Commander in Chief—1683
    Inspector General—2064
    Joint Chiefs of Staff
      Chairman—1363
      Vice Chairman—2199
    Secretary—2184

Appointments and Nominations—Continued
  Defense Department—Continued
    Southern Command, Commander in Chief—2069
  District of Columbia Superior Court, associate judge—1772
  Education Department
    Assistant Secretary (Human Resources and Administration)—2195
    Regional Representatives—1976
    Rehabilitation Services Administration, Commissioner—1440
  Energy Department
    Assistant Secretaries
      Energy Efficiency and Renewable Energy—1777
      Fossil Energy—1429
    Under Secretary—1880
  Environmental Protection Agency, Regional Administrators—2111
  Export-Import Bank of the U.S., Board of Directors, member—2012
  Federal Council on the Aging, members—1998
  Federal Deposit Insurance Corporation
    Chair—2007
    Members—2084
    Vice Chair—2084
  Federal Home Loan Mortgage Corporation, Board of Directors, members—2153
  Federal National Mortgage Association, Board of Directors, members—1759
  General Services Administration, Deputy Regional Administrator—2153
  Health and Human Services Department
    Indian Health Service, Director—1425
    National Institutes of Health, Director—1325
    Social Security Administration, Commissioner—1325
    U.S. Office of Consumer Affairs
      Deputy Director—2200
      Director—2200
  Housing and Urban Development Department, Government National Mortgage Association, President—1345
  Intergovernmental Relations Advisory Commission, members—1771
  International Monetary Fund, U.S. Executive Director—1586
  J. William Fulbright Foreign Scholarship Board, members—1977
  Justice Department
    Assistant Attorney General (Tax Division)—1836
    Special Counsel (Financial Institutions Fraud)—1699
  Labor Department
    Assistant Secretaries
      Mine Safety and Health Administration—1425
      Veterans Employment and Training Service—1425
    Inspector General—1360
  Legal Immigration Reform Commission, Chair—2173
  National Aeronautics and Space Administration, Chief Financial Officer—2203

Appointments and Nominations—Continued
National Credit Union Administration, Board of Directors, member—1829
National Foundation on the Arts and the Humanities
Institute of Museum Services, Director—1360
National Endowment for the Arts, Chair—1350
Navy Department
Assistant Secretaries
Financial Management—2153
Installation and Environment—2092
Under Secretary—1685
North American Free Trade Agreement Task Force, Chairman—1389, 1391
North Atlantic Treaty Organization, Supreme Allied Commander, Europe—1683
Office of the U.S. Trade Representative, Deputy U.S. Trade Representative—1748
Peace Corps, Deputy Director—1522
Science and Technology Policy Office, Associate Directors
International Affairs and National Security—1354
Science—1354
Senior Executive Service positions—1426, 1438, 1904, 1917
Small Business Administration
Chief Counsel for Advocacy—2199
Deputy Administrator—1360
Regional Director—2203
Smithsonian Institution, John F. Kennedy Center for the Performing Arts, Board of Directors, members—2139
State Department
Ambassadors
Angola—1933
Austria—1456
Bahamas—1748
Belgium—1456
Brunei—1533
Djibouti—1880
Haiti—1456
Jamaica—1742
Morocco—1748
Nepal—1829
Norway—1400
Papua New Guinea—1456
Poland—1625
Solomon Islands—1456
Spain—1359
Sweden—1748
Switzerland—1824
Vanuatu—1456
Deputy Secretary—2206
Transportation Department
Federal Aviation Administration, Deputy Administrator—1824
National Highway Traffic Safety Administration, Administrator—2111
Treasury Department
Assistant Secretary (Public Affairs and Public Liaison)—1543
Deputy Assistant Secretary (Federal Finance)—1543
Treasurer of the United States—2054

Appointments and Nominations—Continued
Treasury Department—Continued
U.S. Mint, Director—2202
United Nations, U.S. Representatives
Commission on the Status of Women—1829
Human Rights Commission—1808
International Atomic Energy Agency—1829
U.S. Appeals Court, judges—1349, 1596, 2007
U.S. Arms Control and Disarmament Agency, Director—1699
U.S. District Court, judges—1349, 1596, 1809, 1837, 1864, 1951, 2007, 2012, 2030
U.S. Information Agency
Associate Directors
Education and Cultural Affairs—1933
Management—1730
TV and Film Service Director—1933
U.S. International Development Cooperation Agency
Agency for International Development, Assistant Administrators
Africa—1344
Europe and the Newly Independent States—1829
Latin America and the Caribbean—1425
Legislation and Public Affairs—1829
Overseas Private Investment Corporation, Board of Directors, members—1462
U.S. Tax Court, judge—1462
Veterans Affairs Department
Assistant Secretary (Public and Intergovernmental Affairs)—1425
Under Secretary—1633
White House Conference on Aging, Executive Director—1808
White House Conference on Small Business Commission, Chair and members—1475
White House Office
Assistants to President
Congressional Affairs—2194
Deputy Chiefs of Staff—2139, 2203
Intergovernmental Affairs—1349
Scheduling and Advance, Director—1595
Deputy Assistants to President
Intergovernmental Affairs—1449
Political Affairs, Deputy Director—1449
Deputy Counsel to President—2054
Special Adviser to President for North American Free Trade Agreement—1436
Special Assistant to President and Deputy Press Secretary—2173
World Conservation Union, U.S. Representative—1824

Bill Signings

Agriculture, Rural Development, Food and Drug Administration, and Related Agencies Appropriations Act, 1994, statement—1799
Brady bill, providing for a waiting period before handgun purchases and establishment of a national criminal background check system, remarks—2079
Colorado Wilderness Act of 1993
Remarks—1376

Bill Signings—Continued
Colorado Wilderness Act of 1993—Continued
Statement—1377
Continuing appropriations resolutions, statements—1642, 1800
Department of Defense Appropriations Act, 1994, statement—1958
Department of the Interior and Related Agencies Appropriations Act, 1994, statement—1958
Departments of Commerce, Justice, and State, the Judiciary, and Related Agencies Appropriations Act, 1994, statement—1837
Departments of Labor, Health and Human Services, and Education, and Related Agencies Appropriations Act, 1994, statement—1799
Departments of Veterans Affairs and Housing and Urban Development, and Independent Agencies Appropriations Act, 1994, statement—1854
Emergency Supplemental Appropriations for Relief From the Major, Widespread Flooding in the Midwest Act of 1993
Remarks—1365
Statement—1368
Energy and Water Development Appropriations Act, 1994, statement—1856
Foreign operations, export financing, and related appropriations legislation, statement—1641
Government Performance and Results Act of 1993, remarks—1310
Government Securities Act Amendments of 1993, statement—2187
Hatch Act Reform Amendments of 1993
Remarks—1694
Statement—1696
Hazard Mitigation and Relocation Assistance Act of 1993, statement—2110
International Parental Kidnapping Crime Act of 1993, statement—2093
National and Community Service Trust Act of 1993, remarks—1543
National Child Protection Act of 1993, remarks—2192
North American Free Trade Agreement Implementation Act, remarks—2139
Omnibus Budget Reconciliation Act of 1993, remarks—1355
Persian Gulf war veterans health care legislation, statement—2193
Preventive Health Amendments of 1993, statement—2185
Religious Freedom Restoration Act of 1993, remarks—2000
Resolution Trust Corporation Completion Act, statement—2188
Romania, most-favored-nation trade status legislation, statement—1884
Rural Electrification Loan Restructuring Act of 1993, statement—1877
Small Business Guaranteed Credit Enhancement Act of 1993, statement—1378
South African Democratic Transition Support Act of 1993, remarks—2060

Bill Signings—Continued
Treasury, Postal Service, and General Government Appropriations Act, 1994, statement—1855
Unemployment Compensation Amendments of 1993, statement—2070
Wool and mohair subsidies phaseout legislation, statement—1878

Communications to Congress

Angola, U.S. national emergency with respect to UNITA, message—1611
Armenia, investment treaty with the U.S., message transmitting—1449
Biological diversity convention, message transmitting—2029
Bosnia-Herzegovina
Conflict resolution, letter—1781
No-fly zone report, letter—1740
Caribbean Basin Initiative, message transmitting report—2071
Chemical and biological weapons proliferation, U.S. national emergency
Letter—1397
Letter transmitting notice—1975
Chemical weapons convention, message transmitting—2061
China and Taiwan, rhinoceros and tiger trade, message—1931
Cyprus conflict reports, letters—1393, 1913
Czech Republic, taxation convention with the U.S., message transmitting—1798
District of Columbia, budget requests, message transmitting—1485
Ecuador, investment treaty with the U.S., message transmitting—1468
Federal budget
Deferrals, messages—1740, 2028
Penny-Kasich proposal, letter—2026
Proposed constitutional amendment, letter—1916
Rescissions, message—1879
Federal Labor Relations Authority, message transmitting report—1829
Federal Prevailing Rate Advisory Committee, message transmitting report—1776
General Agreement on Tariffs and Trade, letter—2180
Haiti
Economic sanctions
Letters—1782, 1991
Message—1769
U.S. national emergency, message transmitting notice—1640
Health care reform, proposed legislation, letter—1834
Iran, U.S. national emergency
Message—1950
Message transmitting notice—1879
Iraq
Compliance with United Nations Security Council resolutions, letters—1586, 2073
U.S. national emergency, message—1307
Israel, taxation convention with the U.S., message transmitting protocol—1775

Communications to Congress—Continued
Kazakhstan, investment treaty with the U.S., message transmitting—1450
Korea, South, fishery agreement with the U.S., message transmitting—1915
Kyrgyzstan
Investment treaty with the U.S., message transmitting—1450
Trade with the U.S., letter—2156
Libya, U.S. national emergency, letter transmitting notice—2093
Mine safety and health, message transmitting report—1554
Moldova, investment treaty with the U.S., message transmitting—1451
National Corporation for Housing Partnerships, message transmitting report—1698
National Institute of Building Sciences, message transmitting report—1698
National Science Foundation, message transmitting report—1554
Naval petroleum reserves, message—1706
Netherlands, tax convention with the U.S., message transmitting protocol—1807
North American Free Trade Agreement
Bipartisan cooperation, letter—1998
Congressional approval, letters—1625, 1998
Implementation, letter transmitting report—2206
Legislation, message transmitting—1892
Supplemental documents, message transmitting—1894
Norway, whaling activities, message—1684
Panama
Fish imports to the U.S., message—1758
Government assets held by the U.S., message—1940
Peru, trade with the U.S., letter—1364
Poland, fishery agreement with the U.S., message transmitting—1797
Railroad Retirement Board, message transmitting report—2053
Russia
Fishery agreement with the U.S., message transmitting—2028
Trade with the U.S., message—1640
Saint Lawrence Seaway Development Corporation, message transmitting report—1554
Serbia and Montenegro, economic sanctions, letter—2134
Slovak Republic, taxation convention with the U.S., message transmitting—1798
Somalia, U.S. military operations, message transmitting report—1739
Strengthening America's shipyards, message transmitting report—1645
Transportation Department, messages transmitting reports—1776, 1828
United Nations
International trade law convention, message transmitting—1345
U.S. Government activities, message transmitting report—2011

Communications to Congress—Continued
U.S. Armed Forces, use in international operations, letter—1770
Weapons proliferation activities, measures to restrict participation of U.S. persons, message—1639

Communications to Federal Agencies

See also Presidential Documents Published in the Federal Register (Appendix D)
Agency rulemaking procedures, memorandum—1635
AIDS, Federal workplace policies and programs, memorandum—1641
Child pornography, letter—1952
Combined Federal Campaign, memorandum—1393
Freedom of Information Act, memorandum—1685
North American Free Trade Agreement, implementation, memorandum—2206
President's Community Enterprise Board establishment, memorandum—1460
Report of regulations reviewed, memorandum—1636

Interviews With the News Media

See also Addresses and Remarks
Exchanges with reporters
Blair House—2142
Bryn Mawr, PA—2163
Cleveland, OH—1457
Grand Hyatt Washington Hotel—1791
Lexington, KY—1894
Mellon Auditorium—2172
New Haven, CT—1729
San Francisco, CA—1677
Seattle, WA—2012, 2020, 2022, 2032, 2034, 2035
Sheraton Washington Hotel—2102
U.S. Capitol—1326
White House—1297, 1310, 1312, 1333, 1340, 1354, 1360, 1389, 1405, 1412, 1429, 1431, 1436, 1444, 1454, 1455, 1463, 1490, 1526, 1555, 1592, 1624, 1629, 1632, 1633, 1642, 1643, 1647, 1715, 1730, 1738, 1749, 1772, 1800, 1809, 1818, 1827, 1838, 1881, 1885, 1904, 1906, 1960, 1977, 2001, 2005, 2046, 2054, 2055, 2065, 2068, 2091, 2127, 2133, 2147, 2190
Interviews
Arab media—1477
Israeli media—1480
Louisiana media—1334
Media roundtable—1966
"Meet the Press"—1920
MTV—1546
Nevada media—1315
Newspaper editors—1297, 1302
Radio reporters—1763
Radio talk show hosts—1548
San Diego, CA, television reporters
KFMB—1806
KGTV—1804
KNSD—1805
"The Home Show"—2150

Interviews With the News Media—Continued
Joint news conferences
   Australia, Prime Minister Keating—1491
   Caribbean leaders—1407
   Egypt, President Mubarak—1819
   Guatemala, President De Leon—2075
   Israel, Prime Minister Rabin—1961
   Italy, Prime Minister Ciampi—1526
   Japan, Prime Minister Hosokawa—1619
   Korea, South, President Kim—2056
   Philippines, President Ramos—2047
   Spain, Prime Minister Gonzalez—2128
   Turkey, Prime Minister Ciller—1749
News conferences
   No. 24 (August 30)—1407
   No. 25 (September 14)—1491
   No. 26 (September 17)—1526
   No. 27 (September 27)—1619
   No. 28 (October 14)—1742
   No. 29 (October 15)—1749
   No. 30 (October 15)—1755
   No. 31 (October 25)—1819
   No. 32 (November 10)—1942
   No. 33 (November 12)—1961
   No. 34 (November 22)—2047
   No. 35 (November 23)—2056
   No. 36 (November 30)—2075
   No. 37 (December 6)—2128
   No. 38 (December 15)—2173

Letters and Messages

   See also Communications to Congress; Communications to Federal Agencies; Resignations and Retirements
   Christmas, message—2201
   Colombia, death of Pablo Escobar, message to President Gaviria—2092
   Hanukkah, message—2138
   Hungary, death of Prime Minister Antall, message to President Goncz—2165
   Kwanzaa, message—2207
   Labor Day, message—1437
   Rosh Hashana, message—1462
   U.S. Arms Control and Disarmament Agency, letter to Director on his swearing-in—2179
   Yom Kippur, message—1595

Meetings With Foreign Leaders and International Officials

   Asia-Pacific Economic Cooperation leaders—2025, 2032, 2034, 2035, 2214
   Australia, Prime Minister Keating—1490, 1491
   Bahamas, Prime Minister Ingraham—1407
   Barbados, Prime Minister Sandiford—1407
   Belize, Prime Minister Esquivel—2075
   Bosnia-Herzegovina, President Izetbegovic—1455
   Canada, Prime Minister Chrétien—2012
   China, President Jiang—2022
   Colombia, President Gaviria—2211
   Costa Rica, President Calderon—2075
   Egypt, President Mubarak—1818, 1819

Meetings With Foreign Leaders and International Officials—Continued
   El Salvador, President Cristiani—2075
   Estonia, President Meri—1623
   Guatemala, President De Leon—2075
   Guyana, President Jagan—1407
   Haiti
      President Aristide—2133
      Prime Minister Malval—2133
   Holy See, Pope John Paul II—1370, 1371
   Honduras, President Callejas—2075
   Ireland, Deputy Prime Minister Spring—2213
   Israel
      Foreign Minister Peres—1475, 1643
      Prime Minister Rabin—1475, 1477, 1480, 1960, 1961, 2210
   Italy, Prime Minister Ciampi—1526
   Jamaica, Prime Minister Patterson—1407
   Japan, Prime Minister Hosokawa—1619, 2020
   Jordan, Crown Prince Hassan—1643
   Korea, South, President Kim—2055, 2056, 2064, 2214
   Latvia, President Ulmanis—1623
   Lebanon, Prime Minister Hariri—2211
   Lithuania, President Brazauskas—1623
   Mozambique, President Chissano—2211
   Nicaragua, President Chamorro—2075
   North Atlantic Treaty Organization, Secretary General Woerner—2211
   Palestine Liberation Organization
      Chairman Arafat—1475, 1477, 1480
      Executive Committee member Abbas—1475
   Panama, President Endara—2075
   Philippines, President Ramos—2046, 2047
   Russia
      Foreign Minister Kozyrev—1475, 1632
      Prime Minister Chernomyrdin—1429
   Spain, Prime Minister Gonzalez—2127, 2128
   Sweden, Prime Minister Bildt—2091
   Syria, Foreign Minister Farouk al-Shara—2212
   Thailand, Prime Minister Chuan—2214
   Trinidad and Tobago, Prime Minister Manning—1407
   Turkey, Prime Minister Ciller—1749
   United Kingdom, Foreign Minister Hurd—2210
   United Nations
      General Assembly President Insanally—2211
      Secretary-General Boutros-Ghali—2211

Resignations and Retirements

   See also Statements by the President
   Defense Department
      Joint Chiefs of Staff, Chairman—1637
      Secretary—2177, 2178
   Michel, Representative Robert—1684
   State Department, Deputy Secretary—1932
   White House Office, Assistants to President
      Intergovernmental Affairs—1349
      Legislative Affairs—2054

Statements by the President

   See also Appointments and Nominations; Bill Signings; Resignations and Retirements

Statements by the President—Continued
  Arts and humanities awards recipients—1693
  California, rebuilding the Cypress Freeway—1683
  Campaign finance reform, House of Representatives action—2053
  Coal strike, tentative agreement—2138
  Commerce Department appropriations—1776
  Cuba, meeting with released political prisoner Mario Chanes de Armas—1347
  Deaths
    Doolittle, General James H.—1625
    Peale, Norman Vincent—2205
  Democratic national health care campaign chair—1392
  Education reform legislation, House of Representatives action—1747
  Federal Government
    Acquisition, recycling, and waste prevention—1781
    Pollution prevention provisions, Executive order on compliance—1340
    Procurement reforms—1826
  General Agreement on Tariffs and Trade
    Audiovisual services—1748
    Support by Majority Leader Gephardt—2198
  Germany, ratification of Maastricht Treaty—1771
  Haiti, return of President Aristide—1863
  India, U.S. assistance to earthquake victims—1646
  Jamaica, U.S. Ambassador nomination withdrawal—1742
  Jordan, Michael, retirement—1698
  March on Washington for Jobs and Freedom, 30th anniversary—1402
  Midwest flooding, recovery cost-share adjustment—1565
  National Commission to Ensure a Strong Competitive Airline Industry report—1392
  National service legislation—1315, 1456
  Nobel Peace Prize award to Nelson Mandela and F.W. de Klerk—1758

Statements by the President—Continued
  North American Free Trade Agreement
    Endorsements—1738, 1975
    Implementation—2092
    Supplemental agreements—1376
    Task Force Chairman—1391
  North Atlantic Treaty Organization, Supreme Allied Commander, Europe—1683
  Northern Ireland, peace process—1868, 2179
  Organized crime in the U.S. and Italy—2155
  Pacific Northwest timber sales agreement—1325
  Puerto Rico, referendum on commonwealth status—1997
  Russia, actions by President Yeltsin—1553
  South Africa, economic sanctions—1594
  Supreme Court of the U.S., confirmation of Associate Justice—1314
  Surgeon General, confirmation—1448
  Technology reinvestment project—2070, 2110
  United Nations High Commissioner for Human Rights, establishment—2194
  White House staff changes—1349

Statements Other Than Presidential

  See also Checklist (Appendix C)
  Baltic countries, meeting with leaders—1623
  China, nuclear testing—1694
  Drug control policy—1892
  Germany, telephone conversation with Chancellor Kohl—1448
  Haiti, death of Justice Minister Malary—1749
  North American Free Trade Agreement, message to Latin American leaders—2011
  Russia, telephone conversations with President Yeltsin—1448, 1693, 2202
  Somalia, attack on United Nations forces—1598
  South Africa, transition to democracy—1456

Heterick Memorial Library
Ohio Northern University

DUE	RETURNED	DUE	RETURNED
1.		13.	
2.		14.	
3.		15.	
4.		16.	
5.		17.	
6.		18.	
7.		19.	
8.		20.	
9.		21.	
10.		22.	
11.		23.	
12.		24.